SIDREA Series in Accounting and Business Administration

This is the official book series of SIDREA - the Italian Society of Accounting and Business Administration. This book series is provided with a wide Scientific Committee composed of Academics by SIDREA. It publishes contributions (monographs, edited volumes and proceedings) as a result of the double blind review process by the SIDREA's thematic research groups, operating at the national and international levels. Particularly, the series aims to disseminate specialized findings on several topics – classical and cutting-edge alike – that are currently being discussed by the accounting and business administration communities. The series authors are respected researchers and professors in the fields of business valuation; governance and internal control; financial accounting; public accounting; management control; gender; turnaround predictive models; non-financial disclosure; intellectual capital, smart technologies, and digitalization; and university governance and performance measurement.This book series is indexed in Scopus.

Nicola Castellano • Francesco De Luca
Giuseppe D'Onza • Marco Maffei • Andrea Melis
Editors

Environmental, Social, Governance (ESG)

Risk, Performance, Monitoring

Springer

Editors
Nicola Castellano
University of Pisa
Pisa, Italy

Francesco De Luca
University of Chieti-Pescara
Pescara, Italy

Giuseppe D'Onza
Department of Economics
and Management
University of Pisa
Pisa, Italy

Marco Maffei
University of Naples Federico II
Naples, Italy

Andrea Melis
Department of Business and Economics
University of Cagliari
Cagliari, Italy

ISSN 2662-9879 ISSN 2662-9887 (electronic)
SIDREA Series in Accounting and Business Administration
ISBN 978-3-031-76617-6 ISBN 978-3-031-76618-3 (eBook)
https://doi.org/10.1007/978-3-031-76618-3

This Springer imprint is published by the registered company Springer Nature Switzerland AG
The registered company address is: Gewerbestrasse 11, 6330 Cham, Switzerland

Preface

SIDREA, Società Italiana dei Docenti di Ragioneria e di Economia Aziendale, is the Italian Society of Accounting and Business Administration Academics, which includes over 700 members, all professors (full, associate, assistant professors) in the scientific disciplinary sector of Accounting and Business Administration (the Italian Economia Aziendale). As a non-profit association, SIDREA aims to promote the development of the scientific basis of accounting and business administration culture and the principles of good governance of companies of all types, from private and public companies to non-profit companies, to public administrations. Moreover, the Association, drawing on the scientific heritage of Italian Accounting and Business Administration traditions, intends to provide its contribution by engaging with the institutions in charge to make decisions that affect companies' functioning, their development conditions, and their competitiveness. Additionally, SIDREA put its efforts in impacting on and supporting the system of academic research and higher education in the business administration field.

The pursuit of these objectives is implemented by SIDREA through a wide range of actions and activities both at national and international level as promoted by the Association's bodies (Members' Assembly and Board of Directors), and thanks to the active collaboration of its members. In this regard, it is worth remembering that the Association includes among its members prominent academics with extensive experience in professional and research bodies both at national and international level who can contribute to the achievement of the goals set by the Association. The pursuit of SIDREA's goals occurs, in fact, through the organization and promotion of debates and research, participation in initiatives and projects, collaboration with public and private entities, the establishment of committees and study groups, and the formulation of opinions and views on business issues. Moreover, with specific reference to the subject of financial and non-financial accounting and reporting, the Association includes among its members renowned scholars engaged in the development of important research on related topics and in participating in institutional and professional bodies that deal with the same issues.

For this reason and among others, SIDREA has established a Special Interest Working group (SIW), namely "Environmental, Social, Governance (ESG): risks, performance, control", coordinated by Professors Nicola Castellano, Francesco De Luca, Giuseppe D'Onza, Marco Maffei, and Andrea Melis. This SIW is specifically aimed at investigating the area of environmental, social, and governance factors and how they impact companies, internal control systems, risk management policies, and performance measurement. This topic is currently the object of a lively debate both at theoretical and empirical levels. If, on the one hand, ESG factors are at the centre of the current debate between voluntary and mandatory non-financial/sustainability reporting, on the other hand, the consideration of ESG factors within companies' performance posits the question about the potential extent to which companies are integrating ESG factors in their organizational and decisional processes, through their internal control systems, risk management policies, and performance measurement.

The work of this SIW surely represents a means for SIDREA to express its institutional opinion and provide some cutting-edge research evidence on a topic that fully belongs to its tradition of studies. In fact, even if ESG-related topics could involve several disciplines outside business administration (such as chemistry, engineering, and law), the SIW carried on its task thoroughly and consistently with the mandate received from the Board of Directors of SIDREA by focusing on the Accounting and Business Administration perspectives, under the lens of the pervasive and systemic approach typical of the tradition of the studies of this discipline. A wide array of methodological approaches is adopted, basing on innovative and alternative perspectives, to the extent that they are consistent with the principles of the Italian Economia Aziendale.

Therefore, I am very pleased to introduce this book that involves 114 authors and comprises 39 chapters, across 5 Parts, which underwent a double-blind reviewing process and provides several insights with relevant implications for international academics, practitioners, regulators, and students as well.

Ancona, Italy Stefano Marasca

Introduction

This volume is the output of SIDREA's (Società Italiana dei Docenti di Ragioneria ed Economia Aziendale) special interest research group "Environmental, Social and Governance (ESG): Risks, Performance and Control". The research group was established after the COVID-19 pandemic to encourage social cohesion among SIDREA members by organizing opportunities to meet face-to-face. The SIDREA executive board supported our proposal, and about 180 members joined the research group.

The foundations of the special interest research group were laid in October 2022 during SIDREA's biennial national conference. The aim of the group was to examine ESG sustainability issues in a variety of entities (e.g. large listed corporations, small and medium private enterprises, and non-profit organizations) from different perspectives, including cultural, governance, implementation, management, materiality, measurement, performance, practices, relevance, reporting, reputation, risk management, strategy and value, and so on. We encouraged the use of a range of different theories and methodologies and innovative and alternative approaches to help advance understanding of ESG sustainability issues, as long as they were consistent with the principles of Economia Aziendale. After two years of in-person and remote meetings, two workshops, seminars given by experts in the field, one-to-one feedback, draft papers, and double-blinded reviews, we are pleased to present our contribution to the debate on ESG.

This volume was stimulated by the European Commission's Green Deal Industrial Plan for a predictable and simplified regulatory environment and the more recent Net-Industry Act aimed at promoting investment in the production capacity of products that are key to meeting the European Union's (EU's) climate neutrality goals. Following on from these, several companies started to review their business models and processes to align with the principles set down by the European Commission. At the same time, the EU continues to support and encourage corporate social responsibility. In many companies, ESG is not fully integrated into all aspects of the business. The contributions in this volume emphasize the need for ESG integration into all business areas, including risk management, financial management, and management control. They acknowledge the divide between ESG theory, regulations, and practice and highlight the need for greater efforts at the firm level to realize corporate social responsibility.

In putting together this volume, our aim was to identify opportunities and critical issues associated with integrating ESG factors into business models. With this aim in mind, this volume contains 39 original studies that address a plethora of research questions concerning ESG and sustainability-related issues. In addressing these questions, a wide array of methodological approaches has been adopted, encompassing exploratory case studies and archival-based quantitative analyses. Some of the research questions are explorative in nature. Examples include: How do companies include ESG/sustainability into their business models, cultures, and strategies? What is the role of sustainability values and ESG culture in the development of sustainability-oriented business models? How do companies integrate social and environmental sustainability criteria into executive remuneration design? And how do companies integrate sustainability into their management control tools and enterprise risk management? The empirical studies in this volume are generally theory-building. Some adopt an inductive, qualitative research design, either longitudinal or comparative (either across companies in different countries or based on a multiple case study method in the same country). Others focus on an in-depth analysis of a single case study. Some other research questions addressed in this volume involve theory-testing, and the studies utilize deductive, quantitative research methods, focusing on relatively large samples of listed companies in Italy or in other European countries. The first stream of these studies focuses on financial (e.g. a company's market value) or non-financial (e.g. a company's reputation) outcomes of the presence of specific sustainable corporate governance mechanisms (e.g. the presence of a sustainability-related board committee or chief sustainability officer or integration of sustainability criteria into executive remuneration contracts). These studies address the same research question: What is the impact of having a specific sustainability corporate governance mechanism? The second stream of quantitative studies addresses research questions related to the more general relationship between ESG-related performance and a company's value. They ask: Is ESG-related performance associated with a company's market value? And how, and to what extent, is the relationship between ESG practices/performance and a company's financial performance affected by external factors (e.g. the global pandemic crisis, regulations) and internal factors (e.g. sustainability-related committees and information systems)?

This volume is structured into five parts.

Part I "ESG Values, Culture and Strategy: Embedding Sustainability in Corporate Practices" examines the role and contribution of ESG values and sustainability culture in the development of sustainability-oriented business models and strategies and the enhancement of ESG results and scores. Part I comprises six chapters, which include both theoretical and empirical studies that analyse these factors individually or in combination by adopting a variety of research methods. Aureli and Bartolini examine the influence of ESG values on the development of sustainability business models by examining the case of a benefit corporation (BC). Their study indicates that a sustainability business model is a natural consequence of being a BC, independently of any external pressures. In small companies, the opportunity to incorporate the business owner's personal vision directly into the company's goals and processes favours the adoption of business models based on sustainable development principles. Cervi and Di Carlo find that when ESG values are incorporated into an organization's mission statements, this helps to provide a clear direction for business strategies, employee behaviours, and innovations, which have a positive impact on ESG scores. Furthermore, they highlight that purpose-driven companies (i.e. those with an ESG focus in their mission statements) are more likely to excel in terms of sustainability and responsible corporate behaviour. In a similar vein, Veneziani, Rocca, Torelli, and Caccialanza find that the incorporation of ESG themes into organizational core values facilitates the adoption of sustainable business models and the improvement of ESG performance. They note that the absence of ESG values from organizational culture supports the implementation of control mechanisms in the supply chain. In their case study, they find that product quality is fundamental to enhancing ESG performance. Doronzo and Esposito examine the relationship between cultural values and ESG practices in energy companies. They show that when business performance is not affected by ESG performance, organizations where "masculinity" and "power distance" are highly valued are more likely to engage in greenwashing practices. Di Fabio and Roncagliolo examine the association between staff training activities (design and implementation) and an organization's sustainability culture, focusing on staff training activities in two Italian companies. Their study indicates that the integration of long-term environmental, social, and economic values into training coincides with the adoption of a sustainability-related concept of performance. Furthermore, they show that when companies focus only on financial performance, they fail to consider sustainability targets, and sustainability goals are excluded from staff training. The development of a sustainable culture is important in university education. Verna and D'Andreamatteo analyse ESG topics in university curricula and students' understanding of sustainability. They report that the teaching of sustainability in universities focuses more on theoretical than practical aspects of the topic. To mitigate this issue, the authors suggest the use of a holistic approach to the design, management, evaluation, and improvement of ESG teaching programmes based on the involvement and collaboration of teachers, students, institutional bodies, and social partners.

Part II "ESG Governance, Value Relevance and Corporate Reputation" focuses on key sustainable corporate governance mechanisms (e.g. sustainability-linked executive remuneration contracts, sustainability-related committees, or chief sustainability officers), either exploring the design of these mechanisms or their relationship with a company's market value, reputation, or ESG-related risk rating. Part II comprises nine chapters, which include studies that adopt a variety of research methods, depending on the specific research question(s) and phenomena under analysis. There are three inductive, qualitative, theory-building, and archival-based studies (Aresu, Rombi, and Khalfaoui; Melis, Gravellu, and Wasli; Aura and Leandri). Aresu et al. and Melis et al. seek to open the black box on executive remuneration contracts and explore how CEOs are financially incentivized to integrate social and environmental sustainability into a company's strategy and management. Aresu et al. conduct a longitudinal analysis via an in-depth examination of sustainability-related incentive components (criteria, weights, KPIs, etc.) of the CEOs of the largest non-financial listed companies in Italy. Melis et al. conduct a comparative analysis of aspects of remuneration design and the remuneration process (e.g. the involvement of remuneration- and sustainability-related committees, external consultants, and independent assurance) that lead to the remuneration contracts of CEOs of large non-financial listed companies in France, Germany, and Italy. Aura and Leandri describe the complex relationship between a company's ESG-related performance and its perceived sustainability reputation. By using a multiple case study explorative approach, the authors focus their analysis on the three better perceived Italian listed companies operating in the energy industry, with the Italian state as the main shareholder. There are six deductive, theory-testing, quantitative, and archival-based studies in Part II. These studies help to enhance our understanding of the impact of sustainable corporate governance mechanisms and ESG-related ratings. Florio, Panfilo, and Fiandrino conduct an empirical analysis of a large sample of European listed companies, investigating whether a company's ESG performance and sustainable corporate governance mechanisms (sustainability-linked executive remuneration and sustainability-related committee) influence a company's ESG-related risk rating. Ginesti, Martino, and Zampella, as well as Rizzato, Tonelli, and Devalle, focus on the impact of the presence of a sustainability-related committee in Italian companies. They examine the impact of this advisory and monitoring mechanism on a company's market value (i.e. its value relevance) and environmental risk management, respectively. In their analysis on the effect of sustainable corporate governance mechanisms, Carbone, Manzi, Saggese, and Sarto examine how the presence of a sustainability-related board committee and a chief sustainability officer influences a company's reputation (i.e. the extent to which a company is perceived as more sustainable). Casciello, Fiondella, Prisco, and Santonastaso investigate the value relevance of ESG-related performance and its pillars (environmental, social, and governance) on a sample of European non-financial listed companies. Finally, Latella and Veltri examine the relationship between a company's market value and its ESG-related performance, focusing on a sample of small-cap listed energy companies in Europe.

Part III "ESG Reporting and Risk Management: Strategies and Implications for Corporate Governance" focuses on issues, strategies, and implications related to ESG reporting, risk management, and risk disclosure and on how they affect corporate governance. Part III comprises seven chapters and includes studies that share an empirical approach but adopt several different research methods. The first three chapters focus on ESG issues within the context of risk management and risk disclosure strategies. Specifically, they investigate the extent and the effect of the inclusion of ESG issues within enterprise risk management (ERM), the possible inclusion of ESG risks in a corporate governance rating model, and the extent of

ESG risk management policies disclosure. The next four chapters share insights on sustainability report practices with specific reference to the variables that affect the double materiality assessment process; the interaction between ESG measurement, sustainability reporting, and its impact on stakeholders and management control systems; and the voluntary integration of climate information in management reports. In the first chapter, Crovini, Højrup, M. S. Jensen, Sørensen, and S. R. Jensen address the question of whether and how sustainability has been integrated into ERM. They focus on a single case study of an energy trading company located in Denmark and analyse how the 2021 energy crisis and green transition impacted its ERM. Drawing from an analysis of multiple data sources, such as interviews, meeting attendance annual reports, sustainability reports, and the company's website, they report that the company changed its focus from making profit to managing risks. However, financial risks are embedded in ESG issues, as sustainability risk management has become an integral part of ERM, being flexible and agile. In the second chapter, Magli and Nobolo explore the possibility of including aspects of ESG associated with ESG risks within a national corporate governance rating (CGR) model. They demonstrate the applicability of the CGR model using a sample of national and innovative start-ups. Their findings show that the inclusion of aspects of ESG in the model makes it more comprehensive, innovative, and analytical, specifically with regard to issues, such as shareholder protection, analysis of "risk appetite", remuneration plans, and compliance with gender quotas in management and control bodies. Moreover, in an empirical test of a sample of innovative start-ups, Magli and Nobolo identify shortcomings and errors in the model's metrics. The third chapter investigates the extent to which ESG risks and mitigation actions are disclosed by companies to meet the expectations of investors and the institutional environment. Demartini and Soriano analyse 10-K forms of four major aerospace and defence (A&D) companies in the US market and focus on three attributes (width, depth, and mitigation). They provide evidence that companies consider meeting the expectations of the sustainable investor, ensuring data security, attracting talent, and embracing new technologies, as well as proactively defining mitigation tools, as relevant themes for their risk management processes. The fourth chapter explores the double materiality assessment (DMA) process, as the starting point of sustainability reporting. Vito, Leto, Bernini, and D'Onza present a comparative analysis of three Italian companies that voluntarily undertake a DMA. The analysis focuses on various topics, such as the objectives of companies that choose to perform a DMA, the approaches they follow in its implementation, the role of stakeholders' engagement in each of the approaches adopted, and the organizational units involved in the process. They document differences in the objectives of the companies, with some companies' aims not limited only to compliance with sustainability reporting standards. They also find differences in the approaches followed (technical-rational vs. critical-dialogic) and in the roles of stakeholders in the DMA process. In the fifth chapter, Chiucchi, Ciccola, Giuliani, and Guidi investigate the interaction between ESG measurement, sustainability reporting, and management control systems by focusing on four characteristics: aim (decision-making support or external communication), temporal dimension (ex ante, ongoing, ex post), level of formalization, and organizational aspects. Through the collection of data from semi-structured interviews with key informants, direct observations, documentary research, and a field study involving seven Italian companies from various industries, they provide evidence that ESG measurement is predominantly used for external purposes, such as sustainability reporting and obtaining certifications, rather than improving management control systems. The sixth chapter aims to contribute to the scientific debate about climate risk, reporting novel insights into the voluntary integration of climate information in management reports of Italian listed firms. Caputo, Leopizzi, Lippolis, and Pizzi explore a representative sample of Italian companies to assess the degree of attention paid by Italian companies to climate information. Based on descriptive and empirical analyses, they show that many companies are beginning to incorporate climate information into their narrative disclosures. Interestingly, industries with a substantial climate footprint are at the forefront of this shift towards narrative strategies. However, the widespread adoption appears to be driven by concern about reputational risk. The seventh chapter examines how sustainability reporting contributes to the progression of sustainability initiatives by investigating the factors that influence their adoption and observing how they have evolved over time. Della Porta, De Nicola, and Salvatore focus on a single case study involving an agri-food company. Through the lens of the performativity approach, they explore how impactful narratives and stakeholders' responses shape the trajectory and significance of sustainability reporting and influence the construction of desired realities. Their study reveals the need to enhance environmental management accounting and internal sustainability measurement processes, which are deemed more effective in advancing sustainability efforts.

Part IV "ESG Performance Measurement and Management: Impact on Financial and Corporate Outcomes" focuses on the relationships between different measures of ESG performance, such as ESG scores, and environmental and corporate financial performance in Europe. Part IV comprises seven chapters: six employ empirical approaches with different research methods tailored to the specific research questions and phenomena being analysed, while one adopts a qualitative approach based on a case study. Some studies investigate whether ESG performance is financially driven, whereas others explore whether financial performance is ESG driven. Loprevite, Raucci, and Ricca investigate the impact of various dimensions of financial performance, such as solvency, liquidity, and profitability, on ESG performance. They also test the joint effect of financial performance and the presence of a Corporate Social Responsibility (CSR) committee responsible for decision-making on CSR strategy. Carnevale and Di Tommaso, on the other hand, explore the effect of ESG performance on economic and market performance by focusing on the European energy sector. They examine whether renewable energy companies experience lower economic and market performance compared to the traditional energy companies, thus addressing the question "Does being sustainable pay off?". Ferri,

Meucci, Spagnuolo, and Zagaria investigate the role of corporate ESG performance in shaping corporate performance, with a specific focus on M&A operations. They test whether, in the context of EU listed firms, the acquiring firm improves its ESG performance one year after an M&A transaction by acquiring more sustainable targets. Other studies investigate sustainability performance by disentangling ESG measures into its components and focusing on one component. Calciolari and Ruberti, by questioning the validity of environmental indicators, investigate whether aggregate environmental scores and measures of management efforts aimed at addressing material environmental risks impact the financial solvency of pharmaceutical and chemical companies in the same way. Likewise, Barresi, Bertoni, and Rossi explore whether a specific measure of environmental performance, such as total greenhouse gas emissions, affects oil and gas companies' financial performance. They also focus on the power of countries' institutional characteristics to reinforce the association between carbon emissions and financial performance. Although the environmental pillar of ESG remains the most investigated, studies are increasingly focusing on the consequences of implementing the social dimension of corporate sustainability performance. Drawing on such studies and considering the lack of knowledge about the potential effects of the social dimension of business practices on corporate financial performance, Spagnuolo, Casciello, and Carbone investigate whether the social performance of European non-financial firms is associated with their market-based financial performance. They also test whether the COVID-19 pandemic reinforced or weakened this association. Lavorato, Piedepalumbo, and Lamboglia adopt a qualitative case study approach and examine the role of information systems in supporting ESG strategy development and performance monitoring. They investigate whether information systems play an important role in integrating ESG issues into performance measurement and control systems.

Part V "ESG Implementation and Practices: Challenges, Strategies and Case Studies" explores various aspects of ESG. These fall into the following categories: ESG regulations and accountability, ESG and business models, and ESG and management control tools and practices. Spanò, Allini, Salerno, and Marcenaro examine ESG regulations in the EU and discuss their adequacy in promoting ESG-based holistic management of firms, value creation, and accountability. They use the metaphor of Sisyphus (the mythological hero condemned to a meaningful task for eternity) to illustrate how the risk of juridification arising from the proliferation of norms can lead to approaches of mere accomplishment, rather than promoting substantive commitment of companies to sustainability. The challenges associated with the inclusion of ESG into companies' business models attract much research interest, as testified by numerous contributions on this topic that span very different contexts: banks, non-governmental organizations, and industries. In the banking sector, Baldissera finds a strong commitment to ESG. The asset management policies of the bank investigated in Baldissera's study are focused on sustainability. Accordingly, the bank aligns its investment process and investment advisory services by combining the financial evaluation of products with ESG metrics. Bartolacci, Cardoni, and Soverchia analyse the introduction of a green banking strategy into a cooperative bank and find that managers have different perceptions about its strategic implications, depending on which E, S, or G factor is involved, with the social perspective being the most challenging of the three. The social perspective is also central in the study by Romolini, Fissi, Gori, and Sances, which is more than reasonable in contexts similar to the Dynamo Camp foundation. The creation of social value is embedded in the business model of the foundation. Interestingly, the activity of the foundation also has a strong environmental impact, with its presence fostering a green transition throughout the surrounding area. Palazzi, Sentuti, Cesaroni, and Del Baldo illustrate the importance of networks in developing sustainable business models, and they emphasize the roles of actors, activities, and resources in particular. They conclude that the success of a sustainable business model in small companies or in cooperatives must be part of a comprehensive network-related sustainable business model. The contribution by Vitolla, Marrone, Raimo, and Rubino is somewhat complementary to the previous one, as it discusses the main internal pros and cons related to the adoption of circular economy initiatives. They find that human capital and relationships can benefit from environmentally sustainable initiatives, provided that it is possible to hire qualified personnel. In the seventh study, Leotta, Rizza, Ruggeri, and Messina focus on the transition towards ESG-related accountability and managerial practices and how they can provide effective support for decision-making. Aprile and Bovo shed some light on the impact of institutional forces on the implementation and use of ESG indicators. They find that the pressure exerted by the major players in the supply chain (mimetic isomorphism) is stronger than that exerted by requirements to comply with mandatory regulations (normative isomorphism). Testarmata, Giosi, Meo, Brunelli, and Centini develop a conceptual framework addressing the tension between business sustainability and the associated configuration of management control systems. Their findings reveal effective sustainable management systems. Part V concludes with a chapter prepared by Sallustio, who was invited as an expert in the field to hold a seminar addressing the research theme of the SIDREA group.

The main contribution of this volume is twofold. First, the previous literature on emerging ESG risks and changes has not comprehensively considered the complexity of risk management. This volume provides an in-depth analysis of how sustainability can be integrated into executive incentives and risk management processes, offering insights into the identification and mitigation of ESG risks. In addition, it sheds light on internal sustainability reporting, emphasizing the need to develop a discourse on materiality and to promote linkage with management control systems. Second, this volume emphasizes that financial performance is no longer a standalone indicator. ESG indicators explain financial performance, and financial performance drives ESG performance. In this regard, this volume highlights how research is moving in the direction of ESG responsibility and helping to reshape business models and promote a more mature corporate culture.

The incorporation of ESG into business models poses several research challenges and opportunities for future research. One challenge concerns the importance of cultural variables for the successful development and implementation of sustainability strategies. Regarding these topics, there is a large gap between "what we know" and "what we need to know" about the relationship between ESG values, organizational culture, and the development and execution of sustainability strategy. Most certainly, research on the roles that C-suite values and corporate culture play in favouring/hindering sustainability strategy development and execution processes represents an interesting area for future investigations.

Moreover, little is known about the strength of the relationship between ESG measurement, sustainability reporting, and management control systems. In the aftermath of the introduction of new and more extensive mandatory disclosure requirements, a number of questions arise: How do companies practically address the materiality assessment between double and dynamic approaches to materiality? How does this affect the design of internal control systems? How do internal control systems incorporate ESG aspects into risk management policies?

Sustainability-related performance measurements and incentives represent another challenge for future research. For example, how do we measure sustainable performance? As accounting scholars, we are aware of the impact of performance measurements on incentives. Examples of open research questions that future studies could (and, possibly, should) examine are the following: Should sustainability criteria be integrated into executive remuneration design? Should they be? How can we incentivize corporate executives to manage companies in a sustainable way? How do we design and integrate sustainable corporate governance mechanisms, or ensure that corporate executives are adequately advised about sustainable corporate performance and adequately monitored to ensure they pursue it?

Future research could also investigate the relationship between ESG performance and financial performance. Thus far, studies addressing this issue have explored how various aspects of ESG performance influence, or are influenced by, corporate financial performance, emphasizing that the integration of ESG into business strategies is significantly associated with the financial performance of the business. However, this association varies, according to both industry and economic contexts. We encourage studies of specific industries and economic contexts, especially those with high environment impacts, such as the energy and oil and gas sectors.

This publication could be useful to academics across national boundaries, providing essential specific reading for scholars interested in understanding the different characteristics of ESG. The Italian perspective on how ESG could be managed and controlled by corporate entities could also serve as a stimulus for international scholars to investigate ESG-related practices and issues in specific national contexts.

This publication volume may also be of interest to policymakers, large companies, small and medium-sized enterprises, and practitioners who could benefit from knowledge of operational ESG practices that involve risk management, performance measurement, and management control. An awareness of both good and bad practices could encourage them to identify appropriate incentives for each type of corporate entity and context and contribute to the achievement of international sustainability agendas. The valuable insights in this volume provide a great opportunity to think about and reassess how to address one's own efforts.

We hope that this volume will also prove useful to students, offering them an opportunity to connect research to teaching. We encourage academics to develop specialized courses on the topics covered in this volume to help disseminate knowledge and educate professionals in the field.

We owe an intellectual debt to the SIDREA community, and we extend our deepest appreciation to all the authors and reviewers for their invaluable work. Without their enthusiasm and expertise, the publication of this volume would have not been possible.

The editors
Nicola Castellano
Francesco De Luca
Giuseppe D'Onza
Marco Maffei
Andrea Melis

Contents

Part I ESG Values, Culture, and Strategy: Embedding Sustainability in Corporate Practices

1 **Benefit Corporations and Business Models for Sustainability. The Case of Way2Global** 3
Selena Aureli and Monica Bartolini

2 **The Relationship Between Mission Statements and ESG** 27
Silvia Cervi and Emiliano Di Carlo

3 **Transition of Food Systems Business Models and Sustainable Performance: The Story of a Family Firm** 49
Monica Veneziani, Laura Rocca, Riccardo Torelli, and Andrea Caccialanza

4 **The Interaction Effects Between Cultural Values, ESG, and Green Innovation** 69
Emanuele Doronzo and Paolo Esposito

5 **Staff Training Through the ESG Lens: Insights from Case Studies** 91
Costanza Di Fabio and Elisa Roncagliolo

6 **ESG Concerns and Teaching Processes in Higher Education, an Experimental Approach** 109
Ida Verna and Antonio D'Andreamatteo

Part II ESG Governance, Value Relevance and Corporate Reputation

7 **The Evolution of CSR Contracting in Italian Non-financial Listed Companies** 131
Simone Aresu, Luigi Rombi, and Mariem Khalfaoui

8 Exploring the Integration of Sustainability in Executive Remuneration Design: Evidence from Large Non-financial Listed Companies in France, Germany, and Italy 155
Andrea Melis, Carla Gravellu, and Nouha Wasli

9 ESG and Corporate Reputation in Energy Sector Companies 183
Caterina Aura and Eleonora Leandri

10 ESG Performance, Corporate Governance Mechanisms, and ESG Risk Rating: Evidence from Europe 201
Cristina Florio, Silvia Panfilo, and Simona Fiandrino

11 CSR Board Committees and Value Relevance in Italian Listed Companies 225
Gianluca Ginesti, Ilaria Martino, and Annamaria Zampella

12 The Role of the Sustainability Committee in the Environmental Risk Management: Evidence from Italian Public Companies 241
Fabio Rizzato, Alberto Tonelli, and Alain Devalle

13 CSR Managers and ESG Performance: An Empirical Research 253
Emmadonata Carbone, Maria Angela Manzi, Sara Saggese, and Fabrizia Sarto

14 The Value Relevance of Environmental, Social, Governance Performance 273
Raffaela Casciello, Clelia Fiondella, Martina Prisco, and Rosalinda Santonastaso

15 Is the Firm Value Affected by the ESG Performance? A Study on Small-Capitalized European Listed Energy Companies 299
Pasquale Latella and Stefania Veltri

Part III ESG Reporting and Risk Management: Strategies and Implications for Corporate Governance

16 The Integration of Sustainability into the Risk Management Process and the Impact of the Energy Crisis and Green Transition: Insights from a Danish Energy Trading Company 319
Chiara Crovini, Emma Mørkbak Højrup, Max Strunck Jensen, Karoline Strøm Sørensen, and Sander Randrup Jensen

17 The Influence of ESG Risks on Corporate Governance Rating 337
Francesca Magli and Alberto Nobolo

18 ESG Risk Identification and Mitigation Under the SEC Regulation in the Aerospace and Defence Sector 367
Paola Demartini and Silvia Soriano

19 Double Materiality in Corporate Sustainability: Insights from Italian Companies 387
Diletta Vito, Lorenzo Leto, Francesca Bernini, and Giuseppe D'Onza

20 Investigating the Interaction Between ESG Measurement, Sustainability Reporting, and Management Control Systems 411
Maria Serena Chiucchi, Roberta Ciccola, Marco Giuliani, and Michele Guidi

21 Financial Reporting and Climate Information: The Italian Case 431
Fabio Caputo, Rossella Leopizzi, Stella Lippolis, and Simone Pizzi

22 Exploring the Relevance of Sustainability Reporting Using a Performativity Approach: A Case Study in the Agrifood Sector 449
Armando Della Porta, Manuel De Nicola, and Claudia Salvatore

Part IV ESG Performance Measurement and Management: Impact on Financial and Corporate Outcomes

23 Does Financial Performance Drive ESG Performance? Empirical Evidence from European Listed Companies 471
Salvatore Loprevite, Domenico Raucci, and Bruno Ricca

24 Does ESG Performance Affect Firms' Performance? Evidence from European Energy Companies 495
Concetta Carnevale and Caterina Di Tommaso

25 Please, Help Me to Improve: The Role of Targets' E, S & G Scores in M&A Operations 521
Luca Ferri, Fiorenza Meucci, Flavio Spagnuolo, and Claudia Zagaria

26 Why Go Industry-Specific with ESG Indicators? Testing their Validity and Explanatory Power for Financial Performance 545
Stefano Calciolari and Massimo Ruberti

27 The Association Between Environmental and Financial Performance in the Oil and Gas Industry: An Institutional Approach 567
Samantha Barresi, Michele Bertoni, and Paola Rossi

28 **Does the COVID-19 Pandemic Reward Firms Performing Better on Corporate Social Matters?** 595
Flavio Spagnuolo, Raffaela Casciello, and Emmadonata Carbone

29 **Role of Information Systems in Controlling and Monitoring ESG Performance: Evidence from an Empirical Study** 621
Domenica Lavorato, Palmira Piedepalumbo, and Rita Lamboglia

Part V ESG Implementation and Practices: Challenges, Strategies and Case Studies

30 **ESG Regulation and Accountability: Shall We Really Imagine Sisyphus Happy?** 641
Rosanna Spanò, Alessandra Allini, Francesca Salerno, and Edoardo Marcenaro

31 **Tools for Implementing ESG Factors in Asset Management Banking Policies: The Case of Fideuram-Intesa Sanpaolo Private Banking S.p.A.** 659
Annalisa Baldissera

32 **The Integration of ESG Issues in Community Banking: Contextual Factors and Strategic Managerial Perceptions** 683
Francesca Bartolacci, Andrea Cardoni, and Michela Soverchia

33 **Integrating ESG into a Business Model: A Case Study from a Non-profit Organization** 705
Alberto Romolini, Silvia Fissi, Elena Gori, and Michele Sances

34 **Integrating ESG into the Business Model Through a Network Approach. Insights from a Case Study** 719
Federica Palazzi, Annalisa Sentuti, Francesca Maria Cesaroni, and Mara Del Baldo

35 **Barriers and Benefits of Implementing Circular Economy Models: A Case Study Analysis** 739
Filippo Vitolla, Nicola Raimo, Arcangelo Marrone, and Michele Rubino

36 **Transforming ESG Accountability Practices into Managerial Ones** 759
Antonio Leotta, Carmela Rizza, Daniela Ruggeri, and Mariastella Messina

37 **Implementing ESG in a Family Business Operating in a Sensitive Industry in the Light of Institutional Theory** 781
Roberto Aprile and Sergio Bovo

38 A Systems Perspective on Sustainability Management Systems: Lessons for SMEs 799
Silvia Testarmata, Alessandro Giosi, Beatrice Meo, Sandro Brunelli, and Maria Lisa Centini

39 Towards the Identification of KPIs for 'Credible' Climate Transition Planning by EU Non-financial Borrowers in Hard-to-Abate Sectors 827
Riccardo Sallustio

Contributors

Alessandra Allini Department of Economics, Management, Institutions (DEMI), University of Naples "Federico II", Naples, Italy

Roberto Aprile University of Bergamo, Bergamo, Italy

Simone Aresu Dipartimento di Scienze Economiche ed Aziendali, Università degli Studi di Cagliari, Cagliari, Italy

Caterina Aura Department of Business Administration and Law, University of Calabria, Rende, Italy

Selena Aureli Department of Management, Alma Mater Studiorum - Bologna University, Bologna, Italy

Annalisa Baldissera Department of Law, University of Brescia, Brescia, Italy

Samantha Barresi Department of Economics, Business, Mathematics, and Statistics "Bruno de Finetti", University of Trieste, Trieste, Italy

Francesca Bartolacci University of Macerata, Macerata, Italy

Monica Bartolini Department of Management, Alma Mater Studiorum - Bologna University, Bologna, Italy

Francesca Bernini Department of Economics and Management, University of Pisa, Pisa, Italy

Michele Bertoni Department of Economics, Business, Mathematics, and Statistics "Bruno de Finetti", University of Trieste, Trieste, Italy

Sergio Bovo Alma Petroli SpA, Ravenna, Italy

Sandro Brunelli Dipartimento di Management e Diritto, Università degli Studi di Roma Tor Vergata, Roma, Italy

Andrea Caccialanza Università Cattolica del Sacro Cuore, Piacenza, Italy

Stefano Calciolari Università degli Studi di Milano-Bicocca, Milan, Italy

Fabio Caputo Dipartimento di Scienze dell'Economia, Università del Salento, Lecce, Italy

Emmadonata Carbone Department of Economics, Management, Institutions (DEMI), University of Naples "Federico II", Naples, Italy

Andrea Cardoni University of Perugia, Perugia, Italy

Concetta Carnevale Dipartimento di Culture, Educazione e Società, Università della Calabria, Arcavacata, Italy

Raffaela Casciello Università degli Studi di Napoli Federico II, Naples, Italy
Department of Economics, Management, Institutions (DEMI), University of Naples "Federico II", Naples, Italy

Maria Lisa Centini KPMG, Roma, Italy

Silvia Cervi University of Rome Tor Vergata (Department of Management and Law), Rome, Italy

Francesca Maria Cesaroni Department of Economics Society, Politics, University of Urbino, Urbino (PU), Italy

Maria Serena Chiucchi Department of Management, Università Politecnica delle Marche, Ancona, Italy

Roberta Ciccola Department of Management, Università Politecnica delle Marche, Ancona, Italy

Chiara Crovini Aalborg University Business School, Aalborg, Denmark

Antonio D'Andreamatteo University G. d'Annunzio of Chieti Pescara, Department of Management and Business Administration, Chieti, Italy

Manuel De Nicola Department of Communication Sciences, University of Teramo, Teramo, Italy

Mara Del Baldo Department of Economics Society, Politics, University of Urbino, Urbino (PU), Italy

Armando Della Porta Department of Business Economics, University G. d'Annunzio, Chieti-Pescara, Italy

Paola Demartini Department of Business Studies, Roma Tre University, Rome, Italy

Alain Devalle Dipartimento di Scienze Economico-sociali e matematico-statistiche, Università di Torino, Turin, Italy

Emiliano Di Carlo University of Rome Tor Vergata (Department of Management and Law), Rome, Italy

Costanza Di Fabio Dipartimento di Economia, Università degli Studi di Genova, Genova, Italy

Caterina Di Tommaso Dipartimento Jonico In Sistemi Giuridici Ed Economici Del Mediterraneo: Società, Ambiente, Culture, Università degli Studi di Bari, Bari, Italy

Giuseppe D'Onza Department of Economics and Management, University of Pisa, Pisa, Italy

Emanuele Doronzo Department of Economics, University of Rome "Tor Vergata", Roma, Italy

Paolo Esposito WSB University, Gdańsk, Poland
Department of Business and Economic Studies, Department of Business and Economic Studies, University of Naples "Parthenope", Naples, Italy

Luca Ferri Department of Economics, Management, Institutions (DEMI), University of Naples "Federico II", Naples, Italy

Simona Fiandrino Department of Management, University of Turin, Turin, Italy

Clelia Fiondella Università degli Studi della Campania Luigi Vanvitelli, Capua, Italy

Silvia Fissi University of Florence, Florence, Italy

Cristina Florio Department of Management, University of Verona, Verona, Italy

Gianluca Ginesti Department of Economics, Management, Institutions (DEMI), University of Naples Federico II, Naples, Italy

Alessandro Giosi Dipartimento di Scienze Umane, Università LUMSA, Roma, Italy

Marco Giuliani Department of Management, Università Politecnica delle Marche, Ancona, Italy

Elena Gori University of Florence, Florence, Italy

Carla Gravellu Department of Business and Economics, University of Cagliari, Cagliari, Italy

Michele Guidi Department of Management, Università Politecnica delle Marche, Ancona, Italy

Emma Mørkbak Højrup Aalborg University Business School, Aalborg, Denmark

Max Strunck Jensen Aalborg University Business School, Aalborg, Denmark

Sander Randrup Jensen Aalborg University Business School, Aalborg, Denmark

Mariem Khalfaoui Dipartimento di Scienze Economiche ed Aziendali, Università degli Studi di Cagliari, Cagliari, Italy

Rita Lamboglia University of Naples "Parthenope", Naples, Italy

Pasquale Latella Department of Business Administration and Law, University of Calabria, Arcavacata di Rende, Italy

Domenica Lavorato University of Naples "Parthenope", Naples, Italy

Eleonora Leandri Department of Business Administration and Law, University of Calabria, Rende, Italy

Rossella Leopizzi Dipartimento Jonico In Sistemi Giuridici Ed Economici Del Mediterraneo: Società, Ambiente, Culture, Università degli Studi di Bari Aldo Moro, Bari, Italy

Antonio Leotta Department of Economics and Business, University of Catania, Catania, Italy

Lorenzo Leto Department of Economics, University of Genoa, Genoa, Italy

Stella Lippolis Dipartimento Jonico In Sistemi Giuridici Ed Economici Del Mediterraneo: Società, Ambiente, Culture, Università degli Studi di Bari Aldo Moro, Bari, Italy

Salvatore Loprevite University "Dante Alighieri", Reggio Calabria, Italy

Francesca Magli Dipartimento di Scienze Economico-Aziendali e Diritto per l'Economia, Università degli Studi di Milano-Bicocca, Milan, Italy

Maria Angela Manzi Department of Economics, Management, Institutions (DEMI), University of Naples "Federico II", Naples, Italy

Edoardo Marcenaro Enel Grids srl, Rome, Italy

Arcangelo Marrone LUM University, Casamassima, BA, Italy

Ilaria Martino Department of Economics, Management, Institutions (DEMI), University of Naples Federico II, Naples, Italy

Andrea Melis Department of Business and Economics, University of Cagliari, Cagliari, Italy

Beatrice Meo Dipartimento di Scienze Umane, Università LUMSA, Roma, Italy

Mariastella Messina Department of Economics and Business, University of Catania, Catania, Italy

Fiorenza Meucci Department of Economics, Management, Institutions (DEMI), University of Naples "Federico II", Naples, Italy

Alberto Nobolo Dipartimento di Scienze Economico-Aziendali e Diritto per l'Economia, Università degli Studi di Milano-Bicocca, Milan, Italy

Federica Palazzi Department of Economics Society, Politics, University of Urbino, Urbino (PU), Italy

Silvia Panfilo Venice School of Management, Ca' Foscari University of Venice, Venice, Italy

Palmira Piedepalumbo University of Rome "La Sapienza", Rome, Italy

Simone Pizzi Dipartimento di Scienze dell'Economia, Università del Salento, Lecce, Italy

Martina Prisco Università degli Studi di Napoli Federico II, Naples, Italy

Nicola Raimo LUM University, Casamassima, BA, Italy

Domenico Raucci University "G. d'Annunzio", Chieti-Pescara, Italy

Bruno Ricca University of Messina, Messina, Italy

Carmela Rizza Department of Economics and Business, University of Catania, Catania, Italy

Fabio Rizzato Dipartimento di Management "Valter Cantino", Università di Torino, Turin, Italy

Laura Rocca Università degli Studi di Brescia, Brescia, Italy

Luigi Rombi Dipartimento di Scienze Economiche ed Aziendali, Università degli Studi di Cagliari, Cagliari, Italy

Alberto Romolini International Telematic University Uninettuno, Rome, Italy

Elisa Roncagliolo Dipartimento di Economia, Università degli Studi di Genova, Genova, Italy

Paola Rossi Department of Economics, Business, Mathematics, and Statistics "Bruno de Finetti", University of Trieste, Trieste, Italy

Massimo Ruberti Università degli Studi di Milano-Bicocca, Milan, Italy

Michele Rubino LUM University, Casamassima, BA, Italy

Daniela Ruggeri Department of Economics and Business, University of Catania, Catania, Italy

Sara Saggese Department of Economics, Management, Institutions (DEMI), University of Naples "Federico II", Naples, Italy

Francesca Salerno Company: ENEL S.p.A, Rome, Italy

Riccardo Sallustio Green and Sustainable Finance at Luiss "Guido Carli" University, Rome, Italy

Claudia Salvatore Department of Public Health, University of Naples Federico II, Naples, Italy

Michele Sances International Telematic University Uninettuno, Rome, Italy

Rosalinda Santonastaso Università degli Studi della Campania Luigi Vanvitelli, Capua, Italy

Fabrizia Sarto Department of Economics, Management, Institutions (DEMI), University of Naples "Federico II", Naples, Italy

Annalisa Sentuti Department of Economics Society, Politics, University of Urbino, Urbino (PU), Italy

Karoline Strøm Sørensen Aalborg University Business School, Aalborg, Denmark

Silvia Soriano Department of Business Studies, Roma Tre University, Rome, Italy

Michela Soverchia University of Macerata, Macerata, Italy

Flavio Spagnuolo Department of Economics, Management, Institutions (DEMI), University of Naples "Federico II", Naples, Italy

Rosanna Spanò Department of Economics, Management, Institutions (DEMI), University of Naples "Federico II", Naples, Italy

Silvia Testarmata Dipartimento di Scienze Umane, Università LUMSA, Roma, Italy

Alberto Tonelli Dipartimento di Management "Valter Cantino", Università di Torino, Turin, Italy

Riccardo Torelli Università Cattolica del Sacro Cuore, Piacenza, Italy

Stefania Veltri Department of Business Administration and Law, University of Calabria, Arcavacata di Rende, Italy

Monica Veneziani Università Cattolica del Sacro Cuore, Piacenza, Italy
Università degli Studi di Brescia, Brescia, Italy

Ida Verna University G. d'Annunzio of Chieti Pescara, Department of Management and Business Administration, Chieti, Italy

Diletta Vito Department of Economics and Management, University of Pisa, Pisa, Italy

Filippo Vitolla LUM University, Casamassima, BA, Italy

Nouha Wasli Department of Business and Economics, University of Cagliari, Cagliari, Italy

Claudia Zagaria Department of Economics, University of Campania "Luigi Vanvitelli", Capua, Italy

Annamaria Zampella Department of Economics, Management, Institutions (DEMI), University of Naples Federico II, Naples, Italy

Part I
ESG Values, Culture, and Strategy: Embedding Sustainability in Corporate Practices

Chapter 1
Benefit Corporations and Business Models for Sustainability. The Case of Way2Global

Selena Aureli and Monica Bartolini

1.1 Introduction

In the post-COVID-19 economy, social expectations that businesses shall consider the impact of their decisions on people and the environment have been reinforced (OECD, 2020; McKinsey, 2022). In line with the United Nation's SDGs (UN, 2015), more and more business leaders have decided to join the cause of a regenerative capitalism that occurs through sustainability. Yet, building a better society and a healthier planet is actually thriving. Prioritizing long-term resilience and responsibility, rather than focusing on efficiency and short-term shareholders' value maximization, represents a challenge that may require a revision of existing business models (BMs) and mainstream assumption that customer value creation shall be captured in the form of economic value for investors.

To this regard, a new concept of BM has been coined by some pioneering researchers (Stubbs & Cocklin, 2008; Schaltegger et al., 2012; Bocken et al., 2014; Bocken, 2021), usually referred as Business Model for Sustainability (BMfS) or Sustainable Business Models (SBMs). An SBM can be defined as a business fulfilling three criteria (Schaltegger et al., 2016a, p. 6):

(1) A multiple value proposition in favour of customers and all other stakeholders
(2) The goal of creating and delivering a value portfolio to consider multiple stakeholders' needs
(3) The generation of economic value for the business itself and the commitment to respect and strengthen other forms of capital and, more precisely, natural and social capital.

S. Aureli (✉) · M. Bartolini
Department of Management, Alma Mater Studiorum - Bologna University, Bologna, Italy
e-mail: selena.aureli@unibo.it; monica.bartolini4@unibo.it

N. Castellano et al. (eds.), *Environmental, Social, Governance (ESG)*, SIDREA Series in Accounting and Business Administration,
https://doi.org/10.1007/978-3-031-76618-3_1

This concept of SBM is strongly rooted in stakeholder theory, because it assumes that stakeholders' collaboration is necessary to address sustainability issues and, consequently, enterprises shall offer multiple values to multiple stakeholders (Hörisch et al., 2014; Freudenreich et al., 2020).

Scrutinizing the BM in light of sustainability is extremely relevant because it allows us to understand how actual business practices add value to various stakeholders, including customers, shareholders, the local community, central and local governments, the natural environment, and even future generations (Bocken et al., 2014). While external subjects may detect possible greenwashing or window-dressing patterns not translating into concrete actions when analysing the BM, managers and entrepreneurs increase their awareness in their attempt to "walk their talk" (Schoeneborn et al., 2020) and address the opportunities and problems in doing so (Charles et al., 2017).

Most of the literature on SBMs focused on BM transformation of large or incumbent firms (Boons & Lüdeke-Freund, 2013; Frishammar & Parida, 2019; Lüdeke-Freund et al., 2019). Therefore, the debate mainly referred to challenges associated with the development of sustainable characteristics of existing products and the search for new customers groups, distribution channels, financial sources, and supply partners in line with sustainability aspirations (Biloslavo et al., 2020). Academic research on SBMs also focuses on sustainable new ventures and start-ups, but this stream of research is more limited (Voinea et al., 2019; Retolaza et al., 2009; De Lange, 2017). Another under-investigated field of research concerns sustainability aspects infused in the BM of benefit corporations (BCs), despite their statutory mission to balance profit-making purposes with their transparency and sustainability objectives (Baudot et al., 2019, 2020).

Benefit corporations are for-profit companies with the mission of having a positive impact on the environment and/or society. Their dual purpose has attracted the attention of academic literature, which has recalled the conceptual model of hybrid organizations (Rawhouser et al., 2015; Gamble et al., 2020; Ferlito and Faraci, 2022) and has investigated its governance implications (Ebrahim et al., 2014). Effects of the dual purpose on the BM are less explored instead, even though we might assume that this hybrid logic influences strategic choices leading to differences in the route to value creation, delivery, and capture (Ocasio & Radoynovska, 2016).

Given this gap in the literature, this chapter aims to investigate how merging the goal of "making money" with the one of "doing good" (Gazzola et al., 2019; Mion & Loza Adaui, 2020; Mion et al., 2021) shapes business modelling towards sustainability (Ferlito & Faraci, 2022). Using stakeholder theory as theoretical framework that underpins and explains sustainability practices (Hörisch et al., 2014; Freudenreich et al., 2020), this chapter adopts the conceptual model of Schaltegger et al. (2016a) for SBMs to assess the sustainability orientation of BCs. This conceptual model has been applied to a single case study, regarding a BC operating in the service sector. The company under investigation has been a BC since it was founded. It is a small-sized company that publishes its annual impact report as required by the Italian legislation, has obtained the B Corp certification, and discloses a proper integrated report every year.

The study suggests that the hybrid mission of BCs clearly affects their business model. BCs do not require external pressure to implement sustainable practices. An SBM comes out as the natural consequence of being a BC. In addition, two factors have facilitated the design of the BM in line with the sustainable goals in our case study: (1) the small size of the company, which allows for the full incorporation of the entrepreneur's personal vision in the company goals and processes, and (2) the reporting process that favoured greater strategical awareness deriving from the process of setting the impact assessment and the integrated report in place.

In the following paragraph, this chapter introduces the main literature background, involving both the BCs' peculiarities and their sustainable business models. We also address the linkage between accounting and business models' studies, highlighting that adopting a sustainable BM requires different accounting approaches and tools. The third section describes the methodology adopted for this case-based research, while the fourth section describes the case and the related findings. Finally, the fifth section concludes by presenting the main theoretical and practical implications of this study, as well as its limitations.

1.2 Literature Review

1.2.1 Benefit Corporations

A benefit corporation (BC) is not a new type of business organization but a qualification that any type of company can decide to obtain by amending the corporate purpose in its articles of association. Born in the USA in 2011, the BC is a legal entity recognized by the government, which simultaneously pursues profit objectives and contributes to the society's and the environment's well-being. BCs' legal status imposes the simultaneous pursuit of different economic, social, and environmental goals (Baudot et al., 2019, 2020; Battilana & Lee, 2014; Rawhouser et al., 2015). Such status requires taking into consideration additional interests to the financial ones of their shareholders. Like other business corporations, a BC aims to make profit for shareholders (Bartolini et al., 2023), but to achieve that goal, it conducts business in a socially and environmentally sustainable and responsible way.

According to Hiller (2013), BCs have five distinctive characteristics: (1) provide a common benefit to address both economic and social responsibilities (they have a public purpose in their bylaws), (2) have a specific annual disclosure with specific impacts auditable by an independent third party (a duty of accountability), (3) have broader goals beyond profit-making for shareholders on a voluntary basis (the destination of profits benefits other stakeholders), (4) have greater transparency, and (5) pursue common benefit through concrete actions as part of core business operations. These five aspects are consistent with the CSR framework by Crane et al., (2008) and make BCs an interesting subject for observation through the sustainability lens.

Hiller (2013) states that becoming a BC can be considered a way to implement corporate social responsibility (CSR) because of its strong social commitment. However, it is important to remark that BCs are not social enterprises and also differ from B Corps.

In Italy, the BC legal form was introduced in 2015 and whatever type of company might become a benefit corporation, i.e. "purpose-oriented company" (Muñoz et al., 2018). So, BCs are usually for-profit companies that change their status. On the contrary, social enterprises are usually not-for-profit companies that do not have a specific legal form in several countries. Most importantly, a social enterprise is mainly a revenue-generating organization whose primary purpose is to have a social impact. Grassl (2012) suggests that in social enterprises the profit motive is secondary to the delivery of the social mission and, hence, their business model is mainly infused by the goal of generating positive externalities for society (Yunus et al., 2010).

BCs may be awarded a B Corp certification, which is issued by a private entity named B Lab (Gazzola et al., 2019; Mion & Loza Adaui, 2020; Mion et al., 2021) when an applying company meets certain requirements, showing its commitment to society and the environment, and pays a fee.

To become a certified B Corp (a 3-year certification that guarantees high standards of transparency, as well as social and environmental performance), companies must undertake a process called B Impact Assessment (BIA), which evaluates five broad categories: environment, workers, customers, community, and governance (Castellini et al., 2019; Liute & De Giacomo, 2022). It requires companies to be in constant dialogue with their stakeholders (Gazzola et al., 2019; Burger-Helmchen & Siegel, 2020).

Being a certified B Corp seems trendy among many large for-profit companies that apply for this certification to use the B mark logo and prove their commitment to society and the environment. BCs instead do not need to obtain this certification to show their social purpose. Their five key characteristics (Hiller, 2013) already signal their social and environmental commitment. However, this signal may need to be appropriately amplified, for example, by getting the B Corp certification in order to reach stakeholders (Galli et al., 2021). The reason for getting a certification is also grounded on the decreasing trust consumers have in corporations' communications. Marketers have overused terms such as "green", "responsible", and "sustainable" to describe their products, thus generating consumers' distrust. In other words, the more these terms are used, the less meaning they have in the absence of standards to back their claims. This also frustrates businesses that try to honestly distinguish themselves based on their socially and environmentally sustainable business practices. Third-party certifications can positively contribute to consumer trust. B Corp certification is among the few existing standards that comprehensively assess a company's overall approach to sustainability performance, distinguishing between a truly "good company" and mere marketing. Consumers not only prefer purchasing from a "good company"; they also like working for such socially and environmentally oriented businesses.

Given BCs' dual purpose (i.e. profit on the one side, and public common benefits, on the other), they are considered legal organizational forms that fully incorporate sustainability (Marchini et al., 2023). Coherently, academia has started investigating the linkages between being a BC and CSR practices (Marchini et al., 2023) and devoted attention to either management aspects or BCs' reporting practices. Management aspects are interesting because they are affected by some peculiar BCs' characteristics; specifically, such characteristics should shape a firm's business model, its strategic approach, its CSR practices, and consequently its competitive advantage (Dupire & M'Zali, 2018). At the same time, BCs' reporting requirements, such as the publication of a yearly impact assessment, call for specific research on how their disclosure practices may favour transparency, accountability, and stakeholder engagement (Nigri & Del Baldo, 2018).

1.2.2 Sustainable Business Models

BCs' key elements and particularly their dual purpose should affect their business model, but what is a BM? There are dozens of different definitions for BM and researchers have proposed several component breakdowns of the business over the last decade (Amit & Zott, 2001; Casadesus-Masanell & Ricart, 2010; Chesbrough & Rosenbloom, 2002; Johnson et al., 2008; Morris et al., 2005; Osterwalder & Pigneur, 2010; Teece, 2010; Zott et al., 2011). Nevertheless, most of them share the idea that a BM refers to the activities through which companies create, deliver, and capture value. Such understanding of how a company does business (Beattie & Smith, 2013) is usually described through three main elements (Osterwalder & Pigneur, 2010): value proposition, value creation and delivery, and value capture. Each element is addressed by a specific question:

a) *Value creation dimension*—What is offered to the customer and who is the target customer?
b) *Value delivery dimension*—How are activities and processes employed to deliver the promised value?
c) *Value capture dimension*—Why is the revenue model financially viable?

Because of current socio-institutional changes that question what is legitimate to manufacture and consume, together with an increasing demand for businesses' involvement in sustainable development, more and more organizations are attempting to introduce sustainability in their business model (Nidumolu et al., 2009; Schaltegger et al., 2012). Sustainability goals involve changes in the way of doing business and, therefore, a new sustainable business model is to be designed. Management and entrepreneurship studies have flourished in the attempt of providing tools and methods, such as the BM Canvas or the lean start-up approach, to support the redesign of BMs in the light of sustainability (Pieroni et al., 2019; Bocken et al., 2014; Ünal et al., 2019).

The notion of SBM began to populate management journals in the second half of the 2000s (Stubbs & Cocklin, 2008; Nosratabadi et al., 2019; Karuppiah et al., 2023). As reported by Biloslavo et al. (2020), a sustainable BM is usually defined as "a business model that creates competitive advantage through superior customer value and contributes to the sustainable development of the company and society". Therefore, customer value creation and delivery are still at the core of the model with environmental and social benefits somewhat embedded. From the early definitions provided by Schaltegger et al. (2012) and Wells (2013), many others have been developed. A great portion of studies on SBM actually focuses on the conceptualization of SBM (Geissdoerfer et al., 2018; Lozano, 2018).

Another relevant literature stream of studies focuses on the distinctive traits of SBMs and proposes possible archetypes (Bocken et al., 2014; Upward & Jones, 2016). Yet, the most interesting empirical studies deal with how to align organizational structures and the process of value creation, delivery, and capture to sustainable goals (Boons & Lüdeke-Freund, 2013). Freudenreich et al. (2020), who elaborated on the original work of Schaltegger et al. (2016a), pinpointed the following characteristics for SBMs: (i) offering multiple value propositions to all stakeholders (not only to customers); (ii) creating and delivering the corresponding forms of value (a value portfolio of different outcomes) for different stakeholders; and (iii) capturing economic value for the business while maintaining or regenerating natural, social, and economic capital beyond the boundaries of the single organization.

All cited characteristics are strongly rooted in stakeholder theory, which assumes that stakeholders' collaboration is necessary to address sustainability issues. A company that offers multiple values to multiple stakeholders is an organization with a holistic view on how business is done, capable of involving and internalizing societal and environmental concerns of external subjects (Hörisch et al., 2014; Freudenreich et al., 2020). If stakeholders consider ecological and social outcomes valuable, this must be reflected in value creation processes. Ecological and social outcomes must become part of the value created for stakeholders and, consequently, also be fully integrated in the focal business' purpose (Kurucz et al., 2017). What constitutes value is thus not only different for each stakeholder group (Garriga, 2014; Schneider & Sachs, 2017) but may also be a combination of different types of value.

The latter characteristic ("capturing economic value for the business while maintaining or regenerating natural, social and economic capitals beyond the boundaries of the single organization") is the most challenging aspect to address. It requires an integration of business and ethical considerations; in other words, ethical and business decisions are not two separate phenomena. So, although a discussion of ethical considerations is not crucial in the literature on conventional business models, it becomes central in sustainability-oriented business models (Stubbs & Cocklin, 2008; Pedersen et al., 2018). In this context, the integration of ecological and social impacts into the notion of value creation leads to a defining feature of sustainability-oriented business models (Bocken et al., 2014; Lüdeke-Freund & Dembek, 2017; Schaltegger et al., 2016b).

The main assumption of these studies is that existing companies search for a better fit with the new value landscape infused by sustainability goals and end up modifying their BM (Hacklin et al., 2018; Markides, 2013). Therefore, BM innovation often occurs (Cavalcante et al., 2011; Foss & Saebi, 2017; Geissdoerfer et al., 2018). Changes may refer to single aspects of the business model (e.g. the use of recycled materials, thus reducing environmental impacts and offering a new value proposition to customers) or involve a complete revision and replacement of it. The adoption of circular economy principles, for example, always implies the change of the value proposition and the creation of a value network of partners (Urbinati et al., 2017).

BM changes in well-established large multinationals are fundamental to make current production and consumption processes more sustainable. However, as reported by Bocken et al. (2014), it is likely to be new start-ups and small businesses undertaking the more radical innovations. Literature has mainly focused on the former, while "born-sustainable" new ventures are poorly investigated (Retolaza et al., 2009; De Lange, 2017). Among the few studies dedicated to SBMs in start-ups and small businesses, Voinea et al. (2019) show that CSR strategies are strongly rooted in the business values of their entrepreneurs, which are determined by their personalities and organizational experience. This is in line with previous studies (Bakos et al., 2020; Dasanayaka et al., 2022) showing that organization culture and top management commitment are key drivers in SMEs to adopt sustainable practices. So, for example, a start-up might be prompted by the philanthropic drive of its entrepreneur, rooted in their personal priorities and concern for addressing social or environmental needs to determine most of its CSR initiatives (Voinea et al., 2019).

Given that (1) BC literature suggests that BCs' dual mission should affect the firm's value proposition and related strategies, (2) SBM literature advocates that all value creation, value delivery, and value capture processes should change in light of sustainability, and (3) existing research mainly focuses on large companies, this study questions *how distinctive characteristics of BCs affect the BM adopted in terms of sustainability orientation in the context of small-sized businesses.*

1.2.3 How the Accounting Discipline Deals with Business Models

BM is a concept that has entered the accounting discipline only recently. BM terminology and related concepts are likely to engender discomfort among many members of the financial accounting community (Nielsen & Roslender, 2015; Roslender & Nielsen, 2018). When accountants address BM, they need to draw from economic theory or other disciplines (ICAEW, 2010; Maroun, 2017). The BM concept is used by accountants mainly after the development of Integrated Reporting (IR), a new form of reporting designed to account for the transformation (increase or decrease) of six types of capital, identified as inputs to (and also outputs of) a company's BM (Aureli et al., 2020). Reporting the company BM in IR helps stakeholders to understand "the company story" and assess the sustainability of business models and of the whole company (Michalak et al., 2017).

The reluctance of accounting to deal with BM is due to the fact that decades of BM literature that has flourished in the managerial literature has stressed customers' value creation as the core of BM design, while accounting focuses on value creation for shareholders (Bourguignon, 2005; Roslender & Nielsen, 2018). In addition, managerial literature equally examines value creation, value delivery, and value capture. On the contrary, accounting helps explain how the company captures value for shareholders (which represent the main addressees of corporate communication). Coherently, IRs prepared by accountants mainly describe company business models in terms of outcomes generated, disregarding information on inputs and business activities and processes (Melloni et al., 2016).

As Haslam et al. (2015) state, a proper disclosure of a company BM requires a modification in the accounting conceptual framework that governs the purpose of financial disclosure. The purpose should change from communicating value creation for shareholders to show the positive influence of company activities on various stakeholders such as customers, suppliers, local communities, employees and investors (Michalak et al., 2017). Some accounting researchers explicitly acknowledge the potential of BM disclosure in assessing company value creation for multiple stakeholders as demonstrated by the case of Apple Inc (Lehman & Haslam, 2013), where the analysis of the BM led to the understanding that the company's value capture involved the displacement of costs to and margin capture from suppliers, which is very risky and not sustainable. Similarly, Bini et al. (2018) show that BM disclosure may reveal how companies create value from an economic, social, and environmental perspective, contributing to understand a company's engagement in sustainability.

Managerial accounting is surely more familiar with the concept of value creation (Bourguignon, 2005), which is the basis of the BM concept (Nielsen & Roslender, 2015). Activity-based costing is one of the most popular means of implementing customer value in organizations (Bourguignon, 2005). Activity-based management, target costing, and customer-oriented performance measurement deal with the creation of customer value. Moreover, as highlighted by previous literature, management accounting supports organizational changes usually associated with BM modification (Velu & Stiles, 2013). The problem is that a shift to more sustainable BMs demands experimentation and investments that cannot be decided based on deterministic financial concepts, such as net present value. Adopting a sustainable BM (and not doing mere greenwashing practices) requires different reasoning and accounting tools. Accounting is a cognitive model that offers an economic representation of reality and therefore should be in line with actual business operations (Fig. 1.1).

Regarding this aspect, Metting (2016) introduces a framework that identifies three possible scenarios of accounting changes associated with any kind of BM transformation. One approach is to make small changes in the company processes (defined as first-level changes) and after every change immediately adapt management

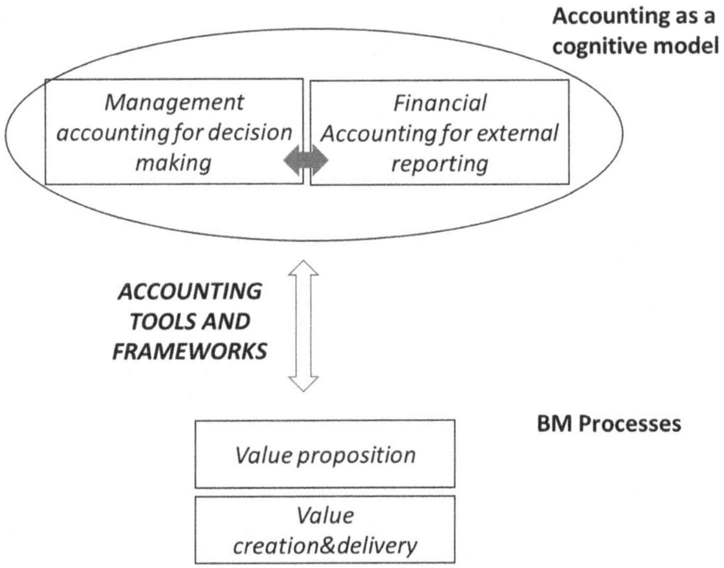

Fig. 1.1 Relationship between BM's elements and accounting

accounting (defined as a second-level change). This iterative approach reduces the size and duration of conceptual representational gaps, but it is possible only if information systems are flexible (as in smaller firms) and when the change is limited to some aspects of the BM. A second approach is to adopt a sequential pattern, which means keeping management accounting constant in the long term, until the new BM is in place. This approach avoids pressures on information systems to change and avoids extensive discussion on how accounting should improve to represent the reality, so that all resources are dedicated to the business processes. The third approach is more radical and consists in changing management accounting before the BM, i.e. using accounting to drive the change. This applies to companies with visionary leaders that conceive future BMs and introduce new KPIs, reporting structures, or measurement tools to create cognitive flexibility and catalyse changes.

1.3 Methodology

The analysis involves a qualitative approach (Flick, 2009) and relies on a single case study methodology (Yin, 2018; Siggelkow, 2007), which is preferable when there is a new phenomenon to be explored (Eisenhardt & Graebner, 2007) and the research questions focus on "how" a phenomenon takes place. In addition, this research strategy is in line with previous studies that have conducted either single or multiple case studies (Paiola et al., 2021; Lippolis et al., 2023).

The case study is explorative by nature. This can be considered appropriate when aiming at a better understanding of a variety of aspects involved in the analysis. We believe that our instrumental case (Stake, 1998) can facilitate the understanding of some more general issues through small sample research, mainly when studying a phenomenon at its early stage.

Furthermore, we have chosen this approach because it allows us to implement a combination of different techniques of analysis, which is necessary when dealing with complex and variable information and data sources (Hartley, 1994).

To ensure greater accuracy, credibility, and validity (Creswell & Tashakkori, 2007), hence bolstering the reliability of the case study findings, three principles of data collection were employed: (a) using multiple sources of data/evidence; (b) creating a database, which is a formal assembly of evidence distinct from the final case study report, assisting the researcher in organizing and documenting the data collected; and (c) maintaining a chain of evidence explicitly linking the questions asked, the data collected, and the conclusions drawn (Yin, 2009).

The analysis involves a combination of secondary data (an array of company disclosures in the form of integrated reports, press releases, public presentations, impact assessments as required by the law, the corporate website, etc.), as well as primary data, that is, direct interviews undertaken with the CEO of the company analysed. The former are official documents that, as in the study of Poponi et al. (2019), allow for a more comprehensive understanding of company practices. The latter were extremely helpful in understanding the motivations for setting up a BC and an SBM. Interviews were recorded, transcribed, and sent to the interviewee for validation (Voss et al., 2002; Voss, 2010). Following the work of Ferlito and Faraci (2022), we encouraged narrative storytelling about the firm's background and BM to elicit information-rich statements. To better ground the analysis in the business reality, contextual research was also carried out (Whitman & Woszczynski, 2004).

In pursuing reliability and validity of qualitative studies, Patton (1987) advocates the use of triangulation as a way to strengthen a study by combining methods. Johnson (1997) provides a list of strategies including data triangulation (the use of multiple data sources to help understand a phenomenon), methods triangulation (the use of multiple research methods to study a phenomenon), investigator triangulation (the use of multiple researchers in collecting and interpreting data to achieve a greater neutrality from personal opinions, ideas, and beliefs), and theory triangulation (the use of multiple theories and perspectives to help interpret and explain the data). In this study, all the suggested strategies were implemented, with the exception of theory triangulation.

The case study selection is based on a theoretical convenience sampling strategy (Voss, 2010). Italy was selected because it is one of the first EU countries to adopt the BC legal form and there are several studies that have mapped the numbers and practices of BCs. A small-sized company was preferred because SMEs represent the backbone of the Italian economy but are less explored compared to large corporations, in both the BC and the SBM literature. In addition, due to their limited reach and considerable financial and human resource constraints, it is particularly interesting to understand how such smaller businesses can effectively achieve social and environmental goals (Nigri & Del Baldo, 2018; Ferlito & Faraci, 2022).

In detail, Way2Global, an Italian SME, is explored in this chapter. The choice of Way2Global was due to several factors. First of all, this company was established as a BC since its inception when the main owner-entrepreneur decided to start a new venture after a previous bankruptcy. Second, the selection was encouraged by the outstanding effort of this enterprise towards sustainability, encompassing both the BM and the strategies related to disclosure and communication. More precisely, Way2Global has obtained several awards in recent years, which makes it a real best practice. Way2Global publishes its impact assessment (or impact report) as required by the Italian legislation, but also has disclosed an IR since 2021 through its website. The company has also obtained the B Corp certification by the B Lab, gaining, in that context, also an acknowledgement as an Impact Business Model (IBM), that is, when a business makes a positive impact as a way of doing business on one or more of its stakeholders. Such acknowledgement is linked to the governance of Way2Global, how the company runs the business and protects its mission, and its ability to formally consider stakeholders in decision-making through the corporate structure or corporate governing documents.

Last but not least, to gain a full involvement of the management, the selection of this case has been also based on the company's willingness to take part in the study and its expectation of gaining benefits from developing a research network. This attitude guaranteed extensive access and positively contributed to deepening our analysis.

1.4 Case Description and Findings

1.4.1 Description of the Case Study

Way2Global's story is a story of rebirth—the story of a small Italian female start-up. It is a language service provider set up as a BC that wants to contribute to the current challenge of addressing society concerns and uses integrated reporting and non-financial disclosure as a driver for spreading a new culture of sustainability.

Way2Global has been funded as a BC in 2017 by Laura Gori, its CEO, following a previous entrepreneurial experience started in 1988 as Trans-Edit Group. Despite the major disruptions of globalization and digital transformation, Trans-Edit Group grew into one of the top 100 global forces in its industry, but it was at the very peak of its achievements when Laura Gori was overwhelmed by personal problems. She was not able to continue leading its "profit-making machines" and, at the same time, she discovered the word of BCs. She joined the Italian community of BCs to learn more about BCs and this new approach of doing business motivated her to restart from scratch, funding a new enterprise named Way2Global.

In 2018, Way2Global cofounded AssoBenefit (https://assobenefit.org/) to promote and support BCs, before obtaining the B Corp certification in 2019.

Laura Gori describes BCs and Way2Global as follows: "We are visionary, trailblazing triple-bottom-line businesses that have sustainability embedded in our business plan as the backbone of our corporate strategy, [aiming] to restore, renew and grow people, planet, and profit. We are committed to the highest standards of ESG performance and pursue business to the benefit of all stakeholders, workers, community, environment, and customers. We are committed to generating value for the world that outweighs the resources we use to run our business operations as we generate these businesses, which means boldly giving back more to society and the planet than we actually take from them. We strive to act as generations of shared values".

According to Way2Global's vision, being a BC means embedding sustainability and the SDGs of the UN 2030 agenda into the company mission and its business plan. It means taking on a new perspective and starting to measure the value of the business according to its ability to take care of the planet and to respond to the great challenges of humanity, despite being a small enterprise.

The three pillars of Way2Global's mission reported in the documents are Sustainability, Governance, and Digital. This is in line with the three major axes of the next-generation EU: Digital Innovation, the Green New Deal, and Sustainable Governance.

1.4.2 Key Characteristics of the SBM of Way2Global

1.4.2.1 Value Proposition of Way2Global

When asked to describe the BM of Way2Global, Laura Gori reports that "Our unique BM combines the dynamism and innovativeness of a start-up with the solidity and experience of three decades of industry leadership. The BM is designed to merge a strong international vocation with our vision of being a BC and our mission of social re-foundation". Being a BC "is a disruptive paradigm shift in the evolution of business towards a regenerative business model. BCs are a wonderful and perfect solution to respond to the urgent challenges of transforming economy into a more equitable, inclusive and sustainable system" (Laura Gori, CEO of Way2Global).

The company vision and its dual purpose is synthetized by its payoff reported in all documents: "Beyond borders for a better world". They aim to contribute to the advent of a fairer and more inclusive world by offering professional translation services to connect people across borders, languages, and cultures. With "translations that connect", Way2Global offers a lever for being successful across borders to its clients and also promotes understanding and cohesion. Translations are considered as a lever of sustainability and the company uses business to produce common benefits and make the world a better place.

1.4.2.2 Value Delivery

Way2Global creates value for both clients and other key stakeholders, whose relevance is highlighted in red in their impact assessment report (see figure below). Clients are as important as employees, shareholders, linguists (who are professional service providers), the BCs community, other institutional partners, and the environment. Way2Global offers them both tangible and intangible forms of value, from services to knowledge and monetary rewards. Therefore, financial value distribution among selected stakeholder categories is monitored accurately. In Fig. 1.2, a value distribution chart is represented. It is an infographic tool to show how generous an enterprise is in distributing the financial value generated. Having the community of linguists and employees among the key stakeholders, Way2Global hands out 65% of the generated value to them, whereas only 8% of the revenue is distributed to shareholders, and the remaining 4% is reinvested in the company.

Many projects were carried out in 2021 to make value delivery real; here are the main ones:

- Green Translations, that is the creation of the world's first decarbonized translation service
- Language Industry 4.0, to facilitate the advent of AI and technological innovation with social impact, as promoters of Open Innovation, Technology Transfer, and Capacity Building projects for the linguist community and academia, aiming to democratize and make accessible knowledge and resources that are revolutionizing the field (like deep learning, big data, and neural networks)
- Way2Academy, the Open Education project created to retrain the translation community, predominantly female, to the use of new enabling technologies. It was the response of Way2Global to the gender digital gap exacerbated by the pandemic, which places women at risk of disqualification from a market revolutionized by digitalization
- Made in B Italy, a project created to enhance the primacy of Italy as an early adopter of the BC model through the introduction of the B Corp legal form

Female empowerment, gender equality, and inclusivity are important pillars of Way2Global's strategy.

Thus, they participated in the W20 (Women 20) women's engagement group that finalized gender equality instances for the G20, translated and promoted the book *100 Women for All* against gender-based violence, supported the Pink Helmets project for Afghan female refugees, and took part in the Italian B Corp communication campaign "Unlock the Change" to spread the concept of sustainable development. Last but not least, they worked as ambassadors of "The Cities of Women" project, which led in March 2022 to the Dubai Charter and the book *Made in B Italy* delivered to the EXPO Dubai to promote the BC model as a lever for women's empowerment and entrepreneurship.

Stakeholders' engagement is another key activity to ensure value delivery. "We are constantly involved in engaging all stakeholders to identify, first, and

Fig. 1.2 Way2Global stakeholders and value distribution (sourced from Way2Global 2021 IR, pp. 17 and 34)

communicate, then, what they perceive as relevant information. A transition towards sustainable business starts by measuring your impact, but continues by adopting non-financial disclosure and, more precisely, IR tools in our case" (Laura Gori, CEO of Way2Global). Coherently, all the value-creating projects mentioned above have been clearly described in their IR.

1.4.2.3 Value Capture

As said, Way2Global uses integrated reporting as a driver for spreading a new culture of sustainability in society and enhancing the engagement with any subject interested in sustainability. They implement the IIRC framework and its six-capital model to assess the value created by their business.

Way2Global actually aims to increase the value of all capitals (not only financial capital for shareholders) linked to different stakeholders' needs, according to Laura Gori. The CEO believes that Way2Global's BM generates several benefits:

- Efficiency, thanks to the collaborators' motivation
- Alliance with suppliers and customers
- Better positioning/reputation
- Innovativeness

These benefits generate economic value, as demonstrated by the increase in financial capital. At the same time, other types of capital flourished, which are related to different stakeholders needs. "Way2Global is able to capture economic value for the business while maintaining or regenerating natural, social, and economic capitals for other subjects beyond the boundaries of our organization" (Laura Gori, CEO of Way2Global).

Figure 1.3 shows how Way2Global business was able to create value in terms of all six types of capital as built in the IR framework, to the benefit of all stakeholders. In 2021, the company was able to increase the number of satisfied customers up to 374 (relational capital) while promoting and facilitating remote working to all

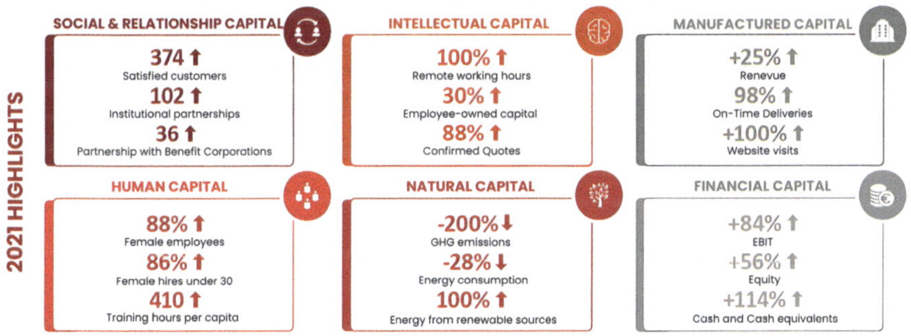

Fig. 1.3 Regeneration of Way2Global's six types of capital (sourced from Way2Global 2021 IR, p. 3)

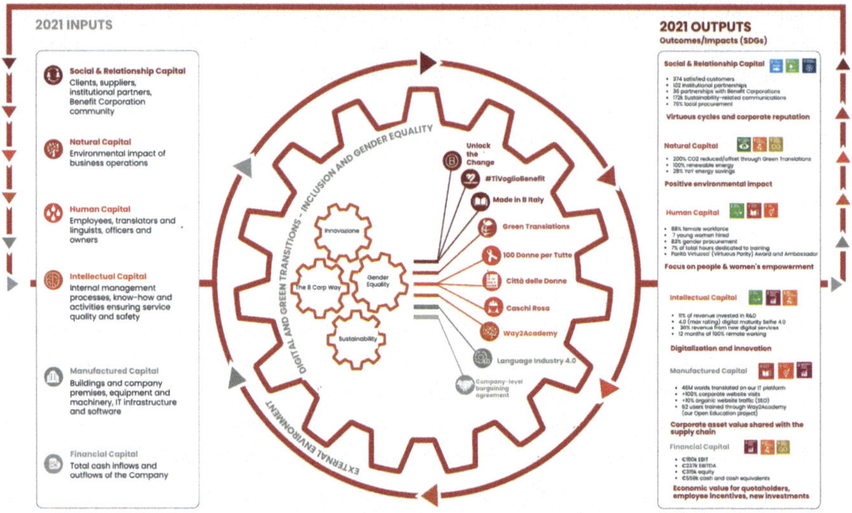

Fig. 1.4 The Way2Global SBM and its linkages with SDGs (sourced from Way2Global IR of 2021, p. 28)

employees (100%). In so doing, the latter could enjoy a better work-life balance (intellectual capital). Employees are key stakeholders to the company. In addition, it was able to raise the number of female and young workers (human capital). With reference to environmental capital, the company achieved a reduction of greenhouse gases emissions by 200% and energy used by 28%, with 100% of total energy used coming from renewable sources. Finally, the company was able to increase its earnings before interest and taxes by 84% (financial capital). The largely satisfactory financial performance testifies to how the sustainability orientation also leverages the competitive advantage gained by the company (Cantele & Zardini, 2018). This addresses the concern about BCs' capability to deliver value to all stakeholders without compromising value creation for shareholders.

Figure 1.4 provides evidence of Way2Global commitment to both maintaining and strengthening all forms of capital. The SBM of Way2Global depicted in the figure also highlights the connection among capital exploitation, the stakeholders' needs addressed, and their broader answer to calls from society for sustainable development (showing how the outputs generated thanks to their SBM are linked to the SDGs).

1.4.3 *The Value of Reporting*

According to Laura Gori, measuring and reporting business activities and their impacts is a key ingredient for implementing a really sustainable business. She believes that the first step to adopt a regenerative change is to start measuring: "If you don't measure, you can't improve as you have no baseline to start from. At

Way2Global, we started our journey into BCs drafting the annual impact report, as required by the Italian legislation, and the B impact assessment, i.e. the free digital online tool offered by B-Lab to help businesses evaluate their positive impact in terms of governance, as well as on workers, communities, environment, and customers".

The following step undertaken by Way2Global was towards IR. They opted for a gradual approach. First, the company appointed an impact manager responsible for monitoring their ESG compliance. Second, they drafted an annual impact evaluation report to be published on the corporate website and to be made available to all stakeholders. Third, Laura Gori in person attended an executive education course in 2020 to develop a skill set in integrated thinking, value creation, accountable strategic leadership, civil economy, and non-financial disclosure. After having passed a written and oral exam, she gained the certification of Chief Value Officer[1] from Bureau Veritas and with her team, she was able to draft the first IR of Way2Global. The IR is now prepared annually and embeds the impact report. For a small company like Way2Global, this also means voluntarily complying with the new requirements of the EU CSR Directive.

The reporting journey favoured greater strategic awareness. The process of setting the impact assessment and the IR in place helped the company to think holistically and put adequate attention to all stakeholders. "Each year we go through a process that proactively considers the needs of anyone that has a stake in our organization. We focus on the group of stakeholders who are considered the most relevant in terms of fostering connections, trust and confidence and whom we aim at and buy in for organisational initiatives".

1.4.4 Findings and Discussion

From the case analysis, some interesting evidence emerged.

First, the BC status and how the funding entrepreneur conceives the meaning and role of being a BC strongly affect the key elements of the BM. According to the BMfS' elements theorized by Freudenreich et al. (2020), Way2Global offers multiple value propositions (or a "value portfolio") to several stakeholders as its goal is to help clients expand their business internationally while creating relations and connections among different subjects that favour sustainable development at the same time. Several stakeholders are addressed by Way2Global with its business, not only customers, but also service providers (professional partners), employees, and the community at large.

---

[1]In Italy, Cepas-Bureau Veritas certifies the accomplishment of competences and knowledge to operate as "Chief Value Officer e Valutatore d'Impatto"; this is the professional profile (manager or consultant) who creates the organizational conditions for drafting sustainability or integrated reports. They collect the necessary data and take care of the creation and communication processes.

Its value creation process is grounded on the collaboration with employees and service providers (mainly professional translators). Value is created with them and for them because internal activities and supply–chain relations are designed to offer them knowledge, well-being, financial security, health, support, protection, and work-life balance. The four key pillars (Innovation, Gender equality, Sustainability, and what they call "the B Corp way") that inform internal processes pave the way for several organizational programmes (e.g. "Green translations", "Way2Academy") that operationalisze and deliver concrete and material value to employees, customers, suppliers, and also local community. As theorized by Schaltegger et al. (2016a), there are different kinds of value exchanged between the company and its stakeholders. In this case, stakeholders are both recipients and co-creators of value in a joint value creation process, which is in line with stakeholder theory. Operations and processes generate economic value for the business itself while respecting and strengthening other forms of capital, more precisely, social, human, and intellectual capital, as demonstrated by the metrics reported in the company's IR.

Second, our case study shows that the dual purpose embedded in the BC status is the greatest lever for designing a BM in light of sustainability; it is stronger than the B Corp certification process. "The double bottom line" focusing on profit and social benefit (Wilburn & Wilburn, 2014) informs the company activities in light of principles of social responsibility, while the path for being certified as a B Corp merely favours a more fine-grained reflection on existing processes. Previous studies have demonstrated that the requirements necessary for the B Corp certification activate new business pathways and push companies to change or revise their BM in light of sustainability and circular economy (Poponi et al., 2019). However, the "B Corp effect" might be relevant only or mainly in traditional for-profit businesses that become aware of social responsibility and start to rebalance their mission and business activities to purse both profit and non-profit objectives during the certification process. BCs already have the twofold aim of reconciling business performances (economic and financial) with ethical behaviour.

In conclusion, it can be stated that BCs are born with missions and strategies oriented to social and environmental aspects and, therefore, it is almost natural for them to include structures and procedures in business practices that facilitate CSR. Assessing and reporting their results is compulsory (via the yearly impact assessment), and this process helps them to revise and improve. BCs are "walk-and-talk" type of organizations (Schoeneborn et al., 2020). While SMEs often implement strategies, structures, and procedures in their core business processes that facilitate CSR—walk practices—but are not able to prepare documents and disclose to customers and other stakeholders their impacts—talk practices—(Wickert et al., 2016), BCs effectively implement and disclose their ESG practices over time. Talk practices mainly operate in a recursive logic, informing and shaping walk initiatives, and then providing feedback to influence future practices (Schons & Steinmeier, 2016; Schoeneborn et al., 2020).

Contrary to the stream of studies stating that pressures from external stakeholders have significant impacts on the implementation of an SBM, our study supports the assumption of Ferlito and Faraci (2022) that benefit corporations have an internally driven proactive behaviour towards sustainability. Our case study is particularly illustrative since in the language service sector there is no evidence of striking negative environmental and social impacts contested by the society. Adopting an SBM came from the company's core values.

1.5 Concluding Remarks

Our study investigates how distinctive characteristics of BCs affect the elements of their BM in terms of sustainability orientation with specific reference to the case of small businesses. Relying on the assessment criteria for SBMs theorized by Freudenreich et al. (2020) and subsequently further developed by Schaltegger et al. (2016a), we found that BCs' dual purpose is strongly related to a company's vision and mission; they function together as guidelines in the design of all BMs' elements, from value creation to value delivery and value capture.

From a theoretical standpoint, this study contributes to the scant existing literature about SBMs and, more precisely, on BMs design for BCs. According to Kirst et al. (2021), research on BCs related to Italian cases is limited to a few papers by only a few authors. In addition, this study provides insights to respond to concerns in the academic literature about BCs' capability to deliver value to all stakeholders without compromising value creation for shareholders. The originality of this study relies on the limitations of previous studies that take for granted that the purpose of creating a "general public benefit" embedded in BCs makes them sustainable entities, without investigating how internal processes and business elements are affected. Our chapter is an attempt to make explicit how the hybrid mission of BCs shapes their BMs in a way that creates a material positive impact on society and the environment.

As for practical implications, this study provides operators with a "best practice" that might inspire managers and entrepreneurs of SMEs, where implementing sustainable practices is particularly challenging, because of resource constraints, cultural issues, and lack of knowledge and competence, to name a few. In addition, Way2Global is an interesting case for teaching purposes, both in the BM and the sustainability reporting disciplines.

However, this study is not free of limitations. Being based on a single case study, the findings of the study may suffer from generalizability. Nevertheless, results are likely to have a wider applicability, especially in the SMEs' domain, as well as in BCs.

Acknowledgements The authors would like to thank Laura Gori, CEO of Way 2Global, for her support and assistance in data collection, which made the study possible.

References

Amit, R., & Zott, C. (2001). Value creation in e-business. *Strategic Management Journal, 22*(6–7), 493–520.

Aureli, S., Del Baldo, M., Lombardi, R., & Nappo, F. (2020). Nonfinancial reporting regulation and challenges in sustainability disclosure and corporate governance practices. *Business Strategy and the Environment, 29*(6), 2392–2403.

Bakos, J., Siu, M., Orengo, A., & Kasiri, N. (2020). An analysis of environmental sustainability in small & medium-sized enterprises: Patterns and trends. *Business Strategy and the Environment, 29*(3), 1285–1296.

Bartolini, M., Aureli, S., & Tinti, S. (2023). Resilience to Covid-19 pandemic crisis as Benefit Corporation – The case of an Italian SME. *Piccola Impresa Small Business, 1*, 109–134. https://doi.org/10.14596/pisb.3594

Battilana, J., & Lee, M. (2014). Advancing research on hybrid organizing - Insights from the study of social enterprises. *Academy of Management Annals, 8*(1), 397–441.

Baudot, L., Dillard, J., & Pencle, N. (2019). The emergence of benefit corporations: A cautionary tale. *Critical Perspectives on Accounting, 67*, 102073. https://doi.org/10.1016/j.cpa.2019.01.005

Baudot, L., Dillard, J., & Pencle, N. (2020). Hybrid organizations and an ethic of accountability: The role of accountability systems in constructing responsible hybridity. *Accounting, Auditing & Accountability Journal, 35*(3), 598–626.

Beattie, V., & Smith, S. J. (2013). Value creation and business models: Refocusing the intellectual capital debate. *The British Accounting Review, 45*(4), 243–254.

Biloslavo, R., Bagnoli, C., Massaro, M., & Cosentino, A. (2020). Business model transformation toward sustainability: The impact of legitimation. *Management Decision, 58*(8), 1643–1662.

Bini, L., Bellucci, M., & Giunta, F. (2018). Integrating sustainability in business model disclosure: Evidence from the UK mining industry. *Journal of Cleaner Production, 171*, 1161–1170.

Bocken, N. (2021). Sustainable business models. In W. Leal Filho, A. M. Azul, L. Brandli, A. Lange Salvia, & T. Wall (Eds.), *Decent work and economic growth. Encyclopedia of the UN Sustainable Development Goals*. Springer.

Bocken, N. M. P., Short, S. W., Rana, P., & Evans, S. (2014). A literature and practice review to develop sustainable business model archetypes. *Journal of Cleaner Production, 65*, 42–56.

Boons, F., & Lüdeke-Freund, F. (2013). Business models for sustainable innovation: State-of-the-art and steps towards a research agenda. *Journal of Cleaner Production, 45*, 9–19.

Bourguignon, A. (2005). Management accounting and value creation: The profit and loss of reification. *Critical Perspectives on Accounting, 16*(4), 353–389.

Burger-Helmchen, T., & Siegel, E. J. (2020). Some thoughts On CSR in relation to B Corp Labels. *Entrepreneurship Research Journal, 10*(4), 20200231.

Cantele, S., & Zardini, A. (2018). Is sustainability a competitive advantage for small businesses? An empirical analysis of possible mediators in the sustainability–financial performance relationship. *Journal of Cleaner Production, 182*, 166–176.

Casadesus-Masanell, R., & Ricart, J. E. (2010). From strategy to business models and onto tactics. *Long Range Planning, 43*(2–3), 195–215.

Castellini, M., Marzano, M., & Riso, V. (2019). How B-Corporations' mobilize IC (unawares) to create value. Evidence from the Italian ecosystem. *Corporate governance e scenari di settore delle imprese*, 82–88.

Cavalcante, S., Kesting, P., & Ulhøi, J. (2011). Business model dynamics and innovation: (re) establishing the missing linkages. *Management Decision, 49*(8), 1327–1342.

Charles, O. H., Jr., Schmidheiny, S., & Watts, P. (2017). *Walking the talk: The business case for sustainable development*. Routledge.

Chesbrough, H., & Rosenbloom, R. S. (2002). The role of the business model in capturing value from innovation: Evidence from Xerox Corporation's technology spin-off companies. *Industrial and Corporate Change, 11*(3), 529–555.

Crane, A., McWilliams, A., Matten, D., Moon, J., & Siegel, D. S. (Eds.). (2008). *The Oxford handbook of corporate social responsibility*. OUP.

Creswell, J. W., & Tashakkori, A. (2007). Differing perspectives on mixed methods research. *Journal of Mixed Methods Research, 1*(4), 303–308.

Dasanayaka, C. H., Gunarathne, N., Murphy, D. F., & Nagirikandalage, P. (2022). Triggers for and barriers to the adoption of environmental management practices by small and medium-sized enterprises: A critical review. *Corporate Social Responsibility and Environmental Management, 29*(4), 749–764.

De Lange, D. E. (2017). Start-up sustainability: An insurmountable cost or a life-giving investment? *Journal of Cleaner Production, 156*, 838–854.

Dupire, M., & M'Zali, B. (2018). CSR strategies in response to competitive pressures. *Journal of Business Ethics, 148*, 603–623.

Ebrahim, A., Battilana, J., & Mair, J. (2014). The governance of social enterprises: Mission drift and accountability challenges in hybrid organizations. *Research in Organizational Behavior, 34*, 81–100.

Eisenhardt, K. M., & Graebner, M. E. (2007). Theory building from cases: Opportunities and challenges. *Academy of Management Journal, 50*(1), 25–32.

Ferlito, R., & Faraci, R. (2022). Sustainable Hybrid Business Model of Benefit Corporation: The Case of an Italian Film Production Company. *Sustainability, 14*(10), 5836. https://doi.org/10.3390/su14105836

Flick, U. (2009). *An introduction to qualitative research*. Sage Publications.

Foss, N. J., & Saebi, T. (2017). Fifteen years of research on business model innovation: How far have we come, and where should we go? *Journal of Management, 43*(1), 200–227.

Freudenreich, B., Lüdeke-Freund, F., & Schaltegger, S. (2020). A stakeholder theory perspective on business models: Value creation for sustainability. *Journal of Business Ethics, 166*, 3–18. https://doi.org/10.1007/s10551-019-04112-z

Frishammar, J., & Parida, V. (2019). Circular business model transformation: A roadmap for incumbent firms. *California Management Review, 61*(2), 5–29. https://doi.org/10.1177/0008125618811926

Galli, D., Torelli, R., & Tibiletti, V. (2021). Signaling the adoption of the benefit corporation model: A step towards transparency. *Sustainability, 13*(12), 6967.

Gamble, E. N., Parker, S. C., & Moroz, P. W. (2020). Measuring the integration of social and environmental missions in hybrid organizations. *Journal of Business Ethics, 167*, 271–284.

Garriga, E. (2014). Beyond stakeholder utility function: Stakeholder capability in the value creation process. *Journal of Business Ethics, 120*, 489–507.

Gazzola, P., Grechi, D., Ossola, P., & Pavione, E. (2019). Certified benefit corporations as a new way to make sustainable business: The Italian example. *Corporate Social Responsibility and Environmental Management, 26*(6), 1435 1445.

Geissdoerfer, M., Vladimirova, D., & Evans, S. (2018). Sustainable business model innovation: A review. *Journal of Cleaner Production, 198*, 104–416.

Grassl, W. (2012). Business models of social enterprise: A design approach to hybridity. *ACRN Journal of entrepreneurship Perspectives, 1*(1), 37–60.

Hacklin, F., Björkdahl, J., & Wallin, M. W. (2018). Strategies for business model innovation: How firms reel in migrating value. *Long Range Planning, 51*(1), 82–110.

Hartley, J. (1994). Case studies in organisational research. In C. Cassell & G. Symon (Eds.), *Qualitative methods in organisational research* (pp. 209–216). Sage.

Haslam, C. J., Tsitsianis, N., Andersson, T., & Gleadle, P. (2015). Accounting for business models: Increasing the visibility of stakeholders. *Journal of Business Models, 3*(1), 62–80.

Hiller, J. S. (2013). The benefit corporation and social responsibility. *Journal of Business Ethics, 118*(2), 287–301.

Hörisch, J., Freeman, R. E., & Schaltegger, S. (2014). Applying stakeholder theory in sustainability management: Links, similarities, dissimilarities, and a conceptual framework. *Organization & Environment, 27*(4), 328–346.

ICAEW. (2010). Business models in accounting: The theory of the firm and financial reporting. Retrieved November 1, 2020, from http://www.icaew.com/~/media/corporate/files/technical/financial%20reporting/information%20for%20better%20markets/bmia%20published%20report.ashx

Johnson, M. W., Christensen, C. M., & Kagermann, H. (2008). Reinventing your business model. *Harvard Business Review, 86*(12), 50–59.

Johnson, R. B. (1997). Examining the validity structure of qualitative research. *Education, 118*(2), 282–292.

Karuppiah, K., Sankaranarayanan, B., & Ali, S. M. (2023). A systematic review of sustainable business models: Opportunities, challenges, and future research directions. *Decision Analytics Journal*, 100272.

Kirst, R. W., Borchardt, M., de Carvalho, M. N. M., & Pereira, G. M. (2021). Best of the world or better for the world? A systematic literature review on benefit corporations and certified B corporations contribution to sustainable development. *Corporate Social Responsibility and Environmental Management, 28*, 1822–1839.

Kurucz, E. C., Colbert, B. A., Lüdeke-Freund, F., Upward, A., & Willard, B. (2017). Relational leadership for strategic sustainability: Practices and capabilities to advance the design and assessment of sustainable business models. *Journal of Cleaner Production, 140*, 189–204.

Lehman, G., & Haslam, C. (2013). Accounting for the Apple Inc business model: Corporate value capture and dysfunctional economic and social consequences. *Accounting Forum, 37*(4), 245–248.

Lippolis, S., Ruggieri, A., & Leopizzi, R. (2023). Open Innovation for sustainable transition: The case of Enel "Open Power". *Business Strategy and the Environment, 32*(7), 4202–4216.

Liute, A., & De Giacomo, M. R. (2022). The environmental performance of UK-based B Corp companies: An analysis based on the triple bottom line approach. *Business Strategy and the Environment, 31*(3), 810–827.

Lozano, R. (2018). Sustainable business models: Providing a more holistic perspective. *Business Strategy and the Environment, 27*(8), 1159–1166.

Lüdeke-Freund, F., & Dembek, K. (2017). Sustainable business model research and practice: Emerging field or passing fancy? *Journal of Cleaner Production, 168*, 1668–1678.

Lüdeke-Freund, F., Gold, S., & Bocken, N. M. P. (2019). A review and typology of circular economy business model patterns. *Journal of Industrial Ecology, 23*(1), 36–61.

Marchini, P. L., Tibiletti, V., Fellegara, A. M., & Mazza, T. (2023). Pursuing a strategy of 'common benefit' in business: The adoption of the benefit corporation model in Italy. *Business Strategy and the Environment, 32*(4), 1481–1503.

Markides, C. C. (2013). Business model innovation: What can the ambidexterity literature teach us? *Academy of Management Perspectives, 27*(4), 313–323.

Maroun, W. (2017). Accounting for revenue using an accountability and business model framework: The case of the South African Institute of Chartered Accountants' professional examinations. *South African Journal of Accounting Research, 31*(3), 240–254.

McKinsey. (2022). COVID-19: Implications for business, April 13, 2022 | Executive Briefing. https://www.mckinsey.com/capabilities/risk-and-resilience/our-insights/covid-19-implications-for-business

Melloni, G., Stacchezzini, R., & Lai, A. (2016). The tone of business model disclosure: An impression management analysis of the integrated reports. *Journal of Management and Governance, 20*(2), 295–320.

Metting, T. (2016). Reference lost – First explorations on the use of MACS in business model transformation. *Paper presented at the Conference 'Digital Enterprise Computing' (DEC) 2016, Böblingen, Germany.*

Michalak, J., Rimmel, G., Beusch, P., & Jonäll, K. (2017). Business model disclosures in corporate reports. *Journal of Business Models, 5*(1), 51–73.

Mion, G., & Loza Adaui, C. R. (2020). Understanding the purpose of benefit corporations: An empirical study on the Italian case. *International Journal of Corporate Social Responsibility, 5*(1).

Mion, G., Loza Adaui, C. R., & Bonfanti, A. (2021). Characterizing the mission statements of benefit corporations: Empirical evidence from Italy. *Business Strategy and the Environment, 30*, 1–13.

Morris, M., Schindehutte, M., & Allen, J. (2005). The entrepreneur's business model: Toward a unified perspective. *Journal of Business Research, 58*(6), 726–735.

Muñoz, P., Cacciotti, G., & Cohen, B. (2018). The double-edged sword of purpose-driven behavior in sustainable venturing. *Journal of Business Venturing, 33*(2), 149–178.

Nidumolu, R., Prahalad, C. K., & Rangaswami, M. R. (2009). Why sustainability is now the key driver of innovation. *Harvard Business Review, 87*(9), 56–64.

Nielsen, C., & Roslender, R. (2015). Enhancing financial reporting: The contribution of business models. *The British Accounting Review, 47*(3), 262–274.

Nigri, G., & Del Baldo, M. (2018). Sustainability reporting and performance measurement systems: How do small-and medium-sized benefit corporations manage integration? *Sustainability, 10*(12), 4499.

Nosratabadi, S., Mosavi, A., Shamshirband, S., Zavadskas, E. K., Rakotonirainy, A., & Chau, K. W. (2019). Sustainable business models: A review. *Sustainability, 11*(6), 1663.

Ocasio, W., & Radoynovska, N. (2016). Strategy and commitments to institutional logics: Organizational heterogeneity in business models and governance. *Strategic Organization, 14*, 287–309.

OECD. (2020). COVID-19 and Responsible Business Conduct. https://www.oecd.org/coronavirus/policy-responses/covid-19-and-responsible-business-conduct-02150b06/

Osterwalder, A., & Pigneur, Y. (2010). *Business model generation: A handbook for visionaries, game changers, and challengers* (Vol. 1). John Wiley & Sons.

Paiola, M., Schiavone, F., Grandinetti, R., & Chen, J. (2021). Digital servitization and sustainability through networking: Some evidences from IoT-based business models. *Journal of Business Research, 132*, 507–516.

Patton, M. Q. (1987). *How to use qualitative methods in evaluation*. Sage.

Pedersen, E. R. G., Gwozdz, W., & Hvass, K. K. (2018). Exploring the relationship between business model innovation, corporate sustainability, and organizational values within the fashion industry. *Journal of Business Ethics, 149*, 267–284.

Pieroni, M. P., McAloone, T. C., & Pigosso, D. C. (2019). Business model innovation for circular economy and sustainability: A review of approaches. *Journal of Cleaner Production, 215*, 198–216.

Poponi, S., Colantoni, A., Cividino, S. R., & Mosconi, E. M. (2019). The stakeholders' perspective within the B corp certification for a circular approach. *Sustainability, 11*(6), 1584.

Rawhouser, H., Cummings, M., & Crane, A. (2015). Benefit corporation legislation and the emergence of a social hybrid category. *California Management Review, 57*, 13–35.

Retolaza, J. L., Ruiz, M., & San-Jose, L. (2009). CSR in business start-ups: An application method for stakeholder engagement. *Corporate Social Responsibility and Environmental Management, 16*, 324–336.

Roslender, R., & Nielsen, C. (2018). Accounting through the business model. *Journal of Business Models, 6*(2), 78–83.

Schaltegger, S., Hansen, E. G., & Lüdeke-Freund, F. (2016a). Business models for sustainability: Origins, present research, and future avenues. *Organization & Environment, 29*(1), 3–10.

Schaltegger, S., Lüdeke-Freund, F., & Hansen, E. G. (2012). Business cases for sustainability: The role of business model innovation for corporate sustainability. *International Journal of Innovation and Sustainable Development, 6*(2), 95–119.

Schaltegger, S., Lüdeke-Freund, F., & Hansen, E. G. (2016b). Business models for sustainability: A co-evolutionary analysis of sustainable entrepreneurship, innovation, and transformation. *Organization & Environment, 29*(3), 264–289.

Schneider, T., & Sachs, S. (2017). The impact of stakeholder identities on value creation in issue-based stakeholder networks. *Journal of Business Ethics, 144*, 41–57.

Schoeneborn, D., Morsing, M., & Crane, A. (2020). Formative perspectives on the relation between CSR communication and CSR practices: Pathways for walking, talking, and t (w) alking. *Business & Society, 59*(1), 5–33.
Schons, L., & Steinmeier, M. (2016). Walk the talk? How symbolic and substantive CSR actions affect firm performance depending on stakeholder proximity. *Corporate Social Responsibility and Environmental Management, 23*(6), 358–372.
Siggelkow, N. (2007). Persuasion with case studies. *Academy of Management Journal, 50*(1), 20–24.
Stake, R. (1998). Case studies. In N. Denzin & Y. Lincoln (Eds.), *Strategies of qualitative inquiry* (pp. 88–90). Sage.
Stubbs, W., & Cocklin, C. (2008). Conceptualizing a "sustainability business model". *Organization & Environment, 2*(21), 103–127.
Teece, D. (2010). Business models, business strategy and innovation. *Long Range Planning, 43*(2–3), 172–194.
UN -United Nations- (2015). https://sustainabledevelopment.un.org/ and https://sdgs.un.org/partnerships
Ünal, E., Urbinati, A., Chiaroni, D., & Manzini, R. (2019). Value creation in circular business models: The case of a US small medium enterprise in the building sector. *Resources, Conservation and Recycling, 146*, 291–307.
Upward, A., & Jones, P. (2016). An ontology for strongly sustainable business models: Defining an enterprise framework compatible with natural and social science. *Organization & Environment, 29*, 97–123.
Urbinati, A., Chiaroni, D., & Chiesa, V. (2017). Towards a new taxonomy of circular economy business models. *Journal of Cleaner Production, 168*, 487–498.
Velu, C., & Stiles, P. (2013). Managing decision-making and cannibalization for parallel business models. *Long Range Planning, 46*(6), 443–458.
Voinea, C. L., Logger, M., Rauf, F., & Roijakkers, N. (2019). Drivers for sustainable business models in start-ups: Multiple case studies. *Sustainability, 11*(24), 6884.
Voss, C. (2010). Case research in operations management. In *Researching operations management* (pp. 176–209). Routledge.
Voss, C., Tsikriktsis, N., & Frohlich, M. (2002). Case research in operations management. *International Journal of Operations & Production Management, 22*, 195–219. https://doi.org/10.1108/01443570210414329
Wells, P. E. (2013). *Business models for sustainability*. Edward Elgar Publishing.
Whitman, M. E., & Woszczynski, A. B. (2004). Exemplary works on information systems research. In M. Whitman & A. Woszczynski (Eds.), *The handbook of information systems research* (pp. 1–14). IGI Global. https://doi.org/10.4018/978-1-59140-144-5
Wickert, C., Scherer, A. G., & Spence, L. J. (2016). Walking and talking corporate social responsibility: Implications of firm size and organizational cost. *Journal of Management Studies, 53*(7), 1169–1196.
Wilburn, K., & Wilburn, R. (2014). The double bottom line: Profit and social benefit. *Business Horizons, 57*(1), 11–20.
Yin, R. K. (2009). *Case study research. Design and methods* (4th ed.). Sage.
Yin, R. K. (2018). *Case study research and applications: Design and methods* (6th ed.). Sage.
Yunus, M., Moingeon, B., & Lehmann-Ortega, L. (2010). Building social business models: Lessons from the Grameen Experience. *Long Range Planning, 43*, 308–325.
Zott, C., Amit, R., & Massa, L. (2011). The business model: Recent developments and future research. *Journal of Management, 37*(4), 1019–1042.

Chapter 2
The Relationship Between Mission Statements and ESG

Silvia Cervi and Emiliano Di Carlo

2.1 Introduction

"I wanted to go back to the very genesis of this company: [. . .] In '92, we used to talk even about our mission – for example as having a PC in every home and desk. [. . .] We had more or less achieved it. Then what? What's next? [. . .] Our mission of empowering every person and every organisation on the planet to achieve more can't be just a set of words. It has to in some sense capture the very essence of who we are in all of the decisions we make".[1] These are words of Satya Nadella, Microsoft's CEO, who attributes the company's turnaround to a renewed focus on its purpose. He assesses that the sense of purpose in mission and culture are two main pillars for companies.

As Drucker states, "A business is not defined by its name, statutes, or articles of incorporation. It is defined by the business mission [. . .]. Only a clear definition of the mission and purpose of the organisation makes possible clear and realistic business objectives" (1973, pp. 115–122). He defines the mission statement as the strategical element through which a firm sets goals, takes decisions, and organizes resources, managing for a successful performance.

> A corporate mission consistent with the principle of the common good becomes a practical way of introducing business ethics at the top of a company (Melé, 2009).

Santos et al. (2015) analyse the importance of social enterprises in the actual corporate scenario: "Welcome to a world where business requirements meet

[1] https://www.cnet.com/tech/tech-industry/microsofts-ceo-on-helping-a-faded-legend-find-a-sense-of-purpose/.

S. Cervi (✉) · E. Di Carlo
University of Rome Tor Vergata (Department of Management and Law), Rome, Italy
e-mail: silvia.cervi@uniroma2.it; dicarloe@uniroma2.it

N. Castellano et al. (eds.), *Environmental, Social, Governance (ESG)*, SIDREA Series in Accounting and Business Administration,
https://doi.org/10.1007/978-3-031-76618-3_2

increasing societal demands. Many executives have become keenly aware over the last decades that the business of their business may have to be more than business, since they are asked to address an ever stronger set of societal expectations". The role of the mission statement[2] is almost clear for practitioners and academics (Pearce, 1982; Pearce & David, 1987; Powers, 2012). It is considered an important strategic means companies must define and through which they communicate their purpose (King & Cleland, 1979; Pearce, 1982).

The actual debate about corporate purpose rounds on the awareness that companies have a social role to respect, and their value creation depends not only on economic results but also on social and environmental issues. Sustainable and economic aspects of the business must be balanced to guarantee the survival and growth of companies (Coda, 1988). They act responsibly only if they focus on the well-being of the communities in which they live and operate (De Woot, 2017). The growing awareness about the social role of companies pushes many scholars to focus on internal stakeholders' participation in the mission development process (Bart & Baetz, 1998). In addition, companies being aware that environmental, social, and governance (ESG) factors influence reputation and performance pay increasing attention to ESG issues and modify purpose and mission statements (Carroll, 1991; Coelho et al., 2003; Avi-Yonah, 2005). Consequently, the need to communicate their social commitment becomes strong (Lash & Wellington, 2007; Stubbs & Cocklin, 2008) and reinforced by the stringent non-financial disclosure requirements mandated by regulators (i.e. European Non-Financial Reporting Directive—NFRD).

According to mandatory disclosures of environmental, social, and governance information and considering the mission statement as a "business card" (Kotler & Murphy, 1981; Aaker, 1984; Bartlett & Ghoshal, 1993), companies tend to incorporate ESG issues into their mission statements. In line with this approach, many scholars show that mission statements that incorporate ESG considerations lead to increase the stakeholder engagement and the sustained creation of long-term value (Zumente & Bistrova, 2021). Thus, a link between purpose, mission statements, and performance (financial and non-financial) is almost clear.

The mission statement has been analysed in several fields. For example, through the analysis of a sample of 61 Fortune 500 companies' mission statements, Pearce and David (1987) show a positive relationship between the inclusion of desired mission statement components and firm financial performance. Bart and Baetz (1998) find that the mission statement development process is positively correlated with the return on assets and the percentage change in sales, defining mission statements as a powerful influencer on financial performance. Scholars have also

[2] As literature suggests (Bartkus & Glassman, 2007; Guiso et al., 2015; Lin et al., 2019), with the term "mission statements" authors intend the mission itself and other qualitative information available from companies' websites, contained in specific sections (i.e. "our culture", "our values", "our history"). Considering some academics and practitioners have used the terms "mission", "vision", "philosophy", "values" and "goals" interchangeably (David, 1989; Levin, 2000), in this chapter a broad "mission statements" definition is used (Leuthesser & Kohli, 1997; Pearce & Roth, 1988).

analysed ESG factors from different points of view. For example, there are several research studies on the impact of ESG on investment decisions (Amel-Zadeh & Serafeim, 2018; Serafeim, 2018; Zaccone & Pedrini, 2020; Zumente & Lāce, 2021), the provision of ESG data according to the growing non-financial disclosure (Ioannou & Serafeim, 2017; Grewal et al., 2019; D'Apice et al., 2021), and the influence of ESG on purpose (Barby et al., 2021; Mayer, 2021). ESG scores are the primary tools used to assess a company's performance in the realms of environmental, social, and governance issues (Friede et al., 2015). Through ESG scores, companies pay attention to the social and environmental impact of their business activity (Clement et al., 2023).

However, to our knowledge, there is no existing literature on the influence of mission statement's textual content on ESG scores. No references either to the influence of ESG scores on the textual content of mission statements. In other words, there seem to be no literature contributions affirming or refuting the association between ESG-oriented textual references into mission statements and high ESG scores of companies. Missing answers also apply to the inverse relationship, i.e. whether high ESG scores are associated with mission statements that are rich in ESG textual references. Therefore, the chapter intends to answer to the following research questions: *Do companies with a mission statement that contains textual references to environmental, social, and governance factors have higher ESG scores? Vice versa, do companies with higher ESG scores have a mission statement with textual references to environmental, social, and governance factors?* Thus, through a systematic literature review on mission statements and ESG, we want to explore whether and how textual contents of mission statements reflect ESG scores, and vice versa.

Results suggest that there could be a significant relationship between textual content of mission statements and ESG scores: companies that incorporate references to ESG themes in their mission statements may tend to achieve higher ESG scores. Vice versa, companies with a higher ESG score tend to include ESG textual references in their mission statements.

The reminder of this chapter is organized as follows. The next section presents the theoretical framework of mission statements and its evolution in the literature. Section 2.3 is based on the concept of ESG, focusing the attention on the relative actual regulation and the main metric to evaluate the environmental, social, and governance contribution of companies (ESG scores). Section 2.4 is dedicated to an explanation of the research method. Section 2.5 considers the analysis of the relationship between mission statements and ESG, especially with respect to the potential influence of the textual content of the former on the ESG scores. The conclusions and findings are discussed in Sect. 2.6. The last section summarizes the potential implications for researchers, practitioners, and investors, discusses the limitations of the study, and proposes future research.

2.2 The Evolving Role of Mission Statements: Defining Purpose and Stakeholder Engagement

The management literature has examined the mission statement for decades, analysing it from different points of view, as its impact on firm performance (Pearce & David, 1987; Klemm et al., 1991; Atrill et al., 2005; Collins & Rukstad, 2008; Palmer & Short, 2008; David et al., 2014) and its definition as a strategic, organizational, and motivational tool (King & Cleland, 1979; David, 1989; Matejka et al., 1993; Powers, 2012; David et al., 2014). In general, mission statements are recognized as the first step in strategic management and represent a declaration of the "reason for being" of organizations (Pearce, 1982; Pearce & David, 1987; Campbell & Yeung, 1991). Several contributions affirm the benefits associated with having a well-defined mission (Bart & Baetz, 1998; Analoui & Karami, 2002; Atrill et al., 2005; Braun et al., 2012).

In a more specific way, most research studies on mission statements have been dedicated to the analysis of its textual content and characteristics (Want, 1986; Bartkus et al., 2004; Baral & Pokharel, 2016; Lin et al., 2019), showing that differences in the content of mission statements determine differences in performance. In particular, short mission statements that do not express financial goals, identify the cultural values of the firm, and define its purpose are related to a more satisfying performance (Bart & Baetz, 1998). To establish a standard for the textual composition, Klemm et al. (1991) define specific requirements—purpose, strategic objectives, quantified planning objectives, and business definition—for mission statements. David (1989) reviews 75 mission statements from a survey of 1000 firms in *Business Week* and defines a practical framework to evaluate and write mission statements. He develops the determination of nine important components of a mission: customers, products or services, location, technology, concern for survival, philosophy, self-concept, concern for public image, and concern for employees.

Generally, scholars agree that, to spread and metabolize the mission statement throughout the organization (McGinnis, 1981), its content must clarify which is the business of the firm and which it should be (Campbell & Yeung, 1991). A well-written mission statement allows the firm to diffuse its purpose to its community of stakeholders (Penco et al., 2019) and to define roles and responsibilities, transforming goals into a work structure, with an impact on corporate policies (Hirota et al., 2010). Through the monitoring of performance, it also helps to achieve the purpose (King & Cleland, 1979). Every organization, profit and non-profit, has its own unique purpose, which must be reflected in a mission statement: organizational goals, objectives, and activities of companies should derive from the mission statement, which "should flow from and be in congruence with the values of the organisation" (Vogt, 1994, p. 29). Bart (1997a) states that the mission statement provides a sense of purpose and direction. The power of mission statements consists in the achievement of inspiration and motivation of employees to exceptional performance and in the definition of resource allocation. To do so, the mission statement has to be made up of three parts, as the target audience (key market), the product or service offered on the market (contribution), and the uniqueness of the offered product (distinction). This is how the mission statement reveals the purpose of the firm. An effective mission statement defines the fundamental scope that differentiates a company from others (Pearce, 1982).

Nowadays, the purpose of companies is a topic commonly argued in the academic and institutional context (Polman, 2016; Business Roundtable, 2019; Link, 2019; Lipton et al., 2019; Mayer, 2021). The discussion starts with the concept of firm: there is a conscious tendency to consider it not as a separate entity, but as a tool of someone's desire (shareholders or stakeholders). In this context, the concept of purpose is becoming more and more important. Collins and Porras (1996) define purpose not as a description of the company's organization or the presentation of target customers, but it represents the soul of companies. As illustrated by David Packard giving to HP employees in 1960, purpose regards deeper reasons for companies, not just making money: purpose is not a goal, but a reason of being.

For the actual debate (shareholder vs stakeholder capitalism) the purpose is the creation of economic and social progress under a sustainable and responsible point of view (De Woot, 2017). Therefore, the purpose is "the good cause" (Donna, 2020) intended as a sense of the existence of the company that requires the simultaneous consideration of social and environmental impacts of its activity.

According to the thought of the Italian Doctrine Economia Aziendale (Zappa, 1962; Onida, 1971), it is necessary to emphasize that in order to respect their social role companies must satisfy the interests of all stakeholders and overall well-being. Profit becomes a means to survive and grow. When a company assumes profit as the supreme good, negative consequences will be generated to its long-term survival and growth, mining competitiveness, social consensus, and economic results (Coda, 1988, p. 127). "The conflict for prioritization" between financial and social goals could create tensions (Zahra et al., 2009), whose resolution could force companies to make wrong choice, such as maintaining the balance between value destruction and creation and intentionally avoiding profit (Santos, 2012). The risk is to harm their primary source of survival and development. Companies must pay attention to profit to guarantee their survival and development but must balance it with social aspects to contribute to the common good (Di Carlo, 2017).

As Santos (2012) writes, (SE[3]) managers can find a balance between the value creation (social logic) and value capture (market logic), trying to exploit resource-scarce environments as much as possible without disadvantaging groups of

[3]"A SE is an organisation that trades, not for private gain, but to generate positive social and environmental externalities" (Santos, 2012). The main characteristics of SEs are the adoption of profit-generating business activity and the pursuit of social goals (Laville & Nyssens, 2001; Mair & Marti, 2006; Peredo & McLean, 2006). Thus, SEs differ from private sector organizations because they prioritize social change over private wealth creation that seek to maximize profit for personal ends. Typical social goals include reducing poverty, inequality, homelessness, carbon emissions, and unemployment (Murphy & Coombes, 2009). Santos et al. (2015) identify SEs several sectors, such as education (e.g. Khan Academy, which provides low-cost online education programmes),

stakeholders. Doherty et al. (2014) explain that "SEs need to manage conflicting, and competing, commercial and social logics as well as the demands of multiple stakeholder groups". Managers can create value for society and stakeholders by looking at governance, organizational structure, HR processes, and performance management systems (Santos et al., 2015). In terms of governance, the model for social enterprises suggests that the presence of social stakeholders in governance bodies can favour the comprehension of their needs. Regarding the organizational structure, it is seen as an important tool for organizing the complexity of the work in order to achieve a combination of social and financial results. Santos et al. (2015) suggest recruiting people who believe in social and environmental issues and propose that the combination of social and environmental key performance indicators (KPIs) should represent a predominant performance measurement system, overcoming the separate evaluation of financial performance and CSR reporting processes.

In line with growing awareness about the social role of companies, many scholars focus on internal stakeholder participation in the mission development process. The inclusion in mission statements of some specific elements relative to the relationship between firms and stakeholders is analysed by several studies (Pearce & David, 1987; Ireland et al., 1992; Vogt, 1994; Becchetti et al., 2022). Bart and Baetz (1998) show that the amount of internal stakeholder involvement is positively and significantly correlated with higher sales returns and significantly higher levels of influence on employee behaviour. In this context, the need to listen to stakeholders becomes mandatory and determines the expansion of the boundaries of stakeholder identity, in line with the growing importance of the external environment of the firm. This broad consideration of stakeholders is widely discussed in institutional, corporate, and academic tables. An example is the Statement on the Purpose of a Corporation, a document of the American Business Roundtable (August 19, 2019), signed by 181 of the most influential CEOs of US companies. It highlights the need to consider social aspects in the purpose of companies, without prioritizing profit. Thus, the degree to which internal stakeholders are involved is an important consideration when a mission statement is developed.

The transition from value creation for shareholders to value creation for stakeholders (Freeman et al., 2007; Harrison et al., 2020) determines that firms can ensure their long-term survival only when they integrate the goal of making profit along with active concern for social issues and the protection of the environment (Elkington, 1997; Lash & Wellington, 2007; Aaker, 1984; Mirvis et al., 2010; Porter & Kramer, 2011). The starting point is the change of the idea of what a firm is. They are a combination of values that characterize the environment in which they live (Brunelli & Di Carlo, 2020). Subsequently, companies must have a mission that includes economic, social, and environmental objectives that will help them contribute to the growth of the community.

---

microfinance (e.g. Grameen Bank, providing loans to the very poor), and environment (e.g. South Pole Carbon Ltd., the global leader for developing emission-reduction projects).

2.3 The Development of Corporate Responsibility Through ESG Scores and Purpose-Driven Business

ESG factors are the main criteria to evaluate companies in terms of sustainability. New forms of regulation have been introduced to facilitate disclosure on sustainability, encouraging companies to include ESG performance in their annual reports. For example, the European Union (EU) has stepped forward sustainability reporting by enacting in 2014 the European Non-Financial Reporting Directive (Directive 2014/95/EU of October 22, 2014, hereafter, NFRD) amending Directive 2013/34/EU as regards disclosure of non-financial and diversity information by certain large companies and groups. According to the European Commission, "a strategic approach to corporate social responsibility is increasingly important for competitiveness. It can bring benefits in terms of risk management, cost reduction, access to capital, customer relations, human resource management, and innovation capacity" (European Competitiveness Report, 2008, p. 4).

In line with increasing institutional and regulatory attention (Lash & Wellington, 2007; Whiteman et al., 2012; Grewal et al., 2019; Christensen et al., 2021; D'Apice et al., 2021; Dryzek, 2022) companies are required to disclose information about their performance, policies, and risks in terms of environmental, social, and governance issues (De Giuli et al., 2024). Although some studies evidence that "when it is mandated by regulation, that disclosure becomes less worthy for investors" (D'Apice et al., 2021, p. 1507), the non-financial disclosure becomes more and more important, and all listed firms must include a sustainability statement in their financial reports (Santamaria et al., 2021). Considering that the general objective of the NFD is to improve transparency, credibility, and comparability of sustainability information, "companies must now demonstrate that they are performing better on the environmental and social fronts as well as in terms of governance" (Clement et al., 2023, p. 2). With the aim of including ESG requirements in the decision-making process (Cicchiello et al., 2022), mandatory disclosure rules tend to align the interests of companies with those of their stakeholders, showing the importance of evaluating quality and quantity disclosure for ESG factors (Santamaria et al., 2021).

ESG criteria are also a valuation tool for investors (Alda, 2021; D'Apice et al., 2021; Gangi et al., 2022). Studies show that companies that invest in ESG factors guarantee a greater profit than companies that do not (Garcia et al., 2017). This process drives present returns, as well as future growth and opportunity (Porter et al., 2019). The increasing power of environmental, social, and governance issues is evidenced by the acceptance of investors, not only to receive a potential lower financial return, but also to receive a negative differential in exchange for social return on investment. In addition, the generation of social returns for investors takes time, manifesting their medium-long-term orientation (Doherty et al., 2014). Thus, the emerging ESG approach is surely linked to the financial performance of companies, but it also underscores an increasing connection with sustainable results. Indeed, the consideration and implementation of social goals have an impact on the acquisition of financial resources. Although socially and environmentally conscious firms (with particular reference to SEs) have greater financial flexibility and can refer to multiple sources of legitimacy (Dart, 2004; Certo & Miller, 2008), sustainable value creation is perceived to be less attractive to traditional banks and venture capital organizations because of likely lower profit generation (Sud et al., 2009). Doherty et al. (2014) resolve these tensions by dual pricing strategies and the generation of social returns at the expense of financial returns on investment. In addition, new fields of social finance (such as loans at preferential terms for SEs, philanthropic venture capital, social impact bond) have been created. Specific categories of funds are financed by investors interested in organizations that create social value and at the same time generate financial returns (Santos et al., 2015).

Therefore, many studies evidence an encouraging impact of ESG issues on the corporate financial performance (CFP), suggesting the ability of the non-financial disclosure to provide significant advantages (Xie et al., 2019; Chen & Xie, 2022; Wagner & Wiśnicki, 2022).

The main tool through which companies are evaluated in terms of sustainability is ESG scores (Ribando & Bonne, 2010; Friede et al., 2015). Through ESG scores, companies are evaluated in three main categories: environmental issues (e.g. environmental impact, resource consumption, impact on biodiversity, waste management), social issues (e.g. impact on the community and suppliers, working conditions, gender diversity; Becchetti et al., 2022), and governance issues (e.g. the organization's transparency, its relationship with shareholders and board of directors, executive compensation, and board diversity) (Ribando & Bonne, 2010).

To express as much as possible the non-financial performance, the ESG score is the best available measure for evaluating CSR activities (Cini & Ricci, 2018), helping companies to improve their reputation (Arouri et al., 2019), reducing legislative pressure on their activities (Gartenberg et al., 2019; Christensen et al., 2021), minimizing financial risk (Chollet & Sandwidi, 2018), and attracting more capital (Chen et al., 2023). ESG scores provide a quantitative assessment of companies' commitment in the management of their social and environmental impact.

In recent years, the link between ESG scores and financial performance has been extensively investigated. Research shows a positive relationship between these two elements: the MSCI rating agency (2020, "Comparing Risk and Performance for Absolute and Relative ESG Scores") confirms that higher profitability is correlated with higher ESG scores and lower levels of risk. This positive link is also due to the positive relationship between the ESG disclosure required by the regulation and the ESG scores (Cicchiello et al., 2022). Indeed, EU firms with higher ESG scores tend to more respect the ESG disclosure regulation. This could be attributed to the increased external pressure from stakeholders after the enactment of the NFD. By increasing the importance of non-financial information for the evaluation of long-term performance (Giron et al., 2022), most of the world's largest companies have started reporting non-financial information to demonstrate their ethical standards and commitment to environmental, social, and governance issues (Pérez, 2015).

ESG scores also represent a smart tool for comparing companies that are sustainability-oriented (Clement et al., 2023). ESG factors influence reputation and performance of firms and modify mission statements and purpose (Carroll, 1991;

Coelho et al., 2003; Avi-Yonah, 2005). Consequently, governance bodies have been strongly focused on corporate purpose, also pushed by investors who need a reason for their investment based on ESG factors (Barby et al., 2021). Thus, companies tend to adopt the "triple bottom line" as approach for their purpose's orientation, generating profit, caring for people, and protecting the planet (Elkington, 1997; Bansal, 2005; Mirvis et al., 2010; Becchetti et al., 2022). As mission statements are the heart of the governance and represent the initial step of the strategic planning process (Pearce & David, 1987), companies insert ESG issues in their purpose and communicate their ESG commitment and outcomes in their mission statements (Lash & Wellington, 2007; Stubbs & Cocklin, 2008).

2.4 Methodology

To achieve a comprehension of the literature about mission statements and ESG, a systematic literature review is adopted and following Alegre et al. (2018), we began by defining the research objectives. The research investigated the theoretical and practical approach to mission statements and ESG factors, the identification of the relationship between mission statements and ESG scores, and the classification of mission statements and the literature on ESG scores.

To do that, we searched for documents included in the "Web of Science" database, containing specific terms that refer to mission and ESG in the topic. We created the following query:

("Mission" OR "Mission Statement*") AND ("ESG" OR "Environmental, social and governance" OR "ESG performance*" OR "ESG disclosure" OR "Environmental, social and governance performance*" OR "ESG rating*" OR "ESG score*" OR "ESG factor*" OR "corporate social responsibility" OR "CSR" OR "sustainab*" OR "sustainab* performance").

This first selection returned 3940 documents. Then we filtered the research to documents written in English in the areas of environmental sciences, green sustainable science technology, environmental studies, management, business, economics, business finance, ethics, and social issues. We decided to consider only articles, review articles, book chapters, and book reviews. The documents obtained were 1253.

Refined the selection, we narrowed the search to high-quality peer-reviewed journals, chosen based on the last available ABS Ranking: the filtered journals were classified with 3,4,4* from ABS ranking 2021. We obtained 168 documents.

To check whether the documents really explained the relationship between mission statements and ESG factors, we reviewed each abstract one by one and decided to refuse all documents that did not specifically refer to this theme. Thus, we were left with 29 documents from high-quality journals in the areas of environmental sciences, green sustainable science technology, environmental studies, management, business, economics, business finance, ethics, and social issues, which were written

Table 2.1 Flow chart of the systematic literature review process

Research objectives	– Analyze the theoretical and practical approach to mission statements and ESG factors – Identify the relationship between mission statements and ESG scores – Classify mission statements and ESG scores literature			
Initial inclusion criteria	Documents included in Web of Science database	Documents contain the attached query in "topic"		**3940**
Subsequent inclusion criteria	Written in English	Articles, review articles, book chapters, book reviews	In categories of environmental sciences, green sustainable science technology, environmental studies, management, business, economics, business finance, ethics, social issues	**1253**
Additional inclusion criteria	Documents published in 3/4/4* ABS 2021 ranking journals			**168**
Additional inclusion criteria	Documents that directly deal mission statements and ESG factors			**29**

Source: elaboration of the authors

in English and that deal specifically with mission statement and environmental, social, and governance issues.

There are no limitations in terms of time and identity of all documents. The 29 documents were published in 14 journals from a variety of management disciplines, including entrepreneurship, such as *Journal of Business Venturing*; management and organizational subjects, such as *California Management Review, Management and Organization Review*, *International Journal of Management Reviews*, and *Journal of Business Research*; economics, such as *Labour Economic* and *World Development*; social issues and nonprofit, such as *Nonprofit and Voluntary Sector Quarterly*; business ethics, such as *Journal of Business Ethics*; environmental issues, such as *Business Strategy and the Environment, Ecological Economics*; industry and innovation matters, such as *IEEE Transactions on Engineering Management, Industry and Innovation*, and *Technovation.* The process of the systematic literature review is showed in Table 2.1.

2.5 The Possible Relationship Between the Content of the Mission Statement and ESG Scores

The connection between mission statements, theories of corporate value creation, and attention to ESG is evident. Zumente and Bistrova (2021) assess that companies become more aware of ESG issues if their mission statements integrate sustainability concepts. Considering a sample of companies in Central and Eastern Europe (CEE), the authors note that companies are increasingly recognizing the importance of ESG factors and are actively integrating sustainability principles into their mission statements.

This evolution in mission statements represents a profound change in corporate culture and strategy. It reflects a deeper shift towards a stronger focus on a long-term shareholder value orientation, seen as the ultimate goal closely related to achieving high ESG scores. By explicitly including references to ESG contributions in their mission statements, these companies signal their commitment to sustainable business practices. In addition, companies recognize that, by including ESG factors, they not only fulfil their ethical responsibilities, but also improve their financial performance and competitiveness in the market (Esposito et al., 2023). The alignment of profit and social impact can be considered a driver of long-term competitive advantage (Santos, 2012): companies that care more about ESG issues become strong competitors for classical commercial firms, representing attractive acquisition targets for multinationals (e.g. the acquisition operations of The Body Shop by L'Oréal and Ben & Jerry's by Unilever).

Therefore, in recent years, the landscape of corporate values and purpose has undergone a profound transformation. The traditional notion that a business exists solely to maximize profits for its shareholders is no longer the prevailing mindset. Instead, a growing awareness that emphasizes the importance of ethical, sustainable, and responsible business practices has emerged. In this context, mission statements, long considered mere statements of intent or purpose, have now become critical tools to communicate a company's commitment to ESG principles. The mission statement answers central questions such as "why the company exists", "what its purpose is", and "for whom, how, and in what time frame it creates value" (Di Carlo, 2017).

Approving the mission statement as the official manifesto of the purpose of a company (Rajasekar, 2013), the growing of sustainable issues has increased interest in the composition of mission statements (David, 1989; Klemm et al., 1991; Ireland et al., 1992; Bart et al., 2001; Fritz & Von Schnur Bein, 2019). Literature on mission statements is quite abundant, both prescriptive (e.g. Pearce & Roth, 1988; Ireland et al., 1992) and descriptive (e.g. David, 1989; Bart, 1997a; Leuthesser & Kohli, 1997). Important works tend to focus on elements that should be included or that are commonly included in the mission statement and on the impact it can have on the firm performance (e.g. Pearce & David, 1987; Bart, 1997b; Bart & Baetz, 1998; O'Gorman & Doran, 1999; Bart et al., 2001; Bart & Hupfer, 2004). Although it is evident that the integration of ESG themes into mission statements is gaining traction, there is no homogeneous answer to the real importance of the textual content of mission statements for ESG performance, in particular for ESG scores, yet. From the analysis of the literature on mission statements[4] and ESG, a link

[4]To understand whether a mission statement contains textual references related to the theme of environmental, social, and governance theme and has a high ESG score, it is possible to consider mission statements published on company websites. As the literature suggests (Bartkus &

between textual contents of the mission statement and ESG scores, and vice versa, has already been established. However, this study creates a coherent theoretical framework and develops the following propositions.

- Proposition 1: *Companies with a mission statement that contains textual references related to social, environmental, and governance issues (e.g. "emissions", "pollution", "recycling", "renewable energy") have a higher ESG score.*
  - Proposition 1a: *Companies with a mission statement containing textual references related to environmental issues (e.g. "emissions", "pollution", "recycling", "renewable energy") have a higher E score.*
  - Proposition 1b: *Companies with a mission statement containing textual references related to social issues (e.g. "human rights", "stakeholders", "gender equality", "community") have a higher S score.*
  - Proposition 1c: *Companies with a mission statement containing textual references related to governance issues (e.g. "ethics", "corruption", "diversity", "independence") have a higher G score.*
- Proposition 2: *Companies with a higher ESG score have mission statements that contain textual references related to social, environmental, and governance issues.*
  - Proposition 2a: *Companies with a higher E score have a mission statement that contains textual references related to environmental issues (e.g. "emissions", "pollution", "recycling", "renewable energy").*
  - Proposition 2b: *Companies with a higher S score have a mission statement that contains textual references related to social issues (e.g. "human rights", "stakeholders", "gender equality", "community").*
  - Proposition 2c: *Companies with a higher G score have a mission statement that contains textual references related to governance issues (e.g. "ethics", "corruption", "diversity", "independence").*

Glassman, 2007; Guiso et al., 2015; Lin et al., 2019), taking into account also other qualitative information available from company websites, contained in specific sections (i.e. "our culture", "our values", "our history"). Considering that some academics and practitioners have used the terms "mission", "vision", "philosophy", "values", and "goals" interchangeably (David, 1989; Levin, 2000), a broad definition is preferred (Leuthesser & Kohli, 1997; Pearce & Roth, 1988).

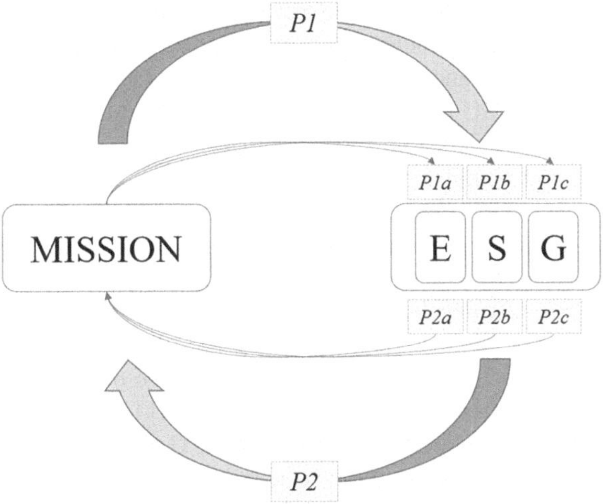

Source: elaboration of authors

In conclusion, the contemporary corporate world is witnessing a significant evolution in the role of mission statements: this change reflects a broader transformation in corporate culture, where long-term shareholder value is closely linked to responsible and sustainable business practices. Consequently, companies with mission statements that incorporate textual references related to the theme of environmental, social, and governance tend to receive higher ESG scores. This trend reinforces the idea that purpose-driven companies are more likely to excel in terms of sustainability and responsible corporate behaviour. In addition, also the current disclosure makes clear that companies need to set not only economic but also sustainable goals. The importance of setting ESG goals becomes a prerequisite for companies to achieve high ESG scores. As these variables are the main tools for non-financial assessment of companies, high ESG scores also lead to improved financial performance. Therefore, in the absence of stringent non-financial disclosure, companies' focus on the composition of the mission statement in relation to ESG factors was low.

Nowadays, with the introduction of the above-mentioned disclosure (in this regard, reference is made to the new sustainability financial reporting standard IFRS S1, which from 1 January 2024 requires the highlighting of sustainability-related risks and benefits that could affect access to financing, cost of capital, and cash flows in the short, medium, and long term), companies tend to pursue sustainable objectives, from which a change in the mission statement derives, leading to better financial performance. The importance of ESG issues for a good financial and non-financial performance is confirmed also by the emergence of new legal forms (low profit limited liability company, benefit corporation, flexible purpose corporation). They are created to overcome some typical limitations of ESG-focused companies, including those related to raising capital (Lasprogata & Cotten 2003).

To extend the practical impact of the research, a content analysis of a sample of collected mission statements could be useful to obtain a glossary coming only from official corporate sources and make a frequency analysis of the most used terms, attributing each to the ESG pillars. In this step, the support of sustainability experts (CSR scholars, social leaders, and ESG providers) could be required to define the most appropriate and complete ESG glossary derived from the collected mission statements. For ESG scores, specific providers are available to present a company's ESG performance based on publicly available data and determine the company's ESG score. They provide two types of data: (1) ESG scores, considered in general, and (2) ESG scores, divided by three pillars of ESG, environmental, social, and governance scores. For the first type of data, there are different categories related to general ESG themes, such as emission, innovation, and resource use for the E pillar; community, human rights, product responsibility, workforce for the S pillar; and CSR strategy, management, and shareholders for the G pillar. For the second type of data, there are different subthemes for the categories of each pillar (emissions, waste, biodiversity, environmental management systems for the emission category of the E pillar; diversity and inclusion, career development and training, working conditions, health, and safety for the S pillar; and shareholder rights and takeover defences for the shareholders category of the G pillar). These scores could be then compared with the results obtained from the analysis of the composition of the mission to evidence any relationship between these two variables (mission, independent variable, and ESG score, dependent variable).

Taking into account these results, it could be possible to perform several analyses on the potential influence of the textual composition of mission statements on ESG scores. Therefore, considering that the scope of the study would be to show how the textual references of mission statements are related to the ESG scores, several scenarios are possible. If the mission statement contains explicit references to ESG, it becomes possible: (1) the mission proves to be a tool for guiding companies towards environmental, social, and governance choices, thus influencing the ESG score: in this case, it would mean that the textual references proposed in the mission have a concrete impact on the company's strategic and operational choices; (2) if the mission does not influence the ESG score, as despite the reference to environmental, social, and/or governance issues in the mission's content, the company has a low ESG score; it is possible that the company implements greenwashing policies rather than making ESG choices only to follow current popular business management strategies, which guarantee a positive impact on public opinion. If the mission statement does not contain textual references related to the environmental, social, or governance theme but the firm has a high ESG score, the company acts according to the logic of concrete social responsibility, implementing strategies aimed at environmental, social, and governance choices, but does not expose such decisions in the mission. This deficit may require a new communication strategy, which, upstream, may risk recalibrating internal governance systems.

2.6 Conclusions

An important theoretical and practical question is based on the following: "Does the mission statement matter?" Looking at the literature, the answer is positive. The critical role of mission statements in shaping the strategic direction and purpose of companies is clear, particularly in the context of ESG considerations. Several important conclusions can be drawn from the research provided.

- Mission statements highlight the sense of purpose: they represent strategic tools useful for decision-making and resource allocation within an organization, playing a pivotal role in shaping corporate culture and performance of companies.
- Here is a current transformation of the concept of purpose: from profit maximization to a broader perspective inclusive of social and environmental responsibilities: the purpose of a company should extend beyond financial gains and consider the well-being of all stakeholders.
- Regulations and directives, such as the European Non-Financial Reporting Directive (NFRD), are increasingly compelling companies to disclose information about their ESG performance. This focus on ESG factors influences corporate purpose and mission statements as companies strive to align with sustainability goals. ESG scores represent a critical performance metric that evaluates the commitment of a company to environmental, social, and governance issues. Investors, regulators, and stakeholders to assess sustainability efforts and ethical standards.
- A purpose-driven approach, aligning mission statements with ESG principles, is associated with improved corporate financial performance, reputational benefits, and stakeholder satisfaction. Well-defined mission statements that incorporate ESG values can inspire and motivate employees, drive innovation, and enhance competitiveness.
- There is a significant relationship between textual contents of mission statements and ESG scores. Companies that incorporate references to environmental, social, and governance themes in their mission statements tend to achieve higher ESG scores. This trend indicates a commitment to sustainability and responsible business practices. Vice versa, considering the mandatory non-financial disclosure, companies with a higher ESG score tend to include environmental, social, and governance textual references in their mission statements.

In conclusion, research underscores the deep influence of mission statements on purpose, culture, and performance, especially in the context of ESG considerations. It highlights the evolving nature of corporate purpose and the importance of mission statements in reflecting this transformation: alignment of mission-driven values and ESG principles can lead to greater corporate value creation and sustainability.

2.7 Originality and Limitations

Analysing the existing literature on mission statements and ESG, the research finds a homogeneous theoretical answer about the reciprocal association between textual contents of mission statements and ESG scores.

The chapter makes a theoretical and practical contribution. The theoretical one is evidenced by the fact that studies on CSR are becoming increasingly valuable and represents an integral part of corporate culture. Certainly, in recent decades, driven by public opinion, social responsibility issues have grown, and corporate groups have become more actively involved in social issues, drawing up the non-financial declaration. However, the commitment to achieving multiple goals simultaneously facilitates the emergence of competing interests between various categories of stakeholders. Therefore, ethical dilemmas are difficult to solve. In this context, the mission is even more valuable as it becomes the company's statement of intent and can also represent "a practical way to introduce ethics into business at the top of the company [. . .] and in the company as a whole toward the common good" (Melé, 2009, p. 239). Following a strict "stakeholder" point of view, the consideration of the common good determines several positive effects on different actors (Brunelli & Di Carlo, 2020). Companies would like to be orientated to good governance, based on purely ethical principles and objectives; potential investors could obtain a benefit thanks to the possibility of distinguishing companies according to the mission; also, agencies involved in rating companies would have to include among the measurement variables also the evaluation of mission statements according to the degree to which it is orientated. In line with this orientation and considering the mission statement as the manifesto of the firm's purpose, its textual composition becomes relevant, as it increasingly consists of ESG references.

From a practical point of view, the major contribution is for governance aspects. Indeed, considering the latter as the body on which the elaboration of the mission depends and the consequent strategic definition, this study provides executive support for (1) imprinting a corporate orientation that is inclined towards social responsibility and improving ESG scores; (2) correctly composing the mission with environmental, social and governance references; (3) defining ESG strategies to be implemented, monitoring their respective progress; and (4) assessing the importance that CSR practices have on corporate governance orientation.

The limitation comes from the fact that the influence of mission statements on ESG has been studied from a theoretical point of view through a systematic literature review. Therefore, it could be necessary to understand, through an empirical analysis, whether this relationship really exists. Future studies could develop a content analysis of a mission statement's sample, create a glossary, and make a frequency analysis of the most used terms, attributing each to the ESG pillars.

In addition, future studies could also test this relationship and whether it varies according to variables such as the sector in which the company operates, the country of origin, and the composition of the Board. It could be possible also through the research method of multiple case studies.

References

Aaker, D. A. (1984). How to select a business strategy. *California Management Review, 26*(3), 167–175.

Alda, M. (2021). The environmental, social, and governance (ESG) dimension of firms in which social responsible investment (SRI) and conventional pension funds invest: The mainstream SRI and the inclusion of ESG. *Journal of Cleaner Production, 298*, 126812.

Alegre, I., Berbegal-Mirabent, J., Guerrero, A., & Mas-Machuca, M. (2018). The real mission of the mission statement: A systematic review of the literature. *Journal of Management & Organization, 24*(4), 456–473.

Amel-Zadeh, A., & Serafeim, G. (2018). Why and how investors use ESG information: Evidence from a global survey. *Financial Analysts Journal, 74*(3), 87–103.

Analoui, F., & Karami, A. (2002). CEOs and development of a meaningful mission statement. *Corporate Governance, 2*, 13–20.

Arouri, M., Gomes, M., & Pukthuanthong, K. (2019). Corporate social responsibility and M&A uncertainty. *Journal of Corporate Finance, 56*, 176–198.

Atrill, P., Omram, M., & Pointon, J. (2005). Company mission statements and financial performance. *Corporate Ownership Control, 2*, 28–35.

Avi-Yonah, R. S. (2005). The cyclical transformations of the corporate form: A historical perspective on corporate social responsibility. *Delaware Journal of Corporate Law, 30*, 767.

Bansal, P. (2005). Evolving sustainability: A longitudinal study of corporate sustainable development. *Strategic Management Journal, 26*, 197–218.

Baral, N., & Pokharel, M. P. (2016). How sustainability is reflected in the S&P 500 companies' strategic documents. *Organization & Environment*, 1–20.

Barby, C., Barker, R., Cohen, R., Eccles, R. G., Heller, C., Mayer, C., Roche, B., Serafeim, G., Stroehle, J., Younger, R., & Zochowski, T. (2021). Measuring purpose: An integrated framework. Available at SSRN 3771892.

Bart, C. K. (1997a). Sex, lies, and mission statements. *Business Horizons, 40*(6), 9–18.

Bart, C. K. (1997b). Industrial firms and the power of mission. *Industrial Marketing Management, 26*(4), 371–383.

Bart, C. K., & Baetz, M. C. (1998). The relationship between mission statements and firm performance: An exploratory study. *The Journal of Management Studies, 35*(6), 823–853.

Bart, C. K., Bontis, N., & Taggar, S. (2001). A model of the impact of mission statements on firm performance. *Management Decision, 39*(1), 19–35.

Bart, C. K., & Hupfer, M. (2004). Mission statements in Canadian hospitals. *Journal of Health Organization and Management, 18*(2), 92–110.

Bartkus, B. R., & Glassman, M. (2007). Do firms practice what they preach? The relationship between mission statements and stakeholder management. *Journal of Business Ethics, 83*, 207–216.

Bartkus, B. R., Glassman, M., & McAfee, R. B. (2004). A comparison of the quality of European, Japanese and U. S. mission statements: A content analysis. *European Management Journal, 22*, 393–401.

Bartlett, C. A., & Ghoshal, S. (1993). Beyond the M-form: Toward a managerial theory of the firm. *Strategic Management Journal, 14*(S2), 23–46.

Becchetti, L., Bobbio, E., Prizia, F., & Semplici, L. (2022). Going deeper into the S of ESG: A relational approach to the definition of social responsibility. *Sustainability, 14*(15), 9668.

Braun, S., Wesche, J. S., Frey, D., Weisweller, S., & Paus, C. (2012). Effectiveness of mission statements in organizations - A review. *Journal of Management Organization, 18*, 430–444.

Brunelli, S., & Di Carlo, E. (2020). Accountability, ethics and sustainability of organizations. New theories, strategies and tools for survival and growth. In *Accounting, finance, sustainability, governance & fraud: Theory and application* (pp. 23–43). Springer.

Business Roundtable. (2019). Statement of the purpose of a corporation.

Campbell, A., & Yeung, S. (1991). Creating a sense of mission. *Long Range Planning, 24*(4), 10–20.
Carroll, A. B. (1991). The pyramid of Corporate Social Responsibility: Toward the moral management of organizational stakeholders. *Business Horizons*, 39–48.
Certo, S. T., & Miller, T. (2008). Social entrepreneurship: Key issues and concepts. *Business Horizons, 51*(4), 267–271.
Chen, Y., Li, T., Zeng, Q., & Zhu, B. (2023). Effect of ESG performance on the cost of equity capital: Evidence from China. *International Review of Economics & Finance, 83*, 348–364.
Chen, Z., & Xie, G. (2022). ESG disclosure and financial performance: Moderating role of ESG investors. *International Review of Financial Analysis, 83*, 102291.
Chollet, P., & Sandwidi, B. W. (2018). CSR engagement and financial risk: A virtuous circle? International evidence. *Global Finance Journal.*
Christensen, H. B., Hail, L., & Leuz, C. (2021). Mandatory CSR and sustainability reporting: Economic analysis and literature review. *Review of Accounting Studies, 26*(3), 1176–1248.
Cicchiello, A. F., Marrazza, F., & Perdichizzi, S. (2022). Non-financial disclosure regulation and environmental, social, and governance (ESG) performance: The case of EU and US firms. *Corporate Social Responsibility and Environmental Management.*
Cini, A. C., & Ricci, C. (2018). CSR as a driver where ESG performance. *Symphonya. Emerging Issues in Management, 1*(1), 68–75.
Clement, A., Robinot, É., & Trespeuch, L. (2023). The use of ESG scores in academic literature: A systematic literature review. *Journal of Enterprising Communities: People and Places in the Global Economy.*
Coda, V. (1988). Fisiologia e patologia nel finalismo dell'impresa. *Aggiornamenti sociali, 2/3*, 125–215.
Coelho, P. R. P., McClure, J. E., & Spry, J. A. (2003). The social responsibility of corporate management: A classical critique. *Mid – American Journal of Business.*
Collins, D. J., & Rukstad, M. G. (2008). Can you say what your strategy is? *Harvard Business Review, 86*, 82–88.
Collins, J. C., & Porras, J. I. (1996). Building your company's vision. *Harvard Business Review, 74*, 65–78.
D'Apice, V., Ferri, G., & Intonti, M. (2021). Sustainable disclosure versus ESG intensity: Is there a cross effect between holding and SRI funds? *Corporate Social Responsibility and Environmental Management, 28*(5), 1496–1510.
Dart, R. (2004). The legitimacy of social enterprise. *Nonprofit Management and Leadership, 14*(4), 411–424.
David, F. R. (1989). How companies define their mission. *Long Range Planning, 22*(1), 90–97.
David, M. E., David, F., & David, F. R. (2014). Mission statement theory and practice: A content analysis and news direction. *International Journal of Business, Marketing, and Decision Sciences, 7*(1).
De Giuli, M. E., Grechi, D., & Tanda, A. (2024). What do we know about ESG and risk? A systematic and bibliometric review. *Corporate Social Responsibility and Environmental Management, 31*(2), 1096–1108.
De Woot, P. (2017). *Responsible innovation*. Routledge.
Di Carlo, E. (2017). *Interesse primario dell'azienda come principio-guida e bene comune.* Giappichelli.
Doherty, B., Haugh, H., & Lyon, F. (2014). Social enterprises as hybrid organizations: A review and research agenda. *International Journal of Management Reviews, 16*(4), 417–436.
Donna, G. (2020). La "buona causa" dell'impresa. *Impresa Progetto. Electronic Journal of Management, 3.*
Drucker, P. F. (1973). *Management: Tasks, responsibilities, practices*. Harper & Row.
Dryzek, J. S. (2022). *The politics of the earth: Environmental discourses*. Oxford University Press.
Elkington, J. (1997). The triple bottom line. *Environmental Management: Readings and Cases, 2*, 49–66.

Esposito, P., Ahmad, Z., Riso, V., & Mustafa, N. (2023). Beyond the business case? Retracing the walk of corporate social responsibility and financial performance relationship in the Oil and Gas sector. *Corporate Social Responsibility and Environmental Management*.

European Competitiveness Report. (2008). Renewed EU strategy 2011-14 on Corporate Social Responsibility of enterprises. COM (2008). 774. SEC (2008). 2853.

European Union, European Non-Financial Reporting Directive (Directive 2014/95/EU of October 22, 2014).

Freeman, R. E., Martin, K., & Parmar, B. (2007). Stakeholder capitalism. *Journal of Business Ethics, 74*(4), 303–314.

Friede, G., Busch, T., & Bassen, A. (2015). ESG and financial performance: Aggregated evidence from more than 2000 empirical studies. *Journal of Sustainable Finance & Investment, 5*(4), 210–233.

Fritz, T. M., & Von Schnur Bein, G. (2019). Beyond socially responsible investing: Effects of mission-driven portfolio selection. *Sustainability*.

Gangi, F., Varrone, N., Daniele, L. M., & Coscia, M. (2022). Mainstreaming socially responsible investment: Do environmental, social and governance ratings of investment funds converge? *Journal of Cleaner Production, 353*, 131684.

Garcia, A. S., Mendes-Da-Silvia, W., & Orsato, R. (2017). Sensitive industries produce better ESG performance: Evidence from emerging markets. *Journal of Cleaner Production. Elsevier Ltd., 150*, 135–147.

Gartenberg, C., Prat, A., & Serafeim, G. (2019). Corporate purpose and financial performance. *Organization Science, 30*(1), 1–18.

Giron, A., Kazemikhasragh, A., Cicchiello, A. F., & Panetti, E. (2022). Company characteristics and sustainability reporting: Evidence from Asia and Africa. *International Journal*.

Grewal, J. D., Riedl, E. J., & Serafeim, G. (2019). Market reaction to mandatory nonfinancial disclosure. *Management Science*.

Guiso, L., Sapienza, P., & Zingales, L. (2015). The value of corporate culture. *Journal of Financial Economics, 117*(1), 60–76.

Harrison, J. S., Philipps, R. A., & Freeman, R. E. (2020). On the 2019 business roundtable 'statement on the purpose of a corporation'. *Journal of Management, 46*(7), 1223–1237.

Hirota, S., Kubo, K., Miyajima, H., Hong, P., & Won Park, Y. (2010). Corporate mission, corporate policies and business outcomes: Evidence from Japan. *Management Decision, 48*(7), 1134–1153.

Ioannou, I., & Serafeim, G. (2017). The consequences of mandatory corporate sustainability reporting. *Harvard Business School research working paper* (11-100).

Ireland, D., Hitt, M., & Williams, J. C. (1992). Self-confidence and decisiveness: Prerequisites for effective management in the 1990s. *Business Horizons, 35*, 36–43.

King, W. R., & Cleland, D. I. (1979). *Strategic planning and policy*. Van Nostrand Reinhold.

Klemm, M., Sanderson, S., & Luffman, G. (1991). Mission statement: Selling corporate values to employees. *Long Range Planning, 24*, 73–78.

Kotler, P., & Murphy, P. E. (1981). Strategic planning for higher education. *The Journal of Higher Education, 52*(5), 470–489.

Lash, J., & Wellington, F. (2007). Competitive advantage on a warming planet. *Harvard Business Review, 85*(3), 94–102.

Lasprogata, G. A., & Cotten, M. N. (2003). Contemplating enterprise: The business and legal challenges of social entrepreneurship. *American Business Law Journal, 41*, 67.

Laville, J. L., & Nyssens, M. (2001). 18 The social enterprise. *The Emergence of Social Enterprise, 4*, 312.

Leuthesser, L., & Kohli, C. (1997). Corporate identity: The role of mission statements. *Business Horizons, 40*(3), 59–67.

Levin, I. M. (2000). Vision revisited: Telling the story of the future. *The Journal of Applied Behavioral Science, 36*(1), 91–107.

Lin, Q., Huang, Y., Zhu, R., & Zhang, Y. (2019). Comparative analysis of mission statements of Chinese and American Fortune 500 companies: A study from the perspective of linguistics. *Sustainability, 11*(18), 4905.
Link, I. (2019). Purpose & profit.
Lipton, M., Rosenblum, S. A., Cain, K. L., Niles, S. V., Blackett, A. S., & Iannone, K. C. (2019). It's time to adopt the new paradigm. In *Post on: Harvard Law School Forum on Corporate Governance and Financial Regulation*.
Mair, J., & Marti, I. (2006). Social entrepreneurship research: A source of explanation, prediction, and delight. *Journal of World Business, 41*(1), 36–44.
Matejka, K., Kurke, L. B., & Gregory, B. (1993). Mission impossible? Designing a great mission statement to ignite your plans. *Management Decision, 31*(4).
Mayer, C. (2021). The future of the corporation and the economics of purpose. *Journal of Management Studies, 58*(3), 887–901.
McGinnis, V. J. (1981). The mission statement: A key step in strategic planning. *Business, 31*(6), 39–43.
Melé, D. (2009). Integrating personalism into virtue-based business ethics: The personalist and the common good principles. *Journal of Business Ethics, 88*, 227–244.
Mirvis, P., Bradley, G., & Kinnicutt, S. (2010). Vision, mission, values: Guideposts to sustainability. *Organizational Dynamics, 39*, 316–324.
Murphy, P. J., & Coombes, S. M. (2009). A model of social entrepreneurial discovery. *Journal of Business Ethics, 87*, 325–336.
O'Gorman, C., & Doran, R. (1999). Mission statements in small and medium-sized businesses. *Journal of Small Business Management, 37*(4), 59–66.
Onida, P. (1971). *Economia d'azienda*. Utet.
Palmer, T. B., & Short, J. C. (2008). Mission statements in U.S. colleges of business: An empirical examination of their content with linkages to Configurations and Performance. *Academy of Management Learning Education, 7*, 454–470.
Pearce, J., II. (1982). The company mission as a strategic tool. *Sloan Management Review, 23*, 74–85.
Pearce, J., II, & David, F. R. (1987). Corporate mission statements: The bottom line. *Academy of Management Executive, 1*, 109–114.
Pearce, J., II, & Roth, K. (1988). Multi Nationalization of the Mission Statement. *SAM Advanced Management Journal*, (Summer), 39–44.
Penco, L., Profumo, G., & Tutore, I. (2019). Mission statements and the sustainability communication. *Symphonya. Emerging Issues in Management, 2*, 95–108.
Peredo, A. M., & McLean, M. (2006). Social entrepreneurship: A critical review of the concept. *Journal of World Business, 41*(1), 56–65.
Pérez, A. (2015). Corporate reputation and CSR reporting to stakeholders: Gaps in the literature and future lines of research. *Corporate Communications: An International Journal, 20*(1), 11–29.
Polman, P. (2016). Re-establishing trust: Making business with purpose the purpose of business. *Re-imagining Capitalism*, 17–31.
Porter, M., Serafeim, G., & Kramer, M. (2019). Where ESG fails. *Institutional Investor, 16*(2).
Porter, M. E., & Kramer, M. R. (2011). Creating shared value. *Harvard Business Review, 89*(1–2), 62–77.
Powers, E. L. (2012). Organizational mission statement guidelines revisited. *International Journal of Management Information Systems, 16*, 281–290.
Rajasekar, J. (2013). A comparative analysis of mission statement content and readability. *Journal of Management Policy and Practice, 14*(6), 131–147.
Ribando, J. M., & Bonne, G. (2010). *A new quality factor: Finding alpha with ASSET4 ESG data* (p. 31). Starmine Research Note, Thomson Reuters.
Santamaria, R., Paolone, F., Cucari, N., & Dezi, L. (2021). Non-financial strategy disclosure and environmental, social and governance score: Insight from a configurational approach. *Business Strategy and the Environment, 30*(4), 1993–2007.

Santos, F., Pache, A. C., & Birkholz, C. (2015). Making hybrids work: Aligning business models and organizational design for social enterprises. *California Management Review, 57*(3), 36–58.
Santos, F. M. (2012). A positive theory of social entrepreneurship. *Journal of Business Ethics, 111*(3), 335–351.
Serafeim, G. (2018). Investors as Stewards of the Commons? *Journal of Applied Corporate Finance, 30*(2), 8–17.
Stubbs, W., & Cocklin, C. (2008). Conceptualizing a sustainable business model. *Organization & Environment, 21*, 103–127.
Sud, M., Vansandt, C. V., & Baugous, A. M. (2009). Social entrepreneurship: The role of institutions. *Journal of Business Ethics, 85*, 201–216.
Vogt, J. (1994). Demystifying the mission statement. *Nonprof World, 12*(1), 29–32.
Wagner, N., & Wiśnicki, B. (2022). The importance of emerging technologies to the increasing of corporate sustainability in shipping companies. *Sustainability, 14*(19), 12475.
Want, J. H. (1986). Corporate mission. *Management Review*, 46–50.
Whiteman, G., Walker, B., & Perego, P. (2012). Planetary boundaries: Ecological foundations for corporate sustainability. *Journal of Management Studies, 50*, 307–336.
Xie, J., Nozawa, W., Yagi, M., Fujii, H., & Managi, S. (2019). Do environmental, social, and governance activities improve corporate financial performance? *Business Strategy and the Environment, 28*(2), 286–300.
Zaccone, M. C., & Pedrini, M. (2020). ESG factor integration into private equity. *Sustainability, 12*(14), 5725.
Zahra, S. A., Filatochev, I., & Wright, M. (2009). How do threshold firms sustain corporate entrepreneurship? The role of boards and absorptive capacity. *Journal of Business Venturing, 24*(3), 248–260.
Zappa, G. (1962). *L'economia delle aziende di consumo*. Giuffrè.
Zumente, I., & Bistrova, J. (2021). ESG importance for long-term shareholder value creation: Literature vs. practice. *Journal of Open Innovation: Technology, Market, and Complexity, 7*(2), 127.
Zumente, I., & Lāce, N. (2021). ESG rating – Necessity for the investor or the company? *Sustainability, 13*(16), 8940.

Chapter 3
Transition of Food Systems Business Models and Sustainable Performance: The Story of a Family Firm

Monica Veneziani, Laura Rocca, Riccardo Torelli, and Andrea Caccialanza

3.1 Introduction

The study will focus on the awareness of sustainability issues in a specific business sector, such as food, which is particularly relevant in Italy. The aim of the analysis is to understand what tools the company uses, in a medium-term time horizon, to adopt a sustainable business model and increase ESG performance. The role of different incentives and pressures is studied to underline the relevance of participation in that process of ecological transition.

Finally, the study attempts to identify, on an experimental basis, the link between the sustainability of the process and the economic-financial performance of the whole company.

The case study will focus on a family firm based in Italy and it represents a *unicum* in the "grain" business that is growing from a "financial" grain business to a "sustainable" grain business.

M. Veneziani (✉)
Università Cattolica del Sacro Cuore, Piacenza, Italy

Università degli Studi di Brescia, Brescia, Italy
e-mail: monica.veneziani@unibs.it

L. Rocca
Università degli Studi di Brescia, Brescia, Italy

R. Torelli
Università Cattolica del Sacro Cuore, Piacenza, Italy

A. Caccialanza
Università Cattolica del Sacro Cuore, Piacenza, Italy

Università di Bologna, Bologna, Italy

N. Castellano et al. (eds.), *Environmental, Social, Governance (ESG)*, SIDREA Series in Accounting and Business Administration,
https://doi.org/10.1007/978-3-031-76618-3_3

The chapter is structured as follows. Firstly, a literature review identifies the research gap and then the methodology explains the case study selection and how the data were analysed. Then the results focus on the content analysis of the documents and the website's disclosure, followed by the company's financial statement analysis over ten years. Finally, contributions and limitations of the study are discussed.

3.2 Literature Review

Several studies have previously observed a growing propensity to adopt more sustainability-oriented approaches to production (Adams et al., 2021). This search for models for more efficient and sustainable production systems requires constant commitment and investment in an approach that aims to involve an ever-widening number of stakeholders (Herremans et al., 2016; Yacob et al., 2019). The transition to sustainable production models is often operationalized through the implementation and development of successful examples of circular economy models (Dey et al., 2020; Morea et al., 2022). That consideration presumes the involvement of different production categories that aim to valorize and use as input each other's co-products and by-products (Silvestri et al., 2021). In these contexts, it has been demonstrated the importance of the strong commitment of the focal company to ensure a long-term investment and commitment (Pohlmann et al., 2020). Accordingly with Velasco-Muñoz et al. (2021), the agricultural systems are valuable examples of productions that balance the need to produce for an increasing (population) demand with natural sources preservation in a broad sense, representing one of the key challenges of our society. The importance of these aspects becomes even clearer when looking at the ambitious targets set by the UN 2030 Agenda and the need to monitor actual progress (Pizzi et al., 2020, 2021; Sachs et al., 2022).

To place this contribution in the existing strand of literature devoted to the analysis of best practices at the agrifood supply chain level, previous studies were collected that had this increasing granularity and focused on sustainability performance disclosure and reporting quality, circular supply chain management practices, food and/or agriculture supply chain management practices, and cereals supply chain management practices.

Secondly, contributions were organized by thematic areas of interest preparatory to the next phase of content analysis. To group these themes consistently, a grouping system was developed that borrowed the areas of interest identified in the Seuring and Müller (2008) study on sustainable supply chains, namely, *legal demands/ regulation*, *customer demands*, *response to stakeholders*, *competitive advantage*, *environmental and social pressure groups,* and *reputation loss*. To these, it was deemed appropriate to add two additional thematic topic areas further explored in the literature regarding sustainable supply chain management (Kamble et al., 2018; Helfaya & Whittington, 2019): *coordination and networking activities* and *risk mitigation*.

Table 3.1 Literature review. Source: Adapted from Seuring and Müller (2008)

Pressures and incentives	Sustainability performance disclosure and reporting quality	Circular supply chain management practices	Food and/or agriculture supply chain management practices	Cereals supply chain management practices
Legal demands/ regulation	Ernstberger and Grüning (2013); Accounting Directive 2013/34/EU; Directive 2014/95/EU; Dlgs 254/2016; Idemudia and Kwakyewah (2018); Alshbili et al. (2021)	Wiek et al. (2011); Dentchev et al. (2017)	Fiandrino et al. (2019); Farm to Fork strategy, 2020	Hamprecht et al. (2005); Labarthe et al. (2021)
Customer demands	Romero et al. (2019); Rustam et al. (2020); van Langen et al. (2021)	Abbey et al. (2015); Lambert (2014); Prieto-Sandoval et al. (2018)	Charlebois (2008); Garner and Ayala (2018)	Altamore et al. (2020); Łaba et al. (2022)
Response to stakeholders	Isenmann and Kim (2006); Islam and Deegan (2008); Tilt (2010); Herremans et al. (2016); Higgins et al. (2015); Romero et al. (2019)	Manetti (2011); Manetti and Toccafondi (2012); Hahn and Kühnen (2013); Amran et al. (2014); Braun et al. (2021); van Langen (2021); Ernst et al. (2022)	Devalle et al. (2021)	Courtonne et al. (2016)
Competitive advantage	Agostini et al. (2022)	Loorbach (2007); Walsh and Sulkowski (2010); Crous et al. (2021); Pizzi et al. (2021); Manninen and Huiskonen (2022)	Beske et al. (2014); Camanzi and Giua (2020); Adams et al. (2021)	Cacchiarelli and Sorrentino (2018); Cacchiarelli and Sorrentino (2019); Galli et al. (2017)
Environmental and social pressure groups	Antonini et al. (2020); Ernst et al. (2022).	Geissdoerfer et al. (2017); Mies and Gold (2021)	Boyer (2022)	Le Heron and Hayward (2002); Grippo et al. (2019)
Reputation loss	Yang et al. (2021); Baah et al. (2021)	Veleva et al. (2017); Ethirajan et al. (2021)	Esposito et al. (2020); Agnusdei and Coluccia (2022)	Scandizzo (2011)

(continued)

Table 3.1 (continued)

Pressures and incentives	Sustainability performance disclosure and reporting quality	Circular supply chain management practices	Food and/or agriculture supply chain management practices	Cereals supply chain management practices
Coordination and networking activities	Adams et al. (2021)	Kamble et al. (2018); Stranieri et al. (2019); Zaid et al. (2020)	Bhagat and Dhar (2011); Zucchella and Previtali (2019); Stranieri et al. (2019); Camanzi and Giua (2020)	Stanco et al. (2020); Ciliberti et al. (2023)
Risk mitigation	Antonini et al. (2020); Rustam et al. (2020)	Tchankova (2002); Hoyt and Liebenberg (2011); Kern et al. (2012); Bridge (2016); Kouloukoui et al. (2019); Helfaya and Whittington (2019)	Ali and Gölgeci (2020).	Ivanov and Das (2020); Amicarelli et al. (2023)

Table 3.1 shows the references identified for each topic area and each strand of literature deepened by this exploratory case study.

Literature has highlighted different mechanisms that can effectively promote the adoption of circular business models; three of that are discussed in this chapter.

Firstly, the waste loss is proposed as relevant. In particular, Tanveer et al. (2021) have stressed the need for the reduction of agrifood waste in order to promote closed-loop supply chains and target the zero hunger and responsible consumption and production goals. Kumar et al. (2022) contribute to this debate developing sustainable performance assessment framework through integrated triple bottom line (TBL) and circular economy practice.

Secondly, within the specific agro-food context, Neri et al. (2021) emphasize the need to find performance measurement systems that value a sufficiently large number of themes and at the same time are cost-effective in their use by the widest possible number of companies, starting with the focal firms in supply chains.

A third suggested element may regard logistics operations that have, as well, to deal with this new perspective. As proposed by Bloemhof et al. (2015) green logistics plays a relevant role in food production and current strategies may face barriers to the effective improvement.

The case study analysed will show pragmatically the adoption and evolution of those three sustainable and circular practices. We highlight (i) the practices the company has undertaken to valorize the by-products and co-products of the cereal chain within its feed and energy supply chain, (ii) the promotion of short supply chains with cultivation contracts stipulated with farmers, and (iii) the effort to integrate its logistics by exploiting the advantages of inter-modality and reducing environmental impact.

It can be noted as the analysis of a detailed case study can contribute to the existing debate enriching the literature on the promotion of circular business models in the food sector, specifically in the cereal one. This case is also relevant because it allows us to understand how the integration of sustainability practices has been undertaken in the medium and long term.

3.3 Methodology

The case selection was based on the ability of the case to offer theoretical insights to understand how the transition to a sustainable and circular business model takes place, *in practice*. In this sense, Cereal Docks can be considered an unusually revelatory case (Yin, 2017), because it has a historical background in the food sector; it is a family firm, not listed, which adopts a sustainable approach over time, but it is also an enterprise that is capable of innovative solutions and flexible adjustments towards circularity. Thus, our case was selected because of the opportunity it offered of developing a concept by learning about various hypotheses and their observable implications in a specific context (Eisenhardt & Graebner, 2007).

Our research covers a period from the foundation to the recent years of transition to a sustainable and circular business model. To analyse data, we adopted an iterated, inductive approach (Langley, 1999; Langley et al., 2013) based on the iteration between data and literature, rather than from a well-defined theoretical framework (Corbin & Strauss, 2008). Multiple sources are used in that process: archival analysis and website's examination.

Thematic analysis was conducted on an inductive basis, as the research aimed to explore the subject. Initially, institutional documents, such as sustainability reports, balance sheets, income statements, and website, were independently analysed by the four authors to identify the themes related to Table 1's pressures and incentives. To ensure the rigour of the thematic analysis, the identified themes were discussed among the authors. They were applied to all sustainability reports, and their usefulness for analysis was confirmed by all authors. Once the themes were identified, a coding section was constructed by two authors for using NVivo. The following documents or sources were analysed, with the support of NVivo software: the company's website (as of 8 September 2023), the 2021 impact report, the 2022 impact report, the sustainability report for 2014/2017, the sustainability report for 2018/2020, and the sustainability report for 2022.

Then, a financial statement analysis over ten years was undertaken by another author to identify the economic and financial evolution of the company (Collier, 2015; Gibson, 2011; Kieso et al., 2019). That is due to, on an experimental basis, trying to identify if there is a link between the sustainability of the process and the transition to circular business model and the economic-financial performance, focusing on a specific product or process.

3.4 Presentation of the Cereal Docks Case Study and Its Relevance in the Agrifood Context

The history of this company began when Mauro Fanin, the founder, transformed Aurora Snc into Cereal Docks Srl in 1993. The small company, focused on the harvesting and drying of corn, soon started investing in new technologies and equipment. The timeline of the progressive expansion of volumes and activities can effectively resume the milestones of this growth and the progressive evolution of the approach to a circular and innovative business model. In 2000, it has been transformed in a joint stock company and started processing the oil seed in their first extraction plan. This step will be the first move towards ever greater vertical integration of activities; in fact, in 2007 both refinery and transesterification plant began operations in the Camisano facility. As it also became active in international markets, the *Cereal Docks International* was founded in order to ensure the supply of raw materials necessary for corporate demand. As the volume increased in 2012 the Camisano Vicentino' facility extraction plant was opened. A broader product diversification occurred in 2013, when the *Cereal Docks Food* was founded and started to operate in the lecithin and oil sector. In 2016, the new extraction plant began operations in the Porto Marghera facility and after the significant expansion the productive facilities began full operations. That plant has been completely renovated and integrated with three logistics structures (sea/railway/road), while the facility in Camisano was improved for higher performance. At international level the origination plant in Romania was also fitted with a railway station and the facility in Fiorenzuola became a strategic warehouse for product distribution. On the logistic side, in 2019 Cereal Docks Spa acquired an abandoned industrial area in Summaga, reinforcing the role of Portogruaro as the strategic hub for Group logistics. This logic of continuous intermodal integration follows the example of a diversification of the transport vehicles used and it is aimed at reducing the use of road vehicles. Accordingly with this approach, in 2023, Cereal Docks Group joined the ALIS—Sustainable Inter-modality Logistics Association, confirming the commitment to an association that promotes synergies and innovation on logistical side.

In 2016, *Demethra Biotech* was also founded and the start-up company *ATP R&D* began operations in the biotech industry. This step represents a further diversification of activities within the group, which is therefore no longer limited to the agrifood categories but is expanding into technological innovation.

In 2017, *Cereal Docks Organic* was founded to develop the organic market and two years later took over a rental contract and management of the company branch in the Roverchiara plant. This facility is fully dedicated to the production of oils and organic panels, texturized vegetable proteins, and micronized meals for food uses. This milestone is consequent to the establishment of organic references in the group's product portfolio and reaffirms the progressive transition.

As well in 2017 the *Mantegna Academy*, the group's business school, was instituted to manage training and promotion of the group's human resources. Two years later the Mantegna Academy launched the *Carta Bianca* project, "art in the company", and the campus project dedicated to students preparing their university theses in the company. These two initiatives jointly represent the progressive approach to structured stakeholders' engagement processes. This also represents a system of proactive stakeholder engagement (Brulhart et al., 2019).

In 2018, the new facility at via dell'Innovazione in Camisano Vicentino began full operations. This new headquarters was built to foster process efficiency and to concentrate all new business, governance, and management control for the entire *Cereal Docks Group* in a single place.

In 2022, the *Grey Silos Venture*, the corporate venture capital of *Cereal Docks Group*, was launched with the aim of supporting innovative start-ups, production processes, and new business models in the agrifood sector. At the end of the same year, the acquisition of *Ital Green Oil*, a firm operating in the transformation of oil seeds, was also announced, confirming its growth capacity also with merge and acquisition (M&A) operations. With the technical partner X-Farm Technologies the *App Sistema Green*® was also announced. The purpose of this tool is to foster the existing company brand *Sistema Green*® increasing the control and tracking their suppliers' supply chains. Similar initiative has been performed through the Cereal Docks' *Alimento Italia* ®. These references are present on organized distribution channels and provide to final consumers information about the genuineness of raw materials or ingredients used and the certainty of their origin from Italian Non-GMO seeds. Thanks to the verification code or the QR code on the product label, it is possible to retrace the entire production chain, accordingly with similar cases in food industry (Tayal et al., 2021).

These few main milestones summarize the evolution of an Italian family food company that has proposed as its claim "*transform to sustain the future*". Therefore, this sustainability approach has been embraced in a multidimensional perspective that comprehends the social, economic, and environmental dimensions. In its current set-up, the group operates within a variety of production industries, such as, in a non-exhaustive list, animal feed, food, refining, cosmetic, biotechnologies, and chemical and pharmaceutical.

This strategic product and market differentiation has allowed the valorization of various by-products and co-products in a circular economy logic that is going to be taken up within the chapter. Parallel to the conception and development of this governance and group structure, the group has also implemented a systematic performance measuring system aimed at the evaluation of non-financial impacts as well. This commitment has been reflected in the reporting and publication of sustainability reports every three years since 2014 (2014/2017; 2018/2020). The measurement of internal impacts also corresponds to a declared commitment to the goals set internationally by the UN 2030 agenda, as demonstrated by the second three-year sustainability report.

3.5 Empirical Analysis and Discussion

3.5.1 Content Analysis

To thoroughly comprehend the underlying elements, drivers, and motivations behind the previously mentioned sustainable practices and circular economy practices, as well as the relevant strategic nodes, a content analysis was conducted on key corporate communication tools with reference to sustainability practices. The coding method was developed based on elements highlighted in previous literature as potential sources of pressure and/or incentives (see Table 3.1 for reference) and the results are discussed using the same reference.

3.5.2 Legal Demand and Regulation

The role of legal dimensions and regulations plays a marginal and indirect role in this case study. Beyond the aspect of communication and sustainability reporting considering new obligations stemming from European reference standards, there are elements of pressure attributed to regular but solely related to certain mandatory safety and quality certifications (e.g. HACCP), as explicitly evident in the company's communicative style across all analysed sources. The narrative regarding the steps taken over time towards achieving a sustainable and circular business model clearly conveys that these actions result from a deliberate choice by the company's management, driven by a well-structured long-term strategy and deep-seated values. We are in the realm of voluntarism rather than regulatory obligation. This difference is readily appreciable from the diversity of actions undertaken, which range over time from targeted interventions for specific stakeholder categories to radical changes in the way of producing and viewing the company's production chain ("Sistema Green® is Cereal Docks' brand that since 2012 describes a cultivation system that combines environmental, social, and economic sustainability. Italian agricultural companies that join the Cereal Docks supply chain, gathered under the Sistema Green umbrella, adhere to specific production protocols that guarantee product nationality, absence of GMOs, and control of greenhouse gas emissions", Sustainability Report 2018–2020).

3.5.3 Customer Demands

The role of the customer appears to be influential and pivotal in the analysed company and represents one of the most recurring and constant elements throughout the years examined in this research. The theme of product quality and safety is, in fact, the second most prominent element after certifications (which are closely related). In the company's narrative, it is repeatedly emphasized that there can be no sustainable product and production process without them also being of high quality and safe, especially for the customer. The most prevalent theme, certifications, confirms what has just been mentioned: the company explicitly states in its official documents the need to provide concrete and reliable evidence to its customers that the products created by the company are primarily safe and conform to very high quality standards ("Our quality and sustainability offices work synergistically to ensure control over the supply chain in terms of quality, safety, traceability, and any requirements emerging from the market", Sustainability Report 2018–2020). This customer-centric focus has led the company over time to consider entering segments not yet served, such as the organic market, and to communicate more effectively and widely about the positive and significant efforts being made operationally and strategically to ensure a genuinely responsible, ethical, and sustainable business model.

3.5.4 Response to Stakeholders

As previously outlined for the company's approach towards customers, it is evident that the analysed company invests significant resources in striving for high levels of safety and product quality to respond to the various stakeholders it deals with. A particular focus for this company is on the various actors in the supply chain, for which it aims to act as a leading entity and promoter of good practices. However, we are dealing with more of an autonomous action by the company based on its values and strategies rather than a response or reaction to external actions. This proactive approach has some limits, particularly evident when analysing the processes related to materiality analysis, both for reporting and for the improvement and redirection of its practices. From all the documents analysed, it is clear that engagement with various stakeholder groups exists but is rather indirect and formal. Methods such as online questionnaires are mostly used, rather than tools for meetings and discussions capable of bringing out the deeper values, requests, and sentiments of stakeholders ("A representation of internal and external stakeholders filled out an online questionnaire", Sustainability Report 2018–2020). This aspect is currently lacking but appears in the company's plans as an area for future improvement.

3.5.5 Competitive Advantage

The company's sustainability actions and communications also have a clear commercial and competitive purpose. It is evident from the language used in various company documents that achieving a leading position in the market, in the supply chain, and being a first mover is one of the driving objectives. The use of numerous recognized certifications and the presence in uncovered market segments (e.g. the organic segment), combined with the utilization of significant process and product innovations, make it clear that the company aims to leverage its strengths to attain a unique competitive position and a significant presence in its reference markets ("It represents a turning point for Cereal Docks Organic, which takes over the production plant in Roverchiara (VR) entirely dedicated to organic production, with the aim of expanding its presence in this market", Sustainability Report 2018–2020). The numerous M&A operations carried out by the company also confirm the strong desire to lead not only in the reference market but also in the production chain, taking control of various steps within it.

3.5.6 Environmental and Social Pressure Groups

New demands and pressures from external groups regarding the impacts and negative externalities produced by the company play a key role in its development and transformation. A temporal analysis reveals that over the years, the company has consistently sought to address and deal with weaknesses in its activities, or more accurately, vulnerabilities subject to external scrutiny. It is clear that the company has consistently integrated social and environmental objectives into its corporate purpose, first through individual limited actions and later through a fundamental shift in its core values. The transition to a benefit corporation and adherence to the B Impact Assessment for B Corps highlight in company documents that the ultimate goal has evolved from purely economic and financial objectives to a common benefit purpose. In the latest sustainability report and impact report, the company states that "... the ultimate purpose of the company is to ensure nourishment and well-being for people, animals, and the environment to maintain ecosystem equilibrium." In addition to a value commitment, there is also substantial commitment backed by a considerable number of process and product certifications that the company has held for years.

3.5.7 Reputation Loss

These certifications form the basis of a corporate credibility system that relies on third-party verification of corporate operations ("Since 2012, third-party certifications have become indispensable for the market, providing the industry with guarantees of safe, traceable, and certified origin products," Sustainability Report 2014–2017). This is achieved not only through an extensive and established certification system but also through deliberate quality and clarity of communication, as stated by top management in the Sustainability Report 2014–2017 ("This commitment must be recognized and rewarded by the market. To make all this happen, it is important not only to do but also to promote and communicate sustainability"). Over the referenced time period in this document, it becomes clear that one of the primary

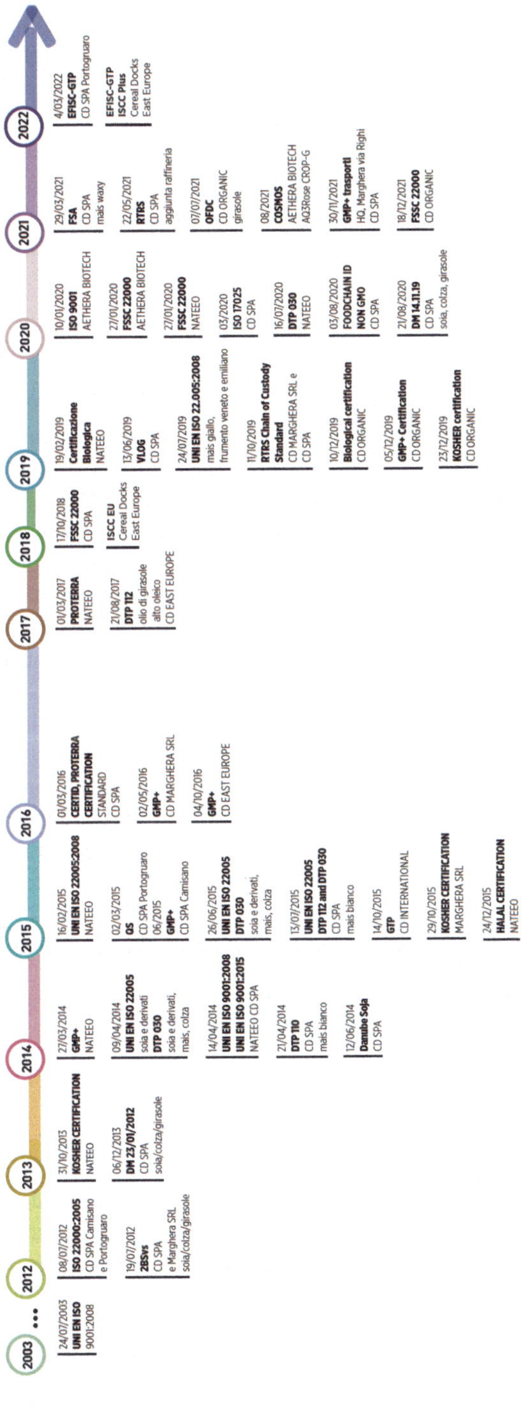

Fig. 3.1 Certifications (source: Cereal Docks Sustainability Report 2022)

objectives of reporting and communication practices in the socio-environmental context is to protect corporate legitimacy, reputation, and credibility (see Fig. 3.1 for certifications over time). Communicative efforts are therefore focused on strongly and clearly highlighting the positive actions the company is undertaking or planning for the future. This approach shifts over the years to become more nuanced in the subsequent sustainability balance sheet (2018–2020) and fades away in the 2022 edition, where the goal of common benefit and proactivity based on solid corporate values emerges as a key determinant.

3.5.8 Coordination and Networking Activities

The aforementioned values also include the entities with which the company collaborates within its supply chain. It is clear that the ambitious goal is to create and maintain efficiency and sustainability throughout the entire supply chain, starting from the early stages in the fields: "Sistema Green is Cereal Docks' brand that since 2012 describes a cultivation system that combines environmental, social, and economic sustainability, with the aim of creating value for Italian agricultural supply chains and the products originating from those supply chains. Italian agricultural companies that join the Cereal Docks supply chain, gathered under the Sistema Green umbrella, adhere to specific production protocols that guarantee product nationality, absence of GMOs, and control of greenhouse gas emissions. In addition, Sistema Green ensures placement certainty and promotes compliance with health and safety obligations in workplaces" (Sustainability Report 2022). Furthermore, the company's commitment lies in valorizing, supporting, and promoting the local community and the businesses operating within it. Several references in the analysed documents are for local companies cooperating in various stages of the supply chain, and there is a clear preference for the local and traditional system ("The Cereal Docks Group has always shown interest in its local territory, aware of the importance and impact the company has on the local fabric" Sustainability Report 2022).

3.5.9 Risk Mitigation

Finally, although it does not emerge as a crucial element, the desire to mitigate social and environmental risks is among the factors promoting sustainable and virtuous behaviours. In particular, the company seeks to minimize dependence on external energy sources by investing substantial resources in on-site electricity generation plants, even though waste materials or semi-finished products are recovered. It is often mentioned that disruptive events such as COVID-19, the Russo-Ukrainian war, and ongoing socio-economic crises have influenced the company's short-term management strategies and choices towards projects aimed at risk reduction and mitigation, especially in terms of supply difficulties (raw materials and energy) and price volatility.

Table 3.2 Main financial performance data (source: authors' elaboration)

Cereal Docks	2022	2021	2020	2019	2018	2017	2016	2015	2014	2013
Net sales (thousands)	1.359.652 €	1.000.054 €	817.937 €	529.113 €	783.415 €	708.742 €	602.730 €	460.969 €	523.526 €	511.674 €
Production values	1.405.821	1.026.562	844.308	543.376	803.102	731.731	618.214	504.640	551.096	525.115
EBIT	62.294	50.105	21.645	31.548	58.484	9.606	38.710	34.649	21.549	−5.950
Net income	48724	37183	16541	21914	40652	4015	23924	21810	8701	−12785
Net financial costs/Net sales	−0.1%	−0.1%	−0.2%	−0.2%	−0.3%	−0.4%	−0.8%	−1.1%	−1.3%	−1.3%
Labour costs/Net sales	1.2%	1.4%	1.7%	1.5%	1.3%	1.3%	1.4%	1.6%	1.3%	1.2%
Amortization and depreciation/Net sales	1.9%	1.7%	2.6%	1.9%	1.7%	1.8%	1.9%	2.1%	1.6%	1.6%
Debt ratio	1.5	1.3	1.6	1.6	2.5	3.9	3.6	2.2	5.6	7.4
Coverage net fixed assets	1.4	1.2	1.4	1	1	0.8	0.9	0.6	0.6	0.6
ROI	7.7%	7.1%	4.7%	7.3%	11.7%	1.9%	8.6%	9.5%	6.6%	−1.8%
ROE	17.5%	13.8%	10.3%	15.5%	39.9%	4.1%	32.1%	44.8%	21.7%	−24.1%

3.5.10 Financial Analysis

From a financial perspective, the Group Cereal Docks presents in the last ten years of analysis a significant economic and financial improvement.

The very high debt ratio in 2013 indicates that debts were 7.4 times greater than equity (Table 3.2). This situation progressively improves over the years until it reaches decidedly more sustainable values from 2019. In 2022, the debts are only 1.5 times greater than equity.

The improvement in the financial situation is also evidenced by the continuous decrease in the incidence of net financial costs on net sales (or turnover).

The structure of financial resources compared with the composition of investments shows a clear improvement over time and reaches the balance position from 2018 onwards. In previous years, however, long-term investments were also partly financed by short-term financing. This situation of imbalance is evident especially in the first three years of the analysis.

From an economic point of view, the turnover tends to grow over the ten years, going from 511 thousand euros in 2013 to more than one million three hundred thousand euros in 2022. The only two years of decline were 2015 and 2019. Membership of the Group to the agro-industrial supply chain has allowed it to continue its activity also in 2020, the most acute period of the first wave of COVID, thus meeting a demand that has not suffered any declines. The same growth trend is given by production value.

Apart from 2013 in which a negative operating income and a net loss emerged, in the following years the typical business result is always positive with a good percentage impact on turnover. The growth in turnover, in general, is therefore accompanied by a less than proportional increase in cost of sales. The only exception is 2020 in which labour costs and internal structural costs are high.

The ROI confirms the good economic growth of the typical business over the ten years; the percentage values are always significant except for 2013, in which a negative indicator was recorded, and 2017 which shows the lowest value.

The ROE is satisfactory and highlights fluctuating but always high values, with the sole exception of 2017. By interpreting the debt situation and the ROI trend as a system, it is observed that the ROE depends on both the ability of the typical business to produce income and the effect of financial leverage. This effect decreases from 2019 as debts decrease.

Overall, it can be said that the Group Cereal Docks is solid from a financial point of view, with a good balance between investments and debts and continuously growing economically. The typical business contributes increasingly to the production of income; financial costs decrease their weight: all this impacts the net profit which reaches its maximum value in 2022, the year with the highest turnover and EBIT value. The Group continues to focus on the innovation of procedures, processes, and products with the aim of increasing efficiencies in terms of costs and, at the same time, to expand the range of products and services offered to customer.

The Group's commitment to R&D and investments in the sustainability of product lines have allowed it to obtain various certifications which have certainly contributed to the business growth. With the certifications obtained from 2019 onwards (see Fig. 3.1), the path traced by the strategy aimed at integrated sustainability of the business is clear.

It is not possible to identify a precise link between performance and a particular strategic choice but in general it can be stated that the underlying choice to invest and focus on the integrated sustainability of the business, improving it over time, has allowed the achievement of satisfactory economic and financial performances.

3.6 Conclusion

The work falls within the research strand of accounting for sustainability and, in particular, within the gaps in the literature on the lack of studies that investigate in deep how the increasing of sustainability consciousness will increase the ESG performance and then the financial one (Daugaard & Ding, 2022; Huang, 2021; Khan, 2022). The aim of this chapter is to present a development of the literature with respect to the promotion of sustainable and circular business model, thanks to the discussion of successful initiative promoted by this focal Italian food company. The chapter contributes to understanding the challenges of the transition from a "financial" grain to a "sustainable" grain, using a relevant case study (Yin, 2017). It seems that the evolution towards sustainability, stakeholder's engagement, and the need for a wider "control" over the supply chain (i.e. with M&A) is capable of increasing both the ESG and the financial performances of the whole company. As far as is known, there are no examples in the literature that have a combination of taking into account the cereal sector, studying a family firm, and examining a longitudinal experience of transition to a sustainable and circular business model. Moreover, the application of financial analysis could be considered an experimental investigation. The limitations are that of case studies, a case that could not be easily generalized but it could be recognized as a *best practice*. Future research will deepen the hypothesis of correlation of ESG and financial performances using other types of data, such as ESG KPIs evolution and interviews with key managers and stakeholders.

References

Abbey, J. D., Meloy, M. G., Guide, V. D. R., Jr., & Atalay, S. (2015). Remanufactured products in closed-loop supply chains for consumer goods. *Production and Operations Management, 24*(3), 488–503.

Adams, D., Donovan, J., & Topple, C. (2021). Achieving sustainability in food manufacturing operations and their supply chains: Key insights from a systematic literature review. *Sustainable Production and Consumption, 28*, 1491–1499.

Agnusdei, G. P., & Coluccia, B. (2022). Sustainable agrifood supply chains: Bibliometric, network and content analyses. *Science of the Total Environment*, 153704.

Agostini, M., Costa, E., & Korca, B. (2022). Non-financial disclosure and corporate financial performance under directive 2014/95/EU: Evidence from Italian listed companies. *Accounting in Europe, 19*(1), 78–109.

Ali, I., & Gölgeci, I. (2020). Managing climate risks through social capital in agrifood supply chains. *Supply Chain Management: An International Journal, 26*(1), 1–16.

Alshbili, I., Elamer, A. A., & Moustafa, M. W. (2021). Social and environmental reporting, sustainable development and institutional voids: Evidence from a developing country. *Corporate Social Responsibility and Environmental Management, 28*(2), 881–895.

Altamore, L., Ingrassia, M., Columba, P., Chironi, S., & Bacarella, S. (2020). Italian consumers' preferences for pasta and consumption trends: Tradition or innovation? *Journal of International Food & Agribusiness Marketing, 32*(4), 337–360.

Amicarelli, V., Lombardi, M., Varese, E., & Bux, C. (2023). Material flow and economic cost analysis of the Italian artisan bread production before and during the Russia-Ukraine conflict. *Environmental Impact Assessment Review, 101*, 107101.

Amran, A., Lee, S. P., & Devi, S. S. (2014). The influence of governance structure and strategic corporate social responsibility toward sustainability reporting quality. *Business Strategy and the environment, 23*(4), 217–235.

Antonini, C., Beck, C., & Larrinaga, C. (2020). Subpolitics and sustainability reporting boundaries. The case of working conditions in global supply chains. *Accounting, Auditing & Accountability Journal, 33*(7), 1535–1567.

Azizul Islam, M., & Deegan, C. (2008). Motivations for an organisation within a developing country to report social responsibility information: Evidence from Bangladesh. *Accounting, Auditing & Accountability Journal, 21*(6), 850–874.

Baah, C., Opoku-Agyeman, D., Acquah, I. S. K., Agyabeng-Mensah, Y., Afum, E., Faibil, D., & Abdoulaye, F. A. M. (2021). Examining the correlations between stakeholder pressures, green production practices, firm reputation, environmental and financial performance: Evidence from manufacturing SMEs. *Sustainable Production and Consumption, 27*, 100–114.

Beske, P., Land, A., & Seuring, S. (2014). Sustainable supply chain management practices and dynamic capabilities in the food industry: A critical analysis of the literature. *International Journal of Production Economics, 152*, 131–143.

Bhagat, D., & Dhar, U. R. (2011). Agriculture supply chain management: A review. *IUP Journal of Supply Chain Management, 8*(3).

Bloemhof, J. M., van der Vorst, J. G., Bastl, M., & Allaoui, H. (2015). Sustainability assessment of food chain logistics. *International Journal of Logistics Research and Applications, 18*(2), 101–117.

Boyer, C. (2022). Towards new accounts of the soil. Practical application of a genuine ecological accounting from the organisation to the socio-ecosystem. In *9th CSEAR Emerging Scholars Colloquium.*

Braun, A. B., Visentin, C., da Silva Trentin, A. W., & Thomé, A. (2021). List of relevant sustainability indicators in remediation processes and their validation by stakeholders. *Journal of Cleaner Production, 317*, Article 128440.

Bridge, S. (2016). Self-employment: Deviation or the norm? *Journal of Management & Organization, 22*(6), 764–778.

Brulhart, F., Gherra, S., & Quelin, B. V. (2019). Do stakeholder orientation and environmental proactivity impact firm profitability? *Journal of Business Ethics, 158*, 25–46.

Cacchiarelli, L., & Sorrentino, A. (2018). Market power in food supply chain: Evidence from Italian pasta chain. *British Food Journal.*

Cacchiarelli, L., & Sorrentino, A. (2019). Pricing strategies in the Italian retail sector: The case of pasta. *Social Sciences, 8*(4), 113.

Camanzi, L., & Giua, C. (2020). SME network relationships and competitive strategies in the agri-food sector: Some empirical evidence and a provisional conceptual framework. *European Business Review*.

Charlebois, S. (2008). The gateway to a Canadian market-driven agricultural Economy: A framework for demand chain management in the food industry. *British Food Journal*.

Ciliberti, S., Frascarelli, A., & Martino, G. (2023). Matching ecological transition and food security in the cereal sector: The role of farmers' preferences on production contracts. *Frontiers in Sustainable Food Systems, 7*, 42.

Collier, P. M. (2015). *Accounting for managers*. Chapter 7. Wiley Publications, UK.

Corbin, J., & Strauss, A. (2008). *Basics of qualitative research* (3rd ed.). Sage.

Courtonne, J. Y., Longaretti, P. Y., Alapetite, J., & Dupré, D. (2016). Environmental pressures embodied in the French cereals supply chain. *Journal of Industrial Ecology, 20*(3), 423–434.

Crous, C., Battisti, E., & Leonidou, E. (2021). Non-financial reporting and company financial performance: A systematic literature review and integrated framework. *EuroMed Journal of Business, 17*(4), 652–676.

Daugaard, D., & Ding, A. (2022). Global drivers for ESG performance: The body of knowledge. *Sustainability, 14*(4), 2322.

Dentchev, N. A., Haezendonck, E., & Van Balen, M. (2017). The role of governments in the business and society debate. *Business & Society, 56*(4), 527–544.

Devalle, A., Gromis di Trana, M., Fiandrino, S., & Vrontis, D. (2021). Integrated thinking rolls! Stakeholder engagement actions translate integrated thinking into practice. *Meditari Accountancy Research, 29*(4), 943–965.

Dey, P. K., Malesios, C., De, D., Budhwar, P., Chowdhury, S., & Cheffi, W. (2020). Circular economy to enhance sustainability of small and medium-sized enterprises. *Business Strategy and the Environment, 29*(6), 2145–2169.

Eisenhardt, K. M., & Graebner, M. E. (2007). Theory building from cases: Opportunities and challenges. *Academy of Management Journal, 50*(1), 25–32.

Ernst, R. A., Gerken, M., Hack, A., & Hülsbeck, M. (2022). SMES' reluctance to embrace corporate sustainability: The effect of stakeholder pressure on self-determination and the role of social proximity. *Journal of Cleaner Production, 335*, Article 130273.

Ernstberger, J., & Grüning, M. (2013). How do firm-and country-level governance mechanisms affect firms' disclosure? *Journal of Accounting and Public Policy, 32*(3), 50–67.

Esposito, B., Sessa, M. R., Sica, D., & Malandrino, O. (2020). Towards circular economy in the agri-food sector. A systematic literature review. *Sustainability, 12*(18), 7401.

Ethirajan, M., Arasu, M. T., Kandasamy, J., Kek, V., Nadeem, S. P., & Kumar, A. (2021). Analysing the risks of adopting circular economy initiatives in manufacturing supply chains. *Business Strategy and the Environment, 30*(1), 204–236.

Fiandrino, S., Busso, D., & Vrontis, D. (2019). Sustainable responsible conduct beyond the boundaries of compliance: Lessons from Italian listed food and beverage companies. *British Food Journal, 121*(5), 1035–1049.

Galli, F., Venturi, F., Bartolini, F., Gava, O., Zinnai, A., Chiara, S., Andrich, G., & Brunori, G. (2017). Shaping food systems towards improved nutrition: A case study on Tuscan Bread Protected Designation of Origin. *International Food and Agribusiness Management Review, 20*(4), 533–552.

Garner, B., & Ayala, C. (2018). Consumer supply-chain demands and challenges at farmers' markets. *British Food Journal*.

Geissdoerfer, M., Savaget, P., Bocken, N. M., & Hultink, E. J. (2017). The circular economy–A new sustainability paradigm? *Journal of Cleaner Production, 143*, 757–768.

Gibson, C. H. (2011). *Financial statement analysis*. South-Western Cengage Learning.

Grippo, V., Romano, S., & Vastola, A. (2019). Multi-criteria evaluation of bran use to promote circularity in the cereal production chain. *Natural Resources Research, 28*, 125–137.

Hahn, R., & Kühnen, M. (2013). Determinants of sustainability reporting: A review of results, trends, theory, and opportunities in an expanding field of research. *Journal of Cleaner Production, 59*, 5–21.
Hamprecht, J., Corsten, D., Noll, M., & Meier, E. (2005). Controlling the sustainability of food supply chains. *Supply Chain Management: An International Journal, 10*(1), 7–10.
Helfaya, A., & Whittington, M. (2019). Does designing environmental sustainability disclosure quality measures make a difference? *Business Strategy and the Environment, 28*(4), 525–541.
Herremans, I. M., Nazari, J. A., & Mahmoudian, F. (2016). Stakeholder relationships, engagement, and sustainability reporting. *Journal of Business Ethics, 138*, 417–435.
Higgins, C., Milne, M. J., & Van Gramberg, B. (2015). The uptake of sustainability reporting in Australia. *Journal of Business Ethics, 129*(2), 445–468.
Hoyt, R. E., & Liebenberg, A. P. (2011). The value of enterprise risk management. *Journal of Risk and Insurance, 78*(4), 795–822.
Huang, D. Z. (2021). Environmental, social and governance (ESG) activity and firm performance: A review and consolidation. *Accounting & Finance, 61*(1), 335–360.
Idemudia, U., & Kwakyewah, C. (2018). Analysis of the Canadian national corporate social responsibility strategy: Insights and implications. *Corporate Social Responsibility and Environmental Management, 25*(5), 928–938.
Isenmann, R., & Kim, K. C. (2006). Interactive sustainability reporting. Developing clear target group tailoring and stimulating stakeholder dialogue. In S. Schaltegger, M. Bennett, & R. Burritt (Eds.), *Sustainability accounting and reporting* (pp. 533–555). Springer.
Ivanov, D., & Das, A. (2020). Coronavirus (COVID-19/SARS-CoV-2) and supply chain resilience: A research note. *International Journal of Integrated Supply Management, 13*(1), 90–102.
Kamble, S. S., Gunasekaran, A., & Gawankar, S. A. (2018). Sustainable Industry 4.0 framework: A systematic literature review identifying the current trends and future perspectives. *Process Safety and Environmental Protection, 117*, 408–425.
Kern, D., Moser, R., Hartmann, E., & Moder, M. (2012). Supply risk management: Model development and empirical analysis. *International Journal of Physical Distribution & Logistics Management, 42*(1), 60–82.
Khan, M. A. (2022). ESG disclosure and firm performance: A bibliometric and meta analysis. *Research in International Business and Finance, 61*, 101668.
Kieso, D. E., Weygandt, J. J., & Warfield, T. D. (2019). *Intermediate accounting*. Chapter 24. Wiley Publications, UK.
Kouloukoui, D., Sant'Anna, Â. M. O., da Silva Gomes, S. M., de Oliveira Marinho, M. M., de Jong, P., Kiperstok, A., & Torres, E. A. (2019). Factors influencing the level of environmental disclosures in sustainability reports: Case of climate risk disclosure by Brazilian companies. *Corporate Social Responsibility and Environmental Management, 26*(4), 791–804.
Kumar, M., Sharma, M., Raut, R. D., Mangla, S. K., & Choubey, V. K. (2022). Performance assessment of circular driven sustainable agri-food supply chain towards achieving sustainable consumption and production. *Journal of Cleaner Production, 372*, 133698.
Łaba, S., Cacak-Pietrzak, G., Łaba, R., Sułek, A., & Szczepański, K. (2022). Food losses in consumer cereal production in Poland in the context of food security and environmental impact. *Agriculture, 12*(5), 665.
Labarthe, P., Coléno, F., Enjalbert, J., Fugeray-Scarbel, A., Hannachi, M., & Lemarié, S. (2021). Exploration, exploitation and environmental innovation in agriculture. The case of variety mixture in France and Denmark. *Technological Forecasting and Social Change, 172*, 121028.
Lambert, D. M. (2014). *Supply chain management: Processes, partnerships, performance* (4th ed.). Supply Chain Management Institute.
Langley, A. (1999). Strategies for theorizing from process data. *Academy of Management Review, 24*(4), 691–710.
Langley, A., Smallman, C., Tsoukas, H., & Van de Ven, A. H. (2013). Process studies of change in organization and management: Unveiling temporality, activity, and flow. *Academy of Management Journal, 56*(1), 1–13.

Le Heron, K., & Hayward, D. (2002). The moral commodity: Production, consumption, and governance in the Australasian breakfast cereal industry. *Environment and Planning A, 34*(12), 2231–2251.

Loorbach, D. (2007). *Transition management. New mode of governance for sustainable development.* International Books.

Manetti, G. (2011). The quality of stakeholder engagement in sustainability reporting: Empirical evidence and critical points. *Corporate Social Responsibility and Environmental Management, 18*(2), 110–122.

Manetti, G., & Toccafondi, S. (2012). The role of stakeholders in sustainability reporting assurance. *Journal of Business Ethics, 107*, 363–377. https://doi.org/10.1007/s10551-011-1044-1

Manninen, K., & Huiskonen, J. (2022). Factors influencing the implementation of an integrated corporate sustainability and business strategy. *Journal of Cleaner Production, 343*, Article 131036.

Mies, A., & Gold, S. (2021). Mapping the social dimension of the circular economy. *Journal of Cleaner Production, 321*, 128960.

Morea, D., Fortunati, S., Cappa, F., & Oriani, R. (2022). Corporate social responsibility as a catalyst of circular economy? A case study perspective in Agri-food. *Journal of Knowledge Management*, (ahead-of-print).

Neri, A., Cagno, E., Lepri, M., & Trianni, A. (2021). A triple bottom line balanced set of key performance indicators to measure the sustainability performance of industrial supply chains. *Sustainable Production and Consumption, 26*, 648–691.

Pizzi, S., Caputo, A., Corvino, A., & Venturelli, A. (2020). Management research and the UN sustainable development goals (SDGs): A biblio-metric investigation and systematic review. *Journal of Cleaner Production, 276*, 124033.

Pizzi, S., Rosati, F., & Venturelli, A. (2021). The determinants of business contribution to the 2030 Agenda: Introducing the SDG Reporting Score. *Business Strategy and the Environment, 30*(1), 404–421.

Pohlmann, C. R., Scavarda, A. J., Alves, M. B., & Korzenowski, A. L. (2020). The role of the focal company in sustainable development goals: A Brazilian food poultry supply chain case study. *Journal of Cleaner Production, 245*, Article 118798.

Prieto-Sandoval, V., Jaca, C., & Ormazabal, M. (2018). Towards a consensus on the circular economy. *Journal of Cleaner Production, 179*, 605–615.

Romero, S., Ruiz, S., & Fernandez-Feijoo, B. (2019). Sustainability reporting and stakeholder engagement in Spain: Different instruments, different quality. *Business Strategy and the Environment, 28*(1), 221–232.

Rustam, A., Wang, Y., & Zameer, H. (2020). Environmental awareness, firm sustainability exposure and green consumption behaviors. *Journal of Cleaner Production, 268*, 122016.

Sachs, J., Kroll, C., Lafortune, G., Fuller, G., & Woelm, F. (2022). *Sustainable development report 2022*. Cambridge University Press.

Scandizzo, S. (2011). A framework for the analysis of reputational risk. *The Journal of Operational Risk, 6*(3), 41.

Seuring, S., & Müller, M. (2008). From a literature review to a conceptual framework for sustainable supply chain management. *Journal of Cleaner Production, 16*(15), 1699–1710.

Silvestri, L., Forcina, A., Di Bona, G., & Silvestri, C. (2021). Circular economy strategy of reusing olive mill wastewater in the ceramic industry: How the plant location can benefit environmental and economic performance. *Journal of Cleaner Production, 326*, 129388.

Stanco, M., Nazzaro, C., Lerro, M., & Marotta, G. (2020). Sustainable collective innovation in the agri-food value chain: The case of the "Aureo" wheat supply chain. *Sustainability, 12*(14), 5642.

Stranieri, S., Orsi, L., Banterle, A., & Ricci, E. C. (2019). Sustainable development and supply chain coordination: The impact of corporate social responsibility rules in the European Union food industry. *Corporate Social Responsibility and Environmental Management, 26*(2), 481–491.

Tanveer, U., Ishaq, S., & Gough, A. (2021). Circular economy in agri-food sector: food waste management perspective. In *Challenges and opportunities of circular economy in agri-food sector: Rethinking waste* (pp. 55–75).

Tayal, A., Solanki, A., Kondal, R., Nayyar, A., Tanwar, S., & Kumar, N. (2021). Blockchain-based efficient communication for food supply chain industry: Transparency and traceability analysis for sustainable business. *International Journal of Communication Systems, 34*(4), e4696.

Tchankova, L. (2002). Risk identification–basic stage in risk management. *Environmental Management and Health, 13*(3), 290–297.

Tilt, C. A. (2010). *Corporate responsibility, accounting and accountants* (pp. 11–32). Springer Berlin Heidelberg.

van Langen, S. K., Vassillo, C., Ghisellini, P., Restaino, D., Passaro, R., & Ulgiati, S. (2021). Promoting circular economy transition: A study about perceptions and awareness by different stakeholders groups. *Journal of Cleaner Production, 316*, 128166.

Velasco-Muñoz, J. F., Mendoza, J. M. F., Aznar-Sánchez, J. A., & Gallego-Schmid, A. (2021). Circular economy implementation in the agricultural sector: Definition, strategies and indicators. *Resources, Conservation and Recycling, 170*, 105618.

Veleva, V., Bodkin, G., & Todorova, S. (2017). The need for better measurement and employee engagement to advance a circular economy: Lessons from Biogen's "zero waste" journey. *Journal of Cleaner Production, 154*, 517–529.

Walsh, C., & Sulkowski, A. J. (2010). A greener company makes for happier employees more so than does a more valuable one: A regression analysis of employee satisfaction, perceived environmental performance and firm financial value. *Interdisciplinary Environmental Review, 11*(4), 274–282.

Wiek, A., Withycombe, L., & Redman, C. L. (2011). Key competencies in sustainability: A reference framework for academic program development. *Sustainability Science, 6*(2), 203–218.

Yacob, P., Wong, L. S., & Khor, S. C. (2019). An empirical investigation of green initiatives and environmental sustainability for manufacturing SMEs. *Journal of Manufacturing Technology Management, 30*(1), 2–25.

Yang, Y., Orzes, G., Jia, F., & Chen, L. (2021). Does GRI sustainability reporting pay off? An empirical investigation of publicly listed firms in China. *Business & Society, 60*(7), 1738–1772.

Yin, R. K. (2017). *Case study research and applications: Design and methods* (6th ed.). SAGE Publications, Inc.

Zaid, M. A., Abuhijleh, S. T., & Pucheta-Martínez, M. C. (2020). Ownership structure, stakeholder engagement, and corporate social responsibility policies: The moderating effect of board independence. *Corporate Social Responsibility and Environmental Management, 27*(3), 1344–1360.

Zucchella, A., & Previtali, P. (2019). Circular business models for sustainable development: A "waste is food" restorative ecosystem. *Business Strategy and the Environment, 28*(2), 274–285.

Chapter 4
The Interaction Effects Between Cultural Values, ESG, and Green Innovation

Emanuele Doronzo and Paolo Esposito

4.1 Introduction

Society is increasing awareness and concern about the environmental practices implemented by companies (Xiao et al., 2022; Santos et al., 2023; Bladt et al., 2024). Given the increasing societal appreciation for environmental practices (Todaro & Torelli, 2024), enterprises are pressured to meet stakeholders' expectations (Ruiz-Blanco et al., 2022; Esposito et al., 2025a). Furthermore, there has been an increasing demand from investors, customers, governments, and business clients for companies to disclose more information about their environmental performance (Zhang et al., 2023). As companies become aware of the potential risks to their image, legitimacy, and reputation, they may be inclined to engage in the practice of exaggerating, deceiving, or embellishing their external communications about their environmental initiatives (Zhang et al., 2023) to cultivate a positive perception (Sun et al., 2023). Enterprises demonstrate good green communication or claim to be environmentally conscious (Rahman & Nguyen-Viet, 2023).

However, it is essential to note that the information enterprises send may not align with their real actions (Pizzetti et al., 2021; Bernini & La Rosa, 2024). Moreover, Gupta and Singh (2024) have shown a growing trend among organizations to acknowledge the competitive advantage of promoting sustainable practices. For this reason, firms often make imprecise environmental assertions and may include

E. Doronzo
Department of Economics, University of Rome "Tor Vergata", Roma, Italy

P. Esposito (✉)
WSB University, Gdańsk, Poland

Department of Business and Economic Studies, University of Naples "Parthenope", Naples, Italy
e-mail: paolo.esposito@uniparthenope.it

N. Castellano et al. (eds.), *Environmental, Social, Governance (ESG)*, SIDREA Series in Accounting and Business Administration,
https://doi.org/10.1007/978-3-031-76618-3_4

erroneous data to appeal to a green example (Gupta & Singh, 2024). Furthermore, Lee and Raschke (2023) underlined an increasing distrust among investors and consumers toward green claims. This mismatch between companies' declarations and ESG actions is known as greenwashing. Greenwashing is a significant danger to sustainable development (Todaro & Torelli, 2024). Delmas and Burbano (2011) studied the different conceptualizations of greenwashing and defined it as the convergence of two distinct behaviors of the enterprises: positive advertising about their environmental contributions and actual scarce environmental performance. In fact, these authors claim that greenwashing can potentially impact consumers. Other authors, such as De Freitas Netto et al. (2020), broaden the previous definition by arguing that greenwashing is a decoupling strategy because companies are engaged in environmental practices without changing their behavior, focusing on the pursuit of economic efficiency. Our research has used this definition of greenwashing because this definition allows for easier operationalization and measurement of the phenomenon.

The literature on greenwashing has extensively studied the factors that contribute to greenwashing (Pizzetti et al., 2021; Mateo-Márquez et al., 2022). There are varying viewpoints on how different factors affect enterprises' involvement in greenwashing (Bladt et al., 2024). This indicates the need for additional research, particularly in empirical studies that analyze extensive datasets by country. This study aims to examine the impact of cultural values on the corporations in greenwashing practices.

The results show that the probability of greenwashing is higher when the companies operate in areas with high masculinity and power distance.

Experimental studies on greenwashing are significant for a wide range of individuals. Regulators and policymakers must create regulations and environmental policies that effectively prevent greenwashing practices. Investors can improve their evaluation of company information, while consumers can decrease their doubt and distrust of non-financial information. Managers can provide more information about their companies' actual actions concerning climate change, which should be trusted and valued by all company stakeholders.

This study makes many contributions to the existing body of knowledge and addresses the need for more research on environmental performance and environmental. This study presents an empirical assessment of the concept of greenwashing within the context of greenwashing literature. The measurement is based on publicly accessible data, making it a valuable resource for future academics and policymakers. It develops the data envelopment analysis (DEA) method provided by Veltri et al. (2023) to detect greenwashing. In addition, this study also offers insights into the theoretical framework around the relationship between cultural values and environmental practices inside organizations.

The chapter is organized as follows: Section 4.2—the literature review and the development of hypotheses; Sect. 4.3—research method, sample selection, empirical models, and variables; and Sect. 4.4—the empirical results and discussion. Finally in Sect. 4.5 we present our conclusion.

4.2 Literature Review

4.2.1 Legitimacy Theory and Greenwashing

Enterprises can obtain legitimacy by conforming to the new context that considers the environmental and social factors relevant, continuing to pursue economic efficiency as their sole aim; in practice, they declare one thing but do another one, implementing a decoupling strategy (de Freitas Netto et al., 2020; Boiral et al., 2023).

The legitimacy theory sustains that this phenomenon can manifest when the enterprises are stressed by simultaneous contradictory pressures of external and internal stakeholders (Suchman, 1995; Guo et al., 2018; De Vries et al., 2015; Bianchi et al., 2022; L'Abate et al., 2023; de Villiers et al., 2024).

In light of what has been said, greenwashing is a decoupling strategy with respect to environmental aspects (Seele & Gatti, 2017; de Freitas Netto et al., 2020; Forcadell & Aracil, 2021; Pedersen & Andersen, 2023).

Thus, the enterprises implement a greenwashing strategy to obtain legitimacy by emphasizing environmental information. It is important to remember that information is the tool that influences perception and determines legitimacy (Suchman, 1995; Hahn & Kühnen, 2013; Testa et al., 2018; Lee & Raschke, 2023).

In fact, recent research shows that companies want to implement innovative standards such as TCFD and SASB to communicate their environmental and social performance, but they also employ communication strategies that can be construed as greenwashing to bolster their credibility (Yang et al., 2020).

4.2.2 Cultural Value and Greenwashing

Many authors argue that stricter regulation reduces the likelihood of enterprises implementing greenwashing strategies (Burbano et al., 2022; Pizzetti et al., 2021; Zhang et al., 2022); Roulet and Touboul (2015) argue that an inverse mechanism may occur. Specifically, these authors sustain that in less regulated contexts where the individual is more empowered, companies may be put under greater pressure to address social and environmental issues because of the lack of effectiveness of the legislator. In this context, stakeholders are more sensitive to unethical behavior of enterprises, which, so, are exposed to increased reputational risk. In conclusion, according to Roulet and Touboul (2015) in less regulated contexts, the probability of greenwashing may be lower.

In addition, empirical analyses by Tang and Demeritt (2018) and Peng et al. (2024) show that companies operating in countries with higher environmental regulations show a modest reduction in emissions. Since individual stakeholders' characteristics can impact managers' actions, it is crucial to consider the role of cultural variables. In fact, the correlation between a nation's environmental performance and Hofstede's cultural dimensions has been demonstrated in many studies (De Mooij & Hofstede, 2010; Dangelico et al., 2020; Ardito et al., 2021). According to the findings of these investigations, masculinity and power distance are especially significant. Indeed, it has been observed that nations that prioritize femininity place more emphasis on environmental factors (Ardito et al., 2021). It is imperative to consider the cultural heritage and position of the manager or entrepreneur. Indeed, a recent investigation by Fu et al. (2023) demonstrates that managers who comprehensively understand the challenges and prospects associated with green investments are more likely to attain favorable economic and environmental outcomes. Conversely, managers who engage in instrumental green activities merely to establish credibility are likelier to employ greenwashing tactics.

Nevertheless, empirical research is scarce examining the correlation between greenwashing and cultural values (Yang et al., 2020). Drawing upon both theoretical and empirical literature, we formulate the following research inquiry:

Can cultural dimensions account for the performance of Italian energy SMEs?

4.3 Methodology

The relationship between efficiency and cultural dimensions is examined in our research using a two-step methodology. The authors compute an efficiency approximation in the initial stage and examine the correlation between efficiency and cultural dimensions in the subsequent stage.

In order to implement a synthetic metric for assessing the performance of enterprises, the authors utilize Data Envelopment Analysis (DEA) method as proposed by Charnes et al. (1992). Data Envelopment Analysis (DEA) computes a business efficiency score by utilizing input and output measurements simultaneously. DEA is a non-parametric approach wherein the score is computed using the input-output data inserted into the mathematical model; therefore, it is not affected by the endogeneity problem (Deidda et al., 2014).

We calculate company scores using input-oriented DEA, as previously described by Veltri et al. (2023). This method compares efficiency scores with and without ESG performance as output.

In the empirical literature, many studies use DEA to assess the overall effectiveness of a business. For example, Esposito et al. (2023) have calculated a score of the economic and social benefits of social enterprises using the DEA method.

The relationship between efficiency score and cultural dimensions is examined in the second phase.

Step 1: Greenwashing score

The following paragraph shows the methodology for calculating the greenwashing score. In the first step, we calculate enterprises' efficiency scores with and without ESG performance and then compare the estimates. The efficiency scores of companies using greenwashing practices should not change in the two cases. We implement the DEA methodology by Veltri et al. (2023). In fact, we employ two input variables (EV/EBITDA and Net Debt/TA) and three output variables (ROE, FCF/Revenue, and ESG scores). We employ ratios instead of absolute measures to avoid scale factors that could impact the calculation of DEA scores, unlike Veltri et al. (2023).

We highlight that the DEA methodology is the most appropriate for our research, as it allows the identification of the occurrence of greenwashing through the relationship between ESG performance and economic performance without making assumptions about the causal relationship that binds them (Capece et al., 2021; Iazzolino et al., 2023).

At this point, we calculated the overall performance scores with or without ESG performance and the variations between them.

Finally, we made the greenwashing score, associating a value of 1 if the delta between the scores was insignificant (the enterprises implement greenwashing strategy) and 0 otherwise.

Step 2: Logistic regression

The authors examine the relationship between the efficacy variable and cultural dimensions by employing logistic regression (LR).

The dependent variability was operationalized by the authors using a dichotomic score, which was computed in the preceding section. Since the dependent variable is binary and the relationship may be susceptible to endogeneity risk, 2SLS LR is the most appropriate empirical method to examine the correlation between cultural dimensions and greenwashing (Angrist et al., 1999; Wooldridge, 2010).

Undoubtedly, one of the factors contributing to endogeneity is the possibility of "reverse causality" affecting the relationship between greenwashing and cultural dimensions (Angrist et al., 1999).

However, the likelihood of this occurring is comparatively remote, given that culture remains static throughout history (Hofstede, 2011). Consequently, the authors opted to employ instrumental variables to assess the cultural dimensions that Nash and Patel (2019) identified.

Table 4.1 presents the measures designated as instrumental variables for the cultural dimensions as outlined by Nash and Patel (2019).

4.4 Empirical Analysis

4.4.1 Data Sample

The authors have focused their research on Italian Energy SMEs because the EU has launched a regulatory process to institutionalize ESG performance. Indeed, on January 5, 2023, the Corporate Sustainability Reporting Directive (CSRD) entered into force. It identifies ESG information that companies must provide, but above all, it extends the reach of the companies involved (van Dijk et al., 2024). The final

Table 4.1 Instrumental variables

Cultural dimension	Instrumental variable	Operationalization
Individualism	Frost	Dichotomic variable that equals 1 if frost is likely to occur, and 0 otherwise
Uncertainty avoidance	Hieratical	Percentage of a country's population following hierarchical religions. Religions classified as hierarchical are: Catholic, Muslim, Orthodox
Power distance	CommHist	Dichotomic variable that equals 1 if the country's government is communist or has been communist, and 0 otherwise
Masculinity	GenDist	GEN_DIST, measures the distance of each country from Italy, the country with the highest masculinity score in our sample
Indulgence	TempAvg	Country's 30-year average temperature (in Celsius)
Short-term vs Long-term orientation	Protestant	Percentage of a country's population following a Protestant religion

This table is an elaboration from Nash and Patel (2019)

sample consists of 402 companies with all financial and ESG data for 2022. The authors, according to the methodology of Veltri et al. (2023), employ two input variables (EV/EBITDA and Revenues/TA) and three output variables (ROE, FCF/Revenue, and ESG scores). The authors preferred to use ratios instead of absolute measures to avoid scale factors that could impact the calculation of DEA scores, unlike Veltri et al. (2023). Tables 4.2 and 4.3 show the descriptive statistics of the sample.

4.4.2 *Findings*

The DEA scores are derived from ESG performance and financial performance. By utilizing this methodology, the authors can estimate whether ESG performance affects energy companies' overall efficacy. The analysis reveals that 121 companies are totally efficient after incorporating the ESG factor. This suggests that these companies' managers consider ESG performance very important. The analysis also shows 50 enterprises with the same efficiency scores with and without ESG performance as output variable in the DEA model. These businesses are those affected by greenwashing. Table 4.4 shows DEA results. Table 4.5 shows the relation between greenwashing score and cultural values. The empirical procedure uses logarithmic regression with instrumental variables (2SLS). Table 4.5 presents the estimated results for 2SLS LR with IV. As elaborated in the methodological section, instrumental variables permit cultural value assessment. Nash and Patel (2019) provided indications for these instrumental variables.

Table 4.2 Descriptive statistics

	N	Mean	St. Dev	ESG_P	EVEBITDA	ROE	FCFSales	MktCap
ESG_P	402	70.93	19.05	1.00				
EVEBITDA	402	12.23	4.05	0.33***	1.00			
ROE	402	18.20	3.53	0.23**	0.38***	1.00		
FCFSales	402	4.48	1.29	0.31***	0.16***	0.10***	1.00	
RevenuesTA	402	5.22	3.71	0.21***	0.02	0.10***	0.23***	1.00
Italian Area	North	244	Center	39	South	119		

Data from public information of companies

The asterisk representation of significance levels is: *Significant at the 10% level; **Significant at the 5% level; ***Significant at the 1% level

Table 4.3 Cultural dimensions

Italian area	Power distance	Individualism	Masculinity	Uncertainty avoidance	Short-term vs long-term orientation	Indulgence
North Italy	51	65	79	30	60	43
Center Italy	65	45	54	44	82	57
South Italy	78	34	56	73	95	70

The analysis is provided by "the Hofstede Centre"—http://geert-hofstede.com/

Empirical analysis aims to determine whether cultural values are the factors that determine greenwashing. Column 1 of Table 4.5 illustrates the estimations.

The "masculinity" and "power distance" estimators are positive and statistically significant in the analysis. As a result, corporations operating in a context characterized by a high degree of masculinity and power distance are more prone to engaging in practices associated with greenwashing.

In conclusion, the model's goodness of measurement was computed by comparing the anticipated and observed outcomes. The model demonstrates a good predictive capability, as evidenced by the 77% accuracy rate of its predictions (Cameron & Trivedi, 2010).

4.5 Conclusions

Recent studies have demonstrated that management emphasizes attaining high environmental, social, and governance (ESG) performance, significantly influencing investor decision-making. Managers may, therefore, be inclined to adopt greenwashing policies, particularly in industries as complex as energy (Veltri et al., 2023). The energy sector, as emphasized by Veltri et al. (2023) and Esposito et al. (2024), is distinguished by both favorable and unfavorable externalities. Furthermore, it furnishes an essential public service, albeit one that may incur expenses for the populace—as the recent energy crisis in Ukraine exemplifies. This study aims to determine whether energy companies, similar to those that prioritize economic performance, have made ESG performance a primary objective.

The analysis reveals that 50 companies implement a greenwashing strategy because their efficiency scores are not affected by ESG performance. This suggests that administrators do not place importance on ESG performance. In conclusion, drawing upon credible theoretical frameworks, the authors postulated the presence of a relation between cultural variables and efficacy. According to the findings of the logistic regression analysis, organizations situated in a context where "masculinity" and "power distance" are highly valued are more likely to engage in greenwashing practices.

Table 4.4 DEA results

Company	DEA score without ESG	DEA score with ESG	Delta score	Greenwashing score
1	0.87	1.00	0.13	0
2	0.88	1.00	0.12	0
3	0.87	1.00	0.13	0
4	0.93	1.00	0.07	0
5	0.91	1.00	0.09	0
6	0.98	1.00	0.02	0
7	0.84	1.00	0.16	0
8	0.85	1.00	0.15	0
9	0.81	1.00	0.19	0
10	0.78	1.00	0.22	0
11	0.95	1.00	0.05	0
12	0.96	1.00	0.04	0
13	0.94	1.00	0.06	0
14	0.98	1.00	0.02	0
15	0.87	1.00	0.13	0
16	0.75	1.00	0.25	0
17	0.91	1.00	0.09	0
18	0.97	1.00	0.03	0
19	0.87	1.00	0.13	0
20	0.92	1.00	0.08	0
21	0.87	1.00	0.13	0
22	0.81	1.00	0.19	0
23	0.76	1.00	0.24	0
24	0.77	1.00	0.23	0
25	0.84	1.00	0.16	0
26	0.91	1.00	0.09	0
27	0.92	1.00	0.08	0
28	0.99	1.00	0.01	0
29	0.91	1.00	0.09	0
30	0.98	1.00	0.02	0
31	0.86	1.00	0.14	0
32	0.79	1.00	0.21	0
33	0.75	1.00	0.25	0
34	0.82	1.00	0.18	0
35	0.93	1.00	0.07	0
36	0.82	1.00	0.18	0
37	0.93	1.00	0.07	0
38	0.98	1.00	0.02	0
39	0.87	1.00	0.13	0
40	0.87	1.00	0.13	0
41	0.86	1.00	0.14	0
42	0.79	1.00	0.21	0

(continued)

Table 4.4 (continued)

Company	DEA score without ESG	DEA score with ESG	Delta score	Greenwashing score
43	0.96	1.00	0.04	0
44	0.75	1.00	0.25	0
45	0.82	1.00	0.18	0
46	0.80	1.00	0.2	0
47	0.91	1.00	0.09	0
48	0.95	1.00	0.05	0
49	0.94	1.00	0.06	0
50	0.91	1.00	0.09	0
51	0.96	1.00	0.04	0
52	0.82	1.00	0.18	0
53	0.95	1.00	0.05	0
54	0.84	1.00	0.16	0
55	0.83	1.00	0.17	0
56	0.87	1.00	0.13	0
57	0.89	1.00	0.11	0
58	0.76	1.00	0.24	0
59	0.82	1.00	0.18	0
60	0.89	1.00	0.11	0
61	0.93	1.00	0.07	0
62	0.99	1.00	0.01	0
63	0.93	1.00	0.07	0
64	0.86	1.00	0.14	0
65	0.87	1.00	0.13	0
66	0.77	1.00	0.23	0
67	0.98	1.00	0.02	0
68	0.95	1.00	0.05	0
69	0.98	1.00	0.02	0
70	0.93	1.00	0.07	0
71	0.83	1.00	0.17	0
72	0.75	1.00	0.25	0
73	0.95	1.00	0.05	0
74	0.85	1.00	0.15	0
75	0.96	1.00	0.04	0
76	0.81	1.00	0.19	0
77	0.87	1.00	0.13	0
78	0.99	1.00	0.01	0
79	0.95	1.00	0.05	0
80	0.86	1.00	0.14	0
81	0.99	1.00	0.01	0
82	0.93	1.00	0.07	0
83	0.92	1.00	0.08	0
84	0.85	1.00	0.15	0

(continued)

Table 4.4 (continued)

Company	DEA score without ESG	DEA score with ESG	Delta score	Greenwashing score
85	0.93	1.00	0.07	0
86	0.75	1.00	0.25	0
87	0.89	1.00	0.11	0
88	0.75	1.00	0.25	0
89	0.87	1.00	0.13	0
90	0.86	1.00	0.14	0
91	0.75	1.00	0.25	0
92	0.75	1.00	0.25	0
93	0.78	1.00	0.22	0
94	0.91	1.00	0.09	0
95	0.95	1.00	0.05	0
96	0.77	1.00	0.23	0
97	0.87	1.00	0.13	0
98	0.83	1.00	0.17	0
99	0.90	1.00	0.1	0
100	0.94	1.00	0.06	0
101	0.96	1.00	0.04	0
102	0.75	1.00	0.25	0
103	0.83	1.00	0.17	0
104	0.88	1.00	0.12	0
105	0.87	1.00	0.13	0
106	0.76	1.00	0.24	0
107	0.97	1.00	0.03	0
108	0.87	1.00	0.13	0
109	0.89	1.00	0.11	0
110	0.93	1.00	0.07	0
111	0.88	1.00	0.12	0
112	0.75	1.00	0.25	0
113	0.81	1.00	0.19	0
114	0.81	1.00	0.19	0
115	0.97	1.00	0.03	0
116	0.96	1.00	0.04	0
117	0.88	1.00	0.12	0
118	0.98	1.00	0.02	0
119	0.99	1.00	0.01	0
120	0.97	1.00	0.03	0
121	0.80	1.00	0.2	0
122	0.85	0.85	0	1
123	0.95	0.95	0	1
124	0.83	0.83	0	1
125	0.81	0.81	0	1
126	0.75	0.75	0	1

(continued)

Table 4.4 (continued)

Company	DEA score without ESG	DEA score with ESG	Delta score	Greenwashing score
127	0.95	0.95	0	1
128	0.87	0.87	0	1
129	0.96	0.96	0	1
130	0.91	0.91	0	1
131	0.89	0.89	0	1
132	0.79	0.79	0	1
133	0.97	0.97	0	1
134	0.90	0.90	0	1
135	0.88	0.88	0	1
136	0.78	0.78	0	1
137	1.00	1.00	0	1
138	1.00	1.00	0	1
139	1.00	1.00	0	1
140	1.00	1.00	0	1
141	1.00	1.00	0	1
142	1.00	1.00	0	1
143	1.00	1.00	0	1
144	1.00	1.00	0	1
145	1.00	1.00	0	1
146	1.00	1.00	0	1
147	1.00	1.00	0	1
148	1.00	1.00	0	1
149	0.89	0.89	0	1
150	0.93	0.93	0	1
151	0.93	0.93	0	1
152	0.92	0.92	0	1
153	0.87	0.87	0	1
154	0.84	0.84	0	1
155	0.91	0.91	0	1
156	0.94	0.94	0	1
157	0.86	0.86	0	1
158	0.76	0.76	0	1
159	0.92	0.92	0	1
160	0.85	0.85	0	1
161	0.78	0.78	0	1
162	0.83	0.83	0	1
163	0.83	0.83	0	1
164	1.00	1.00	0	1
165	1.00	1.00	0	1
166	1.00	1.00	0	1
167	1.00	1.00	0	1
168	1.00	1.00	0	1

(continued)

Table 4.4 (continued)

Company	DEA score without ESG	DEA score with ESG	Delta score	Greenwashing score
169	1.00	1.00	0	1
170	1.00	1.00	0	1
171	1.00	1.00	0	1
172	0.79	0.84	0.04514	0
173	0.74	0.78	0.0372	0
174	0.61	0.64	0.0304	0
175	0.80	0.84	0.04	0
176	0.60	0.63	0.03	0
177	0.78	0.81	0.0388	0
178	0.74	0.77	0.0368	0
179	0.64	0.67	0.032	0
180	0.68	0.71	0.034	0
181	0.71	0.75	0.0356	0
182	0.66	0.69	0.0328	0
183	0.70	0.73	0.0348	0
184	0.74	0.78	0.0372	0
185	0.76	0.80	0.038	0
186	0.70	0.74	0.0352	0
187	0.78	0.81	0.0388	0
188	0.71	0.75	0.0356	0
189	0.63	0.66	0.0316	0
190	0.71	0.75	0.0356	0
191	0.79	0.83	0.0396	0
192	0.72	0.76	0.036	0
193	0.62	0.65	0.0308	0
194	0.78	0.81	0.0388	0
195	0.65	0.68	0.0324	0
196	0.63	0.66	0.0316	0
197	0.64	0.67	0.032	0
198	0.67	0.71	0.0336	0
199	0.74	0.77	0.0368	0
200	0.67	0.71	0.0336	0
201	0.60	0.63	0.03	0
202	0.66	0.69	0.0328	0
203	0.65	0.68	0.0324	0
204	0.73	0.76	0.0364	0
205	0.70	0.74	0.0352	0
206	0.76	0.80	0.038	0
207	0.70	0.73	0.0348	0
208	0.77	0.81	0.0384	0
209	0.74	0.77	0.0368	0
210	0.70	0.74	0.0352	0

(continued)

Table 4.4 (continued)

Company	DEA score without ESG	DEA score with ESG	Delta score	Greenwashing score
211	0.79	0.83	0.0396	0
212	0.78	0.81	0.0388	0
213	0.74	0.78	0.0372	0
214	0.72	0.76	0.036	0
215	0.71	0.75	0.0356	0
216	0.63	0.66	0.0316	0
217	0.70	0.73	0.0348	0
218	0.61	0.64	0.0304	0
219	0.63	0.66	0.0316	0
220	0.67	0.71	0.0336	0
221	0.78	0.82	0.0392	0
222	0.79	0.83	0.0396	0
223	0.67	0.71	0.0336	0
224	0.72	0.76	0.036	0
225	0.79	0.83	0.0396	0
226	0.65	0.68	0.0324	0
227	0.61	0.64	0.0304	0
228	0.80	0.84	0.04	0
229	0.80	0.84	0.04	0
230	0.69	0.72	0.0344	0
231	0.77	0.81	0.0384	0
232	0.78	0.82	0.0392	0
233	0.65	0.68	0.0324	0
234	0.69	0.72	0.0344	0
235	0.71	0.75	0.0356	0
236	0.63	0.66	0.0316	0
237	0.69	0.72	0.0344	0
238	0.74	0.77	0.0368	0
239	0.62	0.66	0.0312	0
240	0.70	0.73	0.0348	0
241	0.70	0.73	0.0348	0
242	0.66	0.69	0.0328	0
243	0.73	0.76	0.0364	0
244	0.66	0.69	0.0328	0
245	0.78	0.82	0.0392	0
246	0.62	0.66	0.0312	0
247	0.78	0.82	0.0392	0
248	0.67	0.71	0.0336	0
249	0.63	0.66	0.0316	0
250	0.69	0.72	0.0344	0
251	0.62	0.65	0.0308	0
252	0.67	0.71	0.0336	0

(continued)

Table 4.4 (continued)

Company	DEA score without ESG	DEA score with ESG	Delta score	Greenwashing score
253	0.62	0.66	0.0312	0
254	0.70	0.73	0.0348	0
255	0.80	0.84	0.04	0
256	0.62	0.66	0.0312	0
257	0.68	0.71	0.034	0
258	0.62	0.65	0.0308	0
259	0.62	0.65	0.0308	0
260	0.62	0.65	0.0308	0
261	0.72	0.76	0.036	0
262	0.80	0.84	0.04	0
263	0.68	0.71	0.034	0
264	0.72	0.76	0.036	0
265	0.74	0.77	0.0368	0
266	0.78	0.82	0.0392	0
267	0.63	0.66	0.0316	0
268	0.68	0.71	0.034	0
269	0.78	0.82	0.0392	0
270	0.66	0.70	0.0332	0
271	0.62	0.66	0.0312	0
272	0.71	0.75	0.0356	0
273	0.72	0.76	0.036	0
274	0.68	0.71	0.034	0
275	0.72	0.76	0.036	0
276	0.77	0.81	0.0384	0
277	0.61	0.64	0.0304	0
278	0.78	0.81	0.0388	0
279	0.61	0.64	0.0304	0
280	0.78	0.82	0.0392	0
281	0.67	0.71	0.0336	0
282	0.66	0.70	0.0332	0
283	0.73	0.76	0.0364	0
284	0.78	0.82	0.0392	0
285	0.74	0.77	0.0368	0
286	0.71	0.75	0.0356	0
287	0.62	0.65	0.0308	0
288	0.74	0.78	0.0372	0
289	0.62	0.65	0.0308	0
290	0.80	0.84	0.04	0
291	0.78	0.82	0.0392	0
292	0.70	0.74	0.0352	0
293	0.65	0.68	0.0324	0
294	0.74	0.77	0.0368	0

(continued)

Table 4.4 (continued)

Company	DEA score without ESG	DEA score with ESG	Delta score	Greenwashing score
295	0.74	0.77	0.0368	0
296	0.60	0.63	0.03	0
297	0.74	0.78	0.0372	0
298	0.62	0.65	0.0308	0
299	0.69	0.72	0.0344	0
300	0.77	0.81	0.0384	0
301	0.77	0.81	0.0384	0
302	0.65	0.68	0.0324	0
303	0.60	0.63	0.03	0
304	0.70	0.74	0.0352	0
305	0.77	0.81	0.0384	0
306	0.63	0.66	0.0316	0
307	0.60	0.63	0.03	0
308	0.66	0.70	0.0332	0
309	0.60	0.63	0.03	0
310	0.73	0.76	0.0364	0
311	0.68	0.71	0.034	0
312	0.66	0.70	0.0332	0
313	0.68	0.71	0.034	0
314	0.75	0.79	0.0376	0
315	0.74	0.78	0.0372	0
316	0.60	0.63	0.03	0
317	0.76	0.80	0.038	0
318	0.80	0.84	0.04	0
319	0.66	0.70	0.0332	0
320	0.72	0.76	0.036	0
321	0.60	0.63	0.03	0
322	0.75	0.79	0.0376	0
323	0.76	0.80	0.038	0
324	0.66	0.69	0.0328	0
325	0.72	0.76	0.036	0
326	0.67	0.71	0.0336	0
327	0.66	0.70	0.0332	0
328	0.63	0.66	0.0316	0
329	0.68	0.71	0.034	0
330	0.66	0.69	0.0328	0
331	0.69	0.72	0.0344	0
332	0.68	0.71	0.034	0
333	0.60	0.63	0.03	0
334	0.74	0.78	0.0372	0
335	0.65	0.68	0.0324	0
336	0.77	0.81	0.0384	0

(continued)

Table 4.4 (continued)

Company	DEA score without ESG	DEA score with ESG	Delta score	Greenwashing score
337	0.78	0.82	0.0392	0
338	0.67	0.71	0.0336	0
339	0.66	0.69	0.0328	0
340	0.68	0.71	0.034	0
341	0.72	0.76	0.036	0
342	0.79	0.83	0.0396	0
343	0.76	0.80	0.038	0
344	0.78	0.81	0.0388	0
345	0.74	0.78	0.0372	0
346	0.71	0.75	0.0356	0
347	0.60	0.63	0.03	0
348	0.69	0.72	0.0344	0
349	0.60	0.63	0.03	0
350	0.69	0.72	0.0344	0
351	0.66	0.69	0.0328	0
352	0.70	0.74	0.0352	0
353	0.62	0.66	0.0312	0
354	0.69	0.72	0.0344	0
355	0.80	0.84	0.04	0
356	0.78	0.82	0.0392	0
357	0.67	0.71	0.0336	0
358	0.72	0.76	0.036	0
359	0.74	0.77	0.0368	0
360	0.63	0.66	0.0316	0
361	0.77	0.81	0.0384	0
362	0.78	0.81	0.0388	0
363	0.67	0.71	0.0336	0
364	0.66	0.70	0.0332	0
365	0.69	0.72	0.0344	0
366	0.62	0.65	0.0308	0
367	0.63	0.66	0.0316	0
368	0.72	0.76	0.036	0
369	0.67	0.71	0.0336	0
370	0.65	0.68	0.0324	0
371	0.78	0.82	0.0392	0
372	0.66	0.70	0.0332	0
373	0.62	0.65	0.0308	0
374	0.75	0.79	0.0376	0
375	0.68	0.71	0.034	0
376	0.63	0.66	0.0316	0
377	0.69	0.72	0.0344	0
378	0.60	0.63	0.03	0

(continued)

Table 4.4 (continued)

Company	DEA score without ESG	DEA score with ESG	Delta score	Greenwashing score
379	0.75	0.79	0.0376	0
380	0.77	0.81	0.0384	0
381	0.70	0.74	0.0352	0
382	0.62	0.65	0.0308	0
383	0.76	0.80	0.038	0
384	0.62	0.66	0.0312	0
385	0.62	0.66	0.0312	0
386	0.65	0.68	0.0324	0
387	0.70	0.73	0.0348	0
388	0.70	0.74	0.0352	0
389	0.78	0.81	0.0388	0
390	0.61	0.64	0.0304	0
391	0.73	0.76	0.0364	0
392	0.72	0.76	0.036	0
393	0.75	0.79	0.0376	0
394	0.65	0.68	0.0324	0
395	0.70	0.73	0.0348	0
396	0.62	0.65	0.0308	0
397	0.75	0.79	0.0376	0
398	0.69	0.72	0.0344	0
399	0.72	0.76	0.036	0
400	0.62	0.66	0.0312	0
401	0.74	0.78	0.0372	0
402	0.72	0.76	0.036	0

The study's contribution is significant as it establishes a robust empirical framework for examining the elements contributing to greenwashing-related behaviors (de Freitas Netto et al., 2020).

Potential avenues for further research include conducting cross-sectoral analyses to determine whether the observed dynamics can be attributed to sector-specific factors or cultural influences.

Greenwashing is an obstacle for firms in terms of improving their competitiveness. Many studies identify that a positive relationship exists between sustainability innovations and firm competitiveness (Esposito et al., 2025b).

Indeed, companies that innovate their processes and products to reduce emissions, for example, improve not only their environmental performance but also their degree of innovation and consequently their competitiveness. Moreover the enterprises that implement greenwashing strategies in the long term will be less competitive regarding their peers. The results of this study also have important implications for policymakers. Indeed, they show that the introduction of more stringent environmental regulations is not a necessary and sufficient factor to ensure the reduction

Table 4.5 Logistic regression

Model	Logistic regression IV 2SLS
Dependent variable	Greenwashing score
Independent variables	
Individualism	−0.21
Uncertainty avoidance	−0.11
Power distance	0.18***
Masculinity	0.31***
Indulgence	0.22
Short-term vs long-term orientation	−0.35

The asterisk representation of significance levels is: * Significant at the 10% level; **Significant at the 5% level; ***Significant at the 1% level

of greenwashing practices. It is necessary for policymakers to implement actions necessary to impact the cultural values of stakeholders so that the reputational cost of greenwashing is as high as possible.

Possible future developments of this work are the application of the methodology to different sectors, contexts, but above all a multiannual analysis on the performance of the scores would give greater robustness to the results identified. Unfortunately, this data was not available at the time of the research.

References

Angrist, J. D., Imbens, G. W., & Krueger, A. B. (1999). Jackknife instrumental variables estimation. *Journal of Applied Econometrics, 14*(1), 57–67.

Ardito, L., Dangelico, R. M., & Messeni Petruzzelli, A. (2021). The link between female representation in the boards of directors and corporate social responsibility: Evidence from B corps. *Corporate Social Responsibility and Environmental Management, 28*(2), 704–720.

Bernini, F., & La Rosa, F. (2024). Research in the greenwashing field: Concepts, theories, and potential impacts on economic and social value. *Journal of Management and Governance, 28*(2), 405–444.

Bianchi, G., Testa, F., Boiral, O., & Iraldo, F. (2022). Organizational learning for environmental sustainability: Internalizing lifecycle management. *Organization & Environment, 35*(1), 103–129.

Bladt, D., van Capelleveen, G., & Yazan, D. M. (2024). The influence of greenwashing practices on brand attitude: A multidimensional consumer analysis in Germany. *Business Strategy and the Environment, 33*(2), 597–625.

Boiral, O., Brotherton, M. C., & Talbot, D. (2023). What you see is what you get? Building confidence in ESG disclosures for sustainable finance through external assurance. *Business Ethics, the Environment & Responsibility.*

Burbano, V. C., Delmas, M. A., & Cobo, M. J. (2022). The past and future of corporate sustainability research. *Organization & Environment, 10860266231213105.*

Cameron, A. C., & Trivedi, P. K. (2010). *Microeconometricsusing stata* (Vol. 2). Stata Press.

Capece, G., Costa, R., & Di Pillo, F. (2021). Benchmarking the efficiency of natural gas distribution utilities in Italy considering size, ownership, and maturity. *Utilities Policy, 72*, 101277.

Charnes, A., Haag, S., Jaska, P., & Semple, J. (1992). Sensitivity of efficiency classifications in the additive model of data envelopment analysis. *International Journal of Systems Science, 23*(5), 789–798.

Dangelico, R. M., Fraccascia, L., & Nastasi, A. (2020). National culture's influence on environmental performance of countries: A study of direct and indirect effects. *Sustainable Development, 28*(6), 1773–1786.

de Freitas Netto, S. V., Sobral, M. F. F., Ribeiro, A. R. B., & Soares, G. R. D. L. (2020). Concepts and forms of greenwashing: A systematic review. *Environmental Sciences Europe, 32*, 1–12.

De Mooij, M., & Hofstede, G. (2010). The Hofstede model: Applications to global branding and advertising strategy and research. *International Journal of Advertising, 29*(1), 85–110.

de Villiers, C., Dimes, R., & Molinari, M. (2024). Determinants, mechanisms and consequences of UN SDGs reporting by universities: Conceptual framework and avenues for future research. *Journal of Public Budgeting, Accounting & Financial Management.*

De Vries, G., Terwel, B. W., Ellemers, N., & Daamen, D. D. (2015). Sustainability or profitability? How communicated motives for environmental policy affect public perceptions of corporate greenwashing. *Corporate Social Responsibility and Environmental Management, 22*(3), 142–154.

Deidda, M., Lupiáñez-Villanueva, F., Codagnone, C., & Maghiros, I. (2014). Using data envelopment analysis to analyse the efficiency of primary care units. *Journal of Medical Systems, 38*, 1–10.

Delmas, M. A., & Burbano, V. C. (2011). The drivers of greenwashing. *California Management Review, 54*(1), 64–87.

Esposito, P., Doronzo, E., & Dicorato, S. L. (2023). The financial and green effects of cultural values on mission drifts in European social enterprises. *Business Strategy and the Environment, 32*(1), 1–29. https://doi.org/10.1002/bse.3115

Esposito, P., Marrasso, E., Martone, C., Pallotta, G., Roselli, C., Sasso, M., & Tufo, M. (2024). A roadmap for the implementation of a renewable energy community. *Heliyon, 10*(7), E282269, CellPress. https://doi.org/10.1016/j.heliyon.2024.e28269

Esposito, P., Doronzo, E., Riso, V., & Tufo, M. (2025a). Sustainability in energy companies under the lens of cultural pressures: when do we talk of greenwashing? *Corporate Social Responsibility and Environmental Management.* https://doi.org/10.1002/csr.3111

Esposito, P., Marrone, A., Pontrelli, V., & Rella, A. (2025b). Exploring drivers and factors of benefit impact reports quality: Retracing a stakeholder theory approach. *Business Strategy and the Environment, 34*(1), 555–569. https://doi.org/10.1002/bse.3974

Forcadell, F. J., & Aracil, E. (2021). A purpose-action framework for Corporate Social Responsibility in times of shock. *Journal of Cleaner Production, 312*, 127789.

Fu, C., Lu, L., & Pirabi, M. (2023). Advancing green finance: a review of sustainable development Abstract Digital. *Economy and Sustainable Development, 1*(1), https://doi.org/10.1007/s44265-023-00020-3.

Guo, R., Zhang, W., Wang, T., Li, C., & Tao, L. (2018). Timely or considered? Brand trust repair strategies and mechanism after greenwashing in China—from a legitimacy perspective. *Industrial Marketing Management, 72*, 127–137.

Gupta, K., & Singh, N. (2024). Visualization of global research trends and future research directions of greenwashing by using bibliometric analysis. *Environment, Development and Sustainability*, 1–21.

Hahn, R., & Kühnen, M. (2013). Determinants of sustainability reporting: A review of results, trends, theory, and opportunities in an expanding field of research. *Journal of Cleaner Production, 59*, 5–21.

Hofstede, G. (2011). Dimensionalizing cultures: The Hofstede model in context. *Online Readings in Psychology and Culture, 2*(1), 2307–0919.

Iazzolino, G., Bruni, M. E., Veltri, S., Morea, D., & Baldissarro, G. (2023). The impact of ESG factors on financial efficiency: An empirical analysis for the selection of sustainable firm portfolios. *Corporate Social Responsibility and Environmental Management.*

L'Abate, V., Vitolla, F., Esposito, P., & Raimo, N. (2023). The drivers of sustainability disclosure practices in the airport industry: A legitimacy theory perspective. *Corporate Social Responsibility and Environmental Management, 30*(4), 1903–1916. https://doi.org/10.1002/csr.2462

Lee, M. T., & Raschke, R. L. (2023). Stakeholder legitimacy in firm greening and financial performance: What about greenwashing temptations?☆. *Journal of Business Research, 155*, 113393.

Mateo-Márquez, A. J., González-González, J. M., & Zamora-Ramírez, C. (2022). An international empirical study of greenwashing and voluntary carbon disclosure. *Journal of Cleaner Production, 363*, 132567.

Nash, R., & Patel, A. (2019). Instrumental variables analysis and the role of national culture in corporate finance. *Financial Management, 48*(2), 385–416.

Pedersen, E. R. G., & Andersen, K. R. (2023). Greenwashing: A Broken Business Model. *Journal of Business Models, 11*(2), 11–24.

Peng, X., Li, J., Tang, Q., Lan, Y. C., & Cui, X. (2024). Do environmental scores become multinational corporations' strategic "greenwashing" tool for window-dressing carbon reduction? A cross-cultural analysis. *Business Strategy and the Environment, 33*(3), 2084–2115.

Pizzetti, M., Gatti, L., & Seele, P. (2021). Firms talk, suppliers walk: Analyzing the locus of greenwashing in the blame game and introducing 'vicarious greenwashing'. *Journal of Business Ethics, 170*(1), 21–38.

Rahman, S. U., & Nguyen-Viet, B. (2023). Towards sustainable development: Coupling green marketing strategies and consumer perceptions in addressing greenwashing. *Business Strategy and the Environment, 32*(4), 2420–2433.

Roulet, T. J., & Touboul, S. (2015). The intentions with which the road is paved: Attitudes to liberalism as determinants of greenwashing. *Journal of Business Ethics, 128*, 305–320.

Ruiz-Blanco, S., Romero, S., & Fernandez-Feijoo, B. (2022). Green, blue or black, but washing–What company characteristics determine greenwashing? *Environment, Development and Sustainability, 24*(3), 4024–4045.

Santos, C., Coelho, A., & Marques, A. (2023). A systematic literature review on greenwashing and its relationship to stakeholders: State of art and future research agenda. *Management Review Quarterly*, 1–25.

Seele, P., & Gatti, L. (2017). Greenwashing revisited: In search of a typology and accusation-based definition incorporating legitimacy strategies. *Business Strategy and the Environment, 26*(2), 239–252.

Suchman, M. C. (1995). Managing legitimacy: Strategic and institutional approaches. *Academy of Management Review, 20*(3), 571–610.

Sun, Z., Sun, X., Wang, W., & Wang, W. (2023). Digital transformation and greenwashing in environmental, social, and governance disclosure: Does investor attention matter? *Business Ethics, the Environment & Responsibility.*

Tang, S., & Demeritt, D. (2018). Climate change and mandatory carbon reporting: Impacts on business process and performance. *Business Strategy and the Environment, 27*(4), 437–455.

Testa, F., Boiral, O., & Iraldo, F. (2018). Internalization of environmental practices and institutional complexity: Can stakeholders pressures encourage greenwashing? *Journal of Business Ethics, 147*, 287–307.

Todaro, D. L., & Torelli, R. (2024). From greenwashing to ESG-washing: A focus on the circular economy field. *Corporate Social Responsibility and Environmental Management.*

van Dijk, L., Hijink, S., & in 't Veld, L. (2024). Corporate Sustainability Reporting. In D. Busch, G. Ferrarini, & S. Grünewald (Eds.), *Sustainable Finance in Europe. EBI Studies in Banking and Capital Markets Law*. Palgrave Macmillan. https://doi.org/10.1007/978-3-031-53696-0_6

Veltri, S., Bruni, M. E., Iazzolino, G., Morea, D., & Baldissarro, G. (2023). Do ESG factors improve utilities corporate efficiency and reduce the risk perceived by credit lending institutions? An empirical analysis. *Utilities Policy, 81*, 101520.

Wooldridge, J. M. (2010). *Econometric analysis of cross section and panel data*. MIT Press.

Xiao, Z., Wang, Y., & Guo, D. (2022). Will greenwashing result in brand avoidance? A moderated mediation model. *Sustainability, 14*(12), 7204.

Yang, Z., Nguyen, T. T. H., Nguyen, H. N., Nguyen, T. T. N., & Cao, T. T. (2020). Greenwashing behaviours: Causes, taxonomy and consequences based on a systematic literature review. *Journal of Business Economics and Management, 21*(5), 1486–1507.

Zhang, K., Pan, Z., Janardhanan, M., & Patel, I. (2023). Relationship analysis between greenwashing and environmental performance. *Environment, Development and Sustainability, 25*(8), 7927–7957.

Zhang, T., Qin, H., & Xu, W. (2022). Environmental regulation, greenwashing behaviour, and green governance of high-pollution enterprises in China. *International Journal of Environmental Research and Public Health, 19*(19), 12539.

Chapter 5
Staff Training Through the ESG Lens: Insights from Case Studies

Costanza Di Fabio and Elisa Roncagliolo

5.1 Introduction

This study examines the ESG dimension of corporate activity focusing in particular on its social dimension, intended as the mutual influence between corporate activity and employees and society in terms of equal opportunities, working conditions, and respect for human rights. Despite its pervasiveness and importance, this dimension has received limited attention in the accounting literature, especially compared to the environmental one (Schönborn et al., 2019). Within the broad area of corporate activities, our study specifically examines the social dimension of staff training activities, which are defined as programmes offered by companies to their employees, either on a compulsory or voluntary basis, to enable them to acquire or improve the skills and knowledge they need to perform their jobs in the company. These activities can have other potential effects, both at the company and individual level, and an overall positive impact on the social context.

This chapter reflects on the attention that companies pay to social issues when designing and implementing staff training. As appropriate performance measurement systems enable companies to set goals in line with their sustainability vision and to the use of resources in line with these goals, it is an issue how companies approach performance measurement and, in particular, what type of costs and benefits companies identify as being associated with staff training activities.

As a result of the implementation of the 2022 Corporate Sustainability Reporting Directive (CSRD), more and more European companies now have to start adopting a more structured approach to collecting and managing data on their ESG impact (Liu & Tian, 2021) and, in many cases, the implementation of sustainable performance

C. Di Fabio · E. Roncagliolo (✉)
Dipartimento di Economia, Università degli Studi di Genova, Genova, Italy
e-mail: roncagliolo@economia.unige.it

N. Castellano et al. (eds.), *Environmental, Social, Governance (ESG)*, SIDREA Series in Accounting and Business Administration,
https://doi.org/10.1007/978-3-031-76618-3_5

measurement systems could be only in its infancy, despite companies' ESG orientation (Marchi, 2019; Hristov et al., 2020; Castellano & Felden, 2021; D'Onza, 2022). We therefore broaden the scope of our observation to include the management vision shaping employee training activities, as an ESG-focused management approach can play a critical role in employee training efforts.

Based on these arguments, we aim at understanding (RQ) *whether the planning phase of staff training activities is influenced by sustainability-related goals, and specifically by the underlying goal of benefiting the social dimension.*

This study adopts a qualitative approach and examines the research question through the cases of two Italian companies characterized by a recent increase in performance, but with different features that may favour a social orientation of their resource allocation decisions, namely a key role of sustainability within the business model. We review publicly available information and conduct semi-structured interviews useful to better understand the experiences and perceptions of subjects directly involved in defining staff training activities and monitoring the associated costs and benefits.

The case analysis reveals that the planning phase of staff training can indeed be influenced by objectives that the company sets itself in terms of the social sustainability of its business and even the higher goal of having a positive impact on society. However, the analysis of the two case studies shows that the influence of sustainability goals on the design of staff training activities depends on the company's view of the concept of performance. In particular, staff training planning is also guided by social sustainability objectives when the company shows that it pursues a performance concept that integrates aspects of financial and ESG performance at the same time. Conversely, staff training planning appears disconnected from sustainability goals when the company pursues a purely financial performance concept. In these cases, the correlation between staff training and performance-related targets may not be established unless there's a necessity to respond to deteriorating financial performance. Here, employee growth and skill development primarily emerge in response to the company's aim to enhance margins, rather than a broader aspiration to create a positive societal impact through training.

This study contributes to the current literature on the ESG dimension of corporate activities and their integration with corporate performance measurement systems. We specifically add to prior research by shedding light on how, in a context informed by ESG-related goals, sustainability awareness can have a key part in planning staff training and developing tailored training programmes suitable to pursue ESG-related aims (Steurer et al., 2005; Talbot et al., 2020). Furthermore, we highlight the relevance of the perspective embraced by each company in directing its staff development endeavours. In this respect, we find that differences in the concept of performance embraced by firms can help explaining differences in orientation of staff training. Specifically, pursuing a sustainability-related concept of performance implies integrating in training planning environmental, social, and economic value over the long term (Mio et al., 2020, 2022), Overall, the chapter contributes to the broader literature focusing on the social dimension of sustainability (Baid &

Jayaraman, 2022; Becchetti et al., 2022) by proposing a focus on employee training activities.

The analysis allows examining the implementation of staff training at different levels, also providing practical implications for actors involved in the training activities.

The remainder of this chapter proceeds as follows. Section 5.2 reviews the academic literature on performance measurement systems in a context informed by ESG-oriented goals, studies on the firm-level determinants of staff training activities, and research on the effects of innovative teaching methods on individuals and society, also introducing our research question. Section 5.3 illustrates the research design and presents selected case studies. Section 5.4 presents the results of the analysis, and Sect. 5.5 provides their discussion. Finally, Sect. 5.6 outlines the contributions arising from this study.

5.2 Literature Review

5.2.1 Investment in Staff Training and Corporate Performance

Training activities require companies to invest resources to provide employees with skills and knowledge necessary to fulfil their position in the company. Research confirms that this investment is associated with organizational performance (Delaney & Huselid, 1996; Harel & Tzafrir, 1999; Storey, 2002) and with both productivity and profitability (d'Arcimoles, 1997; Delgado Ferraz & Gallardo-Vazquez, 2016). Thus, investment in employee training has traditionally been motivated by firms' expected returns in terms of firm performance. However, if we look at the training activities voluntarily offered by companies, they can vary significantly across firms. Activities may vary considerably in terms of hours, teaching methods and range of subjects provided, and teacher training, suggesting that the resources invested may also vary significantly. Comparable companies could decide to invest different resources based on their own expectations of future performance. Of course, a company could decide to invest more than a comparable company if managers believe the investment is needed to improve future financial performance. Nevertheless, ESG-oriented companies may be informed by a holistic perspective (Lozano & von Haartman, 2018) and invest more in training if managers expect it could benefit the social dimension, holding future financial performance constant. Attention to performance measures related to ESG goals is then key to explaining the allocation of resources to employee training.

In particular, companies' efforts to focus on ESG-related metrics for setting targets *ex ante* and assessing performance *ex post* should be seen in the light of the global call for corporate sustainability, which refers to "company's activities - by definition voluntary - demonstrating the inclusion of social and environmental concerns in business operations and in interactions with stakeholders" (van Marrewijk & Werre, 2003, p. 107). As corporate sustainability is a multifaceted issue characterized by "pluralistic goals, ambiguity, uncertainty, emergence, and context dominance" (Searcy, 2009), contributing to sustainability implies integrating environmental, social, and economic value over the long term through appropriate management tools (Mio et al., 2020, 2022), also by tailoring these tools to specific circumstances (Steurer et al., 2005). From this perspective, sustainability awareness can play a key role in the development of sustainability management tools (Talbot et al., 2020).

Appropriate performance measurement systems enable companies to set goals in line with their sustainability vision and to plan the use of resources in line with these goals. Thus, systems that include the positive externalities produced by companies on society within a holistic concept of profit are likely to push companies to employ more resources for implementing staff training activities. Nonetheless, an increasing number of companies have started to perceive an urgent need to collect and manage data on their activities' ESG impact only recently, in particular after the implementation of the CSRD, which requires disclosure of the risks and opportunities related to sustainability issues, expands the scope of application of previous ESG disclosure requirements, and introduces sustainability standards, thus affecting internal decision-making and resource allocation (Liu & Tian, 2021). As this new wave is still in its infancy, in many cases companies have no sustainable performance measurement systems yet, despite their ESG orientation.

5.2.2 Determinants of Staff Training and the Role of the Social Dimension

As firm's characteristics could explain investment in staff training activities, the literature has investigated the firm-level characteristics that explain staff training activities (Garavan et al., 2021). Hansson (2007) provides insights into this topic with a survey conducted in 1999 on 5824 private sector organizations in 26 countries, mostly based in Europe. The intensity of staff training (percentage of the wage bill spent on training) is around 3% and the average incidence of staff training is around 44% of employees trained. Staff training is positively associated with a management analysis of training needs, the existence of a written training policy, and the level of education of the workforce.

However, the main driver of the corporate efforts on training are managers (Hansson, 2007), whose culture and attention to a safe and attractive working environment are crucial. This point is supported by a longitudinal study of 172 firms, which highlights that high-performing companies increase their investment in employee training if they are led by professional managers and have high-quality human capital (Sung & Choi, 2023). Furthermore, human capital quality and technology change work as predictors of the level of staff training investment, consistent with findings in the Russian context (Roshchin & Travkin, 2017).

Studies on SMEs further examine the issue, revealing that, due to limited financial resources, staff training in SMEs is often informal, unplanned, and short-term oriented (MacMahon & Murphy, 1999; Hill & Stewart, 2000). However, there is a positive association between the use of formal, structured, and development-oriented training and size, particularly for firms with 20–99 employees (Kotey & Folker, 2007). Mixed results emerge looking at family firms. Compared to non-family firms, family firms show a slower pattern of adoption of structured programmes, as formal programmes do not seem to increase significantly until the firm reaches a critical growth stage (Kotey & Folker, 2007). By contrast, Reid and Harris (2002) provide evidence that attention to employee training is higher when the firm is family owned/managed; their survey of 212 Irish SMEs also suggests that HR functions play a crucial role in determining companies' investments on training, while workforce and ownership features seem less relevant. Beyond firm-level determinants, emerging research emphasizes the sustainability perspective in human resource management (Delgado Ferraz & Gallardo-Vazquez, 2016; Macke & Genari, 2019). In the light of the stakeholders' theory (Freeman et al., 2010; Donaldson & Preston, 1995), managing a company should encompass the attempt to satisfy interests considered at the social level. In such a broader perspective, managers' decisions must take into account the needs of the wider social context, which includes all individuals associated with the company, including employees. Sustainable HR managers should ensure effective stakeholder engagement and develop policies and actions aimed at achieving long-term business success that contributes to well-being at work and benefits society (Bondarouk & Brewster, 2016). To this end, activities that develop employees' competencies and skills and improve industrial relations and job retention are valuable examples of sustainable HR management (Avery & Bergsteiner, 2011).

Based on these arguments, we aim to explore (RQ) *whether the planning phase of staff training activities is influenced by sustainability-related goals, and specifically by the underlying goal of benefiting society.*

5.3 Research Design

5.3.1 Data Collection and Analysis

To answer our research question, the study adopts a qualitative approach. We examine the sustainability perspective of staff training activities through an in-depth examination of two case studies. The case study method is a valuable source for this purpose as it provides insights into a relatively under-researched research topic (Scapens, 2004; Stoner & Holland, 2004) and allows for the evaluation of more detailed information and contextual issues that may stimulate interesting reflections.

In particular, the case study approach entails the examination of both publicly available information and semi-structured interviews. With regard to publicly available information, we analyse the corporate financial statements and the disclosure on staff training in the latest annual report and, where available, in the sustainability report of the selected companies. We then integrate this information with the results of semi-structured interviews to better understand the experiences and perceptions of professional actors involved in staff training.

The interviews allow us to understand the content, organization, and objectives of the training activities and also provide a space for interviewees to express their views on the benefits and costs of training. We conducted interviews with individuals directly involved in defining staff training and monitoring its costs and benefits, such as the Chief HR Officer and the Head of Diversity & Inclusion, Learning and People Engagement.

In addition, to improve the quality of the interviews and to facilitate the interviewees' preparation, we emailed them in advance the form containing the topics to be covered in the interview. In particular, the interviews focus on (i) by whom and how staff training activities are planned, (ii) what are the strategic objectives of staff training programmes, (iii) what is the content and how are staff training courses organized, and (iv) whether and how companies monitor the costs and benefits of staff training activities.

The interviews are conducted by both two researchers in June and July 2023 and last an average of one hour. They are not audiotape-recorded to favour the confidence of respondents and to encourage them to be open in their comments (Stoner & Holland, 2004). Information was collected in notes, which were integrated by both two researchers with as many details as possible immediately after the interviews to avoid data loss.

We implement our research design by examining two case studies of two Italian companies: company A and company B.[1]

5.3.2 *The Two Cases*

The selected companies have different characteristics, but both of them are relevant examples to examine the specific research questions of this study.

Company A is a listed company operating in the energy sector. Although it represents a traditional manufacturing sector, this company has implemented a specific strategy to increase the production of energy from renewable sources. Therefore, the sustainability issue should play a key role in its business model.

By contrast, company B is unlisted, and it operates in the IT industry. It provides a valuable example of a company involved in a high-technology industry with a

[1] We respect the anonymity of the two companies involved as they have provided us with confidential data and information.

Table 5.1 Key figures from the 2019–2021 financial statements

	Company A			Company B		
	2021	2020	2019	2021	2020	2019
Total assets	6.003.848	4.526.948	4.602.810	69.095	54.147	49.548
Revenues	1.038.182	973.695	1.021.594	29.278	23.209	25.424
EBITDA	434.383	465.236	491.411	−381	1.621	1.248
Net profit	174.450	109.540	32.771	−4.076	−2.678	−3.052
Number of employees	796	767	753	130	113	113

Data in EUR/000

labour-intensive production process. Therefore, the personal knowledge and skills of the employees should be a critical success factor in this company.

The two companies differ significantly in terms of size and economic performance (Table 5.1).[2] In particular, Company A is larger and has a higher number of employees. However, in both companies, we can highlight an improvement in performance over the three-year period examined, following the pandemic crisis.

The two companies also differ in their approach to the sustainability issue. Company A produces an annual sustainability report, several years ahead of the introduction of mandatory non-financial reporting for large listed companies.[3] In addition, from 2021 it explicitly integrates the ESG criteria and the achievement of the Sustainable Development Goals of the United Nations into its strategic plan, revealing a strong commitment to integrating sustainability into its business model. Regarding staff training, in the last issued sustainability report, Company A states that it provides an average of more than 6 days of staff training in the year per employee and that more than 97% of employees are involved in staff training activities. The staff training programmes in this company are grouped into five basic areas: (i) Technical Specialist/on the job, (ii) Managerial, (iii) Health and Safety, (iv) Languages, and (v) Compliance.

On the other hand, Company B is not yet directly involved in ESG reporting, and it does not prepare a sustainability report. However, in its latest separate annual report, Company B presents its HR policy and it explicitly confirms the importance of the professional development of its employees as a strategic objective to be achieved. To this end, it discloses that it provides targeted and appropriate training in line with the company's needs, in particular for newly recruited staff and for existing staff who need to increase their skills in relation to the products and technologies that constitute the company's core business. The management plan also included the stipulation of growth plans for key employees. Other tools used by Company B to enhance the professional skills of its employees encompass (i) a selection by the HR management of the best resources from both the market and

[2] The source of these data is the AIDA Bureau VanDijk database.

[3] The Non-Financial Reporting Directive (Directive 2014/95/EU, also called "NFRD") introduced a requirement for certain large companies to provide a non-financial report. In Italy, the NFRD has been implemented with legislative decree n. 254/2016, applicable from 1 January 2017.

leading universities and (ii) a remuneration system based on the principles of selectivity and meritocracy, linked to the achievement of individual objectives.

5.4 Results

5.4.1 The Influence of ESG-Related Issues on Staff Training Planning

In terms of the logic that informs the planning of staff training activities, in Company A we observe a strong link between strategic planning and staff training; since 2018, the link has become particularly strong as the company has adopted a new leadership model linked to the strategic plan. The leadership model is built by identifying the values and skills needed to implement the strategic plan. The acquisition of the values and skills is entrusted to training, while the assessment of the extent to which the values and skills are also applied is carried out through an evaluation process that includes (i) self-assessment, (ii) assessment by the referring manager, and (iii) comparison between the evaluated employee and the referring manager on how the practical implementation of the acquired values and skills has occurred throughout the year.

Referring to the design process, the identification of the contents is primarily based on input from top management. In addition, the HR function complements that process through a bottom-up dynamic that involves collecting feedback from employees who attend the courses. The HR function specifically asks employees if there are topics they would like to delve into and, based on these indications, proceeds to refine the contents if necessary.

Top management consciously used staff training to not only achieve specific learning outcomes, but also as a tool to connect with all employees, especially during the pandemic, and to disseminate culture. During the pandemic, specific innovations in communication channels and methods were used to meet the need for connection. Courses were organized online and the company created events called "evolving talks", which were used to overcome language barriers (multiple languages) and often addressed sensitive social issues (such as harassment, bullying). These talks continued after the pandemic and were organized in the context of events on topical social issues (human rights, refugees, gender equality, and disability) and with the participation of expert speakers.

Furthermore, to promote maximum participation, the company has worked on the accessibility of the lessons. Specifically, it has sought to adapt the delivery and utilization methods according to the course content. On the one hand, there are still in-person lessons, either in a physical classroom or in a virtual one, which require the presence and participation of the students. On the other hand, the company has been able to provide various online courses, some of which are pre-recorded and accessible to employees through a specific platform that is available 24/7; in this case, the utilization methods are extremely flexible and allow the students to manage their listening according to their own schedule. In this regard, the interviewees emphasize that surprisingly employees make use of the video recordings on their days off.

Company B's strong financial orientation is evident in its approach to ESG. ESG issues are not pervasive in the planning process; when discussing this point, the company shows a compliance-driven approach. First, it especially refers to the environmental dimension, which—in its view—is currently adequately preserved as it avoids actions potentially damaging the environment. Secondly, with regard to the social dimension, the company refers to equal pay and equal opportunities, emphasizing that these elements are managed by the HR function.

For the design, delivery, and evaluation of training effectiveness, the company follows a specific procedure (ISO 9001) as part of the quality processes of certified companies. This procedure imposes a set of constraints on the planning and execution of educational activities, including the recording of activities, the delivery of training, and the verification of the effectiveness of the training provided through a survey that requires feedback from learners and interviews with responsible managers.

Training needs are identified in relation to business requirements. Typically, needs arise in correspondence with aspects of new hires, technological or product-related developments, and language skills upgrading. The company's strategy also significantly influences this, and the training offer caters to needs related to development directions (such as business objectives, for example, the interest in improving margins and the attention to strengthening control over order progress).

Complementary to this top-down approach, Company B also adopts a bottom-up perspective in identifying needs, primarily based on intercepting the needs of department heads. After identifying the training needs of a specific department, the HR function conducts a survey to identify similar needs in other departments.

The organization of training activities is also multifaceted and varies according to the content to be conveyed. For technical training, Company B mainly uses online courses based on generalist e-learning platforms, as well as courses whose content is structured ad hoc according to the specific needs of the company. Academics are also involved in these training activities through the development of in-presence courses. For team-building training, face-to-face courses are mainly used, organized by expert trainers who are able to ensure the involvement of participants, even using innovative techniques.

5.4.2 Connections Between Staff Training Planning and the Concept of Performance

Our analysis provides many elements to identify a strong consistency between the aims of staff training planning and the concept of performance adopted by the two companies. During the interview, Company A establishes, in many cases, a direct connection between training and the achievement of expected financial performance objectives; further, financial performance is framed within a broader concept of value creation, tied to global sustainability objectives. Overall, the company consciously presents employee training as a tool to achieve both improved financial performance and positive social outcomes. Company B presents a concept of financial performance and does not link staff training activity with performance-related targets unless training is specifically needed to react to the erosion of margins attributable to the employees' lack of business administration fundamentals.

More in detail, Company A establishes a direct connection between training and the achievement of financial performance objectives. In particular, the company highlights the link between the leadership model and the strategic plan, which has resulted in a strong connection between strategic objectives and training in a broad sense. Specifically, the company refers to its growth through acquisitions in France; in line with the strategic objectives for acquiring other companies identified in the strategic plan, the leadership model has highlighted inclusivity goals to achieve integration with the acquired entity and its employees. Training to achieve integration is training that has a direct impact on performance and effectively translates income expectations into financial statements and results.

However, this company also frames financial performance within a broader concept of value creation, tied to global sustainability objectives, and emphasizes its alignment with the goals outlined in the 2030 Agenda for Sustainable Development, adopted by all United Nations Member States. Particularly, the company identifies sustainability as both *content and possibly a mode of implementation of the content.*

Indeed, the target audience for the training initiatives is particularly wide-ranging, relying on cultural and scientific dissemination associations abroad as well, in countries where the acquired companies are based, to better reach the research and education world (elementary schools, middle schools, high schools). The content focuses not only on the company and its business, but also on sustainability, inclusiveness, and awareness of one's individual and collective role in the social context.

The company engages artists and scientific and cultural animators and collaborates with them to define the content of the initiatives in France and Spain. For the initiatives in Italy, the training activities are instead carried out by the employees themselves, who also act as trainers. Training is seen as an activity that brings growth benefits for the trainers as well (*serving as an opportunity for growth for our people*). Additionally, the benefit in terms of engagement is emphasized (*it is a source of pride to be able to vote for one's testimony*); the individuals who interact with schools are referred to as "role models".

Concerning the benefit generated by staff training activities, the company adopts a qualitative perspective for its identification. This is based on feedback given by employees who act as trainers; in particular, feedback is gathered immediately after the training experience and again two or three months after the last intervention. In this respect, the company notes that the feedback shows a significant individual benefit (*we have received absolutely enthusiastic comments*) and that, for the trainers, the experience is so positive that it becomes part of a subsequent journey (*about 90% of people who start this kind of programme want to continue it further; for example, we have involved a total of 30 people*). The eagerness to continue seems to be motivated not only by the enjoyable experience but also by the value that trainers attribute to sharing their personal stories and simultaneously representing their company.

The benefits can be tracked at the level of the whole organization, as the evaluation questionnaires also aim to verify any changes in people's behaviour because of the training activity. In this way, it is possible to monitor whether and how the training content has been transferred to people's behaviour and habits, and to identify areas for further improvement.

The company bases its decisions on the dissemination of a management model based on individual awareness of the management of personal resources:

> We consider that every person is a manager; each person manages resources, primarily their own personal resources such as time, relationships, knowledge, and energy. Therefore, all training on soft skills is directed towards everyone and is framed in accordance with our managerial model.

Although not measured, the company also considers a societal benefit, particularly in terms of improving the culture of sustainability in connection with the sustainable development goals, even among children and in areas characterized by a challenging social fabric or underdeveloped conditions, with the precise aim of contributing to reducing these difficulties.

Concerning costs, again the company adopts a generally qualitative approach. It believes that its employees must dedicate considerable time to training preparation; the hours spent on the preparation of the lessons that staff teach in schools include both individual and collective work, as well as the management of activities that are considered to be "quite demanding". Quantification of costs comes into play when activities are assigned to external personnel or when there is a need to cover transportation costs or the set-up of suitable training facilities.

Company B focuses on the financial side of corporate performance and mostly locates staff training activities within firm-oriented issues. Although the company recognizes a "general benefit" of employee training, it does not address its potential links with financial performance and/or an expanded concept of performance that includes sustainability. In general, the company has a soft approach to measuring the benefits of training.

> How do I measure how much more effective it is in developing that language? Well, I mean these types of measurements become really complicated.

It is nonetheless interesting that, despite the lack of awareness of setting and tracking a performance target, the company responds to the erosion of project performance through training, when the erosion of project margin is due to the technical designers' lack of awareness of aspects affecting profitability. More generally, the company reflects on the training deficiencies that have led to the high level of problems; it is often the management that indicates the need for new courses.

In general, the question of the approach to measuring the benefits has revealed a certain difficulty and a certain displacement, which has been resolved for the moment by pointing out the questionable usefulness for the company of certain courses, such as team-building courses (*What do we do? Do we measure how well people get along? No, we don't succeed much*). The issue of measurement overlaps, from the company's perspective, with that of certification (*We measure with certifications, that is, wherever there is an associated certification*).

Training is subject to retrospective reporting by the HR function (number of employees, employees involved in training, training hours, and a list of courses), but it is not part of the ongoing and ex post monitoring objectives:

> at the moment, we do not monitor it, meaning that we have the information, but it is not one of the data points we have set targets for.

The generated benefit is identified at the organizational level within the company. Specifically, the company considers the benefit in terms of (i) increased autonomy generally observed during the performance of job tasks and (ii) more structured work that is more easily coordinated by the project manager. Regarding the increased autonomy of the staff, this organizational benefit is particularly emphasized with reference to onboarding training, i.e. the training of newly hired employees.

As for the coordination of the reference manager, in further specifying this benefit, the interviewees referred not only to purely organizational aspects but also to the benefit identified in terms of the number of working hours that managers can avoid dedicating to training their subordinates and instead devote to their typical tasks (*the benefit of relieving the burden of training these individuals... So here we have a double benefit*) and engage solely in on-the-job training starting from an adequate foundational level. The interviewees specify that, with regard to this benefit, they do not know:

> if it can be said to be measurable, but it is quite evident, we are not measuring it, but there is fairly clear evidence that there is a saving of time and resources.

Benefits are also monitored at an individual level, measured by the development of awareness of critical aspects of the design phase.

The organizational benefit (autonomy, more structured work) and the individual benefit (awareness of the project) are evaluated in a soft manner by the overseeing project manager. Regarding project awareness, it should be noted that in this company, this awareness mainly concerns the implications of choices made by technical designers on profit margins (*awareness of project aspects which were fundamentally focused on marginality, as you may recall*).

> The training that is clearly being conducted anticipates the benefits that the company expects to see.

The individual benefit at employee level, for the individual participating as a learner, is monitored by the company in terms of the skills plan declared by the individual and confirmed or denied by the responsible manager. The comparison of these data can reveal the need for a training path, which can be resolved through continuous training, implicitly included in the solution of the problems inherent in the daily tasks, or through specifically organized courses. Regarding costs, the company takes into account in the HR function budget the resources it intends to allocate to courses held by external instructors.

5.5 Discussion

Our cases reveal two different approaches to planning staff training. Specifically, when ESG issues are pervasive in corporate culture, as in Company B, staff training planning does not incorporate social sustainability objectives and the company shows a compliance-driven approach even if revealing a "soft" and not structured interest in its employees' satisfaction and well-being.

When ESG issues are pervasive in corporate culture, with managers actively committed to creating an attractive working environment (Hansson, 2007; Sung & Choi, 2023), the objectives of social sustainability shape planning employee training initiatives. This is the case of Company A, which adopts a strategic vision that integrates financial and ESG aspects and shows a strong connection between strategic planning and staff training. The strategic plan is tightly linked to the leadership model identifying values and skills required for implementing the strategic plan, in line with the view that, in a context informed by ESG-related goals, sustainability awareness can have a key part in developing sustainability management tools (Talbot et al., 2020). This company also locates the staff training activities within a broader concept of value creation, tied to global sustainability objectives; this orientation is particularly aligned with the business model, in which the sustainability issue plays a key role. Consistently, the target audience for the training initiatives is particularly wide-ranging and training contents are focused not only on the business but also on sustainability, inclusivity, and awareness of one's individual and collective role in the social context. Although not measured, indeed, the company also considers a societal benefit, particularly in terms of improving the culture related to sustainability in connection with the sustainable development goals, even among children and in areas characterized by a challenging social fabric or underdeveloped conditions, with the precise aim of contributing to the reduction of these difficulties.

Furthermore, in Company A training is seen as an activity that brings growth benefits for employees who act as trainers and teaching methods are coherent with this perspective. For instance, the assessment of the extent to which values and skills are also applied is carried out through a structured evaluation process informed by a strong orientation towards self-assessment and dialogue (feedback), and social orientation is also reflected by teaching methods, which have evolved into more inclusive, participative, and flexible classes. This evidence suggests that in these contexts there is an interest in tailoring in original ways staff training to specific needs and situations (Steurer et al., 2005), for instance by selecting specific teaching methods (e.g. opting for participative methods for training aimed at improving the integration of employees and team building) (Milne & McConnell, 2001; Opdecam

& Everaert, 2012; Riley & Ward, 2017; Jackson & Meek, 2021; Oosthuizen et al., 2021; Saxena et al., 2022; Twyford & Dean, 2023).

Our evidence suggests the significance of the performance perspective embraced by the company in directing its staff development endeavours. In this respect, we find that differences in the concept of performance embraced by firms can help explaining differences in approaches adopted when planning staff training, in line with the view that the sustainability-related concept of performance can affect internal decision-making and resource allocation (Liu & Tian, 2021). For instance, Company A explicitly establishes a direct connection between training and the achievement of performance-related targets and it consciously employs staff training as a tool to achieve both better financial performance and positive social outcomes, in line with the idea that contributing to sustainability implies integrating environmental, social, and economic value over the long term through appropriate management tools (Mio et al., 2020, 2022).

Instead, in scenarios where financial objectives take precedence, the linkage between staff training and performance-related goals may not even be established unless there's a pressing need to rectify financial margin erosion. This is the case of Company B, which focuses on the financial side of corporate performance and does not link staff training activity and performance unless training is specifically needed to react to the erosion of margins attributable to the engineers' lack of business administration fundamentals. In Company B training is subject to retrospective reporting by the HR function, but it does not become part of ongoing and ex post monitoring objectives. Similarly, measuring benefits produced by staff training is not a relevant issue and often overlaps, from the company's perspective, with certification. Nonetheless, benefits at the organizational level are identified: the company considers (i) increased autonomy generally observed during the performance of job tasks and (ii) more structured work that is more easily coordinated by the project manager. The benefit is also identified at the individual level, measured in terms of the development of awareness regarding key aspects of the design phase, which is crucial to a company operating in the high-technology industry with employees representing a critical success factor.

5.6 Conclusions

This study reflects on the attention that companies devote to social issues when designing and implementing staff training activities and focuses on whether the planning phase is influenced by sustainability-related goals, and specifically by the underlying goal of benefiting the social dimension. In doing so, we also look at how companies approach performance measurement and, in particular, which type of costs and benefits companies individuate as related to staff training activities.

This study enriches the existing research on the ESG aspect of corporate operations and its alignment with corporate performance evaluation frameworks. Specifically, we extend prior literature by showing how objectives concerning the social sustainability of a company's operations can shape its dedication to planning employee training initiatives, potentially yielding positive outcomes for both employees and society at large. In this respect, our findings extend the research remarking that, in a context informed by ESG-related goals, sustainability awareness can have a key part in developing sustainability management tools (Talbot et al., 2020) also by tailoring these tools to specific needs (Steurer et al., 2005).

Moreover, we underscore the significance of the performance perspective embraced by each company in directing its staff development endeavours. In this respect, we find that differences in the concept of performance embraced by firms can help explain different approaches to planning staff training. Specifically, pursuing a sustainability-related concept of performance implies integrating environmental, social, and economic value over the long term through appropriate management tools (Mio et al., 2020, 2022), for instance in the planning phase of employees' training. Instead, staff training planning is unrelated to sustainability goals in cases where the company pursues a purely financial performance concept. In addition, if financial objectives take precedence, the link between staff training and performance-related goals may not even be established unless there's a pressing need to react to declining financial performance.

More generally, this chapter seeks to advance the broader literature on the social facet of sustainability (Baid & Jayaraman, 2022; Becchetti et al., 2022) by focusing on employee training initiatives within corporate strategies.

From a practical perspective, the study supports companies that already implement staff training in improving their activities and related monitoring mechanisms (management control systems). Second, findings can suggest a far-seeing perspective supporting other companies in organizing staff training programmes. Specifically, the study offers insights into incorporating ESG criteria during the planning stages and underscores the importance of incorporating a socially oriented perspective in the formulation of staff training programmes.

The results and implications of this study should be considered in light of the following limitations. First, staff training is a complex phenomenon that challenges the identification and measurement of benefits, both at the company and the social level. In addition, the analysis covers a limited number of cases, thus placing a limit on the broader generalizability of our findings.

References

Avery, G. C., & Bergsteiner, H. (2011). Sustainable leadership practices for enhancing business resilience and performance. *Strategy & Leadership, 39*(3), 5–15.

Baid, V., & Jayaraman, V. (2022). Amplifying and promoting the "S" in ESG investing: The case for social responsibility in supply chain financing. *Managerial Finance, 48*(8), 1279–1297.

Becchetti, L., Bobbio, E., Prizia, F., & Semplici, L. (2022). Going deeper into the S of ESG: A relational approach to the definition of social responsibility. *Sustainability, 14*(15), 9668.

Bondarouk, T., & Brewster, C. (2016). Conceptualising the future of HRM and technology research. *The International Journal of Human Resource Management, 27*(21), 2652–2671.

Castellano, N., & Felden, C. (2021). Management control systems for sustainability and sustainability of management control systems. *Management Control, 2*, 5–10.
d'Arcimoles, C. H. (1997). Human resource policies and company performance: A quantitative approach using longitudinal data. *Organization Studies, 18*(5), 857–874.
D'Onza, G. (2022). L'orientamento delle aziende ad uno sviluppo sostenibile: quale contributo da parte dei sistemi di management e controllo? *Management Control, 1*, 5–15.
Delaney, J. T., & Huselid, M. A. (1996). The impact of human resource management practices on perceptions of organizational performance. *Academy of Management Journal, 39*(4), 949–969.
Delgado Ferraz, F. A., & Gallardo-Vazquez, D. (2016). Measurement tool to assess the relationship between corporate social responsibility, training practices and business performance. *Journal of Cleaner Production, 129*, 659–672.
Donaldson, T., & Preston, L. E. (1995). The stakeholder theory of the corporation: Concepts, evidence, and implications. *Academy of Management Review, 20*(1), 65–91.
Freeman, R. E., Harrison, J. S., Wicks, A. C., Parmar, B. L., & De Colle, S. (2010). *Stakeholder theory: The state of the art*. Cambridge University Press.
Garavan, T. N., McCarthy, A., Lai, Y., Clarke, N., Carbery, R., Gubbins, C., Sheehan, M., & Saunders, M. N. (2021). Putting the system back into training and firm performance research: A review and research agenda. *Human Resource Management Journal, 31*(4), 870–903.
Hansson, B. (2007). Company-based determinants of training and the impact of training on company performance: Results from an international HRM survey. *Personnel Review, 36*(2), 311–331.
Harel, G. H., & Tzafrir, S. S. (1999). The effect of human resource management practices on the perceptions of organizational and market performance of the firm. *Human Resource Management, 38*(3), 185–199.
Hill, R., & Stewart, J. (2000). Human resource development in small organizations. *Journal of European Industrial Training, 24*(2/3/4), 105–117.
Hristov, I., Chirico, A., & Ranalli, F. (2020). Un approccio sistemico alla teoria della creazione di valore sostenibile: un modello concettuale. *Management Control, 2*, 81–104.
Jackson, D., & Meek, S. (2021). Embedding work-integrated learning into accounting education: The state of play and pathways to future implementation. *Accounting Education, 30*(1), 63–85.
Kotey, B., & Folker, C. (2007). Employee training in SMEs: Effect of size and firm type—Family and nonfamily. *Journal of Small Business Management, 45*(2), 214–238.
Liu, L., & Tian, G. G. (2021). Mandatory CSR disclosure, monitoring and investment efficiency: Evidence from China. *Accounting & Finance, 61*, 595–644.
Lozano, R., & von Haartman, R. (2018). Reinforcing the holistic perspective of sustainability: Analysis of the importance of sustainability drivers in organizations. *Corporate Social Responsibility and Environmental Management, 25*(4), 508–522.
Macke, J., & Genari, D. (2019). Systematic literature review on sustainable human resource management. *Journal of Cleaner Production, 208*, 806–815.
MacMahon, J., & Murphy, E. (1999). Managerial effectiveness in small enterprises: Implications for HRD. *Journal of European Industrial Training, 23*(1), 25–35.
Marchi, L. (2019). Governo delle aziende e creazione di valore: da una prospettiva finanziaria ad una prospettiva economico-sociale. *Management Control, 1*, 5–16.
Milne, M., & McConnell, P. (2001). Problem-based learning: A pedagogy for using case material in accounting education. *Accounting Education, 10*(1), 61–82.
Mio, C., Costantini, A., & Panfilo, S. (2022). Performance measurement tools for sustainable business: A systematic literature review on the sustainability balanced scorecard use. *Corporate Social Responsibility and Environmental Management, 29*(2), 367–384.
Mio, C., Panfilo, S., & Blundo, B. (2020). Sustainable development goals and the strategic role of business: A systematic literature review. *Business Strategy and the Environment, 29*(8), 3220–3245.

Oosthuizen, H., De Lange, P., Wilmshurst, T., & Beatson, N. (2021). Teamwork in the accounting curriculum: Stakeholder expectations, accounting students' value proposition, and instructors' guidance. *Accounting Education, 30*(2), 131–158.

Opdecam, E., & Everaert, P. (2012). Improving student satisfaction in a first-year undergraduate accounting course by team learning. *Issues in Accounting Education, 27*(1), 53–82.

Reid, R. S., & Harris, R. I. (2002). The determinants of training in SMEs in Northern Ireland. *Education+ Training, 44*(8/9), 443–450.

Riley, J., & Ward, K. (2017). Active learning, cooperative active learning, and passive learning methods in an accounting information systems course. *Issues in Accounting Education, 32*(2), 1–16.

Roshchin, S., & Travkin, P. (2017). Determinants of on-the-job training in enterprises: The Russian case. *European Journal of Training and Development, 41*(9), 758–775.

Saxena, D. R., Tupkar, N. J., & Lonkar. (2022). Innovations in current teaching methods: A review. *International Journal of Advanced Research in Science, Communication and Technology, 2*, 152–154.

Scapens, R. W. (2004). Doing case study research. In C. Humphrey & B. Lee (Eds.), *The real life guide to accounting research* (pp. 257–279). Elsevier.

Schönborn, G., Berlin, C., Pinzone, M., Hanisch, C., Georgoulias, K., & Lanz, M. (2019). Why social sustainability counts: The impact of corporate social sustainability culture on financial success. *Sustainable Production and Consumption, 17*, 1–10.

Searcy, C. (2009). Corporate sustainability performance measurement: Lessons from system of systems engineering. In *2009 IEEE International Conference on Systems, Man and Cybernetics* (pp. 1057–1060).

Steurer, R., Langer, M. E., Konrad, A., & Martinuzzi, A. (2005). Corporations, stakeholders and sustainable development I: A theoretical exploration of business–society relations. *Journal of Business Ethics, 61*, 263–281.

Stoner, G., & Holland, J. (2004). Using case studies in finance research. In C. Humphrey & B. Lee (Eds.), *The real life guide to accounting research* (pp. 37–56). Elsevier.

Storey, D. J. (2002). Education, training and development policies and practices in medium-sized companies in the UK: Do they really influence firm performance? *Omega, 30*(4), 249–264.

Sung, S. Y., & Choi, J. N. (2023). What drives firms to invest in training and developing employees? Time-dependent effects of firm internal and external contingencies. *The International Journal of Human Resource Management, 34*(2), 223–252.

Talbot, D., Raineri, N., & Daou, A. (2020). Implementation of sustainability management tools: The contribution of awareness, external pressures, and stakeholder consultation. *Corporate Social Responsibility and Environmental Management, 28*(1), 71–81.

Twyford, E., & Dean, B. A. (2023). Inviting students to talk the talk: Developing employability skills in accounting education through industry-led experiences. *Accounting Education*, 1–23.

Van Marrewijk, M., & Werre, M. (2003). Multiple levels of corporate sustainability. *Journal of Business Ethics, 44*, 107–119.

Chapter 6
ESG Concerns and Teaching Processes in Higher Education, an Experimental Approach

Ida Verna and Antonio D'Andreamatteo

6.1 Introduction

Environmental, social, and governance (ESG) principles have been described as "an investment philosophy that pursues long-term value growth, and it is a comprehensive, concrete, and down-to-earth governance method" (Li et al., 2021, p. 2). Organizations around the globe are benefiting from this relatively new framework both to strengthen their relationships with investors and to change their corporate behavior toward sustainability. In addition, scholars have portrayed universities as "the engine of transformational sustainability" (Purcell et al., 2019) and have acknowledged their "transformative role" in addressing the new challenges being faced by companies and society (p. 267). The "education for sustainable development" has a role in this ongoing process and is intended to "engage learners in thinking critically and creatively about the future as well as in considering the systematic changes that are needed to improve quality of life across the globe" (Scott et al., 2012 in Mader et al., 2013, p. 282). Relatedly, Scott et al. (2012) have called for a shift toward real-word, problem-based, and transdisciplinary programs in research and teaching.

Although the inclusion of environmental, social, and governance factors in universities' strategies and processes is an increasingly perceived need among internal and external stakeholders, little attention has yet been paid in the scholarly

---

This chapter is the result of the joint work of both authors who share the overall approach. Nonetheless, paragraphs: 1, 2, and 8 are attributed to D'Andreamatteo, while paragraphs 3, 4, 5, 6, and 7 are attributed to Verna.

I. Verna (✉) · A. D'Andreamatteo
University G. d'Annunzio of Chieti Pescara, Department of Management and Business Administration, Chieti, Italy
e-mail: ida.verna@unich.it

N. Castellano et al. (eds.), *Environmental, Social, Governance (ESG)*, SIDREA Series in Accounting and Business Administration,
https://doi.org/10.1007/978-3-031-76618-3_6

literature to how higher education can implement transformation plans that effectively include these factors in its various missions (Mader et al., 2013; Purcell et al., 2019).

With reference to teaching, Mader et al. (2013) claimed that attention to sustainability in the curriculum is often linked more to "formal" than "substantial" aspects regarding the inclusion of these factors.

In this sense, our study highlights the need for concrete and holistic approaches that can foster greater staff and student awareness of ESG factors and in this direction contribute more generally to the "building" of a safer and more sustainable society. Consistently, after a brief review of the diffusion of ESG principles in higher education, the study proposes an approach, "L'Ascolto," a framework based on some TQM principles and methods, deemed useful for improving teaching quality and promoting ESG principles. The focus on the needs of the "customer," the dynamic approach related to processes, the systemic logic involving "everything and everyone," knowledge sharing, training, and continuous improvement are all principles that, combined with some TQM methods, provide a solid foundation for innovating teaching processes and promoting ESG orientation. "L'Ascolto" is currently being experimented within an Italian public university.

The chapter is organized as follows: Sect. 6.2 shows insights from previous literature, and Sects. 6.3–6.7 describe the holistic experimental approach "L'Ascolto" and propose how to use it to substantially integrate ESG factors in the first mission of universities. The last section introduces conclusions and study limitations.

6.2 Higher Education, Sustainability, and ESG Concerns

Sustainable development is a key construct. As early as 1987, Brutland conceptualized it as "development that meets the needs of the present without compromising the ability of future generations to meet their own needs" (1987, p. 6), calling for the recognition of the needs of humans, species, and ecosystems and the design of a broad strategic framework to achieve sustainable development. The initial framework has evolved over the decades and has recently been given even more global significance. Indeed, in 2015, world leaders adopted a set of goals (Sustainable Development Goals—SDGs) to be met by 2030, encompassing a wide range of social, economic, and environmental challenges to promote a more sustainable and equitable future for all (United Nations, 2015).

ESG framework is very close to sustainable development, although it is not identical. ESG is a specific construct used to assess and measure the environmental, social, and governance performance of companies and investments. The concept is now used pervasively (Larcker et al., 2022), but in many cases uncritically and overstating its impact on improving business and society performance (Serafeim, 2021). Further, there is a lack of agreement on the purpose of ESG—i.e., what problem it is supposed to solve—and there is overconfidence in the effectiveness of current rating and ranking systems designed to measure ESG quality (Larcker et al., 2022).

Solving sustainability and ESG issues requires the commitment of individuals, companies, civil society organizations, and governments at all levels: local, national, and global. Among these actors, higher education is believed to play a critical role. For instance, many have acknowledged the critical role of universities in creating a sustainable future (Cortese, 2003; Purcell et al., 2019; Žalėnienė & Pereira, 2021), also conceptualizing a new fourth mission, "co-creation for sustainability," in which universities creatively collaborate with other societal actors to build a more sustainable world and address place-based needs (Trencher et al., 2014). However, in the early 2000s, these organizations were unprepared for this critical task (Cortese, 2003). Moreover, only recently have universities started prioritizing their ESG activities and related disclosure (Gagnon & Ming, 2022; Lima et al., 2023).

Higher education can address challenges arising from sustainability issues and ESG concerns from multiple perspectives that correspond to governance, their operations, and each different mission, whether education, research, or public engagement (Michel, 2019).

Several barriers hinder universities' progress toward greater sustainability and effective contribution to society. First, the lack of engagement by academics is related to the incentive mechanisms in use within higher education, which still overvalue research outputs with respect to teaching and the third mission (Trencher et al., 2014). In addition, the lack of formal institutional sustainability policies could slow down the implementation of sustainable development initiatives within universities (Leal Filho et al., 2018).

Some solutions have proven effective in overcoming barriers. For example, pioneering initiatives (Ng, 2019) have consisted in promoting collaboration and knowledge sharing among universities internationally; promoting the commitment of top management; encouraging students to engage in on-campus sustainability development initiatives as well as shared activities with local stakeholders; improving the design and legitimacy of sustainability policies by engaging key internal and external stakeholders; and incorporating targeted learning outcomes and objectives into the curriculum.

Although all university missions are relevant, the remainder of the section deepens ESG concerns in relation to education and teaching, including how universities design and implement curricula, courses, and extracurricular activities to promote students' academic and personal development. Introducing sustainability into such a mission requires appropriate Education Policy (Ng, 2019). However, as Scott (2014) pointed out, it is not enough to plan for the integration of social, cultural, economic, and environmental aspects into the curriculum, and good ideas must be implemented in practice. In other words, the how is as central as the what, but studies have not yet proposed a method that can overcome some of the current barriers in implementing sustainability and ESG, within and across the university's first mission.

First, studies have stressed the advantages and limitations of ESG rankings as a means of comparing organizations' environmental, societal, and governance performance. Zhutiaeva et al. (2023) proposed a group of indicators and criteria deemed useful for assigning an ESG rating to universities. Although the education dimension is evaluated, the focus appears to be restricted to the organization of environmental education programs (at least two events with a minimum of 50 participants, held in each department), to the promotion of the quality and safety of educational services (the presence of quality standards for educational services as a common effort and responsibility of all faculties and branches), and to student self-governance (the coordination and development of youth policies, the presence of non-profit organizations working at the university, and the creation of several youth training projects). While all these aspects are valuable in assessing the involvement of universities with environmental and societal factors, and related activities should be at the core of each university, we believe that they can only partially grasp the complexity of incorporating ESG concerns into educational processes. Relatedly, even with a high score in these criteria and indicators, the degree of achieved sustainability may be overestimated compared to the actual and radical change in universities.

Second, studies have shown how universities are testing ways to prioritize in their curricula the most important challenges facing humanity, namely, climate change, conflicts, inequality, and poverty, among others. Regarding sustainability in general, scholars have long been interested in how to integrate it into higher education (Rusinko, 2010). Rusinko (2010) is among the first to have proposed a way to integrate sustainability into higher education. She outlined four possibilities: achieving sustainability integration using existing structures, in either a narrow (discipline-specific) or broad (cross-disciplinary) way, rather than achieving the goal through new structures, again with a narrow or broad focus. Further, Lidgren et al. (2006) pointed to a "systemic approach" as promising for identifying barriers and solutions to integrating sustainable development into courses and curricula. This calls for the development and use of new indicators; the establishment of multidisciplinary competencies favoring intra-university learning; a more active engagement in the dialogue with both internal and external stakeholders (primarily with the students); the identification of sustainability as a top priority; and the clarification of the paradigm shift required by teachers. Finally, Cebrián et al. (2013) proposed an integrative theoretical framework encompassing all higher education missions. They suggested that embedding sustainability in higher education requires the promotion of organizational learning, a continuous process of individual learning, which in turn spreads to the community. This learning process also involves social and cultural aspects.

Regarding accounting specifically, scholars have emphasized the role of business schools and accounting academics in promoting the desired change (Çalıyurt, 2022; Sheehan et al., 2022). Sheehan et al. (2022) recently suggested a new environmental, social, and governance learning model to teach accounting students how to contribute to improving corporate ESG performance in their future career. This new model is deemed necessary by the authors, in a context that is still dominated by a professional view in which the goal is "shareholder value maximization." In contrast, at the corporate level, future accountants should be prepared to actively advocate ESG initiatives well beyond legal and regulatory obligations. Berg and Lyngstadås (2023) insist on the contribution of the accounting curriculum in developing sustainable literacy and propose ways to include sustainability in introductory management accounting courses while strengthening student's critical thinking skills and improving their employability. Although these proposals are of paramount relevance, they are also very context-specific (a single curriculum or even a course), which makes us feel that they do not, by themselves, ensure substantial and not just formal inclusion of ESG as a concern of higher education as a whole. A more holistic strategy (Too & Bajracharya, 2015) and approach is needed to engage all the actors in ESG, and activate that paradigm shift, i.e., cultural change, already considered necessary by prior literature (e.g., Cebrián et al., 2013; Lidgren et al., 2006).

While acknowledging the value of the abovementioned suggestions and proposals, we argue for the lack of a system that enables the simultaneous consideration of all the relevant aspects in the planning and implementation stages. The following paragraphs describe ways in which "L'Ascolto" approach and platform can allow us to overcome the perceived limitations and barriers and foster the university mission of creating, disseminating, and implementing an environmental, social, and governance culture through teaching and learning, in order to foster the evolution of each disciplinary content toward a multidisciplinary approach in dealing with sustainability.

6.3 A Substantive Approach to ESG Factors and a Cultural Revolution

The analysis of the literature has shown that universities are paying greater attention to ESG factors, but this has not been accompanied by the development of implementation models that can be practically applied to university teaching. There is a gap in the literature regarding "how" such institutions could effectively implement ESG factors in the university's first mission. In this respect, one possible implementation approach is proposed: the web platform "L'Ascolto" (Verna, 2012; Verna et al., 2019; Verna, 2020; Verna & Verna, 2021).

In order to clarify the reasons for choosing this approach, an analysis is proposed with respect to the evidence that has emerged from the literature, that is, with respect to the critical issues that hinder an effective implementation of ESG factors in university teaching.

First, reference was made to a need for transition from formal inclusion in DC and teaching design to substantial implementation of these factors in all university teaching processes. It should be noted that a curriculum and teachings design that is closely related to the management, evaluation, and improvement of teaching processes, considered as a whole, is not a design that "thinks for itself." In this case, if ESG factors were implemented using such an approach, they would not be the result of a mere formal act (Mader et al., 2013), but a part of a holistic management of teaching and the actors involved in it.

In addition, some authors (Sheehan et al., 2022) point out the need to contaminate disciplines with ESG as an "evolutionary" element of the disciplines themselves.

Ultimately, there is a need to overcome the "sad" attitude of "subservience to the norm" or adaptation to a cultural orientation and allow ESG principles to become a "high vantage point" in approaching disciplines. In this sense, the choice of *how* to deal with the ESG "problem" in university teaching could go beyond implementation, extending to the "way of thinking" about disciplines. The outcome of an approach to teaching that considers ESG principles pervasively, not just inclusively, could set these factors as part of the change, in the way teaching is designed, managed, and evaluated and in the approach to disciplines, leading to a real "cultural revolution" in the social context.

In this sense, the "L'Ascolto" approach appeared to respond in a timely manner to the critical issues highlighted in the literature by offering specific (and replicable) implementation methods.

"L'Ascolto" is an experimental project of the G. d'Annunzio University, which funded the development of the platform and the subsequent experimentation in the Degree Courses, DCs, of the University itself. The experimentation began in 2021, in the Department of Business Administration, in the Digital Marketing Degree Course and in the Corporate Finance curriculum, and allowed for the assessment of students' satisfaction, who wished for its dissemination in all the DCs of the department. Also, the interest aroused by "L'Ascolto" from other Italian universities close to experimentation has led us to consider the possibility of an extended experimentation that could allow us to verify the actual effectiveness of this approach with respect to the implementation of these ESG factors. Although the proposed work is limited by an experimentation that has not yet been implemented, with respect to these ESG factors, it is believed that the contribution offered by the presentation of "L'Ascolto" may represent a new point of view on the possible implementation of these ESG factors in university teaching processes and their social implications.

Drawing on the above, the holistic approach named L'Ascolto® is proposed. Its purpose is the continuous improvement of the quality of teaching, pursued jointly by all the actors who access it at different times and in different ways, but with a common goal: the co-creation of value (Verna, 2023, in press).

In order to understand whether, and at what level, this holistic approach makes it possible to address and overcome critical issues related to the effective implementation of ESG factors in university teaching, the following paragraphs provide an analysis of the aims and characteristics of the holistic approach "L'Ascolto" (Fig. 6.1).

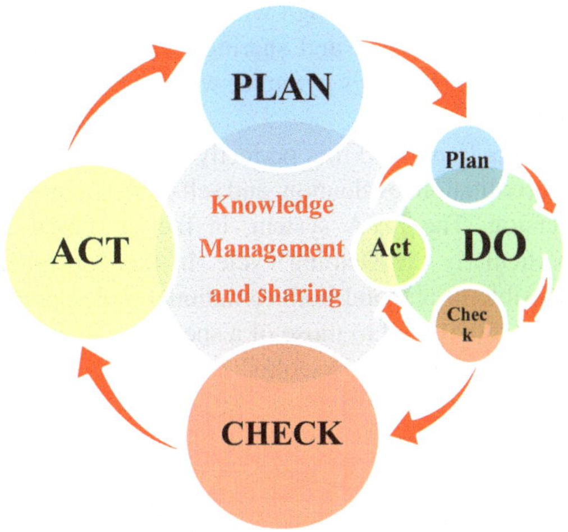

Fig. 6.1 "L'Ascolto," a holistic approach to university teaching (Verna et al., 2019)

6.4 A Holistic Approach to University Teaching for the Substantial Integration of ESG Factors

Considering ESG factors in teaching in a pervasive way, in our opinion, requires a holistic approach that considers actors and processes as a single, dynamic, continuous learning system, evolving toward new knowledge, to be acquired and returned to the context, enriched with new meanings.

To pursue these goals, the "L'Ascolto" approach is proposed, whose framework (Verna, 2012; Verna et al., 2019; Verna, 2020; Verna & Verna, 2021) is the result of combining the philosophy of Total Quality Management, TQM, with Kolb's systems theory and the logic of experiential learning. In particular, the basis of the development of the framework is the need to consider the complexity of teaching, i.e., the dynamic relationships between processes and actors, as an inseparable system of interrelated, constantly evolving parts. In this sense, systemic theory represents a solid conceptual basis for the development of the definition of an approach to teaching, considering its systemic unity (Verna, 2012), its relationships and interdependencies, and dynamic evolutions with respect to the needs of the context (top-down and button-up).

On these theoretical bases and with a view to defining a concrete approach to improving the educational system as a whole, the philosophy and methods of Total Quality Management, TQM, were combined with systemic theory. Specifically, two TQM methods were combined: Deming's PDCA cycle (Verna, 2012) and QFD (Verna, 2014a, 2014b), which offer training actors a unified approach to the overall processes of curriculum and individual course planning (Plan/QFD), connected management of all teaching processes, evaluation, and continuous improvement. This holistic approach was combined with Kolb's experiential learning theory to guide the teacher in following the "Deming/Kolb" cycle (Verna, 2020) for knowledge creation from the teaching-learning experience.

The language through which the "L'Ascolto" platform enables knowledge creation, management, and sharing is the result of combining J. Biggs' constructive alignment (Bloom's pyramid) with qualitative and quantitative assessment and self-assessment tools.

This framework fits perfectly with the theory behind the operation of our AVA (accreditation, evaluation, and self-assessment) system, also in its most recent AVA3 version. The AVA system, in fact, is based on the principles of total quality, particularly the Deming cycle. In this sense, the "L'Ascolto" approach makes it possible to respond both to national and supranational orientations (EHEA, 2015, 2018, 2020) and to those of a specific teaching and learning context (button-up).

Specifically, "L'Ascolto" is an evolution of the Teaching Evaluation Model (TEM) based exclusively on the Deming cycle and aimed at the continuous improvement of individual university courses (Verna, 2012). TEM experimentation over the years (Verna & Perozzi, 2014) has led to an integration of this approach with another quality method (Verna, 2014a, 2014b), i.e., Quality Function Deployment—QFD. Subsequent reflections on the complexity of teaching and the context in which it operates allowed the approach to be extended to the overall training processes, i.e., to the course of study and to the individual courses considered as a whole (Verna et al., 2019; Verna, 2020). The result was a holistic approach to the design, management, evaluation, and improvement of teaching processes, translated into a web platform, "L'Ascolto" (Verna & Verna, 2021), whose aim is to offer training actors a tool for creating, managing, and sharing knowledge.

This holistic approach to teaching processes gives rise to a system of knowledge, managed in a systematic and structured way by the "L'Ascolto" web platform. The goal is to return this knowledge to the teachers themselves for their own continuous self-training, for the development of "disciplinary knowledge," for guiding continuous improvement of student learning, for innovating research in the educational field, in short, for a cultural revolution of the social context.

To understand the working logic of this approach and how it can allow for the design, implementation, and evaluation of ESG factors in university teaching processes, a presentation of the holistic approach "L'Ascolto" is proposed in the following paragraph.

6.5 Design, Implementation, and Evaluation of ESG Factors in University Teaching Processes

Formal inclusion of ESG factors in the design of curricula and courses may become a substantial implementation if the approach used for this purpose considers the actors and teaching processes as an inseparable system of interrelated parts, in continuous evolution (holistic approach).

If ESG factors are viewed as an endeavor to be carried out at the design stage, a purely formal act that does not involve teaching-learning processes, and is therefore not assessable in students' learning outcomes or in the development of teachers' professionalism, leading to a pure intellectual exercise of those designing a training course. If, on the contrary, ESG principles become part of a holistic approach to teaching, in which the design stage is closely related to the management, evaluation, and improvement stages of training processes, ESG factors can become an inseparable part of a unique body of knowledge derived from the teaching-learning experience of the actors themselves (Verna, 2020; Verna et al., 2021).

Looking at Fig. 6.2, we can see that it can be ideally divided into two parts. The first part of the figure highlights the design phase of the course of study and individual courses, called the Plan phase. In this phase, the expected learning outcomes (LO) that must be present in the student at the end of the course of study are defined. At this stage, the Chair of the course of study can integrate ESG factors into the competence profile of the course of study. Although this phase may represent a mere formal inclusion of these factors in the overall teaching design, the continuous cycle that links the design to the subsequent phases allows for immediate implementation (DO phase), evaluation (Check phase), and improvement of what has been designed. In this sense, the formal inclusion of ESG factors can be transformed, over time, into a concrete experience of student training and teachers' and institutional bodies' (i.e., the Chair of the course of study) self-training.

The second part of Fig. 6.2, in fact, represents the phases of management, evaluation, and improvement of all teaching processes. We can see that the design phase is followed by the implementation of teaching strategies (Do). In this phase, the undisputed protagonist is the teacher who concretely implements the teaching-learning processes, implementing the teaching strategies defined in the design phase and experimenting with their effectiveness.

The subsequent evaluation phase (Check), in itinere, which evaluates students' learning and teachers' self-evaluation, allows the improvement process to be informed and directed toward the effective achievement of the LOs. Student learning assessment tests (in itinere) accompanied by course satisfaction tests that monitor critical areas of teaching quality, combined with teacher self-assessment tests, are managed by the platform by offering the teacher aggregated data, useful for guiding improvement (Act phase). The Act phase closes the improvement circle, with the identification and elimination of the obstacles found in the teaching processes, in order to achieve these objectives effectively. In a nutshell, the PDCA process followed by the actors in the pursuit of the quality of teaching has been described. This continuous PDCA process, which involves all actors in a repeated and coordinated manner over time, could lead to the transition from the stage of "mere formal inclusion" of these factors in the design of the course of study to their concrete implementation.

Figure 6.2 shows, in summary, how all the didactic processes are interrelated in "L'Ascolto" and aimed at one single purpose: the creation, management, and sharing of knowledge. Teachers create knowledge from the teaching-learning experience; this knowledge is managed in a structured and systematic manner by the platform

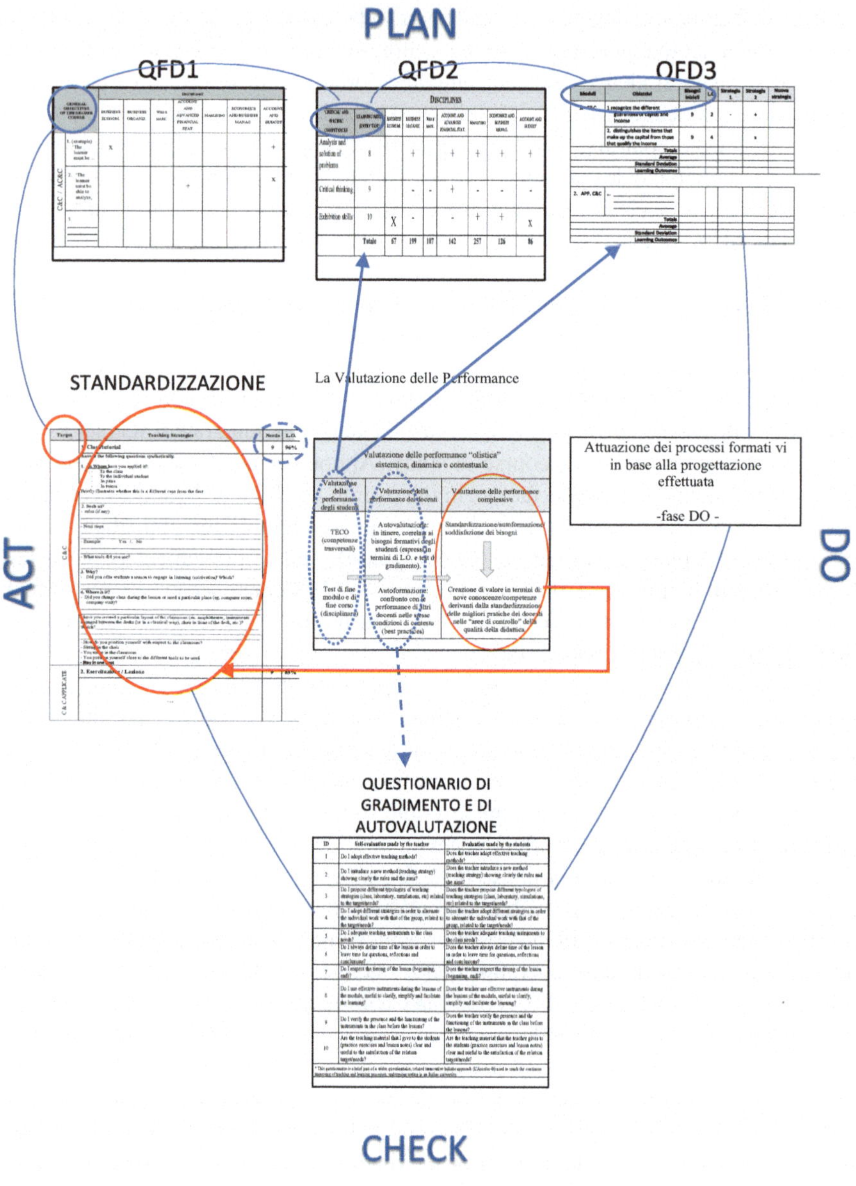

Fig. 6.2 The holistic approach "L'Ascolto" (Verna et al., 2021)

and is shared among teachers (who operate under the same context conditions) for their own continuous self-training, i.e., the continuous improvement of the quality of teaching (student learning).

In the following paragraphs, an analysis of the ways in which the holistic approach "L'Ascolto" could enable a concrete implementation of ESG factors in university teaching processes and possible outcomes is proposed.

6.6 A Web Platform for Listening to and Satisfying "ESG Needs" in University Teaching

As mentioned in the previous paragraph, the PDCA cycle begins with the design phase of the DC and the individual courses. At this stage, PDCA is used in conjunction with QFD, Quality Function Deployment. The first part of Fig. 6.2 (design) shows the overall design phase of a curriculum and the courses (which compose it) implemented using QFD.

Specifically, at this stage, it is the Chair of the DC who defines the expected learning outcomes, the LOs of the DC that will form the professional profile of the figure to be trained. In the design phase (DC and teachings), the inclusion of ESG factors can be easily achieved through the QFD1 and QFD2 matrices. The first matrix, QFD1, makes it possible to highlight the relationship between the general objectives to be achieved in that curriculum and the disciplines that make up the course of study. The QFD2 matrix relates the soft skills provided in the degree course and the disciplines that make up the DC.

As noted above, in defining the DC's LOs, the Chair considers ESG factors as an integral part of the pathway. In this sense, the QFD1 matrix highlights the more or less strong relationship between the general objectives (inclusive of ESG factors) and the disciplines that make up the training course. The QFD2 matrix, on the other hand, highlights the more or less strong relationships between the disciplines (composing the DC) and the soft skills that will have to contribute to the training of the professional figure defined in the DC. Objectives and skills thus defined are related to the design phase carried out by the teachers with QFD3. In relation to these general references (general course objective and soft skills), teachers develop the specific design. In this sense, ESG factors also enter the individual course (syllabus) design in an increasingly specific way. Specifically, at this stage, the general course objective is developed into particular objectives, to which the teaching strategies and the design of in-progress learning assessment tests are linked. In this sense, ESG factors are becoming an increasingly "thought-out" and inseparable part of the discipline being delivered.

It should also be noted that the design phase is closely linked to listening to the training needs of students, teachers, institutional bodies, and other stakeholders. As already pointed out, the most important aspect of the holistic approach of "L'Ascolto" is precisely listening to the needs of the training actors, from which the platform derives its name.

6.6.1 Listening to Actors' Needs and Implementing ESG Factors in University Teaching

If concrete implementation of ESG factors is to be achieved, then it is necessary to listen to the needs that must be met to reach this goal. It is the systemic and dynamic listening to the needs of the actors that guides the continuous improvement of the teaching processes toward the achievement of the general objectives designed in the DC and in the individual courses. In the design phase of a DC, the definition of the LOs must be linked to listening to institutional bodies and stakeholders in order to define an attractive course of study, capable of offering concrete employment opportunities.

Specifically, in the QFD1 matrix, stakeholder listening is broken down into objectives and related to the disciplines, while in QFD2, stakeholder listening is outlined in terms of soft skills and related to both the course disciplines and the initial training needs, expressed by learners entering the DC (i.e., TECO test). Figure 6.3 shows how "L'Ascolto" produces, during the first year, a design whose ESG factors are formally included. The subsequent Do, Check, and Act phases, however, allow for the substantial implementation of these factors, which in subsequent years, starting from the Plan phase, show an increasingly clear and profound integration of ESG factors.

At the same time, with respect to the LOs thus defined, it is necessary to listen to the students' training needs in order to understand the distance (gap) between what has been defined in the design (of the DC and of the individual courses) and the students' training (at the entry and in itinere). Students can practically represent the focus of the teaching-learning process, when listening to their training needs is closely related to the objectives/skills of the DC and the teachings, and when listening is repeated over time. With the L'Ascolto platform, students' needs are listened to, both at admission to the DC and at the entrance, in itinere, and exit from individual courses. In order for the student gap to be filled, it is also important to listen to the training needs necessary for the teacher to meet the students' needs.

This is where the Do phase (Fig. 6.3) begins, in which teachers design their own teaching (QFD3) by connecting to the macro design (QFD1 and QFD2). In the implementation phase of individual courses, teachers develop the teaching strategies defined in the Plan phase (Biggs, 2003). The definition of strategies also concerns ESG objectives that, when successful (Check phase), are standardized (Act phase) and then returned to shared teachers. Sharing is intended to nurture teacher self-education, enhance student learning, and develop disciplinary/interdisciplinary research (ESG) and educational improvement/innovation for ESG teaching.

In this sense, it becomes difficult to think that the implementation of ESG factors in university teaching processes can be avoided using a holistic approach, in which actors and processes are linked in a systemic and dynamic way.

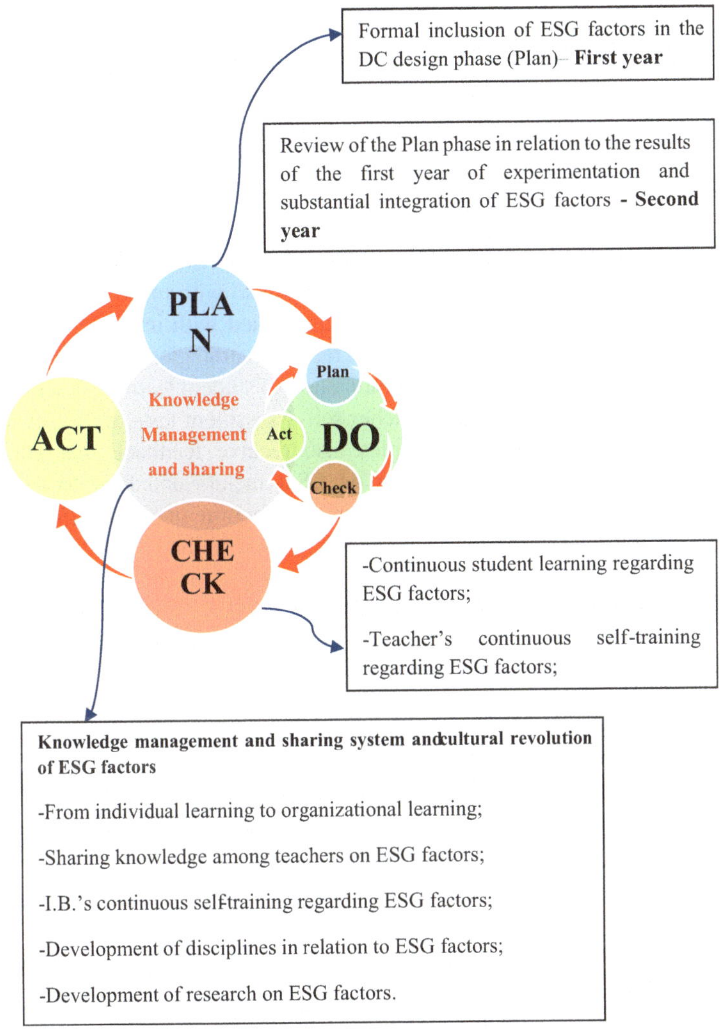

Fig. 6.3 Cultural revolution on ESG factors: from university teaching to the social context

Actors are aware of their active and collaborative role in the satisfaction of their needs, expressed in the design phase (QFD1, QFD2, and QFD3), pursued in the management phase of the teaching processes, evaluated in the results achieved (student learning, teachers' and institutional bodies' self-training), and improved in the pursuit of effective implementation (knowledge creation, management, and sharing). Ultimately, listening to the actors' needs can be accomplished through their active and shared participation in the use of the platform.

6.6.2 Meeting Actors' Needs and Assessing ESG Learning/Teaching

In *L'Ascolto*, evaluation is a key strategic process of listening to students' and teachers' training needs in a connected and continuous way over time (systemic and dynamic listening), informing the teacher of any critical issues arising in the teaching-learning process, and thus of opportunities for improvement. The assessment phase "listens" to the students' needs (with respect to LOs) offering teachers useful information for improvement. In this way, also with respect to ESG factors, listening to the students' needs becomes consolidated with improvement, through the definition and experimentation of new teaching strategies. In addition, teacher listening is implemented through the combination of student learning assessment test results with course satisfaction and teacher self-assessment tests. In this evaluation/self-assessment process, ESG principles also receive feedback that allows the teacher to develop continuous training on ESG factors and how to teach-learn them. Teacher self-assessment and student satisfaction questionnaires will also highlight specific ESG items, which make teacher self-training and student learning improvement even more impactful. The type of evaluation present in *L'Ascolto* is holistic, i.e., an expression of the result of the overall educational processes, assessed in itinere, with respect to the actors who implemented them and their mutual relationships. The inclusion of ESG factors in an approach involving such an assessment could lead to more specific feedback than the one offered by ranking systems, as an expression of the level of implementation of these factors, in the teaching processes being delivered (or delivered).

The final phase, Act, allows for the definition of the corrective actions to be implemented to reduce or eliminate the gap between the training existing in the student at the time of evaluation (in itinere) and the "pending" one (Plan phase). If the strategies adopted are effective, the teacher is not only able to close the *students' gap with respect to the defined objectives, but can also fill his or her own* training *gap*. In particular, the teacher develops the specific professionalism needed to bridge the students' educational *gap*.

It is easy to see how, if the ESG variable is included in this process, the strategies that enabled student learning achievement and teacher self-training will be standardized for sharing. In this way, other teachers will have the opportunity to practically apply these principles with effective strategies in a specific context of needs (disciplinary, learning, and teaching).

6.7 Creating, Managing, and Sharing Knowledge for a "Disciplinary and Cultural Revolution"

The PDCA cycle just described starts, therefore, from educational design and continues through the subsequent phases, up to the Plan phase with feedback useful for reducing the gap between the training promised and the training delivered.

Figure 6.3 schematically shows the abovementioned points, highlighting how the holistic approach L'Ascolto can allow a substantial implementation of ESG factors in university teaching processes.

In this continuous PDCA cycle, ESG factors formally appear in the design phase of the DC and individual courses and then become an integral part of the teaching processes, resulting in the choice of teaching strategies that enable their implementation in the processes. These factors are subsequently evaluated in terms of concrete student learning, in the Check phase (in itinere), as part of the planning (objectives/needs). The Act phase closes and reopens the PDCA cycle and, in the case of student non-learning, directs the teacher toward improvement actions.

The result of this perpetual cycle is the creation, management, and sharing (in a structured, systematic, and selective way) of the knowledge derived from the processes just mentioned (best practices). The success of teaching strategies in achieving the objectives/competences defined in the design phase is standardized and shared among teachers who teach under the same context conditions (students' objectives/needs). Specifically, this knowledge system informs and "trains" (self-training) teachers about these best practices and the concrete possibilities for improvement that can be implemented, in the design and management phases of the teaching processes being delivered, thus enabling concrete implementation of ESG factors.

Thus, the most important aspect of the entire PDCA process is the creation of knowledge (Verna, 2020) that is returned to the actors, in terms of teacher self-training, evolution and innovation of disciplines, continuous improvement in student learning, and ultimately cultural evolution of the social context. In particular, teacher self-training takes place in both the design and improvement phases, when the platform offers the teacher the best strategies adopted by other teachers who have been operating under the same context conditions (training objectives-student needs) achieving success in learning. This self-training continues in the subsequent phases, where the platform supports the teacher by proposing solutions (adopted by other teachers who have found themselves in the same conditions) that are useful for solving students' learning problems. In the event that ESG factors were integrated into such an approach, teacher self-training, promoted by the platform through knowledge sharing, would also lead to a professional development of the teacher with respect to ESG factors. Moreover, teacher self-training on ESG factors would be integrated with the disciplines (students' objectives-needs) and not separated from them. Consequently, if ESG factors become an integral part of a knowledge system derived from a holistic approach to teaching, the result can only be the evolution of disciplinary contents, leading to a real cultural change in the social context, where these factors are part of the change.

Ultimately, the creation, management, and sharing of knowledge fuels the sharing of effective teaching strategies for the implementation of ESG factors (ESG education), the "evolution" of disciplinary content, contaminated by these principles, and in this sense also the experimental research on ESG in the educational field. In this vein, we refer to "cultural revolution," that is, when the inclusion of these factors extends from a mere formal consideration in the design phase to a substantial implementation in teaching processes, extending to the professional development of the teacher, the continuous learning of students, the evolution of disciplines, and scientific research in education.

L'Ascolto, as a system of management and sharing of knowledge deriving from a holistic approach to teaching processes, was tested in two Master of Sciences' programs (Digital Marketing and Corporate Finance curricula) held by the University of G. d'Annunzio University of Chieti Pescara. This first experimentation concerned the use of the platform and its functions to promote the coherence between the objectives of the Master's degree course and those of the single courses, as well as between those objectives, the teaching strategies, and learning assessment, both in the design phase and during and at the end of course delivery. The first results that emerged from the "L'Ascolto" experimentation in 2021 made it possible to ascertain the high satisfaction of the students who appreciated an ongoing, anonymous evaluation centered on the teaching objectives. The students acknowledged a greater awareness of the level of learning achieved. Furthermore, students appreciated the possibility of immediately overcoming any learning difficulties, precisely by virtue of constant listening to their needs with respect to the objectives of the course combined with flexibility in teaching methods of teachers (Verna, 2020). The students also hoped for an extension to all teachings of the Department of Business Economics. These results highlight the approach used by "L'Ascolto" to achieve interdisciplinary learning objectives; hence, it may work to include ESGs learning objectives throughout the whole degree and coherently among all the disciplines.

6.8 Conclusion

In the previous sections, we described a new approach, "L'Ascolto" (Verna & Verna, 2021), which is being tested in a public Italian university and which may offer a way to integrate ESG concerns in the first mission of all universities, with reference to all disciplines and internationally.

Prior literature has already highlighted the need for a systemic approach and a paradigm shift on the part of teachers (Lidgren et al., 2006), based on a continuous learning process, at the individual and organizational level (Cebrián et al., 2013). However, the aforementioned studies have not yet suggested how to move from mere planning or, at best, from a merely formal implementation to a substantive implementation of ESG interests in the first university mission.

Our study sought to make a concrete contribution to the inclusion of environmental, social and governance factors in university curricula and teaching processes, employing the web tool "L'Ascolto," based on a holistic approach to teaching (Verna, 2012; Verna et al., 2019; Verna, 2020). The use of a holistic experimental approach based on a web platform allows for the incorporation of ESG factors in the training projects of the entire Degree Course and specific courses, the subsequent management of these factors in teaching-learning processes, and the evaluation and improvement of the results achieved. In addition, "L'Ascolto" represents an implementation tool that enables the development of sustainable education that can extend from universities to the overall cultural and social context. In fact, "L'Ascolto" allows teachers, students, institutional bodies, and social partners to contribute at different times and in different ways to the design, management, evaluation, and improvement of teaching quality. In this sense, the inclusion of objectives related to ESG factors in university curricula would extend to the processes of management, evaluation (student learning, teacher skill development), and continuous improvement of teaching processes to pursue all educational objectives, of which ESG factors are an integral part. Although "L'Ascolto" represents both as a holistic methodological approach and as an operational tool, a concrete opportunity for the dissemination of the culture of sustainability in universities (and from them to the context of reference), experimentation is needed to evaluate the results that can be achieved with the inclusion of ESG factors into the "L'Ascolto" platform. The initial results suggest that a trial that includes ESG factors could lead to positive results of the same type. Future research will therefore focus on evaluating the effects of using a holistic, web-based experimental approach on the design, management, evaluation, and improvement of ESG factors in academic curricula.

References

Berg, T., & Lyngstadås, H. (2023). We're only in it for the money? Developing sustainable literacy through management accounting curriculum. *Accounting Education*, 1–20. https://doi.org/10.1080/09639284.2023.2270475

Biggs, J. (2003). Aligning teaching and assessing to course objectives. *Teaching and Learning in Higher Education: New Trends and Innovations, 2*(4), 13–17.

Çalıyurt, K. T. (2022). The role of the curriculum in business schools in the widespread use of ESG reporting. In K. T. Çalıyurt (Ed.), *New approaches to CSR, sustainability and accountability* (Vol. III, pp. 3–6). Springer Nature. https://doi.org/10.1007/978-981-16-9364-9_1

Cebrián, G., Grace, M., & Humphris, D. (2013). Organisational learning towards sustainability in higher education. *Sustainability Accounting, Management and Policy Journal, 4*(3), 285–306. https://doi.org/10.1108/SAMPJ-12-2012-0043

Cortese, A. D. (2003). The critical role of higher education in creating a sustainable future.

EHEA. (2015). Yerevan Communiqué. Retrieved from http://ehea.info/media.ehea.info/file/2015_Yerevan/70/7/YerevanCommuniqueFinal_613707.pdf

EHEA. (2018). Paris Communiqué. Retrieved from http://www.ehea.info/media.ehea.info/file/2018_Paris/77/1/EHEAParis2018_Communique_final_952771.pdf

EHEA. (2020). Recommendations to National Authorities for the Enhancement of Higher Education Learning and Teaching in the EHEA. BFUG Advisory Group 2 on Learning and Teaching.

Gagnon, D., & Ming, H. (2022). *Higher education is investing in ESG*. Retrieved July 15, 2023, from https://info.kpmg.us/content/dam/info/en/news-perspectives/pdf/2022/higher-education-is-investing-in-esg.pdf

Larcker, D. F., Tayan, B., & Watts, E. M. (2022). Seven myths of ESG. *European Financial Management, 28*(4), 869–882. https://doi.org/10.1111/eufm.12378

Leal Filho, W., Brandli, L. L., Becker, D., Skanavis, C., Kounani, A., Sardi, C., Papaioannidou, D., Paço, A., Azeiteiro, U., & de Sousa, L. O. (2018). Sustainable development policies as indicators and pre-conditions for sustainability efforts at universities: Fact or fiction? *International Journal of Sustainability in Higher Education, 19*(1), 85–113.

Li, T.-T., Wang, K., Sueyoshi, T., & Wang, D. D. (2021). ESG: Research progress and future prospects. *Sustainability, 13*(21) Art. 21. https://doi.org/10.3390/su132111663
Lidgren, A., Rodhe, H., & Huisingh, D. (2006). A systemic approach to incorporate sustainability into university courses and curricula. *Journal of Cleaner Production, 14*(9–11), 797–809. https://doi.org/10.1016/j.jclepro.2005.12.011
Lima, C. D. S., Kieling, D. L., Veiga Ávila, L., Paço, A., & Zonatto, V. C. D. S. (2023). Towards sustainable development: A systematic review of the past decade's literature on the social, environment and governance and universities in Latin America. *International Journal of Sustainability in Higher Education, 24*(2), 279–298. https://doi.org/10.1108/IJSHE-09-2021-0394
Mader, C., Scott, G., & Abdul Razak, D. (2013). Effective change management, governance and policy for sustainability transformation in higher education. *Sustainability Accounting, Management and Policy Journal, 4*(3), 264–284. https://doi.org/10.1108/SAMPJ-09-2013-0037
Michel, J. O. (2019). Sustainability in higher education. In W. Leal Filho (Ed.), *Encyclopedia of sustainability in higher education* (pp. 1–7). Springer International Publishing. https://doi.org/10.1007/978-3-319-63951-2_455-1
Ng, A. W. (2019). Sustainability and education policy. In W. Leal Filho (Ed.), *Encyclopedia of sustainability in higher education* (pp. 1–8). Springer International Publishing. https://doi.org/10.1007/978-3-319-63951-2_482-1
Purcell, W. M., Henriksen, H., & Spengler, J. D. (2019). Universities as the engine of transformational sustainability toward delivering the sustainable development goals: "Living labs" for sustainability. *International Journal of Sustainability in Higher Education*.
Rusinko, C. A. (2010). Integrating sustainability in higher education: A generic matrix. *International Journal of Sustainability in Higher Education, 11*(3), 250–259.
Scott, G. (2014). Quality management of education for sustainability in higher education. In Z. Fadeeva, L. Galkute, C. Mader, & G. Scott (Eds.), *Sustainable development and quality assurance in higher education: Transformation of learning and society* (pp. 230–254). Palgrave Macmillan UK. https://doi.org/10.1057/9781137459145_11
Scott, G., Tilbury, D., Sharp, L., & Deane, E. (2012). Partner Institutions Australian National University Sustainable Futures Leadership Academy.
Serafeim, G. (2021). ESG: Hyperboles and reality. *Harvard Business School Research Paper Series Working Paper*, 22–031.
Sheehan, N. T., Fox, K. A., Klassen, M., & Vaidyanathan, G. (2022). Threshold concepts and ESG performance: Teaching accounting students reconceptualized fundamentals to drive future ESG advocacy. *Accounting Education*, 1–25. https://doi.org/10.1080/09639284.2022.2122727
Too, L., & Bajracharya, B. (2015). Sustainable campus: Engaging the community in sustainability. *International Journal of Sustainability in Higher Education, 16*(1), 57–71. https://doi.org/10.1108/IJSHE-07-2013-0080
Trencher, G., Yarime, M., McCormick, K. B., Doll, C. N. H., & Kraines, S. B. (2014). Beyond the third mission: Exploring the emerging university function of co-creation for sustainability. *Science and Public Policy, 41*(2), 151–179. https://doi.org/10.1093/scipol/sct044
United Nations. (2015). General Assembly Resolution A/RES/70/1. *Transforming Our World, the 2030 Agenda for Sustainable Development.* Retrieved June 1, 2023, from http://www.un.org/ga/search/view_doc.asp?symbol=A/RES/70/1&Lang=E
Verna, I. (2012). *Il ciclo di Deming nella didattica universitaria.* Il Teaching Evaluation Model TEM, Aracne.
Verna, I. (2014a). Il performance management nelle università italiane. Un'indagine empirica, RIREA "Rivista Italiana di Ragioneria e di Economia Aziendale", monografia sottoposta a doppio referaggio anonimo, Roma, ISBN 978-8866590828.
Verna, I. (2014b). The Quality Function Deployment and the customer satisfaction. The case of Universities. *European Scientific Journal, Agosto, Vol I, Special Edition*, ISSN 1857-7881 (print) e ISSN 1857-7431 (online), pp. 189–202.

Verna, I. (2020). Flexibility in learning and teaching styles in an accounting course. "Deming Towards Kolb". *International Business Research, 13*(11), 1–77. https://doi.org/10.5539/ibr.v13n11p77

Verna, I. (2023). "Progettazione 'dinamica' dei Corsi di Studio, gestione 'sistemica' dei processi formativi e valutazione 'contestuale' delle performance di docenti e studenti. Una piattaforma web per la co-creazione di valore". Relazione presentata al *XL Convegno Nazionale AIDEA 2023 "L'Aziendalismo crea valore! Il ruolo dell'accademia nelle sfide della società"*.

Verna, I., & Perozzi D. (2014). Applying TEM Model (Teaching Evaluation Model) in Academic course in accounting: a comparison across five years. *European Scientific Journal Special Edition, 1*(6), 330–344.

Verna, I., Antonucci, G., Sargiacomo, M., & Venditti, M. (2019). Listening as 'guiding tool' in the continuous improvement of university education: A holistic approach. *European Scientific Journal, 15*(25), 57–78.

Verna, I., Ianni, L., D'Andreamatteo, A., & Venditti, M. (2021). Un approccio olistico alla misurazione della performance nella formazione universitaria. Un modello sperimentale: l'Ascolto. In A. Paolini & L. Del Bene (Eds.), *Monitorare la performance delle università statali e utilizzarne gli esiti per generare valore pubblico*. GdL SIDREA, Franco Angeli.

Verna, I., & Verna, D. (2021). "L'Ascolto un approccio olistico alla formazione superiore", Deposito presso SIAE, Società Italiana degli Autori ed Editori, applicativo, server web.

Žalėnienė, I., & Pereira, P. (2021). Higher education for sustainability: A global perspective. *Geography and Sustainability, 2*(2), 99–106. https://doi.org/10.1016/j.geosus.2021.05.001

Zhutiaeva, S. A., Usanov, A. Y., & Selezneva, A. V. (2023). ESG rankings to confirm the commitment of universities to the SDGs. In I. A. Rumyantseva, H. Anyigba, E. Sintsova, & N. Vasilenko (Eds.), *Finance, economics, and industry for sustainable development* (pp. 235–243). Springer Nature Switzerland. https://doi.org/10.1007/978-3-031-30498-9_21

Part II
ESG Governance, Value Relevance and Corporate Reputation

Chapter 7
The Evolution of CSR Contracting in Italian Non-financial Listed Companies

Simone Aresu, Luigi Rombi, and Mariem Khalfaoui

7.1 Introduction

Companies face new demands and are under external pressure to be accountable to all stakeholders and create long-term rather than short-term value. Supporters of the stakeholder perspective advocate corporate governance mechanisms that encourage boards to serve the interests of all stakeholders (e.g. employees, communities, and the environment) and shareholders (Cohen et al., 2023; Kaplan & Ramanna, 2021).

CSR contracting refers to integrating such concerns into the environmental- and social-related targets of executive remuneration contracts (Cohen et al., 2023; Flammer et al., 2019). By adopting CSR contracting, companies and their stakeholders can monitor the short- and long-term goals reached by key figures (e.g. CEOs) in sustainability-oriented initiatives and outputs, motivating their current behaviours towards sustainability.

CSR contracting is still a subject of debate among scholars. CSR contracting, on the one hand, enhances value (e.g. Flammer et al., 2019) and produces positive social and environmental effects (e.g. Bose et al., 2023; Derchi et al., 2023; Tsang et al., 2021). On the other hand, according to prior literature (Bebchuk & Tallarita, 2022), CSR contracting leads to flaws and dangers for stakeholders due to its metrics tied to limited dimensions of stakeholders' welfare and to a restricted subset of stakeholders. Also, CSR contracting is not subjected to effective scrutiny by outsiders, as outside observers might not assess (e.g. due to lack of time and/or expertise) whether its use provides beneficial incentives or primarily operates as a

S. Aresu (✉) · L. Rombi · M. Khalfaoui
Dipartimento di Scienze Economiche ed Aziendali, Università degli Studi di Cagliari, Cagliari, Italy
e-mail: simonearesu@unica.it; luigi.rombi@unica.it; mariem.khalfaoui@unica.it

N. Castellano et al. (eds.), *Environmental, Social, Governance (ESG)*, SIDREA Series in Accounting and Business Administration,
https://doi.org/10.1007/978-3-031-76618-3_7

mechanism to enhance executives' discretion on their payoffs (Bebchuk & Tallarita, 2022).

Since the current literature has mainly focused on quantitative analyses of the presence (e.g. Hong et al., 2016), content (e.g. Maas, 2018), and outcome (e.g. Flammer et al., 2019) of CSR contracting, it could have possibly neglected a more nuanced analysis of its design evolution (Velte, 2024). In addition, the scant literature (e.g. Flammer et al., 2019; Hong et al., 2016; Keddie & Magnan, 2023; Ott & Endrikat, 2023) focused on a unique institutional setting, namely Anglo-Saxon countries (i.e. the United States). Little is known about the detailed design of CSR contracting in non-Anglo-Saxon countries. This chapter aims to fill this gap by highlighting how Italian non-financial listed companies design environmental, social, and governance-related KPIs over time. Rather than investigating one specific element of the remuneration design, we consider multiple elements (e.g. KPIs types and weights, KPIs targets) and their relationships. Specifically, we analysed those companies constituting the FTSE-MIB index from 2011 to 2023, dividing the sustainability-related remuneration design into short- and long-term incentive plans.

The chapter is structured as follows. The next section describes the concept and characteristics of CSR contracting. Subsequently, the sample, methodology used, and the main results are presented. To conclude, we discuss the observed issues and provide the practical implications and limits of the study.

7.2 The Integration of Sustainability Criteria into Executives' Remuneration Plans: Related Literature

Companies adopt sustainability-oriented mechanisms at the company- (e.g. within their business model) or the individual-level, as in the case of a remuneration policy for their corporate officers. Although executive remuneration packages are still mainly focused on financial-related key performance indicators (hereafter KPIs), non-financial and, more recently, sustainability-related KPIs are increasing (e.g. Qin & Yang, 2022; Tsang et al., 2021).

Including sustainability-related targets within the remuneration package is commonly known as CSR contracting. CSR contracting refers to using sustainability-related KPIs defined at the company-level (e.g. reduction of CO_2 emissions), to align the interest of shareholders and managers to selected stakeholders (Flammer et al., 2019; Ikram et al., 2019). By including stakeholders' interests in the remuneration package, companies address different goals; for instance, employees' health and safety and environmental objectives (e.g. reducing waste) (Hong et al., 2016; Maas & Rosendaal, 2016; Yang, 2023).

Prior studies have shown that CSR contracting has become more prevalent over time (e.g. Aresu et al., 2023; Cohen et al., 2023; Flammer et al., 2019) and that it varies significantly across the organisational hierarchy (i.e. top managers, mid-level managers, and all other employees) and in different industries (e.g. Derchi et al., 2023; Ikram et al., 2019).

Companies may voluntarily adopt CSR contracting due to country-, industry-, and company-specific features. In terms of country-specific features, for instance, the use of CSR contracting was proven to increase in those countries with higher shareholder protections and social and environmental (e.g. U.S. State Climate Adaptation and Resilience Plan) regulatory pressure (e.g. Aresu et al., 2023; Cohen et al., 2023; Hazarika et al., 2022; He et al., 2023). Prior literature (e.g. Cohen et al., 2023; Derchi et al., 2023; Flammer et al., 2019; Hazarika et al., 2022; Maas & Rosendaal, 2016) also highlighted the effect of industry-specific features on CSR contracting, such as the higher presence in emission-intensive sectors (e.g. oil and gas) or the pressure to conform to competitors' behaviours.

In terms of company-specific features, companies may adopt CSR contracting, for instance, to build trust with different stakeholders (Qin & Yang, 2022). Also, corporate governance-related mechanisms seem to affect the adoption and effectiveness of CSR contracting, such as CEO's experience and power, board diversity and independence (e.g. Abdelmotaal & Abdel-Kader, 2016; Al-Shaer & Zaman, 2019; He et al., 2023; Homroy et al., 2023; Qin & Yang, 2022).

Different features, such as the beneficial stakeholders, the nature, the time frame, the KPI's target, and its weight, can impact CSR contracting design (Yang, 2023).

Beneficial stakeholders (i.e. those that can benefit from CSR-oriented initiatives and outputs) are heterogeneous (e.g. employees, investors) and their different time horizons (e.g. short- vs. long-term oriented) can create potential conflicts (Cohen et al., 2023). This heterogeneity leads to difficulties in including unique sustainability measures in CSR contracting that fit all the stakeholders' expectations. The more diverse stakeholders' interests are, the more challenging it is to address all of them by incentivising executives to pursue specific stakeholders-oriented goals.

The company may choose different KPIs according to the stakeholders' prioritised interests (Yang, 2023). The nature of these KPIs, which refers to their general content (Maas & Rosendaal, 2016), can be classified as environmental- (e.g. related to carbon emissions), governance- (e.g. related to board diversity), and social-oriented (e.g. related to employees' welfare). Also, KPIs' nature can be generally related to an overall ESG performance (e.g. positioning in ESG market indexes).

The time frame is the time horizon related to the incentive achievement and can be short-term (one year) or long-term (e.g. three years). The choice of the time frame may be affected by the stakeholders' pressure to achieve specific short- or long-term goals (Flammer et al., 2019).

The target of the KPIs refers to the value or range to which the payout is connected. Companies can define targets through a quantitative value (e.g. 5% reduction of injury frequency rate) or without a precise formula or value (e.g. reducing the injury frequency rate).

Finally, KPIs' weight represents the portion of sustainability-oriented KPIs within a specific incentive plan. It can impact the CSR contracting substantive or symbolic role, signalling the extent to which sustainability-related goals are crucial in the overall remuneration or a mere legitimisation tool adopted by the company (Bebchuk & Tallarita, 2022; Cucari et al., 2023; Yang, 2023).

CSR contracting design can be challenging for different reasons. Sustainability-related criteria introduce new KPIs with different measurements, targets, and time horizons. Potential problems include, for instance, the missing link between sustainability-related strategic plans and targets within the incentive plans and the absence or complexity of sustainability-related targets. These targets are vaguely defined, easy to achieve, and difficult for outsiders to verify (Bebchuk & Tallarita, 2022; Hartikainen et al., 2021).

7.3 Sample and Methodology

7.3.1 Sample

We follow these steps to create our analysis sample.

First, we selected all the companies listed in the FTSE-MIB index, which includes the 40 most liquid and capitalised companies and captures approximately 80% of the domestic market capitalisation between 2011 and 2023 (latest available month: May 2023). Due to the peculiarities of the financial sector, we excluded companies in the financial and real estate sectors from our analysis according to the FTSE classification. The total number of unique non-financial companies in the FTSE-MIB index from January 2011 to May 2023 was 46. Due to the changes in the index, whose constituent's eligibility is quarterly validated,[1] we selected for our analysis only those companies that were consistently members of the index in the majority of months from January 2011 to May 2023. Therefore, among the 149 months from January 2011 to May 2023, we analysed only those companies that were present at least half the time, even with discontinuity. With this step, we excluded from the analysis 21 companies.

Finally, as foreign listed companies can be included as constituents of the FTSE-MIB index, we excluded five companies (Ferrari, Fiat/Fiat Chrysler, Fiat Industrial/CNH Industrial, ST Microelectronics, and Tenaris) as listed in foreign countries and did not apply the Italian corporate governance code in most of the analysed years. The final sample resulted in 20 Italian non-financial listed companies.

Importantly, we started gathering data from the Remuneration Reports (Italian and English versions) that began to be published in 2012, referring to fiscal year 2011, until the latest available data in 2023, to gather the information from unique, comparable reports. Also, we downloaded further documents relevant to this study: corporate governance reports, sustainability reports, and strategic plans (when available).

[1]For the methodology of eligibility of constituents, see the website of Italian Stock Exchange (www.borsaitaliana.it).

7.3.2 Methodology

Following prior literature (e.g. Cai et al., 2022; Hyndman & Liguori, 2023), data have been hand-collected using a document analysis approach. Document analysis is a procedure used in qualitative research based on documents' in-depth examination to elicit meaning, gain understanding, and achieve empirical knowledge (Bowen, 2009). In this study, documents have been used to track the changes and development of CSR contracting.

First, we downloaded all the available remuneration reports, a total of 231 documents.[2] We then filtered only the information on CSR contracting, defined as the range of incentives based on environmental-, social-, and governance-related goals, that can be summarised under the general term of "sustainability-related goals". Instead of relying on pre-selected keywords to identify this information, we meticulously reviewed the entire list of KPIs adopted and selected sustainability-related ones. The authors found a collective agreement in the few uncertain cases (e.g. KPIs related to the quality of internal processes). Among the directors, we analysed only the CEO's short- and long-term incentive plans. When the CEO also served other roles (e.g. General Director), we also examined the incentive plans related to the other roles performed by the person serving as CEO. At the national level, we reviewed the content of the different applicable corporate governance codes issued during the analysis period. Specifically, we analysed the content of the corporate governance codes issued in 2011, 2014, 2015, 2018, and 2020 (Italian Corporate Governance Committee, 2011, 2014, 2015, 2018, 2020).

Second, we defined a list of items on CSR contracting to check throughout the report to gather comparable information among the companies analysed (see Table 7.1).

Specifically, we analysed whether the company justified the inclusion of sustainability-related targets throughout the remuneration report. We also examined whether the payment was in cash or shares (e.g. stock grants and options). We also checked for the weight of CSR contracting within the incentive plan, the name and, whenever available, the weight of each KPI adopted within CSR contracting, the KPI's target, minimum and maximum values according to the remuneration policy, and the degree of achievement of each target. We finally collected data on the existence of any entry gate (i.e. the presence of a paramount financial or non-financial target whose achievement is fundamental to making the short- or long-term incentive plan applicable).

[2] The final number is not, as expected, 240 documents (12 years analysed times 20 companies) as we excluded: Luxottica in the years 2019–2023, after the merger with Essilor as the company started to follow the French Corporate Governance code; Pirelli in 2016 and 2017 (the company delisted from the Italian Stock Exchange on November 2015 and returned to the stock market on October 2017); and Mediaset in 2022 and 2023 (report drawn in accordance with the Dutch Corporate Governance code).

Table 7.1 The definition and a real-life example of items analysed, related to CSR contracting

Item	Definition	Example (from a report)
Motivation	It expresses the reason behind CSR contracting	PRYSMIAN, 2022, long-term plan: "It fosters the alignment of interests towards sustainable value creation in the mid-to long-term, reinforcing the retention of key resources"
Form of payment	Payment is either cash- or share-based	SNAM, 2017, long-term plan: "Plan with annual granting and three-year vesting period"
CSR contracting (and KPIs) weight	The portion of CSR contracting (and of their specific KPIs) within a specific incentive plan	A2A, 2021, short-term plan: "Sustainability (weight 23%)"
KPIs formula	The formula used to measure a KPI	ENI, 2018, short-term plan: "Severity incident rate: Total recordable injuries weighted for severity/hours worked × 1,000,000"
KPIs target	The value or percentage to be reached	Terna, 2017, long-term plan: "Dow Jones Sustainability Index (DJSI) positioning: 100% is reached if the firm position is in the second decile of the index; Non inclusion in DJSi (0%), inclusion in DJSI (80%), position in the first decile of the index (130%), Positioning in the 1st decile of the index for all years of the Plan and inclusion into the "Gold Class" for at least one of the three years (150%)"
KPIs achievement	The degree of achievement of a specific result to which the payout is linked	Italgas, 2022, short-term plan. "Diversity and Inclusion: percentage of women in managerial positions at 31/12/2022. Target: 22%, Achieved: 24.7%"
Entry gate	A paramount financial or non-financial target whose achievement is fundamental to making the incentive applicable	Saipem, 2022, short-term plan: "Adjusted Net Financial Position at December 31, 2022 and Total Recordable Injury Frequency Rate at December 31, 2022"

Data were gathered considering short-term bonuses (i.e. those based on one-year targets) and long-term incentive plans (i.e. those based on more than one-year targets, like three-year targets).

7.4 Results

Table 7.2 (panels A and B) shows the main results on the use and evolution of CSR contracting and its main features. Specifically, Panel A refers to short-term incentive plans, while Panel B refers to long-term ones.

Table 7.2 (Panel A) The evolution and main features of CSR contracting within short-term incentive plans. (Panel B) The evolution and main features of CSR contracting within long-term incentive plans

Company	First year of adoption	Weight of CSR contracting (evolution)	KPIs content	Target design	Target achievement
Panel A					
Enel	2012	From 5–10% range to 30%	Mostly social KPIs used (e.g. injuries frequency rate)	Provided since 2015 (min, target, and max values)	Mostly achieved at the target level or overachieved
Eni	2012	Moved from 30% (in 2013) to 25%	Since 2015, one social (related to incident rate) and one environmental (GHG emissions intensity) KPI used	Mostly expressed as a multiplier in relation to fixed remuneration	Mostly achieved and expressed as a performance score (not the actual value)
Saipem	2012	From 10% to 20%	Many KPIs used, mostly social (e.g. total recordable injuries frequency rate) and environmental-oriented (e.g. GHG emissions)	Not provided	Mostly achieved at the target level or overachieved. Information provided, in particular, since 2019
Snam	2013	From 10% to 20%	Both social (e.g. injury frequency rate) and related to the inclusion and positioning in sustainable indexes (e.g. FTSE4GOOD)	Provided since 2014 (first only target values, then also min and max), with targets communicated ex post	Mostly achieved at above target levels
Buzzi Unicem	2015	Always 8%	One social KPI: lost time injury frequency rate	Not shown for confidential reasons	First not provided, then since 2020, achieved
A2A	2017	Moved from 5% to 23%	At first, generically related to sustainability, then more specific with social (e.g. D&I) and environmental dimensions	Mostly unavailable in the remuneration policy and disclosed since 2021, in the year of achievement	Mostly overachieved and shown as a deviation from the target value (target = 100%)
Italgas	2017	From 15% to 25%	Mostly social and environmental-oriented (e.g. injury frequency rate, energy intensity)	Provided since 2021 (min, target, and max)	Mostly achieved and expressed as a performance score or the actual value

(continued)

Table 7.2 (continued)

Company	First year of adoption	Weight of CSR contracting (evolution)	KPIs content	Target design	Target achievement
Prysmian	2017	From 10–15% range to 20–30% range	Mostly social-oriented (e.g. % women hired; injuries frequency rate)	Provided since 2020 as a target range	Provided since 2020, mostly achieved and shown as the actual value achieved
Terna	2017	From 15% to 25%	Mostly social-oriented (on workplace safety)	Mostly provided (min, target, and max values)	Mostly overachieved and shown as a deviation from the target value (target = 100%)
Finmeccanica/ Leonardo	2018	10%	First inclusion in the DJSI, then injury frequency rate added	ON/OFF target or provided as a target value	Sometimes not provided, sometimes achievement disclosed
Moncler	2018	Constantly 10%	Mostly unclear, based on the sustainability plan	Not provided	Not provided
Pirelli	2019	From 10% to 15%	Mainly two KPIs used: the value of the "green performance" revenues and D&I (women hiring objective)	Not provided	Not provided
Telecom Italia	2020	From 20% to 22%	Mostly social-oriented (e.g. employee engagement) and on customer satisfaction	Provided (min, target, and max values), with targets communicated ex post	Achieved mostly at the target level or overachieved
Atlantia	2021	Constantly 20%	Based on the internal ESG agenda and the external rating of ESG performance	Not provided	Not provided
Recordati	2022	Always 5%	Vaguely expressed: ESG initiative linked to sustainability plan	Not provided for confidential reasons	Mostly yes (ON/OFF)
Diasorin	2023	Always 10%	Vaguely related to the ESG strategic plan	ON/OFF target	Not available info (plan too recent)

Salvatore Ferragamo	2023	Constantly 20%	Mainly environmental-oriented (e.g. improvement on recycled material)	Mostly provided as the target value	Not available info (plan too recent)
Panel B					
Pirelli	2012	From 10% to 20%	Until 2021, only related to positioning in ESG indexes, then environmental KPIs added (CO2 emissions reduction)	Not always provided (e.g. for confidential reasons)	Mostly unclear info
Terna	2016	From 10% to 15%	Inclusion in ESG indexes	Mostly provided (min, target, and max values)	Achieved
Snam	2017	From 10% to 20%	First only environmental-related, then a social KPI added (on gender gap)	Mostly provided (min, target, and max values)	Achieved
Enel	2018	From 10% to 25%	First only environmental KPIs (until 2020), then 1 social and 1 environmental	Provided (min, target, and max values)	Achieved
Buzzi Unicem	2020	Constantly 50%	One environmental KPI used: CO2 emissions intensity	Mostly not provided	Mostly not available info (plan too recent)
Eni	2020	Constantly 35%	Only environmental KPIs used (e.g. related to circular economy)	Provided (min, target, and max values)	Not available info (plan too recent)
Italgas	2020	From 15% to 20%	First on indexes' inclusion and environmental-related, then environmental-related only (e.g. reduction of CO2 emissions)	Mostly provided (min, target, and max values)	Not available info (plan too recent)
Moncler	2020	Constantly 15%	First only environmental KPIs (until 2021), then also related to diversity and the inclusion in ESG indexes	Mostly provided (min, target, and max values)	Not available info (plan too recent)
Prysmian	2020	From 20–30% range to 20%	Both social (e.g. leadership index) and environmental (e.g. recycled waste) KPIs	Mostly provided as a target range	Mostly achieved

(continued)

Table 7.2 (continued)

Company	First year of adoption	Weight of CSR contracting (evolution)	KPIs content	Target design	Target achievement
Atlantia	2021	Constantly 30%	Both environmental (e.g., carbon footprint) and social (e.g., work safety)	First mostly not provided, then provided as a target value	Not available info (plan too recent)
Finmeccanica/ Leonardo	2021	Constantly 20%	Always 1 social (related to female new hires) and 1 environmental (related to emissions' intensity)	Provided as a target range	Not available info (plan too recent)
A2A	2022	Constantly 20%	Environmental-related, on renewable sources	Provided (target = 100%)	Not available info (plan too recent)
Telecom Italia	2022	From 30% to 20%	1 social-oriented and 1 environmental-oriented KPI	Provided (min and max deviations from target)	Not available info (plan too recent)
Saipem	2023	Constantly 20%	Both social (e.g. on D&I) and environmental-oriented (e.g. avoided GHG emissions)	Not provided	Not available info (plan too recent)
Salvatore Ferragamo	2023	Constantly 20%	Both social- (e.g. on gender pay gap) and environmental-oriented (e.g. renewable energy)	Provided (min, target, and max values)	Not available info (plan too recent)

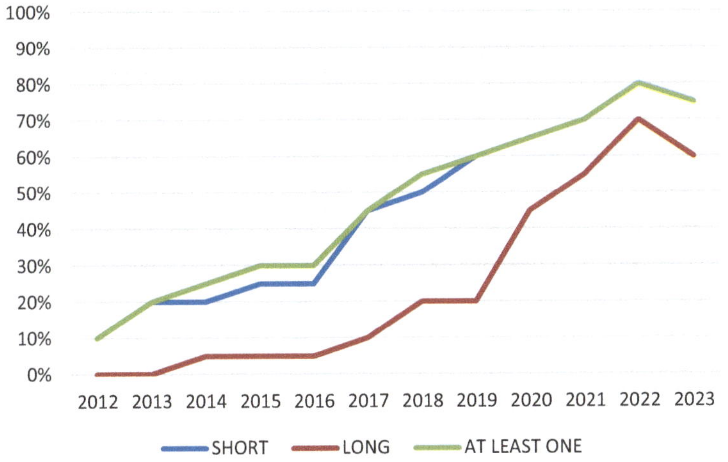

Fig. 7.1 The percentage of companies adopting CSR contracting in variable remuneration. Source: Authors' elaboration

In the period analysed, within short-term incentive plans, 17 companies out of 20 have adopted CSR contracting at least once (Campari, Luxottica, and Mediaset never adopted CSR contracting in the period analysed). Five companies (Campari, Diasorin, Luxottica, Mediaset, and Recordati) have never inserted CSR contracting within long-term incentive plans.

Considering short-term variable remuneration (i.e. one-year time horizon), cash was the most common way to implement CSR contracting. Only in a few cases, some companies paid their executives with a cash/share mix (e.g. Prysmian, Italgas).

Considering long-term variable remuneration (i.e. three to five years' time horizon), share-based remuneration was the most typical form of payment. Specifically, companies chose to integrate sustainability into their executives' stock-option plans (e.g. Telecom Italia) or the stock grants (e.g. Atlantia). In limited cases, companies used cash in the long-term variable remuneration (e.g. Buzzi Unicem and Pirelli).

In the sample analysed, 11 companies out of 20 started to adopt CSR contracting in the short-term variable remuneration before 2019. Also, an average company included CSR contracting in its CEO's long-term incentive plan five years later, compared to the short-term plan year. Only two companies, Pirelli and Terna, included CSR contracting in the long-term variable remuneration before including it in the short-term variable remuneration (7 and 1 year before, respectively). Then, other companies, Atlantia and Salvatore Ferragamo, adopted CSR contracting within the same year in short- and long-term variable remuneration.

In general, as shown in Fig. 7.1, there has been a positive evolution as more and more companies have started to link social and environmental goals in both short- and long-term variable remuneration. In line with prior literature (e.g. Maas & Rosendaal, 2016), CSR contracting is more frequent in short-term rather than long-term incentive plans, emerging in long-term plans mostly since 2020 in several companies, such as Buzzi Unicem, Eni, Leonardo, Prysmian, Saipem, and Snam.

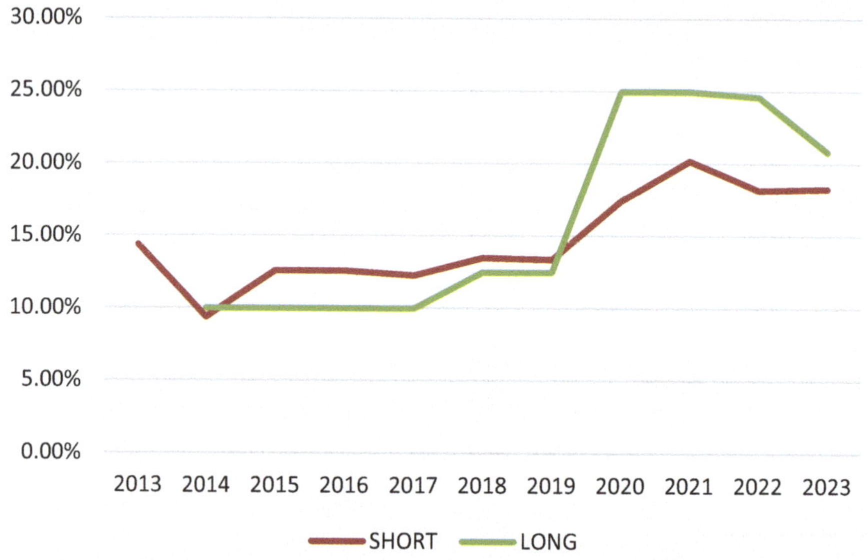

Fig. 7.2 The weight of CSR contracting as a percentage of variable remuneration. Note: 2012 is omitted in the graph as none of the companies adopting CSR contracting disclosed the weight of sustainability-related KPIs in both short- and long-term incentive plans. 2013, for long-term plans only, is missing for the same reason. Source: Authors' elaboration

Only two companies (Eni and Saipem) started to use CSR contracting in 2012. Eni, for instance, started to use CSR contracting in 2012 in the short-term incentive plan with a weight of 30% (within the variable remuneration component). It first diminished to 10% in 2014 but then increased to 25% in the period 2015–2023. At the end of the period analysed, 15 companies out of 20 had included CSR in at least one variable component of the remuneration (i.e. short- or long-term).

Also, it seems that typically, once adopted, companies continue to use CSR contracting without interruptions. In our sample, only one company (Prysmian Spa) interrupted its use in 2018, stating that "sustainability goals, already considered important by the company, will be reintroduced to the MBO system in 2019, together with targets focused more on individual roles and the performance of Business Units" (Prysmian Spa, Remuneration Report 2018).

In addition, as shown in Fig. 7.2, the average weight of sustainability-related goals in the variable part has increased[3] from 15% to 18% in the short-term incentive plans and from 10% to 21% in the long-term incentive plans. Terna, for instance, moved from a 15% weight in 2017 to a 25% weight in the latest years, considering

[3] Although companies mostly disclose the exact weight of sustainability-related variable remuneration and relative KPIs, some companies provided the weight as a range or provided only a list of KPIs. As an example, Prysmian short-term variable remuneration weighted between 10% and 15% of variable remuneration, with a list of 4 KPIs. In these cases, an average value was computed to estimate the weight of each KPI.

short-term incentive plans. Enel adopted CSR contracting in its long-term incentive plans with a 10% weight in 2018, then moved to a 25%.

Enel registered the highest weights within short-term variable remuneration plans from 2020 to 2023, Eni had the highest weight in 2013, and Saipem in 2021, allocating 30% of the short-term incentive plan to sustainability-related remuneration. Referring to the long-term plans, the highest weight was registered in Buzzi Unicem from 2020 to 2022, with 50% of long-term variable remuneration linked to sustainability-related KPIs. Other companies, such as Eni in 2020–2023, Telecom Italia in 2022, and Atlantia in 2021–2022, had between 30% and 35% of long-term variable remuneration linked to sustainability-related KPIs.

In terms of KPIs, there has been an evolution in the measurement of the KPIs adopted, as shown in Fig. 7.3. Specifically, at the beginning of the analysis period (e.g. 2012 and 2013), the sustainability-related KPIs and their weights were often vague and generally related to sustainability. For example, in 2013, Saipem assigned a bonus (weight 10%) in the short-term variable remuneration plan linked to a target called "sustainability in terms of health and safety". However, throughout the analysis period, companies refined sustainability-related KPIs and inserted several specific measures to embrace sustainability into the CEO's variable remuneration. The same company, for example, in 2020 assigned to the short-term variable remuneration plan a sustainability-related bonus (weight 25%) linked to several KPIs on employees' health and safety (Total Recordable Injury Frequency Rate),

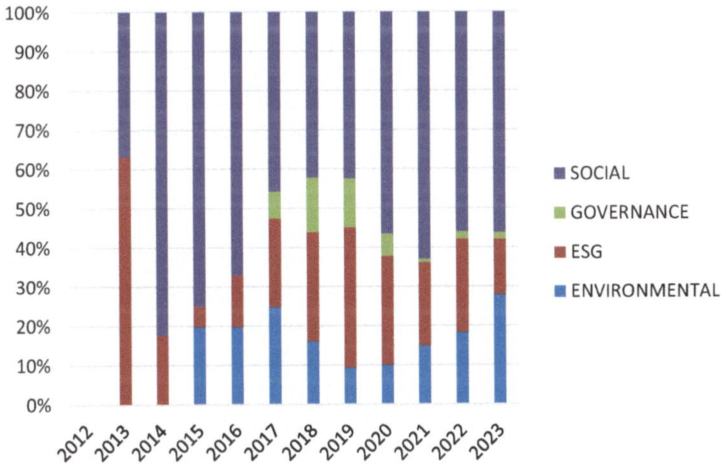

Fig. 7.3 **(Panel A)** A breakdown of the KPIs adopted each year in short-term variable remuneration plans. Environmental, Social, and Governance categories are defined according to the classification of Principles for Responsible Investment (2012). Source: Authors' elaboration. **(Panel B)** A breakdown of the KPIs adopted each year in long-term variable remuneration plans. Environmental, Social, and Governance categories are defined according to the classification of Principles for Responsible Investment (2012). Source: Authors' elaboration

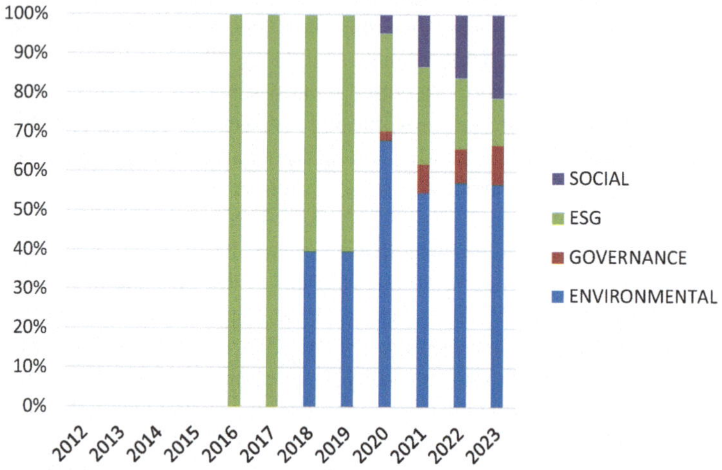

Fig. 7.3 (continued)

environmental protection (e.g. implementing specific initiatives of energy efficiency), and on improving diversity and risk management.

As shown in Fig. 7.3, the evolution of KPIs is different for short- and long-term variable remuneration.

In the case of short-term variable remuneration, KPIs adopted were mostly generically related to ESG (e.g. identified as a "sustainability target") at first, with a residual part of KPIs related to social issues (e.g. employees' health and safety).[4] Social KPIs were present in most cases, while environmental- (e.g. percentage of renewable energy used/produced by the company) and governance-related KPIs (e.g. anti-corruption training activities) were present in very few cases. Still, environmental-related KPIs have grown over the years compared to governance-related ones.

Regarding long-term variable remuneration, the ESG category mainly refers to sustainability index positioning. In only one case, Snam, in 2017, the KPI was a generic "Sustainability" target that the company did not clarify. As shown in Fig. 7.3 (Panel B), after 2019, there has been a change in KPIs adopted in long-term variable remuneration with environmental KPIs, mostly related to the footprint of the company (e.g. reduction of CO2 emission, reduction of waste) being used in most cases. The adoption of social- (e.g. reduction of gender gap) and governance-related KPIs (e.g. the percentage of women at the executive level) increased but remains a residual part.

[4]ESG-related KPIs can refer to generic sustainability-related initiatives or represent "mixed" KPIs that comprise environmental, governance, and social features, such as the positioning in ESG indexes. Generic sustainability-related KPIs were more common in the first years analyzed, being then substituted by "mixed" ESG KPIs.

Also, most companies adopted outcome-oriented KPIs (e.g. Lost Time Injury Frequency Rate, cumulative avoided GHG emissions over three years). Among the few cases of process-oriented KPIs, Italgas in 2017 assigned a short-term bonus also based on the number of institutional investors met during the year.[5]

Notably, many companies use a few sustainability-related KPIs that CEOs should focus on to increase their bonuses. For instance, Leonardo relied during 2018–2020 only on one sustainability-related KPI within the short-term bonus: the inclusion in the Dow Jones sustainability index. Limited cases utilised a broad list of social and environmental KPIs. As an example, in 2021, Prysmian relied on five KPIs to monitor its sustainability-related goals within the short-term remuneration plan: frequency rate of injuries, percentage of women hired (split considering both desk workers and management positions), investment plans for CO2 emission reduction, and positioning in sustainability indexes.

In line with prior studies (e.g. Bebchuk & Tallarita, 2022; Maas & Rosendaal, 2016; Yang, 2023), social KPIs are the most frequently used, followed by environmental KPIs. Also, there are cases with only environmental-related or social-related KPIs, or cases using both social- and environmental-related KPIs. In line with prior studies in different institutional contexts (e.g. Bebchuk & Tallarita, 2022; Maas & Rosendaal, 2016), among the KPIs adopted, the most common social-related KPIs refer to the health and safety of employees, often measured through the injuries frequency rate (e.g. Saipem in 2018, short-term plan) or the lost time injury frequency rate (e.g. Atlantia in 2022, long-term plan). Relatively fewer cases incorporated KPIs related to diversity, equity, and inclusion targets, such as the percentage of women hired (e.g. Prysmian in 2023, short-term plan) and the manager gender pay gap (e.g. Salvatore Ferragamo in 2023, long-term plan).

The most common environmental KPIs were related to reducing CO2 or GHG emissions and adopting renewable energies. Specifically, Snam in 2018 adopted in the long-term incentive plan a KPI called "reduction of gas emissions", measuring the reduction of natural gas emissions over three years, compared to the results recorded at the end of 2016. KPIs on emissions can be expressed either in absolute numbers (e.g. CO2 kg) or, more commonly, as a percentage (e.g. reduction in %). Importantly, companies have started to measure emissions in relative terms by calculating emission intensity as a ratio between emissions and the amount of production (or revenues). For instance, in 2020–2022, ENI used a KPI called "GHG emissions intensity upstream Scope 1 and Scope 2", calculated as the ratio of GHG emissions and gross hydrocarbon production on an operated basis. Interestingly, KPIs related to GHG/CO2 emissions are mostly limited to Scope 1 and Scope 2 emissions (e.g. Saipem in 2023, short-term plan; Enel in 2021–2023, long-term plan). In terms of renewable energies, for instance, A2A added one

[5]Outcome-oriented means that KPIs measure a specific outcome/output (e.g. GHG emissions' actual reduction) while process-oriented means that KPIs measure a process/initiative that will lead to a final outcome/output (e.g., number of projects related to circular economy).

sustainability-related KPI into its CEO's long-term incentive plan: the installed capacity from renewable sources.

In addition to the prior social-oriented or environmental-oriented KPIs, companies track their sustainable progress with more general, investor-oriented KPIs. Specifically, in line with prior literature (e.g. Maas & Rosendaal, 2016), a standard indicator used by companies has been the presence and the positioning in sustainability indexes created by external agencies, such as the Dow Jones Sustainability Index and the FTSE4GOOD index (e.g. Terna in the period 2016–2021, that measures, within the CEO's long-term incentive plan, its average positioning in the Dow Jones Sustainability Index in three years).

An explicit formula is sometimes missing in terms of KPIs' measurement (e.g. Recordati in 2022, short-term incentive plan), while there are cases of formulas explicitly provided (e.g. ENI in both short- and long-term incentive plans).

Furthermore, in many cases analysed, there is no generic motivation behind CSR contracting (i.e. generally linked to a sustainability-related strategy and business model), with the risk of disconnection from crucial corporate objectives. Indeed, only a handful of cases actively establish the linkage between the KPIs and the corporate strategy. As an example, ENI, in the 2023 remuneration report, justifies the choice of a KPI related to upstream GHG net emissions, arguing that it reflects Eni's commitment to reducing GHG emissions in line with the medium-/long-term objectives that will lead the company to decarbonise all products and processes by 2050.

In terms of targets, the information is often missing or unclear.[6] However, companies have improved their disclosure in recent years, presenting targets as actual, minimum, and maximum values to be reached. For instance, a positive evolution has been registered in Enel (short-term incentive plan) and Atlantia (long-term incentive plan). Targets' design is generally more detailed in long-term incentive plans, often providing minimum, maximum, and target values. Usually, targets are known ex post (i.e. when companies provide the prior year's remuneration data for the payment) rather than ex ante (i.e. when companies provide their policy). For instance, from 2013 to 2017, Snam designed its CEO's short-term bonus, linking it with the following KPI: number of accidents occurring per million hours worked during the year. However, there were no targets when presenting the KPI within the remuneration policy; the targets are only known ex post and related to the result achieved. Also, targets are often presented not as actual values of a specific KPI (e.g. GHG emissions reduction of 20%) but as a multiplier in relation to fixed remuneration. For instance, in 2017, ENI specified that, in relationship to the CEO's short-term incentive plan, the "target level of share of incentive payable in the year (65%) is equal to 98% of fixed remuneration (min 83% and max 146%), while the target level of the deferred portion (35%) of the total incentive is equal to 68% of fixed remuneration (min 38% and max 181%)" but without presenting the 2017

[6]A target design was considered as clear when the relationship between a specific KPI value (e.g. minimum and maximum values) and its relative pay-out was defined by the company (e.g. by disclosing minimum and maximum pay-outs and/or by interpolation).

specific targets of the two sustainability-related KPIs adopted within the plan: CO2 emissions and severity incident rate. In a few cases, companies declared not to include targets for confidential reasons (e.g. Buzzi Unicem in its 2021 report).

Interestingly, targets are likely to be reached and "above target" achievements are frequent. Very few cases have seen companies explicitly stating that they have not reached CSR targets. For instance, in the 2023 report explaining the achievement of the 2022 goals, ENI admitted not to have achieved the 2022 targets related to the KPI "severity incident rate". In long-term incentive plans, the plan is often too recent to investigate the ex post achievement of a sustainability-related goal.

7.5 Discussion and Conclusions

Although the previous versions of the Italian Corporate Governance Code (2011, 2014, 2015, and 2018) vaguely mentioned the concept of sustainability, the latest version (2020) explicitly introduced the concept of sustainable success. With the 2020 revised version of the code, companies are recommended to create businesses with a purpose that "consists of creating long-term value for the benefit of the shareholders, taking into account the interests of other stakeholders relevant to the company" (Corporate Governance Code, 2020, p. 4). In addition, the relationship between variable remuneration and performance objectives has also been clarified (Corporate Governance Code, 2020, Art. 5, Recommendation 27). Specifically, it is recommended that these performance objectives should be consistent to promote the company's sustainable success and include non-financial parameters, where relevant.

In recent years, companies have started to include CSR contracting in both components of variable remuneration (i.e. short- and long-term). Also, the number and content of KPIs adopted signal an increased attention towards different dimensions (i.e. social and environmental) of sustainability issues. This positive evolution seems to highlight, thus, the greater attention by the business community towards incorporating sustainability-oriented goals within corporate governance mechanisms. In particular, following the latest Corporate Governance Code revision (2020), Italian companies seem to have increased the weight and content of CSR contracting, made targets more specific (especially in long-term incentive plans), and promptly presented their achievement in the following years.

The positive evolution of CSR contracting frequency and design may reflect the institutional and media pressure (e.g. via international sustainability-related agreements like the 2016 Paris Agreement and the UN Sustainable Development Goals) to embrace sustainability within business-related behaviours and initiatives. Specific agreements and initiatives can be indirect turning points affecting company-level mechanisms, including non-financial reporting and CSR contracting. In Italy, for instance, Legislative Decree n. 254/2016, adopted by the Italian Parliament, enacting Directive 2014/95/EU regarding the disclosure of non-financial and diversity information, has led to higher pressure to incorporate non-financial information in reporting (e.g. Korca et al., 2021).

However, it must be acknowledged that, in the current situation, there is still a lot of room for improvement in adopting CSR contracting by Italian non-financial listed companies.

First, in the current forms of CSR contracting's adoption, it is often unclear why companies choose to integrate sustainability and why a specific set of stakeholders (e.g. employees) has been prioritised over others (e.g. local communities). Based on the available reports, the link between specific KPIs within CSR contracting and short- and long-term goals at the corporate level is far from clear. Companies should define and disclose the motivation behind CSR contracting and link its use to corporate strategy. To validate the internal adoption of CSR, it is recommended that companies clarify the importance of certain KPIs in achieving specific strategic goals of sustainable development and how they are linked with the corporate strategy and the business model. This clarification may also be helpful to validate the adoption of CSR externally, as stakeholders not considered in the KPIs adopted should understand why their interests have been perceived as less critical by the company. Also, through a specific link between the KPIs and the corporate strategy, all those external entities from the company (e.g. investors and analysts) should be able to understand whether the adoption of CSR contracting is effectively incentivising the executives towards a more strategic, sustainable purpose rather than being a mere window-dressing tool to gift executives without any tangible purpose.

Second, another issue that companies are facing is the balance of short- and long-term sustainability goals. Corporate goals differ in their time horizon, and it may be helpful to restructure short- and long-term incentive plans to contain objectives whose achievement can be effectively measurable and feasible in that time horizon (Downie & Bourdon-Leblanc, 2023). On the one hand, there seems to be a learning curve of sustainability-related issues' integration into the variable remuneration component, as most companies adopted CSR contracting first in their short-term incentive plans and then in the long-term incentive plans (Downie & Bourdon-Leblanc, 2023). However, companies provided no clear explanation of why sustainability has been integrated first in the short- and only later in the long-term component. Although some companies differentiate between KPIs used in the short- and long-term incentive plans, a clear explanation of this choice is missing. For instance, in 2020–2022, Buzzi Unicem used the Lost Time Injury Frequency Rate as a KPI within the CEO's short-term bonus. On the other hand, CO2 emissions reduction was adopted as a KPI in the long-term incentive plan. Still, the company does not clarify the choice to use different KPIs in different plans, and a stakeholder could only speculate that specific goals on environmental protection might be reachable only in the long-term, given the need to make further investments that take some time to provide outcomes (Downie & Bourdon-Leblanc, 2023).

The preference for typically relying, at first, on short-term incentive plans can be risky. Although short-term components may be a more straightforward tool to introduce sustainability into a remuneration package, it should be noticed that they are more vulnerable than long-term components as they may be based on excessively discretionary, internal (i.e. with no relative performance evaluation against a peer group) goals that cannot be meaningfully reviewed or assessed by outside observers (Bebchuk & Tallarita, 2022; Downie & Bourdon-Leblanc, 2023; Ritz, 2022). Also, as CSR contracting does not immediately exert a significant effect (Derchi et al., 2021), one could speculate that the introduction of sustainability within the short-term has been done only for legitimacy purposes, as short-term components can depict sustainability as an immediate need of the company in the eyes of the stakeholders.

Third, it is undeniable that the concept of sustainability itself is challenging to measure as it comprises not only different activities and impacts (e.g. direct and indirect CO2 emissions) but also different stakeholders (e.g. employees, local and national communities) whose interests are often in contrast and difficult to measure (Bebchuk & Tallarita, 2022). This seems to be a relevant issue for the companies analysed, as KPIs adopted often tackle only a specific sub-group of stakeholders rather than different groups (Yang, 2023). Stakeholders' salience is different; for instance, employees' health and safety can represent a critical risk in particular industries (e.g. oil and gas) but less of a concern in other industries (e.g. media). Targeting different KPIs to different stakeholders can help embrace the heterogeneous interests of the latter. For instance, considering only the natural environment as a stakeholder can be limited while tackling multiple stakeholders can be more helpful. For example, Buzzi Unicem's long-term plan in 2020–2022 aimed only at environmental sustainability by adopting a KPI named "CO2 emissions of the Group". On the other hand, Enel's long-term incentive plan 2021–2023 aimed to manage environmental and social issues by adopting two different KPIs, "GHG emissions' intensity" and "the percentage of women in management succession plans". Along the same line, it should be noted that some companies chose to integrate sustainability so that their externalities may still be negative, but the reward would still be present. It is the case, for example, of those companies that chose to measure the health and safety of their employees in terms of time lost due to employees' injuries. In this case, the link between the sustainability-related reward and the sustainable outcome may be weak, as the incentive aims at treating the employees' health and safety in terms of the company's efficiency (i.e. time lost) rather than ensuring employees' safety.

Fourth, when designing an incentive plan, it is pivotal to present the target and do it in a timely manner. In the current situation, although there has been an improvement in recent years, targets are often missing. Also, when included, they are frequently not measured in terms of the specific KPI value/percentage but in generic percentage terms (where target = 100%) or in terms of a multiplier of the fixed remuneration, thus highlighting the reward but not the target. Then, importantly, companies typically do not disclose ex ante the targets related to those KPIs called to embrace sustainability in the remuneration plan. While this may be due to confidentiality purposes, as disclosing such targets may be considered sensitive information, it should be noted that, at most, a target range would be beneficial to all the stakeholders (e.g. potential investors) called to evaluate the effectiveness of the incentive plan (Bebchuk & Tallarita, 2022; Maas, 2018). Wherever targets are provided ex post, as often happened, those stakeholders called to evaluate their effectiveness have already made their choices, attenuating the incentives' purpose.

Finally, targets should be challenging for the incentive to be effective. In most cases analysed, all sustainability-related objectives, especially in the short-term incentive plans, were over-performed, meaning that achieving the objective was beyond the target. On the one hand, this could be interpreted as a positive outcome of CSR contracting as it signals that executives are effectively driving companies towards more sustainable businesses. On the other hand, one could argue that the variable part of the remuneration plan is not working effectively as an incentive but as an easy-to-achieve goal, resembling more a gift to executives rather than an actual challenge in linking personal with broader organisational objectives.

The flaws highlighted can lead to a low-quality design of CSR contracting that inefficiently incentivises CEOs to address CSR-related issues (Albuquerque et al., 2024; Yang, 2023). Overall, CSR contracting design can still improve to become an effective form of integration of sustainability into executives' remuneration. Specifically, there may be some corporate governance mechanisms that can help improve its design. Based on additional exploratory analysis, those companies where the sustainability-related committee members are also (with at least one member) within the remuneration committee tend to improve CSR contracting design.[7] However, further analysis is needed to detect whether and how sustainability-related and remuneration committee members interact and effectively contribute to a better, high-quality CSR contracting design (Yang, 2023).

The improvement suggested in this section can make this mechanism, whose positive consequences have been highlighted by prior literature (e.g. Cohen et al., 2023; Flammer et al., 2019; Qin & Yang, 2022), a crucial one in improving environmental and social performance both in the short- and long-term, contributing to the recently recognised principle (Italian Corporate Governance Committee, 2020) of sustainable success. Indeed, CSR contracting can play a positive role in helping executive directors and managers (e.g. mid-level managers) accomplish corporate sustainability-related goals, such as net-zero emissions.

This chapter aims to contribute to the studies on the evolution of sustainable corporate governance practices due to changes in recommendations (e.g. corporate governance codes' revisions) by providing critical practical implications to understand whether CSR contracting is effective or based on undemanding, discretionary goals set by corporate leaders to exert their power and legitimise themselves given

[7] Among the 17 companies that adopted CSR contracting, we analysed whether and how sustainability was integrated within the board specific sub-committees and whether sustainability-related committee's members were also in the remuneration committee. Specifically, we found that 4 out of 17 companies never had a sustainability-related committee with at least one member also sitting in the remuneration committee. These 4 companies also poorly designed CSR contracting (e.g. in terms of targets' design).

the more substantial scrutiny they face on ESG issues. Also, companies can benefit from the study's empirical evidence by identifying the factors contributing to best-practice initiatives in adopting CSR contracting. Analysts, consultants, and investors can avail the results of our research to evaluate and compare effective and ineffective CSR practices, disentangling those companies tackling sustainability seriously from those merely legitimising the adoption of a novel practice that is useless and potentially harmful due to the insensitivity of the remuneration package to the actual outcome. Finally, policymakers can use our results when defining norms and recommendations (e.g. corporate governance codes) that can interact with the self-regulatory, internal corporate governance, and monitoring mechanisms in place.

The study is not free from limitations. First, we considered only the FTSE-MIB segment, thus not providing a complete picture of the state and evolution of CSR contracting in the Italian context. Second, the interplay between financial and sustainability-related KPIs (and their features in terms of weight and targets) has not been explored in detail. Third, being a qualitative study, we have not investigated the significant implications of CSR contracting regarding financial and social-environmental corporate performance. Finally, further investigation is needed at the company-level to detect whether and how sustainability is effectively integrated into a company's strategy and, therefore, whether and how organisational processes can pursue sustainable objectives together with financial ones.

Acknowledgements The three authors gratefully acknowledge the financial support of Fondazione di Sardegna. Luigi Rombi gratefully acknowledges that this study was funded by the European Union - *NextGenerationEU*, in the framework of the *GRINS -Growing Resilient, INclusive and Sustainable* project (GRINS PE00000018 – CUP F53C22000760007). The views and opinions expressed are solely those of the authors and do not necessarily reflect those of the European Union, nor can the European Union be held responsible for them.

References

Abdelmotaal, H., & Abdel-Kader, M. (2016). The use of sustainability incentives in executive remuneration contracts: Firm characteristics and impact on the shareholders' returns. *Journal of Applied Accounting Research, 17*(3), 311–330.

Albuquerque, A., Carter, M. E., Guo, Z. M., & Lynch, L. J. (2024). Complexity of CEO compensation packages. *Journal of Accounting and Economics*, 101709.

Al-Shaer, H., & Zaman, M. (2019). CEO compensation and sustainability reporting assurance: Evidence from the UK. *Journal of Business Ethics, 158*, 233–252.

Aresu, S., Hooghiemstra, R., & Melis, A. (2023). Integration of CSR criteria into executive compensation contracts: A cross-country analysis. *Journal of Management, 49*(8), 2766–2804.

Bebchuk, L. A., & Tallarita, R. (2022). The perils and questionable promise of ESG-based compensation. *Journal of Corporation Law, 48*, 37.

Bose, S., Burns, N., Minnick, K., & Shams, S. (2023). Climate-linked compensation, societal values, and climate change impact: International evidence. *Corporate Governance: An International Review, 31*(5), 759–785.

Bowen, G. A. (2009). Document analysis as a qualitative research method. *Qualitative Research Journal, 9*(2), 27–40.

Cai, W., Bai, M., & Davey, H. (2022). Implementing environmental protection tax in China: An alternative framework. *Pacific Accounting Review, 34*(3), 479–513.

Cohen, S., Kadach, I., Ormazabal, G., & Reichelstein, S. (2023). Executive compensation tied to ESG performance: International evidence. *Journal of Accounting Research, 61*(3), 805–853.

Cucari, N., D'Angelo, E., Sardanelli, D., Surace, F., & Di Silvestre, S. (2023). Substance and symbol in ESG-linked executive compensation: Evidence from Italian listed companies. *SINERGIE, 41*(2), 103–127.

Derchi, G. B., Davila, A., & Oyon, D. (2023). Green incentives for environmental goals. *Management Accounting Research, 59*, 100830.

Derchi, G. B., Zoni, L., & Dossi, A. (2021). Corporate social responsibility performance, incentives, and learning effects. *Journal of Business Ethics, 173*, 617–641.

Downie, M., & Bourdon-Leblanc, J. (2023). *Short-term or long-term: Considerations for metric selection, Hugessen Consulting Report.*

Flammer, C., Hong, B., & Minor, D. (2019). Corporate governance and the rise of integrating corporate social responsibility criteria in executive compensation: Effectiveness and implications for firm outcomes. *Strategic Management Journal, 40*(7), 1097–1122.

Hartikainen, H., Järvenpää, M., & Rautiainen, A. (2021). Sustainability in executive remuneration-A missing link towards more sustainable firms? *Journal of Cleaner Production, 324*, 129224.

Hazarika, S., Kashikar, A., Peng, L., Röell, A., & Shen, Y. (2022). *ESG-linked pay around the world - trends, determinants, and outcomes, working paper.*

He, Q., Nguyen, J. H., Qiu, B., & Zhang, B. (2023). *Climate regulatory risks and executive compensation: Evidence from US State-Level SCAP Finalization, working paper.*

Homroy, S., Mavruk, T., & Nguyen, V. D. (2023). ESG-linked compensation, CEO skills, and shareholder welfare. *The Review of Corporate Finance Studies, 12*(4), 939–985.

Hong, B., Li, Z., & Minor, D. (2016). Corporate governance and executive compensation for corporate social responsibility. *Journal of Business Ethics, 136*, 199–213.

Hyndman, N., & Liguori, M. (2023). 'Be a game changer and keep the ball rolling': Exploring linkages between football clubs, charitable foundations and doing good. *Accounting, Auditing & Accountability Journal, 37*(2), 502–529.

Ikram, A., Li, Z. F., & Minor, D. (2019). CSR-contingent executive compensation contracts. *Journal of Banking & Finance, 151*, 105655.

Italian Corporate Governance Committee. (2011). *Corporate governance code.* Borsa Italiana.

Italian Corporate Governance Committee. (2014). *Corporate governance code.* Borsa Italiana.

Italian Corporate Governance Committee. (2015). *Corporate governance code.* Borsa Italiana.

Italian Corporate Governance Committee. (2018). *Corporate governance code.* Borsa Italiana.

Italian Corporate Governance Committee. (2020). *Corporate governance code.* Borsa Italiana.

Kaplan, R. S., & Ramanna, K. (2021). Accounting for climate change. *Harvard Business Review, 99*(6), 120–131.

Keddie, S. L., & Magnan, M. (2023). Are ESG performance-based incentives a panacea or a smokescreen for excess compensation? *Sustainability Accounting, Management and Policy Journal, 14*(3), 591–634.

Korca, B., Costa, E., & Farneti, F. (2021). From voluntary to mandatory non-financial disclosure following Directive 2014/95/EU: An Italian case study. *Accounting in Europe, 18*(3), 353–377.

Maas, K. (2018). Do corporate social performance targets in executive compensation contribute to corporate social performance? *Journal of Business Ethics, 148*, 573–585.

Maas, K., & Rosendaal, S. (2016). Sustainability targets in executive remuneration: Targets, time frame, country and sector specification. *Business Strategy and the Environment, 25*(6), 390–401.

Ott, C., & Endrikat, J. (2023). Exploring the association between financial and nonfinancial carbon-related incentives and carbon performance. *Accounting and Business Research, 53*(3), 271–304.

Principles for Responsible Investment. (2012). *Integrating ESG into executive pay. Guidance for investors and companies.*

Qin, B., & Yang, L. (2022). CSR contracting and performance-induced CEO turnover. *Journal of Corporate Finance, 73*, 102173.

Ritz, R. A. (2022). Linking executive compensation to climate performance. *California Management Review, 64*(3), 124–140.

Tsang, A., Wang, K. T., Liu, S., & Yu, L. (2021). Integrating corporate social responsibility criteria into executive compensation and firm innovation: International evidence. *Journal of Corporate Finance, 70*, 102070.

Velte, P. (2024). Archival research on sustainability-related executive compensation. A literature review of the status quo and future improvements. *Corporate Social Responsibility and Environmental Management*, in press.

Yang, L. (2023). Compensation Committee CSR-related expertise, CSR contracting quality, and performance implications. *Journal of Management Accounting Research, 35*(3), 197–223.

Chapter 8
Exploring the Integration of Sustainability in Executive Remuneration Design: Evidence from Large Non-financial Listed Companies in France, Germany, and Italy

Andrea Melis, Carla Gravellu, and Nouha Wasli

8.1 Introduction

It has been over a century since the landmark ruling case of 1919, known as Dodge vs. Ford, in the United States, where it was established that a company's primary objective is to serve the interests of its shareholders above any alternative social objectives. Since then, however, the social, economic, and political scenario has substantially changed. The shareholder primacy model has been under scrutiny. Building upon the ideas of stakeholder theory (Freeman, 1984), and following an extensive and ongoing debate, the concept that corporate purpose should extend beyond solely serving company's shareholders and embrace a broader range of stakeholders has received considerable recognition in recent years. Important business leaders' public statements (e.g. Business Roundtable, 2019; the 'Davos Manifesto', 2019) clearly indicate that large companies are experiencing strong societal pressures to prioritize the long-term welfare of their stakeholders, rather than focus on short-term shareholder value. In response, companies adopt publicly observable initiatives and policies that show their attention to social and environmental issues (e.g. Aresu et al., 2023).

Considering the significant attention society gives to executive remuneration (e.g. Berrone & Gomez-Mejia, 2009; The Guardian, 2014; Melis et al., 2015; Financial Times, 2023), and answering the recent call by Dechow (2023), this study aims to explore how companies integrate sustainability criteria into executive remuneration contracts. This corporate governance practice has the potential to serve as a means of conveying a favourable signal to stakeholders that the company's

A. Melis (✉) · C. Gravellu · N. Wasli
Department of Business and Economics, University of Cagliari, Cagliari, Italy
e-mail: melisa@unica.it

N. Castellano et al. (eds.), *Environmental, Social, Governance (ESG)*, SIDREA Series in Accounting and Business Administration,
https://doi.org/10.1007/978-3-031-76618-3_8

strategic commitment embraces sustainability issues (Berrone & Gomez-Mejia, 2009; Ritz, 2022). It may help maintain (or retain) trust with diverse stakeholders and, eventually, improve the company's long-term overall performance (e.g. Flammer et al., 2019). Specifically, companies may choose to adopt an executive remuneration contract that explicitly integrates environmental and social performance targets into the remuneration design. In this contract, the variable component of the expected remuneration is linked to the achievement of sustainability-related performance targets, such as improving the level of employee involvement or the reduction of the intensity of greenhouse gas emissions (e.g. Hong et al., 2016; Flammer et al., 2019; Aresu et al., 2023; Ikram et al., 2023; Cohen et al., 2023). Prior research documented that the adoption of this form of executive remuneration contract represents a 'response to demands of society' (Baraibar-Diez et al., 2019, p. 1457) and is mainly driven by societal, environmental, and social regulatory pressures (Aresu et al., 2023). Pressure from institutional investors also plays a pivotal role in this process (Focke, 2022) as this remuneration practice is increasingly encouraged at the international level, under the initiative of the United Nations (see Principles for Responsible Investment, 2012). Leading institutional investors stated that for sustainability-related initiatives to be truly meaningful, they should be included in the executive remuneration contract: 'To get away from ESG box checking and ensure that ESG considerations are truly embedded in corporate strategies, we need to incentivise ... to embrace them' (Cevian Capital, 2021). Otherwise, as a U.S. business leader pointed out, '...those targets will always be far down the list of executives' priorities—if even on the list' (The Guardian, 2014). Prominent board consultants have also advocated for the adoption of this remuneration practice (e.g. Burchman & Sullivan, 2017). Important national policies, such as the French corporate governance code, have also recommended 'incorporating one or more criteria related to social and environmental responsibility' (Code de gouvernement d'entreprise des sociétés cotées, 2018, para 24.1).

Despite the importance and growing prevalence of this remuneration practice on a global scale (Cavaco et al., 2020), prior research has primarily focused on the outcomes resulting from the mere adoption of this remuneration contract (e.g. Almici, 2023; Flammer et al., 2019; Cavaco et al., 2020; Derchi et al., 2021; Tsang et al., 2021; Bose et al., 2023; Qin & Yang, 2022), generally treating it as a 'black box'.[1] Little or no in-depth analysis of how companies design the sustainability-related incentive and reward mechanisms for their executives was conducted. This is an important lacuna in the literature as there is the risk that the implementation of corporate governance practices goes unquestioned (Stathopoulos & Talaulicar, 2023).

As for any other element in executive remuneration design (e.g. Jensen & Murphy, 1990; Melis et al., 2012), the main question is more nuanced than whether

[1] The few in-depth studies focused on a very limited number of companies. Specifically, Kolk and Perego (2014) explored four Dutch companies, Hartikainen et al. (2021) seven Finnish companies, while Ritz (2022) focused on five oil and gas companies.

integrating sustainability criteria into executive remuneration contracts is, per se, a good corporate governance practice. The integration of sustainability criteria into the executive remuneration contract may serve different purposes, depending on the details in its design (e.g. relevance and weight of the performance indicators chosen, verifiability of the results achieved, etc.). In performance-based executive remuneration plans, 'the devil is in these details' (Bebchuk et al., 2002, p. 792). Some institutional investors, indeed, warn that sustainability-related indicators in executive remuneration contracts are often 'very subjective, fluffy and easily gamed' (Financial Times, 2023). An important open question is, therefore, whether these 'details' help incentivize corporate executives to manage the company in a way that pursue stakeholders' welfare, or whether they result in the executives prioritizing their own individual interests at the expense of the aggregate stakeholders' welfare (Bebchuk & Tallarita, 2022), merely giving lip service to sustainability (Lenihan & Brennan, 2023). Indeed, the scant empirical literature on the topic documented that the design, not the mere adoption, of this form of executive remuneration contract plays an important role in a company's future sustainability performance (Yang, 2023).

To address this important gap in the literature, this study will adopt the conceptual lenses provided by stakeholder-agency theory (e.g. Hill & Jones, 1992) and undertake a detailed investigation of the design of the sustainability criteria in the variable component of the CEO remuneration of large non-financial companies listed in the major E.U. economies, namely Germany, France, and Italy.

The remainder of this work is organized as follows. Section 8.2 presents the conceptual framework. Then, in Sect. 8.3, the research design is illustrated. Key findings are presented in Sect. 8.4, while we discuss our main findings and provide some concluding remarks in Sect. 8.5.

8.2 Conceptual Framework

This study adopts a stakeholder-agency theoretical perspective, which takes agency theory and stakeholder theory as starting points and provides a generalized theory of agency that encompasses the implicit and explicit contractual relationships between all stakeholders (Hill & Jones, 1992). Among stakeholders, corporate executives are the only group who has direct control over the corporate decision-making process and enters either a formal or informal 'contractual' relationship with all others (e.g. employees, suppliers, Hill & Jones, 1992). This unique role suggests that corporate executives can be considered as 'the agents of other stakeholders' (Hill & Jones, 1992, p. 134). However, similarly to what happens in the shareholder-manager agency context, when acting as agents on behalf of stakeholders, corporate executives cannot be assumed to have, on their own, adequate incentives to pursue the stakeholders' welfare in managing the company (Bebchuk & Tallarita, 2022).

One way of minimizing the agency problem that arises from a divergence of interests involves introducing interest alignment mechanisms into the stakeholders-manager agency relationship (Hill & Jones, 1992). By providing sustainability-related incentives, boards of directors rely on the agency theory-based premise that incentives extrinsically motivate executives, align their behaviour with organizational objectives, and lead to the expected organizational performance (e.g. Ott & Endrikat, 2023). The integration of social and environmental criteria into the executive remuneration contract could serve this purpose to the extent that it is grounded in effective performance measurement. This involves the selection of appropriate performance indicators to be included in the incentive contract as well as the choice of how to combine these indicators (e.g. Baker, 1992).

A large stream of literature on incentives and rewards has analysed this problem and provided guidance on the executive remuneration design. Three main principles can be extracted from this vast multidisciplinary literature (see, e.g., Milgrom & Roberts, 1992; Melis et al., 2011, for a review). First, sustainability criteria, as any other criteria integrated into the executive remuneration design, should be relevant to a company's business model. Sustainability criteria and their quantification (i.e. metrics or key performance indicators, hereafter KPIs) should be aligned with corporate strategy, which in turn is expected to aim at long-term value (e.g. Principles for Responsible Investment, 2012; Ritz, 2022). Second, KPIs should be included in the executive contract to the extent they provide additional information about an executive's performance. KPIs used to quantify sustainability criteria should, therefore, be 'actionable' to avoid exposing executives to uncontrollable risk (Kolk & Perego, 2014). This property captures the influenceability of a KPI through an executive's action and decisions, that is, the extent to which the executive who is beneficiary of the remuneration contract can substantially influence it. An executive is unlikely to be incentivized if s/he cannot identify a clear relationship between his/her actions and the organization's target measured by the chosen KPI (Lenihan & Brennan, 2023). At the same time, as sustainability-related targets, like any other targets, can be subject to managerial opportunism, their measurement should be not under control of the executive (e.g. Ritz, 2022), but independently verified (Principles for Responsible Investment, 2012). Third, using a balanced scorecard approach, incentives, and consequently KPIs, should be well-balanced across multiple strategic criteria (Principles for Responsible Investment, 2012) and avoid an excessive focus on limited dimensions of the value of a restricted subset of stakeholders (e.g. Ritz, 2022). As the notion of a company's stakeholders is not necessarily confined to those groups vital for the achievement of corporate objectives, but also expands to encompass all those who may be impacted by the company's activities, for larger companies, this notion potentially encompasses the entire society (Friedman & Miles, 2006, pp. 13–14). Failing to incorporate the breadth of stakeholders' interests in the executive remuneration contract is likely to come at the expense of aggregate stakeholders' value (Bebchuk & Tallarita, 2022). This is because, due to the classic multitasking problem (Holmstrom & Milgrom, 1991), the integration of a KPI is likely to incentivize executives to focus on some specific tasks, thereby diverting their attention and effort away from others (Bebchuk & Tallarita, 2022).

8.3 Research Design

8.3.1 Sample and Data Gathering

The initial sample consisted of all French, German, and Italian companies listed, respectively, on the CAC 40, DAX 40, and FTSE MIB 40 during the 2022 financial year. Companies belonging to financial industries under the Industry Classification Benchmark (e.g. banks and real estate companies) were excluded from the sample due to their peculiarities. Three companies were found to be listed on more than one Stock Exchange under analysis. They were not excluded from the analysis. However, they were not assigned to a single country of reference, but to a category named 'cross-listed' companies. Thus, the preliminary sample consisted of 92 non-financial companies, of which 32 were listed on the Paris Stock Exchange, 32 on the Frankfurt Stock Exchange, 25 on the Borsa Italiana, and 3 cross-listed.

The next step was to check whether those companies included sustainability-related criteria in the remuneration contracts of their executives. The analysis focuses on remuneration contracts having as the beneficiary the Chief Executive Officer. This individual was identified as the highest-ranking executive in each company regardless of whether the company uses 'chief executive officer' as a designation (such as Chair of the Management Board in German companies, or Directeur General in French companies). We found that 86 companies (approx. 93%) integrate sustainability-related criteria into their executive remuneration contract. Specifically, 31 French companies (approx. 97%), 30 German companies (approx. 94%), 22 Italian companies (88%), and the three cross-listed companies comprise our final sample.

Data on CEO remuneration contracts were hand-collected from corporate reports on the company's website. Given the heterogeneity of documents available in European companies, different reports (remuneration reports, annual reports, universal registration documents,[2] non-financial reports, sustainability-related reports, and integrated reports) were used. Most documents were in English; however, the original language version was checked in case of unclear or incomplete information.

8.3.2 Data Analysis

First, we focused on the decision-making process as it is likely to affect the remuneration design (e.g. Bebchuk et al., 2002; Melis et al., 2012). Specifically, we examined the presence and role of: (a) the remuneration committee, which advises the board of directors on executive remuneration issues; (b) the external remuneration consultant, which may support the remuneration committee,

[2] For French companies, the universal registration document is the equivalent of a firm's annual report.

enhancing the effectiveness of the remuneration design as well as serving as a tool to legitimize the executive remuneration contract; (c) the sustainability-related committee, which provides advice and oversight on sustainability issues (García-Sánchez et al., 2019; Peters & Romi, 2015), possibly including the integration of sustainability criteria into the executive remuneration contract (Develay et al., 2023); and (d) the external auditor, which may contribute to enhancing the verifiability of the KPIs in the remuneration contract, by providing an external independent assurance audit, that may (or may not) include the KPIs and targets in the remuneration contract.[3] This was found to enhance how readers interpret sustainability-related information and its subsequent impact on the reputation of a company's social responsibility (hereafter CSR) (Birkey et al., 2016).

Second, to examine how sustainability criteria were integrated in the remuneration contract, we analysed the following key elements of the remuneration design: the rationale, time horizon, weight, method of payment, nature, and measurement of the sustainability performance indicators. The rationale helps an outside stakeholder to understand the reason why a company chooses this form of remuneration, providing information, for example, of which stakeholders the company seeks to address by incentivizing its sustainability strategy. The time horizon represents the incentive's time length that may influence the CEO's performance towards different priorities within the company's sustainability strategy. The weight reflects the significance of sustainability-related criteria in the overall performance-based compensation. A relatively low (high) weight may reflect a symbolic (substantial) commitment towards sustainability (Flammer et al., 2019). The method of payment (cash- or equity-based) shows whether the CEO is incentivized to hold a shareholders' interest or not. The nature and measurement of the sustainability-related KPIs enabled us (and any outside stakeholder) assessing whether KPIs are actionable by the CEO and if the CEO is incentivized to achieve an absolute level of sustainability performance or their performance evaluation is relative, i.e. benchmarked against a peers' group.

Third, to identify which stakeholders and sustainability-related dimensions are covered in the executive remuneration contract, in line with Bebchuk and Tallarita (2022), we considered the following stakeholders: Environment, Employees, Customers, Suppliers, and Community. Furthermore, drawing from the Principles for Responsible Investment (2012), we identified an additional stakeholder group, named 'Stakeholder Dialogue'. This stakeholder group covers all KPIs that do not pertain to social or environmental matters (e.g. Compliance with regulations or Image and reputation). Due to the large variety of KPIs found, we grouped them into dimensions considering the stakeholders' interests covered (e.g. CO2 emissions reduction investments and CO2 emissions to power generation were grouped in carbon emissions reduction). This classification allowed us to assess whether the

[3] In this assessment, we considered the audit of qualitative KPIs (e.g. a company's CSR strategy, initiative, or an in-house developed index) as not applicable (NA) when there was no clear information on whether it was audited or not.

remuneration is well-balanced among a company's stakeholders and in line with the rationale stated for the plan.

Last but not least, to understand the relevance of the KPIs in the remuneration contract, we investigated whether the sustainability dimension measured by the KPI was included in the company's materiality analysis (e.g. in the materiality matrix).

8.4 Empirical Evidence on the Integration of Sustainability Criteria into Executive Compensation Contracts

8.4.1 Remuneration Process

The process of identifying, integrating, and assuring the sustainability criteria in the executive remuneration contracts involves several parties. Our analysis reveals that most companies (all Italian, 93% French, and 86% German companies) exhibit having a remuneration committee involved in the executive remuneration design. French and Italian companies generally have a sustainability-related committee, while only 40% of German companies do. Interestingly, among companies with a sustainability-related committee (approx. 78%), this committee is directly involved in integrating sustainability criteria in the executive remuneration design only in approx. one-third of the cases. This means this process sees the involvement of the sustainability committee in only about one-fourth of the total cases, except for French companies, where this committee was involved in almost half of the companies. An external remuneration consultant was involved in 62% of the companies analysed (see Table 8.1).

Companies generally have their sustainability information assured by an external auditor, either (more frequently) in a limited form or (less frequently) in a reasonable form. Interestingly, some companies opted for a limited assurance with a reasonable audit of selected items. However, this assurance does not necessarily include the sustainability-related KPIs and targets in the executive remuneration contract. As illustrated in Table 8.2 (Panel A), almost 30% (10%) of the total companies audit all (some) sustainability-related KPIs and targets in the annual bonuses. Among these,

Table 8.1 Parties involved in the CEO remuneration design process

	Companies involving a Remuneration Committee		Companies involving a Sustainability-related Committee		Companies involving an External Consultant	
	n°	%	n°	%	n°	%
France	29	93.5	15	48.4	21	67.7
Germany	26	86.7	2	6.7	13	43.3
Italy	22	100.0	6	27.3	18	81.8
Cross-listed	3	100.0	–	–	2	66.7
Total	80	93.0	23	26.7	54	62.8

Table 8.2 External assurance of sustainability-related KPIs in the CEO remuneration contract

	Companies with all KPIs assured		Companies with some KPIs assured	
	n°	%	n°	%
Panel A. Annual bonuses.				
France	16	51.6	4	12.9
Germany	4	16.0	2	8.0
Italy	2	9.1	1	4.5
Cross-listed	2	66.7	1	33.3
Total[a]	24	29.6	8	9.9
Panel B. Long-term incentive plans.				
France	16	66.7	–	–
Germany	6	28.6	2	9.5
Italy	4	25.0	–	–
Cross-listed	2	100.0	–	–
Total[b]	29	50.9	2	3.5

[a] 33 companies (approx. 41%) did not disclose whether the KPIs were audited or not. Ten companies (approx. 12%) were considered as not applicable (NA) because of the nature of KPIs (e.g. indices) or the lack of a clear disclosure

[b] A total of 21 companies (approx. 37%) did not disclose whether the KPIs were audited or not, while 10 companies (approx. 17%) were considered not applicable

the great majority are French, while a significant number of German and Italian companies choose not to disclose this information. Almost 50% (3.5%) of the companies have all (some) sustainability-related KPIs and targets in the long-term remuneration plans audited, with important differences across countries. Specifically, the great majority of French companies fully audited these data, while only 29% and 25% of German and Italian companies, respectively, have these data fully externally audited (see Table 8.2, Panel B).

This remuneration process has as an outcome the integration of the sustainability criteria in the executive remuneration contract. Box 8.1 shows a real-life example of this form of remuneration.

Box 8.1 The Integration of Sustainability Criteria in the CEO Annual Cash-based Bonus. The Case of Eni spa

Rationale of the plan
Financial and non-financial targets related to short- and long-term variable remuneration, including equity-based compensation, are defined in a manner consistent with the four-year Strategic Plan and with the expectations of shareholders and stakeholders, in order to foster a strong results oriented focus and combine operational and financial soundness with social and environmental sustainability.

(continued)

Box 8.1 (continued)

Design of KPIs

KPI description		**Weight (%)**	**Measure of KPI**	**Rationale of the KPIs**
KPI 1	Severity Incident Rate	12.5	Absolute	The indicator Severity Incident Rate (SIR) reflects Eni's HSE priorities and the central importance of our commitment to individual safety. The prevention and risk minimization are cornerstones of Eni's operations in our commitment to achieving constant improvements in safety for all workers and to expressing this commitment in the process of assessing the performance of senior management.
KPI 2	Hydrocarbon Production	12.5	Absolute	The indicators of hydrocarbon production and incremental installed capacity of Renewables make it possible to balance the development of the upstream business with the development objectives of renewable energy connected to the strategy of decarbonizing operations and products.
KPI 3	Incremental Renewable Installed Capacity	12.5	Absolute	
KPI 4	GHG emissions intensity Scope 1 and Scope 2—equity	12.5	Absolute	The Upstream GHG emission intensity indicator (tCO2 eq./kboe) reflects Eni's commitment to reducing GHG emissions, in line with the medium-long-term objectives that will lead the Company to decarbonize all products and processes by 2050. Eni aims to eliminate the carbon footprint associated with its activities, which also involves the gradual reduction of the emission intensity of Scope 1 and Scope 2 upstream emissions, considering for this purpose both the production operated and that not operated.
Total Weight (%)		50.0		

Source: Our elaboration based upon the company's Remuneration and Annual Reports, 2022

8.4.2 Design of Sustainability Criteria in Annual Bonuses

We found that approx. 93% of companies integrated sustainability-related criteria in their executive remuneration plan with an annual time horizon. Specifically, all French and cross-listed companies, which are also listed on the Paris Stock Exchange, 22 Italian companies (88%), and 25 German companies (approx. 83%), have adopted this form of remuneration.

Table 8.3 shows our findings about the design of sustainability criteria in short-term incentive plans. Annual bonuses are always paid in cash, regardless of the company's country of origin. The typical company in our sample includes three sustainability-related KPIs in executive annual bonuses. Companies, on average, use 2.8 KPIs, ranging from a minimum average of 2.3 for Italian companies, passing through 2.6 for German companies, to reach 3 for French companies.

Companies report KPIs in a more or less generic way. For instance, indicators such as Sustainability, ESG, or Corporate Social Responsibility may contain different environmental or social measures and targets, both quantitative and qualitative. A case in point is provided by Renault, which included in its sustainability-related KPIs both quantitative Health and Safety (hereafter H&S) targets, and initiatives such as the development of the circular business economy and the launch of the 'ReKnow' University (Renault, 2023). Generic indicators such as Diversity or DE&I (Diversity, Equity, and Inclusion) may cover a wide and unclear spectrum of dimensions when compared to the specific metrics (e.g. Women in managerial positions or Women in the workforce). The use of the latter would help to clarify the specific sustainability dimension the company aims to cover.

A large variety of KPIs was found. The most frequent KPIs are related to carbon emission reduction (e.g. CO2 emission reduction, Scope 1 and Scope 2, Implementation of a carbon management programme), customer satisfaction, H&S (e.g. Safety, Workplace Accident Frequency Rate), and the increase of Women in managerial positions.

Among those companies that disclose the weight given to sustainability criteria,[4] the average weight is approx. 19% of the total amount of the short-term variable remuneration, ranging from a minimum of 3.8% to a maximum of 50%, with no material differences among the three countries under study.

A very small number of companies opted to measure the relative performance of their executives against a peer group. Sustainability-related KPIs adopted are absolute in 99% of the cases, meaning that the target achievement only depends on the company's performance measurement (e.g. Workplace accident frequency rate reduction over previous years). This evidence may show that companies choose sustainability criteria and targets focusing on their specific companies' objectives. Even if uncommon, we found examples of relative KPIs in French and Italian companies, such as employee engagement measurement through surveys, of which

[4]In our sample, cases of missing data or partial disclosure were very limited among Italian firms (5%). Instead, it was more frequent among French and German firms (32% and 48%, respectively).

Table 8.3 Design of sustainability criteria in annual bonuses

	Method of payment (%)		Average weight (%)	Minimum weight (%)	Maximum weight (%)	Average n° of KPIs per company	Measure of KPI (%)	
	Cash	Equity					Absolute	Relative
France	100.0	–	19.4	10.0	15.0	3.2	99.0	1.0
Germany	100.0	–	18.8	3.8	35.0	2.6	100.0	–
Italy	100.0	–	19.8	5.0	50.0	2.3	98.0	2.0
Cross-listed	100.0	–	15.0	10.0	20.0	4.7	100.0	–
Total	100.0	–	19.2	3.8	50.0	2.8	99.1	0.9

the results were compared with specific peer groups (e.g. Danone, 2023; Moncler Group, 2023).

8.4.3 Stakeholders and Sustainability-Related Dimensions in Annual Bonuses

On average, companies tend to address approximately two stakeholders in their annual bonuses. The stakeholder group most prioritized is Employees (85%), followed by the Environment (approx. 68%), Stakeholder Dialogue (approx. 24%), Customers (approx. 21%), Suppliers (approx. 13%), and the Community (approx. 9%) (see Table 8.4). We observe a similar trend across industries with regard to their emphasis on the Environment and Employees. However, specific patterns emerge within certain sectors for the other groups of stakeholders. Customers are prioritized by companies operating in the Telecommunications, Consumer Discretionary, and Consumer Staples industries. The Community is mostly covered by companies within the Basic Materials and Telecommunications sectors, while Suppliers receive attention mainly from companies in the Basic Materials and Health Care sectors.

Table 8.5 provides a breakdown analysis of the specific dimensions that companies address within the relevant stakeholder groups. Employees-related matters mostly encompass dimensions of employee involvement, gender diversity, and health and safety. Within employee involvement, approx. 19% of companies address the two dimensions of employee engagement and their training and education (e.g. young employees and anti-corruption). One out of four companies covers the dimension of gender diversity in managerial positions. There are significant differences among countries, with this dimension holding particular importance in the French context compared to Germany and Italy. Approx. 19% of companies have KPIs oriented to the reduction of work-related accidents. Interestingly, this dimension seems to carry greater significance within French and Italian companies than in German companies.

Table 8.4 Stakeholders addressed in annual bonuses

	French companies		German companies		Italian companies		Cross-listed companies		Total	
	n°	%	n°	%	n°	%	n°	%	n°	%
Environment	26	83.9	15	60.0	11	52.4	2	66.7	54	67.5
Employees	30	96.8	18	72.0	18	85.7	2	66.7	68	85.0
Customers	5	16.1	3	12.0	7	33.3	2	66.7	17	21.3
Community	5	16.1	–	–	2	9.5	–	0.0	7	8.8
Suppliers	4	12.9	3	12.0	3	14.3	–	0.0	10	12.5
Stakeholder Dialogue	7	22.6	8	32.0	3	14.3	1	33.3	19	23.8

Table 8.5 Sustainability-related dimensions in annual bonuses

	French companies		German companies		Italian companies		Cross-listed companies		Total	
	n°	%	n°	%	n°	%	n°	%	n°	%
Environment										
GHG Emissions reduction										
Carbon Emissions Reduction	10	32.3	7	28.0	7	33.3	1	33.3	25	31.3
Carbon Emission Reduction—Scope 1	6	19.4	2	8.0	1	4.8	1	33.3	10	12.5
Carbon Emission Reduction—Scope 2	5	16.1	2	8.0	1	4.8	–	–	8	10.0
Carbon Emission Reduction—Scope 3	2	6.5	1	4.0	–	–	–	–	3	3.8
Hydrocarbon production	–	–	–	–	1	4.8	–	–	1	1.3
Innovation process	1	3.2	–	–	–	–	–	–	1	1.3
Carbon management programme	3	9.7	1	4.0	–	–	–	–	4	5.0
Digital Development linked to CO2 Roadmap	1	3.2	–	–	–	–	–	–	1	1.3
CDP Rating	2	6.5	1	4.0	–	–	–	–	3	3.8
SBTi Accreditation	1	3.2	–	–	–	–	–	–	1	1.3
Energy Management										
Energy Policy	–	–	1	4.0	–	–	–	–	1	1.3
Renewable Energies	4	12.9	1	4.0	4	19.0	–	–	9	11.3
Energy Consumption	1	3.2	1	4.0	1	4.8	–	–	3	3.8
Energy Intensity	–	–	–	–	1	4.8	–	–	1	1.3
Energy Efficiency	1	3.2	–	–	–	–	–	–	1	1.3
Diversification of Supply Gas	–	–	1	4.0	–	–	–	–	1	1.3
Circular Economy										
Circular Economy	3	9.7	–	–	–		–	–	3	3.8
Sustainable Products	–	–	5	20.0	–	–	1	33.3	6	7.5
Product Durability	–	–	–	–	1	4.8	–	–	1	1.3
Revenues from Sustainable Products	1	3.2	–	–	–	–	–	–	1	1.3
Waste Management	4	12.9	–	–	1	4.8	–	–	5	6.3
Low-Impact Materials	4	12.9	–	–	2	9.5	–	–	6	7.5
Environment Protection										
Biodiversity	2	6.5	–	–	1	4.8	–	–	3	3.8
Water use	2	6.5	1	4.0	1	4.8	–	–	4	5.0
Gas Leakage Reduction	–	–	1	4.0	1	4.8	–	–	2	2.5
Ecosystem Empowering	1	3.2	–	–	–	–	–	–	1	1.3
Environmental Management	–	–	1	4.0	–	–	–	–	1	1.3
Animal Welfare	1	3.2	–	–	–	–	–	–	1	1.3
Climate Change	4	12.9	–	–	–	–	1	33.3	5	6.3

(continued)

Table 8.5 (continued)

	French companies		German companies		Italian companies		Cross-listed companies		Total	
	n°	%	n°	%	n°	%	n°	%	n°	%
Employees										
Employee Involvement										
Employee Commitment	2	6.5	1	4.0	–	–	–	–	3	3.8
Talent Development	6	19.4	2	8.0	1	4.8	–	–	9	11.3
Employee Engagement	9	29.0	3	12.0	2	9.5	1	33.3	15	18.8
Integrity	1	3.2	2	8.0	–	–	–	–	3	3.8
Training and Education	10	32.3	3	12.0	2	9.5	–	–	15	18.8
Employer Attractiveness	–	–	3	12.0	–	–	–	–	3	3.8
People Care	1	3.2	–	–	–	–	1	33.3	2	2.5
Compliance	1	3.2	–	–	–	–	–	–	1	1.3
Traceability and Transparency	1	3.2	–	–	1	4.8	–	–	2	2.5
Employee Satisfaction	2	6.5	3	12.0	2	9.5	–	–	7	8.8
Diversity and Inclusion (D&I)										
D&I	1	3.2	4	16.0	1	4.8	–	–	6	7.5
Diversity	3	9.7	3	12.0	–	–	–	–	6	7.5
Cultural diversity	1	3.2	–	–	–	–	–	–	1	1.3
Disabled Workforce	2	6.5	–	–	–	–	–	–	2	2.5
International Profiles Diversity	1	3.2	–	–	–	–	1	33.3	2	2.5
Equity										
Equality	–	–	3	12.0	2	9.5	–	–	5	6.3
Living Wages policy	–	–	1	4.0	–	–	–	–	1	1.3
Gender Equality	–	–	1	4.0	–	–	–	–	1	1.3
Gender Pay Gap	1	3.2	–	–	1	4.8	–	–	2	2.5
Gender Diversity										
Gender Diversity	4	12.9	1	4.0	–	–	1	33.3	6	7.5
Gender Diversity—Managerial Positions	15	48.4	2	8.0	2	9.5	1	33.3	20	25.0
Gender Diversity—Workforce	2	6.5	1	4.0	3	14.3	1	33.3	7	8.8
Health and Safety (H&S)										
Safety	–	–	2	8.0	–	–	2	66.7	4	5.0
Workplace Accidents	8	25.8	1	4.0	6	28.6	–	–	15	18.8
Reported Accidents	1	3.2	–	–	–	–	–	–	1	1.3
Recordable Injuries	2	6.5	–	–	1	4.8	–	–	3	3.8
Severe Accidents	–	–	–	–	2	9.5	–	–	2	2.5
Fatal Accidents	2	6.5	–	–	1	4.8	–	–	3	3.8
Prevention of Accidents	1	3.2	1	4.0	–	–	–	–	2	2.5
Lost Time Injury Frequency Rate	3	9.7	–	–	–	–	1	33.3	4	5.0
Lost Days Rate	–	–	–	–	1	4.8	–	–	1	1.3

(continued)

Table 8.5 (continued)

	French companies		German companies		Italian companies		Cross-listed companies		Total	
	n°	%	n°	%	n°	%	n°	%	n°	%
Tier 1 and Tier 2 Accidents	1	3.2	–	–	–	–	–	–	1	1.3
Costumers										
Costumers Involvement										
Satisfaction	4	12.9	3	12.0	3	14.3	3	100.0	13	16.3
Awareness	–	–	–	–	1	4.8	–	–	1	1.3
Experience Quality	2	6.5	–	–	2	9.5	1	33.3	5	6.3
Sustainable Products										
Safety and Security	2	6.5	1	4.0	1	4.8	–	–	4	5.0
Sustainable Products	–	–	1	4.0	–	–	–	–	1	1.3
Traceability and Transparency	1	3.2	–	–	1	4.8	–	–	2	2.5
Revenues from Sustainable Products	1	3.2	–	–	–	–	–	–	1	1.3
Community										
Endowments and Initiatives										
Donations to Local Communities	1	3.2	–	–	–	–	–	–	1	1.3
Health Care initiatives in Low/Middle income countries	2	6.5	–	–	–	–	–	–	2	2.5
Digital Divide Reduction	–	–	–	–	1	4.8	–	–	1	1.3
Underprivileged People Training	1	3.2	–	–	–	–	–	–	1	1.3
Community Engagement										
Integration with Local Communities	1	3.2	–	–	–	–	–	–	1	1.3
Local Communities Engagement	–	–	1	4.0	–	–	–	–	1	1.3
Suppliers										
Sustainable Value Chain										
Sustainable Supply Chain	4	12.9	2	8.0	1	4.8	–	–	7	8.8
Traceability and Transparency	1	3.2	–	–	1	4.8	–	–	2	2.5
Suppliers Involvement										
Suppliers Engagement	1	3.2	–	–	1	4.8	–	–	2	2.5
Risk Management Programme	–	–	1	4.0	–	–	–	–	1	1.3
Stakeholder Dialogue										
ESG Indices										
ESG Indices	2	6.5	–	–	–	–	–	–	2	2.5
DJSI Index	–	–	–	–	2	10.0	–	–	2	2.5
Ftse4Good Index	–	–	–	–	1	4.8	–	–	1	1.3
Sustainalytics Index	–	–	–	–	1	4.8	–	–	1	1.3
Corporate Governance										

(continued)

Table 8.5 (continued)

	French companies		German companies		Italian companies		Cross-listed companies		Total	
	n°	%	n°	%	n°	%	n°	%	n°	%
Gender Diversity—Governing Bodies	1	3.2	1	4.0	–	–	–	–	2	2.5
Compliance to Regulations/ Corporate Governance Code	2	6.5	1	4.0	1	4.8	1	33.3	5	6.3
Sustainable Finance	–	–	–	–	1	4.8	–	–	1	1.3
Implementation of ESG Strategy	–	–	3	12.0	–	–	–	–	3	3.8
Definition of ESG targets	–	–	2	8.0	–	–	–	–	2	2.5
Creation of CSR Committee	1	3.2	–	–	–	–	–	–	1	1.3
Inclusion of CSR Roadmap in Budgets and Bonuses	1	3.2	–	–	–	–	–	–	1	1.3
Enlargement of the governance structure to improve sustainability performance	–	–	1	4.0	–	–	–	–	1	1.3
Improvement of governance process with stakeholders	–	–	1	4.0	–	–	–	–	1	1.3
Quality of Succession Plans Confirmed by the Appointments and Corporate Governance Committee	1	3.2	–	–	–	–	–	–	1	1.3
Corporate Reporting and Reputation										
Reporting	–	–	2	8.0	1	4.8	–	–	3	3.8
Image and Reputation	2	6.5	1	4.0	–	–	–	–	3	3.8
Strategic Communication	–	–	1	4.0	–	–	–	–	1	1.3

Note: one company may have more than one KPI related to a general dimension (e.g. the same company may include KPIs related to both Talent Development and Employee Satisfaction)

The Environment is mostly addressed within the framework of carbon emission reduction (approx. 31% of companies), with a uniform commitment across countries, followed by Scope 1 and 2 emissions, with notable prevalence among French companies. In the area of energy management, 11% of companies consider the dimension of renewable energies, particularly in the French and Italian contexts. Although there is generally less emphasis on the other areas, the circular economy dimension receives attention with variations among countries. German companies engage within the dimension of sustainable products, while French and Italian companies prioritize aspects related to low-impact materials.

The Stakeholder Dialogue comprises various dimensions, none of which seems dominant among companies. Equivalent attention is given to issues such as the inclusion of ESG indices, and topics related to corporate governance, e.g., assuring compliance with regulations and the Corporate Governance Code, as well as corporate reporting and reputation. Customers are mostly considered within the dimensions of their satisfaction and the quality of their experience. Establishing a sustainable supply chain is the main dimension companies use to engage with their Suppliers. Lastly, a limited number of companies address the Community stakeholder by implementing initiatives aimed at helping or engaging with local communities.

We found that companies generally cover stakeholder dimensions that are relevant to their business model and stakeholders of interest. The sustainability-related KPIs in the remuneration contracts were associated to stakeholder dimensions covered in the company's materiality analysis. Moreover, apart from very limited cases (e.g. Lost Time Injury Frequency Rate, Lost Days Rate), companies' efforts are directed to impact sustainability issues rather than to avoid ESG risks.

8.4.4 Design of Sustainability Criteria in Long-Term Incentive Plans

We found that approx. two-thirds of the companies integrated sustainability criteria in their CEOs' long-term incentive plans (hereafter LTIPs). Indeed, 24 French (approx. 77%), 19 German (approx. 63%), and 12 Italian companies (approx. 55%) engage in this practice.

Table 8.6 illustrates the design of sustainability criteria. Across countries, the time horizon of the remuneration plan can vary from 3 to 5 years. Most French and Italian companies adopt a 3-year time horizon, whereas German companies display more variation. The method of payment varies between cash and equity. Specifically, approximately 77% of Italian companies adopt equity as a payment method. On the other hand, in Germany, about half of the companies decide to pay in cash, and the other half opt for equity payment. All French companies opt for equity payment.

The typical company adopts two sustainability-related KPIs. The average in LTIPs (2) is lower when compared to annual bonuses. In French and German companies, the average number of sustainability-related KPIs goes down to 1.8, while Italian companies choose a slightly higher number (2.5).

The average weight shows little variation among countries. The average weight in French and Italian companies is 22% and approx. 20%, respectively. German companies allocate relatively higher weights reaching an average of approx. 27%. Overall, weights given to sustainability criteria in LTIPs are greater, and generally better disclosed, than those in the annual bonuses.

Most of the companies in the sample adopt absolute sustainability-related targets. None of the German and Italian companies measures the sustainability performance of their CEOs against a peer group. Only one French company, Schneider Electric, combined three external ESG indices into a Sustainability External and Relative Index, which measures the long-term sustainability performance of the group (Schneider Electric, 2023).

Table 8.6 Design of sustainability criteria in LTIPs

	Method of payment (%)		Average weight (%)	Minimum weight (%)	Maximum weight (%)	Average n° of KPIs per company	Measure of KPIs (%)		Average n° of years of the plan
	Cash	Equity					Absolute	Relative	
France	–	100.0	22.0	10.0	40.0	1.9	92.5	7.5	3.1
Germany	47.6	52.4	26.5	15.0	50.0	1.8	100.0	–	3.9
Italy	23.1	76.9	20.4	10.0	35.0	2.6	100.0	–	3.1
Cross-listed	50.0	50.0	33.3	33.3	33.3	2.8	100.0	–	3.5
Total	23.3	76.7	23.1	10.0	50.0	2.0	95.8	4.2	3.4

8.4.5 Stakeholders and Sustainability-Related Dimensions in Long-Term Incentive Plans

The typical company covers two stakeholders (approx. 1.8 on average) in their LTPIs. The distribution of target stakeholders reveals similarities and differences across countries. For all companies, there is a predominant focus on the Environment (approx. 91% of the cases) and Employees, accounting for approx. 56% of the companies. However, for the remaining stakeholders, each country has its own specificities. French companies tend to prioritize these two stakeholder groups exclusively, while German companies display a wider range of engagement with various stakeholders. Italian companies, in addition to their attention to the Environment and Employees, also demonstrate commitment to Stakeholder Dialogue (see Table 8.7). Uniform patterns were observed across industries. Environment and Employees emerge as the most addressed stakeholder group. Moreover, our analysis reveals some specificities related to industries. For instance, the Basic Materials and Energy sectors exclusively focus on the Environment and Employees in the long term. Meanwhile, the Consumer Staples and Telecommunications sectors place considerable emphasis on Customers. In the Healthcare sector, there is a focus on Customers, the Community, and heightened attention to Suppliers.

Table 8.8 illustrates the performance dimensions addressed for each stakeholder group. For the Environment group, the most frequent dimension is carbon emission reduction. Approximately one-third of the total sample incorporates this dimension in their LTIPs. One-third of the companies encompass Scope 1 carbon emissions, while approx. 12% of the companies use the CDP (Carbon Disclosure Project) rating as a relevant dimension. Another important area covered is energy management, where approx. 11% of the companies disclose the use of renewable energy sources. These dimensions exhibit variations across the three countries. Most German companies prioritize the reduction of Scope 1 greenhouse gas emissions. 21% of French companies focus on Scope 1, while an equal percentage direct their efforts towards Scope 2. Meanwhile, Italian companies, apart from their pursuit of carbon emission reduction, also place significant importance on CDP ratings and the use of renewable energy sources. The circular economy is relatively less addressed, as well as environment protection that French companies cover exclusively, yet slightly.

Table 8.7 Stakeholders addressed in LTIPs

	French companies		German companies		Italian companies		Cross-listed companies		Total	
	n°	%	n°	%	n°	%	n°	%	n°	%
Environment	22	91.7	17	89.5	11	91.7	2	100.0	52	91.2
Employees	13	54.2	11	57.9	8	66.7	–	–	32	56.1
Customers	2	8.3	4	21.1	–	–	–	–	6	10.5
Community	–	–	1	5.3	–	–	–	–	1	1.8
Suppliers	–	–	3	15.8	1	8.3	–	–	4	7.0
Stakeholder Dialogue	3	12.5	2	10.5	4	33.3	1	50.0	10	17.5

Table 8.8 Sustainability-related dimensions in LTIPs

	French companies		German companies		Italian companies		Cross-listed companies		Total	
	n°	%	n°	%	n°	%	n°	%	n°	%
Environment										
GHG Emissions Reduction										
Carbon Emissions Reduction	6	25.0	8	42.1	6	50.0	1	50.0	21	36.8
Carbon Emission Reduction—Scope 1	5	20.8	10	52.6	3	25.0	1	50.0	19	33.3
Carbon Emission Reduction—Scope 2	5	20.8	8	42.1	2	16.7	–	–	15	26.3
Carbon Emission Reduction—Scope 3	3	12.5	1	5.3	–	–	–	–	4	7.0
CAFE Compliance	–	–	–	–	–	–	1	50.0	1	1.8
CDP Rating	3	12.5	–	–	3	25.0	1	50.0	7	12.3
Off-setting of Remaining Scope 1 and 2 Emissions	–	–	1	5.3	–	–	–	–	1	1.8
Energy Management										
Renewable Energies	3	12.5	–	–	3	25.0	–	–	6	10.5
Energy Consumption	2	8.3	–	–	–	–	–	–	2	3.5
Circular Economy										
Circular Economy	1	4.2	–	–	–	–	–	–	1	1.8
Sustainable Products	–	–	3	15.8	–	–	1	50.0	4	7.0
Low-Impact Materials	3	12.5	1	5.3	1	8.3	–	–	5	8.8
Waste Management	2	8.3	1	5.3	2	16.7	–	–	5	8.8
Environment Protection										
Animal Welfare	1	4.2	–	–	–	–	–	–	1	1.8
Biodiversity	2	8.3	–	–	–	–	–	–	2	3.5
Climate Change	1	4.2	–	–	–	–	–	–	1	1.8
Ecosystem Empowering	1	4.2	–	–	–	–	–	–	1	1.8
Water Use	3	12.5	–	–	–	–	–	–	3	5.3
Employees										
Employee Involvement										
Talent Development	–	–	1	5.3	–	–	–	–	1	1.8
Employee Engagement	3	12.5	2	10.5	1	8.3	–	–	6	10.5
Training and Education	1	4.2	1	5.3	1	8.3	–	–	3	5.3
Employer Attractiveness	–	–	1	5.3	–	–	–	–	1	1.8
Employee Satisfaction	–	–	3	15.8	–	–	–	–	3	5.3
Diversity and Inclusion (D&I)										
D&I	1	4.2	–	–	–	–	–	–	1	1.8
Diversity	1	4.2	1	5.3	–	–	–	–	2	3.5
Disabled Workforce	1	4.2	–	–	–	–	–	–	1	1.8
International Profiles Diversity	–	–	–	–	1	8.3	–	–	1	1.8
Equity										

(continued)

Table 8.8 (continued)

	French companies		German companies		Italian companies		Cross-listed companies		Total	
	n°	%	n°	%	n°	%	n°	%	n°	%
Bloomberg GEI Index	–	–	–	–	1	8.3	–	–	1	1.8
Gender Pay Gap	–	–	–	–	1	8.3	–	–	1	1.8
Equal Pay Certification	–	–	–	–	2	16.7	–	–	2	3.5
Gender Diversity										
Gender Diversity	1	4.2	–	–	–	–	–	–	1	1.8
Gender Diversity—Managerial positions	8	33.3	6	31.6	4	33.3	1	50.0	19	33.3
Gender Diversity—Workforce	–	–	–	–	1	8.3	–	–	1	1.8
Health and Safety (H&S)										
Workplace Accidents	–	–	1	5.3	–	–	–	–	1	1.8
Recordable Injuries	1	4.2	–	–	–	–	–	–	1	1.8
Severe Accidents	–	–	1	5.3	1	8.3	–	–	2	3.5
Fatal Accidents	–	–	1	5.3	–	–	–	–	1	1.8
Lost Time Injury Frequency Rate	1	4.2	1	5.3	–	–	–	–	2	3.5
Sick Leave	–	–	1	5.3	–	–	–	–	1	1.8
Customers										
Customers Involvement										
Satisfaction	1	4.2	3	15.8	–	–	–	–	4	7.0
Awareness	1	4.2	–	–	–	–	–	–	1	1.8
Community										
Endowments and Initiatives										
Health Care Initiatives in Low/Middle Income Countries	–	–	3	15.8	–	–	–	–	3	5.3
Support to Farmers in Low/Middle Income Countries	–	–	1	5.3	–	–	–	–	1	1.8
Underserved Communities Support	–	–	1	5.3	–	–	–	–	1	1.8
Social Matters										
Tax Control Framework	–	–	–	–	1	8.3	–	–	1	1.8
Suppliers										
Sustainable Value Chain										
Sustainable Supply Chain	1	4.2	2	10.5	–	–	–	–	3	5.3
Stakeholder Dialogue										
ESG Indices										
ESG Indices	–	–	1	5.3	–	–	–	–	1	1.8
DJSI Index	1	4.2	–	–	4	33.3	1	50.0	6	10.5
Ftse4Good Index	–	–	–	–	2	16.7	–	–	2	3.5
Sustainalytics Index	–	–	–	–	1	8.3	–	–	1	1.8
Ecovadis Score	1	4.2	–	–	–	–	–	–	1	1.8

(continued)

Table 8.8 (continued)

	French companies		German companies		Italian companies		Cross-listed companies		Total	
	n°	%	n°	%	n°	%	n°	%	n°	%
Euronext Vigeo Index	1	4.2	–	–	–	–	–	–	1	1.8
Gresb Index	–	–	–	–	1	8.3	–	–	1	1.8
MSC Index	–	–	–	–	1	8.3	–	–	1	1.8

Note: one company may have more than one KPI related to a general dimension (e.g. the same company may include KPIs related to both DJSI and Ftse4Good Index)

Within the Employees stakeholder group, the most covered area is gender diversity, often measured as the representation of women in managerial positions. Employee involvement is also a significant area, with approximately 11% of companies actively engaging in employee participation practices. French and German companies pay relatively limited attention to Equity issues, which are more relevant for Italian companies. The stakeholder group Customers, is not extensively addressed across most companies, except for German companies, where 16% of them consider customer satisfaction. German companies show the highest level of commitment to their communities compared to the other companies in the sample. Additionally, Italian companies incorporate ESG indices into their stakeholder dialogue, with the most frequently employed index being the Dow Jones Sustainability. Suppliers do not seem to have an importance in the long run among the three countries. Last but not least, similarly to what emerged in annual bonuses, companies typically address stakeholder dimensions that are relevant to their business model and the stakeholders they prioritize. They also focus on assessing the social and environmental impact of their activities, rather than attempting to mitigate their ESG risks.

8.5 Concluding Remarks

This study undertook a detailed investigation of how sustainability criteria are integrated into the design of the variable component of CEO remuneration. Using a sample of large non-financial companies listed in Germany, France, and Italy, the three main economies within the European Union, we found that this executive remuneration practice has become prevalent, reaching a state of 'mainstream' adoption within the vast majority, if not all, of the large companies examined across the countries under analysis. Its diffusion is even higher than what emerged in leading US companies (Bebchuk & Tallarita, 2022). The stated aim of this remuneration practice is generally to align CEO actions with the company's strategy by combining financial and sustainability-related matters in the best interest of both shareholders and stakeholders.

Boards of directors seem to prefer including key performance indicators (KPIs) that are relevant and, to some extent, tailored to the company's business strategy. These KPIs include various dimensions which primarily (and more frequently) assess the social or environmental impact of the company's activities and, may also (though less frequently) evaluate the potential social and environmental risks encountered by the company in its activities. They are also usually actionable by the CEO, i.e. they are influenced by the CEO's performance. The remuneration process generally involves a remuneration committee that often operates with the advisory support of an external remuneration consultant, while a sustainability committee is occasionally involved in. An external independent assurance is frequently provided, but there are still many cases where the KPIs included in the executive remuneration contract are not independently verified, i.e. fully audited by an external independent auditor.

The measurement of the achievement of sustainability-related targets is generally conducted using absolute targets and KPIs. This occurs, to some extent, at the expense of integrating sustainability criteria choosing relative targets and KPIs that would help investors and other stakeholders to compare companies with their peer groups. This could be because relevant KPIs for corporate strategy execution may be very different, being industry- and, in some cases, even company-specific. Lack of uniformity and comparability in the choice of sustainability-related KPIs seems to recall the history of financial KPIs. While uniformity and comparability of these indicators are nowadays expected and somehow taken for granted, it was not the case when their use emerged in the twentieth century (Dechow, 2023). We are arguably still in the process that companies are trying to make sense of their business, and both companies and their stakeholders need to improve their ability to get a better understanding of these metrics (Dechow, 2023). Once the accounting and reporting infrastructure, including those of internal management control systems, is fully implemented, an improvement may be expected in uniformity and comparability.

Despite the diverse range of stakeholder groups and the numerous ways corporate activities can impact them, sustainability criteria predominantly focus on limited aspects concerning only a subset of relevant stakeholders. In line with the US-based evidence (see Bebchuk & Tallarita, 2022), it emerged that while the stated aim of this form of executive remuneration is broad, with the implicit or explicit assumption of serving as an incentive mechanism to ensure the pursuit of stakeholders' welfare, in fact, most of the times, the incentive design has a relatively narrow scope. Sustainability-related KPIs focus chiefly on a restricted group of stakeholders, generally Employees and the Environment; they cover Customers to some extent, but include to a much smaller extent other stakeholders, such as Suppliers and Community. This lack of balance might reflect, in line with the stakeholder-agency perspective, the different relevance of specific stakeholder groups in relation to the company's strategy. However, for each stakeholder group considered, companies generally choose to address specific dimensions that represent only part of what these stakeholders care about, rather than the totality of such stakeholders' welfare. With respect to Employees, for instance, companies often choose KPIs related to health and safety or diversity and inclusion, but none of them incentivizes its CEO to increase employees' salaries (using, e.g., an executive-to-worker pay ratio as KPI). In addition, the use of some specific commonly used KPIs (e.g. those related to workers' health and safety) may also raise some concerns about whether and how companies are truly integrating sustainability issues in the CEO remuneration contract. By tying CEO remuneration to a company's safety performance, for example, a CEO would have a stronger incentive to prioritize workplace safety and take initiatives to prevent accidents, injuries, or potential health risks. However, financially incentivizing a CEO to pursue a safe work environment raises the question of why this incentive is needed. Safety should be a fundamental aspect of any business operation and CEOs already have a legal, and possibly moral, responsibility to ensure a safe work environment. We invite boards of directors to consider including such important sustainability-related issues in the remuneration contract as entry gates, i.e. necessary conditions to be met before becoming eligible for the performance-based remuneration. We also suggest corporate stakeholders, including investors, analyse the details of how sustainability-related criteria are integrated into remuneration design, rather than solely focusing on the mere adoption of sustainability-related criteria in the remuneration contract. Such details may impact the incentives provided to the recipient of the remuneration contract.

From an optimal contracting perspective, the lack of balance among the stakeholders' interests considered may be a theoretical necessity, as an incentive contract can hardly exhaustively incentivize targets that address all the interests and needs of all individuals and groups affected by a company's activities (Bebchuk & Tallarita, 2022). However, together with the lack of disclosure on some important elements of the executive remuneration design (e.g. target level and, to a lesser extent, the specific weight) and process (independent external audit of qualitative KPIs), this lack of balance raises some doubts about the overall effectiveness of the executive remuneration contracts to achieve the stated purpose and address all the stakeholder-executive agency relationships. If data becomes available, future studies could examine these important 'details' in the remuneration design and address the concerns (see, e.g., Bebchuk & Tallarita, 2022; Keddie & Magnan, 2023) that this form of executive remuneration might provide self-interested executives a powerful mechanism to increase their own financial reward without creating substantial value for stakeholders while potentially diluting executives' incentives to create value to shareholders.

In addition, this study focused on large, listed companies headquartered in highly developed European 'collaborative' countries (Fainshmidt et al., 2018) with a relatively high level of social and environmental regulatory pressure. While this choice enabled us to deepen our analysis, the investigation of smaller less visible companies or those listed in diverse institutional environments (e.g. market-based, emergent), where the phenomenon examined may have different characteristics, would provide a more comprehensive picture. Last but not least, due to its exploratory approach, this study did not analyse the antecedents of executive remuneration design or its outcomes. It could not address, *inter alia*, whether and how, for example, the adoption of this form of executive remuneration results in a reorganization of a company's internal processes. While these considerations impose some limitations on the interpretation of our results, they also offer interesting avenues for future research in the relatively uncharted field of the integration of sustainability criteria into executive remuneration contracts.

Acknowledgements This study was funded by the European Union - NextGenerationEU, in the framework of the GRINS -Growing Resilient, INclusive and Sustainable project (GRINS PE00000018 – CUP F53C22000760007). The views and opinions expressed are solely those of the authors and do not necessarily reflect those of the European Union, nor can the European Union be held responsible for them.

References

Almici, A. (2023). Does sustainability in executive remuneration matter? The moderating effect of Italian firms' corporate governance characteristics. *Meditari Accountancy Research, 31*(7), 49–87.

Aresu, S., Hooghiemstra, R., & Melis, A. (2023). Integration of CSR criteria into executive compensation contracts: A cross-country analysis. *Journal of Management*, 49(8), 2766–2804.

Baker, G. P. (1992). Incentive contracts and performance measurement. *Journal of Political Economy, 100*(3), 598–614.

Baraibar-Diez, E., Odriozola, M., & Fernandez-Sanchez, J. (2019). Sustainable compensation policies and its effect on environmental, social, and governance scores. *Corporate Social Responsibility and Environmental Management, 26*(6), 1457–1472.

Bebchuk, L., Fried, J., & Walker, D. (2002). Managerial power and rent extraction in the design of executive compensation. *University of Chicago Law Review, 69*, 751–846.

Bebchuk, L., & Tallarita, R. (2022). The perils and questionable promise of ESG-based compensation. *Journal of Corporation Law, 48*(1), 37–75.

Berrone, P., & Gomez-Mejia, L. (2009). Environmental performance and executive compensation: An integrated agency-institutional perspective. *Academy of Management Journal, 52*, 103–126.

Birkey, R. N., Michelon, G., Patten, D. M., & Sankara, J. (2016). Does assurance on CSR reporting enhance environmental reputation? An examination in the US context. *Accounting Forum, 40*(3), 143–152.

Bose, S., Burns, N., Minnick, K., & Shams, S. (2023). Climate-linked compensation, societal values, and climate change impact: International evidence. *Corporate Governance: An International Review, 31*(5), 759–785.

Burchman, S., & Sullivan, B. (2017). It's time to tie executive compensation to sustainability. *Harvard Business Review*, August, 17th.

Business Roundtable. (2019). *Business roundtable redefines the purpose of a corporation to promote "an economy that serves all Americans"*. Retrieved July 31, 2023, from https://www.businessroundtable.org/business-roundtable-redefines-the-purpose-of-a-corporation-to-promote-an-economy-that-serves-all-americans

Cavaco, S., Crifo, P., & Guidoux, A. (2020). Corporate social responsibility and governance: The role of executive compensation. *Industrial Relations, 59*(2), 240–274.

Cevian Capital. (2021). *Cevian Capital requires ESG targets in management compensation plans*. Press Release, March 3. Retrieved July 31, 2023, from https://www.ceviancapital.com/wp-content/uploads/2021/03/03.03.2021-Cevian-Capital-Requires-ESG-Targets-in-Management-Compensation-Plans.pdf

Code de gouvernement d'entreprise des sociétés cotées (2018), Paris: AFEP-MEDEF.

Cohen, S., Kadach, I., Ormazabal, G., & Reichelstein, S. (2023). Executive compensation tied to ESG performance: International evidence. *Journal of Accounting Research, 61*(3), 805–853.

Danone, S. A. (2023). *Universal Registration Document.*

Davos Manifesto. (2019). The Universal Purpose of a Company in the Fourth Industrial Revolution. *World Economic Forum*. Retrieved July 31, 2023, from https://www.weforum.org/agenda/2019/12/davos-manifesto-2020-the-universal-purpose-of-a-company-in-the-fourth-industrial-revolution/

Dechow, P. M. (2023). Understanding the sustainability reporting landscape and research opportunities in accounting. *The Accounting Review, 98*(5), 481–493.

Derchi, G. B., Zoni, L., & Dossi, A. (2021). Corporate social responsibility performance, incentives, and learning effects. *Journal of Business Ethics, 173*, 617–641.

Develay, E., Wang, Y., & Giamporcaro, S. (2023). The effectiveness of CSR Committees' characteristics and CSR contracting. *Academy of Management Proceedings, 1*, 14174.

Fainshmidt, S., Judge, W. Q., Aguilera, R. V., & Smith, A. (2018). Varieties of institutional systems: A contextual taxonomy of understudied countries. *Journal of World Business, 53*(3), 307–322.

Financial Times. (2023). *Investors warn 'fluffy' ESG metrics are being gamed to boost bonuses*, September 15th. Retrieved from https://www.ft.com/content/25aed60d-1deb-4a41-8f39-00c92702b663

Flammer, C., Hong, B., & Minor, D. (2019). Corporate governance and the rise of integrating corporate social responsibility criteria in executive compensation: Effectiveness and implications for firm outcomes. *Strategic Management Journal, 40*(7), 1097–1122.

Focke, M. (2022). Do sustainable institutional investors influence senior executive compensation structures according to their preferences? Empirical evidence from Europe. *Corporate Social Responsibility and Environmental Management, 29*(5), 1109–1121.

Freeman, R. (1984). *Strategic management: A stakeholder approach*. Pitman.

Friedman, A., & Miles, S. (2006). *Stakeholders: Theory and practice*. Oxford University Press.

García-Sánchez, I. M., Hussain, N., Martínez-Ferrero, J., & Ruiz-Barbadillo, E. (2019). Impact of disclosure and assurance quality of corporate sustainability reports on access to finance. *Corporate Social Responsibility and Environmental Management, 26*(4), 832–848.

Hartikainen, H., Järvenpää, M., & Rautiainen, A. (2021). Sustainability in executive remuneration-A missing link towards more sustainable firms? *Journal of Cleaner Production, 324*, 1–11.

Hill, C., & Jones, T. (1992). Stakeholder-agency theory. *Journal of Management Studies, 29*(2), 131–154.

Holmstrom, B., & Milgrom, P. (1991). Multitask principal–agent analyses: Incentive contracts, asset ownership, and job design. *The Journal of Law, Economics, and Organization, 7*(special issue), 24–52.

Hong, B., Li, Z., & Minor, D. (2016). Corporate governance and executive compensation for corporate social responsibility. *Journal of Business Ethics, 136*, 199–213.

Ikram, A., Li, Z., & Minor, D. (2023). CSR-contingent executive compensation contracts. *Journal of Banking & Finance, 151*(June).

Jensen, M., & Murphy, K. (1990). CEO incentives: It's not how much you pay, but how. *Harvard Business Review, 3*, 138–153.

Keddie, S. L., & Magnan, M. (2023). Are ESG performance-based incentives a panacea or a smokescreen for excess compensation? *Sustainability Accounting, Management and Policy Journal, 14*(3), 591–634.

Kolk, A., & Perego, P. (2014). Sustainable bonuses: Sign of corporate responsibility or window dressing? *Journal of Business Ethics, 119*, 1–15.

Lenihan, O., & Brennan, N. M. (2023). Do boards effectively link firm objectives to CEO bonus performance measures? *Journal of Management and Governance*, 1–28.

Melis, A., Carta, S., & Gaia, S. (2011). *I compensi basati su azioni. Principi, teorie ed evidenze empiriche*. Giuffrè Editore.

Melis, A., Carta, S., & Gaia, S. (2012). Executive remuneration in blockholder-dominated firms. How do Italian firms use stock options? *Journal of Management and Governance, 16*, 511–541.

Melis, A., Gaia, S., & Carta, S. (2015). Directors' remuneration: A comparison of Italian and UK non-financial listed firms' disclosure. *The British Accounting Review, 47*(1), 66–84.

Milgrom, P., & Roberts, J. (1992). *Economics, organization and management*. Prentice Hall.

Moncler Group. (2023). *Remuneration Report*.

Ott, C., & Endrikat, J. (2023). Exploring the association between financial and nonfinancial carbon-related incentives and carbon performance. *Accounting and Business Research, 53*(3), 271–304.

Peters, G. F., & Romi, A. M. (2015). The association between sustainability governance characteristics and the assurance of corporate sustainability reports. *Auditing: A Journal of Practice & Theory, 34*(1), 163–198.

Principles for Responsible Investment. (2012). *Integrating ESG Issues into Executive Pay*. United Nations Global Compact & Finance Initiative.

Qin, B., & Yang, L. (2022). CSR contracting and performance-induced CEO turnover. *Journal of Corporate Finance, 73*, 1–24.

Renault Group. (2023). *Universal Registration Document*.

Ritz, R. A. (2022). Linking executive compensation to climate performance. *California Management Review, 64*(3), 124–140.

Schneider Electric SE. (2023). *Universal Registration Document*.

Stathopoulos, K., & Talaulicar, T. (2023). The case for robust academic research on corporate governance. *Corporate Governance: An International Review, 31*(3), 400–404.

The Guardian. (2014). *An insider's view: Why more companies should tie bonuses to sustainability*. August 11th. Retrieved August 4, 2023, from https://www.theguardian.com/sustainable-business/2014/aug/11/executive-compensation-bonusessustainability-goals-energy-water-carbon-dsm

Tsang, A., Wang, K. T., Liu, S., & Yu, L. (2021). Integrating corporate social responsibility criteria into executive compensation and firm innovation: International evidence. *Journal of Corporate Finance, 70*, 1–27.

Yang, L. (2023). Compensation committee CSR-related expertise, CSR contracting quality, and performance implications. *Journal of Management Accounting Research, 35*(3), 197–223.

Chapter 9
ESG and Corporate Reputation in Energy Sector Companies

Caterina Aura and Eleonora Leandri

9.1 Introduction

Through the in-depth analysis of some case studies, the contribution developed in this chapter offers food for thought with which to stimulate a correct interpretation of the current corporate challenges linked to sustainability reporting and compliance with ESG criteria, which improve corporate reputation. Today, more than once, small and large companies must equip themselves with adequate tools to evaluate ESG factors and the related risks involved. The acronym ESG (Environmental, Social, and Governance) refers to the actions a company takes to contribute to the planet's current environmental and social challenges. ESG represent the 3 pillars of sustainability for the European Union, useful for verifying, measuring, and supporting the sustainability commitment of a company or organization (Galli & Torelli, 2021). Sustainability is a key component of a company's reputation and represents the most important economic challenge globally today. A constant, attentive commitment by companies to compliance with ESG criteria is not only and exclusively a way to create value, but a way to improve the image toward the outside; furthermore, public discussions of a company's ESG issues serve to build a consistent ESG reputation, which can lead to higher financial performance (Nicolas et al., 2024).

In these terms, sustainability is a decisive component of a company's reputation, representing one of the most important economic challenges globally today; sustainability, through an efficient knowledge management system, improves corporate reputation, guarantees business continuity, and implements the company's ability to produce and share value in the long term (Arduini et al., 2024). Being sustainable

C. Aura (✉) · E. Leandri
Department of Business Administration and Law, University of Calabria, Rende, Italy
e-mail: caterina.aura@unical.it; eleonora.leandri@unical.it

N. Castellano et al. (eds.), *Environmental, Social, Governance (ESG)*, SIDREA Series in Accounting and Business Administration,
https://doi.org/10.1007/978-3-031-76618-3_9

and adapting to ESG criteria is also essential to preserve one's reputation and to consolidate bonds of trust with potential stakeholders (Winit et al., 2023). This not only increases opportunities for collaboration, but also facilitates access to financing and liquidity. Companies that show low levels of ESG performance will have low credit, reputational and financial standing and will be perceived as at risk by investors (Pollice & Sponziello, 2024). As ESG (environmental, social, governance) issues have become a rightful part of analyzing the risk associated with investments and contractual relationships with partners, suppliers, and other types of third parties, correct estimation is important. Only by integrating ethical, social, and environmental issues into their strategies can companies improve their economic-financial performance, their commitment to sustainability, and therefore be more competitive and attract more investors. Improving ESG performance also improves corporate reputation. Starting from these premises, the chapter proposes an analysis on the topic of corporate reputation and its connection with ESG indicators. Specifically, we discuss how companies (in our case some companies in the energy sector), attentive to the risks linked to ESG factors manage to improve their corporate reputation. In fact, in the study by Maaloul et al. (2023), it is shown that companies that manage and disclose information on ESG issues have a better reputation, which in turn reduces debt financing costs. As a basis for analysis in the chapter, the ranking drawn up in Italy by "Reputation Science," a leading company in reputation analysis and management, is used. The company has developed a new "ESG Perception Index" tool useful for providing an overall picture of the companies perceived as most sustainable. The doctrine covered by the ESG Index has strongly focused on the resolution of social and environmental problems (Clement et al., 2023), which have accelerated the process of sustainable development, the only way to guarantee rational and long-lasting growth over time, preserving the planet and safeguarding the future of future generations.

In the following paragraphs, the sustainability report is discussed to subsequently introduce the analysis. After examining the framework proposed by the ESG Global Perception Index, we proceed with the analysis of the sustainability balance sheet of some companies in the energy sector which, based on the "ESG Perception Index" are positioned as the top ten most sustainable companies in Italy. Subsequently we tried to understand the reason for this ranking. The companies selected for the survey all belong to the energy sector and are characterized by being large listed companies, particularly attentive to the issue of sustainability, and therefore perceived as more sustainable. These are companies that, especially in recent years, have tried to contribute significantly to the process of sustainable growth, carrying out projects aimed at minimizing the impact on the environment, guaranteeing better working conditions, promoting economic and social development.

Finally, the results and conclusions are presented. What emerges from the investigation confirms the initial hypotheses. Specifically, from the analysis of case studies and their comparison, it is possible to demonstrate, through empirical evidence, how the use of corporate strategies in line with the objectives of the 2030 Agenda and therefore the ESG criteria can rapidly improve the reputation of companies, favoring higher ratings and consolidating the relationship of trust with their stakeholders.

9.2 Literature Review

The theoretical foundations and conceptual justifications of most ESG studies, academic and otherwise, are quite ancient and relate to corporate social responsibility (Irigaray & Stocker, 2022). Today, corporate social responsibility and environmental, social, and governance (ESG) criteria have emerged as guiding frameworks for companies to integrate sustainability and ethical practices into their core operations. They are of profound interest especially if analyzed as factors determining the reputation of companies. Despite the difference in roles, they are complementary in the definition of responsible and sustainable business practices. Environmental, social, and governance (ESG) integration has gained popularity since it was first introduced by the United Nations in 2004 (Eccles & Stroehle, 2018). Today it is considered one of the most innovative and used sustainability parameters globally. Over time, "the responsible attitude and virtuous behavior of companies" have evolved and grown above all thanks to Directive 2014/95/EU defined as NFRD (Non-Financial Reporting Directive), which made the communication of non-financial data in the financial statements mandatory, social sheet mandatory, at least for large companies, since 2017. In the study by Cicchiello et al. (2023), the effect of European regulation on non-financial reporting on the performance, commitment, and effectiveness of companies in environmental, social, and governance (ESG) matters is analyzed, demonstrating that NFRD regulation supports the adoption of ESG strategies that benefit society as a whole. Even companies that did not have the obligation have moved in this direction and have decided to deliberately draw up their own sustainability report, above all to improve their reputation externally. In November 2022, the European Parliament created the Corporate Sustainability Reporting Directive ("CSRD" or "Directive"), requiring companies to regularly report information on their social and environmental impact. In recent years, many scholars have analyzed the evolution of sustainability reporting present in the literature, also outlining future changes in the organizational and professional field in the face of the progressive incorporation of "sustainability practices" within corporate reporting (Abela, 2022; Lai & Stacchezzini, 2021).

Studies on sustainability and its various dimensions, environmental, economic, social, and cultural, have been at the center of the various scientific disciplines for at least two decades and, the recent global pandemic, due to the spread of Covid-19, with its disastrous consequences (Broadstock et al., 2021; Ferriani & Natoli, 2021; Savio et al., 2023), has contributed to focusing scholarly efforts on identifying concrete sustainability practices. CSR has been and still is at the center of important studies by various disciplines. To provide a measure of the meaning and value of the CSR dimension, ESG criteria were created. The turning point for a new path on sustainable finance issues occurred in 2015, with the adoption of the international

Agenda (Agenda 2023) on sustainable development. Research on the topic has also increased significantly following the signing by the 198 UN countries of the 2030 Agenda, an action plan for the prosperity of the planet and people which provides for the achievement of 17 objectives by the participating countries particularly ambitious (Wilburn & Wilburn, 2020; Baratta et al., 2023). This plan is part of multiple dynamics, ranging from quality education, to decent work, from the fight against climate change, to the adoption of new and more rational models of production and consumption, and so on. The 17 SDGs (Sustainable Development Goals) are at the heart of the 2030 Agenda for Sustainable Development that the Member States of the United Nations adopted in 2015 (Halkos & GKampoura, 2021). "The years 2022–2023 mark the halfway point for the implementation of the 2030 Agenda, offering a unique opportunity to analyze implementation challenges during the 7 years of SDG implementation so far and provide recommendations for the second half of the period towards 2030 (Biermann et al., 2022)."

At a certain point it was necessary to integrate the economic/financial aspects with organizational and operational aspects of an environmental, social, and governance nature. The SDGs, which play the role of broad objectives relating to broader contexts, have been combined with specific indicators for measuring sustainability performance, i.e. the ESGs. In the study by Delgado Ceballos et al. (2023), sustainable development goals are linked to corporate-level sustainability and ESG factors concluding that sustainability interventions can help solve the major ESG challenges contained in the SDGs. The need to integrate ESG factors into the financial sector therefore becomes a consolidated practice. As financial markets have begun to recognize the importance of pursuing sustainability outcomes in business, the concept of materiality has also gained traction in relation to environmental, social, and governance factors (MacNeil & Esser, 2022).

This represents a result partly due to regulatory evolution, which through the various directives of the European Commission has practically outlined its future obligation for all companies, and partly to the fact that "good sustainability practices" are increasingly considered useful tools to encourage the creation of value. The strong acceleration of sustainable growth dynamics has led to a notable development of sustainable and responsible investments, with the consequent appearance of ESG rating agencies. These agencies have the function of identifying and selecting those companies most in line with the new market expectations (Perrini & Iantosca, 2021). These are agencies called upon to evaluate the sustainability performance of companies and which, due to the ever-increasing importance that this activity is assuming, represent a point of reference for corporate organizations and financial markets in the current scenario. Even within academic studies, which are increasingly oriented toward examining the topic of sustainability in greater depth, there is a notable proliferation of qualitative-quantitative analyses regarding corporate sustainability assessments and their link with the results of activities and ESG indicators. As widely stated, ESG is a broader version of CSR (Saini et al., 2023), which in the past was already considered a green area under development (Lindgreen et al., 2009), very complex due to its different peculiarities, determined by the different analysis contexts such as the country, the sector, and the analysis time

(Kleine & Hauff, 2009). The criteria are developed in the wake of the dimensions on which CSR is based and, in this approach, analyses arise in the literature that evaluate the impact of CSR on the financial performance and social status of a company (Lech, 2013; Jha & Cox, 2015; Thuy et al., 2021, Baran et al., 2022). Today, ESG factors are becoming an indispensable objective for sustainability which is now becoming a consolidated practice by companies, together with the integration of ethical, social, and environmental values into their corporate strategies and business models with a view to sustainable finance (Widyawati, 2020). Investments in ESG-related activities are capable of strengthening the company's reputation and satisfying stakeholder expectations. "ESG in-vesting has moved from a niche topic to a central parameter for many investors in recent years" (Deutsche Bank 2022). Companies adopt ESG criteria to respond to different needs; for example, managers adopt them as a strategic lever (Zerbini, 2017; Park & Jang, 2021), to differentiate themselves from the competition (MBeji et al., 2021; Porter & Kramer, 2006; Serra Cantallops et al., 2018), improve company value and promote sustainability (Freeman, 1984), reduce costs (Porter et al., 2019), have positive effects on employees (Agarwal et al., 2012), improving their behavior and productivity (Park, 2020), also building customer loyalty (Kim & Park, 2017) and improving reputation (Murè et al., 2021). The trend suggests a moderately positive relationship between social and financial performance (Griffin & Mahon, 1997; Stanwick & Stanwick, 1998; Orlitzky et al., 2003; Bird et al., 2007; Barnett & Salomon, 2006; Van Beurden & Gossling, 2008; Yang, 2010).

In recent decades, in the field of sustainability, ESG factors have managed to acquire such relevance that they are currently considered pillars of company performance in the context of corporate economics. This is a line of research particularly appreciated by scholars and which, especially in the current context, represents one of the most debated topics precisely because of its direct connection with the topic of sustainability. It is understood that the scientific contributions that have followed one another over the decades have been able to capture various aspects, highlighting both the considerable advantages that can derive for companies that adopt "responsible behavior" and how the latter are able to guarantee better corporate performance. According to Arru and Ruggieri (2016), "the benefits linked to these practices, however, do not end in this relationship, also including the consolidation of the license to operate, the reduction of business risk, the increase in efficiency, tax breaks, in-crease in visibility, success and reputation, development of the ability to anticipate environmental trends, increase in staff motivation and involvement, increase in the level of safety and the ability to prevent crises." Assessing the ESG impact of a company therefore means observing whether and how it is able to produce positive value for the environment and its stakeholders.

In particular, the Environmental Principles evaluate the commitment adopted by a company in the use of clean energy and in defending environmental sustainability. The Social criteria, referring to the social impact of the company, examine its relationship with the community in which it operates (people, employees, suppliers, and customers). The term Governance concerns the ethical principles that regulate the management of the business system, such as respect for rights, inclusiveness, remuneration logic, and respect for minorities. The ways in which ESG information is communicated to stakeholders is so significant that the majority of investors make decisions also considering non-financial data (Sroka, 2013). The communication of information relating to the three ESG pillars is fundamental for a correct evaluation of stakeholders who are continuously engaged in close commercial relationships with companies. "Currently there are different metrics and different types of certification aimed at identifying and communicating to stakeholders the impact generated in the economic, environmental and social fields, however they present different limitations and there is no single reference standard" (Maggi, 2022). The new reputational challenge is played, in fact, along the lines of ESG. In fact, companies that face ESG controversies experience a significant negative effect on corporate value and an increase in risk, which can be reversed if the ESG score increases (Brighi et al., 2023). There can be no reputation linked to sustainability if there is no clear mapping of stakeholders (suppliers, collaborators and consultants, media, trade associations, territorial associations, and institutions). ESG sustainability reports are, in fact, aimed at all company stakeholders and are used to evaluate the performance and environmental, social, and governance impact of a company (Marcello & Loia, 2024). We are aware that it is the perception that stakeholders have of the reputation of a business organization which determines their propensity to make decisions (purchase, investment, etc.) regarding that company and its products. Building an ESG-proof reputation therefore means showing sensitivity and knowledge, even if not necessarily technical, toward business processes that impact all three ESG areas. It is not just about being and acting sustainably; it is equally important to know how to communicate externally, making all the commitment made by the company to pursue this mission shine through. The company's main stakeholders will then evaluate, based on this information, whether or not to undertake relationships with the company. Unfortunately, barriers to unlocking valuable ESG data for small businesses cause market inefficiencies that impact estimated financial costs and reputation (Akgun et al., 2021). There are numerous studies that investigate the link between CSR, reputation, and the economic-financial performance of companies (Burke & Logsdon, 1996; Ellen et al., 2006; Margolis & Walsh, 2003).

Some statistical surveys highlight how, especially in recent years, consumers' attention toward their purchases has significantly increased. An increasingly responsible attitude is spreading, based on conscious choices, the result of an accurate evaluation of the quality of the products, their origin, the production methods, the ethical behavior adopted or not by companies. In fact, it is precisely the culture underlying corporate organizations that can and, indeed, today, must make the difference. Businesses, as open and dynamic systems, are asked not only to know how to adapt to the transformations of society but also to know how to anticipate and stimulate change, and therefore to be innovative. Furthermore, companies interact with a variety of subjects, from whom they receive impulses and to whom they in turn transfer others. In such a dense network of relationships, and in such a complex scenario as the current one, it is inevitable that the expectations of the various corporate stakeholders are also very high. In the current global scenario, in which climate change represents a real threat, reviewing one's business models by directing

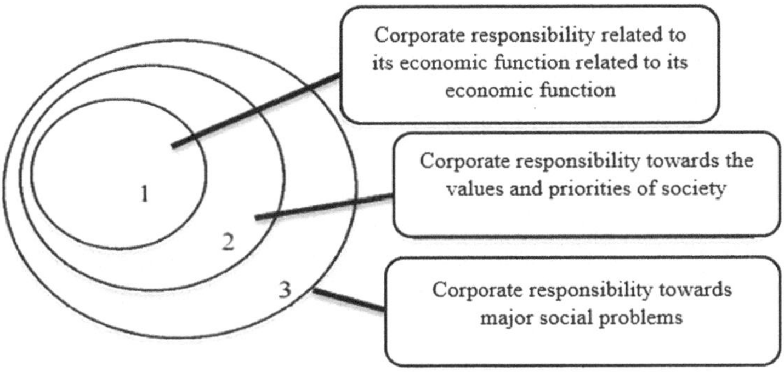

Fig. 9.1 Concentric circles model. Source: Nigro and Petracca, 2016

them toward the concrete pursuit of sustainable development objectives offers corporate organizations an extraordinary opportunity to attract investors and enter new markets. The inclusion of ESG—Environmental, Social, and Governance—factors in company assets is therefore fundamental, even when not mandatory, to improve the company's image and reputation externally. In fact, these are factors capable of significantly influencing the reputation of companies and their consequent ability to attract resources. Business studies, in which stakeholder theory and CSR—Corporate Social Responsibility—now represent pillars, highlight how in the current global market companies can no longer be oriented only toward profit maximization. Current challenges require the adoption of strategies capable of integrating ethical, social, and environmental issues, which have long been considered, according to numerous scientific contributions, capable of improving corporate performance (Barnett & Salomon, 2006; Luo & Bhattacharya, 2006; Giacomello, 2012; Arru & Ruggieri, 2016) and favor the acquisition of a competitive advantage. Environmental protection, the reduction of CO_2 emissions, waste management, the well-being, health and safety of workers, the management of fair working hours and wages, the implementation of ethical choices are just some examples of important factors which, if included in company policies and adequately represented in social balance sheets, can contribute to strengthening the image of companies, promoting their lasting success over time.

In the model of concentric circles (Fig. 9.1) published by the Committee for Economic Development (CED), in 2016, within the report "Corporate Social Responsibility" it is stated that "the company works thanks to public consensus and its fundamental purpose is to constructively serve the needs of society to the satisfaction of society."

The social, environmental, and ethical aspects of the company combine with each other in order to stimulate a favorable economic and social situation, from which both internal subjects and stakeholders can benefit.

Thanks to CSR, the inclusion of good sustainable development practices in the core business of companies, it is possible to promote the stability of profits in the long term, making organizations less prone to ambiguous behavior and less vulnerable to changes in political-social values, from increase in unemployment and discrimination.

We therefore confirm the importance of CSR as indicated in the concentric circle model, as a general ethic that pushes a company to adopt policies and practices that support sustainability without forgetting, however, that without the aspects measured by ESG, it cannot be emphasized for a long time, as the market requires quantitative measurement of impacts. Here we must not over-look the ESG aspects which refer to the rational and quantitative aspect of the long-term growth strategy and which should motivate a company's sustainability program. In summary, while CSR focuses primarily on the social aspects of corporate engagement, ESG broadens the vision to include environmental impact and corporate governance. Both approaches are important to ensure sustainable management of companies in the current economic environment and ensure a positive corporate reputation.

9.3 The Social Balance Sheet in European Legislation

Reporting on non-financial aspects relating to sustainability has become increasingly important and interesting for companies, to the point of drawing up the "Sustainability Report." The success of companies is no longer measured exclusively by their financial results, but also by their responsibility toward society (Primec & Belak, 2017). However, it should be noted that the interest in "the responsible attitude of companies" has grown strongly over time not only because the adoption of virtuous behavior can be ethically appreciable but also because enhancing the aspects of the ethical-socio-environmental sphere has become mandatory, at least for large companies, since 2017. In fact, retracing the evolutionary process of European legislation, Directive 2014/95/EU of the European Commission, known by the acronym NFRD (Non-Financial Reporting Directive), adopted in 2014 and implemented in Italy in 2016, represented a significant change of pace on the topic of sustainability reporting. Non-financial reporting represents the first legal step toward the implementation of socially responsible corporate governance, whose global trend began in the 1950s, and (Primec & Belak, 2022) introducing the obligation for companies to report how sustainability issues influence their performance, position, and development (the "outside-in" perspective) and their impact on people and the environment (the "inside-out" perspective). The directive imposed the obligation on all "large companies that constitute entities of public interest and which, at the balance sheet date, have an average number of employees employed during the financial year equal to 500." In reality, driven by this legislation, many other companies, other than those required by law, have already voluntarily started to independently draw up their own sustainability report. These are companies that, aware of the importance of the topic, have deemed it useful to firmly disclose their commitment to sustainability, thus also anticipating subsequent regulatory developments. Developments that did not take long to wait given that, in November 2022, the European Parliament adopted the Corporate Sustainability Reporting Directive ("CSRD" or "Directive"), i.e. the Directive with the new rules for corporate sustainability reporting. Directive that will make companies more accountable to the public by obliging them to regularly disclose information on their social and environmental impact. Reporting and its now mandatory nature will therefore make sustainability an integral part of every business process and companies will have to be able to communicate their policy effectively. Sustainability which until some time ago represented a great opportunity is transformed into the real discriminating factor on which the possibility of being present on the market or not will depend. These are in fact the reasons that have pushed many scholars to concentrate their efforts, especially in recent years, on the evolution of sustainability reporting, also outlining possible future changes in the organizational and professional field in the face of the progressive and ever-increasing incorporation of sustainability in the context of corporate reporting (Abela, 2022; Lai & Stacchezzini, 2021; Larrinaga & Bebbington, 2021). Currently, the perception of the company image represents the factor that most influences stakeholders' decisions compared to the various technical ratings, which is why it is essential to measure it. Companies involved in ESG scandals suffer serious reputational and, consequently, financial damage (Aouadi & Marsat, 2018; Shakil, 2021; Liu et al., 2023). The analysis of the communication of risks connected to ESG variables by companies is important to understand their point of view.

9.4 The Case Studies: Eni, Enel, and Terna

In this section, the sustainability reports of Eni, Enel, and Terna are examined with the aim of evaluating the relationship between corporate reputation and ESG indicators. These three companies were chosen because they are companies recognized at a national and international level for the particular attention they show in implementing activities that respect the environment, local communities, and the work carried out by their employees. These companies are in fact able to integrate their business activities with sustainability issues, thus managing to adopt ethically responsible behavior toward the entire community. The approach of the three companies is summarized in their respective Sustainability Reports (years 2020/2021); the document, which is mandatory, is divided into three different sections, corresponding to the triple line of analysis (economic, social, and environmental). Specifically, it is demonstrated, through the analysis of these documents, how companies that pay more attention and therefore invest more resources in ESG factors are able to improve their corporate reputation. Previous studies, in different fields, such as banking (Galletta et al., 2022), have examined the impact between ESG factors and reputation, demonstrating that higher ESG scores reduce bank operational risk. As already reiterated previously, analyzing the impact of the integration of ESG criteria in the evaluation of corporate reputation is fundamental because the perception that stakeholders have of a company's reputation is often decisive in their purchase and investment decisions. In these terms, sustainability is a decisive component of a company's reputation, representing one of the most important economic challenges globally today. A constant and attentive commitment on the part of companies to compliance with ESG criteria is not only and exclusively a way of creating value, but rather a way of improving the image toward the outside.

9.5 The Methodology

In Italy, "Reputation Science," a leading company in the analysis and management of reputation, has developed a new tool "ESG Perception Index" useful for providing a general picture of the companies perceived as the most sustainable. An analysis is proposed, based on company reports, and the "ESG Perception Index" for the measurement of companies in the three areas of ESG, compared with some corporate reputation data, on a sample of companies belonging to the energy sector. The research methodology adopted is based on a qualitative approach. After the reconstruction of a theoretical reference framework, we will proceed with the analysis of the sustainability balance sheet of some companies in the energy sector which, on the basis of the "ESG Perception Index" are positioned among the top ten most sustainable companies in Italy, all belonging to the energy sector and characterized by being large listed companies, particularly attentive to the issue of sustainability, so much so that they are considered the most sustainable. These are companies which, especially in recent years, have sought to contribute significantly to the process of sustainable growth, placing projects aimed at minimizing the impact on the environment, ensuring better working conditions, to promote economic and social development.

As reported on the online site, "ESG Perception Index" (Fig. 9.2) is the index developed by Reputation Science, to measure the perception of sustainability of companies.

9.6 Analysis and Discussion: Financial Statements Compared

The data shown in Fig. 9.2 shows Enel, Eni, and Terna in order of position. These companies are part of the energy sector and, according to what is assessed by the Perception Index, are the best performing in terms of actions relating to the sphere of ESG dimensions, and therefore of perception of sustainability. The analysis model we are going to observe "evaluates the proximity of the brand to the 17 pillars of sustainability defined by the UN and produces for each an indicator (from 0 to 100) based on qualitative-quantitative and structural parameters: in addition to the volume of content that report the association between the brand and sustainability, the reputational impact of this content on the brand also weighs on the score, the

Fig. 9.2 ESG Perception Index. Source: https://www.esgreputation.it

association of the brand identity with sustainability on search engines and how much the company talks about sustainability through its proprietary channels such as website and social profiles." The unit of measurement of online reputation is represented by an aggregate index which is expressed in R. The R value applied to each individual web content detected takes into consideration 104 distinct parameters including global parameters relating to the domain and specific parameters of each link. All the results of the analysis are subjected to consultative re-reading. The trend of the ESG Global Perception Index over time allows us to understand trends and random or structural changes in companies which are useful for predictive analysis and for the identification of a specific evolving trend line.

The index calculated by ESG global on the top200 shows that between October 2022 and April 2023, (Fig. 9.3) the sustainability reputation of the companies included is declining; specifically, a peak was reached in the first half of 2023 and then in the second part of the year there was a significant decline of 69%. This situation can be seen if we observe the 200 companies included in the ESG Perception Index sample.

If, however, we look specifically at the top 10 companies (Fig. 9.4) which also include Enel, Eni, and Terna, we note that they are still the driving force as they show a better reputation for sustainability, and alone, they obtain an ESG Global Perception Index equal to at R340,061, which represents 35% of the entire inclusive basket of over 200 companies. A percentage up by 11 points compared to the last half-yearly survey in October 2022. The global index settles at higher levels than

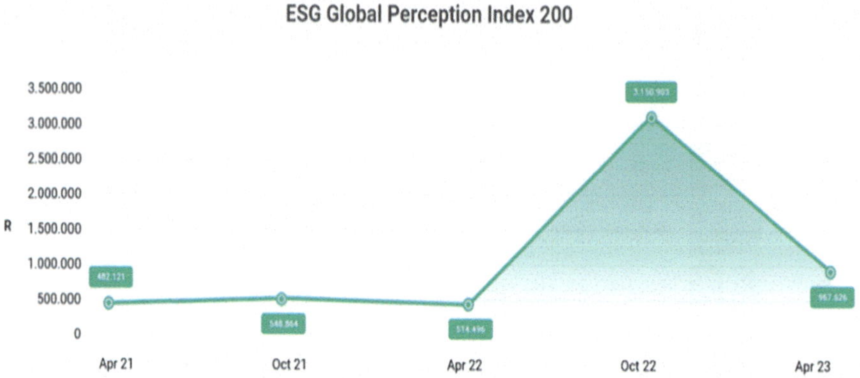

Fig. 9.3 ESG Perception Index200 in the period between April 2021 and April 2023. Source: https://www.esgreputation.it October 2021

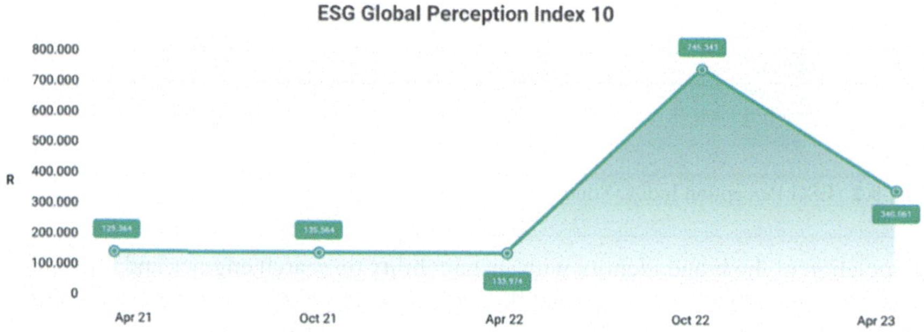

Fig. 9.4 ESG Perception Index10 in the period between April 2021 and April 2023. Source: https://www.esgreputation.it October 2021

those recorded a year earlier (514,496 R) despite the decline recorded in the semester under analysis. The half-yearly trend is particularly dynamic starting from April 2022 when compared with the stationarity trend found in previous index surveys.

This shows that despite the energy crisis and the conflict of the Russia-Ukraine bloc, companies operating in the energy sector are always among the first on the list from a reputation point of view.

If we compare the sustainability reports of the first three companies firstly for questions of practicality and then above all of homogeneity, as they operate in the same sector we realize why they are classified according to this logic.

For example, Enel holds the record thanks to the now historic permanence of some sustainability indices such as FTSE4Good, Dow Jones and for a series of other initiatives that support waste recycling according to the circular economy paradigm such as “Enel in circulation,” which aims to transform waste into works of art, and a series of other initiatives. Furthermore, between April and October 2022, it was awarded at the CEO for Life Lundbeck Awards for making a free psychological support and support service available to employees during the pandemic. The initiatives for the redevelopment of power plants, the partnerships to support electric mobility, and the "Piazza dei Mestieri" social entrepreneurship project have also achieved great reputational impact.

Eni second in the ranking enjoys this position thanks to its green initiatives such as Plenitude, which is a "Benefit company or an Italian company 100% controlled by Eni SpA, which integrates the sale and marketing of gas and electricity for families and companies with the production of renewable energy and the management of charging points for electric vehicles." Among the actions most focused on sustainability, we find the Eni Award, which is considered an international point of reference for research in the fields of energy and the environment. Eni has also given greater importance to green projects which emphasize the sustainable activities of the six-legged dog by seeking new foreign stakeholders as partners for the supply of gas, a purely Italian strategy useful for freeing its supplies from Moscow.

Terna, on the other hand, ranks third, due to the large investment of 10 billion euros in actions aimed at promoting the energy transition and also because it was judged as the best company/employer in the utilities segment. It also inaugurated its own Academy for research and training, signed a partnership with Pirelli for the development of sustainable mobility and took part in the Stanford University program for education and awareness on energy issues.

9.7 Conclusions

The objective of the research was to provide a contribution on the topic of CSR and ESG criteria of companies, highlighting how CSR is directly linked to ESG indicators, which have become increasingly discriminating in the choices made by both investors and consumers during their approach to companies in which to invest or establish lasting relationships. Through an in-depth analysis of the most recent developments on the topic and the analysis of some case studies, we intended to try to strengthen the thesis according to which companies which, through concrete projects, adopt virtuous behavior toward the planet and people, have a greater probability of establishing themselves as sustainable companies. The research work that was presented attempted to limit and analyze the most significant activities implemented by the companies observed and which contributed to their positioning among the top positions of the companies perceived as most sustainable. Observed companies that have adopted an ESG approach are reaping benefits across all sectors, improving their reputation. Environmental, social, and governance factors have become an integral part of corporate strategies. The data expressed in the sustainability reports of these companies are very important for stakeholders because today they represent the only evaluation tool, together with ESG criteria, to evaluate them from a reputational point of view. By observing the data from the ESG Global Perception Index ranking, we understood that in the relationship between ESG and reputation, the most sustainable companies from a reputational point of view are those operating in the energy sector. The most represented cluster among the

20 companies perceived as most sustainable on the web is the one dedicated to energy (40%): a figure that confirms the weight of this sector in the ESG Perception Index. The ESG Global Perception Index, while on the one hand highlighting the strong growth in brand communication in the ESG field, on the other shows the sharp decline in reputation regarding sustainability. The only sector that is not affected by the decline in reputation is the energy sector. The supremacy of the energy sector is probably clearly visible and perceived because this sector today is certainly one of the main suspects among the anthropogenic causes of global warming. Furthermore, energy is central to almost every major challenge and opportunity facing the world today. Whether it's jobs, security, climate change, food production, or increasing incomes, access to energy is essential. Companies operating in this sector probably feel more burdened by these responsibilities toward the planet, which is why they move with greater commitment, through sustainability actions imposed by the famous 2030 Agenda Objectives, which currently represent the "document" that best manages to explain the way in which sustainability must be applied to guarantee healthy, tolerable, and lasting growth, through the involvement of central governments, local institutions, businesses, and citizens. Sustainable energy is an opportunity to transform lives, the economy, and the planet. Over the last decade, sustainability has rapidly penetrated all different areas of society. In fact, it has found wide application not only in environmental protection practices, in the mechanisms for reducing CO2 emissions, in the use of new energy sources but also in the dynamics of education and training, in the inclusion of the most vulnerable categories, in working conditions, in relations with institutions, in the methods of access to resources, and in those of distribution of wealth. All these conditions, if validly underlined and valorized, make companies more sustainable and the related brands are perceived by stakeholders as the best and most sustainable, improving their image and therefore their reputation. Finally, the results suggest that ESG control is important not only from a macro sustainability point of view, but also from the point of view of the risk-return relationship of the individual company (Brighi et al., 2023), therefore also reputational. Implementing CSR and ESG can improve the company's image in the eyes of consumers, employees, investors, and other stakeholders. Demonstrating commitment to social responsibility and positive impact on the environment and society can generate trust and loyalty. Modern consumers expect companies to be both socially and environmentally responsible. Adopting CSR and ESG practices allows companies to meet these expectations, strengthening customer trust, improving corporate reputation, and increasing consumer loyalty. Having ethical and sustainable policies, scrupulously managing environmental issues and caring about the well-being of employees can reduce the chance of legal problems or reputational damage. Studying aspects of CSR by integrating its quantitative measurement through ESG has become a priority for many companies, not only for the good of the planet, but also for the long-term success and reputation of the company it-self.

References

Abela, M. (2022). A new direction? The "mainstreaming" of "sustainability reporting". *Sustainability Accounting, Management and Policy Journal, 13*(6), 1261–1283.

Agarwal, U. A., Datta, S., Blake-Beard, S., & Bhargava, S. (2012). Linking LMX, innovative work behavior and turnover intentions: The mediating role of work engagement. *Career Development International, 17*(3), 208–230.

Akgun, O. T., Mudge, T. J., III, & Townsend, B. (2021). How company size bias in ESG scores impacts the small cap investor. *The Journal of Impact and ESG Investing, 1*(4), 31–44.

Aouadi, A., & Marsat, S. (2018). Do ESG controversies matter for firm value? *Evidence from International Data, Journal of Business Ethics, Springer, 151*(4), 1027–1047.

Arduini, S., Manzo, M., & Beck, T. (2024). Corporate reputation and culture: The link between knowledge management and sustainability. *Journal of Knowledge Management, 28*(4), 1020–1041. https://doi.org/10.1108/JKM-02-2023-0139

Arru, B., & Ruggieri, M. (2016). The benefits of corporate social responsibility in the creation of sustainable value: The role of expertise resources and reputational capital. *Business Economics Online, 7*(1), 17–41.

Baran, M., Kuźniarska, A., Makieła, Z. J., Sławik, A., & Stuss, M. M. (2022). Does ESG reporting relate to corporate financial performance in the context of the energy sector transformation? Evidence from Poland. *Energies, 15*(2), 477. https://doi.org/10.3390/en15020477

Baratta, A., Cimino, A., Longo, F., Solina, V., & Verteramo, S. (2023). The impact of ESG practices in industry with a focus on carbon emissions: Insights and future perspectives. *Sustainability, 15*(8), 6685.

Barnett, M. L., & Salomon, R. M. (2006). Beyond dichotomy: The curvilinear relationship between social responsibility and financial performance. *Strategic Management Journal, 27*(11), 1101–1122.

Biermann, F., Hickmann, T., Sénit, C.-A., Beisheim, M., Bernstein, S., Chasek, P., Grob, L., Kim, R. E., et al. (2022). Scientific evidence on the political impact of the sustainable development goals. *Nature Sustainability, 5*, 795–800.

Bird, R. D., Hall, A., Momentè, F., & Reggiani, F. (2007). What corporate social responsibility activities are valued by the market? *Journal of Business Ethics, 76*, 189–206.

Brighi, P., Della Bina, A. C. F., & Valeria, V. (2023). L'orientamento Esg delle imprese europee. Controversie, valore e rischi. *BANCARIA, 6*, 15–33.

Broadstock, D. C., Chan, K., Cheng, L. T., & Wang, X. (2021). The role of ESG performance during times of financial crisis: Evidence from COVID-19 in China. *Finance Research Letters, 38*, 101716.

Burke, L., & Logsdon, J. M. (1996). How corporate social responsibility pays off. *Long Range Planning, 29*(4), 495–502.

Cicchiello, A. F., Marrazza, F., & Perdichizzi, S. (2023). Normativa sulla divulgazione non finanziaria e performance ambientale, sociale e di governance (ESG): il caso delle aziende europee e statunitensi. *Responsabilità sociale d'impresa e gestione am-bientale, 30*(3), 1121–1128.

Clément, A., Robinot, É., & Trespeuch, L. (2023). The use of ESG scores in academic literature: A systematic literature review. *Journal of Enterprising Communities: People and Places in the Global Economy.*

Delgado-Ceballos, J., Ortiz-De-Mandojana, N., Antolín-López, R., & Montiel, I. (2023). Connecting the sustainable development goals to firm-level sustainability and ESG factors: The need for double materiality. *BRQ Business Research Quarterly, 26*(1), 2–10. https://doi.org/10.1177/23409444221140919

Eccles, R. G., & Stroehle, J. (2018). Exploring social origins in the construction of ESG measures. Electron SSRN Journal

Ellen, P. S., Webb, D. J., & Mohr, L. A. (2006). Building corporate associations: Consumer attributions for corporate socially responsible programs. *Journal of the Academy of Marketing Science, 34*, 147–157.

Ferriani, F., & Natoli, F. (2021). ESG risks in times of Covid-19. *Applied Economics Letters, 28*(18), 1537–1541.

Freeman, R. E. (1984). *Strategic management: A stakeholder approach*. Cambridge University Press.

Galletta, S., Mazzù, S., & Naciti, V. (2022). A bibliometric analysis of ESG performance in the banking industry: From the current status to future directions. *Research in International Business and Finance, 62*, 101684.

Galli, D., & Torelli, R. (Eds.). (2021). *Il valore della sostenibilità: modelli emergenti di rendicontazione non finanziaria tra le imprese italiane leader ESG*. FrancoAngeli.

Giacomello, L. (2012). Environmental innovation as a strategic factor: An analysis in the furniture sector.

Griffin, J. J., & Mahon, J. F. (1997). The corporate social performance and corporate financial performance debate: Twenty-five years of incomparable research. *Business & Society, 36*(1), 5–31. https://doi.org/10.1177/000765039703600102

Halkos, G., & Gkampoura, E.-C. (2021). Where do we stand on the 17 Sustainable Development Goals? An overview on progress. *Economic Analysis and Policy, 70*, 94–122, ISSN 0313-5926. https://doi.org/10.1016/j.eap.2021.02.001

Irigaray, H. A. R., & Stocker, F. (2022). ESG: New concept for old problems. *Cadernos EBAPE. BR, 20*, 1–4.

Jha, A., & Cox, J. (2015). Corporate social responsibility and social capital. *Journal of Banking & Finance, 60*, 252–270.

Kim, W. C., & Park, J. W. (2017). Examining structural relationships between work engagement, organizational procedural justice, knowledge sharing, and innovative work behavior for sustainable organizations. *Sustainability, 9*, 205.

Kleine, A., & Hauff, M. (2009). Sustainability-driven implementation of corporate social responsibility: Application of the integrative sustainability triangle. *Journal of Business Ethics, 85*, 517–533.

Lai, A., & Stacchezzini, R. (2021). Organizational and professional challenges amid the evolution of sustainability reporting: A theoretical framework and an agenda for future research. *Meditari Accountancy Research, 29*(3), 405–429.

Larrinaga, C., & Bebbington, J. (2021). The pre-history of sustainability reporting: A constructivist reading. *Accounting, Auditing & Accountability Journal, 34*(9), 162–181.

Lech, A. (2013). Corporate social responsibility and financial performance. Theoretical and empirical aspects. *Comparative Economic Research Central and Eastern Europe, 16*, 49–62.

Lindgreen, A., Swaen, V., & Maon, F. (2009). Introduction: Corporate social responsibility implementation. *Journal of Business Ethics, 85*, 251–256.

Liu, J., Ge, Z., & Wang, Y. (2023). Role of environmental, social, and governance rating data in predicting financial risk and risk management. *Corporate Social Responsibility and Environmental Management, 31*(1), 260–273.

Luo, X., & Bhattacharya, C. B. (2006). Corporate social responsibility, customer satisfaction, and market value. *Journal of Marketing, 70*(4), 1–18.

Maaloul, A., Zéghal, D., Ben Amar, W., & Mansour, S. (2023). The effect of environ-mental, social, and governance (ESG) performance and disclosure on cost of debt: The mediating effect of corporate reputation. *Corporate Reputation Review, 26*(1), 1–18.

MacNeil, I., & Esser, I. M. (2022). From a financial to an entity model of ESG. *European Business Organization Law Review, 23*(1), 9–45.

Maggi, D. (2022). Methods and opportunities for applying the new paradigm of ESG metrics to social enterprise. https://hdl.handle.net/11579/157482.

Marcello, R., & Loia, A. M. (2024). L'integrazione dei fattori esg nel processo di risk governance: pianificazione strategica e disclosure. *Società & contratti, bilancio & revisione, 2*, 84–103.

Margolis, J. D., & Walsh, J. P. (2003). Misery loves companies: Rethinking social initiatives by business. *Administrative Science Quarterly, 48*, 268–305.
MBeji, R., Yousfi, O., Loukil, N., & Omri, A. (2021). Board diversity and corporate social responsibility: Empirical evidence from France. *Journal of Business Ethics, 173*(1), 133–155.
Murè, P., Spallone, M., Mango, F., Marzioni, S., & Bittucci, L. (2021). ESG and reputation: The case of sanctioned Italian banks. *Corporate Social Responsibility and Environmental Management, 28*(1), 265–277.
Nicolas, M. L., Desroziers, A., Caccioli, F., & Aste, T. (2024). ESG reputation risk matters: An event study based on social media data. *Finance Research Letters, 59*, 104712.
Nigro, C., & Petracca, M. (2016). *Corporate social responsibility: From its origins to the situationist approach, focus on isomorphism and decoupling processes*. Giappicchelli.
Orlitzky, M., Schmidt, F. L., & Rynes, S. L. (2003). Corporate social and financial performance: A meta-analysis. *Organization Studies, 24*(3), 403–441.
Park, K. O. (2020). How CSV and CSR affect organizational performance: A productive behavior perspective. *International Journal of Environmental Research and Public Health, 17*, 2556.
Park, S. R., & Jang, J. Y. (2021). The impact of ESG management on investment decision: Institutional investors' perceptions of country-specific ESG criteria. *International Journal of Financial Studies, 9*(3), 48. https://doi.org/10.3390/ijfs9030048
Perrini, F., & Iantosca, A. (2021). I rating ESG: amarli o odiarli? *Economia & management: la rivista della Scuola di Direzione Aziendale dell'Università L. Bocconi, 1*, 19–22.
Pollice, F., & Sponziello, M. (2024). Capitolo ii le norme che regolano le società benefit. Le società benefit e I fattori ESG per la valorizzazione del patrimonio culturale in Ita-lia: Società Benefit and ESG Standard for the enhancement of Cultural Heritage in Italy, 47.
Porter, M. E., & Kramer, M. R. (2006). Strategy & society: The link between competitive advantage and corporate social responsibility. *Harvard Business Review, 84*(12), 78–92.
Porter, M., Serafeim, G., & Kramer, M. (2019). Where ESG fails. Institutional Investor. https://www.institutionalinvestor.com/article/b1hm5ghqtxj9s7/Where-ESG-Fails
Primec, A., & Belak, J. (2017). Corporate governance and management: Institutional and formal approach for achieving socially responsible and corporate governance of a higher quality. In *Proceedings of the paradoxes of leadership and governance in the postmodern society, 5th international OFEL conference on Corporate Governance, Management and Entrepreneurship, Dubrovnik, Croatia, 7–8 April 2017* (pp. 154–164). CIRU—Governance Research and Development Centre.
Primec, A., & Belak, J. (2022). Sustainable CSR: Legal and managerial demands of the new EU legislation (CSRD) for the future corporate governance practices. *Sustainability, 14*(24), 16648. https://doi.org/10.3390/su142416648
Saini, M., Aggarwal, V., Dhingra, B., Kumar, P., & Yadav, M. (2023). ESG and financial variables: A systematic review. *International Journal of Law and Management, 65*(6), 663–682. before printing No. before printing. https://doi.org/10.1108/IJLMA-02-2023-0033
Savio, R., D'Andrassi, E., & Ventimiglia, F. (2023). A systematic literature review on ESG during the COVID-19 pandemic. *Sustainability, 15*(3), 2020.
Serra-Cantallops, A., Peña-Miranda, D. D., Ramón-Cardona, J., & Martorell-Cunill, O. (2018). Progress in research on CSR and the hotel industry (2006–2015). *Cornell Hospitality Quarterly, 59*(1), 15–38.
Shakil, M. H. (2021). Environmental, social and governance performance and financial risk: Moderating role of ESG controversies and board gender diversity. *Resources Policy, 72*, 102144, ISSN 0301-4207. https://doi.org/10.1016/j.resourpol.2021.102144
Stanwick, P. A., & Stanwick, S. D. (1998). The relationship between corporate social performance, and organizational size, financial performance, and environmental performance: An empirical examination. *Journal of Business Ethics, 17*(2), 195–204.
Sroka, R. (2013). Association of stock exchange issuers, GES and Crido Business Consulting. Warszawa, pp. 49–63.

Thuy, C. T. M., Khuong, N. V., Canh, N. T., & Liem, N. T. (2021). Corporate social responsibility disclosure and financial performance: The mediating role of financial statement comparability. *Sustainability, 13*, 10077.

Van Beurden, P., & Gössling, T. (2008). The worth of values–a literature review on the relation between corporate social and financial performance. *Journal of Business Ethics, 82*, 407–424.

Widyawati, L. (2020). A systematic literature review of socially responsible investment and environmental social governance metrics. *Business Strategy and the Environment, 29*(2), 619–637.

Wilburn, K., & Wilburn, R. (2020). ESG reporting using UN sustainable development goals. *Journal of Strategic Innovation & Sustainability, 15*(2).

Winit, W., Ekasingh, E., & Sampet, J. (2023). How disclosure types of sustainability performance impact consumers' relationship quality and firm reputation. *Sustainability, 15*(1), 803.

Yang, F. J., Lin, C. W., & Chang, Y. N. (2010). The linkage between corporate social performance and corporate financial performance. *African Journal of Business Management, 4*(4), 406.

Zerbini, F. (2017). CSR initiatives as market signals: A review and research agenda. *Journal of Business Ethics, 146*(1), 1–23.

Chapter 10
ESG Performance, Corporate Governance Mechanisms, and ESG Risk Rating: Evidence from Europe

Cristina Florio, Silvia Panfilo, and Simona Fiandrino

10.1 Introduction

Environmental, Social, and Governance (ESG)[1] risks have become increasingly prominent in recent years. According to the Global Risk Report 2024 (World Economic Forum, 2024), environmental risk caused by extreme weather events is the top risk most likely to present a material crisis on a global scale in 2024. Climate and environmental risks are the core focus of global risks perceived over the next decade, and at the same time, they are those risks that firms, regulators, and civil society are least prepared to face. Moreover, misinformation and disinformation that widen societal and political divides are perceived as an emerging risk for the following years (World Economic Forum, 2024). Overall, ESG risks are stretching the capacity to respond to critical global challenges to their limit; therefore, supportive actions from different actors have become urgent.

[1] In line with previous research (Lewellyn & Muller-Kahle, 2023; Gillan et al., 2021), we interchange the terms ESG, sustainability, and Corporate Social Responsibility (CSR), although these three terms have specific constructs. ESG concerns a firm's business activity's environmental, social, and governance aspects. Sustainability refers to fulfilling the needs of current generations without compromising the needs of future generations while ensuring a balance between economic growth, environmental issues, and social well-being. CSR refers to voluntary social and environmental activities companies engage in by considering stakeholders' interests.

C. Florio (✉)
Department of Management, University of Verona, Verona, Italy
e-mail: cristina.florio@univr.it

S. Panfilo
Venice School of Management, Ca' Foscari University of Venice, Venice, Italy

S. Fiandrino
Department of Management, University of Turin, Turin, Italy

N. Castellano et al. (eds.), *Environmental, Social, Governance (ESG)*, SIDREA Series in Accounting and Business Administration,
https://doi.org/10.1007/978-3-031-76618-3_10

According to a recent survey conducted by PwC (Chalmers et al., 2021), global investors are paying increasing attention to ESG risks and opportunities facing the companies they can invest in. Nearly 80% of the respondents maintained that ESG was an essential factor in their investment decisions, and about 50% expressed the intention to divest from companies that did not take sufficient action on ESG issues. Similarly, a survey conducted by the Morgan Stanley Institute for Sustainable Investing (Morgan Stanley, 2021) shows that the interest in ESG investing jumped from 71% in 2015 to 85% in 2019 among the general population of investors and from 84% to 95% among millennial investors.

Following the increased attention to sustainability issues, large, listed companies are progressively addressing ESG objectives in their corporate strategy and managerial decision-making processes to enhance their ESG performance. Corporate governance mechanisms are introduced to monitor managers and align their interests with other stakeholders (Radu & Smaili, 2022). One such governance mechanism is appointing a sustainability committee that supports the board of directors to better meet stakeholder demands by implementing an appropriate sustainability strategy (Radu & Smaili, 2022). Another more recent governance mechanism is the implementation of ESG-linked executive compensation policies that integrate ESG criteria into executive compensation contracts (Aresu et al., 2022; Adu et al., 2021). This means that pay-for-performance incentives are linked to sustainability-related targets, such as energy efficiency, greenhouse gas emissions reduction, diversity, equity and inclusion, and employee engagement (Flammer et al., 2019). Notably, the PwC survey found that almost 70% of respondents believe ESG goals should be embedded into executive compensation targets (Chalmers et al., 2021).

While examining the importance of ESG in reducing the overall firm risk has become a popular area of research (Bax et al., 2023), there is little evidence of the relationship between companies' ESG performance and the external market assessment of their ESG risks. Furthermore, although the introduction of the sustainability committee and ESG-based executive compensation is growing, academic studies have mainly investigated the effect of these governance mechanisms on ESG performance as measured and communicated by the company (Gebhardt et al., 2022; Haque & Ntim, 2020; Baraibar-Diez et al., 2019; Haque, 2017), however without examining their effect on the external market assessment of a company's ESG risks. Therefore, scant empirical research tests whether ESG performance and sustainability-linked corporate governance mechanisms improve companies' ESG risk evaluation (i.e., rating).

This research aims to fill this knowledge gap by investigating, first, whether companies with higher ESG performance enjoy a lower level of (market-assessed) ESG risk and, second, whether the market assigns a lower ESG risk rating to those companies that opted for including sustainability-based incentives in executive management compensation schemes and appointing a sustainability committee compared to those lacking such ESG-related corporate governance mechanisms.

Previous literature supports our research objectives with these relevant arguments. First, pursuing sustainable business practices generates reputational and social capital, reducing firm risk (Albuquerque et al., 2019). Therefore, we expect a negative relationship between ESG performance and ESG risk rating. Second, "*sustainable compensation policy tends to motivate executive management to design and implement carbon reduction initiatives, which in turn can mitigate climate-related risks and improve long term financial prospects of a firm*" (Haque, 2017, p. 361). Third, the sustainability committee encourages directors to implement a sustainability strategy and monitors related results and outcomes (Radu & Smaili, 2022). Consistent with these arguments, we anticipate a negative relationship between these corporate governance mechanisms and ESG risk rating.

To test whether ESG performance, ESG executive compensation, and sustainability committee are negatively associated with companies' ESG risk rating assigned by external stakeholders, we run regression analyses on a sample of 304 companies listed in the European Union (EU) for which we manually collected data on the ESG risk rating from Sustainalytics and corporate governance and financial data from Thomson Reuters Eikon Refinitiv. The EU represents an intriguing setting for this analysis because the EU Commission implemented several regulations to favor sustainability transition and published the Corporate Sustainability Reporting Directive (CSRD; EU, 2022), the Corporate Sustainability Due Diligence Directive (EU, 2024), and the European Sustainability Reporting Standards (ESRS; Fiandrino, 2023). Thus, companies are pressured to enhance their sustainability efforts and can react to these regulations by addressing sustainable board characteristics (Mio et al., 2020; Velte, 2023). However, no evidence has been collected on how the market perceives ESG-related corporate governance initiatives, while only a few studies have addressed ESG performance in Europe (Winschel & Stawinoga, 2019).

Our findings show that ESG performance is negatively related to companies' ESG risk rating and that the presence of the sustainability committee favors lower levels of companies' ESG risk rating. Conversely, ESG-linked executive compensation does not affect ESG risk rating.

This study contributes to the literature on ESG performance and corporate governance by exploring the role of specific sustainability-focused governance mechanisms (i.e., ESG-linked executive compensation and a sustainability committee at the board of directors' level) in supporting a firm's external evaluation of ESG risks. First, it significantly contributes to the recent stream on the effect of ESG performance on unmanaged ESG risk, demonstrating that higher sustainability performance negatively affects the risk rating provided by third independent parties. Second, it extends prior empirical evidence that the market rewards those companies that appoint committees dedicated to a specific task (Florio & Leoni, 2017), which in this case is sustainability-related.

Our research has practical implications as well. Empirically identifying strategic mechanisms to lower the level of unmanaged ESG risk, the research can support companies in enhancing ESG performance and establishing the sustainability committee because it is rewarded by a better external assessment of a company's ESG risks from investors and other stakeholders. Conversely, the lack of a significant relationship between ESG-linked executive compensation and ESG risk rating may demonstrate that stakeholders need greater transparency on such a mechanism to evaluate a company with a lower risk rating. In turn, this may support recent international regulations concerning the reporting of companies' sustainability policies, governance, and practices, especially in the EU, where the ESRS GOV-3 *Integration of sustainability-related performance in incentive schemes* obliges companies under the scope of the CSRD to disclose detailed information also about the integration of their sustainability-related performance in incentive schemes to members of the administrative, management, and supervisory bodies (European Commission, 2023). The lack of a significant association between ESG-linked executive compensation and ESG risk rating may also signal that the market waits until ESG targets are satisfied before rewarding the company.

The remainder of this study proceeds as follows: Section 10.2 describes the theoretical background, while Sect. 10.3 presents prior research on ESG performance, ESG-linked executive compensation, and sustainability committee to formulate the hypotheses to be tested. Section 10.4 addresses the research design adopted, while Sect. 10.5 illustrates the descriptive statistics and discusses the results from the regression analysis. Finally, Sect. 10.6 formulates concluding remarks, including research limitations and avenues for further research.

10.2 Theoretical Background

During the last decades, academics have provided normative Corporate Social Responsibility (CSR) theories, dictating under which rationale executives and managers should make decisions (Smith, 2003).

The shareholder theory by Friedman (1970) posits that businesses are legally and economically obliged to prioritize profit maximization for their shareholders. In his view, "*[t]here is one and only one social responsibility of business—to use its resources and engage in activities designed to increase its profits so long as it [...] engages in open and free competition, without deception or fraud.*" Therefore, the company's sole responsibility is to increase its profits, while social and environmental initiatives are secondary. In line with this perspective, some research suggests that ESG practices destroy value by bearing expenses that decrease financial performance and shareholder value (Lys et al., 2015).

However, several past scandals (e.g., Enron in the United States, Gescartera Brokerage House in Spain, Vivendi in France) have urged business leaders to leave such a shareholder-centered approach that has driven business decisions for several decades and adopt a stakeholder approach to governance instead. Prioritizing stakeholders is even more demanding than maximizing shareholder wealth. It involves attention to the interests and well-being of all those who contribute to achieving the organization's objectives (Phillips et al., 2003).

The stakeholder theory by Freeman (1984) suggests that the purpose of any business is to create value for stakeholders, including shareholders and employees, customers, suppliers, debtholders, regulatory authorities, etc. Stakeholder theory is descriptive, normative, managerial, and instrumental (Freeman et al., 2010). First, it presents a model describing the corporation as a constellation of cooperative and competitive interests possessing intrinsic value. Its fundamental basis is normative because it involves accepting stakeholders as "persons or groups with legitimate interests" in procedural and/or substantive aspects of corporate activity. Stakeholder theory is managerial because it addresses how companies can create value and trade with each other. Finally, stakeholder theory is instrumental because its framework examines the connections between stakeholder management and achieving various corporate performance goals (Freeman et al., 2010). In fact, addressing stakeholders' reciprocal interests allows the company to reduce information asymmetry and better identify risks and opportunities (Freeman et al., 2010).

Considering the instrumental rationale of the stakeholder theory, the risk-reducing impact of ESG activities that may result from meeting the needs of various stakeholders can alleviate agency costs and lead to lower financial risks (Masulis & Reza, 2015). Furthermore, high ESG performance can build up moral capital and motivate stakeholders to be more loyal and less inclined to react to negative news, leading to lower financial risks. Conversely, low ESG performance can lead to adverse effects in terms of loss of revenues, decrease in share price, and shrink in customer loyalty (Champagne et al., 2022). For instance, Volkswagen, Nike, and Boeing have suffered financial setbacks following an event related to ESG issues. For instance, after the first Boeing aircraft crash in 2018, Boeing's stock price declined 15% while its Credit Default Swap (CDS) spread climbed 17% (Henisz & McGlinch, 2019).

Prior research finds that ESG activities increase corporate financial performance (Margolis & Walsh, 2003; Waddock & Graves, 1997), mitigate stock price crash risk (Feng et al., 2022), and contribute 7.3% less to systemic risk (Eratalay & Cortés Angel, 2022). Better ESG practices lead to lower financial distress and default risk and positively affect financial stability (Boubaker et al., 2020). Moreover, high ESG commitment strengthens the relationship between companies and stakeholders in times of crisis, implying that ESG activities constitute a form of insurance-like protection against downside risk (Godfrey et al., 2009). Firms with high social capital, measured by ESG performance, are mainly found to obtain higher stock returns, profitability, growth, and sales per employee during the financial crisis compared to low-ESG firms (Lins et al., 2017). They also outperformed low-ESG firms in non-crisis periods, confirming that ESG activities are a risk management tool (Lins et al., 2017). Furthermore, ESG performance can shape up in the eyes of lenders as an additional insurance on credit risk because greater awareness of ESG issues is strongly and significantly associated with better creditworthiness (Brogi et al., 2022; Henisz & McGlinch, 2019).

Most empirical evidence shows that systematic risk is lower for firms with higher CSR scores, that is, firms reaching better performance across community, diversity, employee relations, environment, product, and human rights attributes (Albuquerque et al., 2019). According to Champagne et al. (2022), companies with better ESG performance should be able to decrease their exposure to ESG risks by better managing their relations with stakeholders. However, so far, there is no evidence of such a relationship. Similarly, there is no evidence of the relationship between governance mechanisms driving decision-making processes and managerial decisions that could reduce companies' unmanaged ESG risks. Therefore, we aim to fill this research gap by investigating whether ESG performance, ESG-linked executive compensation, and the presence of a CSR committee affect ESG risk rating as attributed by a third independent party.

10.3 Hypothesis Development

10.3.1 ESG Performance and ESG Risk Rating

Few studies investigate the effects of ESG performance on exposure to ESG risks. For instance, the study of Champagne et al. (2022) tests whether companies with better extra-financial performance (e.g., investing in CSR activities or projects) can reduce their exposure to ESG risks linked to adverse ESG events. The results show that ESG performance is inversely related to the likelihood that the firm will face adverse ESG events, thus lowering ESG risk. However, different CSR activities are found to generate opposite effects. On the one hand, technical CSR activities, such as labor relations or product quality, oriented to primary stakeholders (employees, customers, suppliers, and investors), are associated with lower ESG risk. On the other hand, institutional CSR activities, such as philanthropy and community-related activities mainly focused on secondary stakeholders (regulators, community, and business partners), are associated with higher risk because firms adopt sustainable practices to compensate for or insure against ESG risk.

Moreover, focusing on the relationship between companies' ESG profile and systemic risk, considering the EU and the US markets separately, Bax et al. (2023) demonstrate that companies with high ESG scores tend to exhibit low systemic risk, indicating a positive effect of ESG scores. In other words, "*higher ESG performance could lead to more prudent and sustainable actions conducting to a reduction in the overall risk*" (Bax et al., 2023; p. 1407). In line with such evidence, in this study, we anticipate that companies with better ESG performance are rewarded with a lower ESG risk rating. Accordingly, we formulate the following hypothesis:

Hypothesis 1: There is a negative association between ESG performance and ESG risk rating.

10.3.2 ESG-linked Executive Compensation and ESG Risk Rating

Because executives should address the interests of all stakeholders (Hill & Jones, 1992), ESG-linked executive compensation is widely recognized as the governance mechanism to align executives' behavior toward improving economic, social, and environmental sustainability (Almici, 2023). Therefore, ESG-linked executive compensation can protect stakeholders' interests in the strategic decision-making and resource allocation processes. In fact, by tying executive compensation to sustainability goals, chief executive officers and other executives can be incentivized to satisfy stakeholders' interests and sustainability goals. For this reason, ESG-linked executive compensation can be a tool for efficient incentive contracting (Cohen et al., 2023); it can effectively align executives' incentives with companies' socially responsible actions.

Several studies have investigated the effects of ESG-linked executive compensation (Winschel & Stawinoga, 2019). Academic research has primarily focused on the advantages and benefits of establishing ESG-linked executive compensation to improve sustainability performance, suggesting that integrating ESG objectives into executive compensation facilitates the convergence of different interests through the orientation of companies toward sustainability (Almici, 2023). Most researchers find a positive and statistically significant relation between ESG executive compensation and ESG performance (Elsayed & Elbardan, 2018). For instance, Haque (2017) examines the effects of board characteristics and sustainable compensation policy on carbon performance and finds that ESG-based compensation policy improves carbon performance. Similarly, Baraibar-Diez et al. (2019) show that sustainable compensation policies positively affect ESG performance, referring to a sample of European listed companies. Haque (2017) provides similar evidence because, in the long run, sustainability compensation policies tend to incentivize senior management to design and take action on carbon reduction initiatives that can reduce climate risk and enhance companies' profitability over time. In turn, Flammer et al. (2019) show that adopting CSR-based contracts leads not only to an increase in the long-term orientation and firm value but also to a reduction in emissions, facilitating the development of green innovations. Their results suggest that managers focus on stakeholders' interests, thus minimizing the agency problem. Finally, the recent research of Almici (2023) based on a sample of Italian listed companies provides similar evidence suggesting that embedding sustainability in executive compensation positively affects firms' ESG performance. The study also shows that specific corporate governance characteristics can positively impact the relationship between sustainability goals and ESG performance. ESG-based executive compensation policies positively impact ESG performance when the latter is retrieved by companies' reports (Almici, 2023; Elsayed & Elbardan, 2018). By minimizing the goal incongruence between companies and stakeholders, executive compensation potentially reduces information asymmetries (Velte, 2016) and improves a firm's evaluation by market players. Furthermore, incentives linked to sustainability-related targets can motivate executives to undertake social and environmental initiatives (Haque & Ntim, 2020; Haque, 2017), thus potentially enhancing sustainable business practices with a long-term social and environmental perspective (Baraibar-Diez et al., 2019).

Based on the above arguments, adopting an ESG-linked executive compensation policy allows for *"responding to a large number of stakeholders with different demands"* (Baraibar-Diez et al., 2019; p. 1457). Therefore, we argue that investors and stakeholders should positively reward companies that have adopted this aligning mechanism by assigning lower ESG risk ratings. Hence, our second hypothesis is formulated as follows:

Hypothesis 2: There is a negative association between the presence of ESG-linked executive compensation policy and ESG risk rating.

10.3.3 Sustainability Committee and ESG Risk Rating

The increasing importance of focusing on long-term value creation and cultivating stakeholder relationships (Freeman, 1984) has led companies to establish committees with sustainability expertise. These committees assume proposing and consultative functions to the board of directors (Gennari & Salvioni, 2019). Sustainability committees aim to contribute to the board's decision-making processes with a long-term perspective and a stakeholder orientation.

The sustainability committee also has a monitoring role as the board specifically charges it to orientate the company to CSR actions (Velte & Stawinoga, 2020). It addresses policies and practices that relate to the sustainable growth of the company and reviews the company's annual sustainability report (Valle et al., 2019). Furthermore, this committee addresses companies' responsibility to stakeholders and balances conflicting interests among stakeholders, thus assuming a coordinating function (Gennari & Salvioni, 2019). Therefore, companies have started designating sustainability committees to consider sustainability issues from the perspective of risks, strategic opportunities, and commitments to stakeholders (Liao et al., 2015).

In turn, academics have started to investigate the effectiveness of the sustainability committee, providing mixed empirical evidence. García-Sánchez et al. (2019) show that the sustainability committee mediates the responsibility of independent directors regarding corporate sustainability and nurtures the development of strategies to enhance environmental and social performance. Conversely, other studies question whether the sustainability committee is a symbolic initiative rather than an effective monitoring tool. For example, Chams et al. (2019) show that the presence of a sustainability committee in a firm does not make the firm sustainable, while the literature review on European archival research leads Velte (2023) to conclude that a substantive implementation of sustainable board governance reflects better CSR efforts and increased CSR performance.

In line with stakeholder theory, establishing a sustainability committee can be a response to growing stakeholder demands to monitor sustainability activities and evaluate sustainability outcomes. Furthermore, according to Gennari and Salvioni (2019; p. 763), "*the board's commitment to value creation in the long-term is more visible to financial markets and external stakeholders than when the responsibility for social issues is assigned to other committees (e.g. audit, remuneration) or to the board as a whole.*" Therefore, we argue that having a sustainability committee at the board level can result in a lower ESG risk rating assigned by an external independent party representing the whole of the stakeholders. Hence, our third hypothesis is formulated as follows:

Hypothesis 3: There is a negative association between the presence of the sustainability committee and ESG risk rating.

10.4 Research Design

10.4.1 Empirical Model and Variables Definition

To test our hypotheses, we employed the following linear regression models:

ESG risk rating $= \beta_0 + \beta_1$***ESG score*** $+ \beta_2$***Board size*** $+ \beta_3$***Board independence*** $+ \beta_4$***Board diversity*** $+ \beta_5$***ROA*** $+ \beta_6$***Size*** $+ \beta_7$***GDP*** $+ \varepsilon$ ***(Model 1)***

ESG risk rating $= \beta_0 + \beta_1$***ESG pay*** $+ \beta_2$***Sustainability committee*** $+ \beta_3$***Board size*** $+ \beta_4$***Board independence*** $+ \beta_5$***Board diversity*** $+ \beta_6$***ROA*** $+ \beta_7$***Size*** $+ \beta_8$***GDP*** $+ \varepsilon$ ***(Model 2)***

We estimated Model 1 for testing H1 and Model 2 for testing H2 and H3. In both models, the dependent variable refers to the end of 2022, while independent variables are lagged to reduce endogeneity concerns. In both models, ε represents the residual or that portion of the endogenous variable that is not explained by the exogenous regressors. Furthermore, all models include industry-fixed effects.

ESG risk rating is the dependent variable and represents the market-assessed ESG risk of a company. It gives investors an overall company score based on assessing how much of a company's exposure to ESG risk is unmanaged. Sustainalytics, a global leader in sustainability analysis, provides the rating. In detail, the ESG risk rating score is the sum of unmanaged risk for each of the company's material ESG issues. The unmanaged risk is calculated as the difference between the company's overall exposure to ESG risks and managed ESG risks, where the exposure to ESG risk is assessed by the Sustainalytics research analyst team considering the potential impact of 20 material ESG issues on each of 138 Sustainalytics-defined sub-industries. In contrast, the managed risk score is determined by multiplying the material ESG issues' management score by the material ESG issues' manageable risk score. *ESG risk rating* potentially ranges from 0 to 100, classified into five categories: Negligible risk (0–10); Low risk (10–20); Medium risk (20–30); High risk (30–40); and Severe risk (40+). For instance, in 2022, Hermès was classified in the first category, Telefonica SA was ranked in the second category, EssilorLuxottica SA was classified in the third category, Thyssenkrupp AG was ranked in the fourth cluster while there was only one company in the severe risk category: Pge Polska Grupa Energetyczna SA. The more the ESG risk remains unmanaged, the higher the variable *ESG risk rating*.

The test variable in Model 1 is *ESG score*, which addresses the company's ESG performance based on verifiable reported data in the public domain. Thomson Reuters Eikon Refinitiv provides this score by measuring a firm's ESG performance and commitment across the ten main ESG themes: resource use, emissions, environmental product innovation, workforce, human rights, community, product responsibility, management, shareholders, and CSR strategy. It relies on publicly available sources, such as company websites, annual reports, CSR reports, and audited reports. For these reasons, in the last few years, increasing reference has been made to the ESG score provided by Refinitiv (Abdelmotaal & Abdel-Kader, 2016; Almici, 2023). *ESG score* ranges from 0 to 100. The more ESG issues are addressed, the higher the ESG score.

The test variables in Model 2 are the binary variables *ESG pay* and *Sustainability committee. ESG pay* addresses whether there is an ESG-based executive compensation policy. In detail, if the senior executive's compensation is linked to sustainability targets, *ESG pay* equals 1; it equals 0 otherwise. In turn, *Sustainability committee* indicates whether the company has a CSR committee or a team responsible for addressing ESG issues within the organization and, thus, for decision-making on the company's sustainability strategy. The variable equals 1 if there is a sustainability committee and 0 otherwise.

Finally, we included several control variables in both models that aim to capture governance-, accounting-, and country-related aspects. The model controls for the number of directors on the board (*Board size*), the percentage of independent directors on total board members (*Board independence*), and the percentage of women on the board on total board members (*Board diversity*). We also included a measure of performance defined as the ratio between net profit over total assets (*ROA*) and firm size, measured by the logarithm of total assets (*Size*). Finally, we included the Gross Domestic Product in the natural logarithm (*GDP*). To alleviate endogeneity concerns, we computed all the control variables as the average from 2019 to 2021. Table 10.1 describes the variables used.

10.4.2 Sample Selection and Data Collection

We tested our hypotheses on a sample of EU-listed firms. The European setting is unique because of its intensive regulative focus on sustainable business practices. As Velte (2023; p. 48) suggested, *"the EU has published a proposal for a new directive on sustainable board duties and incentives. Mandatory sustainable board duties regarding sustainable value chains (sustainable value chain management), mandatory gender quotas and sustainability-related compensation packages for executive directors may complement current sustainable finance and reporting reform initiatives and promote firms' sustainability transformation."* Because of such pressure on EU companies to enhance their efforts toward sustainability, they represent an interesting research sample to investigate the current approaches to leading and monitoring efforts of the board of directors toward sustainability strategies. Our sample includes financial and nonfinancial companies, as it is a common practice in ESG-focused studies (Bolton & Kacperczyk, 2021; Champagne et al., 2022).

Our dependent variable, *ESG risk rating*, refers to the year 2022. We relied on freely available data and hand-collected this variable from Sustainalytics's website

Table 10.1 Variables description

Variables	Description	Source
Dependent variable		
ESG risk rating	Unmanaged risk for a company on material ESG issues. Year-end, 2022.	Sustainalytics's website
Independent variables		
ESG score	Score based on the company's self-reported environmental, social, and corporate governance information. Year-end, 2021.	Refinitiv Eikon (ESG Score)
Environmental score	Score based on the company's impacts on living and non-living natural systems, including the air, land, and water, as well as complete ecosystems. Year-end, 2021.	Refinitiv Eikon (Environmental Pillar Score)
Social score	Score based on the company's capacity to generate trust and loyalty with its workforce, customers, and society, using best management practices. Year-end, 2021.	Refinitiv Eikon (Social Pillar Score)
Governance score	Score based on the company's systems and processes, which ensure that its board members and executives act in the best interests of its stakeholders. Year-end, 2021.	Refinitiv Eikon (Governance Pillar Score)
ESG pay	Dummy variable equal to 1 if the company has adopted an ESG-based executive compensation policy and 0 otherwise. Year-end, 2020.	Refinitiv Eikon (Compensation Policy Elements/Policy ESG Related Compensation)
Sustainability committee	Dummy variable equal to 1 if the company has designated a sustainability committee, and 0 otherwise. Year-end, 2020.	Refinitiv Eikon (CSR Sustainability Committee)
Control variables		
Board size	Total number of board members at the end of the fiscal year. Average annual data, 2019–2021.	Refinitiv Eikon (Board Size)
Board independence	Percentage of independent members on the board of directors. Average annual data, 2019–2021.	Refinitiv Eikon (Value – Board Structure/Independent Board Members)
Board diversity	Percentage of females on the board of directors. Average annual data, 2019–2021.	Refinitiv Eikon (Value – Board Structure/Board Diversity)
ROA	Net income over total assets ratio. Average annual data, 2019–2021.	Refinitiv Eikon (Net income after taxes and Total Assets, Reported)
Size	Natural logarithm of total assets. Average annual data, 2019–2021.	Refinitiv Eikon (Total Assets, Reported)
Industry	Categorical variable as reported in Table 10.3.	Refinitiv Eikon (GICS Sector)
GDP	Natural logarithm of the average gross domestic product at purchaser's prices from 2019 to 2021.	Worldbank's website

Table 10.2 Sample distribution by country

Country	Frequency	Percent
Austria	13	4.28
Belgium	12	3.95
Czech Republic	2	0.66
Denmark	6	1.97
Finland	12	3.95
France	65	21.38
Germany	62	20.39
Greece	4	1.32
Hungary	1	0.33
Ireland	14	4.61
Italy	13	4.28
Luxembourg	5	1.64
Malta	1	0.33
Netherlands	20	6.58
Poland	12	3.95
Portugal	3	0.99
Spain	18	5.92
Sweden	41	13.49
Total	**304**	**100.00**

in April 2023. The initial population included 312 EU-listed firms. Then, we collected data on the test variables (*ESG score*, *ESG pay*, and *Sustainability committee)* and the control variables related to corporate governance *(Board size, Board independence*, and *Board diversity)* and accounting *(ROA* and *Size)* from Thomson Reuters Eikon Refinitiv. After inquiring Refinitiv, we removed 8 observations due to missing data. The final sample comprises 304 firms from 18 EU countries across 19 sectors. The sample is thus well diversified in terms of industry representation. Finally, we hand-collected each country's Gross Domestic Product from the Worldbank's website. Tables 10.2 and 10.3 summarize the distribution by country and industry.

10.5 Findings

10.5.1 Descriptive Statistics, Univariate Analyses, and Preliminary Tests

This section presents the descriptive statistics of the variables used, focusing on the dependent variable (*ESG risk rating*) and the main independent variables (*ESG score, ESG pay*, and *Sustainability committee*). As reported in Table 10.4, the average *ESG risk rating* for EU companies is 19.306, with a standard deviation of 6.69, which means that data is not spread far from the mean. Table 10.5 adds to the

Table 10.3 Sample distribution by industry

Industry	Frequency	Percent
Commercial Services	12	3.95
Communications	13	4.28
Consumer Durables	12	3.95
Consumer Non-Durables	17	5.59
Consumer Services	12	3.95
Distribution Services	3	0.99
Electronic Technology	14	4.61
Energy Minerals	5	1.64
Finance	71	23.36
Health Services	5	1.64
Health Technology	21	6.91
Industrial Services	10	3.29
Non-Energy Minerals	11	3.62
Process Industries	17	5.59
Producer Manufacturing	31	10.20
Retail Trade	12	3.95
Technology Services	12	3.95
Transportation	7	2.30
Utilities	19	6.25
Total	**304**	**100**

Table 10.4 Descriptive statistics

	Obs.	Mean	St. dev.	Min	Max
ESG risk rating	304	19.306	6.680	4.677	45.255
ESG score	304	72.738	13.043	34.870	95.510
Environmental score	304	69.575	19.321	0.000	99.760
Social score	304	75.251	15.510	25.660	98.320
Governance score	304	71.687	17.088	13.470	96.500
ESG pay	304	0.655	0.476	0.000	1.000
Sustainability committee	304	0.875	0.331	0.000	1.000
Board size	304	11.513	3.889	3.333	22.000
Board independence	304	61.233	23.809	0.000	100.000
Board diversity	304	35.506	10.343	0.000	63.157
ROA	304	0.043	0.055	−0.120	0.412
Size	304	16.821	1.735	12.876	23.887
GDP	304	7.092	1.029	2.800	8.299

variable description by presenting the distribution of the sampled companies according to the *ESG risk rating* classes defined by Sustainalytics. It allows observing that the average *ESG risk rating* falls in the "low" risk category, meaning that sampled companies have a relatively low level of ESG risk left unmanaged. Most companies (159 out of 304) obtain an *ESG risk rating* between 11 and 20, while 109 companies report a "medium" *ESG risk rating*, ranging from 21 to 30. Sixteen

Table 10.5 Descriptive statistics of ESG risk rating grouped according to Sustainalystics' intervals

ESG risk rating categories	Obs.	Mean	S. d.	Min	Max
Negligible risk (0–10)	16	8.428	1.376	4.677	9.998
Low risk (10–20)	159	15.236	2.748	10.096	19.913
Medium risk (20–30)	109	24.255	2.864	20.039	29.942
High risk (30–40)	19	32.753	2.461	30.080	38.646
Severe risk (40+)	1	45.255	0.000	45.255	45.255
Total	304	19.305	6.680	4.677	45.255

observations report a "negligible" *ESG risk rating* lower than 10. Finally, only one observation falls within the "severe" risk class, scoring higher than 40. According to Sustainalytics, such a company faces severe ESG risk exposure, which could compromise its business activities. Moving to independent variables, the average *ESG score* is equal to 72.738 out of 100, but it ranges considerably (from 34.87 to 95.51).

Considering the environmental, social, and governance pillars separately, companies show the highest level of commitment to social activities as the mean equals 75.251. For the environment pillar, companies achieve 69.575 in mean, while for the governance aspects, the mean is 71.687. Furthermore, 65.5% of sampled companies adopt an ESG compensation policy (*ESG pay*), while 87.5% have a *Sustainability committee*.

Regarding control variables, the mean *Board size* is 11.51 directors, with 61.23% independent directors (*Board independence*) and 35.50% females (*Board diversity*). Concerning companies' performance, *ROA* averages 4.3% but ranges from −12% to 41.2%.

Table 10.6 presents the Pearson correlations matrix between the dependent and independent variables. *ESG score, Sustainability committee*, *Board size*, *Board diversity,* and *ROA* present a statistically significant correlation at a 10% p-value with *ESG risk rating*. Although some independent variables are significantly correlated, our model is unaffected by multicollinearity issues. The average Variance Inflation Factor is 1.32 for Model 1 and 1.26 for Model 2, thus well below conventional thresholds (Stock & Watson, 2020).

Finally, before running our primary regression analysis, we tested whether the association found by prior literature (Baraibar-Diez et al., 2019; Elsayed & Elbardan, 2018; Haque, 2017; Radu & Smaili, 2022) between *ESG pay and Sustainability committee* (independent variables) and companies' *ESG score* (dependent variable) is confirmed in our sample. Table 10.7 shows the results, highlighting that both the variables *ESG pay* and *Sustainability committee* have a strong positive significant association with *ESG score* (p-value <0.001). Introducing an ESG-based executive compensation and a sustainability committee increases the *ESG score* by 5.016 and 12.908 points, respectively (see Table 10.7, column 3). Results support prior evidence that the presence of sustainability incentives and committees increases ESG performance. This represents a premise to extend prior literature investigating whether these ESG-related corporate governance mechanisms also affect ESG risk rating.

Table 10.6 Pearson correlation

	(1)	(2)	(3)	(4)	(5)	(6)	(7)	(8)	(9)	(10)	(11)	(12)	(13)
ESG risk rating (1)	1.000												
ESG score (2)	−0.0988*	1.000											
Environmental score (3)	−0.0554	0.7625*	1.000										
Social score (4)	−0.0793	0.8421*	0.5911*	1.000									
Governance score (5)	−0.0735	0.6361*	0.1919*	0.2899*	1.000								
ESG pay (6)	−0.0215	0.3706*	0.2505*	0.2562*	0.3663*	1.000							
Sustainability committee (7)	−0.1172*	0.4593*	0.3698*	0.4435*	0.2304*	0.1647*	1.000						
Board size (8)	0.1210*	0.3711*	0.3360*	0.3515*	0.1581*	0.1916*	0.2779*	1.000					
Board independence (9)	−0.0664	0.1503*	0.0517	0.0778	0.2340*	0.0638	0.0794	−0.2348*	1.000				
Board diversity (10)	−0.1070*	0.2733*	0.2226*	0.1593*	0.2777*	0.2982*	0.2108*	0.0759	0.0437	1.000			
ROA (11)	−0.1315*	−0.2072*	−0.1734*	−0.1528*	−0.1140*	−0.0984*	−0.0815	−0.2915*	0.0770	0.0015	1.000		
Size (12)	0.0281	0.2774*	0.2851*	0.1843*	0.1891*	0.0362	0.1043*	0.3930*	−0.0268	0.0105	−0.2778*	1.000	
GDP (13)	−0.0065	0.3391*	0.2430*	0.2616*	0.2695*	0.2802*	0.1695*	0.3673*	−0.0621	0.2887*	−0.1425*	−0.0217	1.000

* $p < 0.1$

Table 10.7 Preliminary analysis of the association between ESG compensation policy, the Sustainability committee, and ESG performance

	(1) ESG_score	(2) ESG_score	(3) ESG_score
	Coeff. (p-value)	Coeff. (p-value)	Coeff. (p-value)
ESG pay	**5.400*** **		**5.016*** **
	(0.0002)		(0.0002)
Sustainability committee		**13.205*** **	**12.908*** **
		(0.0000)	(0.0000)
Board size	**0.502** **	0.251	0.217
	(0.0178)	(0.2192)	(0.2764)
Board independence	**0.106*** **	**0.096*** **	**0.085*** **
	(0.0002)	(0.0003)	(0.0012)
Board diversity	**0.156** **	**0.151** **	0.099
	(0.0167)	(0.0131)	(0.1019)
ROA	**−23.466***	**−24.815** **	**−21.777***
	(0.0552)	(0.0320)	(0.0543)
Size	**2.420*** **	**2.488*** **	**2.415*** **
	(0.0000)	(0.0000)	(0.0000)
GDP	**2.213*** **	**2.437*** **	**2.014*** **
	(0.0020)	(0.0003)	(0.0023)
constant	−4.000	−10.982	−7.019
	(0.6642)	(0.2056)	(0.4106)
N_obs	304	304	304
df_res	278	278	277
N_X	25	25	26
R2	0.38	0.44	0.47
AdjR2	0.32	0.39	0.42
RMSE	10.414	9.857	9.625
F_test	24.2	31.6	30.9
Industry FE	YES	YES	YES

* $p < 0.1$, ** $p < 0.05$, *** $p < 0.001$

10.5.2 Multivariate Analyses

Model 1 tests whether ESG performance affects the ESG risk rating. Results in Table 10.8 (first column) show that a higher *ESG score* decreases the level of *ESG risk rating* (p-value <0.001). Thus, Hypothesis 1 is confirmed. A one-unit increase in the *ESG score* is associated with a 0.127-unit decrease in the *ESG risk rating*. Among control variables, *ROA* presents a strong negative statistically significant relation with the dependent variable. At the same time, *Size* is positively associated with *ESG risk rating* (p-value <0.05). We also decomposed the *ESG score* into environmental, social, and governance dimensions. The additional models (columns 2, 3, and 4, respectively) indicate that the strong negative association is driven by a company's social and environmental performances (p-value <0.001). The

Table 10.8 Multivariate analysis of the association between ESG performance and ESG risk rating

	(1) ESG risk rating	(2) ESG risk rating	(3) ESG risk rating	(4) ESG risk rating
	Coeff. (p-value)	Coeff. (p-value)	Coeff. (p-value)	Coeff. (p-value)
ESG score	**−0.127*** **			
	(0.0001)			
Board size	−0.006	−0.031	0.002	−0.078
	(0.9590)	(0.7884)	(0.9835)	(0.5013)
Board independence	−0.020	**−0.030***	**−0.027***	**−0.029***
	(0.1884)	(0.0507)	(0.0741)	(0.0628)
Board diversity	−0.048	**−0.058***	**−0.065***	**−0.064***
	(0.1670)	(0.0969)	(0.0577)	(0.0711)
ROA	**−23.631*** **	**−21.557*** **	**−22.408*** **	**−20.943*** **
	(0.0004)	(0.0013)	(0.0007)	(0.0019)
Size	**1.025*** **	**0.860*** **	**0.926*** **	**0.798*** **
	(0.0001)	(0.0013)	(0.0005)	(0.0032)
GDP	0.150	−0.061	0.008	−0.068
	(0.6943)	(0.8736)	(0.9837)	(0.8610)
Environmental score		**−0.053*** **		
		(0.0086)		
Social score			**−0.095*** **	
			(0.0001)	
Governance score				−0.033
				(0.1410)
constant	14.241***	14.100***	15.716***	14.607***
	(0.0038)	(0.0050)	(0.0015)	(0.0039)
N_obs	304	304	304	304
df_res	278	278	278	278
N_X	25	25	25	25
R2	0.16	0.13	0.15	0.11
AdjR2	0.08	0.05	0.08	0.03
RMSE	5.558	5.651	5.571	5.699
F_test	7.4	5.8	7.1	5.1
Industry FE	YES	YES	YES	YES

* $p < 0.1$, ** $p < 0.05$, *** $p < 0.001$

relationship between *ROA* and *Size* is confirmed as per the primary model. Furthermore, in the models looking at the individual dimensions, *Board independence* and *Board diversity* also emerge as significant drivers for reducing the *ESG risk rating* (p-value <0.1).

Model 2 tests whether the *ESG pay* and *Sustainability committee* are associated with companies' *ESG risk rating*. Results in Table 10.9 show that only the sustainability committee strongly significantly affects ESG risk rating (p-value <0.01). In

Table 10.9 Multivariate analysis of the association between the Sustainability committee, ESG compensation policy, and ESG risk rating

	(1) ESG risk rating	(2) ESG risk rating	(3) ESG risk rating
	Coeff. (p-value)	Coeff. (p-value)	Coeff. (p-value)
ESG pay	−0.604		−0.493
	(0.4397)		(0.5207)
Sustainability committee		**−3.755*****	**−3.726*****
		(0.0006)	(0.0007)
Board size	−0.070	0.009	0.012
	(0.5441)	(0.9398)	(0.9172)
Board independence	**−0.034****	**−0.029***	**−0.028***
	(0.0284)	(0.0569)	(0.0687)
Board diversity	**−0.068***	**−0.057***	−0.052
	(0.0562)	(0.0985)	(0.1426)
ROA	**−20.603*****	**−20.792*****	**−21.090*****
	(0.0023)	(0.0016)	(0.0015)
Size	**0.716*****	**0.710*****	**0.718*****
	(0.0067)	(0.0060)	(0.0056)
GDP	−0.138	−0.122	−0.080
	(0.7229)	(0.7460)	(0.8336)
constant	14.812***	16.073***	15.683***
	(0.0036)	(0.0012)	(0.0017)
N_obs	304	304	304
df_res	278	278	277
N_X	25	25	26
R2	0.11	0.14	0.14
AdjR2	0.03	0.07	0.06
RMSE	5.715	5.600	5.606
F_test	4.8	6.7	5.9
Industry FE	YES	YES	YES

* $p < 0.1$, ** $p < 0.05$, *** $p < 0.001$

other words, having appointed a sustainability committee reduces ESG unmanaged risks by 3.726 points. Therefore, we can confirm our Hypothesis 3, but not Hypothesis 2. Among the control variables, *ROA, Board Independenc*e, and *Size* are found to affect the dependent variable. In detail, companies with higher profitability and more independent directors on the board present a lower *ESG risk rating*. In contrast, the bigger the company, the higher the ESG risk rating, which aligns with the idea that the bigger the size, the higher the business complexity.

Finally, we run an additional robustness analysis.[2] Specifically, we re-run the models by splitting companies into high versus low *ESG risk rating*. To this purpose, we defined a dummy variable *high ESG risk rating* equal to 1 for companies

[2]Untabulated results are available upon request.

belonging to medium, high, or severe classes according to Sustainalytics definitions, 0 otherwise. Overall results are consistent: they exhibit that *ESG score* and *Sustainability committee* are negatively associated with *high ESG risk rating* (Hypothesis 1 and 2 supported), but *ESG pay* is not (Hypothesis 3 not supported). They thus confirm the findings of our main models.

10.6 Conclusions

In this study, we analyze the impact of ESG performance, ESG-linked executive compensation, and sustainability committees on companies' ESG risk rating assigned by third independent parties. We consider ESG performance and two corporate governance mechanisms—ESG-linked executive compensation policy and sustainability committee—as critical governance factors that, according to stakeholder theory, may affect managers' behavior and, eventually, influence stakeholders' external evaluation concerning companies' ESG risk profile.

In line with prior literature (Radu & Smaili, 2022), a preliminary analysis confirmed that the two sustainability-focused governance mechanisms identified are positively associated with a higher company's sustainability performance. Our main findings show that ESG performance and the presence of the sustainability committee reduce companies' ESG risk rating. Conversely, results do not offer significant evidence of the relationship between ESG-linked executive compensation and the ESG risk rating. One possible explanation for this result is that including ESG targets per se might not be enough for the market players to award the company with a lower ESG risk rating. For such a purpose, information on reaching such targets may be critical. Stakeholders may also need greater transparency on such a mechanism to evaluate a company with a lower risk rating.

Overall, our study contributes to the recent stream on the effect of ESG performance on (ESG) risk management (e.g., Champagne et al., 2022) as we empirically demonstrate that higher sustainability performances and the presence of a sustainability committee negatively affect the risk rating provided by third independent parties. In other words, they are two strategic mechanisms to lower unmanaged ESG risk.

The study is not free from limitations. The independent variable *ESG pay* measures the mere presence of an ESG-based executive compensation policy without detailing specific ESG targets included in compensation contracts. The dependent and test variables are gathered from a single source, although criticism is increasing about diverging ESG ratings (Berg et al., 2022; Christensen et al., 2022). Furthermore, this empirical analysis relies on single-year observations and a relatively small sample due to secondary sources' data availability on the ESG risk rating. Future studies may extend the investigation to broader international settings and timeframes.

Despite these limitations, the current research provides new evidence that, in the EU, a higher ESG performance and the sustainability committee drive a lower ESG risk profile measured according to a third independent market party. Such evidence brings practical implications, as it provides companies with a confirmation that investing in sustainability initiatives and embedding sustainability in the corporate governance structure is rewarded by the market with a lower ESG risk rating.

References

Abdelmotaal, H., & Abdel-Kader, M. (2016). The use of sustainability incentives in executive remuneration contracts: Firm characteristics and impact on the shareholders' returns. *Journal of Applied Accounting Research, 17*(3), 311–330. https://doi.org/10.1108/JAAR-12-2013-0123

Adu, D. A., Flynn, A., & Grey, C. (2021). Executive compensation and sustainable business practices: The moderating role of sustainability-based compensation. *Business Strategy and the Environment, 31*, 1–39. https://doi.org/10.1002/bse.291338

Albuquerque, R., Koskinen, Y., & Zhang, C. (2019). Corporate social responsibility and firm risk: Theory and empirical evidence. *Management Science, 65*, 4451–4469. https://doi.org/10.1287/mnsc.2018.3043

Almici, A. (2023). Does sustainability in executive remuneration matter? The moderating effect of Italian firms' corporate governance characteristics. *Meditari Accountancy Research, 31*(7), 49–87. https://doi.org/10.1108/MEDAR-05-2022-1694

Aresu, S., Hooghiemstra, R., & Melis, A. (2022). Integration of CSR criteria into executive compensation contracts: A cross-country analysis. *Journal of Management, 49*(8), 2766–2804. https://doi.org/10.1177/01492063221110200

Baraibar-Diez, E., Odriozola, M. D., & Fernandez Sanchez, J. L. (2019). Sustainable compensation policies and its effect on environmental, social, and governance scores. *Corporate Social Responsibility and Environmental Management, 26*(6), 1457–1472. https://doi.org/10.1002/csr.1760

Bax, K., Bonaccolto, G., & Paterlini, S. (2023). Do lower environmental, social, and governance (ESG) rated companies have higher systemic impact? Empirical evidence from Europe and the United States. *Corporate Social Responsibility and Environmental Management, 30*(3), 1406–1420. https://doi.org/10.1002/csr.2427

Bax, K., Sahin, Ö., Czado, C., & Paterlini, S. (2023). ESG, risk, and (tail) dependence. *International Review of Financial Analysis, 87*, 102513. https://doi.org/10.1016/j.irfa.2023.102513

Berg, F., Kölbel, J. F., & Rigobon, R. (2022). Aggregate confusion: The divergence of ESG ratings. *Review of Finance, 26*(6), 1315–1344. https://doi.org/10.1093/rof/rfac033

Bolton, P., & Kacperczyk, M. (2021). Do investors care about carbon risk? *Journal of Financial Economics, 142*(2), 517–549. https://doi.org/10.1016/j.jfineco.2021.05.008

Boubaker, S., Cellier, A., Manita, R., & Saeed, A. (2020). Does corporate social responsibility reduce financial distress risk? *Economic Modelling, 91*, 835–851. https://doi.org/10.1016/j.econmod.2020.05.012

Brogi, M., Lagasio, V., & Porretta, P. (2022). Be good to be wise: Environmental, Social, and Governance awareness as a potential credit risk mitigation factor. *Journal of International Financial Management & Accounting, 33*(3), 522–547. https://doi.org/10.1111/jifm.12156

Chalmers, J., Cox, E., & Picard, N. (2021). The economic realities of ESG. PricewaterhouseCoopers (PwC). October 28. Retrieved from https://www.pwc.com/gx/en/services/audit-assurance/corporate- reporting/esg-investor-survey.html

Champagne, C., Coggins, F., & Sodjahin, A. (2022). Can extra – Financial ratings serve as an indicator of ESG risk? *Global Finance Journal, 54*, 100638. https://doi.org/10.1016/j.gfj.2021.100638

Chams, N., & García-Blandón, J. (2019). Sustainable or not sustainable? The role of the board of directors. *Journal of Cleaner Production, 226*, 1067–1081. https://doi.org/10.1016/j.jclepro.2019.04.118

Christensen, D. M., Serafeim, G., & Sikochi, A. (2022). Why is corporate virtue in the eye of the beholder? The case of ESG ratings. *The Accounting Review, 97*(1), 147–175. https://doi.org/10.2308/TAR-2019-0506

Cohen, S., Kadach, I., Ormazabal, G., & Reichelstein, S. (2023). Executive compensation tied to ESG performance: International evidence. *Journal of Accounting Research, 61*(3), 805–853.

Elsayed, N., & Elbardan, H. (2018). Investigating the associations between executive compensation and firm performance: Agency theory or tournament theory. *Journal of Applied Accounting Research, 19*(2), 245–270. https://doi.org/10.1108/JAAR-03-2015-0027

Eratalay, M. H., & Cortés Angel, A. P. (2022). The impact of ESG ratings on the systemic risk of European blue-chip firms. *Journal of Risk and Financial Management, 15*, 153. https://doi.org/10.3390/jrfm15040153

EU. (2022). Directive (EU) 2022/2464 of the European Parliament and of the Council of 14 December 2022 amending Regulation (EU) No 537/2014, Directive 2004/109/EC, Directive 2006/43/EC and Directive 2013/34/EU, as regards corporate sustainability reporting. https://eur-lex.europa.eu/legal-content/EN/TXT/?uri=CELEX%3A32022L2464

EU. (2024). Directive (EU) 2024/1760 of the European Parliament and of the Council of 13 June 2024 on corporate sustainability due diligence and amending Directive (EU) 2019/1937 and Regulation (EU) 2023/2859. https://eurlex.europa.eu/eli/dir/2024/1760/oj

European Commission. (2023). Commission Delegated Regulation (EU) 2023/2772 of 31 July 2023 supplementing Directive 2013/34/EU of the European Parliament and of the Council as regards sustainability reporting standards. https://eur-lex.europa.eu/legal-content/EN/TXT/?uri=CELEX%3A32023R2772

Feng, J., Goodell, J. W., & Shen, D. (2022). ESG rating and stock price crash risk: Evidence from China. *Finance Research Letters, 46*, 102476. https://doi.org/10.1016/j.frl.2021.102476

Fiandrino, S. (2023). *La sostenibilità aziendale in ottica sistemica- relazionale. Evoluzione concettuale e analisi di casi aziendali.* Giappichelli Editore, Torino.

Flammer, C., Hong, B., & Minor, D. (2019). Corporate governance and the rise of integrating corporate social responsibility criteria in executive compensation: Effectiveness and implications for firm outcomes. *Strategic Management Journal, 40*, 1097–1122. https://doi.org/10.1002/smj.3018

Florio, C., & Leoni, G. (2017). Enterprise risk management and firm performance: The Italian case. *The British Accounting Review, 49*(1), 56–74. https://doi.org/10.1016/j.bar.2016.08.003

Freeman, R. E. (1984). *Strategic management: A stakeholder approach.* Pitman.

Freeman, R. E., Harrison, J. S., Wicks, A. C., Parmar, B. L., & de Colle, S. (2010). *Stakeholder theory: The state of the art.* Cambridge University Press.

Friedman, M. (1970). The social responsibility of business is to increase its profits. *The New York Times Magazine, 9*, 26–32. https://www.nytimes.com/1970/09/13/archives/a-friedman-doctrine-the-social-responsibility-of-business-is-to.html

García-Sánchez, I. M., Gómez-Miranda, M. E., David, F., & Rodríguez-Ariza, L. (2019). Board independence and GRI-IFC performance standards: The mediating effect of the CSR committee. *Journal of Cleaner Production, 225*, 554–562. https://doi.org/10.1016/j.jclepro.2019.03.337

Gebhardt, M., Thun, T. W., Seefloth, M., & Zülch, H. (2022). Managing sustainability—Does the integration of environmental, social and governance key performance indicators in the internal management systems contribute to companies' environmental, social and governance performance? *Business Strategy and the Environment, 32*(4), 2175–2192. https://doi.org/10.1002/bse.3242

Gennari, F., & Salvioni, D. M. (2019). CSR committees on boards: The impact of the external country level factors. *Journal of Management and Governance, 23*(3), 759–785. https://doi.org/10.1007/s10997-018-9442-8

Gillan, S. L., Koch, A., & Starks, L. T. (2021). Firms and social responsibility: A review of ESG and CSR research in corporate finance. *Journal of Corporate Finance, 66*, 101889. https://doi.org/10.1016/j.jcorpfin.2021.101889

Godfrey, P. C., Merrill, C. B., & Hansen, J. M. (2009). The relationship between corporate social responsibility and shareholder value: An empirical test of the risk management hypothesis. *Strategic Management Journal, 30*, 425–445. https://doi.org/10.1002/smj.750

Haque, F. (2017). The effects of board characteristics and sustainable compensation policy on carbon performance of UK firms. *The British Accounting Review, 49*, 347–364. https://doi.org/10.1016/j.bar.2017.01.001

Haque, F., & Ntim, C. G. (2020). Executive compensation, sustainable compensation policy, carbon performance and market value. *British Journal of Management, 31*(3), 525–546. https://doi.org/10.1111/1467-8551.12395

Henisz, W. J., & McGlinch, J. (2019). ESG, material credit events, and credit risk. *Journal of Applied Corporate Finance, 31*(2), 105–117. https://doi.org/10.1111/jacf.12352

Hill, C. W., & Jones, T. M. (1992). Stakeholder-agency theory. *Journal of Management Studies, 29*(2), 131–154. https://doi.org/10.1111/j.1467-6486.1992.tb00657.x

Lewellyn, K., & Muller-Kahle, M. (2023). ESG leaders or laggards? A configurational analysis of ESG performance. Business & Society, 63, 00076503231182688. https://doi.org/10.1177/00076503231182688

Liao, L., Luo, L., & Tang, Q. (2015). Gender diversity, board independence, environmental committee and greenhouse gas disclosure. *The British Accounting Review, 47*(4), 409–424. https://doi.org/10.1016/j.bar.2014.01.002

Lins, K. V., Servaes, H., & Tamayo, A. (2017). Social capital, trust, and firm performance: The value of corporate social responsibility during the financial crisis. *Journal of Finance, 72*(4), 1785–1824. https://doi.org/10.1111/jofi.12505

Lys, T., Naughton, J. P., & Wang, C. (2015). Signaling through corporate accountability reporting. *Journal of Accounting and Economics, 60*, 56–72. https://doi.org/10.1016/j.jacceco.2015.03.001

Margolis, J. D., & Walsh, J. P. (2003). Misery loves companies: Rethinking social initiatives by business. *Administrative Science Quarterly, 48*(2), 268–305. https://doi.org/10.2307/3556659

Masulis, R. W., & Reza, S. W. (2015). Agency problems of corporate philanthropy. *The Review of Financial Studies, 28*(2), 592–636. https://doi.org/10.1093/rfs/hhu082

Mio, C., Fasan, M., Marcon, C., & Panfilo, S. (2020). The predictive ability of legitimacy and agency theory after the implementation of the EU directive on non-financial information. *Corporate Social Responsibility and Environmental Management, 27*(6), 2465–2476. https://doi.org/10.1002/csr.1968

Morgan Stanley. (2021). Sustainable signals: Individual investors and the COVID-19 pandemic. Morgan Stanley Institute for Sustainable Investing. CRC 3854109 10/2021. https://www.morganstanley.com/assets/pdfs/2021-Sustainable_Signals_Individual_Investor.pdf

Phillips, R., Freeman, R. E., & Wicks, A. C. (2003). What stakeholder theory is not. *Business Ethics Quarterly, 13*(4), 479–502. https://doi.org/10.5840/beq200313434

Radu, C., & Smaili, N. (2022). Alignment versus monitoring: An examination of the effect of the CSR committee and CSR-linked executive compensation on CSR performance. *Journal of Business Ethics, 180*(1), 145–163. https://doi.org/10.1007/s10551-021-04904-2

Smith, H. J. (2003). The shareholders vs. stakeholders debate. MIT Sloan Management Review. https://sloanreview.mit.edu/article/the-shareholders-vs-stakeholders-debate/

Stock, J. H., & Watson, M. W. (2020). *Introduction to econometrics* (4th ed.). Pearson.

Valle, I. D. D., Esteban, J. M. D., & Pérez, Ó. L. D. F. (2019). Corporate social responsibility and sustainability committee inside the board. *European Journal of International Management, 13*(2), 159–176. https://doi.org/10.1504/EJIM.2019.098145

Velte, P. (2016). Sustainable management compensation and ESG performance—The German case. *Problems and Perspectives in Management, 14*(4), 17–24. https://doi.org/10.21511/ppm.14(4).2016.02

Velte, P. (2023). Does sustainable board governance drive corporate social responsibility? A structured literature review on European archival research. *Journal of Global Responsibility, 14*(1), 46–88. https://doi.org/10.1108/JGR-05-2022-0044

Velte, P., & Stawinoga, M. (2020). Do chief sustainability officers and CSR committees influence CSR-related outcomes? A structured literature review based on empirical-quantitative research findings. *Journal of Management Control, 31*(4), 333–377. https://doi.org/10.1007/s00187-020-00308-x

Waddock, S. A., & Graves, S. B. (1997). The corporate social performance-financial performance link. *Strategic Management Journal, 18*, 303–319. https://doi.org/10.1002/(SICI)1097-0266(199704)18:4<303::AID-SMJ869>3.0.CO;2-G

Winschel, J., & Stawinoga, M. (2019). Determinants and effects of sustainable CEO compensation: a structured literature review of empirical evidence. *Management Review Quarterly, 69*, 265–328. https://doi.org/10.1007/s11301-019-00154-9

World Economic Forum. (2024). The global risk report 2024. 19th Edition. https://www.weforum.org/publications/global-risks-report-2024/

Chapter 11
CSR Board Committees and Value Relevance in Italian Listed Companies

Gianluca Ginesti, Ilaria Martino, and Annamaria Zampella

11.1 Introduction[1]

Pressures from local communities and international policy makers have increased the attention on corporate social responsibility (CSR) and firms have progressively improved CSR internal governance mechanisms (Peters et al., 2019; Radu & Smaili, 2021). Firms have voluntary established CSR board sub-committees aimed at handling the complexity of ethics and accountability matters to create sustainable value in the long term (Erhemjamts et al., 2013; Burke et al., 2019). Scholars claim that the CSR board committee has more than a mere coordination function of firm's social actions (Gennari & Salvioni, 2019), since it is actively involved in strategic corporate decisions that are likely to affect stakeholders' and investors' expectations (Radu & Smaili, 2021; Ginesti et al., 2023). For example, the CSR board committee may help the board of directors to improve monitoring mechanisms to foster higher quality environmental and social policies that in turn may impact investors' investment decisions (Amel-Zadeh & Serafeim, 2018). This is because, companies engaged in CSR polices are environmentally friendly and address better ethical needs of a wider range of partners (Ginesti et al., 2023). Moreover, companies with higher CSR engagement improve their reputation and benefit from higher investment efficiency (Benlemlih & Bitar, 2018), with a positive influence on

[1] While all authors contributed to this study, Gianluca Ginesti mainly focused on the research idea and covered the theoretical and practical implications of the results. Annamaria Zampella mainly focused on the theoretical background, the development of the empirical strategy, and Ilaria Martino primarily focused on predictions and interpretation and discussions of statistical results.

G. Ginesti · I. Martino (✉) · A. Zampella
Department of Economics, Management, Institutions (DEMI), University of Naples Federico II, Naples, Italy
e-mail: ilaria.martino@unina.it

N. Castellano et al. (eds.), *Environmental, Social, Governance (ESG)*, SIDREA Series in Accounting and Business Administration,
https://doi.org/10.1007/978-3-031-76618-3_11

firms' value, as well as of analyst following (Jo & Harjoto, 2011). Therefore, scholars argue that when companies "do well by doing good" they meet the expectations of various stakeholders and may thus have positive effects on market value (Freeman et al., 2010; Porter & Kramer, 2011; Becchetti et al., 2012). Bollen (2007) also argues that investors may derive utility from their investment choices in companies that are consistent with their personal values or societal concerns. Hart and Zingales (2017) question that if shareholders follow social factors in their own life, why would they not want the companies they invest in to do the same? Consequently, top management may adopt CSR strategies to be in line with the recent sentiment of investors (Renneboog et al., 2008) on sustainability. Conversely, there is also evidence that forcing firms to increase spending in social and sustainability policies is likely to negatively impact on shareholders' value (Manchiraju & Rajgopal, 2017).

All these argumentations suggest that CSR policies are value relevant for investment decisions (Jain et al., 2016; Amel-Zadeh & Serafeim, 2018; Serafeim & Yoon, 2022; Zhou et al., 2022) and, thus the presence of the CSR board committee has theoretical and practical implications (Radu & Smaili, 2021). Despite an increasing interest in literature on the effect of ESG metrics on capital markets (Serafeim & Yoon, 2022) to the best of our knowledge, little is known about the role of CSR board committee on the value relevance of companies' accounting information. Taking into account the recent academic and policy debate on the role of CSR for firm's value creation and investors' expectations (Burke et al., 2019; Zhou et al., 2022), we investigate whether the presence of CSR board committee strengths the value relevance of Italian listed firms. Further, we explore the moderating effect of CSR board committee on the relationships between accounting numbers, ESG score, and market price.

Using a sample of 413 firms listed on Italian stock exchange in Milan over the period 2017–2021 (2065 firm-year observations), we find that the presence of CSR board committee increases the value relevance of corporate information, suggesting that investors recognize the importance of CSR board committee in their capital allocation.

Our results provide contributions to the current academic and policy debate. Unlike most of the prior studies that have generally focused on the antecedents and effects of ESG corporate reporting, we provide fresh empirical evidence about the ability of CSR governance mechanisms to affect capital markets. This is important, since empirical investigations on whether investors may take advantage of firms' CSR engagement remain inconclusive (Becchetti et al., 2012; Manchiraju & Rajgopal, 2017). Second, we document that the presence of CSR board committees positively moderates the impact of *earnings and book value per share*, as well as ESG score.

In terms of practical implications, our research offers renewed insights about which governance characteristics are likely to influence the value relevance of accounting number and corporate information. Therefore, the results of our study may help companies and investors in identifying corporate governance architecture that can improve the management of the CSR strategies which is able to create shared value.

This research is structured as follows. The next section reports the institutional background and literature review, followed by hypothesis. Section 11.3 describes the methodology, including the sample, data collection, variables, and empirical models. This is followed by Sect. 11.4, which illustrates the results, offering additional analyses and robustness tests. Section 11.5 discusses the conclusions.

11.2 Background and Predictions

The CSR board committee is a sustainability governance mechanism, which shows the commitment of firms toward social and environmental issues (Liao et al., 2015). A board sub-committee relies on specific expertise, supporting the board of directors to deal with complex issues and promptly monitor business practices (Dixon-Fowler et al., 2017; Ginesti et al., 2023). The need of a board CSR committee arises from the increasing pressure that firms are facing to transform their business model into a more sustainable-oriented ones (Ginesti et al., 2023). In particular, the changes in societal norms and stakeholders' expectations have been a first important driver for promoting social responsibilities among firms and thus the presence of board CSR committees is considered a useful way to increase the corporate reputation on social and environmental matters (Kolev et al., 2019).

Despite an increasing interest of international regulations and local authorities on the role, composition, and duties of CSR board committees (Elmaghrabi, 2021), there is a common view that it represents a CSR governance mechanism responsible for setting CSR-oriented goals, sustainability policies, as well as the monitoring of the CSR strategies (Ricart et al., 2005). Adopting the lens of stakeholder theory (Freeman, 1984; Freeman et al., 2010), firms choose to set up such sub-board committee to manage sustainability-related risks and opportunities in a more proactive manner (García-Sánchez et al., 2019). In this way, they can better address the needs of a broader range of stakeholders (Mallin & Michelon, 2011) and investors' capital allocations (Amel-Zadeh & Serafeim, 2018). This is because the higher engagement in CSR activities enables managers to adopt a holistic approach to solving business problems and meeting wider stakeholders' interests (Costa et al., 2015; Elmaghrabi, 2021; Ginesti et al., 2023).

Moreover, the presence of CSR committee allows companies to improve corporate strategies that balance financial and non-financial goals (Liao et al., 2015; Velte & Stawinoga, 2020). Due to the importance of the role of CSR board committee at the corporate governance level, many studies have found that CSR board committee positively influences firms' CSR performance (Spitzeck, 2009; Shaukat et al., 2016; Cucari et al., 2018; Radu & Smaili, 2021) and market value (Dal Maso et al., 2017; Nekhili et al., 2017; Amel-Zadeh & Serafeim, 2018; Nandy et al., 2023; Orazalin et al., 2024). The CSR board committee generally monitors activities regarding CSR-related aspects and management's targets on CSR activities, even promoting a higher level of corporate transparency and disclosure quality (García-Sánchez et al., 2019). For example, Mallin et al. (2013) suggest a positive effect of stakeholders' orientation of corporate governance structure, which includes CSR board committees on financial and non-financial disclosure. In this regard, the greater ability of firms to communicate to their stakeholders, including investors, the improvement of their corporate social responsibility performance, enables them to enhance their CSR reputation and image. Consequently, strengthened corporate reputation helps to address investor uncertainty and their related confidence in firm's actions with an impact on stock market reaction (Ramchander et al., 2012).

In academic research, theoretical implications of CSR board committee have been investigated by using different perspectives, including the stakeholder theory (Freeman, 1984, Freeman et al., 2010). The perspective of stakeholder theory may support the value relevance of CSR for investment decisions since it is plausible that investors recognize the importance of considering a wide range of stakeholders' interests in implementing the business activities (Jain et al., 2016; Radu & Smaili, 2021). Hence, the presence of a CSR board sub-committee assures a strong commitment toward CSR and therefore a lower firm risk (Mishra & Modi, 2013; Albuquerque et al., 2019; Serafeim & Yoon, 2022) and a better value creation (Cohen et al., 2017; Suto & Takehara, 2020; Lu et al., 2021; Zhou et al., 2022). Thus, the presence of CSR board sub-committee into firms' governance structure is pivotal to demonstrate the effort of top management to address the current interests off all stakeholders, including shareholders (Ginesti et al., 2023). In line with this idea, Lourenço et al. (2014) argue that market valuation of companies could be explained by non-financial information that provide evidence of the company's effort in terms of social responsibility-related activities. Raimo et al. (2021) argue that the provision of non-financial disclosure to investors gives them access to a range of information about past and future companies' performance, which are not frequently available in the market. This leads to a reduction of information asymmetry among investors. Moreover, De Villiers and Van Staden (2011) argue that non-financial disclosure represents a key tool for investors to consider extra-financial indicators in their assessment of corporate risks. All these argumentations are in line with the study of Wang and Li (2016), who demonstrate that the value relevance of CSR information is a key content of non-financial information. In this regard, a number of studies show the positive relationship between firms' CSR performance (either disclosed by the firm itself) and market valuation of equity (Shevlin, 1996; Moneva & Cuellar, 2009; Cordazzo et al., 2020). This is because a good CSR performance enhances the corporate reputation that in turn can increase the value relevance of cash flow and net income (Hussainey & Salama, 2010; Lourenço et al., 2014; Wong & Zhang, 2022). Overall, Rao and Tilt (2016) show that the improvement of corporate transparency relies on the adequate governance structure that implies the presence of CSR board committee.

Therefore, extant literature provides theoretical and empirical evidence that CSR board committee is crucial in determining the implementation of CSR policies, which have several beneficial effects for firms. Hence, in line with the stakeholder theory, it is reasonable to expect an increasing recognition of CSR by investors. In particular, the presence of the CSR board committee may enable firms to provide relevant information about their social and sustainability operations, leading investors to take appropriate decisions that would reduce the risks and uncertainties perceived by capital markets (García-Sánchez et al., 2019). Based on this, we argue that the presence of a CSR board committee would reinforce the corporate attitude toward social actions, accountability, and transparency. Hence, firms with a CSR board committee will meet the expectations of shareholders in terms of value creation, leading to an increase of value relevance in capital market. On these bases, we propose the following hypothesis:

H1: *The CSR board committee positively affects the value relevance of Italian listed companies.*

11.3 Methodology, Sample Selection, and Data Collection

We analyze a sample of Italian listed firms, and we collected accounting and financial data from the ORBIS database and information on the presence of CSR committee, as well as ESG scores from Refinitiv.

We start our sample selection process by selecting 413 firms listed on Italian stock exchange over the period 2017–2021 (2065 firm-year observations). From this initial sample, we removed firm-years observations as outliers (35) in line with Cook's distance methodology (Jobson, 1991) and financial firms (345). This criterion leads to a final sample of 337 unique firms, obtaining 1685 firm-years observations.

Table 11.1 displays the sample selection process and the composition of our sample by number of observations and industry sector.

To develop our empirical analysis, we rely on value relevance methodology based on Ohlson model (Barth et al., 2001; Holthausen & Watts, 2001). The Ohlson model is widely adopted in value relevance research, since it considers the ability of earnings and the book value of equity to explain market value as a proxy for the informativeness of firms' financial statements. Our study employs statistically significant regression coefficients as measures of the value relevance of the variables employed (Song et al., 2010).

To decide whether a fixed effects model, random effects model, or OLS model is more appropriate to our panel dataset, we performed several diagnostic tests, such as Hausman test and Breusch-Pagan Lagrange multiplier test (Onali et al., 2017). The results of these tests suggest that the OLS model is preferable. Our regression analyses are based on the following model (1):

$$P_{i,t} = \alpha + \beta_1 EPS_{i,t} + \beta_2 BVPS_{i,t} + \varepsilon \qquad (11.1)$$

where for firm i at time t, P is the market price after the end of the financial period under examination (i.e., 30 April). This ensures that the accounting information is in the public domain and has been "absorbed" by investors (Tsalavoutas et al., 2012). EPS is the net income per share, and BVPS is the book value of common equity per share; ε is the error term.

Table 11.1 Sample selection and composition

Panel A: Sample selection	N	
Initial sample	2065	
Outliers—Cook's distance	(35)	
Financial services	(345)	
Final sample	1685	
Panel B: Composition	**N**	**%**
Agriculture	5	0.002
Hotels and restaurants	15	0.007
Public administration	30	0.014
Administrative services	245	0.120
Arts	35	0.017
Mining	10	0.005
Manufacturing	675	0.332
Retail trade	70	0.034
Wholesale	110	0.054
Constructions	25	0.012
Water supply	10	0.005
Energy	90	0.044
Real estate	65	0.032
Healthcare	25	0.012
ICT	220	0.108
Transport	40	0.020
Other services	15	0.007
Total	**1685**	**1**

We estimate incremental regression models to test for the impact of our variables of interest and our control variables in the following model (2):

$$P_{i.t} = \alpha + \beta_1 EPS_{i,t} + \beta_2 BVPS_{i,t} + \beta_3 CSRc_{i,t} + \beta_4 ESG_{i,t} + \beta_5 EPS_{i,t} {}^* CSRc_{i,t} + \beta_6 BVPS_{i,t} {}^* CSRc_{i,t} + \beta_7 ESG_{i,t} {}^* CSRc_{i,t} + \beta_8 ROE_{i,t} + \beta_9 LEV_{i,t} + \beta_{10} SIZE_{i,t} + \varepsilon \quad (11.2)$$

where $CSRc_{i,t}$, is a dummy variable that takes the value of "1" (one) if the firm has voluntarily established a CSR committee and "0" (zero) otherwise (Radu & Smaili, 2021; Ginesti et al., 2023); ESG is the Environmental, Social, and Governance score obtained from Refinitiv; the interaction variables are used to understand if the presence of the CSRc improves the value relevance of accounting variables (i.e., ESP and BVPS) and ESG score. Finally, we also include several control variables that are likely to impact on dependent variables, such as firm's profitability (ROE), firm's leverage (LEV), and firm's size (SIZE).

The detailed calculation of all variables used in our empirical analysis is reported in Table 11.2.

Table 11.2 Variables construction, measurement, and data source

Variable	Measurement
P	Market price after the end of the financial period under examination (i.e., 30 April).
EPS	Earnings over number of outstanding shares at the end of year t
BVPS	Book value of equity over number of outstanding shares at the end of year t
CSRc	A dummy variable which takes the value of "1" when a firm has established CSR board committee and the value "0" otherwise
ESG	Environmental, social, and governance score that varies between 0 and 100 (where 100 is the best score)
ROE	Net income divided by equity at the end of year t
LEV	Total debt divided by total assets at the end of year t
SIZE	Log of total assets at the end of year t

11.4 Results

11.4.1 Descriptive Statistics

Table 11.3 shows the descriptive statistics of the variables used in the analysis. Panel A shows descriptive statistics for the whole sample, while Panel B and Panel C depict, respectively, descriptive statistics for firms with a CSR board committee and firms without a CSR board committee.

In Panel A, the variable P ranges between 0.15 and 132.50, as the sample includes both the small and large Italian firms; the mean is 5.41. EPS (in thousands of euros) has a mean of 1.15 and BVPS has a mean of 2.81.

Regarding our main variable of interest, our sample includes around 51% of observations in which companies have established a board CSR committee (CSRc). Firms in the sample have a mean of ESG score of 50.70, suggesting that on average Italian listed companies do not show high ESG scores, despite there are companies that have registered top tier ESG score.

Lastly, the control variables ROE, LEV, and SIZE have, respectively, a mean of 8.39, 0.62, and 5.15.

Regarding Panel B and Panel C, we have investigated if the differences between the variables are statistically significant, so we have computed the t-test. The results of this test (untabulated) show that significant differences exist between the variables P, EPS, BVPS, ESG, E, and S.

Table 11.4 reports the Pearson correlations between all variables. The variable P is positively and significantly correlated with EPS, BVPS, ESG, ROE, and SIZE, while it is negatively and significantly correlated with LEV. Furthermore, we control for the potential multi-collinearity of the employed independent variables by computing the variance inflation factors (VIFs). The results obtained indicate absence of collinearity among the regressors.

Table 11.3 Descriptive statistics

Variables	Min	Max	Mean	Dev. Std.
Panel A. Total sample				
P	0,15	132,50	5,41	13,12
EPS	−54,93	7,62	1,15	3,33
BVPS	−51,05	44,46	2,81	5,76
CSRc	0	1	0,51	0,50
ESG	0	99,87	50,70	28,02
E	0	99,76	22,45	31,05
S	0	98,96	20,31	31,35
G	0	99,86	24,50	30,22
ROE	−98,76	88,77	8,39	20,01
LEV	0	5,18	0,62	1,79
SIZE	1,67	8,73	5,15	1,17
Panel B. Firms with a CSRc				
P	0,22	132,50	5,65	13,10
EPS	−43,22	7,62	1,61	3,30
BVPS	,39,45	44,46	3,01	2,99
ESG	10,15	99,87	55,20	26,12
E	11,43	99,76	58,20	27,21
S	10,91	98,96	53,56	27,33
G	11,34	99,86	54,15	26,02
ROE	−16,25	88,77	9,44	19,17
LEV	0	3,12	0,60	1,80
SIZE	1,71	8,73	5,11	1,15
Panel C. Firms without a CSRc				
P	0,15	120,60	5,23	12,98
EPS	−54,93	5,67	1,10	3,31
BVPS	−51,05	30,25	2,10	3,00
ESG	0	75,15	38,91	28,01
E	0	78,56	38,23	28,00
S	0	69,54	38,98	27,67
G	0	70,11	39,03	27,98
ROE	−98,76	59,56	6,95	20,02
LEV	1,67	5,18	0,65	1,79
SIZE	1,67	8,52	4,97	1,16

11.4.2 Regression Results

Table 11.5 reports the results of our analysis and confirms that the estimated coefficients for EPS and BVPS are positively related to market price across Model (1) and Model (2). In particular, the marginal effect of the OLS regression, a one-standard deviation increase in EPS is associated with an increase in the dependent variable P of 1,89, while an increase in BVPS is associated with an increase of P of 1,21. These findings are consistent with prior literature that has investigated the

Table 11.4 Pearson correlation

	P	EPS	BVPS	CSRc	ESG	ROE	LEV	SIZE
P	1							
ESP	0,15***	1						
BVPS	0,11***	0,13***	1					
CSRc	0,03	−0,04	0,01	1				
ESG	0,15***	0,10***	0,17***	0,01	1			
ROE	0,16***	0,16***	−0,01	−0,03	0,16**	1		
LEV	−0,08***	−0,05	−0,17***	−0,03	−0,06**	0,23***	1	
SIZE	0,23***	0,25***	0,23***	0,02	0,24***	0,07**	−0,11***	1

*p-value < 1% ***, p-value < 5% **, p-value < 10% **

Table 11.5 Regression results

Variables	Mod, (1)	VIF	Mod, (2)	VIF
P (Constant)	1,04(39,17)***	–	0,32(3,90)***	–
EPS	0,57(19,09)***	1,48	0,20(6,16)***	1,48
BVPS	0,21(7,17)***	1,48	0,05(2,02)**	1,48
CSRc	–	–	0,23(7,84)***	1,09
ESG	–	–	0,41(27,53)***	1,04
CSRc*EPS	–	–	0,32(2,70)**	1,64
CSRc*BVPS	–	–	0,12(2,81)**	1,59
CSRc*ESG	–	–	0,61(6,52)***	2,11
ROE	–	–	0,08(2,79)**	1,44
LEV	–	–	−0,03(−0,07)	1,10
SIZE	–	–	0,02(1,74)*	1,11
Obs,	1685 firm-year observations			
Adj, R^2	0,60	0,84		
F test	1060,80***	838,87***		

*Note: p-value < 1% ***, p-value < 5% **, p-value < 10% **

value relevance of earnings and book values (i.e., Barth et al., 2001; Holthausen & Watts, 2001) and with other studies that have investigated the value relevance of ESG/CSR disclosure (i.e., Cordazzo et al., 2020; Aureli et al., 2020; Cahan et al., 2016) and ESG/CSR performance (i.e. Choi et al., 2020; Jain et al., 2016; Middleton, 2015; Hassel et al., 2005).

In Model (2), we gradually introduce our variable of interest (CSRc) and the results show that the presence of CSR board committees positively affects the value relevance of Italian listed firms (p-value <1%). Moreover, the presence of CSR board committee positively moderates the relationship between EPS, BVPS as well as ESG and market price (p-value <5%). These results suggest that investors have particular interest in firms' commitment toward CSR activities, transparency, and accountability (Doh et al., 2010). Furthermore, our findings suggest that the presence of CSR board committee may improve governance mechanisms that can increase shareholders' wealth and thus the long-term survival of the companies (Becchetti et al., 2012; Liao et al., 2015; Jaggi et al., 2018; Jaggi et al., 2018). This is in line with prior studies that suggest that the presence of CSR committee leads to a better firms' CSR performance. Moreover, the presence of CSR governance mechanisms can offer better non-financial information that lead to reduce information asymmetry and investors' perceived risk (Mishra & Modi, 2013; Jain et al., 2016; Serafeim & Yoon, 2022).

As in Rao and Tilt (2016) and Wang and Li (2016), our results show that the presence of CSR board committee strengthens the value relevance of ESG score, since the interaction effect between the coefficient of CSRc and ESG is positive and significant (p-value $<1\%$).

11.4.3 Robustness Tests and Additional Analyses

In this section we provide robustness tests and additional analyses to increase the theoretical and practical implications of our results.

First, since CSRc may be endogenously determined, and bias the regression results, we addressed this potential problem by using an instrumental variable in the two-stage least squares regression. Assuming that the voluntary establishment of CSRc might be influenced by firm size and economic and financial performance (Jaggi et al., 2018), we first regressed CSRc on Size, LEV, and ROE, obtaining the predicted value of CSRc:

$$\mathrm{CSRc} = \alpha + \beta_1 \mathrm{Size} + \beta_2 \mathrm{LEV} + \beta_3 \mathrm{ROE} + \varepsilon \tag{11.3}$$

In the second stage, we used the predicted value of CSRc in place of its actual value in the main regression analysis, Model (1). We conducted 2-SLS regression tests with the predicted values of CSRc, obtaining the following equation:

$$\mathrm{P} = \alpha + \beta_1 \mathrm{EPS}_{i,t} + \beta_2 \mathrm{BVPS}_{i,t} + \beta_3 \widehat{CSRc} + \beta_4 \mathrm{ESG} + \beta_5 EPS * \widehat{CSRc} + \beta_6 BVPS * \widehat{CSRc} + \beta_7 ESG * \widehat{CSRc} + \beta_8 \mathrm{ROEi,t} + \beta_9 \mathrm{LEVi,t} + \beta_{10} \mathrm{SIZEi,t} + \varepsilon \tag{11.4}$$

The results (untabulated) confirm those obtained in the main analysis.

Second, we winsorized the financial variables at the 99th percentile and our main results (untabulated) continue to hold.

Third, we controlled whether the CSR committee has a different impact on the key element of ESG score and thus we replace in Model (2) the ESG score by introducing the "Environmental" score (E), "Social" score (S), and "Governance" (G). Our results are reported in Table 11.6 and show that, in the marginal effect of the OLS regression, a one-standard deviation increase in E is associated with an increase in the dependent variable P of 3,41, and an increase in S is associated with an

Table 11.6 Additional analysis

Variables	Mod, (3)	VIF
P (Constant)	−0,89(−0,43)	–
EPS	0,03(1,69)*	1,74
BVPS	0,01(2,64)**	1,63
CSRc	0,20(8,12)***	1,10
E	0,11(2,65)**	1,05
S	0,21(3,19)***	1,10
G	0,00(0,54)	1,11
CSRc*EPS	0,21(2,70)**	1,63
CSRc*BVPS	0,11(2,80)**	1,60
CSRc*E	0,31(2,51)**	1,85
CSRc*S	0,40(3,01)***	1,84
CSRc*G	0,00(0,51)	2,01
ROE	0,03(3,01)***	1,44
LEV	−0,01(−0,67)	1,10
SIZE	0,23(12,54)***	1,11
Obs,	1685 firm-year observations	
Adj, R^2	0,85	
F test	733,16***	

*Note; p-value < 1% ***, p-value < 5% **, p-value < 10% **

increase of P of 6,58, while an increase in G is associated with an increase of P of 0,03. These results suggest that social and human capital could be considered as key drivers of firm's value and thus social disclosure is value relevant for investors (Qiu et al., 2016). This evidence is also consistent with emerging findings that show that globally investors consider firm's social performance important for their investment decisions (Marsat & Williams, 2014). Moreover, this finding mirrors the value attached to social screens by the global SRI sector (Renneboog et al., 2008) and corroborates the predictions of scholars (Friedman & Miles, 2001) on the importance for stakeholders of corporate social reputation. A lower coefficient of the E score is probably due to the investors' concerns about a potential increase in costs related to the adoption of environmental policies costs at the expense of financial performance (Misani & Pogutz, 2015). Additionally, the market is short-term oriented, and investors often do not consider longer-term environmental information when making investment decisions (Hassel et al., 2005). In addition, Choi et al. (2020) suggest that environmental issues are value relevant only for firms that operate in "environmentally sensitive" industries, and thus our results should be interpreted with caution.

We do not find any significant impact of G on market price, possibly because in Italian setting there is a corporate governance disclosure regime that meets the need of investors.

Finally, the CSRc positively moderates the relationship between E, S, P, and market price.

11.5 Conclusions

Our study is a first attempt to understand whether the presence of a CSR board committee improves the value relevance of companies' accounting numbers and information. We test this hypothesis on a sample of Italian listed companies over the period 2017–2021. We provide evidence that CSR board committees positively impact on companies' value relevance, suggesting that the recent international policy debate arising from the new social and environmental concerns on corporate sustainability is of importance for investors' judgments.

Beyond the theoretical implications, our analysis has also practical implications. For example, our results shed light on the dynamics and outcomes of stock market reaction, when a CSR board committee operates within the corporate governance structure. Therefore, our study is of interest for policymakers, companies, and investors interested to understand mechanisms through which CSR governance bodies may affect the shareholders' decisions and wealth.

Our study is not free of limitations and thus our results should be interpreted with cautions. First, our study focuses only on Italian context, which is characterized from underdeveloped capital markets and weaker shareholder protection (La Porta & Lopez-de-Silanes, 1998) than Anglo-American contexts. Second, our results may be affected by confounding events in capital markets related to the long-term effect of Covid-19 pandemic on accounting numbers. Finally, we do not consider the impact of other potential corporate governance variables that may concurrently affect the value relevance.

Overall, this study opens the way for future research on effects of CSR governance mechanisms on corporate transparency and capital markets, especially in the view of the novel international laws and regulations on sustainability corporate issues. For example, future studies may investigate how the composition, expertise, and frequency of CSR committee meetings impact investors' reactions.

References

Albuquerque, R., Koskinen, Y., & Zhang, C. (2019). Corporate social responsibility and firm risk: Theory and empirical evidence. *Management Science, 65*(10), 4451–4469.

Amel-Zadeh, A., & Serafeim, G. (2018). Why and how investors use ESG information: Evidence from a global survey. *Financial Analysts Journal, 74*(3), 1–17.

Aureli, S., Gigli, S., Medei, R., & Supino, E. (2020). The value relevance of environmental, social, and governance disclosure: Evidence from Dow Jones sustainability world index listed companies. *Corporate Social Responsibility and Environmental Management, 27*(1), 43–52.

Barth, M. E., Beaver, W. H., & Landsman, W. R. (2001). The relevance of the value relevance literature for financial accounting standard setting: Another view. *Journal of Accounting and Economics, 31*(1–3), 77–104.

Becchetti, L., Ciciretti, R., Hasan, I., & Kobeissi, N. (2012). Corporate social responsibility and shareholder's value. *Journal of Business Research, 65*(11), 1628–1635.

Benlemlih, M., & Bitar, M. (2018). Corporate social responsibility and investment efficiency. *Journal of Business Ethics, 148*, 647–671.

Bollen, N. P. (2007). Mutual fund attributes and investor behavior. *Journal of Financial and Quantitative Analysis, 42*(3), 683–708.

Burke, J. J., Hoitash, R., & Hoitash, U. (2019). The heterogeneity of board-level sustainability committees and corporate social performance. *Journal of Business Ethics, 154*(4), 1161–1186.

Cahan, S. F., De Villiers, C., Jeter, D. C., Naiker, V., & Van Staden, C. J. (2016). Are CSR disclosures value relevant? Cross-country evidence. *European Accounting Review, 25*(3), 579–611.

Choi, H., Han, I., & Lee, J. (2020). Value relevance of corporate environmental performance: A comprehensive analysis of performance indicators using Korean data. *Sustainability, 12*(17), 7209.

Cohen, J., Holder-Webb, L., & Khalil, S. (2017). A further examination of the impact of corporate social responsibility and governance on investment decisions. *Journal of Business Ethics, 146*, 203–218.

Cordazzo, M., Bini, L., & Marzo, G. (2020). Does the EU directive on non-financial information influence the value relevance of ESG disclosure? Italian evidence. *Business Strategy and the Environment, 29*(8), 3470–3483.

Costa, C., Lages, L. F., & Hortinha, P. (2015). The bright and dark side of CSR in export markets: Its impact on innovation and performance. *International Business Review, 24*(5), 749–757.

Cucari, N., Esposito De Falco, S., & Orlando, B. (2018). Diversity of board of directors and environmental social governance: Evidence from Italian listed companies. *Corporate Social Responsibility and Environmental Management, 25*(3), 250–266.

Dal Maso, L., Liberatore, G., & Mazzi, F. (2017). Value relevance of stakeholder engagement: The influence of national culture. *Corporate Social Responsibility and Environmental Management, 24*(1), 44–56.

De Villiers, C., & Van Staden, C. J. (2011). Where firms choose to disclose voluntary environmental information. *Journal of Accounting and Public Policy, 30*(6), 504–525.

Dixon-Fowler, H. R., Ellstrand, A. E., & Johnson, J. L. (2017). The role of board environmental committees in corporate environmental performance. *Journal of Business Ethics, 140*, 423–438.

Doh, J. P., Howton, S. D., Howton, S. W., & Siegel, D. S. (2010). Does the market respond to an endorsement of social responsibility? The role of institutions, information, and legitimacy. *Journal of Management, 36*(6), 1461–1485.

Elmaghrabi, M. E. (2021). CSR committee attributes and CSR performance: UK evidence. *Corporate Governance: The International Journal of Business in Society, 21*(5), 892–919.

Erhemjamts, O., Li, Q., & Venkateswaran, A. (2013). Corporate social responsibility and its impact on firms' investment policy, organizational structure, and performance. *Journal of Business Ethics, 118*(2), 395–412.

Freeman, R. E. (1984). *Strategic management: A stakeholder approach*. Pitman.

Freeman, R. E., Harrison, J. S., Wicks, A. C., Parmar, B. L., & De Colle, S. (2010). Stakeholder theory: The state of the art. *Academy of Management Annals, 4*(1), 403–445.

Friedman, A. L., & Miles, S. (2001). Socially responsible investment and corporate social and environmental reporting in the UK: An exploratory study. *The British Accounting Review, 33*(4), 523–548.

García-Sánchez, I., Gómez-Miranda, M., David, F., & Rodríguez-Ariza, L. (2019). Board independence and GRI-IFC performance standards: The mediating effect of the CSR committee. *Journal of Cleaner Production, 225*, 554–562.

Gennari, F., & Salvioni, D. M. (2019). CSR committees on boards: The impact of the external country level factors. *Journal of Management and Governance, 23*(3), 759–785.

Ginesti, G., Campa, D., Allini, A., & Maffei, M. (2023). The role of CSR committee characteristics on R&D investments. *International Business Review, 32*, 102147.

Hart, O., & Zingales, L. (2017). Serving shareholders doesn't mean putting profit above all else. *Harvard Business Review, 12*, 2–6.

Hassel, L., Nilsson, H., & Nyquist, S. (2005). The value relevance of environmental performance. *European Accounting Review, 14*(1), 41–61.

Holthausen, R. W., & Watts, R. L. (2001). The relevance of the value-relevance literature for financial accounting standard setting. *Journal of Accounting and Economics, 31*(1–3), 3–75.

Hussainey, K., & Salama, A. (2010). The importance of corporate environmental reputation to investors. *Journal of Applied Accounting Research, 11*(3), 229–241.

Jaggi, B., Allini, A., Macchioni, R., & Zagaria, C. (2018). The factors motivating voluntary disclosure of carbon information: Evidence based on Italian listed companies. *Organization & Environment, 31*(2), 178–202.

Jaggi, B., Allini, A., Macchioni, R., & Zampella, A. (2018). Do investors find carbon information useful? Evidence from Italian firms. *Review of Quantitative Finance and Accounting, 50*, 1031–1056.

Jain, A., Jain, P. K., & Rezaee, Z. (2016). Value-relevance of corporate social responsibility: Evidence from short selling. *Journal of Management Accounting Research, 28*(2), 29–52.

Jo, H., & Harjoto, M. A. (2011). Corporate governance and firm value: The impact of corporate social responsibility. *Journal of Business Ethics, 103*(3), 351–383.

Jobson, J. D. (1991). Confidence regions for the mean-variance efficient set: An alternative approach to estimation risk. *Review of Quantitative Finance and Accounting, 1*, 235–257.

Kolev, K. D., Wangrow, D. B., Barker, V. L., III, & Schepker, D. J. (2019). Board committees in corporate governance: A cross-disciplinary review and agenda for the future. *Journal of Management Studies, 56*(6), 1138–1193.

La Porta, R., & Lopez-de-Silanes, F. (1998). Capital markets and legal institutions. In *Beyond the Washington consensus: Institutions matter* (pp. 73–92).

Liao, L., Luo, L., & Tang, Q. (2015). Gender diversity, board independence, environmental committee and greenhouse gas disclosure. *The British Accounting Review, 47*(4), 409–424.

Lourenço, I. C., Callen, J. L., Branco, M. C., & Curto, J. D. (2014). The value relevance of reputation for sustainability leadership. *Journal of Business Ethics, 119*, 17–28.

Lu, H., Oh, W. Y., Kleffner, A., & Chang, Y. K. (2021). How do investors value corporate social responsibility? Market valuation and the firm specific contexts. *Journal of Business Research, 125*, 14–25.

Mallin, C. A., & Michelon, G. (2011). Board reputation attributes and corporate social performance: An empirical investigation of the US best corporate citizens. *Accounting and Business Research, 41*(2), 119–144.

Mallin, C., Michelon, G., & Raggi, D. (2013). Monitoring intensity and stakeholders' orientation: How does governance affect social and environmental disclosure? *Journal of Business Ethics, 114*, 29–43.

Manchiraju, H., & Rajgopal, S. (2017). Does corporate social responsibility (CSR) create shareholder value? Evidence from the Indian Companies Act 2013. *Journal of Accounting Research, 55*(5), 1257–1300.

Marsat, S., & Williams, B. (2014). Does the market value social pillar?. Available at SSRN 2419387.

Middleton, A. (2015). Value relevance of firms' integral environmental performance: Evidence from Russia. *Journal of Accounting and Public Policy, 34*(2), 204–211.

Misani, N., & Pogutz, S. (2015). Unraveling the effects of environmental outcomes and processes on financial performance: A non-linear approach. *Ecological Economics, 109*, 150–160.

Mishra, S., & Modi, S. (2013). Positive and negative corporate social responsibility, financial leverage, and idiosyncratic risk. *Journal of Business Ethics, 117*(2), 431–448.

Moneva, J. M., & Cuellar, B. (2009). The value relevance of financial and non-financial environmental reporting. *Environmental and Resource Economics, 44*, 441–456.

Nandy, M., Kuzey, C., Uyar, A., Lodh, S., & Karaman, A. S. (2023). Can CSR mechanisms spur GRI adoption and restore its lost value relevance? *Journal of Applied Accounting Research, 24*(4), 609–634.

Nekhili, M., Nagati, H., Chtioui, T., & Rebolledo, C. (2017). Corporate social responsibility disclosure and market value: Family versus nonfamily firms. *Journal of Business Research, 77*, 41–52.

Onali, E., Ginesti, G., & Vasilakis, C. (2017). How should we estimate value-relevance models? Insights from European data. *The British Accounting Review, 49*(5), 460–473.

Orazalin, N. S., Ntim, C. G., & Malagila, J. K. (2024). Board sustainability committees, climate change initiatives, carbon performance, and market value. *British Journal of Management, 35*(1), 295–320.

Peters, G. F., Romi, A. M., & Sanchez, J. M. (2019). The influence of corporate sustainability officers on performance. *Journal of Business Ethics, 159*(4), 1065–1087.

Porter, M. E., & Kramer, M. R. (2011). Creating shared value: Redefining capitalism and the role of the corporation in society. *Harvard Business Review, 89*(1/2), 62–77.

Qiu, Y., Shaukat, A., & Tharyan, R. (2016). Environmental and social disclosures: Link with corporate financial performance. *The British Accounting Review, 48*(1), 102–116.

Radu, C., & Smaili, N. (2021). Alignment versus monitoring: An examination of the effect of the CSR committee and CSR-linked executive compensation on CSR performance. *Journal of Business Ethics, 180*, 1–19.

Raimo, N., Caragnano, A., Zito, M., Vitolla, F., & Mariani, M. (2021). Extending the benefits of ESG disclosure: The effect on the cost of debt financing. *Corporate Social Responsibility and Environmental Management, 28*(4), 1412–1421.

Ramchander, S., Schwebach, R. G., & Staking, K. I. M. (2012). The informational relevance of corporate social responsibility: Evidence from DS400 index reconstitutions. *Strategic Management Journal, 33*(3), 303–314.

Rao, K., & Tilt, C. (2016). Board composition and corporate social responsibility: The role of diversity, gender, strategy and decision making. *Journal of Business Ethics, 138*, 327–347.

Renneboog, L., Ter Horst, J., & Zhang, C. (2008). Socially responsible investments: Institutional aspects, performance, and investor behavior. *Journal of Banking & Finance, 32*(9), 1723–1742.

Ricart, J. E., Rodríguez, M. Á., & Sanchez, P. (2005). Sustainability in the boardroom: An empirical examination of Dow Jones sustainability world index leaders. *Corporate Governance: The International Journal of Effective Board Performance, 5*(3), 24–41.

Serafeim, G., & Yoon, A. (2022). Stock price reactions to ESG news: The role of ESG ratings and disagreement. *Review of Accounting Studies, 28*(3), 1–31.

Shaukat, A., Qiu, Y., & Trojanowski, G. (2016). Board attributes, corporate social responsibility strategy, and corporate environmental and social performance. *Journal of Business Ethics, 135*, 569–585.

Shevlin, T. (1996). The value-relevance of nonfinancial information: A discussion. *Journal of Accounting and Economics, 22*(1–3), 31–42.

Song, C. J., Thomas, W. B., & Yi, H. (2010). Value relevance of FAS No, 157 fair value hierarchy information and the impact of corporate governance mechanisms. *The Accounting Review, 85*(4), 1375–1410.

Spitzeck, H. (2009). The development of governance structures for corporate responsibility. *Corporate Governance: The International Journal of Business in Society, 9*(4), 495–505.

Suto, M., & Takehara, H. (2020). Corporate social responsibility intensity, management earnings forecast accuracy, and investor trust: Evidence from Japan. *Corporate Social Responsibility and Environmental Management, 27*(6), 3047–3059.

Tsalavoutas, I., André, P., & Evans, L. (2012). The transition to IFRS and the value relevance of financial statements in Greece. *The British Accounting Review, 44*(4), 262–277.

Velte, P., & Stawinoga, M. (2020). Do chief sustainability officers and CSR committees influence CSR-related outcomes? A structured literature review based on empirical-quantitative research findings. *Journal of Management Control, 31*(4), 333–377.

Wang, K. T., & Li, D. (2016). Market reactions to the first-time disclosure of corporate social responsibility reports: Evidence from China. *Journal of Business Ethics, 138*(4), 661–682.

Wong, J. B., & Zhang, Q. (2022). Stock market reactions to adverse ESG disclosure via media channels. *The British Accounting Review, 54*(1), 101045.

Zhou, G., Liu, L., & Luo, S. (2022). Sustainable development, ESG performance and company market value: Mediating effect of financial performance. *Business Strategy and the Environment, 31*(7), 3371–3387.

Chapter 12
The Role of the Sustainability Committee in the Environmental Risk Management: Evidence from Italian Public Companies

Fabio Rizzato, Alberto Tonelli, and Alain Devalle

12.1 Introduction and Literature

Frequent corporate social and environmental disasters (e.g. corporate governance scandals, human rights issues and exploitative supply chain working conditions) are increasingly affecting corporate reputations, stakeholder relations and financial results, highlighting that strategy implementation and long-term corporate success depend on the effective management of environmental, social and governance (ESG) issues. ESG issues may represent threats or opportunities for companies and must be properly identified, measured (Nicholls, 2020) and reported (Adams, 2017; Adams & Larrinaga, 2019) to reduce negative external impacts and exploit any potential opportunities they offer (Adams, 2015; Adams et al., 2013). Thus, to ensure effective reporting of sustainability matters, standard setters have issued new regulations to facilitate high-quality sustainability information (Jørgensen et al., 2022). This means that corporations must manage pressures regarding ESG issues, which today greatly affect their reputations. For instance, Brogi et al.'s (2022) study highlighted that lenders view business models, attitudes and approaches to ESG issues as additional insurance against credit risk, since greater awareness of ESG issues is strongly and significantly associated with better creditworthiness. The integration of ESG issues (e.g. the volatility of financial assets) into financial risk processes and measures may be useful for risk prediction and forecasting. In fact, ESG issues have implications for corporations because they are directly linked to ESG risks. To avoid

F. Rizzato · A. Tonelli (✉)
Dipartimento di Management "Valter Cantino", Università di Torino, Turin, Italy
e-mail: alberto.tonelli@unito.it

A. Devalle
Dipartimento di Scienze Economico-sociali e matematico-statistiche, Università di Torino, Turin, Italy

N. Castellano et al. (eds.), *Environmental, Social, Governance (ESG)*, SIDREA Series in Accounting and Business Administration,
https://doi.org/10.1007/978-3-031-76618-3_12

the negative consequences of such risks, enterprises must equip themselves with enterprise risk management processes (i.e. monitoring systems with which various parties, such as risk managers, internal auditors, external auditors and risk committees, engage) to identify any risks to the companies' strategies. Linked to this, Chairani and Siregar's (2021) study demonstrated that proper enterprise risk management is influenced by ESG issues. Therefore, corporate governance processes should be updated to include ESG matters. ESG risks, together with other corporate risks, expose firms to reputational and operational damage (González Sánchez & Morales de Vega, 2018; Humphrey et al., 2012; Young & Thyil, 2014; Xie et al., 2019), so companies have increasingly established sustainability or corporate social responsibility (CSR) committees within their governance structures to effectively address sustainability issues (Birindelli et al., 2018). As highlighted in the academic literature, such matters need to be addressed to support companies' long-term success (Fahad & Rahman, 2020; Jarboui et al., 2023; Orazalin et al., 2023). ESG risk management practices and their incorporation into strategy, accounting and reporting have developed rapidly, emerging as particularly interesting issues (Adams, 2017; Landi et al., 2022) and influencing more than 60,000 SMEs aiming to transition. These companies operate in industries that are undergoing significant transformation, and defining an appropriate set of risks is critical for achieving informed change management and preserving going concern. The Net Balance Foundation (2011) highlighted their poor management of ESG risks, showing that only 70% of 50 companies had policies in place to manage ESG issues and only 36% focused on ESG in their company visions and value statements. Furthermore, it is believed that some business managers are not sufficiently aware that ESG risks can impact their businesses (Adams, 2017).

Nevertheless, although ESG issues are wide ranging, they tend to be linked largely to the environment. ESG covers three types of issues: environmental (issues such as climate change and pollution), social (issues such as violations of human rights) and governance (issues such as gender equality on boards of directors). The Global Risk Report 2023 (WEF, 2023) stated that, in the next 10 years, 6 environmental risks will become consistently and predominantly relevant to the environment and society. They relate to the mitigation of climate change, in terms of climate change adaptation, natural disasters, extreme weather events, biodiversity losses and ecosystem collapses. These risks have potentially severe consequences. Such events exacerbate ecosystem deterioration, threaten supply chains across the globe and undermine climate crisis mitigation. Thus, it is important to focus on the environmental perspective. In addition, constraints on sustainable investments, risk management processes and concern about these issues may influence firms as going concerns, given that environmental sensitivity is framed as a vital condition. Thus, it is widely accepted that climate and environmental risks will become core global risks over the next few years. For instance, Sharfman and Fernando (2008) highlighted that effective environmental risk management leads to a lower cost of capital, a shift from equity to debt financing and higher tax benefits associated with the ability to add debt, while Lee and Choi revealed that firms' carbon risk management decreases the cost of debt capital in financial markets. Furthermore, firms mainly exposed to environmental risk and characterised by proper risk management achieve improved environmental performance and market value (Dal Maso et al., 2023). Environmental risk management is also a signal of well-being for banks, which are generally proactive in requiring environmental risk management procedures and reporting to enhance accounting (Dobler et al., 2014).

In relation to such premises, various regulatory changes have recently obliged Italian companies to establish organisational, administrative and accounting arrangements (Article 2086 of the Civil Code), which must be appropriate to the nature and size of the company, able to detect company crises and losses of going concern in a timely manner and capable of facilitating the prompt adoption and implementation of regulatory tools for overcoming such crises and recovering going concern. A company with adequate arrangements should be equipped to detect corporate risk factors and assess the impact of individual events on its financial and economic equilibrium, which is the minimum goal the regulations have set in terms of preventing corporate crises and promptly identifying corporate risks. However, various researchers (e.g. Malik et al., 2020) have claimed that the mere presence of a board-level risk committee does not mitigate enterprise risk, although the existence of a structurally strong board is crucial for effective enterprise risk management and governance. This regulatory intervention, by promoting consideration of ESG factors, is leading to the redesign of corporate governance to facilitate the detection and management of sustainability risks alongside traditional economic and financial risks. It also enhances stakeholder capitalism by fostering the sustainable success of companies listed on regulated markets through common benefit objectives and appropriate company models. If companies consider ESG risks and expand their corporate visions to include the pursuit of sustainability goals in their relevant operations and structures, it follows that their corporate structures must be evaluated in terms of their governance and control of ESG issues as well as the potential impact of sustainability risks on their capital or economic–financial balances. Velte and Stawinoga (2020) claimed that the literature on sustainability officers and CSR committees is highly significant. The literature has focused on corporate governance mechanisms in general (Koutoupis et al., 2021; Lagasio & Cucari, 2019; Malik et al., 2020) and their effect on ESG matters (e.g. environmental disclosure; Helfaya & Moussa, 2017; Lagasio & Cucari, 2019). Hence, it is worth analysing ESG risks and the impact of sustainability committees on ESG practices in more depth. So far, researchers have focused on corporate environmental performance and its relationship to firm risk by highlighting its negative influence (Xue et al., 2020).

Therefore, in this study, the authors hypothesised that the presence of a sustainability committee would lead to a greater focus on environmental risk management. Due to the growing prevalence of environmental risks, among others, that influence companies' actual and future establishment of sustainability committees, the objective of this study was to understand whether corporations may better manage such risks by introducing proper governance structures. In other words, the aim was to answer the question *'Does the presence of a sustainability committee positively or negatively affect the management of environmental risks?'* The authors focused on the Italian context due to the latest regulatory changes requiring Italian companies to equip themselves with organisational, administrative and accounting arrangements.

This study contributes to the literature by providing additional insights into ESG risk management, helping to position future research. Moreover, it provides the basis for developing an environmental risk management index by to assist companies in determining whether they are subject to transition risks, aware that their businesses could be affected, consider the intensity of climate change risks and recognise the future implications of ESG risks for their businesses. Regarding practical implications, the study may be useful for helping companies understand whether ad hoc CSR committees are suitable for managing climate change risks, especially if those risks are configured as proper corporate risks equivalent to other risks. The originality of the study lies in the growing relevance of ESG risk management given that ESG practices should be developed as a vital source of long-term orientation and must be rooted in each company's corporate governance structure. Moreover, it describes an Italian context recently influenced by the need to comply with the latest regulatory changes.

This chapter is structured as follows: Sect. 12.2 explains the methodology for the study, Sect. 12.3 presents the results, and Sect. 12.4 provides the discussion and conclusion.

12.2 Methodology

The authors adopted a quantitative methodology to identify whether the presence of corporate governance committees helped companies manage environmental risks. The authors considered the governance variable in depth by investigating whether firms that had already strengthened their governance structures by electing sustainability committees succeeded in improving attitudes towards the management of such risks. The authors focused on identifying determinants of this sensitivity towards ESG risks. Recent environmental events in Italy, such as reduced rainfall, widespread fires, flooding and storms, led us to delve into the Italian context. Specifically, the authors aimed to identify the factors that are crucial for environmental risk management and have broad societal and corporate implications. The initial sample comprised 456 Italian companies, but due to the unavailability of some data, the authors reduced the sample to 453 companies. Data were gathered from Refinitiv—a database widely used in sustainability and financial accounting research (Akbas et al., 2018) that contains a large amount of international company data. The analysis covered a multi-year period ranging from 2017 (coinciding with the inception of the Task Force on Climate-Related Financial Disclosures (TCFD)) to 2022 (the last year for which data were available). The adoption of this wide range of years enabled us to conduct panel data analysis, which is a methodology characterised by reduced estimation and omitted variable bias that is highly accurate from an inferential point of view (Hsiao & Pesaran, 2008). Authors ran the panel data analysis using Stata 17, with a strongly balanced model of 453 companies. The equation for the panel data analysis was as follows:

$$\begin{aligned} Environmental\ Risk\ Management_{it} &= B_0 + B_1\ SustComm_{it} + B_2\ ROE_{it} \\ &+ B_3\ Leverage_{it} + B_5\ LnTotAss_{it} + \mu_t + \omega_i + \varepsilon_{it}. \end{aligned}$$

The dependent variable was *environmental risk management* (EnvRiskMan), which the authors determined by considering the following dummy variables (Xue et al., 2020):

- Recognition of climate change as a source of risk: does the company recognise climate change as a relevant risk to the business?
- Specific climate-related risk management process: does the company maintain a specific climate-related risk management process?
- Climate-related risks integrated into risk management: does the company integrate climate-related risks into its company-wide risk management programme?
- Financial exposure to transition risk: does the company disclose assets or business activities vulnerable to transition risk?
- Climate change commercial risks and opportunities: is the company aware that climate change can represent commercial risks and/or opportunities? This includes the development of new products/services to overcome the threats of climate change to a company's existing business model. Some companies view climate change as a business opportunity and develop new products/services accordingly.
- Climate change risks and opportunities strategy: does the company detail how it incorporates climate change risks and opportunities into its strategy (e.g. mitigation, new products and research and development)?

The authors processed the data using a dichotomous approach; that is, if disclosure was present, the value of the variable was 1, but otherwise 0. 'Not available' (NA) data derived from missing Refinitiv information. The authors neutralised the presence of NA data by adopting the following formula, excluding them from the ratio's computation:

$$EnvironmentalRiskManagement = \frac{\sum_{i=1}^{n} d_{it}}{\left(\sum_{i=1}^{n} d_{it}\right) - NA}$$

SustComm was the independent variable, which the authors drew from Refinitiv to answer the following question: 'Does the company have a CSR committee/team or a board-level/senior management committee responsible for decision-making regarding CSR strategy?' Once again, the authors considered this variable using a dichotomous approach: the variable had a value of 0 if the company has a sustainability committee and 1 if a committee had been elected.

The control variables were *return on equity* (ROE) (Capelli et al., 2021; Teng et al., 2021) for the profitability of the company, *leverage* (Lev) (Asante-Appiah &

Lambert, 2022; Naveed et al., 2021; Teng et al., 2021; Zhang, 2023) for the company's indebtedness, and the natural logarithm of total assets (LnTotAss) as a measure of firms' sizes (Champagne et al., 2022).

12.3 Results

The descriptive statistics of the model are shown in Table 12.1.

The average value for the EnvRiskMan variable was 0.28822, suggesting that, although the companies cared about climate change, the proper management of these matters was not deeply rooted within them. However, when considering this result across years, the authors observed that this value increased, peaking in 2021, with a mean value of about 0.31. Nevertheless, the mean value for the variable SustComm (the variable highlighting the presence (or not) of a sustainability committee) was close to 0.75, showing that most of the sample companies relied on the presence of such committees. This result is justified, since addressing ESG issues is becoming essential for ensuring companies' long-term success. The adjusted R^2 of the model was 0.3166, highlighting the reliability of the analysis.

To test the assumptions of the data panel analysis, the first check was to verify the absence of perfect multicollinearity. This check showed that there was no significant correlation between the independent variables, ensuring that the authors avoided generating distortion in the regression parameters and errors. Authors checked the presence of multicollinearity twice, first by verifying Pearson's correlations (Table 12.2), and second, by examining the VIFs (Table 12.3).

Table 12.1 Descriptive statistics

Variable	Obs	Mean	Std. Dev.	Min.	Max.
EnvRiskMan	549	0.288221	0.3901214	0	1
SustComm	564	0.7358156	0.4412893	0	1
ROE	1059	0.0935527	0.2371431	−3.1905	0.749
Lev	1169	3.756936	0.5567939	0	66.86047
LnTotAss	884	2.088715	2.455222	15.45683	27.69775

Table 12.2 Pearson's correlations

	EnvRiskMan	SustComm	ROE	Lev	LnTotAss
EnvRiskMan	1.000				
SustComm	0.3818	1.000			
ROE	0.0295	0.0957	1.000		
Lev	0.0294	0.0397	−0.2382	1.000	
LnTotAss	0.3778	0.2745	−0.1218	0.6368	1.000

Table 12.3 VIFs

Variable	VIF	1/VIF
LnTotAss	1.88	0.532275
Lev	1.81	0.553986
SustComm	1.13	0.884821
ROE	1.07	0.932167

Table 12.4 Random-effects regression model

EnvRiskMan	Coefficient	Std. err.	*p*-value	95% conf.	interval
SustComm	0.2072231	0.0446253	0.000	0.1197591	0.2946871
ROE	−0.1231559	0.1154763	0.286	−0.3494852	0.1031735
Lev	−0.0153592	0.0046582	0.001	−0.024489	−0.0062294
LnTotAss	0.0912313	0.0147101	0.000	0.0624001	0.1200625
_cons	−1.760187	0.3043901	0.000	−2.356781	−1.163593

Correlations among the variables were all below 0.5, indicating the absence of multicollinearity. Regarding the VIFs, the results once again showed the absence of multicollinearity, because all the values were below 2.

Authors also had to check for heteroscedasticity. Thus, the authors performed Breusch–Pagan and Cook–Weisberg tests, which ensured the absence of heteroscedasticity. This confirmed that environmental risk management variability was consistent across values for all the independent variables.

The first step before performing the analysis was to identify the most appropriate model: a fixed-effects model or a random-effects model. A Hausman test confirmed that for this analysis, a random-effects model would be more accurate than a fixed-effects model because prob. $> chi^2 = 0.2761$. Thus, the authors used a random-effects model (Table 12.4).

The aim of using this model was to verify whether EnvRiskMan was affected by the presence of a sustainability committee, which allowed us to confirm or reject our hypothesis. Table 12.4 shows that the presence of a sustainability committee affected environmental risk management. The coefficient was statistically significant and positively correlated, given that the beta coefficient was 0.20722 and the p-value was null. This meant that going from not having a sustainability committee to electing one increased the value for EnvRiskMan by 0.20722. Thus, the random-effects model demonstrated the importance of electing a committee to focus entirely on sustainability matters to strengthen the management of environmental and climate change risks. There was also an incentive to establish sustainability committees, since the result confirmed that they would enable firms to better manage climate change matters. In other words, the presence of sustainability committees encouraged companies to pay more attention to climate change matters alongside other corporate risks. LnTotAss was another significant variable, showing that an increase of 1% in LnTotAss reflected an improvement of 0.09123 in the management of climate risks. Thus, the larger the company, the more sensitive it was to climate change matters. Larger, more structured companies may generate climate controversies because they are more widely involved with the environment. Another significant variable was Lev, which had a negative relationship with the dependent variable. Profitability had no implications in terms of affecting companies' perceptions of climate change risks. It is reasonable to assume that higher returns for shareholders do not affect attitudes towards climate change.

12.4 Discussion and Conclusion

Nowadays, it is common and widely acknowledged that attention to ESG issues is vital for maintaining companies as on-going concerns. However, such a perspective must be deeply rooted in companies to ensure their longevity. ESG issues are intertwined with a corresponding risk that is mainly linked to the environmental perspective. The Global Risk Report 2023 (WEF, 2023) stated that, in the next 10 years, 6 environmental risks will become consistently and predominantly relevant for the environment and society (e.g. for mitigating climate change in terms of related climate change adaptation, natural disasters, extreme weather events, biodiversity losses and ecosystem collapses). Birindelli et al. (2018) claimed that sustainability committees have become a common means to better manage and address sustainability issues. However, academia has focused largely on corporate governance mechanisms and ESG matters (e.g. environmental disclosure and environmental performance) without delving into more specific nuances (Helfaya & Moussa, 2017; Koutoupis et al., 2021; Lagasio & Cucari, 2019; Malik et al., 2020; Xue et al., 2020). Moreover, researchers have argued that some directors are not well informed about and aware of ESG risks and frame them only as potential emerging or not significant risks (Adams, 2017). However, environmental risks have been categorised as among the main corporate risks that could spread their effects in corporations that are insensitive towards environmental risks. For instance, firms unprepared for sustainable investments and risk management processes could be unexpectedly hit by adverse circumstances. Therefore, in view of the increasing attention companies are giving and/or will have to give to ESG issues (especially ESG risks), the relevance of this study is in deeply investigating the role of corporate governance structures in the management of environmental risks. The objective of this research was to determine the influence of sustainability committees on the adequate management of environmental risks. Descriptive statistics showed that most of the sample companies had elected sustainability committees, demonstrating that this is becoming a common managerial practice among Italian public companies. Furthermore, the descriptive statistics regarding the variable for measuring sensitivity towards environmental risks yielded only meagre average results, approximately equal to 0.3, highlighting that firms are largely unprepared to tackle environmental risks. However, the trend compared with the first year of the analysis increased, demonstrating firms' growing inclination to adopt such managerial procedures.

Based on the results of the multivariate analysis, it is arguable whether the presence of a sustainability committee may determine proper environmental risk management. Together with size of the firm (identified by adopting the natural logarithm of total assets), the results of the analysis revealed positive and significant associations between the independent and dependent variables. The correspondence between the presence of a sustainability committee and the measure for assessing the management of environmental risks is debatable, as rooted governance structures cover not only historic governance issues but also the expanding boundaries of ESG topics. Nevertheless, earlier governance structures could be suitable for managing ESG issues. Before the advent and exponential growth of ESG issues, with all their academic and practical implications, the Italian Civil Code required companies to meet the standard (Art. 2428) in terms of disclosing environmental issues. Therefore, the establishment of sustainability committees for managing environmental risks is necessary because there is a positive relationship between the management of environmental risks and the presence of a sustainability committee. In addition, Article 2086 of the Italian Civil Code requires companies to adopt organisational, administrative and accounting arrangements suitable for identifying crises other than losses of going concern. Once again, this justifies the need for sustainability committees to manage environmental risks.

The current chapter makes theoretical contributions and has practical implications. Theoretically, the study deepens the investigation of ESG risk management, helping to position future research in terms of the implications of sustainability committees and procedures for managing environmental risks. Furthermore, it provides the basis for an environmental risk management index to assess whether a company faces transition risks. Such an index would be helpful for evaluating companies' awareness of the potential impacts of climate change risks and for gauging the intensity of such effects. Additionally, it could show how companies account for ESG risks and their future implications for their businesses. From a practical perspective, this study highlights the importance of electing a sustainability committee even though, in the Italian context, disclosure of ESG risks was already mandated. In this regard, it can help firms become aware of the significance of ESG risks in various industries and understand whether they should be framed at the same level as other risks.

In the future, researchers could replicate the study for a specific industry to determine the significant sectors in which environmental risk issues affect business activities. In addition, the same analysis could be expanded to other geographical areas. The environmental risk perspective could encompass the risks that affect governance and social issues to present a more comprehensive picture of ESG issues. The study could also be strengthened by narrowing down each variable included in the environmental risk management score and re-conducting the study. For instance, a study considering financial exposure to transition risks and whether the presence of a sustainability committee leads to better disclosure of a firm's vulnerability to transition risks would be valuable. Lastly, the sustainability committee variable could be strengthened by considering other governance factors (e.g. the presence of independent directors).

This study has some limitations. Firstly, the authors did not unpack the components of the environmental risk score, treating it as an overall score without focusing on a single element (e.g. whether awareness of ESG risks could influence awareness of a company's transition risk). Addressing this issue could constitute a future research avenue. Secondly, other limitations were the limited time-span of 6 years and the restriction of the sample to Italian companies, which may have undermined the generalisability of the results. In addition, some variables were influenced by missing values.

References

Adams, C. (2015). *Understanding integrated reporting: The concise guide to integrated thinking and the future of corporate reporting. Do Sustainability*. Routledge.

Adams, C. A. (2017). Conceptualising the contemporary corporate value creation process. *Accounting, Auditing & Accountability Journal, 30*(4), 906–931. https://doi.org/10.1108/AAAJ-04-2016-2529

Adams, C. A., Coulson, A. B., Emmelkamp, T., Greveling, R., Klüth, G., & Nugent, M. (2013). *Capitals background paper for IR*. IIRC.

Adams, C. A., & Larrinaga, C. (2019). Progress: Engaging with organisations in pursuit of improved sustainability accounting and performance. *Accounting, Auditing and Accountability Journal, 32*(8), 2367–2394.

Akbas, F., Markov, S., Subasi, M., & Weisbrod, E. (2018). Determinants and consequences of information processing delay: Evidence from the Thomson Reuters institutional brokers' estimate system. *Journal of Financial Economics, 127*(2), 366–388.

Asante-Appiah, B., & Lambert, T. A. (2022). The role of the external auditor in managing environmental, social, and governance (ESG) reputation risk. *Review of Accounting Studies, 28*, 1–53.

Birindelli, G., Dell'Atti, S., Iannuzzi, A. P., & Savioli, M. (2018). Composition and activity of the board of directors: Impact on ESG performance in the banking system. *Sustainability, 10*(12), 4699.

Brogi, M., Lagasio, V., & Porretta, P. (2022). Be good to be wise: Environmental, social, and governance awareness as a potential credit risk mitigation factor. *Journal of International Financial Management & Accounting, 33*(3), 522–547.

Capelli, P., Ielasi, F., & Russo, A. (2021). Forecasting volatility by integrating financial risk with environmental, social, and governance risk. *Corporate Social Responsibility and Environmental Management, 28*(5), 1483–1495.

Chairani, C., & Siregar, S. V. (2021). The effect of enterprise risk management on financial performance and firm value: The role of environmental, social and governance performance. *Meditari Accountancy Research, 29*(3), 647–670. https://doi.org/10.1108/MEDAR-09-2019-0549

Champagne, C., Coggins, F., & Sodjahin, A. (2022). Can extra-financial ratings serve as an indicator of ESG risk? *Global Finance Journal, 54*, 100638.

Dal Maso, L., Gianfagna, L., Maglione, F., & Lattanzi, N. (2023). Going green: Environmental risk management, market value and performance. *Corporate Social Responsibility and Environmental Management, 31*(1), 122–132.

Dobler, M., Lajili, K., & Zéghal, D. (2014). Environmental performance, environmental risk and risk management. *Business Strategy and the Environment, 23*(1), 1–17.

Fahad, P., & Rahman, P. M. (2020). Impact of corporate governance on CSR disclosure. *International Journal of Disclosure and Governance, 17*(2–3), 155–167.

González Sánchez, M., & Morales de Vega, M. E. (2018). Corporate reputation and firms' performance: Evidence from Spain. *Corporate Social Responsibility & Environmental Management, 25*(6), 1231–1245. https://doi.org/10.1002/csr.1634

Helfaya, A., & Moussa, T. (2017). Do board's corporate social responsibility strategy and orientation influence environmental sustainability disclosure? UK evidence. *Business Strategy and the Environment, 26*(8), 1061–1077.

Hsiao, C., & Pesaran, M. H. (2008). Random coefficient models. In *The econometrics of panel data: Fundamentals and recent developments in theory and practice* (pp. 185–213).

Humphrey, J. E., Lee, D. D., & Shen, Y. (2012). Does it cost to be sustainable?. *Journal of Corporate Finance, 18*(3), 626–639.

Jarboui, A., Dammak Ben Hlima, N., & Bouaziz, D. (2023). Do sustainability committee characteristics affect CSR performance? Evidence from India. *Benchmarking: An International Journal, 30*(2), 628–652. https://doi.org/10.1108/BIJ-04-2021-0225

Jørgensen, S., Mjøs, A., & Pedersen, L. J. T. (2022). Sustainability reporting and approaches to materiality: Tensions and potential resolutions. *Sustainability Accounting, Management and Policy Journal, 13*(2), 341–361. https://doi.org/10.1108/SAMPJ-01-2021-0009

Koutoupis, A., Kyriakogkonas, P., Pazarskis, M., & Davidopoulos, L. (2021). Corporate governance and COVID-19: A literature review. *Corporate Governance: The International Journal of Business in Society, 21*(6), 969–982.

Lagasio, V., & Cucari, N. (2019). Corporate governance and environmental social governance disclosure: A meta-analytical review. *Corporate Social Responsibility and Environmental Management, 26*(4), 701–711.

Landi, G. C., Iandolo, F., Renzi, A., & Rey, A. (2022). Embedding sustainability in risk management: The impact of environmental, social, and governance ratings on corporate financial risk. *Corporate Social Responsibility and Environmental Management, 29*(4), 1096–1107.

Malik, M. F., Zaman, M., & Buckby, S. (2020). Enterprise risk management and firm performance: Role of the risk committee. *Journal of Contemporary Accounting & Economics, 16*(1), 100178.

Naveed, K., Voinea, C. L., Ali, Z., Rauf, F., & Fratostiteanu, C. (2021). Board gender diversity and corporate social performance in different industry groups: Evidence from China. *Sustainability, 13*(6), 3142.

Nicholls, J. A. (2020). Integrating financial, social and environmental accounting. *Sustainability Accounting, Management and Policy Journal, 11*(4), 745–769.

Orazalin, N., Kuzey, C., Uyar, A., & Karaman, A. S. (2023). Does CSR contribute to the financial sector's financial stability? The moderating role of a sustainability committee. *Journal of Applied Accounting Research, 25*, 105–125. Vol. ahead-of-print No. ahead-of-print. https://doi.org/10.1108/JAAR-12-2022-0329

Sharfman, M. P., & Fernando, C. S. (2008). Environmental risk management and the cost of capital. *Strategic Management Journal, 29*(6), 569–592.

Teng, X., Wang, Y., Wang, A., Chang, B. G., & Wu, K. S. (2021). Environmental, social, governance risk and corporate sustainable growth nexus: Quantile regression approach. *International Journal of Environmental Research and Public Health, 18*(20), 10865.

Velte, P., & Stawinoga, M. (2020). Do chief sustainability officers and CSR committees influence CSR-related outcomes? A structured literature review based on empirical-quantitative research findings. *Journal of Management Control, 31*(4), 333–377.

WEF, World Economic Forum. (2023). Global risks report 2023. https://www.weforum.org/reports/global-risks-report-2023/

Xie, J., Nozawa, W., Yagi, M., Fujii, H., & Managi, S. (2019). Do environ-mental, social, and governance activities improve corporate financial performance? *Business Strategy and the Environment, 8*(2), 286–300.

Xue, B., Zhang, Z., & Li, P. (2020). Corporate environmental performance, environmental management and firm risk. *Business Strategy and the Environment, 29*(3), 1074–1096.

Young, S., & Thyil, V. (2014). Corporate social responsibility and corporate governance: Role of context in international settings. *Journal of Business Ethics, 122*(1), 1–24.

Zhang, D. (2023). Does green finance really inhibit extreme hypocritical ESG risk? A greenwashing perspective exploration. *Energy Economics, 121*, 106688.

Chapter 13
CSR Managers and ESG Performance: An Empirical Research

Emmadonata Carbone, Maria Angela Manzi, Sara Saggese, and Fabrizia Sarto

13.1 Introduction

Prompted by the stakeholders' pressures to take sustainable initiatives, over the past years, firms have globally improved their sensitivity to the role played for the overall society and have replied to the increasing request of actions as socially responsible organizations (Tsang et al., 2023). As a result, they have strengthened their attention on Environmental, Social and Governance (ESG) issues and adopted proactive ESG strategies (García-Sánchez et al., 2020; Friede et al., 2015). Indeed, as reported by the Global Sustainable Investment Review, in 2018 the ESG integration grew by 69% over the previous 2 years (Global Sustainable Investment Alliance, 2018) and more recently, in non-US markets, sustainable investment assets have increased by 20% since 2020 (Global Sustainable Investment Alliance, 2022).

Alongside such pressures, a fruitful academic debate has also flourished on sustainability practices and how corporate governance is able to integrate sustainability issues into the firm decision-making process (Jain & Jamali, 2016). In this vein, research has pointed out that board characteristics can affect corporate social performance and ESG outcomes (Valle et al., 2019; García-Sánchez et al., 2020). This is especially true for gender diversity, independent directors (Fernández-Temprano & Tejerina-Gaite, 2020; Rao & Tilt, 2021; Alsayegh et al., 2020), board size and meetings (García-Sánchez et al., 2020; Alsayegh et al., 2020;

E. Carbone (✉) · M. A. Manzi · S. Saggese · F. Sarto
Department of Economics, Management, Institutions (DEMI), University of Naples "Federico II", Naples, Italy
e-mail: emmadonata.carbone@unina.it; mariaangela.manzi@unina.it; sara.saggese@unina.it; fabrizia.sarto@unina.it

N. Castellano et al. (eds.), *Environmental, Social, Governance (ESG)*, SIDREA Series in Accounting and Business Administration,
https://doi.org/10.1007/978-3-031-76618-3_13

Cuadrado-Ballesteros et al., 2017), audit committee and CEO duality (Naciti, 2019; Crifo et al., 2019; Cucari et al., 2018).

More recently, scholarly attention has been attracted by the potential implications of institutionalized sustainability bodies related to board and executive expertise for ESG performance (Velte & Stawinoga, 2020). Indeed, listed companies tend to voluntarily institutionalize the Chief Sustainability Officer (CSO) and Corporate Social Responsibility (CSR) committee in order to improve their sustainable management systems (Fernández et al., 2011; Velte & Stawinoga, 2020; Jaggi et al., 2018; Mackenzie, 2007).

Specifically, the CSO is a top manager whose primary duty is to promote and implement the CSR strategy (Fu et al., 2020; Strand, 2013). Indeed, for example, when in 2004 Linda Fisher was appointed as the first CSO of a publicly traded company (i.e. DuPont), the firm announced that the new role would have been responsible for 'advancing DuPont's progress in achieving sustainable growth, DuPont environmental and health programs, the company's product stewardship programs, and global regulatory affairs'.

The CSR committee is instead responsible for providing advice and assistance to the board about social and environmental issues (Velte & Stawinoga, 2020). In this vein, it is in charge of supporting the board of directors in monitoring firms' CSR practices and performance, ensuring compliance with regulations and managing ESG risks (Mahmood et al., 2018; Cucari et al., 2018; Valle et al., 2019). Moreover, it supports the board in fulfilling its duties towards the shareholders by guiding the sustainable growth and development of the company (Danvila del Valle et al., 2013). From a different standpoint, the CSR committee assists the top management in the formulation and implementation of CSR principles and practices, by also revising the company's annual sustainability report and ensuring its credibility (Qaderi et al., 2022). Therefore, such a governance body not only leads the CSR policies and strategies, but it also drives the company's inclusion in sustainability indexes (Danvila del Valle et al., 2013).

Despite literature has explored the effects of such roles on CSR-related outcomes (Velte and Stawinoga, 2020), studies have provided inconclusive findings (Baraibar-Diez & Odriozola, 2019; Derchi et al., 2021; Fu et al., 2020; Rodrigue et al., 2013). Additionally, while research has mainly focused on the influence of CSO and CSR committee on CSR disclosure, assurance and performance (Adel et al., 2019; Ruhnke & Gabriel, 2013; Martinez-Ferrero & Garcia-Sanchez, 2017; Rodrigue et al., 2013), limited attention has been devoted to the effect of the presence of both such bodies on ESG reputation.

Therefore, by relying on a sample of non-financial Italian listed companies, this study aims to fill these gaps by empirically examining if the presence of CSO and CSR committee can affect the ESG rating measured in terms of the ESG Global Perception Index.

13.2 Literature Review

Literature has emphasized that several board characteristics can play a key role in CSR performance (Valle et al., 2019). Specifically, some studies have investigated the board composition in terms of gender diversity and the presence of independent directors (Fernández-Temprano & Tejerina-Gaite, 2020; Rao & Tilt, 2021; Alsayegh et al., 2020). Other research has focused on the effects of board size and frequency of board meetings on ESG outcomes (García-Sánchez et al., 2020; Alsayegh et al., 2020; Cuadrado-Ballesteros et al., 2017). Still, others have explored the influence of audit committee and CEO duality on environmental and sustainability performance (Naciti, 2019; Crifo et al., 2019; Cucari et al., 2018).

Aside from these studies, more recent research has examined whether institutionalized sustainability bodies in board and executive management influence ESG performance (Velte & Stawinoga, 2020).

Indeed, although as still an emerging phenomenon, more and more listed companies are trying to improve their sustainable management systems by voluntarily institutionalizing the CSR committee and the CSO (Fernández et al., 2011; Velte & Stawinoga, 2020; Jaggi et al., 2018; Mackenzie, 2007).

In this regard, the literature claims that the CSO is responsible for ensuring that overall working conditions, firm procedures and production processes comply with social and environmental issues (Strand, 2013, 2014).

Turning to the CSR committee, Hussain et al. (2018, 418) posit that it 'symbolises the board's orientation and commitment towards sustainable development', emphasizing the firm's intention to make sustainability a key core strategy (Ricart et al., 2005; Amran et al., 2014). Indeed, the literature highlights that such committee supports the board in addressing social and environmental issues (Velte & Stawinoga, 2020) as well as in monitoring firms' CSR practices and performance to comply with regulations and to properly manage ESG risks (Mahmood et al., 2018; Cucari et al., 2018; Valle et al., 2019). At the same time, scholars suggest that it supports the board in handling the firm's sustainable growth (Danvila del Valle et al., 2013), applying CSR principles and revising the CSR report to warrant the related credibility (Qaderi et al., 2022). Thereby, the CSR committee plays a key role not only in leading the CSR policies and strategies, but also in driving the company's inclusion in sustainability indexes (Danvila del Valle et al., 2013). Indeed, as noted by Mackenzie (2007, 940), the CSR committee 'reviews the company's adoption of external codes and inclusion in CSR indices' such as the 'FTSE4Good'.

Extensive literature has investigated the establishment of these roles by assessing their implications for CSR-related outcomes (Velte & Stawinoga, 2020). However, there are still some gaps to fill. First of all, previous studies on the effect of both CSO and CSR committee have yielded mixed results. While some authors have documented that establishing a CSR committee and a CSO is able to improve CSR outcomes (Cucari et al., 2018; Helfaya & Moussa, 2017; Baraibar-Diez & Odriozola, 2019; Derchi et al., 2021; Hussain et al., 2018; Fu et al., 2020), others have suggested that these figures do not produce any significant effect (Rankin et al.,

2011; Rodrigue et al., 2013). Second, despite the literature has mainly explored the effect of CSO and CSR committee on CSR reporting and disclosure (e.g. Liao et al., 2015; Adel et al., 2019; Michelon, 2011), assurance (e.g. Ruhnke & Gabriel, 2013; Martinez-Ferrero & García-Sánchez, 2017) and performance (e.g. Berrone & Gomez-Mejia, 2009; Rodrigue et al., 2013), there is still a lack of empirical research investigating the implications of both mechanisms (i.e. CSO and CSR committee) for ESG reputation.

With this in mind, in order to shed light on the implications of CSO and CSR for ESG rating, the following section discusses in depth the role of such governance bodies.

13.2.1 The Chief Sustainability Officer and CSR Committee

The ongoing discussion on sustainability issues has profoundly broadened the scope of corporate governance which has to support the formulation and implementation of CSR strategies and build a sustainable management system able to provide a solid structure for a good ESG reputation. Due to the relevance of the issue, companies are seeking to institutionalize managerial roles and governance mechanisms devoted to CSR (Velte & Stawinoga, 2020): CSO and CSR committee.

With regard to managerial roles, firms are increasingly adding a new executive position, the CSO, at the top of the corporate hierarchy at the C-suite level, next to CEO, COO and CFO, in order to address increasingly complex social and environmental requirements (Svejenova et al., 2017). Literature has documented that CEOs who introduced the CSO position in their firms declared that their purpose was to include sustainability within their corporate and competitive strategies (Strand, 2014). Indeed CSOs, who are often also called chief ethics officers and chief environmental officers, are primarily responsible for CSR practices and related performance, reporting their actions directly to the CEO or the board of directors (Strand, 2013, 2014). Although their tasks might vary according to the firm internal (e.g. stages of firm) and external characteristics (e.g. firm industry), they usually elaborate, execute and monitor the CSR strategy while reviewing the related business practices (Miller & Serafeim, 2014). They analyse internal and external social needs and propose competitive strategies able to obtain both a firm's sustainable development and profit growth (Velte & Stawinoga, 2020). In doing so, they usually foster the organizational culture towards sustainable orientation, by also performing employee training programs focused on CSR issues (Miller & Serafeim, 2014).

Turning to the CSR committee, also called ethics/sustainability/environmental/ESG one, this body is usually a sub-committee within the corporate board. Its establishment is generally suggested by corporate governance codes and in very few countries (e.g. India) it has become mandatory (Baraibar-Diez & Odriozola, 2019; Khan et al., 2023; Jarboui et al., 2022). In Italy, for instance, it represents a voluntary committee, and the corporate governance code advises its appointment only to firms belonging to the FTSE-Mib index of the Milan Stock Exchange (CGC, 2018).

Looking at the CSR committee tasks, it plays a crucial role in supporting the board with regard to both the formulation of the CSR strategy and the monitoring of the related executions/outcomes.

On the one side, it has the responsibility of identifying and proposing to the board the CSR policies, initiatives and strategies to be followed (Baraibar-Diez & Odriozola, 2019; Orazalin et al., 2024). In doing so, it acts to make sure that the formulated strategy prioritizes the CSR-related concerns, thus incorporating sustainability into the companies' strategic direction and operations (Martinez-Ferrero and García-Sánchez, 2017), while ensuring that the established corporate objectives are in line with the stakeholders' interests (Peters & Romi, 2014; García-Sánchez et al., 2019). Therefore, the CSR committee is not only in charge of ensuring that the company strategy is committed to sustainability concerns, but it should also guarantee that the strategy is translated into concrete action plans (Michelon & Parbonetti, 2012; Amran et al., 2014).

On the other side, the CSR committee contributes to the board oversight effectiveness by managing risks and opportunities related to CSR, while protecting both the stakeholders' interests and shareholder value (Burke et al., 2019; Peters & Romi, 2015; Spira & Bender, 2004). Indeed, it oversees the managerial implementation of the company's CSR and sustainability agenda (Danvila del Valle et al., 2013) and has also the authority to monitor the overall firm activities compliance with its CSR and ethical standards (Mahmood et al., 2018; Cucari et al., 2018; Valle et al., 2019). Therefore, it allows the fulfilment of regulations and obligations to stakeholders (García-Sánchez et al., 2019). In doing so, the CSR committee reviews and monitors the sustainability performance as well as the related disclosure (Qaderi et al., 2022). It is also in charge of revising the company annual sustainability report and ensuring its quality and credibility (Qaderi et al., 2022; Cucari et al., 2018). Therefore, the CSR committee is responsible for disseminating sustainability reports and promoting CSR disclosures to keep a connection between the firm and stakeholders (Adel et al., 2019; García-Sánchez et al., 2019; Baraibar-Diez & Odriozola, 2019; Fuente et al., 2017).

13.2.2 The Impact of CSO and CSR Committee on ESG Reputation

To assess the effect of CSO and CSR committee roles on ESG perception reputation, the present research relies on the legitimacy theory (Suchman, 1995).

Suchman (1995, 574) defines legitimacy as the 'generalized perception or assumption that the actions of an entity are desirable, proper, or appropriate within some socially constructed system of norms, values, beliefs, and definitions'. In line with this view, legitimacy theory posits that companies (as any other social institutions) operate in society through the implicit social contract and the fitting of companies' behaviours to these social contracts affects their development, long-term success and survival (Gray et al., 1995).

Indeed, social contracts motivate managers and related companies to go beyond institutional compliance and adopt structures, processes and practices that meet society's expectations in order to reduce the so-called 'legitimacy gap' (Sawyer et al., 2010; Fernando & Lawrence, 2014), as the difference between the external stakeholders' expectations about how a firm should behave and how it does behave (Lindblom, 1994). In this regard, companies are required to cope with social demand by satisfying society's expectations and fulfilling its main values which, far from static, constantly evolve over years (Shocker & Sethi, 1973). In particular, as the global attention towards CSR issues increases, companies might try to change their behaviour to decrease this legitimacy gap between them and the public (Suchman, 1995) and demonstrate that their strategies ground in socially responsible values (Dyllick & Muff, 2016).

Building on the legitimacy theory, a number of studies have investigated several ways though which firms aim to fill the legitimacy gap such as the sustainability reporting and disclosure as well as sustainable incentive and governance structure (Ali et al., 2021; Campbell, 2003; Boiral, 2013; Rodrigue et al., 2013; Berrone & Gomez-Mejia, 2009; Velte, 2023; Liao et al., 2019; Prior et al., 2008; Eliwa et al., 2021). Indeed, looking at this latter dimension, a concrete action to be made to gain legitimacy for the CSR orientation of corporate initiatives is enriching governance mechanisms with bodies dedicated to CSR issues such as the CSO and the CSR committee (Jaggi et al., 2018).

With regard to the CSO, as this manager may encourage the firm to engage in the CSR strategy and to aligning the business model with sustainability objectives (Liao et al., 2015; Baraibar-Diez & Odriozola, 2019), its establishment might be perceived in a good way by the external society, thus positively affecting the firm reputation and the credibility in terms of ESG targets (Velte & Stawinoga, 2020). Such view is also in line with Strand (2014) who documents that firms facing environmental crises may hire CSOs to remediate organizational legitimacy.

Looking at the CSR committee, as this body at the board level is often called to assess, approve and control the firm's CSR disclosure and reporting, its appointment enhances the credibility of the CSR report. This signaling demonstrates that monitoring activities related to CSR are effectively conducted (Prinsloo & Maroun, 2021).

In light of these arguments, we therefore expect that the presence of CSO and CSR committee positively influences the ESG rating. Therefore, we formulate the following hypotheses:

H1: The presence of a CSO fosters the ESG rating.
H2: The presence of a CSR committee fosters the ESG rating.

13.3 Methodology

13.3.1 Sample

To empirically test our hypotheses, we rely on a sample of non-financial companies listed on the Milan Stock Exchange at the end of 2019 (i.e. 341). We decided to focus on the Italian context as it is theoretically interesting for the following reasons. First of all, thanks to several country's distinctive features (e.g. a strong emphasis on the needs of employees and local communities, Del Baldo, 2015), Italian firms are particularly sensitive to CSR issues (Ormazabal & Sarriegi, 2014) that they care by setting strategic actions and adopting a strong stakeholders' engagement (Perrini et al., 2007). Moreover, compared to other European settings (e.g. France, UK, Germany and Spain), Italy is one of the countries where the CSR committee is often adopted. Indeed, if we consider only the firms belonging to the FTSE-Mib index of the Milan Stock Exchange, for which the establishment of the committee is suggested by the Corporate Governance Code, its adoption almost reaches 90% (Minciullo et al., 2021).

Thereby, focusing on the Italian context, we constructed our dataset by gathering information from multiple sources (i.e. the AIDA database, and hand-collected information from corporate financial, social and governance reports).

13.3.2 Dependent Variable

As for our dependent variables, we captured the ESG reputation through two different measures. The first one (*ESG_GPI_P*) was a dummy variable equal to 1 if the company in our sample was present in the ESG Global Perception Index, and 0 otherwise. The index comprises the top Italian 200 companies perceived as more sustainable and it is developed and disseminated by Reputation Science, a leading company in Italy for reputation analysis and management. Among different available ESG rankings (e.g. Asset4; Birindelli et al., 2018), we chose this one as it specifically analyses the shareholder's perception of ESG actions by grounding on the ONU sustainability agenda.

Moreover, among the companies included in the ranking, we analysed the index score for each firm in our sample. This variable (*ESG_GPI*) was calculated by transforming the ESG Global Perception Index, which varies from 0 to 100, in a score ranging from 0 (lowest ESG perception) to 1 (highest ESG perception). Specifically, the score is built by assessing the proximity of each analysed brand to the 17 pillars of sustainability as defined by the ONU and produces, for each company, an indicator that is based on qualitative-quantitative and structural parameters. The aggregated index is the measure of online reputation and is called 'R'. It considers the amount of content reporting the association between the brand and sustainability, the reputational impact of such content on the brand, the association of brand identity and sustainability on web searching sources, as well as the amount of sustainability information that the company discloses through online channels (e.g. website, social profiles). The result is an expression of the perception generated from the beginning to the last 6 months because the contents remain online, and the past influences the current perception.

13.3.3 Independent and Control Variables

We examined the influence of CSR bodies[1] on the ESG rating by using two independent variables that are not included in the ESG perception index as they do not appear among the ONU sustainability pillars. First, we used a dummy variable (*CSO*) equal to 1 if the firm had a CSO position, and 0 otherwise (Fu et al., 2020). We defined CSOs as executives who take primary responsibility for corporate sustainability or issues related to CSR/environmental/social/ESG performance (Strand, 2013, 2014). Second, we captured the presence of a CSR committee through a dummy variable (*CSR_COM*) coded 1 if the firm had a committee within the board specifically devoted to the CSR/environmental/social/ESG issues and 0 otherwise (Radu & Smaili, 2021).[2] Furthermore, following previous studies (Bravo, 2018; Birindelli et al., 2018; Fu et al., 2020; Tijani & Ahmadi, 2022), we controlled for governance and firms' characteristics by adding the following variables (*VAR_CTRL*): the business size expressed as the number of company's employees in log form (*SIZE*), the company classification in terms of industry (*INDUSTRY*) by using the ATECO code, the number of directors on the board in log form (*BOARD_SIZE*), the percentage of independent directors (*INDEP_DIR_PERC*) and the profitability (*AV_ROE*) expressed as the 5 years average of the return on equity ratio.

13.3.4 Model Specification

To test our hypotheses, the statistical analyses related to the relationship between the CSR bodies and the presence of the company in the ESG Global Perception Index were conducted through a logit regression *(1)* considering the involvement of a binary dependent variable. To this aim, we used the following empirical specification:

---

[1] To complete the analysis and generalize the results, we considered any manager and/or committee within the company that deals with CSR issues regardless of name (e.g., ESG manager, sustainability manager, sustainability committee).

[2] In the case of a committee that performed both the audit/risk committee function and the CSR one, we considered the dummy equal to 1.

$_{(1)}$ $ESG\_GPI\_P_i = \beta 0 + \beta 1^{*}CSO_i$ or $CSR\_COM_i + \sum_j \beta_{ij}^{*} VAR\_CTRL_{ij} + \varepsilon_i$

Differently, to test the relationship between the CSR bodies and ESG performance, we employed an Ordinary Least Square (OLS) regression *(2)*, specified in the following empirical model:

$_{(2)}$ $ESG\_GPI_i = \beta 0 + \beta 1^{*}CSO_i$ or $CSR\_COM_i + \sum_j \beta_{ij}^{*} VAR\_CTRL_{ij} + \varepsilon_i$

13.4 Findings

13.4.1 Descriptive Statistics and Correlations

Table 13.1 presents the descriptive statistics of the sample of Italian listed companies and the correlation of our variables. As shown, among the top 200 most sustainable companies under the ESG Global Perception Index, 14% belongs to our sample of Italian listed firms. The correlation matrix indicates that both our variables of interest, CSO and CSR committee, are positively correlated with the presence of the company in the ESG Global Perception Index ($p < 0.05$). No suspicions of multicollinearity emerge.

Focusing on the companies included in the ESG Global Perception Index, Table 13.2 shows the descriptives and correlations. As reported, the perception level is on average quite high (around 0.38) and a large proportion of companies present a CSO (*CSO*) (38%) and a CSR committee (*CSR_COM*) (74%). Both CSO and CSR committee variables are positively correlated with the score of the ESG Global Perception Index, although only the CSO-ESG_GPI correlation is statistically significant ($p < 0.05$).

13.4.2 Regressions Analysis

Tables 13.3 and 13.4 show the results of our regressions. To improve the consistency and strength of the relationship, we first regressed the dependent variable only on the main independent one and then we added the control variables. To exclude potential biases, we used standard errors for significance tests of estimated coefficients (Greene, 2011). Moreover, computing the variance inflation factor (VIF), we concluded that multicollinearity was not a concern in our sample since it was below the cut-off of 5 (Hair et al., 2010).

Table 13.3 shows the results of our logit regression. In line with our predictions, the presence of a CSO (*CSO*) (Model 2: $\beta 1 = 3.690$, $p < 0.01$) (H1) or a CSR committee (*CSR_COM*) (Model 4: $\beta 1 = 2.971$, $p < 0.01$) (H2) positively influences the probability of the company to be included in the ESG Global Perception Index list (*ESG_GPI_P*).

As for our OLS regression, findings in Table 13.4 also highlight a positive and statistically significant relationship between CSO (*CSO*) (Model 2: $\beta 1 = 0.170$,

Table 13.1 Descriptive statistics and correlations: sample of total Italian listed companies

Sample of total Italian listed companies										
Variable	Mean	S.D.	1	2	3	4	5	6	7	8
1. ESG_GPI_P	0.138	0.345	1							
2. CSO	0.067	0.251	0.503*	1						
3. CSR_COM	0.185	0.389	0.577*	0.414*	1					
4. SIZE	1112.34	7,614,104	0.233*	0.201*	0.193*	1				
5. INDUSTRY	506630.5	207158.8	−0.065	−0.038	−0.064	−0.020	1			
6. AV_ROE	5.638	13.527	0.073	−0.032	0.043	0.013	−0.224*	1		
7. BOARD_SIZE	1.985	0.518	0.281*	0.159*	0.254*	0.080	−0.083	−0.026	1	
8. INDEP_DIR_PERC	0.628	0.230	0.080	0.140*	0.098	0.093	0.000	−0.063	0.207*	1

N = 341
$P < 0.05$

Table 13.2 Descriptive statistics and correlations: sample of Italian listed companies in the ESG Global Perception Index

Sample of Italian listed companies in the ESG global perception index										
Variable	Mean	S.D.	1	2	3	4	5	6	7	8
1. ESG_GPI	0.381	0.193	1							
2. CSO	0.383	0.491	0.449*	1						
3. CSR_COM	0.745	0.441	0.263	0.361*	1					
4. SIZE	5547	19578.48	0.170	0.125	0.136	1				
5. INDUSTRY	472990.4	213118.2	−0.004	0.043	0.219	−0.011	1			
6. AV_ROE	8.109	11.517	0.024	−0.196	−0.285	−0.038	−0.299*	1		
7. BOARD_SIZE	2.349	0.504	−0.250	−0.051	0.017	−0.056	−0.096	−0.090	1	
8. INDEP_DIR_PERC	0.674	0.213	0.199	0.208	0.297*	0.192	0.383*	−0.215	−0.228	1

$N = 47$

$p < 0.05$

Table 13.3 Results of Logit Regression Model

	ESG_GPI_P			
	Model 1	Model 2	Model 3	Model 4
CSO	3.580***	3.690***		
	(0.543)	(0.701)		
CSR_COM			3.322***	2.971***
			(0.390)	(0.416)
SIZE		0.000**		0.000**
		(0.000)		(0.000)
INDUSTRY		−0.000		−0.000
		(0.000)		(0.000)
AV_ROE		0.032**		0.024
		(0.014)		(0.017)
BOARD_SIZE		1.656***		1.248**
		(0.488)		(0.530)
INDEP_DIR_PERC		−0.511		−0.040
		(0.878)		(1.088)
CONSTANT	−2.299***	−5.868***	−3.099***	−5.865***
	(0.195)	(1.154)	(0.296)	(1.220)
N	341	341	341	341
R-squared	0.202	0.330	0.322	0.387

Standard errors in parentheses.
* $p < 0.10$, ** $p < 0.05$, *** $p < 0.01$

$p < 0.01$) or CSR committee (*CSR_COM*) (Model 4: $\beta1 = 0.117$, $p < 0.05$) and the level of company ESG reputation (*ESG_GPI*).

Taking together, these results support both H1 and H2. This suggests that both CSO and CSR committees orientate the board to promote ESG strategies (Fu et al., 2020; Strand, 2013), leading companies to implement more sustainable policies and improving their sustainability reputation (Mahmood et al., 2018; Cucari et al., 2018; Valle et al., 2019).

Considering that, by construction, the dependent variable ESG_GPI lies between 0 and 1, with uncensored extremes (since it cannot assume values greater than 1 or less than 0) (Villadsen & Wulff, 2018), we replicated the latter analysis through the fractional regression model to corroborate the results which remain consistent as shown in Table 13.5.

We delved further to test the strength of our results through a post hoc analysis. In particular, we split the sample into firms having (or not) a CSO (panel A) and a CSR committee (panel B). Table 13.6 shows the results obtained by comparing the means of the samples. The analyses corroborate our previous findings as we found statistically significant differences for both the CSR governance mechanisms and their effect on ESG reputation, expressed by the ESG score.

Table 13.4 Results of OLS Regression Model

	ESG_GPI			
	Model 5	Model 6	Model 7	Model 8
CSO	0.177***	0.170***		
	(0.053)	(0.060)		
CSR_COM			0.116**	0.117**
			(0.050)	(0.059)
SIZE		0.000		0.000
		(0.000)		(0.000)
INDUSTRY		−0.000		−0.000
		(0.000)		(0.000)
AV_ROE		0.002		0.001
		(0.003)		(0.003)
BOARD_SIZE		−0.076		−0.088
		(0.064)		(0.072)
INDEP_DIR_PERC		0.077		0.093
		(0.108)		(0.098)
CONSTANT	0.314***	0.443***	0.295***	0.464**
	(0.032)	(0.165)	(0.036)	(0.186)
N	47	47	47	47
R-squared	0.202	0.278	0.069	0.167

Standard errors in parentheses.
* $p < 0.10$, ** $p < 0.05$, *** $p < 0.01$

Table 13.5 Robustness check

	ESG_GPI			
	Model 1	Model 2	Model 3	Model 4
CSO	0.462***	0.446***		
	(0.138)	(0.149)		
CSR_COM			0.313**	0.319**
			(0.136)	(0.152)
SIZE		0.000		0.000
		(0.000)		(0.000)
INDUSTRY		−0.000		−0.000
		(0.000)		(0.000)
AV_ROE		0.005		0.003
		(0.007)		(0.007)
BOARD_SIZE		−0.201		−0.230
		(0.162)		(0.178)
INDEP_DIR_PERC		0.208		0.245
		(0.273)		(0.247)
CONSTANT	−0.486***	−0.148	−0.538***	−0.099
	(0.088)	(0.415)	(0.104)	(0.460)
N	47	47	47	47
R-squared	0.023	0.032	0.008	0.020

Standard errors in parentheses.
* $p < 0.10$, ** $p < 0.05$, *** $p < 0.01$

Table 13.6 T-test

Panel A: CSO			
	CSO = 0 (29) mean	CSO = 1 (18) mean	Difference (mean) T-test
ESG_GPI	0.313	0.490	−0.177***
Panel B: CSR_COM			
	CSR COM = 0 (12) mean	CSR COM = 1 (35) mean	Difference (mean) T-test
ESG_GPI	0.295	0.411	−0.116**

13.5 Conclusions

13.5.1 Discussion

The objective of this study is to empirically explore the influence of CSOs and CSR committees on ESG rating. After analysing a sample of non-financial Italian listed companies at the end of 2019 through both logit and OLS regression models, findings document that the establishment of a CSO and CSR committee positively affects the ESG ratings in terms of ESG perception.

These results suggest that having the CSO and CSR committee might be appreciated by stakeholders, thus improving their perception of the company's commitment and attention towards CSR strategy (Liao et al., 2015). Indeed, there is the possibility that the appointment of a CSO, who usually drives the company towards ESG-oriented strategic and action plans (Miller & Serafeim, 2014; Kanashiro & Rivera, 2019), might signal to the external society the company's CSR orientation with positive implication for its credibility and reputation. Moreover, from a different standpoint, the results might be interpreted in light of the increased CSR report's credibility as the presence of the CSR committee demonstrates that the monitoring activities related to CSR are effectively carried out (Prinsloo & Maroun, 2021).

13.5.2 Theoretical and Practical Implications

On the basis of our results, our research exerts theoretical, managerial and policy makers implications.

First of all, it provides contributions to the literature on the effects of the CSR committee and CSO, corroborating research reporting that such mechanisms foster CSR performance (Berrone & Gomez-Mejia, 2009; Rodrigue et al., 2013). Moreover, it advances prior studies by interpreting the CSR performance in terms of ESG rating. In doing so, it also extends the literature on governance and ESG rating as it employs a not yet explored proxy of ESG reputation. From a different standpoint, our study fills a gap in the literature by investigating the Italian setting on which, to the best of our knowledge, no empirical studies are exploring the implications of the above-mentioned CSR bodies (Argento et al., 2019; Celentano et al., 2020; Cantino et al., 2019; Gennari & Salvioni, 2019).

From the managerial standpoint, our findings demonstrate that setting up specific corporate governance bodies dedicated to CSR issues helps to guide the management in pursuing such objectives. Thus, taking into consideration that these governance mechanisms increase reputation, our study is of interest to companies geared to demonstrate their attention towards CSR. Indeed, our research suggests that the presence of a CSO and CSR committee helps in being included in a sustainability index and achieving a high score in terms of positive impact. At the same time, our results are also able to support firms by showing how to design the board structure in order to improve the effectiveness of CSR strategies and ESG reputation.

Finally, our research suggests to policy makers and regulators how to sustain and prompt the companies' orientation towards CSR issues by stressing the relevance of appointing the figure of CSO and the CSR committee, as it demonstrates that these corporate bodies are beneficial for ESG reputation.

Notwithstanding such contributions, some limitations might in turn create opportunities for future research. First, we only focus on the presence/absence of the CSO and CSR committee, while we do not address their characteristics. Future studies might explore not only their demographic attributes (e.g. gender and age), but also their background and expertise in terms of sustainability. Second, our study does not examine the interplay among the CSO, CSR committee and board. Thereby, further research could explore which board characteristics lead to the appointment of CSO and CSR committee, which might, in turn, influence ESG performance.

Moreover, we investigate the ESG performance in terms of reputation, without considering if the presence of the CSR committee and CSO effectively promotes ESG strategies and actions. Future research could assess if the bodies' legitimization effect is the result of (mere) symbolic initiatives or rather operational efforts towards CSR that satisfy the stakeholders' demands (Peters & Romi, 2015; Al-Shaer & Zaman, 2019).

Finally, our ESG reputation proxy is retrieved from the Reputation Science Observatory which, although calculated through a reliable methodology considering more than 100 parameters, is not free of subjective influences. Therefore, it would be interesting to analyse our tested relationships by adopting alternative ESG ratings (e.g. KLD rating, Bloomberg ESG score).

References

Adel, C., Hussain, M. M., Mohamed, E. K., & Basuony, M. A. (2019). Is corporate governance relevant to the quality of corporate social responsibility disclosure in large European companies? *International Journal of Accounting & Information Management, 27*(2), 301–332.

Ali, I., Lodhia, S., & Narayan, A. K. (2021). Value creation attempts via photographs in sustainability reporting: A legitimacy theory perspective. *Meditari Accountancy Research, 29*(2), 247–263.

Alsayegh, M. F., Abdul Rahman, R., & Homayoun, S. (2020). Corporate economic, environmental, and social sustainability performance transformation through ESG disclosure. *Sustainability, 12*(9), 3910.

Al-Shaer, H., & Zaman, M. (2019). CEO compensation and sustainability reporting assurance: Evidence from the UK. *Journal of Business Ethics, 158*, 233–252.

Amran, A., Lee, S. P., & Devi, S. S. (2014). The influence of governance structure and strategic corporate social responsibility toward sustainability reporting quality. *Business Strategy and the Environment, 23*(4), 217–235.

Argento, D., Culasso, F., & Truant, E. (2019). From sustainability to integrated reporting: The legitimizing role of the CSR manager. *Organization and Environment, 32*(4), 484–507.

Baraibar-Diez, E., & Odriozola, M. D. (2019). CSR committees and their effect on ESG performance in UK, France, Germany, and Spain. *Sustainability, 11*(18), 5077.

Berrone, P., & Gomez-Mejia, L. R. (2009). Environmental performance and executive compensation: An integrated agency-institutional perspective. *Academy of Management Journal, 52*(1), 103–126.

Birindelli, G., Dell'Atti, S., Iannuzzi, A. P., & Savioli, M. (2018). Composition and activity of the board of directors: Impact on ESG performance in the banking system. *Sustainability, 10*(12), 4699.

Boiral, O. (2013). Sustainability reports as simulacra? A counter-account of A and A+ GRI reports. *Accounting, Auditing & Accountability Journal, 26*(7), 1036–1071.

Bravo, F. (2018). Does board diversity matter in the disclosure process? An analysis of the association between diversity and the disclosure of information on risks. *International Journal of Disclosure and Governance, 15*, 104–114.

Burke, J. J., Hoitash, R., & Hoitash, U. (2019). The heterogeneity of board-level sustainability committees and corporate social performance. *Journal of Business Ethics, 154*, 1161–1186.

Campbell, D. (2003). Intra-and intersectoral effects in environmental disclosures: Evidence for legitimacy theory? *Business Strategy and the Environment, 12*(6), 357–371.

Cantino, V., Devalle, A., Fiandrino, S., & Busso, D. (2019). The level of compliance with the Italian legislative decree No. 254/2016 and its determinants: Insights from Italy. *Financial reporting*, (2019/1).

Celentano, A., Lepore, L., Pisano, S., D'Amore, G., & Alvino, F. (2020). The joint effect of board independence and CSR committee on CSR disclosure: Evidence from Italian listed companies. *Corporate Governance: Examining Key Challenges and Perspectives, 13*, 319–328.

Corporate Governance Committee (CGC). (2018). Corporate governance code. https://www.borsaitaliana.it/comitato-corporate-governance/codice/codiceeng2018.en.pdf

Crifo, P., Escrig-Olmedo, E., & Mottis, N. (2019). Corporate governance as a key driver of corporate sustainability in France: The role of board members and investor relations. *Journal of Business Ethics, 159*(4), 1127–1146.

Cuadrado-Ballesteros, B., Martínez-Ferrero, J., & García-Sánchez, I. M. (2017). Board structure to enhance social responsibility development: A qualitative comparative analysis of US companies. *Corporate Social Responsibility and Environmental Management, 24*(6), 524–542.

Cucari, N., Esposito De Falco, S., & Orlando, B. (2018). Diversity of board of directors and environmental social governance: Evidence from Italian listed companies. *Corporate Social Responsibility and Environmental Management, 25*(3), 250–266.

Danvila del Valle, I., Diez Esteban, J. M., & Péres, O. L. D. F. (2013). Corporate social responsibility and sustainability committee inside the board. *European Journal of International Management, 13*(2), 159–176.

Del Baldo, M. (2015). A state of the art of corporate social responsibility diffusion in Italy: Limits and potentials. In *Corporate social responsibility in Europe: United in sustainable diversity* (pp. 435–468).

Derchi, G. B., Zoni, L., & Dossi, A. (2021). Corporate social responsibility performance, incentives, and learning effects. *Journal of Business Ethics, 173*, 617–641.

Dyllick, T., & Muff, K. (2016). Clarifying the meaning of sustainable business: Introducing a typology from business-as-usual to true business sustainability. *Organization & Environment, 29*(2), 156–174.

Eliwa, Y., Aboud, A., & Saleh, A. (2021). ESG practices and the cost of debt: Evidence from EU countries. *Critical Perspectives on Accounting, 79*, 102097.

Fernández, J. L., Luna Sotorrio, L. L., & Baraibar Díez, E. (2011). The relation between corporate governance and corporate social behaviour: A structural equation model analysis. *Corporate Social Responsibility and Environmental Management, 18*(2), 91–101.

Fernández-Temprano, M. A., & Tejerina-Gaite, F. (2020). Types of director, board diversity and firm performance. *Corporate Governance: The International Journal of Business in Society, 20*(2), 324–342.

Fernando, S., & Lawrence, S. (2014). A theoretical framework for CSR practices: Integrating legitimacy theory, stakeholder theory and institutional theory. *Journal of Theoretical Accounting Research, 10*(1), 149–178.

Friede, G., Busch, T., & Bassen, A. (2015). ESG and financial performance: Aggregated evidence from more than 2000 empirical studies. *Journal of Sustainable Finance & Investment, 5*(4), 210–233.

Fu, R., Tang, Y., & Chen, G. (2020). Chief sustainability officers and corporate social (ir)-responsibility. *Strategic Management Journal, 41*(4), 656–680.

Fuente, J. A., García-Sanchez, I. M., & Lozano, M. B. (2017). The role of the board of directors in the adoption of GRI guidelines for the disclosure of CSR information. *Journal of Cleaner Production, 141*, 737–750.

García-Sánchez, I. M., Aibar-Guzmán, B., Aibar-Guzmán, C., & Azevedo, T. C. (2020). CEO ability and sustainability disclosures: The mediating effect of corporate social responsibility performance. *Corporate Social Responsibility and Environmental Management, 27*(4), 1565–1577.

García-Sánchez, I. M., Gómez-Miranda, M. E., David, F., & Rodríguez-Ariza, L. (2019). Board independence and GRI-IFC performance standards: The mediating effect of the CSR committee. *Journal of Cleaner Production, 225*, 554–562.

Gennari, F., & Salvioni, D. M. (2019). CSR committees on boards: The impact of the external country level factors. *Journal of Management and Governance, 23*(3), 759–785.

Global Sustainable Investment Alliance. (2018). Global sustainable investment alliance review 2018. https://www.gsi-alliance.org/wp-content/uploads/2019/03/GSIR_Review2018.3.28.pdf

Global Sustainable Investment Alliance. (2022). Global sustainable investment Alliance review 2022. https://www.gsi-alliance.org/members-resources/gsir2022/

Gray, R., Kouhy, R., & Lavers, S. (1995). Corporate social and environmental reporting: A review of the literature and a longitudinal study of UK disclosure. *Accounting, Auditing & Accountability Journal, 8*(2), 47–77.

Greene, W. H. (2011). *Econometric analysis*. Pearson.

Hair, H. F., Anderson, R. E., Tatham, R. L., & Black, W. C. (2010). *Multivariate data analysis*. Prentice Hall.

Helfaya, A., & Moussa, T. (2017). Do board's corporate social responsibility strategy and orientation influence environmental sustainability disclosure? UK evidence. *Business Strategy and the Environment, 26*(8), 1061–1077.

Hussain, N., Rigoni, U., & Orij, R. P. (2018). Corporate governance and sustainability performance: Analysis of triple bottom line performance. *Journal of Business Ethics, 149*(2), 411–432.

Jaggi, B., Allini, A., Macchioni, R., & Zampella, A. (2018). Do investors find carbon information useful? Evidence from Italian firms. *Review of Quantitative Finance & Accounting, 50*(4), 1031–1056.

Jain, T., & Jamali, D. (2016). Looking inside the black box: The effect of corporate governance on corporate social responsibility. *Corporate Governance: An International Review, 24*(3), 253–273.

Jarboui, A., Hlima, N. D. B., & Bouaziz, D. (2022). Do sustainability committee characteristics affect CSR performance? Evidence from India. *Benchmarking: An International Journal, 30*(2), 628–652.

Kanashiro, P., & Rivera, J. (2019). Do chief sustainability officers make companies greener? The moderating role of regulatory pressures. *Journal of Business Ethics, 155*, 687–701.

Khan, A., Afeef, M., Ilyas, M., & Jan, S. (2023). Does CSR committee drive the association between corporate social responsibility and firm performance? International evidence. *Managerial Finance, 50*(1), 50–74.

Liao, L., Chen, G., & Zheng, D. (2019). Corporate social responsibility and financial fraud: Evidence from China. *Accounting & Finance, 59*(5), 3133–3169.

Liao, L., Luo, L., & Tang, Q. (2015). Gender diversity, board independence, environmental committee and greenhouse gas disclosure. *The British Accounting Review, 47*(4), 409–424.

Lindblom, C. K. (1994). The implications of organizational legitimacy for corporate social performance and disclosure. In *Critical Perspectives on Accounting Conference, New York*.

Mackenzie, C. (2007). Boards, incentives and corporate social responsibility: The case for a change of emphasis. *Corporate Governance: An International Review, 15*(5), 935–943.

Mahmood, Z., Kouser, R., Ali, W., Ahmad, Z., & Salman, T. (2018). Does corporate governance affect sustainability disclosure? A mixed methods study. *Sustainability, 10*(1), 207.

Martinez-Ferrero, J., & Garcia-Sanchez, I. (2017). Sustainability assurance and assurance providers: Corporate governance determinants in stakeholder-oriented countries. *Journal of Management & Organization, 23*(5), 647–670.

Michelon, G. (2011). Sustainability disclosure and reputation: A comparative study. *Corporate Reputation Review, 14*, 79–96.

Michelon, G., & Parbonetti, A. (2012). The effect of corporate governance on sustainability disclosure. *Journal of Management & Governance, 16*, 477–509.

Miller, K., & Serafeim, G. (2014). *Chief sustainability officers: Who are they and what do they do?*. Working paper. Harvard Business School.

Minciullo, M., Pedrini, M., & Zaccone, M. C. (2021). *L'integrazione della sostenibilità nella governance: quando la forma diventa sostanza?* Egea.

Naciti, V. (2019). Corporate governance and board of directors: The effect of a board composition on firm sustainability performance. *Journal of Cleaner Production, 237*, 1–8.

Orazalin, N., Kuzey, C., Uyar, A., & Karaman, A. S. (2024). Does CSR contribute to the financial sector's financial stability? The moderating role of a sustainability committee. *Journal of Applied Accounting Research, 25*(1), 105–125.

Ormazabal, M., & Sarriegi, J. M. (2014). Environmental management evolution: Empirical evidence from Spain and Italy. *Business Strategy and the Environment, 23*(2), 73–88.

Perrini, F., Russo, A., & Tencati, A. J. (2007). CSR strategies of SMEs and large firms: Evidence from Italy. *Journal of Business Ethics, 74*(3), 285–300.

Peters, G. F., & Romi, A. M. (2014). Does the voluntary adoption of corporate governance mechanisms improve environmental risk disclosures? Evidence from greenhouse gas emission accounting. *Journal of Business Ethics, 125*, 637–666.

Peters, G. F., & Romi, A. M. (2015). The association between sustainability governance characteristics and the assurance of corporate sustainability reports. *Auditing: A Journal of Practice & Theory, 34*(1), 163–198.

Prinsloo, A., & Maroun, W. (2021). An exploratory study on the components and quality of combined assurance in an integrated or a sustainability reporting setting. *Sustainability Accounting, Management and Policy Journal, 12*(1), 1–29.

Prior, D., Surroca, J., & Tribó, J. A. (2008). Are socially responsible managers really ethical? Exploring the relationship between earnings management and corporate social responsibility. *Corporate Governance: An International Review, 16*(3), 160–177.

Qaderi, S. A., Ghaleb, B. A. A., Hashed, A. A., Chandren, S., & Abdullah, Z. (2022). Board characteristics and integrated reporting strategy: Does sustainability committee matter? *Sustainability, 14*(10), 6092.

Radu, C., & Smaili, N. (2021). Alignment versus monitoring: An examination of the effect of the CSR committee and CSR-linked executive compensation on CSR performance. *Journal of Business Ethics, 180*(4), 1–19.

Rankin, M., Windsor, C., & Wahyuni, D. (2011). An investigation of voluntary corporate greenhouse gas emissions reporting in a market governance system: Australian evidence. *Accounting, Auditing & Accountability Journal, 24*(8), 1037–1070.

Rao, K. K., & Tilt, C. (2021). Gender and CSR decisions: Perspectives from Australian boards. *Meditari Accountancy Research, 29*(1), 60–85.

Ricart, J. E., Rodríguez, M. Á., & Sanchez, P. (2005). Sustainability in the boardroom: An empirical examination of Dow Jones sustainability world index leaders. *Corporate Governance: The International Journal of Business in Society, 5*(3), 24–41.

Rodrigue, M., Magnan, M., & Boulianne, E. (2013). Stakeholders' influence on environmental strategy and performance indicators: A managerial perspective. *Management Accounting Research, 24*(4), 301–316.

Ruhnke, K., & Gabriel, A. (2013). Determinants of voluntary assurance on sustainability reports: An empirical analysis. *Journal of Business Economics, 83*(9), 1063–1091.

Sawyer, K. R., Johnson, J., & Holub, M. (2010). The necessary illegitimacy of the whistleblower. *Business & Professional Ethics Journal, 29*(1), 85–107.

Shocker, A. D., & Sethi, S. P. (1973). An approach to incorporating societal preferences in developing corporate action strategies. *California Management Review, 15*(4), 97–105.

Spira, L. F., & Bender, R. (2004). Compare and contrast: Perspectives on board committees. *Corporate Governance: An International Review, 12*(4), 489–499.

Strand, R. (2013). The chief officer of corporate social responsibility: A study of its presence in top management teams. *Journal of Business Ethics, 112*(4), 721–734.

Strand, R. (2014). Strategic leadership of corporate sustainability. *Journal of Business Ethics, 123*, 687–706.

Suchman, M. C. (1995). Managing legitimacy: Strategies and institutional approaches. *The Academy of Management Review, 20*(3), 571–610.

Svejenova, S., Alvarez, J. L., Mazza, C., Meyer, R., Krücken, G., & Walgenbach, P. (2017). Changing the C-suite: New chief officer roles as strategic responses to institutional complexity. In *New themes in institutional analysis: Topics and issues from European research* (pp. 135–161). Edward Elgar Publishing.

Tijani, A., & Ahmadi, A. (2022). An empirical study of the relationship between the busy outside directors and indicators of ESG performance. *Decision Science Letters, 11*(3), 323–332.

Tsang, A., Frost, T., & Cao, H. (2023). Environmental, social, and governance (ESG) disclosure: A literature review. *The British Accounting Review, 55*(1), 101149.

Valle, I. D. D., Esteban, J. M. D., & Pérez, Ó. L. D. F. (2019). Corporate social responsibility and sustainability committee inside the board. *European Journal of International Management, 13*(2), 159–176.

Velte, P. (2023). Chief sustainability officer expertise, sustainability-related executive compensation and corporate biodiversity disclosure: Empirical evidence for the European capital market. *Journal of Global Responsibility, 14*(2), 241–253.

Velte, P., & Stawinoga, M. (2020). Do chief sustainability officers and CSR committees influence CSR-related outcomes? A structured literature review based on empirical-quantitative research findings. *Journal of Management Control, 31*(4), 333–377.

Villadsen A. R., Wulff J. (2018). Fractional regression models in strategic management research. In Academy of Management Proceedings, 2018(1), 11217. : Academy of Management.

Chapter 14
The Value Relevance of Environmental, Social, Governance Performance

Raffaela Casciello, Clelia Fiondella, Martina Prisco, and Rosalinda Santonastaso

14.1 Introduction

In recent years, European Union (EU) firms have experienced an unprecedented pressure to develop business initiatives coherent with Environmental, Social, Governance (ESG) paradigm. Several actions, programs, and plans have been endorsed to enhance sustainable growth among Member States. Following the agreement on the 2030 Agenda, the European Commission (EC) issued the "*European Green Deal*" to achieve carbon neutrality by 2050 (EC, 2019) and the "*European Pillar of Social Rights Action Plan*" to enhance inclusion and equal opportunities for all citizens (EC, 2021a, 2021b). Regarding governance issues, the EC also published the "*Sustainable Corporate Governance*" initiative aiming to improve the EU regulatory framework on corporate governance by enabling firms to focus on long-term sustainable value creation rather than short-term benefits (EC, 2022). Therefore, European firms, especially the listed ones, have experienced significant pressure to adopt sustainable practices to protect the environment, safeguard human rights, and grant fair and ethic corporate governance practices. Considering that stakeholders expect companies to adopt a more sustainable development paradigm in their business strategies and the negative consequences for the corporate market value of ESG controversies (Aouadi & Marsat, 2018), the ESG performance has become a pivotal element in assessing the firm's value.

R. Casciello · M. Prisco
Università degli Studi di Napoli Federico II, Naples, Italy
e-mail: raffaela.casciello@unina.it; martina.prisco@unina.it

C. Fiondella · R. Santonastaso (✉)
Università degli Studi della Campania Luigi Vanvitelli, Capua, Italy
e-mail: clelia.fiondella@unicampania.it; rosalinda.santonastaso@unicampania.it

N. Castellano et al. (eds.), *Environmental, Social, Governance (ESG)*, SIDREA Series in Accounting and Business Administration,
https://doi.org/10.1007/978-3-031-76618-3_14

Recent studies have widely investigated the effect of ESG performance on firm's financial performance. However, previous studies explored the association between the ESG performance, considered as a whole, and the market-based performance, thus ignoring the possibility that only some pillars may be significantly associated with it. To date, results on the connection between of the ESG performance on the financial performance of the firm provided mixed evidence (e.g., Ahmad et al., 2021; Friede et al., 2015; Han et al., 2016; Velte, 2017). More importantly, these studies neglected the possibility that the strength of the association of single pillar and shareholder value may be different according to the nature of the pillar (e.g., Zhao et al., 2018; Yoon et al., 2018). This paper aims to investigate such literature gap and contribute to the existent stream of research.

The interest in investigating the value relevance of ESG performance stems from several reasons. First, in recent years, investors and market participants have increasingly focused their attention on the sustainability nature of companies' strategic choices. In fact, they are taking greater account of how companies manage ESG risks and their sustainability performance (e.g., Friede et al., 2015; Khan et al., 2016). Second, the strengthening of international non-financial reporting regulations, such as the Non-Financial Reporting Directive (2014/95/EU) and the Corporate Sustainability Reporting Directive (CSRD), has put additional pressure on firms to provide accurate and transparent sustainability disclosure to meet the needs of different stakeholders' groups (Kurunmäki & Miller, 2006; Schmitz & Glänzel, 2016). Furthermore, studying whether ESG performance disclosure is value relevant could contribute to understand the underlying motivations behind the adoption of greenwashing strategies and the pursuit of opportunistic corporate or personal goals.

Data on corporate ESG performance are collected using the London Stock Exchange Group database (LSEG), previously known as Refinitiv Eikon from Thomson Reuters. It is considered one of the largest database for data on firm's environmental, social, and governance performance and it is widely adopted in academic research on sustainability topics (e.g., De Villiers et al., 2022). We develop Ohlson's (1995) model to achieve our research goal, controlling for additional firm-level features affecting market-based performance. The study focuses on EA listed non-financial firms that provided information on ESG performance over the period 2015–2022. This time frame is particularly significant as it includes the effects of the 2030 Agenda 2030, which has encouraged institutions to enhance the sustainability growth within the EA boundaries. We select 2022 as final year due to the data availability.

Based on a sample of 81 listed non-financial firms, results show that investors significantly value the performance related to the three pillars of sustainability: environmental, social, and corporate governance, thus indicating that all ESG dimensions are crucial drivers of a firm's market-based performance. The findings are also robust to several statistical tests, such as the two-stage least squares (2SLS) regression models, for addressing potential endogeneity issues.

The remainder of the paper is structured as follows: Section 14.2 presents the theoretical framework and hypothesis development. Section 14.3 describes the methodology of the study. Section 14.4 provides empirical results while Sect. 14.5 shows findings from additional robustness tests. Section 14.6 provides conclusions.

14.2 Theoretical Framework and Hypothesis Development

14.2.1 Theoretical Framework

This study uses the value enhancing theory to explain the association between ESG practices and market-based performance (e.g., Brammer & Millington, 2004; Malik, 2015; Yoon et al., 2018; Zhou et al., 2022). Such framework emphasizes the contribution of management actions to increase firm profitability and financial performance, thereby ultimately improving shareholder value. These actions might refer to a wide number of initiatives such as strategic investments and cost-cutting interventions that are all aimed at generating higher returns (Servaes et al., 2009; Veldman & Gaalman, 2015).

In line with such theoretical framework, we argue that by developing ESG practices firms benefit from several advantages in terms of innovation, operating efficiency improvements, and competitive differentiation (e.g., Al-Hiyari et al., 2023; Cheng et al., 2023; Macchioni et al., 2024; Meira et al., 2023; Shin et al., 2023; Tang, 2022) contributing to increase their market value. Under the value enhancing theory, we particularly shed light on the role of ESG practices as a strategic driver to increase firm market value. In the subsequent subparagraphs, we highlight more precisely how the wider ESG performance and each single practice might affect the market-based performance in line with the value enhancing theory.

14.2.2 ESG Performance and Market-Based Performance

The call for sustainable growth has seen a swift rise in recent years. The Agenda 2030 of United Nations (2015), established in 2015, has significantly propelled the goals of sustainable growth, positively impacting the environment, society, and individuals. In line with the Sustainable Development Goals defined by the Agenda, in 2019, the EC introduced the Green Deal, aiming to facilitate Europe's transition to carbon neutrality by the year 2050.

Under such pressures, firms have notably developed their ESG practices in order to satisfy stakeholders' instances on related issues. In doing so, firms not only align with stakeholders' needs, but also support the corporate growth (Hu et al., 2023). In this regard, previous studies have highlighted several channels through which ESG performance affects firm market value, such as the reduction of equity costs and business risks, the increase in firm's reputation, and the acquisition of new competitive advantages through an improved corporate image (e.g., Amel-Zadeh & Serafeim, 2018; Bui et al., 2020; Van Duuren et al., 2016; El Ghoul et al., 2017;

Friede et al., 2015; Khan, 2022; Miralles-Quirós et al., 2019; Nekhili et al., 2019; Pulino et al., 2022; Qureshi et al., 2023; Tarmuji et al., 2016; Zhao et al., 2018). This is also confirmed by several survey data addressed to directors and executives that have declared the relevance of ESG performance for their business to achieve a better financial performance (e.g., Wu & Tham, 2023). Coherent with such reasoning, we develop our first hypothesis as follows:

H1: ESG performance is positively associated with market-based performance.

14.2.3 Environmental Performance and Market-Based Performance

Climate change has become a serious concern for nations, individuals, and companies as well. Firms are accused of contributing to worsen such an emergency because the fuel-based consumption has increased greenhouse gas emissions and air pollution over years. To date, firms are requested to develop environmental-friendly practices.

Investors are more likely to support more environmental-friendly initiatives if these latter ones help to receive a return. Existent literature argues that more environmental-friendly firms not only better meet the expectations of stakeholders, but they are also more likely to face new sources of opportunities. Accordingly, consumers are more willing to pay a premium price for the sold goods if they respect and preserve environment (e.g., Al-Najjar & Anfimiadou, 2011; Shao et al., 2022; Shi & Jiang, 2023; Wang et al., 2014; Yadav et al., 2016; Yang et al., 2021). The higher expenses for implementing environmental-friendly investments are remunerated by higher prices of sold goods, guaranteeing the benefit-cost trade-off balance. Therefore, the environmental performance may be used strategically to better compete with other firms in the sector. If the environmental-friendly initiatives allow more efficient use of inputs, such as raw materials and energy, firms may also experience a reduction of environmental burden, industrial waste, and operational costs, contributing to generate new competitive advantages (e.g., Farza et al., 2021; Iqbal et al., 2022; Hao et al., 2022; Dai & Xue, 2022; Zhang & Fu, 2023).

Based on the above arguments, investors are more likely to positively react to the environmental-friendly initiatives. Accordingly, they contribute to improve the firm image and the operational efficiency. We then expect that environmental performance is positively associated with market-based performance and develop our second hypothesis as follows:

H2: Environmental performance is positively associated with market-based performance.

14.2.4 Social Performance and Market-Based Performance

The growing focus on addressing key social issues, including the protection of human rights, the fight against discrimination, and the promotion of equal opportunities, has garnered significant attention from global regulatory bodies, such as the United Nations (2015) and the European Commission (2019). In recent times, the aspect of social performance has also emerged as a primary concern for firms. The company operates through the presence of individuals whose actions and activities enable it to nurture business activity. Through social performance, firms meet expectations of a wide range of stakeholders, such as employees, customers, local communities, and the government (Wood, 1991; Hillman & Keim, 2001). Indeed, employees represent one of the main groups of stakeholders demanding for an adequate social performance. For the purpose of this study, it is important to notice that the way through which firms manage and maintain relationships with employees can also influence their financial performance. Good policies improve the commitment of employees to the organization reducing the lower turnover and the absenteeism, thus increasing productivity (Berman et al., 1999; Delery & Doty, 1996; Kang et al., 2016; Kumar et al., 2016). Firms may invest in several fields to strengthen the relationships with employees, such as health and safety, training and development, and diversity and equal opportunities. These initiatives generate trust and loyalty among employees, creating new competitive advantages by distinguishing the firm from its competitors (Berman et al., 1999; Greening & Turban, 2000; Soana, 2011). Customers are also other relevant stakeholders that call for a better social performance to the firm (Rhouma et al., 2012). Firms investing in product quality and safety improve the perceptions and the satisfaction of customers that, in turn, support sales and firm profitability (Cek & Eyupoglu, 2020; Dhaliwal et al., 2011; Gao & Bansal, 2013; Garcia-Sanchez et al., 2008; Mishra & Suar, 2010; Pulino et al., 2022; Tenucci & Supino, 2020).

Following these argumentations, we expect that social performance is more likely to sustain firm's growth, allowing the firm to achieve higher profits and increase its competitiveness. These factors are extremely relevant for investors and market participants for making capital allocation decisions so that we expect to influence positively the market-based performance. On the contrary, corporate activities which are socially irresponsible damage firm's image and reputation, thus eroding the firm's value. We then expect that the social performance is also value relevant for investors, thus developing our third hypothesis as follows:

H3: Social performance is positively associated with market-based performance.

14.2.5 Governance Performance and Market-Based Performance

The governance performance refers to a wide range of firm-level features including, among others, board of directors' functions and structure, directors' compensations policy, corporate vision, strategy and rights granted to shareholders (e.g., Zheng et al., 2023). In other terms, governance performance concerns the exercise of power within the organization and the distribution of responsibilities. Therefore, it is inherently related to firm's outcomes (Klettner et al., 2014). More precisely, the corporate performance is an expression of firm's fiduciary and moral responsibilities toward their stakeholders (Aguilera et al., 2007), which have the potential to influence their perceptions and behaviors toward the organization (Gill, 2008; Yoon et al., 2018). Accordingly, good governance performance can improve firm's reputation and image with positive consequences for corporate performance (e.g., Li & Yang, 2012; Paoloni et al., 2023; Ifada et al., 2024). It might also foster the investors' trust and promote capital investment in the firm (e.g., Cek & Eyupoglu, 2020). Furthermore, it is also argued that directors and executives are willing to invest in a better governance performance if this enhances sympathy toward the company to the extent to achieve prestige and financial returns (Barnea & Rubin, 2010).

Following these arguments, the governance performance is expected to be positively associated with market-based performance, thus developing our hypothesis as follows:

H4: Governance performance is positively associated with market-based performance.

14.3 Methodology

14.3.1 Sample Selection

The sample is composed of EA listed non-financial companies from 20 countries[1] which provided data on ESG performance as well as on the individual E, S and G pillar performances for the period 2015–2022. The choice to investigate such a long period is aimed at consolidating the robustness of results concerning the value relevance of ESG performance. Furthermore, we chose to conclude the analysis in the last year available for data collection to provide the most up-to-date empirical

[1] The 20 EA countries are: Austria (AT), Belgium (BE), Denmark (DK), Finland (FI), France (FR), Germany (DE), Greece (GR), Hungary, (HU), Ireland (IE), Italy (IT), Luxembourg (LU), Malta (MT), Netherlands (NL), Poland (PL), Portugal (PT), Romania (RO), Slovenia (SI), Spain (ES), Sweden (SE), United Kingdom (GB).

Table 14.1 Sample selection steps

Sample selection steps	Number of companies
Active EA listed non-financial companies from 20 countries during the period 2015–2022	1,945
Excluding the companies with no recent IAS-compliant financial statements data and with missing data on E, S, G single pillars performance	−1,864
Final sample	**81**

evidence possible. We extracted ESG-related, governance, and corporate accounting data from the LSEG database. The country-level data were extracted from the World Bank and Euro Area Statistics' online databases.

The initial sample consisted of all EA listed non-financial companies from 20 countries, totaling about 1945 entities from the LSEG database. Then, we excluded all companies lacking recent IFRS-compliant financial statements data and those with missing data on the E, S, G pillars performances. The final sample included 81 EA listed non-financial companies with 312 firm-year observations.

Below, we provided the reasons for such a significant reduction in the number of companies in our sample and discuss the limitations. During the period under investigation (2015–2022), the disclosure of ESG performance was still voluntary for many EA listed non-financial companies, excluding large listed companies with more than 500 employees, for which the Non-Financial Reporting Directive mandated sustainability reporting obligations starting in 2017. This regulatory context certainly influenced the availability of data on ESG performance in databases for EA listed non-financial companies. Furthermore, the decision to exclude companies without complete financial data, ESG performance data, and control variables' data was necessary to ensure the reliability and validity of observations over the timespan of the extracted sample. The limited number of companies for which the LSEG database provides ESG performance information from 2015 to 2022 is note worthy and merits further reflection. This phenomenon could indicate that, among other things, a lack of shared and consistent commitment over time to provide sufficient information on corporate ESG performance.

However, the selection of companies that provided comprehensive financial and ESG performance data covering the years 2015–2022 helps to address the research questions, considering the pervasiveness of ESG performance reporting practices over time.

Table 14.1 contains the sample selection steps.

Continuous variables are winsorized at the first and 99th percentiles to moderate the influence of outliers.

14.3.2 Research Method

To assess if the corporate ESG performance of EA listed non-financial firms during the period 2015–2022 is value relevant, we adopted the traditional value relevance model based on Ohlson (1995). The Ohlson's (1995) model, an influential framework in financial accounting research, measures the value relevance of financial statements' numbers by regressing the corporate market value on the basis of corporate earnings and book value of equity. The underlying assumption for this model is that stakeholders, especially investors and market participants, rely upon these two accounting measures for gaining information about the corporate financial health and profitability (Ohlson, 1995). Specifically, we performed the following base model (1):

$$MVS_{i,t} = \alpha_0 + \alpha_1 EPS_{i,t} + \alpha_2 BVPS_{i,t} + \varepsilon_i \tag{14.1}$$

where i is the company and t is the year. *MVS* is the market value per share at the end of the fiscal year, *EPS* is the net income per share, and *BVPS* is the book value of common equity per share. All variables were deflated by the number of shares outstanding to avoid the scale effect (Aledo et al., 2019; Barth & Clinch, 2009; Easton, 1999; Venter et al., 2014).

To test the research hypotheses, we ran four Ordinary Least Square (OLS) regression models (model 2, model 3, model 4, model 5) by adding the independent variables step by step and measuring the incremental value relevance by comparing the R^2 (Beisland, 2009; Brown et al., 1999; Collins et al., 1997).

First, we introduced the ESG performance proxy (*ESG_score*) in the base model, resulting in model (2), as follows:

$$MVS_{i,t} = \alpha_0 + \alpha_1 EPS_{i,t} + \alpha_2 BVPS_{i,t} + \alpha_3 ESG\_score_{i,t} + \varepsilon_i \tag{14.2}$$

where i is the company and t is the year. *ESG_score* is the independent proxy measuring the yearly corporate ESG performance. The *ESG_score* proxy is provided by LSEG database, and it is an overall company score based on the self-reported information in the environmental, social, and corporate governance pillars. It is a versatile and trustworthy measure to capture ESG performance, as confirmed by many sustainability management and accounting studies (Rajesh, 2020; Gong et al., 2019; Ioannou & Serafeim, 2012; Semenova & Hassel, 2015). The ESG score results from weighted heterogeneous variable aggregation, including, for example, the innovation adopted to reduce environmental impact and improve job satisfaction, diversity, safety, equality, and protection of human rights; the sustainable use of resources; carbon dioxide emissions; equal treatment of shareholders and integration of sustainability objectives into the corporate strategy.

Second, we added some control variables, described below, capturing firm-specific characteristics that demonstrated to be significantly associated with corporate sustainability performance (Naciti, 2019).

Third, we included dummy variables for capturing year, country, and industry fixed effects, as indicated in the following model (3):

$$\begin{aligned} MVS_{i,t} = {} & \alpha_0 + \alpha_1 EPS_{i,t} + \alpha_2 BVPS_{i,t} + \alpha_3 ESG\_score_{i,t} + \alpha_4 Leverage_{i,t} \\ & + \alpha_5 Size_{i,t} + \alpha_6 EBIT + \alpha_7 ROA_{i,t} + \alpha_8 CFO_{i,t} + \alpha_9 Indep\_Board_{i,t} \\ & + \alpha_{10} Board\_Div_{i,t} + \alpha_{11} AuditB\_Com_{i,t} + \alpha_{12} AuditC\_Indep_{i,t} \\ & + \alpha_{13} CSR_{i,t} + \alpha_{14} GDP\_GWT_{i,t} + \alpha_{15} Y2015 + \alpha_{16} Y2016 + \alpha_{17} Y2017 \\ & + \alpha_{18} Y2018 + \alpha_{19} Y2019 + \alpha_{20} Y2020 + \alpha_{21} Y2021 + \alpha_{22} Y2022 + \\ & < Country\_FE > + < Industry\_FE > + \varepsilon_i \end{aligned} \tag{14.3}$$

where i is the company and t is the year. We use the leverage, firm size, and EBIT as control variables for two main reasons: they demonstrated to be significantly associated with corporate ESG performance (Ho et al., 2021; Darnall et al., 2010, Chang & Kuo, 2008; Artiach et al., 2010) and they account for the part of variability of the market performance depending on the variability of financial leverage, firm size, and profitability (Bowman, 1980; Ghosh & Sherman, 1993; Bae & Jeong, 2007; Brimble & Hodgson, 2007; Filip & Raffournier, 2010). In fact, they are the most used control variables in value relevance models (Dimitrov & Jain, 2008; Sinkin et al., 2008). *Leverage* is the firm's financial leverage, measured as total debt divided by total assets at fiscal year-end. It is a relevant driver for the market value of debt (Bowman, 1980) and influences the market participants' capital allocation decisions (Ghosh & Sherman, 1993). *Size* is the firm size, measured as the natural logarithm of the revenues at fiscal year-end. The larger the company, the greater the market visibility, which, in turn, influences the value relevance of corporate accounting numbers for market participants (e.g., Bae & Jeong, 2007; Brimble & Hodgson, 2007). *EBIT* is earnings before interest and taxes scaled by total assets at fiscal year-end and it measures the corporate profitability. Higher accounting earnings, excluding losses, are associated with improved stock returns, as more profitable companies attract investor attention and achieve better market valuations (Filip & Raffournier, 2010). We included in the model also *ROA*, *CFO*, *Indep_Board*, *Board_Div*, *AuditB_Com*, *CSR*, and *GDP_GWT* as control variables. *ROA*, the return on assets ratio, demonstrated to be negatively associated with sustainability performance (Jyoti & Khanna, 2021). *CFO* is the proxy of cash flow from operations scaled by total asset and it is positively associated with the sustainability performance (Jia & Li, 2022). *Indep_Board* is the percentage of independent board members as reported by the company and it is negatively associated with the corporate sustainability performance (Naciti, 2019). The presence of women on board of directors is associated with a greater focus on the pursuit of CSR goals (Martınez-Ferrero et al., 2021) and better sustainability performance (Naciti, 2019). Therefore, we included the *Board_Div* proxy, the percentage of female on the board of directors as reported by the company, as control variable. Since the presence of an audit committee improves the sustainability performance due to its increasingly concern about the risk of misleading the stakeholders expectations about the corporate commitment toward sustainability aims (Yorke et al., 2023), we included in the model the *AuditB_Com* proxy. It is a dummy variable equals to 1 if the company has an audit board committee and 0 otherwise. We also included in the model *CSR*, a dummy variable equal to 1 if the company has a corporate social responsibility committee or team and 0 otherwise. Companies with a CSR committee demonstrated to have better sustainability and corporate social responsibility performance (Velte & Stawinoga, 2020; Radu & Smaili, 2021). To capture the variability of financial performance due to economic cycles of expansion and recession, we included in the model *GDP_GWT* the annual growth of gross domestic product.

To assess if the performance about each single E-S-G pillar is value relevant in EA listed non-financial firms between 2015–2022, we ran the same regression models indicated above (2–3) by replacing the *ESG_score* proxy with the three single pillars proxies, *E_score*, *S_score*, and *G_score*, as indicated in the following models (4–5):

$$MVS_{i,t} = \alpha_0 + \alpha_1 EPS_{i,t} + \alpha_2 BVPS_{i,t} + \alpha_3 E\_score_{i,t} + \alpha_4 S\_score_{i,t} + \alpha_5 G\_score_{i,t} + \varepsilon_i \tag{14.4}$$

$$\begin{aligned} MVS_{i,t} = {} & \alpha_0 + \alpha_1 EPS_{i,t} + \alpha_2 BVPS_{i,t} + \alpha_3 E\_score_{i,t} + \alpha_4 S\_score_{i,t} \\ & + \alpha_5 G\_score_{i,t} + \alpha_6 Leverage_{i,t} + \alpha_7 Size_{i,t} + \alpha_8 Profitability + \alpha_9 ROA_{i,t} \\ & + \alpha_{10} CFO_{i,t} + \alpha_{11} Indep\_Board_{i,t} + \alpha_{12} Board\_Div_{i,t} \\ & + \alpha_{13} AuditB\_Com_{i,t} + \alpha_{14} AuditC\_Indep_{i,t} + \alpha_{15} CSR_{i,t} \\ & + \alpha_{16} GDP\_GWT_{i,t} + \alpha_{17} Y2014 + \alpha_{18} Y2015 + \alpha_{19} Y2016 + \alpha_{20} Y2017 \\ & + \alpha_{21} Y2018 + \alpha_{22} Y2019 + \alpha_{23} Y2020 + \alpha_{24} Y2021 + \alpha_{25} Y2022 + \\ & < Country\_FE > + < Industry\_FE > + \varepsilon_i \end{aligned} \tag{14.5}$$

E_Score, S_Score, and *G_Score* are provided by the LSEG database. The Environmental Pillar score, *E_score*, measures a "*company's impact on living and non-living natural systems, including the air, land, and water, as well as complete ecosystems. It reflects how well a company uses best management practices to avoid environmental risks and capitalize on environmental opportunities to generate long term shareholder value*" (LSEG glossary). Therefore, we use the E_Score to measure the yearly corporate environmental performance. The Social Pillar score, S_score, measures a "*company's capacity to generate trust and loyalty with its workforce, customers, and society, through its use of best management practices. It reflects the company's reputation and the health of its license to operate, which are key factors in determining its ability to generate long term shareholder value*" (LSEG glossary). Therefore, we use the S_Score to measure the yearly corporate social performance. The Corporate Governance pillar score, G_score, instead, measures a "*company's systems and processes, which ensure that its board members and executives act in the best interests of its long-term shareholders. It reflects a company's capacity, through its use of best management practices, to direct and control its rights and responsibilities through the creation of incentives, as well as checks and balances to generate long term shareholder value*" (LSEG glossary). Therefore, we use the G_Score to measure the yearly corporate governance performance.

Appendix A provides the description of variable used in the analyses.

14.4 Results

14.4.1 Descriptive Statistics

Table 14.2 shows the results of descriptive statistics. On average, the *MVS* of all companies is around 64.10. EPS has a mean of 1.72 and BVPS has a mean of 81.96. Regarding the other variable, the *ESG_score, ESG_Cscore, E_score, S_score*, and *G_score* yield a mean of 31.19, 30.66, 25.17, 33.18, and 34.12, respectively.

Looking at the financial control variables, *Leverage* has a mean of 0.25 which implies that the companies have low leverage, with much more equity than debt while *Size* has a mean of 19.96 which indicates that our sample is dominated by large and medium-sized firms. The mean values of *EBIT, ROA*, and *CFO* are 0.03, 0.01, and 0.04, respectively. Regarding the governance control variables, the mean values

Table 14.2 Descriptive statistics of variables used in the value relevance analysis

	Mean	SD	Min	Max
MVS	64.10	220.40	0	1714.34
BVPS	81.96	656.73	−42.99	9770.28
EPS	1.72	183.18	−2539.09	2476.73
ESG_score	31.19	17.11	1.80	80.35
ESG_Cscore	30.66	16.80	1.80	80.35
E_score	25.17	21.64	0	90.83
S_score	33.18	20.55	1.40	88.61
G_score	34.12	18.66	3.55	89.40
Leverage	0.25	0.43	0	7.86
Size	19.96	1.95	14.44	25.17
EBIT	0.03	0.50	−11.58	0.86
ROA	0.01	0.28	−3.18	0.99
CFO	0.04	0.18	−2.79	0.45
Indep_Board	35.06	30.63	0	100
Board_Div	19.82	16.58	0	75
AuditB_Com	0.81	0.39	0	1
CSR	0.36	0.48	0	1
GDP_GWT	1.83	3.40	−9.40	13.6

Note. The appendix provides details on the construction of variables used in all models

Table 14.3 Variance inflation factors test

Variable	VIF	1/VIF
ROA	4.88	0.20
Profitability	4.64	0.22
Audit_Com	2.47	0.40
Indep_Board	2.19	0.46
ESG_Score	2.07	0.48
CSR	1.64	0.61
AuditB_Com	1.60	0.63
Size	1.56	0.64
Leverage	1.49	0.67
BVPS	1.31	0.76
CFO	1.24	0.81
EPS	1.17	0.86
Board_Div	1.08	0.93
GDP_GWT	1.04	0.96
Mean VIF	2.03	

Note. The appendix provides details on the construction of variables used in all models

of *Indep_Board, Board_Div, AuditB_Com,* and *CSR* are 35.06, 19.82, 0.81, and 0.36, respectively. The average *GDP_GWT* is 1.83% which implies that, on average, the economy has been expanding at a rate of 1.83% from 1 year to another.

Furthermore, the (untabulated) results of the Pearson correlations show that the dependent variable, *MVS,* is positively and significantly correlated with *BVPS, EPS, Indep_Board, AuditB_Com,* and *CSR.* Nevertheless, the correlations between the independent variables suggest that our analysis does not suffer from multicollinearity because all correlation coefficients are lower than 0.8 (Hair et al., 2006). Moreover, the results of the variance inflation test, shown in Table 14.3, confirm that there are no collinearity issues among the variables used in regression models.

14.4.2 Regression Results

Table 14.4 shows the results of OLS regression models (1), (2), and (3).

Regarding the base model (1) where we regress *BVPS* and *EPS* on *MVS*, the results show a significant and positive association between these variables (p-value 1%); the adjusted R^2 is 43%.

Next, we report model (2) that adds *ESG_score* to the base model (1). The coefficients of the base model remain consistent and the variable *ESG_score* is statistically significant.

In the next column, we provide the results of full model (3) that adds the control variables that might affect the value relevance of ESG performance. Considering the limited scope of our sample, the findings indicate a significant and positive association between *ESG_score* and *MVS* (p-value 5%). This outcome implies that companies boasting higher ESG_scores tend to possess higher market value. Therefore,

Table 14.4 Value relevance including basic variables, controls, and interest variables

	Mod (1)	Mod (2)	Mod (3)
BVPS	0.23*** (22.67)	0.22*** (17.42)	0.09*** (11.60)
EPS	0.11*** (3.31)	0.09** (2.09)	0.03** (1.99)
ESG_score		0.60* (1.86)	3.58*** (2.69)
Leverage			−50.07 (−1.45)
Size			−47.79*** (−4.00)
EBIT			17.93 (0.28)
ROA			−16.03 (−0.18)
CFO			−465.76*** (−3.51)
Indep_Board			5.13*** (5.07)
Board_Div			−0.53 (−0.46)
AuditB_Com			−176.03 (−1.58)
CSR			81.68* (1.91)
GDP_GWT			6.61 (0.93)
Constant	45.99 (7.21)	32.94 (1.33)	1053.93*** (3.85)
Year fixed effects			YES
Industry fixed effects			YES
Country fixed effects			YES
F	267.44***	106.60***	18.38***
Adj R^2	0.43	0.51	0.80
Observations	312	312	312

Note. Table 14.4 reports the results of the OLS regression models with year, industry, and country fixed effects (Mod.1; Mod2; Mod.3). The appendix provides details on the construction of variables used in all models. The symbols ***, **, and * denote two-sided significance at the 1%, 5%, and 10% levels, respectively

the base hypothesis (H1) is supported. This view is consistent with the value enhancing theory, which considers sustainability activities to be important to increase firm market value. The growing significance of ESG issues to capital-market participants highlights that non-financial information represents a factor explaining the variation in the market value of firms (e.g., Aureli et al., 2020; De Villiers et al., 2017; Lombardi et al., 2019) because the market value of firm reflected

Table 14.5 Value relevance including basic variables, controls, and interest variables

	Mod (4)	Mod (5)
BVPS	0.22*** (17.26)	0.10*** (7.58)
EPS	0.09** (2.11)	0.03 (0.95)
E_score	0.47* (1.66)	1.07** (1.97)
S_score	1.49* (1.87)	1.64** (1.99)
G_score	0.70** (1.96)	2.56*** (2.82)
Leverage		−42.34 (−1.32)
Size		−51.65*** (−5.21)
EBIT		12.30 (0.20)
ROA		−9.28 (−0.11)
CFO		−323.56*** (2.95)
Indep_Board		3.99*** 6.28
Board_Div		−0.77 (−0.82)
AuditB_Com		12.72 (0.34)
CSR		93.64*** (2.62)
GDP_GWT		4.03 (0.64)
Constant	37.74 (1.39)	945.24*** (4.55)
Year fixed effects		YES
Industry fixed effects		YES
Country fixed effects		YES
F	64.87***	18.50***
Adj R2	0.51	0.78
Observations	312	312

Note. Table 14.5 reports the results of the OLS regression models with year, industry, and country fixed effects (Mod.4; Mod5). The appendix provides details on the construction of variables used in all models. The symbols ***, **, and * denote two-sided significance at the 1%, 5%, and 10% levels, respectively

ESG performance that it is considered an intangible asset by investors (Kaspereit & Lopatta, 2016). Furthermore, these findings are consistent with empirical studies that have identified a positive correlation between sustainability performance and market value (Jadoon et al., 2021; Lins et al., 2017; Lopatta & Kaspereit, 2014).

Looking at the control variables, the coefficients of the *Size, CFO, Indep_Board,* and *CSR* are all statistically significant. The adjusted R^2 increases up to 80%.

Table 14.5 presents the results for environmental, social, and corporate governance pillars. model (4) includes the *E_score, S_score,* and *G_score* to the base model (1). The coefficients of *E_score, S_score,* and *G_score* are positive and statistically significant. model (5) adds the control variables to the Model (4). The coefficients of *E_score, S_score,* and *G_score* remain positive and statistically significant. This suggests that a higher score in environmental, social, and governance performance is associated with a higher market value for firms.

Empirical evidence supports the view that companies' efforts toward environmental objectives are favorably perceived by investors, enhancing market share valuation. Indeed, environmental performance bolsters the firm's competitiveness due to the stimulus it provides for product innovation (e.g., Brännlund & Lundgren, 2009). Moreover, the growing awareness among capital-market investors about the importance of social factors as indicators of potential future risk and return results in an elevation of the firm's value (e.g., Servaes & Tamayo, 2013). Finally, a good governance proves advantageous for the firm's value as it mitigates conflicts between managers and shareholders through effective oversight, thus maintaining positive relationships (e.g., Yoon et al., 2018). Therefore, Hypotheses 2, 3, and 4 are supported.

14.5 Robustness Tests

To increase the robustness of our analysis, we performed several additional tests. In detail, we re-estimated model (3) by using an alternative measure of ESG performance, such as the ESG Combined Score (*ESG_Cscore*). The *ESG_Cscore* is provided by LSEG database, and it overlays the LSEG ESG Score with ESG controversies to provide a comprehensive evaluation on the company's sustainability impact and conduct.

The results reported in Table 14.6 show a positive and significant relationship between *ESG_Cscore* and *MVS* in model (6) and full model (7).

Furthermore, we performed a two-stage least squares (2SLS) instrumental variable (IV) estimation approach to confirm that our results are insensitive to endogeneity concerns which could arise from omitted variable bias or reverse causality. Hence, we re-estimated model (3) and Model (5) performing IV 2SLS regressions. We identify *ESG_score, E_score, S_score,* and *G_score* as the instrumented variable, while *Indep_Board, Board_Div, AuditB_Com,* and *CSR* as

Table 14.6 Regression robustness results (alternative measure of ESG performance)

	Mod (6)	Mod (7)
BVPS	0.22*** (17.43)	0.10*** (7.81)
EPS	0.09** (2.09)	0.03 (0.78)
ESG_Cscore	0.69** (1.98)	1.79* (1.66)
Leverage		−38.50 (−1.19)
Size		−52.31*** (−5.27)
EBIT		27.12 (0.44)
ROA		−25.15 (−0.30)
CFO		−309.36*** (−2.78)
Indep_Board		3.50*** (5.63)
Board_Div		−0.34 (−0.38)
AuditB_Com		1.61 (0.04)
CSR		84.68** (2.36)
GDP_GWT		4.01 (0.63)
Constant	30.37 (1.23)	905.87*** (4.28)
Year fixed effects		YES
Industry fixed effects		YES
Country fixed effects		YES
F	106.75***	18.51***
Adj. R^2	0.51	0.77
Observations	312	312

Note. Table 14.6 reports the results of the OLS regression models with year, industry, and country fixed effects (Mod.4; Mod5). The appendix provides details on the construction of variables used in all models. The symbols ***, **, and * denote two-sided significance at the 1%, 5%, and 10% levels, respectively

instrumental variables. The results, shown in Table 14.7 confirm a positive and significant relation between ESG performance and market value (model 3) as well as between each dimension of ESG performance and market value (model 5). Therefore, the inferences drawn from the 2SLS approach align with those from our primary analyses and further confirm the robustness of main findings.

Table 14.7 Results of two-stage least squares tests

	Mod (8)	Mod (9)
BVPS	0.13*** (8.64)	0.13*** (6.43)
EPS	0.02 (0.42)	0.02 (0.31)
ESG_score	13.34*** (4.01)	
E_score		10.16* (1.65)
S_score		16.43* (1.70)
G_score		2.26* (1.68)
Leverage	−19.25 (−0.45)	31.61 (−0.62)
Size	−98.35*** (−5.98)	46.46 (−1.03)
EBIT	103.42 (1.28)	111.01 (1.12)
ROA	−133.22 (−1.21)	98.40 (−0.65)
CFO	−162.73 (−0.92)	131.05 (−0.65)
GDP_GWT	4.74 (0.54)	1.16 (−0.10)
Constant	1481.04*** (4.96)	432.71 (0.46)
Year fixed effects	YES	YES
Industry fixed effects	YES	YES
Country fixed effects	YES	YES
Wald Chi2	520.25	421.70
Prob > Chi2	0.00	0.00
Adj. R^2	0.69	0.61
Observations	312	312

Note. Table 14.7 reports the results of the 2SLS regression models with year, industry, and country fixed effects (Mod.4; Mod5). The appendix provides details on the construction of variables used in all models. The symbols ***, **, and * denote two-sided significance at the 1%, 5%, and 10% levels, respectively

Furthermore, given the challenges associated with measurement and estimation errors in studies pertaining to sustainability investment (Chegut et al., 2011), we conducted additional sensitivity and robustness tests. Specifically, we mitigated potential endogeneity concerns by employing lagged values for our dependent variable, MVS. Consequently, we re-evaluated model (3). The (untabulated) results align closely with those reported in Table 14.2.

14.6 Conclusion

This paper aims to examine the value relevance of ESG performance in EA listed non-financial firms. Results show that investors consider value relevant each dimension of ESG performance. Therefore, our results provide strong support that ESG performance and each E-S-G pillars are valuable predictors of firm market-based performance.

The results contribute to previous research on the economic effects of the ESG performance on corporate performance. Although this has been a well-debated issue in recent years, most of the studies explore the impact of the overall performance (i.e., the ESG performance), excluding how the single dimensions (i.e., environmental, social, and governance performance) affect the firm's value. In mitigating such literature gap, our study provides a better understanding on the effect of the single component of ESG performance on firm's value. Furthermore, from a theoretical point of view, our results are supportive of the value enhancing theory as underpinning framework to explain the impact of ESG performances on market-based performance.

This study offers valuable practical implications. It suggests that promoting ESG initiatives within organizations can lead to improved economic performance, as investors positively assess each dimension—environmental, social, and governance performance. In this vein, managers should bolster ESG performance not only to enhance shareholder value but also to attract additional potential investments, thereby fostering sustainable growth. Given that ESG dimensions influence various aspects of a firm, such as its relationship with the environment, consumers, employees, or governance structure, managers should prioritize those dimensions that effectively improve the balance between expenses and revenues to enhance firm profitability. However, the positive impact of ESG initiatives on investment attractiveness may raise the risk of managers resorting to opportunistic behaviors, accentuating positive news while downplaying negative ones. Because ESG initiatives demand significant investment and long-term commitment, it becomes cost-effective and profitable for them to resort to greenwashing practices, thereby evading real investment in ESG initiatives.

Therefore, our research also offers valuable insights for policymakers. Governments need to recognize firms engaging in greenwashing practices and subsequently devise appropriate regulatory measures to mitigate them. For instance, state and local authorities should enhance incentive and penalty mechanisms to deter all forms of greenwashing. Additionally, the government should intensify oversight of units involved in the ESG assurance process, including audit committees, external and internal auditors, to mitigate greenwashing practices effectively.

Based on the argument that companies implementing ESG initiatives enjoy increased market-based returns, the findings of this study should capture investors' attention as they provide insights into companies likely to offer superior returns on invested capital. Consequently, our study underscores the importance of steering financial investors toward a shared awareness of sustainability issues in their investment decisions, aiming to incentivize the support of more sustainable businesses. This need persists despite the recent focus the EU has placed on the ESG agenda.

This research has some limitations, mainly related to the size of the sample. First, the companies of the sample might not sufficiently represent the broader population, potentially skewing the perceived trends, behaviors, or performances of EA listed non-financial firms. Second, this small sample size could constrain the ability to infer the findings to the population of all EA listed non-financial companies. Third, employing such a limited sample size improves the risk of overfitting in statistical models, which could cause these models to align too closely with our specific dataset, diminishing their applicability to a broader context. However, by selecting companies that have disclosed thorough financial and ESG performance data across several years (2015–2022), we aim to address our research questions by considering the extent of corporate ESG performance reporting practices over time.

Fourth, generalizability could be an issue when extending our results to other countries. Our sample uses data from EA area in which heterogeneity across countries is mitigated. For years, the EC has implemented various actions and programs to promote sustainable growth aligned with the ESG framework. This has put significant pressure on European Union firms to improve their ESG performance. While our results are relevant in this context, they might not directly translate to other regions where business environments and factors such as capital market characteristics vary. Therefore, it would be beneficial to conduct further research in different settings to validate our findings and understand the dynamics between ESG performance and market-based performance in various contexts.

Fifth, our study employs the LSEG database to examine the value relevance of ESG performance. Future studies could benefit from utilizing alternative databases to compare similar ESG measurements, thereby determining if variations in databases yield divergent outcomes. Additionally, it could prove insightful for subsequent research to analyze individual subcategories within the environmental, social, and governance pillars, as opposed to aggregating all subcategories, to gain a more nuanced understanding of each ESG component's impact.

Finally, further studies may deepen the topic of the value relevance of ESG performance by investigating if there are some factors, internal or external to the company, that can convey this relationship, by strengthening or weakening it.

Acknowledgments Raffaela Casciello and Martina Prisco gratefully acknowledge that this study was funded by the European Union—*NextGenerationEu*, in the framework of the *GRINS—Growing, Resilient, INclusive and Sustainable* project (MUR Project Code: PE00000018 - CUP E63C22002140007). The views and opinions expressed in this study are solely those of the authors and do not necessarily reflect those of the European Union. The European Union is not responsible for them.

Appendix A

Variable	Description
MVS	Market value per share at the end of the reporting period.
BVPS	Book value of common equity per share.
EPS	Net income per share.
ESG_score	The overall company score based on the self-reported information in the environmental, social, and corporate governance pillars.
E_Score	A measure of the company's impact on living and non-living natural systems, including the air, land, and water, as well as complete ecosystems. It reflects how well a company uses best management practices to avoid environmental risks and capitalize on environmental opportunities to generate long-term shareholder value (Thomson Reuters glossary). It is the measure of the yearly corporate environmental performance.
S_Score	A measure of the company's capacity to generate trust and loyalty with its workforce, customers, and society, through its use of best management practices, reflecting the company's reputation and the health of its license to operate, which are key factors in determining its ability to generate long-term shareholder value (Thomson Reuters glossary). It is the measure of the yearly corporate social performance.
G_Score	The company's systems and processes ensure that its board members and executives act in the best interests of its long-term shareholders, reflecting a company's capacity, through its use of best management practices, to direct and control its rights and responsibilities through the creation of incentives, as well as checks and balances to generate long-term shareholder value (Thomson Reuters glossary). It is the measure of the yearly corporate governance performance.
Leverage	Total debt divided by total assets at fiscal year-end.
Size	The logarithm of the revenues at fiscal year-end.
EBIT	Total revenues for the fiscal year minus total operating expenses plus operating interest expense, unusual expense/income and non-recurring items, supplemental, total for the same period.
ROA	Ratio of earnings before interest and taxes upon book value of assets.
CFO	Operating cash flow scaled by total assets.
Indep_Board	The percentage of independent board members as reported by the company.
Board_Div	The percentage of female directors on board.
AuditB_Com	Dummy variable equal to 1 if the company has an audit board committee and 0 otherwise.
CSR	Dummy variable equal to 1 if the company has a corporate social responsibility committee or team and 0 otherwise.
GDP_GWT	The annual growth of gross domestic product.

References

Aguilera, R. V., Rupp, D. E., Williams, C. A., & Ganapathi, J. (2007). Putting the s back in corporate social responsibility: A multilevel theory of social change in organizations. *Academy of Management Review, 32*(3), 836–863.

Ahmad, N., Mobarek, A., & Roni, N. N. (2021). Revisiting the impact of ESG on financial performance of FTSE350 UK firms: Static and dynamic panel data analysis. *Cogent Business & Management, 8*(1), 1900500.

Aledo, J., García Lara, J. M., González, M. T., & Grambovas, C. A. (2019). An empirical assessment of proposed solutions for resolving scale problems in value relevance accounting research. *Accounting & Finance, 60*(4), 3905–3933.

Al-Hiyari, A., Ismail, A. I., Kolsi, M. C., & Kehinde, O. H. (2023). Environmental, social and governance performance (ESG) and firm investment efficiency in emerging markets: The interaction effect of board cultural diversity. *Corporate Governance: The International Journal of Business in Society, 23*(3), 650–673.

Al-Najjar, B., & Anfimiadou, A. (2011). Environmental policies and firm value. *Business Strategy and the Environment, 21*(1), 49–59.

Amel-Zadeh, A., & Serafeim, G. (2018). Why and how investors use ESG information: Evidence from a global survey. *Financial Analysts Journal, 74*(3), 87–103.

Aouadi, A., & Marsat, S. (2018). Do ESG controversies matter for firm value? Evidence from international data. *Journal of Business Ethics, 151*, 1027–1047.

Artiach, T., Lee, D., Nelson, D., & Walker, J. (2010). The determinants of corporate sustainability performance. *Accounting & Finance, 50*(1), 31–51.

Aureli, S., Gigli, S., Medei, R., & Supino, E. (2020). The value relevance of environmental, social, and governance disclosure: Evidence from Dow Jones sustainability world index listed companies. *Corporate Social Responsibility and Environmental Management, 27*(1), 43–52.

Bae, K. H., & Jeong, S. W. (2007). The value-relevance of earnings and book value, ownership structure, and business group affiliation: Evidence from Korean business groups. *Journal of Business Finance & Accounting, 34*(5), 740–766.

Barnea, A., & Rubin, A. (2010). Corporate social responsibility as a conflict between shareholders. *Journal of Business Ethics, 97*(1), 71–86.

Barth, M. E., & Clinch, G. (2009). Scale effects in capital markets-based accounting research. *Journal of Business Finance & Accounting, 36*(3–4), 253–288.

Beisland, L. A. (2009). A review of the value relevance literature. *The Open Business Journal, 2*(1), 7–27.

Berman, S. L., Wicks, A. C., Kotha, S., & Jones, T. M. (1999). Does stakeholder orientation matter? The relationship between stakeholder management models and firm financial performance. *The Academy of Management Journal, 42*(5), 488–506.

Bowman, R. G. (1980). The importance of a market-value measurement of debt in assessing leverage. *Journal of Accounting Research, 18*(1), 242–254.

Brammer, S., & Millington, A. (2004). The development of corporate charitable contributions in the UK: A stakeholder analysis. *Journal of Management Studies, 41*(8), 1411–1434.

Brännlund, R., & Lundgren, T. (2009). Environmental policy without costs? A review of the porter hypothesis. *International Review of Environmental and Resource Economics, 3*(2), 75–117.

Brimble, M., & Hodgson, A. (2007). On the intertemporal value relevance of conventional financial accounting in Australia. *Accounting and Finance, 47*(4), 599–622.

Brown, S., Lo, K., & Lys, T. (1999). Use of R2 in accounting research: Measuring changes in value relevance over the last four decades. *Journal of Accounting and Economics, 28*(2), 83–115.

Bui, T., Ali, M. H., Tsai, F. M., Iranmanesh, M., Tseng, M., & Lim, M. K. (2020). Challenges and trends in sustainable corporate finance: A bibliometric systematic review. *Journal of Risk and Financial Management, 13*(11), 264.

Cek, K., & Eyupoglu, S. (2020). Does environmental, social and governance performance influence economic performance? *Journal of Business Economics and Management, 21*(4), 1165–1184.

Chang, D., & Kuo, L. R. (2008). The effects of sustainable development on firms' financial performance – An empirical approach. *Sustainable Development, 16*(6), 365–380.
Chegut, A., Schenk, H., & Scholtens, B. (2011). Assessing SRI fund performance research: Best practices in empirical analysis. *Sustainable Development, 19*(2), 77–94.
Cheng, L. T., Lee, S. K., Li, S. K., & Tsang, C. K. (2023). Understanding resource deployment efficiency for ESG and financial performance: A DEA approach. *Research in International Business and Finance, 65*, 101941.
Collins, D. W., Maydew, E. L., & Weiss, I. S. (1997). Changes in the value-relevance of earnings and book values over the past forty years. *Journal of Accounting and Economics, 24*(1), 39–67.
Dai, D., & Xue, Y. (2022). The impact of green innovation on a firm's value from the perspective of enterprise life cycles. *Sustainability, 14*(3), 1226.
Darnall, N., Henriques, I., & Sadorsky, P. (2010). Adopting proactive environmental strategy: The influence of stakeholders and firm size. *Journal of Management Studies, 47*(6), 1072–1094.
De Villiers, C., Hsiao, P. C. K., & Maroun, W. (2017). Developing a conceptual model of influences around integrated reporting, new insights and directions for future research. *Meditari Accountancy Research, 25*(4), 450–460.
De Villiers, C., Jia, J., & Li, Z. (2022). Corporate social responsibility: A review of empirical research using Thomson Reuters Asset4 data. *Accounting & FinanceVolume, 62*(4), 4523–4568.
Delery, J. E., & Doty, D. H. (1996). Modes of theorizing in strategic human resource management: Tests of universalistic, contingency, and configurational performance predictions. *Academy of Management Journal, 39*(4), 802–835.
Dhaliwal, D. S., Li, O. Z., Tsang, A., & Yang, Y. G. (2011). Voluntary nonfinancial disclosure and the cost of equity capital: The initiation of corporate social responsibility reporting. *The Accounting Review, 86*(1), 59–100.
Dimitrov, V., & Jain, P. C. (2008). The value-relevance of changes in financial leverage beyond growth in assets and GAAP earnings. *Journal of Accounting, Auditing & Finance, 23*(2), 191–222.
Easton, P. D. (1999). Security returns and the value relevance of accounting data. *Accounting Horizons, 13*(4), 399–412.
El Ghoul, S., Guedhami, O., & Kim, Y. (2017). Country-level institutions, firm value, and the role of corporate social responsibility initiatives. *Journal of International Business Studies, 48*(3), 360–385.
European Commission. (2019). The European Green Deal. https://eur-lex.europa.eu/legal-content/EN/TXT/HTML/?uri=CELEX:52019DC0640
European Commission. (2021a). Proposal for a Directive of The European Parliament and of The Council on Corporate Sustainability Due Diligence and amending Directive (EU) 2019/1937.
European Commission. (2021b). The European pillar of social rights action plan. https://op.europa.eu/webpub/empl/european-pillar-of-social-rights/en/
European Commission. (2022). Proposal for a Directive of the European Parliament and of the Council on Corporate Sustainability Due Diligence and amending Directive (EU) 2019/1937.
Farza, K., Ftiti, Z., Hlioui, Z., & Louhichi, W. (2021). Does it pay to go green? The environmental innovation effect on corporate financial performance. *Journal of Environmental Management, 300*, 113695.
Filip, A., & Raffournier, B. (2010). The value relevance of earnings in a transition economy: The case of Romania. *The International Journal of Accounting, 45*, 77–103.
Friede, G., Busch, T., & Bassen, A. (2015). ESG and financial performance: Aggregated evidence from more than 2000 empirical studies. *Journal of Sustainable Finance & Investment, 5*(4), 210–233.
Gao, J., & Bansal, P. (2013). Instrumental and integrative logics in business sustainability. *Journal of Business Ethics, 112*(2), 241–255.
García-Sánchez, I., Prado-Lorenzo, J., Rodríguez-Domínguez, L., & Gallego-Álvarez, I. (2008). Social responsibility in Spain: Practices and motivations in firms. *Management Decision, 46*(8), 1247–1271.

Ghosh, D. K., & Sherman, R. G. (1993). Leverage, resource allocation and growth. *Journal of Business Finance & Accounting, 20*(4), 575–582.

Gill, A. (2008). Corporate governance as social responsibility: A research agenda. *Berkeley Journal of International Law, 26*(2), 452–478.

Gong, M., Gao, Y., Koh, L., Sutcliffe, C., & Cullen, J. (2019). The role of customer awareness in promoting firm sustainability and sustainable supply chain management. *International Journal of Production Economics, 217*, 88–96.

Greening, D. W., & Turban, D. B. (2000). Corporate social performance as a competitive advantage in attracting a quality workforce. *Business & Society, 39*(3), 254–280.

Hair, J. F., Black, W. C., Babin, B. J., Anderson, R. E., & Tatham, R. L. (2006). *Multivariate data analysis* (6th ed.). Pearson Prentice Hall.

Han, J. J., Kim, H. J., & Yu, J. (2016). Empirical study on relationship between corporate social responsibility and financial performance in Korea. *Asian Journal of Sustainability and Social Responsibility, 1*, 61–76.

Hao, X., Chen, F., & Chen, Z. (2022). Does green innovation increase enterprise value? *Business Strategy and the Environment, 31*(3), 1232–1247.

Hillman, A. J., & Keim, G. D. (2001). Shareholder value, stakeholder management, and social criteria: what's the bottom line? *Strategic Management Journal, 22*(2), 125–139.

Ho, L., Bai, M., Lu, Y., & Qin, Y. (2021). The effect of corporate sustainability performance on leverage adjustments. *The British Accounting Review, 53*(5), 100989.

Hu, A., Yuan, X., Fan, S., & Wang, S. (2023). The impact and mechanism of corporate ESG construction on the efficiency of regional green economy: An empirical analysis based on signal transmission theory and stakeholder theory. *Sustainability, 15*(17), 13236.

Ifada, L. M., Hendar, H., & Mohd Saleh, N. (2024). Board governance model, institutions, financial performance, and environmental performance: Stakeholder supremacy or coordinationproblems? *Corporate Social Responsibility and Environmental Management, 31*(5), 3869–3883.

Ioannou, I., & Serafeim, G. (2012). What drives corporate social performance? The role of nation-level institutions. *Journal of International Business Studies, 43*(9), 834–864.

Iqbal, N., Xu, J. F., Fareed, Z., & Wan, G. (2022). Financial leverage and corporate innovation in Chinese public−listed firms. *European Journal of Innovation Management, 25*(1), 299–323.

Jadoon, I. A., Ali, A., Ayub, U., Tahir, M., & Mumtaz, R. (2021). The impact of sustainability reporting quality on the value relevance of corporate sustainability performance. *Sustainable Development, 29*(1), 155–175.

Jia, J., & Li, Z. (2022). Corporate sustainability, earnings persistence and the association between earnings and future cash flows. *Accounting & Finance, 62*(1), 299–336.

Jyoti, G., & Khanna, A. (2021). Does sustainability performance impact financial performance? Evidence from Indian service sector firms. *Sustainable Development, 29*(6), 1086–1095.

Kang, D. U., Yu, G. J., & Lee, S. J. (2016). Disentangling the effects of the employee benefits on employee productivity. *Journal of Applied Business Research, 32*(5), 1447–1458.

Kaspereit, T., & Lopatta, K. (2016). The value relevance of SAM's corporate sustainability ranking and GRI sustainability reporting in the European stock markets. *Business Ethics: A European Review, 25*(1), 1–24.

Khan, M. A. (2022). ESG disclosure and firm performance: A bibliometric and meta analysis. *Research in International Business and Finance, 61*, 1–9.

Khan, M., Serafeim, G., & Yoon, A. (2016). Corporate sustainability: First evidence on materiality. *The Accounting Review, 91*(6), 1697–1724.

Klettner, A., Clarke, T., & Boersma, M. (2014). The governance of corporate sustainability: Empirical insights into the development, leadership and implementation of responsible business strategy. *Journal of Business Ethics, 122*, 145–165.

Kumar, S., Duhan, M., & Haleem, A. (2016). Evaluation of factors important to enhance productivity. *Cogent Engineering, 3*(1), 1145043.

Kurunmäki, L., & Miller, P. (2006). Modernizing government: 'The calculating self, hybridization and performance measurement. *Financial Accountability and Management, 22*(1), 87–106.

Li, Y., & Yang, H. I. H. (2012). Disclosure and cost of equity capital: An analysis at the market level. Research Collection School of Accountancy, pp. 1–54.

Lins, K. V., Servaes, H., & Tamayo, A. (2017). Social capital, trust, and firm performance: The value of corporate social responsibility during the financial crisis. *The Journal of Finance, 72*(4), 1785–1824.

Lombardi, R., Trequattrini, R., Cuozzo, B., & Cano-Rubio, M. (2019). Corporate corruption prevention, sustainable governance and legislation: First exploratory evidence from the Italian scenario. *Journal of Cleaner Production, 217*, 666–675.

Lopatta, K., & Kaspereit, T. (2014). The world capital markets' perception of sustainability and the impact of the financial crisis. *Journal of Business Ethics, 122*(3), 475–500.

Macchioni, R., Fiondella, C., & Prisco, M. (2024). The value relevance of environmental innovation: Evidence from European Union context. *Journal of Cleaner Production, 446*, 141246.

Malik, M. (2015). Value-enhancing capabilities of CSR: A brief review of contemporary literature. *Journal of Business Ethics, 127*, 419–438.

Martínez-Ferrero, J., Lozano, M. B., & Vivas, M. (2021). The impact of board cultural diversity on a firm's commitment toward the sustainability issues of emerging countries: The mediating effect of a CSR committee. *Corporate Social Responsibility and Environmental Management, 28*(2), 675–685.

Meira, E., Cunha, F. A. F. D. S., Orsato, R. J., Miralles-Quirós, M. M., & Miralles-Quirós, J. L. (2023). The added value and differentiation among ESG investment strategies in stock markets. *Business Strategy and the Environment, 32*(4), 1816–1834.

Miralles-Quirós, M. M., Miralles-Quirós, J. L., & Hernández, J. R. (2019). ESG performance and shareholder value creation in the banking industry: International differences. *Sustainability, 11*(5), 1404.

Mishra, S., & Suar, D. (2010). Does corporate social responsibility influence firm performance of Indian companies? *Journal of Business Ethics, 95*(4), 571–601.

Naciti, V. (2019). Corporate governance and board of directors: The effect of a board composition on firm sustainability performance. *Journal of Cleaner Production, 237*, 117727.

Nekhili, M., Boukadhaba, A., Nagati, H., & Chtioui, T. (2019). ESG performance and market value: The moderating role of employee board representation. *The International Journal of Human Resource Management, 30*, 1–27.

Ohlson, J. A. (1995). Earnings, book values, and dividends in equity valuation. *Contemporary Accounting Research, 11*(2), 661–687.

Paoloni, P., Lombardi, R., & Principale, S. (2023). The impact of gender diversity on corporate social responsibility knowledge: Empirical analysis in European context. *Journal of Knowledge Management, 27*(9), 2484–2498.

Pulino, S. C., Ciaburri, M., Magnanelli, B. S., & Nasta, L. (2022). Does ESG disclosure influence firm performance? *Sustainability, 14*(13), 1–18.

Qureshi, O. A., Trepci, E., Shahzad, A. A., Manandhar, P., & Rodriguez-Ubinas, E. (2023). Quantitative assessment of the HVAC system of zero-energy houses of the solar decathlon Middle East 2021. *Energy Reports, 9*, 1050–1060.

Radu, C., & Smaili, N. (2021). Alignment versus monitoring: An examination of the effect of the CSR committee and CSR-linked executive compensation on CSR performance. *Journal of Business Ethics, 180*, 1–19.

Rajesh, R. (2020). Exploring the sustainability performances of firms using environmental, social, and governance scores. *Journal of Cleaner Production, 247*, 119600.

Rhouma, A. B., Francoeur, C., & Robin, G. (2012). International corporate sustainability barometer 2012: Sustainability management in France. In *Corporate sustainability in international comparison* (pp. 70–93). Springer International Publishing.

Schmitz, B., & Glänzel, G. (2016). Hybrid organizations: Concept and measurement. *International Journal of Organizational Analysis, 24*(1), 18–35.

Semenova, N., & Hassel, L. G. (2015). On the validity of environmental performance metrics. *Journal of Business Ethics, 132*(2), 249–258.

Servaes, H., & Tamayo, A. (2013). The impact of corporate social responsibility on firm value: The role of customer awareness. *Management Science, 59*(5), 1045–1061.

Servaes, H., Tamayo, A., & Tufano, P. (2009). The theory and practice of corporate risk management. *Journal of Applied Corporate Finance, 21*(4), 60–78.

Shao, J., Li, W., Aneye, C., & Fang, W. (2022). Facilitating mechanism of green products purchasing with a premium price—Moderating by sustainability-related information. *Corporate Social Responsibility and Environmental Management, 29*(3), 686–700.

Shi, J., & Jiang, Z. (2023). Willingness to pay a premium price for green products: Does a reference group matter? *Environment, Development and Sustainability, 25*(8), 8699–8727.

Shin, J., Moon, J. J., & Kang, J. (2023). Where does ESG pay? The role of national culture in moderating the relationship between ESG performance and financial performance. *International Business Review, 32*(3), 102071.

Sinkin, C., Wright, C. J., & Burnett, R. D. (2008). Eco-efficiency and firm value. *Journal of Accounting and Public Policy, 27*(2), 167–176.

Soana, M.-G. (2011). The relationship between corporate social performance and corporate financial performance in the banking sector. *Journal of Business Ethics, 104*(1), 133–148.

Tang, H. (2022). The effect of ESG performance on corporate innovation in China: The mediating role of financial constraints and agency cost. *Sustainability, 14*(7), 3769.

Tarmuji, I., Tarmuji, N. H., & Maelah, R. (2016). The impact of environmental, social and governance practices (ESG) on economic performance: Evidence from ESG score. *International Journal of Trade, Economics and Finance, 7*(3), 67–74.

Tenucci, A., & Supino, E. (2020). Exploring the relationship between product-service system and profitability. *Journal of Management and Governance, 24*(3), 563–585.

United Nations. (2015). Transforming our world: The 2030 agenda for sustainable development. https://sustainabledevelopment.un.org/content/documents/21252030%20Agenda%20for%20Sustainable%20Development%20web.pdf

Van Duuren, E., Plantinga, A., & Scholtens, B. (2016). ESG integration and the investment management process: Fundamental investing reinvented. *Journal of Business Ethics, 138*, 525–533.

Veldman, J., & Gaalman, G. J. (2015). Competitive investments in cost reducing process improvement: The role of managerial incentives and spillover learning. *International Journal of Production Economics, 170*, 701–709.

Velte, P. (2017). Does ESG performance have an impact on financial performance? Evidence from Germany. *Journal of Global Responsibility, 8*(2), 169–178.

Velte, P., & Stawinoga, M. (2020). Do chief sustainability officers and CSR committees influence CSR-related outcomes? A structured literature review based on empirical-quantitative research findings. *Journal of Management Control, 31*, 333–377.

Venter, E. R., Emanuel, D., & Cahan, S. F. (2014). The value relevance of mandatory non-GAAP earnings. *Abacus, 50*(1), 1–24.

Wang, L., Li, S., & Gao, S. (2014). Do greenhouse gas emissions affect financial performance? – An empirical examination of Australian public firms. *Business Strategy and the Environment, 23*(8), 505–519.

Wood, D. (1991). Corporate social performance revisited. *The Academy of Management Review, 16*(4), 691–717.

Wu, Y., & Tham, J. (2023). The impact of executive green incentives and top management team characteristics on corporate value in China: The mediating role of environment. *Social and Government Performance. Sustainability, 15*(16), 12518.

Yadav, P. L., Han, S. H., & Rho, J. J. (2016). Impact of environmental performance on firm value for sustainable investment: Evidence from large US firms. *Business Strategy and the Environment, 25*(6), 402–420.

Yang, M., Chen, H., Long, R., Wang, Y., Hou, C., & Liu, B. (2021). Will the public pay for green products? Based on analysis of the influencing factors for Chinese's public willingness to pay a price premium for green products. *Environmental Science and Pollution Research, 28*(43), 61408–61422.

Yoon, B., Lee, J. H., & Byun, R. (2018). Does ESG performance enhance firm value? Evidence from Korea. *Sustainability, 10*(10), 3635.

Yorke, S. M., Donkor, A., & Appiagyei, K. (2023). Experts on boards' audit committee and sustainability performance. *Journal of Cleaner Production, 414*, 137553.

Zhang, R., & Fu, W. (2023). Multiple large shareholders and corporate environmental performance. *Finance Research Letters, 51*, 103487.

Zhao, C., Guo, Y., Yuan, J., Wu, M., Li, D., Zhou, Y., & Kang, J. (2018). ESG and corporate financial performance: Empirical evidence from China's listed power generation companies. *Sustainability, 10*(8), 2607.

Zheng, M., Feng, G. F., Jiang, R. A., & Chang, C. P. (2023). Does environmental, social, and governance performance move together with corporate green innovation in China? *Business Strategy and the Environment, 32*(4), 1670–1679.

Zhou, G., Liu, L., & Luo, S. (2022). Sustainable development, ESG performance and company market value: Mediating effect of financial performance. *Business Strategy and the Environment, 31*(7), 3371–3387.

Chapter 15
Is the Firm Value Affected by the ESG Performance? A Study on Small-Capitalized European Listed Energy Companies

Pasquale Latella and Stefania Veltri

15.1 Introduction

Nowadays, investors are not only interested in the financial and market performance of a firm, instead they also look at their environmental, social, and governance (ESG) performance (Wei et al., 2023). Firms are required to focus on non-financial aspects of their activities not only by stakeholders but also by regulators. For instance, the Paris agreement commits firms to cut their emissions, incentivizing them to achieve a better environmental performance. Nevertheless, regulation has been mainly focused on disclosure of non-financial information (NFI). The Directive 2014/95/ EU (Non-Financial Reporting Directive—NFRD) has introduced the obligation for large undertakings to disclose ESG information. It has been issued to increase transparency, credibility, and comparability of NFI disclosed (Cicchiello et al., 2023; La Torre et al., 2020). Recently, a new Directive, the Corporate Sustainability Reporting Directive (CSRD), has been issued with the purpose to overcome the main limits associated with the NFRD (Mazzotta & Veltri, 2022). The ESG performance of companies has been studied by many authors. Some studies focused on which factors affect more the sustainability performance of the firms (Birindelli et al., 2018; Menicucci & Paolucci, 2022), but most of the research investigated whether the ESG performance may affect firm value, with mixed results (Adamkaite et al., 2023; Ahmad et al., 2021; Baboukardos, 2018). Our study aims at analyzing the association between ESG performance and firm value investigating a sample of small-capitalized firms, so adding evidence to this stream of the literature. To the best of

P. Latella (✉) · S. Veltri
Department of Business Administration and Law, University of Calabria, Arcavacata di Rende, Italy
e-mail: pasquale.latella@unical.it; stefania.veltri@unical.it

N. Castellano et al. (eds.), *Environmental, Social, Governance (ESG)*, SIDREA Series in Accounting and Business Administration,
https://doi.org/10.1007/978-3-031-76618-3_15

our knowledge, this is the first empirical study on this issue focused solely on small-capitalized listed firms.

The need to research the association between ESG and firm performance is particularly urgent in controversial sectors like the energy sector, which is characterized by a high ESG risk (Iazzolino et al., 2023; Veltri et al., 2023). On the one hand, the energy firms, including oil & gas, electricity, renewable energy, and consumable fuels, have significant environmental impacts. If not properly managed, their production processes can contribute to air pollution, accidents, and injuries. These organizations are constantly under scrutiny from civil societies, elite groups, and governments, which have the task to promulgate various regulations with the aim to minimize potential environmental risks (Jain et al., 2020). Consequently, energy companies have increasingly embraced sustainability actions to gain legitimacy, benefiting an improvement in terms of financial performance (Forgione et al., 2020). On the other hand, energy companies may adopt opportunistic behavior and disclose unreliable information about their sustainable activities. As a result, stakeholders may not perceive their sustainability actions as sincere and this could translate in a negative impact of ESG performance on market value (Kaupke & zu Knyphausen-Aufseß, 2022).

The few extant empirical research on energy sector do not offer univocal results, providing findings going from negative (e.g., Kaupke & zu Knyphausen-Aufseß, 2022), to neutral (e.g., Adamkaite et al., 2023) and positive association between ESG and market performance (e.g., Zhao et al., 2018; Gong et al., 2020).

Furthermore, the studies are mainly focused on the US context and large-capitalized listed firms. Our work aims to fill this gap by focusing on the European listed small-capitalized energy firms for the 5-year period 2017–2021, which followed the enactment of EU Directive within the European countries, so adding knowledge to the literature stream on the association between ESG and market company performance.

The chapter is organized as follows. Section 15.2 outlines the theoretical framework, while Sect. 15.3 provides an overview of the state of art in this research field and the hypotheses development. In Sect. 15.4, we describe the methodology including the sample, the research variables, and the model. Section 15.5 shows the results. In Sect. 15.6, we discuss the findings. Limitations and avenues for future research are provided in Sect. 15.7.

15.2 Theoretical Framework

Several theories, such as stakeholder theory (Freeman, 1984), legitimacy theory (Suchman, 1995), value creation theory (Cai et al., 2012), were used to explain the relationship between ESG performance and firm value.

A social theory that supports the impact of ESG performance on firm performance, suggesting a positive association, is stakeholder theory (Kumar et al., 2022). According to this theory, firms have a responsibility not only toward their shareholders but also toward various stakeholders. They should take into consideration the interests and needs of these stakeholders, not just focus on maximizing profits (Yin et al., 2023). Companies that adopt effective sustainable practices generate a positive impact on the environment and society, which is recognized by stakeholders and ultimately enhances company performance (Ademi & Klungseth, 2022).

We relied on the stakeholder theory as we thought that it explains best the linkage between ESG performance and firm value in the context of energy firms, supporting a positive impact, driven by an enhancement of firm reputation in the eyes of the stakeholders. This is particularly relevant for energy firms which constantly face public concerns. To address these concerns and meet societal expectations, they may actively adopt substantial ESG practices. Indeed, not only does a strong ESG performance help energy companies build trust with communities, but it also reduces regulatory risks and enhances their social license to operate. By taking these actions, energy companies can position themselves for long-term success by adapting to evolving market dynamics and reducing their reliance on finite resources, thus positively impacting firm value. To conclude, from a theoretical standpoint, adopting ESG-related practices should bring benefit effects in terms of firm value for energy companies.

15.3 State of Art

While existing research has often found a positive relationship between ESG and firm value (Alareeni & Hamdan, 2020; Karishma & Tripathi, 2023), the direction of the ESG/firm value association has been less clear for controversial sectors.

Empirically speaking, the relationship between the ESG factors and firm market value or financial performance of energy firms has been widely analyzed in the literature with conflicting results, meaning that whether and to what extent ESG influences firm performance remains an empirical question that deserves more investigation. Authors investigated the impact of ESG disclosure or ESG performance on firm value. Among the first ones, we can include the articles of Behl et al. (2022), Hasan et al. (2022), and Wasiuzzaman et al. (2022) that provide evidence of a negative association between ESG disclosure and firm performance. In detail, Behl et al. (2022) found, on a sample of energy firms, that the relationship between the ESG disclosure scores and Tobin Q varies in the short run with respect to the long run. Precisely, it was negative in the short run and positive in the long run. A negative relationship between Tobin Q and the ESG disclosure scores has been also proved by Hasan et al.'s (2022) work. The authors investigated this relationship on multiple samples grouped by industry finding a negative association for energy and utility firms. Wasiuzzaman et al. (2022) analyzed the impact of ESG disclosure on firm's profitability, considering the moderating effect of the national culture, proxied with the Hofstede's cultural dimensions. By using the instrumental variables regression technique, they proved a significant negative association between ESG and firm's profitability, which is significantly moderated by the cultural dimensions of power distance and long-term orientation. Among the studies analyzing the impact of ESG performance on firm performance for firms belonging to sensitive industries, we can include the studies of Lin et al. (2015), Miralles-Quirós et al. (2018), Yoon et al. (2018), Vásquez-Ordóñez et al. (2023), Ionescu et al. (2019), Gong et al. (2020), Shahbaz et al. (2020), Lech (2013), Kaupke & zu Knyphausen-Aufseß (2022), and Cowan et al. (2012).

Lin et al. (2015) concluded that the association between ESG performance and financial performance is positive for firms which belong to environmental sensitive industries, while deteriorates for firms which do not operate in environmental sensitive industries. Miralles-Quirós et al. (2018) showed that investors positively valued the CSR performance of Brazilian firms. Precisely, the overall CSR performance had a positive and significant effect as well as the environmental and the governance ones, whereas social performance had a positive but not significant effect. Interestingly, they further proved that environmental performance did not have a significant impact on firm value for those firms operating in environmental sensitive industries. Gong et al. (2020) tested the impact of CSR performance on firm value in the energy industry, specifically focusing on the managerial ability components of the CSR. Their results suggest that the positive impact of CSR on firm value is mainly driven by the managerial ability components. By using a combination of quantitative and qualitative approaches, Vásquez-Ordóñez et al. (2023) showed that there is not strong enough evidence to conclude that Tobin Q for energy companies is affected by the single ESG dimensions. Similarly, Ionescu et al.'s (2019) work, focused on firms from travel and tourism industry, found a weak positive relationship between environmental scores and firm value. The explanation provided is that for firms operating in environmental sensitive industries, the concerns about environmental practices are already reflected in share prices. Based on a sample of firms from an emerging market (i.e., Korea), Yoon et al. (2018) achieved results which are in contrast with the aforementioned studies. The analysis they carried out provided them with a negative and significant effects of all the ESG scores (i.e., both combined and the single pillars), when the ESG scores interact with a variable representing sensitive industries, on firm value. Shahbaz et al. (2020) found no impact on the association between ESG performance and on the firm performance, proxied by Tobin Q for a sample of energy firms. The same result is found by Lech (2013) for a sample of Polish energy companies. The works of Kaupke and zu Knyphausen-Aufseß (2022) and Cowan et al. (2012), which focused on the oil and gas industry (i.e., a sub-industry of energy), also showed mixed results, while the study of Cowan et al. (2012) provided evidence of a positive impact of the environmental strengths on the firm performance, proxied by Tobin Q. The study of Kaupke and zu Knyphausen-Aufseß (2022) found a negative impact of ESG performance on Tobin Q.

All considering, the majority the aforementioned studies have been conducted on large cap energy companies, so highlighting a research gap of the ESG/firm value association for small cap energy companies.

15.3.1 Hypothesis Development

Based on the description above, our work aims to contribute to the existing literature on the relationship between ESG performance and firm market value. The stakeholder theory explains how implementing effective ESG practices, whether they are environmental, social, or governance-oriented, enhances corporate reputation. This, in turn, leads to an increase in firm value. Accordingly, we formulated the following research hypothesis:

H_1. The overall ESG performance of the European listed small-capitalized energy firms positively affects firm market value.

Among the scrutinized studies on energy firms, only a few have managed to disentangle environmental practices, social practices, and governance practices. Vásquez-Ordóñez et al. (2023), Behl et al. (2022), and Shahbaz et al. (2020), which investigated the impact of the single pillars (i.e., environmental, social, and governance), did not find any differences among them. Both theory and former studies do not suggest that a specific ESG component contributes more to firm performance than others (Velte, 2017).

Consistently, we posited that environmental, social, and governance performance have the same impact on firm value. Specifically, we formulated the following additional research hypotheses:

H_2. The environmental performance of the European listed small-capitalized energy firms positively affects firm market value;

H_3. The social performance of the European listed small-capitalized energy firms positively affects firm market value;

H_4. The governance performance of the European listed small-capitalized energy firms positively affects firm market value.

Figure 15.1 illustrates the linkage between firm ESG practices and firm value according to the adopted theoretical framework.

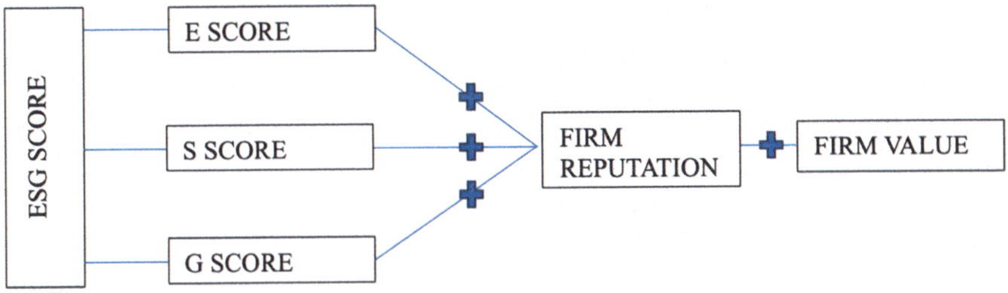

Fig. 15.1 Conceptual model for the relationship between ESG practices and firm value

15.4 Methodology

15.4.1 Sample Selection

The research has been carried out on the small cap European listed energy companies. The choice to focus the research on the European listed markets was motivated by the in-depth regulatory process embarked on by the EU to institutionalize ESG performance disclosure within corporate reporting practices (Manes-Rossi & Nicolò, 2022). As part of the CSR strategy for 2011–2014, the EU released the NFRD, imposing specific non-financial disclosure requirements on all public interest entities with more than 500 employees, also creating a "reporting cut-off point" between the European region and the other geographical contexts (EU, 2014). As already mentioned, the NFRD has been followed by the CSRD, which the regulator issued recently, with the aim to overcome some limits of NFRD (Mazzotta & Veltri, 2022). These circumstances make Europe an appropriate context to conduct the research.

We chose to narrow the sample just to energy firms as we wanted to focus on an environmental sensitive industry. Energy is among those industries which are supposed to generate a major socio-environmental impact (Garcia et al., 2017). Indeed, this industry accounts for one third of the total pollutants, hence energy firms should implement sustainability practices (Kumar et al., 2022). We focused on small cap companies as empirical literature is mainly focused on large-capitalized firms, so investigating small-capitalized firms adds knowledge to the literature stream focused on the relationship between ESG performance and firm market value. We decided to conduct our research for 5-year period 2017–2021.

Operationally speaking, we first selected European listed energy firms whose market cap is below 2 billion according to Refinitiv Eikon's data as the market capitalization of small cap companies goes from 300 million to 2 billion (Forbes, 2022). Given that the European equity markets are small, we also take into consideration firms with a market capitalization lower than 300 million.

To select energy firms, we relied on the Global Industry Classification Standard (GICS). It is a global classification system which involves four tiers: sectors, industry group, industry, and sub-industry. To identify energy firms, we relied on the GICS industry group classification level.

Among the companies selected, we further screened the sample by selecting only the firms for which information on ESG scores was available for at least one of the sampled years.

These criteria provide us with a sample of 48 European small cap energy firms. Selecting only small cap firms implies, especially for ESG-related data, the missingness of values. Therefore, our panel data is unbalanced.

Table 15.1 provides an overview of sampled companies classified by country, while Fig. 15.2 shows the classification of sampled firms by GICS industry (a sub-level of the GICS industry group).

Table 15.1 Sample firms by country

Country	Sample firms
United Kingdom	13
Norway	7
Sweden	5
France	3
Netherlands	3
Spain	2
Germany	2
Russia	2
Austria	2
Italy	2
Greece	2
Luxembourg	1
Poland	1
Romania	1
Jersey	1
Belgium	1

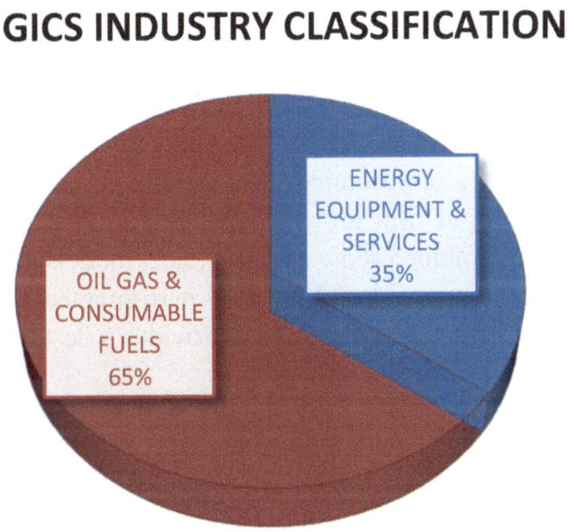

Fig. 15.2 Sample firms by GICS industry

15.4.2 Research Variables

To study the association between ESG performance and market value performance we employed a panel data model, being our analysis carried out on cross-sectional and time-series data, meaning that are observed data for the same firms in a 5-year period. Nevertheless, we evaluated the correctness to employ panel model with statistical tests. In our model the dependent variable (firm value) is proxied with Tobin's Q. It is an accounting-and-marked based measure, which allows to take into consideration both market and accounting performance. We used the log variable to normalize the distribution. Our explicative independent variable (ESG performance) is proxied with ESG ratings provided by Refinitiv Eikon, which provides an influential measure of ESG performance available to the entire financial community

Table 15.2 Variables' definition

Variables	Definition
Dependent variables	
TOBIN	$\text{Log}\left(\frac{\text{MARKET VALUE OF EQUITY+TOTAL LIABILITIES}}{\text{BOOK VALUE OF EQUITY+TOTAL LIABILITIES}}\right)$
Independent variables	
ESG	ESG combined score collected from Refinitiv Eikon
ENVIRONMENTAL SCORE	Environmental pillar score collected from Refinitiv Eikon
SOCIAL SCORE	Social pillar score collected from Refinitiv Eikon
GOVERNANCE SCORE	Governance pillar score collected from Refinitiv Eikon
Controls	
CAPEX	Capital Expenditure/Total Assets
LEVERAGE	Total Liabilities/Total Assets
ROA	Net Income/Total Assets
TOTAL ASSETS	Natural logarithm of total assets

and based on company-reported data (Forgione et al., 2020). In our regression equations, to avoid estimation biases, we controlled for a number of factors that could affect the relationship between ESG performance and market value, identified on the basis of empirical literature (e.g., Kaupke & zu Knyphausen-Aufseß, 2022; Adamkaite et al., 2023). In detail, we controlled for firm size via total assets, for risk via leverage, for profitability via Return on Assets, and also include capital expenditure as measure of firm growth. We carried out both a panel model considering the overall ESG combined score and also panel models in which ESG pillars (environment, social, or governance) stand for ESG performance, to investigate which ESG pillars impacts most firm value. Table 15.2 provides a description of how variables are defined.

15.4.3 Methodology and Preliminary Analyses

There are three models which allow to perform a static panel data analysis (Ademi & Klungseth, 2022):

1) pooled ordinary least squares (OLS) regression;
2) fixed-effects regression;
3) random-effects regression.

To choose which of the aforementioned models fit best our data, we performed three tests. The F test is used to choose between the fixed effect model and the pooled OLS model. Contrary to the fixed effect (FE) model, the pooled OLS model does not take into account some individual characteristics of observations. Under the null hypothesis, the restricted model, which is the pooled OLS, is valid, whereas if the null hypothesis is rejected, then the FE model is valid. Given the very low p-value for all the models, the null is rejected and the FE model is chosen in all the four cases.

The Breusch and Pagan-Lagrange Multiplier Test is a $\chi 2$ test to choose between pooled OLS and random-effects (RE) model. Under the null, all the variances among

Table 15.3 Tests' p-value

Test	P-value (1)	P-value (2)	P-value (3)	P-value (4)
F Test	4.64e-15	5.642e-15	< 2.2e-16	< 2.2e-16
Lagrange Multiplier Test	3.544e-16	4.701e-16	8.34e-09	1.01e-07
Hausman Test	0.2289	0.1472	0.008	0.762

Table 15.4 Descriptive statistics

Variables	Obs	Mean	Median	Sd. Dev.	Min.	Max.
TOB	240	−0.009	−0.03	0.523	−1.948	1.699
ESG	181	43.972	45.06	19.520	1.840	83.54
ENV	181	38.754	40.53	24.062	0.000	93.01
SOC	181	48.261	49.25	24.367	1.200	92.82
GOV	181	50.317	49.84	23.944	4.060	95.26
LEV	240	0.297	0.24	0.338	0.000	2.57
ROA	240	−0.016	0.007	0.244	−1.617	1.88
CAP	234	0.065	0.042	0.065	0.000	0.38
TA	240	20.60	20.59	1.365	17.853	24.59

statistic units are 0, hence the RE model is valid. Given the very low p-value for all the models, the null is rejected and the RE model is chosen in all the four cases.

Hausman Test is a test to choose between FE model and RE model. The FE model is valid under both the null and the alternative hypotheses, whereas the RE model is valid under the null. Given the high p-value, the null is not rejected (except for *model 3*), and the RE model is chosen. Table 15.3 shows the p-value of the tests for each model. The first two models are based on the full sample, whereas the others refer to the models carried out on the sub-sample of oil and gas firms.

15.5 Analysis

15.5.1 Descriptive Statistics

Table 15.4 provides descriptive statistics for all the variables for the full sample. Looking at the mean score, it can be noticeable that sampled firms perform better on the governance pillar than the environmental and social pillars.

15.5.2 Correlation Matrix

Table 15.5 reports the Pearson correlation matrix among the variables examined. As we can observe, the correlation among the ESG score and firm value is positive and statistically significant suggesting that the ESG scores may have a positive impact on

Table 15.5 Correlation matrix

	TOB	ESG	ENV	SOC	GOV	LEV	ROA	CAP	TA	VIF
TOB	1									
ESG	0.174**	1								1.56
ENV	0.18**	0.83***	1							2.19
SOC	0.15**	0.88***	0.72***	1						2.01
GOV	0.05	0.69***	0.42***	0.51***	1					1.49
LEV	0.24***	0.11	0.06	0.06	0.13*	1				1.61
ROA	−0.04	−0.03	0.03	−0.05	−0.03	−0.4***	1			1.51
CAP	0.08	−0.003	−0.15**	−0.11	0.19***	−0.07	−0.04	1		1.15
TOAS	−0.3***	0.4***	0.49***	0.32***	0.38***	0.06	−0.03	−0.09	1	2.31

firm value. For what concerns the single pillars, environmental and social scores are positively correlated with firm value, instead no significant correlation has been found between Tobin Q and the governance pillar score. The matrix (Table 15.5) shows that the correlations between the independent variables were not strong, except for the ESG score and the environmental and social one which however were used into different regression models. The value of the variance inflation factor (VIF test) demonstrates that multicollinearity was not a serious issue because it was far below the critical value.

15.5.3 Full Sample Results

Given the results of the tests in the 4.3 subsection, we carried out random effect for all the models (*model 3*). Table 15.6 reports the results of the regression.

Our results, for the overall ESG performance and the environmental performance, align with stakeholder theory. This theory posits that stakeholders tend to trust the ESG practices actually implemented by energy firms whose managers exhibit ethical behavior. Consequently, this leads to an increase in the market value of the firm.

Table 15.6 Random-effects model on the total sample

	(1)	(1.1)	(2)	(2.1)
ESG	0.008*** (0.003)	0.005* (0.003)		
ENV			0.008*** (0.003)	0.007** (0.003)
SOCIAL			0.002 (0.003)	0.0007 (0.003)
GOV			−0.001 (0.002)	0.0002 (0.002)
TOTAL ASSET	−0.18*** (0.06)	−0.17*** (0.05)	−0.21*** (0.07)	−0.16*** (0.05)
LEVERAGE	0.46*** (0.12)	0.55*** (0.16)	0.49*** (0.12)	0.32* (0.17)
CAPEX	1.24* (0.69)	1.03 (0.81)	1.52** (0.68)	0.42 (0.84)
ROA	0.02 (0.11)	0.12 (0.2)	0.04 (0.10)	0.12 (0.21)
Constant	3.11** (1.27)	3.14*** (0.99)	3.82*** (1.32)	2.79*** (1.02)
Observations	175	134	175	134
R^2	0.34	0.23	0.37	0.14
Adjusted R^2	0.24	0.2	0.26	0.09
Year fixed-effects	YES	NO	YES	NO
Country fixed-effects	YES	NO	YES	NO

Notes: *p < 0.1; **p < 0.05; ***p < 0.01

Indeed, it is noticeable that the ESG scores have a significant and positive impact on firm value as proxied by the natural logarithm of the Tobin Q. Precisely, given the logarithmic transformation of the dependent variable, we can state that if the overall ESG score increases by one unit, keeping constant all the other variables, the firm value proxied by Tobin Q increases by 0.8%. The same holds for environmental performance. H1 and H2 were, then, not rejected.

This result is consistent with the main literature on the association between firm value and ESG scores (Karishma & Tripathi, 2023) and with some studies focused on energy firms (e.g., Zhao et al., 2018; Gong et al., 2020). The neutral impact of social and governance performance on firm performance is consistent with the studies of Shahbaz et al. (2020) and Lech (2013).

Models 1.1 and 2.1 report the results with all the independent variables lagged. We carried out this model to see if the impact of ESG performance on Tobin Q is delayed. We found consistent results with the main analysis (without lags).

15.5.4 Sub-sample Results

To verify if these results are valid also for the oil and gas industry, the most numerous subgroup within the energy industry group, we carried out the regression for this sub-sample. Table 15.7 shows the results of the regression model.

Contrary to the previous studies, which found either a negative (Kaupke & zu Knyphausen-Aufseß, 2022) or a positive (Cowan et al., 2012) impact of ESG factors on firm value for oil and gas firms, we provided evidence of no impact.

15.5.5 Endogeneity Test

To address potential endogeneity concerns between ESG performance and firm value, an endogeneity test was performed by using lagged ESG-related variables as the instrumental variables (consistently with Chen et al., 2023). Table 15.8 reports the results of the estimation by means of instrumental variables, where it is observed that the regression coefficient both for the overall ESG performance and for the single pillars remains consistent with the previous results despite with a less level of significance. Consequently, the conclusions drawn are still valid even after accounting for endogeneity concerns.

15.6 Discussion

The energy sector is one of the most problematic in terms of environmental damages as it contributes to one third of the total pollutant (Kumar et al., 2022), thus sustainability practices must be implemented to limit their impacts. On the ground

Table 15.7 Random-effects and fixed-effects regression model on oil & gas firms

	(3)	(4)
ESG	0.003 (0.003)	
ENV		0.001 (0.002)
SOCIAL		0.002 (0.003)
GOV		−0.002 (0.002)
TOTAL ASSET	−0.42*** (0.08)	−0.22*** (0.07)
LEVERAGE	0.32*** (0.11)	0.48*** (0.11)
CAPEX	1.44** (0.6)	1.52** (0.60)
ROA	−0.01 (0.10)	−0.001 (0.11)
Constant		4.16*** (1.48)
Observations	106	106
R^2	0.6	0.55
Adjusted R^2	0.36	0.42
Year fixed-effects	YES	YES
Country fixed-effects	NO	YES

Notes: *p < 0.1; **p < 0.05; ***p < 0.01

Table 15.8 Random-effects model with instrumental variable estimation

	(1)	(2)
ESG	0.008* (0.005)	
ENV		0.01** (0.005)
SOCIAL		−0.002 (0.005)
GOV		−0.002 (0.005)
TOTAL ASSET	−0.16*** (0.053)	−0.20*** (0.06)
LEVERAGE	0.47*** (0.13)	0.51*** (0.14)
CAPEX	0.36 (0.87)	1.15 (0.98)
ROA	−0.01 (0.11)	0.006 (0.12)
Constant	2.81*** (1.03)	3.66*** (1.20)
Observations	127	127
R^2	0.27	0.26
Adjusted R^2	0.24	0.22

of the stakeholder theory, this study investigated the impact of ESG performance, proxied with Refinitiv ESG ratings, on firm value, as proxied by Tobin Q, for 48 small cap energy listed companies from 2017 to 2021. The results were consistent with H1 and H2, suggesting in detail that the ESG performance as well as the environmental performance positively impacted firm value.

For what concerns ESG performance and environmental performance, the results supported the stakeholder theory, according to which ESG investing allows companies to improve their reputation, obtaining a competitive advantage with respect to its peers and benefiting in terms of financial performance and market valuation (Ademi & Klungseth, 2022). Instead, no impact has been found for social and governance performance. Furthermore, when testing the same hypotheses on the sub-sample of oil and gas firms, we didn't find any significant impact of either the overall ESG performance or the single pillars.

Small cap firms are subject of interest, also in the eyes of the regulator. The new European regulation (i.e., CSRD) extends the obligation to report non-financial information also to listed small-and-medium enterprises (SMEs). This constitutes an important novelty as SMEs represent the overwhelming majority of enterprises worldwide and exert a considerable influence on the economy (Cardoni et al., 2022). They contribute to the 70% of global pollution, whereas larger firms produce only the 30% (Bakos et al., 2020). Thus, imposing the requirement for companies to disclose non-financial information may incentivize them to decrease their environmental impact in order to maintain a positive perception among their stakeholders. Additionally, this new regulation is advantageous for investors, as they depend on ESG ratings, which are determined based on companies' ESG disclosure, to assess the non-financial performance of the companies in which they invest.

Despite their limitations, ESG ratings are relevant to investors as they show non-financial risks and opportunities associated with investments (Shahbaz et al., 2020). However, the disagreement among different ESG rating providers can confuse investors. Therefore, it is recommended to achieve more convergence on certain indicators identified through collaboration with policymakers and consistent regulatory requirements.

After observing the descriptive statistics of the ESG scores and individual pillar scores, it is evident that there is room for improvement. Specifically, the environmental scores are the lowest among the three pillars. To address this, policymakers might consider implementing regulations specifically tailored to the environmentally sensitive industries. These regulations would require firms within these industries to take actions to improve their environmental performance.

Moreover, energy companies that are leaders in implementing ESG strategies, such as Enel, serve as excellent examples of how high-quality financial performance and strong ESG performance can go hand in hand. This serves as a motivation for smaller companies to follow suit and prioritize good ESG practices, especially considering that financial performance is often a concern for firms.

The contribution of our paper is manifold. First, it addresses the need for more industry-specific analyses pointed out by several authors (Pacelli et al., 2022), focusing on the energy sector, a controversial and environmentally sensitive sector, scarcely investigated in the empirical literature (Kaupke & zu Knyphausen-Aufseß, 2022). Second, this paper considers European listed energy companies instead of focusing on USA energy companies, so considering an institutional context characterized by non-financial regulation (Manes-Rossi & Nicolò, 2022). Thirdly, the study focuses on the small cap listed energy sector, rarely investigated in empirical literature.

15.7 Limitations and Future Research

Notwithstanding its contribution, our study suffers from some limitations. First, the sustainability performance has been measured by the Refinitiv ESG score, thus caution should be used in interpreting results, as most often used ESG ratings differ significantly in their outcome (Kaupke & zu Knyphausen-Aufseß, 2022). Second, because we used the Refinitiv ESG score as a measure of ESG performance, only publicly listed companies were included in the sample, as companies that are not publicly listed do not receive Refinitiv ESG ratings. Third, the analysis is limited to a specific industry. Fourth, our sample is small, due to the presence of a high number of missing values. Indeed, ESG ratings are not available for the entire 5-year period. Furthermore, additional control variables may be added to the model. For instance, controlling for ownership structure may be relevant as lots of energy firms are owned by central states or local governments.

Future research may consider carrying out the analysis on small cap firms which belong to other environmental sensitive industries to test if the results still hold. Furthermore, future works may extend the sample and the timeframe of the analysis as ESG data are increasingly available. Future studies could also consider employing different measures of both ESG performance and firm performance.

Credit Authorship and Contribution Statement Conception and design of study: P. Latella, S. Veltri; acquisition of data: P. Latella; analysis and/or interpretation of data: P. Latella, S. Veltri; introduction and literature review: S. Veltri; methodology and empirical results: P. Latella; conclusion and discussion: P. Latella, S. Veltri; revising the manuscript critically for important intellectual content: S. Veltri.

References

Adamkaite, J., Streimikiene, D., & Rudzioniene, K. (2023). The impact of social responsibility on corporate financial performance in the energy sector: Evidence from Lithuania. *Corporate Social Responsibility and Environmental Management, 30*(1), 91–104.

Ademi, B., & Klungseth, N. J. (2022). Does it pay to deliver superior ESG performance? Evidence from US S&P 500 companies. *Journal of Global Responsibility, 13*(4), 421–449.

Ahmad, N., Mobarek, A., & Roni, N. N. (2021). Revisiting the impact of ESG on financial performance of FTSE350 UK firms: Static and dynamic panel data analysis. *Cogent Business & Management, 8*(1), 1900500.

Alareeni, B. A., & Hamdan, A. (2020). ESG impact on performance of US S&P 500-listed firms. *Corporate Governance: The International Journal of Business in Society, 20*(7), 1409–1428.
Baboukardos, D. (2018). The valuation relevance of environmental performance revisited: The moderating role of environmental provisions. *The British Accounting Review, 50*(1), 32–47.
Bakos, J., Siu, M., Orengo, A., & Kasiri, N. (2020). An analysis of environmental sustainability in small & medium-sized enterprises: Patterns and trends. *Business Strategy and the Environment, 29*(3), 1285–1296.
Behl, A., Raghu Kumari, P. S., Makhija, H., & Sharma, D. (2022). Exploring the relationship of ESG score and firm value using cross-lagged panel analyses: case of the Indian energy sector. *Annals of Operations Research, 313*, 231–256.
Birindelli, G., Dell'Atti, S., Iannuzzi, A. P., & Savioli, M. (2018). Composition and activity of the board of directors: Impact on ESG performance in the banking system. *Sustainability, 10*(12), 4699.
Cai, Y., Jo, H., & Pan, C. (2012). Doing well while doing bad? CSR in controversial industry sectors. *Journal of Business Ethics, 108*, 467–480.
Cardoni, A., Kiseleva, E., & Bellucci, A. (2022). The quality of SMEs stakeholder communication during strategic crises: The case of Italian unlisted SMEs. *Business Strategy and the Environment, 32*(6), 1–17.
Chen, S., Song, Y., & Peng, G. (2023). Environmental, social, and governance (ESG) performance and financial outcomes: Analyzing the impact of ESG on financial performance. *Journal of Environmental Management, 345*, 118829.
Cicchiello, A. F., Marrazza, F., & Perdichizzi, S. (2023). Non-financial disclosure regulation and environmental, social, and governance (ESG) performance: The case of EU and US firms. *Corporate Social Responsibility and Environmental Management, 30*(3), 1121–1128.
Cowan, A., Welch, S., & Welch, O. (2012). An empirical investigation of the link between performance and corporate social responsibility in the oil and gas industry. *Oil, Gas & Energy Quarterly, 61*, 35–45.
EU (European Directive). (2014). Directive of the European Parliament and of the Council of 22 October 2014 amending Directive 2013/34/EU as regards disclosure of non-financial and diversity information by certain large undertakings and groups, 2014/95/EU. https://eur-lex.europa.eu/legal-content/IT/TXT/?uri=celex%3A32014L0095
Forbes. (2022). Small-cap stocks. https://www.forbes.com/advisor/investing/small-cap-stocks/
Forgione, A. F., Laguir, I., & Staglianò, R. (2020). Effect of corporate social responsibility scores on bank efficiency: the moderating role of institutional context. *Corporate Social Responsibility and Environmental Management, 27*(5), 2094–2106.
Freeman, R. E. (1984). Strategic management: A stakeholder approach.
Garcia, A. S., Mendes-Da-Silva, W., & Orsato, R. J. (2017). Sensitive industries produce better ESG performance: Evidence from emerging markets. *Journal of Cleaner Production, 150*, 135–147.
Gong, Y., Yan, C., & Ho, K. C. (2020). The effect of managerial ability on corporate social responsibility and firm value in the energy industry. *Corporate Social Responsibility and Environmental Management, 28*(2), 581–594.
Hasan, I., Singh, S., & Kashiramka, S. (2022). Does corporate social responsibility disclosure impact firm performance? An industry-wise analysis of Indian firms. *Environment, Development and Sustainability, 24*, 10141–10181.
Iazzolino, G., Bruni, M. E., Veltri, S., Morea, D., & Baldissarro, G. (2023). The impact of ESG factors on financial efficiency: An empirical analysis for the selection of sustainable firm portfolios. *Corporate Social Responsibility and Environmental Management, 30*(4), 1917–1927.
Ionescu, G. H., Firoiu, D., Pirvu, R., & Vilag, R. D. (2019). The impact of ESG factors on market value of companies from travel and tourism industry. *Technological and Economic Development of Economy, 25*(5), 820–849.

Jain, N. K., Panda, A., & Choudhary, P. (2020). Institutional pressures and circular economy performance: The role of environmental management system and organizational flexibility in oil and gas sector. *Business Strategy and the Environment, 29*(8), 3509–3525.

Karishma, J., & Tripathi, P. S. (2023). Mapping the environmental, social and governance literature: A bibliometric and content analysis. *Journal of Strategy and Management, 16*(3), 397–428.

Kaupke, K., & zu Knyphausen-Aufseß, D. (2022). Sustainability and firm value in the oil and gas industry—A vicious circle? *Corporate Social Responsibility and Environmental Management, 30*(3), 1129–1144.

Kumar, A., Gupta, J., & Das, N. (2022). Revisiting the influence of corporate sustainability practices on corporate financial performance: An evidence from the global energy sector. *Business Strategy and the Environment, 31*(7), 3231–3253.

La Torre, M., Sabelfeld, S., Blomkvist, M., & Dumay, J. (2020). Rebuilding trust: Sustainability and non-financial reporting and the European Union regulation. *Meditari Accountancy Research, 28*(5), 701–725.

Lech, A. (2013). Corporate social responsibility and financial performance. Theoretical and empirical aspects. *Comparative Economic Research, 16*(3), 49–62.

Lin, C. S., Chang, R. Y., & Dang, V. T. (2015). An integrated model to explain how corporate social responsibility affects corporate financial performance. *Sustainability, 7*(7), 8292–8311.

Manes-Rossi, F., & Nicolo', G. (2022). Exploring sustainable development goals reporting practices: From symbolic to substantive approaches—Evidence from the energy sector. *Corporate Social Responsibility and Environmental Management, 29*(5), 1799–1815.

Mazzotta, R., & Veltri, S. (2022). Dalla voluntary alla mandatory disclosure dell'informativa societaria di natura non finanziaria. *Strategie, governance e valutazione d'azienda, 1312*, 1–206.

Menicucci, E., & Paolucci, G. (2022). Board diversity and ESG performance: Evidence from the Italian banking sector. *Sustainability, 14*(20), 13447.

Miralles-Quirós, M., Miralles-Quirós, J., & Valente Gonçalves, L. (2018). The value relevance of environmental, social, and governance performance: The Brazilian case. *Sustainability, 10*(3), 574.

Pacelli, V., Pampurini, F., & Quaranta, A. G. (2022). Environmental, social and governance investing: Does rating matter? *Business Strategy and the Environment, 32*(1), 30–41.

Shahbaz, M., Karaman, A. S., Kilic, M., & Uyar, A. (2020). Board attributes, CSR engagement, and corporate performance: What is the nexus in the energy sector? *Energy Policy, 143*, 111582.

Suchman, M. C. (1995). Managing legitimacy: Strategic and institutional approaches. *Academy of Management Review, 20*, 571–610.

Vásquez-Ordóñez, L. R., Lassala, C., Ulrich, K., & Ribeiro-Navarrete, S. (2023). The impact of corporate social responsibility on the financial performance of renewable energy firms. *Economic Research-Ekonomska Istraživanja, 36*(2), 2174152.

Velte, P. (2017). Does ESG performance have an impact on financial performance? Evidence from Germany. *Journal of Global Responsibility, 80*(2), 169–178.

Veltri, S., Bruni, M. E., Iazzolino, G., Morea, D., & Baldissarro, G. (2023). Do ESG factors improve utilities corporate efficiency and reduce the risk perceived by credit lending institutions? An empirical analysis. *Utilities Policy, 81*, 101520.

Wasiuzzaman, S., Ibrahim, S. A., & Kawi, F. (2022). Environmental, social and governance (ESG) disclosure and firm performance: Does national culture matter? *Meditari Accountancy Research, 31*(5), 1239–1265.

Wei, Y., Liu, Q., & Luo, J. (2023). How does corporate social responsibility have influence on firms' access to trade credit. *Accounting & Finance, 63*(1), 1321–1349.

Yin, X.-N., Li, J.-P., & Su, C.-W. (2023). How does ESG performance affect stock returns? Empirical evidence from listed companies in China. *Heliyon, 9*(5), e16320.

Yoon, B., Lee, J., & Byun, R. (2018). Does ESG performance enhance firm value? Evidence from Korea. *Sustainability, 10*(10), 3635.

Zhao, C., Guo, Y., Yuan, J., Wu, M., Li, D., Zhou, Y., & Kang, J. (2018). ESG and corporate financial performance: empirical evidence from China's listed power generation companies. *Sustainability, 10*(8), 2607.

Part III
ESG Reporting and Risk Management: Strategies and Implications for Corporate Governance

Chapter 16
The Integration of Sustainability into the Risk Management Process and the Impact of the Energy Crisis and Green Transition: Insights from a Danish Energy Trading Company

Chiara Crovini, Emma Mørkbak Højrup, Max Strunck Jensen, Karoline Strøm Sørensen, and Sander Randrup Jensen

16.1 Introduction

Sustainability scholars have emphasized that companies are responsible for major environmental, social, and governance (ESG) issues impacting society and the natural environment (Lenssen et al., 2014; Anderson & Anderson, 2009). In fact, various risks can occur as a result of sustainability challenges. For instance, some risk factors are related to human activity, technological development, physical infrastructure, economic development, political governance, and natural disasters (Dentchev et al., 2013, pp. 142–143). However, one of the most relevant sustainability risks is represented by consumption, which is intended to increase the demand for commodities (Lenssen et al., 2014).

Since the beginning of 2021, the energy market in Europe has become even more volatile and a lot more exposed to uncertainty, which has caused a huge increase in electricity prices. The reason behind this is what has been called "the perfect storm," which is a combination of factors that have influenced the supply of energy production. Extreme climate conditions around Europe and very low water levels in the reservoirs of hydropower plants are some of the reasons that have significantly impacted the decreased electricity production (von der Leyen, 2022). Hence, Europe has entered what many call an "energy crisis," where prices in many countries have risen exponentially. Some companies and actors have had the role of managing and balancing the grid. At the same time, all this uncertainty unfolds and affects the market. Other companies have been on the verge of bankruptcy, needing governmental support due to the high operating costs (Rosemain & Thomas, 2022).

C. Crovini (✉) · E. M. Højrup · M. S. Jensen · K. S. Sørensen · S. R. Jensen
Aalborg University Business School, Aalborg, Denmark
e-mail: chiarac@business.aau.dk

N. Castellano et al. (eds.), *Environmental, Social, Governance (ESG)*, SIDREA Series in Accounting and Business Administration,
https://doi.org/10.1007/978-3-031-76618-3_16

Therefore, the changes in the energy market could be seen as both threats and opportunities to businesses due to the increased risk and uncertainty.

The main purpose of the book chapter is twofold: it aims to analyze if and how sustainability has been integrated into the risk management process, and how the 2021 energy crisis and green transition have impacted the risk management process and practices of an Energy Trading company located in Denmark.

The book chapter specifically answers the call made by Anton and Nucu (2020) and Lenssen et al. (2014) to explore the challenges of shifting to sustainability risk management in the energy sector and in the context of the financial crisis, in this case, brought by the 2021 energy crisis, and political turbulence and effects of the Ukraine war.

Specifically, this study aims to investigate the following research question (RQ):

> How has sustainability been integrated into the risk management process, and how has the 2021 energy crisis and green transition strategy impacted the risk management practices?

Drawing upon the studies by Lenssen et al. (2014) and Tekathen and Dechow (2013), the empirical investigation is based on a single case study. The primary data source is qualitative in the form of face-to-face and online semi-structured interviews, and these are supplemented by publicly available information and reports, such as information retrieved in the company website, the annual reports of the case company presenting also sustainability information, and the annual reports of the parent company.

The case company belongs to the energy field in Denmark, which is the frontrunner in Europe in managing ESG risks and fostering sustainability (Ministry of Foreign Affairs of Denmark, 2022; Environmental Performance Index, 2022; Madsen & Ulhøi, 2016).

From the analysis of the non-financial information contained in the annual reports of the company and the parent company, there emerged that sustainability (in its three areas, "E" environmental, "S" social, and "G" governance) is perfectly embedded in the company's strategy, business model, and risk management. Accordingly, although the main risk categories identified by the company represent traditional risks (i.e., market risk, liquidity risk, and credit risk), their description is clearly linked to ESG issues and to the company's strategy and business model aiming to move energy into Net Zero future.

Findings also show that the company has a structured and homogenous risk management system that can adapt and focus on the most crucial threats. The firm has economically fared well through the energy crisis, and the ERM system has contributed to this, incorporating ESG risks. Another positive element is the essential role sustainability has begun to play in the energy sector, where higher demand and increasing focus on green alternatives harmonize with the company's business strategy.

The company's ability to stay agile and adapt to the given situation has put it in a privileged position to deal with the increased uncertainty of the energy crisis and the green transition strategy that have magnified existing risks and uncertainties. Risks related to media coverage, regulatory risks, and cyber-attacks are also some risks that are not necessarily new. Still, their impact has become significantly greater, such as in the case of cyber-attacks happening more frequently than before the energy crisis. Overall, the company has changed its focus, from making a profit to managing risks.

The study contributes to the literature on SRM (Lenssen et al., 2014; Anderson & Anderson, 2009), by focusing on a company belonging to a sector and a country that have been particularly sensitive to ESG issues and green transition. In addition, the case company represents a unique case as the strategy and business model have been changed to integrate sustainability issues within the business management and specifically into the risk management process.

The chapter is structured as follows: Section 16.2 introduces the literature review on the organizational structure of risk management, focusing on the energy sector and specifically concentrates on the evolution toward sustainability risk management. Section 16.3 describes the research design, data collection, and analysis. Section 16.4 presents the findings of the case study, while the last section deals with the discussion, concluding remarks, contributions, limitations, and further avenues for research.

16.2 Literature Review

16.2.1 From Enterprise Risk Management (ERM) to Sustainability Risk Management (SRM)

The debate around risk, uncertainty, and risk management became particularly important after the 2008 economic and financial crisis (Crovini et al., 2018). However, risk is inherent to business, and its management has always been crucial for firms (Crovini et al., 2021).

Since the beginning of the twenty-first century, there has been increasing interest in a more holistic and systematic view of risk management, where the earlier mentioned risk silos should become more integrated and the rest of the organization (Arena et al., 2010; Crovini, 2019). This led to the introduction of Enterprise Risk Management (ERM), which has become a leading paradigm in the risk management literature, intending to evaluate, identify, and manage risk at an enterprise level (Anton & Nucu, 2020; Arena et al., 2017; McShane, 2018). Frameworks like COSO (2004, 2017) and ISO (2009) emerged to show how to address risk in an "integrated" way (Arena et al., 2017; Crovini et al., 2021); where for example, the COSO framework focuses on aligning the overall cooperate strategic objectives with the organizational structure but also managerial reporting and control procedures (Tekathen & Dechow, 2013).

ERM offers a way to link risk management in an organization with business strategy, decision-making, and objective setting (Arena et al., 2010). Tekathen and Dechow (2013) analyzed a German company that interestingly presented an opposite representation of that offered by COSO. They observed that ERM fostered risk identification and accountability. They based their framework of analysis on Arena et al. (2010) and on four theoretical coordinates: context, risk rationalities, technologies in use, and expertise. The context represents the external and internal drivers potentially influencing and constituting management practices. Risk rationalities revolve around specific risk conceptualization. Tekathen and Dechow (2013, p. 102) define risk rationalities by drawing on Arena et al. (2010) and Rose and Miller (1992) as the "domain for the formulation and justification of idealized schemes for representing reality, analyzing it and rectifying it." Risk rationalities represent the "Companies' efforts to conceptualize uncertainty into manageable and communicable risks, and to appropriately distribute tasks for dealing with them" (Arena et al., 2010, p. 662). Technologies are the tools and the procedures to practice ERM. Tekathen and Dechow (2013, p. 102) define technologies as exploring "the multiplicity of tools and procedures enrolled in order to practice ERM," and they divide them into scopic systems and network systems to differentiate the electronic from non-electronic ways of communicating and translating risks throughout the organization. Finally, expertise is represented by risk experts and owners that can have different functions according to their roles in the organization (Kaplan & Mikes, 2016). Understanding the relationship between the involved actors is also important to understanding organizational ERM (Arena et al., 2010).

Over the past few years, the debate has shifted toward sustainability risk management (SRM) considering all the emerging issues that have impacted the environment, social, and governance matters (Lenssen et al., 2014; Anderson & Anderson, 2009). Specifically, scholars have emphasized companies' crucial role in resolving sustainability challenges, calling for a holistic approach to sustainability risks, involving strategy, changes in the business model, and a more responsible corporate decision-making process. This holistic approach also involves risk management, as it represents a crucial process to identify, assess, and manage ESG risks (Lenssen et al., 2014; Dentchev et al., 2013).

Anderson and Anderson (2009, p. 26) argued that SRM needs to be a critical part of ERM. In 2018, COSO issued a new framework to develop guidance to help entities understand the full spectrum of these risks and manage and disclose them effectively. In this regard, some companies have adopted the ESG Risk Framework, which is based on the principles of protecting the environment, respecting human rights and promoting good corporate governance (see, for example, the Swiss Re company). Anderson and Anderson (2009, p. 36) pointed out, "If companies don't identify, analyze, and mitigate environmental risk problems at a much faster pace than that used today, they will not survive." Therefore, it is evident that, nowadays, sustainability is supposed to be embedded in the risk management process.

Lenssen et al. (2014) developed a conceptual framework that considers a granulated governance perspective to manage ESG risks. They articulated the framework on five levels: individual, organizational, sectorial, national, and supranational level. They argued that sustainability challenges and risks should be addressed considering different dimensions and that the company has a role and impact on the whole society, which also influences its operations. However, the study calls for further empirical research exploring the five governance levels, to better understand how sustainability risks are managed.

Therefore, this study aims to extend the debate by empirically investigating the organizational dimension of SRM in the energy sector, where research in the risk management field is still underexplored.

16.2.2 Risk Management in the Energy Sector

The literature related to risk management in the energy market varies a lot because it has been researched concerning different types of risk. In the past, research focused on managing and mitigating financial risks, where a lot of attention has been given to market risks due to the amount of volatility in the energy market (Denton et al., 2003; Linsmeier et al., 2002). Nijman (2012) investigated the impacts and outcomes of different financial legislations given the new incentives they have created, whereas others focused on quantifying the risks.

As the paradigm in the energy sector has shifted toward the green transition and renewable energy sources, considering the increasing focus on climate change (Arnold & Yildiz, 2015), so has the risk management literature within this sector. Scholars still focus on financial risk management, which is an overarching focus area. However, the aim seems to have changed to find ways to lower the investment risks usually associated with renewable energy sources (Hain et al., 2018). Other aspects of the literature have been focusing on solutions and policies in hopes of "de-risking" renewable energy investments to create more favorable investments opportunities with higher investment returns (Apak et al., 2011; Polzin et al., 2019; Taghizadeh-Hesary & Yoshino, 2019).

Taghizadeh-Hesary and Yoshino (2019) highlighted the increasing impact that weather and climate risks can have on the energy sector in the future due to their relationship with climate change and renewable energy sources since most of these renewable energy projects are dependent on climate or sunlight. Long-term changes in weather patterns or temperatures can, therefore, have both direct and indirect consequences for the energy sector (Schaeffer et al., 2012; Solaun & Cerdá, 2019; Taghizadeh-Hesary & Yoshino, 2019; Wieczorek-Kosmala, 2020). Here, financial tools like weather derivatives have been used to manage weather risk, attracting interest from the energy sector (Brockett et al., 2005).

The prominence of ERM has also been investigated in the energy sector, where different conclusions were drawn. Kleffner et al. (2003) pointed out that companies in the energy sector seem more inclined to adopt ERM due to the energy market's high degree of volatility. Lechner and Gatzert (2018) concurred that companies from the energy sector are more likely to implement ERM systems. Their reasoning is the potential impact of historical scandals, i.e., the Enron scandal, regulatory restrictions, and potentially just a better risk understanding than other industries (Lechner & Gatzert, 2018). However, Paape and Speklé (2012) did not find evidence that the energy sector has a more fully developed ERM system than companies in other sectors. The number of investigations on ERM in the energy sector is few compared to some of the other research areas mentioned, where Anton and Nucu (2020) called for further research in this sector in order to enlarge the body of knowledge on ERM due to the higher exposure to risk that companies in this sector have compared to some other sectors.

16.3 Research Design

16.3.1 The Fieldwork of Analysis

The empirical investigation focuses on one case company. The company belongs to the energy trading field located in Denmark that is the frontrunner in Europe in managing ESG risks and fostering sustainability (Ministry of Foreign Affairs of Denmark, 2022; Environmental Performance Index, 2022; Madsen & Ulhøi, 2016). This international company helps move energy from source to use powering homes, businesses, and societies as they transition to a new and sustainable energy future.

In 2021 the company traded power across 24 European countries and gas across 16 countries. They also have subsidiaries in the UK, Germany, and Singapore and branches in Norway and Sweden. The firm expects to expand its presence further over the next years—both across Europe and globally.

From the analysis of the information provided on the website and in the narrative information of the annual reports, the company has implemented a new strategy over the past few years, focusing on renewable energy trading with ambitious goals to become the best renewable energy trader in Europe. The strategy pursues net zero emissions and focuses on trading renewable energy to ensure efficiency and deliver green energy to the market. Their business model revolves around asset management and power and gas trading, but, interestingly, their focus is also on empowering their employees (i.e., the "S," social element of ESG issues) and governance bodies (i.e., the "G" of the ESG issues) to meet the company's strategic objectives.

When managing risks, the company links them to their business model. Specifically, their risks are market risk (including commodity price risk and currency risk), credit risk, and liquidity risk. The firm follows the parent company's risk policy, designed to manage, identify, and mitigate these risks.

16.3.2 Data Collection and Analysis

As mentioned above, this research is a single case study (Scapens, 1990; Lukka & Kassanen, 1995; Granlund & Lukka, 1998). The primary data source is qualitative in the form of face-to-face and online semi-structured interviews, supplemented with the analysis of publicly available information and reports, such as the company's annual reports disclosing also sustainability information and the annual reports of the parent company. The analysis of the non-financial information was used to triangulate the data gathered from other sources. The interviewees included members from the risk management departments, employees with a portfolio position, trading analysts, and a finance director (see Appendix 1). The interviews lasted max 30 min; they were recorded and transcribed afterward. The number of interviews was considered enough due to the empirical saturation (Glaser & Strauss, 1967). The same themes and topics repeatedly emerged, and there were no new content or contrasting opinions (i.e., inductive thematic saturation, Saunders et al., 2018).

The semi-structured interviews were based on an interview guide informed by the literature (Lenssen et al., 2014; Anderson & Anderson, 2009; Arena et al., 2010; Tekathen & Dechow, 2013), and publicly available information about the company. The interview guide was split into four areas:

1) Organizational responsibilities of the interview partner,
2) Risk management, organizational structure, processes & perceptions, impact of energy crisis, and green transition strategy,
3) Responsibilities in the context of risk management, and
4) Confrontation with sustainability and its integration into risk management.

The interviews were coded into some categories to facilitate the analysis. The first categories were based on the following theoretical coordinates (Tekathen & Dechow, 2013): context (internal and external), risk rationalities, technologies and impact on the communication with and between risk experts. The risk owners also had a category, as well as the information about how integrated the SRM system is. Furthermore, other categories cover the organizational structure, the impact of the energy crisis, and sustainability/green transition. The areas where our case matches the theory contribute to strengthening the internal validity of the case study (Yin, 2018). Pattern matching is predominant in the discussion part of the chapter, where we are matching for rivaling explanations in the risk management literature. We also use another version of pattern matching called explanation building (Yin, 2018).

16.4 Findings

16.4.1 The Context

Context is the first element that impacts risk management practices, and it is important to focus on external and internal factors (Tekathen & Dechow, 2013).

The case company has strict policies regarding risk management. The parent company disclosed risk management information in their annual report for the first time in 2006, but it first mentioned ERM in 2018. In 2020, they changed it to the current framework, which integrates sustainability and focuses on ESG issues, as they wanted to steer the company in the right direction in light of this situation with rising commodity prices. They wanted a bottom-up style and to listen more to the employees closer to the market. So, the focus on risk management has increased recently and the name ERM signals that the management at the business unit level is more involved in the risk decisions the leadership team makes (Arena et al., 2017). These decisions are aligned to a sustainability strategy that aims to energize a greener, fairer future toward net zero emissions.

Since the energy crisis began in 2021, it has been more expensive to buy electricity as an end consumer, but it has also been more expensive for the case company (Credit Risk Manager). They must pay bigger margins, meaning they should pay a larger amount in cash to secure the deal, influencing how they trade. The markets have become less liquid, meaning that not everyone can pay the invoices.

The interviews showed that the overall risk management process has not changed and that they carry out the usual activities but with increasing attention to aspects that the energy crisis can impact, such as sustainability and climate change, representing the core of the company's business model.

The PPA Team Portfolio manager stated:

> The green transition is what drives their business. If solar and wind power did not exist, the company would not exist. If we did not build windmills and solar cells, then we would not have had the opportunity to grow.

Therefore, this external factor is crucial to keep growing as a company. Over the years, the customers, both B2B and end consumers, have started to value the green transition.

> . . .the other side is that consumers, especially large consumers, have started to demand green electricity on long contracts because they can see that being green is something consumers value. (PPA Team Portfolio Manager)

Hence, an impact of the 2021 energy crisis is that the case company gets more customers that value the green transition and sustainability, as smaller companies cannot afford to operate in the market anymore.

In addition to being a part of the green transition, the case company also supports developing and trading new products in new areas. This strategy exposes the company to more risks. So even though the case company facilitates green transition, they are slowly facing more operational risks. However, the company is aware of these types of risks, and they rely on previous experience to manage them.

Sustainability has, therefore, not affected the case company negatively. Without the green transition and the increasing focus on renewable energy, the company would not survive in the market.

As a trading house, the case company depends on free markets and liberalization so they can act in the market and be part of optimizing the green transition. But during this energy crisis, the case company has been exposed to some external uncertainties from a political perspective. There have been some political initiatives around the crisis, for instance, on price caps on gas and electricity. Still, politicians have also talked about what they call a solidarity contribution, which is an additional tax on energy trades (Finance Director).

Hence, the uncertainty around political interference has been the biggest problem for the case company. During the crisis, one of our interviewees thought that the biggest winner in this crisis must have been the green transition because it gave great incentives to build a lot of windmills and solar cells so we could get independent of gas. But this did not turn out to be the case. Instead, people became scared of building new windmills and solar cells as political uncertainty made it almost impossible (Finance Director). Based on this, no one was willing to build anything because they did not know what they could earn from investing in new windmills and solar cells.

> The actual market price depends on what politicians think that day. (Finance Director)

Therefore, the green transition in Europe has been stopped for a couple of months in 2021–2022 because no one was willing to develop anything because they did not know the prices.

The Ukraine invasion in 2022 also caused a lot of uncertainty. The media and news impacted the everyday work of the case company, bringing new risks. Employees could see that whenever Putin said something, the market either went up or down.

> So, there will also be a lot of such media risk, and this becomes difficult when the market we are operating in gets sensitive toward the news. But this type of risk is not new. It has always been present, but during these times, it has become more important to focus on it since it can have huge consequences. (Power Trading Analyst)

Hence, the case company has increased its focus on the news because the impact has been a lot bigger during the energy crisis than before. It has also impacted the individual trader, as they might close the deal faster than they would have done before.

However, it is not just the media risk that has had a bigger impact on the case company. Also, the so-called cyber-attacks have had an increasing impact. Cyber risk has always been critical but has now become a greater risk. After the invasion, the company experienced many more cyber-attacks than before, so the focus on this type of risk has also increased due to these external events (Operational Risk Manager).

16.4.2 Risk Rationalities

In the wake of the 2021 energy crisis, the risk management of the case company has been challenged and put under pressure. This has meant that the current risk management practices in different front-office departments had to be reworked or reconfigured to the increasing volatility, liquidity, and price exposures (PPA Team Portfolio Manager) because of the increasing economic value of risk (Green Desk: Portfolio Manager & Analyst).

The energy crisis and the path toward green transition have magnified many risks and brought them into the light, but the risks the firm is exposed to are the same (Operational Risk Manager). Still, the content of these risk categories has also included aspects related to ESG issues. The energy crisis increased prices and volatility, changing the company's risk exposure. This economic pressure stressed the risk systems, exposures, counterparties, and how to deal with risks, but the risk departments managed the stress well as they already knew those risks (Credit Risk Manager). As mentioned above, the case company embeds sustainability (in its three areas, "E" environmental, "S" social, and "G" governance) in their risk management process, which can be defined as SRM.

The energy crisis meant previous models for calculating VaR and other key risk figures had to be updated and reconfigured to fit the increasingly unpredictable environment. The unpredictability created a conflict between how the traders saw the market and how the frameworks and models configured it. Hence, strategies to mitigate and hedge risk exposure changed, shifting the focus from margins on exchanges to direct contracts with counterparties, so from market risk to credit risk (PPA Team Portfolio Manager). The increased focus on risk in the trading departments also meant that inefficient parts of risk practices previously overlooked had to be reconfigured and improved, where, for example, the gas asset trading management department changed the risk framework from including Premium at Risk (PaR) in the transport capacities part of the framework to only having VaR, because it could better capture the reality of volatility and correlation in prices in the environment (Head of Structured Trading & Asset Management).

In the green desk department, prices have increased from 20 cents to over 8 euros, more than a 4000% since the start of 2021 (Green Desk: Portfolio Manager & Analyst). This price increase required the market risk department to better measure the risk exposure from trading on the green certificate market, but it has been difficult as the market is not very transparent, and there is no exchange for the certificates. Before the price increase, the market risk department was aware of the risk exposure that green desk traders undertook themselves, but the costs of trying to implement a new measure on an illiquid market without an exchange outweighed the benefits. However, they have now implemented a framework as a result of the energy crisis.

Sustainability has also had an influence, where operational risk has encountered new risk exposures to the compliance risk as sustainability introduces new ways of doing things, raising new system defects (Operational Risk Manager). Looking at the broader picture, the ERM policies have not changed much because of the energy crisis, although there has been a new focus on cash as a policy for liquidity and cash holdings is being developed to strengthen the umbrella of risk policies.

Overall, the case company has tried to improve the agile and adaptive risk management structure embedding sustainability. The analyst from the speculative trading department described how the crisis has not inhibited trading but it has changed how they trade and how they had to be adaptive as the focus shifted toward risks (Power Trading Analyst). This progressive transition from profit to ESG risks was natural as the risk management structure could handle and support the changes in the trading department (Credit Risk Manager).

> Our business model takes advantage of being a speedboat in the market, navigating through uncertainty and adapting to the situation (Head of Structured Trading & Asset Management).

As mentioned above, this capability was made possible by focusing more on risks and not only on making profits. The energy crisis and the green transition put more emphasis on risk exposures and the front-office. Previously, the finance department had the freedom to do whatever it wanted in pursuit of profits, but the agenda changed, and it now monitors cash and liquidity risk more carefully (Finance Director).

16.4.3 Technologies and the Communication Between Risk Experts

From the empirical analysis and the information in the annual reports, technology and digital capabilities were fundamental to pursue the new strategy toward Net Zero emission and green transition. The case company has a network of different systems and data collected and distributed from a central Enterprise Resource Planning (ERP) system (i.e., the scopic system). All these IT systems are integral for the day-to-day work of all employees, and there is an enormous amount of data flowing in and out of the ERP system through different reports and information channels (Credit Risk Manager). The ERP system plays a central role in the company's day-to-day business as all trades are registered (approximately 7.4 million transactions in 2021). Both front- and back-office depend on the systems because of internal data and information flows and the need to exchange data with the market. Therefore, the company is supposed to have good IT support, updating the systems continuously. If there are any issues with reports or systems, the operational risk department helps fix the issue, so they are responsible for keeping the systems up to date in terms of risk (Operational Risk Manager).

The ERP system is a hub for risk information and reports, where files, reports, and data are uploaded every day and are easily and freely accessible through different internal systems (PPA Team Portfolio Manager). For example, traders are supplied with price data and other information to easily calculate the VaR of different trades and positions (Power Trading Analyst). As mentioned, many different systems manage operational risks, like Endure, Brandy, and Nexus, which are related to the financial reporting system (SAP). Furthermore, when booking a trade, they use ETRM software that feeds the trades into different valuations for product control, risk, and financial reporting, ensuring the trades are captured correctly. They can also withdraw risk management information from the different systems for KPIs, enabling them to track different trends and events, indicating the movement of operational risks (Operational Risk Manager).

Apart from all these data, models, and systems credit risk department also uses data from big analysis bureaus like Moody's and Standard & Poor's to calculate their credit risks through different variables and systems. The risks are conveyed throughout the different departments through the ERP system in daily reports (Credit Risk Manager). Daily risk reports are a concise and formal way of bringing all the risk information from risk departments to the front-office traders, and managers use them to talk about risks daily (Head of Structured Trading & Asset Management). The reports contain information on risk numbers and measures, such as VaR, P&L, and drawdown, keeping traders updated on their limits and risk exposures.

The energy crisis and the new sustainability strategy tested the company's technologies and IT systems, and they were also stressed and pressured by an increasing number of cyber-attacks and the unstable market, but the company was able to handle them and the tools in the ERP system have been essential (Credit Risk Analyst and Operational Risk Manager). Overall, the energy crisis has challenged the IT systems and slowed the automatization of the models, which have been reconfigured and constantly monitored.

From the empirical findings, there emerged that scopic systems are surrounded by network systems through social interactions and communication between employees. Many of the interviewees' everyday work consists, to a certain extent, of communication about risks with colleagues. In many situations, these conversations happen in person, and it is also pointed out that they occur naturally because it is advantageous for both parties because they are often dependent on each other. The risk information is useful for formulating processes or frameworks to execute and make risks count. The Green Desk department has a strong interest in having a good relationship with market risk and credit risk officers to provide a complete overview of specific activities (Green Desk: Portfolio Manager & Analyst). The Finance Director also mentioned how the 2021 energy crisis has increased the liquidity risk and affected financial planning.

It has also been pointed out that general communication about risk has risen due to the 2021 energy crisis and the new strategy, thus requiring more coordination (Power Trading Analyst). More structured and formal settings for individuals to speak about their perceptions or opinions about some specific risks are also set up. The Operational Risk Manager also refers to what they call "Speak Up," where everyone in the organization can report if they discover an issue, which can be solved collectively to prevent it from happening again (Operational Risk Manager). Accordingly, the PPA Team Portfolio Manager describes the risk management at the case company as an eco-system:

> Risk management is more like an eco-system, where several people have shares in one activity, thus sharing responsibilities and information about that.

This enhanced communication can be seen between the market and credit risk departments, which interact with many different actors and departments because they need to act upon many different risks.

Consequently, different procedures are in place to facilitate this broad communication. Risk reports are also issued daily (PPA Team Portfolio Manager), facilitating all information about risks and uncertainties. The risk departments also have different lines of reporting and communicating with the relevant risk experts, where the market risk department has a daily dialog with them (Credit Risk Manager).

Overall, the case company has a lot of different technologies within different parts of the organization, resulting in a good translation into risk management practices, which seems to be a natural part of every process. This view is reinforced by the Head of Structured Trading and Asset Management, who has 10 years of experience in the energy sector:

> . . . it's not because it's something we're forced to do. Managing risks, and ESG issues, is a natural part of the job, regardless of whether it was now or in the past. (. . .) so it's more natural that you have to consider risks if you work in a team like mine. (Head of Structured Trading and Asset Management)

He further elaborated that this natural way of including risk in everything is industry-specific and related to the energy sector.

16.5 Discussions and Conclusions

This study answers the call to further research in the field of risk management, specifically SRM (Anderson & Anderson, 2009; Lenssen et al., 2014). In particular, this research extends the analysis in the energy trading sector, by considering the impact of new emerging risks stemming from the 2021 energy crisis (Anton & Nucu, 2020) and on the integration of sustainability into an existing risk management process.

From the documental analysis, there emerged that although the main risk categories identified by the company represent traditional risks (i.e., market risk, liquidity risk, and credit risk), their content is closely related to ESG risks, to the company's strategy and business model aiming to move energy into Net Zero future. Hence, the findings are aligned with Anderson and Anderson (2009), who argue that SRM is part of the ERM process and that, in this case, it is perfectly embedded. In fact, the company has an enterprise-wide view, where SRM is a central part of their strategy and business model, and almost every employee is a risk manager.

When the 2021 energy crisis emerged, the company adjusted its focus from profit to risk. As mentioned earlier, the company is agile and flexible, also because the industry is characterized by a lot of volatility and historical crises (Lechner & Gatzert, 2018), which could have made them more resistant to uncertain times and made their ERM/SRM setup more ready for crises. The 2021 energy crisis and the green transition strategy did not bring new risks, but it has changed the magnitude of the risks and the extent of the risk exposures.

The ERP system (*technologies in use*) has a significant and central role in the everyday work of all employees as a hub for facilitating risk data and providing actors in the organization with insightful risk information. If this system does not work, the employees will have difficulty doing their job since everything is collected in the ERP system and every transaction is registered there (Tekathen & Dechow, 2013). The IT system allows many different actors throughout the organization to become risk owners by allowing them to easily engage with access to report risk and other actors' information about risks (Tekathen & Dechow, 2013). This enabled the employees to become what Tekathen and Dechow (2013) defined as "expert risk owners," who have risk knowledge and report based on it. The risk information flow that the scopic systems provide allows them to constantly be informed and report on risks, and the network systems allow them to get broader information about risks and knowledge from other departments. The company tried to establish this political culture where failure can be openly spoken of as not always blameworthy, and they know where to direct their focus. Hence, technology has been used to increase the attention to the social and governance matters.

Regarding theoretical contributions, this case study furthers the debate on the SRM literature (Lenssen et al., 2014; Anderson & Anderson, 2009), by focusing specifically on the energy sector (Anton & Nucu, 2020) and on the organizational level (Lenssen et al., 2014). The case company presents a well-functioning and integrated SRM system that has helped the firm fare well through the energy crisis. In particular, the study analyzes the structure of the process, which encompasses the relation to organizational structure, information flow, processes, and integration with the ERP system.

The case company represents a good example, as the risk management process seems to have been a key factor in this successful navigation of the energy crisis (Crovini, 2022). Another positive aspect is the bigger role sustainability is playing in the energy sector, where higher demand and increasing focus on green alternatives harmonizes with the business strategy and business model. In addition, this case is peculiar because even though the main risk categories identified by the company represent traditional risks (i.e., market risk, liquidity risk, and credit risk), their description retrieved in the analysis of the non-financial information in the annual reports is clearly linked to ESG issues and to the company's strategy and business model striving to pursue sustainable development and green transition.

Hence, the study has practical implications for risk experts willing to integrate their daily risk activities into a more structured and integrated SRM process by drawing inspiration from good communication and interaction between the different risk experts with clear responsibilities.

Regarding the limitations of the study, the case company is part of a multinational group. The empirical investigation focused on the company acting as an independent business unit. Hence, the analysis can be further extended by involving the parent company in the UK. Even though the case company has a risk management department, thus representing an eligible case study for our research, the parent company has the control and the strategic direction of the subsidiary. In addition, we could interview traders, people from the risk management departments, and the Finance Director. Even though more actors are involved, we have chosen to focus on two of the most relevant departments when it comes to risk since the case company is a trading company, and these two departments work with risks on a daily basis.

Appendix 1 List of Interviews

Interviewees	Time and length
PPA team portfolio manager	18/11/2022 00:15:57
Power trading analyst	18/11/2022 00:22:33
Credit risk manager	18/11/2022 00:25:00
Head of structured trading and asset management	19/11/2022 00:16:27
Operational risk manager	20/11/2022 00:16:47
Green desk analyst	20/11/2022 00:15:03
Green desk portfolio manager	20/11/2022 00:16:03
Operational risk manager	21/11/2022 00:15:02
Finance director	21/11/2022 00:25:49
Head of structured trading and asset management	22/11/2022 00:13:27
Green desk analyst	22/11/2022 00:17:03
PPA team portfolio manager	22/11/2022 00:20:10
Green desk portfolio manager	23/11/2022 00:17:00

References

Anderson, D. R., & Anderson, K. E. (2009). Sustainability risk management. *Risk Management and Insurance Review, 12*(1), 25–38.

Anton, S. G., & Nucu, A. E. A. (2020). Enterprise risk management: A literature review and agenda for future research. *Journal of Risk and Financial Management, 13*(11), 281.

Apak, S., Atay, E., & Tuncer, G. (2011). Financial risk management in renewable energy sector: Comparative analysis between the European Union and Turkey. *Procedia-Social and Behavioral Sciences, 24*, 935–945.

Arena, M., Arnaboldi, M., & Azzone, G. (2010). The organizational dynamics of Enterprise risk management. *Accounting, Organizations and Society, 35*(7), 659–675.

Arena, M., Arnaboldi, M., & Palermo, T. (2017). The dynamics of (dis)integrated risk management: A comparative field study. *Accounting, Organizations and Society, 62*, 65–81.

Arnold, U., & Yildiz, Ö. (2015). Economic risk analysis of decentralized renewable energy infrastructures – A Monte Carlo simulation approach. *Renewable Energy, 77*, 227–239.

Brockett, P. L., Wang, M., & Yang, C. (2005). Weather derivatives and weather risk management. *Risk Management and Insurance Review, 8*(1), 127–140.

COSO. (2004) Enterprise risk management — Integrated framework. http://www.coso.org/documents/COSO_ERM_ExecutiveSummary.pdf

COSO. (2017). Enterprise risk management. Integrating with strategy and performance.

COSO. (2018). Enterprise risk management. Applying enterprise risk management to environmental, social and governance-related risks.

Crovini, C. (2019). *Risk management in small and medium enterprises*. Routledge.

Crovini, C. (2022). Crisis management and risk management in SMEs: Towards an integrated early warning system. In T. Henschel, & S. Durst (Eds.), *Crisis management for small and medium-sized enterprises (SMEs) strategies for external crises (Management for professionals)* (pp. 215–233). Springer Nature. https://doi.org/10.1007/978-3-030-91727-2

Crovini, C., Ossola, G., & Britzelmaier, B. (2021). How to reconsider risk management in SMEs? An advanced, reasoned and organized literature review. *European Management Journal. Elsevier Ltd, 39*(1), 118–134.
Crovini, C., Ossola, G., & Marchini, P. L. (2018). Cyber risk: The new enemy for risk management in the age of globalisation. *Management Control, 2*, 135–155.
Crovini, C., Santoro, G., & Ossola, G. (2021). Rethinking risk management in entrepreneurial SMEs: Towards the integration with the decision-making process. *Management Decision, 59*(5), 1085–1113.
Dentchev, N. A., Vander Velpen, K., & Izquierdo, E. (2013). *How to breed gazelles: Creating business for growth.* Kluwer.
Denton, M., Palmer, A., Masiello, R., & Skantze, P. (2003). Managing market risk in energy. *IEEE Transactions on Power Systems, 18*(2), 494–502.
Environmental Performance Index. (2022). https://epi.yale.edu/epi-results/2022/component/epi
Glaser, B. G., & Strauss, A. S. (1967). *The discovery of grounded theory: Strategies for qualitative research.* De Gruyter.
Granlund, M., & Lukka, K. (1998). It is a small world of management accounting practices. *Journal of Management Accounting Research, 10*(1), 153–179.
Hain, M., Schermeyer, H., Uhrig-Homburg, M., & Fitchner, W. (2018). Managing renewable energy production risk. *Journal of Banking and Finance, 97*, 1–19.
ISO. (2009). ISO 31000 Risk management – Principles and guidelines.
Kaplan, R. S., & Mikes, A. (2016). Risk management—The revealing hand. *Journal of Applied Corporate Finance, 28*(1), 8–18.
Kleffner, A. E., Lee, R. B., & McGannon, B. (2003). The effect of corporate governance on the use of enterprise risk management: Evidence from Canada. *Risk Management and Insurance Review, 6*(1), 53–73.
Lechner, P., & Gatzert, N. (2018). Determinants and value of enterprise risk management: Empirical evidence from Germany. *The European Journal of Finance, 24*(10), 867–887.
Lenssen, J.-J., Dentchev, A., & N. & Roger, L. (2014). Sustainability, risk management, and governance: Towards an integrative approach. *Corporate Governance, 14*(5), 670–684.
Linsmeier, T. J., Thornton, D. B., Venkatachalam, M., & Welker, M. (2002). The effect of mandated market risk disclosures on trading volume sensitivity to interest rate, exchange rate, and commodity price movements. *The Accounting Review, 77*(2), 343–377.
Lukka, K., & Kassanen, E. (1995). The problem of generalizability: Anecdotes and evidence in accounting research. *Accounting, Auditing and Accountability Journal, 8*(5), 71–90.
Madsen, H., & Ulhøi, J. P. (2016). Corporate environmental initiatives in small and medium sized enterprises and their outcomes: A longitudinal study. *Business Strategy and the Environment, 25*, 92–101.
McShane, M. (2018). Enterprise risk management: History and a design science proposal. *The Journal of Risk Finance, 19*(2), 137–153.
Ministry of Foreign Affairs of Denmark. (2022). https://indien.um.dk/en/news/what-makes-denmark-named-worlds-most-sustainable-country
Nijman, L. (2012). The impact of the new wave of financial regulation for European energy markets. *Energy Policy, 47*, 468–477.
Paape, L., & Speklé, R. F. (2012). The adoption and design of enterprise risk management practices: An empirical study. *European Accounting Review, 21*(3), 533–564.
Polzin, F., Egli, F., Steffen, B., & Schmidt, T. S. (2019). How do policies mobilize private finance for renewable energy? – A systematic review with an investor perspective. *Applied Energy, 236*, 1249–1268.
Rose, N., & Miller, P. (1992). Political power beyond the state: Problematics of government. *The British Journal of Sociology, 43*(2), 173–205.
Rosemain, M., & Thomas, L. (2022, July 19). France to pay $10 billion to take full control of EDF. Reuters. https://www.reuters.com/markets/europe/france-offers-12-euros-per-share-take-full-control-edf-2022-07-19/

Saunders, B., Sim, J., Kingstone, T., Baker, S., Waterfield, J., Bartlam, B., Burroughs, H., & Jinks, C. (2018). Saturation in qualitative research: Exploring its conceptualization and operationalization. *Quality and Quantity, 52*(4), 1893–1907.

Scapens, R. W. (1990). Researching management accounting practice: The role of case study methods. *The British Accounting Review, 22*(3), 259–281.

Schaeffer, R., Szklo, A. S., de Lucena, A. F. P., Borba, B. S. M. C., Nogueria, L. P. P., Fleming, F. P., Troccoli, A., Harrison, M., & Boulahya, M. S. (2012). Energy sector vulnerability to climate change: A review. *Energy, 38*(1), 1–12.

Solaun, K., & Cerdá, E. (2019). Climate change impacts on renewable energy generation. A review of quantitative projections. *Renewable and Sustainable Energy Reviews, 116*, 109415.

Taghizadeh-Hesary, F., & Yoshino, N. (2019). The way to induce private participation in green finance and investment. *Finance Research Letters, 31*, 98–103.

Tekathen, M., & Dechow, N. (2013). Enterprise risk management and continuous re-alignment in the pursuit of accountability: A German case. *Management Accounting Research, 24*, 100–121.

von der Leyen, U. (2022). 2022 state of the union address. https://ec.europa.eu/commission/presscorner/detail/en/speech_22_5493

Wieczorek-Kosmala, M. (2020). Weather risk management in energy sector: The polish case. *Energies, 13*(4), 945.

Yin, R. K. (2018). *Case study research and applications: Design and methods* (6th ed.). SAGE Publications, Inc.

Chapter 17
The Influence of ESG Risks on Corporate Governance Rating

Francesca Magli and Alberto Nobolo

17.1 Introduction

In today's dynamic business landscape, where sustainability and ethical practices are increasingly important, understanding the interplay between environmental, social, and governance (ESG) risks and corporate governance ratings has become paramount for investors, regulators, and corporate leaders alike.

In recent years, there has been a paradigm shift in how businesses perceive their responsibilities; they now consider them to extend beyond mere profit maximization. ESG factors have emerged as crucial metrics for evaluating a company's sustainability practices. Moreover, new regulatory interventions, requiring all European companies to adhere to mandatory ESG standards, have induced firms to modify their corporate governance (CG) systems not only to comply with the law but also to enhance ESG factors (Brooks & Oikonomou, 2018). CG and ESG factors are closely linked; companies rely on CG, while ESG principles are used to ensure that companies operate in line with their ethical values.

Moreover, ESG results should be an integral part of good corporate governance, and good corporate governance ensures that companies are accountable for their actions. By understanding how corporate governance and ESG factors are linked, companies can ensure that their operations align with their ethical values and that they are taking a proactive approach to ESG factors (Magli, 2023).

Corporate governance, as well as being crucial to a company's management, is a phrase whose definition has become increasingly broad over time, to the point of including ownership, mandatory and voluntary regulation, and even sustainability

---

F. Magli (✉) · A. Nobolo
Dipartimento di Scienze Economico-Aziendali e Diritto per l'Economia, Università degli Studi di Milano-Bicocca, Milan, Italy
e-mail: francesca.magli@unimib.it

N. Castellano et al. (eds.), *Environmental, Social, Governance (ESG)*, SIDREA Series in Accounting and Business Administration,
https://doi.org/10.1007/978-3-031-76618-3_17

aspects (Magli, 2011). Corporate governance is undergoing a period of transformation as companies grapple with an array of challenges and adapt to emerging trends. By addressing regulatory complexity, navigating shareholder activism, and prioritizing cybersecurity and data privacy, companies can strengthen their governance frameworks and enhance resilience in an uncertain environment.

Other corporate governance issues have recently emerged, reinforcing calls for improvements in the frameworks addressing risk and crisis management as well as related issues such as audit quality, stock price manipulation, and insider trading. Finally, they have called greater attention to ESG principles and their role when investors make their investment and voting decisions (OECD, 2021).

For better corporate governance around the world, 2023 saw the announcement of the G20/OECD Principles of Corporate Governance (OECD, 2023). These are a set of principles that help policy makers to evaluate and improve the legal, regulatory, and institutional frameworks for corporate governance, with the aim of supporting economic efficiency, sustainable growth, and financial stability. The review of these principles in the OECD debate considers a range of priority areas, such as the management of environmental, social, and governance risks. These Principles provide a new chapter on sustainability and resilience, addressing not only disclosure (information and communication) but also the role of shareholders, boards, and stakeholders (ownership and governance) (Hobbs, 2023).

ESG considerations have become increasingly prominent in the corporate world, with companies recognizing the importance of integrating sustainability and ethical practices into their operations. However, as the landscape evolves, various trends and challenges emerge, shaping the way businesses perceive and address ESG risks. ESG emerged from developed countries such as European states and the USA. ESG investing is arguably the most popular and fastest-growing investment strategy of the twenty-first century (Fonseca, 2020).

The most important ESG trends are:

- The rise of stakeholder capitalism: There is a growing recognition among businesses that they must prioritize the interests of all stakeholders, including employees, customers, communities, and the environment, rather than solely focusing on shareholders. This shift toward stakeholder capitalism is driving companies to adopt more holistic approaches to ESG management by considering the broader impacts of their actions on society and the planet.
- Increased ESG disclosure and reporting: Investors, regulators, and consumers are demanding greater transparency and accountability from companies regarding their ESG performance. As a result, there has been a significant increase in ESG disclosure and reporting, with many companies voluntarily publishing sustainability reports and participating in ESG ratings and rankings. This trend is driven by the recognition that transparent disclosure can enhance trust, attract investment, and mitigate reputational risks.
- Integration of ESG into investment decisions: Institutional investors and asset managers are increasingly incorporating ESG factors into their investment decision-making processes. ESG integration strategies seek to identify companies

with strong sustainability practices and mitigate risks associated with environmental and social issues. This trend is reshaping capital markets, incentivizing companies to improve their ESG performance to attract investment and reduce their cost of capital.

A number of important challenges remain. First, despite efforts to develop frameworks and standards for ESG reporting, there remains a lack of standardization and consistency in how companies measure, report, and disclose their ESG performance. This inconsistency makes it challenging for investors to compare companies' ESG practices accurately and assess their sustainability risks and opportunities.

Second, the increasing focus on ESG has led to concerns about greenwashing, where companies exaggerate or misrepresent their sustainability efforts to improve their public image. Additionally, some companies may prioritize ESG initiatives that yield short-term benefits or are easy to implement, rather than addressing more significant environmental and social challenges. This dilution of ESG efforts undermines the credibility of sustainability initiatives and hinders progress toward genuine impact.

Third, ESG risks are complex and interconnected, spanning multiple dimensions, including climate change, human rights, supply chain management, and corporate governance. Addressing these risks requires a comprehensive understanding of the interdependencies and trade-offs involved, as well as collaboration across internal functions, industry sectors, and value chains. However, many companies struggle to effectively identify, assess, and manage these multifaceted risks, resulting in gaps in their ESG strategies and performance.

In our analysis, we want to directly connect ESG issues with corporate governance practices, using a qualitative analysis methodology that ultimately expresses a simple score; that is, a rating.

The corporate governance rating (CGR) indicates the level of corporate governance practices prevailing in the organization. It serves as an opinion on how a corporation is being managed. CGR plays a crucial role in evaluating the effectiveness of governance practices within organizations.

The main aim of this chapter will be to increase the relevance and significance of the sustainability/ESG issue within a CGR model to better represent the effectiveness of governance. CGR is important to improve or analyze corporate reputation. The CG rating score can be used by investors, such as institutional investors (who play an increasingly significant role in the capital market), to evaluate which company to invest in. Moreover, where companies have a low score, it can become an incentive for corporate management to pay more attention to corporate governance issues (Khanchel, 2007: 741).

We argue that our study's findings offer actionable insights for policymakers and practitioners. In particular, the practical significance of our study consists in enabling organizations to manage risks actively, build stakeholder trust, make informed strategic decisions, access capital, ensure regulatory compliance, gain competitive advantage, and create long-term value—all in a better way. By systematically identifying and addressing ESG risks, organizations safeguard their reputation, minimize operational disruptions, and capitalize on emerging opportunities in sustainability-focused markets. By integrating governance and ESG considerations, companies can navigate the complexities of the real modern business landscape and thrive in an increasingly sustainability-focused world.

Through rigorous empirical analysis, our research strengthens the empirical foundation upon which future studies can build, advancing the scientific understanding of the topic. The empirical significance of analyzing the CGR model and taking into account ESG issues is supported by evidence demonstrating improvements in financial performance, risk management, cost of capital, stakeholder trust, market value, and regulatory compliance, as found in previous studies (see Gompers et al., 2003; Klapper & Love, 2004; Karamanou & Vafeas, 2005; Bebchuk et al., 2009).

The theoretical significance of using corporate governance ratings updated with ESG risks lies in their ability to advance governance principles to address broader societal and environmental challenges, align organizational objectives with stakeholder expectations, and enhance organizational legitimacy and long-term viability. By integrating governance and ESG considerations, organizations can strengthen their governance frameworks, mitigate risks, and create sustainable value for stakeholders and society as a whole.

The chapter is divided as follows. The next section deals with previous literature on the main topics. Subsequently, we illustrate our methodology by describing the structure and evolution of the CGR model and creating our sample. Finally, we offer our findings, discussion, and conclusion.

17.2 ESG, Corporate Governance, and the Corporate Governance Rating: A Literature and Theoretical Review

The practice and development of ESG in companies are relatively mature activities. As a result, there is a wealth of literature on ESG research (Li et al., 2021; Savio et al., 2023). It focuses mainly on the social origin of the name and the construction of ESG measures (Eccles & Viviers, 2011; Eccles & Stroehle, 2018), the importance of ESG measures/metrics in socially responsible investment (Escrig-Olmedo et al., 2010; Gerard, 2019; Widyawati, 2020), ESG investment themes (Daugaard, 2020; Horan et al., 2022; O'Connor, 2022), the influence of the ESG score on measuring corporate sustainability performance (Drempetic et al., 2020; Khaled et al., 2021), and the importance and role of ESG factors in financial decision-making and control processes (Ziolo et al., 2019; Tsang et al., 2023). In terms of specific issues, the combination of ESG and the COVID-19 pandemic (Adams & Abhayawansa, 2022; Savio et al., 2023), ESG and investment and stock returns, ESG and gender studies (Dello Strologo et al., 2022; Romano & Petruccioli, 2020; Manita et al., 2018), ESG in specific industries (Legrand & Matthew-Bolofinde, 2022), and ESG ratings

(De Jong & Di Bartolomeo, 2022; van Zanten & Huij, 2022) has all been investigated.

In these analyses, for example, Escrig-Olmedo et al. (2010) offered an exhaustive overview of the different criteria for evaluation used by sustainability indices and ESG agencies, whereas Gerard (2019) and Widyawati (2020) undertook critical reviews of ESG/ESG metrics and socially responsible investment.

On the topic of ESG investments, Daugaard's (2020) study contributed to the challenge by systematically exploring the literature to reveal a richer array of topics: the heterogeneous nature of ESG investing, its costs and motivations, and its management literature origins. Meanwhile, Horan et al. (2022) presented a model of ESG Intensity describing the degree of interest or commitment an investor has in ESG/sustainable investing. The model ranges from disinterest (characterized by an exclusive focus on traditional financial objectives) to a singular, perhaps exclusive, focus on a specific impact (characterized by intentional proxy voting, company engagement, and active ownership).

Drempetic et al. (2020) analyzed the influence of the ESG score on measuring corporate sustainability performance. They used Thomson Reuters ASSET4 ESG ratings to analyze the influence of firm size, a company's available resources for providing ESG data, and the availability of a company's ESG data on the company's sustainability performance. Their results raise the question of whether the way the ESG score measures corporate sustainability gives an advantage to larger firms with more resources while not providing investors with the information needed to make decisions based on their beliefs. Other researchers that analyzed this sub-topic include Khaled et al. (2021), who showed that there are particular Sustainable Development Goals (SDGs) and targets that are more relevant to the business sector than others. They also investigated how firm-specific characteristics can help explain variation in corporate sustainability performance, and found that profitable, larger, and less leveraged companies are more likely to exhibit better corporate sustainability performance.

In terms of the importance and role of ESG factors in financial decision-making and control processes, Ziolo et al. (2019) investigated which ESG criteria are incorporated into financial institutions' decision-making processes and verified the level of sustainability of financial systems in selected OECD (The Organization for Economic Cooperation and Development) countries.

Regarding ESG and COVID-19, Adams and Abhayawansa (2022) critically examined the call for "harmonization" of sustainability reporting frameworks and standards that occurred alongside an increase in ESG investing during the COVID-19 pandemic. Savio et al. (2023) provided a systematic literature review examining the combination of ESG and the COVID-19 pandemic.

The relation between ESG, investment, and stock returns was analyzed by Riches and Brands, whereas Dello Strologo et al. (2022) analyzed ESG and gender studies, in particular the status of SDGs implementation in Eurozone countries to identify the best-performing nations and study their implemented policies. Romano and Petruccioli (2020) performed a systematic review of the literature on gender diversity management, inclusive cultures, and current challenges.

Recently, ESG in specific industries was analyzed by Legrand and Matthew-Bolofinde (2022). They explain that the concept and rationale behind ESG is analyzed with an emphasis on the criteria and limitations of ESG scores. For these scholars, there is a potential misalignment between the ESG criteria and the ability to achieve ambitious SDGs based on the narrow, environmentally based view on sustainability in the hotel sector.

In terms of ESG ratings, van Zanten and Huij (2022) evaluated if two types of sustainability ratings (an SDG score and ESG ratings) adequately capture companies' sustainability performance. They analyzed whether these sustainability ratings aligned with how investors, regulators, and climate scientists—as three key stakeholders—judge corporate unsustainability.

As we can see, most of these studies are recent. However, Corporate Governance studies date back much further. There are numerous studies on corporate governance (Demb & Neubauer, 1992; Blair, 1995; Shleifer & Vishny, 1997; Kose & Senbet, 1998; Airoldi & Forestieri, 1998; Becht et al., 2002; Zattoni, 2006; Huse, 2007; Hermalin & Weisbach, 2012) as well as on the relationship between effective governance and performance (Demstez & Villalonga, 2001; Weich, 2023; Anderson & Reeb, 2003; Burkart et al., 2003; Jaskeiwicz et al., 2005; Daines et al., 2010; Coles et al., 2001; De Andres et al., 2005; Bhagat & Black, 2002; Coles & Hoi, 2003; Giovannini, 2010; Dalton & Dalton, 2010).

The first studies cited focused on all corporate governance issues, in particular around or immediately after significant corporate scandals. In the studies that analyze the ways in which governance influences performance, some analyze the ownership structure. Demstez and Villalonga (2001) deduce from their empirical analysis that performance always depends on the ownership structure; therefore, concentration and shareholding fragmentation both seem to influence company value. Weich, in a 2003 study on a sample of listed Australian companies, identifies ownership as a significant variable that explains performance. In the context of family businesses, Anderson and Reeb (2003) identified that families are present in a third of the entire population of S&P 500 companies and that companies controlled by families perform better than non-family-controlled companies. Furthermore, their statistical analysis confirms that company performance increases when a family member is the company CEO. Among other types of owners, Jaskeiwicz et al. (2005) found that venture capitalists increase company profits. When analyzing the types of directors, Bhagat and Black (2002) and Coles et al. (2001) found a negative correlation between outsider directors and performance. Bhagat and Black (2002) used accounting performance measures while Coles et al. (2001) used market value added. Giovannini, in a 2010 analysis of a sample of 56 companies listed on the Milan Stock Exchange between 1999 and 2005, found how the presence of independent directors influences company value.

The main novelties in the study of Corporate Governance are certainly the analyses of corporate governance that consider the application of the G20/OECD principles. Since the previous iteration of these principles was expressed in 2015, several themes, including sustainability, concentration of ownership, institutional investors, and digitalization, have influenced the scope of corporate governance. The objective of the 2023 review of these Principles was to update the Recommendations in light of recent developments in capital markets and corporate governance practices, and to ensure their continued relevance and usefulness as the main global reference standard (OECD, 2023). There are, however, few references in the literature on these G20/OECD principles application (Botez, 2023, Botez et al., 2023, Havel et al., 2023, Larionova, 2022).

According to Li et al. (2021), there are literature reviews on the role and performance of corporate governance in ESG (Yoshikawa et al., 2021) and discussions of the relationship between corporate governance and corporate social responsibility (Aluchna & Roszkowska-Menkes, 2019).

According to Bucchetti and Arduino, it is necessary to examine the role of CG in ESG outcomes by exploring CG themes, ESG indicators, and the employed theories, countries, methodologies, and models used to address endogeneity. A multitude of factors collectively impact ESG outcomes positively. These include the presence of female directors, the involvement of institutional investors, the inclusion of independent directors, the presence of certain distinctive CEO characteristics, the design of a strategically structured directors' compensation scheme, and the establishment of a dedicated sustainability committee. Conversely, it appears that family ownership could potentially exert a detrimental effect on ESG performance (Buchetti & Arduino, 2022). Despite the evidence concerning the CG determinants of ESG outcomes, several underexplored areas may remain, such as the potential influence of directors' expertise in specific ESG-related sectors and the effects of CEO tenure.

Few articles comprise Corporate Governance Rating literature. Of those that exist, most are articles by rating agencies (Standard & Poor's, 2002; ICRA, 2004) while only a small minority are academic. The latter particularly focus on the theme of rating model type that is, whether it is based on a single index (Gompers et al., 2003; Briano-Turrent & Rodriguez-Ariza, 2016), on different indices (Larcker et al., 2007; Black et al., 2006; Mansour et al., 2020), or on a list of relevant factors using a questionnaire/survey (Garay & Gonzalez, 2008; Klapper & Love, 2004; Durnev & Kim, 2005; Black et al., 2006).

Previous analysis on the empirical relevance is, for example, a meta-analysis conducted by Bebchuk et al. (2009) that found that companies with higher governance ratings tend to have higher profitability, market valuation, and stock returns. In terms of enhanced risk management, a study by Gompers et al. (2003) found that companies with stronger governance practices experience lower stock return volatility, suggesting that they have greater resilience to external shocks, including ESG-related events. Empirical evidence suggests that companies with higher governance ratings benefit from lower financing costs. Karamanou and Vafeas (2005) found that firms with better governance practices are perceived as less risky by investors, leading to lower costs of debt and equity capital.

By integrating governance and ESG considerations, organizations can enhance their sustainability performance, mitigate risks, and create long-term value for shareholders and stakeholders. Several studies have documented a positive relationship between corporate governance ratings, ESG performance, and market value. Klapper and Love (2004) found that companies with higher governance ratings tend to have higher market valuations, suggesting that investors place a premium on good governance practices.

Unfortunately, there are no academic articles or articles from rating agencies that analyze the link between CG rating and ESG factors/risks in detail.

One of the limits of the study of this link certainly lies in the fact that the ESG rating, as an instrument, already addresses identifying a score that represents the company's ability to deal with ESG problems. Some studies have tried to analyze how ESG ratings can be used to increase corporate governance when shareholders care about social and environmental outcomes (Chaigneau & Sahuguet, 2023). Unfortunately, some scholars consider ESG ratings as imperfect measures of ESG performance and they rely on more standardized methodologies (Chaigneau & Sahuguet, 2023).

Given this gap in the literature, this leads us to think that including the ESG risks issue in the CG Rating model could be used successfully to better represent the company's ability or inability both to be ethical and to obtain good financial performance.

In order to provide context, outline the scope of existing research, and identify gaps or areas where further investigation is needed, we first selected what we considered to be the most suitable theory and then searched and reviewed the existing theoretical literature.

The most suitable theory, in the context of also examining the introduction of ESG elements in corporate governance rating, is stakeholder theory (Martin et al., 2020). Stakeholder theory (Freeman, 1984) is a management and organizational theory that posits that organizations should consider the interests of all stakeholders, not just shareholders, in their decision-making processes and operations. The theory suggests that organizations are not only accountable to shareholders but also to a broader set of stakeholders who can significantly affect or be affected by the organization's actions. The main aspects of stakeholder theory include the requirement to consider multifaceted stakeholder groups; the interconnectedness of stakeholder interests (for example, decisions that benefit shareholders may have adverse effects on employees or the environment); the importance of a normative perspective in order to advocate for the ethical consideration of stakeholders' interests in organizational decision-making; the long-term orientation; value creation for stakeholders (aligning business objectives with the interests of all stakeholders); dynamic engagement and dialogue with stakeholders to understand their evolving needs and expectations; and legitimacy and trust being gained through transparent and responsible business practices.

Stakeholder theory provides a valuable lens through which to understand the integration of the corporate governance rating with ESG issues. This theoretical perspective emphasizes the importance of considering the interests of all stakeholders, including shareholders, employees, customers, suppliers, communities, and the environment, in organizational decision-making processes.

The following explains how stakeholder theory could inform the integration of corporate governance rating with ESG issues:

- Recognition of stakeholder interests: Integrating ESG considerations into corporate governance rating acknowledges the concerns and expectations of various stakeholders regarding environmental sustainability, social responsibility, and ethical governance practices. By addressing ESG issues, organizations demonstrate a commitment to balancing the diverse interests of stakeholders and promoting long-term sustainability.
- Enhanced stakeholder engagement: Integrating ESG issues into a corporate governance rating provides an avenue for stakeholder engagement and dialogue on sustainability-related matters. By soliciting input from stakeholders and incorporating their perspectives into governance practices, organizations can build trust, foster collaboration, and enhance legitimacy.
- Alignment of governance practices with stakeholder expectations: Integrating ESG considerations into a corporate governance rating ensures that governance practices reflect broader societal and environmental concerns. By evaluating governance effectiveness in addressing ESG risks, organizations can demonstrate responsiveness to stakeholder expectations and enhance their reputation as responsible corporate citizens.
- Management of stakeholder relationships: Integrating ESG issues into a corporate governance rating enables organizations to identify and address stakeholder concerns related to environmental impacts, social practices, and governance transparency. By actively managing stakeholder relationships through transparent disclosure and proactive risk mitigation, organizations can build stronger partnerships and enhance their social license to operate.
- Long-term value creation: Integrating ESG considerations into a corporate governance rating promotes sustainable value creation by addressing environmental risks, social inequalities, and governance weaknesses that can undermine long-term organizational performance. By incorporating ESG issues into governance practices, organizations can mitigate risks, seize opportunities, and contribute positively to the well-being of stakeholders and the broader community.

In summary, stakeholder theory provides a framework for understanding the integration of ESG issues into a corporate governance rating by emphasizing stakeholder interests, engagement, alignment of governance practices, management of stakeholder relationships, and long-term value creation. By embracing stakeholder perspectives and incorporating ESG considerations into governance processes, organizations can enhance their resilience, legitimacy, and sustainability in an increasingly complex and interconnected world.

Our literature review revealed that there are no studies that have analyzed CGR and ESG aspects from the perspective of stakeholder theory. However, two studies have addressed the corporate governance rating within the stakeholder theory while also acknowledging sustainability aspects (such as the sustainability report or CSR disclosure in company annual reports). They are:

- Almagtome, A., Khaghaany, M., and Önce, S. (2020), in which the analysis of 125 firm-years of data suggests that the company provides more CSR disclosure if it has a better corporate governance rating or larger total assets. The paper also reveals that social, environmental, and economic indicators, as pillars of sustainable development, are not the result of corporate governance practices or of stakeholder pressure alone but represent a holistic reflection of the accumulated effects of various factors related to both corporate governance practices and stakeholder theory.

- Chan, M.C., Watson, J., and Woodliff, D. (2014), which investigates the association between mechanisms used by companies to enhance relations with stakeholders. Consistent with stakeholder theory and controlling for industry profile, firm size, stockholder power/dispersion, creditor power/leverage, and economic performance, their analysis of the annual reports for a sample of 222 listed companies suggests that firms providing more CSR information have better corporate governance ratings, are larger, belong to higher-profile industries, and are more highly leveraged.

Our work is therefore highly innovative, as it investigates ESG, corporate governance, and stakeholders via the same tool, the CGR.

17.3 Methodology: Corporate Governance Rating Models

One of the most interesting tools with which to analyze corporate governance in depth is the Corporate Governance Rating (CGR). This is a tool that can be organized as a questionnaire, as an index, or as a set of indices where a summarized single score represents the effectiveness of a company's corporate governance. The objective of CGR is to evaluate a company's business conduct, practices, and disclosure standards quality in terms of fairness and transparency, from the perspective of its financial stakeholders (ICRA, 2004). To do this, it is necessary to analyze a considerable amount of information, including that contained in such sources as the CG report, the Articles of Association, the meeting regulations, the minutes of the meetings of the board of directors and of the board committees, the annual reports, offer documents, and the minutes of the annual general meeting and extraordinary general meetings. These are all documents that are taken into consideration in our analysis and from which data is taken to implement the answers to the various metrics in our CGR model.

To create the best CG rating model, we analyzed the characteristics of international CG rating models, in particular those of Governance Metrics International Ratings (MSCI_GMI), Institutional Shareholders Services (ISS), and Standard and Poor's (S&P) (Table 17.1). Table 17.1 provides a comparison of rating agencies including rating scale (given in tenths or hundredths), parameters, aggregate in different classes or areas, and the number of analytical questions.

After a careful analysis of the rating models of the most renowned agencies, we have identified the most important key variables of corporate governance. They are: ownership structure; governance structure with particular emphasis on board

Table 17.1 Rating systems comparison

Rating agency	Rating system		
	Scores	Sections	Questions/ analytical issues
MSCI_GMI	1–10	7 (Corporate board structure and independence; director positions and committee assignments; executive compensation; director compensation; audit fees; corporate ownership; takeover defenses)	450
Institutional Shareholder Services (ISS)	1–100	8 (Board of Directors [structure and composition]; internal and external audit; statute provisions; state laws; anti-takeover provisions; executive and director compensation; ownership; director education)	61
Standard & Poor's (S&P)	1–10	4 (Ownership structure and external influences; shareholders' rights and stakeholder relations; transparency; disclosure and audit; board structure and effectiveness)	98

Note: This table represents the rating system comparison between MSCI_GMI, ISS, and S&P, with the analysis of scores range, sections analyzed, and the number of analytical issues

structure and processes; stakeholder relationship; financial transparency; ethical practices; and information disclosure (ICRA, 2004; Standard & Poor's, 2002).

An appropriate approach for a corporate governance rating system to adopt is first to have a rating [model] of the corporate governance in a given country, from a country perspective. In fact, there is no one model of corporate governance that works in all countries and all companies. Indeed, there exist many different codes of "best practice" that consider differing legislation, board structures, and business practices in individual countries. Consequently, corporate governance cannot be dealt with in an abstract model, as it is a product of national cultural and political systems (Donker et al., 2008: 84).

Corporate governance rating systems should provide, therefore, a useful indication of the corporate governance environment in specific countries, and in individual companies within those countries (Mallin, 2001: 257).

Considering the importance of the governance rating model and of the country perspective, our study therefore focuses on creating and using a more suitable model in order to better represent Italian companies.

17.3.1 The Evolution of the CGR Model: The Importance of ESG Risk Factors

As we have already mentioned, some researchers have analyzed the relationship between corporate governance and ESG. Existing research emphasizes that corporate governance significantly influences firms' non-financial reporting (NFR), particularly across a range of ESG outcomes (Buchetti & Arduino, 2022).

By keeping ESG indicators under control it is possible to address the risks arising from them more easily and quickly, such as climate change, socio-demographic change, technological evolution, violations of human and workers' rights, environmental damage and negative impact on the environment, violation of the integrity of corporate conduct, etc.

The idea of introducing this new analysis into the existing CGR model led us to identify documents or regulations that would allow the introduction of new metrics/parameters into the model, useful for the creation of a more innovative and explanatory model of the effectiveness of the CG.

In particular, the innovations introduced after 2020 and especially in 2022/23:

- Consider of the neutrality of the various Corporate Governance models desired by the Corporate Governance Code
- Intensify of the implications of equality and gender quotas on Corporate Governance
- Add the lessons of the COVID-19 Pandemic in order of ESG risks and the related implications for the controls and risks committee
- Assess the role of the non-financial declaration on corporate disclosure and
- Consider the implications of the new Corporate Crisis Code on the roles of corporate bodies

Even if not all of them can be traced back to ESG issues directly, we can say that they can be linked. We will mention all of them, focusing above all on explaining their connection with ESG risks.

17.3.2 The New Structure of the Italian CGR Model

Corporate governance systems have different features depending on the country concerned; in order to test the typical characteristics of corporate governance in Italian companies, we developed our own Corporate Governance Rating (CGR) model.

Our CG rating model differs from others (Standard and Poor's, ISS, etc.—see Table 17.2) by drawing greater attention to the features peculiar to the Italian governance system. There is more information on family business characteristics, on peculiar control and management bodies for the traditional model of governance (not found in other scoring systems), on transparency, and on the protection of minority rights as set forth in the Code of Conduct for Italian listed companies.[1]

[1]This CGR model, designed in 2008 and subsequently updated, will become, in 2024, a fundamental tool used for the analysis of the corporate governance rating of companies in the new Governance Observatory of Department of Business and Law - University of Milan Bicocca.

Table 17.2 Rating systems comparison with our CGR model

	Rating system		
Rating agency	Scores	Sections	Questions/ analytical issues
MSCI_GMI	1–10	7 (Corporate board structure and independence; director positions and committee assignments; executive compensation; director compensation; audit fees; corporate ownership; takeover defenses)	450
Institutional Shareholder Services (ISS)	1–100	8 (Board of directors [structure and composition]; internal and external audit; statute provisions; state laws; anti-takeover provisions; executive and director compensation; ownership; director education)	61
Standard & Poor's (S&P)	1–10	4 (Ownership structure and external influences; shareholders' rights and stakeholder relations; transparency; disclosure and audit; board structure and effectiveness)	98
Italian CGR model	–23.8—46.6	3 (Ownership; corporate governance structure; corporate disclosure)	194

Note: This table represents the rating system comparison between Italian CGR model and the international rating agencies

The objective of the CGR is to analyze the effectiveness of corporate governance. Below, we discuss the steps for building the model, to identify and define all the variables considered important in the assessment of corporate governance.

Our most recent CGR model consists of 194 metrics, which represent a summary of the management and governance procedures adopted by a company. This structure is an evolution of three previous models created and tested: one in 2009 that had 91 metrics and 8 categories (shareholder composition, board of directors, committees, internal control committee, protection of shareholder rights, quality of corporate information, board of statutory auditors, and auditing company) (Magli & Nobolo, 2009); a second in 2013 (Magli et al., 2014) with three categories (like the current model) and 177 metrics; and a third in 2020 that incorporated new legislation, in particular the new Corporate Governance Code (2020) and the D. Lgs. 49/2019 which transposes the "Shareholders' Rights" EU Directive 828/2017.

The aim of the latest model is to include some new aspects relevant to CG, such as:

- Further intensifying the implications of equality and gender quotas on Corporate Governance
- Further intensifying the lessons of the COVID-19 pandemic regarding ESG risks and the related implications on the controls and risks committee
- Assessing the role of the non-financial declaration on corporate disclosure and
- Incorporating ESG factors relevant to corporate governance

In the 2013 model, the three main categories analyzed were ownership, governance, and corporate disclosure. Each of these categories was assigned a different weight in relation to its relevance for the whole system of corporate governance and was divided into subclasses/sections. From 2023, some of the subclasses changed in number. The explanations of the changes can be found below.

The first category, "Ownership," examines the company ownership structure and includes 61 metrics grouped into three subclasses:

- Shareholder composition, with 35 metrics and a weight of 33.3%
- Shareholders' meeting, with 8 metrics and a weight of 33.3% and
- Shareholder protection, with 18 metrics and a weight of 33.3%

Within the Ownership macro-section, we have only modified the subsection "Shareholder protection," which now includes 18 questions rather than 11. The protection of shareholders is one of the cornerstones of many new regulations concerning corporate governance; but we also know that minorities are strongly protected under ESG legislation. Therefore, the seven new added questions are:

1. Is the 231 Organizational Model[2] adopted?
2. Is there an investor relator present?
3. Is there a dedicated section on the company website?
4. Is the right to vote across borders guaranteed?
5. Can members participate in the meeting electronically?
6. Can members vote by proxy?
7. Can members/shareholders include items on the agenda of the meeting?

The second category, called "Corporate Governance," focuses on the analysis of the company governance structure, underlining the characteristics of various governing bodies and entities in charge of the audit. This category consists of 107 metrics divided into 7 sections:

- Board of directors, with 49 metrics and a weight of 35%
- Executive committee, with 5 metrics and a weight of 5%
- Control & Risk committee, with 18 metrics and a weight of 5%
- Appointments committee, with 9 metrics and a weight of 5%
- Remuneration committee, with 17 metrics and a weight of 5%
- Board of statutory auditors, with 15 metrics and a weight of 25% and
- Auditors, with 5 metrics and a weight of 20%

In this section, the main changes were already implemented in the previous version. The most relevant, in relation to the introduction of the new Corporate

[2]The Organization, Management, and Control Model in accordance with the Italian Legislative Decree n. 231/2001 consists of a range of rules, protocols, tools, and behaviors functional to providing the Company with an effective and adequate organizational, management, and control system suitable for identifying and preventing risks of committing relevant crimes pursuant to Legislative Decree 231/2001 by persons of the entity or functionally related to the entity in the interest or for the benefit of the Company.

Governance Code of Conduct of 2020, concerned first the role of the management body and its responsibility in choosing the governance model (traditional, one-tier, or two-tier) and its responsibility in appointing a committee that approves the company's industrial plan (these added 2 metrics); and second, the composition of the board of directors (BoD), investigating an increase in the minimum quota of independent directors (1/3 of the management body). This metric, being already present, has therefore only been modified.

The new questions relating to the 2022–2023 period instead concerned various subsections.

In particular, the "administrative body" subsection introduced these questions:

1. Has the number of independent directors on the Board of Directors increased in the last 5 years?
2. Has the number of independent directors on the Board of Directors increased in the last 10 years?
3. Is the criterion of gender equality in the composition respected, pursuant to the legislation in force pro tempore?
4. Are "Alarm signals," as referred to in art. 3 of the Business Crisis Code, constantly monitored?
5. Does the Board of Directors define the nature and level of risk compatible with the strategic objectives of the company?

The "Control and Risk Committee" subsection introduced these questions:

1. Is a procedure in place for identifying risks (the so-called risk assessment) and evaluating and hierarchizing them, as well as researching and implementing a risk response?
2. Are indicators such as "risk appetite"—risk propensity/acceptable risk—and "risk severity" monitored?
3. Is there at least one risk owner to whom responsibility and management of one or more risks can be assigned?

The "Remuneration Committee" subsection introduced this question:

1. Are there remuneration plans linked to performance objectives including non-financial parameters?

The "Supervisory body" subsection introduced these questions:

1. Is the criterion of gender equality in the composition respected, pursuant to the legislation in force pro tempore?
2. Do you evaluate the adequacy of the organizational, administrative, and accounting structures regarding the timely detection of crises?

As we can see from these new questions, the gender makeup of the board and of the supervisory body is investigated; the update outlined by the "Golfo-Mosca" Italian law of 2011, extended by the 2020 law of the State (n. 160/2019), is added. It is represented by a new metric that evaluates whether the company's BoD and supervisory body respect the quotas suggested by the law, i.e., by having two fifths of their members be female (instead of one third as previously established).

The third and final category, "Corporate Disclosure," covers corporate economic and financial communication, and it is composed of 25 metrics contained within a single section. The highest score is assigned to the information that each company provides on its website or within the various documents issued during the year, such as statutes; semi-annual or quarterly financial reports; information on ownership, corporate bodies, and share price; press releases; curricula and directors' remuneration; reports on corporate governance; details of shareholders' meetings; website "contacts" sections; and procedures for internal dealing, management of confidential information, and transactions with related parties.

The new questions in this section are:

1. Does the company adhere to the regulations of the self-discipline code?
2. Is there information in the NFS (Non-Financial Statement) about the company organization and management model, about the company policies undertaken and their expected and achieved result?
3. Is there information in the NFS about the main risks the company faces and the methods for managing them?
4. Are there references in the NFS to environmental and social aspects affecting the company, respect for human rights, and the fight against corruption as required by law?

These questions reflect in particular the NFS, also called NFI (non-financial information). The companies falling within the scope of NFRD (Non-Financial Reporting Directive—2014/95/EU) are large Public Interest Entities, with more than 500 employees as of the financial statement's date. All these requests are mandatory for these companies but are optional for all others, in order to give greater communication to stakeholders. Considering the environmental, social, and employee issues, human rights, and bribery and corruption issues, the NFRD requires companies to disclose information about their business model, policies (including implemented due diligence processes), outcomes, risks and risk management, and Key Performance Indicators relevant to the business.

Our CGR model includes other technical aspects that regard weights and range score.

Weights are important because they help to better identify the relevance of some parameters in comparison with others. For this reason, in the first section ("Ownership"), we have the same weight for the three subsections, while in the "Corporate Governance" section, we have different weights. The greatest weight is afforded to the Board of Directors (35%), followed by the Board of Statutory Auditors (25%) and the External Auditors (20%). The committees, made up of BoD members, score much lower and the same as each other, i.e. 5%.

The score for each metric/parameter is a number that can be calculated on the basis of a legend present in the questionnaire, summarized in the table below (Table 17.3).

Table 17.3 Metric score

Type	Score	Comments and/or examples
Characteristic identification	Range – 1 / 1	A negative score (−1) allows us to stress the negative elements that signal abnormalities
Percentage evaluation	Range −1 / 1	Where a score is based on the percentage detected, for example, "the share of the largest shareholder," the share is compared with a benchmark
Numerical evaluation	No. or range – 1 / 1	A number, or, in the case of comparison with a benchmark parameter, the range score is applied; for example: "Number of positions held by independent directors." If the number detected is <10, it is assigned a score of 0; however, if the number is >10, it is assigned a score of −1.

Note: This table represents the different types of score range, in particular the denomination and examples

Table 17.4 Rating classes

CLASS	SCORE	
	from	to
A	32.52	46.6
B	18.44	32.52
C	4.36	18.44
D	−9.72	4.36
E	−23.8	−9.72

Note: The table represents the class and the scores attributed to various rating classes

At the end of analysis process, the company obtains an evaluation in CG rating classes. There are five rating classes, among which rating class A is the highest score the entity can achieve, and rating class E is the lowest score (Table 17.4).

17.3.3 Sample

In order to analyze whether the defined corporate governance model can be more useful and exhaustive in explaining the good governance of a company (thanks to the inclusion of ESG aspects), we apply it to a sample of companies never previously analyzed.

The choice of this sample did not concern the comparison of large or small companies (Magli et al., 2014), or companies with shareholder concentration-diffusion (Magli et al., 2013), which feature in studies we have previously carried out. This sample is made up of more technological and innovative companies or startups. They were selected from the list of innovative SMEs (https://www.mimit.gov.it/it/impresa/competitivita-e-nuove-imprese/start-up-innovative) made available by the Italian "Ministry of Business and Made in Italy." In particular, we included those that are most structured at a legislative level, i.e. those that have the majority of their company documentation published online.

The sample analyzed represents Italian startup companies, which, however, are already strongly structured; so much so that they are all joint-stock companies. They were all founded between 2011 (the oldest) and 2021. Each startup has its own sector of activity and specific objectives. Some focus on artificial intelligence and machine learning, while others specialize in medical technology or e-commerce, or rent and manufacturing. We chose startups because they are oriented toward innovation and the search for original solutions to existing problems or new market needs, quickly adapting to changes, therefore possessing greater resilience or the ability to overcome crises without long-term negative consequences.

Our interest in these simple and new companies is motivated by trying to use the CG rating model for very recent companies that, with their consolidated and strong structure, can represent, in a simple score, their corporate governance capacity. Moreover, we wanted to analyze startups, which are enterprises more subject to risks, because we would like to identify a CGR model in order to analyze the entire range of companies, including businesses with completely different structural characteristics. Interestingly, since all of them are joint-stock companies, they prepare and communicate large numbers of informative documents from which it was possible to derive the necessary information to fill out the CG rating questionnaire.

The sample is quite varied. It includes two companies that deal with Real Estate/Rent and in particular with proptech (a portmanteau of the words "property" and "technology"): Casavo, and short-term rent experts Clean BnB.

The Casavo SpA company purchases properties quickly, upgrades them, and puts them back on the market using data and technological tools to present direct purchase offers and reduce the time it takes to sell properties. Casavo's goal is to change the way we sell and buy homes thanks to technology. Clean BnB SpA is a company that rents other people's properties for short periods. Clean BnB apartments welcome guests from all over the world and the owner will receive monthly income. Clean BnB SpA will take care of all the related services, i.e., ensuring the visibility of the property online, managing bookings with synchronization toward the main online channels (Airbnb, Booking, Expedia, Homeaway), welcoming guests, cleaning, providing linen, managing the property (reporting and paying the profit to the owner), and undertaking bureaucratic management (relating to the opening of the business in the municipality/region, and periodic communication of guests in a website of the state police).

The others are from different sectors; however, they are all connected in some way to technology. Crowd Fund Me SpA is one of the main Italian crowd-investing platforms (for Equity Crowdfunding, Real Estate Crowdfunding, and Corporate Debt). The portal offers the possibility of investing in unlisted companies, carefully selected from among those with the greatest growth potential: investors, both retail and institutional, thus have the opportunity to diversify their portfolio by investing in unlisted assets.

Digital Magics SpA is an accelerator and incubator of innovative startups and scaleups that offer content and services with high technological value (fintech and insurtech, Internet of Things, health, travel, e-commerce, enterprise software, martech and adtech, foodtech, transportation, AI, and Blockchain).

D-Orbit is the market leader in space logistics and transportation, with a history of space-proven technologies and successful missions.

Energica Motor SpA is an innovation, design, and production company in the field of 100% electric mobility. In April 2022, Energica was acquired by Ideanomics (a global group on Nasdaq) and given the mission to accelerate the commercial adoption of electric vehicles.

Kolinpharma SpA is a company in the neutraceutical sector, that is, the meeting place between nutrition and pharmaceuticals. They offer products with high functional content, capable of interacting synergistically with the physiological functions of the organism, to stimulate the biological reaction of the human body and protect people's well-being. They have 7 industrial patents in Italy, 6 in 12 other European countries, 6 in the United States, and 1 in Israel.

Matica Fintec SpA designs, develops, and sells technological solutions for banking (financial cards with 3D customization, microchip coding, RFID, etc.) and government institutions (laser technologies, holographic security protection, color thermal sublimation, etc.) possessing the highest security standards.

Sostravel.com SpA is a digital tourism company listed on Euronext Growth Milan and OTCQB. It manages the sostravel and flio apps, and the www.sostravel.com and www.amareitalia.com platforms, offering booking services, digital itineraries, information on flights and airports, car rentals, and experiences. The company operates its proprietary Lost Luggage Concierge service and is expanding into ad hoc telemedicine services for travelers.

UCapital SpA is the holding company of a global fintech ecosystem active in the finance, technology, and media sectors. The Group is made up of: UCapital SpA; UCapital24 SpA (listed on Euronext Milan, it is the first global fintech social network, which also manages a web TV with headquarters both in Milan and in New York); UCapital Global PLC, present in the Euronext Paris list, which operates both as Asset & Wealth Management and as Investment Banking focusing in particular on startups and SMEs throughout Europe; and Trade Capital Italia, an Italian SIM, company specialized in trading services.

This is the composition of the sample (Table 17.5):

The most important CG documents used to answer questions for the implementation of the model were: Statute, Corporate Governance and investor relations sections on websites; minutes of the shareholders' meetings; procedures relating to the management and dissemination of privileged information and share capital transactions; procedures for transactions with related parties; internal dealing procedures; financial statements; sustainability reports; Insiders Register Procedures; impact reports; ethical codes; organizational models; and corruption prevention and transparency plans.

Table 17.5 Sample

Company name	Sector	Date of establishment
Casavo SpA	Real estate	2017
Clean BnB SpA	Rent	2016
Crowd Fund Me SpA	Crowd investing	2017
Digital Magics SpA	Hub for innovation	2017
D-Orbit SpA	Aerospace logistics	2011
Energetica Motor Company SpA	Motorcycle industry	2015
Kolinpharma SpA	Nutraceuticals	2013
Matica Fintec SpA	Fintech	2019
Sostravel SpA	Tour operator	2018
UCapital SpA	Investment company	2021

Note: The table represents sectors and date of establishment of the various startups included in the sample

17.4 Findings and Discussion

The results have not been illustrated in detail for individual companies, apart from in the tables that we can see below, to benefit from observing an overall vision (see Table 17.6).

Most of these innovative companies have developed the ESG theme and the corporate governance structure in more or less the same way. The analysis of the model integrating the ESG parameters, compared with the previous model (which did not take these factors into consideration), generally reports higher values. This result cannot always be seen as evidence of voluntarily high levels of CSR (corporate social responsibility) given that some parameters are mandatory as they are required by law; if not present, they take on negative values. The fact that these companies are all startups from the last decade, even if, as already mentioned, they are all structured as large companies or joint-stock companies, highlights some characteristics of newly founded companies, that is, many of these are unable to comply with all the dictates of particularly voluntary rules.

All the companies in the analyzed sample show higher scores in the model with ESG than in the one without ESG.

Many of them show higher scores in the first section, where the increasing scores strongly depend on the "Shareholder protection" section (a fundamental subsection in the ESG context), which provides positive responses (with a value of +1) to all four questions relating to respect for voting rights, as well as to the adoption of the 231 organizational model (as seen in the cases of Casavo, D-Orbit, Energica Motor Company, and Matica Fintec).

In terms of comparisons with other previous studies (Magli et al., 2013, 2014), we cannot make a comparison regarding the questionnaires with the ESG parameters incorporated given that at the time of those investigations, the ESG issue was not yet so relevant and researched in the main corporate documents/corporate information.

Table 17.6 Result scores

Enterprise	Year	Type CG score	Section 1	Section 2	Section 3	Total
CASAVO SpA.	2022	ESG	6.4	9.2	−0.8	14.8
		No ESG	4.8	8.4	−0.8	12.4
	2021	ESG	6.0	5.2	−0.8	10.4
		No ESG	4.4	8.4	−0.8	12.0
CLEAN BnB SpA.	2022	ESG	8.0	8.4	−0.4	16.0
		No ESG	6.4	6.8	−0.6	12.6
	2021	ESG	8.0	8.4	−0.4	16.0
		No ESG	6.4	6.8	−0.6	12.6
CROWD FUND ME SpA.	2022	ESG	7.6	6.8	−0.8	13.6
		No ESG	6.0	5.6	−0.8	10.8
	2021	ESG	7.6	7.2	−0.8	14.0
		No ESG	6.0	6.0	−0.8	11.2
DIGITAL MAGICS SpA.	2022	ESG	7.2	8.4	−0.4	15.2
		No ESG	5.6	8.4	−0.4	13.6
	2021	ESG	7.2	8.4	−0.4	15.2
		No ESG	5.6	8.4	−0.4	13.6
D-ORBIT SpA.	2022	ESG	6.0	5.6	−2.0	9.6
		No ESG	4.4	6.8	−2.0	**9.2**
	2021	ESG	6.0	5.6	−2.0	9.6
		No ESG	4.4	6.8	−2.0	**9.2**
ENERGICA MOTOR COMPANY SpA.	2022	ESG	5.2	9.2	−0.4	14.0
		No ESG	3.6	8.8	−0.6	11.8
	2021	ESG	6.0	9.6	−0.2	15.4
		No ESG	4.4	9.2	−0.4	13.2
KOLINPHARMA SpA.	2022	ESG	6.0	12.0	−0.8	**17.2**
		No ESG	4.4	11.2	−0.4	15.2
	2021	ESG	6.0	12.0	−0.8	**17.2**
		No ESG	4.4	11.2	−0.4	15.2
MATICA FINTEC SpA.	2022	ESG	6.8	8.4	−0.2	15.0
		No ESG	4.0	7.6	−0.4	11.2
	2021	ESG	6.4	8.4	−0.2	14.6
		No ESG	3.6	7.6	−0.4	10.8
SOSTRAVEL SpA.	2022	ESG	5.2	8.8	−1.2	12.8
		No ESG	3.6	8.0	−0.8	10.8
	2021	ESG	7.2	8.4	−0.4	15.2
		No ESG	3.6	8.4	−0.8	11.2
UCAPITAL SpA.	2022	ESG	7.2	8.0	−0.4	14.8
		No ESG	5.6	7.6	−0.4	12.8
	2021	ESG	7.2	8.4	−0.4	15.2
		No ESG	5.6	8.0	−0.4	13.2

Note: The table represents the result scores for all the startups analyzed. In particular, for all of them the first line represents the CGR model with ESG metrics analyzed in 2022; the second line represents the CGR model without ESG metrics analyzed in 2022. In the last lines for all companies, the third represents the CGR model with ESG metrics analyzed in 2021; the fourth line represents the CGR model without ESG metrics analyzed in 2021

The comparison of this "Ownership" section with previous studies highlights that in the 2013 family-non-family business analysis the "shareholder protection" subsection did not obtain high scores, as the entire "Ownership" section, that it had a low score for family businesses. This may be due to the reduced need for higher levels of protection of family business, since the members of the family are themselves shareholders in the firm (Magli et al., 2013).

While in the 2014 PMI-large and listed companies analysis, the peculiarities of the companies revealed that it was the listed companies that obtained a higher score in the "ownership protection" subsection. The motivation is, more or less the same as for the previous study, small and medium-sized enterprises are often not public companies and the main shareholders are also the directors of the company (Magli et al., 2014).

In today's study, even the Governance section, in the ESG model compared to the non-ESG one, is superior for the majority of the companies analyzed. Benefits are particularly highlighted in the "Control and Risk Committee" section, where, for the majority of the assessed companies, the risks are identified and there is attention to aspects related to "risk appetite" (Clean BnB, Crowd Fund Me, D-Orbit, Kolinpharma, Matica Fintec, and Sostravel.com); however, almost no company (even among those cited for risk communication) has yet addressed the risk owner aspect.

Remaining in the governance context, expanded with new questions related to ESG and with different subsections, we find some companies (Energica Motor Company, Kolinpharma, and Sostravel.com) that also respond positively to the creation of remuneration plans linked to performance objectives set in the subsection "Remuneration Committee." Furthermore, one company improves its score due to an increase in independent directors (Clean BnB). However, there are some companies that, for this section in the model featuring ESG parameters, record decreasing scores; in particular, they fail to comply with gender quotas (not within the BoD/administrative body but within the supervisory body) (Casavo, D-Orbit, and UCapital). In the latter cases, however, the reduction in the score for these parameters is irrelevant given that other metrics increase in the same or in other subsections, compensating for the decrease.

The comparison of this "Corporate governance" section with previous studies (Magli et al., 2013, 2014) highlights slightly different results compared to the comparative analyses in the previous subsection "Ownership."

In fact, while previously the characteristics of shareholders of family businesses were similar to the characteristics of shareholders of SMEs, we now notice how the problem shifts to the compulsory corporate bodies for large companies and originates different comparisons. In this case, in fact, we observe that in the 2013 family-non-family business analysis, we have high values in the "governance" subsection for both family and non-family businesses. Large companies such as Parmalat or Mediaset were investigated among the family businesses. The reason concerns the good practice of creating committees within the BdD (Board of Directors) (Magli et al., 2013).

In the 2014 PMI-large and listed companies analysis, however, the peculiarities of the companies revealed that it was the listed companies that obtained a higher score as they had the "obligation" to create committees in the BdD. In fact, SMEs had a drastic reduction in value in the CGR rating given that they did not have strong suggestions and therefore did not organize committees (Magli et al., 2014).

In today's study, the third section relating to disclosure often appears without particular changes. For some companies (Casavo, Clean BnB, and Matica Fintec) this section offers the benefits of a better score mainly because the company adheres to the new self-discipline code, which we know is not a mandatory regulation but is nevertheless one strongly followed and applied by companies in general, especially listed ones.

As regards the comparison between the 2 years 2021–2022 (see Table 17.6), there are no particular changes either in the representations of the model with ESG factors or in the previous model. The prevailing changes that are highlighted also concern very specific parameters, such as the metric that asks if the debt is less than twice the net worth and less than four times the Gross Operating Income (Matica Fintec); or the variable metric that asks if there is a clear "definition of independence requirements" in the subsection "Control Body," which in 2021 only applied to two companies (Sostravel.com and UCapital). For only one company, however, did the only difference between 2021 and 2022 concern the Disclosure section, where for the year 2022 the company's financial statements are not published on the site (Energica Motor Company).

The general analysis highlights that all the companies in the sample have a type C rating (from 4.36 to 18.44); with a range that, regarding the model with ESG, goes from 9.6 for D-Orbit SpA to 17.2 for Kolinpharma SpA, and without ESG, goes from 9.2 for D-Orbit SpA to 15.2 for Kolinpharma SpA (in Table 17.6, their scores are in bold).

The highest-scoring company is Kolinpharma SpA. This company operates in the nutraceutical sector, which links nutrition and pharmaceuticals. It is where substances are selected and products with high functional content are formulated. These products are then capable of interacting synergistically with the physiological functions of the organism. It is a company officially recognized as an "innovative start up" that invests in Research & Development and employs highly qualified research personnel.

The least-performing company appears to be D-Orbit SpA. D-Orbit is a company in full expansion that has managed, since 2011, to develop and make the market understand what is meant by space logistics. The company dedicated its first resources to the study of a device for removing space debris from orbit, through a Horizon 2020 loan, which gave rise to the D-Orbit Decommissioning Device (D3), an intelligent engine specialized in satellite decommissioning maneuvers. Most of its customers are institutional clients such as the Italian Space Agency (ASI) and the European Space Agency (ESA).

17.5 Concluding Remarks

In this study, we analyzed the application of the new Italian CGR model, which we revisited in order to consider the effect of the main ESG issues on a sample of innovative startups.

After updating the model based on the main ESG themes and adding some specific parameters to the different subsections of the model, we applied the new model to the new sample.

The objective of this analysis was twofold. First, we sought to update the CGR model with the most current directives on corporate governance, including ESG issues, to try to identify to what extent (if at all) the new model could better illustrate the governance of a company. For this reason, we applied both the new model and the previous model in our analysis.

Second, we wanted to apply the model to types of samples not previously analyzed (Magli et al., 2013, 2014). This was in order to be able to determine whether this model could also represent the good corporate governance of "different" companies; in this case, ones newly founded but equally large in terms of legal structure (all joint-stock companies).

As regards the application of the CGR model that considers ESG aspects, we always found more positive scores than were achieved with the application of the previous model. In particular, we note the highest difference score (3.8) between the two models for the company Matica Fintec SpA, followed by Clean BnB SpA (3.4). These differences for both companies concern all three sections (ownership, governance, and disclosure) even if the largest difference is found in the ownership section. The aspects of greater shareholder protection, and in particular the assurance of shareholders being able to vote even if not directly present at the meeting, have strengthened the important ESG aspect of protecting minority shareholders. The company with the least difference is D-Orbit (0.4).

The application of the model to this sample tells us that the model can still be used, as most of the required parameters/metrics can be identified. The only difficulty, which we also noted for other samples analyzing small-sized companies, is the completeness of the information in the "corporate governance" section regarding the existence of committees. As we know, in the case of small and medium-sized enterprises there is neither the obligation nor the suggestion to follow the indications of the Self-Regulatory Code; the same is true for this sample which, although it is made up of companies with complex legal structures, features companies that are still startups. Unfortunately, the relevance of these parameters (which for 3 committees, excluding the executive one, went unanswered as the committees are not present) led to a reduction in the score of 15% (because each committee represents 5% in terms of weight). However, the comparison in this sample led to differences being highlighted especially in the first and second sections.

Another aspect of this difficulty is related to disclosure. Due to the characteristics of the sample, which is made up of joint-stock companies and highly technological companies, it is necessary to communicate all the information requested of a listed company. While the first section benefits above all from the greater consideration and defense of minority shareholders, or from other aspects such as the application of the 231 organizational, the second section benefits from compliance with the percentages, suggested by national regulations, of independent directors adopted, gender quotas, and other aspects such as preparation of remuneration plans linked to performance objectives, implementation of risk management, and supervision of the warning signals identified in article 3 of the new Italian Crisis Code.

The main limitation affecting this analysis is the impossibility of comparing it with the analyses performed on previous samples. This impossibility manifests in two problems. The first concerns the fact that we could only compare the values of the previous model (without ESG issues) as it applied to innovative companies within the previous samples. The second concerns the fact that our previous analyses feature samples with different characteristics, for example strictly assessing ownership concentration and not always only the dimensional aspects of the companies.

The second important limitation of this study concerns the fact that in previous analyses we have always compared samples composed of businesses with opposing characteristics (for example, family and non-family businesses, or SMEs and listed companies), but in this case we examined only innovative businesses.

References

Adams, C., & Abhayawansa, S. (2022). Connecting the COVID-19 pandemic, environmental, social and governance (ESG) investing and calls for 'harmonisation' of sustainability reporting. *Critical Perspectives on Accounting, 82*, 102309. https://doi.org/10.1016/j.cpa.2021.102309

Airoldi, G., & Forestieri, G. (1998). *Corporate governance: analisi e prospettive del caso italiano, [Corporate governance: Analysis and perspectives of the Italian case]*. ETASlibri.

Almagtome, A., Khaghaany, M., & Önce, S. (2020). Corporate governance quality, stakeholders' pressure, and sustainable development: An integrated approach. *International Journal of Mathematical, Engineering and Management Sciences, 5*(6), 1077–1090.

Aluchna, M., & Roszkowska-Menkes, M. (2019). Integrating corporate social responsibility and corporate governance at the company level. *Towards a conceptual model. Engineering Economics, 30*, 349–361. https://doi.org/10.5755/j01.ee.30.3.17511

Anderson, R. C., & Reeb, D. M. (2003). Founding family ownership and firm performance: Evidence from the S&P 500. *The Journal of Finance, 58*(3), 1301–1328.

Bebchuk, L. A., Cohen, A., & Ferrell, A. (2009). What matters in corporate governance?. *Review of Financial Studies, 22*(2), 783–827.

Becht, M., Bolton, P., & Roell, A. (2002). Corporate governance and control, National Bureau of economic research. Available at SSRN: https://ssrn.com/abstract=343461 or https://doi.org/10.2139/ssrn.343461.

Bhagat, B., & Black, B. (2002). The non correlation between board independence and long term firm performance? *The Journal of Corporation Law, 57*, 232–272.

Black, P., Mccormick, R., James, M., & Pedder, D. (2006). Learning how to learn and assessment for learning. *Research Papers in Education, 21*, 119–132. https://doi.org/10.1080/02671520600615612

Blair, M. (1995). *Ownership and control: Rethinking corporate governance for the twenty-first century*. Brookings Institution.

Botez, I. (2023). The general framework of the corporate governance codes for the G20 & 25 European Countries: An overview on corporate governance of bucharest stock exchange. *Journal of Financial Studies & Research, 2023*, 488942. https://doi.org/10.5171/2023.488942
Botez, I., Jansen, A., & Fratiloiu, B. (2023). The new corporate governance landscape and its impact on the companies' future. *Ecoforum Journal, 12*(2), 1–15.
Briano-Turrent, G. D. C., & Rodriguez-Ariza, L. (2016). Corporate governance ratings on listed companies: An institutional perspective in Latin America. *European Journal of Management and Business Economics, 25*(2), 63–75. https://doi.org/10.1016/j.redeen.2016.01.001
Brooks, C., & Oikonomou, I. (2018). The effects of environmental, social and governance disclosures and performance on firm value: A review of the literature in accounting and finance. *The British Accounting Review, 50*(1), 1–15. https://doi.org/10.1016/j.bar.2017.11.005
Buchetti, B., & Arduino F. R. (2022). A systematic literature review on corporate governance and ESG research: Trends and future directions. SSRN Electronic Journal. https://doi.org/10.2139/ssrn.4286866.
Burkart, M., Panunzi, F., & Shleifer, A. (2003). Family firms. The. *Journal of Finance, 58*(5), 2167–2201.
Chaigneau, P., & Sahuguet, N. (2023). Executive compensation with socially responsible shareholders S&P Global Market. Intelligence. https://doi.org/10.2139/ssrn.4345102.
Chan, M. C., Watson, J., & Woodliff, D. (2014). Corporate governance quality and CSR disclosures. *Journal of Business Ethics, 125*(1), 59–73.
Coles, J., & Hoi, C. (2003). New evidence on the market for directors: Board membership and Pennsylvania senate bill 1310. *Journal of Finance, 58*(1), 197–230.
Coles, J. W., McWilliams, V. B., & Sen, N. (2001). An examination of the relationship of governance. *Journal of Management, 27*(1), 23–50.
Daines, R. M., Gow, I. D., & Larcker, D. F. (2010). Rating the ratings: How good are commercial governance ratings? *Journal of Financial Economics, 98*, 439–461.
Dalton, D. R., & Dalton, C. M. (2010). Integration of micro and macro studies in governance research: CEO duality, board composition, and financial performance. *Journal of Management—Special Issue: Bridging Micro and Macro Domains, 37*(2), 404–411. https://doi.org/10.1177/0149206310373399
Daugaard, D. (2020). Emerging new themes in environmental, social and governance investing: A systematic literature review. *Accounting and Finance, 60*(2), 1501–1530. https://doi.org/10.1111/acfi.12479
De Andres, P., Azafora, V., & Lopez, F. (2005). Corporate boards in OECD countries: Size, composition, functioning and effectiveness. *Corporate Governance: An International Review, 13*, 197–210.
De Jong, M., & Di Bartolomeo, D. (2022). *Risks related to environmental, social and governmental issues (ESG)*. Palgrave Macmillan.
Dello Strologo, A., Paoloni, N., & D'Andrass, E. (2022). Recognizing progress on SDG 5 of the 2030 agenda in Europe: Guidelines for development in support of gender equality. In P. Paoloni & R. Lombardi (Eds.), *Organizational resilience and female entrepreneurship during crises. SIDREA series in accounting and business administration* (pp. 95–110). Springer. https://doi.org/10.1007/978-3-030-89412-2_8
Demb, A., & Neubauer, F. (1992). *The corporate board: Confronting the paradoxes*. Oxford University Press.
Demstez, H., & Villalonga, B. (2001). Ownership structure and corporate performance. *Journal of Corporate Finance, 7*, 209–233.
Donker, H., Poff, D., & Zahir, S. (2008). Corporate values, codes of ethics, and firm performance: a look at the canadian context. *Journal of Business Ethics, 82*, 527–537.
Drempetic, S., Klein, C., & Zwergel, B. (2020). The influence of firm size on the ESG score: Corporate sustainability ratings under review. *Journal of Business Ethics, 167*, 333–360. https://doi.org/10.1007/s10551-019-04164-1

Durnev, A., & Kim, E. H. (2005). To steal or not to steal: Firm attributes, legal environment, and valuation. *The Journal of Finance, 60*, 1461–1493. https://doi.org/10.1111/j.1540-6261.2005.00767.x
Eccles, R. G., & Stroehle, J. C. (2018). Exploring social origins in the construction of ESG measures, SSRN. https://doi.org/10.2139/ssrn.3212685.
Eccles, N. S., & Viviers, S. (2011). The origins and meanings of names describing investment practices that integrate a consideration of ESG issues in the academic literature. *Journal of Business Ethics, 104*(3), 389–402. https://doi.org/10.1007/s10551-011-0917-7
Escrig-Olmedo, E., Muñoz-Torres, M. J., & Fernández-Izquierdo, M. Á. (2010). Socially responsible investing: Sustainability indices, ESG rating and information provider agencies. *International Journal of Sustainable Economy, 2*(4), 442–461.
Fonseca, J. (2020). The rise of ESG investing: How aggressive tax avoidance affects corporate governance & ESG analysis. *Illinois Business Law Journal, 25*, 1–18.
Freeman, R. E. (1984). *Strategic management: A stakeholder approach*. Pitman Publishing.
Garay, U., & Gonzalez, M. (2008). Corporate governance and firm value: The case of Venezuela. *Corporate Governance: An International Review., 16*, 194–209. https://doi.org/10.1111/j.1467-8683.2008.00680.x
Gerard, B. (2019). ESG and Socially responsible investment: A critical review. *Beta Scandinavian Journal of Business Research, 33*(01), 61–83. https://doi.org/10.18261/issn.1504-3134-2019-01-05
Giovannini, R. (2010). Corporate governance, family ownership and performance. *Journal of Management and Governance, 14*(2), 145–166.
Gompers, P., Ishii, J., & Metrick, A. (2003). Corporate governance and equity prices. *Quarterly Journal of Economics, 118*, 107–155.
Havel, B., Lasák, J., & Pihera, V. (2023). Czech corporate governance in the light of its history and the influence of the G20/OECD corporate governance principles. *European Business Organization Law Review, 24*, 167–200. https://doi.org/10.1007/s40804-022-00253-3
Hermalin, B. E., & Weisbach, M. S. (2012). Information disclosure and corporate governance. *Journal of Finance, 67*, 195–234.
Hobbs, A. (2023). EMEIA board priorities 2023: How to shape tomorrow's board agenda today. Available at www.ey.com/en_fi
Horan, S., Dimson, E., Emery, C., Blay, K., & Yelton, G. (2022). Practical applications of the state of ESG investing: A portfolio management perspective. *Practical Applications, 2022*, pa521. https://doi.org/10.3905/pa.2022.pa521
Huse, M. (2007). *Board, governance and value creation*. Cambridge University Press.
ICRA. (2004). ICRA's corporate governance rating methodology, ICRA rating feature. Available at www.icraindia.com
Jaskeiwicz, P., González, V., Menedez-Requejo, S., & Schiereck, D. (2005). Long run IPO performance analysis of German and Spanish family owned business. *Family Business Review, 18*(3), 179–202.
Karamanou, I., & Vafeas, N. (2005). The association between corporate boards, audit committees, and management earnings forecasts: an empirical analysis. *Journal of Accounting Research, 43* (3), 453–486.
Khaled, R., Ali, H., & Mohamed, E. K. A. (2021). The sustainable development goals and corporate sustainability performance: Mapping, extent and determinants. *Journal of Cleaner Production, 311*, 127599. https://doi.org/10.1016/j.jclepro.2021.127599
Khanchel, I. (2007). Corporate governance: Measurement and determinant analysis. *Managerial Auditing Journal, 22*, 740–760. https://doi.org/10.1108/02686900710819625
Klapper, L. F., & Love, I. (2004). Corporate governance, investor protection and performance in emerging markets. *Journal of Corporate Finance, 10*, 703–728. https://doi.org/10.1016/S0929-1199(03)00046-4
Kose, J., & Senbet, L. W. (1998). *Corporate governance and board effectiveness*. NYU Stern.

Larcker, D. F., Richardson, S. A., & Tuna, I. (2007). Corporate governance, accounting outcomes, and organizational performance. *The Accounting Review, 82*(4), 963–1008.

Larionova, M. (2022). A brief history of the G20 institutional dynamics (2008–21). *International Organisations Research Journal, 17*(2), 250–274. (in English). https://doi.org/10.17323/1996-7845-2022-02-11

Legrand, W., & Matthew-Bolofinde, A. (2022). ESG, SDGs, and hospitality: Challenges and opportunities in activating sustainability. In C. N. Berrones-Flemmig, F. Contreras, & U. Dornberger (Eds.), *Business in the 21st century* (pp. 25–39). Emerald Publishing Limited. https://doi.org/10.1108/978-1-80382-787-220221003

Li, T. T., Wang, K., Sueyoshi, T., & Wang, D. D. (2021). ESG: Research progress and future prospects. *Sustainability, 13*, 11663. https://doi.org/10.3390/su132111663

Magli, F. (2011). *Proprietà, governance e performance. [Ownership, governance and performance].* Giappichelli editore.

Magli, F. (2023). *Corporate governance systems: Latest innovations and insight in the Italian context.* McGraw Hill.

Magli, F., & Nobolo, A. (2009). Corporate Governance e sistema dualistico: alcune criticità nelle Società per Azioni Bancarie. In corporate governance: governo, controllo e struttura finanziaria [Corporate Governance and the Dualistic System: Some Critical Issues in Banking Joint Stock Companies. In corporate governance: government, control and financial structure proceedings of the 2008 conference] Il Mulino publisher.

Magli, F., Nobolo, A., & Ogliari, M. (2014). Italian corporate governance rating model: Is it useful in testing all types of corporate governance? *Corporate Ownership & Control, 11*(3), 321–335. https://doi.org/10.22495/cocv11i3conf1p2

Magli, F., Nobolo, A., & Vallone, C. (2013). CGR model to explore relationship between governance and performance in family and non-family businesses. In *The Firm's role in the economy: Does a growth-oriented business model exist?* Cacucci.

Mallin, C. (2001). Institutional investors and voting practices: an international comparison. *Corporate Governance: an international review, 9*(2), 118–126.

Manita, R., Bruna, M. G., Dang, R., & Houanti, L. (2018). Board gender diversity and ESG disclosure: Evidence from the USA. *Journal of Applied Accounting Research, 19*(2), 206–224. https://doi.org/10.1108/JAAR-01-2017-0024

Mansour, M., Hashim, H. A., & Salleh, Z. (2020). Dataset for corporate governance index of Jordanian non-financial sector firms. *Data in Brief, 30*, 1–5.

Martin, B., Brindisi, C., & Kay, I. (2020). The stakeholder model and ESG, Harvard law school forum on corporate governance. https://corpgov.law.harvard.edu/2020/09/14/the-stakeholder-model-and-esg/

O'Connor, B. (2022). *ESG investing handbook: Insights and developments in environmental, social and governance investment.* Harriman House.

OECD. (2021). the future of corporate governance in capital markets following the COVID-19 crisis. https://www.oecd-ilibrary.org/sites/efb2013c-en/index.html?itemId=/content/publication/efb2013c-en&_csp_=40913905

OECD. (2023). *G20/OECD principles of corporate governance 2023.* OECD Publishing. https://doi.org/10.1787/ed750b30-en

Romano, A., & Petruccioli, R. (2020). Gender diversity management, culture inclusive e sfide dell'attualità. Una review sistematica della letteratura [Looking back and looking forward: Equity challenges and gender diversity management. A literature review]. *Education Sciences & Society*, 1. https://doi.org/10.3280/ess1-2020oa9477.

Savio, R., D'Andrassi, E., & Ventimiglia, F. A. (2023). Systematic literature review on ESG during the COVID-19 pandemic. *Sustainability, 15*, 2020. https://doi.org/10.3390/su15032020

Shleifer, A., & Vishny, R. (1997). A survey of corporate governance. *The Journal of Finance, 52*(2), 737–783.

Standard & Poor's. (2002). *Standard & Poor's corporate governance scores: Criteria, methodology and definitions.* McGraw Hill.

Tsang, A., Frost, T., & Cao, H. (2023). Environmental, Social, and Governance (ESG) disclosure: A literature review. *British Accounting Review, 55*(1), 101149. https://doi.org/10.1016/j.bar.2022.101149

Van Zanten, J. A., & Huij, J. (2022) ESG to SDG: Do sustainable investing ratings align with the sustainability preferences of investors, regulators, and scientists? (November 6, 2022). https://doi.org/10.2139/ssrn.4186680.

Weich, E. (2023). The relationship between ownership structure and performance in listed Australian companies. *Australian Journal of Management, 28*(3), 287–305.

Widyawati, L. (2020). A systematic literature review of socially responsible investment and environmental social governance metrics. *Business Strategy and the Environment, Wiley Blackwell, 29*(2), 619–637. https://doi.org/10.1002/bse.2393

Yoshikawa, T., Nippa, M., & Chua, G. (2021). Global shift towards stakeholder-oriented corporate governance? Evidence from the scholarly literature and future research opportunities. *Multinational Business Review, 29*, 321–347. https://doi.org/10.1108/MBR-10-2020-0200

Zattoni, A. (2006). *Assetti proprietari e corporate governance, [Ownership and corporate governance]*. EGEA.

Ziolo, M., Filipiak, B. Z., Bąk, I., & Cheba, K. (2019). How to design more sustainable financial systems: The roles of environmental, social, and governance factors in the decision-making process. *Sustainability, 11*, 5604. https://doi.org/10.3390/su11205604

Chapter 18
ESG Risk Identification and Mitigation Under the SEC Regulation in the Aerospace and Defence Sector

Paola Demartini and Silvia Soriano

18.1 Introduction

The increasing focus on sustainability concerns and changes in regulations regarding the communication and measurement of ESG issues necessitate significant efforts from companies. This includes implementing new management and control systems (Semenova, 2021; Harasheh & Provasi, 2023) and developing effective communication tools (Arvidsson & Dumay, 2022; Tsang et al., 2022). These efforts are linked, on the one hand, to the need to respond effectively to the information needs of investors and stakeholders, whose decision-making is increasingly driven by the relevance of ESG factors (Amel-Zadeh & Serafeim, 2018; Demartini & Pagliei, 2023) and, on the other hand, to the need to meet the challenges of a new regulatory scenario (Redondo Alamillos & de Mariz, 2022; Yosifova & Petrova-Kirova, 2022).

In this regard, ESG risk identification and mitigation is considered a focal point for companies to maintain adequate competitiveness and respond to multiple institutional pressures (Cohen, 2023; Zioło et al., 2023). The purpose of our research is to investigate the key ESG risks that companies need to disclose.

In line with our research aim, first, we decided to focus on the U.S. context, where it exists a mandatory approach to risk disclosure, which is more detailed than in other regulations (Campbell et al., 2014; Cordazzo et al., 2017; Brown et al., 2018; Rose, 2020).

Beginning in 2005, the Securities and Exchange Commission (SEC) mandated firms to include a risk factor section in their Form 10-K to discuss '*the most significant factors that make the company speculative or risky*' (Campbell et al.,

P. Demartini · S. Soriano (✉)
Department of Business Studies, Roma Tre University, Rome, Italy
e-mail: paola.demartini@uniroma3.it; ssoriano@uniroma3.it

N. Castellano et al. (eds.), *Environmental, Social, Governance (ESG)*, SIDREA Series in Accounting and Business Administration,
https://doi.org/10.1007/978-3-031-76618-3_18

2014). In 2018 and 2019, the SEC released new rules to update the disclosure obligations that apply to publicly traded companies stating that disclosure should discuss the most significant factors, including *emerging environmental, social, and governance risks* (Ho, 2020).

In addition, since the risks identified by companies are linked to the sector they belong and their business model, we considered it worthy to adopt a sector-specific approach to provide an accurate and in-depth analysis (Antoncic, 2019). Then, we decided to develop our inquiry addressing the Aerospace and Defence sector (A&D).

There are many reasons for choosing the A&D sector. These reasons include its specific weight in the global economic context (Deloitte, 2023;[1] Ahmad et al., 2021; Khan, 2023; Ghadge et al., 2010), the specificity of the sector's activity, which by its very nature has a controversial relationship with sustainable development (Singh et al., 2022), the presence of European players competing with U.S. companies in the global market and, finally, the identification of a research gap linked to the lack of studies on the relationship between this sector and ESG risks.

Our analysis begins with the selection of the four U.S. champions in the A&D sector and through the construction of a framework aimed at detecting the quality of disclosure of ESG risks (Beretta & Bozzolan, 2004, 2008; Jia et al., 2016; Truant et al., 2017) and the presence and type of instruments used to mitigate them.

More specifically, this framework, which is the result of our re-elaboration of the model already developed in the paper by Beretta and Bozzolan in 2004, is characterised by the presence of three dimensions of analysis, namely 'Width', 'Depth', and 'Mitigation'; the third represents the element of innovation with respect to the models already elaborated in the literature. All the information classified within the model was collected through a manual content analysis (Krippendorf, 1980) to correctly interpret and categorise the information collected during the analysis process (Guthrie & Abeysekera, 2006).

Our findings reveal that disclosures about ESG risks suffer from the limitations already highlighted on disclosure of risks in the 10-k form, namely, to be generic and, in some cases boilerplate (Harper Ho, 2020). Furthermore, it has been confirmed that a 'mimetic approach' has been adopted by companies, as shown by previous studies on voluntary sustainability reporting (Martínez-Ferrero & García-Sánchez, 2017). This mimetic approach stems from the desire of companies to meet both the regulatory requirements and the stakeholders' expectations by trying to minimise both information and litigation costs and conforming to the quantity and quality of ESG information disclosed by competitors.

Our research contributes to the emerging field of ESG risk disclosure by providing a structured analysis of the current level of mandatory disclosure under the SEC regulation. Specifically, we focus on A&D companies, which are global players and knowledge-intensive business services (KIBS), making them worthy of investigation (Muller & Doloreux, 2009).

[1] https://www2.deloitte.com/us/en/pages/manufacturing/articles/aerospace-and-defense-industry-outlook.html.

The paper's final contribution is to provide insights for future research on the different approaches taken by U.S. and EU regulators in defining the content of companies' mandatory ESG risk disclosures.

This chapter is structured as follows: Sect. 18.2 illustrates the theoretical background and purpose of the research, focusing on both the relationship between risk management and risk disclosure and the SEC's increased regulatory focus on ESG risk factors and risk mitigation disclosure; Sect. 18.3 focuses on the research design, describing the selection of the sample and the construction of the analytical framework; the findings, interpreted across the three dimensions of ESG issues in terms of both risk and impact, are presented in Sect. 18.4; and Sect. 18.5 highlights our conclusions and some implications for future research directions.

18.2 Theoretical Background and Context

18.2.1 From ESG Risk Management to ESG Risk Disclosure and Vice Versa

In previous years, formal, rigorous risk management was once the lonely domain of commercial banks and insurance companies; it has since spread to investment banks, asset managers, corporations, and governments (Power, 2004). Meanwhile, it has also become the subject of increasing interest to shareholders, bondholders, lenders, rating agencies, regulators, and policymakers. Risk management has evolved, including risk mitigation efforts on the market, operational risks and processes, reputational risks and, in the last year, shifting attention towards arising risks such as cyber security, climate change and, more broadly, ESG risks (Antoncic, 2019).

On the one hand, the evolution of risk management is linked to the characteristics of the firm and the context that require greater attention to the issue of risk, but also to the capabilities developed internally, as suggested by the resource based view (Barney & Clark, 2007; Madhani, 2010), according to which risk management can be conceived as a dynamic capability,[2] which is shaped by the firm's resources and which also shapes the future organisational resources (Mishra et al., 2019).

On the other hand, the importance of risk management is also connected to external pressure from investors and regulators, which, in recent years, has highlighted the need to disclose more information about emerging risks. Consequently, as institutional theory suggests (Zucker, 1987; Ball & Craig, 2010), there is an obvious need for companies to translate, inside the organisation, the macro changes taking place outside. Particularly, ESG risks have been fuelled by growing recognition of their impacts on corporations and society. Governments and

[2] Dynamic capabilities: 'the organizational and strategic routines by which firms achieve new resource configurations as markets emerge, collide, split, evolve, and die' (Eisenhardt & Martin, 2000).

multilateral institutions, including the United Nations (UN), the International Organization of Securities Commissions (IOSCO), standard-setters such as the International Sustainability Standards Board (ISSB) and the Global Reporting Initiative (GRI), are all promoting ESG disclosure to help capital markets more accurately price ESG risks and encourage companies to become more accountable for the external impacts of their operations.

However, it should be emphasised that this request for more information is exercised by different bodies with distinct purposes and approaches. This pressure from institutions and the financial market drives companies both to invest in sustainability communication and integrate sustainability into their strategic plans and management. Such behaviour has been studied thoroughly, and scholars agree that isomorphism (i.e. coercive, normative, and/or mimetic) is the main theoretical lens to understanding this journey towards greater environmental and social responsibility (Martínez-Ferrero & García-Sánchez, 2017).

The first step towards corporate social responsibility is generally accomplished by drawing up a sustainability report (Dienes et al., 2016).

Although sustainability reporting is primarily designed for communicating with the stakeholders, the standards provide themes of attention, guidelines, and metrics that prompt companies to question the relevance of ESG themes in their business management. In most organisations, this process starts with identifying, assessing, responding to and monitoring ESG risks and opportunities. It can translate into a next step that leads to the board's assumption of a strategic position and, consequently, the activation of sustainability-oriented management (Arif et al., 2021). This assumption of responsibility is key to reorienting the system of corporate controls, within which ESG risk management activities, as above stated, have become increasingly important.

Regardless of how much harmonisation there will be on ESG standards, it is clear that mandatory sustainability reporting will increase significantly worldwide over the next few years and that this will impact corporate management systems (Christensen et al., 2021).

Since, as of today, companies listed on the U.S. financial markets are already subject to disclosure requirements on main corporate risk factors and how they are managed, for the purposes of our research, we believe it is essential to delve into this context.

18.2.2 The SEC's Current and New Rules About ESG Risk Factors and Risk Mitigation Disclosure

The SEC requires companies to publish 10-K forms so investors can make informed investment decisions. The 10-K includes five distinct sections:

- *Business*. This provides an overview of the company's main operations, including its products and services.
- *Risk factors*. These outline any and all risks the company faces or may face in the future.

- *Selected financial data*. This section details specific financial information about the company over the last 5 years.
- *Management's discussion and analysis* of financial condition and results of operations. Also known as MD&A, this gives the company an opportunity to explain its business results from the previous fiscal year.
- *Financial statements and supplementary data*. This includes the company's audited financial statements. A letter from the company's independent auditor certifying the scope of their review is also included in this section.

In 2018 and 2019, the SEC released new rules to update the disclosure obligations that apply to publicly traded companies under Regulation S-K. The SEC's current guidance on risk factors disclosure advises that disclosure should discuss the 'most significant' factors that make the company's securities speculative or risky and should be organised and concise. This includes also how companies provide information to investors about risk, including emerging environmental, social, and governance (ESG) risks (Ho, 2020).

Over 85% of companies in the S&P 500 already produce voluntary sustainability reports, so some of this ESG information is already publicly available to investors, although their quality and comparability are uneven across firms. Moreover, voluntary sustainability reports are also subject to different materiality and reliability standards than those that apply to public filings. These factors have led most investors to rely primarily on the more limited ESG information companies provide in their public filings, which is more accessible and is reported in a consistent investment analysis.

Nonetheless, researchers and practitioners (Ho, 2020) question whether ESG information is under-reported in public U.S. filings, which happens in part because of companies' failure to identify ESG information as material and in part because of a lack of integration between the corporate risk management, internal controls, and reporting functions that apply to public filings, and those through which voluntary reports are produced (Jones, 2023).

18.3 Research Design

In the following section, both the rationale for our choice of analysis context and the process of designing our framework are described.

18.3.1 Why the Aerospace and Defence Sector Is Worthy of Investigation

Since the interest of our analysis was in the identification and the mitigation of ESG risks in companies' risk disclosure, we decided to focus our attention on analysing the A&D sector in the U.S. market.

Starting with the definition of the sector provided by the Sustainable Accounting Standards Board (SASB) through the Sustainable Industry Classification System® (SICS®), we chose to analyse this sector for several reasons, including, on the one hand, its weight and impact on society (Deloitte, 2023) and, on the other hand, the fact that is an under-researched sector from the point of view of risk mitigation and management tools, especially ESG ones.

Looking more closely at the reasons for our choice, it is necessary to highlight how the global A&D market, which is expected to grow from $795.92 billion in 2022 to $855.62 billion in 2023 at a compound annual growth rate (CAGR) of 7.5%, has a significant specific weight in technological innovation (Ahmad et al., 2021; Khan, 2023) and supply chain (Ghadge et al., 2010). This specific weight is generated by the nature of the sector itself, which has a complex supply chain with multiple tiers of suppliers and requires the use of advanced technologies and a very high level of security and confidentiality of data and information. At the same time, the specific weight is due to the nature of the challenges that companies operating in this sector have faced and will have to face. In fact, as the '2023 aerospace and defence industry outlook' points out: 'supply chain disruptions and talent shortages may be the biggest risks or challenges for A&D organizations in 2023'. Furthermore, companies operating in this sector need to increase their level of digital technologies and capabilities, by developing a 'digital thread linking engineering, supply chain, production and aftermarket' (Deloitte, 2023).

We have also identified previous research dealing with the main risks of the sector, addressing a variety of issues including: technological innovation and using blockchain as a tool that can generate potential opportunities (Ahmad et al., 2021); the elaboration of a risk management framework for aerospace supply chain systems (Ghadge et al., 2010); and the elaboration of a framework of critical success factors for the implementation of Industry 4.0 in the A&D industry (Khan, 2023). On the contrary, we have noticed an almost complete absence of studies aimed at investigating the weight that the specific category of ESG risks has in this sector and the possible existence of specific ways of managing them.

Existing studies have approached the issue of sustainability in the A&D sector either by focusing on the increased attention investors are paying to ESG issues, considering the A&D sector only from the perspective of business ethics breaches and of the potential impact on company value and earnings (Glazerman & Cohen, 2020), or from a corporate governance perspective, examining the drivers for aerospace companies to engage in corporate environmental responsibility (CER) and its impact, with the aim of showing how greater involvement in environmental policy by aerospace industries enhances competitive advantage and market value (Gangi et al., 2022).

Ultimately, the decision to focus on the analysis of the A&D sector is not only linked to its significance but also to the fact that while there is a clear acknowledgement of the importance of implementing sustainable solutions within companies in the A&D sector, in all three aspects (environmental, social, and governance), what is missing is a structured analysis of the actual and current level of disclosure of ESG

Table 18.1 Selected companies

Lockheed Martin	2023	US$ 67.60	122,000	US$ 52.5	NYSE
Raytheon Technologies	2022	US$ 67.07	182,000	US$ 158.86	NYSE
Boeing	2022	US$ 66.61	156,000	US$ 137.1	NYSE
Northrop Grumman	2022	US$ 36.60	95,000	US$ 43.76	NYSE

Source: Our elaboration from Wikipedia and the 10-k forms of each company

risks, as well as the implementation of specific solutions to mitigate or respond to them.

From our perspective, the lack of studies addressing these issues is also directly related to the controversial link between sustainability and the A&D sector. This ambiguity occurs particularly in terms of investment preferences, which are increasingly shifting towards sustainable investment choices and are characterised by the decision not to invest in A&D stocks 'because the A&D firms are involved in manufacturing military weapons, which is identified as a "negative" category impacting the ESG scores of such firms'. However, today, according to Singh et al. (2022), the impact of the Russia-Ukraine conflict on financial markets has led to a recalibration of investment priorities and an increase in investment in the A&D sector.

This last aspect, together with the role of the A&D sector in a global context increasingly focused on ensuring a sustainable future, convinced us of the importance of conducting a study capable of tackling challenging themes such as what ESG risks the companies perceive as the most relevant and how they declare to mitigate them.

18.3.1.1 The Selected Companies

In our analysis we have selected the top companies (i.e. Lockheed Martin, Raytheon Technologies,[3] Northrop Grumman, and Boeing) in the A&D sector listed in the U.S. market (yahoo finance, 2023; DefenceNews, 2023).[4] In the following Table 18.1, the main data of the selected companies are presented.

We have chosen to use Form 10-K, an integral part of the Annual Report, as the basis for collecting the data concerning Item 1A, which contains the risk factors described in Item 105 of Regulation S-K, i.e. information on the principal risks faced by the company, generally listed in order of importance.

Ultimately, the forms analysed for the selected companies are dated 31/12/2022 so that the negative impact of the pandemic can be partially excluded, as the documents only contain references to its residual effects.

[3]Raytheon Technologies changed its name to RTX in June 2023.

[4]https://finance.yahoo.com/news/12-best-aerospace-defense-stocks-155436380.html; https://people.defensenews.com/top-100/.

18.3.2 The Framework of Analysis

We have decided to approach the analysis using a framework that would allow us to answer our research question, i.e., to understand not only whether and how much information on ESG risks is disclosed in the 10-K, but also which risks are disclosed, what their significance is, and how the company intends to respond to and/or mitigate them. For the construction of the framework, we broadly followed the approach of previous literature, which has dealt with the analysis of risk reporting from the point of view of the characteristics of risk disclosure, as well as the possible determinants of risk disclosure (Beretta & Bozzolan, 2004; Jia et al., 2016; Elshandidy et al., 2018).

The first work (Beretta & Bozzolan, 2004) is a key tool for setting up a conceptual model of a multidimensional nature, based on the principle that: 'the quantity of disclosure is not a satisfactory proxy for the quality of disclosure'. Therefore, the authors propose a framework, which they use for the analysis of 'four different but complementary dimensions (the content of information disclosed, the economic sign attributed to expected impacts, the type of measures used to quantify and qualify the expected impacts, the outlook orientation of risk communication and the managerial approach to the management of risks)'.

The second work (Jia et al., 2016), building on the framework developed and tested by Beretta and Bozzolan, proposes the use of a finer-grained approach to examine the 'quality', 'quantity', and 'richness' (width and depth) of risk management disclosure, by applying semantic content analysis to all the dimensions and sub-dimensions of the framework, in order to obtain a more detailed analysis of risk management disclosure.

Finally, before going into the details about our model, it is worth noting that we have used, as a starting point to identify the ESG risks, the labels provided by the SASB[5] in its sector standards and materiality map. This choice is motivated by the desire for consistency with the U.S. context, since the SASB labels make it possible both to identify the ESG risks that are most likely to affect cash flows, access to finance and the cost of capital and to highlight those that are most relevant to investors (SASB, 2023).[6]

Now that we have described the fundamentals of our frame, we can move on to a detailed description of it. It classifies the information according to three dimensions and eleven sub-dimensions (see Table 18.2).

The dimensions and sub-dimensions consist of:

[5]In June 2021, the SASB and the London-based International Integrated Reporting Council announced their combination to form the Value Reporting Foundation (VRF). In August 2022, the IFRS Foundation consolidated the VRF and Climate Disclosure Standards Board with its own newly formed International Sustainability Standards Board (ISSB) and all the open SASB Standards projects were transitioned to the ISSB.

[6]https://sasb.org/standards/materiality-finder/.

Table 18.2 Analysis framework representation

WIDTH dimension	DEPTH dimension	MITIGATION
• Material label (as for SASB) E → (Energy management; Waste & hazardous materials management) S → (Social Capital: Data security; Product quality & safety) G → (Business Model and Innovation: Product design & lifecycle management; Materials sourcing & efficiency; Leadership and Governance: Business ethics) • Not Material label (as for SASB) E → (Physical impacts of climate change) S → (Human Capital: Employee health & safety; Employee engagement, diversity & inclusion) • Our label (emerging from disclosure) E → (New environmental laws, regulations, and policies; Other environmental risks, i.e. reputational risk) S → (Human Capital: Attracting talent) G → (Business Model and Innovation: New technologies, digital transformation, and property rights; Leadership and Governance: Litigation costs)	• Risk description (Parts of the 10-K form that justify the choice of classification) • Time Historical Forward-looking • Type of measure Financial Non-financial Quantitative Qualitative • Economic sign: Positive Negative • Type of impact: Direct on financial results Indirect (through drivers)	• Type of intervention (Type of intervention taken or planned to be taken if the identified risk occurs or will occur) • Time Ex ante Ex post • Type of measure Financial Non-financial Qualitative Quantitative

- Width (material label as for SASB, not material label as for SASB, our label)
- Depth (risk description, time, type of measure, economic sign, and type of impact)
- Mitigation (type of intervention, time, and type of measure)

The first dimension (WIDTH) represents the first level of data classification, which is initially subdivided according to a logic of belonging to environmental (E), social (S), or governance (G) issues and then assigned to different types of labels. The labels are divided into: material labels according to the materiality map constructed by the SASB for the A&D sector; labels that fall within the SASB model but are considered non-material at the sector level and for which we have found significant information for the purposes of our analysis; and finally, labels that we have introduced based on our content analysis after examining the 10-Ks.

Looking at the details of the three themes, within the environmental theme (E), we identified five labels.

- **'Energy Management'** and **'Waste & Hazardous Materials Management'**, which are material labels under the SASB model. Their materiality can be explained by the fact that, on the one hand, 'energy is a critical input to A&D manufacturing processes and an entity's energy mix, may influence the cost and reliability of energy supply and, ultimately, affect the entity's cost structure and regulatory risk' (SASB industry standard, 2023); and on the other hand, 'A&D product manufacturing may generate hazardous process waste', therefore, 'entities face regulatory and operational challenges in managing waste, as some wastes are subject to specific regulations pertaining to their transport, treatment, storage, and disposal' (SASB industry standard, 2023).
- **'Physical impacts of climate change'**, which is a non-material label according to the SASB model, but which we considered to be related to a risk spotted in the analysed sample and highly relevant to our analysis.
- **'New Environmental laws, regulations and policies'** and **'Other Environmental risks'** are labels introduced by us. In particular, the first deals with tracking and classifying information on risks and impacts generated by changes in the sustainability regulatory landscape; the second is a residual category in which we have included and analysed data on risks and impacts related to the failure to meet stakeholder expectations in relation to companies' strategies, objectives, and commitment to sustainability issues.

Within the social theme (S), we identified two sub-dimensions and five labels.

- The first sub-dimension is **'Social Capital'**, which includes the labels **'Data security'** and **'Product Quality & Safety'**, both of which are material according to the SASB model. Their materiality can be explained by the fact that on the one hand, the companies in the sector analysed 'may develop sensitive military and advanced aviation products and may therefore be at a high risk for cyber-attacks' and be subject to potential 'regulatory action, legal action, or adversely impact revenues and brand value' (SASB industry standard, 2023); on the other hand, 'product safety is an important consideration for A&D entities given the industry's key role in commercial aviation and military operations', in fact, 'incidents could result in financial impacts, including increased costs, regulatory penalties, or brand-value impacts that could adversely affect market share' (SASB industry standard, 2023).

In addition, regarding this sub-dimension, and considering the labels that make it up, it should be stressed that the concept of social capital should be understood as a concept of social responsibility, mainly related to the impact that the company's activity can have on its stakeholders at the societal level, and only as a reflection on the company's results.

- The second sub-dimension is **'Human Capital'**, which includes two non-material labels within the SASB model: **'Employee Health & Safety'** and

'Employee Engagement, Diversity & Inclusion'; and we have introduced one label: **'Attracting talent'**, under which we include data on the risks and impacts associated with one of the sector's key challenges: attracting and retaining new talent capable of responding to the constant need for innovation.

Finally, within the governance theme (G), we identified two sub-dimensions and five labels.

- The first sub-dimension is **'Business Model and Innovation'**, which includes two labels considered material by the SASB, i.e. **'Product Design & Lifecycle Management'** and **'Materials Sourcing & Efficiency'**. Their materiality is linked to the importance of companies in this sector being able to respond to customer and societal demand for more sustainable products and services; it is connected to their exposure to 'supply chain risks when critical materials are used in products', and it is bound to the 'potential for financial impacts stemming from supply disruptions and volatile input prices' (SASB industry standard, 2023). This sub-dimension also includes a label we have introduced**: 'New technologies, digital transformation and property rights'**, under which data is collected related to the dimension of technological innovation, which we believe is an indispensable factor in the sustainability risks faced by companies in this sector that they need to be able to manage and mitigate.
- The second sub-dimension is **'leadership and Governance'**, which includes both a material label according to the SASB: **'Business ethics'**, which refers to the fact that companies operating in the sector analysed are 'vulnerable to regulatory scrutiny of business ethics' (SASB industry standard, 2023) due to the particular nature of the operations they carry out; and we introduced a label: **'litigation costs'**, which, while referring to ESG issues, addresses them from purely a governance perspective, looking at the potential risks of penalties, claims, and lawsuits.

The second dimension (DEPTH) is intended to provide a deeper information of all the information embedded in the different themes and labels. More specifically, the data collected are analysed according to the sub-dimensions described below.

A. **'Risk description'**, which briefly lists the parts of the 10-K form that justify the initial and subsequent choice of classification.
B. **'Time'**, which allows data to be distinguished by time to understand whether the identified risk is historical or forward-looking.
C. **'Type of measure'**, where the type of measure implemented within the company is specified, highlighting whether it is a financial measure, i.e. with a direct impact on the company's financial results in terms of both costs and cash flow or a non-financial measure, i.e. with an indirect impact on the company's performance generated by the use of drivers such as reputation or competitiveness; and where it is, also, highlighted whether the measure is quantitative or qualitative in nature, based on the presence or absence of quantification elements of the risks within the 10-K form.

D. **'Economic sign'**, which makes it possible to highlight the economic sign of the expected impact of the risk. In the case of an impact characterised by a reduction in revenue and/or an increase in costs, it is classified as negative, and vice versa, it is classified as positive.
E. **'Type of impact'**, in which the risk is classified according to the type of impact generated, specifying whether the impact is direct or indirect.

The third and final dimension (MITIGATION) represents the most innovative part of our model, as it aims to analyse the type of mitigation and/or reaction that the company expects to have to the potential occurrence of the classified risks; therefore, it serves to understand the type of attitude that the company has towards ESG risks, highlighting its possible proactivity or wait-and-see attitude, allowing us to comprehend the issues on which the company intends to adopt the second one. More specifically, the data is analysed according to the sub-dimensions described below.

a. **'Type of intervention'**, in which the type of intervention that has been taken or that is planned to be taken if the specific identified risk occurs is specified. Therefore, the concept of intervention is understood as the act or fact of acting in response to something to influence its outcome.
b. **'Time'**, which makes it possible to understand whether the intervention is or will be implemented before (ex-ante) or after (ex-post) the possible occurrence of the impact of the risk event.
c. **'Type of measure'**, which classifies interventions according to whether they are financial or non-financial and qualitative or quantitative, following a logic like that used for the dimension DEPTH, subcategory C.

Given the complexity and multi-dimensionality of the framework described above, which requires the classification of information that is both quantitative and qualitative in nature and therefore cannot be categorised by software to be properly completed, we decided to use a manual content analysis, which would allow us to adequately understand the quality of risks and impacts reported in the 10-K forms. Accordingly, we read the whole section of 'risk factors' in the 10-k form for each company, then we gathered in an excel spreadsheet the statements corresponding to the coded dimensions. To minimise the risk of limited objectivity in the interpretation of the data and to verify the correctness of their classification and evaluation, we activated a manual keyword search and a double-checking mechanism between the researchers.

This methodology, which is widely used in the context of corporate disclosure studies and, more specifically, in risk reporting analysis (Ibrahim & Hussainey, 2019), was chosen not only because is a technique characterised by codifying qualitative and quantitative information into pre-defined categories in order to derive patterns in the presentation and reporting of information (Guthrie & Abeysekera, 2006), but also because it permits repeatability and interpretation of data according to their context (Krippendorf, 1980).

18.4 Findings

In the following section, our main findings are presented and discussed, while analytical evidence based on our framework of analysis is available at request.

18.4.1 Environmental

If we break down the analysis of the results by ESG theme, we can see that, regarding the **environmental theme** (see Diagram 18.1 environmental risks), the analysis shows that there is almost complete agreement between the information considered by the companies as material risks and that considered as such by the SASB materiality map, with the exception of the 'energy management' label, on which no company provides any information, in our opinion, because the information on this does not seem to be in line with the risks that can be included in the 10-K form, while more information on energy management and future objectives is included in the sustainability reports.

Moreover, the most innovative element found in our analysis of the environmental dimension is the inclusion of the expectations of the sustainable investor among the financial and non-financial risk factors, with the identification of mitigating tools in accordance with the nature of the risk and, therefore, exclusively on an ongoing basis. This perspective, albeit with a negative view of the risk of failure to meet expectations, emerges from the information collected under the residual label of

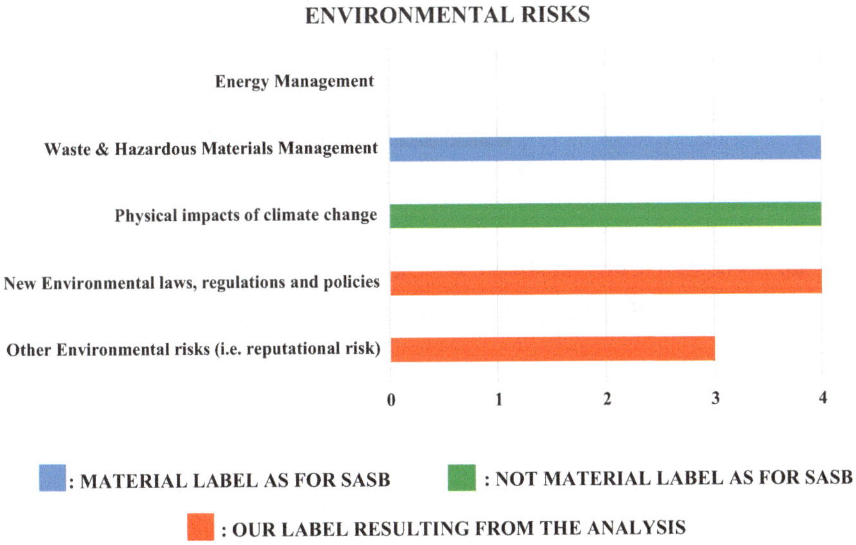

Diagram 18.1 Number of companies disclosing information about environmental risks

'other environmental risks', demonstrating the growing need for A&D companies to embark on a path of commitment to sustainability objectives, not only to respond to institutional pressure but also to try to overcome the negative relationship between investment preferences and the sector itself.[7] Finally, the risks are, in most cases, considered from a forward-looking perspective[8] and are expected to have a negative impact on financial performance, although non-quantitative information is provided, and the mitigation and response tools are almost always characterised by both a wait-and-see and a proactive attitude.[9]

18.4.2 Social

With regard to the **Social themes** (see Diagram 18.2 social risks), it should be noted that there is no complete coincidence between the risks considered by the companies as material and the SASB materiality map. Information provided on labels such as 'Data security' and 'Product Quality & Safety' are provided as expected and in line

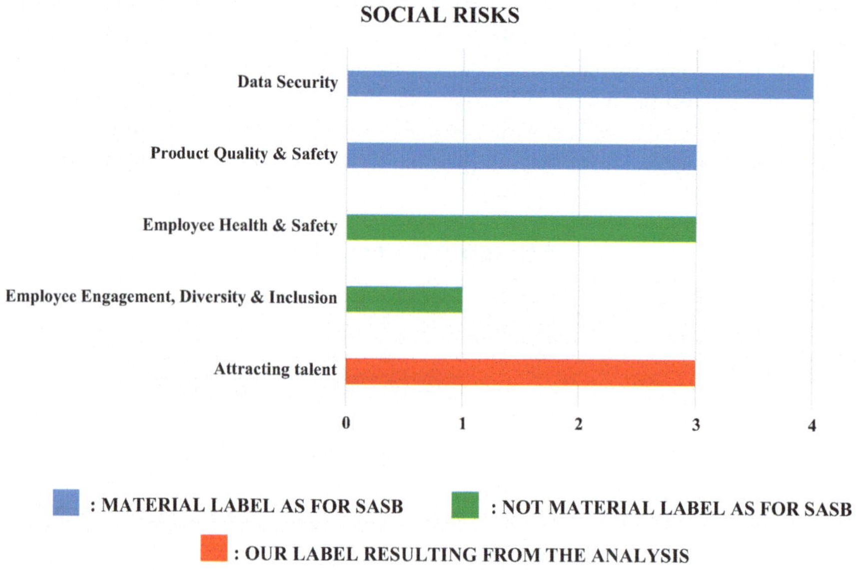

Diagram 18.2 Number of companies disclosing information about social risks

[7]No information was found for 'Lockheed Martin' that could be categorised under the residual label.

[8]Except for the label: **'Waste & Hazardous Materials Management'.**

[9]Purely wait-and-see attitude for the label: **'Waste & Hazardous Materials Management'.**

with the SASB map. In addition, labels concerning the risks related to Human Capital (i.e. Employee Health and Safety, Employee Engagement, and Diversity and Inclusion) are perceived by the companies as the main challenges for the business, while they are not material risks for the A&D sector following the SASB guidance. However, information on the mitigation of those risks is missing.

The most noteworthy elements concern the labels: 'Data security' and 'Attracting talent' risk mitigation.

As for data security, a greater proactivity on the part of companies in the area of risk mitigation and management emerges, both because it is a typical risk of the sector and because it concerns an issue with respect to which companies are seeking to constantly invest in the search for new security tools. To ensure their competitiveness, companies must abandon the wait-and-see attitude that characterises their behaviour concerning the risks inherent in the introduction of new environmental regulations.

Concerning the theme of 'Attracting talent', all companies except one declare they depend on the recruitment and retention of qualified personnel, and failure to attract, train, and retain such personnel could seriously harm the business. However, as for the mitigation of the risk, the information provided is generic and focuses on the relevance of successfully managing the short- and long-term transfer of critical knowledge and skills, including leadership development and succession planning throughout the business.

18.4.3 Governance

If we break down the analysis with regard to the **governance dimension** (see Diagram 18.3 governance risks), we find that companies particularly highlight risks related to supply chain management and supply chain disruption risk, also highlighted by industry sources (2023 aerospace and defence industry outlook), which are reported under the label 'Material Sourcing & Efficiency'. Surprisingly, no firms signal the topic Product Design & Lifecycle Management as the main risk; however, it is sometimes referred to in the label we have introduced as 'New technologies, digital transformation and property rights' based on what is highlighted by industry reports (Deloitte, 2023).

The risk that emerges as most relevant is related to the identification and adoption of new technologies in line with evolving knowledge and customer expectations. Companies are aware that design, manufacture, and service products that incorporate advanced technologies involve risks to respect the timing of delivery or to achieve required regulatory approval. For these reasons, companies adopt a proactive approach to risk mitigation and state that they invest substantial amounts in research and development efforts to pursue advancements in a wide range of technologies, products, and services. With reference to the label 'Business Ethics', we note the awareness of companies that operate in an industry subject to tight government controls and the need to mitigate this risk through employee training programmes

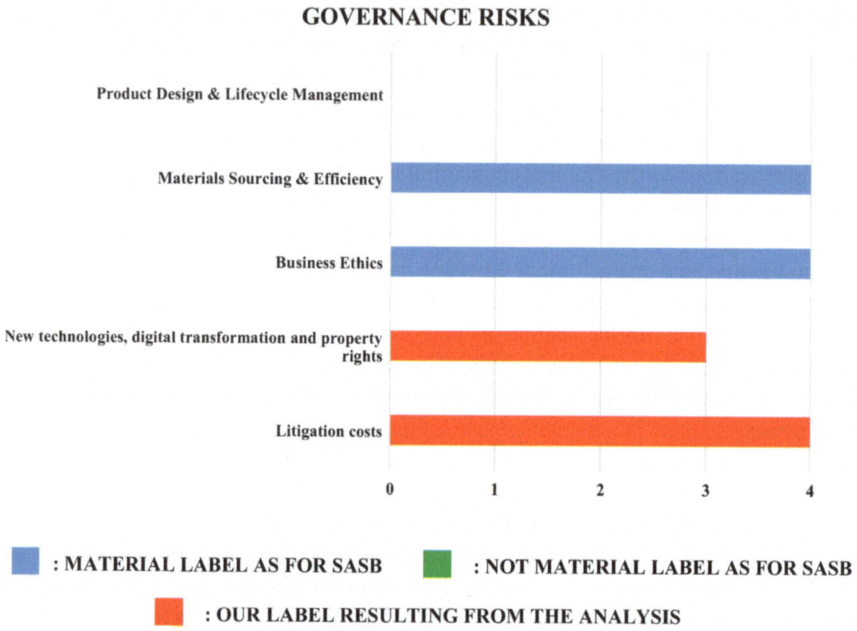

Diagram 18.3 Number of companies disclosing information about governance risks

and compliance control systems that also cover the supply chain. Finally, the label 'Litigation costs', addressing the potential risks of penalties, claims, and lawsuits, emerges as relevant, even if it is not material according to the SASB.

18.5 Concluding Remarks and Future Research

Our concluding remarks address the main findings that have emerged from our analysis.

Our analysis of the 10-K forms of top A&D companies shows that the description of material risks and impacts follows the approach identified by the SEC, which recommends that disclosure should discuss the 'most significant' factors that make the company's securities speculative or risky. Consistently, companies provide information that is forward-looking in nature and that is expected to have a negative impact on the company's financial performance.

With regard to mitigation actions, it is difficult to identify proactivity on the part of companies. In general, the behaviour is passive, indicating possible mitigation actions only when the event that represents a threat occurs but cannot be reasonably estimated ex-ante in terms of occurrence and magnitude of impact. In addition, for some identified risks, no mitigation action is presented because they are either outside the direct control of the company or are completely uncertain and, therefore, not subject to any type of assessment in terms of mitigation/reaction.

We believe that this behaviour is due to the willingness of companies to focus only on those risks with a high degree of uncertainty, which are difficult to predict and mitigate through risk management techniques; this can be explained by the company's liability associated with the Form 10-K and therefore the desire to make clear what is beyond the company's control in order to reduce potential lawsuits and litigation costs.

This would also explain the great uniformity of the information provided by companies in the same sector, which can be explained in light of a mimetic attitude, in order to respond formally to the demands of regulators and investors, but to reduce the cost of information and not to expose themselves to reputational risks or breaches of privacy that could be detrimental to the company's competitiveness. On the other hand, such an attitude also leads to boilerplate information, i.e. information that protects the company, but has no value for analysts and investors.

Proactivity in risk mitigation emerges only for some specific issues: the new regulatory and financial market expectations on ESG risks, ensuring data security, attracting talent, and embracing new technologies. This demonstrates the relevance of risks concerning knowledge governance that characterises the industry and that, from our viewpoint, will require specific deepening at the level of industry-specific ESG standards.

These topics, which are vital for KIBSs, are currently under-investigated and underdeveloped according to current standards such as the European Sustainability Reporting Standards (ESRS, 2023),[10] ISSB standards (2023),[11] and GRI standards. They require in-depth analysis at the sector-specific level.

U.S. and European regulators are taking different approaches to defining the content of companies' ESG disclosures. The different perspectives depend on the primary interests of the governments. In a nutshell, we talk about protecting the stock market in the U.S. and supporting the green transition in Europe.

If the objective is to ensure the efficient functioning of the stock market in line with efficient market theory (Demartini, 2004), the primary interest of the regulator is to ensure that investors have all the information to allocate resources rationally according to their preferences in terms of expected returns, risk, and sensitivity to ESG issues. If, on the other hand, the aim is to promote environmental and social policies in line with the European Green Deal, the primary purpose of the EU Corporate Sustainability Reporting Directive (CSRD) becomes to support the transition process of companies by facilitating the inflow of financial resources from banks, sustainable investors and the allocation of government incentives (Palea & Drogo, 2020).

---

[10] https://www.efrag.org/lab6.

[11] https://www.ifrs.org/supporting-implementation/supporting-materials-for-ifrs-sustainability-disclosure-standards/.

Accordingly, it is worth noting that while US regulation requires companies to provide information about risks, such as factors that could materially affect their results (i.e. cash flows, earnings, and financial position) in the interest of investors, European regulation applies a double materiality approach, requiring companies to provide information about their impact on society as well.

As a result, as we have seen in our analysis, US companies will seek to provide information on the key factors that make the company speculative or risky in order to avoid potential shareholder litigation. European companies, on the other hand, will need to provide ESG information that is material from a risk/opportunity perspective in order to demonstrate how they intend to meet the ESG targets set out in the regulations and in their strategic plans.

Building on these findings, we envisage two possible avenues for future research.

The first concerns the global harmonisation of ESG disclosure. The primary interests of regulators are not aligned, which is reflected in the current debate on the harmonisation of accounting for ESG information and it creates complexity for standard-setters, users, and providers of ESG information.

The second strand of research concerns the impact of new regulatory scenarios on control systems and risk management. As stated in our theoretical background, there is a mutual influence between risk management and risk disclosure, which is noteworthy to be investigated for its practical and research implications. In order to adequately address this latter topic, an in-depth approach using case studies and action research methodologies will be required.

Disclaimer The data that support the findings of this study are available from the corresponding author, upon reasonable request.

References

Aerospace & Defence. (2023). Sustainability Accounting Standard. INDUSTRY STANDARD | VERSION 2023-06.

Ahmad, R. W., Hasan, H., Yaqoob, I., Salah, K., Jayaraman, R., & Omar, M. (2021). Blockchain for aerospace and defense: Opportunities and open research challenges. *Computers & Industrial Engineering, 151*, 106982.

Amel-Zadeh, A., & Serafeim, G. (2018). Why and how investors use ESG information: Evidence from a global survey. *Financial Analysts Journal, 74*(3), 87–103.

Antoncic, M. (2019). Why sustainability? Because risk evolves and risk management should too. *Journal of Risk Management in Financial Institutions, 12*(3), 206–216.

Arif, M., Sajjad, A., Farooq, S., Abrar, M., & Joyo, A. S. (2021). The impact of audit committee attributes on the quality and quantity of environmental, social and governance (ESG) disclosures. *Corporate Governance: The International Journal of Business in Society, 21*(3), 497–514.

Arvidsson, S., & Dumay, J. (2022). Corporate ESG reporting quantity, quality and performance: Where to now for environmental policy and practice? *Business Strategy and the Environment, 31*(3), 1091–1110.

Ball, A., & Craig, R. (2010). Using neo-institutionalism to advance social and environmental accounting. *Critical Perspectives on Accounting, 21*(4), 283–293.

Barney, J. B., & Clark, D. N. (2007). *Resource-based theory: Creating and sustaining competitive advantage*. OUP Oxford.

Beretta, S., & Bozzolan, S. (2004). A framework for the analysis of firm risk communication. *The International Journal of Accounting, 39*(3), 265–288.

Beretta, S., & Bozzolan, S. (2008). Quality versus quantity: The case of forward-looking disclosure. *Journal of Accounting, Auditing & Finance, 23*(3), 333–376.

Brown, S. V., Tian, X., & Wu Tucker, J. (2018). The spillover effect of SEC comment letters on qualitative corporate disclosure: Evidence from the risk factor disclosure. *Contemporary Accounting Research, 35*(2), 622–656.

Campbell, J. L., Chen, H., Dhaliwal, D. S., Lu, H. M., & Steele, L. B. (2014). The information content of mandatory risk factor disclosures in corporate filings. *Review of Accounting Studies, 19*, 396–455.

Christensen, H. B., Hail, L., & Leuz, C. (2021). Mandatory CSR and sustainability reporting: Economic analysis and literature review. *Review of Accounting Studies, 26*(3), 1176–1248.

Cohen, G. (2023). ESG risks and corporate survival. *Environment Systems and Decisions, 43*(1), 16–21.

Cordazzo, M., Papa, M., & Rossi, P. (2017). The interaction between mandatory and voluntary risk disclosure: A comparative study. *Managerial Auditing Journal, 32*(7), 682–714.

Demartini, P. (Ed.). (2004). *Informazione, imprese e mercati finanziari efficienti: spunti di riflessione in una prospettiva multidisciplinare* (Vol. 358). FrancoAngeli.

Demartini, P. & Pagliei, C. (2023). Can we trust ESG ratings? Management Control, Special issue 2.

Dienes, D., Sassen, R., & Fischer, J. (2016). What are the drivers of sustainability reporting? A systematic review. *Sustainability Accounting, Management and Policy Journal, 7*(2), 154–189.

Eisenhardt, K. M., & Martin, J. A. (2000). Dynamic capabilities: What are they? *Strategic Management Journal, 21*(10–11), 1105–1121.

Elshandidy, T., Shrives, P. J., Bamber, M., & Abraham, S. (2018). Risk reporting: A review of the literature and implications for future research. *Journal of Accounting Literature, 40*(1), 54–82.

Gangi, F., Mustilli, M., Daniele, L. M., & Coscia, M. (2022). The sustainable development of the aerospace industry: Drivers and impact of corporate environmental responsibility. *Business Strategy and the Environment, 31*(1), 218–235.

Ghadge, A., Dani, S., & Kalawsky, R. (2010). A framework for managing risks in the aerospace supply chain using systems thinking. In *2010 5th international conference on system of systems engineering* (pp. 1–6). IEEE.

Glazerman, G., & Cohen, J. (2020). "Non-financial" is a misnomer but Doesn't have to be a missed opportunity. *Journal of Applied Corporate Finance, 32*(2), 108–116.

Guthrie, J., & Abeysekera, I. (2006). Content analysis of social, environmental reporting: What is new? *Journal of Human Resource Costing & Accounting, 10*(2), 114–126.

Harasheh, M., & Provasi, R. (2023). A need for assurance: Do internal control systems integrate environmental, social, and governance factors? *Corporate Social Responsibility and Environmental Management, 30*(1), 384–401.

Harper Ho, V. (2020). Non-financial reporting & corporate governance: Explaining American divergence & its implications for disclosure reform. *Accounting, Economics, and Law: A Convivium, 10*(2), 20180043.

Ho, V. H. (2020). Disclosure overload? Lessons for risk disclosure & ESG reporting reform from the regulation SK concept release. *Villanova Law Review, 65*, 67.

Ibrahim, A. E. A., & Hussainey, K. (2019). Developing the narrative risk disclosure measurement. *International Review of Financial Analysis, 64*, 126–144.

Jia, J., Munro, L., & Buckby, S. (2016). A finer-grained approach to assessing the "quality" ("quantity" and "richness") of risk management disclosures. *Managerial Auditing Journal, 31*(8/9), 770–803.

Jones, R. C. (2023). Sustainability reporting and Practitioners' responsibilities. *The CPA Journal, 93*(7/8), 42–47.

Khan, L. (2023). *A framework of critical success factors for implementation of industry 4.0 in aerospace and defense industries*. (Doctoral dissertation University of Central Florida Orlando, Florida).

Krippendorf, K. (1980). *Content analysis: An introduction to its methodology*. Sage Publications.

Madhani, P. M. (2010). Resource based view (RBV) of competitive advantage: An overview. In P. Madhani (Ed.), *Resource based view: Concepts and practices* (pp. 3–22).

Martínez-Ferrero, J., & García-Sánchez, I. M. (2017). Coercive, normative and mimetic isomorphism as determinants of the voluntary assurance of sustainability reports. *International Business Review, 26*(1), 102–118.

Mishra, B. K., Rolland, E., Satpathy, A., & Moore, M. (2019). A framework for enterprise risk identification and management: The resource-based view. *Managerial Auditing Journal, 34*(2), 162–188.

Muller, E., & Doloreux, D. (2009). What we should know about knowledge-intensive business services. *Technology in Society, 31*(1), 64–72.

Palea, V., & Drogo, F. (2020). Carbon emissions and the cost of debt in the eurozone: The role of public policies, climate-related disclosure and corporate governance. *Business Strategy and the Environment, 29*(8), 2953–2972.

Power, M. (2004). The risk management of everything. *The Journal of Risk Finance, 5*(3), 58–65.

Redondo Alamillos, R., & de Mariz, F. (2022). How can European regulation on ESG impact business globally? *Journal of risk and Financial Management, 15*(7), 291.

Rose, A. M. (2020). A response to calls for SEC-mandated ESG disclosure. *Washington University Law Review, 98*, 1821.

Semenova, N. (2021). Management control systems in response to social and environmental risk in large Nordic companies. *International Journal of Corporate Social Responsibility, 6*, 1–11.

Singh, A., Patel, R., & Singh, H. (2022). Recalibration of priorities: Investor preference and Russia-Ukraine conflict. *Finance Research Letters, 50*, 103294.

Truant, E., Corazza, L., & Scagnelli, S. D. (2017). Sustainability and risk disclosure: An exploratory study on sustainability reports. *Sustainability, 9*(4), 636.

Tsang, A., Frost, T., & Cao, H. (2022). Environmental, social, and governance (ESG) disclosure: A literature review. *The British Accounting Review, 55*, 101149.

Yosifova, D., & Petrova-Kirova, M. (2022). The new EU corporate sustainability reporting framework in the context of GRI standards. In *Economic and social development: Book of proceedings* (pp. 85–95).

Zioło, M., Bąk, I., & Spoz, A. (2023). Incorporating ESG risk in companies' business models: State of research and energy sector case studies. *Energies, 16*(4), 1809.

Zucker, L. G. (1987). Institutional theories of organization. *Annual Review of Sociology, 13*(1), 443–464.

Webliography

Yahoo Finance (2023). https://finance.yahoo.com/news/12-best-aerospace-defense-stocks155436380.html

DefenceNews (2023). https://people.defensenews.com/top-100/

Sasb (2023). https://sasb.org/standards/materiality-finder/

ESRS (2023). https://www.efrag.org/lab6

ISSB (2023). https://www.ifrs.org/supporting-implementation/supporting-materials-for-ifrs-sustainability-disclosure-standards/

Deloitte (2023). https://www2.deloitte.com/us/en/pages/manufacturing/articles/aerospace-and-defense-industry-outlook.html

Chapter 19
Double Materiality in Corporate Sustainability: Insights from Italian Companies

Diletta Vito, Lorenzo Leto, Francesca Bernini, and Giuseppe D'Onza

19.1 Introduction[1]

In recent years, an increasing number of firms have published information on sustainability matters to satisfy the demand of a growing number of stakeholders and demonstrate firms' commitment toward sustainable goals. In doing so, they apply the materiality principle (KPMG, 2013).

The Corporate Sustainability Reporting Directive (CSRD) has introduced the concept of double materiality to determine the environmental, social, and governance (ESG) matters to be reported in sustainability statements. Particularly, the double materiality requires companies to report both on how sustainability issues affect their financial performance, position, and development (the "outside-in" perspective) and on their impact on people and the environment (the "inside-out" perspective) (European Commission, 2021).

We are grateful to the Coordinators and members of the SIDREA GdS *Environment, Social, Governance (ESG): rischi, performance, controllo* for helpful comments and suggestions. All errors or omissions are the sole responsibility of the authors.

[1]All the authors contributed to the research and to the writing of the chapter. Specifically, Dr. Diletta Vito wrote Sects. 19.2.1, 19.2.2, 19.4.1, 19.4.3 and 19.5, Dr. Lorenzo Leto wrote Sects. 19.3, 19.4.2 and 19.4.4, Prof. Francesca Bernini wrote Sect. 19.2.3, and Prof. Giuseppe D'Onza wrote Sect. 19.1.

D. Vito (✉) · F. Bernini · G. D'Onza
Department of Economics and Management, University of Pisa, Pisa, Italy
e-mail: diletta.vito@ec.unipi.it; francesca.bernini@unipi.it; giuseppe.donza@unipi.it

L. Leto
Department of Economics, University of Genoa, Genoa, Italy
e-mail: lorenzo.leto@edu.unige.it

N. Castellano et al. (eds.), *Environmental, Social, Governance (ESG)*, SIDREA Series in Accounting and Business Administration,
https://doi.org/10.1007/978-3-031-76618-3_19

Double materiality aims to enhance the relevance and transparency of sustainability reports and increase accountability by making the reports more focused on "what matters" and reducing insignificant information for stakeholders (Lai et al., 2017; Puroila & Mäkelä, 2019; GRI, 2016).

Most of the research on materiality focuses on its key role in determining what information to include and what to exclude in financial statements. For this purpose, standard setters (i.e. IASB, 2018) require preparers to understand what information could influence the decisions of the primary users of financial disclosure, namely the investors, lenders, and other creditors (Brennan & Gray, 2005).

Studies on materiality in sustainability reporting (Edgley et al., 2015; Puroila & Mäkelä, 2019; Dechow, 2023) have highlighted that the principle of materiality requires a reconfiguration in the passage from financial to sustainability reporting. Indeed, the audience of sustainability reports goes beyond investors to include a variety of stakeholders having different views and expectations. Moreover, the logic underpinning such disclosure may differ from the market logic that benefits investors (Edgley et al., 2015) which typically characterizes materiality in financial reporting. These studies also indicate that the materiality assessment process is even more flexible than those applied to prepare and audit financial reporting. This can produce both advantages and disadvantages in terms of the relevance of this report.

With a few exceptions (Higgins et al., 2014; Edgley et al., 2015; Lai et al., 2017), to date, little has been written about how companies conduct materiality assessment in the context of sustainability reporting. These arguments provide a motivation for this study that helps to answer the recent calls for more empirical research on double materiality assessment in the context of sustainability reporting (Baumüller & Sopp, 2021; Fiandrino et al., 2022).

Edgley's study (2014) has highlighted the malleable nature of the materiality concept in the financial reporting context. Particularly, she maintains that its conceptualization and operationalization largely depend on the contextual factors in which the materiality assessment is applied. Researchers agree that decisions on materiality fundamentally remain a matter of judgment and may be legitimately used to accommodate practical problems emerging in specific circumstances (D'Onza, 2021; Macchioni & Maffei, 2021). Other studies have also highlighted that materiality is a social and behavioral phenomenon that varies among companies depending on *who* participates in constructing the meaning of materiality and *to whom* the information is addressed (Carpenter et al., 1994; Eccles et al., 2014; Lai et al., 2017).

All these considerations support the argument that it is likely that the double materiality assessment (DMA) process is unstructured and can be adapted to different situations to achieve diverse objectives. Thus, the exploration of company practices can provide interesting insights to extend our knowledge of this new phenomenon. This is a second motivation encouraging the development of our research.

This study explores *how* the DMA process is performed in three Italian companies focusing on four key aspects of such a process that have been identified basing on the literature review on double materiality presented in Sect. 19.2.2. Particularly, this analysis explores (I) the objectives companies intend to achieve by adopting this assessment, (II) the assessment approaches, (III) the role of stakeholder engagement in the DMA process, and (IV) the organizational units involved.

This study contributes to the literature in different ways. First, it adds to prior research on materiality in the context of sustainability reporting cited in Sect. 19.2.2 by investigating how companies are implementing the double materiality assessment processes. In doing so, the study proposes a theoretical framework to analyze the DMA through four aspects: objectives, approaches, role of stakeholder engagement, and organizational units involved that we have identified based on the review of the relevant literature in this field. Second, it contributes to extending studies on stakeholder engagement (Kujala et al., 2022; O'Riordan & Fairbrass, 2014) within the context of corporate social responsibility to understand how the involvement of stakeholders can improve the DMA process. Third, as mentioned above, this study contributes to answering the recent call for more empirical research on double materiality.

Regarding the practical contribution, the study offers valuable guidance for companies to support practitioners in the implementation of double materiality assessment processes and provides real-world examples. Furthermore, the results of this study can be used by auditors to develop their assurance activities over the DMA process and by standard setters to improve regulations and guidelines.

The chapter is structured as follows: Sect. 19.2 analyzes the recent literature on this topic and provides a brief description of double materiality within the new EU Directive and European Sustainability Reporting Standards (ESRS); Sect. 19.3 outlines the methodology employed; Sect. 19.4 delves into the case studies; Sect. 19.5 discusses the findings along with their implications.

19.2 Research Background

19.2.1 Single Materiality in the Context of Financial Reporting and Auditing

Materiality has been extensively analyzed in accounting research as it is a key qualitative characteristic for the relevance of financial information for external stakeholders (Brennan & Gray, 2005). Materiality has also been analyzed vastly in auditing studies (Messier et al., 2005).

The review of this literature allows us to outline some key characteristics of materiality that are also relevant in the context of sustainability reporting.

One of the most cited definitions of financial materiality dates to 1952 and describes materiality as *a statement, fact, or item whereby its disclosure or the method of giving it expression would be likely to influence the judgment of a reasonable person* (Kohler, 1952, p. 317).

Subsequent definitions (e.g. IFAC, 2005; IASB, 2018) have identified "the reasonable person" (i.e., the primary users of financial statements) by substantially confirming this materiality concept.[2] In line with these definitions, researchers have indicated that the assessment of materiality is a subjective and complex process that requires preparers to place in the perspective of the users to understand what matters to them. Then, these expectations should lead to the production and the disclosure of financial information by avoiding those that are irrelevant to users' decision-making processes (Hicks, 1964; Messier et al., 2005; D'Onza 2021; Macchioni & Maffei, 2021).

This view underlines a kind of moral responsibility underpinning the concept of materiality (Edgley, 2014), as the company should publish all relevant information irrespective of its impact on users. Moreover, the adoption of such a principle should lead the company to limit the information only to those that really matter to the users and avoid insignificant and boilerplate reporting.

Studies on financial materiality have also highlighted that materiality assessments are highly subjective; *professional judgment* plays a fundamental role in them, despite the presence of standards and guidance (Messier et al., 2005). Literature in this field has amply highlighted that preparers and auditors use the malleability nature of this concept to accommodate practical problems (Edgley, 2014). Thus, materiality is inherently secretive, paternalistic, and materialistic and, in some cases, only nominally serves the interests of users of financial information (Brennan & Gray, 2005).

These considerations highlight that materiality is a subjective rather than an objective fact. Such a characteristic is reinforced when materiality is translated from financial to sustainability reporting because, as discussed in the next Sections, preparers should apply their perceptions, opinions, and experience to adapt the materiality assessment process to different objectives.

19.2.2 Double Materiality in the Context of Sustainability Reporting

With the issuance of the CSRD that has proposed the double materiality approach, a growing debate among academics and practitioners is developing about the multiple aspects characterizing this approach. Such a debate has focused on three main interconnected issues: the shifting from a single to a double materiality perspective, the identification and assessment of material matters, and the impact on the company's decision-making process.

Regarding the first issue, studies have argued that this change does not only involve a terminological shift of the materiality concept, but it stems from the necessity to embrace a broader range of stakeholders' interests than in the case of

[2]According to the IASB, information is material if omitting, misstating, or obscuring it could reasonably be expected to influence the decisions that the primary users of general-purpose financial statements make based on those financial statements (IASB, 2018).

financial reporting (e.g., Baumüller & Sopp, 2021; Christensen et al., 2021). They also indicate that this shift reflects the extended reporting scope of sustainability reporting, and it is linked with the need to ensure a more holistic view of a company's economic, ecological, and social performance.

Some commentators argue that the implementation of the double materiality approach can imply higher costs for producing and disclosing sustainability information that can outweigh the benefits (Baumüller & Sopp, 2021). Consequently, a cost/benefit analysis may lead practitioners to give more importance to one dimension of materiality, which, in the beginning stage, is likely to be the traditional financial materiality. Other commentators (Haaker & Freiberg, 2021) argue that the core of the question in such a shift is which relevant time horizon should be considered for making materiality assessments. The double materiality serves the aim of providing investors with information about how a company creates, preserves, or erodes value over the short, medium, and long term. Even if a primarily financial perspective is taken, the concept of double materiality extends this perspective beyond the short-term focus of financial statements to embrace social and environmental issues that can influence financial results in the long term.

The second issue is related to the identification and assessment of material matters (Baumüller & Sopp, 2021; Clark, 2021; de Villiers et al., 2022; Giner & Luque-Vílchez, 2022). Regarding this aspect, a sub-issue concerns the method used to perform double materiality. Several researchers emphasize the need for stakeholder engagement by suggesting that companies may identify material issues by relying on stakeholders' perceptions (Fiandrino et al., 2022; Jones et al., 2016; Torelli et al., 2020). These studies highlight the opportunity to intensify the dialogue with stakeholders to better define and prioritize their information needs. In this way, companies can avoid the risk and cost of missing relevant information, as well as the information overload that occurs when they assess as material certain information that is overly specific and relevant only to a niche of stakeholders (Baumüller & Sopp, 2021; Crovini et al., 2021; Fiandrino et al., 2022). However, relying on stakeholder engagement during the judgment on material matters is not without challenges. For example, Fasan and Mio (2017) point out a conflicting vision of the materiality determination process, in which different stakeholder groups compete to have their issues classified as material, at the expense of other stakeholders. Specifically, their work suggests that the higher the number of the company's stakeholders, the more difficult it will be for the board of directors to decide and disclose sustainability information.

Another sub-issue regards the challenge for preparers of sustainability reports to avoid an oversimplification of the variety of views and expectations of multiple stakeholders in the definition of material sustainability topics. In line with the CSRD requirements, the literature has clarified the need to adopt a broader approach to double materiality by considering material all the matters that may affect the sustainability of the systems in which firms operate (e.g., the environment and society), irrespective of whether these impacts have financially material consequences for the firm (Dechow, 2023).

This approach encloses an ideological conflict between the investors' financial interests and other stakeholders' needs, which leads to a trade-off that may be hard to balance in practice. Moreover, this trade-off adds more complexity to performing double materiality assessment and can also increase the costs for producing sustainability information companies (Giner & Luque-Vílchez, 2022; Clark, 2021; Dechow, 2023; Puroila & Mäkelä, 2019).

Puroila and Mäkelä (2019) point out that the presence of multiple ways to consider, value, and measure the different aspects of sustainability information leads to a lack of universal criteria to encompass all varieties of sustainability issues. Consistent with this, studies support the technical-rational approach to develop structural materiality analysis and suggest relying on quantitative methods for prioritizing sustainability issues (Calabrese et al., 2019).

However, while the technical-rational approach is widely accepted and reinforced by the common use of the materiality matrix for reporting, it is not immune from limitations. For instance, Puroila and Mäkelä (2019) argue that the technical-rational approach portrays the assessment as a neutral and value-free measurement, comparing issues against one another without accounting for the issue related to commeasuring different aspects. Furthermore, the materiality matrix presents the multiple stakeholders as having a unified understanding of what is considered important in corporate sustainability, thereby overlooking the differences and conflicting views among them. The authors claim that rather than relying on the technical-rational approach, which considers materiality as binary, material or immaterial, a "true" stakeholder engagement in materiality assessment for sustainability reporting must explicitly consider a wide variety of issues. They prompt an approach that highlights debate, dialogue, and pluralism in values and goals related to corporate sustainability where varying points of interest are expressed and respected, and conflict can be fostered, instead of unifying stakeholder views with a (false) compromise. The authors name this approach as a critical-dialogic approach, drawing inspiration from the critical-dialogic accounting proposed by Brown and Dillard (2014).

Finally, the last issue is related to the usefulness of double materiality analysis to the company's decision-making processes. In this light, some authors examine the strategic role of double materiality (Beske et al., 2019; Whitehead, 2017). These studies indicate that double materiality analysis may help companies identify the topics that matter to stakeholders and include these assessments in the strategy-setting processes. In this way, firms may increase their legitimacy by meeting stakeholder expectations more effectively.

Besides the strategic role, other studies suggest that materiality considerations may help companies enhance their internal management systems, such as risk management and performance measurement (Fiandrino et al., 2022). This is because a thorough assessment of material matters can provide valuable insights into the most significant risks and opportunities, allowing companies to allocate resources and develop initiatives to mitigate risks and capture opportunities. By integrating materiality into risk management processes, companies can make more informed and targeted decisions to protect and enhance their long-term performance.

Taken together, this evidence highlights an open question in the literature, specifically regarding how the assessment of materiality has empirically evolved to understand the extent, speed, and nature of companies' responsiveness and accountability toward stakeholders' expectations.

19.2.3 The Principle of Double Materiality in the CSRD and ESRS

Starting in 2020, EFRAG was entrusted by the European Commission with the development of the new EU sustainability reporting standards. EFRAG recently approved the final version of the ESRS, which establishes the rules and the requirements for companies to report on the impacts, opportunities, and risks related to sustainability, following the CSRD.

The ratification of the standards marks an important step forward in the definition of a new sustainability reporting system in Europe. Companies involved in the new ESG reporting system must provide a sustainability report regarding their strategies and business models, governance and organization, opportunities and risks related to sustainability, as well as policies, objectives, plans of action, and performances. Stakeholder engagement is critical to the company's ongoing due diligence process and sustainability materiality assessment.

The purpose of sustainability reporting in the EFRAG framework is to provide relevant, faithful, comparable, and reliable information on the material impacts produced by the company's sustainability actions on relevant stakeholders, including the environment, as well as on the risks and opportunities these sustainability commitments generate regarding the companies' ability to create value.

Because of this new perspective of ESG reporting, the concept of double materiality comes into play, also changing the way companies approach sustainability. Before the advent of the new regulations, the materiality analysis was conducted through a materiality matrix useful for defining the sustainability issues that are considered relevant, according to the peculiarities of the entity and its strategy, as well as to the expectations of its stakeholders. To identify the relevant issues, companies generally refer to the Sustainable Development Goals of the UN Agenda 2030 and the indicators proposed by the GRI. It is important to note that identifying the relevant impacts of a company's activity is, on one side, entrusted to the board of directors, and, on the other, it is completed and informed by a dialogue with affected stakeholders. For this reason, it should represent a real strategic activity.

EFRAG provides a more complex definition of double materiality,[3] which represents the basis for sustainability reporting (ESRS 1–2). The concept of double

[3]The previous Directive 2013/34/UE and the NFRD required to report the impacts that sustainability produced on companies' performances, position and development, and on their impact on people and the environment.

materiality encompasses two strictly interrelated dimensions: impacts and financial materiality. EFRAG guidelines (Appendixes of ESRS1) point out that companies and their sustainability reporting, at the same time, impact the external ecosystem (inside-out materiality) and are affected by external factors that can create or destroy value for entities (outside-in materiality). Inside-out materiality is recognized as impact materiality, while outside-in materiality is identified as financial materiality. In this perspective, double materiality is considered the "mathematical union" of these two dimensions. A sustainability issue is consistent with the double materiality principle if it meets the impact perspective of materiality, the financial perspective, or both two perspectives (ESRS1). Since the two dimensions of materiality are interrelated, companies are incentivized to include the concept of sustainability in their business model and, therefore, to enhance or redefine their performance measurement and risk management systems.

ESRS 1 approaches materiality starting with a process of materiality assessment that aims to identify material impacts, risks, and opportunities regarding environmental, social, and governance issues from the impact or the financial materiality perspective or both. An issue is considered as "material" if it meets the criteria of impact materiality and/or the criteria of financial materiality (Fig. 19.1). Ultimately, the assessment process aims to identify the issues to be reported in the sustainability report. To support the materiality assessment, EFRAG shows a list of material topics

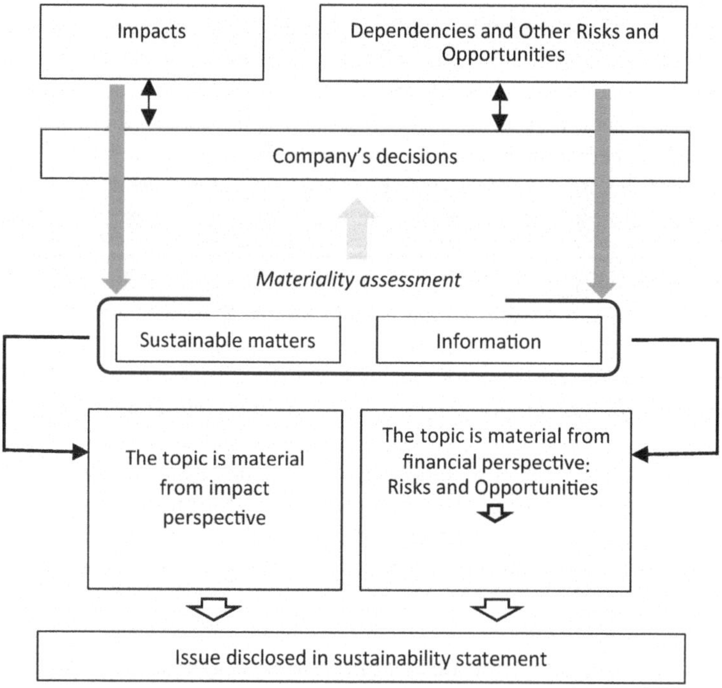

Fig. 19.1 Impacts and financial materiality. Source: adapted from Sanchez Danes et al. (2023)

and information that should be reported, under the perspective of double materiality, which is organized into topics (i.e. ESG), sub-topics (i.e. climate change), and sub-sub-topics (i.e. emissions).

The materiality of the impacts pertains to the actual or the potential, positive or negative, material impacts that an organization's activity produces on society and the environment over the short, medium, and long term. It includes impacts that are caused by the company and those directly linked to its operations, products, or services along the entire value chain. In particular, the impacts to be considered are not restricted to the most evident links between the organization and the other entities nor to direct contractual linkages.

The assessment of impact materiality consists of a three-step process that starts from the analysis of the context where the company realizes its activities, defines its business relationships and the impacts that the activities produce on its key stakeholders. The second step consists of the recognition of the actual and potential impacts. This step contemplates the engagement of affected stakeholders and/or other sustainability experts. When negative impacts are detected, impact materiality should be assessed by using parameters including both the severity of actual impacts, shaped by scale (level of seriousness), scope (width), and remediability (possibility of restoring the environment or the affected people) of the impact, and the severity of potential negative impacts. The materiality of positive impacts is measured on the scale and scope of the actual impacts and the scale, scope, and likelihood of the potential impacts. The materiality of both positive and negative impacts should be assessed, and both negative and positive material impacts should be reported. The third step assesses the materiality of the impacts to identify the material matters to be reported in the sustainability statement. To define the eligibility of a matter for being included in the reports, EFRAG suggests companies determine adequate thresholds.

Financial materiality regards the effects of sustainability on financial parameters. The inclusion of financial materiality in the sustainability reports represents an extension of the concept of materiality which aims to enclose information about sustainability outcomes on financial statements.

The assessment of the financial materiality aims to identify sustainability issues that are relevant for primary users of financial reports and that are useful for potential investors in making decisions related to financing the company. A piece of information is material if its omission may compromise the decision-making of sustainability statement users. The issue of sustainability is relevant from a financial point of view if it determines or can determine substantial effects on cash flows, cost of capital, or access to financing of the company, CAPEX, and other financial items.

Risks and opportunities from the perspective of financial materiality may arise from impacts and dependencies on natural and social resources or factors, such as exposure to climate hazards or regulation changes that refer to systemic risk. In the financial materiality perspective, risks contribute to generate a negative deviation in future expected positive cash flows or to increasing deviations in future expected negative cash flows and/or contribute to negative deviation from an expected change in capital that is not documented in the financial statement, while opportunities have the opposite effects. To evaluate the materiality of these risks and opportunities, companies should consider the combination of the possibility that the risk or the opportunity occurs and the potential magnitude of their financial effects, by adopting adequate thresholds.

Finally, the assessment will involve the so-called "material impacts or risks arising from actions to address sustainability matters."

Although double materiality emerges in the field of disclosure studies, it also significantly impacts companies' attempts toward sustainability. Thus, it is reasonable to consider the new perspectives proposed by CRSD as an incentive for companies to consider ESG commitment not only as a response to stakeholders' pressure (Ferrón-Vílchez et al., 2021) or as a lever to maintain or develop competitiveness on the markets (Cennamo et al., 2009) but also as a strategy capable of impacting on performances and value. From this perspective, the development of performance measurement and risk management systems can be encouraged by the regulatory framework that orients companies toward double materiality.

19.3 Research Design and Methodology

19.3.1 The Theoretical Framework for Case Analysis

To guide the analysis and interpretation of data collected in our case studies, the research project focuses on four key aspects of the double materiality assessment process, which have been identified through the review of the literature reported in Sect. 19.2.2. These aspects are: (I) the objectives companies want to achieve through the adoption of this assessment, (II) the approaches firms employ for its implementation, (III) the role of stakeholder engagement in the DMA process, and (IV) the organizational units involved in the process.

The first element regards the objectives that companies seek to achieve through the double materiality assessment process. Previous studies on materiality in the context of sustainability reporting (Lai et al., 2017; Baumüller & Sopp, 2021) indicate some potential objectives that companies can achieve in performing the DMA process.

At a basic level, this assessment may be performed to meet regulatory requirements with reporting standards. Specifically, this objective may be limited to the identification of those ESG topics that matter for the organization and its stakeholders with the exclusive intent to help preparers define the content of sustainability reports. A second objective may consist of applying the DMA to identify risks and opportunities and what really matters for stakeholders to support not only reporting issues but also to receive inputs for the sustainability strategy formulation. In this perspective, this assessment becomes a governance tool and informs decision-making processes regarding the allocation of companies' resources (Fiandrino et al., 2022). A third objective may regard the use of the DMA process for the enhancement of risk management or performance measurement systems or both. Thus, the DMA process, also through the involvement of stakeholders, can help the company to identify ESG key performance and risk indicators in order to extend the monitoring of performance and risks to the environmental and social dimensions of the company's business model (Guix & Font, 2020; Edgley et al., 2015; George et al., 2016).

The second element the research team has analyzed in this chapter regards the approaches used to perform the double materiality assessment process. Studies indicate that this process can be performed through two different approaches: a quantitative "technical-rational" or a qualitative "critical-dialogic" (Puroila & Mäkelä, 2019). These approaches differ in terms of dynamics, reasons, and organizational units involved.

The technical-rational approach, which is still the one most supported by the literature, aims to translate the sustainability issues into measurable components (Calabrese et al., 2019). This approach is compromise-oriented since it accommodates the diverse interests of stakeholders by balancing the differences between them to meet their information needs. It is guided by corporate strategies and leans on established industry norms, viewing sustainability mainly through the lens of risk management and business opportunity (Boiral & Henri, 2017).

The critical-dialogic approach, on the other hand, emphasizes a more inclusive stakeholder engagement, recognizing the diversity and pluralism of stakeholder perspectives (Puroila & Mäkelä, 2019). It promotes a more democratic and transparent process, where materiality is not merely a technical exercise but a sociopolitical construct that embraces experimental learning and ongoing debate. This approach aims to better address the broader complexities of sustainable development and connected societal impacts.

Closely related to the approaches that companies follow, the third element analyzed in this study regards the way stakeholders are engaged and the influence they exercise during the development of the double materiality assessment (Puroila & Mäkelä, 2019). Specifically, in the interaction with their stakeholders, companies must choose which group of stakeholders should involve in the analysis of sustainability matters, the level of their involvement, and how to use their inputs in the DMA process. Furthermore, this study examines the challenges and complexities of engaging various stakeholders, each with distinct interests and viewpoints, to understand how these elements together influence the outcomes and effectiveness of double materiality assessments (Fasan & Mio, 2017).

Finally, a fourth element regards the identification of organizational units that have the responsibility to carry out the DMA process. Previous studies on the analysis of materiality in the context of sustainability reporting (Lai et al., 2017; Stubbs & Higgins, 2014) indicate that the organizational units involved may differ among companies. Specifically, the DMA process can be managed by a single department (e.g. CSR, investor relation, communication) or by an inter-departmental team composed of members with different expertise. Identifying who holds the task for conducting the DMA could improve the understanding of what skills and competencies the company use to achieve the planned objectives and develop the approaches used to carry out such evaluations.

19.3.2 Cases Selection, Data Collection, and Analysis

This study explores the DMA process in the context of preparing and disclosing sustainability information. To conduct this research, we employed a multiple-case study analysis to gain an extensive and in-depth description of how companies are implementing the new concept of double materiality assessment in their real-life context (Yin, 2014).

We developed our analysis in a single country (i.e., Italy) to avoid the results of our analysis being influenced by the political, cultural, and regulatory differences existing in different countries. Prior studies on sustainability practices (Mio et al., 2015) show that differences in cultural variables may influence sustainability reporting practices, especially in a regime of voluntary reporting.

Italian context is considered suitable for analyzing companies' behaviors in terms of sustainability. In fact, literature (Clementino & Perkins, 2021) recognizes that Italian companies are reactive to ESG-related issues (Ormazabal & Sarriegi, 2014) and, at the same time, the number of companies that implement sustainability reporting and assurance is increasing (Larrinaga et al., 2020; Romolini et al., 2014). Moreover, Italy is a civil law country where particular attention to stakeholders' involvement is recognized. This approach toward a dialogue with stakeholders is also reflected in how Italian companies manage and approach sustainability (Habisch et al., 2011).

In this study, we adopted the theoretical sampling as suggested by Eisenhardt and Graebner (2007). Thus, we selected cases for their richness concerning the theme of double materiality assessment and for the ease of accessing the key internal stakeholders and organizational documents. It was a prerequisite for choosing the cases that they have either recently conducted or are currently conducting the double materiality assessment. Moreover, we chose to select cases for which double materiality assessment is voluntary at the time of the research but is expected to become mandatory within the next 3 years according to the CSRD requirement.

Following our research objectives and following Yin's (2014) guidance, we opted for three case studies. The selected case studies are all Italian companies, each operating in distinct industrial sectors, under the recommendation by Eisenhardt and Graebner (2007) (more details in Table 19.1).

Concerning the data collection, we used multiple data sources to enhance the validity of the research (Eisenhardt, 1989). Initially, we collected data through semi-structured interviews, each lasting approximately 45 min, with three key individuals from each organization (see Table 19.1), resulting in a total of nine interviews.

Specifically, the interviewees were identified by asking the companies to indicate those persons who are responsible for preparing the sustainability reports and carrying out the DMA process. These persons differ among companies. In company 1, they are the sustainability director (an independent member of the Board of directors), the CFO and the risk manager. For company 2, we interviewed the CFO, the communication department, and the controller, while for company 3 the interviews were conducted with the sustainability director (an independent member

Table 19.1 Case studies' description

		Company 1	*Company 2*	*Company 3*
Case studies general information	*Ownership Structure*	Listed Company	Joint venture	Private Company
	Major Shareholders	Founder family	Founder family	Founder families
	Dimension (No. of employees)	200	1500	7000
	Industry	Light mechanical	Consumer goods	Tissue papers
	Interviewees	Sustainability director, investor relator and risk manager	CFO, communication department and controller	Sustainability director, CSR department and controller

Source: Authors' elaboration

of the Board of directors), the CSR department and the controller. All the interviews line that took place between March and September 2023 were conducted online using common video-conferencing tools.

To facilitate the interviews, we developed a questionnaire that included both closed and open-ended questions. This questionnaire was sent to the interviewees prior to the scheduled meetings. The list of questions was grouped into six sections, which specifically regard:

a) General information about the company and the way the sustainability issues are approached;
b) Information regarding the sustainability reporting process;
c) The double materiality assessment process and the objectives pursued through DMA;
d) The approach followed to perform the DMA process;
e) The way stakeholders are engaged in sustainability and DMA process;
f) Questions on the organizational units involved.

Each section includes detailed questions. For example, the questions regarding stakeholder engagement include the following: *Does the company include stakeholders in the sustainability reporting process? Which stakeholders? Have been identified after a mapping? What tools are used to engage stakeholders? How is the company using stakeholders' inputs?*

The interviews were recorded, transcribed, and coded using the theoretical framework outlined in Sect. 19.3.1. Specifically, the research team performs a thematic analysis for coding the interviews' transcriptions (Gioia et al., 2013) and then to identify and report themes regarding the four key aspects of the DMA process: objectives, approaches, stakeholder engagement, and organizational units involved. The research team used a mixed method for coding. To verify and validate data obtained through the interview, the research team also analyzed the organization's sustainability reports and other internal documents (e.g., internal procedures for the DMA process) when available and made accessible to researchers.

19.4 Case Studies Analysis

19.4.1 The Objectives of Double Materiality Assessment

The companies analyzed aim to achieve different objectives in conducting the double materiality assessment process. Our analysis reveals that compliance with the sustainability reporting standards constitutes the first objective that companies intend to achieve through the DMA.

For example, the interviewees working for Company 3 indicated that "*the double materiality assessment that the company is currently performing in a voluntary way will serve to address future regulatory reporting standards.*" Similarly, the CFO of Company 1, even though it has not yet completed the double materiality assessment, recognized that "*this task is essential for the company and must be completed within the next 3 years to proactively prepare and ensure compliance with evolving regulatory standards.*"

Some of the interviewees indicated that using the results of the DMA process only to comply with the ESRS is not efficient as, in this way, the costs of this process outweighed the benefits. In this respect, the sustainability director of Company 3 stated that "*we will not repeat this task in the upcoming years just to comply with ESRS. It proved to be expensive in terms of time and resources.*" This decision is linked to how Company 3 is using the outcomes of the double materiality assessment: "*at the moment, the company is not incorporating the results of the double materiality assessment as input for the decision-making process.*" However, he recognized that "*if the company will use the double materiality assessment as input for its sustainability strategy, we should repeat the DMA process on a regular basis.*"

The CFO of Company 2 stated that "*Our CEO views the materiality analysis as a source of data that can help the development of the sustainability strategy. We decided to incorporate the suggestions from our consultants... and use double materiality to identify the most relevant environmental, social, and governance (ESG) matters for our primary stakeholders...in this way, once we understand what matters for them, we can redesign our sustainability strategy.*" Despite Company 2 recognizing that the DMA process "*is challenging and time-consuming,*" it expects to yield benefits for the company's long-term results in terms of enhanced value and reputation.

Concerning the connection between double materiality assessment and management systems, interviews highlighted a two-sided relationship. The sustainability director of Company 1 indicates "*the objective is to use the results of our double materiality analysis to orientate risk management and performance measurement systems toward sustainability.... Now, risk and performance indicators are only financially oriented... In this way, we can develop at the board level an ESG mindset by integrating strategy, risk, and performance measurement systems.*" In this case, even though double materiality assessment is at the beginning, the objective is that it will serve as a management tool supporting strategy formulation as well as risk management and performance measurement systems. Conversely, Company 3 adopted an opposite approach, where management systems provide input to double materiality assessment. In this regard, the head of the sustainability department mentioned "*the sustainability team uses the risk identification previously undertaken by the company's risk management function for conducting the double materiality analysis.... specifically, to analyze the impact of ESG issues on the external ecosystem (inside-out materiality).*" He suggested that this process was initially adopted to lower the cost of the analysis.

19.4.2 The Approaches to Double Materiality

The analysis of the interviews' findings indicates that companies are evaluating different approaches to perform the DMA process. The uncertainty regarding the approaches to follow may depend on the motivations driving companies to report on ESG matters. For example, Company 1 has decided to voluntarily publish sustainability reporting driven by requests for ESG information coming from its institutional investors. This company, whose double materiality assessment has not yet been completed, has decided to start with this category of stakeholders to identify the material sustainability matters.

As claimed by the investor relator: "*the reason behind this choice is that in the last years, institutional investors are demanding more information on how the company is managing the ESG risks linked with its business model...thus, involving them is an opportunity to know what they expect our company does for sustainability... before understanding what information they want to be disclosed.*" Specifically, as Company 1 produces loudspeakers, the interviews with institutional investors have revealed their increasing expectations that the company manages the sustainability issues at the end of the life of its products to minimize environmental impacts (for example, through the recycling and reuse of rare-hearth minerals) and protect the company's reputation. To date, the assessment of these stakeholders' needs was carried out qualitatively, as suggested by the critical-dialogic approach, by gathering impressions directly from stakeholders and not turned them into metrics.

For Company 2, the double materiality analysis follows a technical-rational approach, evidenced by the creation of a materiality matrix and the adoption, in its development, of CSRD guidelines. Not by chance, the company employed a structured approach to sustainability reporting based on the GRI standards. The company carried out materiality analysis in four steps: (1) stakeholder mapping, (2) stakeholder engagement, (3) synthesis and interpretation of results, and (4) synching with SDGs. To develop the matrix, the company adopted a structured stakeholder engagement process as described in Sect. 5.2. As the Communication Department Director affirmed: "*it was a significant effort, as we had to conduct a survey involving over 400 stakeholders. Fortunately, the high response rate enabled us to map their expectations satisfactorily."*

Despite having shown a longer commitment to sustainability principles than the others, dating back over 15 years, Company 3 has only recently completed its first double materiality assessment. The company has demonstrated a commitment to sustainability that extends beyond compliance and regulatory mandates. As noted by the sustainability director: "*when the company set its objectives in 2008, specifically related to decarbonization (an ambitious target for an energy-intensive business with no public interest and solely family-owned investors) it reflected a decision initiated and promoted only by the founders."*

Company 3, to conduct the double materiality analysis, uses a methodological approach based on the novelties introduced by the GRI 3 and adapts it to integrate the guidelines for building double materiality according to the ESRS. Specifically, it implements a structured process divided into four steps: 1. understanding of the context of reference; 2. identification of the impacts; 3. assessment of their significance; 4. prioritization.

Although Company 3 has adopted a technical-rational approach in developing a materiality matrix, it has also conducted interviews to understand the significance of each identified issue and impact. In these interviews, as the sustainability director of the company claimed: "*stakeholders, including suppliers, customers, NGOs, local communities, and investors, were asked to assess key issues based on their economic, environmental, and societal impacts. The evaluation focused on the scope, relevance, and remediation potential of these impacts."*

This method of directly and fully gathering stakeholders' perspectives and opinions aligns more with a critical-dialogic approach.

19.4.3 The Role of Stakeholder Engagement

Stakeholder engagement is an activity in the DMA process that the company analyzed is putting in place. Our results suggest that in all three cases, stakeholders were pivotal in raising sustainability awareness across organizations. However, several differences emerged between the three organizations.

The first difference is related to the group of stakeholders whose perceptions and interests seem to prevail over those of the other groups. Company 1 recognized the prevailing interests of investors, Company 2 focused more on costumers, but they also involve suppliers and other stakeholders' categories (such as owners and banks), while Company 3 primarily involved internal stakeholders but subsequently extend the analysis to external stakeholders.

The companies' emphasis on specific stakeholder groups resulted in different sustainability priorities. For instance, Company 1 draws attention to environmental impacts and certification maintenance (e.g., ISO). Company 2 identified high relevance in factors such as packaging and plastic use, as well as product quality and safety. Company 3 prioritizes factors like the proper management of resources, reduction of emissions into the atmosphere, and the health and safety of workers.

The second difference refers to the extent to which stakeholder engagement was conducted. Company 1 did not adopt a structured process to investigate stakeholders' perceptions. In this case, the company relied on informal meetings with investors, which revealed that their interests were shifting toward sustainability matters. On the contrary, Company 2 conducted a clearly defined stakeholder engagement process. Firstly, the company identified, mapped, and prioritized the most relevant stakeholders to engage in the materiality analysis. Then, the company conducted surveys with a sample of each group of identified stakeholders. Finally, it analyzed the answers and identified the materiality topics relevant to the respondents. Similarly, Company 3 conducted one-to-one interviews with the company's stakeholders and management to assess impacts, risks, and opportunities.

Despite the differences mentioned above, our analysis highlighted dialogue with stakeholders as a common element of stakeholder engagement within the three cases, albeit with different applications. Company 1 regularly meets with investors to investigate their interests and gain awareness of potential preference shifts. Company 3 stated that "*the dialogue with stakeholders is continuous. We discuss the most relevant topics and carry out numerous engagement initiatives. In this regard, the company selects the most appropriate methods and tools depending on the topics covered, frequency and intensity of the relationships and level of knowledge on the topics.*" Company 2 considers the dialogue with stakeholders a corporate value that inspires the corporate strategies to create a sustainable system able to promptly respond to current social and environmental challenges. In this regard, the company said that "w*e have a distinctive feature, which is an open dialogue with stakeholders and, more generally, with the world outside, to be inspired and channel its action in the right way.*"

Finally, companies pointed out that stakeholder engagement is not without challenges. All three cases emphasized the complexity of balancing stakeholders' interests and preferences, particularly in situations where they were geographically distant. In the case of Company 1, the most relevant challenge is balancing the interests of investors (located in Europe) with the interests of suppliers (located in the East). The differences in country regulations, cultures, and values often translate into different and conflicting preferences. In this regard, the investor relator of Company 1 stated: "*often, we must balance different and conflicting interests. It's not an easy task, but we must necessarily try to resolve this trade-off because it is only in this way that we can pursue our goal of value creation.*" Similarly, Company 2 emphasized that balancing interests and values is a daily challenge for the company due to its ownership structure, which combines an Italian family as major shareholders with an American multinational company as a key partner. As the CFO stated: "*this peculiarity has a significant impact on financial and sustainability reporting since it is evident that two different perspectives will need to be taken into account, and they often do not closely coincide.*"

19.4.4 The Organizational Units Involved in the Double Materiality Assessment

Regarding the organizational units involved in the double materiality assessments, in Company 1 the definition of responsibility and the interaction among different units/persons is an ongoing process. As said in Sects. 19.4.2 and 19.4.3, the investor relator has conducted interviews with institutional investors and is continuing the process by engaging other stakeholders: suppliers and customers. The company had appointed an independent director whose role is to guide the board of directors and management in integrating sustainability practices into the company's business strategies. The risk manager is also involved in the process to provide the independent director with information about how ESG risks are managed. The objective for the near future involves strong coordination among these individuals to integrate the results of the materiality assessment into the strategic and operational plans.

Company 2 has created a dedicated Sustainability Team, made up of three people with different educational backgrounds (i.e., environmental engineering, communication science, and business administration) within the communications department responsible for performing the double materiality assessment. As highlighted by the interviewees, this team plays a crucial role in spreading the sustainability culture throughout the organization, aligning related activities across different teams, and monitoring related KPIs. The controller is also involved in the process of designing and improving the performance measurement of ESG objectives. The sustainability team is also in charge of collecting, analyzing, and reporting sustainability information and data used to develop sustainability reports.

Company 3 changed the organizational units responsible for sustainability reporting over the years. Initially, the responsibility was held by the Human Resources department. However, in 2015, the company shifted the responsibility to a newly established CSR office within the Communications department. Further advancing its commitment, Company 3 introduced a department dedicated exclusively to environmental sustainability, staffed with specialists in carbon footprint reporting and ESG indicators. This department is currently responsible for conducting the double materiality assessment.

19.5 Discussion and Conclusions

The analysis of DMA processes in the selected Italian companies shows a variegate and dynamic landscape of objectives, approaches, the role of stakeholder engagement, and the organizational units involved. This is probably due to the time of our study, since DMA is still in a nascent stage and there are no established practices, organizations are exploring several possible alternatives to perform the DMA process.

Regarding the *objectives* of the DMA process, in line with Baumüller and Sopp (2021), our findings indicate that even though organizations perform double materiality assessments to demonstrate compliance with the ESRS, this represents only the minimum and initial objective. Our results indicate that the organization's view of DMA goes beyond the regulatory compliance as they are working to link the DMA with sustainability strategy decision-making and sustainability-oriented management control systems.

These results provide support to prior studies suggesting that materiality assessment may be used to reinforce the orientation of organizations' strategies, risk management, and performance measurement toward ESG goals (Guix & Font, 2020; Edgley et al., 2015; George et al., 2016). Our findings indicate that while the outputs of the DMA process can help to identify what really matters for stakeholders to redesign company's sustainability strategy, the linkage between DMA and internal management systems can follow different ways and directions. With specific regard to risk management and performance measurement systems, when companies have already developed these systems taking into consideration the ESG issues, the information provided by these systems can support the inside-out materiality assessment (DMA) to analyze the company's impact on people and environment. In other circumstances, when these systems are designed to focus on financial risks and performance, the DMA process can provide inputs to expand the risk and performance analysis incorporating ESG issues in these systems. In line with the considerations of a recent study on materiality in the context of sustainability reporting (Fiandrino et al., 2022), we believe that our results can help the development of future studies that aim to investigate how to incorporate ESG issues into risk management and performance measurement systems.

Consistently with prior research (e.g., Calabrese et al., 2019; Puroila & Mäkelä, 2019), our study confirms the prevalence of the technical-rational approach to perform DMA. Despite literature highlighting the adoption of material matrices has weaknesses (Puroila & Mäkelä, 2019), our analysis reveals a predominance in the use of these tools, in line with the technical-rational approach. However, the analysis reveals that companies are aware of the necessity to include a more qualitative approach (i.e., critical-dialogic) to better address the broader complexities of sustainable development and also consider qualitative issues that cannot be translated into metrics and quantitative indicators.

Moreover, the study highlights that companies acknowledge stakeholders as influential in shaping sustainability priorities. Indeed, all three cases relied on stakeholder engagement practices to identify material issues, in accordance with suggestions of prior literature (Fiandrino et al., 2022; Jones et al., 2016; Torelli et al., 2020). In this respect, the relevance of the dialogue between companies and their stakeholders is well recognized and used in all cases to overcome challenges of balancing diverse interests (Baumüller & Sopp, 2021; Crovini et al., 2021; Fiandrino et al., 2022).

Regarding the organizational units involved in the DMA process, overall, our analysis reveals that companies are modifying their organizational structures to integrate sustainability by including the DMA in their business processes. The paths that organizations follow in this change may diverge among companies. Our analyses show that companies (in our study Company 1 and 3) have voluntarily appointed a sustainability director to increase the Board expertise regarding sustainability. This can help to favor the integration of CSR in company strategies, and in this perspective, the results of DMA can provide useful inputs for strategy setting. Similarly to recent empirical research (Risi et al., 2022), our results also indicate that the integration of CSR in business operations can be achieved either through the establishment of a centralized CSR department which has the responsibility for DMA and other CSR processes or by following a decentralized model in which different organizational units (i.e. investor relator, risk managers, controller) cooperate in implementing DMA and other CSR practices.

By conducting an explorative analysis, this study can offer insights to develop future research. First, the framework used in this study to examine the DMA process enriches the proposals of theoretical frameworks (e.g. Eccles & Krzus, 2014) that future studies may use to perform the analysis of double materiality in the context of sustainability reporting, also using quantitative research methods helping the generalizability of results. Second, it also provides initial insights into the integration of stakeholder engagement in the DMA process. Our finding indicates that this can represent an initial stage in the process of involving the analysis of stakeholders' expectations into the organization sustainability strategies and to favor the greater orientation of management systems, like risk management and performance measurement toward ESG (Leto & Vito, 2023). Future studies can expand on this analysis, as the integration of ESG into management systems can pave the way for future research projects.

From a practical perspective, this study can be useful for companies, regulators, and standard setters. Companies can use these findings to design and implement the ESRS guideline regarding double materiality. The analysis of our case studies can also be used to perform benchmarking and to improve the DMA process. The study also provides valuable insights for regulators and standard setters by highlighting how companies are translating policies and requirements into real-world practices.

This study also has limitations that may provide avenues for future studies. It examines only three companies, which might limit the diversity of experiences and perspectives. Their specific contexts, industry landscapes, and governance structures might limit the generalizability of these insights to other organizations. Including a more extensive range of cases across various industries or regions could offer a broader understanding of challenges and best practices in adopting double materiality. Furthermore, the study delves into the early stages of adopting double-materiality assessments, but it might lack a comprehensive exploration of the challenges and complexities encountered throughout the implementation process. A deeper examination of barriers, failures, or resistance within the organizations could provide a more nuanced understanding.

References

Baumüller, J., & Sopp, K. (2021). Double materiality and the shift from non-financial to European sustainability reporting: Review, outlook and implications. *Journal of Applied Accounting Research, 23*(1), 8–28. https://doi.org/10.1108/JAAR-04-2021-0114

Beske, F., Haustein, E., & Lorson, P. C. (2019). Materiality analysis in sustainability and integrated reports. *Sustainability Accounting, Management and Policy Journal, 11*(1), 162–186. https://doi.org/10.1108/SAMPJ-12-2018-0343

Boiral, O., & Henri, J. F. (2017). Is sustainability performance comparable? A study of GRI reports of mining organizations. *Business & Society, 56*(2), 283–317.

Brennan, N., & Gray, S. J. (2005). The impact of materiality: Accounting's best kept secret. *Asian Academy of Management Journal of Accounting and Finance (AAMJAF), 1*(1), 1–30.

Brown, J., & Dillard, J. (2014). Integrated reporting: On the need for broadening out and opening up. *Accounting, Auditing & Accountability Journal, 27*(7), 1120–1156. https://doi.org/10.1108/AAAJ-04-2013-1313

Calabrese, A., Costa, R., Ghiron, N., & Menichini, T. (2019). Materiality analysis in sustainability reporting: A tool for directing corporate sustainability towards emerging economic, environmental and social opportunities. *Technological and Economic Development of Economy, 25*, 1–23. https://doi.org/10.3846/tede.2019.10550

Carpenter, G. S., Glazer, R., & Nakamoto, K. (1994). Meaningful brands from meaningless differentiation: The dependence on irrelevant attributes. *Journal of Marketing Research, 31*(3), 339–350. https://doi.org/10.2307/3152221

Cennamo, C., Berrone, P., & Gomez-Mejia, L. R. (2009). Does stakeholder management have a dark side? *Journal of Business Ethics, 89*(4), 491–507. https://doi.org/10.1007/s10551-008-0012-x

Christensen, H. B., Hail, L., & Leuz, C. (2021). Mandatory CSR and sustainability reporting: Economic analysis and literature review. *Review of Accounting Studies, 26*(3), 1176–1248. https://doi.org/10.1007/s11142-021-09609-5

Clark, C. (2021). How do standard setters define materiality and why does it matter? *Business Ethics: A European Review, 30*, 378–391. https://doi.org/10.1111/beer.12351

Clementino, E., & Perkins, R. (2021). How do companies respond to environmental, social and governance (ESG) ratings? Evidence from Italy. *Journal of Business Ethics, 171*, 379–397. https://doi.org/10.1007/s10551-020-04441-4

Crovini, C., Schaper, S., & Simoni, L. (2021). Dynamic accountability and the role of risk reporting during a global pandemic. *Accounting, Auditing & Accountability Journal, 35*(1), 169–185. https://doi.org/10.1108/AAAJ-08-2020-4793

D'Onza, G. (2021). Il principio di materiality nel bilancio e nella revisione contabile: una parentesi ancora aperta. In D. Mancini, G. D'Onza, & C. Caserio (Eds.), *Sistemi informativi e revisione aziendale, Scritti in onore di L. Marchi*. Giappichelli Editore, Torino. ISBN 978-88-921-9530-1.

de Villiers, C., La, T. M., & Molinari, M. (2022). The global reporting Initiative's (GRI) past, present and future: Critical reflections and a research agenda on sustainability reporting (standard-setting). *Pacific Accounting Review, 34*(5), 728–747. https://doi.org/10.1108/PAR-02-2022-0034

Dechow, P. M. (2023). Understanding the sustainability reporting landscape and research opportunities in accounting. *Accounting Review, 98*(5), 481–493. https://doi.org/10.2308/TAR-2023-0145

Eccles, R. G., Ioannou, I., & Serafeim, G. (2014). The impact of corporate sustainability on organizational processes and performance. *Management Science, 60*(11), 2835–2857.

Eccles, R. G., & Krzus, M. P. (2014). *The integrated reporting movement: Meaning, momentum, motives, and materiality*. John Wiley & Sons. ISBN: 978-1-118-64698-4.

Edgley, C. (2014). A genealogy of accounting materiality. *Critical Perspectives on Accounting, 25*(3), 255–271. https://doi.org/10.1016/j.cpa.2013.06.001

Edgley, C., Jones, M. J., & Atkins, J. (2015). The adoption of the materiality concept in social and environmental reporting assurance: A field study approach. *The British Accounting Review, 47*(1), 1–18. https://doi.org/10.1016/j.bar.2014.11.001
Eisenhardt, K. M. (1989). Building theories from case study research. *Academy of Management Review, 14*(4), 532–550. https://doi.org/10.5465/amr.1989.4308385
Eisenhardt, K. M., & Graebner, M. E. (2007). Theory building from cases: Opportunities and challenges. *Academy of Management Journal, 50*(1), 25–32. Scopus. https://doi.org/10.5465/AMJ.2007.24160888
European Commission. (2021). Proposal for a directive of the European Parliament and of the Council amending directive 2013/34/EU, Directive 2004/109/EC, Directive 2006/43/EC and Regulation (EU) No 537/2014, as regards corporate sustainability reporting, COM (2021) 189 final, 2021/ 0104 (COD).
Fasan, M., & Mio, C. (2017). Fostering stakeholder engagement: The role of materiality disclosure in integrated reporting. *Business Strategy & the Environment (John Wiley & Sons, Inc), 26*(3), 288–305. https://doi.org/10.1002/bse.1917
Ferrón-Vílchez, V., Valero-Gil, J., & Suárez-Perales, I. (2021). How does greenwashing influence managers' decision-making? An experimental approach under stakeholder view. *Corporate Social Responsibility and Environmental Management, 28*(2), 860–880. https://doi.org/10.1002/csr.2095
Fiandrino, S., Tonelli, A., & Devalle, A. (2022). Sustainability materiality research: A systematic literature review of methods, theories and academic themes. *Qualitative Research in Accounting & Management, 19*(5), 665–695. https://doi.org/10.1108/QRAM-07-2021-0141
George, R. A., Siti-Nabiha, A. K., Jalaludin, D., & Abdalla, Y. A. (2016). Barriers to and enablers of sustainability integration in the performance management systems of an oil and gas company. *Journal of Cleaner Production, 136*, 197–212. https://doi.org/10.1016/j.jclepro.2016.01.097
Giner, B., & Luque-Vílchez, M. (2022). A commentary on the "new" institutional actors in sustainability reporting standard-setting: A European perspective. *Sustainability Accounting, Management and Policy Journal, 13*(6), 1284–1309. https://doi.org/10.1108/SAMPJ-06-2021-0222
Gioia, D. A., Corley, K. G., & Hamilton, A. L. (2013). Seeking qualitative rigor in inductive research: Notes on the Gioia methodology. *Organizational Research Methods, 16*(1), 15–31. https://doi.org/10.1177/1094428112452151
GRI Standards. (2016). Consolidated set of GRI sustainability reporting Standards. Global sustainability Standards board. Accessed January 7, 2024, from http://www.ekvilib.org/wp-content/uploads/2018/03/GRI-standardi-2016.pdf
Guix, M., & Font, X. (2020). The materiality balanced scorecard: A framework for stakeholder-led integration of sustainable hospitality management and reporting. *International Journal of Hospitality Management, 91*, 102634. https://doi.org/10.1016/j.ijhm.2020.102634
Haaker, A., & Freiberg, J. (2021). Empfehlungen des Sustainable-Finance-Beirate? *NWB Internationale Rechnungslegung, 17*(4), 120–121.
Habisch, A., Patelli, L., Pedrini, M., & Schwartz, C. (2011). Different talks with different folks: A comparative survey of stakeholder dialog in Germany, Italy, and the US. *Journal of Business Ethics, 100*(3), 381–404. https://doi.org/10.1007/s10551-010-0686-8
Hicks, E. L. (1964). Materiality. *Journal of Accounting Research, 2*(2), 158–171. https://doi.org/10.2307/2489998
Higgins, C., Stubbs, W., & Love, T. (2014). Walking the talk(s): Organisational narratives of integrated reporting. *Accounting, Auditing & Accountability Journal, 27*(7), 1090–1119. https://doi.org/10.1108/AAAJ-04-2013-1303
IASB. (2018). Conceptual framework for financial reporting 2018.
International Federation of Accountants (IFAC). (2005). Environmental management accounting.
Jones, P., Comfort, D., & Hillier, D. (2016). Managing materiality: A preliminary examination of the adoption of the new GRI G4 guidelines on materiality within the business community. *Journal of Public Affairs, 16*(3), 222–230. https://doi.org/10.1002/pa.1586

Kohler, E. (1952). *A dictionary for accountants*. Prentice Hall.

KPMG. (2013). The KPMG survey of corporate responsibility reporting 2013. Accessed January 7, 2024, from www.kpmg.com/Global/en/IssuesAndInsights/ArticlesPublications/corporateresponsibility/Documents/corporate-responsibility-reporting-survey-2013.pdf

Kujala, J., Sachs, S., Leinonen, H., Heikkinen, A., & Laude, D. (2022). Stakeholder engagement: Past, present, and future. *Business & Society, 61*(5), 1136–1196. https://doi.org/10.1177/00076503211066595

Lai, A., Melloni, G., & Stacchezzini, R. (2017). What does materiality mean to integrated reporting preparers? An empirical exploration. *Meditari Accountancy Research, 25*(4), 533–552. https://doi.org/10.1108/MEDAR-02-2017-0113

Larrinaga, C., Rossi, A., Luque-Vilchez, M., & Núñez-Nickel, M. (2020). Institutionalization of the contents of sustainability assurance services: A comparison between Italy and United States. *Journal of Business Ethics, 163*, 67–83. https://doi.org/10.1007/s10551-018-4014-z

Leto, L., & Vito, D. (2023). Il contributo dei sistemi di RM e PM alla sostenibilità integrata: Il caso B&C Speakers. *Management Control, 3*, 113–139. https://doi.org/10.3280/MACO2023-003006

Macchioni, R., & Maffei, M. (2021). Riflessioni sull'applicazione del principio di «materiality». In D. in Mancini, G. D'Onza, & C. Caserio (Eds.), *Sistemi informativi e revisione aziendale, Scritti in onore di L. Marchi*. Giappichelli Editore, Torino. ISBN 978-88-921-9530-1.

Messier, W. F., Jr., Martinov-Bennie, N., & Eilifsen, A. (2005). A review and integration of empirical research on materiality: Two decades later. *Auditing: A Journal of Practice & Theory, 24*(2), 153–187. https://doi.org/10.2308/aud.2005.24.2.153

Mio, C., Venturelli, A., & Leopizzi, R. (2015). Management by objectives and corporate social responsibility disclosure: First results from Italy. *Accounting, Auditing & Accountability Journal, 28*(3), 325–364. https://doi.org/10.1108/AAAJ-09-2013-1480

O'Riordan, L., & Fairbrass, J. (2014). Managing CSR stakeholder engagement: A new conceptual framework. *Journal of Business Ethics, 125*(1), 121–145. https://www.jstor.org/stable/24033158

Ormazabal, M., & Sarriegi, J. M. (2014). Environmental management evolution: Empirical evidence from Spain and Italy. *Business Strategy and the Environment, 23*(2), 73–88. https://doi.org/10.1002/bse.1761

Puroila, J., & Mäkelä, H. (2019). Matter of opinion: Exploring the socio-political nature of materiality disclosures in sustainability reporting. *Accounting, Auditing & Accountability Journal, 32*(4), 1043–1072. https://doi.org/10.1108/AAAJ-11-2016-2788

Risi, D., Wickert, C., & Ramus, T. (2022). Coordinated enactment: How organizational departments work together to implement CSR. *Business & Society, 62*, 000765032211102. https://doi.org/10.1177/00076503221110213

Romolini, A., Fissi, S., & Gori, E. (2014). Scoring CSR reporting in listed companies: Evidence from Italian best practices. *Corporate Social Responsibility and Environmental Management, 21*(2), 65–81. https://doi.org/10.1002/csr.1299

Sanchez Danes, G., Heintges, S., Mazzeo, P., Villacorta, V., & Trouvain, E. (2023). *Implementation guidance for the materiality assessment*. EFRAG.

Stubbs, W., & Higgins, C. (2014). Integrated reporting and internal mechanisms of change. *Accounting, Auditing & Accountability Journal, 27*(7), 1068–1089. https://doi.org/10.1108/AAAJ-03-2013-1279

Torelli, R., Balluchi, F., & Furlotti, K. (2020). The materiality assessment and stakeholder engagement: A content analysis of sustainability reports. *Corporate Social Responsibility and Environmental Management, 27*(2), 470–484. https://doi.org/10.1002/csr.1813

Whitehead, J. (2017). Prioritizing sustainability indicators: Using materiality analysis to guide sustainability assessment and strategy. *Business Strategy and the Environment, 26*(3), 399–412. https://doi.org/10.1002/bse.1928

Yin, R. K. (2014). *Case study research: Design and methods* (5th ed.). SAGE.

Chapter 20
Investigating the Interaction Between ESG Measurement, Sustainability Reporting, and Management Control Systems

Maria Serena Chiucchi, Roberta Ciccola, Marco Giuliani, and Michele Guidi

20.1 Introduction

During the past few years, the emerging environmental and social challenges have increased the demand for organizations to prioritize and actively pursue corporate sustainability. In this competitive environment, the relevance of the measurement of Environmental, Social, and Governance (ESG) aspects has increasingly arisen driven by the growing significance of environmental issues, social responsibility, and effective governance. The integration and systematic assessment of ESG aspects into organizational practices are crucial for considering the impact of operations on societal well-being. Consequently, the ESG measurement has become important for the management and disclosure of organizational impacts and contributions on the environment and society (Arvidsson & Dumay, 2022; Nielsen, 2023) having implications for both sustainability reporting and management control systems (Maas et al., 2016).

Sustainability reporting is an essential tool for ESG disclosure (Camilleri, 2015) as it concerns the process of preparation and disclosure of information, on a voluntary or mandatory basis, regarding the environmental, social, economic, and corporate governance dimensions (Erkens et al., 2015) and has become an integral component of corporate reporting. In this context, ESG measurement plays a pivotal role in shaping sustainability reporting by providing quantifiable and measurable data that enhance transparency and inform stakeholders (S&P Global, 2022). Along similar lines, several authors have argued that effective management control systems

M. S. Chiucchi (✉) · R. Ciccola · M. Giuliani · M. Guidi
Department of Management, Università Politecnica delle Marche, Ancona, Italy
e-mail: m.s.chiucchi@univpm.it; r.ciccola@univpm.it; m.giuliani@univpm.it; m.guidi@univpm.it

N. Castellano et al. (eds.), *Environmental, Social, Governance (ESG)*, SIDREA Series in Accounting and Business Administration,
https://doi.org/10.1007/978-3-031-76618-3_20

can enhance the implementation of sustainability strategies and, by incorporating ESG measurement, drive organizations towards achieving their ESG goals (Beusch et al., 2022; Crutzen & Herzig, 2013; Lueg & Radlach, 2016).

While recent studies have begun to explore the relationship between sustainability reporting and management control systems (de Villiers et al., 2016; Herremans & Nazari, 2016; Lozano et al., 2016; Traxler et al., 2020), a thorough understanding of how ESG measurement and its characteristics interact with these elements is still lacking (Traxler et al., 2020).

This study aims to investigate the interaction between ESG measurement, sustainability reporting, and management control systems. Specifically, it explores four of the characteristics of ESG measurement, such as its aim (decision-making support or external communication), temporal dimension (ex-ante, ongoing, and ex-post), level of formalization (formal and informal systems), and the organizational aspects, in relation to sustainability reporting and management control systems. To achieve this objective, a field study involving seven Italian companies has been developed.

The remainder of the chapter is organized as follows. Section 20.2 reviews prior studies on ESG measurement, sustainability reporting, and management control systems. Then, following the explanation of our research design in Sect. 20.3, we present the main findings in Sect. 20.4. Section 20.5 is dedicated to discussion and concluding remarks.

20.2 Literature Review

A notable trend in contemporary business is the proactive enhancement of sustainability practices by companies in response to growing concerns about the social and environmental impact of business operations (Adams & Frost, 2008; Bebbington & Unerman, 2018; Kim et al., 2023). This trend is driven by the acknowledgement of the need to meet stakeholder demands for harm reduction and the creation of social good (Baron, 2005; Calculli et al., 2021; D'Souza et al., 2022), as well as by the need of investors for ESG metrics that capture these sorts of environmental and social management challenges and signal how these issues will be internalized within the company (Cort, 2020).

While large companies have traditionally been the primary targets of such calls, the current landscape witnesses a broader embrace of sustainability principles across diverse business sectors. These aspects underscore the importance for every organization to thoroughly plan its sustainability strategy and implement coherent actions at an operational level. Equipping organizations with suitable tools and measures is equally crucial to guide the company towards sustainability. Consequently, companies are investing in data collection systems and integrating environmental, social, and governance performance data into decision-making, risk management, and performance measurement processes (Adams & Frost, 2008).

Sustainability reporting has emerged as a significant focus within the accounting literature, driven by the increasing recognition of its role in ESG disclosure

(Camilleri, 2015). Sustainability reporting involves the voluntary or mandatory disclosure of information related to corporate environmental, social, economic, and governance dimensions (Erkens et al., 2015). While sustainability reporting is predominantly seen as a means for communicating with external stakeholders, recent research emphasizes its internal relevance, positing it as a valuable tool for measuring sustainability performance and supporting decision-making within organizations (Traxler et al., 2020; Crutzen & Herzig, 2013; Lueg & Radlach, 2016).

Conversely, the measurement of sustainability issues has the function of guiding management decisions for the implementation of corporate sustainability strategies. This is achieved by conveying essential information, such as ESG performance metrics or reports to managers mainly to support internal decision-making and improve sustainability performance. According to this approach, sustainability performance measurement is "the process of collecting, analyzing and communicating sustainability performance information to support better management decisions" (Maas et al., 2016: 239).

The measurement of ESG aspects is essential for the management and disclosure of sustainability practices and initiatives. Scholars have fundamentally identified two distinct approaches to sustainability measurement, namely the outside-in approach and the inside-out approach (Maas et al., 2016; Schaltegger & Wagner, 2006) which "differ in their driving forces behind sustainability accounting" (Burritt & Schaltegger, 2010: 832). The outside-in approach is "reporting-driven" and focuses on meeting stakeholder expectations or addressing specific requests from third parties such as rating agencies or media groups. Measurement and management activities are finalized primarily for sustainability reporting and communication with stakeholders. The emphasis is on transparency, disclosure, and aligning sustainability practices with external expectations. The inside-out approach, on the other hand, involves using sustainability measurement to support management in executing their corporate sustainability strategy by providing essential information, such as sustainability performance metrics and reporting (Walkiewicz et al., 2021). These approaches reveal the significance of both sustainability reporting and management control systems in the context of the ESG measurement.

The integration of ESG metrics into sustainability reporting is driven by both strategic considerations within firms and evolving regulatory standards (Benameur et al., 2024). ESG metrics are integral to corporate reporting frameworks, serving not only as compliance tools but also as strategic assets that enhance a firm's reputation and competitive advantage (Buallay, 2019). Companies may measure ESG for reasons beyond sustainability reporting, such as obtaining environmental certifications, thus implementing it only afterwards, when they believe they have reached a sufficient level of maturity or are under pressure from external stakeholders (Guidi et al., 2024).

Recent advancements in sustainability reporting standards, such as the launch of the European Sustainability Reporting Standards (ESRS) and IFRS Sustainability Disclosure Standards, signify a major shift towards the standardization of ESG reporting practices. This shift is further reinforced by the increasing tendency of already established standards, such as those by the Global Reporting Initiative

(GRI), to promote interoperability guidelines (GRI & EFRAG, 2023). By standardizing the metrics and methodologies used in sustainability reporting, these frameworks ensure that ESG disclosures are comprehensive and comparable across different regulatory environments (Dinh et al., 2023). These developments not only standardize ESG disclosures but also emphasize the strategic importance of sustainability within corporate governance frameworks, thereby enhancing transparency, accountability, and stakeholder trust in the long term (Papoutsi & Sodhi, 2020).

Regarding the linkages between ESG measurement and management control systems, in the pursuit of sustainability, several scholars have argued that management control systems can facilitate the integration of social and environmental dimensions alongside the financial aspects (Gerged et al., 2023; Riccaboni & Leone, 2010). Defined as comprehensive systems, rules, practices, values, and activities implemented by management to direct employee behaviour (Malmi & Brown, 2008), management control systems form a package of processes and mechanisms guiding employees towards objectives aligned with the organization's strategies (Crabtree & Gasper, 2020; Malmi & Brown, 2008; Bedford & Malmi, 2015), tying performance measurement with incentives and organizational structure (Cheng et al., 2023). The implementation of sustainability indicators in management control systems can increase ESG performance (Gebhardt et al., 2023) and firm value (Harasheh & Provasi, 2023) and support the management of related risks (Semenova, 2021). In this regard, companies should implement changes to their management control systems to answer to the rising pressure from regulatory bodies and stakeholders on sustainability matters (Ferretti et al., 2024). For instance, introducing stakeholder-related metrics for emissions, human rights, customer health, employee empowerment, and industry associations in their management compensation systems (Yeh et al., 2024). Therefore, the tension between traditional management control systems focused on growth and profitability and the imperatives of social and environmental sustainability has spurred research at the intersection of sustainability and management control systems (Gerged et al., 2023; Gunarathne et al., 2023; Lueg & Radlach, 2016) to deepen the role that management control tools can play in supporting companies in facing the challenges posed by the ESG-focused transformation (Vannoni et al., 2024). The discussion on measurement approaches for sustainability and ESG aspects leads also to the complex dynamics between sustainability reporting and management control systems (de Villiers et al., 2016; Kaur & Lodhia, 2018; Mio et al., 2016). Scholars posit that integrating sustainability reporting into management control systems can enhance organizational sustainability performance (Herremans & Nazari, 2016; Maas et al., 2016). Moreover, it is suggested that management control systems may facilitate the implementation of sustainability reporting practices through specific tools like the Balanced Scorecard or organizational roles such as that of management accountants (de Villiers et al., 2016). Questions persist regarding the actual utilization of sustainability report indicators for planning, goal setting, and monitoring, which is crucial for the effectiveness of management control systems in steering organizations towards sustainability (Crutzen & Herzig, 2013).

In conclusion, the literature suggests a complex relationship between ESG measurement, sustainability reporting, and management control systems. To explore this relationship, the present study considers four characteristics of ESG measurement, related to sustainability reporting and management control systems, that have been addressed by the previous research mentioned above: the aim, distinguishing between internal and external purposes (Bebbington & Unerman, 2018; Burritt & Schaltegger, 2010; D'Souza et al., 2022); the temporal dimension, intended as the moment when environmental, social, and governance factors are assessed along the control process (Maas et al., 2016; Schaltegger & Wagner, 2006; Walkiewicz et al., 2021); the level of formalization in terms of structured frameworks, tools, processes, and methodologies employed to systematically capture, assess, and report ESG aspects (Crabtree & Gasper, 2020; Malmi & Brown, 2008; Traxler et al., 2020); the organizational aspects which refer to the roles, responsibilities, and structures dedicated to sustainability (Ascani et al., 2021; Cheng et al., 2023; Kaur & Lodhia, 2018).

20.3 Research Method

To achieve the aim of this research, a field study was conducted. Drawing from Lillis and Mundy (2005: 120), a field study represents a qualitative research method which employs "limited-depth studies conducted at a non-random selection of field sites, thus lying somewhere between in-depth cases and broad-based surveys". This method can be considered "a research design that embraces a relatively small number of companies, as opposed to a wide-ranging survey or intensive case enquiries in two or three companies" (Roslender & Hart, 2003: 6).

The field study is considered suitable to explore "complex phenomena in a confined domain" (Lillis & Mundy, 2005: 131). It relies on data collection which is less strict compared to questionnaire-based research and less intensive compared to the case study method. Accordingly, the field study allows, at the same time, to obtain a broad and general view of the phenomenon under investigation and its actual extension (Granlund & Malmi, 2002) and to go deeper into some specific topics.

Since our study is aimed at exploring the relationship between ESG measurement, sustainability reporting, and management control systems, adopting the field study method enables us to capture the nuances of how these components interact and influence each other within a specific organizational context. On the one hand, compared to an in-depth case study the field study allows to gather insights into the wide range of practices characterizing the disclosure and use of ESG information through the investigation of the experience of several organizations. On the other hand, given the emerging nature of the phenomenon investigated, surveys would not be adequately flexible and exhaustive to identify emergent issues and examine thoroughly aspects deemed relevant.

Table 20.1 Sample analysed

Company	Industry
A	Retail
B	Shoe sole manufacturing
C	Facility management
D	Building material
E	Shoe manufacturing
F	Industrial component manufacturing
G	Industrial paints manufacturing

The case organizations have been selected using purposeful sampling (Patton, 1990). As this study aims to provide a comprehensive view of the relationship between ESG measurement, sustainability reporting, and management control systems, the research is focused on organizations that at least have implemented sustainability reports as a corporate disclosure or/and have implemented a sustainability management control system/performance measurement system. Seven companies got involved in this research; the companies differ in size and belong to different industries as represented in Table 20.1.

The primary source of data collection was semi-structured interviews conducted both at the organization's headquarters and online. Thanks to its flexibility the semi-structured interview allows the interviewers to adapt to the specific situation and thus reach a detailed understanding of the topic investigated, as well as of emergent issues (Kreiner & Mouritsen, 2005; Qu & Dumay, 2011). In doing so, the semi-structured interview facilitates a comparative analysis of the experiences of the different companies investigated. Interviews were conducted from April 2022 to June 2023.

Since we were interested in analysing the relationship between ESG measurement, sustainability reporting, and management control systems, the main informants were the actors with key positions in such processes (Pettigrew, 1990), that is in our case the sustainability managers, the management accountants, the CFOs, other members of the Administration, Finance, and Control function. Each interview lasted from 30 to 60 min and was tape-recorded and immediately transcribed. The interviews were focused on the following topics: (1) general information about sustainability reporting and management control systems oriented towards sustainability; (2) ESG measurement practices; and (3) ESG certifications and rating systems.

Interviews were triangulated with direct observation and field notes during visits to the organization, which allowed us to keep track of informal conversations with the main informants (Van de Ven & Johnson, 2006). Moreover, we conducted documentary research about both internal and public documents such as internal reports, annual reports, codes of conduct, company websites, etc.

The collected data were then analysed according to the insights that emerged in the literature review. The data were coded to delineate the purposes and characteristics of ESG measurement and the complex relationship with sustainability reporting and management control systems. The codes used in this examination referred to the four characteristics of ESG measurement mentioned in the previous section: aim, temporal dimension, level of formalization, and organizational aspects.

20.4 Findings

The findings are presented according to four characteristics of ESG measurement mentioned in the previous section: the aim (decision-making support or external communication), the temporal dimension (ex-ante, ongoing, and ex-post), the level of formalization (formal and informal systems), and the organizational aspects of the ESG measurement.

20.4.1 The Aim of the ESG Measurement

Company A is a prominent Italian retail enterprise that has strategically positioned sustainability at the core of its operations, reflecting a commitment to environmental and social responsibility. The company actively engages in ESG measurements primarily for external purposes, namely sustainability reporting and engagement in certification processes (i.e. alignment with ISO standards). The primary goal of sustainability reporting is to move beyond simple financial metrics and convey the multifaceted value created by the company. The report has become an integral part of the company's identity, reflecting its commitment to transparency and sustainability. Concerning the ESG certifications, initiatives include the implementation of an environmental management system and the adherence to occupational health and safety standards. ESG measurement also serves managerial purposes, but this is limited to critical initiatives that require ad hoc monitoring such as emissions or paper consumption.

For Company B, the aim of ESG measurement serves both internal and external purposes. Internally, ESG metrics are used to inform strategic decisions, assess the success of sustainability initiatives, and align business operations with the company's holistic vision. Externally, ESG measurement serves the purpose of sustainability reporting, allowing the company to communicate its commitment to environmental, social, and governance values to external stakeholders such as customers, investors, and regulatory bodies.

The primary aim of ESG measurement within Company C is centred around sustainability reporting and certifications. The emphasis of the company's ESG measurement approach lies in generating data and insights for the sustainability reporting process and obtaining relevant certifications, revealing a commitment to demonstrating the company's sustainability performance to external stakeholders and adhering to recognized standards.

In the case of Company D, ESG measurement primarily serves external purposes. The company's focus on obtaining ISO and EPD certifications indicates a commitment to meeting external standards demanded by architect customers. These certifications are essential for sustainability reporting and are likely used as a means to enhance the company's reputation, comply with external demands, and secure market share. While internal actions are taken to ensure compliance, the primary aim is to meet the expectations of external stakeholders through formal certifications. The company prefers obtaining environmental certifications, over communicating sustainability information through corporate disclosures, given their greater verifiability and considering the value assigned by third parties.

> The centrality of certifications is important because it falls within the logic of sustainability reporting. The risk is that a company claims to be sustainable on its own without any third-party validation. For us, it is fundamental to have a certification that reflects sustainability because the recognition from a third-party entity strengthens the company's claim (HR & Marketing Manager, Company D).

Company E uses ESG measurement mostly for external purposes. The aim is to assess and enhance the company's corporate identity, gain legitimacy, and align operations with evolving values. Top-down leadership is emphasized, indicating a commitment to using ESG metrics for internal decision-making and organizational culture. Externally, the company recognizes the importance of sustainability reporting to communicate its efforts in social responsibility to customers, employees, and the local community. ESG measurement, consequently, serves as a tool for external reputation management. The desire to communicate these dimensions to customers was also combined with that of comparison with peer companies.

> It was a form of attention to the customer but, on the other hand, it represented an opportunity to measure us also with respect to our competitors (CFO, Company E).

Company F is a company specializing in the production of industrial components. Sustainability is one of the main pillars of its corporate strategy, encompassing energy efficiency, waste reduction, and responsible sourcing, demonstrating a comprehensive approach to environmental stewardship. The overarching objective of ESG measurement within Company F is twofold, aiming at both external reporting and bolstering internal decision-making processes. Externally, the company utilizes ESG metrics to enhance transparency and communicate its sustainability performance to stakeholders through a comprehensive sustainability reporting. Internally, ESG measurement supports decision-making processes, providing valuable insights that contribute to strategic planning and performance management, as confirmed by the periodic meetings involving the CEO and the top management for evaluating the alignment of the company's sustainability performance with its strategic goals and for identifying areas of improvement.

For Company G, the aim of ESG measurement mostly serves internal purposes. The use of environmental Key Performance Indicators (KPIs) in management control systems indicates a focus on operational excellence and product efficiency. The annual internal review of these KPIs suggests an ongoing commitment to improving internal processes.

20.4.2 *The Temporal Dimension of the ESG Measurement*

The temporal dimension of ESG measurement refers to the moment when ESG factors are assessed along the management control process. The "ex-ante" control involves verifying the coherence between operational objectives with long-term objectives. The "ongoing" control entails periodically forecasting and verifying that results align with planned objectives and implementing corrective actions. The "ex-post control" is conducted at the end of a period to compare planned objectives with actual results and identify areas of improvement for the next period.

In analysing the ESG measurement attributes, the interviews reveal that Company A uses ESG metrics primarily ex-post to monitor specific initiatives, while ex-ante, during the planning stage, and ongoing, when controlling the implementation of their sustainable strategy, ESG measures are less relevant when compared to the financial ones.

Company B is actively incorporating ESG measures into its comprehensive sustainability shift. The ex-ante phase involves strategic planning to integrate sustainability into the company's core identity and strategy, aligning with environmental, social, and governance dimensions. Ongoing efforts include the measurement of sustainability indicators across the three ESG categories to ensure that the company's products reflect reduced environmental and social impact. The ex-post dimension involves assessing the success of ESG integration as a strategic advantage, differentiating Company B in the market.

Company C engages primarily in the ex-ante phase with the creation of an "Integrated Strategic Plan" for Sustainability demonstrating a commitment to translating strategy into actions for sustainable value generation.

For Company D, ESG measurement is prominently featured in its sustainability strategy, particularly with a strong focus on environmental factors. The ex-ante dimension involves the anticipation of ISO and EPD certifications, aligning with governance and environmental criteria. Ongoing actions include internal measurements to ensure compliance with legal and environmental standards, with a strong emphasis on obtaining certifications to demonstrate commitment to ESG principles. The ex-post assessment involves evaluating how well ESG considerations, especially environmental ones, have contributed to maintaining market share.

In the case of Company E, the luxury shoe manufacturer, ESG measurement becomes integral to its sustainability initiatives. The ex-ante phase involves recognizing the growing importance of corporate sustainability, especially from a social responsibility perspective. Initiatives undertaken include ESG metrics related to social responsibility, aiming to gain legitimacy with employees, customers, and the local community. The ex-post dimension involves assessing the success of ESG integration, particularly in terms of social responsibility, and the impact on the company's corporate identity.

For Company F, the temporal dimension encompasses ex-ante, ongoing, and ex-post phases, reflecting a comprehensive approach to sustainability measurement. Company F stands out for its embracing of both retrospective and prospective approaches. This dual focus on both consumptive evaluation and goal setting shows that ESG metrics support informed decision-making in the realm of sustainability.

Company G, the industrial paints manufacturer, incorporates ESG measurement into its sustainability strategy with a primary focus on eco-efficiency. The ex-ante phase involves aligning ESG measures, especially environmental considerations, with the company's internal emphasis on enhancing operational excellence. Ongoing efforts include the integration of environmental KPIs into the sustainability strategy, with an annual internal review of these indicators. The ex-post dimension involves a proactive stance towards voluntary sustainability reporting to align with upcoming regulatory changes, demonstrating the company's commitment to governance aspects of ESG.

20.4.3 The Degree of Formalization of the ESG Measurement

The level of formalization of the ESG measurement consists of the extent to which structured frameworks, tools, processes, and methodologies are employed to systematically capture, assess, and report ESG aspects.

Company A lacks a formal sustainability performance measurement system; it carries out ad hoc measurements of some KPIs produced during the Sustainability Reporting process to monitor specific aspects such as emissions and paper consumption. Thus, the absence of a structured performance measurement system is compensated by ad hoc rather than routine monitoring of specific initiatives. These ESG data are not reported to the top management regularly, but they are monitored ad hoc for specific decisions.

> At this moment we do not have sustainability performance measurement systems, but certainly from all the experience we have had, with specific projects in different fields, we do have monitoring underway. I would speak more of ad hoc measurement, when there is a need to monitor a phenomenon, such as emissions or the amount of paper consumed (Management accountant, Company A).

Company B is amid a comprehensive sustainability shift, actively engaging in both formal and informal aspects of ESG measurement. On the formal side, the company strategically plans to integrate sustainability into its core identity and strategy, aligning with economic, social, and environmental dimensions. This includes the use of formal frameworks and indicators to assess the company's environmental and social impact, emphasizing their significance in the mission and values. The ongoing efforts involve the establishment and tracking of formal ESG metrics to ensure the reduction of environmental and social impact in its products. In the ex-post phase, the assessment will involve evaluating the success of these formal ESG measures as a strategic advantage in differentiating the company. Informally, Company B is also fostering a culture of sustainability, encouraging employee engagement, and incorporating social responsibility practices beyond formal metrics.

Company C does not engage in a formalized ESG measurement process based on formal accounting tools. Although the company's ESG measurement process is not formalized, the interviews indicate that sustainability reporting has played a crucial role in fostering a culture of sustainability measurement within functions where it was previously absent. The reporting process has not only stimulated the production of new data but also uncovered information that did not exist before. It has instilled a culture of measurement in functions where it was lacking, prompting the company to establish structures for systematic data collection.

Company D primarily focuses on environmental impacts. Formal aspects pertain to obtaining ISO and EPD certifications and recognized standards in governance and environmental practices. Additionally, Company D exhibits an informal aspect by undertaking voluntary social sustainability initiatives, showcasing an additional layer of commitment to ESG values beyond formal requirements.

In the case of Company E, both formal and informal aspects of ESG measurement are seamlessly integrated into its sustainability initiatives. Initiatives undertaken include formal ESG metrics related to social responsibility, aligning with the company's commitment to gaining legitimacy with employees, customers, and the local community. Informally, Company E's approach likely includes employee engagement programmes, community partnerships, and other socially responsible practices that contribute to its overall sustainability narrative.

Within company F, the ESG measurement process is formalized with a structured and organized methodology for ESG monitoring. Specifically, KPIs related to ESG aspects are monitored quarterly, with periodic meetings involving cross-functional teams, including the CEO, to define action plans for achieving set objectives. Also, several KPIs from the sustainability reporting process have been incorporated into the company's Management by Objectives (MBO) system, directly influencing variable compensation for managers. Objectives such as reducing pollutant emissions and managing energy and water consumption are tied to performance-based compensation. This alignment ensures coherence between sustainability goals and the overall business objectives.

> There are quarterly data collections for sustainability indicators which are followed by periodic meetings within the company which are transversal among the functions that are involved. Faced with each of these indicators, we don't just take the data, look at them and say we were good or not, but there are action plans that are aimed at achieving these objectives and which are therefore followed in their development quarter after quarter and the CEO always attends these meetings (CFO, Company F).

Company G demonstrates a balanced approach to both formal and informal ESG measurement. On the formal side, the company aligns its sustainability strategy with eco-efficiency goals, incorporating KPIs to measure environmental impacts. These KPIs are integrated into the sustainability strategy and undergo annual internal reviews, reflecting the formal aspect of the company's commitment to ESG measures. Simultaneously, although they recognize the implementation of sustainability reporting as an initiative to be undertaken, it is secondary to the actuation of initiatives that produce operational benefits.

> The thing is that we were supposed to prepare the sustainability report for the past year, but there were other priorities, and now we are going to resume the project and try to carry it out next year (Sustainability Manager, Company G).

This recognizes the importance of informal aspects of ESG measurement in driving operational excellence, such as involving continuous improvement processes and employee engagement beyond what is captured in formal reports.

20.4.4 The Organizational Aspects of the ESG Measurement

The organizational aspects of the ESG measurement refer to the internal implications in terms of roles, functions, and responsibilities.

Looking at organizational aspects, Company A has established a Sustainability Group composed of the managers of the main organizational functions, aiming to facilitate cross-functional collaboration and enhance engagement in sustainability projects. This initiative addresses challenges related to fragmented responsibilities among the different functions—as the company did not have a dedicated Sustainability Department—fostering a more cohesive and integrated approach to sustainability. The sustainability reporting process is under the responsibility of the Director of Public Relations.

For Company B, the responsibility for ESG measurement is distributed across various corporate functions. The initiative is championed by owner-managers, especially the COO, indicating a top-level commitment to sustainability. In terms of elaboration, departments such as sustainability, operations, and marketing may collaborate to ensure alignment with the company's core identity and strategy. Primary stakeholders are engaged in the materiality assessment of sustainability topics to understand the alignment with the internal perception.

> We've involved the employees, suppliers and customers because they're the most important stakeholders for us, so, they are the ones we measure ourselves with daily so for us they were the ones who most of all could give us major contributions (COO, Company B).

From an organizational standpoint, within company C, ESG measurement and sustainability reporting process are guided and coordinated by the sustainability manager. The company's focus on certifications concerning quality, environment, health, and safety such as ISO certifications is aligned with the pivotal role of "Management Systems" Department, which deals with internal audit processes for certifications.

In the case of Company D, the organizational structure for ESG measurement appears to be influenced by external stakeholders, particularly architect customers demanding ISO and EPD certifications. The process involves collaboration between compliance, quality assurance, and possibly marketing departments to ensure adherence to standards and certification requirements. The data produced is used by owner-managers and key decision-makers to maintain market share and uphold the company's reputation.

Company E's organizational approach to ESG measurement involves top-down leadership, as owner-managers occupying top management roles are actively involved in shaping the company's sustainability initiatives. Corporate functions such as marketing, human resources, and operations are involved in the development and implementation of sustainability metrics. The data generated is used by top management to assess the success of sustainability initiatives and their impact on corporate identity. Additionally, departments like marketing may use this data to communicate the company's sustainability efforts to external stakeholders.

Company F is characterized by the integration of sustainability into the various core business functions, without the existence of a distinct sustainability department in place. However, the company recently established an inter-council committee, the Control and Risks Committee, with a sustainability focus. The sustainability reporting process is under the responsibility of the administrative and financial function.

For Company G, the organizational aspect of ESG measurement revolves around the sustainability manager, indicating a specific role dedicated to overseeing ESG initiatives. Corporate functions such as operations, finance, and sustainability are likely involved in the elaboration of ESG metrics, with the sustainability manager playing a central role. The generated data and KPIs undergo internal review by the management team. While not currently shared externally, the company expresses a proactive stance in planning for sustainability reporting, such as involving collaboration between the sustainability manager, finance, and other relevant functions. The data produced is used internally for operational assessment and future strategic planning to align with upcoming regulatory changes.

20.5 Discussion and Conclusions

By conducting a field study involving seven Italian companies, this study has investigated the dynamic relationship between ESG measurement, sustainability reporting, and management control systems. To investigate this interaction, four characteristics of ESG measurement have been analysed, such as its aim, temporal dimension, level of formalization, and organizational aspects.

The findings show that the companies in the study predominantly use ESG measurement for external purposes. First, companies engage with ESG measurement for sustainability reporting, aimed at improving transparency about ESG aspects, enhancing company reputation, and strengthening stakeholder trust. Second, companies are committed to obtaining certifications to meet external standards demanded by main stakeholders. The pursuit of certifications and adherence to external standards play a significant role in shaping the ESG strategies of certain companies. This external validation is a driving force behind their ESG initiatives. Finally, two companies engage with ESG measurement for both external and internal purposes, i.e. supporting decision-making processes, while only within one company ESG measurement serves internal purposes linked to operational excellence and product efficiency.

A critical dimension in understanding ESG measurement is the temporal aspect. Most companies involved in the field study, with few exceptions, display a comprehensive approach, incorporating ESG aspects across all phases along the control process, namely ex-ante, ongoing, and ex-post. This suggests a holistic integration of ESG into the process that evolves from initial goal setting to implementation and assessment. The degree of formalization in ESG measurement processes varies among the companies. Company F has a highly formalized process with structured quarterly KPI monitoring. The company also incorporates specific KPIs derived from the sustainability report into the company MBO system, demonstrating a deep integration of these metrics into core business processes. Companies A and C have a less formalized approach relying on ad hoc monitoring of KPIs derived from the sustainability report. The findings reveal also that most companies adopt informal approaches to embed ESG values into the company culture or foster employees' engagement.

Regarding the organizational aspects, many companies have established specific roles to coordinate their ESG measurement efforts, especially for sustainability reporting, i.e. sustainability managers. This demonstrates a trend towards centralizing ESG responsibilities within dedicated roles to enhance focus and coordination. The findings also show a cross-functional collaboration between multiple departments such as marketing, operations, and human resources typically involved in the development and implementation of ESG metrics. Additionally, the findings underscore a significant emphasis on top-level commitment and involvement in sustainability initiatives. Companics B and E, for instance, highlight the role of top management, including COOs and other senior leaders, in driving ESG strategies. This top-down approach is critical for embedding sustainability into the corporate culture and ensuring alignment with the company's core identity and strategy.

In summary, the findings underscore a dynamic landscape of ESG measurement, sustainability reporting, and management control systems where companies adopt different approaches based on their objectives, temporal considerations, organizational structures, and level of formality. The results of the field study show the prevalent use of ESG measurement for external purposes, particularly for enabling the sustainability reporting process, to enhance transparency, reputation, and stakeholder trust. This finding aligns with the studies suggesting that external accountability and stakeholder demands significantly shape corporate ESG strategies (Camilleri, 2015; Erkens et al., 2015). This aspect, along with the use of ESG measurement for the pursuit of certifications and adherence to external standards, reveals the adoption of the outside-in approach described by Maas et al. (2016), where external validation drives sustainability practices.

Most of the companies studied, except for Company F, do not employ specific management control tools for ESG measurement, and the key management accounting actors, such as management accountants, are not primarily involved in the ESG processes. Instead, there appears to be a prevalence of informal controls (Riccaboni & Leone, 2010). These findings differ from the study of Ferretti et al. (2024), which highlights that the evolving nature of ESG demands provokes significant changes within management control systems as a response to sustainability pressures. However, our analysis shows that sustainability reporting catalysed the introduction of ESG control practices within the analysed organizations. Yet, these companies have begun to use ESG information often derived from sustainability reports in a holistic, multi-temporal (ex-ante, ongoing, and ex-post) manner to support decision-making processes and integrate these insights into their strategic planning systems. These findings resonate with recent studies which have recognized the internal relevance of sustainability reporting (Traxler et al., 2020; Herremans & Nazari, 2016). Company G represents a singular exception in this study as the organization has adopted an inside-out approach. This approach might be attributed to the company's distinctive emphasis on environmental efficiency as a core aspect of its products.

An interaction that emerges between the four characteristics of ESG measurement, sustainability reporting, and management control systems is the one linking the aim of ESG measurement and its temporal dimension. Companies that prioritize external purposes, such as sustainability reporting and obtaining certifications, tend to adopt a comprehensive temporal approach. For example, Company B integrates ESG considerations from the strategic planning stage (ex-ante), through continuous monitoring (ongoing), to post-implementation assessment (ex-post). This suggests that companies driven by the need for transparency and stakeholder engagement recognize the importance of embedding ESG considerations throughout the operational cycle to ensure accuracy and accountability in their reporting, aligning with the findings of Maas et al. (2016), who emphasize the importance of a multi-phase approach in achieving comprehensive ESG integration. Conversely, companies with a primarily internal focus on ESG measurement, such as Company G, adopt a more selective temporal approach. While Company G employs ex-ante and ongoing phases to align ESG measures with internal processes and enhance operational efficiency, it is less proactive in ex-post reporting. This selective use of temporal dimensions indicates a prioritization of internal decision-making over external communication, which is consistent with Burritt and Schaltegger's (2010) inside-out approach.

This study offers various contributions to the literature. It provides empirical evidence about the complex interaction between ESG measurement, sustainability reporting, and management control systems by highlighting how these elements interact to shape corporate sustainability strategies and measurement practices. This integration addresses the intersection of sustainability and management practices. By demonstrating that companies with comprehensive temporal approaches (ex-ante, ongoing, and ex-post) achieve better integration of ESG practices, the study supports and extends the work of Maas et al. (2016) on the importance of a multi-phase ESG integration. Additionally, this study contributes to prior studies by proposing potential attributes through which this relationship can be analysed, namely the aim, the temporal dimension, the level of formalization, and organizational aspects of ESG measurement. It also contributes to studies that aim to bridge the gap between internal and external reporting (de Villiers et al., 2016; Mio et al., 2016; Traxler et al., 2020) by highlighting the role of sustainability reporting as a catalyst for ESG control practice.

This study has also managerial implications. First, it suggests how to create synergies between ESG measurement, sustainability reporting, and management control systems, highlighting the factors that can favour or hinder these linkages. Therefore, this research illustrates levers and barriers related both to technical aspects—i.e., tools, techniques, and indicators—and organizational aspects, i.e., actors and functions involved in ESG measurement. Companies can enhance their ESG strategies by adopting a comprehensive temporal approach that integrates ESG considerations at every stage: planning (ex-ante), implementation (ongoing), and assessment (ex-post). This practice leads to more accurate reporting, better decision-making, and improved sustainability performance. The study underscores the importance of formalizing ESG measurement processes to ensure consistent oversight and alignment with strategic sustainability goals.

To handle and incorporate ESG practices effectively, businesses ought to think about facilitating cross-functional collaboration to integrate ESG reflections throughout the organization. Companies should also aim for a well-rounded strategy that considers both the internal and external goals of ESG measurement. This entails leveraging ESG data to improve communication and transparency with external stakeholders, hence boosting stakeholder trust and business reputation.

The present research is not without limitations. The focus on the established practices within a small number of organizations may overlook emerging or innovative approaches to ESG measurement and its integration into sustainability reporting and management control systems. Additionally, the exploratory nature of the research provides initial insights but may lack the depth required to establish causality among ESG measurement, sustainability reporting, and management control systems. Thus, more and in-depth research is needed in these directions.

As sustainability becomes increasingly central to corporate strategy, advancing research on this topic is imperative for developing robust frameworks that support both internal decision-making and external accountability. Ultimately, the pursuit of comprehensive ESG integration will not only enhance organizational transparency and performance but also contribute significantly to global sustainability efforts.

References

Adams, A., & Frost, G. (2008). Integrating sustainability reporting into management practices. *Accounting Forum, 32*, 288–302.

Arvidsson, S., & Dumay, J. (2022). Corporate ESG reporting quantity, quality and performance: Where to now for environmental policy and practice? *Business Strategy and the Environment, 31*(3), 1091–1110.

Ascani, I., Ciccola, R., & Chiucchi, M. S. (2021). A structured literature review about the role of management accountants in sustainability accounting and reporting. *Sustainability, 13*(4), 2357.

Baron, D. P. (2005). Competing for the public through the news media. *Journal of Economics & Management Strategy, 14*(2), 339–376.

Bebbington, J., & Unerman, J. (2018). Achieving the United Nations sustainable development goals: An enabling role for accounting research. *Accounting, Auditing & Accountability Journal, 31*(1), 2–24.
Bedford, D. S., & Malmi, T. (2015). Configurations of control: An exploratory analysis. *Management Accounting Research, 27*, 2–26.
Benameur, K. B., Mostafa, M. M., Hassanein, A., Shariff, M. Z., & Al-Shattarat, W. (2024). Sustainability reporting scholarly research: A bibliometric review and a future research agenda. *Management Review Quarterly, 74*(2), 823–866.
Beusch, P., Frisk, J. E., Rosén, M., & Dilla, W. (2022). Management control for sustainability: Towards integrated systems. *Management Accounting Research, 54*, 100777.
Buallay, A. (2019). Between cost and value: Investigating the effects of sustainability reporting on a firm's performance. *Journal of Applied Accounting Research, 20*(4), 481–496.
Burritt, R. L., & Schaltegger, S. (2010). Sustainability accounting and reporting: Fad or trend? *Accounting, Auditing & Accountability Journal, 23*(7), 829–846.
Calculli, C., D'Uggento, A. M., Labarile, A., & Ribecco, N. (2021). Evaluating people's awareness about climate changes and environmental issues: A case study. *Journal of Cleaner Production, 324*, 129244.
Camilleri, M. A. (2015). Environmental, social and governance disclosures in Europe. *Sustainability Accounting, Management and Policy Journal, 6*(2), 224–242.
Cheng, M. M., Perego, P., & Soderstrom, N. S. (2023). Sustainability and management accounting research. *Journal of Management Accounting Research, 35*(3), 1–11.
Cort, T. (2020). ESG risk depends on management control quality. In D. C. Esty & T. Cort (Eds.), *Values at work*. Palgrave Macmillan.
Crabtree, A., & Gasper, D. (2020). Conclusion: The sustainable development goals and capability and human security analysis. In *Sustainability, capabilities and human security* (pp. 169–182).
Crutzen, N., & Herzig, C. (2013). A review of the empirical research in management control, strategy and sustainability. *Accounting and Control for Sustainability, 26*, 165–195.
D'Souza, C., Ahmed, T., Khashru, M. A., Ahmed, R., Ratten, V., & Jayaratne, M. (2022). The complexity of stakeholder pressures and their influence on social and environmental responsibilities. *Journal of Cleaner Production, 358*, 132038.
De Villiers, C., Rouse, P., & Kerr, J. (2016). A new conceptual model of influences driving sustainability based on case evidence of the integration of corporate sustainability management control and reporting. *Journal of Cleaner Production, 136*, 78–85.
Dinh, T., Husmann, A., & Melloni, G. (2023). Corporate sustainability reporting in Europe: A scoping review. *Accounting in Europe, 20*(1), 1–29.
Erkens, M., Paugam, L., & Stolowy, H. (2015). Non-financial information: State of the art and research perspectives based on a bibliometric study. *Comptabilité Contrôle Audit, 21*(3), 15–92.
Ferretti, P., Gonnella, C., & Martino, P. (2024). Integrating sustainability in management control systems: An exploratory study on Italian banks. *Meditari Accountancy Research, 32*(7), 1–34.
Gebhardt, M., Thun, T. W., Seefloth, M., & Zülch, H. (2023). Managing sustainability—Does the integration of environmental, social and governance key performance indicators in the internal management systems contribute to companies' environmental, social and governance performance? *Business Strategy and the Environment, 32*(4), 2175–2192.
Gerged, A. M., Albitar, K., & Al-Haddad, L. (2023). Corporate environmental disclosure and earnings management—The moderating role of corporate governance structures. *International Journal of Finance & Economics, 28*(3), 2789–2810.
Granlund, M., & Malmi, T. (2002). Moderate impact of ERPS on management accounting: A lag or permanent outcome? *Management Accounting Research, 13*(3), 299–321.
GRI & EFRAG. (2023). GRI-ESRS interoperability index.
Guidi, M., Vitali, S., Giuliani, M., & Chiucchi, M. S. (2024). Understanding the interplay between sustainability strategy and the approach to sustainability reporting in SMEs. *Journal of Management & Organization*, 1–20.

Gunarathne, N., Lee, K. H., & Hitigala Kaluarachchilage, P. K. (2023). Tackling the integration challenge between environmental strategy and environmental management accounting. *Accounting, Auditing & Accountability Journal, 36*(1), 63–95.

Harasheh, M., & Provasi, R. (2023). A need for assurance: Do internal control systems integrate environmental, social, and governance factors? *Corporate Social Responsibility and Environmental Management, 30*(1), 384–401.

Herremans, I. M., & Nazari, J. A. (2016). Sustainability reporting driving forces and management control systems. *Journal of Management Accounting Research, 28*(2), 103–124.

Kaur, A., & Lodhia, S. (2018). Stakeholder engagement in sustainability accounting and reporting: A study of Australian local councils. *Accounting, Auditing & Accountability Journal, 31*(1), 338–368.

Kim, N. K. W., Choi, S., Jung, T., & Park, S. (2023). How does demand uncertainty from climate change exposure affect the firms' cost structures? Examining the real effects of climate change on the firms' operational decisions. *Corporate Social Responsibility and Environmental Management, 30*(6), 2969–2989.

Kreiner, K., & Mouritsen, J. (2005). The analytical interview. In *The art of science* (pp. 153–176).

Lillis, A. M., & Mundy, J. (2005). Cross-sectional field studies in management accounting research—Closing the gaps between surveys and case studies. *Journal of Management Accounting Research, 17*(1), 119–141.

Lozano, R., Nummert, B., & Ceulemans, K. (2016). Elucidating the relationship between sustainability reporting and organisational change management for sustainability. *Journal of Cleaner Production, 125*, 168–188.

Lueg, R., & Radlach, R. (2016). Managing sustainable development with management control systems: A literature review. *European Management Journal, 34*(2), 158–171.

Maas, K., Schaltegger, S., & Crutzen, N. (2016). Integrating corporate sustainability assessment, management accounting, control, and reporting. *Journal of Cleaner Production, 136*, 237–248.

Malmi, T., & Brown, D. A. (2008). Management control systems as a package—Opportunities, challenges and research directions. *Management Accounting Research, 19*(4), 287–300.

Mio, C., Marco, F., & Pauluzzo, R. (2016). Internal application of IR principles: Generali's internal integrated reporting. *Journal of Cleaner Production, 139*, 204–218.

Nielsen, C. (2023). ESG reporting and metrics: From double materiality to key performance indicators. *Sustainability, 15*(24), 16844.

Papoutsi, A., & Sodhi, M. S. (2020). Does disclosure in sustainability reports indicate actual sustainability performance? *Journal of Cleaner Production, 260*, 121049.

Patton, M. Q. (1990). *Qualitative evaluation and research methods*. SAGE Publications, Inc.

Pettigrew, A. M. (1990). Longitudinal field research on change: Theory and practice. *Organization Science, 1*(3), 267–292.

Qu, S. Q., & Dumay, J. (2011). The qualitative research interview. *Qualitative Research in Accounting & Management, 8*(3), 238–264.

Riccaboni, A., & Leone, E. L. (2010). Implementing strategies through management control systems: The case of sustainability. *International Journal of Productivity and Performance Management, 59*(2), 130–144.

Roslender, R., & Hart, S. J. (2003). In search of strategic management accounting: Theoretical and field study perspectives. *Management Accounting Research, 14*(3), 255–279.

S&P Global. (2022). Transparency and impact: The essential principles of ESG.

Schaltegger, S., & Wagner, M. (2006). Integrative management of sustainability performance, measurement and reporting. *International Journal of Accounting, Auditing and Performance Evaluation, 3*(1), 1–19.

Semenova, N. (2021). Management control systems in response to social and environmental risk in large Nordic companies. *International Journal of Corporate Social Responsibility, 6*(1), 13.

Traxler, A. A., Schrack, D., & Greiling, D. (2020). Sustainability reporting and management control–a systematic exploratory literature review. *Journal of Cleaner Production, 276*, 122725.

Van de Ven, A. H., & Johnson, P. E. (2006). Knowledge for theory and practice. *Academy of Management Review, 31*(4), 802–821.

Vannoni, V., Palazzi, F., Sentuti, A., & Sgrò, F. (2024). The role of the management control system in supporting ESG-focused transformation in financial intermediaries: A case study of an Italian Bank. *International Journal of Economics and Finance, 16*(1), 22–32.

Walkiewicz, J., Lay-Kumar, J., & Herzig, C. (2021). The integration of sustainability and externalities into the "corporate DNA": A practice-oriented approach. *Corporate Governance: The International Journal of Business in Society, 21*(3), 479–496.

Yeh, T. T., Xiao, Y., & Daniel, S. J. (2024). Stakeholder influences on management control systems for ESG governance and reporting in the global automotive industry. *Journal of Corporate Accounting & Finance, 35*(2), 103–120.

Chapter 21
Financial Reporting and Climate Information: The Italian Case

Fabio Caputo, Rossella Leopizzi, Stella Lippolis, and Simone Pizzi

21.1 Introduction

The last few years have been interested by an intense debate about the need to enhance financial markets' transparency (CONSOB, 2022). In detail, many initiatives have been launched by regulators and by the main international stock exchanges to encourage companies to integrate their traditional reporting practices with more sophisticated accountability tools (EY, 2021). Furthermore, this paradigm shift has been also driven by the pressures made by analysts and professional investors on companies. Therefore, the current scenario is characterized by a higher degree of transparency because of the co-existence of normative and coercive pressures made by regulators and stakeholders (Chung & Cho, 2018; La Torre et al., 2020).

One of the main reporting areas interested by this paradigm shift is represented by the information about the environmental, social, and governance (ESG) impacts generated by companies. Contrarily to the past, stakeholders are more interested in exploring the ESG dimensions because of the increasing awareness about the potential externalities related to the anthropic impacts caused by companies. Within this scenario, a pivotal role is covered by investors as evidenced by the rapid growth of investment funds and market portfolios developed considering ESG criteria. Furthermore, the relevance of the topic has been also underlined by the empirical evidence collected by academics, which have identified a substantial positive

F. Caputo (✉) · S. Pizzi
Dipartimento di Scienze dell'Economia, Università del Salento, Lecce, Italy
e-mail: fabio.caputo@unisalento.it

R. Leopizzi · S. Lippolis
Dipartimento Jonico In Sistemi Giuridici Ed Economici Del Mediterraneo: Società, Ambiente, Culture, Università degli Studi di Bari Aldo Moro, Bari, Italy

N. Castellano et al. (eds.), *Environmental, Social, Governance (ESG)*, SIDREA Series in Accounting and Business Administration,
https://doi.org/10.1007/978-3-031-76618-3_21

correlation between the adoption of sustainable practices and companies' financial returns (Eccles et al., 2020). Therefore, academics agreed about the need to rethink the traditional theoretical paradigms about corporate social responsibility and sustainable development because of the institutionalization of the ESG practices (Pizzi et al., 2023; Shabana et al., 2017).

However, extracting information about ESG dynamics considering traditional reporting tools represents a critical task for investors and analysts. As evidenced in previous research, ESG information cover a critical role in financial valuation because of they could describe intangible assets and potential value drivers (Edmans, 2023). In this regard, many companies have started to disclose their ESG data on voluntary or mandatory basis to engage in a more effectively way with stakeholders. A relevant contribution was provided by the European Commission, which was one of the first regulators to introduce specific requirements about sustainability reporting to intercept investors' informative needs (Venturelli & Caputo, 2017). In addition, the high degree of attention paid by the European Commission to the topic is confirmed by the recent development of the Corporate Sustainability Reporting Directive (CSRD), which will introduce more strict requirements about sustainability reporting (KPMG, 2022a).

As evidenced by the latest trends in financial and sustainability accounting, climate change represents one of the main ESG topics able to influence companies' financial ratios (IVSC, 2022; Pizzi, 2022). In this regard, many companies started to include specific information about climate risks in their management reports. In fact, according to previous literature, the transparency of information could help mitigate these climate risks. Indeed, important information failures limit understanding of climate risks and their financial impact on companies (Amar et al., 2022). The need to consider climate risk has been also underlined by the recent initiatives launched by the European Financial Reporting Advisory Group, which introduced in December 2022 the European Sustainability Reporting Standards (Pizzi, 2022). Furthermore, another contribution has been provided by the IFRS Foundation and by the Security Exchange Commission (SEC), which has started to develop new standards to enhance financial markets' transparency. Interestingly, despite substantial and symbolic differences between standards, the three proposals agree about the need to pay specific attention to climate reporting (KPMG, 2022b).

However, despite the relevant contribution provided by the main sustainability reporting standard setters, the main political and scientific debates about climate change reporting underlined the need to integrate this information into traditional financial reports (Kaplan & Ramanna, 2022; Moreno & Caminero, 2022). This evidence is confirmed by the choice made by the European Commission to introduce strict requirements about the integration of the sustainability declarations within management reports (KPMG, 2022a). Therefore, the next years will be characterized by the development of new accountability tools based on the integration of financial and sustainability reports within a common umbrella.

According to this evidence, the chapter aims to contribute to the scientific debate about climate risk reporting with novel insights about the voluntary integration of climate information within the management reports prepared by the Italian listed firms. For our purposes, we will explore a representative sample of Italian companies to understand the degree of attention paid by Italian companies to an emerging topic. The identification of the climate information has been favored by the existence of a standalone section about risk reporting in the management reports ("*Relazione sulla Gestione*") (Adamo & Di Cagno, 2021).

The contribution to the scientific debate is twofold. The first contribution consists of the collection of novel insights about climate risk reporting (Cosma et al., 2022; Lombardi et al., 2022), with a specific focus on an institutional context characterized by an intense debate about sustainability reporting and regulation. Regarding the second contribution, the chapter will contribute to the development of a novel research field about the integration of ESG information within financial reports (Acunzo & Abate, 2021; Fiume et al., 2022; Kaplan & Ramanna, 2022).

The chapter is structured as follows. Section 21.2 consists of a literature review about accountability processes and sustainability risk reporting. Section 21.3 describes the methodology adopted by the authors while Sect. 21.4 reports the empirical evidence collected through the analysis. Finally, in Sect. 21.5, we will develop a critical analysis about the main insights of our research.

21.2 Literature Review and Research Question

21.2.1 ESG Risks Disclosure

By analyzing the top 10 global risks by severity announced by the World Economic Forum (2022), five of these are environmental ones and the first one is the climate action failure. In particular, climate change risk represents an urgent global issue for world organizations (Mateo-Márquez et al., 2020; Principale, 2023). The issue is obviously a priority also for the European Union that fixed the target reducing to zero emissions by 2050, through a series of measures (European Commission, 2020). At the same time, academics give growing importance to the issue in their studies (He et al., 2022).

Nowadays, risk management has become a fundamental part of internal control to identify, measure, and assess the different kinds of risk that a company has to face. Furthermore, among the different kinds of risks that a company must face, the so-called non-financial risks or ESG risks have become crucial to manage in an adequate way the negative effects of unsustainable practices, such as penalties, not compliance, and so on (Spedding & Rose, 2008).

The relevance of the topic is also confirmed by the recent initiatives launched by the Committee of Sponsoring Organizations of the Treadway Commission (COSO) and by the World Business Council for Sustainable Development (WBCSD). The two organizations have published a guidance to help entities understand the potential effects of ESG risks and to integrate and disclose them effectively (COSO & WBCSD, 2018). In the guidance, the theme "climate change" is expressed into four key issues that are carbon emissions, product carbon footprint, financing environmental impact, and climate change vulnerability.

In mitigating risks, a pivotal role is covered by corporate disclosure because of the need to engage effectively with internal and external stakeholders. Disclosing information about risks is particularly relevant for stakeholders because of it could support the comprehension of the opportunity, prospect, hazard, danger, harm, threat, or exposure that could impact the company in the future (Linsley & Shrives, 2006). In this regard, many studies were developed to investigate the usefulness of risk management disclosure, the extent and quality of risk management disclosure, and the determinants of risk management disclosure.

One of the main issues considered by academics is represented by risk disclosure quality. In particular, many studies were developed about potential semantic proxies able to summarize risk disclosure quality. Beretta and Bozzolan (2004) highlighted the importance of semantic properties of disclosure, proposing a multidimensional model for measuring the quality of risk disclosure. Another research published by Neri et al. (2018), which mixed qualitative and quantitative elements, developed an index of the measurement of the quality of risk disclosure considering a mixed method based on quantitative and qualitative estimations. Furthermore, Leopizzi et al. (2020) using a content analysis, evaluate the level of non-financial risk disclosure after the introduction of the Directive 2014/95/EU on non-financial information and the effectiveness of non-financial risk management.

Part of the literature investigated the factors that influence the extent of risk disclosure. For example, these studies found as determinants of company size and industry (Beretta & Bozzolan, 2004), company size and level of risk (Linsley & Shrives, 2006), the number of executive directors and of independent directors in relation to the extent of risk disclosure (Abraham & Cox, 2007) and other governance and ownership characteristics.

With specific reference to the relationship between climate risks disclosure and corporate characteristics, research developed on the subject is quite rare. Some recent research papers suggested that there was a positive relationship between firm size and financial performance, but a negative association with the level of indebtedness (Kouloukoui et al., 2018, 2019). Also referring to German DAX30 companies, a recent study based on a content analysis of climate-related corporate disclosures from 2018 to 2020—linked to the recommendations of the Task Force on Climate-related Financial Disclosures (TCFD)—shows that there are poor reporting rates in the corporate governance domain, and carbon-sensitive companies report relevant information on climate issues more than others (Braasch & Velte, 2023).

The extent of climate risk disclosure has been also analyzed together with pandemic disclosure in the study of Adams and Abhayawansa (2021). They examined what and how information on pandemic and climate risks is reported by organizations, to suggest considerations for a conceptual framework for non-financial reporting (NFR) to encompass ESG risks. The study shows that little attention has been given to pandemic risks and that disclosures on climate-related risks focus predominantly on "risks" of increased regulation. The information, indeed, seems to be diffused across different corporate reporting with no integration.

This evidence is in line with the emerged exigence, already highlighted, to systematize this information in a unique umbrella to allow comparison and easy identification of the information for stakeholders.

In summary, it is possible to highlight that generally the literature on the disclosure of climate-related topics analyzes mainly companies' impact on the climate rather than companies' exposure to climate-related risks (Andrew & Baker, 2020; Hahn et al., 2015), and the energy and resource sectors have been the most studied. Many studies, indeed, have just the aim of quantifying disclosure (Leopizzi et al., 2023; Panfilo & Krasodomska, 2022).

21.2.2 Institutional Background and Hypothesis Development

As evidenced in the previous section, the relevance of non-financial information for investors has been highlighted in previous studies (Lombardi, 2021), according to which there is a positive link between disclosing ESG information and the financial performance of a company. In fact, the tendency of international institutions is to integrate ESG information into the financial statements (Reichlin, 2021). Furthermore, as previously evidenced, climate change represents one of the main ESG topics able to influence companies' financial ratios. Moreover, considering that according to previous literature the transparency of information could help mitigate these climate risks, many companies disclosed about climate risks in their reports (Amar et al., 2022).

Furthermore, the Financial Stability Board's Taskforce on Climate-Related Financial Disclosures (TCFD) has set a high-level framework for disclosing climate risks and opportunities in financial reports. These recommendations and guidelines provided valuable advice for companies to disclose adequate climate-related information in corporate reporting, such as climate-related risks, opportunities, key performance indicators (KPIs). The establishment of an international working group, the Task Force on Climate-related Financial Disclosures (TCFD), at COP 21 (2015) is considered an important international policy effort by financial regulators to address the challenge of climate-related financial risks.

Specifically, the recommendations of the TCFD (2017) are divided into four thematic areas: governance, strategy, risk management, metrics and targets. The recommendations from TCFD cover four key areas. First, in terms of governance, they aim to encourage organizations to disclose their decisions regarding climate-related risks and opportunities, focusing on the oversight of the Board of Directors and the role of management. Second, concerning strategies, the TCFD provides three recommendations, urging companies to specify climate-related risks and opportunities, assess their impacts, and assess the strategy's resilience. Third, with regard to risk management, three recommendations address risk identification, assessment, management processes, and integration into overall risk management. Lastly, in the realm of metrics and targets, TCFD calls for the disclosure of metrics used, greenhouse gas emissions data, and climate objectives, providing transparency on key parameters to address climate change risks.

The Task Force recommended that companies include climate-related financial disclosures in their annual financial reports, but recognized companies may include such information in other types of reports. Over the years, the percentage of companies that disclosed information in financial reports or integrated reports increased from 45% in fiscal year 2017 to 71% (TCFD, 2020). Nevertheless, the number of companies that have decided to be compliant to these recommendations is not so high. In Italy, for instance, recent studies (Principale & Pizzi, 2023) show that most of Italian companies decided not to adopt the TCFD recommendations, even if previous results show that companies that have already adopted TCFD have inevitably an advantage to approach to the disclosure about ESG risks.

The European Commission has spurred ESG risk disclosure by introducing the Non-Financial Reporting Directive (NFRD) and the Corporate Sustainability Reporting Directive. Specifically, EU Directive 2014/95 mandates the disclosure of "non-financial and diversity information" in the annual report or a separate document. Regarding non-financial risks, it requires the disclosure of primary risks related to the company's operations, including those tied to its business relationships, products, or services that may have adverse impacts in these areas, along with how the company manages these risks. The CSRD builds upon this, stipulating that non-financial information should now be integrated into the management report rather than being presented separately from the financial statement. This aligns with the global trend of incorporating sustainability information into financial reports, reflecting the international political and scientific consensus (Kaplan & Ramanna, 2022; Moreno & Caminero, 2022).

Given the context outlined above, this research focuses on examining the disclosure of climate-related risks within management reports. In light of the unsatisfactory outcomes observed in previous studies, particularly concerning the level of compliance among companies, we have chosen not to assess adherence to the TCFD recommendations or compliance with the specific risk disclosure requirements of the Directive. Instead, our objective is to ascertain the mere presence of climate-related information within the management reports, especially in anticipation of the forthcoming introduction of the CSRD. To address this, we aim to fill the existing knowledge gap regarding climate risk reporting by conducting an in-depth evaluation of the current state of climate reporting practices in Italy, with a particular emphasis on the information conveyed within management reports.

21.3 Sampling and Methods

21.3.1 Sampling Strategy

A comprehensive examination of 111 Italian companies operating in non-financial sectors was conducted for the purpose of this study (Table 21.1). The choice to

Table 21.1 Sample description

Industry	Total
Aerospace	2
Automotive	5
Chemicals	2
Construction and engineering	5
Electronics	9
Energy	8
Food and beverage	5
Healthcare and pharma	5
Logistics and transport	7
Machine and plant	9
Manufacturing	15
Media and publishing	7
Oil and gas	2
Retailers	3
Services	9
Steel	1
Technology	1
Telecommunications	3
Textile	5
Utilities	8
Total	**111**

exclude financial companies has been driven by the opportunity to explore a homogeneous sample of companies because of the existence of several differences between financial and non-financial companies (Caputo et al., 2021; Venturelli et al., 2018).

The criteria for sample selection were informed by the regulatory guidelines articulated in CONSOB documentation, which delineates the obligations of entities to adhere to sustainability reporting standards. More specifically, the sample exclusively comprised Italian Public Interest Entities (PIEs) that had consistently published sustainability reports for every fiscal year within the period from 2017 to 2021. This specific criterion guided our sample selection process, ensuring the inclusion of entities possessing a discernible degree of familiarity with ESG performance and the associated risks (Leopizzi et al., 2020).

21.3.2 Empirical Model

The analysis was constructed using an empirical approach centered on Poisson regressions. Poisson regression is a statistical methodology well-suited for text analysis due to its capacity to accommodate discrete variables, such as the count of observations, the number of words, and sentence length (Cazier & Pfeiffer, 2016;

Li et al., 2011). Moreover, opting for Poisson regression over the conventional ordinary least squares (OLS) method offers several advantages, including addressing issues associated with zero values in the dependent variable and mitigating estimation bias arising from heteroskedasticity in the error term, as elucidated by Paniagua et al. (2018).

21.3.2.1 Dependent Variable

The dependent variable considered in the present study is represented by the total number of references to climate issues in companies' financial reports (WORDS). The data collection was conducted using a research protocol based on the following steps: (a) report identification, (b) data collection, and (c) data validation. The report identification was favored by the existence of a freely available repository to collect listed companies' corporate disclosure. In this regard, we avoid potential bias related to the identification of the document considering the corporate website. The second step consists of data collection. The data collection was conducted using digital devices to count the number of explicit reminders to climate risks and opportunities. Finally, a set of tests were developed to validate the data collected. In particular, we manually checked the existence of potential criticisms related to the adoption of the concept "climate" to describe other dynamics such as the relationship with employees and the political issues.

21.3.2.2 Independent and Control Variables

As evidenced in the previous sections, the paper aims to contribute to the scientific debate with novel insights about the integration of climate information within traditional financial reports. In order to actively contribute to the debate, we chose to explore the interlinkages between climate disclosure and the exposure to environmental and climate risks.

For our purposes, using the data provided by the international database AIDA BvD, we considered as independent variables the data released by Trucost about environmental risks. In detail, the Trucost's environmental valuation coefficients are numerical factors that symbolize the typical monetary value of harm incurred, encompassing the external expenses linked to an organization's externalities, which in turn affects human, natural, and built capital. Therefore, the higher the level of exposure to the Trucost indicator, the greater the economic damage associated with the occurrence of the adverse event (Trucost, 2015).

According to this evidence, we considered four alternative perspectives. The first perspective consists of the exposure to environmental risks (T_ENV) while the second perspective regards the specific sub-indicator about the exposure to monetary loss related to GHG emissions (T_GHG). The third perspective regards the sectorial risks (T_SEC), which could assume values lower, higher, or equal to the score assigned to each company. Finally, we developed a performance indicator based on

Table 21.2 Variables' description

Variable	Mean	Std. Dev.	Min	Max
Dependent variable				
WORDS	30.829	42.585	0	264
Independent variable				
T_ENV	4.379	6.269	0.25	30.2
T_GHG	1.905	3.693	0.09	26.28
T_SEC	1.645	3.964	0.096	29.649
T_PER	1.336	0.909	0.442	7.452
Control variables				
SIZE	13.756	2.044	6.411	18.638
ROE	7.516	12.889	−38.61	60.4
DE	0.878	0.893	0	4.6
EPS	−0.51	1.377	−4.343	1.994

the ratio between companies' GHG risks and the sectorial' GHG risks (T_PER). In this regard, we will consider the effects related to the choice made by companies to overperform or underperform in comparison with their comparables.

Finally, we integrated our empirical analysis with a set of control variables to avoid potential endogeneity issues. Consistently with previous accounting research, we considered the effects related to corporate dimensions (SIZE), financial returns (ROE), the debt-to-equity ratio (DE), and the earning per share (EPS).

The variables considered in the empirical model are summarized in Table 21.2.

21.4 Results

21.4.1 Descriptive Analysis

The descriptive analysis (Table 21.3) reveals that the most virtuous sectors are the Energy, the Utilities, and the Logistic and Transport. Although the existence of other sectors with score equal to 100%, the data about the three sectors are particularly relevant because of their relevance within the sample and, subsequently, within Italian financial markets. The greater attitude to disclose this information is probably explained by their interlinkages with climate issues. In this regard, previous studies underlined their pivotal role within the public policies about climate mitigation (Leopizzi et al., 2023; Lippolis et al., 2023).

Regarding the less virtuous sectors, the analysis reveals the scarce attitude to disclose climate information by Machine and Plant, Chemicals, and Retailers. The lack of information by Retailers is related to their characteristics while the insights about Machine and Plant and Chemicals reveal the existence of alternative behaviors by preparers. Surprisingly, in the textile sector, only the 60% of the companies disclosed climate information despite the high degree of pressure made by

Table 21.3 Descriptive analysis. Focus on climate disclosure

Industry	Climate information	No information	Sample size
Energy	100,00%	0,00%	8
Utilities	100,00%	0,00%	8
Logistics and transport	100,00%	0,00%	7
Automotive	100,00%	0,00%	5
Telecommunications	100,00%	0,00%	3
Aerospace	100,00%	0,00%	2
Oil and gas	100,00%	0,00%	2
Steel	100,00%	0,00%	1
Technology	100,00%	0,00%	1
Electronics	88,89%	11,11%	9
Manufacturing	86,67%	13,33%	15
Media and publishing	85,71%	14,29%	7
Construction and engineering	80,00%	20,00%	5
Healthcare and pharma	80,00%	20,00%	5
Services	66,67%	33,33%	9
Food and beverage	60,00%	40,00%	5
Textile	60,00%	40,00%	5
Machine and plant	55,56%	44,44%	9
Chemicals	50,00%	50,00%	2
Retailers	33,33%	66,67%	3
Total	81,98%	18,02%	111

stakeholders and non-governmental organizations. In fact, the textile sector is one of the most impactful sectors on climate (Luque & Herrero-García, 2019). Therefore, collecting data about climate could be relevant for investors interested in extending their portfolio with textile companies.

The analysis of the confidence interval revealed that the sample is characterized by a high degree of heterogeneity in terms of information disclosed by the observed companies (Table 21.4). In detail, we found that the standard deviation within certain sectors such as the Aerospace or the Energy is significantly higher than other sectors. Therefore, the dynamics related to the disclosure of climate information by companies are probably also influenced by managers' attitudes toward ESG issues. Regarding the Oil&Gas and the Utilities sectors, it is necessary to provide independent reflections because of their specificities (Imperiale et al., 2023). The two sectors are significantly exposed to reputational risks associated with their anthropic impacts. In this regard, the high degree of heterogeneity is explained by the accountability strategies adopted by managers to face the issues related to stakeholder pressures. In this regard, despite the relevance of the topic, certain managers could choose to avoid potential reputational risks through the adoption of "opaque" narrative approach to describe the effects related to climate change (Amar et al., 2022).

Table 21.4 Confidence interval analysis. N.B. We excluded from our analysis the Steel and Technology sectors

	95% confidence interval mean					
	Mean	Lower	Upper	Std. Dev.	Min.	Max.
Aerospace	54.500	114.279	−5.279	43.134	24.000	85.000
Automotive	21.800	39.542	4.058	20.241	4.000	53.000
Chemicals	2.000	5.920	−1.920	2.828	0.000	4.000
Construction and engineering	28.400	62.734	−5.934	39.170	0.000	97.000
Electronics	16.444	29.025	3.864	19.256	0.000	52.000
Energy	65.000	103.594	26.406	55.696	7.000	151.000
Food and beverage	27.200	57.197	−2.797	34.223	0.000	72.000
Healthcare and pharma	15.800	26.011	5.589	11.649	0.000	27.000
Logistics and transport	39.429	65.828	13.029	35.636	5.000	98.000
Machine and plant	17.556	33.344	1.767	24.167	0.000	60.000
Manufacturing	22.933	37.778	8.088	29.334	0.000	99.000
Media and publishing	19.714	37.646	1.783	24.205	0.000	65.000
Oil and gas	135.500	387.355	−116.355	181.726	7.000	264.000
Retailers	3.000	8.880	−2.880	5.196	0.000	9.000
Services	17.667	36.093	−0.760	28.205	0.000	86.000
Telecommunications	9.667	15.899	3.434	5.508	6.000	16.000
Textile	8.600	18.777	−1.577	11.610	0.000	28.000
Utilities	80.125	119.344	40.906	56.597	6.000	168.000

21.4.2 Correlation Analysis

A correlation analysis (Table 21.5) was conducted to exclude potential statistical issues related to heteroskedasticity and multicollinearity issues (Baltagi, 2005; Certo & Semadeni, 2006). The absence of statistically significant correlations greater than 0.6 confirms the robustness of our analysis (Kalnins, 2018).

21.4.3 Empirical Analysis

The empirical analysis (Table 21.6) reveals interesting insights about the relationship between climate disclosure and environmental dynamics.

The Eq. 1 confirms the existence of a positive relationship with SIZE ($\beta = 0.721$; $p < 0.01$) and DE ($\beta = 0.0.692$; $p < 0.01$) while the relationship with ROE ($\beta = -0.052$; $p < 0.01$) and EPS ($\beta = -0.184$; $p < 0.01$) is negative. The insights can be summarized in the existence of a direct connection with company resources, confirming that large companies are interested to legitimate their behaviors adopting a more narrative approach in their corporate disclosure to engage in a more effective way with their stakeholders (Gulluscio et al., 2020).

Table 21.5 Correlation analysis

Variables	(1)	(2)	(3)	(4)	(5)	(6)	(7)	(8)	(9)
(1) WORDS	1.000								
(2) SIZE	0.398*	1.000							
(3) ROE	0.058	−0.050	1.000						
(4) DE	−0.082	−0.036	0.118	1.000					
(5) EPS	0.085	0.283	0.300	0.134	1.000				
(6) T_ENV	−0.026	0.164	0.149	−0.167	−0.059	1.000			
(7) T_GHG	−0.004	0.127	0.119	−0.148	0.058	0.767*	1.000		
(8) T_SEC	−0.048	0.078	0.109	−0.134	0.092	0.671*	0.964*	1.000	
(9) T_PER	0.167	0.184	0.005	−0.099	−0.113	0.156	0.067	−0.082	1.000

*** $p < 0.01$, ** $p < 0.05$, * $p < 0.1$

Table 21.6 Empirical analysis

	(1)	(2)	(3)	(4)	(5)
SIZE	0.721***	0.748***	0.703***	0.705***	0.73***
	(0.021)	(0.021)	(0.026)	(0.022)	(0.021)
ROE	−0.052***	−0.045***	−0.054***	−0.05***	−0.052***
	(0.006)	(0.006)	(0.006)	(0.006)	(0.006)
DE	0.692***	0.489***	0.679***	0.63***	0.623***
	(0.08)	(0.085)	(0.081)	(0.081)	(0.081)
EPS	−0.184***	−0.247***	−0.207***	−0.22***	−0.217***
	(0.023)	(0.025)	(0.024)	(0.025)	(0.024)
T_ENV		−0.035***			
		(0.005)			
T_GHG			0.034		
			(0.033)		
T_SEC				0.094**	
				(0.044)	
T_PER					−0.066***
					(0.025)
_cons	−7.225***	−7.386***	−6.989***	−7.104***	−7.198***
	(0.352)	(0.337)	(0.375)	(0.347)	(0.345)
Pseudo R^2	0.701	0.726	0.706	0.707	0.708

Standard errors are in parentheses

The conjoint evaluation of the insights related to Eqs. 2 and 3 provides interesting reflections about the interlinkages with environmental performance. On a hand, the Eq. 2 reveals the existence of a negative relationship between the disclosure of climate information and the exposure to environmental risks ($\beta = -0.035; p < 0.01$). Pollutant companies are probably less interested to disclose climate information than sustainable companies because of the existence of reputational risks related to the disclosure of unfavorable information (Imperiale et al., 2023). Thus, contrarily to sustainability reporting, the analysis reveals that there is a less greenwashing risk in financial reporting practices. On the other hand, we did not identify statistically significant relationship with the variable T_GHG. The absence of statistically significant relationship is probably related to the stakeholders' difficult to estimate the anthropic impacts generated by a company in terms of GHG (Rankin et al., 2011).

The absence of statistically significant results in Eq. 3 is partially mitigated by the insights collected in Eq. 4. In detail, we found that companies that operate in environmentally sensitive sectors characterized by a high degree of GHG emissions disclose more climate information than the other ($\beta = -0.094; p < 0.05$). Therefore, the need to provide information about climate risks is driven by sectorial dynamics instead of internal evaluation, revealing the existence of a potential isomorphic behaviors adopted by companies. In fact, as evidenced in previous accounting studies, many companies adequate their accountability practices following the behaviors adopted by their comparables (Martínez-Ferrero & García-Sánchez, 2017).

Considering the theoretical misalignment between Eqs. 3 and 4, we considered in Eq. 5 an alternative indicator based on the synthesis of the two indicators considered in the previous models. Interestingly, the analysis highlighted that T_PER is negatively associated with WORDS ($\beta = -0.066$; $p < 0.01$). This result is particularly relevant because of it sheds the lights on the effects related to the performance achieved by the companies in comparison with their sector of origin. In detail, we found that companies that have achieved an evaluation behind the score achieved by their sector of origin did not disclose information about their climate impacts. In this regard, the analysis reveals the existence of relevant differences between financial and sustainability reporting practices in terms of potential legitimacy strategies (Wagenhofer, 2023). In fact, previous sustainability reporting research reveals that many highly pollutant companies disclose their climate information to legitimate their behaviors (Caputo et al., 2021).

21.5 Discussion and Concluding Remarks

Companies play a pivotal role in the context of climate change mitigation, as they are instrumental in addressing the adverse consequences of this global challenge. In recent years, there has been a growing demand from investors and stakeholders for climate-related information. Despite the increasing adoption of sophisticated accountability tools, whether mandated or voluntary, by companies worldwide, there remains a dearth of comprehensive knowledge about corporate climate strategies.

The heightened awareness of climate-related concerns has led to a broader acceptance of sustainability reports among companies. However, investors have indicated that gaining a nuanced understanding of the primary drivers of environmental and climate impacts necessitates the development of instruments directly linked to financial indicators. The absence of a clear connection between financial and non-financial dynamics poses a significant impediment to effective stakeholder engagement from an Environmental, Social, and Governance (ESG) perspective.

In light of these considerations, this chapter seeks to contribute to the evolving discourse on climate reporting by offering fresh insights into the integration of ESG data within conventional financial statements. Our analysis has unveiled that many companies are beginning to incorporate climate information into their narrative disclosures. Notably, sectors characterized by a substantial climate footprint are at the forefront of this shift toward narrative strategies. This widespread adoption is driven by their vulnerability to reputational risks.

Our study employs both descriptive and empirical analyses, employing Poisson regressions. The empirical findings illuminate the multifaceted factors influencing the choice to disclose climate-related information. We observe a positive influence of exposure to environmental risks on the disclosure of such information, while the performance achieved by a company relative to its sector has a negative effect. Consequently, our analysis corroborates the existence of diverse accountability mechanisms stemming from varying motivations behind the decision to disclose pertinent information to stakeholders. Concerning sectoral dynamics, we also find that companies with climate risks exceeding their sector's average are less inclined to divulge such information. This suggests a pressing need for these companies to legitimize their operations, mirroring the dynamics observed with environmental risks.

The theoretical contributions of our findings extend the body of research on climate-related information by introducing novel insights into the integration of ESG elements into traditional financial reporting. Despite the increasing attention of accounting scholars to ESG risk reporting in recent years, only a limited number of studies have approached this topic from a financial reporting perspective.

From a practical standpoint, this chapter serves as a valuable resource for practitioners, policymakers, and regulators seeking to comprehend the landscape of climate-related disclosure and anticipate the potential impact of forthcoming regulatory developments in this domain. The future integration of sustainability-related information within the management reports will represents a critical task for practitioners because of the need to evaluate non-financial topics through a financial-based lens. In this regard, the disclosure of climate-related risks will require an additional effort because of the need to monetize risks and opportunities related to sustainability issues. Therefore, despite the attempt made by a wide number of companies to disclose sustainability information on a voluntary basis using a narrative approach, identifying quantitative metrics will represent a critical task for practitioners.

It is important to note that our research focuses on the examination of climate-related risk disclosure within management reports. Given the suboptimal compliance levels observed in previous studies, particularly in terms of companies adhering to the Task Force on Climate-related Financial Disclosures (TCFD) recommendations and the specific risk disclosure requirements of the Directive, we deliberately refrained from evaluating such compliance in this study. Consequently, this limitation creates an avenue for future research to explore adherence to the stringent TCFD requirements, specifically within the context of financial reporting.

References

Abraham, S., & Cox, P. (2007). Analysing the determinants of narrative risk information in UK FTSE 100 annual reports. *British Accounting Review, 39*(3), 227–248. https://doi.org/10.1016/j.bar.2007.06.002

Acunzo, G., & Abate, E. (2021). Sugli impatti del cambiamento climatico sull'informativa finanziaria secondo gli IFRS. *Rivista Italiana Di Ragioneria e Di Economia Aziendale.*

Adamo, S., & Di Cagno, N. (2021). *Il Bilancio d'esercizio Delle Imprese Societarie.* Cacucci Editore.

Adams, C. A., & Abhayawansa, S. (2021). Connecting the COVID-19 pandemic, environmental, social and governance (ESG) investing and calls for "harmonisation" of sustainability reporting. *Critical Perspectives on Accounting, 148*, 148–162. https://doi.org/10.1016/j.cpa.2021.102309

Amar, J., Demaria, S., & Rigot, S. (2022). Enhancing financial transparency to mitigate climate change: Toward a climate risks and opportunities reporting index. *Environmental Modeling and Assessment, Springer Science and Business Media Deutschland GmbH, 27*(3), 425–439. https://doi.org/10.1007/s10666-021-09800-7

Andrew, J., & Baker, M. (2020). Corporate social responsibility reporting: The last 40 years and a path to sharing future insights. *Abacus, 56*(1), 35–65. https://doi.org/10.1111/abac.12181

Baltagi, B. H. (2005). *Econometric analysis of panel data* (3rd ed., Ed. John Wiley & Sons Ltd). John Wiley & Sons, 2008

Beretta, S., & Bozzolan, S. (2004). A framework for the analysis of firm risk communication. *International Journal of Accounting, 39*(3), 265–288. https://doi.org/10.1016/j.intacc.2004.06.006

Braasch, A., & Velte, P. (2023). Climate reporting quality following the recommendations of the task force on climate-related financial disclosures: A focus on the German capital market. *Sustainable Development, 31*(2), 926–940. https://doi.org/10.1002/sd.2430

Caputo, F., Pizzi, S., Ligorio, L., & Leopizzi, R. (2021). Enhancing environmental information transparency through corporate social responsibility reporting regulation. *Business Strategy and the Environment, John Wiley and Sons Ltd, 30*(8), 3470–3484. https://doi.org/10.1002/bse.2814

Cazier, R. A., & Pfeiffer, R. J. (2016). Why are 10-K filings so long? *Accounting Horizons, 30*(1), 1–21. https://doi.org/10.2308/acch-51240

Certo, S. T., & Semadeni, M. (2006). Strategy research and panel data: Evidence and implications. *Journal of Management, Sage Publications Sage CA: Thousand Oaks, CA, 32*(3), 449–471. https://doi.org/10.1177/0149206305283320

Chung, J., & Cho, C. H. (2018). Current trends within social and environmental accounting research: A literature review. *Accounting Perspectives, 17*(2), 207–239. https://doi.org/10.1111/1911-3838.12171

CONSOB. (2022). Principali Tendenze in Tema Di Investimenti Sostenibili e Criptoattività.

Cosma, S., Principale, S., & Venturelli, A. (2022). Sustainable governance and climate-change disclosure in European banking: The role of the corporate social responsibility committee. *Corporate Governance (Bingley), Emerald Group Holdings Ltd., Department of Sciences of the Economy, Università del Salento, Lecce, Italy, 22*(6), 1345–1369. https://doi.org/10.1108/CG-09-2021-0331

COSO and WBCSD. (2018). Applying Enterprise Risk Management to Environmental, Social and Governance-related Risks – World Business Council for Sustainable Development (WBCSD). Accessed September 15, 2023, from https://www.wbcsd.org/Programs/Redefining-Value/Making-stakeholder-capitalism-actionable/Enterprise-Risk-Management/Resources/Applying-Enterprise-Risk-Management-to-Environmental-Social-and-Governance-related-Risks

Eccles, R. G., Lee, L.-E., & Stroehle, J. C. (2020). The social origins of ESG: An analysis of innovest and KLD. *Organization and Environment, SAGE Publications Inc, 33*(4), 575–596. https://doi.org/10.1177/1086026619888994

Edmans, A. (2023). The end of ESG. *Financial Management, 52*(1), 3–17. https://doi.org/10.1111/fima.12413

European Commission. (2020). European Climate Law (Vol. 0036, pp. 1–58).

EY. (2021). *The evolving non-financial reporting landscape.*

Fiume, R., Onesti, T., Cordero di Montezemolo, G., & Strada, M. (2022). Dialogue with standard setters. Climate change and financial reporting. *Financial Reporting, 1*, 155–166. https://doi.org/10.3280/fr2022-001005

Gulluscio, C., Puntillo, P., Luciani, V., & Huisingh, D. (2020). Climate change accounting and reporting: A systematic literature review. *Sustainability, MDPI AG, 12*(13), 5455. https://doi.org/10.3390/su12135455

Hahn, T., Pinkse, J., Preuss, L., & Figge, F. (2015). Tensions in corporate sustainability: Towards an integrative framework. *Journal of Business Ethics, 127*(2), 297–316. https://doi.org/10.1007/s10551-014-2047-5

He, R., Luo, L., Shamsuddin, A., & Tang, Q. (2022). Corporate carbon accounting: A literature review of carbon accounting research from the Kyoto protocol to the Paris agreement. *Accounting and Finance, John Wiley and Sons Inc, 62*(1), 261–298. https://doi.org/10.1111/acfi.12789

Imperiale, F., Pizzi, S., & Lippolis, S. (2023). Sustainability reporting and ESG performance in the utilities sector. *Utilities Policy, Pergamon, 80*, 101468. https://doi.org/10.1016/j.jup.2022.101468

IVSC. (2022), IVSC ESG survey results: Unlocking the value of ESG.

Kalnins, A. (2018). Multicollinearity: How common factors cause type 1 errors in multivariate regression. *Strategic Management Journal, 39*(8), 2362–2385. https://doi.org/10.1002/smj.2783

Kaplan, R., & Ramanna, K. (2022). Accounting for climate change. *Harvard Business Review, 99*(6), 120–131.

Kouloukoui, D., Gomes, S. M. D. S., Marinho, M. M. D. O., Torres, E. A., Kiperstok, A., & de Jong, P. (2018). Disclosure of climate risk information by the world's largest companies. *Mitigation and Adaptation Strategies for Global Change, 23*(8), 1251–1279. https://doi.org/10.1007/s11027-018-9783-2

Kouloukoui, D., Sant'Anna, Â. M. O., da Silva Gomes, S. M., de Oliveira Marinho, M. M., de Jong, P., Kiperstok, A., & Torres, E. A. (2019). Factors influencing the level of environmental disclosures in sustainability reports: Case of climate risk disclosure by Brazilian companies. *Corporate Social Responsibility and Environmental Management, 26*(4), 791–804. https://doi.org/10.1002/csr.1721

KPMG. (2022a). The new CSRD: What does this mean for you?

KPMG. (2022b). Comparing sustainability reporting proposals.

La Torre, M., Sabelfeld, S., Blomkvist, M., & Dumay, J. (2020). Rebuilding trust: Sustainability and non-financial reporting and the European Union regulation. *Meditari Accountancy Research, Emerald Group Publishing Ltd, 28*, 701–725. https://doi.org/10.1108/MEDAR-06-2020-0914

Leopizzi, R., Iazzi, A., Venturelli, A., & Principale, S. (2020). Nonfinancial risk disclosure: The "state of the art" of Italian companies. *Corporate Social Responsibility and Environmental Management, 27*(1), 358–368. https://doi.org/10.1002/csr.1810

Leopizzi, R., Palmi, P., & Di Cagno, P. (2023). Sustainability reporting and electric utilities: A bibliometric analysis. *Utilities Policy, 84*, 101651. https://doi.org/10.1016/j.jup.2023.101651

Li, E. X., Ramesh, K., & Shen, M. (2011). The role of newswires in screening and disseminating value-relevant information in periodic sec reports*. SSRN Electronic Journal. https://doi.org/10.2139/ssrn.1465158.

Linsley, P. M., & Shrives, P. J. (2006). Risk reporting: A study of risk disclosures in the annual reports of UK companies. *The British Accounting Review, Academic Press, 38*(4), 387–404. https://doi.org/10.1016/J.BAR.2006.05.002

Lippolis, S., Ruggieri, A., & Leopizzi, R. (2023). Open innovation for sustainable transition: The case of Enel "open power". *Business Strategy and the Environment, John Wiley and Sons Ltd, 32*(7), 4202–4216. https://doi.org/10.1002/BSE.3361

Lombardi, R. (2021). The going-concern in non-financial information. In *The going-concern-principle in non-financial disclosure* (pp. 79–96). Springer. https://doi.org/10.1007/978-3-030-81127-3_3

Lombardi, R., Schimperna, F., Paoloni, P., & Galeotti, M. (2022). The climate-related information in the changing EU directive on non-financial reporting and disclosure: First evidence by Italian large companies. *Journal of Applied Accounting Research, Emerald Group Holdings Ltd, 23*(1), 250–273. https://doi.org/10.1108/JAAR-04-2021-0117

Luque, A., & Herrero-García, N. (2019). How corporate social (ir) responsibility in the textile sector is defined, and its impact on ethical sustainability: An analysis of 133 concepts. *Corporate Social Responsibility and Environmental Management.*, Wiley, 111 River St, Hoboken 07030-5774, NJ USA, *26*(6), 1285–1306. https://doi.org/10.1002/csr.1747

Martínez-Ferrero, J., & García-Sánchez, I. M. (2017). Coercive, normative and mimetic isomorphism as determinants of the voluntary assurance of sustainability reports. *International Business Review, Elsevier Ltd, 26*(1), 102–118. https://doi.org/10.1016/j.ibusrev.2016.05.009

Mateo-Márquez, A. J., González-González, J. M., & Zamora-Ramírez, C. (2020). The influence of countries' climate change-related institutional profile on voluntary environmental disclosures. *Business Strategy and the Environment, John Wiley and Sons Ltd, 30*(2), bse.2690. https://doi.org/10.1002/bse.2690

Moreno, A. I., & Caminero, T. (2022). Application of text mining to the analysis of climate-related disclosures. *International Review of Financial Analysis, 83*, 102307. https://doi.org/10.1016/j.irfa.2022.102307

Neri, L., Elshandidy, T., & Guo, Y. (2018). Determinants and impacts of risk disclosure quality: Evidence from China. *Journal of Applied Accounting Research, 19*(4), 518–536. https://doi.org/10.1108/JAAR-07-2016-0066

Panfilo, S., & Krasodomska, J. (2022). Climate change risk disclosure in Europe: The role of cultural-cognitive, regulative, and normative factors. *Accounting in Europe, Routledge, Ca' Foscari University of Venice, Venice, Italy, 19*(1), 226–253. https://doi.org/10.1080/17449480.2022.2026000

Paniagua, J., Rivelles, R., & Sapena, J. (2018). Corporate governance and financial performance: The role of ownership and board structure. *Journal of Business Research, Elsevier Inc., 89*, 229–234. https://doi.org/10.1016/j.jbusres.2018.01.060

Pizzi, S. (2022). *La Standardizzazione Dell'informativa Di Sostenibilità*. Stato Dell'arte e Profili Evolutivi. Cacucci Editore.

Pizzi, S., Principale, S., Fasiello, R., & Imperiale, F. (2023). The institutionalization of social and environmental accounting practices in Europe. *Journal of Applied Accounting Research, 24*(5), 816–838. https://doi.org/10.1108/JAAR-07-2022-0190

Principale, S. (2023). The current scenario on sustainable corporate governance: Theoretical and practical evidence. In *SIDREA series in accounting and business administration* (Vol. F203, pp. 43–62). Springer Nature. https://doi.org/10.1007/978-3-031-30354-8_3/COVER

Principale, S., & Pizzi, S. (2023). The determinants of TCFD reporting: A focus on the Italian context. *Administrative Sciences, 13*(2), 61.

Rankin, M., Windsor, C., & Wahyuni, D. (2011). An investigation of voluntary corporate greenhouse gas emissions reporting in a market governance system: Australian evidence. *Accounting, Auditing and Accountability Journal, 24*(8), 1037–1070. https://doi.org/10.1108/09513571111184751

Reichlin, L. (2021). IFRS ® foundation meeting investors' needs for sustainability-related information.

Shabana, K. M., Buchholtz, A. K., & Carroll, A. B. (2017). The institutionalization of corporate social responsibility reporting. *Business & Society, SAGE Publications Ltd, 56*(8), 1107–1135. https://doi.org/10.1177/0007650316628177

Spedding, L. S., & Rose, A. (2008). Business risk management handbook: A sustainable approach (p. 738).

TCFD. (2017). Recommendations of the task force on climate-related financial disclosures i letter from Michael R. Bloomberg.

TCFD. (2020), Task force on climate-related financial disclosures 2020 status report.

Trucost. (2015). *Trucost's valuation methodology*.

Venturelli, A., & Caputo, F. (2017). *Informativa Non Finanziaria e Regulation: Tendenze Evolutive e Relative Implicazioni Alla Luce Dell'emanazione Del D. Lgs 254/16*. McGraw Hill.

Venturelli, A., Cosma, S., & Leopizzi, R. (2018). Stakeholder engagement: An evaluation of european banks. *Corporate Social Responsibility and Environmental Management, 25*(4), 690–703. https://doi.org/10.1002/csr.1486

Wagenhofer, A. (2023). Sustainability reporting: A financial reporting perspective. *Accounting in Europe, 21*, 1–13. https://doi.org/10.1080/17449480.2023.2218398

World Economic Forum. (2022). *The global risks report 2022 17th Edition*.

Chapter 22
Exploring the Relevance of Sustainability Reporting Using a Performativity Approach: A Case Study in the Agrifood Sector

Armando Della Porta, Manuel De Nicola, and Claudia Salvatore

22.1 Introduction

Studies on sustainability accounting have seen a notable surge in recent years (Adams & Frost, 2008; Burritt & Schaltegger, 2010; Hsiao et al., 2022). Organizations are increasingly acknowledging the significance of being accountable with regard to economic aspects and also with respect to environmental and social impacts (Buhr, 2007). To this end, a radical change is needed, but the pathways to enable a consistent transformation remain somewhat unclear, as does the role of accounting in facilitating this transition (Egan & Tweedie, 2018; D'Onza, 2022). In this context, an expanding body of research is dedicated to comprehending how companies implement sustainability concepts using accounting tools and the hurdles they face (Contrafatto et al., 2019).

Sustainability reporting is one of the pivotal tools in the accounting domain. Despite extensive studies, several questions persist regarding the reasons behind its adoption and how it evolves to shape the reality it serves (O'Dwyer & Unerman, 2016). To gain a deeper understanding of the relevance of sustainability reporting, scholars have suggested a more in-depth examination of the factors that lead to its

A. Della Porta (✉)
Department of Business Economics, University G.d'Annunzio, Chieti-Pescara, Italy
e-mail: armando.dellaporta@unich.it

M. De Nicola
Department of Communication Sciences, University of Teramo, Teramo, Italy
e-mail: mdenicola@unite.it

C. Salvatore
Department of Public Health, University of Naples Federico II, Naples, Italy
e-mail: claudia.salvatore@unina.it

N. Castellano et al. (eds.), *Environmental, Social, Governance (ESG)*, SIDREA Series in Accounting and Business Administration,
https://doi.org/10.1007/978-3-031-76618-3_22

adoption and how they change over time (Busco et al., 2018; Contrafatto, 2014; Contrafatto et al., 2019). Analyzing these aspects can offer clearer insights into its ability to drive significant organizational shifts toward sustainability.

Aligned with the growing demand for theory-driven empirical investigations (O'Dwyer & Unerman, 2016), we have adopted a performativity approach (Mackenzie, 2006; Marti & Gond, 2018) to explore the relevance of sustainability reporting. In broad terms, performativity refers to the ability of speech acts, discourse, and networks to enact actions (Austin, 1962; Callon, 2007; MacKenzie, 2006). Performativity-based analysis allows to shift the research focus from analyzing whether concepts accurately reflect reality to assess how they induce effects that modify and conform reality with their contained descriptions (MacKenzie, 2006; Callon, 2007; Gond et al., 2016). Accounting, encompassing matters of measurement is intricately linked to the concept of performativity (Vosselman, 2022; Yu & Huber, 2023). To describe accounting as performative implies that it plays a role in shaping reality (Burchell et al., 1980; Hines, 1988; Miller & Power, 2013; Power, 2021).

Based on these considerations, this study seeks to assess the performativity of sustainability reporting through a case study focused on a company operating in the agrifood industry—specifically, a major Italian virgin olive oil producer referred herein as GreenGold for anonymity. The agrifood sector has relevant impacts in various areas, such as human rights, fair labor, land use, waste, water cycles, climate change, and animal rights (Bebbington & Larrinaga, 2014; Schaltegger, 2018; Spence & Rinaldi, 2014). Agrifood companies have a unique position in recognizing the connections between environmental, social, and economic aspects better than others. They operate in a sector with a significant ecological impact and could be considered potential innovators in aligning corporate activities with global ecological and societal indicators (Bebbington et al., 2019; Gibassier & Alcouffe, 2018; Schaltegger, 2018).

In the period from February to December 2023, we conducted semi-structured interviews with the top management of GreenGold to identify and interpret the evolution of sustainability reporting at GreenGold. We also benefited from additional documents the company provided, as well as from other sources and technical analyses we extracted from the Internet, to get more awareness about sustainability perception in this industry.

This chapter contributes, through a case study analysis, to shed more light on the internal and external conditions (Gibassier & Alcouffe, 2018) that characterize the adoption of sustainability reporting, its evolution over time and, consequently, its relevance. By employing the performative perspective, we highlight the motivations (and the intentions) underpinning the sustainability reporting adoption and the resultant effects. This allows us to offer a comprehensive, contextualized view of the conditions that influence performativity of sustainability reporting inside and beyond organizational boundaries (O'Dwyer & Unerman, 2016; Gibassier & Alcouffe, 2018; Contrafatto et al., 2019).

The paper is organized as follows: In Sect. 22.2, we provide a summary of existing studies that have explored the relevance of sustainability reporting. In

Sect. 22.3, we analyze the theoretical framework adopted in this chapter. In Sect. 22.4, we describe the research methodology. In Sect. 22.5, we detail the case study, and in Sect. 22.6, we discuss findings, implications, and conclusions.

22.2 The Relevance of Sustainability Reporting: A Review

Understanding the relevance of management and accounting concepts and tools, namely their potential impact on organizations and their environment, has become a subject of significant concern (Castellano & Felden, 2021). Some authors argue that this issue has evolved into a distinct research topic (Kieser et al., 2015). Regarding sustainability reporting, the literature is quite fragmented in analyzing the various conditions involved in producing internal and external impacts (Herzig & Schaltegger, 2006; Hahn & Kuhnen, 2013; Nazari et al., 2015; Hsiao et al., 2022).

Some studies emphasize the importance of information reliability and management control systems as necessary conditions to enhance the accuracy and the reliability of the reported information (Durden, 2008; Gond et al., 2012; Traxler et al., 2020). Other studies focus on the quality of Environmental, Social, and Governance (ESG) information disclosed, and the alignment between strategies and the Sustainable Development Goals (SDGs) (Schaltegger, 2018; Silva et al., 2019; Cinquini & De Luca, 2022). From this perspective, sustainability reporting, besides measuring the socio-environmental performance of an organization and communicating it externally, could facilitate the adoption of more ambitious sustainability objectives and, in turn, guide change (Hopwood et al., 2005; Contrafatto & Burns, 2013; Traxler et al., 2020).

Literature on the topic also suggests that the mere adoption of sustainability reporting has a positive external impact on stock market especially for large, publicly listed companies (Kaspereit & Lopatta, 2014; Velte, 2021).

Gibassier and Alcouffe (2018) encourage scholars to extend their focus beyond the boundaries of an organization and examine how a business entity can implement accounting tools to advance sustainability in its own industry and also to better comprehend the influence of both internal and external stakeholders on their development (Greco et al., 2021). Other studies propose to focus on the evolutionary dynamics of sustainability reporting in order to better understand the boundary conditions shaping sustainability reporting's relevance over time (O'Dwyer & Unerman, 2016; Maughan, 2023). Some recent studies suggest that sustainability reporting has an evolutionary nature, characterized by progressive and multi-stage implementation involving phases of experimentation, redesign, and abandonment (Belal & Owen, 2015; Contrafatto, 2014; Contrafatto et al., 2019). These studies have emphasized the importance of external changes in influencing the evolution (design and adaptation) of sustainability reporting (Contrafatto et al., 2019) and the importance of building trust in this tool through ongoing, constructive dialogues that center around its role within organizational strategy, values, and culture (Busco et al., 2018; Contrafatto et al., 2019). This line of research aligns with O'Dwyer and

Unerman (2016) who suggest delving deeper into the dynamics of how sustainability reporting gains or loses relevance in specific contexts. It involves examining the evolution of sustainability reporting across time to better understand the internal and external conditions that contribute to its ascendancy or, conversely, its decline (Vinnari & Laine, 2013; Belal & Owen, 2015; Contrafatto et al., 2019). To achieve aims like this, numerous scholars in the management and accounting field have highlighted the merits of adopting a performativity perspective (Carter et al., 2010; Gond et al., 2016; Vosselman, 2022; Yu & Huber, 2023).

22.3 Theoretical Framework

The core concept of "performativity" appears straightforward but holds deeper implications. Initially coined by Austin (1962), the concept challenged the idea that language merely mirrors reality by suggesting that words possess the power to effect change in the world. From this perspective, performativity represents a linguistic turn toward the broader theme of effectiveness, illustrating how signs like words and numbers have the power to shape the world without solely relying on human agency. According to Austin (1962), language is not purely descriptive; saying something also entails doing something. He differentiates between illocutions and perlocutions: the former immediately create realities that correspond to the speaker's intentions (e.g., a formal announcement by a public authority), while the latter generate activities that may or may not realize these intentions (e.g., the announcement of a new company strategy made by a CEO). These concepts are fundamental in the theory of speech acts because they distinguish between the act of speaking and the effects or reactions that the act can have on the recipient. More basically illocutionary acts refer to actions carried out when making a statement, giving an order, making a request, or expressing an opinion. They are actions performed with the act of speaking itself, which have effects on the recipient. Perlocutionary acts refer to the effects that a verbal action has on the recipient or audience, such as persuading them, convincing them, threatening them, annoying them, or making them laugh. They are the effects or reactions that the perlocutionary act can provoke in the listener. They rely on the effects, which are influenced by circumstances—a concept Austin termed as felicitous conditions. Perlocutionary acts direct performativity toward the recipient of speech acts, requiring the ongoing reconstruction of felicitous conditions for the speech acts to effectively resonate with the receiver. Notably, not all performative utterances are successful; unsuccessful utterances are deemed as infelicitous rather than incorrect. The effectiveness of a performative utterance relies on meeting felicitous conditions, which may pertain to the individual (sincerity of the utterer) or the institutional context (e.g., authorized personnel that pronounce husband and wife). Failure to satisfy these conditions renders the utterance unhappy, losing its effectiveness (Baker & Modell, 2019). These conditions are contextual and subject to change; therefore, they require continuous efforts for construction and reconstruction, making perlocutionary performativity an ongoing journey rather than a destination (Garud & Gehman, 2019).

Given the importance of these felicitous (Austin, 1962) or boundary conditions (Marti & Gond, 2018), the linguistic turn was later followed by a material turn that highlighted the impact of statements as not solely dependent on language but also on their association with humans, non-humans, and the material world (Callon, 2007; MacKenzie, 2006; Barad, 2003). For economics to become a performative discourse, it requires a diverse network of both humans and non-humans (e.g., calculative practices) (Callon, 2007). The performativity of financial economic models or accounting is perlocutionary, contingent on meeting specific conditions for the model to shape the world as intended. When these conditions are not met, the models may generate practices that deviate from their predictions and potentially undermine the models themselves.

While illocutionary performatives bring something into existence, the perlocutionary ones alter an ongoing situation (Butler, 2010). Callon (2010) suggests that an illocution can be seen as a specific instance of a perlocution: a scenario where no overflows (breakdowns or disruptions) occur because all the necessary conditions are fulfilled.

According to Callon (2010), illocutionary performativity is uncommon. As Austin (1962) indicates, misfires—speech acts failing to achieve the intended outcomes—are more common. Misfires give rise to concerns, generating controversies and tensions that render the effects of the initial speech unpredictable.

On the contrary, perlocutionary performativity has a more fluid, open-ended, and dynamic perspective and is not limited to a binary assessment (success or failure) (D'Adderio et al., 2019). Vosselman (2022) draws a parallel between performativity seen as a destination and an ongoing journey. Performativity is seen as a destination when its intentions are successfully realized. Conversely, it is an ongoing journey when the alignment between accounting and "the world" is transient, susceptible to disruption by various influences.

For instance, according to Vosselman (2022), considering accounting as an act of calculation (e.g., assessing social and environmental impacts in a sustainability report) can yield the intended effects envisaged by those performing the calculations. If it delivers all anticipated effects, this act of calculation embodies a performative illocution. Therefore, illocutionary performativity conforms with the intention of who performs the calculation. However, once the calculation is carried out, unforeseen outcomes might emerge. This shifts the nature of the calculation into a performative perlocution, thereby allowing various effects while striving to meet specific favorable conditions. In essence, performativity relies on contextual boundaries (Marti and Gond, 2018) and functions within a sphere of influence that is not dominant (Butler, 2010). Consequently, it becomes crucial to focus on exploring the conditions that impact the performativity of perlocutionary acts. MacKenzie (2006) delineates four types of performativity that Marti and Gond (2018) turn into a process, a journey of a theory intended to transform reality in its image. Firstly, *generic performativity* occurs when an aspect of economics (a theory, model, concept, procedure, dataset, etc.) is used by participants in economic processes.

Secondly, *effective performativity* emerges when this aspect has an impact on economic processes. Thirdly, there's *Barnesian performativity*, where practical use of this aspect aligns economic processes with their depiction in economics. Here the theory has reached its intended destination. This contrasts with counter-performativity (the fourth type), which diverges economic processes from their depiction in economics, where the theory finds itself in a more fluid and dynamic situation. MacKenzie's concept of counter-performativity delves into the challenges posed by the boundary conditions required by a model. For instance, the 1987 stock market crash serves as an example of counter-performativity. That event disrupted the functioning of the Black–Scholes–Merton model by invalidating its key parameter, implied volatility. It led to the emergence of a new reality in options trading that contradicted the model's principles.

Considering the above, in the following sections, we will illustrate the sustainability reporting journey at GreenGold using the typologies outlined by Mackenzie (2006).

22.4 Methodology

This case study delves into the motivational and organizational dynamics surrounding the adoption of sustainability reporting by GreenGold, a prominent producer of extra virgin olive oil in Italy. The selection of this company was intentional, to specifically target a business that operates in the agrifood sector, specifically, in a high sensitive field such that of olive oil production. Recognized nationally and internationally for its excellence, the company has received many awards for its unwavering commitment to quality and sustainability. Intriguingly, despite being two-centuries old, the company had never considered to create a sustainability report to communicate the measures substantiating its sustainability efforts to stakeholders until 2020. Using the performativity perspective discussed above, this study investigates the organizational dynamics that led GreenGold to believe in the importance of sustainability reporting and to voluntarily invest significant resources in its preparation. The choice of a case study, particularly an explanatory one, became imperative to address the "how" and "why" questions of sustainability reporting (O'Dwyer & Unerman, 2016). This approach offers an opportunity to explore in-depth the motivations, challenges, and strategies adopted by an organization in the making of sustainability reporting. Through a theoretically informed case study, we can discern and encapsulate the complexity and richness of interactions among various actors and factors that contribute to its relevance (Campbell & Yin, 2018). The case study is based on interviews and documentary analysis (Qu & Dumay, 2011). The members of the company's team appointed to craft the sustainability reporting were interviewed, namely the General Manager, the Production Manager, and the Quality Manager. Nine interviews, each lasting about an hour, were conducted between February and December 2023. We interviewed four times the General Manager, three times the Production Manager, and two times the Quality

Manager. To ensure the spontaneity of the conversation, interviewees were granted anonymity. The interviews were recorded and later transcribed, along with notes taken during the conversation, using NVivo software. In the first interview, information was provided about the research objectives and, more generally, on the topics that would be addressed. In subsequent interviews, conducted in the form of semi-structured interviews, the themes were discussed more specifically based on the following key points:

- Motivations behind the sustainability reporting process
- Existence of internal conditions (skills, competencies, and databases necessary) for measurements
- Degree of internal involvement of staff from various functions and any resistances
- Response of key stakeholders to the publication of the reporting

During the interviews, the interviewees were given the freedom to provide additional information and considerations. The transcripts of the interviews were carefully reviewed by each author for further verification, and a synthesis of the most significant parts for the development of the case was prepared. This synthesis was subsequently shared among the research group members to serve as the basis of the writing of a final report, which was then discussed with the interviewees. Finally, the data collected from the semi-structured interviews were triangulated with internal documents, financial data, and sustainability data.

22.5 The Case Study

The empirical study focuses on the implementation of sustainability reporting at GreenGold, in the years 2020 and 2021. This chapter traces the development of its performativity journey.

GreenGold is a family-owned business that is part of a select group of Italian producers. It has deep roots, tracing back ten generations to 1780 when the founder operated a water-powered stone mill to process wheat and olives into flour and oil. Throughout its history, GreenGold has maintained a strong commitment to sustainability in its production practices. In 1954, the ninth generation of the family joined the business, propelling its growth throughout Italy by introducing the world's first olive oil with a geographical origin certification. Over the years, the president has become an advocate for the finest "Made in Italy." GreenGold has been recognized with numerous awards for its quality.

Olive oil production accounts for two-thirds of GreenGold's overall revenue, which approaches nearly 150 million euros. It is followed by flour production (around 20 million euros), wine (approximately 5 million euros), and other products developed by the brewery. The core business is extra virgin olive oil, which is also exported to the United States, where the company has a commercial branch, and Asia, particularly in China. Exports constitute 25% of the production.

The owner's philosophy is deeply grounded in authentic values that shape the conduct of business operations. GreenGold firmly believes that all participants in the olive oil industry should assess their performance, considering not only economic but also environmental and social aspects, adhering to the triple-bottom line approach (Durden, 2008). The case aims to show that sustainability reporting, as envisioned by GreenGold's top management, goes beyond its conventional role as a tool (comparable to a camera, in Mackenzie's terms) used for merely recording social performance and its benefits. Instead, it is conceptualized as an engine driving sustainable transformation, exerting influence not only on internal but also on external decision-making processes. Essentially, its goal is to catalyze a process of behavioral change among crucial stakeholders (customers, retailers, and financial institutions). The performativity of sustainability reporting stems from its capacity to instigate behavioral change and enhance sustainable performances both within and beyond the organization. Sustainability reporting is expected to function as a performative illocution (Austin, 1962), representing an intentional act of calculation (Vosselman, 2022) with the potential to mold the world in its own image, contingent upon the presence of the right conditions. The subsequent sections delve into three pivotal moments of its journey toward the intended destination (Garud & Gehman, 2019; Vosselman, 2022).

22.5.1 The "Legitimation" Moment

GreenGold's decision to publish a sustainability report was not driven by a response to other companies or as a reaction to occasional reputation-related issues reported in the sector's press. These concerns occasionally raised questions about the integrity and ethical practices of operators in the Italian olive supply chain.

Rather, the decision was prompted by the letter addressed in 2020 to CEOs by Larry Fink (Fink, 2020), the CEO of BlackRock, the world's largest investment fund. In this letter, Fink took a clear stance in favor of companies adopting sustainable practices and stakeholder management. He emphasized the importance of disclosing ESG indicators as critical parameters for evaluating companies. BlackRock's commitment to environmental sustainability translated into a serious warning and a strong recommendation to embrace sustainable reporting: "We will be increasingly inclined to vote against management when companies have not made sufficient progress... Last year, BlackRock voted against or withdrew its confidence in 4,800 top managers from 2,700 different companies...Important progress in improving disclosure has already been made—and many companies already do an exemplary job of integrating and reporting on sustainability—but we need to achieve more widespread and standardized adoption."

Fink's message was clear in reevaluating sustainability reporting: only those who adhere to strict standards of financial, tax, social, environmental, and economic reporting will have access to favorable financing conditions.

"These words—commented the General Manager of GreenGold—shed light on the tasks of the actors of olive oil industry: to be truly sustainable and demonstrate it tangibly through a reporting. This entails oversee food processes, carefully consider the supply chain but also to reduce CO2 emissions not just by purchasing mere green certificates, but by concretely demonstrating continuous improvements within the processes themselves."

The decision to reevaluate the significance of ESG reporting and invest resources in it was influenced by Fink's words.

Up until that point, GreenGold continued to see itself as sustainable without feeling the need to create a report to showcase its sustainability to a broader audience. The company's enduring culture, shaped over more than two centuries of market success, stood as evidence of its sustainability.

The General Manager gained full support from the family ownership. Fink's ideas mobilized individuals and inspired action. To facilitate the actual drafting of the report, a dedicated working group was appointed, which included the General Manager and other members from the Quality and Production sector, with the methodological assistance from a consultancy company.

The initial meetings focused on selecting a framework for translating sustainability into measurable parameters. The consultant recommended adopting the GRI Standard as it is the most widely used framework for sustainability reporting. The GRI Standard covers a wide range of sustainability-related topics, including environmental impact, workers' rights, human rights protection, social responsibility, and supply chain management.

The General Manager promptly agreed, viewing the GRI framework as the optimal choice for effectively communicating GreenGold's dedication to sustainability to stakeholders.

Management control and information system (SAP) was unable to provide with the non-financial data required by the GRI:

"We cannot translate the concept of sustainability by asking the controller for help. The controller knows how to do financial reporting. He records a power invoice for €50,000. He does not record consumption in kilowatts, perhaps by division, by processing phase," remarked the Production Manager.

Over time, the company concentrated on enhancing processes by obtaining numerous ISO certifications, without involving management control to bridge the gap between non-financial and financial indicators. Even the SAP system could not provide the necessary information to implement sustainability reporting.

"Our experience stems from a 20-year certification system, giving us a strong credibility in both environmental aspects—as we held the 14001 certification—and social accountability, having the SA8000 certification. We were also certified for food safety, holding all the primary certifications available in the market" said the General Manager—however, these were ad hoc measurements, not systematic, conducted for specific reasons."

The decision to adopt sustainability reporting, authored by Fink's letter, has been implemented concretely within the company's specific context by a dedicated team. This moment can be viewed as an expression of "generic performativity." Through

Fink's voice, ESG measures challenged the existing status quo and gained support, legitimacy, and technical expertise (Marti & Gond, 2018). The General Manager and his team embraced this challenge with their profound knowledge and expertise in production and IT processes. GreenGold was the first in the olive oil industry to embrace the challenge of sustainability reporting to set an example for all stakeholders, emphasizing the importance of initiating significant changes in both production and business practices.

After gaining legitimacy, the next step was to implement the measurements required by the GRI framework.

22.5.2 The "Embodiment" Moment

The "embodiment" moment refers to a stage where an abstract concept or idea is transformed into a tangible and visible form, in an intentional act of calculation (similar to a speech act, see Vosselman, 2022, p. 144). In this context, it relates to the process of translating the sustainability concept into concrete measurements and data that can be incorporated into a sustainability report. The abstract notion of sustainability becomes tangible and visible through the use of indicators, calculations, and measurable data.

In subsequent meetings, the General Manager, in consultation with the advisor, clarified the intent of calculation. The purpose of sustainability reporting was not about business case but rather about measuring the social and environmental impacts produced by the company's operations. The objective was to convey to stakeholders, through the GRI framework, that GreenGold had consistently adhered to its mission of prioritizing practices focused on quality and sustainability over profit-driven practices that could compromise the former. It was deemed necessary to expedite such a transformation across the entire sector. From a performativity perspective, this moment was crucial because it aimed to transition from generic to effective performativity (Mackenzie, 2006). The company's sustainability concept had to be translated into an intentional act of calculation (Vosselman, 2022), which did not previously exist and had to produce effects. Until then the concept of sustainability was separated from its measurement. As pointed out by the General Manager, "Over the years, GreenGold has refined the idea of sustainability, has developed the guiding concept, but has not supported it with a coherent and systematic measurement system."

This embodiment of sustainability concept into an intentional act of calculation was accomplished through a "socio-technical assemblage" (Callon, 2007) that brought together individuals from various areas of expertise, as well as GreenGold's guiding concept of sustainability, the GRI model, sets of activities and social interactions, language, social norms and conventions, and material devices. The General Manager, who served as the group's coordinator, had in-depth knowledge of IT and agrifood processes due to previous experience with leading Italian agrifood companies. The consultant provided templates (detailed Excel files) and essential methodologies (algorithms) for conducting measurements. Other team members from the quality and production sector were well-versed in collecting and calculating the required data to fill out the templates provided by the GRI consultant. Through meetings, emails, and phone calls, this diverse group collaborated to create the company's first sustainability report within approximately 6 months. The working team began with defining the company's sustainability concept as the foundation for performing the measurements.

"We began with the concept of sustainability adopted at GreenGold. It is rooted in the Brundtland definition, which asserts our commitment to meet current needs without compromising future ones. We make the most efficient use of all the resources that nature provides, from the soil throughout the entire lifecycle of our products, emphasizing value creation and prioritizing product quality and people's well-being. It means that for agrifood companies like GreenGold, preserving the soil is crucial under specific conditions. To maintain soil healthy, one must tend to every aspect of it. It's no coincidence that traditional farmers used to keep stables with animals that produced manure to fertilize the soil. Soil richness and fertility cannot be sustained through chemical fertilizers alone. Preserving these aspects demands a deep understanding of agricultural processes, coupled with profound respect for both nature and the individuals who cultivate the land. This is our guiding principle" said the General Manager.

Starting with the Brundtland definition and adhering to the methodological guidance provided by the consultant in alignment with GRI standards, the working team conducted an initial materiality analysis to pinpoint priorities and strategic themes in the social, environmental, and governance domains. A substantial convergence emerged between the company's priorities, as expressed in the definition of sustainability given, and those of the stakeholders. Priorities revolved around worker safety and well-being, product quality, consumers' safety, efficient use of resources, pollution prevention, and climate change mitigation. Well-being of the workforce was assessed through indicators related to accident reduction, increased training hours, inclusivity, and gender equality. Product quality was substantiated with references to ISO and SA certifications, as well as various national and international awards received over time. Efficiency in resource utilization was demonstrated through measurement of fuel and lubricant consumption, water leakages, energy consumption for water movement, energy savings from advanced technologies, and reductions in emissions of carbon dioxide, methane, and nitrogen oxide, as well as total waste reduction.

Translating the concept of sustainability into numerical data was imperative for effecting internal and external changes, as well as for communicating with stakeholders and potential investors.

"When we started working on the reporting to translate it into concrete measurements, we had numerous meetings. I noticed that the operators, spontaneously, began turning off the lights without the need for specific instructions, something the previous service directives had failed to achieve. By discussing concrete measurements, we made sustainability 'cool,' modern, and essential for both the company and the environment. Before, there was a lack of formalization; informality prevailed. People conducted their tasks but were unaware of the outcomes they were generating. Those responsible for measuring energy consumption monitored it, but its significance was limited. Similarly, those tracking production times for a product recorded the data, yet it remained underutilized."

To date, GreenGold has produced two sustainability reports, one for the year 2020 and another for 2021. In the introduction of the second report, it is stated, "... The second sustainability report, the first of its kind in the world for an olive oil company, has helped us realize the actual value of this project. Thc first assessment allowed us to measure ourselves, and this second one has enabled us to change our practices and to make improvements."

The main results achieved in 2021, compared to 2020, are as follows:

- Commitment to controlling electricity consumption and streamlining production processes resulted in a 5% reduction in overall electricity consumption per kilogram of product produced compared to the previous year.
- Carbon dioxide emissions were reduced by 9% for the core olive oil business, 12% for beer production, and 9% for wine production.
- Gender equality has been achieved among employees and workers, both in terms of basic salary and average salary.
- Training hours for all employees increased from an average of 15 h per employee to 86.

  The accident indicator shows a decrease of approximately 34%.

"We are sustainable at 77%," stated the General Manager after reviewing the numbers. "When people at GreenGold encountered the sustainability reporting, a transformation occurred. At that juncture, they grasped our true trajectory and gained a profound understanding of the essence of sustainability," articulated the General Manager. The reporting had demonstrated energy savings, improved workplace safety performance, a reduction in accidents, increased training hours, savings in water consumption, in lubricants, in fuels, and in CO2 emissions.

All of the above profoundly altered the perspectives of the actors involved in the company's operations and facilitated a more nuanced comprehension of their actions. The measurement practices mandated by the reporting process necessitated a comprehensive examination of actions and their consequences. Consequently, there was an enhanced understanding of the links between activities and the environment. The intricacies of the activities, their implications, and their effects were now evident and unambiguous. In subsequent meetings, all participants shared a heightened awareness. The practice of sustainability reporting reshaped participants' viewpoints by elucidating the interdependencies between the company and the ecosystem in which it operated. "We realized," said the Production Manager, "that we were not operating in a market but in an environment. And the measures that described the effectiveness of this relationship were not just profits. We also had to believe in these new measures."

The reliability of the numerical data was essential for the performativity of the report. To ensure reliability, an independent audit firm was engaged. The firm scrutinized the process of defining the relevant topics in the sustainability report, compared the financial data within the report with the financial statements, conducted interviews and discussions with staff to understand the data collection, aggregation, processing, and transmission processes. They subsequently certified the report as compliant with the GRI Standards in all significant aspects.

22.5.3 *The "Stakeholder Delusion" Moment*

Notably, GreenGold is the only company in the extra olive oil industry in Italy to have started a sustainability report. In addition, the General Manager decided to assess not only the internal impact of their reports but also to assess the external impact of the reports. Despite the company's genuine efforts, consumers were not acknowledging their commitment. The meticulous reporting of GreenGold has not effectively conveyed this message to their customers. The General Manager said that their competitors appeared more sustainable without investing in sustainable communication. "Being sustainable isn't just about purchasing green certificates and solar panels. Some competitors have bought green certificates from various parts of the world, but that isn't sustainability. Claiming to be sustainable just because you've installed solar panels, as another competitor did, isn't a genuine commitment to sustainability. These examples haven't received attention in newspapers or specialized magazines. Until now, sustainability has been misunderstood by the olive oil sector" the General Manager pointed out.

One key issue is that consumers often do not distinguish between producers and bottlers. "Here's the scenario: some people, seeking to save a few cents, continue to prefer purchasing products not directly from us but from retailers lacking direct experience with olives. These retailers buy bulk oil from various global sources and bottle it. We also procure oil from Spain, but owning a million olive trees, we know precisely what we're buying and its quality" commented the General Manager.

Regarding retailers, the Quality Manager clarified that: "It was struggling to convince others that olive oil is an exceptionally unique product. Many companies, both producers, and particularly bottlers, persist in regarding olive oil as a mere commodity. However, at GreenGold we firmly believe that olive oil transcends this status. It is the only product worldwide that remains unadulterated within its packaging without the use of preservatives, as mandated by law. Moreover, it is the sole product subject to subjective taste evaluations by consumers, who may express unfavourable judgments. Such assessments can lead to penalties and, in some instances, even criminal charges if the infractions recur over time and involve substantial quantities of oil. This distinct product is semi-fresh and cannot be warehoused like canned goods. Prolonged exposure to sunlight results in oxidation and the loss of its inherent properties. Regrettably, this aspect is frequently underestimated by major retailers."

Another source of disappointment came from the financial system. The General Manager said: "We aspire to see the global industrial system shifting toward evaluating the financial balance sheet through the sustainability performance lens:

I aim to achieve a triple AAA rating based on my sustainability achievements disclosed in the reporting. Regrettably, such a rating doesn't exist yet. The fact that we've reduced workplace accidents by 34% should ideally translate into savings regarding insurance costs. The reductions in CO2 emissions, as well as reduced fuel and lubricant consumption, should theoretically result in tax benefits and environmental disposal contributions. The reduction in energy consumption achieved through process enhancements should naturally lead to a reduction in energy costs. Unfortunately, banks, for the most part, still remain sceptical about thc impact of these metrics. We have not yet succeeded in obtaining lower borrowing costs, despite the improvements show-cased in the sustainability report."

Lastly some disappointments came from Larry Fink's recent clarifications in his 2023 letter (Fink, 2023), addressed not only to CEOs but also to investors, where he now downplays the significance of ESG information. While he still underscores the importance of pursuing decarbonization models, Fink restricts the role of asset managers to vehicles for decisions ultimately made by governments, companies, and investors. In his 2023 annual letter, Larry Fink highlights that "for long-term investment, it is necessary to have a long-term view of the factors that will influence performance, including demographics, government policies, technological advancements, and the transition to a low-carbon economy." However, he adds, "we are not the environmental police." Nevertheless, the primary objective remains the returns demonstrated in the financial statements.

These "disappointments" have not diminished the "faith" in the sustainability measures. In the most recent interview, the General Manager clarified that, in the near future, he aims to systematize socio-environmental measurements (environmental management accounting), a process that has not occurred previously. Additionally, he intends to enhance these measures by leveraging artificial intelligence. As for sustainability reporting, the project is currently on hold. The last report dates back to 2021. The stakeholders' less than positive response triggered a reflection on the cost–benefit aspect of sustainability reporting in the GRI format with independent certification. Currently, the General Manager prefers to wait and adhere to the structural choices of sustainability reporting that will be mandated by the regulator, that will make it compulsory for GreenGold starting from 2025.

22.6 Discussion and Conclusions

As mentioned earlier, we have utilized the perspective of performativity to delve deeper into how impactful narratives and stakeholder responses shape the direction and importance of sustainability reporting, ultimately influencing the creation of desired realities. This perspective proves valuable as it transcends the mere technical dimension of sustainability reporting construction, highlighting instead the motivations behind its adoption and the impacts it generate. The analysis conducted thus far has shown that external influence led the General Manager of GreenGold to choose to communicate socio-environmental performance through a report. Persuasive statements from BlackRock's CEO, Fink, persuaded the General Manager to enhance and systematize socio-environmental measurement practices. Fink reevaluated the importance of external communication and reconsidered the approach to sustainability reporting. Until then, GreenGold had never acknowledged the significance of this document. From a performativity standpoint, GreenGold needed to establish what Austin (1962) refers to as "felicitous conditions" to enable sustainability reporting to produce the desired effects. Consequently, a challenge arose at GreenGold to transition from ad hoc measurements for specific purposes to adopting a systematic approach aimed at creating sustainability reporting capable of influencing both internal and external changes. Following Mackenzie (2006), a pivotal moment was the legitimization of reporting within GreenGold. The adoption of reporting at GreenGold was enthusiastically embraced as a strategic step for a company genuinely committed to sustainability. It rapidly garnered support from both management and staff, who acknowledged its importance in shaping the internal and external reality and not only in merely recording the organizations'action (akin to a camera). Mackenzie (2006) views this phase of legitimization as a form of generic performativity. Yet, technical limitations within management control and the existing SAP system hindered the data required for measurements. Despite this, the General Manager's expertise and a specialized team made up for these shortcomings. The subsequent phase involved shaping the reporting to achieve the desired effects. The selection of the GRI framework compelled GreenGold to detail comprehensive socio-environmental measurements. This phase significantly contributed to embedding the company's sustainability beliefs and changing behaviors. Evaluating emissions and waste made these areas visible, manageable, and valuable. According to interviewees, integrating environmental considerations into daily operations gradually altered habits, such as "turning off lights at the end of work hours." It also transformed the approach to production and logistics. Monitoring performance in these sectors proved beneficial, boosting confidence in GreenGold's sustainability practices and highlighting the positive correlation between sustainable actions and financial aspects. Following Mackenzie (2006), we can define this phase as effective performativity, wherein accounting tools and practices, such as sustainability reporting, influence and shape behaviors and decisions within an organization. Essentially, it represents a level of performativity where accounting tools effectively create tangible impacts, influence actors' behaviors, and contribute to shaping organizational reality. But these positive effects did not go further; they did not reach what Mackenzie defines as Barnesian performativity. Barnesian performativity refers to the ability of accounting practices and tools to establish and solidify social and organizational realities that reflect the conceptions and interests of the involved actors. Barnesian performativity would imply that the reporting itself, along with the sustainable practices it aims to represent, actively influences and transforms the attitudes, behaviors, and decision-making structures of organizations and their stakeholders. In other words, sustainability reporting should have a significant impact in shaping corporate practices and perceptions, as well as in generating concrete changes toward more sustainable practices. However, sustainability reporting may not achieve Barnesian performativity if its impacts do not result in substantial and lasting changes in organizational practices and stakeholder behaviors. For example, if despite sustainability reporting, companies continue to adhere to unsustainable practices, or if stakeholders do not change their behavior in response to the information provided by the report, then the reporting may not be considered Barnesianly performative. Sustainability reporting at GreenGold failed to generate external effects that would alter the attitudes of primary stakeholders (consumers, retailers, and banks), who were the intended audience. The General Manager viewed sustainability reporting as a performative illocution, a standalone act capable of shaping the world in its image, a transformative engine rather than passive camera. From this perspective, sustainability reporting and measurements lacked the capacity to serve as engines capable of changing primary stakeholders' behaviors. They lacked the power to alter structural conditions, as noted by Baker and Modell (2019), thus falling short of achieving Barnesian performativity (MacKenzie, 2006). These stakeholders resisted GreenGold's sustainability approach. According to Felin and Foss (2009), sustainability accounting practices can become fully performative (Barnesian) only if they reinforce relatively unchanging realities that inherently favor such approaches. Unfortunately, the behaviors of consumers, banks, major retailers, and especially competing companies are not yet aligned with GreenGold's sustainability ideals. Consumers and bottlers still prioritize prices, not appreciating the value of sustainability. Furthermore, recent statements from Fink (2023) have partly revised the strong assertions made in 2020 which emphasized the central importance of sustainability reporting. The lack of external success of the reporting led the General Manager to assess the cost–benefit aspect of reporting. The internal positive impacts stemmed from the assessment of socio-environmental metrics, leading to a reduced reliance on the entire costly and, unfortunately, inefficient Global Reporting Initiative (GRI) framework. By concentrating on specific socio-environmental measurements, GreenGold can streamline and tailor its efforts, avoiding unnecessary complexities linked to the comprehensive GRI framework. The sustainability reporting at GreenGold is currently halted in 2021. Despite believing in reporting, the General Manager awaits regulatory choices for non-financial communication that will be enforced from 2025 onward. Meanwhile, he has opted to enhance environmental management accounting (EMA) measurements and expand internal management control using artificial intelligence, thanks to his technical proficiency.

The GreenGold case illustrates that the measurement exercise conducted for two consecutive years (2020 and 2021) undoubtedly helped better internalize sustainability beliefs and enacting internal changes, reinforcing the notion that GreenGold operates in an environment, not simply in a market. From this viewpoint, sustainability reporting achieved its goal. The certified GRI reporting undeniably has reinforced sustainability beliefs and incentivized internal changes. From this perspective, performativity resembles a self-fulfilling prophecy (Power, 2021; Vosselman, 2022), where Fink's words set this cycle in motion. However, the GreenGold case demonstrates how accounting performativity has not extended beyond rooting beliefs and promoting internal changes. This case reveals an unsuccessful one-way journey from illocution to destination. Sustainability reporting has not fully reached its intended destination. The cold response from stakeholders limited the full performativity of sustainability reporting and paved the way for a socio-technical rearrangement that enhanced environmental management accounting within management control. This led to a new socio-technical assemblage centered on environmental management accounting, putting sustainability reporting on standby, thereby limiting its relevance, showing how performativity is embedded in continuous socio-technical rearrangement (Callon, 2007, p. 17).

22.7 Limitations and Recommendations for Future Study

The main limitations of the present research concern the following aspects. Firstly, the GreenGold case may be too specific and unique to its context. Although it provides detailed insights into the procedural dynamics characterizing sustainability reporting, the findings may lack generalizability. To address this limitation, further exploration of the intriguing perspective offered by this study on the role of performativity in explaining the emergence and decline of sustainability reporting is warranted. This could deepen our understanding of the entire process. Future studies might incorporate additional case studies to encourage international comparisons within the same industry or across sectors where sustainability concepts and tools, such as environmental management accounting and sustainability reporting, find felicitous conditions for promoting the intended change. Alternatively, research could delve into the conditions leading to counter effects, such as cases where the socio-material assemblage is unsuccessful (counter-performativity).

Furthermore, as the findings in this paper are predominantly based on the medium size of the company under scrutiny, future studies might delve into larger-sized enterprises. Moreover, inquiries could assess whether internal factors, like the existence of an ethical committee within the organizational structure (Ginesti et al., 2023), or corporate social responsibility (CSR) incentive systems (Aresu et al., 2023), could be deemed "felicitous" and positively influence the performativity of sustainability reporting.

Thirdly, future research could investigate whether (and which) personality traits of top managers can be regarded as well as "felicitous" conditions.

References

Adams, C. A., & Frost, G. R. (2008). Integrating sustainability reporting into management practices. *Accounting Forum, 32*(4), 288–302.

Aresu, S., Hooghiemstra, R., & Melis, A. (2023). Integration of CSR criteria into executive compensation contracts: A cross-country analysis. *Journal of Management, 49*(8), 2766–2804.

Austin, J. L. (1962). *How to do things with words*. Oxford University Press.

Baker, M., & Modell, S. (2019). Rethinking performativity. A critical realist analysis of accounting for corporate social responsibility. *Accounting, Auditing and Accountability Journal, 32*(4), 930–956.

Barad, K. (2003). Posthumanist performativity: Toward an understanding of how matter comes to matter. *Signs: Journal of Women in Culture and Society, 28*(3), 801–831.

Bebbington, J., & Larrinaga, C. (2014). Accounting and sustainable development: An exploration. *Accounting, Organizations and Society, 39*(6), 395–413.

Bebbington, J., Osterblom, H., Crona, B., Jouffray, J. B., Larrinaga, C., Russell, S., & Scholtens, B. (2019). Accounting and accountability in the anthropocene. *Accounting, Auditing and Accountability Journal, 33*(1), 152–177.

Belal, A., & Owen, D. L. (2015). The rise and fall of stand-alone social reporting in a multinational subsidiary in Bangladesh: A case study. *Accounting, Auditing & Accountability Journal, 28*(7), 1160–1192.

Buhr, N. (2007). Histories of and rationales for sustainability reporting. In J. Unerman, J. Bebbington, & B. O'Dwyer (Eds.), *Sustainability accounting and accountability* (pp. 57–69). Routledge.

Burchell, S., Clubb, C., Hopwood, A., Hughes, J., & Nahapiet, J. (1980). The roles of accounting in organizations and society. *Accounting, Organizations and Society, 5*(1), 5–2.

Burritt, R. L., & Schaltegger, S. (2010). Sustainability accounting and reporting: Fad or trend? *Accounting, Auditing & Accountability Journal, 23*(7), 829–846.

Busco, C., Giovannoni, E., Granà, F., & Izzo, M. F. (2018). Making sustainability meaningful: Aspirations, discourses and reporting practices. *Accounting Auditing and Accountability Journal, 31*(8), 2218–2246.

Butler, J. (2010). Performative agency. *Journal of Cultural Economy, 3*(2), 147–161.

Callon, M. (2007). What does it mean to say that economics is performative? In D. MacKenzie, F. Muniesa, & L. Siu (Eds.), *Do economists make markets? On the Performativity of Economics* (pp. 311–357). Princeton University Press.

Callon, M. (2010). Performativity, misfires and politics. *Journal of Cultural Economy, 3*(2), 163–169.

Campbell, D. T., & Yin, R. K. (2018). *Case study research and applications: Design and methods* (6th ed.). Sage Publications.

Carter, C., Clegg, S., & Kornberger, M. (2010). Re-framing strategy: Power, politics and accounting. *Accounting, Auditing, Accountability Journal, 23*(5), 573–594.

Castellano, N., & Felden, C. (2021). Management control Systems for Sustainability, and Sus-tainability of management control systems. *Management Control, 2*, 5–11.

Cinquini, L., & De Luca, F. (Eds.). (2022). *Non-financial disclosure and integrated reporting theoretical framework and empirical evidence* (SIDREA series in accounting and business administration (SSABA)). Springer.

Contrafatto, M. (2014). The institutionalization of social and environmental reporting. *Accounting Organizations and Society, 39*(6), 414–432.

Contrafatto, M., & Burns, J. (2013). Social and environmental accounting, organisational change and management accounting: A processual view. *Management Accounting Research, 24*(4), 349–365.

Contrafatto, M., Costa, E., & Pesci, C. (2019). Examining the dynamics of SER evolution: An institutional understanding. *Accounting, Auditing & Accountability Journal, 32*(6), 1771–1800.

D'Adderio, L., Glaser, V., & Pollock, N. (2019). Performing theories, transforming organizations: A reply to Marti and Gond. *Academy of Management Review, 44*(3), 676–679.

D'Onza, G. (2022). L'orientamento delle aziende ad uno sviluppo sostenibile: quale contributo da parte dei sistemi di management e controllo? *Management Control, 1*, 5–15.

Durden, C. (2008). Towards a socially responsible management control system. *Auditing & Accountability Journal, 21*(5), 671–694.

Egan, M., & Tweedie, D. (2018). A 'green' accountant is hard to find: Can accountants contribute to sustainability management initiatives? *Accounting, Auditing and Accountability Journal, 31*(6), 1749–1773.

Felin, T., & Foss, N. J. (2009). Social reality, the boundaries of self-fulfilling prophecy, and economics. *Organization Science, 20*(3), 654–668.

Fink, L. (2020). A fundamental reshaping of finance. https://www.blackrock.com/corporate/investor-relations/2020-larry-fink-ceo-letter

Fink, L. (2023). Larry Fink's annual Chairman's letter to investors. https://www.blackrock.com/corporate/investor-relations/larry-fink-annual-chairmans-letter

Garud, R., & Gehman, J. (2019). Performativity: Not a destination but an ongoing journey. *Academy of Management Review, 44*(3), 679–684.

Gibassier, D., & Alcouffe, S. (2018). Environmental management accounting: The missing link to sustainability? *Social and Environmental Accountability Journal, 38*(1), 1–18.

Ginesti, G., Campa, D., & Spano' R., Allini M., Maffei M. (2023). The role of CSR committee characteristics on R&D investments. *International Business Review, 32*(5), 102147.

Gond, J. P., Cabantous, L., Harding, N., & Learmonth, M. (2016). What do we mean by performativity in organizational and management theory? The uses and abuses of performativity. *International Journal of Management Review, 18*(4), 440–463.

Gond, J.-P., Grubnic, S., Herzig, C., & Moon, J. (2012). Configuring management control systems: Theorizing the integration of strategy and sustainability. *Management Accounting Research, 23*(3), 205–223.

Greco, G., Sciulli, N., & D'Onza, G. (2021). The influence of stakeholder engagement on sustainability reporting: Evidence from Italian local councils. *Public Management Review, 17*, 465–488.

Hahn, R., & Kuhnen, M. (2013). Determinants of sustainability reporting: A review of results, trends, theory, and opportunities in an expanding field of research. *Journal of Cleaner Production, 59*, 5–21.

Herzig, S., & Schaltegger, S. (2006). Corporate sustainability reporting: An overview. In S. Schaltegger, M. Bennett, & R. Burritt (Eds.), *Sustainability accounting and reporting* (pp. 301–324). Springer.

Hines, R. D. (1988). Financial accounting: In communicating reality, we construct reality. *Accounting, Organizations and Society, 13*(3), 251–261.

Hopwood, B., Mellor, M., & O'Brien, G. (2005). Sustainable development: Mapping different approaches. *Sustainable Development, 13*(1), 38–52.

Hsiao, P.-C. K., de Villiers, C., Horner, C., & Oosthuizen, H. (2022). A review and synthesis of contemporary sustainability accounting research and the development of a research agenda. *Accounting and Finance, 62*(4), 4453–4483.

Kaspereit, T., & Lopatta, K. (2014). The value relevance of SAM's corporate sustainability ranking and GRI sustainability reporting in the European stock markets. *Business Ethics: A European Review, 25–1*, 1–24.

Kieser, A., Nicolai, A., & Seidl, D. (2015). The practical relevance of management research: Turning the debate on relevance into a rigorous scientific research program. *The Academy of Management Annals, 9*(1), 143–233.

MacKenzie, D. (2006). *An engine, not a camera*. The MIT Press.

Marti, E., & Gond, J. P. (2018). When do theories become self-fulfilling? Exploring the boundary conditions of performativity. *The Academy of Management Review, 43–3*, 487–508.

Maughan, R. (2023). Adopting and adapting sustainability accounting: Fit and faith in a family business. *Accounting, Auditing & Accountability Journal, 36*(9), 1–31.

Miller, P., & Power, M. (2013). Accounting, organizing and economizing: Connecting accounting research and organizational theory. *Academy of Management Annals, 7*(1), 555–603.

Nazari, J. A., Herremans, I. M., & Warsame, H. A. (2015). Sustainability reporting: External motivators and internal facilitators. *Corporate Governance, 15*(3), 375–390.

O'Dwyer, B., & Unerman, J. (2016). Fostering rigour in accounting for social sustainability. *Accounting, Organizations and Society, 49*, 32–40.

Power, M. (2021). Modelling the microfoundations of the audit society: Organizations and the logic of the audit trail. *Academy of Management Review, 46*(1), 6–32.

Qu, S. Q., & Dumay, J. (2011). The qualitative research interview. *Qualitative Research in Accounting and Management, 8*(3), 228–264.

Schaltegger, S. (2018). Linking environmental management accounting: A reflection on (missing) links to sustainability and planetary boundaries. *Social and Environmental Accountability Journal, 38*(1), 19–29.

Silva, S., Nuzum, A.-K., & Schaltegger, S. (2019). Stakeholder expectations on sustainability performance measurement and assessment. A systematic literature review. *Journal of Cleaner Production, 217*, 204–215.

Spence, L. J., & Rinaldi, L. (2014). Governmentality in accounting and accountability: A case study of embedding sustainability in a supply chain. *Accounting, Organizations and Society, 39*(6), 433–452.

Traxler, A. A., Schrack, D., & Greiling, D. (2020). Sustainability reporting and management control—A systematic exploratory literature review. *Journal of Cleaner Production, 276*, 122725.

Velte, P. (2021). Archival research on integrated reporting: A systematic review of main drivers and the impact of integrated reporting on firm value. *Journal of Management and Governance, 26*, 997–1061.

Vinnari, E., & Laine, M. (2013). Just a passing fad? The diffusion and decline of environmental reporting in the Finnish water sector. *Accounting, Auditing & Accountability Journal, 26*(7), 1107–1134.

Vosselman, E. (2022). The performativity of accounting: Advancing a Posthumanist understanding. *Qualitative Research in Accounting & Management, 19*(2), 137–161.

Yu, L., & Huber, C. (2023). How accounting research understands performativity: Effects and processes of a multi-faceted notion. *Qualitative Research in Accounting & Management, 20*(5), 704–738.

Part IV
ESG Performance Measurement and Management: Impact on Financial and Corporate Outcomes

Chapter 23
Does Financial Performance Drive ESG Performance? Empirical Evidence from European Listed Companies

Salvatore Loprevite, Domenico Raucci, and Bruno Ricca

23.1 Introduction

The pressures of international organizations, investors, and stakeholders for fair and sustainable economic development increasingly ask companies for the integration of Environmental, Social, and Governance (ESG) issues into investment policies and decision-making processes to support responsible value creation (van Duuren et al., 2016; Zumente & Bistrova, 2021; Cornell & Shapiro, 2021).

From a managerial perspective, the complexity of relationships with stakeholders increases, requiring companies to combine financial and sustainability results in facing a wide range of responsibilities related to the three ESG pillars and to meet the expectations of shareholders who are more interested in maximizing profits and value. Thus, research interest in the link between ESG Performance (ESGP) and Financial Performance (FP) is also growing: Is there a link between ESGP and FP? Does ESGP drive FP or does FP drive ESGP? (Brammer & Millington, 2008; Scholtens, 2008; Chams et al., 2021).

To answer these questions, which have important theoretical and practical implications, a growing literature has addressed this topic studying the relationships in both of above cause-and-effect directions (i.e., ESGP on FP and FP on ESGP). The

S. Loprevite (✉)
University "Dante Alighieri", Reggio Calabria, Italy
e-mail: s.loprevite@unidarc.it

D. Raucci
University "G. d'Annunzio", Chieti-Pescara, Italy
e-mail: domenico.raucci@unich.it

B. Ricca
University of Messina, Messina, Italy
e-mail: bruno.ricca@unime.it

N. Castellano et al. (eds.), *Environmental, Social, Governance (ESG)*, SIDREA Series in Accounting and Business Administration,
https://doi.org/10.1007/978-3-031-76618-3_23

conflicting findings mean that the scientific debate is still unsolved (Chams et al., 2021; Eliwa et al., 2019; Duque-Grisales & Aguilera-Caracuel, 2021; Bruna et al., 2022; Berg et al., 2022; DasGupta, 2022; Nurim et al., 2022).

The link between ESGP and FP was studied by mainly analyzing the impact that ESGP has on FP (Eliwa et al., 2019; Bruna et al., 2022; Friede et al., 2015; Velte, 2017; Huang, 2021; Zhao & Strotmann, 2015; Zhao & Murrell, 2022), while the influence of FP on ESGP has been comparatively less explored in literature (Brammer & Millington, 2008; Scholtens, 2008; Chams et al., 2021; DasGupta, 2022; Preston & O'Bannon, 1997; Singh et al., 2022). This lack of literature is not defensible, as delving into the causes of ESGP to understand whether it is financially-driven is a relevant aspect to investigate. Such insight contributes to a better evaluation of ESG results by considering a possible conditional cause. Therefore, apart from its theoretical relevance, this can contribute significantly to better managerial control of ESG results. For these reasons, we choose to fit our research into this more limited literature strand, investigating the role of FP, measured through accounting-based metrics, in determining company ESGP.

With regard to the reference framework, we referred to the *Slack Resource Theory* (Waddock & Graves, 1997; Orlitzky et al., 2003) to deal with the question of whether a better FP potentially results in the availability of slack resources that can be used to enhance ESGP (Preston & O'Bannon, 1997). To avoid exclusively focusing on financial resources, we consider the level of investment in intangibles and the presence of a Corporate Social Responsibility (CSR) Committee, which can be taken as an intangible resource related to organizational culture and governance (Huarng & Yu, 2024), as control variables.

Concerning the methodology, we analyze the impact of FP on ESGP by a *dynamic panel regression* (Arellano & Bond, 1991). The dynamic specification of the process implies the presence of the lagged dependent variable among the regressors that allows for consistent and unbiased estimates of the other parameters in the model. The analysis is conducted on a sample of 262 European listed companies, with a panel dataset that refers to the years 2010–2022. Moreover, adopting a holistic approach to measuring the two performances, we use:

- Three comprehensive scores constructed through statistical-mathematical synthesis techniques implemented on a large set of financial ratios, for FP;
- The Thomson Reuters ESG Score, which is a metric that summarizes the three dimensions of this performance, for ESGP.

Within the scant literature investigating the FP → ESGP relationship, this study is the first attempt to overcome the conceptual limitations associated with partial measurements of FP (Bruna & Ben, 2021; Baboukardos, 2018; Endrikat et al., 2014; Dragomir, 2018; Horváthová, 2010). Furthermore, to examine the relationship more in-depth, we consider the joint effect of FP with the presence of a CSR Committee specifically responsible for decision-making on CSR strategy. The scientific value of the chapter is also enhanced using a dynamic panel regression and the level of investment in intangibles resulting in financial statements as a control variable.

The remainder of the paper is structured as follows:

The following section summarizes the theoretical frameworks and hypotheses development. Section 23.3 sets out the research design: sample, variables, and methods. Section 23.4 exposes data processing and findings. Section 23.5 presents the robustness analysis, while Sect. 23.6 discusses and concludes.

23.2 Literature Review and Hypotheses Development

23.2.1 Theoretical Frameworks

The lack of conclusive results on the ESGP-FP link keeps the issue of its nature and the direction of causality open, starting from the basic question of whether organizations that engage in ESG practices achieve higher FP and/or whether it is the more profitable and better FP organizations that engage more in ESG practices (Preston & O'Bannon, 1997; Waddock & Graves, 1997; Peloza, 2009).

Most literature has focused on the impacts of ESGP on FP, finding a negative, neutral, or positive association between them within several classic theoretical frameworks (Duque-Grisales & Aguilera-Caracuel, 2021; Endrikat et al., 2014; Iazzolino et al., 2023), such as *Neoclassical Theory*, *Agency Theory,* and *Stakeholder Theory* (Preston & O'Bannon, 1997; Jensen, 2001; King & Lenox, 2001; Freeman, 1984).[1] On the contrary, literature investigating the role of FP as an antecedent factor that drives companies to invest in ESG practices is a much narrower strand of research. These studies adopt the interpretative lens of the *Slack Resources Theory* (Waddock & Graves, 1997; Orlitzky et al., 2003) to support the hypothesis that firms with higher FP have more financial resources to invest in ESG practices. Rooted within the organizational slack view of discretionary resources, the *Slack Resource Theory* proposes that better FP potentially results in the availability of slack resources allowing the firm to invest in different current or potential assets and capabilities. Slack resources can be of different types, both tangible and intangible, and can include human resources, innovation and technology-related resources, and other economic-financial resources, etc. (McGuire et al., 1988; Surroca et al., 2010; Shahzad et al., 2016). According to the proponents, the investments made with this type of non-committed resources have a discretionary and strategic nature and, although they do not immediately pay off, they allow the company to adapt to internal and external pressures deriving from environmental changes (Waddock & Graves, 1997; Kraatz & Zajac, 2001; Bansal, 2005). From this perspective, some scholars argue that the availability of slack resources (financial or

[1] Another line of research explores the possibility that the relationship would be reciprocal causal, forming a continuous virtuous circle (Zhao & Murrell, 2022; Orlitzky et al., 2003; Surroca et al., 2010). From this perspective, it is considered that if improved ESGP leads to better FP, at the same time FP successfully allows to spend more on ESG practices because the companies can afford it (Busch & Friede, 2018).

other) provides companies with greater management margins to invest in extra activities, such as research projects, but also to engage in the improvement of ESGP (Orlitzky et al., 2003; Surroca et al., 2010; Cheng et al., 2014; Chiu & Sharfman, 2011; Kock et al., 2012). In line with these theoretical assumptions, several empirical studies have pointed to the existence of a positive FP → ESGP relationship (Chams et al., 2021; Nurim et al., 2022; McGuire et al., 1988; Zhang et al., 2018; Aguilera-Caracuel et al., 2015; Seifert et al., 2004), despite there being no lack of authors who theorize a negative relationship between the two performances by interpreting the slack resource paradigm from the hypothesis of managerial opportunism (Preston & O'Bannon, 1997; Shahzad et al., 2016).

Although slack resources can be of different types, literature on the FP → ESGP relationship has mainly used financial slack resources, operationalized using accounting or market-based measures to consider excess resources within companies (Peloza, 2009; Margolis & Walsh, 2003; Melo, 2012; El Khoury et al., 2023). Many of the studies using FP measures as proxies for slack (Clarkson et al., 2011; Schreck, 2011) assume that high levels of FP result in available slack resources (Preston & O'Bannon, 1997), and that is because the literature has viewed FP as a precursor to slack resources since slack is more likely to appear in companies with high FP (Endrikat et al., 2014). This assumption is also confirmed by empirical reviews on a positive relationship between slack resources and FP (Daniel et al., 2004). On the contrary, a smaller number of studies based on *Slack Resource Theory* criticize this prevailing focus on FP suggesting conceptualizing the heterogeneous and multidimensional nature of slack resources combining financial with other tangible and intangible resources (Shahzad et al., 2016). This is because the availability of intangible resources, including innovation, human, reputation, organizational culture, and other similar resources, could be a powerful predictor of better ESGP (Surroca et al., 2010).

Based on the above theoretical framework, as will be explained hereafter, in this chapter we study the role of FP as a determinant of ESGP by combining it with slack resources of another nature, namely investments in Intangibles (INT) found in financial statements and the presence of a CSR Committee as an intangible resource related to organizational culture and governance.

23.2.2 Hypotheses Development

According to the *Slack Resource Theory*, financial slack expresses an endowment of resources greater than those necessary to meet immediate obligations resulting from bad planning or good organizational performance in prior periods (Voss et al., 2008). These resources can be discretionally used for various purposes making companies responsive to sustainable development issues and more inclined to engage in ESG practices and investments (Waddock & Graves, 1997; McGuire et al., 1988). Schaltegger and Synnestvedt (2002) argue that sustainability practices are perceived as a "luxury" good in which companies evaluate investments only when a certain level of FP is achieved and compatible with the will to satisfy the pressures of stakeholders. Following the slack resources paradigm, companies with low FP and scarce financial resources tend to focus their investments on maximizing profitability, as this is the main focus of shareholders for whom ESG practices are not a corporate priority (Barnea & Rubin, 2010; Artiach et al., 2010; Parmar et al., 2010). Instead, companies with a better financial structure enjoy a greater availability of slack resources (Brammer & Millington, 2008) as well as a series of benefits related to opportunities for access to credit and a lower cost of capital, due to lower levels of risk. This greater financial availability, expressed by a higher FP, is a significant driver of the potential for expanding investment types and the propensity to incorporate ESG practices (Shahzad et al., 2016).

This role of corporate financial status has been variously emphasized in research on FP as an antecedent of ESGP. For example, Chams et al. (2021) defined financial status as a "catalyst" of resources to support ESGP, while McGuire et al. (1988) conceptualized its role as a "predictor" of ESGP.

In these perspectives, the prevailing empirical evidence found a positive effect of FP on ESGP (Chams et al., 2021; DasGupta, 2022; Nurim et al., 2022; Zhang et al., 2018; Aguilera-Caracuel et al., 2015; Seifert et al., 2004; Artiach et al., 2010). In particular, Artiach et al. (2010) found that FP, as measured by free cash flow and corporate profitability, is positively correlated with sustainability performance. Seifert et al. (2004) and Chams et al. (2021) showed that free cash flows and Tobin's Q, used as proxies for FP, positively influence ESGP. Zhang et al. (2018) proved the positive relationship between cash and cash equivalents and CSR performance. DasGupta (2022) pointed out that the FP shortfall, taken as a proxy for the company's past performance (historical aspiration level) and the past performance of other "comparable" organizations (social aspiration level), has a strong positive influence on a firm's ESGP. On the contrary, few studies found a negative relationship between the two variables (Shahzad et al., 2016; Chiu & Sharfman, 2011; Julian & Ofori-Dankwa, 2013).[2]

We believe that in the literature finding a positive link between FP and ESGP there is a lack of insights concerning the role of different FP dimensions, for which it may be useful to distinguish:

[2]For example, Julian and Ofori-Dankwa (2013) report that greater financial resources available, measured with ROS, ROE, and Net Profitability, is negatively associated with corporate social performance. These results, which contrast the prevailing perspective of a positive FP → ESGP relationship, are explainable by the interpretation of the slack resource paradigm from the hypotheses of *managerial opportunism (Preston & O'Bannon,* 1997*)* and *impression management* (Talbot & Boiral, 2015). Through this interpretation, it is assumed that top management may employ the discretionary resources for personal purposes. For example, as noted by Preston and O'Bannon (1997), if the company has a short-term compensation scheme, a high FP may tempt the managers to cash in by reducing investments in ESG practices to take advantage, to increase their short-term private gains. Instead, when FP weakens, managers may attempt to offset it by engaging in ESG programs. In this way, they try to justify their disappointing results using the typical logic of impression management.

- The dimension related to the financial structure, in its solvency and liquidity profiles, that relates to the availability of monetary resources and access credit possibilities to support the investments required by the commitment to ESG practices;
- The profitability dimension, which is not necessarily linked in the short run to the availability of financial resources, should be more sensitive to the logic of impression management.

To use effective measures of the various dimensions of the FP above, we refer to recent literature contributions that propose integrating FP measurements according to a holistic approach based on comprehensive scores (Bruna et al., 2022; Ricca et al., 2022). This latter line of research, originating with the affirmation of the ESGP scores, extends the use of overall scores to FP measurements as they are considered more capable of summarizing the complexity of FP through holistic measures capturing the interconnections between the financial structure and the dynamics of corporate revenues, expenses, and profitability (Bruna et al., 2022).

Moving from the above literature, and consistent with our aim of exploring the use of various overall FP scores to distinguish the impact of different FP dimensions on ESGP, we test the following hypothesis:

- **HP.1.** FP is positively associated with ESGP, but with a significantly different relationship for the financial dimension (*solvency* and *liquidity*) compared to the profitability dimension.

Recent ESG literature studies the presence of a CSR Committee within corporate governance as an organizational mechanism that is gaining relevance (Michelon & Parbonetti, 2012; Fuente et al., 2017; Bifulco et al., 2023). The constitution and composition of this Committee are not formalized, as there are often mainly norms or recommendations issued at a national or institutional level that suggest its creation (Baraibar-Diez & Odriozola, 2019). However, the presence of a CSR Committee demonstrates organizational alignment and companies' true commitment to implementing both business strategies and ESG practices, translating them into investments to address sustainability risks and opportunities (Baraibar-Diez & Odriozola, 2019; Peters & Romi, 2015; Velte & Stawinoga, 2020). Several studies show how the presence of a CSR Committee improves the levels of ESG disclosure (Venturelli et al., 2020; Cucari et al., 2018), fostering a higher level of assurance statement content (Rossi & Tarquinio, 2017). Moreover, numerous studies reveal how the characteristics of these Committees and the conditions for their effective functioning allow for higher ESGP (Hussain et al., 2018; Burke et al., 2019; Elmaghrabi, 2021; Jarboui et al., 2023), although a more limited number of studies highlight that the market value of companies with a CSR Committee does not differ significantly from those without this board (Bifulco et al., 2023; Panwar et al., 2023; Panwar et al., 2018). At the general level, then, the positive influences from the presence of the CSR Committee are variously theorized by studies and are also confirmed by empirical research investigating the role of the CSR Committee as mediator/moderator of relationships between Governance boards and ESGP (Bifulco et al., 2023; García-Sánchez et al., 2019; Martínez-Ferrero et al., 2021). Concerning the mediator/moderator role of the CSR Committee in the relationship between FP and ESGP, we find only the study by Bifulco et al. (2023), in which the authors use a CSR Committee as a moderating variable in the ESGP → FP relationship.[3] In contrast, there are no studies investigating the mediation/moderation role of a CSR Committee in the inverse FP → ESGP relationship, which we explore in this research. Thus, regarding research on the FP → ESGP relationship, there is a lack of studies exploring the potential influence of the presence of a CSR Committee.

In the perspective of the FP → ESGP relationship, we believe it is possible to hypothesize that the presence of this Committee can take an active role in sustainability policies, acting as a mechanism for monitoring the investment in ESG practices and thus fostering the improvement of ESGP. On this basis, we test the following further research hypothesis:

– **HP.2**. The presence of a CSR Committee improves the relationship of FP on ESGP.

Since the role of intangible resources in improving a firm's ESGP has been widely highlighted in literature (Huarng & Yu, 2024; Surroca et al., 2010; Gao et al., 2022; Khan et al., 2019; Huang, 2022), to make our analysis more effective by considering an additional factor that may affect the dependent variable ESGP, we also include the level of INT as a control variable in the tests of our research hypotheses (see Sect. 23.3.2).

23.3 Research Design

23.3.1 Sample

Our analysis covers the period from 2010 to 2022, for a total of 13 years.[4] To prevent distortions due to missing values, we decided to use a strongly *balanced panel data*.[5] We extracted the sample from a population of non-financial companies by Refinitiv® Eikon Datastream, excluding financial companies due to their different balance sheet structure and different financial performance measures. Starting from 3415 non-financial companies (44,395 firm-year observations) listed throughout the period of analysis and based in countries adopting the Euro as their single currency, we excluded all firms with missing data over the analysis period (3153 companies;

[3] The authors, assuming the stock price as a market measure of FP, hypothesize that the presence of a CSR Committee may produce an improvement in the ESGP → FP relationship. However, their results do not support such hypothesis, since they found this variable does not play a strongly significant moderating role in the investigated relationship.

[4] We start from 2010 given that before this period the coverage of the data for analysis is very low in Refinitiv Eikon Datastream®, particularly for ESG data. The financial year 2022 is the last with data available at the time of our study.

[5] A panel is called "balanced" if all units are observed in each observation period.

Table 23.1 Sample selection

Description	No. of observations
Non-financial firm-year observations available in Refinitiv® Eikon Datastream for the period 2010–2022	44,395
Dropped observations for missing financial or ESG data	40,989
Final non-financial firm-year observations (t = 2010, 2022; 262 companies)	3406

Table 23.2 Sample of companies by sector and country

Sector	Firms	Market	Firms
Basic materials	37	Austria	10
Consumer discretionary	48	Belgium	11
Consumer staples	21	Finland	20
Energy	15	France	57
Health care	20	Germany	94
Industrials	68	Greece	4
Technology	19	Ireland	5
Telecommunications	11	Italy	17
Utilities	23	Luxembourg	1
		Netherlands	16
		Portugal	5
		Spain	22
Total	262	Total	262

40,989 firm-year observations) (Table 23.1). After the above selection, we obtained a non-probabilistic sample of 262 European listed companies (3406 firm-year observations), composed as detailed in Table 23.2.

23.3.2 *Variables*

All data for the variables used to implement our analysis and listed in the following sections are extracted from Refinitiv® Eikon Datastream. All continuous variables used in our models are normalized in the interval 0–100.

23.3.2.1 ESG Performance and Financial Performance

In the analysis models, we denote the dependent variable as "ESGP." For its measure, we use the ESG score by Refinitiv® Eikon Datastream,[6] which is an overall company ESG score based on the self-reported information in the ESG pillars.

[6] ID Code Refinitiv Eikon Datastream: "TRESGS."

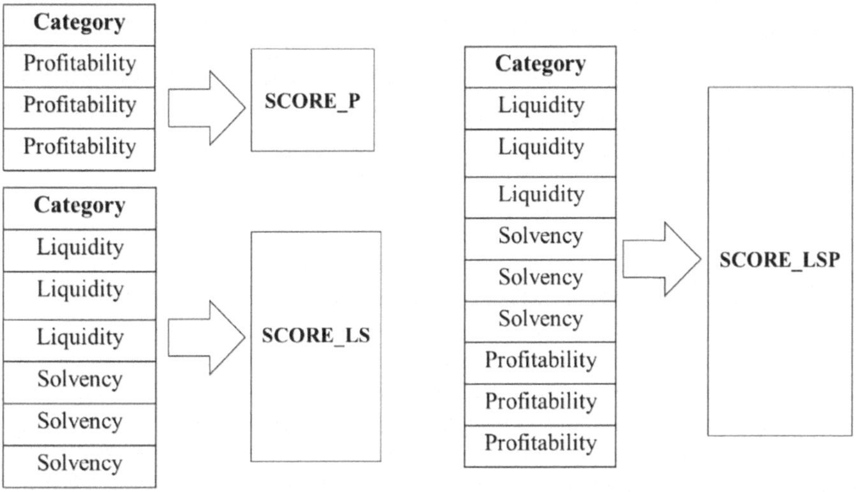

Fig. 23.1 FP scores

Table 23.3 Financial ratios applied to TOPSIS

Dimension	Ratio	ID Code Refinitiv® Eikon Datastream	Polarity
Liquidity	Current ratio (CR)	WC08106	Positive
Liquidity	Quick ratio	WC08101	Positive
Liquidity	Net debt	WC18199	Negative
Solvency	Interest coverage ratio	WC08291	Positive
Solvency	Equity ratio	WC08241	Positive
Solvency	Debt-to-equity ratio	WC08231	Negative
Profitability	ROE	WC01701	Positive
Profitability	ROA	WC08326	Positive
Profitability	Cost of goods ratio	WC08331	Negative

For Financial Performance, we create the following three FP scores (Fig. 23.1):

- Profitability (SCORE_P);
- Solvency and Liquidity (SCORE_LS);
- FP overall (SCORE_LSP).

We use three financial ratios (2 with positive polarity and 1 with negative polarity) to calculate the above scores (Table 23.3) by TOPSIS (Hwang, 1981; Bulgurcu, 2012).

23.3.2.2 Other Variables

Since the dependent variable ESGP is influenced by other factors not correlated with the three FPs, we include the variable INT as a control variable in our regression models, obtained from the "Total Intangible Other Assets Net" (ID Code WC02649) deflated by "Total Assets." (ID Code WC02999). In addition, we create three continuous independent variables (CSR_FP) obtained from the products ($CSR_{it-1}{}^{*}FP_{it-1}$) between FPs and the dichotomous variable "CSR Sustainability Committee" (ID Code CGVSDP005) indicating the presence (=1) or absence of the CSR committee (=0) responsible for decision-making on CSR strategy.

23.3.3 Methodology

In our study, we make use of methodologies known in literature.

As already mentioned, in the first step of analysis we synthesize FPs (Fig. 23.1) calculated from financial ratios (Table 23.3) using the *Technique for Order Preference by Similarity to the Ideal Solution* (TOPSIS) (Hwang, 1981; Lin & Tsai, 2010; Ricca, 2023), a methodology derived from Multi-Criteria Decision-Making (MCDM) based on the rank of alternatives to obtain the best alternative selection, which is the closest to the ideal solution. In other words, the best alternative is the most distant solution from the anti-ideal one. The TOPSIS method considers the distance from both sides (Bulgurcu, 2012).

Since the ESG regulatory landscape was dynamic during the period under review, the static panel regression models have a serious problem of serial correlation and are not suitable for investigating the relationship between FPs and ESGP (Table 23.6). Thus, for the reasons given, we use the dynamic panel regression model to investigate the impact of FPs on ESGP. Furthermore, with the lagged dependent variable (ESGP) included as a regressor in the dynamic panel model it is also possible to capture firms' adjustments toward the degree of persistence of the ESG policy influence (Dang et al., 2015). For this purpose, it is crucial to determine the number of lags (time delays) of the dependent variable (ESGP). Since there is no previous literature to support this, we proceeded empirically considering that the current ESG performance largely depends on the results obtained in previous years. From the empirical tests conducted, we can conclude that an *autoregressive process of second-order* [AR(2)] is much more effective and meaningful.

Therefore, to check HP.1, we estimate the following dynamic panel regression model (Arellano & Bond, 1991; Holtz-Eakin et al., 1988; Arellano & Bover, 1995; Blundell & Bond, 1998):

$$ESGP_{it} = \alpha_{it} + \delta_1 ESGP_{it-1} + \delta_2 ESGP_{it-2} + \beta_1 FP_{it-1} + \lambda_1 INT_{it-1} + \varepsilon_{it} \quad (23.1)$$

Then, to check HP.2, we estimate the following dynamic panel regression model:

$$ESGP_{it} = \alpha_{it} + \delta_1 ESGP_{it-1} + \delta_2 ESGP_{it-2} + \beta_1 FP_{it-1} + \lambda_1 INT_{it-1} + \rho_1 (CSR\,FP_{it-1}) + \varepsilon_{it} \quad (23.2)$$

where, for both equations:

$i = 1, 2, \ldots, 262.$
$t = 1, 2, \ldots, 13.$
α_{it} is the constant.
δ_k, β_1, and λ_1 and ρ_1 are unknown estimated coefficients.
$\varepsilon_{it} = \mu_i + \nu_{it}$ is the error term.

We apply the dynamic panel regression based on Arellano and Bond's Generalized Moment Method (GMM) which allows any endogeneity and serial correlation problems to be captured and corrected (Holtz-Eakin et al., 1988). In particular, the Arellano and Bond estimator uses additional instruments and exploits the orthogonality conditions that exist between the lagged values of ESGP and the disturbance ν_{it} (Arellano & Bond, 1991). The instruments used are the lagged values of the dependent variable ESGP, independent variables FPs, CSR_FPs, and control variable INT. These instruments are significant, and each of them influences ESGP.

23.4 Data Processing and Findings

Preliminarily, using the Levin-Lin-Chu panel unit-root test (Levin et al., 2002) we checked the stationarity for each variable. As shown in Table 23.4, all the variables were found stationary.

The values of kurtosis, skewness, and the Jarque-Bera test (Jarque & Bera, 1980) (H0: the sample was extracted from a population of data distributed as a normal random variable) reported in Table 23.5 (descriptive statistics) highlight that none of the variables involved in the analysis has a normal distribution.

The correlation coefficients (Table 23.6) between ESGP and the three synthesized FPs are all weak and significant at the level of $p < 0.01$.

First, we test the impact of FPs and the control variable INT on ESGP by static panel regression model. As shown in Table 23.7, the tests performed on the three equations confirm the positive and significant impact of first lagged values of FPs on ESG, the overall significance of the model (Wald test), and the fixed effects model

Table 23.4 Check for stationarity: Levin-Lin-Chu unit-root test

Levin-Lin-Chu unit-root test	
	Bartlett kernel
ESGP	−11.5***
Score_LSP	−26.8***
Score_LS	−14.0***
Score_P	−8.4***
CSR × FP_SLP	−17.0***
CSR × FP_SL	−10.7***
CSR × FP_P	−48.4***
INT	−14.3***

Note: Significance levels are as follows: *$p < 0.1$. **$p < 0.05$. ***$p < 0.01$

Table 23.5 Descriptive statistics

Descriptive statistics					
Statistics	ESG_SCORE	Score_LSP	Score_LS	Score_P	INT
Minimum	0.0	0.0	0.0	0.0	0.0
Maximum	100.0	100.0	100.0	100.0	100.0
Mean	65.0	38.2	36.7	49.8	33.1
Median	67.9	35.3	35.6	48.3	28.1
Std. dev.	19.9	15.3	9.9	18.5	25.1
Kurtosis	0.0	0.6	9.5	−0.7	−0.5
Skewness	−0.6	0.5	1.1	0.1	0.6
Test Jarque-Bera	146.2***	166.1***	1090.1***	62.3***	224.0***

Note: Significance levels are as follows: *$p < 0.1$. **$p < 0.05$. ***$p < 0.01$

Table 23.6 Correlation matrix

Variables	ESGP	Score_LSP	Score_LS	Score_P	INT
ESP	1				
Score_LSP	−0.10	1			
Score_LS	−0.17	0.82	1		
Score_P	0.03	0.55	0.50	1	
INT	0.11	−0.01	−0.05	0.03	1

Table 23.7 Fixed effect models

Fixed effect models			
	Dependent: ESGP (t)		
Independent variables	Coefficients		
FP_SLP (t-1)	0.05***		
FP_SL (t-1)		0.11***	
FP_P (t-1)			0.07**
INT (t-1)	0.027**	0.032**	0.032**
Constant	62.19***	60.05***	60.53***
D/W statistic	0.77	0.75	0.70
Wald test	10.82***	11.31***	44.10**
Hausman test	24.57	30.89	19.30

Note: Significance levels are as follows: *$p < 0.1$. **$p < 0.05$. ***$p < 0.01$

(Hausman test), but show positive autocorrelation problems of the residuals (Durbin-Watson statistic). Hence, we will adopt the GMM first difference also to keep the serial correlation problem under control.

Second, before applying the dynamic panel regression model, we wanted to check endogeneity between the three FPs and ESGP by performing a two-step test.

In the first step (Table 23.8), we regressed the FP scores on INT, and the natural logarithm of Total Asset (ln_TA), which represents the firm size, is not fitted in the model (1) and has a significant correlation with ESG and FPs.

Table 23.8 Endogeneity check: First step equations

Endogeneity check: First step equations			
	Dependent variables:		
Independent variables	FP_SL	FP_P	FP_P
ln_TA	-0.62^{***}	-0.47^{***}	-0.39^{***}
INT	-0.05^{*}	-0.04	-0.13
Cons	7.70^{***}	6.77^{***}	7.53^{***}
Hausman	45.89^{***}	87.89^{***}	33.68^{***}

Note: Significance levels are as follows: $*p < 0.1$. $**p < 0.05$. $***p < 0.01$

Table 23.9 Endogeneity check: Second Step equations

Endogeneity check: Second step equations			
Independent variables	Dependent: ESGP (t)		
e_FP_SLP	-0.15		
e_FP_SL		-0.20	
e_FP_P			-0.24
INT	0.02^{**}	0.05^{***}	-0.03^{**}
Cons	70.89^{***}	72.58^{***}	78.01^{***}
D-W	0.39	0.60	0.58

Note: Significance levels are as follows: $*p < 0.1$. $**p < 0.05$. $***p < 0.01$

Instead, in the second step, we estimated three equations, one for each of the FPs (Table 23.9), in which the dependent variable is ESGP, the independents are INT and the FPs residuals (e_FP) obtained by fitting the models from step 1. According to this logic, if in the estimated step 2 models the e_FPs variables are found to be non-significant, we can rule out the presence of endogeneity in FPs.

As mentioned above, we use Model (1) to test HP.1. The results (Table 23.10) reveal that first lagged FP *overall* (FP_SLP) and *Solvency and liquidity* (FP_SL) scores positively impact ESGP, while *profitability* score (FP_P) has a weak and negative impact. Moreover, in all three equations, the impact of INT on ESGP is negative. As usual, the GMM model and its estimators were tested using the Arellano-Bond, Sargan, and Wald tests. As shown in Table 23.10, the p-values of the Sargan test demonstrate the validity of the instrument used in the model as well as the Arellano-Bond test showing the absence of serial correlation problems in the first-differenced errors at order 2.

Finally, we use model (2) to test HP.2. In this case, compared with Eq. (23.1), we included the continuous variable CSR_FP to test the influence of CSR committee presence combined with FP on ESGP. As in the previous case (1), first lagged FP overall (FP_SLP) and "Solvency and liquidity" (FP_SL) scores positively impact the ESGP, while "Profitability" score (FP_P) has a weak and negative impact (Table 23.11). Instead, the previous year's presence of a CSR committee has a significant and negative impact in the equation regarding "solvency and liquidity" (FP_SL) and is weak and positive for overall (FP_SLP) and negative for "profitability" (FP_P). In this case, the first lagged variable INT is always significant and has a positive influence on ESGP.

Table 23.10 Arellano-Bond GMM (two-step) dynamic panel data estimation

Arellano-Bond dynamic panel data estimation			
GMM two-step			
	Dependent: ESGP (t)		
Independent variables	Coefficients		
ESGP (t-1)	0.45***	0.48***	0.65***
ESGP (t-2)	0.04***	0.07***	0.04***
FP_SLP (t-1)	0.17***		
FP_SL (t-1)		0.19***	
FP_P (t-1)			−0.06***
INT (t-1)	−0.09***	−0.12***	−0.11***
Arellano-Bond test for zero autocorrelation in first-differenced errors -H0: No autocorrelation			
Order_1	−9.48***	−9.56***	−9.56***
Order_2	−0.69	−0.37	−0.21
Sargan test of overidentifying restrictions -H0: Overidentifying restrictions are valid			
Sargan test	201.35	200.10	204.02
Wald chi2(6)	121.78***	150.41***	64.86***

Note: Significance levels are as follows: *$p < 0.1$. **$p < 0.05$. ***$p < 0.01$

Table 23.11 Arellano-Bond GMM (two-step) dynamic panel data estimation

Arellano-Bond dynamic panel data estimation			
GMM two-step			
	Dependent: ESGP (t)		
Independent variables	Coefficients		
ESGP (t-1)	0.397***	0.427***	0.519***
ESGP (t-2)	0.270***	0.022***	0.019***
FP_SLP (t-1)	0.162***		
FP_SL (t-1)		0.301***	
FP_P (t-1)			−0.008***
CSRxFP (t-1)	0.005***	−0.125***	−0.024***
INT (t-1)	0.146***	0.173**	0.073***
Arellano-Bond test for zero autocorrelation in first-differenced errors H0: No autocorrelation			
Order_1	−9.14***	−9.38***	−9.31***
Order_2	−0.08	−0.33	−0.27
Sargan test of overidentifying restrictions H0: Overidentifying restrictions are valid			
Sargan test	212.09	210.60	212.41
Wald chi2(6)	547.84***	931.03***	516.37***

Note: Significance levels are as follows: *$p < 0.1$. **$p < 0.05$. ***$p < 0.01$

All three FPs GMM models result significant (see Test Arellano-Bond, Sargan, Wald, Table 23.10) and, as revealed by BKW (Besley, Kuh, and Welsch) diagnostics (Table 23.12), there is no risk of collinearity.

Table 23.12 BKW (Besley, Kuh, and Welsch) collinearity diagnostics

BKW (Besley, Kuh, and Welsch) collinearity diagnostics: proportions of variance						
	lambda	cond	lambda	cond	lambda	cond
ESGP (t-1)	2.322	1.000	2.712	1.000	2.567	1.000
ESGP (t-2)	1.853	1.119	1.617	1.295	1.539	1.292
FP_SLP (t-1)	1.810	1.133				
FP_SL (t-1)			1.219	1.492		
FP_P (t-1)					1.249	1.433
CSRxFP_SLP (t-1)	0.702	1.819	0.570	2.181	0.548	2.164
INT (t-1)	0.584	1.993	0.400	2.820	0.490	3.100

Note: lambda = eigenvalues of the inverse covariance matrix; cond = index of collinearity condition and whereby BKW: cond ≥30 "strong" linear quasi-dependence;10 ≤ cond<30 moderately strong collinearity

23.5 Robustness Analysis

This section presents the results of the robustness analysis we conducted to verify the validity of the results obtained with the first model in Table 23.11. To test the robustness of the results to the variables used, we performed three models.

In Model.1 and Model.2 we applied the dynamic panel regression on two sub-samples obtained by dividing the original sample based on the countries with the average ESGP < or ≥ the overall average (=64.98):

1. **Model.1**—Countries with average ESGP <64.98, 141 companies (Austria, Belgium, Germany, Greece, Ireland, Luxembourg, Netherlands).
2. **Model.2**—Countries with average ESGP ≥64.98, 121 companies (Finland, France, Italy, Portugal, Spain)

For both sub-samples, the relationship between ESGP and FP as measured by R (Pearson's correlation) is negative and weak. However, the one for sub-sample 2 (−0.180) is greater than the one for sub-sample 1 (−0.095). From the results obtained from Models 1 and 2 (Table 23.14 in the Appendix), we can see that in both cases the coefficients of the independent and control variables are significant and have the same sign as the coefficients of the model reported in Table 23.11.

For Model.3 (Table 23.14 in the Appendix), we changed the continuous dependent variable ESGP to an ordinal polychotomous variable (ESG_RATING) using the Refinitiv® Eikon Datastream ESG Rating Methodology, in which ESGP scores are transformed into ratings (D- to A+) by a simple percentile sorting. Subsequently, the ratings, expressed as an ordinal variable, were transformed into conventional non-equidistant real numbers by the inverse of the standardized normal distribution function, through Torgerson's psychometric method (Torgerson, 1958) (see Table 23.13 in the Appendix). This methodology allows the ratings expressed in categorical form to be replaced by continuous values so that the differences between rating categories correspond to the true distances between them (Delvecchio, 2000).

Similarly, in this case, the coefficients of the independent and control variables, calculated by the elaboration of Model.3 (Table 23.14 in the Appendix) are significant and have the same sign as the coefficients of the first model shown in Table 23.11.

23.6 Discussion and Conclusions

This research aimed to investigate the role of FP in determining ESGP, considering the presence of a CSR Committee specifically responsible for corporate commitment to sustainability practices and level of investment in intangibles. For this purpose, we conducted an empirical analysis on a sample of 262 European listed companies, using a panel dataset from Refinitiv® Eikon Datastream covering the years 2010–2022. We regressed FP on ESGP by a *dynamic panel regression through first difference GMM* to capture the dynamic behavior of ESGP including the level of investment in intangibles as a control variable and considering the joint effect of a CSR Committee with FP. Regarding FP, we used some comprehensive scores obtained by TOPSIS to make the distinction between overall FP and its dimensions of "*profitability and solvency,*" and "*liquidity.*"

Research has delved into the causes of ESGP to understand whether it is financially-driven (Brammer & Millington, 2008; Peloza, 2009). Therefore, the study fits into a smaller field of literature on the direction of causality between the two performances, which showed contrasting empirical results regarding the positive or negative signs of the impacts of FP on ESGP (Scholtens, 2008; Chams et al., 2021; DasGupta, 2022; Preston & O'Bannon, 1997; Singh et al., 2022; Shahzad et al., 2016; Chiu & Sharfman, 2011; Julian & Ofori-Dankwa, 2013).

In this narrower field of research, as clarified in the chapter, we have adopted the interpretive lens of *Slack Resources Theory*, which hypothesizes that companies with higher FP have more discretionary financial resources to invest in ESG practices (Waddock & Graves, 1997; Orlitzky et al., 2003; Seifert et al., 2004; Schreck, 2011; Margolis et al., 2009). To deepen the analysis of the possible divergences found by literature in the investigated relationship, we have distinguished the more strictly financial profile of FP (*solvency* and *liquidity*) from the economic one (*profitability*). In this perspective, we tested our first hypothesis (HP.1) by assuming that FP is positively associated with ESGP, but with a significantly different relationship for the financial dimension (*solvency* and *liquidity*) as compared to the *profitability* dimension.

Our findings confirmed this assumption by showing that higher FP levels are positively and significantly associated with ESGP. The positive relationship exists both considering the overall FP and considering the *solvency* and *liquidity* aspects alone, but it is very weak and negative for the Profitability score (i.e., SCORE_P, which is the PF score that encompasses only the profitability ratios). This evidence is in line with the previous studies that found a positive FP → ESGP relationship (Chams et al., 2021; DasGupta, 2022; Nurim et al., 2022; Zhang et al., 2018; Aguilera-Caracuel et al., 2015; Seifert et al., 2004; Artiach et al., 2010) but, most importantly, adds to literature by pointing out that the adequacy of the corporate financial structure, which relates to the availability of monetary resources and/or the better possibility of finding them through access to credit, serves as a driver of

ESGP. On the contrary, in the short term there is no significant relationship with profitability performance, which appears, albeit weakly, sensitive to impression management practices. From a methodological perspective, the use of comprehensive scores for the various FP dimensions allows us to affirm the greater validity of FP overall scores for the study of relationships with ESGP.

In the second instance, we postulated (HP.2) that the presence of a CSR Committee improves the role of FP as a determinant of ESGP (for all FPs). The findings confirmed this hypothesis. This result, which stands in contrast to previous studies showing a non-strongly significant moderating role of a CSR Committee (albeit for the ESGP → FP relationship) (Bifulco et al., 2023), is particularly relevant on a practical level as it highlights the important role that this Committee plays in drawing top management's attention to a commitment to ESG practices. It is also significant scientifically as there are no previous studies related to the impacts of FP on ESGP that have reported this phenomenon.

The results of this research may be subject to further development. For example, future research, based on our methodological framework, could delve into the topic of studying other corporate governance variables as moderating variables, also taking into consideration the possible various relationships of a CSR Committee with the above variables. One could also attempt the use of more complex models of analysis, such as moderated mediation models, which are still scantily applied in the study of the relationship of FP as a determinant of ESGP. More simply, other research could test the conclusions reached here by referring to other samples from different countries.

Appendix

Table 23.13 Refinitiv® Eikon Datastream® Rating

Refinitiv® Eikon Datastream Rating			
Score interval	Rating Refinitiv	ESG_RATING	RAT_EP Rating Torgerson methods
0.917–1	A+	12	4.5839
0.834–0.916	A	11	3.8834
0.751–0.833	A-	10	3.3364
0.667–0.750	B+	9	2.8766
0.584–0.666	B	8	2.4832
0.501–0.583	B-	7	2.1298
0.417–0.500	C+	6	1.8035
0.334–0.416	C	5	1.4729
0.251–0.333	C-	4	1.1446
0.167–0.250	D+	3	0.8339
0.084–0.166	D	2	0.4893
0–0.083	D-	1	0.0000

Table 23.14 Models for robustness check

Arellano-Bond dynamic panel data estimation			
GMM two-step			
Independent variables	Mod.1	Mod.2	Mod.3
	Dependent variable: ESGP		Dependent variable: RAT_EP
	Coefficients		
ESGP (t-1)	0.459***	0.375***	0.333***
ESGP (t-2)	0.028***	0.030*	0.063***
FP_SLP (t-1)	0.203***	0.148***	0.005**
CSRxFP (t-1)	0.015**	0.003**	0.002**
INT (t-1)	0.031**	0.180*	0.004**
Arellano-Bond test for zero autocorrelation in first-differenced errors H0: No autocorrelation			
Order_1	−5.98***	−7.99***	−9.14***
Order_2	−0.70	−1.70*	−0.17
Sargan test of overidentifying restrictions H0: Overidentifying restrictions are valid			
Sargan test	90.03	202.08	207.94
Wald chi2(6)	705.69***	516.37***	1132.90***

References

Aguilera-Caracuel, J., Guerrero-Villegas, J., Vidal-Salazar, M. D., & Delgado-Márquez, B. L. (2015). International cultural diversification and corporate social performance in multinational enterprises: The role of slack financial resources. *Management International Review, 55*, 323–353. https://doi.org/10.1007/s11575-014-0225-4

Arellano, M., & Bond, S. (1991). Some tests of specification for panel data: Monte Carlo evidence and an application to employment equations. *The Review of Economic Studies, 58*, 277–297. https://doi.org/10.2307/2297968

Arellano, M., & Bover, O. (1995). Another look at the instrumental variable estimation of error-components models. *Journal of Econometrics, 68*, 29–51. https://doi.org/10.1016/0304-4076(94)01642-D

Artiach, T., Lee, D., Nelson, D., & Walker, J. (2010). The determinants of corporate sustainability performance. *Accounting and Finance, 50*, 31–51. https://doi.org/10.1111/j.1467-629X.2009.00315.x

Baboukardos, D. (2018). The valuation relevance of environmental performance revisited: The moderating role of environmental provisions. *The British Accounting Review, 50*, 32–47. https://doi.org/10.1016/j.bar.2017.09.002

Bansal, P. (2005). Evolving sustainably: A longitudinal study of corporate sustainable development. *Strategic Management Journal, 26*, 197–218. https://doi.org/10.1002/smj.441

Baraibar-Diez, E., & Odriozola, M. D. (2019). CSR committees and their effect on ESG performance in UK, France, Germany, and Spain. *Sustainability, 11*, 5077.

Barnea, A., & Rubin, A. (2010). Corporate social responsibility as a conflict between shareholders. *Journal of Business Ethics, 97*, 71–86. https://doi.org/10.1007/s10551-010-0496-z

Berg, F., Kölbel, J. F., & Rigobon, R. (2022). Aggregate confusion: The divergence of ESG ratings*. *Review of Finance, 26*, 1315–1344. https://doi.org/10.1093/rof/rfac033

Bifulco, G. M., Savio, R., Paolone, F., & Tiscini, R. (2023). The CSR committee as moderator for the ESG score and market value. *Corporate Social Responsibility and Environmental Management, 30*(6), 3231–3241. https://doi.org/10.1002/csr.2549

Blundell, R., & Bond, S. (1998). Initial conditions and moment restrictions in dynamic panel data models. *Journal of Econometrics, 87*, 115–143. https://doi.org/10.1016/S0304-4076(98)00009-8

Brammer, S., & Millington, A. (2008). Does it pay to be different? An analysis of the relationship between corporate social and financial performance. *Strategic Management Journal, 29*, 1325–1343. https://doi.org/10.1002/smj.714

Bruna, M. G., & Ben, L. B. (2021). CSR & financial performance: Facing methodological and modeling issues commentary paper to the eponymous FRL article collection. *Finance Research Letters, 44*, 102036. https://doi.org/10.1016/j.frl.2021.102036

Bruna, M. G., Loprevite, S., Raucci, D., et al. (2022). Investigating the marginal impact of ESG results on corporate financial performance. *Finance Research Letters, 47*, 102828. https://doi.org/10.1016/j.frl.2022.102828

Bulgurcu, B. K. (2012). Application of TOPSIS technique for financial performance evaluation of technology firms in Istanbul stock exchange market. *Procedia-Social and Behavioral Sciences, 62*, 1033–1040. https://doi.org/10.1016/j.sbspro.2012.09.176

Burke, J. J., Hoitash, R., & Hoitash, U. (2019). The heterogeneity of board-level sustainability committees and corporate social performance. *Journal of Business Ethics, 154*, 1161–1186. https://doi.org/10.1007/s10551-017-3453-2

Busch, T., & Friede, G. (2018). The robustness of the corporate social and financial performance relation: A second-order meta-analysis. *Corporate Social Responsibility and Environmental Management, 25*, 583–608. https://doi.org/10.1002/csr.1480

Chams, N., García-Blandón, J., & Hassan, K. (2021). Role reversal! Financial performance as an antecedent of ESG: The moderating effect of total quality management. *Sustainability, 13*, 7026.

Cheng, B., Ioannou, I., & Serafeim, G. (2014). Corporate social responsibility and access to finance. *Strategic Management Journal, 35*, 1–23. https://doi.org/10.1002/smj.2131

Chiu, S.-C., & Sharfman, M. (2011). Legitimacy, visibility, and the antecedents of corporate social performance: An investigation of the instrumental perspective. *Journal of Management, 37*, 1558–1585.

Clarkson, P. M., Li, Y., Richardson, G. D., & Vasvari, F. P. (2011). Does it really pay to be green? Determinants and consequences of proactive environmental strategies. *Journal of Accounting and Public Policy, 30*, 122–144. https://doi.org/10.1016/j.jaccpubpol.2010.09.013

Cornell, B., & Shapiro, A. C. (2021). Corporate stakeholders, corporate valuation and ESG. *European Financial Management, 27*, 196–207. https://doi.org/10.1111/eufm.12299

Cucari, N., Esposito De Falco, S., & Orlando, B. (2018). Diversity of board of directors and environmental social governance: Evidence from Italian listed companies. *Corporate Social Responsibility and Environmental Management, 25*, 250–266. https://doi.org/10.1002/csr.1452

Dang, V. A., Kim, M., & Shin, Y. (2015). In search of robust methods for dynamic panel data models in empirical corporate finance. *Journal of Banking & Finance, 53*, 84–98. https://doi.org/10.1016/j.jbankfin.2014.12.009

Daniel, F., Lohrke, F. T., Fornaciari, C. J., & Turner, R. A. (2004). Slack resources and firm performance: A meta-analysis. *Journal of Business Research, 57*, 565–574. https://doi.org/10.1016/S0148-2963(02)00439-3

DasGupta, R. (2022). Financial performance shortfall, ESG controversies, and ESG performance: Evidence from firms around the world. *Finance Research Letters, 46*, 102487. https://doi.org/10.1016/j.frl.2021.102487

Delvecchio, F. (2000). *Statistica per la ricerca sociale*. Cacucci editore.

Dragomir, V. D. (2018). How do we measure corporate environmental performance? A critical review. *Journal of Cleaner Production, 196*, 1124–1157. https://doi.org/10.1016/j.jclepro.2018.06.014

Duque-Grisales, E., & Aguilera-Caracuel, J. (2021). Environmental, social and governance (ESG) scores and financial performance of multilatinas: Moderating effects of geographic international diversification and financial slack. *Journal of Business Ethics, 168*, 315–334. https://doi.org/10.1007/s10551-019-04177-w

El Khoury, R., Nasrallah, N., & Alareeni, B. (2023). The determinants of ESG in the banking sector of MENA region: A trend or necessity? *Competitiveness Review: An International Business Journal, 33*, 7–29. https://doi.org/10.1108/CR-09-2021-0118

Eliwa, Y., Aboud, A., & Saleh, A. (2019). ESG practices and the cost of debt: Evidence from EU countries. *Critical Perspectives on Accounting, 79*, 102097. https://doi.org/10.1016/j.cpa.2019.102097

Elmaghrabi, M. E. (2021). CSR committee attributes and CSR performance: UK evidence. *Corporate Governance: The International Journal of Business in Society, 21*, 892–919. https://doi.org/10.1108/CG-01-2020-0036

Endrikat, J., Guenther, E., & Hoppe, H. (2014). Making sense of conflicting empirical findings: A meta-analytic review of the relationship between corporate environmental and financial performance. *European Management Journal, 32*, 735–751. https://doi.org/10.1016/j.emj.2013.12.004

Freeman, R. E. (1984). *Strategic management: A stakeholder approach*. Pitman.

Friede, G., Busch, T., & Bassen, A. (2015). ESG and financial performance: Aggregated evidence from more than 2000 empirical studies. *Journal of Sustainable Finance & Investment, 5*, 210–233. https://doi.org/10.1080/20430795.2015.1118917

Fuente, J. A., García-Sánchez, I. M., & Lozano, M. B. (2017). The role of the board of directors in the adoption of GRI guidelines for the disclosure of CSR information. *Journal of Cleaner Production, 141*, 737–750. https://doi.org/10.1016/j.jclepro.2016.09.155

Gao, J., Li, J., & Luo, Y. (2022). Does the enterprise's choice of intangible capital help to promote its ESG score? *Frontiers in Environmental Science, 10*, 978955.

García-Sánchez, I. M., Gómez-Miranda, M. E., David, F., & Rodríguez-Ariza, L. (2019). Board independence and GRI-IFC performance standards: The mediating effect of the CSR committee. *Journal of Cleaner Production, 225*, 554–562. https://doi.org/10.1016/j.jclepro.2019.03.337

Holtz-Eakin, D., Newey, W., & Rosen, H. S. (1988). Estimating vector autoregressions with panel data. *Econometrica, 56*, 1371–1395. https://doi.org/10.2307/1913103

Horváthová, E. (2010). Does environmental performance affect financial performance? A meta-analysis. *Ecological Economics, 70*, 52–59. https://doi.org/10.1016/j.ecolecon.2010.04.004

Huang, D. Z. X. (2021). Environmental, social and governance (ESG) activity and firm performance: A review and consolidation. *Accounting and Finance, 61*, 335–360. https://doi.org/10.1111/acfi.12569

Huang, D. Z.-X. (2022). An integrated theory of the firm approach to environmental, social and governance performance. *Accounting and Finance, 62*, 1567–1598. https://doi.org/10.1111/acfi.12832

Huarng, K.-H., & Yu, T. H.-K. (2024). Causal complexity analysis of ESG performance. *Journal of Business Research, 170*, 114327. https://doi.org/10.1016/j.jbusres.2023.114327

Hussain, N., Rigoni, U., & Orij, R. P. (2018). Corporate governance and sustainability performance: Analysis of triple bottom line performance. *Journal of Business Ethics, 149*, 411–432. https://doi.org/10.1007/s10551-016-3099-5

Hwang, C. L., & Yoon, K. (1981). Multi objective decision making: Methods and application.

Iazzolino, G., Bruni, M. E., Veltri, S., et al. (2023). The impact of ESG factors on financial efficiency: An empirical analysis for the selection of sustainable firm portfolios. *Corporate Social Responsibility and Environmental Management, 30*, 1917–1927. https://doi.org/10.1002/csr.2463

Jarboui, A., Dammak Ben Hlima, N., & Bouaziz, D. (2023). Do sustainability committee characteristics affect CSR performance? Evidence from India. *Benchmarking: An International Journal, 30*, 628–652. https://doi.org/10.1108/BIJ-04-2021-0225

Jarque, C. M., & Bera, A. K. (1980). Efficient tests for normality, homoscedasticity and serial independence of regression residuals. *Economics Letters, 6*, 255–259. https://doi.org/10.1016/0165-1765(80)90024-5

Jensen, M. C. (2001). Value maximization, stakeholder theory, and the corporate objective function. *Journal of Applied Corporate Finance, 14*, 8–21. https://doi.org/10.1111/j.1745-6622.2001.tb00434.x

Julian, S. D., & Ofori-Dankwa, J. C. (2013). Financial resource availability and corporate social responsibility expenditures in a sub-Saharan economy: The institutional difference hypothesis. *Strategic Management Journal, 34*, 1314–1330. https://doi.org/10.1002/smj.2070

Khan, S. Z., Yang, Q., & Waheed, A. (2019). Investment in intangible resources and capabilities spurs sustainable competitive advantage and firm performance. *Corporate Social Responsibility and Environmental Management, 26*, 285–295. https://doi.org/10.1002/csr.1678

King, A. A., & Lenox, M. J. (2001). Does it really pay to be green? An empirical study of firm environmental and financial performance: An empirical study of firm environmental and financial performance. *Journal of Industrial Ecology, 5*, 105–116. https://doi.org/10.1162/108819801753358526

Kock, C. J., Santaló, J., & Diestre, L. (2012). Corporate governance and the environment: What type of governance creates greener companies? *Journal of Management Studies, 49*, 492–514. https://doi.org/10.1111/j.1467-6486.2010.00993.x

Kraatz, M. S., & Zajac, E. J. (2001). How organizational resources affect strategic change and performance in turbulent environments: Theory and evidence. *Organization Science, 12*, 632–657. https://doi.org/10.1287/orsc.12.5.632.10088

Levin, A., Lin, C.-F., & James Chu, C.-S. (2002). Unit root tests in panel data: Asymptotic and finite-sample properties. *Journal of Econometrics, 108*, 1–24. https://doi.org/10.1016/S0304-4076(01)00098-7

Lin, C.-T., & Tsai, M.-C. (2010). Location choice for direct foreign investment in new hospitals in China by using ANP and TOPSIS. *Quality and Quantity, 44*, 375–390. https://doi.org/10.1007/s11135-008-9199-2

Margolis, J. D., Elfenbein, H. A., & Walsh, J. P. (2009). Does it pay to be good ... and does it matter? A meta-analysis of the relationship between corporate social and financial performance. *SSRN Electronic Journal*, 1–68. https://doi.org/10.2139/ssrn.1866371

Margolis, J. D., & Walsh, J. P. (2003). Misery loves companies: Rethinking social initiatives by business. *Administrative Science Quarterly, 48*, 268–305. https://doi.org/10.2307/3556659

Martínez-Ferrero, J., Lozano, M. B., & Vivas, M. (2021). The impact of board cultural diversity on a firm's commitment toward the sustainability issues of emerging countries: The mediating effect of a CSR committee. *Corporate Social Responsibility and Environmental Management, 28*, 675–685. https://doi.org/10.1002/csr.2080

McGuire, J. B., Sundgren, A., & Schneeweis, T. (1988). Corporate social responsibility and firm financial performance. *The Academy of Management Journal, 31*, 854–872. https://doi.org/10.5465/256342

Melo, T. (2012). Slack-resources hypothesis: A critical analysis under a multidimensional approach to corporate social performance. *Social Responsibility Journal, 8*, 257–269. https://doi.org/10.1108/17471111211234879

Michelon, G., & Parbonetti, A. (2012). The effect of corporate governance on sustainability disclosure. *Journal of Management and Governance, 16*, 477–509. https://doi.org/10.1007/s10997-010-9160-3

Nurim, Y., Harjanto, N., Prabawati, P. I., & Wijaya, N. R. (2022). Stable financial performance as the antecedent of ESG activity and firm value relationship: An evidence from Indonesia. In W. A. Barnett & B. S. Sergi (Eds.), *Quantitative analysis of social and financial market development* (pp. 85–102). Emerald Publishing Limited.

Orlitzky, M., Schmidt, F. L., & Rynes, S. L. (2003). Corporate social and financial performance: A meta-analysis. *Organization Studies, 24*, 403–441. https://doi.org/10.1177/0170840603024003910

Panwar, R., Nawani, S., & Pandey, V. (2018). Legislated CSR: A brief introduction. In *Corporate social responsibility* (pp. 133–146). Emerald Publishing Limited.

Panwar, R., Pandey, V., Suddaby, R., & Vidal, N. G. (2023). Did India's CSR mandate enhance or diminish firm value? *Business & Society, 62*, 401–433.

Parmar, B. L., Freeman, R. E., Harrison, J. S., et al. (2010). Stakeholder theory: The state of the art. *The Academy of Management Annals, 4*, 403–445. https://doi.org/10.5465/19416520.2010.495581

Peloza, J. (2009). The challenge of measuring financial impacts from investments in corporate social performance. *Journal of Management, 35*, 1518–1541. https://doi.org/10.1177/0149206309335188

Peters, G. F., & Romi, A. M. (2015). The association between sustainability governance characteristics and the assurance of corporate sustainability reports. *Auditing: A Journal of Practice & Theory, 34*, 163–198. https://doi.org/10.2308/ajpt-50849

Preston, L. E., & O'Bannon, D. P. (1997). The corporate social-financial performance relationship: A typology and analysis. *Business & Society, 36*, 419–429. https://doi.org/10.1177/000765039703600406

Ricca, B. (2023). *La performance di sostenibilità delle imprese. Un framework di misurazione multidimensionale basato su metodologie statistiche*. Franco Angeli.

Ricca, B., Ferrara, M., & Loprevite, S. (2022). Searching for an effective accounting-based score of firm performance: A comparative study between different synthesis techniques. *Quality and Quantity, 57*(4), 3575–3602. https://doi.org/10.1007/s11135-022-01522-6

Rossi, A., & Tarquinio, L. (2017). An analysis of sustainability report assurance statements. *Managerial Auditing Journal, 32*, 578–602. https://doi.org/10.1108/MAJ-07-2016-1408

Schaltegger, S., & Synnestvedt, T. (2002). The link between 'green' and economic success: Environmental management as the crucial trigger between environmental and economic performance. *Journal of Environmental Management, 65*, 339–346. https://doi.org/10.1006/jema.2002.0555

Scholtens, B. (2008). A note on the interaction between corporate social responsibility and financial performance. *Ecological Economics, 68*, 46–55. https://doi.org/10.1016/j.ecolecon.2008.01.024

Schreck, P. (2011). Reviewing the business case for corporate social responsibility: New evidence and analysis. *Journal of Business Ethics, 103*, 167–188. https://doi.org/10.1007/s10551-011-0867-0

Seifert, B., Morris, S. A., & Bartkus, B. R. (2004). Having, giving, and getting: Slack resources, corporate philanthropy, and firm financial performance. *Business & Society, 43*, 135–161. https://doi.org/10.1177/0007650304263919

Shahzad, A. M., Mousa, F. T., & Sharfman, M. P. (2016). The implications of slack heterogeneity for the slack-resources and corporate social performance relationship. *Journal of Business Research, 69*, 5964–5971. https://doi.org/10.1016/j.jbusres.2016.05.010

Singh, A., Singh, P., & Shome, S. (2022). ESG–CFP linkages: A review of its antecedents and scope for future research. *Indian Journal of Corporate Governance, 15*, 48–69. https://doi.org/10.1177/09746862221089062

Surroca, J., Tribó, J. A., & Waddock, S. (2010). Corporate responsibility and financial performance: The role of intangible resources. *Strategic Management Journal, 31*, 463–490. https://doi.org/10.1002/smj.820

Talbot, D., & Boiral, O. (2015). Strategies for climate change and impression management: A case study among Canada's large industrial emitters. *Journal of Business Ethics, 132*, 329–346. https://doi.org/10.1007/s10551-014-2322-5

Torgerson, W. S. (1958). Theory and methods of scaling.

van Duuren, E., Plantinga, A., & Scholtens, B. (2016). ESG integration and the investment management process: Fundamental investing reinvented. *Journal of Business Ethics, 138*, 525–533. https://doi.org/10.1007/s10551-015-2610-8

Velte, P. (2017). Does ESG performance have an impact on financial performance? Evidence from Germany. *Journal of Global Responsibility, 8*, 169–178. https://doi.org/10.1108/JGR-11-2016-0029

Velte, P., & Stawinoga, M. (2020). Do chief sustainability officers and CSR committees influence CSR-related outcomes? A structured literature review based on empirical-quantitative research findings. *Journal of Management Control, 31*, 333–377. https://doi.org/10.1007/s00187-020-00308-x

Venturelli, A., Pizzi, S., Caputo, F., & Principale, S. (2020). The revision of nonfinancial reporting directive: A critical lens on the comparability principle. *Business Strategy and the Environment, 29*, 3584–3597. https://doi.org/10.1002/bse.2598

Voss, G. B., Sirdeshmukh, D., & Voss, Z. G. (2008). The effects of slack resources and environmental threat on product exploration and exploitation. *The Academy of Management Journal, 51*, 147–164. https://doi.org/10.5465/amj.2008.30767373

Waddock, S. A., & Graves, S. B. (1997). The corporate social performance-financial performance link. *Strategic Management Journal, 18*, 303–319.

Zhang, Y., Li, J., Jiang, W., et al. (2018). Organizational structure, slack resources and sustainable corporate socially responsible performance. *Corporate Social Responsibility and Environmental Management, 25*, 1099–1107. https://doi.org/10.1002/csr.1524

Zhao, X., & Murrell, A. (2022). Does a virtuous circle really exist? Revisiting the causal linkage between CSP and CFP. *Journal of Business Ethics, 177*, 173–192. https://doi.org/10.1007/s10551-021-04769-5

Zhao, D., & Strotmann, A. (2015). *Analysis and visualization of citation networks* (Synthesis lectures on information concepts, retrieval, and services) (Vol. 7, pp. 1–207). Morgan & Claypool Publishers.

Zumente, I., & Bistrova, J. (2021). ESG importance for long-term shareholder value creation: Literature vs. practice. *Journal of Open Innovation: Technology, Market, and Complexity, 7*, 127. https://doi.org/10.3390/joitmc7020127

Chapter 24
Does ESG Performance Affect Firms' Performance? Evidence from European Energy Companies

Concetta Carnevale and Caterina Di Tommaso

24.1 Introduction

Sustainable energy development goals and companies' engagement in environmental, social, and governance (ESG) issues are two of the most relevant questions to the attention of governments, regulators, and stakeholders around the world. International and national institutions highlight that these two themes are closely connected, because energy companies, by their very nature as producers and distributors of energy, have a substantial impact on world sustainability issues. Consequently, the sensitivity of energy companies towards sustainable development issues is fundamental for achieving the goals linked to energy efficiency improvements, usage of renewable energy sources, and GHG emission reduction (United Nation, 2023).

However, the transition process towards cleaner energy is complex and costly, and the current international context, characterized by uncertain economic conditions and high market volatility, exposes energy companies to significant risks. While, on the one hand, it seems imperative for energy companies to give priority to ESG issues, on the other hand, the economic and market dynamics seem to push in favour of economic and stock-market performance (henceforth market performance) even to the detriment of the ESG performance. Hence, it is crucial to understand whether and how managers' choices to enhance companies' commitment to ESG issues affect their economic and market performance, and whether being sustainable pays off.

C. Carnevale (✉)
Dipartimento di Culture, Educazione e Società, Università della Calabria, Arcavacata, Italy
e-mail: concetta.carnevale@unical.it

C. Di Tommaso
Dipartimento Jonico In Sistemi Giuridici Ed Economici Del Mediterraneo: Società, Ambiente, Culture, Università degli Studi di Bari, Bari, Italy

N. Castellano et al. (eds.), *Environmental, Social, Governance (ESG)*, SIDREA Series in Accounting and Business Administration,
https://doi.org/10.1007/978-3-031-76618-3_24

Our study aims to examine the relationship between European energy companies' ESG performance and their economic and market performance. We choose to focus on the European energy sector for several reasons. First, European countries are heavily dependent on fossil fuels and on imports of traditional low-cost energy sources and, as such, they are called to promote important changes in their energy sector. Second, in recent years, European energy companies are experiencing important transformations, affecting all activities within the supply chain (from power generation to trading, including transmission and distribution), due to the use of renewable energy sources and growing pressure from stakeholders. Third, the European Union (EU) is pushing for the advancement of the Paris Agreement and to foster cooperation among countries on climate change, clean energy, and reducing greenhouse gas emissions (European Commission, 2018; European Commission, 2022). Fourth, in the last decade, European energy companies have had to face important exogenous shocks, linked to both global and local economic, geopolitical, and financial dynamics, which have strongly influenced the market and procurement processes. Last but not least, the existing literature provides mixed results on the relationships between firms' ESG performance and their economic and market performance, neglecting specific analyses of the European energy companies and the European energy context.

By testing several econometric models, we verify whether ESG performance affects European energy companies' economic and market performance and whether these relationships are moderated by the different business models adopted by the companies (renewable vs. traditional energy), the economic and financial crises and, finally, the different national capitalism models adopted across European countries.

Our findings show a complex picture. First, we find that European energy companies enjoy relevant benefits from a commitment to improving their ESG performance, but still today renewable energy companies experience a very important disadvantage related to new and immature technologies and markets. Moreover, in the contexts of exogenous and negative shocks, companies do not appear to enjoy the benefits related to the effects of ESG performance on their economic and market performance. During crisis periods, the commitment to ESG issues may result in socially responsible firms becoming more vulnerable and the costs associated with ESG engagement could potentially outweigh the benefits. Finally, our analysis reveals that the different national models of capitalism emerging from economic frameworks can significantly moderate the benefits that ESG efforts generate on a company's economic and market performance. This implies that the EU cannot yet be considered a homogeneous area.

Our research offers several contributions. First, this study provides new empirical evidence on the relationship between ESG performance and a firm's economic and market performance in the energy sector. To the best of our knowledge, this is the first study investigating these relationships by offering a broad analysis perspective on European energy companies. Second, we provide evidence that the different business models (renewable vs. traditional), adopted by European energy companies, highly affect the relationship between ESG performance and the company's economic and market performance. Third, we provide new evidence on the effects that exogenous structural breaks produce on the relationship between European energy companies' ESG performance and their economic and market performance. Finally, our study contributes to filling a gap in the existing literature, as European cross-country differences continue to be under-investigated. Although Europe is one of the most investigated geographical areas concerning ESG issues, there is a lack of studies that, starting from industry-specific analyses, have highlighted how the institutional, economic, and financial differences among the European countries could significantly influence the relationships between the ESG performance and energy companies economic and market performance. To date, Europe offers a very mixed picture in terms of national economic and legislative features. Therefore, a comprehensive analysis of how national, institutional, economic, and financial differences affect these relationships is very important. In order to do this, we adopt the lens of the varieties of capitalism (VoC), which classifies countries based on financial and labour market characteristics.

Our research offers important insight to managers and policymakers. The results could help more enlightened managers resolve the typical conflicts highlighted by the agency theory. By documenting the positive effect of ESG performance on the economic and market performance of energy companies, our study supports managers' choices towards engaging in CSR activities, through which relationships with all stakeholders could be improved and greater social trust obtained. As far as policymakers are concerned, our analysis highlights that the transition process towards renewable energy sources needs more support from European institutions, as renewable energy companies are facing the economic disadvantages associated with immature technologies and markets.

The paper is organized as follows. The next section reviews the existing literature and outlines the related research questions within a broader theoretical background. Section 24.3 explains the research design (sample, data, and estimation models). Section 24.4 discusses the findings. Finally, Sect. 24.5 provides implications and limitations and suggests insights for future research.

24.2 Theoretical Background Literature and Research Questions

To analyse the relationship between CSR performance (henceforth CSP) and firms' economic and market performance researchers developed and used several theories supporting their research hypotheses and evidence. The first, the agency theory, asserts that shareholders' profit maximization is the sole social responsibility of the company, and so the social practices only make sense if they increase the shareholders' profit (Friedman, 1962). According to this theory, the costs related to a firm's engagement in CSR fall directly to the bottom line, reducing the firm's value and its capability to generate profit. Therefore, CSR activities should not exceed the minimum legal standards. Moreover, the use of resources for CSR activities places companies at a competitive disadvantage vis-à-vis competitors whose managers do not pursue a social mission (Jensen & Meckling, 1976). For these reasons, proponents of the agency theory argue that the relationship between CSP and a firm's market value and profitability is negative.

A second theory, widely used by researchers, is the stakeholder theory. According to this theory, the more a company enjoys the trust of its stakeholders, the greater its success will be over time (Freeman, 1984). The commitment to CSR issues helps a company build and maintain relationships of trust with stakeholders, minimize bargaining costs, and increase its competitive advantage (Jones, 1995).

By integrating the stakeholder theory with the resource dependence theory (Pfeffer & Salancik, 1978) and resource-based theory (Barney, 1991), some researchers argued that more favourable relationships with stakeholders not only produce cost savings but also higher revenues (McWilliams & Siegel, 2011). Furthermore, as these relationships improve and trust builds, transaction costs decline, and the firm is exposed to minor risks (Surroca et al., 2010). According to this perspective, a firm's commitment to CSR plays a pivotal role in enhancing relationships with stakeholders and increasing strategic intangible assets such as trust and reputation.

Starting from these arguments, Barnett (2007) developed the concept of stakeholder influence capacity (SIC), that is: "the ability of a firm to identify, act on, and profit from opportunities to improve stakeholder relationships through CSR." Stakeholders perceive companies with a strong SIC as more trustworthy compared to their competitors, and therefore they reward them. For such firms, being socially responsible pays. In contrast, stakeholders consider companies with a low SIC as less trustworthy and they perceive their CSR activities as mere "greenwashing." For such firms, to be socially responsible might not pay (Barnett & Salomon, 2012).

Consequently, proponents of stakeholder theory and resource-based theory argue that the relationship between CSP and a firm's profitability and market value is positive, but only if a firm has a good reputation and enjoys stakeholders' trust.

24.2.1 The Link Between ESG Performance and Economic-Market Performance in the Energy Sector

Despite numerous empirical studies, the relationship between CSP and corporate economic/market performance remains ambiguous (Gillan et al., 2021; Lu et al., 2014). While many studies support a positive correlation, others support negative or inconclusive associations. These results can be attributed to the different metrics used to evaluate CSP and company performance, model specifications, and control variables, as well as disparities across the studied periods, contexts, and industries.

Within this complex framework, the energy sector requires a greater effort of analysis by researchers for at least two reasons. On the one hand, empirical research focusing on energy companies remains very limited. On the other hand, companies in the energy sector are currently experiencing major transformations, affecting all activities within the supply chain. Furthermore, the energy industry plays a crucial role in achieving the Sustainable Development Goals because these companies can significantly contribute to reducing global CO_2 emissions. Thus, many benefits for society can derive from the energy companies' commitment to CSR.

Nevertheless, as Ruggiero & Lehkonen (2017) point out, also regarding energy companies, it is not yet clear if being responsible pays. Filbeck and Gorman (2004) and Sueyoshi and Goto (2009) claim that they do not find a positive relationship between financial and environmental performance. Ruggiero and Lehkonen (2017) find results partially congruent with those provided by Sueyoshi and Goto (2009) and they claim that resource-based theory may not entirely apply to renewable energy companies. The authors point out that carbon intensity seems to play a minimal role in moderating the relationship between the increase of renewable energy and a firm's performance, and this could explain why among the top 100 greenest utilities in the world, only five had a share of renewable energy higher than 20%.

Conversely, other studies show that CSP produces a significant effect on energy companies' performance. Pätäri et al. (2014) claim that CSR concerns negatively affect both profitability and market value, while CSR strengths produce a positive effect only on companies' market value. By comparing the market performance of green energy stocks relative to brown energy stocks, Bouri et al. (2022) find that brown stock returns tend to decrease more than green energy stock returns.

Overall, the existing studies provide mixed results. Therefore, we ask the following research questions:

RQ1a -	*Does ESG performance affect energy companies' economic performance?*

RQ1b -	*Does the business model (renewable vs. traditional energies) moderate the relationship between ESG performance and energy companies' economic performance?*

RQ1c -	*Does ESG performance affect energy companies' market performance?*

RQ1d -	*Does the business model (renewable vs. traditional energies) moderate the relationship between ESG performance and energy companies' market performance?*

24.2.2 *The Effect of ESG Performance During Crisis Periods*

Does a firm's ESG engagement affect its economic and market performance in the context of exogenous shock? Numerous studies demonstrated that the uncertainty related to periods of economic turbulence increases the usefulness of CSP information for investors, especially when confidence in companies and markets is eroded. According to Godfrey et al. (2009), a firm's ESG engagement creates trust and enhances relationships with stakeholders. This helps stabilize the firm's market performance and has a less volatile income stream, even during crisis periods (Atif & Ali, 2021). Other researchers provide evidence that a firm's commitment to CSR can be thought of as an insurance policy that pays off when investors face a severe confidence crisis (Lins et al., 2017). Dyck et al. (2019) show that, during crisis periods, the financial market recognizes a greater value in companies with higher ESG performance, and institutional investors ask companies for greater commitment to ESG performance. In line with Bouri et al. (2022), Dyck et al. (2019) provide evidence that the volatility of green stocks decreases relative to the volatility of brown stocks during crisis periods. Abbassi et al. (2022) argue that a firm's ESG performance becomes more valuable during economic turmoil periods and that a high ESG performance would make the firm appear more credible. The authors claim that the financial crisis stands as a turning point in how the market evaluates firms' ESG performance. ESG performance could play a key role in assuaging information asymmetry problems and in shaping corporate decisions in the aftermath of new economic turmoil periods. Finally, Amiraslani et al. (2023) show that ESG performance pays off in periods when there is a loss of trust in energy industries. The authors demonstrate that markets reward companies with higher ESG performance by offering them better financing conditions.

However, other researchers do not believe that ESG performance is really an effective shield during crisis periods. Buchanan et al. (2018) find evidence that, during crisis, firms engaged in CSR activities experienced more of a decrease in firm value than firms non-engaged in CSR. The authors claim that the costs of CSR engagement can outweigh the benefits when a crisis emerges and that this result is not driven by unobserved industry-level factors. Drago and Carnevale (2020) find that investors (lenders) do not reward European companies engaging in CSR during the crisis periods. Demers et al. (2021) robustly refute the importance of ESG performance in explaining stock returns for US companies during the recent pandemic. Their analyses provide robust evidence that ESG scores did not immunize stocks during the COVID-19 crisis, while industry affiliation and investments in innovative and intangible assets did. Berkman et al. (2021) find that Japanese firms with high CSR ratings experienced significantly lower stock returns than Japanese firms with low CSR ratings during the global financial crisis.

The timeframe considered in our analysis includes three periods of major crises: the sovereign debt crisis in Europe, the COVID-19 crisis, and the Russo-Ukrainian war. As previous studies show, these events produced extreme shocks in financial markets (Chen et al., 2022; Ghosh et al., 2023; Goodell et al., 2023). Furthermore, in May 2022, the Russo-Ukrainian war prompted the European Council to ban imports of Russian oil, diversify energy supply sources, and increase the use of renewable energy sources.

As it is reasonable to expect all these exogenous shocks produce important effects on the economic and market performance of European energy companies, we ask the following research questions:

RQ2a -	*Does a crisis moderate the relationship between ESG performance and energy companies' economic performance?*

RQ2b -	*Does a crisis moderate the relationship between ESG performance and energy companies' market performance?*

24.2.3 The Effect of ESG Performance in the Different Economic National Models

Firms' ESG engagement encompasses multiple dimensions of corporate behaviour and represents a tool to manage the fundamental trade-offs between attention to shareholders and attention to other stakeholders, including institutions. Proponents of the institutional theory argue that such trade-offs crucially depend on the forms and dynamics of economic organizations (firms, networks, markets), which—in turn—are shaped by national rules and mechanisms (Cai et al., 2016). Hence, firms' commitment to ESG issues should be explicitly analysed within a wider field of national economic governance, characterized by specific modes and complementarities between the market, regulations, and relationship between firms and stakeholders (Brammer et al., 2012). Moreover, as outlined by several researchers (Ioannou & Serafeim, 2012; Matten & Moon, 2008), applying the lens of institutional theory to study firms' CSR engagement allows better understanding of business responsibilities between different regions and countries. This is because CSR practices are always contingent on the institutional framework of businesses (Campbell, 2007; Liang & Renneboog, 2017).

To better specify the mechanisms by which national institutional arrangements shape corporate CSR activities, some researchers have adopted a perspective drawn from the broader literature on comparative capitalism, namely the VoC approach (Kang & Moon, 2012; Hall & Soskice, 2001). This offered other researchers a robust theoretical framework for developing cross-country analysis on issues related to companies' ESG performance.

The main conceptual argument underlying the VoC approach is that companies' behaviour depends on the national institutional arrangements that govern: (a) product market competition; (b) the labour market; (c) the financial market; (d) corporate governance mechanisms; (e) the social protection; and (f) the education sector. If they are coordinated in a complementary manner, these arrangements give a distinctive competitive advantage to companies (Amable, 2003). Countries exhibit significantly different features in each of these areas, and institutional complementarities define the different domestic models of capitalism (Gjølberg, 2009; Witt et al., 2018).

For the purposes of this paper, the assumptions underlying the VoC approach are relevant, as the existing empirical evidence shows that the national economy model affects firms' commitment to ESG issues and their economic and market performances. To date, the European Union cannot be considered a homogeneous area, as differences persist in the institutional contexts and spheres of economic governance across European countries. In light of the above, we believe it is important to verify whether these differences affect the link between energy companies' ESG performance and their economic and market performance. Therefore, we posit the following research questions:

RQ3a -	*Does the national model of capitalism moderate the relationship between ESG performance and energy companies' economic performance?*

RQ3b -	*Does the national model of capitalism moderate the relationship between ESG performance and energy companies' market performance?*

24.3 Research Design

24.3.1 Sample Selection

Our study focuses on European energy companies listed during the 2012–2022 period. We perform the screener procedure in Refinitiv aiming to identify companies that: (a) have their headquarters and primary listing market in one of EU27 member states, and (b) are classified in the Global Industry Classification Standard (GICS) as companies belonging to the Energy and Utilities sectors (S&P Global, 2023). We exclude from our dataset: (a) companies classified in GICS as Water Utilities, and (b) companies with missing values in ESG score, accounting, and control variables. Our final sample consists of 97 energy companies, 28 of which are classified as renewable energy companies, located in 17 European countries (Table 24.1).

24.3.2 Regression Variables

24.3.2.1 Dependent Variables

To develop our analysis, we use as dependent variables both accounting and stock-market measures. While accounting-based measures tap only historical aspects of a company's performance, market returns represent investors' evaluations of a

Table 24.1 Sample

Country	No of energy companies with ESG score	No of renewable energy companies with ESG score	No of non-renewable energy companies with ESG score
Austria	4	0	4
Belgium	3	0	3
Czech Republic	1	0	1
Denmark	3	1	2
Finland	2	0	2
France	13	3	10
Germany	21	10	11
Greece	5	1	4
Hungary	1	0	1
Ireland	1	1	0
Italy	5	0	5
Netherlands	4	1	3
Poland	7	0	7
Portugal	5	2	3
Romania	2	0	2
Spain	7	1	6
Sweden	13	8	5
Total	**97**	**28**	**69**

company's ability to generate future economic earnings. Specifically, our dependent variables are *EBITDA_margin* and *MTBV* (market-to-book value ratio) (for details, see Table 24.2). We use the *EBITDA_margin* as an economic performance indicator because it provides a measure of company efficiency and its operational profitability performance, regardless of its size, structure, tax obligations, or depreciation.

Therefore, the *EBITDA_margin* can be useful to evaluate a company's real performance vis-à-vis other competitors in its industry. We use *MTBV* as a measure of market performance because this ratio is widely used in the literature and has two distinct interpretations, both theoretically sound (Blacconiere et al., 2000; Branch et al., 2014). On the one hand, it reflects the value that the market places on a company's common equity and on the managers' ability to use assets effectively. On the other hand, *MTBV* is related to financial risk (Griffin & Lemmon, 2002; Liew & Vassalou, 2000).

24.3.2.2 ESG Measure

To answer our research questions, we use an overall company's ESG performance measure (*ESG_score*). We retrieve ESG performance data from Refinitiv. The Refinitiv ESG database offers one of the most comprehensive ESG databases,

Table 24.2 Variables description

Variables	Description	Source
Dependent variables		
EBITDA_margin	Ratio between earnings before interest, taxes, and depre-cation and the total revenue.	Refinitiv
MTBV	Ratio between the company's market value six months after the fiscal year-end period *t* and the company's book value at the fiscal year-end *t*.	Refinitiv
ESG variables		
ESG_score	Overall ESG score.	Refinitiv
Firm-level variables		
Renewable	Dummy variable equals 1 if more than 60% of the company's revenues derive from renewable energy sources.	Refinitiv
Company_age	Natural logarithm of the number of years since a company was established.	Refinitiv
Size	Natural logarithm of total assets.	Refinitiv
Leverage	Ratio of total debts on total equity.	Refinitiv
R&D_expenses_ratio	Ratio of R&D expense on total revenues.	Refinitiv
Sales_growth	Annual growth of sales (%).	Refinitiv
ROA	Ratio of net income on total assets.	Refinitiv
Payout	Ratio of total amount of dividends paid out to shareholders on net income of the company.	Refinitiv
Interest_exp	Ratio of interest expenses on total revenues.	Refinitiv
Macroeconomic variables		
GDP_growth	Annual growth of a country's GDP.	Refinitiv
Crude_oil_price	Annual mean value of the historical daily closing price of ICE Europe Brent Crude Electronic Energy Future.	Refinitiv
Stoxx_volatility	Annual mean value of the historical closing price of daily EURO STOXX 50 volatility.	Refinitiv
IRS	Interest rate swap 10Y at the last trading day of each year.	Refinitiv
Moderating variables		
Crisis	Dummy variable equals 1 in crisis periods for the European economy.	Authors' elaboration
LME	Dummy variable equals 1 if the firm is headquartered in Ireland.	Authors' elaboration
CME	Dummy variable equal to 1 if firm is headquartered in: Austria, Belgium, Czech Republic, Denmark, Finland, Germany, Hungary, Netherlands, Poland, Romania, and Sweden.	Authors' elaboration
MME	Dummy variable equals 1 if the firm is headquartered in: France, Greece, Italy, Portugal, and Spain.	Authors' elaboration

covering over 12,500 public and private companies globally, of which over 2500 are European companies (Refinitiv, 2022).

Relying on company-reported data, Refinitiv collects and calculates more than 630 company-level ESG performance/risk measures. These data points are grouped into 10 categories. Refinitiv assigns a different weight to each category to take into account the relative importance of each theme to each industry group. The ESG category scores are aggregated to build the environmental, social, and governance pillar scores. The overall ESG score is the weighted sum of the three pillar scores, and it is expressed and normalized to percentages ranging between 0 and 100.

24.3.2.3 Control Variables

Relying on prior studies, we control for a wide range of firm-specific variables (Lee et al., 2016; Mio et al., 2023) and macroeconomic conditions (Baldwin et al., 2017; Carley et al., 2017; Reboredo et al., 2017) that could affect companies economic and market performances.

More precisely, in models devoted to estimate the effects of ESG performance on a company's economic performance, we insert vector *C* that includes: *Renewable, Company_age*, *Size*, *Leverage*, *R&D_expenses_ratio,* and *Sales_growth*. We also insert vector *M* that includes variables such as *GDP_growth*, and *Crude_oil_price*.

In models devoted to estimate the effects of ESG performance on a company's market performance, we insert vector *CF* that includes: *Renewable*, *Company_age*, *Size*, *Leverage*, *R&D_expenses_ratio*, *ROA*, *Payout,* and *Interest_exp*. We also insert vector *MF* that includes: *GDP_growth*, *Crude_oil_price, Stoxx_volatility,* and *IRS*.

Finally, in all estimated models we include country and year dummies to control for unobservable factors.

A complete description of the control variables is reported in Table 24.2.

24.3.3 Regression Models

We begin our analysis by regressing *EBITDA_margin* on ESG performance and the control variables (*RQ1a*). The estimation model is defined by the following Eq. (24.1):

$$EBITDA\ margin_{i,t} = \beta_0 + \beta_1 ESG\_score_{i,t-1} + \beta_2 C_{i,t} + \beta_3 M_t + \varepsilon_{i,t} \tag{24.1}$$

where *EBITDA_margin* is the ratio between earnings before interest, taxes, and deprecation and the total revenue of the *i-th* firm in the year *t*. *ESG_score* is the overall ESG score of the *i-th* firm in the year preceding *t*. Vectors *C* and *M* include the firm-specific information and the macroeconomic control variables as specified in Sect. 24.3.2.3.

To verify whether the company's business model moderates the relationship between the company's ESG performance and its economic performance (*RQ1b*), we include the interaction terms between *ESG_score* and *Renewable* in Eq. (24.1). Our regression model is described by the following Eq. (24.2):

$$EBITDA\ margin_{i,t} = \beta_0 + \beta_1 ESG\_score_{i,t-1} + \beta_2 ESG\_score_{i,t-1} * Renewable + \beta_3 C_{i,t} + \beta_4 M_t + \varepsilon_{i,t} \quad (24.2)$$

To investigate whether ESG performance affects the company's market performance (*RQ1c*), we estimate the model described in Eq. (24.3):

$$MTBV_{i,t+m} = \beta_0 + \beta_1 ESG\_score_{i,t-1} + \beta_2 CF_{i,t} + \beta_3 MF_t + \varepsilon_{i,t} \quad (24.3)$$

where *MTBV* is the ratio between the company's market value of the *i-th* firm six months (m) after the fiscal year-end *t* and the company's book value at the fiscal year-end *t.* We adopt the prudent approach of considering the market value six months after the fiscal year-end period *t* to ensure unbiased estimates. This decision allows us to effectively account for any potential delays in the release of accounting information (Blacconiere et al., 2000; Liang & Yao, 2005). *ESG_score* is the overall ESG score as specified above. Vectors *CF* and *MF* include the firm-specific information and the macroeconomic control variables as specified in the previous Sect. 24.3.2.3.

To understand whether the company's business model moderates the relationship between ESG performance and the company's market performance (*RQ1d*), we estimate the following regression model (Eq. 24.4):

$$MTBV_{i,t+m} = \beta_0 + \beta_1 ESG\_score_{i,t-1} + \beta_2 ESG\_score_{i,t-1} * Renewable + \beta_3 CF_{i,t} + \beta_4 MF_t + \varepsilon_{i,t} \quad (24.4)$$

To investigate whether a crisis moderates the relationship between a company's ESG performance and its economic and market performance (*RQ2a* and *RQ2b*), we estimate the models described in Eq. 24.5 and Eq. 24.6:

$$EBITDA\ margin_{i,t} = \beta_0 + \beta_1 ESG\_score_{i,t-1} + \beta_2 Crisis + \beta_3 ESG\_score_{i,t-1} * Crisis + \beta_4 C_{i,t} + \beta_5 M_t + \varepsilon_{i,t} \quad (24.5)$$

$$MTBV_{i,t+m} = \beta_0 + \beta_1 ESG\_score_{i,t-1} + \beta_2 Crisis + \beta_3 ESG\_score_{i,t-1} * Crisis + \beta_4 CF_{i,t} + \beta_5 MF_t + \varepsilon_{i,t} \quad (24.6)$$

where *Crisis* is a dummy variable (built using OECD CLIs data) equal to one for the years 2012, 2020, and 2022 (OECD, 2023).

Finally, we verify whether the capitalism model adopted by each European country moderates the effect of ESG performance on a company's economic and market performances (RQ3a and RQ3b).

Relying on prior studies (Drago & Carnevale, 2020; Hall & Soskice, 2001), EU countries can be clustered into three different models of capitalism: liberal market economies (LME), coordinated market economies (CME), and Mediterranean market economies (MME). Therefore, to identify the capitalism model of the *i-th* firm's home country in the year *t*, we introduce a dummy variable for each cluster, and we build the vector *VOC* that includes three dummy variables: *LME, CME,* and *MME* (for variables details see Table 24.2). At this step, we include the *VOC* vector and the interaction terms between each variable included in the *VOC* vector and *ESG_Score* variable in our Eq. 24.1 and Eq. 24.3. The new regression models are described as follows (Eq. 24.7 and Eq. 24.8):

$$EBITDA\ margin_{i,t} = \beta_0 + \beta_1 ESG\_score_{i,t-1} + \beta_2 VOC_{i,t} + \beta_3 ESG\_score_{i,t-1} * VOC_{i,t} + \beta_4 C_{i,t} + \beta_5 M_t + \varepsilon_{i,t} \tag{24.7}$$

$$MTBV_{i,t+m} = \beta_0 + \beta_1 ESG\_score_{i,t-1} + \beta_2 VOC_{i,t} + \beta_3 ESG\_score_{i,t-1} * VOC_{i,t} + \beta_4 CF_{i,t} + \beta_5 MF_t + \varepsilon_{i,t} \tag{24.8}$$

24.4 Results

24.4.1 Preliminary Analysis

In this section, we provide the results of the t-test conducted on the dependent variables and the company-level variables (Table 24.3). Findings show that renewable energy companies are significantly less profitable, younger, and smaller with respect to non-renewable energy companies. Furthermore, renewable energy companies have lower MTBV ratios, pay more interest expenses, distribute lower dividends, and exhibit higher sales growth ratios and R&D expenses. Finally,

Table 24.3 Preliminary analysis

	Renewable companies		Non-renewable companies		
Variables	Mean	Std. Dev.	Mean	Std. Dev.	*P*-value
EBITDA_margin	16.31	34.44	20.29	27.65	0.0018***
MTBV	1.71	1.50	3.20	2.05	0.0000***
ESG_score	51.95	21.30	64.55	18.08	0.0000***
Company_age	3.03	0.68	3.33	0.85	0.0000***
Size	19.60	2.20	21.35	2.60	0.0000***
Leverage	28.16	25.49	29.08	25.97	0.6455
R&D_expenses_ratio	0.68	0.74	0.52	0.75	0.0004***
Sales_growth	0.33	0.81	0.16	0.57	0.0006***
ROA	0.71	5.83	2.42	5.72	0.0324**
Payout	0.20	0.27	0.34	0.32	0.0000***
Interest_exp	1.36	0.25	0.33	0.31	0.0000***

renewable energy companies present lower ESG scores. This last result might surprise, as it seems to suggest that renewable energy companies are less interested in ESG issues. We believe that the result can be explained by considering that, unlike non-renewable energy companies, renewable energy companies, by virtue of their business model (a sign of a notable commitment to ESG issues), are less interested in communicating further commitments in ESG issues and/or adopt greenwashing techniques. These choices are reflected in the ESG score assigned by Refinitiv (Refinitiv, 2022) which, it is worth remembering, constructs the companies' ESG scores based on public information released by the companies themselves regarding their ESG performance, commitment, and effectiveness.[1]

24.4.2 *Regression Results*

In this section, we present the results obtained by performing a Pooled Ordinary Least Squares (OLS) regression for the models described in the previous Sect. 24.3.3.

24.4.2.1 The ESG Performance–Economic Performance Relationship

Column 1 of Table 24.4 reports the estimates of the regression model described in Eq. 24.1. The results are very interesting. First, we find that renewable energy companies exhibit a lower *EBITDA_margin* of approximately 0.137% compared to non-renewable energy companies. This outcome, already highlighted in the preliminary analysis, is consistent with the evidence provided by Ruggiero and Lehkonen (2017) and Schabek (2020). We can explain this finding by considering that renewable energy companies are younger and smaller compared to non-renewable energy companies. This implies that renewable energy companies could have a smaller customer base and a limited negotiating power with their suppliers and customers. Furthermore, as many researchers (Alharbi et al., 2023; Iskin et al., 2012; Kempa et al., 2021) also point out, renewable energy companies operate with immature technologies and markets. All these aspects lead renewable energy companies to face higher production costs and lower efficiency levels. Findings also show that ESG performance positively impacts companies' economic performance. Specifically, higher ESG scores increase the profitability of energy companies by about 0.226%. Therefore, in line with the stakeholder theory, our results prove that companies' commitment to ESG issues increases profit opportunities (Naeem et al., 2022).

[1]Results related to descriptive statistics, correlation matrix, and VIF analysis, not reported due to paper length constraints, are available upon request.

Table 24.4 The link ESG performance–economic and market performances

	EBITDA_margin		*MTBV*	
	(1)	(2)	(3)	(4)
Renewable	–0.137***	–0.319***	–0.102***	–0.076***
	(0.028)	(0.100)	(0.033)	(0.000)
ESG_score$_{-1}$	0.226**	0.224**	0.141***	0.151***
	(0.102)	(0.089)	(0.032)	(0.000)
ESG_score$_{-1}$*Renewable		0.007***		0.001***
		(0.002)		(0.000)
Company_age	0.101***	0.055***	0.015***	0.014***
	(0.015)	(0.014)	(0.001)	(0.000)
Size	0.025***	0.025***	0.002***	0.002***
	(0.003)	(0.009)	(0.000)	(0.000)
Leverage	0.061	0.031	–0.062**	–0.063***
	(0.061)	(0.035)	(0.028)	(0.000)
R&D_expenses_ratio	0.231***	0.222***	0.065***	0.065***
	(0.024)	(0.020)	(0.018)	(0.000)
Sales_growth	0.002	0.004		
	(0.021)	(0.020)		
ROA			0.006*	0.006***
			(0.003)	(0.000)
Payout			–0.021	–0.023
			(0.024)	(0.022)
GDP_growth	–0.059	–0.006	–0.050	–0.049
	(0.037)	(0.042)	(0.071)	(0.070)
Crude_oil_price	0.071**	0.077**	0.042***	0.041***
	(0.032)	(0.039)	(0.002)	(0.000)
Interest_exp			0.038	0.040
			(0.050)	(0.047)
Stoxx_volatility			–0.026**	–0.026***
			(0.012)	(0.000)
IRS			–0.151***	–0.150***
			(0.041)	(0.000)
Constant	0.434	2.249	–1.938	–1.928
	(1.434)	(1.723)	(1.466)	(1.501)
Observations	588	588	588	588
R-squared	0.559	0.483	0.412	0.412
Country FE	YES	YES	YES	YES
Year FE	YES	YES	YES	YES

Looking at the control variables we note that older and larger companies and those that allocate a higher proportion of their revenue to R&D activities exhibit greater economic performance. These results can be explained by considering that older and larger companies generally have a consolidated position in their markets and can enjoy a significant advantage in negotiating relationships with suppliers and customers. Moreover, larger companies have more resources to invest in R&D, and this can lead to new competitive advantages and increased efficiency.

Shifting our focus on the macroeconomic factors, we find that *Crude_oil_price* positively impacts the *EBITDA_margin*. This is because higher crude oil prices lead to increased revenue and profits for renewable and non-renewable energy companies. When crude oil prices rise, these companies can sell their products at higher prices, resulting in greater revenue per unit of production and, therefore, higher profits. However, it must be taken into account that the relationship between crude oil prices and energy companies' economic performance is complex because it depends on other factors, such as companies' geographical diversification, hedging strategies, and the use of other energy sources (Pickl, 2019; Reboredo, 2015; Lee & Baek, 2018).

Looking at column 2 of Table 24.4 (Eq. 24.2), we observe that the coefficient of *ESG_score*Renewable* is positive and significant. This result suggests that ESG performance has a stronger positive impact on the economic performance of renewable energy companies compared to non-renewable energy companies. Therefore, we can state that being responsible pays off, and it is particularly beneficial for renewable energy companies.

Overall, our findings support managers' choices and policymakers' initiatives in favour of better management of ESG issues in the energy sector. As renewable energy sources gain prominence and public interest in sustainable practices grows, energy companies that prioritize ESG performance are evaluated more favourably by stakeholders, gain social trust, and achieve better economic outcomes.

However, looking at the magnitudes of *Renewable*, *ESG_score,* and *Renewable*ESG_score* coefficients, a complex picture emerges: (a) being a renewable energy company seems to have a negative impact on economic performance, (b) having good ESG performance increases the company's economic performance, but (c) the net positive effects of ESG performance do not fully offset the disadvantage to be a renewable energy company.

24.4.2.2 The ESG Performance–Market Performance Relationship

The data reported in columns 3 and 4 of Table 24.4 provide a series of key findings on the relationship between companies' ESG performance and their market performance (Eq. 24.3 and Eq. 24.4).

First of all, looking at column 3 we note that renewable energy companies experience a lower market performance compared to non-renewable energy companies. This result is consistent with evidence provided by Ruggiero and Lehkonen (2017) and Schabek (2020), and it can be explained by considering that renewable energy companies are younger, smaller, have higher production costs (Sadorsky, 2012), and operate with young and immature technologies and markets (Alharbi et al., 2023; Iskin et al., 2012; Kempa et al., 2021). Therefore, it is not surprising that renewable energy companies are perceived as riskier companies and that all these factors lead to a higher equity risk premium and a lower MTBV ratio.

The result related to the relationship between ESG performance and market performance is interesting: the *ESG_score* coefficient is highly significant. This means that, ceteris paribus, an increase in ESG performance leads to a market performance improvement of approximately 0.141%. This result is relevant because it underlines that the stock market is not only able to evaluate the energy companies' ESG performance, but it also rewards companies that show greater commitment to ESG issues.

Looking at the control variables we note that older, larger, more profitable companies and those investing in R&D have a better market performance. These results are not surprising because these companies are likely to have better growth prospects and innovation capabilities and enjoy potential competitive advantages. Therefore, these companies are perceived as less risky and, of course, this leads to higher market performance. Likewise, it is no surprise that higher levels of leverage are associated with lower market performance.

Macroeconomic factors indicate that energy companies' market performance is affected by market volatility (*IRS*), and by the price of crude oil. Specifically, higher market volatility could be a signal of economic uncertainty, impacting stock performance and investor confidence in the energy sector. Decreased *IRS* could make stocks more appealing compared to fixed-income investments, potentially fostering growth in the stock market. Conversely, elevated *IRS* might dampen stock-market sentiment, as investors get greater returns from fixed-income investments. Finally, we find that positive movements in oil prices result in an upward trend in the stock prices of all energy companies. This finding is in line with Reboredo (2015) and Lee & Baek (2018), who argue that the increase in oil prices makes non-renewable companies more profitable but, at the same time, it also makes renewable energy more competitive.

Focusing on the results reported in column 4 of Table 24.4 (our Eq. 24.4), we note that the coefficient of *ESG_score*Renewable* is positive and significant, but it is very small (0.001). This means that the impact of ESG performance on the *MTBV* ratio is quite similar when comparing renewable energy companies to non-renewable energy companies. However, it is worth noting that the net effect of ESG performance on renewable energy companies' market performance is very strong and it translates into an increase in market performance of around 0.076 (0.001 + 0.151 − 0.076).

Overall, a clear picture emerges from our findings: (a) being a renewable energy company seems to have a negative impact on market performance, (b) energy companies with better ESG scores perform better, (c) the net positive effects of ESG performance fully offset the disadvantage to be a renewable energy company.

24.4.2.3 The Link Between ESG Performance and Economic-Market Performance During Crisis Periods

As mentioned above, the time frame of our analysis includes three periods of major crises. We therefore estimated the regression models described in Eq. (24.5) and

Table 24.5 ESG performance and crisis

	EBITDA_margin	*MTBV*
	(1)	(2)
Renewable	−0.089***	−0.103***
	(0.028)	(0.025)
ESG_score$_{-1}$	0.225***	0.114***
	(0.005)	(0.002)
Crisis	−0.140**	−0.158**
	(0.067)	(0.063)
ESG_score$_{-1}$*Crisis	−0.002**	−0.003***
	(0.001)	(0.001)
Firms controls	YES	YES
Macro controls	YES	YES
Country FE	YES	YES
Year FE	YES	YES
R-squared	0.446	0.414
Observations	588	588

Eq. (24.6) to take into account the potential effect of a crisis on the relationship between the ESG performance of energy companies and their economic and market performance. Table 24.5 reports the results obtained. We observe that *Crisis* variable exhibits a negative and significant coefficient. This result is not surprising since, during crisis periods, energy consumption decreases, and this reduction negatively affects the revenues for energy companies, pushing the *EBITDA_margin* downward. Similarly, during periods of crisis, the climate of uncertainty in financial markets negatively impacts the future income prospects of energy companies, and this translates into a decrease in their market performance.

We point out another relevant result: the coefficient of *ESG_score*Crisis* variable is negative and significant. This result bears noteworthy implications. Specifically, during crisis periods energy companies do not appear to enjoy the expected benefits of ESG performance. On the contrary, in the context of an exogenous negative shock, a company's engagement in ESG issues seems to even be considered as a wasteful extravagance. In this perspective, higher commitment to ESG issues may result in socially responsible energy companies becoming more vulnerable in times of crisis. Unlike Lins et al. (2017), who argue that during crisis periods companies with high CSR scores increase their value compared to companies with low CSR ratings, our results seem to suggest that the costs associated with ESG commitment could potentially exceed the benefits.

Overall, in line with empirical evidence provided by Buchanan et al. (2018), Drago and Carnevale (2020), Demers et al. (2021), and Berkman et al. (2021), our results highlight that during crisis periods, the complex trade-offs between the company's ESG performance and the challenges posed by financial crises play against the company's engagement in ESG issues and, therefore, it seems that an overinvestment view prevails.

24.4.2.4 The Role of National Economic Systems

Finally, to verify whether the national capitalism models affect the relationship between energy companies' EGS performance and their economic and financial performance, we estimated the models described in Eq. (24.7) and Eq. (24.8), where European energy companies are associated with the *LMEs*, *CMEs*, and *MMEs* clusters, depending on the country where they are based (see Sect. 24.3.3). In Table 24.6 we present the results obtained. In all estimates, the *LMEs* cluster is our control group.

Looking at the *Renewable* and *ESG_score* variables, in line with our previous results, we find that: (a) renewable energy companies exhibit lower economic and market performance compared to non-renewable energy companies, and (b) the ESG performance has a positive effect on economic and market performance across all energy companies.

By shifting our focus on the interaction terms *ESG_score*CME* and *ESG_score*MME*, we find that national capitalism models moderate the relationship between energy companies' ESG performance and their economic and market performance. Specifically, we note that energy companies located in MMEs and CMEs enjoy more benefits from their ESG efforts compared to energy companies located in LMEs.

Table 24.6 The role of national economic systems

	EBITDA_margin	*MTBV*
	(1)	(2)
Renewable	−0.145***	−0.096***
	(0.036)	(0.028)
ESG_score_{-1}	0.280***	0.198***
	(0.002)	(0.001)
CME	−0.169	0.165
	(0.116)	(0.160)
MME	0.322**	0.386**
	(0.158)	(0.171)
ESG_score*CME	0.003***	0.002**
	(0.001)	(0.001)
ESG_score*MME	0.005**	0.005**
	(0.002)	(0.002)
Constant	2.440	−2.613
	(1.895)	(1.936)
Firms controls	YES	YES
Macro controls	YES	YES
Country FE	YES	YES
Year FE	YES	YES
R-squared	0.454	0.432
Observations	588	588

Looking at energy companies engaged in ESG issues and headquartered in MMEs, we point out that they experience better economic and market performances compared to both those located in CMEs and LMEs. Specifically, in MMEs the effect of ESG performance on *EBITDA_margin* and *MTBV* is equal to 0.285 and 0.203, respectively, against 0.283 and 0.200 related to companies located in CMEs. The moderating effect of national capitalism models on the relationship between ESG and economic and market performance becomes even more evident when we compare the energy companies located in MMEs with those located in LMEs (0.285 against 0.280 on *EBITDA_margin* and 0.203 vs 0.198 on *MTBV*). These findings seem to suggest that within the European context, MMEs characteristics are more conducive compared to those of CMEs and especially LMEs to promote good synergism between companies' ESG commitments and business outcomes.

Our results are not unexpected and, consistent with previous studies (Kang & Moon, 2012; Carnevale & Mazzuca, 2014; Kinderman, 2012), prove that differing national capitalism models can moderate the benefits deriving from companies' ESG commitment. In CMEs, and to a greater extent in MMEs, competitive pressures on product markets are more moderate and the relations between stakeholders and companies are based mostly on informal relations and reputational factors. Moreover, CMEs and MMEs also exhibit significantly different features in other economic areas and institutional complementarities compared to countries clustered in LMEs. CMEs and, to a greater extent, MMEs are characterized by major protection on the labour market and social protection, lower sophistication of financial markets, major stock ownership concentration, and creditor rights protection. All these features contribute to favouring companies' engagement in ESG issues to enjoy better relationships with stakeholders. On the other hand, in CMEs and MMEs stakeholders are more aware of their strength and relevance, and they reward the companies that are most committed to ESG issues by consolidating relationships increasingly based on social trust.

24.5 Robustness Tests and Further Analyses[2]

To ensure the robustness and depth of our results, we develop two tests. First, we re-perform our analysis by using the Generalized Method of Moments (GMM). To do this, we introduce $EBITDA\_margin_{-1}$ and $MTBV_{-1}$ as lagged dependent variables in our Eqs. (24.2) and (24.4). The new estimates confirm the outcomes obtained by using OLS estimators. Second, we estimate our Eqs. (24.2) and (24.4) by using alternative measures of the firm's economic and market performance, such as *ROA* and *Market_to_sales* (the ratio between the firm's market value and the total sales). Overall, the outcomes of the new regressions confirm our previous findings.

[2]The results cited in the present section, not reported due to paper length constraints, are available upon request.

Moreover, we develop some further analyses. First, we investigated whether the company's scores in each ESG pillar have a different impact on the company's economic and market performances compared to the overall ESG performance. To achieve this goal, we replaced the overall *ESG_score* in Eqs. (24.2) and (24.4) alternatively with the scores in Environmental (E), Social (S), and Governance (G) pillars of the *i-th* firm in the year preceding *t*. The results reveal that only the E and S pillar scores contribute to enhance the performance of energy firms, while the G pillar score demonstrates no discernible impact on the economic and market performances of energy companies.

Finally, as part of our additional analyses, we re-estimated our Eqs. (24.2) and (24.4) by replacing the overall scores in the E, S, and G pillars with the specific scores reflecting the companies' commitment and performance in each pillar, as defined by Refinitiv. The outcomes confirm our previous conclusion: (a) all other conditions being equal, renewable energy companies benefit from the commitment and performance recorded in environmental and social issues to a greater extent than traditional energy companies; and (b) the commitment and performance scores recorded in G pillar seem do not have a significant impact on the economic and market performances of European energy companies.

24.6 Conclusions

This paper investigates the effect of ESG performance on European energy companies' economic and market performance. We provide several exciting findings. First, consistent with previous studies, we find that, in the European context, renewable energy companies show lower economic and market performance than traditional energy companies. Second, European renewable energy companies enjoy greater benefits from their commitment to ESG issues compared to non-renewable energy companies. Third, during crisis periods the costs associated with companies' ESG engagement outweigh the anticipated benefits. Fourth, cross-country analysis shows that national capitalism models significantly moderate the relationship between energy companies' ESG performance and their economic and market performances.

Overall, our findings depict a clear picture and offer significant insight for managers and policymakers. Enhancing ESG performance helps, at the same time, to comply with the rules issued by European institutions and to improve companies' economic and market performance. Therefore, choosing to be sustainable not only ensures to meet stakeholders' expectations but it also increases the social trust that underpins a company's prospects for success. This is especially true for renewable energy companies, which still suffer from the negative effects deriving from the use of immature technologies. Ceteris paribus, for renewable energy companies to engage in ESG issues pays off more compared to non-renewable energy companies and, in terms of market performance, it can even eliminate the disadvantage from which they start.

Our results highlight another important element that energy company managers should focus on, namely investment in R&D. Unlike exogenous variables on which company managers hardly can act (for example, the trend in crude oil prices), investments in R&D activities represent a very important managers' lever to support a company's competitive advantage. If this aspect seems to be less relevant for non-renewable energy companies, investing in the development of new technologies remains a crucial point for reducing operative costs of renewable energy companies. Actually, the development of technologies through which the costs of producing energy from renewable sources could be reduced should also be relevant for European institutions, which are pushing towards an increase in the share of energy from renewable sources and a reduction in the use of fossil fuels. In this sense we believe that the convergence between the goals of European institutions and those of the managers may provide the right basis for efficiently and effectively addressing huge capitals (both public and private) to finance joint initiatives for the development of technologies intended for the production of clean energy.

Our results provide further insight and policy implications for European regulators. While ESG performance is generally associated with better economic and market performance, our study indicates that the positive effects of ESG performance are not always realized: during crisis periods being engaged in ESG issues seems to strongly penalize the energy companies. While it is evident that managers alone are unlikely to be able to deal with and resolve the effects produced by financial crises, policymakers could instead draft financial and legislative instruments to be implemented whenever such situations arise. Recent events (for example, the Russo-Ukrainian war) have required important financial measures by European States to support the energy costs of companies and households. The beneficiaries of these financial supports were energy consumers, regardless of the energy source used (renewable vs fossil) and the degree of ESG commitment of the energy supplier. In the future, the choices of the European policymakers could instead be oriented differently. If the priority objectives of the European institutions basically consist in promoting both the companies' ESG commitment and a steady increase in the share of renewable energy, European policymakers should consider a stable solution to financially support mostly renewable energy companies committed to ESG issues during times of crisis. By doing so, important goals could be achieved. On the one hand, these initiatives would act as significant levers in favouring an increasingly growing energy companies' commitment to sustainable development issues even in times of crisis. On the other hand, energy companies could enjoy valid support in their choices towards increasing the use of renewable sources.

Our study presents some limitations. First, we focus on the current scenario, and therefore, we may not be able to grasp the extent of changes attributable to the new and continually evolving regulatory interventions and technological innovations that could significantly affect costs and competitiveness of renewable energy companies. Second, our research does not grasp the effects that current global geopolitical changes will generate on the financial market conditions and, therefore, on the decisions that managers and policymakers will have to take. The end of the Russo-Ukrainian war will deliver the world a new global geopolitical order, where the increased role of renewable energy sources in meeting the world's energy needs will help to re-shape the balance and power relations between countries. The push towards a greater use of renewable sources, promoted by the leaders of European countries in the aftermath of the outbreak of the Russo-Ukrainian war, could really accelerate the process towards achieving the Sustainable Development Goal 7.2, related to the share of renewable energy in the global energy mix. Third, this study only uses ESG data provided by Refinitiv. This could have affected our results, since as it is known, the numerous ESG data providers use different methodologies and metrics, and this potentially results in heterogeneous ESG scores.

Future studies could further investigate the results proposed by this work, using ESG data provided by different rating agencies, verifying over time the effects produced by the current economic and energy crisis that is affecting Europe and, finally, investigating whether the measures adopted by European policymakers, to promote the transition process towards a cleaner energy will have produced real benefits for energy companies engaged in ESG issues.

References

Abbassi, W., Boubaker, S., & Louhichi, W. (2022). Why do corporate social responsibility-oriented companies opt for bond debt? Evidence from crisis periods. *International Journal of Finance & Economics (early view)*. https://doi.org/10.1002/ijfe.2741

Alharbi, S. S., Al Mamun, M., Boubaker, S., & Rizvi, S. K. A. (2023). Green finance and renewable energy: A worldwide evidence. *Energy Economics, 118*, 106499. https://doi.org/10.1016/j.eneco.2022.106499

Amable, B. (2003). *The diversity of modern capitalism*. Oxford University Press.

Amiraslani, H., Lins, K. V., Servaes, H., & Tamayo, A. (2023). Trust, social capital, and the bond market benefits of ESG performance. *Review of Accounting Studies, 28*, 421–462. https://doi.org/10.1007/s11142-021-09646-0

Atif, M., & Ali, S. (2021). Environmental, social and governance disclosure and default risk. *Business Strategy and the Environment, 30*, 3937–3959. https://doi.org/10.1002/bse.2850

Baldwin, E., Carley, S., Brass, J. N., & MacLean, L. M. (2017). Global renewable electricity policy: A comparative policy analysis of countries by income status. *Journal of Comparative Policy Analysis, 19*, 277–298. https://doi.org/10.1080/13876988.2016.1166866

Barnett, M. L. (2007). Stakeholder influence capacity and the variability of financial returns to corporate social responsibility. *Academy of Management Review, 32*, 794–816. https://doi.org/10.5465/amr.2007.25275520

Barnett, M. L., & Salomon, R. M. (2012). Does it pay to be *really* good? Addressing the shape of the relationship between social and financial performance. *Strategic Management Journal, 33*, 1304–1320. https://doi.org/10.1002/smj.1980

Barney, J. (1991). Firm resources and sustained competitive advantage. *Journal of Management, 17*, 99–120. https://doi.org/10.1177/014920639101700108

Berkman, H., Li, M., & Lu, H. (2021). Trust and the value of CSR during the global financial crisis. *Accounting and Finance, 61*, 4955–4965. https://doi.org/10.1111/acfi.12721

Blacconiere, W. G., Johnson, M. F., & Johnson, M. S. (2000). Market valuation and deregulation of electric utilities. *Journal of Accounting and Economics, 29*, 231–260. https://doi.org/10.1016/S0165-4101(00)00021-5

Bouri, E., Iqbal, N., & Klein, T. (2022). Climate policy uncertainty and the price dynamics of green and brown energy stocks. *Finance Research Letters, 47*, 102740. https://doi.org/10.1016/j.frl.2022.102740
Brammer, S., Jackson, G., & Matten, D. (2012). Corporate Social Responsibility and institutional theory: New perspectives on private governance. *Socio-Economic Review, 10*, 3–28. https://doi.org/10.1093/ser/mwr030
Branch, B. S., Sharma, A., Chawla, C., & Tu, F. (2014). An updated model of price-to-book. *Journal of Applied Finance, 24*, 73–93.
Buchanan, B., Cao, C. X., & Chen, C. (2018). Corporate social responsibility, firm value, and influential institutional ownership. *Journal of Corporate Finance, 52*, 73–95. https://doi.org/10.1016/j.jcorpfin.2018.07.004
Cai, Y., Pan, C. H., & Statman, M. (2016). Why do countries matter so much in corporate social performance? *Journal of Corporate Finance, 41*, 591–609. https://doi.org/10.1016/j.jcorpfin.2016.09.004
Campbell, J. L. (2007). Why would corporations behave in socially responsible ways? An institutional theory of corporate social responsibility. *Academy of Management Review, 32*, 946–967. https://doi.org/10.5465/amr.2007.25275684
Carley, S., Baldwin, E., MacLean, L. M., & Brass, J. N. (2017). Global expansion of renewable energy generation: An analysis of policy instruments. *Environmental and Resource Economics (Dordrecht), 68*, 397–440. https://doi.org/10.1007/s10640-016-0025-3
Carnevale, C., & Mazzuca, M. (2014). Sustainability report and bank valuation: Evidence from European stock markets. *Business Ethics: A European Review, 23*, 69–90. https://doi.org/10.1111/beer.12038
Chen, Y., Wang, C., & Zhu, Z. (2022). Toward the integration of European gas futures market under COVID-19 shock: A quantile connectedness approach. *Energy Economics, 114*, 106288. https://doi.org/10.1016/j.eneco.2022.106288
Demers, E., Hendrikse, J., Joos, P., & Lev, B. (2021). ESG did not immunize stocks during the COVID-19 crisis, but investments in intangible assets did. *Journal of Business Finance and Accounting, 48*, 433–462. https://doi.org/10.1111/jbfa.12523
Drago, D., & Carnevale, C. (2020). Do CSR ratings affect loan spreads? Evidence from European Syndicated Loan Market. *Sustainability, 12*, 7639. https://doi.org/10.3390/su12187639
Dyck, A., Lins, K. V., Roth, L., & Wagner, H. F. (2019). Do institutional investors drive corporate social responsibility? International evidence. *Journal of Financial Economics, 131*, 693–714. https://doi.org/10.1016/j.jfineco.2018.08.013
European Commission. (2018). Directive (EU) 2018/2001 of the European Parliament and of the Council of 11 December 2018 on the promotion of the use of energy from renewable sources. In: https://eur-lex.europa.eu/legal-content/EN/TXT/PDF/?uri=CELEX:32018L2001
European Commission. (2022). Proposal for a Directive of the European Parliament and of the Council amending Directive (EU) 2018/2001 on the promotion of the use of energy from renewable sources, Directive 2010/31/EU on the energy performance of buildings and Directive 2012/27/EU on energy efficiency. In: https://eur-lex.europa.eu/legal-content/EN/TXT/PDF/?uri=CELEX:52022PC0222
Filbeck, G., & Gorman, R. F. (2004). The relationship between the environmental and financial performance of public utilities. *Environmental and Resource Economics (Dordrecht), 29*, 137–157. https://doi.org/10.1023/B:EARE.0000044602.86367.ff
Freeman, R. E. (1984). *Strategic management: A stakeholder perspective*. Pitman.
Friedman, M. (1962). *Capitalism and freedom*. University of Chicago Press.
Ghosh, B., Pham, L., Teplova, T., & Umar, Z. (2023). COVID-19 and the quantile connectedness between energy and metal markets. *Energy Economics, 117*, 106420. https://doi.org/10.1016/j.eneco.2022.106420
Gillan, S. L., Koch, A., & Starks, L. T. (2021). Firms and social responsibility: A review of ESG and CSR research in corporate finance. *Journal of Corporate Finance, 66*, 101889. https://doi.org/10.1016/j.jcorpfin.2021.101889

Gjølberg, M. (2009). The origin of corporate social responsibility: Global forces or national legacies? *Socio-Economic Review, 7*, 605–637. https://doi.org/10.1093/ser/mwp017

Godfrey, P. C., Merrill, C. B., & Hansen, J. M. (2009). The relationship between corporate social responsibility and shareholder value: An empirical test of the risk management hypothesis. *Strategic Management Journal, 30*, 425–445. https://doi.org/10.1002/smj.750

Goodell, J. W., Gurdgiev, C., Paltrinieri, A., & Piserà, S. (2023). Global energy supply risk: Evidence from the reactions of European natural gas futures to Nord Stream announcements. *Energy Economics, 125*, 106838. https://doi.org/10.1016/j.eneco.2023.106838

Griffin, J. M., & Lemmon, M. L. (2002). Book-to-market equity, distress risk, and stock returns. *The Journal of Finance, 57*, 2317–2336. https://doi.org/10.1111/1540-6261.00497

Hall, P. A., & Soskice, D. (2001). An introduction to varieties of capitalism. In P. A. Hall & D. Soskice (Eds.), *Varieties of capitalism* (pp. 1–68). Oxford University Press.

Ioannou, I., & Serafeim, G. (2012). What drives corporate social performance? The role of nation-level institutions. *Journal of International Business Studies, 43*, 834–864. https://doi.org/10.1057/jibs.2012.26

Iskin, I., Daim, T., Kayakutlu, G., & Altuntas, M. (2012). Exploring renewable energy pricing with analytic network process — Comparing a developed and a developing economy. *Energy Economics, 34*, 882–891. https://doi.org/10.1016/j.eneco.2012.04.005

Jensen, M. C., & Meckling, W. H. (1976). Theory of the firm: Managerial behavior, agency costs and ownership structure. *Journal of Financial Economics, 3*, 305–360. https://doi.org/10.1016/0304-405X(76)90026-X

Jones, T. M. (1995). Instrumental stakeholder theory: A synthesis of ethics and economics. *Academy of Management Review, 20*, 404–437. https://doi.org/10.2307/258852

Kang, N., & Moon, J. (2012). Institutional complementarity between corporate governance and Corporate Social Responsibility: A comparative institutional analysis of three capitalisms. *Socio-Economic Review, 10*, 85–108. https://doi.org/10.1093/ser/mwr025

Kempa, K., Moslener, U., & Schenker, O. (2021). The cost of debt of renewable and non-renewable energy firms. *Nature Energy, 6*, 135–142. https://doi.org/10.1038/s41560-020-00745-x

Kinderman, D. (2012). "Free us up so we can be responsible!" The co-evolution of Corporate Social Responsibility and neo-liberalism in the UK, 1977-2010. *Socio-Economic Review, 10*, 29–57. https://doi.org/10.1093/ser/mwr028

Lee, D., & Baek, J. (2018). Stock prices of renewable energy firms: Are there asymmetric responses to oil price changes? *Economies, 6*, 59. https://doi.org/10.3390/economies6040059

Lee, K., Cin, B. C., & Lee, E. Y. (2016). Environmental responsibility and firm performance: The application of an environmental, social and governance model. *Business Strategy and the Environment, 25*, 40–53. https://doi.org/10.1002/bse.1855

Liang, C.-J., & Yao, M.-L. (2005). The value-relevance of financial and nonfinancial information? Evidence from Taiwan's Information Electronics Industry. *Review of Quantitative Finance and Accounting, 24*, 135–157. https://doi.org/10.1007/s11156-005-6334-1

Liang, H., & Renneboog, L. (2017). On the foundations of corporate social responsibility. *The Journal of Finance, 72*, 853–910. https://doi.org/10.1111/jofi.12487

Liew, J., & Vassalou, M. (2000). Can book-to-market, size and momentum be risk factors that predict economic growth? *Journal of Financial Economics, 57*, 221–245. https://doi.org/10.1016/S0304-405X(00)00056-8

Lins, K. V., Servaes, H., & Tamayo, A. (2017). Social capital, trust, and firm performance: The value of corporate social responsibility during the financial crisis. *The Journal of Finance, 72*, 1785–1824. https://doi.org/10.1111/jofi.12505

Lu, W., Chau, K. W., Wang, H., & Pan, W. (2014). A decade's debate on the nexus between corporate social and corporate financial performance: A critical review of empirical studies 2002–2011. *Journal of Cleaner Production, 79*, 195–206. https://doi.org/10.1016/j.jclepro.2014.04.072

Matten, D., & Moon, J. (2008). "Implicit" and "Explicit" CSR: A conceptual framework for a comparative understanding of corporate social responsibility. *Academy of Management Review, 33*, 404–424. https://doi.org/10.5465/amr.2008.31193458

McWilliams, A., & Siegel, D. S. (2011). Creating and capturing value. *Journal of Management, 37*, 1480–1495. https://doi.org/10.1177/0149206310385696

Mio, C., Fasan, M., & Scarpa, F. (2023). Materiality investor perspectives on utilities' ESG performance. An empirical analysis of ESG factors and cost of equity. *Utilities Policy, 82*, 101555. https://doi.org/10.1016/j.jup.2023.101555

Naeem, N., Cankaya, S., & Bildik, R. (2022). Does ESG performance affect the financial performance of environmentally sensitive industries? A comparison between emerging and developed markets. *Borsa Istanbul Review, 22*(S2), 128–140. https://doi.org/10.1016/j.bir.2022.11.014

OECD. (2023). *OECD Composite Leading Indicators: Reference Turning Points and Component Series*. Retrieved April 5, 2023, from https://www.oecd.org/sdd/leading-indicators/composite-leading-indicators-cli-oecd-december-2022.htm

Pätäri, S., Arminen, H., Tuppura, A., & Jantunen, A. (2014). Competitive and responsible? The relationship between corporate social and financial performance in the energy sector. *Renewable and Sustainable Energy Reviews, 37*, 142–154. https://doi.org/10.1016/j.rser.2014.05.012

Pfeffer, J., & Salancik, G. R. (1978). *The external control of organizations: A resource dependence perspective*. Harper & Row.

Pickl, M. J. (2019). The renewable energy strategies of oil majors – From oil to energy? *Energy Strategy Reviews, 26*, 100370. https://doi.org/10.1016/j.esr.2019.100370

Reboredo, J. C. (2015). Is there dependence and systemic risk between oil and renewable energy stock prices? *Energy Economics, 48*, 32–45. https://doi.org/10.1016/j.eneco.2014.12.009

Reboredo, J. C., Rivera-Castro, M. A., & Ugolini, A. (2017). Wavelet-based test of co-movement and causality between oil and renewable energy stock prices. *Energy Economics, 61*, 241–252. https://doi.org/10.1016/j.eneco.2016.10.015

Refinitiv. (2022). *Environmental, Social and Governance Scores from Refinitiv*. In: https://www.refinitiv.com/en/sustainable-finance/esg-scores#methodology

Ruggiero, S., & Lehkonen, H. (2017). Renewable energy growth and the financial performance of electric utilities: A panel data study. *Journal of Cleaner Production, 142*, 3676–3688. https://doi.org/10.1016/j.jclepro.2016.10.100

S&P Global. (2023). *Global Industry Classification Standard (GICS) Methodology*. Retrieved April 3, 2023, from https://www.spglobal.com/spdji/en/landing/topic/gics/

Sadorsky, P. (2012). Modeling renewable energy company risk. *Energy Policy, 40*, 39–48. https://doi.org/10.1016/j.enpol.2010.06.064

Schabek, T. (2020). The financial performance of sustainable power producers in emerging markets. *Renewable Energy, 160*, 1408–1419. https://doi.org/10.1016/j.renene.2020.06.067

Sueyoshi, T., & Goto, M. (2009). Can environmental investment and expenditure enhance financial performance of US electric utility firms under the clean air act amendment of 1990? *Energy Policy, 37*, 4819–4826. https://doi.org/10.1016/j.enpol.2009.06.038

Surroca, J., Tribó, J. A., & Waddock, S. (2010). Corporate responsibility and financial performance: The role of intangible resources. *Strategic Management Journal, 31*, 463–490. https://doi.org/10.1002/smj.820

United Nation. (2023). *The Sustainable Development Goals Report 2023: Special Edition*. Retrieved July 26, 2023, from https://unstats.un.org/sdgs/report/2023/

Witt, M. A., Kabbach de Castro, L. R., Amaeshi, K., Mahroum, S., Bohle, D., & Saez, L. (2018). Mapping the business systems of 61 major economies: A taxonomy and implications for varieties of capitalism and business systems research. *Socio-Economic Review, 16*, 5–38. https://doi.org/10.1093/ser/mwx012

Chapter 25
Please, Help Me to Improve: The Role of Targets' E, S & G Scores in M&A Operations

Luca Ferri, Fiorenza Meucci, Flavio Spagnuolo, and Claudia Zagaria

25.1 Introduction

As a critical corporate investment, mergers and acquisitions (M&A) have created significant discussion topics in the financial and management fields (Calipha et al., 2010; Malik et al., 2014). M&A operations, especially successful ones, involve significant changes for the acquirers (Agrawal et al., 1992). After mergers and acquisitions, the acquirer can improve its economic and financial strength, but also its commitment to environmental, social, and governance (ESG) issues. Specifically, the paradigm of ESG performance as a measure of sustainable behavior became a key factor in facilitating the deal achievement in M&A transactions (Franklin, 2019; Gillan et al., 2021). Recently, a report issued by PWC (2022) discusses the pivotal role of Corporate Social Responsibility (CSR) commitment in M&A, showing that companies have begun to pay attention to sustainability matters when they formulate their investment strategies to improve their own sustainability awareness.

Previous literature mainly focused on the financial benefits originated by targeting high-sustainable firms, finding evidence of either positive market reactions for acquirers (Yen & André, 2019; Cho et al., 2021; Tampakoudis et al., 2021) or higher bid premiums for sellers (Gomes & Marsat, 2018; Chen & Gavious, 2015; Qiao & Wu, 2019; Ma, 2023). Moreover, other studies focused on the non-financial consequences of M&A deals involving high-sustainable targets. In this regard, Aktas

L. Ferri · F. Meucci (✉) · F. Spagnuolo
Department of Economics, Management, Institutions (DEMI), University of Naples "Federico II", Naples, Italy
e-mail: luca.ferri@unina.it; fiorenza.meucci@unina.it; flavio.spagnuolo@unina.it

C. Zagaria
Department of Economics, University of Campania "Luigi Vanvitelli", Capua, Italy
e-mail: claudia.zagaria@unicampania.it

N. Castellano et al. (eds.), *Environmental, Social, Governance (ESG)*, SIDREA Series in Accounting and Business Administration,
https://doi.org/10.1007/978-3-031-76618-3_25

et al. (2011) provide evidence of increased environmental and social performance for bidders that merge with more socially responsible targets.

Similarly, Tampakoudis and Anagnostopoulou (2020) analyzed how the pre-deal ESG score of a target is value-enhancing for the future financial and non-financial performance of acquirers. More recently, Rahman and Wu (2024) obtained similar results by investigating a sample of Chinese listed firms.

However, the majority of the aforementioned authors highlighted the existence of a lack in literature claiming for further research with the aim to analyze which specific dimension of targets' ESG paradigm can drive the potential improvement in CSR engagement of acquirers.[1] In this paper, we address this underdeveloped issue in M&A literature, aiming to investigate whether and how the post-deal change in the acquirer's ESG score is affected by the pre-deal target's ESG score, also detangling the target's ESG rating into the three constituent pillars. Thus, we examine which ESG factor is pivotal for acquiring firms' performance, given that M&A literature provided evidence for dissimilar impacts of ESG dimensions when they are treated separately (Teti et al., 2022; Cardillo & Harasheh, 2023). The importance of investigating this matter is underscored also by the evolving nature of sustainable practices within the M&A process, necessitating ongoing inquiry (Ahammad, 2023; González-Torres et al., 2020).

Recent anecdotal examples help to clarify the main research question of the present study, developed by an empirical approach. In 2017, Safran SA, a global leader in aerospace and defense, acquired 100% of Zodiac Aerospace SA, through an intra-industry deal. Following the acquisition, Safran SA exhibited a noteworthy improvement in its ESG performance overtime, jumping from an ESG score of 40.42 in 2016—one year before the deal announcement—to 58.00 in 2019—one year after deal completion—and further increased to 74.55 in 2022.[2] In Safran SA's 2018 Integrated Report, the company explicitly acknowledges the anticipation of heightened sustainability awareness and performance, attributing this progress directly to the assimilation of the target's practices: "*With the acquisition of Zodiac Aerospace, Safran has strong assets to fulfil its mission: sustainably contribute to more open, comfortable, safe and clean access to the skies*" (Safran SA, 2018, p. 3).

What emerges from this anecdotal case is that acquirers may intentionally target companies within the scope to improve their sustainability commitment and that—even more importantly—such potential benefits could be achieved as expected. Therefore, in the present study, we aim to provide an empirical investigation of how M&A operations can contribute to the strategic improvement of acquirers' ESG performance due to the targets' environmental, social, and governance practices.

[1] Kayser and Zülch (2024) stressed the necessity of further investigation about single ESG pillar asserting that "*as the number of studies that analyze the influence of companies' single sustainability pillars is still limited, further disentangling of effect and the relevance of companies' single pillars provide promising options for research*" (p. 24).

[2] These scores have been extracted by *Thomson Reuters* database on 15th December, 2023.

To quantitatively address such abovementioned matters, we analyze a set of 132 M&A deals conducted by European non-financial listed companies from 2015 to 2021. Basing our analysis on ordinary least squares (OLS) regression, we develop two models, and we regress the future acquirer' ESG score, respectively, on the ESG score of a target company and on the detangled environmental, social, and governance scores.

Coherently with our expectations, our main findings reveal that companies acquiring more sustainable targets (those with higher ESG score) improve their own ESG score one year after the M&A transaction. These results corroborate previous evidence provided by Aktas et al. (2011), Tampakoudis and Anagnostopoulou (2020), and Rahman and Wu (2024), while adding new insights about the influences of single ESG dimensions in acquirers' sustainability performance. In particular, we show that acquirers' ESG benefits are mainly driven by better governance practices rather than higher social and environmental engagements provided by the targets. As many authors claimed (Aktas et al., 2011; Vastola & Russo, 2021; Cardillo & Harasheh, 2023), such outcome confirms that the effectiveness of targets' corporate governance can be particularly beneficial for acquirers, whereas the latter can more easily learn by the former's corporate practices aimed to improve sustainability behavior.

Moreover, our additional analysis makes the readers aware that companies may incur in potentially unethical behavior (i.e., greenwashing) to satisfy the stakeholders' ESG orientation (Garrow & Valentine, 2012). In particular, we furtherly give evidence that bidders who exhibit in pre-deal period higher levels of greenwashing activities are more likely to acquire targets with higher ESG scores.

The contribution of this study to the literature is threefold. First, it enriches the stream of studies on sustainability in the M&A market (Aktas et al., 2011; Gomes & Marsat, 2018; Arouri et al., 2019; Yen & André, 2019; Caiazza et al., 2021; Cho et al., 2021; Tampakoudis et al., 2021; Teti et al., 2022) since it represents the first work to examine to what extent detangled ESG factors determine the future CSR performance of acquirers. Second, we expand previous literature on the effect of M&A operations on the acquirer's performance, going beyond financial consequences, and closely investigating sustainability outcomes. Finally, we contribute to a better understanding of the ESG paradigm, revealing dissimilarities across ESG pillars when they provide higher CSR engagement to acquirers.

The remainder of the study proceeds as follows. Section 25.2 provides an overview of the literature and the development of hypothesis. Section 25.3 details the sample composition and the methodology employed in the study. Section 25.4 discusses the empirical results and addresses further robustness tests and additional analysis, while Sect. 25.5 concludes by showing the main study implications, the work limitations, and avenues for future research.

25.2 Literature Review and Hypothesis Development

Companies facing prominent investment decisions, such as that concerned with M&A, are incorporating sustainability matters that usually reflect owners' concerns (Amel-Zadeh & Serafeim, 2018). For this reason, researchers started to investigate how sustainability and CSR activities in general might represent a great motivation behind the success of M&A transactions (Gillan et al., 2021; Piñeiro-Chousa et al., 2021). Both acquirers and sellers involved in such operations pay great attention to the ESG measures given that stakeholders are more aware of firms' sustainable actions (Barros et al., 2022). On the one hand, bidders generally tend to deal with sellers that display higher CSR activities to bring higher benefits for their stakeholders and shareholders (Gomes, 2019) and to avoid a negative spillover effect on their reputation (Boone & Uysal, 2020). On the other hand, sellers pay great attention to sustainability matters to obtain higher deal premium from the transaction (Gomes & Marsat, 2018; Qiao & Wu, 2019; Ma, 2023). Furthermore, Krishnamurti et al. (2019) demonstrated that more socially responsible acquirers are more prone to negotiate with sellers closer to their CSR activities, avoiding less sustainable ones. Hence, previous studies confirmed that sustainability issues are involved in M&A operations. However, scholars mainly examined the role played by ESG dimensions in the determination of financial and valuation effects for both bidders and target firms (Gomes & Marsat, 2018; Arouri et al., 2019; Caiazza et al., 2021; Yen & André, 2019; Cho et al., 2021; Tampakoudis et al., 2021; Teti et al., 2022). For this purpose, researchers indicate two different views about the benefits brought by the integration of ESG matters in investment decisions. On one side, the shareholder theory only legitimizes the investments aimed to increase the wealth of firms' shareholders (Friedman, 1970; Jensen, 2002). From this point of view, ESG-related activities and expenses are considered a waste of financial resources burdening shareholders (Deng et al., 2013). For instance, scholars give evidence that managers might overinvest in CSR activities for reputation concerns, sacrificing liquidity for core business investments (Barnea & Rubin, 2010; Buchanan et al., 2018).

Also, reflecting managerial agency problems, the focus on sustainability matters might be considered a time-consuming activity that shifts primary managers' responsibilities toward owners' wealth (Benabou & Tirole, 2010; Ferrell et al., 2016).

A different point of view is taken by the stakeholder theory (Freeman, 1984; Porter & Kramer, 2006), which recognizes how CSR commitment can increase value for shareholders by inducing further benefits for stakeholders' communities. For instance, scholars found that CSR engagement and ESG performance affect positively firm value (Jo & Harjoto, 2011; Mervelskemper & Streit, 2017; Fatemi et al., 2017). Also, Awaysheh et al. (2020) find better operating performance for high-CSR committed firms compared to low ones' peers. More strictly related to M&A empirical literature, the majority of studies on ESG issues for acquirers and sellers' financial performance rely on this latter point of view (Tampakoudis et al., 2021). For instance, Deng et al. (2013) examined US merger operations from 1992 to 2007 and found that acquirers' CSR performance positively affects their long-term operating returns. More recently, scholars observed positive announcement returns for acquirers with higher ESG performance (Krishnamurti et al., 2021; Zhang et al., 2022). Extant research also gave evidence of financial advantages for sellers, brought by ESG engagement. Indeed, studies demonstrate that acquirers either pay a higher bid premium (Gomes & Marsat, 2018; Qiao & Wu, 2019; Ma, 2023) or generally rely on higher target valuation (Chen & Gavious, 2015) when they deal with more sustainable sellers. Moreover, further academicians have shown additional benefits of sustainability in M&A, such as lower arbitrage spreads (Arouri et al., 2019), as well as favorable market reactions around the announcement of the operations (Yen & André, 2019; Cho et al., 2021).

Hence, previous literature on M&A exhaustively talked about the role of CSR engagement for the financial outcomes of acquirers. Conversely, very little has been said about the impact of sustainability issues on their non-financial performance in the post-M&A deal period. In fact, if it is true that dealing with higher sustainable targets may lead to higher economic returns for acquiring firms, it is also true that they might enhance their "*value*" through the integration of targets' capabilities and corporate culture (Haspeslagh & Jemison, 1991; Angwin & Meadows, 2015) that might also be, among other things, a high sustainability orientation.

This study aims to empirically investigate this underdeveloped topic, examining the non-financial consequences for acquirers, as measured by ESG performance scores. To the best of our knowledge, very few works examine the post-deal sustainability dimension of acquirers. For instance, Vastola and Russo (2021) found that after an M&A transaction, a firm can alternatively embed, add, or lose sustainability basing on target sustainability orientation and capabilities. In particular, the authors state that acquirers embed CSR activities when they integrate and co-develop target' capabilities, actively learning from sellers. Secondly, they also show that acquirers add sustainability when they acquire new sustainable technologies, usually through the merger with the target. This is consistent with the streams of studies that investigate the "buying" of sustainability through M&A transactions (Austin & Leonard, 2008; Mirvis, 2008; Wickert et al., 2017). We intend to explore the integration of target sustainability practices in acquirers' ones by investigating the relationship between acquirers' potential change in post-deal ESG scores and the level of ESG performance of targets in the pre-deal stage. Hence, we examine the extent to which targeting firms with higher ESG performance help to improve the future ESG engagement of acquirers. Aktas et al. (2011) investigated a close issue, documenting that the environmental and social performance of the acquirers increase following the acquisition of more socially responsible investing (SRI) aware targets. Therefore, the authors demonstrated that acquirers might learn from the target's ESG practices and experiences. More recently, Tampakoudis and Anagnostopoulou (2020) and Rahman and Wu (2024) show that through the acquisition of targets with high social, environmental, and governance performance, firms might enhance both their corporate sustainability together with their market value, compared to the pre-deal period.

Coherently, focusing closely on non-financial outcomes of M&A operations, we expect to find evidence of improved ESG performance for the acquirers, led by dealing with targets with higher CSR commitment. Such expectation would confirm the role played by targets' sustainability in providing acquirers benefits (Aktas et al., 2011; Yen & André, 2019; Teti et al., 2022), building up a new understanding of ESG rating measures.

Hence, based on the above discussion, we intend to test the following hypothesis:

H_1 *The target's ESG score in the pre-deal stage positively impacts the acquirer's ESG score change in the post-deal period.*

Furthermore, we examine the extent to which each factor that constitutes the ESG paradigm of targets' affects the future sustainability performance of acquirers. In particular, we have been prompted by Tampakoudis and Anagnostopoulou (2020) and Rahman and Wu (2024), who claimed for further investigation on how single Environmental (E), Social (S) and Governance (G) scores of targets might help acquirers to enhance their own ESG performance. Generally speaking, whereas the targets' ESG score may lead to a higher future CSR commitment for acquiring firms, it is possible that one of such detangled elements may not. For instance, the results provided by Aktas et al. (2011) focus on the social and environmental influences of targets, while governance matters are excluded. Also, Arouri et al. (2019) suggested that more socially responsible acquirers are perceived by the market as more capable to complete an M&A operation timely and successfully while influences of environmental and governance concerns are set aside. Conversely, Wickert et al. (2017) demonstrated that the sustainability orientation of acquirers could be led mainly by organizational and governance aspects of target firms, leaving out environmental and social issues.

Regarding the usage of ESG metrics, mixed evidence exists about the role of detangled ESG scores in M&A' deal features and acquirers' performance. Very recently, Cardillo and Harasheh (2023) examined how sustainability divergences between acquirer and target firm affect the deal length in M&A and they found dissimilar impact across constituent pillars of ESG ratings on deal timing. In particular, they found that governance and social discrepancies slow down the deal's success where social score divergences between bidders and sellers do not. Regarding the financial performance of firms, a recent work by Teti et al. (2022) explores the impact of targets' single ESG factors on the value appreciation of acquiring firms. They found that environmental and social scores are not relevant for M&A value creation, whereas better corporate standards affect positively the takeover performance of bidders. These last two studies make us aware of single ESG metrics' importance in affecting M&A concerns.

For this reason, in this research we adopt detangled ESG scores of target firms to evaluate acquirers' non-financial performance in the post-deal period. We are aware that none of the abovementioned studies analyzed targets' E, S, and G dimensions as a single factor while analyzing post-deal CSR benefits for acquirers. However, in line with findings provided by previous scholars on acquirers' sustainability improvement led by sellers' social (Aktas et al., 2011; Arouri et al., 2019), environmental (Aktas et al., 2011), and governance (Wickert et al., 2017; Vastola & Russo, 2021) factors, we expect that the magnitude of each pillar score can improve ESG performance of acquirers after the deal achievement.

We address this issue by formulating the following subsequent hypotheses:

H_{1a} *The target's Environmental score in the pre-deal stage positively impacts the acquirer's ESG score change in the post-M&A deal period.*

H_{1b} *The target's Social score in the pre-deal stage positively impacts the acquirer's ESG score change in the post-M&A deal period.*

H_{1c} *The target's Governance score in the pre-deal stage positively impacts the acquirer's ESG score change in the post-M&A deal period.*

The test of the above hypotheses allows us to examine more in depth the manner in which targets' sustainability is integrated in ESG performance of acquirers in M&A. Given that we posit all the three dimensions improve CSR commitment of buyers, we also intend to find out which factor could be a stronger driver of such benefits. Doing that, we build on very new insights to the current knowledge about ESG performance role in M&A.

25.3 Research Design

25.3.1 Sample Selection

We collect and merge data from different data sources. We start our sample selection process by selecting from *Zephyr* all M&A deals which involve European listed firms during the seven-year period from 2015 to 2021.[3]

To include a deal in our initial sample, the M&A transaction needs to respond to the following three criteria.

First, we select only acquisitions involving at least 50% of the target equity to ensure that all bidders in our sample aim for full control of the targets they are acquiring and to avoid transactions with a small changes in ownership (i.e., M&A operations caused by likely trading activities). Second, we exclude acquisitions with the funding sources coming from debt, that is, categorized as leverage buy-outs to avoid sample bias from a sample that heavily-debt finance. Third, we include in our sample only M&A operations in which the deal value is not less than € 1 million, while we exclude deals involving targets with negative equity. Hence, our procedure identifies an initial sample composed by 353 deals.

Following previous studies, we then exclude deals involving financial firms, since their ESG policies differ from those of other firms[4] (e.g., Tampakoudis & Anagnostopoulou, 2020; Teti et al., 2022; Cardillo & Harasheh, 2023).

[3] We select only the transactions completed before the end of the sample period.

[4] We consider the following to be financial firms: banks, insurance firms, broker/dealers, real estate, and other financial services (Standard Industrial Classification codes 6000–6999).

Table 25.1 Sample selection process

Initial sample: Completed acquisition involving listed acquirers located in European Union countries, between 2015–2021—from Zephyr database	353
Less	
Deals involving financial companies	*74*
Deals involving targets/acquirers with no matching ESG scores—from *Thomson Reuters Database*	*130*
Deals involving targets/acquirers with no matching financial information—from *Orbis (Bureau Van Dijk) Database*	*17*
Final sample	*132*

Note. This table shows the sample selection process. The final sample consists of 132 M&A deals

Lastly, we merged this list of events with the list of ESG scores and financial data collected, respectively, from *Thomson Reuters* and *Orbis* databases. After excluding deals involving companies with ESG and financial missing data, we obtain a final sample of 132 M&A deals (Table 25.1).

Table 25.2 presents the sample composition showing the deals distribution by announcement year (Panel A), by acquirer's industry (Panel B), and by acquirer's country (Panel C). It emerges that our sample is homogeneously distributed announcement year, with a small drop in transactions number in 2020, coherently with the Covid-19 pandemic that slowed down M&A activity (Magnanelli et al., 2022). In addition, Table 25.2 shows that the acquirers in our sample are mainly from the industry *Business Equipment* (30 deals), although all sectors are represented. Finally, it emerges also that our sample is well composed by almost all 27-EU countries, although Italy and France are the most involved representing almost 25% of the total deals.

25.3.2 The Models

We developed two regression analyses in order to test our hypotheses. First, to test the hypothesis H_1, we investigate whether and how the target's ESG score is associated with the change in the acquirer's ESG score after the M&A deal, adopting the following model:[5]

[5]The ESG scores as obtained from *Thomson Reuters* are widely adopted in previous literature as ESG performance measures (Arouri et al., 2019; Gomes & Marsat, 2018; Krishnamurti et al., 2019; Yen & André, 2019; Tampakoudis & Anagnostopoulou, 2020). However, we acknowledge the criticalities that arise when using such metrics. In particular, as pointed out by Sahin et al. (2023), ESG scores are called *non-definitive* whereas their figures may change retroactively (for years data) depending on the extraction date.

Table 25.2 Sample composition

Year	Frequencies	% Events
Panel A: Event distribution by Announcement Year		
2015	26	19.70%
2016	18	13.64%
2017	25	18.94%
2018	13	9.85%
2019	20	15.15%
2020	14	10.60%
2021	16	12.12%
Total	**132**	**100%**
Industry	Frequencies	% Events
Panel B: Event distribution by Acquirer industry		
Consumer Non-Durables	8	6.06%
Consumer Durables	6	4.55%
Manufacturing	4	3.03%
Energy, Oil, and Gas	5	3.79%
Chemicals	10	7.58%
Business Equipment	30	22.72%
Communications	11	8.33%
Utilities	19	14.39%
Wholesale, Retail, Shops	8	6.06%
Healthcare	5	3.79%
Other	26	19.70%
Total	**132**	**100%**
Country	Frequencies	% Events
Panel C: Event distribution by Acquirer country (EU-27)[a]		
Austria	2	1.52%
Belgium	6	4.55%
Bulgaria	4	3.03%
Croatia	10	7.58%
Cyprus	2	1.52%
Denmark	6	4.55%
France	16	12.12%
Germany	13	9.85%
Ireland	6	4.55%
Italy	16	12.12%
Luxembourg	2	1.52%
Netherlands	8	6.06%
Poland	9	6.82%
Portugal	7	5.30%
Romania	3	2.27%
Spain	6	4.55%
Sweden	8	6.06%

(continued)

Table 25.2 (continued)

Country	Frequencies	% Events
Switzerland	2	1.52%
United Kingdom	6	4.55%
Total	**132**	**100%**

Note. This table reports the sample composition. Panel A shows deals' distribution by M&A announcement year. Panel B reports acquirers' industry affiliation based on the Fama-French 12-industry classification. Panel C refers to deal distribution by the acquirer's country (EU-27) with at least one observation. % Events refers to the percentage of deals on the total number of deals included in our final sample (132 deals)

[a] We included the United Kingdom in our sample because Brexit begins on December 31, 2020

$$\Delta ESG\ score_{Acquirer} = \alpha_1 ESG\ score_{Target} + \gamma Controls + \varepsilon \quad (25.1)$$

where:

- $\Delta ESG\ score_{Acquirer}$ is the change of acquirer's ESG score between the year after the deal completion and the year before the announcement;
- $ESG\ score_{Target}$ is the target's ESG score the year before the M&A announcement.

We expect to find that the coefficient α_1 is positive and significant at any conventional level meaning that the target's ESG score is positively associated with the change in the acquirer's ESG score after the M&A deal.

The second regression aims to test the hypothesis H_{1a}, H_{1b}, H_{1c}. We investigate whether and how each ESG dimension drives the change in the acquirers' post-deal ESG performance, through the following model:

$$\Delta ESG\ score_{Acquirer} = \beta_1 E\ score_{Target} + \beta_2 S\ score_{Target} + \beta_3 G\ score_{Target} + \gamma Controls + \varepsilon \quad (25.2)$$

where:

- $E\ score_{Target}$ is the target's Environmental score the year before the M&A announcement;
- $S\ score_{Target}$ is the target's Social score the year before the M&A announcement;
- $G\ score_{Target}$ is the target's Governance score the year before the M&A announcement.

We expect to find that the coefficients β_1, β_2, β_3 are positive and significant at conventional levels meaning that the target's Environmental, Social, and Governance scores are positively associated with the change in the acquirer's ESG score after the M&A deal.

We also include a vector of variables ($\gamma Controls$) in both Eq. (25.1) and Eq. (25.2) to control for various acquirers-specific characteristics that are known to be correlated with the change of bidders' ESG scores (Tampakoudis & Anagnostopoulou,

2020; Teti et al., 2022). In particular, we control for the acquirer profitability ($ROA_{Acquirer}$), measured as the income before tax divided by the average total assets (Bereskin et al., 2018; Kwon et al., 2018), for the acquirer size ($Size_{Acquirer}$), measured as the natural logarithm of the book value of assets (Bereskin et al., 2018), and for the acquirer leverage ($Leverage_{Acquirer}$), measured as the ratio of total liabilities on total assets (Fatemi et al., 2017). For all the control variables, we compute the related change following the same rationale we employed to calculate the change in acquirers' ESG score (i.e., considering values between one year after deal completion and one year before the deal announcement).

In addition, we control for two dummy variables which assume the value of 1 if the target is in the same country (*Domestic*) and industry (*Intra*) of the acquirer and 0 otherwise, because the construction of ESG pillars' scores is very sensitive to industry relatedness and to country level (Lopez de Silanes et al., 2020).

25.4 Results

25.4.1 Descriptive Statistics

Table 25.3 presents the descriptive statistics (mean, standard deviation, minimum, and maximum) of the variables involved in our tests. The results show that there is a high distance between the minimum (min = 5.08) and maximum (max = 90.59) values of the target's ESG score, this indicates significant differences in the ESG performance among target firms. Moreover, results highlight that among the three ESG pillars, the highest mean value is observed for the social score (mean = 61.29), although the highest maximum value is reached at environmental score (max = 96.68). Our descriptive statistics also indicate that on average the acquirers' profitability decreases by 3% after the deal completion, their leverage structure increases by about 8%, while they grow in terms of total assets by more than 20%. Also, in our sample 31% (17%) of deals are domestic (intra-industry) acquisitions.

Table 25.4 presents the correlations between the dependent, independent, and control variables and shows that the only variables with a high correlation are the E score, S score, and G score, which present correlation indices related to the ESG score greater than 0.5.[6] Furthermore, the matrix shows that the correlation between the target's ESG score, as well as individual pillar scores, and the change in acquirer ESG score is positive. This seems to be consistent with our expectation.

[6]Given the relatively high correlation among ESG scores' metrics, we compute the variance inflation factors (VIFs) in the regression analyses to control that the potential interrelationship between explanatory variables does not affect seriously the overall analysis. Despite VIFs lower than 5 would be optimal, the untabulated VIFs' values in the regressions that we run are all less than 10, which is an acceptable threshold to alleviate the multicollinearity problems (García et al., 2015; Salmerón Gómez et al., 2016).

Table 25.3 Descriptive statistics

Variable	Obs.	Mean	Std. Dev	Min	Max
$\Delta ESG\ score_{Acquirer}$	132	0.17	0.28	−0.38	1.10
$ESG\ score_{Target}$	132	55.40	1.71	5.08	90.59
$E\ score_{Target}$	132	54.83	0.30	4.87	96.68
$S\ score_{Target}$	132	61.29	1.27	3.69	95.20
$G\ score_{Target}$	132	54.91	0.81	5.49	91.61
$ROA_{Acquirer}$	132	−0.03	0.78	−0.93	1.22
$Size_{Acquirer}$	132	0.21	0.42	−0.62	2.13
$Leverage_{Acquirer}$	132	0.08	0.44	−0.11	1.14
Domestic	132	0.31	0.47	0	1
Intra	132	0.17	0.38	0	1

Note. This table reports the descriptive statistics (mean, standard deviation, minimum, and maximum) of the main variables. All continuous variables were winsorized at the 1st and 99th percentiles

25.4.2 Regression Analysis

The results of Eq. (25.1), shown in Table 25.5, demonstrate that the target's ESG score is positively associated with the change in the acquirer's ESG score after the M&A deal, since the α_1 coefficient is positive and statistically significant at conventional level. Such result confirms that our hypothesis H_1 is validated. Thus, we corroborate with findings provided by Aktas et al. (2011), Tampakoudis and Anagnostopoulou (2020), and Rahman and Wu (2024) confirming that when acquirers deal with high-sustainable sellers, it is likely that they incorporate their sustainability practices in a beneficial manner, improving their ESG commitment (Mirvis, 2008; Wickert et al., 2017; Vastola & Russo, 2021).

The results of Eq. (25.2), shown in Table 25.6, demonstrate that the target's score for each ESG pillar is positively associated with the change in the acquirer's ESG score after the M&A deal, since the β_1, β_2, β_3 coefficients are positive and statistically significant at any conventional level. Such result confirms that our hypotheses H_{1a}, H_{1b}, H_{1c} are validated. Moreover, findings show that the coefficient β_3 is higher than β_1 and β_2, thus highlighting that the influence of the target's Governance score is stronger than the Environmental and Social scores. In order to verify whether the differences between the coefficients are significant, we also conduct the F-test,[7] which confirms that there is a significant difference between β_3 and β_1 and also between β_3 and β_2, while the difference between β_2 and β_1 is not statistically significant.

This finding indicates an interesting insight. Indeed, such result reveals that acquirers mainly learn from well-governed targets and that such characteristic drives

[7]The F-test can be used to test the null hypothesis that differences in coefficients of independent variables are significative equal to zero (Cooke, 1998).

Table 25.4 Correlation matrix

	1	2	3	4	5	6	7	8	9	10
$\Delta ESGscore_{Acquirer}$	**[a]1.00**									
$ESG\ score_{Target}$	**[a]0.21**	**[a]1.00**								
$E\ score_{Target}$	[a]0.07	**[a]0.59**	**[a]1.00**							
$S\ score_{Target}$	[a]0.18	**[a]0.51**	**[a]0.58**	**[a]1.00**						
$G\ score_{Target}$	[a]0.07	**[a]0.71**	**[a]0.53**	**[a]0.51**	**[a]1.00**					
$ROA_{Acquirer}$	[a]0.02	**[a]−0.24**	[a]−0.17	**[a]−0.17**	**[a]−0.24**	**[a]1.00**				
$Size_{Acquirer}$	**[a]−0.15**	[a]0.13	[a]0.09	**[a]0.11**	[a]0.00	[a]−0.06	**[a]1.00**			
$Leverage_{Acquirer}$	[a]0.06	[a]0.06	[a]−0.05	**[a]−0.12**	[a]−0.08	[a]−0.07	**[a]0.42**	**[a]1.00**		
Domestic	**[b]0.16**	[b]−0.02	[b]0.09	[b]0.04	**[b]−0.06**	[b]−0.07	[b]−0.09	[b]0.05	**[c]1.00**	
Intra	**[b]−0.15**	[b]0.06	[b]0.09	[b]0.01	[b]−0.00	[b]0.12	**[b]−0.10**	[b]−0.04	[c]0.01	**[c]1.00**

Note. This table presents the correlations among the selected variables. Variables are coded with numbers from 1 to 10, in the following order: *$\Delta ESGscore_{Acquirer}$* (1), *$ESG\ score_{Target}$* (2), *$E\ score_{Target}$* (3), *$S\ score_{Target}$* (4), *$G\ score_{Target}$* (5), *$ROA_{Acquirer}$* (6), *$Size_{Acquirer}$* (7), *$Leverage_{Acquirer}$* (8), *Domestic* (9) and *Intra* (10). [a] indicates the level of association between two continuous variables (Pearson correlation). [b] indicates the level of association between one continuous variable and one dichotomous variable (point-biserial correlation). [c] indicates the level of association between two dichotomous variables (Chi-square coefficient). Figures in bold indicate statistically significant correlation at least at 5% or better

Table 25.5 Regression results from Eq. (25.1)

	coeff.	rob. std. err.	*t-stat.*	*p-value*
$ESG\ score_{Target}$	0.11	0.04	2.63	0.01***
Controls				
$ROA_{Acquirer}$	0.07	0.01	6.34	0.00***
$Size_{Acquirer}$	−0.11	0.09	−1.12	0.47
$Leverage_{Acquirer}$	−0.02	0.01	−1.83	0.07*
Domestic	0.08	0.06	1.37	0.77
Intra	−0.14	0.07	−1.91	0.06*
Obs.	**132**			
Year FE	**No**			
Industry FE	**No**			
R^2	**0.151**			
Prob > *F*	**0.000**			

Note. This table reports the results of the OLS regression (Eq. 25.1). Appendix contains details of the construction of all variables. The symbols ***, **, and * denote two-sided significance at the 1%, 5%, and 10% levels, respectively

positively the future sustainability orientation, whereas social and environmental engagement are less prominent factors.

If it is true that acquirers integrate sustainability issues into their investment decisions (Gillan et al., 2021; PWC, 2022), acquiring targets with higher G standards can positively influence the acquirers' strategic achievement toward such greater sustainable orientation. Indeed, governance arrangements especially reflect the organizational culture of firms, their values, and ethical standards (Cartwright & Schoenberg, 2006; Guiso et al., 2015) and hence could be the main drivers of either changes or improvements following the M&A operations. This is particularly evident in our results, which suggest that governance dispositions enable the transfer of overall sustainability values from the targets to the acquirers. Such a process fosters the cultural integration of firms and, subsequently, the aimed adoption of better ESG practices as a whole.[8]

Overall, our results seem to be coherent with previous studies that indicate governance score as main predictor of both M&A deal success (Cardillo & Harasheh, 2023) and acquirers' value-enhancing (Teti et al., 2022).

As regards control variables, they are all significant at conventional level in both models, except for the variable *Domestic* and $Size_{Acquirer}$. In particular, the

[8]In the anecdotal case presented in the introduction section of the paper, we mentioned that Safran SA improved its overtime sustainability performance following the acquisition of Zodiac Aerospace SA. It may be reasonable to believe that part of this improvement can be explained by the integration of governance practices embedded by the acquired company. Indeed, following the transaction, Safran SA integrated pivotal representatives of Zodiac Aerospace SA into the board of directors. Specifically, Olivier Zarrouati—chairman of Zodiac Aerospace SA's management board—became Safran SA's deputy CEO, while Lydie Jallier—Human Resources (HR) Director of Zodiac Aerospace SA has been named Executive HR vice-president in Safran SA.

Table 25.6 Regression results from Eq. (25.2)

	coeff.	rob. std. err.	*t-stat.*	*p-value*
$E\ score_{Target}$	0.13	0.06	2.19	0.03**
$S\ score_{Target}$	0.08	0.03	2.37	0.02**
$G\ score_{Target}$	0.45	0.11	3.88	0.00***
Controls				
$ROA_{Acquirer}$	0.01	0.00	1.82	0.07*
$Size_{Acquirer}$	−0.09	0.06	−1.35	0.70
$Leverage_{Acquirer}$	−0.03	0.01	−2.07	0.04**
Domestic	0.05	0.04	1.26	0.54
Intra	−0.13	0.07	−1.70	0.09*
Obs.	**132**			
Year FE	**No**			
Industry FE	**No**			
R^2	**0.208**			
Prob > *F*	**0.000**			

Note. This table reports the results of the OLS regression (Eq. 25.2). Appendix contains details of the construction of all variables. The symbols ***, **, and * denote two-sided significance at the 1%, 5%, and 10% levels, respectively

coefficient of $ROA_{Acquirer}$ is positive and statistically significant, at 1% and 10%, respectively, in the first model (Eq. 25.1) and in the second model (Eq. 25.2), showing that the higher the change in acquirer profitability, the higher the change in its ESG score after the M&A deal. The coefficient of $Leverage_{Acquirer}$ is negative and statistically significant, at 10% and 5%, respectively, in the first model (Eq. 25.1) and in the second model (Eq. 25.2), highlighting that the change in acquirer's ESG score after the M&A deal is higher when the changes in level of leverage are lower. Finally, the coefficient *Intra* is negative and statistically significant at 10% in both models, showing that the change in the acquirer's ESG score after the M&A deal is lower when the target is in the same industry of the acquirer.

25.4.3 Robustness Tests and Additional Analysis

25.4.3.1 Robustness Test on Endogeneity Concerns

One main concern in our analyses is about potential endogeneity issues arising from likely omitted variables in our empirical models. If this is the case, then it is possible that the change in the acquirers' ESG performance 1 year ahead from the deal completion is explained by factors that are not directly observable in our model and that, therefore, the ESG increase of the acquirers is not due to the M&A transaction but to further (i.e., unobservable) determinants. We address this issue by implementing a robustness test which aims to confirm that M&A operations are an effective and relevant driver for the change in the acquirers' ESG performance.

Specifically, for this purpose, we employ the propensity score matching (PSM) to create a control sample of firms that are "comparable" to the firms in our initial sample (i.e., acquirers), but have not been involved in any M&A transaction (i.e., non-acquirers).

Specifically, the statistical technique of PSM returns, for each treated company (i.e., acquirers), a matched "nearest-neighbor" control firm (i.e., non-acquirers) based on certain matching criteria (Rosenbaum & Rubin, 1985).

Following prior studies in similar contexts (Gomes & Marsat, 2018; Gomes, 2019), we use the firm size (i.e., total assets in million), firm valuation (market-to-book ratio), firm leverage (i.e., total debt on total assets), and firm liquidity (i.e., current assets on current liabilities) as matching criteria. Moreover, we also require both exact financial data year and exact industry matches between companies in the two sub-samples.

Then, for our pooled sample (i.e., composed by M&A-involved and non M&A-involved firms), we rely on model specifications of Eq. (25.1) with the following adjustments. In particular, we replace the independent variable $ESG\ score_{Target}$ with a dummy variable that takes the value of 1 if the firm has been involved in an M&A operation (i.e., *Acquirer*), and 0 otherwise. Coherently, our dependent variable (control variables) will capture the 1 year change in firm's ESG score (respective control variables) for all firms included in the pooled sample. Lastly, we drop *Domestic* and *Intra* as control variables.

Table 25.7 shows results for our robustness test. In particular, Panel A provides descriptive statistics for variables employed as matching criteria, related to the two sub-samples of firms involved in M&A transaction ($Acquirers = 1$) and matched firms not involved in M&A transaction ($Acquirers = 0$). Overall, untabulated *t-tests* do not indicate significative differences across the two sub-samples. We expected such preliminary results given that we use such a variables as matching criteria.

More interestingly, Panel B offers the regression results for our robustness tests. Specifically, we find that the coefficient of *Acquirer* is significant at 1% level (t-stat $= 3.43$ and p-value < 0.01), indicating that being involved in an M&A transaction is associated with a greater positive 1 year change in firm's ESG performance, compared to not being involved in such a transactions. While this evidence confirms the idea that M&A operations are valuable patterns through which firms can augment their sustainable performance as many authors believe (Tampakoudis & Anagnostopoulou, 2020; Vastola & Russo, 2021; Rahman & Wu, 2024), it also allows us to alleviate potential endogeneity matters from our main inferences.

25.4.3.2 Untabulated Robustness Tests

In order to make our results more robust, we perform further robustness tests. For simplicity reasons, we do not tabulate the results of such further analysis.

Table 25.7 Robustness test

	Acquirers = 1		Acquirers = 0	
PSM dimensions	*N*	Mean	*N*	Mean
Panel A. Descriptive statistics for Propensity Score Matching (PSM) criteria				
SIZE	132	474.34	132	475.12
MTB RATIO	132	1.83	132	1.91
LEVERAGE	132	0.27	132	0.27
LIQUIDITY	132	0.09	132	0.12
	ΔESG score			
Dependent variable	Coeff.	rob. std. err.	*t-stat.*	*p-value*
Panel B. Regression results for robustness test				
Acquirer	0.12	0.03	3.43	0.00***
Controls				
ROA	0.12	0.02	6.54	0.00***
Size	0.13	0.08	1.71	0.09*
Leverage	−0.06	0.03	1.88	0.07*
Obs.	**232**			
Year FE	**No**			
Industry FE	**No**			
R^2	**0.132**			
Prob > *F*	**0.0012**			

Note. This table reports the results of our robustness test related to the pooled sample of 264 observations. Panel A provides descriptive statistics for variables used as matching dimensions in PSM model. Year and Industry are used as exact match criteria. Panel B provides results for regression related to the robustness test. *ΔESG score* is the firm's change in ESG score 1 year ahead from the M&A, while *Acquirer is* a dummy variable that takes the value of 1 if the firm has been involved in an M&A operation and 0 otherwise. Control variables are defined as in Appendix. The symbols ***, **, and * denote two-sided significance at the 1%, 5%, and 10% levels, respectively

First, we repeat our main analysis demanding for more fixed effects structure in our models. In particular, we include fixed effects per year and country of the acquirer to control for the differences in the volume of deals with time and also for the country-specific factors related to M&A activity (Perafán-Peñá et al., 2022; Cardillo & Harasheh, 2023).

To run such analysis, we employ more stringent constraints to our initial sample. Specifically, we require at least 5 observations for each acquirer's country.[9] Overall, the untabulated results on 117 deals analysis are qualitatively the same for both the hypotheses tested in our research, and they allow us to alleviate potential macroeconomic biases that potentially could affect our main findings.

[9] Thus, we exclude in our robustness test the following countries: Austria, Bulgaria, Cyprus, Luxembourg, Romania, and Switzerland.

Also, to complement the findings on our first hypothesis (H_1), similarly to Tampakoudis and Anagnostopoulou (2020), we replace from Eq. (25.1) the continuous independent variable of interest $ESG\ score_{Target}$ with a dichotomic variable that takes the value of 1 if the target displays a higher ESG score than the acquirer's ESG score (i.e., $ESG\ greater_{target}$). Keeping equal the rest of model specifications in Eq. (25.1), our results from this test are even more significant (coefficient on $ESG\ greater_{target}$ of 0.16, *t*-statistics = 4.33).

25.4.3.3 Additional Analysis

Our main study arises from the rationale that bidders want to purchase green and sustainable targets to obtain, through the embedding of sellers' practice, a post-acquisition improvement in their sustainability performance to respond to stakeholders' needs (Pfeffer & Salancik, 1978; Vastola & Russo, 2021).

However, one additional motivation surrounding such conjecture may arise from the incentives to incur in *greenwashing* activities. In particular, such phenomenon occurs when managers voluntarily provide misleading information to stakeholders about firms' ESG practices, with the aim to convey the image of a sustainable company (Delmas & Burbano, 2011).

Whereas previous studies suggest that companies may perform greenwashing activities to satisfy the stakeholders' demands for a change in ESG practices (Garrow & Valentine, 2012), we additionally want to test if the pre-deal acquirers' levels of greenwashing can positively affect the decision to acquire a target with greater ESG score.

Similar to Ghitti et al. (2023), we rely on the acquirers' ESG controversy score from *Thomson Reuters* (that ranges from 0 to 100) one year before the deal announcement to proxy for bidders' level of greenwashing. We multiply such raw score by negative one to obtain higher values indicating higher likelihood of greenwashing activities. Then, we regress the ESG score of the targets (i.e., $ESG\ score_{Target}$) on our measure of acquirers' level of greenwashing (i.e., $ESG\ controversial_{Acquirer}$) and on a set of control variables about target-specific characteristics (i.e., we refer to ROA_{Target} as a measure of targets' profitability, to $Size_{Target}$ as a measure of targets' total assets and to $Leverage_{Target}$ which measures targets' leverage).

Table 25.8 shows the results from our additional analysis. Coherently to what we expected, we find that acquirers with a higher level of greenwashing (i.e., higher ESG controversy score) on average decide to purchase target companies with a higher ESG score. The coefficient of $ESG\ controversial_{Acquirer}$ is positive (0.09) and statistically significant (*t-statistics* = 2.00) at 5%.

Overall, we suggest that greenwashing might be a concrete motivation behind the decision of acquirers to target high ESG performant companies (Li et al., 2020; Lu, 2021).

Table 25.8 Regression results from additional analysis

	$ESG\ score_{Target}$			
Dependent variable	coeff.	rob. std. err.	*t-stat.*	*p-value*
$ESG\ controversial_{Acquirer}$	0.09	0.04	2.00	0.05**
Controls				
ROA_{Target}	0.21	0.05	4.11	0.000***
$Size_{Target}$	0.16	0.04	3.12	0.002***
$Leverage_{Target}$	−0.12	0.52	−0.23	0.81
Obs.	**71**[a]			
Year FE	**No**			
Industry FE	**No**			
R^2	**0.094**			
Prob > *F*	**0.0279**			

Note. This table reports the results of the OLS regression as explained in Sect. 25.4.3 (*Additional analysis*). $ESG\ score_{Target}$ is defined in Appendix, while $ESG\ controversial_{Acquirer}$ is the acquirer's ESG controversy score one year before the deal announcement. ROA_{Target} measures target's profitability at the announcement year, $Size_{Target}$ measures the targets' total assets at the announcement year, and $Leverage_{Target}$ is the level of target's leverage at the announcement year. The symbols ***, **, and * denote two-sided significance at the 1%, 5%, and 10% levels, respectively

[a] We rely on a sample of 71 observations, given that the acquirers' ESG controversy score was not available for 61 deals

25.5 Conclusions

We examined whether and how the post-deal change in the acquirer's ESG score is influenced by the target's ESG score. Moreover, detangling the ESG paradigm, the study also investigates how each ESG pillar drives the change in the acquirers' post-deal ESG performance.

Our findings reveal that the increase in the acquirers' ESG score one year after the deal is positively affected by the pre-deal targets' ESG score. More interestingly, we demonstrate that the subsequent increase in acquirers' ESG performance due to the targets' ESG orientation is mainly driven by the inclusion of better governance standards of the targets, rather than by their social and environmental practices' integration. Overall, these findings are consistent with the previous literature on the influence of the target's ESG score on the increase of the acquirer's ESG performance (e.g., Aktas et al., 2011; Tampakoudis & Anagnostopoulou, 2020; Rahman & Wu, 2024), adding new intuitions on the role of each pillar ESG in driving this change. While our robustness tests confirm that M&As can be a significant driver of future corporate sustainability performance, our additional analysis also warns that acquirers are likely to incur in acquisitions of highly sustainable targets for greenwashing purposes, to fulfill the increasing-demand for ESG performance required by companies' investors and stakeholders in general (Li et al., 2020).

Our research has several practical implications. First of all, our inferences advance the idea that M&A operations are successful tools for achieving the sustainable transformation required by more and more stakeholders. Thus, from a managerial point of view, we inform M&A practitioners that the external acquisition of green practices and capabilities is a valid option to achieve such a change. Specifically, we indicate that the quality of targets' corporate governance is the main channel through which managers of acquiring firms can improve ESG engagement for their companies. Overall, this study may also help investors to gain awareness about the importance of firms' ESG performance in making sustainable investment decisions.

Lastly, our study reveals essential hints for both policymakers and regulators. In fact, our study endorses the idea that ESG scores are used by companies to evaluate the sustainability performance of sellers in an M&A market (Teti et al., 2022). For this reason, our results can encourage the former to promote the ESG disclosure on which these metrics and scores are based, rewarding companies that implement higher ethical standards in such contexts. At the same time, we make the latter aware of likely unethical motivation (i.e., greenwashing) that may affect the choice to undertake an M&A operation from the acquirers' perspective. The matter is particularly crucial nowadays, as the current regulation of non-financial disclosure under the *Corporate Sustainability Reporting Directive no. 2464/2022* (CSRD) will disruptively extend the scope of the mandatory ESG information regime to "smaller" companies in the European context. Such a scenario will largely change the processes related to M&A operations as buyers will have a wider range of ESG information to consider and, above all, cover a larger number of potential target companies.

However, this study is not exempt from limitations. Firstly, we focus on short-term improvement of acquirers' ESG performance, while different conclusions might be made by analyzing our research question in long term. We hence encourage further studies on this issue that would provide a more comprehensive view of the role of sustainability in M&A operations. Secondly, our study is affected by a data availability issue,[10] linked to the need to match target and acquirer ESG scores with M&A deals' information. As more data become available, future research may investigate this topic by involving more countries and more years, allowing for a larger sample of events that enhance the generalizability of results obtained.

Acknowledgments Flavio Spagnuolo gratefully acknowledges that this study was funded by the European Union—*NextGenerationEu*, in the framework of the *GRINS—Growing, Resilient, Inclusive, and Sustainable* project (MUR project code: PE00000018–CUP E63C22002140007). The views and opinions expressed in this study are solely those of the authors and do not necessarily reflect those of the European Union. The European Union is not responsible for them.

[10] Despite the absolute number of 132 deals analyzed in our study hinders a complete generalizability of our findings, our final sample is directly comparable with others in in similar contexts. For instance, Aktas et al. (2011) rely on 106 deals between 1997–2007, Tampakoudis and Anagnostopoulou (2020) analyze 100 deals between 2003–2016, while Teti et al. (2022) 76 deals, between 2008–2020.

Appendix. Variables Definition

Variable	Type	Description	Source
$\Delta ESGscore_{Acquirer}$	Continuous variable	The ratio of the difference between the acquirer's ESG scores in the year after the deal completion and the year before the deal announcement to the acquirer's ESG score the year before the M&A announcement.	*Thomson Reuters*
$ESG\ score_{Target}$	Continuous variable	The target's ESG score the year before the M&A announcement.	
$E\ score_{Target}$	Continuous variable	The target's Environmental score the year before the M&A announcement.	
$S\ score_{Target}$	Continuous variable	The target's Social score the year before the M&A announcement.	
$G\ score_{Target}$	Continuous variable	The target's Governance score the year before the M&A announcement.	
$ROA_{Acquirer}$	Continuous variable	The change in acquirer's income before tax divided by the average total assets between one year after the deal completion and one year before the deal announcement.	*Orbis (Bureau Van Dijk)*
$Size_{Acquirer}$	Continuous variable	The change in acquirer's natural logarithm of the book value of assets between one year after the deal completion and one year before the deal announcement.	
$Leverage_{Acquirer}$	Continuous variable	The change in acquirer's ratio of total liabilities on total assets between one year after the deal completion and one year before the deal announcement.	
Domestic	Dichotomic variable	Dichotomic variable, that takes the value of 1 if the target is in the same country of the acquirer, 0 otherwise.	*Zephyr (Bureau Van Dijk)*
Intra	Dichotomic variable	Dichotomic variable, that takes the value of 1 if the target is in the same industry of the acquirer, 0 otherwise.	

References

Agrawal, A., Jaffe, J. F., & Mandelker, G. N. (1992). The post-merger performance of acquiring firms: A re-examination of an anomaly. *The Journal of Finance, 47*(4), 1605–1621.

Ahammad, M. F. (2023). The role of sustainability in mergers & acquisitions: A literature review. *Advances in Mergers and Acquisitions*, 19–30.

Aktas, N., De Bodt, E., & Cousin, J. G. (2011). Do financial markets care about SRI? Evidence from mergers and acquisitions. *Journal of Banking & Finance, 35*(7), 1753–1761.

Amel-Zadeh, A., & Serafeim, G. (2018). Why and how investors use ESG information: Evidence from a global survey. *Financial Analysts Journal, 74*(3), 87–103.

Angwin, D. N., & Meadows, M. (2015). New integration strategies for post-acquisition management. *Long Range Planning, 48*(4), 235–251.

Arouri, M., Gomes, M., & Pukthuanthong, K. (2019). Corporate social responsibility and M&A uncertainty. *Journal of Corporate Finance, 56*, 176–198.

Austin, J. E., & Leonard, H. B. D. (2008). Can the virtuous mouse and the wealthy elephant live happily ever after? *California Management Review, 51*(1), 77–102.

Awaysheh, A., Heron, R. A., Perry, T., & Wilson, J. I. (2020). On the relation between corporate social responsibility and financial performance. *Strategic Management Journal, 41*(6), 965–987.

Barnea, A., & Rubin, A. (2010). Corporate social responsibility as a conflict between shareholders. *Journal of Business Ethics, 97*(1), 71–86.

Barros, V., Matos, P. V., Sarmento, J. M., & Vieira, P. R. (2022). M&A activity as a driver for better ESG performance. *Technological Forecasting and Social Change, 175*, 121338.

Benabou, R., & Tirole, J. (2010). Individual and corporate social responsibility. *Economica, 77*(305), 1–19.

Bereskin, F., Byun, S. K., Officer, M. S., & Oh, J. M. (2018). The effect of cultural similarity on mergers and acquisitions: Evidence from corporate social responsibility. *Journal of Financial and Quantitative Analysis, 53*, 1995–2039.

Boone, A., & Uysal, V. B. (2020). Reputational concerns in the market for corporate control. *Journal of Corporate Finance, 61*, 101399.

Buchanan, B., Cao, C. X., & Chen, C. (2018). Corporate social responsibility, firm value, and influential institutional ownership. *Journal of Corporate Finance, 52*, 73–95.

Caiazza, S., Galloppo, G., & Paimanova, V. (2021). The role of sustainability performance after merger and acquisition deals in short and long-term. *Journal of Cleaner Production, 314*, 127982.

Calipha, R., Tarba, S., & Brock, D. (2010). Mergers and acquisitions: A review of phases, motives, and success factors. *Advances in Mergers and Acquisitions, 9*, 1–24.

Cardillo, G., & Harasheh, M. (2023). Stay close to me: What do ESG scores tell about the deal timing in M&A transactions? *Finance Research Letters*, 103498.

Cartwright, S., & Schoenberg, R. (2006). Thirty years of mergers and acquisitions research: Recent advances and future opportunities. *British Journal of Management, 17*(S1), S1–S5.

Chen, E., & Gavious, I. (2015). Does CSR have different value implications for different shareholders? *Finance Research Letters, 14*, 29–35.

Cho, K., Han, S. H., Kim, H. J., & Kim, S. (2021). The valuation effects of corporate social responsibility on mergers and acquisitions: Evidence from US target firms. *Corporate Social Responsibility and Environmental Management, 28*(1), 378–388.

Cooke, T. E. (1998). Regression analysis in accounting disclosure studies. *Accounting and Business Research, 28*(3), 209–224.

Delmas, M. A., & Burbano, V. C. (2011). The drivers of greenwashing. *California Management Review, 54*(1), 64–87.

Deng, X., Kang, J. K., & Low, B. S. (2013). Corporate social responsibility and stakeholder value maximization: Evidence from mergers. *Journal of Financial Economics, 110*(1), 87–109.

Fatemi, A. M., Fooladi, I., & Garehkoolchian, N. (2017). Gains from mergers and acquisitions in Japan. *Global Finance Journal, 32*, 166–178.

Ferrell, A., Liang, H., & Renneboog, L. (2016). Socially responsible firms. *Journal of Financial Economics, 122*(3), 585–606.

Franklin, J. (2019). ESG now a key factor in M&A. *International Financial Law Review*.

Freeman, R. E. (1984). *Strategic management: A stakeholder approach*. Pitman.

Friedman, M. (1970). The social responsibility of business is to increase its profits. *The New York Times Magazine*. Available at: http://umich.edu/thecore/doc/Friedman.pdf

García, C. B., García, J., López Martín, M. M., & Salmerón, R. (2015). Collinearity: Revisiting the variance inflation factor in ridge regression. *Journal of Applied Statistics, 42*(3), 648–661.

Garrow, N., & Valentine, T. (2012). *Aspects of acquirer behaviour in Australian mergers and acquisitions*. Australian & New Zealand Academy of Management.

Ghitti, M., Gianfrate, G., & Palma, L. (2023). The agency of greenwashing. *Journal of Management and Governance*, 1–37.

Gillan, S. L., Koch, A., & Starks, L. T. (2021). Firms and social responsibility: A review of ESG and CSR research in corporate finance. *Journal of Corporate Finance, 66*, 101889.

Gomes, M. (2019). Does CSR influence M&A target choices? *Finance Research Letters, 30*, 153–159.

Gomes, M., & Marsat, S. (2018). Does CSR impact premiums in M&A transactions? *Finance Research Letters, 26*, 71–80.

González-Torres, T., Rodríguez-Sánchez, J. L., Pelechano-Barahona, E., & García-Muiña, F. E. (2020). A systematic review of research on sustainability in mergers and acquisitions. *Sustainability, 12*(2), 513.

Guiso, L., Sapienza, P., & Zingales, L. (2015). The value of corporate culture. *Journal of Financial Economics, 117*(1), 60–76.

Haspeslagh, P. C., & Jemison, D. B. (1991). *Managing acquisitions: Creating value through corporate renewal* (Vol. 416). Free Press.

Jensen, M. C. (2002). Value maximization, stakeholder theory, and the corporate objective function. *Business Ethics Quarterly, 12*(2), 235–256.

Jo, H., & Harjoto, M. A. (2011). Corporate governance and firm value: The impact of corporate social responsibility. *Journal of Business Ethics, 103*(3), 351–383.

Kayser, C., & Zülch, H. (2024). Understanding the relevance of sustainability in mergers and acquisitions—A systematic literature review on sustainability and its implications throughout deal stages. *Sustainability, 16*(2), 613.

Krishnamurti, C., Shams, S., & Chowdhury, H. (2021). Evidence on the trade-off between corporate social responsibility and mergers and acquisitions investment. *Australian Journal of Management, 46*(3), 466–498.

Krishnamurti, C., Shams, S., Pensiero, D., & Velayutham, E. (2019). Socially responsible firms and mergers and acquisitions performance: Australian evidence. *Pacific-Basin Finance Journal, 57*, 101193.

Kwon, O., Lim, S., & Lee, D. H. (2018). Acquiring startups in the energy sector: A study of firm value and environmental policy. *Business Strategy and the Environment, 27*, 1376–1384.

Li, B., Xu, L., McIver, R., Wu, Q., & Pan, A. (2020). Green M&A, legitimacy and risk-taking: Evidence from China's heavy polluters. *Accounting and Finance, 60*(1), 97–127.

Lopez de Silanes, F., McCahery, J. A., & Pudschedl, P. C. (2020). ESG performance and disclosure: A cross-country analysis. *Singapore Journal of Legal Studies*, 217–241.

Lu, J. (2021). Can the green merger and acquisition strategy improve the environmental protection investment of listed company? *Environmental Impact Assessment review, 86*.

Ma, R. (2023). The sustainable development trend in environmental, social, and governance issues and stakeholder engagement: Evidence from mergers and acquisitions in China. *Corporate Social Responsibility and Environmental Management, 30*(6), 3159–3173.

Magnanelli, B. S., Nasta, L., & Ramazio, E. (2022). Bid premiums and cumulative abnormal returns: An empirical investigation on the consequences of the Covid-19 pandemic. *Finance Research Letters, 49*, 103093.

Malik, M. F., Anuar, M. A., Khan, S., & Khan, F. (2014). Mergers and acquisitions: A conceptual review. *International Journal of Accounting and Financial Reporting, 4*(2), 520.

Mervelskemper, L., & Streit, D. (2017). Enhancing market valuation of ESG performance: Is integrated reporting keeping its promise? *Business Strategy and the Environment, 26*(4), 536–549.

Mirvis, P. H. (2008). Can you buy CSR? *California Management Review, 51*(1), 109–116.

Perafán-Peñá, H. F., Gill-De-Albornoz, B., & Giner, B. (2022). Earnings management of target firms and deal premiums: The role of industry relatedness. *The British Accounting Review, 54*(2), 101038.

Pfeffer, J., & Salancik, G. R. (1978). *The external control of organizations: A resource dependence perspective*. Harper & Row.

Piñeiro-Chousa, J., López-Cabarcos, M. Á., Caby, J., & Šević, A. (2021). The influence of investor sentiment on the green bond market. *Technological Forecasting and Social Change, 162*, 120351.

Porter, M. E., & Kramer, M. R. (2006). The link between competitive advantage and corporate social responsibility. *Harvard Business Review, 84*(12), 78–92.

PricewaterhouseCoopers, P. W. C. (2022). *The importance of ESG and sustainability in M&A (2022)*. Available at: https://www.pwc.com/jp/en/knowledge/thoughtleadership/assets/pdf/sustainability-ma-report-2022.pdf

Qiao, L., & Wu, J. (2019). Pay for being responsible: The effect of Target Firm's corporate social responsibility on cross-border acquisition premiums. *Sustainability (Switzerland), 11*, 5.

Rahman, J., & Wu, J. (2024). M&A activity and ESG performance: Evidence from China. *Managerial Finance, 50*(1), 179–197.

Rosenbaum, P. R., & Rubin, D. B. (1985). Constructing a control group using multivariate matched sampling methods that incorporate the propensity score. *The American Statistician, 39*(1), 33–38.

Safran SA. (2018). *Integrated Report*. Available at: https://www.safran-group.com/finance/publications-results

Sahin, Ö., Bax, K., Paterlini, S., & Czado, C. (2023). The pitfalls of (non-definitive) Environmental, Social, and Governance scoring methodology. *Global Finance Journal, 56*, 100780.

Salmerón Gómez, R., García Pérez, J., López Martín, M. D. M., & García, C. G. (2016). Collinearity diagnostic applied in ridge estimation through the variance inflation factor. *Journal of Applied Statistics, 43*(10), 1831–1849.

Tampakoudis, I., & Anagnostopoulou, E. (2020). The effect of mergers and acquisitions on environmental, social and governance performance and market value: Evidence from EU acquirers. *Business Strategy and the Environment, 29*(5), 1865–1875.

Tampakoudis, I., Noulas, A., Kiosses, N., & Drogalas, G. (2021). The effect of ESG on value creation from mergers and acquisitions. What changed during the COVID-19 pandemic? *Corporate Governance, 21)6*, 1117–1141.

Teti, E., Dell'Acqua, A., & Bonsi, P. (2022). Detangling the role of environmental, social, and governance factors on M&A performance. *Corporate Social Responsibility and Environmental Management, 29*(5), 1768–1781.

Vastola, V., & Russo, A. (2021). Exploring the effects of mergers and acquisitions on acquirers' sustainability orientation: Embedding, adding, or losing sustainability. *Business Strategy and the Environment, 30*(2), 1094–1104.

Wickert, C., Vaccaro, A., & Cornelissen, J. (2017). "Buying" corporate social responsibility: Organisational identity orientation as a determinant of practice adoption. *Journal of Business Ethics, 142*(3), 497–514.

Yen, T. Y., & André, P. (2019). Market reaction to the effect of corporate social responsibility on mergers and acquisitions: Evidence on emerging markets. *The Quarterly Review of Economics and Finance, 71*, 114–131.

Zhang, T., Zhang, Z., & Yang, J. (2022). When does corporate social responsibility backfire in acquisitions? Signal incongruence and acquirer returns. *Journal of Business Ethics, 175*(1), 45–58.

Chapter 26
Why Go Industry-Specific with ESG Indicators? Testing their Validity and Explanatory Power for Financial Performance

Stefano Calciolari and Massimo Ruberti

26.1 Introduction

The urgent need for concrete action to combat climate change is triggering innovation and practice changes in business and economic research (Aghion et al., 2019). In this context, researchers strive to understand the global economy comprehensively while providing solutions to this evolving challenge involving multiple stakeholders, including investors, managers, employees, consumers, and regulators (Madsen & Ulhøi, 2001). However, the current financial regulations prioritise profit and employment objectives, sometimes to the detriment of environmental concerns.

The Environmental, Social, and Governance (ESG) framework has emerged in business literature and practice to complement the profit-maximising function of economic actors with the evolving objectives towards climate and social change. In other words, the ESG framework is expected to enable businesses to incorporate principles and goals beyond mere financial profit in their decisions and practices, with the underlying assumption that such ability attunes companies to the challenges of the modern era.

In support of this new perspective, financial rating agencies have supplemented their traditional assessments with ESG indicators to measure individual companies' risks within the three pillars and their efforts to improve their exposure. These new systems of metrics are crucial for enhancing capital allocation in more sustainable companies, thereby improving the economic landscape without altering free-market conditions. In fact, any of such measurement systems is intended to categorise companies that grow and prosper while respecting the environment (E) and society

S. Calciolari · M. Ruberti (✉)
Università degli Studi di Milano-Bicocca, Milan, Italy
e-mail: massimo.ruberti@unimib.it

N. Castellano et al. (eds.), *Environmental, Social, Governance (ESG)*, SIDREA Series in Accounting and Business Administration,
https://doi.org/10.1007/978-3-031-76618-3_26

(S) and practising socially conscious governance (G): the three pillars of sustainability. As a result, ESG rating agencies elaborate a wide range of information on ESG performance dimensions, which are then generally aggregated into a single *final score* summarising the level of ESG risk a company faces and the managerial effort put in place to deal with such risk.

However, while a synthetic score can speed up market evaluation, it may conceal relevant information. Indeed, measurement and assessment face several challenges: company-level specificities, significant variability between industry sectors, and the institutional heterogeneity of contexts (e.g., national development level) where companies run their business. In addition, the lack of transparency about data collection and assessment algorithms does not help deal with such challenges.

In this regard, this chapter shows to what extent the disaggregated ESG scores provided by the rating agency MSCI can be valuable in understanding the relationship between financial performance and management efforts to address environmental challenges.

We focus our analysis on the environmental rating of pharmaceutical companies and compare it with the one of chemical companies. The motivation for this sample selection is based on two considerations. First, the pharmaceutical sector is a major contributor to health care and thus to the improvement of human life and economic activity: this raises pharmaceutical companies' political and social salience. Second, the environmental impact of this sector is not sufficiently discussed and represents a growing concern (Belkhir & Elmeligi, 2019). Indeed, compared to other chemical production sectors, pharmaceutical manufacturing generates more waste and by-products, and it is the least efficient in terms of carbon emissions per unit of production (Cue & Zhang, 2009). In addition, the negative environmental impacts of the sector extend throughout the life cycle of pharmaceuticals, with residues entering waterways after human consumption (Kümmerer, 2010).

Based on such premises, one would expect environmental sustainability to be a top priority for both the pharmaceutical industry and regulators. However, surprisingly, the pharmaceutical industry is not included in the EU taxonomy (Calciolari et al., 2024). This omission may be a clue to the general underestimation of the industry's environmental impacts and might reduce the incentives for investors and managers to support relevant climate change initiatives in this sector.

The main objective of this study is twofold. First, it empirically assesses whether aggregated ESG metrics are as useful as disaggregated ones to explain the company's financial risk variability. Second, we examine whether the relationship between ESG metrics and financial risk is industry-specific by comparing evidence from two industries with similar manufacturing processes. In particular, we selected pharmaceutical and (nonpharmaceutical) chemical companies for reasons better explained in Sect. 26.4. The second objective is motivated by the fact that raters identify different material topics for different industries, suggesting that ESG evaluations control for each industry's specificities and thus should be equally effective in detecting relationships between ESG and financial performances across sectors.

The chapter is structured as follows: the next section discusses the extant literature on the role and limitations of ESG rating and presents the consequential justification of our study. Section 26.3 describes the ESG assessment methods adopted by MSCI: we focused on this global rating agency due to data availability at the authors' university, while Sect. 26.4 explains the empirical strategy and shows the descriptive statistics of our sample. Section 26.5 shows the results of a multivariate analysis testing the relationship between firms' financial performance and managerial efforts on environmental themes. Finally, Sect. 26.6 is dedicated to the conclusions.

26.2 Background

26.2.1 Nonfinancial Information and ESG Ratings

As the ESG framework has gained prominence, companies and regulators have sought to understand what information companies need to communicate on sustainability. Such information is commonly referred to as 'nonfinancial information' that is disclosed in sustainability reports. This form of corporate communication, occurring either voluntarily or mandatorily, is variegated because it is conceptually broad and due to the variety of stakeholders interested in a business. The potential ESG information users include the surrounding community, employees, financial business partners, social organisations, other business associates, government entities, consumers, and, more importantly, investors (Dragomir, 2011; Gray et al., 2014; Montiel & Delgado-Ceballos, 2014). Different stakeholders are concerned with various aspects of a company's sustainability performance. For example, the surrounding community may be interested in the local environment, such as safety and health risks, local pollution levels, and procedures for addressing complaints on the matter. At the same time, employees are mainly concerned about occupational health, job prospects, professional training, risk management, and disaster prevention. Consumers may seek information about the production processes' respect for human rights, product safety, and global environmental responsibility. Other business associates are interested in the company's policy and management practices related to sustainability. Financial business partners, banks, and investors focus on financial risk management and performance, as well as the financial impact of environmental and social factors (Haidar et al., 2021).

In these conditions, companies seek guidance on disclosing a balanced level of ESG information. However, even an excessive level of disclosure may have adverse effects. Considering that, in addition to financial statements and sustainability reports, further communication channels have already become routine for businesses (e.g., social media interactions and traditional media outlets), information overload is risky due to stakeholders' limitations in processing information effectively. This may result in reduced decision-making efficiency, perplexity, and disengagement (Seo et al., 2019). Too much information can hide essential details, causing stakeholder confusion or misunderstanding. It may also undermine stakeholder trust if they suspect the company is using information overload to hide negative news, pretending to be more transparent than it actually is (a scheme known as 'greenwashing').

In this regard, ESG rating agencies play a fundamental role in sustainable investing and corporate responsibility. These agencies rate companies' ESG performance by evaluating their environmental practices, social initiatives, and governance structures. For instance, Henry Fernandez, CEO of the rating agency MSCI, states that his company's mission includes empowering better investment decisions by providing a wide range of tools that clients can use to make their portfolios and companies more sustainable (MSCI, 2023a). The evaluation process generally relies on a wide range of information, including sustainability reports. The result of this evaluation consists of ESG scores or ratings, which provide a concise assessment of companies' alignment with sustainable and responsible business practices. More specifically, the assessment consists of two conceptually different tasks performed for any company: (a) the identification of ESG risks associated with the business activities; (b) the evaluation and rating of the actual practices enacted to deal with ESG risks.

Responsible investors (Renneboog et al., 2008) rely on these ratings (or scores) to make informed investment decisions: companies with high ESG scores are favoured by responsible investors, who perceive them as well positioned for long-term success and aligned with their values (Lins et al., 2017). High ratings can be a source of pride for companies, favouring a positive perception by investors and partners, customers and labour. In contrast, low ESG ratings can raise red flags, signalling financial and reputational risks such as regulatory challenges, legal issues, or consumer backlash. As a result, ESG rating agencies became catalysts for encouraging companies to improve their sustainability practices and disclosure.

26.2.2 Major Issues Regarding ESG Metrics

On 23rd October 2023, Aswath Damodaran warned: '*ESG scores today measure everything —consequently, they measure nothing*'. (Financial Times, 2023). Despite ESG ratings' growing importance in orienting financial market actors, persistent criticism remains rooted in their information power. Indeed, the scores provided by different rating agencies frequently exhibit substantial inconsistencies (Berg et al., 2022; Chatterji et al., 2016; Christensen et al., 2022). The discrepancies mainly revolve around the lack of correlation and convergence between the indicators proposed by different raters.

There are several explanations for such a situation. Tsang et al. (2022) pointed out three main issues: the significant variations in ESG assessment standards, the disparities in data collection methods, and the overall opacity and divergence in their analytical approaches. Kotsantonis and Serafeim (2019) listed four major problems with ESG data: (1) the extensive range and lack of uniformity in companies' data, metrics, and reporting practices; (2) the lack of transparency among data providers in defining companies' peer groups and the arbitrary ranges of best and worst performance that determine the benchmark for the sample's ESG—ranges derived from defining either companies' reference peer groups or absolute levels of performance; (3) the heterogeneous analytical approaches used to fill substantial data gaps across companies, and the different time frames characterising different ESG metrics; (4) the ESG raters' disagreement on data materiality rising along with the increasing available information. The first two aspects, per se, can significantly alter the ranking of a company's performance, thus undermining the reliability of ESG scores, while the third point may result in significant discrepancies between data sources. The last aspect calls for a better understanding of the materiality notion used to generate ESG metrics.

This chapter focuses on materiality, assuming that general ESG metrics used for any type of company may be less appropriate than industry-specific ESG metrics (Khan et al., 2016). This argument was recently made also in the ESG financial materiality standard developed by the Sustainability Accounting Standard Board (SASB) (Schiehll & Kolahgar, 2021). Already a decade ago, Eccles et al. (2012) highlighted 'the need for sector-specific materiality and sustainability reporting standards'. They argued that the development of industry-specific guidelines identifying material sustainability topics and the related data and key performance indicators (KPIs) would have improved corporate ESG reporting. Such guidelines should recognise that specific topics, such as climate change, are more important in some sectors than others, if not from one company to another. Therefore, environmental performance metrics are complex in terms of ESG assessment and risk management, and a 'one-size-fits-all' approach appears to fall short (Capelle-Blancard & Petit, 2017). Therefore, industry-specific guidelines are expected to better orient companies towards effective ESG best practices and their appropriate disclosure. This industry-level approach identifies common sustainability challenges and opportunities for companies characterised by similar business models, regulatory environments, and product offerings.

26.2.3 Study Justification

The relationship between ESG ratings and financial performance has been analysed from different perspectives. The main body of literature deals with the relationship between ESG performance and profitability, while other research streams focus on the association of ESG ratings with cash flow management, cost of capital, and corporate risk (Saini et al., 2023). The literature results are often inconsistent and strongly influenced by settings and indicators chosen. For instance, as pointed out by Albertini (2013), studies focused on the environmental performance of firms can be grouped into two categories: some works deal with management efforts in terms of actions (e.g., certification or process change), while others focus on the effects of such actions (e.g., reduction of environmental impact). Our study uses a dataset that considers both aspects and focuses on the environmental pillar.

Our study aims to empirically test the limits of ESG metrics in explaining financial performance. In particular, we test the influence of environmental performance (i.e., E pillar) and financial risk using two alternative ESG metrics: (a) Aggregated environmental performance, controlling for aggregated social and governance performance; (b) Environmental *risk management,* controlling for environmental *risk exposure*, aggregated social and governance performance. We performed the analyses with the two alternative metrics using a sample of companies from two industries (pharmaceutical and chemical) and, separately, the groups of companies from each industry.

We focused on the relationship between financial risk and environmental risk management because of the gap in the literature, where this topic is underinvestigated. As recently implied by EBA (2021) ('environmental, social or governance matters [. . .] may have a positive or negative impact on the financial performance or solvency of an entity, sovereign or individual'), the relation between these two dimensions is not clear though relevant in terms of business sustainability.

In our analysis, we try to answer the following three research questions:

RQ1: Are disaggregated environmental performance measures more useful than aggregated ones in explaining financial risk?

RQ2: Are management's efforts to mitigate material environmental risks associated with financial risk?

RQ3: Can environmental performance equally explain companies' financial risk across industries?

We expect to find disaggregated measures more useful in explaining financial risk but not equally valuable for explaining this financial performance across industries. In addition, we expect a positive relationship between environmental risk management and company solvency because more solid and risk-averse companies may be more cautious in dealing with environmental risks. This is coherent with Maaloul et al. (2023), stating that more leveraged firms disclose more ESG information to maintain legitimacy for obtaining debt easily (Fig. 26.1).

26.3 The MSCI Rating Framework

MSCI's ESG ratings result from a systematic approach aimed at identifying industry frontrunners (scoring AAA or AA), moderate performers (A, BBB, BB), and underperformers (scoring B, CCC) based on two assessment dimensions: the business exposure to ESG risks and the actual practices adopted to manage such risks. ESG risks are differently distributed across industries and individual companies.

MSCI's ESG rating model discerns the ESG risks (often referred to as 'Key Issues') that are material for each specific sector, industry or subindustry—based on the Global Industry Classification Standard (GICS®). More specifically, the model articulates the ESG risks by identifying, for each pillar—E (Environmental), S (Social), and G (Governance)—the Key Issues that are most pertinent to each

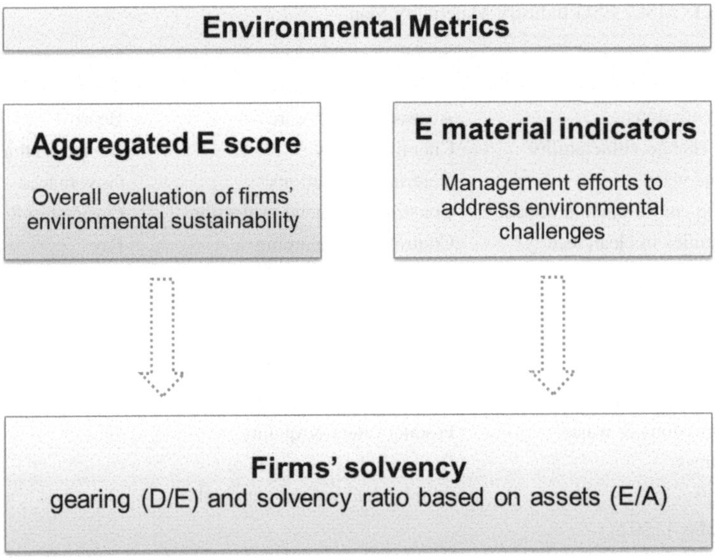

Fig. 26.1 Graphical representation of the investigative research aim. Source: Authors' own elaboration

industry. The approach is synthesised in the ESG Industry Materiality Map (MSCI, 2023b). Each map identifies the key issues specific to an industry and the respective weights determining the relevance assumed in the assessment of each pillar. Therefore, the ESG assessment of two industries, even if similar in production processes, can be differently evaluated in terms of environmental responsibility via its specific materiality map. This process relies on the most up-to-date data, extensive research, and insights gathered through company consultations and publicly available information (MSCI, 2023c). The rest of the section will provide a qualitative description of this model to understand better how we select the disaggregated data in the empirical section.

Table 26.1 lists all the Key Issues included in the overall MSCI's ESG Materiality Map articulated in the three ESG pillars. Each issue has its materiality level (a weight expressed with a percentage) depending on the sector or industry-specific relevance within the rating system: a key issue can be weighted zero per cent if deemed unimportant.

Table 26.2 shows the Materiality Maps of the two industries under investigation: the pharmaceutical industry (including biotechnological companies, hereafter labelled BioPharma) and the chemical one (hereafter Chemicals). Notably, few key issues are considered material (i.e., having a non-zero weight) among the complete list, and only one environmental issue is material for both industries: toxic emissions & waste.

A brief description of these material issues included in the two materiality maps is reported in Table 26.3.

Table 26.1 MSCI ESG Industry Materiality Map

Environmental	Social	Governance
Biodiversity & land use	Access to finance	Accounting
Carbon emissions	Access to health care	Board
Climate change vulnerability	Chemical safety	Business ethics
Electronic waste	Community relations	Governance
Financing environmental impact	Consumer financial protection	Ownership & control
Opportunities in clean tech	Controversial sourcing	Pay
Opportunities in green building	Health & safety	Tax transparency
Opportunities in renewable energy	Human capital development	
Packaging material & waste	Labour management	
Product carbon footprint	Opportunities in nutrition & health	
Raw material sourcing	Privacy & data security	
Toxic emissions & waste	Product safety & quality	
Water stress	Responsible investment	
	Supply chain labour standards	

Source: MSCI (2023)

Table 26.2 MSCI ESG Materiality Map of the two industries

Environmental	Social	Governance
(a) Pharmaceuticals & biotechnology industry		
Toxic Emissions & Waste	Access to health care	Governance
	Human capital development	
	Product Safety & Quality	
(b) Chemical industry		
Carbon emissions	Chemical safety	Governance
Opportunities in clean tech		
Toxic Emissions & Waste		
Water stress		

Source: MSCI (2023)

Coherently with the focus of our study, we selected the environmental pillar, and Table 26.4 explains the assessment methodology for the four environmental material issues in the two investigated industries.

As anticipated, each issue is assessed based on the extent of a company's exposure to the particular risk/opportunity associated with the issue and the management measures taken to mitigate such exposure. While the former mainly depends on exogenous factors (such as industry-specific activities or business processes' reliance on natural resources), the latter directly depends on the company's management willingness and capacity to implement and effectively communicate its ESG practices. Therefore, one should expect the second factor—rather than the first one—to discriminate against virtuous companies.

Table 26.3 Material issues for Chemical and BioPharma companies

Pillar	Industry	Material issue	Companies are evaluated on ...
Environment	Chemicals	Carbon emissions	The carbon intensity of their operations and their efforts to manage climate-related risks and opportunities.
	Chemicals	Opportunities in clean tech	Their clean tech innovation capacity, strategic development initiatives, and revenue generated from clean technologies.
	Chemicals BioPharma	Toxic emissions & waste	The potential environmental contamination and toxic or carcinogenic emissions arising from their operations and the strength of their environmental management systems.
	Chemicals	Water stress	The water intensity of their operations, the water stress in their areas of operation, and their efforts to manage water-related risks and opportunities.
Social	Chemicals	Chemical safety	The possible presence of harmful chemicals in their product portfolio, their potential exposure to strengthening or pending chemical regulations, and their efforts to develop less harmful alternatives.
	BioPharma	Access to health care	Their efforts to expand health care products and services to developing countries and underserved markets (e.g., low regional physician concentration), including equitable pricing mechanisms, patents, capacity advancement, and product donations.
	BioPharma	Human capital development	Their workforce talent requirements and their ability to attract, retain, and develop a highly skilled workforce.
	BioPharma	Product safety & quality	Their exposure to possible recalls or product safety concerns, the strength of their supply chain and sourcing systems, their quality management efforts in manufacturing and their responsible marketing practices.
Governance	Chemicals BioPharma	Governance	Companies' corporate governance and business ethics practices have on investors. All companies are assessed on all governance key issues, including Ownership & Control, board, pay, accounting, business ethics, and tax transparency.

Source: MSCI (2023)

26.4 Methods and Sample

26.4.1 Empirical Strategy

We selected two sectors with similar production processes but politically different markets: the pharmaceutical and chemical industries. The comparison is intended to highlight differences that are unlikely related to the manufacturing processes, thus

Table 26.4 MSCI assessment methodology of the environmental material issues for the two sectors

Toxic emissions & waste	Opportunities in clean tech	Carbon emissions	Water stress
Risk exposure indicators			
Percentage of operations in business segments associated with generating air pollutants and hazardous waste	Business segments addressing clean technologies like energy efficiency or industrial automation	Percentage of operations in business segments with high carbon intensity	Water input of the business lines, asset-weighted
	Operations in markets with policy incentives for relevant technologies	Operations in countries with pending or strong carbon regulation	Operations located in high water stress areas such as Australia, asset-weighted
Risk management indicators			
Policies to increase recycling and address environmental impacts	Clean technology strategy adoption	Carbon efficiency targets and programs	Water optimisation program in own operation, risk assessment
Reduction targets, monitoring, and implementation mechanisms	R&D spending as a proportion of revenue, extent of clean tech focus of R&D spending	Reported carbon efficiency performance	Programs with local communities
Environmental management systems to manage toxic by-products and regular audits	Involvement in, and revenues derived from clean technologies		Water efficiency performance
Performance: Toxic emissions intensity and trend (SOx, NOx, VOC, haz. wastes)			

Note: The grey shadowed column reports the issues material for both industries, while the white shadowed columns report the issue material only for chemical companies
Source: MSCI (2023)

reasonably excluding such factors, but more likely related to the fact that the pharmaceutical industry has a different political salience. We think this is highlighted by the fact that the pharmaceutical industry is not included in the EU taxonomy, while this is not the case for the chemical industry (Calciolari et al., 2024).

As dependent variables, we chose two financial ratios of corporate solvency: leverage (debt/equity) and solvency ratio based on assets (equity/assets). As main regressors, we selected the disaggregated material scores that MSCI assigns to the companies in the sample to measure their ability to manage material environmental risks (such as toxic emissions and waste management). We control for the level of risk exposure of the companies in their material environmental issues and for the year, size, profitability, and the scores of the other two ESG pillars: social and governance. Equation (26.1) stylises the fixed-effects panel used for our estimation.

$$Solvency_{it} = \alpha + \beta\ RiskManagement_{it} + \gamma\ RiskExposure_{it} + \eta\ CV_{it} + \epsilon_{it} \quad (26.1)$$

The subscripts *i and t* indicate, respectively, the firm (or case) and the year of the observation. *RiskManagement* is the main regressor and accounts for the managerial efforts to reduce material Environmental risk, while *RiskExposure* is the control variable accounting for the level of firms' exposure to material Environmental risk; and CV_{it} is a vector of time-varying control variables: Total assets, Number of workers, ROA, Social Score, Governance Score. Finally, ϵ_{it}, is the error term clustered at a company level, while β, γ, η are estimated coefficients, and α a constant term.

26.4.2 The Sample

Our primary source is the MSCI database, providing data over a period spanning from 2013 to 2022. As already mentioned, we selected companies from two sectors: pharmaceutical and biotechnology companies (BioPharma) and chemical companies (Chemicals). We complemented this data with financial variables obtained from the Orbis BvD database. The merge between MSCI and Orbis data was performed using the ISIN code of each company as a unique identifier. Notably, only 4.96% of companies had to be excluded or omitted when merging the two datasets because not all the companies included in one database are also available in the other.

The sample consists of 1250 cases: 781 BioPharma and 469 chemical companies. MSCI has thoroughly evaluated each company in this sample over an average of 4.8 years during the 10-year observation period, with a total number of observations equal to 6039. This extended observation period allows for the exploitation of information entangled in the variability of ESG performance and financial performances over time.

The sample includes companies from all over the world (see Table 26.5). It is worth noting that American companies are the most represented in BioPharma, while Asian companies are predominant in Chemicals and hold the second position in BioPharma.

Table 26.6 provides a longitudinal view of the basic descriptives of the financial control variables for the two industry groups.

Regarding sample size, the number of BioPharma companies ranges from 155 in 2013 to 530 in 2022, while Chemical companies range from 158 in 2013 to 348 in 2022. These figures reflect changes in the composition and inclusion of firms over the observation period and explain the declining numbers in the financial metrics: the two industries are not declining in value, but the widening of MSCI's database has been catching smaller companies over time.

For BioPharma companies, the mean value of total assets starts at $10,181.1 million in 2013 and ends at $5383.0 million in 2022. The average number of employees ranges from 10,894.6 in 2013 to 5346.0 in 2022. Chemical firms show a general downward trend also in the mean values of observed variables. The total

Table 26.5 Regional distribution of BioPharma and chemical firms across industry segments

Geographic region	BioPharma		Chemicals		
	Biotechnology	Pharmaceuticals	Commodity chemicals	Diversified chemicals	Specialty chemicals
Americas	322	119	24	8	63
Asia	57	160	148	26	114
Europe	53	49	17	6	50
Oceania	9	7	2	1	5
Africa	0	5	0	2	3
Sub-Total	441	340	191	43	235
Total	781		469		

Source: MSCI (2023)

assets vary from \$8974.5 million in 2013 to \$7633.6 million in 2022, and the average number of workers or employees ranges from 12,666.2 in 2013 to 10,066.3 in 2022. The average value of ROA of the two industries is very different: chemical companies, on average, are scoring positive results, while the BioPharma profitability ratio is negative.

Table 26.7 presents the key statistics for the two dependent variables of our study:

a) Asset-based Solvency ratio:

$$\frac{\text{Shareholders' equity}}{\text{Total assets}}$$

b) Gearing:

$$\frac{\text{Noncurrent liabilities} + \text{Loans\&short term debt}}{\text{Shareholders' equity}}$$

It also displays the statistics of the main explanatory variable used in the model specifications: the aggregated Environmental pillar score; the only material managerial in common in the two industries (Toxic emissions and waste management); and the further three disaggregated scores, material for the chemical industry only.

For the Solvency ratio, Chemical firms have an average of 49.52% with moderate variability, ranging from −79.36% (indicating potential financial distress) to 99.96% (highlighting solid financial health). In contrast, BioPharma firms exhibit a slightly higher average Solvency ratio of 58.17%, with more variability (ranging from −99.77% to 98.93%).

Regarding the Gearing variable, Chemical firms show an average ratio of 92.15% with significant variability, ranging from 0% (no debt) to 971.67% (indicating substantial debt). BioPharma firms have an average Gearing ratio of 64.07%, with considerable variability (ranging from 0% to 981.58%).

Notably, these two ratios are inversely correlated: a firm is less risky when the solvency ratio is high and gearing is low. This also affects how the regression coefficients are read in the next section.

Table 26.6 Financial metrics comparison between BioPharma and Chemical firms (2013–2022)

Year	BioPharma Firms				Chemical firms			
	N.	Avg. Total Asset[a]	Avg. N. worker	Avg. ROA	N.	Avg. Total Asset[a]	Avg. N. worker	Avg. ROA
2013	155	10,181.09	10,894.60	−8.61%	158	8,974.46	12,666.24	7.42%
2014	188	8,554.55	9,083.50	−8.03%	158	8,699.61	12,439.36	6.74%
2015	242	7,449.07	7,501.70	−7.74%	152	8,407.10	12,198.28	6.63%
2016	283	6,744.69	6,652.70	−12.08%	185	6,968.44	10,801.64	7.14%
2017	291	6,847.89	6,554.40	−12.83%	200	9,217.15	11,196.87	8.27%
2018	374	6,128.75	6,528.30	−10.02%	270	8,255.79	10,532.16	8.08%
2019	407	6,042.07	6,216.00	−11.65%	283	7,931.96	10,169.59	6.70%
2020	472	5,893.00	6,150.50	−9.39%	287	8,459.41	10,579.57	4.75%
2021	563	5,252.47	5,271.40	−12.24%	327	8,067.12	9,843.64	9.70%
2022	530	5,382.96	5,346.00	−13.59%	348	7,633.57	10,066.33	8.88%

[a] Millions of US$

Source: Orbis BvD (2023)

Table 26.7 Descriptive statistics of the two alternative dependent variables and the main explanatory variables used in the different model specifications

		Dependent variables		*Main explanatory variables*				
		Solvency ratio*	Gearing*	Environmental pillar	Toxic emission management	Carbon emissions management	Water stress management	Opportunities in clean tech management
BioPharma	N	3481	3265	3599	3577	3152	1026	4
	Mean	58.17	64.07	4.83	3.14	2.85	3.20	3.65
	Min	−99.77	0.00	0.00	0.00	0.00	0.00	0.00
	Max	98.93	981.58	10.00	10.00	8.20	10.00	7.10
	S.D.	30.20	114.48	1.62	1.21	1.81	2.28	3.67
Chemical	N	2364	2306	2427	2403	2419	2130	2388
	Mean	49.52	92.15	4.24	4.57	4.76	3.55	3.83
	Min	−79.36	0.00	0.30	0.00	0.80	0.00	0.00
	Max	99.96	971.67	8.90	10.00	9.30	10.00	10.00
	S.D.	20.11	107.84	1.50	1.44	2.16	1.54	2.04
Full sample	N	5845	5571	6026	5980	5571	3156	2392
	Mean	54.67	75.70	4.59	3.71	3.68	3.44	3.83
	Min	−99.77	0.00	0.00	0.00	0.00	0.00	0.00
	Max	99.96	981.58	10.00	10.00	9.30	10.00	10.00
	S.D.	26.92	112.62	1.60	1.49	2.19	1.82	2.04

Note: Solvency Ratio and Gearing values are excluded from the next analysis when Equity is negative (3.34% of the observation)
Source: MSCI (2023) and Orbis BvD (2023)

Table 26.8 displays the descriptive statistics of the control variables used in the different model specifications. The main control variables regard the exposure level to material environmental risk companies suffer in the two sectors. Other control variables are the financial proxy of size (total assets and number of workers), profitability (ROA), and the scores in the Social and Governance pillars.

According to the reported average scores in Tables 26.7 and 26.8, chemical companies are more exposed to environmental risks but seem to put more effort into managing their specific environmental issues.

26.5 Results

This section shows the results of our modelling of the relationship between companies' management commitment to addressing material ESG risks and the financial risk measured by two different financial ratios: asset-based Solvency Ratio and Gearing. We analysed whether management's response to material environmental risks influences financial solvency/risk using different models and samples to test the analysis' sensitivity to measurement approach and industry selection.

Our analysis's benchmark consists of using the aggregated Environmental score as main explanatory variable of the two financial ratios. None of the three different sample specifications (see Table 26.12 and 26.13 in the Appendix) show evidence that the Environmental Pillar influences the company's solvency. Therefore, the aggregate metric does not seem to have explanatory power with respect to the considered financial performance.

Further, we replaced the aggregated measure with the disaggregated metrics of the environmental pillar in our models. We analysed the dependent variables with two different model specifications (without and with control variables) using three alternative data settings: (1) the full sample of companies; (2) only BioPharma companies; (3) only Chemical companies.

In the first analytical step, we considered the data set covering both sectors together. It is important to highlight that, when using the whole sample, it is impossible to consider all the material issues for the chemicals industry because the data concerning 'clean tech opportunities' and 'water stress' are both non-material and too scarce for the BioPharma sector. Table 26.9 shows the results of the fixed-effects regressions. Columns 1 and 3 consider the solvency ratio as the dependent variable (respectively, with and without control factors), while columns 2 and 4 consider the gearing ratio. The coefficients of the two exposure variables show the expected signs and are significant, thus supporting the hypothesis that management's environmental efforts influence companies' solvency. However, the effect of Toxic emission management on gearing is not significant in the full model (column 4).

The next step consists of applying the same models separately to the companies of each industry. In this way, it is possible to include further material issues for the Chemicals group and to check whether our previous results (shown in Table 26.9)

Table 26.8 Descriptive statistics of the control variables used in the different model specifications

		Main control variables				*Other control variables*				
		Toxic emission exposure	Carbon emissions exposure	Water stress exposure	Opportunities in Clean Tech exposure	Social Pillar	Governance Pillar	Assets (Mln.$)	Workers	ROA
BioPharma	N	3593	3163	2990	2741	3602	3599	3505	3131	3404
	Mean	5.24	2.40	4.09	1.94	4.25	4.39	6343	6518.64	–11.09%
	Min	0.00	0.00	0.00	0.00	0.40	0.00	0.00	1.00	–99.77%
	Max	8.64	6.10	9.20	7.90	9.30	10.00	197,205.00	152,700.00	82.41%
	SD	1.44	0.57	1.09	2.40	0.77	1.66	21,374.61	18,061.41	28.58
Chemical	N	2418	2417	2150	2415	2427	2426	2368	1902	2364
	Mean	8.27	6.20	6.10	3.75	3.07	5.22	8192	10,776.97	7.57%
	Min	0.70	0.42	1.20	0.00	0.00	0.00	11.80	44.00	–72.63%
	Max	10.00	10.00	10.00	7.90	10.00	10.00	192,164.00	122,404.00	77.48%
	SD	1.49	1.59	1.44	1.42	2.23	2.11	14,742.54	14,943.67	8.75
Full sample	N	6011	5580	5140	5156	6029	6025	5873	5033	5768
	Mean	6.46	4.04	4.93	2.78	3.78	4.72	7089	8127.89	–3.44%
	Min	0.00	0.00	0.00	0.00	0.00	0.00	0.00	1.00	–99.77%
	Max	10.00	10.00	10.00	7.90	10.00	10.00	197,205.00	152,700.00	82.41%
	SD	2.08	2.20	1.59	2.20	1.64	1.90	19,001.68	17,074.52	24.45

Source: MSCI (2023) and Orbis BvD (2023)

Table 26.9 Fixed-effect panel regression results: Whole sample and common material indicator

	(1)	(2)	(3)	(4)
Variables	Solvency ratio	Gearing	Solvency ratio	Gearing
Toxic emission management	0.587**	−3.469**	0.477	−3.250*
	(0.267)	(1.576)	(0.295)	(1.972)
Toxic emission exposure			0.500	−2.512
			(0.419)	(2.309)
Social pillar score			0.183	−1.082
			(0.277)	(1.766)
Governance pillar score			0.0760	0.325
			(0.199)	(1.239)
Total assets			−4.154***	16.62**
			(1.505)	(7.850)
Workers			0.0000685	0.000287
			(0.000117)	(0.000777)
ROA			0.247***	−0.886***
			(0.0317)	(0.196)
Control for year (base = 2013)	YES	YES	YES	YES
Constant	58.06***	72.20***	112.6***	−147.2
	(1.222)	(7.304)	(20.85)	(106.8)
Observations	5619	5520	4752	4677
R-squared	0.017	0.006	0.082	0.028
Number of company	1208	1202	1008	1004

Robust standard errors in parentheses
*** $p < 0.01$, ** $p < 0.05$, * $p < 0.1$

hold for each industry. When analysing the BioPharma group (Table 26.10), results are almost consistent with the full sample: evidence supports a positive relationship between companies' efforts to manage toxic and carbon emissions and financial solvency, but the negative relationship between toxic emission management and gearing is not significant.

When replicating the same analysis on the Chemicals group, results (Table 26.11) show scarce evidence of a relationship between environmental management efforts and financial solvency. In particular, only Carbon emission management and Water stress emission are significantly associated with gearing, but with opposite signs (and the positive sign of the latter is unexpected). Considering that we purposely selected the two sectors characterised by similar production processes, these results suggest that either the relationship between financial performance and environmental sustainability efforts may be industry-sensitive or the environmental sustainability measures are not equally effective in capturing the managerial effort across industries.

The matter of sustainability measurement is not secondary. On the one hand, as already mentioned, Tables 26.12 and 26.13 (in the Appendix) show no evidence supporting the investigated relationships. On the other hand, results on the use of disaggregated ESG metrics show mixed evidence depending on the data set used. This confirms the importance of investigating ESG data at a disaggregated level for

Table 26.10 Fixed-effect panel regression results: BioPharma companies and disaggregated Environmental material indicators

	(1)	(2)	(3)	(4)
Variables	Solvency ratio	Gearing	Solvency ratio	Gearing
Toxic emission management	1.168**	−4.561*	1.100**	−4.717
	(0.456)	(2.606)	(0.505)	(3.329)
Toxic emission exposure			0.545	−2.763
			(0.570)	(3.478)
Social pillar score			0.405	−1.505
			(0.827)	(5.901)
Governance pillar score			0.590	−0.713
			(0.373)	(2.163)
Total assets			−2.567	7.656
			(1.764)	(9.314)
Workers			0.0000930	0.000315
			(0.000096805)	(0.000965)
ROA			0.213***	−0.639***
			(0.0344)	(0.223)
Control for year (base = 2013)	YES	YES	YES	YES
Constant	63.64***	58.70***	92.83***	−26.94
	(1.987)	(11.80)	(23.79)	(121.2)
Observations	3300	3236	2883	2829
R-squared	0.036	0.007	0.085	0.018
Number of company	761	759	649	646

Robust standard errors in parentheses
*** $p < 0.01$, ** $p < 0.05$, * $p < 0.1$

measuring sustainability practices on material themes. In addition, it highlights the priority of defining industry-specific valid measures of sustainability and eventually considering company-specific metrics when appropriate to capture the sustainability value of specific managerial practices.

26.6 Conclusions

With the growing urgency of tackling climate change, companies are at a crossroads where addressing the environmental impact of their operations is paramount. The challenge is to manage environmental, social, and governance (ESG) risks while maintaining robust financial performance. This chapter investigates the relationship between environmental sustainability performance and financial solvency by comparing alternative measures of the environmental dimension applied to different data settings. The results of the study have led to several key takeaways.

First and foremost, it is worth noting that the assessment of the overall environmental pillar, as measured by the aggregated E pillar metrics, does not appear to help predict a company's solvency. This observation holds across different model

Table 26.11 Fixed-effect panel regression results: Chemical companies and disaggregated Environmental material indicators

	(1)	(2)	(3)	(4)
Variables	Solvency ratio	Gearing	Solvency ratio	Gearing
Toxic emission management	−0.149	0.343	−0.156	0.514
	(0.270)	(1.512)	(0.272)	(1.524)
Carbon emission management	0.404*	−3.936*	0.442*	−4.177*
	(0.236)	(2.101)	(0.237)	(2.145)
Water stress management	−0.386	3.381*	−0.362	3.215*
	(0.278)	(1.901)	(0.285)	(1.928)
Clean opportunities management	0.0286	−3.011	−0.0110	−2.868
	(0.412)	(2.641)	(0.415)	(2.683)
Toxic emission exposure			0.389	−4.279
			(0.509)	(3.049)
Carbon emission exposure			−0.517	3.808
			(0.437)	(3.468)
Water stress exposure			0.310	−1.178
			(0.373)	(3.235)
Clean opportunities exposure			−0.367	1.263
			(0.471)	(2.571)
Social pillar score	−0.0908	1.410	−0.110	1.448
	(0.252)	(1.613)	(0.247)	(1.648)
Governance pillar score	−0.185	−0.205	−0.171	−0.311
	(0.214)	(1.935)	(0.216)	(1.948)
Total assets	−5.081*	17.87	−5.067*	17.93
	(2.762)	(13.67)	(2.778)	(13.68)
Workers	0.000101	−0.000241	0.0000804	−0.000122
	(0.000178)	(0.00106)	(0.000168)	(0.00102)
ROA	0.443***	−2.915***	0.437***	−2.895***
	(0.0561)	(0.403)	(0.0552)	(0.402)
Constant	121.1***	−130.9	121.0***	−119.1
	(39.11)	(194.2)	(39.93)	(192.9)
Control for year (base = 2013)	YES	YES	YES	YES
Observations	1669	1653	1667	1651
R-squared	0.181	0.134	0.185	0.136
Number of companies	347	346	347	346

Robust standard errors in parentheses
*** $p < 0.01$, ** $p < 0.05$, * $p < 0.1$

specifications and data settings. Therefore, the overall E pillar score does not help explain a company's financial solvency. This implies that without granular information on the managerial efforts towards environmental sustainability, it is unlikely to predict financial consequences with an aggregated sustainability measure.

Second, results show that the influence of specific management's environmental efforts on a company's relevant financial performance dimension is more detectable. In particular, companies that actively manage material environmental issues tend to have better solvency. However, this result does not hold across different measures of financial risk. In fact, the influence of environmental efforts on gearing does not hold across model specifications, although showing consistently the expected direction.

Third, the study highlights the importance of using industry-specific sustainability metrics. As a matter of fact, different patterns emerge when looking at different sectors, such as Chemicals and BioPharma. In the BioPharma sector, there is a rather consistent positive relationship between efforts to manage material environmental aspects and solvency. Conversely, there is no evidence of such a relationship in the Chemicals sector.

In conclusion, this chapter highlights that industry-specific material issues can be more useful than aggregated ones in explaining financial risk, but environmental performance might explain companies' financial risk differently across industries. As sustainability awareness grows, our findings can contribute to the evolving discourse on how companies can effectively balance ESG considerations with financial performance and how disaggregated values might be valuable to researchers.

Appendix

Table 26.12 Fixed-effect panel regression results. Solvency ratio and Environmental Pillar score in three sample specifications

	(1)	(3)	(2)
Variables	Whole sample	BioPharma	Chemical
Environmental pillar score	0.225	0.205	−0.0220
	(0.330)	(0.411)	(0.472)
Social pillar score	0.183	0.569	0.188
	(0.266)	(0.805)	(0.262)
Governance pillar score	0.0722	0.597	−0.129
	(0.201)	(0.376)	(0.171)
Total assets	−4.057***	−2.399	−6.190***
	(1.501)	(1.752)	(2.370)
Workers	8.23e-05	0.000106	0.000108
	(0.000124)	(0.0000978)	(0.000183)
ROA	0.250***	0.215***	0.392***
	(0.0316)	(0.0343)	(0.0539)
Constant	115.2***	95.07***	138.9***
	(20.50)	(23.16)	(33.39)
Control for year (base = 2013)	YES	YES	YES
Observations	4776	2895	1881
R-squared	0.079	0.081	0.166
Number of companies	1015	652	366

Robust standard errors in parentheses
*** $p < 0.01$, ** $p < 0.05$, * $p < 0.1$

Table 26.13 Fixed-effect panel regression results. Gearing and Environmental Pillar score in three sample specifications

Variables	(1) Whole sample	(3) BioPharma	(2) Chemical
Environmental pillar score	−1.525	−0.565	−2.491
	(2.274)	(2.768)	(3.324)
Social pillar score	−1.118	−2.117	−0.541
	(1.730)	(5.742)	(1.514)
Governance pillar score	0.354	−0.751	0.105
	(1.251)	(2.184)	(1.586)
Total assets	16.47**	7.220	32.18**
	(7.811)	(9.229)	(13.47)
Workers	0.000188	0.000249	−0.000280
	(0.000809)	(0.000969)	(0.00112)
ROA	−0.899***	−0.649***	−2.323***
	(0.195)	(0.222)	(0.357)
Constant	−165.6	−44.09	−366.2*
	(102.9)	(116.8)	(188.2)
Control for year (base = 2013)	YES	YES	YES
Observations	4701	2841	1860
R-squared	0.026	0.016	0.110
Number of companies	1011	649	365

Robust standard errors in parentheses
*** $p < 0.01$, ** $p < 0.05$, * $p < 0.1$

References

Aghion, P., Hepburn, C., Teytelboym, A., & Zenghelis, D. (2019). Path dependence, innovation and the economics of climate change. Handbook on green growth, 6783.

Albertini, E. (2013). Does environmental management improve financial performance? A meta-analytical review. *Organization & Environment, 26*(4), 431457.

Belkhir, L., & Elmeligi, A. (2019). Carbon footprint of the global pharmaceutical industry and relative impact of its major players. *Journal of Cleaner Production, 214*, 185–194.

Berg, F., Koelbel, J. F., & Rigobon, R. (2022). Aggregate confusion: The divergence of ESG ratings. *Review of Finance, 26*(6), 13151344.

Calciolari, S., Cesarini, M., & Ruberti, M. (2024). Sustainability disclosure in the pharmaceutical and chemical industries: Results from bibliometric analysis and AI-based comparison of financial reports. *Journal of Cleaner Production, 447*, 141511.

Capelle-Blancard, G., & Petit, A. (2017). The weighting of CSR dimensions: One size does not fit all. *Business & Society, 56*(6), 919–943.

Chatterji, A. K., Durand, R., Levine, D. I., & Touboul, S. (2016). Do ratings of firms converge? Implications for managers, investors and strategy researchers. *Strategic Management Journal, 37*(8), 15971614.

Christensen, D. M., Serafeim, G., & Sikochi, A. (2022). Why is corporate virtue in the eye of the beholder? The case of ESG ratings. *The Accounting Review, 97*(1), 147175.

Cue, B. W., & Zhang, J. (2009). Green process chemistry in the pharmaceutical industry. *Green Chemistry Letters and Reviews, 2*(4), 193–211.

Dragomir, V. D. (2011). Accounting for sustainability: The quest for a conceptual framework. *International Journal of Critical Accounting, 3*(4), 384398.
EBA. (2021). On management and supervision of ESG risks for credit institutions and investment firms. https://www.eba.europa.eu/sites/default/files/document_library/Publications/Reports/2021/1015656/EBA%20Report%20on%20ESG%20risks%20management%20and%20supervision.pdf
Eccles, R. G., Krzus, M. P., Rogers, J., & Serafeim, G. (2012). The need for sector-specific materiality and sustainability reporting standards. *Journal of Applied Corporate Finance, 24*(2), 6571.
Financial Times. (2023). ESG is beyond redemption: May it RIP. Aswath Damodaran. https://www.ft.com/content/d4082c75-3141-4a58-935b-60a44c22897a.
Gray, R., Adams, C., & Owen, D. (2014). *Accountability, social responsibility and sustainability: Accounting for society and the environment*. Pearson Higher Ed.
Haidar, H. M., Sohail, R. M., & Al Qurashi, S. M. (2021). Emerging trends in sustainability reporting (SR): Comparative literature review in developed, developing and GCC countries. *Open Journal of Business and Management, 9*(6), 26972718.
Khan, M., Serafeim, G., & Yoon, A. (2016). Corporate sustainability: First evidence on materiality. *The Accounting Review, 91*(6), 16971724.
Kotsantonis, S., & Serafeim, G. (2019). Four things no one will tell you about ESG data. *Journal of Applied Corporate Finance, 31*(2), 5058.
Kümmerer, K. (2010). Pharmaceuticals in the environment. *Annual Review of Environment and Resources, 35*, 57–75.
Lins, K. V., Servaes, H., & Tamayo, A. (2017). Social capital, trust, and firm performance: The value of corporate social responsibility during the financial crisis. The. *Journal of Finance, 72*(4), 17851824.
Maaloul, A., Zéghal, D., Ben Amar, W., & Mansour, S. (2023). The effect of environmental, social, and governance (ESG) performance and disclosure on cost of debt: The mediating effect of corporate reputation. *Corporate Reputation Review, 26*(1), 1–18.
Madsen, H., & Ulhøi, J. P. (2001). Integrating environmental and stakeholder management. *Business Strategy and the Environment, 10*(2), 7788.
Montiel, I., & Delgado-Ceballos, J. (2014). Defining and measuring corporate sustainability: Are we there yet? *Organization & Environment, 27*(2), 113139.
MSCI. (2023a). https://www.msci.com/whoweare/corporateresponsibility
MSCI. (2023b). https://www.msci.com/oursolutions/esginvesting/esgratings
MSCI. (2023c). https://www.msci.com/oursolutions/esginvesting/esgindustrymaterialitymap
Renneboog, L., Ter Horst, J., & Zhang, C. (2008). Socially responsible investments: Institutional aspects, performance, and investor behavior. *Journal of Banking & Finance, 32*(9), 17231742.
Saini, M., Aggarwal, V., Dhingra, B., Kumar, P., & Yadav, M. (2023). ESG and financial variables: A systematic review. *International Journal of Law and Management, 65*(6), 663–682.
Schiehll, E., & Kolahgar, S. (2021). Financial materiality in the informativeness of sustainability reporting. *Business Strategy and the Environment, 30*(2), 840855.
Seo, Y., Primovic, M. J., & Jin, Y. (2019). Overcoming stakeholder social media fatigue: A trialogue approach. *Journal of Business Strategy, 40*(6), 4048.
Tsang, A., Frost, T., & Cao, H. (2022). Environmental, social, and governance (ESG) disclosure: A literature review. *The British Accounting Review, 55*, 101149.

Chapter 27
The Association Between Environmental and Financial Performance in the Oil and Gas Industry: An Institutional Approach

Samantha Barresi, Michele Bertoni, and Paola Rossi

27.1 Introduction

During the last two decades, environmental, social, and governance activities have become a critical concern for firms, consumers, governments, and policymakers (Awaysheh et al., 2020; Gregory-Smith et al., 2017; Gull et al., 2022). More in detail, global warming, the potential impact of ecological accidents, and the social alarm surrounding various polluting events highlight society's awareness and concern about the quality of the environment and corporations' role and responsibility in this regard (Berthelot et al., 2003).

Global environmental challenges and the essential role of industrial companies in preventing adverse environmental effects induce businesses to examine the environmental impact of their activities (Qiu et al., 2017; Shen et al., 2019; Slacik et al., 2021). In this sense, the attention of shareholders, regulatory authorities, investors, creditors, and government agencies towards ESG issues has grown exponentially over the last decade (Escrig-Olmego et al., 2013; Devalle et al., 2017; Naeem & Çankaya, 2022). Environmental, social, and governance ratings have become a fundamental aspect of financial, business, and consumer decisions in advanced economies, with their importance lately acknowledged by European and American political leaders, emphasising the need for studies in this area (Apergis et al., 2022; Erhart, 2022).

S. Barresi · M. Bertoni · P. Rossi (✉)
Department of Economics, Business, Mathematics, and Statistics "Bruno de Finetti", University of Trieste, Trieste, Italy
e-mail: prossi@units.it

N. Castellano et al. (eds.), *Environmental, Social, Governance (ESG)*, SIDREA Series in Accounting and Business Administration,
https://doi.org/10.1007/978-3-031-76618-3_27

By this premise, environmental and financial performance cannot be considered disjointed but dually linked. Some researchers like Iwata and Okada (2011) see the first as both a threat and an opportunity simultaneously. Arguably, environmental actions can benefit the companies' financial performance because of reputational and organisational gains. However, achieving good environmental performance by curbing emissions or reducing waste spills can be expensive, thus generating a trade-off between environmental costs and profitability. For this reason, researchers' interest in exploring the relationship between environmental performance (EP) and financial performance (FP) has expanded quickly over the last decade.

The investigation of a possible correlation between EP and FP has been under study and debate among researchers for many years (Friede et al., 2015). Various prominent studies exhibit mixed results when several environmental and financial performance measurements are utilised. For instance, according to the meta-analysis of Horváthová (2010), who analysed 64 studies related to the relationship between EP and FP, about 15% of the studies report a negative effect of environmental performance on financial performance, about 30% report no effect, and 55% report a positive effect.

One of the possible reasons for the conflicting results pointed out by previous studies is the uniqueness of the industry context. However, only some studies have investigated these issues in each specific industrial sector. Research on highly environmentally impactful industries like oil and gas is equally limited. The oil and gas industry is considered one of the major contributors to carbon emissions worldwide and one of the worst ocean polluters because of oil spills. At the same time, oil and gas companies rank among the largest and most profitable in the world (Tarmizi & Brahmana, 2023). Despite the relevance of this topic in the oil and gas sector, few studies have investigated the association between carbon emissions and financial performance. Moreover, no studies differentiate between direct and indirect emissions and analyse the moderator role of institutional characteristics.

In order to cover these gaps, the present study aims to investigate the impact of CO^2 emissions, distinguishing between Scope 1, Scope 2, and Scope 3 emissions, on the financial performance, measured by return on equity and return on asset. Moreover, adopting a cluster analysis, we investigate the moderating role of institutional characteristics on the association between environmental and financial performance. The main results of our study show a positive association between financial performance and environmental performance, measured by carbon emissions, in the oil and gas industry. Separating the carbon emissions in Scope 1, Scope 2, and Scope 3, we demonstrate that direct emissions (Scope 1) and indirect emissions associated with the purchase of electricity, steam, heat, or cooling impact the return on equity, while only the indirect emissions (Scope 2 and Scope 3) influence return on assets. To understand how country-level institutional characteristics moderate the association between environmental performance and financial performance, we categorise the countries into three clusters based on the degree of institutional enforcement within a country, measured by World Bank measures. The main findings indicate that Cluster 1 and Cluster 3 play a moderating role in the association between carbon emissions and financial performance.

This paper is structured as follows. Section 27.2 presents the literature review and the hypothesis development. Section 27.3 describes the data set and research methods. Section 27.4 includes the analysis of the results. Finally, Sect. 27.5 provides conclusions, limitations, and suggestions for future research.

27.2 Literature Review and Hypothesis Development

27.2.1 Theoretical Framework

Historically, enterprises arise to generate profits. This belief was championed by Friedman (1970), who famously stated that the only social responsibility of a business is to increase its profits. However, as time went on, the business concept has also evolved, leading to the development of the theory of corporate sustainability (CS), which is neatly defined by Dyllick and Hockerts (2002, p. 131) as "meeting the needs of a firm's direct and indirect stakeholders, without compromising its ability to meet the needs of future stakeholders as well". Accordingly, CS, which until the late 1980s was typically associated with a company's capacity to sustain consistent corporate financial performance (FP), today has evolved into a tripartite structure that embeds corporate's financial, social, and environmental dimensions (Aydoğan & Kara, 2023).

The current scenario further consolidates the shift towards the Environmental, Social, and Governance (ESG) paradigm. Indeed, a company's overall performance is assessed comprehensively based on economic, environmental, social, and corporate governance aspects. This holistic approach has been gaining importance as individual and institutional investors seek investments with appealing financial returns and an enticing social and environmental impact (Ahmad et al., 2021). In these connections, scholars such as Eccles et al. (2014) claim that highly sustainable companies are less affected by managerial myopia and are capable of attracting long-lasting investors.

These premises entail the existence of a strong connection between environmental, social, governance, and financial performance. Several theories have been proposed to explain this linkage (positive or negative), and in this section, we will explore the assumptions underlying the hypotheses we have posited for the study.

Theoretical foundations favour a positive relationship between environmental, social, governance, and financial performance, including Stakeholder and Natural Resource-Based View (NRBV) theories. The *Stakeholder Theory* devised by Edward Freeman assumes that companies are not only beholden to shareholders but equally to their stakeholders, who are defined as individuals, groups, or organisations that have an interest in the companies' processes and outcomes and can affect or are affected by the achievement of the businesses' goals (Freeman, 1984). Stakeholders count, among others, creditors, customers, employees, shareholders, and debtors. These are the fundamental players of the companies without whom they cannot stand up. In this vision, all parties involved in the company's activities are interconnected and dependent on each other, creating an ecosystem (Parmar et al., 2010). Moreover, embedding stakeholders in environmental strategies, trying to pander to their needs and attentiveness in environmental matters, is a winning solution in line with stakeholder theory. Consumers will be more prone to paying a premium price for sustainable products, and at the same time, employees will tend to be interested in working for sustainable companies. Furthermore, environmental initiatives reduce regulatory pressures on responsible firms (Brown & Dacin, 1997; Hillman & Keim, 2001; Brammer et al., 2007; Castaldo et al., 2009; Misani & Pogutz, 2015).

In conjunction with the theory previously stated, we can find another fundamental theoretical underpinning: the *Natural Resource-Based View Theory.* This theory is an enlargement of the Resource-Based View and includes the environmental effects of companies' resources along with the processes that emerge from them (Hart, 1995; Hart & Dowell, 2011; Andersén, 2021). For enterprises, a way to demonstrate commitment to the stakeholders' needs is, for instance, trying to reduce its environmental footprint. In this connection, proponents of the NRBV theory advocate the positive impact of environmental performance on financial performance. In other words, this view foresees improved EP conducts to better FP (Hart, 1995; Horváthová, 2010; Brahmana & Kontesa, 2021; Tarmizi & Brahmana, 2023). Under this theoretical approach, therefore, companies with a business activity attentive to environmental matters better organise their resources, resulting in an increased competitive advantage over those less environmentally devoted (Brahmana & Kontesa, 2021). As a result, companies that engage in environmental practices yield, under the natural resourced-based view, more economic benefits such as high profits, competitive advantages, and a better allocation of resources than additional costs (Beckmann et al., 2014; Nollet et al., 2016; Trumpp & Guenther, 2017; Xie et al., 2019).

In the context of the oil and gas industry, the stakeholder theory suggests that companies operating in this sector with a meaningful environmental impact are led to creating a positive environment and relationships with the companies' stakeholders in order to avoid the ecological disasters that are detrimental both from an environmental and financial perspective and enhance their social reputation. Moreover, in this industrial setting, sustainable use of natural resources such as oil reserves, combined with responsible practices in extraction, production processes, and general pollution prevention and abatement, can lead to a competitive advantage, as advocated by the NBRV.

Despite the contribution of the above theories to the relationship between ESG performance and financial performance, the complexity of this process could also be explained by the institutional theory that describes the firm's behaviour under different institutional environments. In fact, it is defined as "the rules of the game in a society or, more formally, the humanly devised constraints that shape human interaction" (North, 1990), influencing a firm's decision-making process as well as change of behaviours towards sustainable directions (North, 2005; Delmas & Toffel, 2008). The emergence of uniform characters within an organisation is termed isomorphism, which is achieved through mimetic, coercive, and normative forces (DiMaggio & Powell, 1983). Mimetic isomorphism results from the pressure to emulate the forms and actions of other organisations, particularly those sharing similar characteristics with the company. This tendency is heightened under conditions of uncertainty, where individuals seek to mitigate risks by aligning their actions with those considered representative or common. Coercive isomorphism arises due to external pressures, such as government regulations, compelling organisations to take specific, intended actions. Normative isomorphism occurs when organisations adopt certain systems or standards to gain recognition or certification from professional institutions. According to the neo-institutional theory (Scott, 2001), external and internal forces can influence companies to adopt sustainable activities. Companies located in countries with the same strong institutional factors are more likely to adopt more ethical business conducts and to achieve better environmental performance, confirming the role of normative and coercive forces on the association between environmental performance and financial performance. Companies located in weak institutional factors could have similar environmental practices linked with positive financial performance through mimetic isomorphism.

27.2.2 A Synopsis of the Literature on the Relationship Between Environmental Performance and Financial Performance

The theoretical groundwork formerly sketched has led scholars to explore how environmental, social, and governance factors influence firm performance and to flesh out the study of this relationship through several empirical studies. However, the literature in this area reports mixed findings, varying from positive and negative to no association.

Indeed, several studies conducted on similar samples of American firms in comparable time arcs produced sundry conclusions. In 1996, Klassen and McLaughlin, examining publicly traded firms on the NYSE or AMEX over the period from 1985 to 1991, found significant positive returns for solid environmental management and significant negative returns for weak environmental management, confirming a positive link between environmental and financial performance, as measured by stock market performance. Russo and Fouts (1997), analysing a sample of 243 US firms for the years 1991 and 1992, found that “it pays to be green”, which means that there is a strong positive relationship between environmental performance and financial performance, measured by return on assets when the industry growth rate is reasonable.

In contrast, Cordeiro and Sarkis’s (1997) investigation, analysing a sample of 523 US firms in 1992, discovered a negative association between environmental initiatives and analysts’ earnings estimates. Likewise, Khanna and Damon (1999) identified a negative relationship between environmental and financial performance in the short term, as evaluated by return on investment (ROI), in a sample of 123 U.S. chemical businesses from 1991 to 1993.

Various underlying reasons can explain such a broad and diverse range of outcomes. Different methods may provide dissimilar results in certain circumstances: for instance, Salama (2005) investigated panel data of 201 firms from the UK, finding no significant association between environmental performance and financial performance when OLS regression is used. Still, the study found a significant positive association when using median regression.

In other cases, as in the Iwata and Okada (2011) work conducted on 268 Japanese manufacturing companies from 2004 to 2008, different environmental performance measures are found to affect financial performance differently. According to the authors, waste emissions do not significantly relate to financial performance. On the other hand, greenhouse gas reductions positively affect the financial performance of clean industries and the whole sample, except for dirty industries, where there is no significant relation.

Velte (2017) examined a sample of companies listed on the German Prime Standard (DAX 30, TecDAX, MDAX) from 2010 to 2014, performing a correlation and regression analysis to highlight potential connections between ESG factors, accounting, and market-based measures of financial performance (ROA and Tobin's Q). From the study, it emerges that environmental performance scores positively impact ROA but have no impact on Tobin's Q.

In trying to pinpoint the reasons for the inconsistent results in the literature, scholars like Eccles et al. (2014) argue that according to the parameters used to measure sustainability performance, the impact of corporate sustainability on business processes and outcomes varies. Furthermore, Friede et al. (2015) report an overview of over 2000 empirical works conducted from 1970 to explore the relationship between ESG and FP, showing that almost 90% of the studies find a non-negative ESG-FP relationship. Meanwhile, looking at the individual pillars of ESG, the research winds up with mixed findings. Moreover, this investigation provides one relevant piece of information: the strength of the relationships changes by region. Eventually, authors like Clark et al. (2015) also suggested that various circumstances, such as changes in business practices across markets and industries, can influence the link between ESG and financial performance.

Given this backdrop, it is feasible to encounter a fair number of studies in the current literature focusing on the issues described so far by taking industry-specific analyses. Towards this end, a stream of previous studies with diverse results examines how ESG performance affects business performance in the so-called sensitive industries, like energy, healthcare, and oil and gas, to name a few. Notably, a valuable investigation completed by Constantinescu (2021) analysed the link between sustainability disclosure, as determined by the overall and individual ESG scores, and the value of European entities operating in the healthcare and energy industries. Utilising linear regression models, the research revealed a negative and significant correlation between environmental and financial performance in the energy sector. However, there was no significant influence on the value of healthcare companies.

Kalia and Aggarwal (2023) obtained a similar pattern of results regarding the latter sector. After analysing a sample of global healthcare companies, their findings demonstrated a negative or insignificant relationship between ESG scores and FP in developing economies. On the contrary, ESG matters positively and significantly impacts financial performance in developed economies. This implies that the variations and discrepancies of the yields found in the literature may also depend on the context of the specific country. This is consistent with Pinheiro et al. (2023): their contribution suggests that the country's level of development affects the environmental and governance pillars positively.

Recently, scholars like Makridou et al. (2023) conducted a study investigating the influence of ESG matters on European energy companies' financial performance. The study used the return on assets as a proxy of profitability and examined the overall ESG score and individual ESG factors. The empirical results indicated that energy firms' ESG combined performance score impacted corporate financial performance negatively but not significantly. Upon analysing each ESG pillar separately, it was revealed that there was a significant negative association between firm performance and the environmental dimension. On the other hand, the company's financial performance is positively but not significantly associated with corporate social and governance responsibilities.

To date, the outcomes in this line of research remain contradictory. Moreover, environmentally sensitive sectors like energy, healthcare, and oil and gas are considered highly polluting industries with a significant environmental footprint. Therefore, these industries are expected to focus on sustainability issues with significant costs that may negatively affect their financial performance. Strikingly, although investigations on the nexus between ESGP and CFP are increasing in certain sectors, they remain scarce in crucial environmentally related industries.

27.2.3 *Environmental and Financial Performance: An Insight into the Oil and Gas Industry*

As reviewed thus far, an important number of studies have analysed the linkage between ESG and financial performance both in its wholeness and singularly for each pillar (environmental, social, and governance). Nonetheless, the literature shows a paucity of research about industries that highly impact the environment, such as oil and gas.

The issue has been tackled by a few recent studies that have yielded positive findings regarding the relationship between environmental and financial performance. As a matter of fact, over the last few years, Brahmana and Kontesa (2021) attempted to shed light on this point by analysing the Fortune Global List Oil and Gas companies while also considering the mediating effect of clean technology. The study authors measure environmental performance using CO emissions and oil spills, comparing these to accounting measures of financial performance, such as ROA and ROE. The study revealed a negative correlation between CO emissions, oil spills, other waste spills, and financial performance. This indicates that higher carbon emissions can be detrimental to the financial performance of the oil and gas industry firms. Although, the authors did not find any significant effect of the adoption of clean technology.

The suggestion that a better EP positively influences FP is backed up by the evidence of Tarmizi and Brahmana (2023), who studied how the mediating effects of political connections in oil and gas companies can explain the relationship between environmental and financial performance. The study involved 154 oil and gas companies from the Fortune Global 500. They found a positive relationship between environmental performance, proxied as CO emissions, spill events, fines, and financial performance measured by ROA and ROE. However, the causal relationship between environmental and financial performance was not significant for CO emissions: the researchers concluded that for oil and gas companies, spills and fines are a more important concern for their reputation than emissions. The authors used the number of politicians among the board members to measure the impact of the political connections. Politically connected oil and gas companies tend to outperform non-politically connected firms, but only when measuring environmental performance through oil spills. Furthermore, scholars have found that politicians sitting on the board could help companies reduce the reputational damage generated by oil spills. However, this benefit does not extend to carbon emissions, which do not harm the firms' performances and cannot help when the authorities have already imposed fines.

The main findings of the above studies support the positive relationship model, according to which green regulations drive firms to include environmental investments in their corporate strategies, such as introducing eco-friendly raw materials and implementing technologies that address environmental needs. Thus, we posit the following hypothesis:

H_1: *Financial performance in the oil and gas industry is positively associated with carbon emissions performance.*

H_{1a}: *Financial performance in the oil and gas industry is positively associated with Scope 1, Scope 2, and Scope 3 emissions.*

27.2.4 The Moderating Effect of the Institutional Characteristics

The literature review discussed above proves that environmental performance influences and shapes financial performance. Although the positive effect of EP on FP is largely demonstrated, few studies have also shown insignificant and negative results. These inconsistent findings could be motivated by the interaction of EP with institutional factors. Previous studies demonstrated that the national institutional level could indirectly impact the firm's economic performance and directly the firm's engagement to environmental issues. In the context of oil and gas, Tarmizi and Brahmana (2023) found that oil and gas businesses with more significant political clout would perform better financially in the face of low environmental performance, suggesting that institutional factors could affect the link between EP and FP. Following previous studies about the association between institutional quality and environmental quality (i.e. Gani, 2012; Halkos & Tzeremes, 2013; Abid, 2016; Rizk & Slimane, 2018; Khan & Rana, 2021; Khan et al., 2022), we identify the following Worldwide Governance Indicators (WGI) as measures of national institutional level: voice and accountability, political stability, government effectiveness, regulatory quality, rule of law, and corruption control (Kaufmann et al., 2010).

The Voice and Accountability Index measures the power of citizens to participate in selecting their government, as well as freedom of expression, freedom of association, and freedom of media (Kaufmann et al., 2011). This index can influence environmental performance for two reasons. First, in democratic countries, citizens have more possibilities to select a government with a strong commitment towards the environment, electing political parties with an agenda to ensure environmental well-being (Dunlap et al., 2001). Second, when the government or companies do not resolve environmental problems, independent media expose this issue, exerting pressure on firms to improve their engagement in CSR activities, including environmental performance (Weaver et al., 1999; Hartmann & Uhlenbruck, 2015). These arguments suggest that a high level of voice and accountability is positively associated with environmental performance. A large body of empirical research (i.e. Congleton, 1992; Barrett & Graddy, 2000; Bernauer et al., 2012; Pellegrini & Gerlagh, 2006; Ward, 2008; Halkos & Tzeremes, 2013; Abid, 2016; Adams & Klobodu, 2017; Khan & Rana, 2021) confirms the positive effect of democracy on environmental quality. However, another stream of literature review contradicts this result. For instance, Midlarsky (1998), examining six environmental performance indicators, provided a negative relationship between CO^2 and democracy. The recent study of Khan et al. (2022), examining the link between EP and FP in BRI (Belt and Road Initiative) countries, demonstrated that voice and accountability drive carbon dioxide, suggesting that the level of voice and accountability is not sufficient in these countries to protect environmental quality.

The Political Stability Index refers to the chances of the government being disrupted or toppled through illegal methods, such as violence and terrorism (Kaufmann et al., 2011). Political instability creates uncertainty in the economic environment, negatively affecting macroeconomic performance (Alesina & Perotti, 1996). Firms that operate in times of weak financial performance or unfavourable environments are less likely to invest in environmental activities because the political instability disrupts the long-term economic policies conducive to better economic performance, reducing the expected return of sustainability projects (Fredriksson & Svensson, 2003). Moreover, in politically unstable regions, firms are not held accountable for their actions towards sustainability. From these viewpoints, stable political environments have generally led to increased environmental performance. Some studies have explored the relationship between political stability and environmental performance, finding mixed results (Barrett & Graddy, 2000; Welsch, 2004; Damania et al., 2003; Fiorino, 2011; Halkos & Tzeremes, 2013; Abid, 2016; Khan & Rana, 2021; Khan et al., 2022).

The Government Effectiveness Index measures the public service quality, the level of autonomy from political influence, the quality of policy formulation, and its implementation (Kaufmann et al., 2011). Government effectiveness can influence firms' contribution to the environment in several ways. Governments can encourage firms to adopt sustainable practices by procuring goods and services from firms with strong environmental performance records (Eisner, 2004). In addition, in countries with ineffective governments, the high level of red tape hinders the progress of sustainable corporate development efforts, increasing transaction costs (Keyworth, 2006; Duvanova, 2014) and decreasing firms' performance due to the misallocation of resources (Bozeman & DeHart-Davis, 1999). According to these assumptions, the government's effectiveness should increase the environmental quality. Many empirical studies confirm that in the countries where public services are most effective, firms decrease environmental degradation (i.e. Samimi et al., 2012; Gani & Scrimgeour, 2014; Abid, 2016; Dadgara & Nazari, 2016; Khan & Rana, 2021; Peng et al., 2021). However, a recent study by Khan et al. (2022) found that in BRI countries, government policy reliability and the independence of civil servants from political compressions increase carbon dioxide emissions.

The Regulatory Quality Index refers to the government's ability to create and enforce effective policies and regulations that promote economic and sustainable development. Regulatory quality is closely tied to various economic outcomes, such as reducing wealth inequality and improving the provision of welfare services, which ultimately leads to better economic performance and corporate environmental performance. It is argued that a country or a firm must prioritise sustainability while achieving economic success in order to ensure long-term survival. Therefore, regulatory quality plays a crucial role in both economic and corporate sustainable performance, as it is essential for the smooth functioning of market economies. Furthermore, countries with strong regulatory quality are able to minimise negative environmental impacts (Homer, 2009). The main findings of the empirical research about the relationship between regulatory quality and environmental performance provided evidence that in countries with high regulatory quality, carbon emissions, waste, and pollution decrease (i.e. Halkos & Tzeremes, 2013; Gani, 2012; Abid, 2017; Khan & Rana, 2021; Khan et al., 2022).

The Rule of Law Index measures individuals' level of trust and adherence to societal rules, particularly the quality of contract enforceability, property rights, and bureaucracy efficiency (Kaufmann et al., 2011). In countries, with strong rule of law, companies are encouraged to invest and expand their operations and enhance economic performance, including corporate environmental performance. On the contrary, countries with weak rule of law tend to have limited competition, resulting in a lower contribution to the environment (Deacon, 1999). When organisations operate in stable regulatory systems, they become more mindful of their actions in terms of environmental standards. Additionally, research indicates that firms are more inclined to adhere to standards and regulations when they understand the negative consequences of disregarding social and environmental responsibilities (Gunningham et al., 2004). Previous studies showed a positive influence of the rule of law on environmental performance (i.e. Gani, 2012; Halkos & Tzeremes, 2013; Salman et al., 2019; Khan & Rana, 2021; Khan et al., 2022).

The Corruption Control Index measures the degree and variability to which governmental authority can prevent conflicts of interest and opportunistic actions rooted in corruption. In countries characterised by a strong control of corruption, companies will exhibit ethical conducts. Corruption companies, regardless of whether in the public or private sectors, are willing to participate in bribery to achieve higher and faster profits. Moreover, corruption enables companies to shirk their social responsibilities by employing child labour, evading environmental obligations, and illegally disposing of toxic waste in rivers, thus cutting waste management costs and maximising their own profits (Biswas et al., 2012;). Corruption, oppressive governments, deep-rooted poverty, injustice, severe human rights abuses, and pollution are all interconnected (Frynas, 2009). Failing to adhere to standards can have a detrimental impact on society and the natural environment, ultimately impeding the country's development. Additionally, corruption leads to increased red tape and hampers business expansion. Research indicates that a higher level of corruption leads to environmental degradation (Damania et al., 2003; Welsch, 2004; Pellegrini & Gerlagh, 2006; Gani, 2012; Ozturk & Al-Mulali, 2015; Wang et al., 2018; Habib et al., 2020; Khan & Rana, 2021). On the contrary, some studies found that the control of corruption has no or positive association with carbon emissions (Akhbari & Nejati, 2019; Sulemana & Kpienbaareh, 2020; Khan et al., 2022).

The studies hitherto support the idea that institutional characteristics play a crucial role in impacting environmental performance. As a result, this line of thought offers valuable insights into the possible influential role of institutional factors in the link between environmental and financial performance. Therefore, we formulate the following hypothesis:

H_2: Institutional characteristics influence the relationship between environmental and financial performance in the oil and gas industries.

27.3 Data and Methodology

27.3.1 Sample Selection

To test our hypotheses, we employ a sample of oil and gas firms drawn from the Refinitiv Eikon database, spanning from 2007 to 2021. To ensure the maximum possible geographical coverage, we selected all the companies falling in the "Oil and gas producers" and "Oil equipment and services" categories from the database. After removing companies with missing or abnormal data (such as companies with negative equity), we obtained a cross-sectional sample of 1644 firm-year observations. The sample comprises 229 unique firms from 22 countries, spanning all continents, with the exclusion of Africa (for lack of data). The majority of our observations, amounting to 61.98% of the sample, refer to the United States, Canada, and the United Kingdom. Other countries represented in our sample are

Norway, Australia, the Russian Federation, France, Italy, China, and Japan: along with the first three countries mentioned above, these countries represent 88.08% of our observations.

27.3.2 Dependent Variables

Financial performance is our major dependent variable. Consistently with previous studies, we use reliable accounting measures, like return on assets (ROA) and return on equity (ROE), to gauge it.

ROA is the metric defining the operating return of the assets, and it is computed as the ratio between the operating result (defined as net income before interest expenses and income tax) and the average total assets of the firm. On the other hand, ROE points out the overall performance from the perspective of the equity investors. It is calculated as the ratio between net income (minus preferred dividends) and the simple average of the firm's common equity. Both ratios are extracted from Refinitiv Eikon.

27.3.3 Independent Variables

To assess the environmental performance, we use greenhouse gas emissions retrieved from the Refinitiv Eikon database. More in detail, we use the natural logarithm of the total tonnes of greenhouse gas emissions[1] (CO2_TOTAL), divided among Scope 1 (CO2_SCOPE1, direct emissions from sources that are owned or controlled by the company), Scope 2 (CO2_SCOPE2, indirect emissions from consumption of purchased electricity, heat, or steam which occur at the facility where the resource is generated), and Scope 3 indirect emissions (CO2_SCOPE3 emissions from contractor-owned vehicles, employee business travel, waste disposal, outsourced activities, from product use by customers, from the production of purchased materials, from electricity purchased for resale).

27.3.4 Control Variables

Following previous literature, we include sundry control variables in this study to regulate the relation between the dependent and independent variables. More precisely, we control for firm size (SIZE), measured by the natural logarithm of the

[1] Greenhouse gases measured by our variable are mostly carbon dioxide (CO2), but the data include also emission of methane (CH4), nitrous oxide (N2O), hydrofluorocarbons (HFCS), perfluorinated compound (PFCS), sulfur hexafluoride (SF6), and nitrogen trifluoride (NF3).

market value at the end of the observation year. Financial leverage (LEV) is defined as the ratio between long- and short-term debt and the total assets of the firms. Capital intensity (CAPITAL) is measured as the ratio between net property, plant, and equipment, and total assets. Our model also includes a dummy variable (EMS) indicating whether the company claims to have an ISO 14001 or EMS (environmental management systems) certification.[2] Our aim is to determine whether adherence to formalised environmental standards and procedures can affect the relationship between financial and environmental performance. On the one hand, we expect that such certifications should enhance the company's environmental performance; on the other hand, the costs associated with obtaining a certification could negatively influence financial performance.

27.3.5 Cluster Analysis Variables

We conduct a cluster analysis based on institutional characteristics. By doing this, we uncover connections between various factors and confirm consistent trends in how carbon emissions affect financial performance without depending on specific hypotheses. In line with the study of De Villiers and Marques (2016), our cluster analysis is based on the World Bank (2024) indicators at a national level: voice and accountability, political stability, government effectiveness, regulatory quality, rule of law, and anti-corruption.

The values of these measures range between 22.5 and 2.5, where higher values reflect higher citizen participation, more effective governments, higher regulatory quality, more effective rule of law, and higher corruption control index.

These indicators are based on several hundred variables obtained from different data sources, capturing governance perceptions reported by survey respondents, NGOs, commercial business information providers, and public sector organisations worldwide (Kaufmann et al., 2010).

27.3.6 Regression Models

To test the hypothesis, we estimate ordinary least squares (OLS) regressions to test our hypotheses. The model has been widely applied in prior studies investigating the relationship between carbon emissions and financial performance:

[2]ISO 14000 is a family of standards by the International Organization for Standardization (ISO) related to environmental management that exists to help organizations minimize how their operations negatively affect the environment, comply with applicable laws, regulations, and other environmentally oriented requirements, and continually improve in the above. The ISO 14000 framework encompasses various aspects, from resource usage and waste management to monitoring environmental performance and involving stakeholders in environmental commitments. See https://www.iso.org/standard/60857.html.

$$FP_{it} = \alpha_0 + \alpha_1\, CO_{2t} + \alpha_2\, SIZE_{it} + \alpha_3\, LEVERAGE_{it} + \alpha_4\, CAPITAL_{it} + \alpha_4\, EMSit + \varepsilon_{it} \quad (27.1)$$

Specification 1 included the key explanatory variable, that is total CO_2. Specification 2 included SCOPE 1, whereas specification 3 included SCOPE 2 and specification 4 SCOPE 2. We utilise hierarchical linear models to explore how differences in institutional regulations influence certain effects. Our model incorporates interactions between companies within distinct clusters and their decision to publish a report. Specifically, we analyse the variable of interest (CO_2) in connection with three distinct dummy variables (Cluster1, Cluster2, and Cluster3), each denoting a company's affiliation with a particular cluster. Both interacted variables are binary, and we establish baseline effects when both variables (CO_2 and, respectively, Cluster1, Cluster2, and Cluster3) are absent (set at 0).

$$FP_{it} = \alpha_0 + \alpha_1 CO_{2it} + \alpha_{2\,it} CO_{2it*} CLUSTER\ 1 + \alpha_3\, SIZE_{it} + \alpha_4 LEVERAGE_{it} + \alpha_5\, CAPITAL_{it} + \alpha_6 EMS_{it} + \varepsilon_{it} \quad (27.2)$$

Statistical significance was set at a p-value less than 0.05.

27.4 Results

27.4.1 Cluster Analysis Results

We initially conducted a descriptive analysis to cluster countries based on their institutional characteristics. Employing a k-means cluster analysis, we identify three separate country clusters. These clusters emerge from a non-hierarchical algorithm that considers both the level and variability of institutional characteristics. With reference to the institutional factors, Cluster 1 is characterised by high score levels of the indicators used to define the institutional settings, Cluster 2 by mid-score levels, and Cluster 3 by low score levels.

27.4.2 Descriptive Statistics

Table 27.1 shows a descriptive analysis of the variables in our sample, reporting mean, standard deviation, minimum value, lower quartile, median, upper quartile, and maximum value for all the variables included in our regression analysis. Return on equity, return on assets, and financial leverage have been winsorised at 5% to remove outliers and reduce heteroscedasticity.

The descriptive analysis reported in Table 27.1 shows that the firms in our sample exhibit diversified financial and environmental performances, size, and financial leverage.

Table 27.2 reports the Pearson correlation coefficients of all the variables used in our models. Besides the obvious correlation between ROE and ROA, independent variables that are included separately in our regression equations, the correlation analysis does not highlight any multicollinearity issues. Naturally, there is a high and statistically significant correlation between total emissions and their components (Scope 1, Scope 2, and Scope 3). However, as explained in paragraph 3.6, our models consider these variables separately to study the effects of the single components on the relationship between financial and environmental performance.

The correlation between total greenhouse gas emissions and financial performance is modest but positive and statistically significant, and while this relationship remains true for the Scope 1 and Scope 2 emissions, the correlation between Scope 3 emissions and financial performance is not statistically significant. Size and capital intensity are both positively correlated to total gas emissions, and so is, less intuitively, financial leverage. The presence of an ISO 14000 certification is not correlated with financial performances, while there is a very moderate positive association with emissions: probably a consequence of size, because larger companies tend to emit more greenhouse gases but are also more likely to possess an environmental management system certification.

27.4.3 Results and Discussions

Table 27.3 provides the results of regressions of the pooled sample about the association between environmental performance and financial performance and the effect of dividing the CO_2 into SCOPE1, SCOPE 2, SCOPE 3. Our results reveal that CO2 has a negative association with FP ($p < 0.01$), measured by either ROA or ROE, thus confirming hypothesis 1 (Models 1 and 5).

When carbon emissions are divided among Scope 1, Scope 2, and Scope 3, the results offer some hindsight in the role played by direct and indirect emissions. We did not find any significant relationships between direct (Scope 1) emissions and ROA (Model 2), while there is a negative and significant ($p < 0.1$) association between direct emissions and ROE (Model 6). Indirect emissions, caused by the production and purchase of energy but still under the control of the firm (Scope 2), are instead negatively associated both with ROA and ROE (Models 3 and 7, $p < 0.01$), while indirect emissions outside the firm's control (Scope 3) are negatively associated with financial performance only in the case of ROA (Model 4, $p < 0.01$), but not for ROE (Model 8). The results regarding the impact of Scope 1, Scope 2, and Scope 3 on financial performance partially support $H_{1a.}$ Rather predictably, larger and less leveraged firms exhibit better financial performances (SIZE and LEVERAGE control variables), while the role played by capital intensity appears to be significant only when total emissions are considered (Models 1 and 5). Finally, possession of an environmental management system certification (EMS) seems to be negatively associated with financial performance, probably because of the associated costs, but our results are significant at the 10% level only for ROA and

Scope 2 emissions (Model 3) and for ROE and total carbon emissions (Model 5). These findings confirm partially the hypothesis 1a.

Table 27.4 summarises the results of the regressions that include the institutional variables.

Carbon emissions, which we did not split among the three scopes for this analysis, continue to remain negatively associated with financial performances in all our models, confirming the baseline effect of environmental performance on financial performance.

Model 9 shows that the baseline effect of total carbon emissions is negative and significant (CO2_TOTAL: −1.958, p-value <0.01), indicating that environmental performance is positively associated with financial performance (measured by ROA) regardless of the cluster to which the firms belong. The baseline effect of Cluster 1 is negative and significant (CLUSTER1: −8.684, p-value <0.05), meaning that being located in countries characterised by strong institutional enforcement is negatively associated with financial performances, regardless of firms' carbon emissions. This effect may be due to the higher level of regulatory quality and rule of law that characterises these countries. However, the interaction term is positive and significant (CLUSTER1*CO2: 1.249, p-value <0.05), showing that the financial performance of firms belonging to Cluster 1 countries benefits from lower carbon emissions.

Model 10 shows that the baseline effect of total carbon emissions is negative and significant (CO2_TOTAL: −0.867, p-value <0.01), indicating that environmental performance is positively associated with financial performance (measured by ROA) regardless of the cluster to which the firms belong. The baseline effect of Cluster 2 is positive but not significant (CLUSTER2: 8.171, p-value >0.1), meaning that we could not find any evidence that being located in countries characterised by middle-tier institutional enforcement is associated with financial performances, regardless of firms' carbon emissions. Similarly, the interaction term is negative but not significant (CLUSTER2*CO2: −1.054, p-value >0.1), preventing us from concluding that the financial performance of firms belonging to Cluster 2 countries benefits from lower carbon emissions.

Model 11 shows that the baseline effect of total carbon emissions is negative and significant (CO2_TOTAL: −0.791, p-value <0.05), indicating that environmental performance is positively associated with financial performance (measured by ROA) regardless of the cluster to which the firms belong. The baseline effect of Cluster 3 is positive and significant (CLUSTER3: 7.911, p-value <0.05), meaning that being located in countries characterised by lower institutional enforcement is positively associated with financial performances, regardless of firms' carbon emissions. We can argue that this effect may be ascribed to the looser regulatory framework to which these firms are subject. The interaction term is negative and significant (CLUSTER3*CO2: −1.224, p-value <0.05), showing that lower carbon emissions negatively affect firms belonging to Cluster 3 countries' financial performance.

Models 12–14 investigate the relationship between ROE and environmental performance, with similar results to Models 9–11 with regard to the institutional variables. The main difference is that Model 13 shows that belonging to a middle-tier

(Cluster 2) country is positively and significantly associated with ROE (CLUSTER2: 22.389, p-value <0.1), regardless of carbon emissions. The interaction term, however, is negative but not significant (CLUSTER2*CO2: -2.836, p-value >0.1), preventing us from concluding that the financial performance of firms belonging to Cluster 2 countries benefits from lower carbon emissions.

To summarise, Models 1–8 provide evidence that lower carbon emissions lead to higher financial performance. This result is in line with Brahmana and Kontesa (2021). The main rationale for this association lies in the assumption that firms that are more attentive to their environmental footprint demonstrate a better commitment to their stakeholders' needs and will gain a competitive advantage against those that pollute more, thus leading to better financial performance.

When total emissions are broken down into their components, i.e., Scope 1, Scope 2, and Scope 3 emissions, results are less straightforward and require an interpretation. We could not find any significant association between direct carbon emissions (Scope 1) and ROA. Instead, we found a significant association between direct (Scope 1) emissions and ROE. Therefore, this difference in results may be attributable to the differences between ROA and ROE, namely the non-operating items of the income statement and the financial leverage (controlled by our models and always negatively associated with financial performances). We can theorise that direct carbon emissions are negatively associated with the cost of debt, a claim that could possibly be explained by the issuance of sustainability-linked bonds, whose interest rates increase if issuers do not meet specific emission-curbing targets. Clearly, this result calls for more research on the association between carbon emissions and the cost of debt in the oil and gas industry. Scope 2 emissions generated by the purchase of energy are indirect but still controllable by the firm, which can choose a low-emission energy supplier and advertise this choice to its stakeholders. Scope 2 emissions are negatively associated with both ROA and ROE, and this association is significant, respectively, at the 1% (ROA) and at the 5% (ROE) level (Models 2 and 7). It appears that shifting the burden of carbon-reducing investments to energy suppliers can bear the same benefits and competitive advantages as reducing carbon emissions directly. It is also possible that, in a highly polluting industry such as oil and gas, subject to strong external pressures for reducing its environmental footprint, curbing emissions requires substantial efforts and expensive investments, whose benefits in terms of financial performance would appear only in the long term (Nguyen, 2023). It would be necessary, therefore, to monitor the future evolution of the association between direct emissions and financial performance in this industry. Scope 3 emissions, those generated indirectly by other sources in the firm's value chain (such as the production and transportation of materials, waste disposal, employee commuting, downstream distribution, etc.), are arguably more difficult to control. Nevertheless, they are negatively associated with ROA (Model 4, $p < 1\%$), but no significant results are yielded when financial performance is measured by ROE (Model 8). The results that emerge from Models 1–4, which employ ROA, signal that the association between carbon emissions and financial performance is driven by indirect emissions, both controllable (Scope 2) and non-controllable (Scope 3). Curbing indirect emissions seems to benefit financial performances, although the lack of control on Scope 3 emissions may limit their impact on the financial performance, as the carbon emissions coefficients in Models 3 and 4 show. Models 6–8 produce more contradictory results, possibly attributable to the much greater standard deviation of ROE compared to ROA in our sample (Table 27.1).

The multivariate analysis conducted in Models 9–14 leads us to conclude that institutional variables influence the relationship between environmental and financial performance in oil and gas firms, thus confirming H_2. This result is in line with the previous empirical research about the association between institutional quality and environmental performance (i.e. Khan & Rana, 2021; Khan et al., 2022).

In particular, the financial performance (measured by both ROA and ROE) of firms located in countries with strong institutional quality (Cluster 1) benefits from decreased carbon emissions. The effect is reversed for firms located in countries with lower institutional quality (Cluster 3), while we do not obtain any evidence for firms in middle-tier countries (Cluster 2). These results may be explained by the fact that, in strong institutional settings, stakeholders may pressure oil and gas firms to curb emissions, and firms that meet their stakeholders' expectations typically achieve higher financial performances. This effect, however, is dependent upon the level of institutional quality. In fact, when the levels of citizen participation, government effectiveness, regulatory quality, rule of law, and corruption control drop below a certain degree, the mediating role of institutional variables is either insignificant (Cluster 2) or reversed (Cluster 3). We can, therefore, argue that in a high-quality institutional setting characterised by high regulatory quality and high levels of enforcement, investing in carbon-reducing initiatives is beneficial in terms of financial performance. In weaker institutional settings, the costs of curbing polluting emissions seem to prevail over the benefits in terms of stakeholder satisfaction, thus worsening financial performance.

27.4.4 Additional Analysis: The Role of Corporate Governance Variables

To broaden our analysis, in line with previous literature (Walls et al., 2012), we included some corporate governance variables in our models (untabulated). Namely, we added the size of the board, the percentage of non-executive directors, and a gender diversity indicator, i.e., the percentage of women sitting on the board of directors.

Generally, including these variables in our models does not alter the results we have already commented on in the previous section. The only exception is Model 2 (ROA and Scope 1 emissions), where the inclusion of these additional control variables leads to a negative and significant ($p < 10\%$) coefficient for direct emissions. In our original Model 2 (see Table 27.3), the Scope 1 coefficient was negative but not statistically significant.

When including corporate governance variables in Models 1–4 (ROA and direct and indirect carbon emissions), we observed that board size is negatively correlated to financial performance ($p < 5\%$, with the exception of Model 2—Scope 1 emissions—where significance is at 10%). In Models 5–8, where financial performance is expressed by ROE, the size of the board is not significant. In all models from 1 to 8, the presence of non-executive members on the board of directors is positively and significantly associated with financial performance ($p < 5\%$), while the board diversity is never significant.

In Models 9–11 (ROA and institutional clusters), we had the same effects as in Models 1–4: board size is negatively associated with financial performance ($p < 5\%$), while the percentage of non-executive directors is positively associated with ROA ($p < 1\%$). In Models 12–14 (ROE and institutional clusters), the board size is not significant, while the coefficient related to non-executive members remains positive and statistically significant ($p < 1\%$). Board diversity is not significant in any of the six 9–14 Models.

27.5 Conclusions

The aim of this paper is to investigate the association between carbon emissions, divided into indirect and direct emissions, and economic performance, analysing a sample of 229 companies from 24 countries operating in the oil and gas industry for the business year 2007–2022. Moreover, this study investigates the moderating role of countries' institutional characteristics in the above relationship.

For the direct effect of EP on FP, our results provide evidence of the positive impact of EP on FP, in line with the recommendation based on natural RBV theory and stakeholder theory, which suggests that firms with high environmental performance (low CO_2) perform better financially. When we divide the carbon emissions into Scope 1, Scope 2, and Scope 3, the positive relationship between financial performance and direct and indirect emissions is confirmed. However, Scope 1 is not associated with ROA, and Scope 3 is not associated with ROE. Regarding the moderator role of institutional factors, our results demonstrate that they significantly influence the positive association between EP and FP in countries characterised by strong institutional settings, confirming the prevalence of coercive and normative isomorphism. In these countries, companies recognise the profitability of environmental practices. On the contrary, in countries with weak institutional settings, the institutional factors negatively impact the relationship between EP and FP, indicating the absence of mimetic isomorphism.

This study's contribution is twofold. First, we extend the previous research about the impact of carbon emissions on the company value in the oil and gas sector (i.e., Tarmizi & Brahmana, 2023), analysing the influence of the direct and indirect emissions on return on equity and return on asset. Second, this study offers unique contributions by exploring the moderating role of the country-level institutional setting on the association between carbon emissions and financial performance by grouping companies into three clusters with similar institutional characteristics.

The present study provides some theoretical implications, extending the stakeholder and natural resource-based theories to different types of emissions (direct and indirect emissions). Moreover, this research integrates institutional pressures and environmental performance practices to enhance financial performance in one model. In the literature review, examining environmental performance and its impact on firm performance is unexplored within the framework of institutional pressures. The study's results suggest that organisations as social entities are compelled to address institutional pressures such as normative, coercive, and mimetic forces in order to ensure their survival and competitiveness. Consequently, it demonstrates the necessity to analyse the companies' behaviour from an institutional perspective. Our findings also offer valuable insights for managing the oil and gas industry and policy implications for regulators. Primarily, companies will benefit from investing in addressing environmental issues. Secondly, managerial implications for firms located in high-quality institutional settings are that investing in green technologies benefits all stakeholders and leads to better financial performance. The policy implications for regulators and standard setters are that improving a country's regulatory framework and its enforcement can stimulate oil and gas firms to invest in carbon-reducing technologies to pursue their own self-interest and that of their stakeholders.

Despite its important contributions, this study has several limitations. First, the study focused on the oil and gas industry only, and therefore, the generalisability of its empirical finding and their application across other sectors should be done carefully. Second, institutional factors were taken as a whole through the adoption of cluster analysis to explore the moderating effect, which limits our understanding regarding the moderating effect of each dimension of institutional pressures. Future research could explore the moderating role of each dimension of institutional pressures, as well as across different industries.

Appendix: Tables

Table 27.1 Descriptive analysis of the sample (N = 1644)

Variable	Mean	Std Dev	Min.	Q25	Median	Q75	Max.
ROE	3.56	24.93	−85.15	−2.79	7.43	16.10	56.34
ROA	2.97	10.59	−31.04	−0.11	4.16	7.99	27.56
CO2_TOTAL	6.04	1.14	0.78	5.45	6.10	6.86	8.39
CO2_SCOPE1	5.99	1.19	−0.30	5.52	6.08	6.78	8.38
CO2_SCOPE2	4.85	1.28	−0.30	4.35	4.99	5.65	7.62
CO2_SCOPE3	6.05	1.31	−0.30	6.10	6.10	6.10	9.21
CLUSTER 1	0.82	0.38	0	1	1	1	1
CLUSTER 2	0.06	0.24	0	0	0	0	1
CLUSTER 3	0.11	0.32	0	0	0	0	1
SIZE	4.00	1.04	0.71	3.29	3.94	4.60	6.91
LEVERAGE	36.06	22.11	0	20.27	33.65	50.33	92.68
CAPITAL	0.60	0.25	0	0.43	0.64	0.81	0.99
EMS	0.46	0.50	0	0	0	1	1

Table 27.2 Pearson correlation matrix

	(1)	(2)	(3)	(4)	(5)	(6)	(7)	(8)	(9)	(10)	(11)	(12)	(13)
ROE (1)	1.00												
ROA (2)	0.88	1.00											
	<0.01***												
CO2_TOTAL (3)	0.10	0.12	1.00										
	<0.01***	<0.01***											
CO2_SCOPE1 (4)	0.11	0.13	0.91	1.00									
	<0.01***	<0.01***	<0.01***										
CO2_SCOPE2 (5)	0.08	0.08	0.69	0.66	1.00								
	0.00***	0.00***	<0.01***	<0.01***									
CO2_SCOPE3 (6)	0.03	0.01	0.44	0.44	0.41	1.00							
	0.16	0.76	<0.01***	<0.01***	<0.01***								
CLUSTER 1 (7)	−0.05	−0.05	−0.03	−0.05	−0.05	−0.02	1.00						
	0.04**	0.03**	0.18	0.06*	0.05*	0.32							
CLUSTER 2 (8)	0.06	0.06	0.03	0.04	0.05	0.02	−0.55	1.00					
	0.01**	0.01**	0.17	0.10	0.04**	0.40	<0.01***						
CLUSTER 3 (9)	0.01	0.02	0.01	0.03	0.02	0.01	−0.78	−0.09	1.00				
	0.65	0.49	0.57	0.29	0.43	0.58	<0.01***	0.00***					
SIZE (10)	0.31	0.33	0.62	0.60	0.53	0.28	−0.07	0.09	0.02	1.00			
	<0.01***	<0.01***	<0.01***	<0.01***	<0.01***	<0.01***	0.00***	0.00***	0.38				
LEVERAGE (11)	−0.26	−0.22	0.13	0.12	0.04	0.04	0.01	0.01	−0.02	−0.17	1.00		
	<0.01***	<0.01***	<0.01***	<0.01***	0.08**	0.07**	0.69	0.73	0.46	<0.01***			
CAPITAL (12)	−0.08	−0.07	0.21	0.23	0.11	0.10	0.02	−0.04	0.01	−0.11	0.18	1.00	
	0.00***	0.01**	<0.01***	<0.01***	<0.01***	<0.01***	0.43	0.11	0.80	<0.01***	<0.01***		
EMS (13)	0.01	0.03	0.05	0.06	0.04	0.05	−0.36	0.28	0.22	0.13	−0.01	−0.02	1.00
	0.60	0.23	0.04**	0.01***	0.14	0.05*	<0.01***	<0.01***	<0.01***	<0.01***	0.58	0.36	

Note: ***significant at the 1% level; **significant at the 5% level; *significant at the 10% level

Table 27.3 Summary results of regression analysis—Models 1–8 (N = 1644)

	ROA				*ROE*			
Variable	*Model 1*	*Model 2*	*Model 3*	*Model 4*	*Model 5*	*Model 6*	*Model 7*	*Model 8*
Constant	0.414	−0.547	−0.574	0.768	2.489	0.172	−0.472	−0.102
CO2_TOTAL	−0.940***				−2.367***			
CO2_SCOPE1		−0.428				−1.139*		
CO2_SCOPE2			−0.647***				−1.199**	
CO2_SCOPE3				−0.531***				−0.436
SIZE	3.363***	2.978***	3.104***	2.900***	7.282***	6.357***	6.338***	5.721***
LEVERAGE	−0.051***	−0.057***	−0.058***	−0.060***	−0.168***	−0.183***	−0.186***	−0.193***
CAPITAL	2.151**	1.604*	1.557	1.406	4.734**	3.434	2.909	2.277
EMS	−0.494	−0.441	−0.477*	−0.424	−1.772*	−1.638	−1.699	−1.609
Year variables	Yes	Yes	Yes	Yes	Yes	Yes	Yes	Yes
Adj R2	0.312	0.308	0.311	0.311	0.304	0.300	0.301	0.299

Note: ***significant at the 1% level; **significant at the 5% level; *significant at the 10% level

Table 27.4 Summary results of regression analysis—Models 9–14 (N = 1644)

	ROA			*ROE*		
Variable	*Model 9*	*Model 10*	*Model 11*	*Model 12*	*Model 13*	*Model 14*
Constant	7.814**	0.027	−0.337	19.616***	1.454	0.931
CO2_TOTAL	– 1.958***	– 0.867***	−0.791**	– 4.682***	– 2.170***	– 2.057***
CLUSTER 1	−8.684**			– 20.064***		
CLUSTER1*CO2	1.249**			2.837***		
CLUSTER 2		8.171			22.389*	
CLUSTER 2*CO2		−1.054			−2.836	
CLUSTER 3			7.911**			16.374**
CLUSTER 3*CO2			−1.224**			– 2.547**
SIZE	3.338***	3.339***	3.348***	7.221***	7.212***	7.250***
LEVERAGE	– 0.053***	– 0.052***	– 0.052***	– 0.171***	– 0.171***	– 0.170***
CAPITAL	2.122**	2.238**	2.050**	4.671**	4.978**	4.525*
EMS	−0.817*	−0.716	−0.594	−2.593**	−2.424**	−1.968*
Year variables	Yes	Yes	Yes	Yes	Yes	Yes
Adj R2	0.315	0.313	0.313	0.307	0.307	0.305

Note: ***significant at the 1% level; **significant at the 5% level; *significant at the 10% level

References

Abid, M. (2016). Impact of economic, financial, and institutional factors on CO2 emissions: Evidence from sub-Saharan Africa economies. *Utilities Policy, 41*, 85–94. https://doi.org/10.1016/j.jup.2016.06.009

Abid, M. (2017). Does economic, financial and institutional developments matter for environmental quality? A comparative analysis of EU and MEA countries. *Journal of Environmental Management, 188*, 183–194. https://doi.org/10.1016/j.jenvman.2016.12.007

Adams, S., & Klobodu, E. K. M. (2017). Urbanization, democracy, bureaucratic quality, and environmental degradation. *Journal of Policy Modeling, 39*(6), 1035–1051. https://doi.org/10.1016/j.jpolmod.2017.04.006

Ahmad, N., Mobarek, A., & Roni, N. N. (2021). Revisiting the impact of ESG on financial performance of FTSE350 UK firms: Static and dynamic panel data analysis. *Cogent Business & Management, 8*(1), 1900500. https://doi.org/10.1080/23311975.2021.1900500

Akhbari, R., & Nejati, M. (2019). The effect of corruption on carbon emissions in developed and developing countries: Empirical investigation of a claim. *Heliyon, 5*(9), 1–9. https://doi.org/10.1016/j.heliyon.2019.e02516

Alesina, A., & Perotti, R. (1996). Income distribution, political instability, and investment. *European Economic Review, 40*, 1203–1228. https://doi.org/10.1016/0014-2921(95)00030-5

Andersén, J. (2021). A relational natural-resource-based view on product innovation: The influence of green product innovation and green suppliers on differentiation advantage in small manufacturing firms. *Technovation, 104*, 102254. https://doi.org/10.1016/j.technovation.2021.102254

Apergis, N., Poufinas, T., & Antonopoulos, A. (2022). ESG scores and cost of debt. *Energy Economics, 112*, 106186. https://doi.org/10.1016/j.eneco.2022.106186

Awaysheh, A., Heron, R. A., Perry, T., & Wilson, J. I. (2020). On the relation between corporate social responsibility and financial performance. *Strategic Management Journal, 41*(6), 965–987. https://doi.org/10.1002/smj.3122

Aydoğan, E., & Kara, E. (2023). The analysis of the dynamic relationship between corporate sustainability and financial performance. *Business & Economics Research Journal, 14*(2), 199–216. https://doi.org/10.20409/berj.2023.407

Barrett, S., & Graddy, K. (2000). Freedom, growth, and the environment. *Environment and Development Economics, 5*(4), 433–456. https://doi.org/10.1017/S1355770X00000267

Beckmann, M., Hielscher, S., & Pies, I. (2014). Commitment strategies for sustainability: How business firms can transform trade-offs into win–win outcomes. *Business Strategy and the Environment, 23*(1), 18–37. https://doi.org/10.1002/bse.1758

Bernauer, T., Böhmelt, T., & Koubi, V. (2012). Environmental changes and violent conflict. *Environmental Research Letters, 7*(1), 1–8. https://doi.org/10.1088/1748-9326/7/1/015601

Berthelot, S., Cormier, D., & Magnan, M. (2003). Environmental, disclosure research: Review and synthesis. *Journal of Accounting Literature, 22*(1), 1–44.

Biswas, A. K., Farzanegan, M. R., & Thum, M. (2012). Pollution, shadow economy and corruption: Theory and evidence. *Ecological Economics, 75*, 114–125. https://doi.org/10.1016/j.ecolecon.2012.01.007

Bozeman, B., & DeHart-Davis, L. (1999). Red tape and clean air: Title V air pollution permitting implementation as a test bed for theory development. *Journal of Public Administration Research and Theory, 9*(1), 141–178. https://doi.org/10.1093/oxfordjournals.jpart.a024403

Brahmana, R., & Kontesa, M. (2021). Does clean technology weaken the environmental impact on the financial performance? Insight from global oil and gas companies. *Business Strategy and the Environment, 30*, 3411–3423. https://doi.org/10.1002/bse.2810

Brammer, S., Millington, A., & Rayton, B. (2007). The contribution of corporate social responsibility to organisational commitment. *The International Journal of Human Resource Management, 18*(10), 1701–1719. https://doi.org/10.1080/09585190701570866

Brown, T. J., & Dacin, P. A. (1997). The company and the product: Corporate associations and consumer product responses. *Journal of Marketing, 61*(1), 68–84. https://doi.org/10.2307/1252190

Castaldo, S., Perrini, F., Misani, N., & Tencati, A. (2009). The missing link between corporate social responsibility and consumer trust: The case of fair trade products. *Journal of Business Ethics, 84*(1), 1–15. https://doi.org/10.1007/s10551-008-9669-4

Clark, G. L., Feiner, A., & Viehs, M. (2015). From the stockholder to the stakeholder: How sustainability can drive financial outperformance. Corporate Finance: Valuation. https://api.semanticscholar.org/CorpusID:166867337.

Congleton, R. D. (1992). Political institutions and pollution control. *The Review of Economic and Statistics, 74*(3), 412–421. https://doi.org/10.2307/2109485

Constantinescu, D. (2021). Sustainability disclosure and its impact on firm's value for energy and healthcare industry. *Central European Economic Journal, 8*(55), 313–329. https://doi.org/10.2478/ceej-2021-0022

Cordeiro, J. J., & Sarkis, J. (1997). Environmental proactivism and firm performance: Evidence from security analyst earnings forecasts. *Business Strategy and the Environment, 6*(2), 104–114. https://doi.org/10.1002/(SICI)1099-0836(199705)6:2<104::AID-BSE102>3.0.CO;2-T

Dadgara, Y., & Nazari, R. (2016). The impact of good governance on environmental pollution in south west Asian countries. *Iranian Journal of Economic Studies, 5*(1), 49–63. https://doi.org/10.22099/ijes.2017.23649.1292

Damania, R., Fredriksson, P. G., & List, J. A. (2003). Trade liberalization, corruption, and environmental policy formulation: Theory and evidence. *Journal of Environmental Economics and Management, 46*(3), 490–512. https://doi.org/10.1016/S0095-0696(03)00025-1

De Villiers, C., & Marques, A. (2016). Corporate social responsibility, country-level predispositions, and the consequences of choosing a level of disclosure. *Accounting and Business Research, 46*(2), 167–195. https://doi.org/10.1080/00014788.2015.1039476

Deacon, R. (1999). The political economy of environment-development relationships: A preliminary framework. University of California at Santa Barbara, economics working paper series. Retrieved December 21, 2023, from https://escholarship.org/content/qt8h33b5c0/qt8h33b5c0.pdf?t=krnjf6.

Delmas, M. A., & Toffel, M. W. (2008). Organisational responses to environmental demands: Opening the black box. *Strategic Management Journal, 29*, 1027–1055. https://doi.org/10.1002/smj.701

Devalle, A., Fiandrino, S., & Cantino, V. (2017). The linkage between ESG performance and credit ratings: A firm-level perspective analysis. *International Journal of Business and Management, 12*, 53. https://doi.org/10.5539/ijbm.v12n9p53

DiMaggio, P. J., & Powell, W. W. (1983). The iron cage revisited: Institutional isomorphism and collective rationality in organisational fields. *American Sociological Review, 48*(2), 147–160. https://doi.org/10.2307/2095101

Dunlap, R. E., Xiao, C., & McCright, A. M. (2001). Politics and environment in America: Partisan and ideological cleavages in public support for environmentalism. *Environmental Politics, 10*(4), 23–48. https://doi.org/10.1080/714000580

Duvanova, D. (2014). Economic regulations, red tape, and bureaucratic corruption in post-communist economies. *World Development, 59*, 298–312. https://doi.org/10.1016/j.worlddev.2014.01.028

Dyllick, T., & Hockerts, K. (2002). Beyond the business case for corporate sustainability. *Business Strategy and the Environment, 11*(2), 130–141. https://doi.org/10.1002/bse.323

Eccles, R. G., Ioannou, I., & Serafeim, G. (2014). The impact of corporate sustainability on organizational processes and performance. *Management Science, 60*(11), 2835–2857. https://doi.org/10.1287/mnsc.2014.1984

Eisner, M. A. (2004). Corporate environmentalism, regulatory reform, and industry self-regulation: Toward genuine regulatory reinvention in the United States. *Governance, 17*(2), 145–167. https://doi.org/10.1111/j.1468-0491.2004.00241.x

Erhart, S. (2022). Take it with a pinch of salt—ESG rating of stocks and stock indices. *International Review of Financial Analysis, 83*, 102308. https://doi.org/10.1016/j.irfa.2022.102308

Escrig-Olmedo, E., Muñoz-Torres, M. J., & Fernández-Izquierdo, M. Á. (2013). Sustainable development and the financial system: Society's perceptions about socially responsible investing. *Business Strategy and the Environment, 22*(6), 410–428. https://doi.org/10.1002/bse.1755

Fiorino, D. (2011). Explaining national environmental performance: Approaches, evidence, and implications. *Policy Sciences, 44*(4), 367–389. https://doi.org/10.1007/s11077-011-9140-8

Fredriksson, P. G., & Svensson, J. (2003). Political instability, corruption and policy formation: The case of environmental policy. *Journal of Public Economics, 87*(7–8), 1383–1405. https://doi.org/10.1016/S0047-2727(02)00036-1

Freeman, R. E. (1984). *Strategic management: A stakeholder approach*. Pitman. https://books.google.it/books?id=4PUJAQAAMAAJ

Friede, G., Busch, T., & Bassen, A. (2015). ESG and financial performance: Aggregated evidence from more than 2000 empirical studies. *Journal of Sustainable Finance & Investment, 5*(4), 210–233. https://doi.org/10.1080/20430795.2015.1118917

Friedman, M. (1970). The social responsibility of business. *The New York Times Magazine*, September 13th. In M. Friedman (Ed.), *An economist's protest: Columns on political economy* (pp. 177–184). Thomas Horton & Daughters, 1972.

Frynas, J. G. (2009). Corporate social responsibility in the oil and gas sector. *The Journal of World Energy Law & Business, 2*(3), 178–195. https://doi.org/10.1093/jwelb/jwp012

Gani, A. (2012). The relationship between good governance and carbon dioxide emissions: Evidence from developing economies. *Journal of Economic Development, 37*(1), 77–93. https://doi.org/10.1007/s11356-020-08680-w

Gani, A., & Scrimgeour, F. (2014). Modeling governance and water pollution using the institutional ecological economic framework. *Economic Modelling, 42*, 363–372. https://doi.org/10.1016/j.econmod.2014.07.011

Gregory-Smith, D., Manika, D., & Demirel, P. (2017). Green intentions under the blue flag: Exploring differences in EU consumers' willingness to pay more for environmentally friendly products. *Business Ethics: A European Review, 26*(3), 205–222. https://doi.org/10.1111/beer.12151

Gull, A. A., Saeed, A., Suleman, M. T., & Mushtaq, R. (2022). Revisiting the association between environmental performance and financial performance: Does the level of environmental orientation matter? *Corporate Social Responsibility and Environmental Management, 29*(5), 1647–1662. https://doi.org/10.1002/csr.2310

Gunningham, N., Kagan, R. A., & Thornton, D. (2004). Social license and environmental protection: Why businesses go beyond compliance. *Law & Social Inquiry, 29*(2), 307–341. https://doi.org/10.1111/j.1747-4469.2004.tb00338.x

Habib, S., Abdelmonen, S., & Khaled, M. (2020). The effect of corruption on the environmental quality in African countries: A panel quantile regression analysis. *Journal of the Knowledge Economy, 11*, 788–804. https://doi.org/10.1007/s13132-018-0571-8

Halkos, G. E., & Tzeremes, G. (2013). Carbon dioxide emissions and governance: A nonparametric analysis for the G-20. *Energy Economics, 40*, 110–118. https://doi.org/10.1016/j.eneco.2013.06.010

Hart, S. L. (1995). A natural-resource-based view of the firm. *Academy of Management Review, 20*(4), 986–1014.

Hart, S., & Dowell, G. (2011). A natural-resource-based view of the firm: Fifteen years after. *Journal of Management, 37*(5), 1464–1479. https://doi.org/10.1177/0149206310390219

Hartmann, J., & Uhlenbruck, K. (2015). National Institutional Antecedents to corporate environmental performance. *Journal of World Business, 50*(4), 729–741. https://doi.org/10.1016/j.jwb.2015.02.001

Hillman, A. J., & Keim, G. D. (2001). Shareholder value, stakeholder management, and social issues: What's the bottom line? *Strategic Management Journal, 22*(2), 125–139. https://doi.org/10.1002/1097-0266(200101)22:2<125::AID-SMJ150>3.0.CO;2-H

Homer, A. W. (2009). Coal mine safety regulation in China and the USA. *Journal of Contemporary Asia, 39*(3), 424–439. https://doi.org/10.1080/00472330902944511

Horváthová, E. (2010). Does environmental performance affect financial performance? A meta-analysis. *Ecological Economics, 70*(1), 52–59. https://doi.org/10.1016/j.ecolecon.2010.04.004

Iwata, H., & Okada, K. (2011). How does environmental performance affect financial performance? Evidence from Japanese manufacturing firms. *Special Section – Governing the Commons: Learning from Field and Laboratory Experiments, 70*(9), 1691–1700. https://doi.org/10.1016/j.ecolecon.2011.05.010

Kalia, D., & Aggarwal, D. (2023). Examining impact of ESG score on financial performance of healthcare companies. *Journal of Global Responsibility, 14*(1), 155–176. https://doi.org/10.1108/JGR-05-2022-0045

Kaufmann, D., Kraay, A., & Mastruzzi, M. (2010). The worldwide governance indicators: Methodology and analytical issues. World Bank, working paper series 5430.3.10.1017/S1876404511200046.

Kaufmann, D., Kraay, A., & Mastruzzi, M. (2011). The worldwide governance indicators: Methodology and analytical issues. *Hague Journal on the Rule of Law, 3*, 220–246. https://doi.org/10.1017/S1876404511200046

Keyworth, T. (2006). Measuring and managing the costs of red tape: A review of recent policy developments. *Oxford Review of Economic Policy, 22*(2), 260–273. https://doi.org/10.1093/oxrep/grj016

Khan, M., & Rana, A. T. (2021). Institutional quality and CO2 emission–output relations: The case of Asian countries. *Journal of Environmental Management, 279*, 111569. https://doi.org/10.1016/j.jenvman.2020.111569

Khan, H., Weili, L., & Khan, I. (2022). The role of institutional quality in FDI inflows and carbon emission reduction: Evidence from the global developing and belt road initiative countries. *Environmental Science and Pollution Research, 29*, 30594–30621. https://doi.org/10.1007/s11356-021-17958-6

Khanna, M., & Damon, L. A. (1999). EPA's voluntary 33/50 program: Impact on toxic releases and economic performance of firms. *Journal of Environmental Economics and Management, 37*(1), 1–25. https://doi.org/10.1006/jeem.1998.1057

Klassen, R. D., & McLaughlin, C. P. (1996). The impact of environmental management on firm performance. *Management Science, 42*(8), 1199–1214. https://doi.org/10.1287/mnsc.42.8.1199

Makridou, G., Doumpos, M., & Lemonakis, C. (2023). Relationship between ESG and corporate financial performance in the energy sector: Empirical evidence from European companies. *International Journal of Energy Sector Management, 18*(4), 873–895. https://doi.org/10.1108/IJESM-01-2023-0012

Midlarsky, M. I. (1998). Democracy and the environment: An empirical assessment. *Journal of Peace Research, 35*(3), 341–361. https://doi.org/10.1177/0022343398035003005

Misani, N., & Pogutz, S. (2015). Unraveling the effects of environmental outcomes and processes on financial performance: A non-linear approach. *Ecological Economics, 109*, 150–160. https://papers.ssrn.com/abstract=2533029

Naeem, N., & Çankaya, S. (2022). The impact of ESG performance over financial performance: A study on global energy and power generation companies. *International Journal of Commerce and Finance, 8*(1), 1–25.

Nguyen, L.-T. (2023). The relationship between environmental performance and financial performance: Evidence from an emerging east Asian economy. *International Journal of Disclosure and Governance, 20*(1), 1–14. https://doi.org/10.1057/s41310-022-00152-6

Nollet, J., Filis, G., & Mitrokostas, E. (2016). Corporate social responsibility and financial performance: A non-linear and disaggregated approach. *Economic Modelling, 52*, 400–407. https://doi.org/10.1016/j.econmod.2015.09.019

North, D. C. (1990). *Institutions, institutional change, and economic performance*. Cambridge University Press.

North, D. C. (2005). *Institutions, institutional change and economic performance*. Cambridge University Press.

Ozturk, I., & Al-Mulali, U. (2015). Investigating the validity of the environmental Kuznets curve hypothesis in Cambodia. *Ecological Indicators, 57*, 324–330. https://doi.org/10.1016/j.ecolind.2015.05.018

Parmar, B., Freeman, R., Harrison, J., Purnell, A., & De Colle, S. (2010). Stakeholder theory: The state of the art. *The Academy of Management Annals, 3*, 403–445. https://doi.org/10.1080/19416520.2010.495581

Pellegrini, L., & Gerlagh, R. (2006). Corruption, democracy, and environmental policy: An empirical contribution to the debate. *The Journal of Environment & Development, 15*(3), 332–354. https://doi.org/10.1177/1070496506290960

Peng, G., Zhang, J., & Shi, K. (2021). Determining the effectiveness of pollution control policies implemented by the Chinese government: Distribution fitting and testing of daily PM2.5 data. *Energy & Environment, 33*(8), 1487–1507. https://doi.org/10.1177/0958305X211043528

Pinheiro, A. B., Panza, G. B., Berhorst, N. L., Toaldo, A. M. M., & Segatto, A. P. (2023). Exploring the relationship among ESG, innovation, and economic and financial performance: Evidence from the energy sector. *International Journal of Energy Sector Management, 18*(3). https://doi.org/10.1108/IJESM-02-2023-0008

Qiu, R., Xu, J., & Zeng, Z. (2017). Carbon emission allowance allocation with a mixed mechanism in air passenger transport. *Journal of Environmental Management, 200*, 204–216. https://doi.org/10.1016/j.jenvman.2017.05.036

Rizk, R., & Slimane, M. B. (2018). Modelling the relationship between poverty, environment, and institutions: A panel data study. *Environmental Science and Pollution Research, 25*(31), 31459–31473. https://doi.org/10.1007/s11356-018-3051-6

Russo, M. V., & Fouts, P. A. (1997). A resource-based perspective on corporate environmental performance and profitability. *The Academy of Management Journal, 40*(3), 534–559. https://doi.org/10.2307/257052

Salama, A. (2005). A note on the impact of environmental performance on financial performance. *The Economics of Corporate Social Responsibility, 16*(3), 413–421. https://doi.org/10.1016/j.strueco.2004.04.005

Salman, M., Long, X., Dauda, L., & Mensah, C. N. (2019). The impact of institutional quality on economic growth and carbon emissions: Evidence from Indonesia, South Korea and Thailand. *Journal of Cleaner Production, 241*(20), 118331. https://doi.org/10.1016/j.jclepro.2019.118331

Samimi, A. J., Ahmadpour, M., & Ghaderi, S. (2012). Governance and environmental degradation in MENA region. *Procedia-Social and Behavioral Sciences., 62*, 503–507. https://doi.org/10.1016/j.sbspro.2012.09.082

Scott, W. R. (2001). *Institutions and Organisations* (2nd ed.). Sage Publications.

Shen, F., Ma, Y., Wang, R., Pan, N., & Meng, Z. (2019). Does environmental performance affect financial performance? Evidence from Chinese listed companies in heavily polluting industries. *Quality & Quantity, 53*(4), 1941–1958. https://doi.org/10.1007/s11135-019-00849-x

Slacik, J., Grüb, B., & Greiling, D. (2021). New wine in old bottles: Governing logics for applying sustainability management control systems in Austrian electric utilities. *International Journal of Energy Sector Management, 16*(1), 50–77. https://doi.org/10.1108/IJESM-06-2020-0016

Sulemana, I., & Kpienbaareh, D. (2020). Corruption and air pollution: A comparative study of African and OECD countries. *Air Quality Atmosphere & Health, 13*, 1421–1429. https://doi.org/10.1007/s11869-020-00896-6

Tarmizi, N. F. A., & Brahmana, R. K. (2023). Environmental performance, political connection, and financial performance: Evidence from global oil and gas companies. *Environmental Science and Pollution Research, 30*(4), 11081–11098. https://doi.org/10.1007/s11356-022-22881-5

Trumpp, C., & Guenther, T. (2017). Too little or too much? Exploring U-shaped relationships between corporate environmental performance and corporate financial performance. *Business Strategy and the Environment, 26*(1), 49–68. https://doi.org/10.1002/bse.1900

Velte, P. (2017). Does ESG performance have an impact on financial performance? Evidence from Germany. *Journal of Global Responsibility, 8*(2), 169–178. https://doi.org/10.1108/JGR-11-2016-0029

Walls, J. L., Berrone, P., & Phan, P. H. (2012). Corporate governance and environmental performance: Is there really a link? *Strategic Management Journal, 33*(8), 885–913. https://doi.org/10.1002/smj.1952

Wang, Z., Danish, Z. B., & Wang, B. (2018). The moderating role of corruption between economic growth and CO2 emissions: Evidence from BRICS economies. *Energy, 148*, 506–513. https://doi.org/10.1016/j.energy.2018.01.167

Ward, H. (2008). Liberal democracy and sustainability. *Environmental Politics, 17*(3), 386–409. https://doi.org/10.1080/09644010802055626

Weaver, G. R., Trevino, L. K., & Cochran, P. L. (1999). Integrated and decoupled corporate social performance: Management commitments, external pressures, and corporate ethics practices. *Academy of Management Journal, 42*(5), 539–552. https://doi.org/10.2307/256975

Welsch, H. (2004). Corruption, growth and environment: A cross-country analysis. *Environment and Economic Development, 9*(5), 663–693. https://doi.org/10.1017/S1355770X04001500

World Bank. (2024). Worldwide Governance Indicators. (www.govindicators.org)

Xie, J., Nozawa, W., Yagi, M., Fujii, H., & Managi, S. (2019). Do environmental, social, and governance activities improve corporate financial performance? *Business Strategy and the Environment, 28*(2), 286–300. https://doi.org/10.1002/bse.2224

Chapter 28
Does the COVID-19 Pandemic Reward Firms Performing Better on Corporate Social Matters?

Flavio Spagnuolo, Raffaela Casciello, and Emmadonata Carbone

28.1 Introduction

Most accounting studies have investigated causes, characteristics, and consequences of the pursuit of corporate environmental and governance goals, thus ignoring the social dimension of business practices. Managing the social aspects of business is a topic captivating more and more the attention of researchers, practitioners, and the public alike (Flammer, 2015; Saeidi et al., 2015; Sroufe & Gopalakrishna-Remani, 2019). Over the past decades, Corporate Social Performance (CSP, hereafter)—such as the "*configuration of principles of social responsibility, processes of social responsiveness, and policies, programs, and observable outcomes as they relate to the firm's societal relationships*" (Wood, 1991, p. 693)—has become increasingly essential to fully understand all the corporate outcomes in an integrated manner.

Although an univocal definition of CSP is missing to date, many scholars agree that it represents the outcome of investments made in Corporate Social Responsibility (CSR) measurable by rating agencies or external organizations, since stakeholders cannot acquire complete information on the CSR initiatives on their own (Cho & Lee, 2019; Barnett, 2007). Such activities are usually designed to improve social conditions within or outside the company and promote social good (e.g., Mackey et al., 2007; McWilliams & Siegel, 2001).

Many studies investigated the relationship between CSP and corporate financial performance (CFP) (e.g., Mellahi et al., 2016; Wang et al., 2016; Brower & Dacin, 2020; Sroufe & Gopalakrishna-Remani, 2019), especially under the perspective of CSR (e.g., Baron, 2001; Baron & Diermeier, 2007; Hillman & Keim, 2001).

F. Spagnuolo · R. Casciello (✉) · E. Carbone
Department of Economics, Management, Institutions (DEMI), University of Naples "Federico II", Naples, Italy
e-mail: flavio.spagnuolo@unina.it; raffaela.casciello@unina.it; emmadonata.carbone@unina.it

N. Castellano et al. (eds.), *Environmental, Social, Governance (ESG)*, SIDREA Series in Accounting and Business Administration,
https://doi.org/10.1007/978-3-031-76618-3_28

Notwithstanding, the evidence about the relationship between CSP and CFP is still mixed and sometimes contradictory (Aupperle et al., 1985; Barnett & Salomon, 2006; Lopez et al., 2007). The uncertainty surrounding the link between CSP and CFP stems from conflicting drivers behind CSR decision-making (Cho & Lee, 2019). Moreover, there is a growing consensus about the fact that the CSP-CFP relationship may be dynamic and not consistently predictable (Brower & Dacin, 2020). Therefore, the nature of such relationship, particularly for European listed non-financial companies, remains unresolved. Recent studies on more structured CSP approaches (Bice, 2017; Bondy et al., 2012), the emergence of CSP rating agencies (Avetisyan & Ferrary, 2013), and the increasing pressure to create socially sustainable projects for operational legitimacy (Deephouse et al., 2017) have not reached a definitive conclusion on this issue yet.

The first aim of this study is to investigate whether in the context of European listed non-financial firms in the period 2017–2022 the CSP is significantly associated with the market-based CFP and if the relationship is positive or negative.

Consistent with the "stakeholder theory" (Donaldson & Preston, 1995; Freeman, 1984; Freeman & Reed, 1983; Jones, 1995), engaging in social initiatives not only helps companies maintaining trust and good relationships with stakeholders, but also fosters the corporate reputation on strong ethical commitment (Daily & Huang, 2001). Companies adopting socially sustainable practices often enjoy lower implicit costs and witness an improvement in financial performance (Cornell & Shapiro, 1987). This favorable correlation grounds in the idea that business success is linked to how firms address the multiple needs of stakeholders and local community (Barnett et al., 2006; Vurro & Perrini, 2011). Conversely, negative perceptions of low social sustainability diminish a firm's capacity to attract capital and capture investors' attention (McGuire et al., 1988), since socially sustainable practices lead investors to perceive investments in such firms as riskier (Alexander & Buchholz, 1978; Spicer, 1978).

Consistent with the "shareholder theory" (Friedman, 1970; Clarke & Friedman, 2016; Jensen, 2001), firms are interested in optimizing profits for their shareholders, complying at the same time with relevant regulations and laws. This perspective views the maximization of financial performance as the corporate primary goal. Companies investing in socially responsible initiatives incur substantial expenses. If these investments do not yield a corresponding economic gain, which is not always guaranteed, they might undermine earnings and damage the value creation for shareholders. Therefore, socially responsible investments by drawing resources away from the company's core business reduce corporate efficiency and competitive advantage. In addition, they have a long-term orientation (Haley, 1991; Godfrey, 2005), while shareholders are primarily interested in short-term gains. For such reasons, socially responsible investment and CSP may not be viewed favorably by shareholders (Dunn & Sainty, 2009).

Since the relationship between CSP and market-based CFP can be alternatively positive or negative, for the reasons stated above in light of the stakeholder theory and the shareholder theory, this study aims to investigate the characteristic of such relationship in the context of European listed non-financial companies during the period 2017–2022.

The second half of such period (2020–2022) was characterized by the onset of the COVID-19 pandemic. The spread of the pandemic all over Europe challenged firms and organizations on how to properly manage CSR commitment, especially since the pandemic has damaged the social dimension of individuals in many ways (He & Harris, 2020). During the COVID-19 pandemic, European firms were expected to be more inclined to undertake socially oriented projects or initiatives for ethical, philanthropic, or competitive reasons (He & Harris, 2020). Their commitment to CSR policies may have attracted more of the attention of consumers, shareholders, market participants, investors, and various stakeholders, in those months critical for the social dimension of human life. This may have generated positive outcomes for the market-based CFP of firms.

To date, it is unknown whether firms enhancing their CSP during the COVID-19 pandemic received greater reward from investors, lenders, and other stakeholders, with positive consequences for the market-based CFP.

Therefore, the second aim of this study is to investigate the role of the COVID-19 pandemic in shaping the relationship between CSP and market-based CFP. In posing the research question, four factors have been considered.

First, the COVID-19 pandemic may have heightened the efforts of European companies in pursuing social goals (He & Harris, 2020).

Second, companies showing a tangible commitment to social sustainability, worker well-being, and support for local communities typically attract the interest of investors and consumers (He & Harris, 2020).

Third, investors are increasingly drawn to sustainable and responsible environmental, social, and governance (ESG) investments (Scholtens, 2014; Eccles et al., 2017; Escrig-Olmedo et al., 2017).

Fourth, European institutions have recently introduced initiatives aimed at safeguarding workplaces and workers damaged by the pandemic, as well as protecting personal data and privacy during the diffusion of COVID-19 and implementing remote working measures. The United Nations (UN) too encouraged firms to embrace socially sustainable development to solve the COVID-19 crisis, thus boosting the CSR politics. Hence, based on the above factors, we expect that the COVID-19 pandemic determined a positive relationship between CSP and market-based CFP in European listed non-financial firms.

Research hypotheses are tested through panel fixed-effects regression models. Results demonstrate that CSP is negatively associated with CFP and that the effects of COVID-19 pandemic on the perception of the social dimension were so strong that such relationship turns positive. Moreover, we performed additional analyses on two different firms' subsamples, based on industries' COVID-19 sensitiveness. Specifically, the findings demonstrate that the positive CSP-CFP relationship is significantly stronger in firms operating in industries more exposed to COVID-19 compared to those in less exposed industries. The results suggest that the relationship between CSP and CFP is industry-dependent.

This study contributes to the accounting literature in multiple ways.

First, it addresses the call for more research on the social dimension of sustainability, the least explored pillar among the ESG ones (Nikolakis et al., 2022). Second, this study contributes to disentangle the intricate relationship between CSP and CFP in European listed non-financial firms, thus investigating the effects of the COVID-19 pandemic. Third, it provides the first empirical evidence of the role of the COVID-19 pandemic in restoring centrality to the social dimension of human life in corporate contexts and strategic business decisions. Fourth, it demonstrated that during the COVID-19 pandemic, market participants rewarded firms performing better on corporate social matters.

The chapter is structured as follows. Section 28.2 contains the literature review and presents the research hypotheses. Section 28.3 shows the sample selection and the research methodology. Section 28.4 presents the results of descriptive statistics and regression models, while Section 28.5 shows the robustness tests. Section 28.6 provides discussions and conclusions.

28.2 Literature Review and Research Hypotheses

Social sustainability performance can be defined as the social impacts resulting from an organization's sustainable practices and policies (Daily & Huang, 2001; Wilkinson et al., 2001). It gauges the degree to which growth- and development-enhancing conditions exist within organizations, aiming to achieve diverse social goals (Sroufe & Gopalakrishna-Remani, 2019).

This performance metric serves as a measure of the organization's commitment to various dimensions of social responsibility, responding to the increasing expectations placed on companies beyond mere profitability considerations (Matten & Moon, 2008; Sharma & Henriques, 2005).

Many studies investigated the relationship between CSP and CFP (e.g., Mellahi et al., 2016; Wang et al., 2016; Brower & Dacin, 2020; Sroufe & Gopalakrishna-Remani, 2019), especially under the perspective of CSR (e.g., Baron, 2001; Baron & Diermeier, 2007; Hillman & Keim, 2001). To date, the evidence about the relationship between CSP and CFP is mixed and sometimes contradictory. For example, according to Lopez et al. (2007) the higher the CSP, the lower the CFP in the first years in which sustainability practices are applied; according to Barnett and Salomon (2006) the improvement in CSP is positively associated with the CFP. Instead, Aupperle et al. (1985) declared the absence of relationship between the CSP and the CFP. According to Cho and Lee (2019) the lack of definitive evidence about the relationship between CSP and CFP may be traced back to conflicting motivations influencing the choices of CSR.

Previous studies explored peculiar mechanisms through which the CSP may impact firm performance (Flammer, 2013; Mellahi et al., 2016), thus arguing about the possible time spans to wait for seeing the payoff of the investments in CSP (Wang et al., 2016). Notwithstanding, there is a growing consensus that the relationship between CSP and CFP is dynamic and not always predictable (Brower

& Dacin, 2020). To date, there is no univocal answer regarding the direction of the relationship between CSP and CFP, especially for the European listed nonfinancial companies in recent years characterized by an increasing rationalization of CSP (e.g., Bice, 2017, Bondy et al., 2012), the presence of CSP rating agencies (Avetisyan & Ferrary, 2013), and the pressure to develop social sustainable project to gain legitimacy to operate (Deephouse et al., 2017). Therefore, this study investigates whether in the context of European listed nonfinancial firms in the period 2017–2022, the CSP is significantly associated with market-based CFP.

According to the stakeholder theory (Donaldson & Preston, 1995; Freeman, 1984; Freeman & Reed, 1983; Jones, 1995), firms are morally and ethically obligated to fulfill their commitments to all stakeholders (e.g., employees, customers, suppliers, the local community) both explicitly and implicitly. In turn, corporates' socially responsible actions can serve business interests and enhance financial performance (Rowley & Berman, 2000). As for the market-based perspective, the firm's social attitude is seen as instrumental to corporate effectiveness and, its performance. Organizational behavior and practices aiming to pursue social sustainability can result in improved financial performance (Daily & Huang, 2001). From the stakeholder theory perspective, firms with socially sustainable practices have more low-cost implicit claims and experience an increase in financial performance (Cornell & Shapiro, 1987). This positive relationship rests on the fundamental assumption that success in business is reached also by dealing with the different needs of stakeholders and community (Barnett et al., 2006, Vurro & Perrini, 2011).

By socially acting, firms maintain trust and positive relationships with stakeholders and build a strong reputation for being socially responsible and reliable. As stakeholders are continuously asking them to provide more information on how they identify and manage sustainability issues, firms improve social activities and disclosure to gain the legitimacy to operate. Companies demonstrating their social performance and commitment to stakeholders have a better chance to improve reputation from media exposure (Michelon et al., 2020). In contrast, a lack of socially sustainable practices can also discourage investors, as they perceive a higher risk in investing such firms (Alexander & Buchholz, 1978; Spicer, 1978). Negative perceptions of low social sustainability decrease a firm's ability to attract capital and investors' attention and constrain relationship between companies and the financial community (McGuire et al., 1988). Therefore, based on the above arguments, the relationship between CSP and market-based CFP may be positive.

According to the shareholder theory (Friedman, 1970; Clarke & Friedman, 2016; Jensen, 2001), the primary responsibility of a company is to maximize the profit for its shareholders, while complying with applicable rules and laws. This approach considers the financial performance as the corporate primary objective.

As for the market-based perspective, the social sustainability activities implemented by firms have a long-term orientation; therefore, the CSP may be appreciated in the long run. Generally, long-term institutional shareholders evaluate positively the CSP (Cox et al., 2004; Neubaum & Zahra, 2006). However, shareholders are primarily interested in short-term gains. Since long-term investments in social responsibility soon burden the corporate cost structure and show the results only in the long term (Haley, 1991; Godfrey, 2005), these may not be viewed favorably by shareholders (Dunn & Sainty, 2009). Firms investing in socially responsible initiatives face significant costs. If these costs are not balanced by an equivalent economic return, they can erode profits and reduce shareholder value. In addition, shareholders may interpret socially responsible investment as activities that divert time and focus from the company's core business activities. This may lead to a loss of efficiency and competitiveness in its core business. As resources are diverted from the main goal of generating profit, shareholders may not be interested in CSP. Based on the above arguments, the relationship between CSP and market-based CFP may be negative.

Since the relationship between the CSP and the market-based CFP in European listed nonfinancial companies during the period 2017–2022 can be alternatively positive or negative, each being interpretable in light of the stakeholder theory or the shareholder theory, respectively, we pose a research hypothesis open to both outcomes as follows.

HP1 During the period 2017–2022, the relationship between CSP and market-based CFP in European listed non-financial companies is positive/negative and statistically significant.

The outbreak of the COVID-19 pandemic in 2020 had a significant impact on the global economy (Euronews, 2020), the perception of sociality, health protection, human rights (Tisdell, 2020) and on the consumer ethic (He & Harris, 2020). In many European countries, the imposition of lockdown measures and restrictions on the daily activities of citizens (aimed at protecting personal and community health) led to limitations on personal freedoms, such as the freedom of movement (Fenichel, 2013; Tisdell, 2020). Living for months with restrictions and limitations raised many questions about the balance between protecting public health and respecting individual rights (Acemoglu et al., 2020). The pandemic also highlighted the importance of taking measures to protect human health in several contexts, such as in institutions, public administrations, companies, and other social organizations (Tisdell, 2020). Butcher and Massey (2020) demonstrated that people from Black, Asian, and minority ethnic (BAME) backgrounds were more exposed to the risk of contracting the virus and die for it than other people. This issue not only exacerbated social differences between groups of individuals, but also captured the public's attention to the presence of inequalities and social problems that can no longer be ignored.

The COVID-19 pandemic also generated slowdowns in some production activities all over Europe, thus damaging the productivity of many companies and generating adverse economic consequences for entrepreneurs and shareholders (e.g., Acemoglu et al., 2020; Tisdell, 2020). Obstacles to production activities and the adoption of specific contingency measures significantly impacted workers' working conditions and wages, increasing social inequalities (e.g., Acemoglu et al., 2020; Tisdell, 2020).

Some firms have profited economically from the crisis created by the pandemic, especially by raising the prices (He & Harris, 2020). Yet, in some cases, companies were shown to have a proactive role in combating the spread of the virus, providing concrete support to people in economic difficulty, and protecting the right to health (Lindsay, 2020; Jones, 2020). For example, He and Harris (2020) reported the existence of UK manufacturing companies that converted their traditional production to the production of ventilators, personal protective equipment, and hand sanitizer. Many of them were donated.

The spread of the COVID-19 pandemic has posed challenges to firms and organizations about the CSR, especially in light of the improved sensitivity to social issues of the European community (He & Harris, 2020). During the COVID-19 pandemic, European companies may have been more prone to implement socially oriented projects (or initiatives) for ethical, philanthropic, or competitive purposes (He & Harris, 2020). By publicly adopting CSR policies, these firms may have also attracted the attention of consumers, shareholders, market participants, investors, and many other kinds of stakeholders in order to benefit from higher market-based CFP. Today, it is still unknown if firms improving their CSP during the COVID-19 pandemic may have been more rewarded by investors, lenders, and other stakeholders by experiencing an increase in their market-based CFP. This study investigates if in the context of European listed nonfinancial firms, the COVID-19 pandemic caused the CSP to be significantly associated with the market-based CFP. The association between CSP and market-based CFP may be positive or negative, depending on which phenomenon happens and/or prevails on the other.

During the COVID-19 pandemic, investors might consider CSP as a type of performance that is not particularly relevant compared to financial performance or not worthy of special attention during the capital allocation decisions. In this case, CSP would not be significantly associated with market-based CFP.

Similarly, investors might assume that during the COVID-19 pandemic, companies that strive to demonstrate good CSP are engaging in "greenwashing" strategies on social aspects for opportunistic purposes (Yu et al., 2020). In this case, investors might "punish" these companies, thus causing a decline in their market-based CFP. The CSP would be negatively associated with market-based CFP. Instead, we do believe that in the context of European listed nonfinancial firms, the COVID-19 pandemic caused the CSP to be positively (and significantly) associated with the market-based CFP. Four reasons support our expectation.

First, although social sustainability has always been an important part of responsible business strategies, the COVID-19 pandemic may have intensified the efforts of European companies in pursuing social goals (He & Harris, 2020). During the pandemic, companies have acknowledged their central role in protecting human rights through investments ensuring safety in the workplace, access to medical care, and support to meet economic challenges (He & Harris, 2020).

Second, companies demonstrating a concrete commitment to social sustainability, worker health, and support for local communities usually attract the interest of investors and consumers (He & Harris, 2020), especially of those ones becoming increasingly sensitive to these issues.

Third, investors are showing more and more interest in sustainable and responsible ESG investments (Eccles et al., 2017; Escrig-Olmedo et al., 2017; Scholtens, 2014). By signing the "United Nations Principles for Responsible investment," many large investors made an agreement to make capital allocation choices considering the consequences of investments from an ESG point of view. Since then, the number of ESG-sensitive investors has increased significantly, especially the institutional ones (Eccles et al., 2017; EUROSIF, 2014). Moreover, investing in firms pursuing ESG targets demonstrated to generate competitive returns, thus fueling the market's interest in making sustainable capital allocation choices (Eccles et al., 2017; Kotsantonis et al., 2016). The pandemic may have reinforced this trend, thus prompting investors to evaluate companies not only by their financial performance, but also by their social impact (e.g., employment quality, safety and health, training and development, diversity and opportunity, human rights, community, and product responsibility). These investors often seek investment opportunities in companies that demonstrate sustainable and responsible management of social factors because they help to understand the corporate long-term resilience and sustainability (Eccles et al., 2017).

A recent study by Broadstock et al. (2021) showed that during the COVID-19 pandemic in the context of Chinese listed companies, high ESG investment portfolios surpassed low ESG ones. This evidence indicates that investors chose sustainable investments during the pandemic, especially because ESG performance counteracted financial risk during financial crisis generated by the COVID-19 spread.

Fourth, European institutions have recently introduced initiatives aimed at protecting workplaces and workers affected by the pandemic ("Support to mitigate Unemployment Risks in an Emergency"), protecting personal data and privacy during the implementation of COVID-19 and implementing remote work tracking measures ("General Data Protection Regulation"). The UN encouraged firms to embrace the social sustainable development to recover the economy from the COVID-19 pandemic and build an economic system more resilient to pandemic crises. These measures created additional expectations on companies to strengthen their commitment to solve social issues and on investors and market participants to reward those companies improving the CSP.

Therefore, based on the above arguments, we expect that during the COVID-19 pandemic the relationship between CSP and market-based CFP in European listed non-financial companies is positive, thus posing the following research hypothesis.

HP2 During the COVID-19 pandemic, the relationship between CSP and market-based CFP in European listed non-financial companies is positive.

28.3 Methodology

28.3.1 Sample

The data are collected from the *Thomson Reuters Refinitiv Eikon* database, frequently used for rigorous sustainability- and accounting-based scientific analyses

(De Villiers et al., 2022; Patten, 2015; Richardson, 2015). The initial sample was composed of 2622 European (EU-27) listed non-financial companies over the years 2017–2022, excluding public authorities, states, and governments. Even before the worldwide spread of the COVID-19 pandemic in 2020, this period has been characterized by an increasing pressure to improve the social performance in corporate organizations (Fatima & Elbanna, 2023). The data are collected from 2017 to obtain a symmetric year distribution based on two periods: the pre-COVID-19 pandemic period between 2017 and 2019 and the COVID-19 pandemic period between 2020 and 2022 (Hong et al., 2024; Huang et al., 2024). The initial sample was composed of 2623 non-financial companies. After excluding companies without comprehensive financial and non-financial data (i.e., ESG data), the final sample is composed of 743 companies, encompassing 3792 firm-year observations.[1]

28.3.2 Statistical Models

The first hypothesis (HP1) tests if and how companies' market-based CFP is associated with companies' CSP. Consistent with previous studies (Franco et al., 2020; Lin et al., 2019; Okafor et al., 2021), we empirically address this research question relying on the following panel fixed-effects regression model (Eq. 28. 1)[2]:

$$\text{TOBIN } Q_{i,t}/\text{PTB}_{i,t} = \beta_0 + \beta_1 \text{CSP}_{i,t-1} + \sum Controls_{i,t-1} + \sum \text{FE}_j^y + \varepsilon_{i,t} \tag{28. 1}$$

Two proxies are used for measuring firms' market-based CFP. The first one is Tobin's Q (i.e., *TOBIN Q*), computed as the sum of the market value of the firm and the book value of its debt on its total assets (Harjoto & Jo, 2011; Wang & Qian, 2011; Aouadi & Marsat, 2018). This variable captures the market expectations on the companies' future financial performance, frequently used by scholars to test the CSP-CFP relationship as an indicator of CFP (Luo & Bhattacharya, 2006). The second proxy is the Price-To-Book ratio (i.e., *PTB*), computed as the ratio between firm's market price per share and firm's book value per share (Nguyen, 2018). Similar to Tobin's Q proxy, when PTB returns low values, the market perceives the future firm's profitability as low (i.e., the value of the firm is undervalued and lower CFP). Conversely, when the PTB is high, the firm's stock value is overvalued (i.e., higher CFP). The CSP, the independent variable of our study, is measured through the social pillar score (i.e., *CSP*) provided by *Thomson Reuters Refinitiv*

---

[1] All continuous variables are winsorized at the first and 99th percentiles to mitigate the influence of outliers.

[2] In order to establish the foundation for our reliance on these model specifications, we conducted both the Breusch-Pagan Lagrange multiplier test (1980) and the Hausman test, as introduced by Hausman and Taylor (1981).

Eikon database. This score measures a "company's capacity to generate trust and loyalty with its workforce, customers, and society, through its use of best management practices. It reflects the company's reputation and the health of its license to operate, which are key factors in determining its ability to generate long-term shareholder value" (Thomson Reuters Eikon, 2018). Therefore, it measures the results of the corporate activities for pursuing social objectives[3] (Aktas et al., 2011; Teti et al., 2022). One main concern that arises in statistical analysis is the problem of the endogeneity, occurring when an independent variable may be correlated with the errors of the model. To alleviate part of this endogeneity concern, we use 1-year lagged social pillar score to control for potential reverse causality concerns about CSP-CFP relationship (Lin et al., 2019; Liu et al., 2022). Overall, the significantly positive (negative) coefficient on β_1 in Eq. 28. 1 at any conventional level would indicate that the CSP is positively (negatively) associated with the CFP, and our first hypothesis would be confirmed (HP1).

To test our second hypothesis about the role of the COVID-19 pandemic in shaping the CSP-CFP relationship, we rely on the following equation (Eq. 28.2):

$$\begin{aligned} \text{TOBIN } Q_{i,t}/\text{PTB}_{i,t} = {} & \alpha_0 + \alpha_1 \text{CSP}_{i,t-1} + \alpha_2 \text{COVID} * \text{CSP}_{i,t-1} \\ & + \alpha_3 \text{COVID} + \sum \textit{Controls}_{i,t-1} + \sum \text{FE}_j^y + \varepsilon_{i,t} \end{aligned} \tag{28.2}$$

We add in Eq. (28.2) a dichotomic variable (i.e., *COVID*) that is equal to 1 for years 2020–2022 (i.e., COVID-19 pandemic period) and 0 otherwise (i.e., pre-COVID-19 pandemic period). To accept the second hypothesis (HP2), i.e. during the COVID-19 pandemic the CSP-CFP relationship is positive, it is necessary that the coefficient α_2 on interaction variable *COVID*CSP* is significantly positive at conventional level. Despite that, such circumstance is not sufficient to fully support HP2. In particular, the interpretation of our results in relation to this hypothesis depends also on both signs and magnitude of α_1: whereas α_1 is significantly greater than 0, the HP2 would be supported if and only if $\alpha_2 > \alpha_1$. The set of control variables (*Controls*) is selected consistent with prior academic findings on the determinants of market-based CFP, such as firm size (*SIZE*), measured as the natural logarithm of total assets (Kim & Li, 2021; Li & Chen, 2018; Yu & Van Luu, 2021; Nuber et al., 2020); leverage (*LEVERAGE*), measured as the ratio of total debt to total assets (Li & Chen, 2018; Nuber et al., 2020; Yu & Van Luu, 2021); Altman Z-score (*ZSCORE*) (Altman, 1968); return on equity ratio (*ROE*), computed as the earnings before taxes divided by total stockholders' equity (Ruf et al., 2001); the board size (*BOARD*), measured as the natural logarithm of the number of directors (Yu & Van Luu, 2021); and the corporate social responsibility committee (*CSRCOM*), a dichotomic variable equals to 1 if the firm has a committee on

[3]Although previous literature widely utilized ESG metrics provided by recognized data providers (Krishnamurti et al., 2019; Yen & André, 2019), we are aware that such measures may change retroactively basing on the extraction date (Sahin et al., 2023).

Table 28.1 Variables description

Variable	Type	Description	Source
TOBIN Q	Continuous variable	The ratio between the sum of the market value of the firm and the book value of its debt and firm's total assets for firm *i* at year *t*	Constructed *(Thomson Reuters Refinitiv Eikon)*
PTB	Continuous variable	The ratio between firm's market price per share and firm's book value per share for firm *i* at year *t*	
CSP	Continuous variable	Social pillar score for firm *i* at year *t-1*	*Thomson Reuters Refinitiv Eikon*
COVID	Dummy variable	Dichotomic variable equals to 1 for all observations related to years 2020–2022 (i.e., COVID-19 pandemic period) and 0 otherwise (i.e., pre-COVID-19 pandemic period)	Constructed *(Thomson Reuters Refinitiv Eikon)*
SIZE	Continuous variable	The natural logarithm of the book value of assets for firm *i* at year *t-1*	Constructed *(Thomson Reuters Refinitiv Eikon)*
LEVERAGE	Continuous variable	The ratio of total liabilities on total assets for firm *i* at year *t-1*	*Thomson Reuters Refinitiv Eikon*
ZSCORE	Continuous variable	Altman Z-score for firm *i* at year *t-1*	
ROE	Continuous variable	The ratio of net income on equity for firm *i* at year *t-1*	
BOARD	Continuous variable	The natural logarithm of the number of directors for firm *i* at year *t-1*	
CSRCOM	Dummy variable	Dichotomic variable equals to 1 if the firm has a committee on corporate social responsibility/sustainability and to 0, otherwise, for firm *i* at year *t-1*	

corporate social responsibility/sustainability and 0 otherwise (Yu & Van Luu, 2021). The regression models include *FE* to control for country *j* and year *y* fixed effects under indicated model specifications. All companies' data are provided by the *Thomson Reuters Refinitiv Eikon* database, while Table 28.1 describes all variables employed for the analyses.

28.4 Results

Table 28.2 provides the description of the sample composition by industry (Fama-French 12-industry classification) and country. Most companies operate in the Manufacturing sector (i.e., 1392 observations), in the Business Equipment sector (i.e., 753 observations), or in the Communication sector (i.e., Telephone and TV;

Table 28.2 Sample description

	Frequencies	%
Panel A: distribution by industry		
Industry		
Business Equipment	753	19.86%
Chemicals	234	6.17%
Consumer Durables	178	4.69%
Energy	58	1.53%
Healthcare	63	1.66%
Manufacturing	1392	36.71%
Consumer Nondurables	81	2.14%
Telephone and TV	435	11.47%
Utilities	236	6.22%
Wholesale, Retail, Shops	299	7.89%
Other	63	1.66%
Total	*3792*	*100%*
Panel B: distribution by Country (EU-27)		
Country		
Austria	89	2.35%
Belgium	205	5.41%
Croatia	20	0.53%
Cyprus	54	1.42%
Denmark	7	0.18%
Estonia	25	0.66%
Finland	187	4.93%
France	836	22.05%
Germany	1068	28.16%
Greece	166	4.38%
Ireland	33	0.87%
Italy	453	11.95%
Latvia	13	0.34%
Lithuania	15	0.40%
Luxembourg	76	2.00%
Malta	14	0.37%
Netherlands	176	4.64%
Portugal	33	0.87%
Slovakia	28	0.74%
Slovenia	60	1.58%
Spain	227	5.99%
Sweden	7	0.18%
Total	*3792*	*100*

Notes: This table reports the sample composition. Panel A reports acquirers' industry affiliation based on the Fama-French 12-industry classification. Panel B refers to distribution by the acquirer's country (EU-27) with at least one observation. % Events refers to the percentage of deals on the total number of deals included in our final sample (3792 observations)

435 observations). Considering the geographical origin, the most represented countries in the sample are Germany (i.e., 1068, 28% of observations), France (i.e., 836, 22% of observations), and Italy (i.e., 453, approximately 12% of observations).

Table 28.3 provides descriptive statistics for all the variables employed in the study, distinguished by the COVID-19 pandemic versus pre-COVID-19 pandemic period. These statistics reveal that the financial performance of the companies investigated remains consistent across the two periods, with a slight decrease in the COVID-19 period subsample. Regarding the social performance, CSP increases from 62 to 65. Moreover, the mean value of LEVERAGE is less than 0.30 (for both subsamples), which means that companies under investigation are 70% financed by internal capital. Similarly, the mean ZSCORE of our sample indicates a positive value (i.e., 3.035).

As for governance aspects, the boards of directors of investigated firms are composed, on average, of 11 members, with consistency pre- and during COVID-19 pandemic. Differently, we recognize a low presence of governance mechanisms dedicated to sustainability (i.e., 19% of the overall sample presents a CSR committee).

The Pearson correlation matrix is reported in Table 28.4.

It could be noticed a positive correlation among our CFP measures In addition, the table shows a negative and significant correlation between CSP and both CFP measures. Among other things, while there exists a negative and significant correlation between board size and CFP, the correlation between BOARD and CSP is positive and significant. Overall, multicollinearity is not a problem in our analysis since the untabulated variance inflation factors (VIFs) in our regressions are below the cutoff of 5 (Hair et al., 2010).

Table 28.5 presents the estimation of Eqs. (28. 1) and (28.2), respectively, tabulated in Panel A and Panel B.

Panel A demonstrates that the shareholder perspective prevails over the stakeholders' viewpoint. In fact, the relationship between CSP and CFP is negative and statistically significant at the 99% confidence level. This is true for each dependent variable (i.e., TOBIN Q, models 1 and 3; PTB, models 2 and 4). As proposed in the theoretical background, challenging the assumptions of the stakeholder theory, the shareholder perspective contends that CSR activities are generally perceived as diverging from the interests of shareholders. Considering the primary responsibility of a corporation to generate profits for its shareholders, any allocation of resources toward social or environmental initiatives may be viewed as a deviation from this profit-centric mission. Our results support these arguments and strengthen previous empirical evidence, indicating a negative relationship between CSR and firm value (Crisóstomo et al., 2011), particularly from a market standpoint (Tampakoudis & Anagnostopoulou, 2020).

Examining Panel B reveals results from Eq. (28.2). The findings lend support to HP2, indicating that the COVID-19 pandemic crisis turns positively the relationship between CSP and CFP in European listed non-financial companies. Indeed, the interaction variable CSP*COVID is positive and significantly associated with CFP in all models ($p < 0.1$ in model 1 and model 3, and $p < 0.05$ in model 2 and model 4),

Table 28.3 Descriptive statistics

Panel A: descriptive statistics by *COVID-19* versus *non-COVID-19 period*

	COVID-19 period			*Non-COVID-19 period*			*Full sample*				
	Mean	Median	St.dev.	Mean	Median	St.dev.	Mean	Median	St.dev.	Min	Max
TOBIN Q	1.165	0.655	1.582	1.374	0.744	1.156	1.256	0.702	1.091	0.002	10.371
PTB	1.624	0.939	2.180	1.824	1.008	2.342	1.711	0.966	2.254	0.001	14.411
CSP	65.478	69.927	21.435	62.317	66.151	22.355	63.467	67.438	22.073	6.831	96.360
COVID	0	0	0	1	1	0	0.564	1	0.496	0	1
SIZE	22.521	22.495	1.512	21.820	21.757	1.787	22.075	22.034	1.725	17.997	25.953
LEVERAGE	0.244	0.233	0.154	0.284	0.275	0.162	0.270	0.259	0.161	0.000	0.713
ZSCORE	3.059	2.261	2.971	3.021	2.271	3.047	3.035	2.262	3.019	−1.646	19.511
ROE	0.137	0.130	0.134	0.098	0.118	0.196	0.113	0.122	0.176	−0.746	0.662
BOARD	11.569	12	4.327	10.159	10	4.324	10.672	10	4.378	2	30
CSRCOM	0.236	0	0.425	0.178	0	0.383	0.199	0	0.340	0	1
obs.	*1652*			*2140*			*3792*				
obs. %	*43.57%*			*56.93%*			*100%*				

Notes: This table reports the descriptive statistics (mean, median, standard deviation, minimum, and maximum) for the variables employed in the study. All the variables were winsorized at the first and 99th percentiles

Table 28.4 Pearson correlations

	1	2	3	4	5	6	7	8	9	10
TOBIN Q	**1**									
PTB	**0.842**	**1**								
CSP	**–0.091**	**–0.060**	**1**							
COVID	–0.046	0.044	–0.069	**1**						
SIZE	0.251	0.186	0.578	–0.196	**1**					
LEVERAGE	**–0.198**	–0.038	–0.052	**0.121**	**0.138**	**1**				
ZSCORE	**0.637**	**0.523**	**–0.122**	0.006	**–0.241**	**–0.482**	**1**			
ROE	**0.212**	**0.206**	**0.078**	**–0.105**	**0.077**	**–0.137**	**0.277**	**1**		
BOARD	**–0.224**	**–0.188**	**0.390**	**–0.155**	**0.604**	**–0.096**	**–0.238**	0.013	**1**	
CSRCOM	**–0.068**	–0.040	**0.242**	**–0.070**	**0.296**	**0.128**	**–0.112**	0.019	**0.180**	**1**

Notes: This table displays Pearson's correlations with figures in bold indicating statistical significance at the 95% confidence level or better

while the coefficient on CSP remains negative, in line with results provided by Panel A of Table 28.5. Coherently with our theoretical predictions, the heightened attention toward social initiatives during the COVID-19 pandemic (e.g., Escrig-Olmedo et al., 2017) positively influences the relationship between CSP and market-based CFP. Overall, this result aligns theoretically with the stakeholder perspective, whereas it indicates that companies committed in higher social behaviors enhance their financial performance (Eccles et al., 2017; Martínez-Ferrero & Frías-Aceituno, 2015; Arouri et al., 2019), even boosting their market value (Kaspereit & Lopatta, 2016; Yadav et al., 2016, 2017). One likely motivation could be that investors' preferences may have shifted during the pandemic, with a growing demand for ethically and socially responsible business practices (Humphreys & Trotman, 2022). Thus, companies aligning their CSR efforts with these evolving preferences may also have experienced improved financial outcomes.

28.5 Robustness Tests

To assess the validity of main results, we perform further analyses which strengthen the inferences. First, we adopt a different methodological approach to investigate CSP-CFP relationship and the role of the COVID-19 pandemic in shaping such a relation.

Specifically, we divided all firm-year observations into two subsamples, consisting of observations before and during the COVID-19 pandemic. Table 28.6

Table 28.5 Main analyses

	Tobin's Q (1)	PTB (2)	Tobin's Q (3)	PTB (4)
Panel A: panel analysis from Eq. (28. 1)—the relationship between CSP and CFP				
Intercept	1.215***	34.184***	1.345***	33.343***
CSP	−0.008***	−0.009***	−0.007***	−0.010***
SIZE	0.051***	1.435***	0.050***	1.420***
LEVERAGE	−0.031**	0.023	−0.031**	−0.025
ZSCORE	−0.001	−0.049**	−0.000	−0.042**
ROE	0.014**	0.384**	0.009	0.216
BOARD	0.001	−0.015	−0.009	0.001
CSRCOM	0.003	0.102	0.002	0.092
Year FE	No	No	Yes	Yes
Country FE	No	No	Yes	Yes
Observations	3792	3792	3792	3792
R^2	0.14	0.12	0.18	0.18
Panel A: panel analysis from Eq. (28.2)—the role of COVID-19				
Intercept	1.233***	34.940***	1.205***	33.550***
CSP	−0.022***	−0.011***	−0.015***	−0.007***
CSP* COVID	0.006*	0.007**	0.006*	0.006**
COVID	−0.010*	−0.0304*	0.004	0.092
SIZE	0.051***	1.462***	0.051***	1.424***
LEVERAGE	−0.034**	−0.084	−0.033**	−0.074
ZSCORE	−0.001	−0.052**	−0.000	−0.045**
ROE	0.014**	0.379**	0.019	0.200
BOARD	−0.000	−0.125	0.000	0.002
CSRCOM	0.002	0.082	0.002	0.082
Year FE	No	No	Yes	Yes
Country FE	No	No	Yes	Yes
Observations	3792	3792	3792	3792
R^2	0.14	0.12	0.18	0.18

Notes: This table provides results of panel data for regression explained in Eq. (28. 1). We include country and industry fixed effects in the regression or firm fixed effect under a different specification. Standard errors are clustered at firm level in all models. ***, **, and * indicate statistical significance at the 1%, 5%, and 10% levels (two-tailed), respectively

presents the results of this robustness test, computed for both TOBIN Q and PTB measures as dependent variables. The findings confirm the main results, revealing a negative relationship between CSP and CFP for the sample of firms belonging to the pre-COVID-19 pandemic subsample. However, consistent with the main results for HP2, Panel A of Table 28.6 shows that this relationship is positive and statistically significant during the COVID-19 pandemic.

Second, to make the findings more robust, we examined the CSP-CFP relationship conditionally to industries' COVID-19 sensitiveness. If market participants heavily considered CSP in their investment decisions during COVID-19, it is reasonable to expect this relationship to be stronger in industries severely

Table 28.6 Robustness test: panel analysis on pre-COVID-19 and COVID-19 subsamples

	Tobin's Q (1)	PTB (2)	Tobin's Q (3)	PTB (4)
Panel A: subsample of COVID-19 observations				
Intercept	1.816***	54.405***	1.554***	44.327***
CSP	0.003**	0.018**	0.001*	0.012*
SIZE	0.077	2.306	0.065	1.857
LEVERAGE	−0.054**	−1.617***	−0.051***	−1.566***
ZSCORE	−0.005***	−0.158***	−0.005***	−0.148***
ROE	0.018**	0.615***	0.008	0.318
BOARD	0.001	−0.028	−0.000	−0.018
CSRCOM	0.001	0.234	0.003	0.327
Year FE	No	No	Yes	Yes
Country FE	No	No	Yes	Yes
Observations	1652	1652	1652	1652
R^2	0.20	0.19	0.23	0.22
Panel B: subsample of pre-COVID-19 observations				
Intercept	0.385**	1.330	0.940***	18.425***
CSP	−0.015***	−0.012**	0.014***	−0.010**
SIZE	0.015*	−0.001	0.039***	0.758***
LEVERAGE	0.015	1.020	0.016	1.014
ZSCORE	−0.008***	−0.204***	−0.010***	−0.205***
ROE	0.029*	0.470	0.032**	0.556
BOARD	0.000	0.016	0.001	0.045
CSRCOM	0.023	0.674*	0.019	0.551
Year FE	No	No	Yes	Yes
Country FE	No	No	Yes	Yes
Observations	2140	2140	2140	2140
R^2	0.11	0.12	0.13	0.17

Notes: This table provides results of panel data for our robustness test. Variable definition and measurement are provided in Table 28.2. We include country and industry fixed effects in the regression or firm fixed effect under a different specification. Standard errors are clustered at the firm level in all models. ***, **, and * indicate statistical significance at the 1%, 5%, and 10% levels (two-tailed), respectively

impacted by the pandemic crisis and weaker in industries that were affected only marginally.

Albuquerque et al. (2020) showed that sectors reacted (and were exposed) differently to pandemic crisis. For this reason, we divided the sample into two subsamples based on the industries' sensitivity to COVID-19, and we run our regressions only considering observations belonging to COVID-19 period.

Specifically, we considered industries such as healthcare, chemicals, energy, and utilities as COVID-19-sensitive. The healthcare and chemical sectors emerged as crucial players in addressing the health crisis. Their essential roles in supplying medical resources, developing vaccines, and manufacturing healthcare essentials played a critical part in safeguarding public health (Mazur et al., 2021).

The energy and utility sectors faced significant challenges, with lockdowns and restrictions leading to reduced energy consumption and disrupted supply chains. Fluctuations in energy prices further exacerbated the difficulties faced by companies in these sectors, impacting their operations and financial performance (Mazur et al., 2021).

Therefore, although in different ways, each of these sectors played a distinct role in navigating the complexities of the pandemic and can be considered as more COVID-19-sensitive if compared to the further industries.

Table 28.7 presents the results of post hoc analyses for both TOBIN Q and PTB measures as dependent variables. Panel A and Panel B show findings for firms in COVID-19-sensitive industries and those not COVID-19-sensitive, respectively.

Table 28.7 Post hoc analyses on industries' COVID-19-sensitive subsample

	Tobin's Q (1)	PTB (2)	Tobin's Q (3)	PTB (4)
Panel A: subsample of industries' COVID-19-sensitive observations				
Intercept	26.661***	34.012***	19.993***	24.550***
CSP	0.038**	0.023***	0.015**	0.025**
SIZE	1.128	1.453	0.816	1.010
LEVERAGE	1.525	4.775***	0.383	3.170**
ZSCORE	0.215***	0.338***	0.205***	0.327***
ROE	−0.421	−0.720	−0.107	−0.285
BOARD	0.017	−0.037	−0.022	−0.044
CSRCOM	0.300	0.559	0.540	0.897
Year FE	No	No	Yes	Yes
Country FE	No	No	Yes	Yes
Observations	275	275	275	275
R^2	0.28	0.30	0.35	0.37
Panel B: subsample of industries' non-COVID-19-sensitive observations				
Intercept	48.160***	71.780***	42.516***	63.766***
CSP	0.005**	0.004*	0.001*	0.001
SIZE	2.172	3.282	1.902	2.899
LEVERAGE	0.778*	4.230***	−0.121	2.930***
ZSCORE	0.080***	0.090***	0.059***	0.057*
ROE	0.188	0.418*	0.534***	0.914***
BOARD	−0.003	−0.003	−0.007	−0.009
CSRCOM	−0.142	−0.275	−0.031	−0.109
Year FE	No	No	Yes	Yes
Country FE	No	No	Yes	Yes
Observations	1377	1377	1377	1377
R^2	0.15	0.15	0.26	0.24

Notes: Table 28.6 provides results of panel data for our robustness test. Variable definition and measurement are provided in Table 28.2. We include country and industry fixed effects in the regression or firm fixed effect under a different specification. Standard errors are clustered at the firm level in all models. ***, **, and * indicate statistical significance at the 1%, 5%, and 10% levels (two-tailed), respectively

The results contribute to delve deeper into the interpretation of main findings and unveil the effect of CSP on CFP across different sectors studied. Specifically, for both measures of financial performance, the effect of CSP on financial performance appears positive and statistically significant mainly for the subsample of companies belonging to COVID-19-sensitive industries. This suggests that for these companies, the engagement in corporate social activities leads to "incremental" rewards from market participants if compared to companies in sectors less hit by COVID-19.

28.6 Conclusions

Drawing on the literature concerning the relationship between social activities and CFP (Cellier & Chollet, 2016; Eccles et al., 2017; Kaspereit & Lopatta, 2016; Kruger, 2015; Martínez-Ferrero & Frías-Aceituno, 2015; Sheikh, 2018) and adopting a multifaceted theoretical approach that integrates both stakeholder and shareholder theories, we empirically demonstrate that the COVID-19 pandemic played a significant role in shaping the relationship between CSP and CFP.

In particular, basing the analyses on a sample of 743 European listed non-financial companies in the period 2017–2022, we challenge the relationship between social activities and CFP. In doing so, the findings diverge from the expectation of a positive correlation between social activities and CFP (Chellier & Chollet, 2016). Instead, the results align with previous studies that have reported a negative CSP-CFP relationship (e.g., Kruger, 2015). This aspect challenges the conventional wisdom and prevailing assumptions regarding the positive impact of social initiatives on financial performance. In essence, the results support the arguments stemming from the shareholder theory perspective, asserting that investments in social activities may not necessarily yield financial gains. This insight contributes to the ongoing debate within the literature, emphasizing the need for a nuanced understanding of the intricate interplay between CSR initiatives and financial outcomes.

Conversely, when we scrutinized the issue within the context of the COVID-19 pandemic, a noteworthy shift emerged: the relationship between CSP and CFP turned positive. This phenomenon finds explanation through the lens of the stakeholder theory. As companies actively engage in social initiatives, their reputations ascend, fostering stronger relationships with stakeholders and exerting a positive influence on financial performance (Porter & Kramer, 2019).

During the COVID crisis, various stakeholders, including communities, political entities, investors, and, broadly speaking, the public, intensified their scrutiny of companies' social behaviors. In this heightened awareness, an investment in social initiatives that might not have been advantageous previously then might turn positive. Investors, in particular, play a crucial role in this dynamic, actively seeking socially responsible activities due to their recognized impact on customers, communities, and, consequently, overall performance (He & Harris, 2020; Scholtens, 2014). This is particularly true in the European context, where recent developments have seen European institutions taking proactive measures, introducing initiatives, and implementing mechanisms aimed at safeguarding not only workplaces but also the whole social activities impacted by the pandemic (Rinaldi, 2023).

At the same time, the post hoc analyses reveal that firms belonging to industries considered COVID-19-sensitive benefit more from socially responsible activities compared to those in non-COVID-19-sensitive industries. Given the heightened scrutiny from investors on these firms due to their significant exposure during the pandemic, their social behaviors have the potential to impact financial market performance.

Stemming on these results, the study offers theoretical contributions and has practical implications.

In terms of the theoretical perspective, this study addresses a gap in the literature concerning the impact of the COVID-19 pandemic on the relationship between CSP and CFP. In doing so, it makes three significant contributions. First, it enriches the ongoing and inconclusive debate on CSP and CFP (Gillan et al., 2021) by exploring the role of the COVID-19 pandemic. Second, within the emerging literature on the financial impact of the COVID-19 pandemic (Bai & Ho, 2022), it initiates a discussion on social issues and illustrates that COVID-19 reinforces the potential beneficial role of socially responsible activities. This echoes suggestions that CSR and CSP could be vital resilience factors during periods of heightened economic uncertainty (Albuquerque et al., 2020). Third, on a broader scale, this study contributes to the accounting literature by providing empirical evidence on the role played by corporate commitment in pursuing social sustainability goals. By demonstrating a positive relationship between CSP and market-based financial performance, this study addresses a research gap on the social dimension of sustainability, which is the least explored among the three ESG pillars (Nikolakis et al., 2022).

As for the practical implications, the results of this study may be useful to investors and lenders. Particularly, during times of heightened public sensitivity to social issues, such as the COVID-19 pandemic, companies investing in social sustainability goals not only enhance their image and reputation for ethical commitment to community benefit but also enjoy positive market-based financial performance. These findings are significant for investors and lenders seeking efficient capital allocations.

Furthermore, this study signals to managers that investing in social sustainability goals is not only morally right but also leads to improved financial performance. Enhancing market financial performance generates an undeniable value for the company, enabling the manager to initiate a self-financing process for future investments in social sustainability. This establishes a virtuous circle that benefits individuals, communities, and corporate profitability.

Despite the mentioned contributions, this research is not without limitations. First, although the statistical models correct endogeneity problems because of potential reverse causality concerns in CSP-CFP relationship, the analyses do not resolve completely this issue. For instance, factors that affect both financial and social performance might be omitted in the model, thus leading to biased estimates. Second, the study shows that CSP is related to CFP and not that CSP caused CFP.

Hence, we encourage future research to look for more evidence on the potential causality between CSP and CFP. Also, despite previous studies demonstrated the effectiveness of the Thomson Reuters social pillar (Lahouel et al., 2021), this variable may not capture all dimensions of the social pillar due to inherent limitations associated with archival data. Future research could explore the relationship between CSP and CFP using more innovative measures of CSP, such as survey-based indexes.

Moreover, our examination of the CSP-CFP relationship, along with the role of the COVID-19 pandemic in shaping such a relation, focuses on the European context, which exhibits distinct reactions to COVID-19 (Forman & Mossialos, 2021). Future research might effectively address this issue in different geographical areas, either focusing on country-level differences in EU or exploring the United State of America and the Middle East and North Africa, providing a broader perspective on the role of macroeconomic events in the relationship between social and financial performance.

Acknowledgements The authors gratefully acknowledge that this study was funded by the European Union—*NextGenerationEu*, in the framework of the GRINS—*Growing Resilient, INclusive and Sustainable*—project (Codice Progetto MUR: PE00000018—CUP E63C22002140007). The views and opinions expressed in this study are solely those of the authors and do not necessarily reflect those of the European Union. The European Union is not responsible for them.

References

Acemoglu, D., Chernozhukov, V., Werning, I., & Whinston, M. D. (2020). *Optimal targeted lockdowns in a multi-group SIR model. Economic fluctuations and growth, health economics, public economics*. National Bureau of Economic Research. https://www.nber.org/papers/w27102

Aktas, N., De Bodt, E., & Cousin, J. G. (2011). Do financial markets care about SRI? Evidence from mergers and acquisitions. *Journal of Banking & Finance, 35*(7), 1753–1761.

Albuquerque, R., Koskinen, Y., Yang, S., & Zhang, C. (2020). Resiliency of Environmental and Social Stocks: An analysis of the Exogenous COVID-19 Market Crash. *The Review of Corporate Finance, 9*(3), 593–621. https://doi.org/10.1093/rcfs/cfaa011

Alexander, G. J., & Buchholz, R. A. (1978). Corporate social responsibility and stock market performance. *Academy of Management Journal, 21*, 479–486.

Altman, E. I. (1968). Financial ratios, discriminant analysis and the prediction of corporate bankruptcy. *The Journal of Finance, 23*(4), 589–609.

Aouadi, A., & Marsat, S. (2018). Do ESG controversies matter for firm value? Evidence from international data. *Journal of Business Ethics, 151*, 1027–1047.

Arouri, M., Gomes, M., & Pukthuanthong, K. (2019). Corporate social responsibility and M&A uncertainty. *Journal of Corporate Finance, 56*, 176–198.

Aupperle, K., Carroll, A., & Hatfield, J. D. (1985). An empirical examination of the relationship between corporate social responsibility and profitability. *Academy of Management Journal, 28*, 446–463.

Avetisyan, E., & Ferrary, M. (2013). Dynamics of stakeholders' implications in the institutionalization of the CSR field in France and in the United States. *Journal of Business Ethics, 115*, 115–133.

Bai, M., & Ho, L. (2022). Corporate social performance and firm debt levels: Impacts of the covid-19 pandemic and institutional environments. *Finance Research Letters, 47*, 102968.
Barnett, M. L. (2007). Stakeholder influence capacity and the variability of financial returns to corporate social responsibility. *Academy of Management Review, 32*, 794–816.
Barnett, M. L., & Salomon, R. M. (2006). Beyond dichotomy: The curvilinear relationship between social responsibility and financial performance. *Strategic Management Journal, 27*(11), 1101–1122.
Barnett, M. L., Jermier, J. M., & Lafferty, B. A. (2006). Corporate reputation: The definitional landscape. *Corporate Reputation Review, 9*, 26–38.
Baron, D. P. (2001). Private politics, corporate social responsibility, and integrated strategy. *Journal of Economics and Management Strategy, 10*, 1–75.
Baron, D. P., & Diermeier, D. (2007). Strategic activism and nonmarket strategy. *Journal of Economics & Management Strategy, 16*(3), 599–634.
Bice, S. (2017). Corporate social responsibility as institution: A social mechanisms framework. *Journal of Business Ethics, 143*(1), 17–34.
Bondy, K., Moon, J., & Matten, D. (2012). An institution of corporate social responsibility (CSR) in multi-national corporations (MNCs): Form and implications. *Journal of Business Ethics, 111*, 281–299.
Broadstock, D. C., Chan, K., Cheng, L. T., & Wang, X. (2021). The role of ESG performance during times of financial crisis: Evidence from COVID-19 in China. *Finance Research Letters, 38*, 101716.
Brower, J., & Dacin, P. A. (2020). An institutional theory approach to the evolution of the corporate social performance–corporate financial performance relationship. *Journal of Management Studies, 57*(4), 805–836.
Butcher, B., & Massey, J. (2020). Why are more people from BAME backgrounds dying from coronavirus. *BBC News*, 19.
Cellier, A., & Chollet, P. (2016). The effects of social ratings on firm value. *Research in International Business and Finance, 36*, 656–683.
Cho, S. Y., & Lee, C. (2019). Managerial efficiency, corporate social performance, and corporate financial performance. *Journal of Business Ethics, 158*, 467–486.
Clarke, C., & Friedman, H. H. (2016). 'Maximizing shareholder value': A theory run Amok. *i-manager's Journal on Management, 10*(4), 45–60. Available at SSRN: https://ssrn.com/abstract=2796836
Cornell, B., & Shapiro, A. C. (1987). Corporate stakeholders and corporate finance. *Financial Management*, 5–14.
Cox, P., Brammer, S., & Millington, A. (2004). An empirical examination of institutional investor preferences for corporate social performance. *Journal of Business Ethics, 52*, 27–43.
Crisóstomo, V. L., de Souza Freire, F., & De Vasconcellos, F. C. (2011). Corporate social responsibility, firm value and financial performance in Brazil. *Social Responsibility Journal, 7* (2), 295–309.
Daily, B. F., & Huang, S. C. (2001). Achieving sustainability through attention to human resource factors in environmental management. *International Journal of Operations & Production Management, 21*(12), 1539–1552.
De Villiers, C., Jia, J., & Li, Z. (2022). Corporate social responsibility: A review of empirical research using Thomson Reuters Asset4 data. *Accounting & Finance*, 1–46.
Deephouse, D., Bundy, J., Tost, L., & Suchman, M. (2017). Organizational legitimacy: Six key questions. In R. Greenwood, C. Oliver, & T. B. Lawrence (Eds.), *The SAGE Handbook of Organizational Institutionalism* (pp. 27–54). Sage.
Donaldson, T., & Preston, L. E. (1995). The Stakeholder Theory of the Corporation: Concepts, Evidence, and Implications. *Academy of Management Review, 20*(1), 65–91.
Dunn, P., & Sainty, B. (2009). The relationship among board of director characteristics, corporate social performance and corporate financial performance. *International Journal of Managerial Finance, 5*(4), 407–423.

Eccles, R. G., Kastrapeli, M. D., & Potter, S. J. (2017). How to integrate ESG into investment decision-making: Results of a global survey of institutional investors. *Journal of Applied Corporate Finance, 29*(4), 125–133.

Escrig-Olmedo, E., Rivera-Lirio, J. M., Muñoz-Torres, M. J., & Fernández-Izquierdo, M. Á. (2017). Integrating multiple ESG investors' preferences into sustainable investment: A fuzzy multicriteria methodological approach. *Journal of Cleaner Production, 162*, 1334–1345.

Euronews. (2020). COVID-19: World economy in 2020 to suffer worst year since 1930s Great Depression, says IMF, Accessible at: https://www.euronews.com/2020/04/14/watch-live-international-monetary-fund-gives-world-economic-outlook-briefing-on-covid-19, Accessed 06.05.2020.

EUROSIF. (2014). European SRI Study. http://www.eurosif.org/our-work/research/sri/european-sri-study-2014/. Accessed 18.05.15.

Fatima, T., & Elbanna, S. (2023). Corporate social responsibility (CSR) implementation: A review and a research agenda towards an integrative framework. *Journal of Business Ethics, 183*(1), 105–121.

Fenichel, E. P. (2013). Economic considerations for social distancing and behavioral based policies during an epidemic. *Journal of Health Economics, 32*(2), 440–451.

Flammer, C. (2013). Corporate social responsibility and shareholder reaction: The environmental aware- ness of investors. *Academy of Management Journal, 56*, 758–781.

Flammer, C. (2015). Does corporate social responsibility lead to superior financial performance? A regression discontinuity approach. *Management Science, 61*, 2549–2568.

Forman, R., & Mossialos, E. (2021). The EU Response to COVID-19: From Reactive Policies to Strategic Decision-Making. *Journal of Common Market Studies, 59*(56).

Franco, S., Caroli, M. G., Cappa, F., & Del Chiappa, G. (2020). Are you good enough? CSR, quality management and corporate financial performance in the hospitality industry. *International Journal of Hospitality Management, 88*, 102395.

Freeman, R. E. (1984). Strategic management: A stakeholder theory. *Journal of Management Studies, 39*(1), 1–21.

Freeman, R. E., & Reed, D. L. (1983). Stockholders and stakeholders: A new perspective on corporate governance. *California Management Review, 25*(3), 88–106.

Friedman, M. (1970, September 13). The social responsibility of business is to increase its profits. *New York Times Magazine*, 122–124. http://www.colorado.edu/studentgroups/libertarians/issues/friedman-soc-resp-business.html

Gillan, S. L., Koch, A., & Starks, L. T. (2021). Firms and social responsibility: A review of ESG and CSR research in corporate finance. *Journal of Corporate Finance, 66*, 101889.

Godfrey, P. C. (2005). The relationship between corporate philanthropy and shareholder wealth: A risk management perspective. *Academy of Management Review, 30*(4), 777–798.

Hair, H. F., Anderson, R. E., Tatham, R. L., & Black, W. C. (2010). *Multivariate Data Analysis*. Prentice Hall.

Haley, U. C. (1991). Corporate contributions as managerial masques: Reframing corporate contributions as strategies to influence society. *Journal of Management Studies, 28*(5), 485–510.

Harjoto, M. A., & Jo, H. (2011). Corporate governance and CSR nexus. *Journal of Business Ethics, 100*, 45–67.

Hausman, J. A., & Taylor, W. E. (1981). Panel data and unobservable individual effects. *Econometrica: Journal of the Econometric Society*, 1377–1398.

He, H., & Harris, L. (2020). The impact of Covid-19 pandemic on corporate social responsibility and marketing philosophy. *Journal of Business Research, 116*, 176–182.

Hillman, A., & Keim, G. (2001). Shareholder value, stakeholder management, and social issues: What's the bottom line? *Strategic Management Journal, 22*, 125–139.

Hong, Y., Zhang, R., & Zhang, F. (2024). Time-varying causality impact of economic policy uncertainty on stock market returns: Global evidence from developed and emerging countries. *International Review of Financial Analysis, 91*, 102991.

Huang, W., Wang, H., Wei, Y., & Chevallier, J. (2024). Complex network analysis of global stock market co-movement during the COVID-19 pandemic based on intraday open-high-low-close data. *Financial Innovation, 10*(1), 7.

Humphreys, K. A., & Trotman, K. T. (2022). Judgment and decision making research on CSR reporting in the COVID-19 pandemic environment. *Accounting & Finance, 62*(1), 739–765.

Jensen, M. C. (2001). Value maximization, stakeholder theory, and the corporate objective function. *Journal of Applied Corporate Finance, 14*, 8–21. https://doi.org/10.1111/j.1745-6622.2001.tb00434.x

Jones, T. M. (1995). Instrumental stakeholder theory: A synthesis of ethics and economics. *Academy of Management Review*, 404–437.

Jones, H. (2020). *Huge surge in volunteers to help combat coronavirus loneliness, Metro*, Accessible at: https://metro.co.uk/2020/04/07/huge-surge-volunteers-help-combat-coronavirus-loneliness-12524549/, Accessed 18.04.20.

Kaspereit, T., & Lopatta, K. (2016). The value relevance of SAM's corporate sustainability ranking and GRI sustainability reporting in the European stock markets. *Business Ethics: A European Review, 25*, 1–24.

Kim, S., & Li, Z. F. (2021). *Understanding the Impact of ESG Practices in Corporate Finance*.

Kotsantonis, S., Pinney, C., & Serafeim, G. (2016). ESG integration in investment management: Myths and realities. *Journal of Applied Corporate Finance, 28*(2), 10–16.

Krishnamurti, C., Shams, S., Pensiero, D., & Velayutham, E. (2019). Socially responsible firms and mergers and acquisitions performance: Australian evidence. *Pacific-Basin Finance Journal, 57*, 101193.

Kruger, P. (2015). Corporate goodness and shareholder wealth. *Journal of Financial Economics, 115*, 304–329.

Lahouel, B. B., Zaied, Y. B., Song, Y., & Yang, G. L. (2021). Corporate social performance and financial performance relationship: A data envelopment analysis approach without explicit input. *Finance Research Letters, 39*, 101656.

Li, H., & Chen, P. (2018). Board gender diversity and firm performance: The moderating role of firm size. *Business Ethics: A European Review, 27*(4), 294–308.

Lin, W. L., Law, S. H., Ho, J. A., & Sambasivan, M. (2019). The causality direction of the corporate social responsibility–Corporate financial performance Nexus: Application of Panel Vector Autoregression approach. *The North American Journal of Economics and Finance, 48*, 401–418.

Lindsay, J. (2020). *Aldi donates Easter eggs to food banks and local charities Metro*, https://metro.co.uk/2020/04/04/aldi-donates-easter-eggs-food-banks-local-charities-12507475/. Accessed 18.04.20.

Liu, Y., Kim, C. Y., Lee, E. H., & Yoo, J. W. (2022). Relationship between sustainable management activities and financial performance: Mediating effects of non-financial performance and moderating effects of institutional environment. *Sustainability, 14*(3), 1168.

Lopez, M. V., Garcia, A., & Rodriguez, L. (2007). Sustainable development and corporate performance: A study based on the Dow Jones Sustainability Index. *Journal of Business Ethics, 75*(3), 285–300.

Luo, X., & Bhattacharya, C. B. (2006). Corporate social responsibility, customer satisfaction, and market value. *Journal of Marketing, 70*(4), 1–18.

Mackey, A., Mackey, T., & Barney, J. (2007). Corporate social responsibility and firm performance: Investor preferences and corporate strategies. *Academy of Management Review, 32*, 817–835.

Martínez-Ferrero, J., & Frías-Aceituno, J. V. (2015). Relationship between sustainable development and financial performance: International empirical research. *Business Strategy and the Environment, 24*, 20–39.

Matten, D., & Moon, J. (2008). "Implicit" and "explicit" CSR: A conceptual framework for a comparative understanding of corporate social responsibility. *Academy of Management Review, 33*, 404–424.

Mazur, M., Dang, M., & Vega, M. (2021). COVID-19 and the march 2020 stock market crash. Evidence from S&P1500. *Finance Research Letters, 38*, 101690. 1-8.

McGuire, J. B., Sundgren, A., & Schneeweis, T. (1988). Corporate social responsibility and firm financial performance. *Academy of Management Journal, 31*, 854–872.

McWilliams, A., & Siegel, D. (2001). Corporate social responsibility: A theory of the firm perspective. *Academy of Management Review, 26*(1), 117–127.

Mellahi, K., Frynas, J., Sun, P., & Siegel, D. (2016). A review of the nonmarket strategy literature: Toward a multi-theoretical integration. *Journal of Management, 42*, 143–173.

Michelon, G., Rodrigue, M., & Trevisan, E. (2020). The marketization of a social movement: Activists, shareholders and CSR disclosure. *Accounting, Organizations and Society, 80*, Article 101074.

Neubaum, D. O., & Zahra, S. A. (2006). Institutional ownership and corporate social performance: The moderating effects of investment horizon, activism, and coordination. *Journal of Management, 32*(1), 108–131.

Nguyen, H. V. (2018). Hedging and hedging effectiveness under required disclosures: a study of the impact of derivatives use on capital investment. *Journal of Economics and Finance, 42*, 471–491.

Nikolakis, W., Olaru, D., & Kallmuenzer, A. (2022). What motivates environmental and social sustainability in family firms? A cross-cultural survey. *Business Strategy and the Environment, 31*(5), 2351–2364.

Nuber, C., Velte, P., & Horisch, J. (2020). The curvilinear and time-lagging impact of sustainability performance on financial performance: Evidence from Germany. *Corporate Social Responsibility and Environmental Management, 27*(1), 232–243.

Okafor, A., Adeleye, B. N., & Adusei, M. (2021). Corporate social responsibility and financial performance: Evidence from US tech firms. *Journal of Cleaner Production, 292*, 126078.

Patten, D. M. (2015). An insider's reflection on quantitative research in the social and environmental disclosure domain. *Critical Perspectives on Accounting, 32*, 45–50.

Porter, M. E., & Kramer, M. R. (2019). Creating shared value. In *Managing sustainable business* (pp. 323–346). Springer.

Richardson, A. J. (2015). Quantitative research and the critical accounting project. *Critical Perspectives on Accounting, 32*, 67–77.

Rinaldi, L. (2023). Accounting and the COVID-19 pandemic two years on: insights, gaps, and an agenda for future research. In Accounting Forum (47, 3, pp. 333–364). Routledge.

Rowley, T., & Berman, S. (2000). A brand new brand of corporate social performance. *Business & Society, 39*(4), 397–418.

Ruf, B. M., Muralidhar, K., Brown, R. M., Janney, J. J., & Paul, K. (2001). An empirical investigation of the relationship between change in corporate social performance and financial performance: A stakeholder theory perspective. *Journal of Business Ethics, 32*, 143–156.

Saeidi, S. P., Sofian, S., Saeidi, P., Saeidi, S. P., & Saaeidi, S. A. (2015). How does corporate social responsibility contribute to firm financial performance? The mediating role of competitive advantage, reputation, and customer satisfaction. *Journal of Business Research, 68*, 341–350.

Sahin, Ö., Bax, K., Paterlini, S., & Czado, C. (2023). The pitfalls of (non-definitive) environmental, social, and governance scoring methodology. *Global Finance Journal, 56*, 100780.

Scholtens, B. (2014). Indicators of responsible investing. *Ecological Indicators, 36*, 382–385.

Sharma, S., & Henriques, I. (2005). Stakeholder influences on sustainability practices in the Canadian forest products industry. *Strategic Management Journal, 26*, 159–180.

Sheikh, S. (2018). Is corporate social responsibility a value-increasing investment? Evidence from antitakeover provisions. *Global Finance Journal, 38*, 1–12.

Spicer, B. H. (1978). Investors, corporate social performance and information disclosure: An empirical study. *Accounting Review, 53*, 94–111.

Sroufe, R., & Gopalakrishna-Remani, V. (2019). Management, social sustainability, reputation, and financial performance relationships: An empirical examination of US firms. *Organization & Environment, 32*(3), 331–333.

Tampakoudis, I., & Anagnostopoulou, E. (2020). The effect of mergers and acquisitions on environmental, social and governance performance and market value: Evidence from EU acquirers. *Business Strategy and the Environment, 29*(5), 1865–1875.

Teti, E., Dell'Acqua, A., & Bonsi, P. (2022). Detangling the role of environmental, social, and governance factors on M&A performance. *Corporate Social Responsibility and Environmental Management, 29*(5), 1768–1781.

Thomson Reuters Eikon. (2018). *Thomson Reuters ESG Scores*, 3–16.

Tisdell, C. A. (2020). Economic, social and political issues raised by the COVID-19 pandemic. *Economic Analysis and Policy, 68*, 17–28.

Vurro, C., & Perrini, F. (2011). Making the most of corporate social responsibility reporting: Disclosure structure and its impact on performance. *Corporate Governance: The International Journal of Business in Society, 11*(4), 459–474.

Wang, H., & Qian, C. (2011). Corporate philanthropy and corporate financial performance: The roles of stakeholder response and political access. *Academy of Management Journal, 54*(6), 1159–1181.

Wang, Q., Dou, J., & Jia, S. (2016). A meta-analytic review of corporate social responsibility and corporate financial performance: The moderating effect of contextual factors. *Business & Society, 55*, 1083–1121.

Wilkinson, A., Hill, M., & Gollan, P. (2001). The sustainability debate. *International Journal of Operations & Production Management, 21*, 1492–1502.

Wood, D. (1991). Corporate social performance revisited. *Academy of Management Review, 16*, 691–717.

Yadav, P. L., Han, S. H., & Rho, J. J. (2016). Impact of environmental performance on firm value for sustainable investment: Evidence from large US firms. *Business Strategy and the Environment, 25*, 402–420.

Yadav, P. L., Han, S. H., & Kim, H. (2017). Sustaining competitive advantage through corporate environmental performance. *Business Strategy and the Environment, 26*, 345–357.

Yen, T. Y., & André, P. (2019). Market reaction to the effect of corporate social responsibility on mergers and acquisitions: Evidence on emerging markets. *The Quarterly Review of Economics and Finance, 71*, 114–131.

Yu, E. P., & Van Luu, B. (2021). International variations in ESG disclosure—Do cross-listed companies care more? *International Review of Financial Analysis, 75*, 101731.

Yu, E. P. Y., Van Luu, B., & Chen, C. H. (2020). Greenwashing in environmental, social and governance disclosures. *Research in International Business and Finance, 52*, 101192.

Chapter 29
Role of Information Systems in Controlling and Monitoring ESG Performance: Evidence from an Empirical Study

Domenica Lavorato, Palmira Piedepalumbo, and Rita Lamboglia

29.1 Introduction

In recent years, sustainability has gained strategic importance in the business landscape, driven by the growing awareness among companies that environmental and social factors can pose risks and opportunities that can affect business outcomes (Corsi & Arru, 2018; Morioka & de Carvalho, 2016). The growing strategic importance of ESG-related issues has stimulated interest in incorporating environmental, social and governance (ESG) dimensions into corporate strategies. 'If improvements in social and environmental performance translate into long-term shareholder value, companies will need to ensure that associated activities are fully integrated into strategic processes' (Arjaliès & Mundy, 2013, p. 285). This requires the creation of appropriate management control, performance measurement systems and tools to assess and validate strategic objectives.

A central premise in the management control literature is that organisations should align their management control systems with strategic priorities and directions (Henri, 2006; Langfield-Smith, 1997). Alignment between strategy and management control systems is critical for effective strategy implementation and the achievement of strategic goals, as it reduces risk and uncertainty and ultimately improves organizational performance (Ittner & Larcker, 2001). It has been argued that performance measurement facilitates the effective management of an organisation's strategic competencies by providing essential information about critical business operations (Kaplan & Norton, 1996; Simons et al., 2000).

D. Lavorato · R. Lamboglia
University of Naples "Parthenope", Naples, Italy

P. Piedepalumbo (✉)
University of Rome "La Sapienza", Rome, Italy
e-mail: palmira.piedepalumbo@uniroma1.it

N. Castellano et al. (eds.), *Environmental, Social, Governance (ESG)*, SIDREA Series in Accounting and Business Administration,
https://doi.org/10.1007/978-3-031-76618-3_29

As highlighted in the literature, the relationship between strategy and measurement systems is bidirectional (Goyal et al., 2013; Miraglia, 2012; Williamson et al., 2006). Strategies influence the specific performance management and the measurement tools into which they are translated. However, these tools and performance indicators support managers in decision-making processes related to strategy implementation.

Despite numerous studies that highlight the importance of integrating sustainability aspects at the strategic level to influence ESG performance in the medium and long term (Baumgartner & Rauter, 2017; De Villiers et al., 2016), their alignment with performance management and measurement systems remains insufficiently addressed in practice (Braune et al., 2019; Hristov et al., 2021, 2022).

Several scholars have highlighted the central role of information systems in the practical implementation of sustainability strategies (Gebhardt et al., 2022; Goni et al., 2017). These systems support management by providing various tools to measure management objectives and results (Marchi & De Santis, 2020). Specifically, information systems play a crucial role in supporting decision-making and control processes, significantly enhancing the analysis and measurement of ESG performance (de Villiers et al., 2021). Essentially, they help companies collect, integrate, automate and monitor information related to ESG dimensions (Corsi & Arru, 2018).

Nevertheless, studies focusing on the effective use of information systems for ESG strategy development and performance measurement are scarce (Corsi & Arru, 2018; Goni et al., 2017; Hristov et al., 2022).

To address this research gap, this study investigates how the implementation of an appropriate information system effectively supports ESG strategy development and facilitates performance monitoring and control.

To achieve this research objective, we adopt a qualitative case study method (Yin, 2017) and examine the case of Elyze, a software program designed to collect and monitor ESG data. To ensure robust data triangulation, we collected and analysed both primary and secondary data from various sources, including online documentation, archival documents and in-depth interviews with software developers and users. To ensure the rigour of our qualitative approach, we conducted a qualitative analysis of the data following the method outlined by Gioia et al. (2013). Thematic analysis was used as an analytical tool for a comprehensive examination of the collected data.

This study makes significant contributions to both academic literature and managerial practice. Theoretically, this enriches the discourse on the use of information systems to integrate ESG information and implement ESG performance management and control practices, thereby filling a gap identified in the literature. Practically, by providing empirical evidence, this study helps managers gain deeper insights into how companies use IT tools for ESG performance and metrics.

The remainder of this paper is organised as follows: Sect. 29.2 presents the theoretical background, which includes the mainstream of research relevant to the topic. Section 29.3 describes the methodology used to fulfil the research objectives and conducts a case study. Section 29.4 presents the results. Finally, Sect. 29.5 discusses the results and concludes the paper.

29.2 Literature Review

In recent years, the concept of ESG has gained significant attention in the global competitive and institutional landscape. Companies are under constant pressure from various stakeholders to develop and implement ESG practices (Duque-Grisales & Aguilera-Caracuel, 2021; Jain & Tripathi, 2023). At the same time, it is widely recognised that companies that adopt ESG practices and initiatives enjoy several competitive advantages, in particular reduced capital constraints (Cheng et al., 2014), a lower cost of debt (Eliwa et al., 2021), reduced information asymmetry and a lower cost of capital (Raimo et al., 2021). In this context, the strategic importance of integrating ESG principles into corporate operations becomes clear as it strengthens overall corporate performance (Hristov et al., 2021; Hristov et al., 2022; Marchi, 2020).

ESG encompasses a set of criteria used by investors, stakeholders and society to assess a company's impact on the environment, society and governance practices (Jamali et al., 2017; Mohammad & Wasiuzzaman, 2021). Consequently, ESG is intrinsically linked to the idea that companies should integrate the three dimensions (ESG) into their business strategies and management.

Numerous scholars and practitioners argue that companies cannot effectively pursue ESG strategies without collecting, processing, managing data and monitoring ESG objectives (Rodríguez-Olalla & Avilés-Palacios, 2017; Bebbington & Unerman, 2018; Corsi & Arru, 2021). Therefore, the need to implement management control tools in companies to seamlessly integrate ESG concerns into their decision-making processes is widely recognised (Arjaliès & Mundy, 2013; Maas et al., 2016).

Some scholars have emphasised the need to redesign management control systems to measure the achievement of ESG objectives (D'Onza, 2022). This involves improving both the performance measurement system, which should adopt a more multidimensional approach, and the information system, which should provide reliable data and information (Castellano & Felden, 2021).

Performance measurements have emerged as a critical lever in strategy implementation (Micheli & Mura, 2017). Numerous studies have highlighted the central role of performance measurement in strategy development, communication and review (Franco-Santos et al., 2012; Micheli & Manzoni, 2010). At present, simple measures of financial performance are inadequate for assessing organisational performance. In particular, the assessment of sustainability performance requires the collection, analysis and dissemination of information on sustainability impacts to facilitate internal management decisions, thereby facilitating interactions between businesses, society and the environment (Maas et al., 2016). The use of performance indicators to capture and consolidate information is at the core of sustainability performance measurements (Schöggl et al., 2016).

Companies integrating sustainability require increasingly advanced and complex performance measurement systems that combine financial and non-financial measures to become more holistic in nature (Capalbo et al., 2023). Consequently, the successful implementation of ESG objectives relies on continuous monitoring and reporting facilitated by the development of performance management and control systems that reconcile this perspective with the traditional emphasis on economic and financial variables (Evans et al., 2017; Fadda et al., 2021; Marchi, 2020).

In recent years, the academic literature has placed great emphasis on the external and internal pressures that drive companies to develop and implement systems and tools to manage and monitor ESG objectives (Pondeville et al., 2013; Windolph et al., 2014). These approaches can be explored through two broad lines of research (Garzella & Fiorentino, 2014).

The first line of research is rooted in socio-institutional theory, which examines the institutional mechanisms that influence firms to adopt and implement ESG practices. Typically, companies formulate ESG strategies for ethical, reputational and social reasons or to mitigate the potential negative consequences of non-compliance with sustainability regulations. In addition, some studies argue that companies adopt ESG strategies in response to legitimate stakeholder demands (Suchman 1995). Consequently, companies engage in socially responsible behaviour to adequately address stakeholder concerns and gain legitimacy in their eyes (Suchman, 1995; Lamboglia et al., 2018).

The second line of research, based on the resource-based view (RBV), emphasises the link between ESG strategies and competitive advantage (Hart, 1995; Russo & Fouts, 1997). According to the RBV, sustainability is a distinctive competence essential for companies seeking a sustainable competitive advantage (Russo & Fouts, 1997). Academic studies support the notion that a company's proactive approach to ESG issues is driven by competitive motivations linked to its potential to gain, defend, or renew competitive advantage (Hart, 1995; McWilliams & Siegel, 2011).

The two theoretical approaches can be linked to the main perspectives of sustainability management development outlined in the literature: 'outside-in' and 'inside-out' (Burritt & Schaltegger, 2010; Maas et al., 2016). The outside-in perspective is mainly driven by external pressures and describes the management and measurement of ESG performance based on a company's interactions with its stakeholders. In this scenario, the goal of the measurement system is to satisfy the information expectations of all external parties (Fiorentino et al., 2016). Consequently, a performance measurement system begins by engaging with stakeholders, understanding their expectations and formulating appropriate indicators (Burritt & Schaltegger, 2010).

By contrast, the inside-out perspective, based on the strategic importance of sustainability, views performance measurement as a process that starts with the collection of internal data related to a company's strategy and extends to the communication of information generated to all stakeholders (Arjaliès & Mundy,

2013). The ultimate objective of this approach is to develop a management system capable of reconciling economic, social and environmental objectives (Vitale et al., 2019). Studies in this context have focused on the importance of translating sustainability strategy into performance indicators and the control mechanisms that translate the strategy into indicators (Figge et al., 2002; Hansen & Schaltegger, 2016; Henri & Journeault, 2010). However, they also highlight the role of these indicators in supporting managers in the decision-making processes related to strategy implementation (Burritt et al., 2002).

In line with these perspectives, studies following an outside-in approach have focused on transparency, seeking to disclose sustainable results and establishing legitimacy. Conversely, studies adopting the inside-out approach have prioritised performance improvement, characterised by a strong commitment to sustainable value creation and the adoption of sustainable business practices, avoiding the treatment of sustainability as a mere formal requirement (Gonzalez-Gonzalez & Zamora Ramirez, 2016).

For companies seeking robust sustainability reporting and performance, these two perspectives are complementary and can be integrated into a more advanced sustainability approach known as the 'twin-track' model. In this model, sustainability management tools address both external pressures and the company's strategic imperatives (Burritt & Schaltegger, 2010; Gonzalez-Gonzalez & Zamora Ramirez, 2016; Vitale et al., 2019). Studies analysing this approach show how a performance measurement system can simultaneously satisfy the information needs of both managers and external parties, highlighting the interrelationships between managerial vision and stakeholder perspectives (Henri & Journeault, 2010).

Although numerous studies have suggested that the integration of sustainability aspects at the strategic level is essential for influencing ESG performance in the medium and long term (Baumgartner & Rauter, 2017; De Villiers et al., 2016), the integration of these aspects with ESG management control and performance measurement systems has not been sufficiently addressed from a practical perspective (Braune et al., 2019; Hristov et al., 2021; Hristov et al., 2022). There is limited empirical evidence on the role of management control systems in general, and performance measurement systems in particular, in supporting sustainability strategies and translating them into improved performance (Asiaei et al., 2021; Ghosh et al., 2019; Gond et al., 2012).

Several scholars have highlighted the importance of information systems in the practical implementation of ESG strategies (Arici et al., 2022; Gebhardt et al., 2022; Goni et al., 2017; Hristov et al., 2021). According to these studies, ESG strategies influence control systems, particularly information systems, to meet new internal and external information needs (Corsi & Arru, 2018).

The information system can be viewed as a set of elements and relationships that define the process of information production. It starts with the data describing the phenomena of the company and its environment, with the aim of effectively and efficiently satisfying the internal and external knowledge needs of the company (Marchi, 2003). Through various tools and techniques, information systems help organisations collect, store and analyse data to gain insights and make informed decisions. It supports management through various systems that measure management objectives and results (Marchi & De Santis, 2020). Specifically, the information system plays a critical role in supporting decision-making and control processes by significantly enhancing the analysis and measurement of ESG performance (de Villiers et al., 2021).

Corporate managers recognise the challenges of measuring sustainability impacts and acknowledge that financial, environmental and social objectives are often in conflict (Epstein & Widener, 2010; Hart & Milstein, 2003; Porter & Kramer, 2011). Information systems play a central role in managing this complexity, helping companies to transparently and efficiently collect, integrate, automate and monitor information related to ESG dimensions (Corsi & Arru, 2018). Information systems streamline the collection of rich data on an organisation's ESG activities by drawing information from multiple sources (Galeotti et al., 2022). The collected ESG data are transformed into information that is then used in ESG performance control and measurement systems.

29.3 Methodology

29.3.1 Research Design and Data Analysis

To achieve the research objective, the study adopted a qualitative case study methodology (Yin, 2017). This methodology was chosen because qualitative research is often used to explore phenomena that have not been extensively explored in the literature (Fawcett et al., 2014). Qualitative research becomes particularly relevant when the research question is framed as 'how?' (Yin, 2017), making it suitable for cases where the researcher wishes to explore new topics. The case study under review is classified as an exploratory case, ideal for investigating a subject not fully covered in the existing literature (Yin, 2017; Mills et al., 2009). This approach offered a holistic view of the research problem and facilitated the description, understanding, and explanation of the research situation.

This approach is centred on the case study of ESGnext, with a particular focus on the Elyze software developed by the company. ESGnext, an innovative startup, is dedicated to helping companies effectively manage corporate sustainability to create sustainable value for their businesses. The company's mission is to support other companies in their sustainability journey by elevating sustainability as a strategic element. At the heart of our analysis is Elyze, a software developed by ESGnext. Elyze is a software tool designed to help companies collect, monitor and share sustainability information and to provide an efficient integrated reporting system.

To gain insight into the perspective of a user company, Alfa was selected, an internationally significant company in the metal packaging, paint and ink sectors. Alfa is one of the world's leading companies in this sector, producing approximately 80,000 tonnes of coating products annually. Committed to the development of environmentally friendly products, Alfa places particular emphasis on innovative product formulations. The company is dedicated to creating new formulations based on the principles of reducing environmental impact and minimising the use of fossil fuel-based raw materials.

The decision to investigate ESGnext was driven by its status as one of the few companies in Italy offering software for collecting and sharing sustainability information. However, the choice of the client company, Alfa, serves a dual purpose. First, Alfa was selected because it was one of the first companies to implement and use Elyze to collect and manage sustainability information. Second, Alfa's involvement in the paint and ink sector makes it particularly sensitive to sustainability issues.

A specific analysis protocol was followed for this case study (Yin, 2017). First, a comprehensive literature review was conducted, followed by a systematic collection of evidence. To ensure data triangulation (Yin, 2017) and mitigate distortions due to personal bias or non-objective individual perspectives of the authors, information was collected from different sources: internal documents, materials available on companies' websites, PowerPoint presentations and interviews. The sources of evidence were selected and concatenated (Yin, 2017). In particular, the data and information obtained from the analysis of documents and information available on companies' websites were functional in structuring the interviews, focusing on the aspects of interest.

Before conducting the interviews, preliminary research was conducted to enrich the research team's understanding of the companies' operations and characteristics, the contextual factors surrounding the two companies and the specifics of Elyze software. This research was primarily based on an in-depth analysis of the available data, including internal documents, website information, PowerPoint presentations and videos.

The case study was developed through semi-structured interviews conducted between February and September 2023. Initially, an interview was conducted with the ESGnext project manager to provide an overview of ESGnext and, in particular, the Elyze software. Individuals from ESGnext and the client company were identified for subsequent interviews to meet the research objectives. We interviewed the Chief Executive Officer (CEO), Director and Data Analyst of ESGnext, who provided detailed insights into the activities of ESGnext and the operation of the Elyze software. We then interviewed the Health, Safety, & Environment (HSE) and Sustainability Director of Alfa, a client of ESGnext, who provided valuable client perspectives on the functionality and benefits of using Elyze. More data and information on the sources analysed and interviews are provided in Table 29.1.

For each participant, a focused interview was conducted (Yin, 2017), in which each subject was interviewed according to a scheme of open-ended questions, allowing participants to spontaneously express their personal views on the topic under investigation and the researcher to fully understand the issues at hand (Qu & Dumay, 2011). The interviews were conducted using the Microsoft Teams communication platform. Before starting the individual interviews, the research team introduced themselves, clarified the main objectives of the study and addressed any concerns regarding the confidentiality of the information provided and company

Table 29.1 Summary of analysed sources and interviews

Companies analysed	Sources analysed	Interviewee	Duration of interviews
ESGnext	Documents Corporate website Interviews	• CEO • Director • Project manager • Data analyst	Sixty minutes per interview, conducted in February and April
Alfa		• HSE & sustainability director	Sixty minutes, conducted in September

data collected. With the interviewees' consent, the interviews were videotaped and subsequently transcribed according to the '24-hour rule' (Eisenhardt, 1989).

Qualitative content analysis was used to examine the interview texts to identify key concepts relevant to the research objective. This process followed a multistage approach (Gioia et al., 2013; Merriam & Tisdell, 2015). Each researcher independently reviewed the interviews to ensure an unbiased analysis. The authors collaborated to discuss and establish a common classification of the key concepts. Further quality control was conducted by each author after reading the interview texts. The critical segments essential for the development of the case were synthesised. This synthesis was shared among the members of the research group to produce a final report.

29.3.2 Case Study Description

Elyze is highly customisable software developed by ESGnext to help companies collect, monitor and share sustainability information expressed through ESG indicators. The software offers two deployment options: cloud-based and on-premise. In the cloud version, users gain online access through a login consisting of the user name and password provided by the manufacturing company to the client company. In the on-premises version, the software was installed on the company's existing servers.

Elyze was designed to meet the sustainability criteria of the Global Reporting Initiative (GRI). However, due to its customisable and configurable nature, companies using Elyze have the flexibility to input various key performance indicators (KPIs) essential to their monitoring needs. These KPIs cover sustainability, economic and financial aspects. Within each category of KPIs, data is manually entered, consisting mainly of physical-technical indicators (e.g. energy consumption in kilowatts and water consumption in cubic meters). The data passes through two crucial stages: 'to be validated', where the initial data entry has to be verified and 'validated', where the entered data is double-checked and its accuracy is confirmed. The validated data is then processed using the PowerBI software.

Elyze generates outputs in the form of graphs and/or tables, thereby facilitating the preparation of sustainability reports.

29.4 Results

This section presents the main findings of the case study analysis.

The ESG concept has gained considerable importance and strategic relevance for companies today (Duque-Grisales & Aguilera-Caracuel, 2021; Hristov et al., 2021; Jain & Tripathi, 2023; Marchi, 2020). In line with the growing importance of sustainability, companies are taking action and making efforts to integrate ESG issues into their corporate strategy and management. As discussed below, the interviews highlighted the motivations driving companies to develop and implement systems and tools to manage and control ESG objectives as well as the challenges they face in implementing them. The case study analysis highlights the key role of information systems in the practical implementation of ESG strategies.

According to the respondents, companies choose to implement ESG management systems and tools primarily to comply with sustainability regulations, particularly the legal requirement to produce a sustainability report. In some cases, decisions are made in response to legitimate stakeholder demands. The CEO of ESGnext confirms that '*larger companies tend to see sustainability as a regulatory obligation. For smaller companies, the interest should ideally come from entrepreneurs, but entrepreneurs are often sceptical about ESG issues and see sustainability primarily from a marketing perspective. In practice, the impetus often comes from compliance demands from the supply chain or customers. For example, a small company may supply a large company that requires sustainability information from the entire supply chain*'. In other cases, the decision to implement ESG management systems and tools is driven by institutional pressures that force companies to adapt or by spontaneous imitation behaviour observed in other companies.

In response to external pressures, particularly the need to comply with sustainability reporting regulations, companies choose to implement information systems to support the collection, monitoring and sharing of sustainability information expressed through ESG indicators. The main challenge that companies face in addressing sustainability is their limited capacity or difficulty in measuring and collecting the data required by ESG reporting guidelines. In this respect, the information system is a useful tool for companies, allowing them to '*monitor and track various facets ranging from environmental and social factors to governance, such as employee training or gender-based remuneration disparities*', as affirmed by ESGnext's CEO.

In addition to the inherent challenge of measuring sustainability data per se, one of the most critical issues is the collection and aggregation of ESG data because they originate from different corporate information systems and therefore reside in different databases. The Elyze software addresses this challenge by providing a centralised repository where data can be stored, thus creating a comprehensive historical record of past data. As ESGnext's CEO explains, '*Our goal was to create a single repository where all ESG information could be consolidated, along with supporting documentation*'.

An interesting aspect that emerged from the respondents was that once the software was implemented, companies began to proactively engage with ESG issues and gradually developed an awareness of the strategic importance of sustainability. Consequently, the information system plays a key role in moving companies from reactive to proactive approaches to ESG issues. Central to this shift is the recognition that a proactive approach to ESG issues can serve as a key differentiator for sustainable competitive advantage. Consequently, companies are beginning to view sustainability as a distinctive capability and recognise the imperative to integrate ESG issues into their strategies and management. This evidence is confirmed by the following statement of the ESGnext CEO: '*There is a shift in the mindset of entrepreneurs. Initially, integrating ESG issues into the business feels somewhat obligatory, driven primarily by regulatory compliance. Entrepreneurs are gradually developing a passion for these issues and are beginning to understand their importance and the need to integrate them into their strategy*'.

Respondents described the ESG information system as a true internal management tool. Using the entered and processed data, the software facilitates the measurement and control of ESG performance. Thus, the IS can simultaneously meet the information needs of both managers and external stakeholders through the final preparation of sustainability reports.

With a deeper understanding of the strategic importance of sustainability, the respondents perceived performance measurement as a continuum, starting with the collection of internal data relevant to the company's strategy and culminating in the communication of information generated to all stakeholders. The journey towards strategic integration of sustainability, guided by the adoption of the information system, can be found in the statement of Alfa's HSE & Sustainability Director: '*We have moved from the mere inclusion of ESG information as a "trend" to the realization of the need to restructure the company's business model from an ESG perspective and to seek to mitigate the impact of this change across the organization*'.

On this last point, respondents identified cultural change as the most challenging aspect of implementing ESG performance monitoring and control systems and, more generally, of moving towards sustainability. Integrating sustainability into strategy and management systems requires a change in the company's mindset, which can be difficult to implement and may encounter resistance. This difficulty lies in the fact that the implementation of ESG policies, initiatives and practices can be slow and costly, although the benefits of this process are often not immediately apparent, especially in the short term. Furthermore, the process of implementing sustainability requires a change in the way a company works and views its business development. Indeed, as the Alfa's HSE & Sustainability Director confirm, '*companies tend to achieve better results during periods of generational change or when there is a change in leadership. It is not always easy to understand the implications of certain ESG projects or issues, as these are new concepts that require a change in mentality and in the way the company is perceived*'.

The results show that Elyze helps companies overcome the challenges and difficulties of implementing sustainability in practice by facilitating the integration of ESG issues into strategy and performance measurement systems. According to the ESGnext project manager, '*our goal is to accompany companies on their sustainability journey and try to ensure that sustainability becomes a strategic and not a superficial element for our customers'*.

The implementation of the software begins with an analysis of the data collected and processed by the company through various existing information systems. The data collected from an ESG perspective was evaluated for its relevance and the possibility of correlation with GRI's proposed indicators. Specifically, this assessment focuses on the extent to which the data already collected is GRI-compliant and what data still needs to be collected to meet the company's chosen set of GRI indicators. Essentially, the aim is to understand what data and information are already collected and produced by the company's information systems and what data and information need to be integrated instead, following a transparent, correct and systematic process. Once the basic structure of the software has been defined using a set of indicators, users upload the relevant information. This basic structure is adapted to the specific needs of the company, allowing users to add indicators that are important to the course of management. The flexibility of the IT tool is particularly appreciated by users, as Alfa's HSE and Sustainability Director explains: '*If one day, when I am doing the materiality analysis again, I discover the existence of a GRI that needs to be reported and is specific to my industry but is not currently included in Elyze, I can easily integrate it into the software'*.

The ESG data were entered into the software by the managers of each department. The entered data were validated to ensure transparency and reliability. These two processes, data entry and validation, involve different levels of control, which reduce errors and increase data accuracy. The data entry and validation processes were described in detail by Alfa's HSE and Sustainability Director: '*within our company, two people collect, process and enter data into the software on a monthly basis. Some data is simple and comes directly from invoices, bills etc. In other cases, data is extracted from various management systems. Managers receive these extractions, process and integrate them based on relevant keys. For example, waste data is extracted from waste management software and then aggregated according to GRI standards. Currently, I am the only person responsible for the data validation phase. During this phase, I review the data collected by others to ensure its accuracy and then validate it*'.

The dashboards generated by the software enable management to effectively monitor ESG performance. Each included indicator allowed targets to be set, facilitating the analysis of variance and verification of target achievement. In this way, the software allows management to carry out continuous monitoring, ensuring access to real-time information on targets achieved and missed, as well as corrective actions. As confirmed by Alfa's HSE & Sustainability Director, '*Within our system, we have pages that aggregate and re-aggregate different data by GRI type, a dashboard that provides an overview of selected indicators, and a control tower page that shows the selected indicators with the targets. This allows us to see how we're doing against our targets on a monthly basis'*.

The data generated by the ESG performance monitoring and control software is integrated seamlessly into an internal reporting system, providing critical support for top-level decision-making. In particular, respondents highlighted the usefulness of reports produced as monthly management tools during management meetings. Consequently, the final report supports both directional and strategic decision-making processes, thereby improving overall control. As Alfa's HSE & Sustainability Director claims, '*The management control function has direct access to the tool. Reports are then periodically exported and distributed to individuals associated with the management committee. In addition, the tool plays a vital role in the audit phase of environmental, safety, and quality systems'*.

The use of this tool has a significant impact on internal reporting processes, not only in terms of the content of reports, which has become more complex and detailed, but also in terms of frequency and timeliness. This enables management to access a wide range of information in real time. The software enables continuous reporting, instant alerts, customised dashboards tailored to different analysis and reporting needs, and real-time simulations to ensure the effective control of business activities. The respondents also highlighted the increased effectiveness of internal reporting tools. Unlike traditional tables, which have little communicative impact, the presentation of graphs that change in real time increases the communicative power of internal reporting tools. As affirmed by ESGnext CEO, '*the tool is able to summarize a really deep concept in an image and make it immediately understandable (for example, how many men and women there are in the company)*'.

In essence, both developers and users of the software emphasised that the information system serves as a crucial link between strategy development and practical implementation, as the Alfa's HSE & Sustainability Director stated: '*The software is an integral part of our strategy. It is clear that digitalization plays a crucial role in our sustainability efforts*'.

29.5 Discussion and Conclusion

The aim of this work is to investigate, through an exploratory case study, how the implementation of an appropriate information system effectively supports the development of an ESG strategy and performance control. Our study contributes to the literature on ESG strategy and performance control by filling the existing gap and responding to the call for more empirical studies on the practical integration of sustainability with ESG performance management and control systems (Braune et al., 2019; Hristov et al., 2021; Hristov et al., 2022).

Our results show that the information system has played an increasingly important role in integrating ESG issues into strategies, performance management and control systems.

The case study results reflect a growing tendency for companies to recognise the importance of ESG factors and adopt appropriate systems and tools to integrate them into their strategies. The decision to allocate resources, both economically and intellectually, to the development and implementation of a dedicated information system tailored to the collection, monitoring and analysis of ESG data reveals the concerted efforts and initiatives that companies are undertaking to integrate these factors into their day-to-day operations.

In addition to demonstrating a commitment to sustainability, the analysis highlights the inherent challenges that organisations face in setting and implementing ESG metrics and targets. This highlights the need for a sustained and long-term commitment to sustainability practices, recognising that the integration of ESG considerations requires ongoing commitment and adaptation. This case study highlights how digital transformation and new technologies offer promising opportunities for companies to effectively manage the complexity of ESG considerations. By leveraging modern tools and platforms, companies can streamline their ESG-related efforts and implement more efficient strategies and management processes (Galeotti et al., 2022). This case study focuses on the proposed information system designed to seamlessly integrate sustainability data with traditional economic metrics. Such systems play a crucial role in enabling companies to provide and analyse comprehensive sustainability data in line with the growing demand for transparency and accountability in corporate practices.

The analysis shows that companies' initial approaches to sustainability are driven primarily by external factors. Indeed, companies' initial choice of information systems is mainly driven by external pressures, such as compliance with sustainability regulations, particularly the legal requirement to produce a sustainability report. Other motivations include the response to legitimate requests from stakeholders, institutional pressure and spontaneous imitation by other companies.

Therefore, in line with previous studies, companies initially decide to implement the information system or manage and monitor ESG objectives following a more outside-in approach. Thus, companies adopt software with a focus on communicative aspects with the aim of producing a sustainability report to satisfy compliance needs, gain legitimacy in the eyes of stakeholders and respond to pressures from the external environment that set socio-environmental accountability processes in motion (Burritt & Schaltegger, 2010; Fiorentino et al., 2016).

Once the information system has been implemented, companies become more aware of the strategic relevance of sustainability and begin to integrate ESG issues into their processes. While the initial motivation for implementation is driven by external factors, as the software is implemented and used within a company, the management begins to understand the strategic importance of sustainability. Therefore, management has begun to view software as an internal management tool that can align economic, social and environmental goals (Vitale et al., 2019).

From this perspective, ESG performance monitoring and management systems address both external pressures and the strategic imperatives of the company, consciously steering change towards sustainability (Burritt & Schaltegger, 2010; Gonzalez-Gonzalez & Zamora Ramirez, 2016; Vitale et al., 2019).

Therefore, the current study shows that the implementation of information systems for monitoring and controlling ESG objectives pushes companies towards a more advanced approach to sustainability, known as the 'twin-track model'. The performance measurement system simultaneously satisfies the information needs of both managers and external parties (Henri & Journeault, 2010). In line with the literature, our results show that although external pressures are the dominant motivation for adopting systems and tools to manage and control ESG performance (Fiorentino et al., 2016; Schaltegger and Burritt, 2010), strong internal pressures are equally important (Figge et al., 2002; Hansen & Schaltegger, 2016; Henri & Journeault, 2010).

In particular, the combination of internal and external drivers is pushing companies to seek greater integration between traditional corporate information systems aimed at collecting and analysing economic-financial information and information systems for collecting and measuring ESG data. The integration of information systems is considered a key differentiator in achieving sustainable competitive advantage.

Therefore, in line with previous studies, our results highlight that companies feel the need to implement information systems to help them collect, monitor and share information on sustainability expressed through ESG indicators (Corsi & Arru, 2018). In this regard, information systems facilitate the collection of large amounts of data related to ESG activities and help aggregate this data from different sources (Galeotti et al., 2022).

In addition, our research demonstrates that the use of ESG data collection and analysis software improves the reporting capability of ESG performance measurement tools by integrating internal and external data. Data integration is the biggest challenge faced by companies when measuring ESG performance. By using advanced tools to project results, the information system enables companies to monitor ESG performance on an ongoing basis, allowing them to identify deviations from targets and take the most appropriate corrective action where necessary. Data analysis and reporting tools can identify trends, correlations and performance gaps, allowing companies to make informed decisions and set ESG targets (Marchi & De Santis, 2020). In addition, the analysis contained in the reports provides input for the decision-making processes of top management, management control and audits.

Our study has numerous theoretical and practical implications. From a theoretical perspective, this study enriches the literature on ESG strategy and performance control and provides insights for bridging the gap between ESG strategy formulation and implementation (Gebhardt et al., 2022; Goni et al., 2017). This study responds to the call for more empirical research on the use of information systems for ESG strategy development and performance measurements (Corsi & Arru, 2018; Goni et al., 2017; Hristov et al., 2022).

From a practical perspective, by providing empirical evidence and case studies, this study helps managers better understand how companies use IT tools to improve ESG performance and metrics.

Our study has some limitations. First, the selected research methodology allowed us to conduct an exploratory study on the topic. Although the reasons for choosing this method, as outlined in the previous sections, are valid, the study needs to be extended to other categories of respondents to provide a more complete picture of the issues analysed. Moreover, the interview method is particularly suited to exploratory analyses but has significant limitations in terms of the generalisability of the conclusions. Second, in addition to the viewpoint of software development companies, our analysis captures only the viewpoint of one customer company. Further studies could extend these analyses to additional customers and/or companies, using software to validate or refute our findings. Our findings, which represent the first attempt to describe the contribution of management and IT systems to the implementation of ESG practices, could stimulate further studies aimed at investigating how control practices change in the context of sustainability.

References

Arici, T., Usta, A. T., Cigerim, E., & Gok, M. S. (2022). Mediating role of information systems on strategy and performance: Innovation and competition perspective. *Proceedings on Engineering, 4*(2), 179–190.

Arjaliès, D. L., & Mundy, J. (2013). The use of management control systems to manage CSR strategy: A levers of control perspective. *Management Accounting Research, 24*(4), 284–300.

Asiaei, K., Rezaee, Z., Bontis, N., Barani, O., & Sapiei, N. S. (2021). Knowledge assets, capabilities and performance measurement systems: A resource orchestration theory approach. *Journal of Knowledge Management, 25*(8), 1947–1976.

Baumgartner, R. J., & Rauter, R. (2017). Strategic perspectives of corporate sustainability management to develop a sustainable organization. *Journal of Cleaner Production, 140*, 81–92.

Bebbington, J., & Unerman, J. (2018). Achieving the United Nations sustainable development goals: An enabling role for accounting research. *Accounting, Auditing & Accountability Journal, 31*(1), 2–24.

Braune, E., Charosky, P., & Hikkerova, L. (2019). Corporate social responsibility, financial performance and risk in times of economic instability. *Journal of Management and Governance, 23*(4), 1007–1021.

Burritt, R. L., & Schaltegger, S. (2010). Sustainability accounting and reporting: Fad or trend? *Accounting, Auditing & Accountability Journal, 23*(7), 829–846.

Burritt, R. L., Hahn, T., & Schaltegger, S. (2002). Towards a comprehensive framework for environmental management accounting—Links between business actors and environmental management accounting tools. *Australian Accounting Review, 12*(27), 39–50.

Capalbo, F., Sorrentino, M., Smarra, M., & Ippolito, A. (2023). Il ruolo strategico dei Sistemi di Misurazione delle Performance nelle aziende sanitarie: un caso studio. *Management Control*, 119–142.

Castellano, N., & Felden, C. (2021). Management Control Systems for Sustainability and Sustainability of Management Control Systems. *Management Control, 2021*(2).

Cheng, B., Ioannou, I., & Serafeim, G. (2014). Corporate social responsibility and access to finance. *Strategic Management Journal, 35*(1), 1–23.

Corsi, K., & Arru, B. (2018). Exploring the effects of sustainability on accounting information systems: The role of SBSC. In *Network, smart and open* (pp. 235–255). Springer.

Corsi, K., & Arru, B. (2021). Role and implementation of sustainability management control tools: Critical aspects in the Italian context. *Accounting, Auditing & Accountability Journal, 34*(9), 29–56.

de Villiers, C., Rouse, P., & Kerr, J. (2016). A new conceptual model of influences driving sustainability based on case evidence of the integration of corporate sustainability management control and reporting. *Journal of Cleaner Production, 136*, 78–85.

de Villiers, C., Kuruppu, S., & Dissanayake, D. (2021). A (new) role for business–promoting the United Nations' sustainable development goals through the internet-of-things and blockchain technology. *Journal of Business Research, 131*, 598–609.

D'Onza, G. (2022). L'orientamento delle aziende ad uno sviluppo sostenibile: quale contributo da parte dei sistemi di management e controllo? *Management Control*, 5–15.

Duque-Grisales, E., & Aguilera-Caracuel, J. (2021). Environmental, social and governance (ESG) scores and financial performance of multilatinas: Moderating effects of geographic international diversification and financial slack. *Journal of Business Ethics, 168*(2), 315–334.

Eisenhardt, K. M. (1989). Building theories from case study research. *Academy of Management Review, 14*(4), 532–550.

Eliwa, Y., Aboud, A., & Saleh, A. (2021). ESG practices and the cost of debt: Evidence from EU countries. *Critical Perspectives on Accounting, 79*, 102097.

Epstein, M. J., & Widener, S. K. (2010). Identification and use of sustainability performance measures in decision-making. *Journal of Corporate Citizenship, 40*, 43–73.

Evans, S., Vladimirova, D., Holgado, M., Van Fossen, K., Yang, M., Silva, E. A., & Barlow, C. Y. (2017). Business model innovation for sustainability: Towards a unified perspective for creation of sustainable business models. *Business Strategy and the Environment, 26*(5), 597–608.

Fadda, N., Corsi, K., Marinò, L., & Pischedda, G. (2021). Sustainable-oriented management come fattore di resilienza organizzativa: un caso di studio. *Management Control*, 39–60.

Fawcett, S. E., Waller, M. A., Miller, J. W., Schwieterman, M. A., Hazen, B. T., & Overstreet, R. E. (2014). A trail guide to publishing success: Tips on writing influential conceptual, qualitative, and survey research. *Journal of Business Logistics, 35*(1), 1–16.

Figge, F., Hahn, T., Schaltegger, S., & Wagner, M. (2002). The sustainability balanced scorecard–linking sustainability management to business strategy. *Business Strategy and the Environment, 11*(5), 269–284.

Fiorentino, R., Garzella, S., Lamboglia, R., & Mancini, D. (2016). Strategie di sostenibilità: dalle motivazioni ai sistemi di misurazione della performance. *Management Control*, 116–142.

Franco-Santos, M., Lucianetti, L., & Bourne, M. (2012). Contemporary performance measurement systems: A review of their consequences and a framework for research. *Management Accounting Research, 23*(2), 79–119.

Galeotti, M., Lombardi, R., Paoloni, P., & Roberto, F. (2022). Big data and sustainability reports: The current approach to non-accounting data management. *Management Control, 2022*, 95–116.

Garzella, S., & Fiorentino, R. (2014). An integrated framework to support the process of green management adoption. *Business Process Management Journal, 20*(1), 68–89.

Gebhardt, M., Thun, T. W., Seefloth, M., & Zülch, H. (2022). Managing sustainability—Does the integration of environmental, social and governance key performance indicators in the internal management systems contribute to companies' environmental, social and governance performance? *Business Strategy and the Environment*.

Ghosh, B., Herzig, C., & Mangena, M. (2019). Controlling for sustainability strategies: Findings from research and directions for the future. *Journal of Management Control, 30*(1), 5–24.

Gioia, D. A., Corley, K. G., & Hamilton, A. L. (2013). Seeking qualitative rigor in inductive research: Notes on the Gioia methodology. *Organizational Research Methods, 16*(1), 15–31.

Gond, J. P., Grubnic, S., Herzig, C., & Moon, J. (2012). Configuring management control systems: Theorizing the integration of strategy and sustainability. *Management Accounting Research, 23*(3), 205–223.

Goni, F. A., Chofreh, A. G., Mukhtar, M., Sahran, S., Shukor, S. A., & Klemeš, J. J. (2017). Strategic alignment between sustainability and information systems: A case analysis in Malaysian public higher education institutions. *Journal of Cleaner Production, 168*, 263–270.

Gonzalez-Gonzalez, J. M., & Zamora Ramirez, C. (2016). Voluntary carbon disclosure by Spanish companies: An empirical analysis. *International Journal of Climate Change Strategies and Management, 8*(1), 57–79.

Goyal, P., Rahman, Z., & Kazmi, A. A. (2013). Corporate sustainability performance and firm performance research: Literature review and future research agenda. *Management Decision, 51*(2), 361–379.

Hansen, E. G., & Schaltegger, S. (2016). The sustainability balanced scorecard: A systematic review of architectures. *Journal of Business Ethics, 133*, 193–221.

Hart, S. L. (1995). A natural-resource-based view of the firm. *Academy of Management Review, 20*(4), 986–1014.

Hart, S. L., & Milstein, M. B. (2003). Creating sustainable value. *Academy of Management Perspectives, 17*(2), 56–67.

Henri, J. F. (2006). Management control systems and strategy: A resource-based perspective. *Accounting, Organizations and Society, 31*(6), 529–558.

Henri, J. F., & Journeault, M. (2010). Eco-control: The influence of management control systems on environmental and economic performance. *Accounting, Organizations and Society, 35*(1), 63–80.

Hristov, I., Appolloni, A., Chirico, A., & Cheng, W. (2021). The role of the environmental dimension in the performance management system: A systematic review and conceptual framework. *Journal of Cleaner Production, 293*, 126075.

Hristov, I., Appolloni, A., & Chirico, A. (2022). The adoption of the key performance indicators to integrate sustainability in the business strategy: A novel five-dimensional framework. *Business Strategy and the Environment.*

Ittner, C. D., & Larcker, D. F. (2001). Assessing empirical research in managerial accounting: A value-based management perspective. *Journal of Accounting and Economics, 32*(1–3), 349–410.

Jain, K., & Tripathi, P. S. (2023). Mapping the environmental, social and governance literature: A bibliometric and content analysis. *Journal of Strategy and Management.*

Jamali, D., Karam, C., Yin, J., & Soundararajan, V. (2017). CSR logics in developing countries: Translation, adaptation and stalled development. *Journal of World Business, 52*(3), 343–359.

Kaplan, R. S., & Norton, D. P. (1996). *Using the balanced scorecard as a strategic management system.*

Lamboglia, R., Fiorentino, R., Mancini, D., & Garzella, S. (2018). From a garbage crisis to sustainability strategies: The case study of Naples' waste collection firm. *Journal of Cleaner Production, 186*, 726–735.

Langfield-Smith, K. (1997). Management control systems and strategy: A critical review. *Accounting, Organizations and Society, 22*(2), 207–232.

Maas, K., Schaltegger, S., & Crutzen, N. (2016). Advancing the integration of corporate sustainability measurement, management and reporting. *Journal of Cleaner Production, 133*, 859–862.

Marchi, L. (2003). *I sistemi informativi aziendali*. Giuffrè.

Marchi, L. (2020). Dalla crisi allo sviluppo sostenibile: il ruolo dei sistemi di misurazione e controllo. *Management Control*, 5–16.

Marchi, L., & De Santis, F. (2020). Il processo e la struttura tecnico-informativa del controllo. In *Controllo di gestione. Pianificazione, programmazione e reporting* (pp. 33–71). Giappichelli Editore.

McWilliams, A., & Siegel, D. S. (2011). Creating and capturing value: Strategic corporate social responsibility, resource-based theory, and sustainable competitive advantage. *Journal of Management, 37*(5), 1480–1495.

Merriam, S. B., & Tisdell, E. J. (2015). *Qualitative research: A guide to design and implementation.* John Wiley & Sons.

Micheli, P., & Manzoni, J. F. (2010). Strategic performance measurement: Benefits, limitations and paradoxes. *Long Range Planning, 43*(4), 465–476.

Micheli, P., & Mura, M3. (2017). Executing strategy through comprehensive performance measurement systems. *International Journal of Operations & Production Management, 37*(4), 423–443.

Mills, A. J., Durepos, G., & Wiebe, E. (Eds.). (2009). *Encyclopedia of case study research*. Sage publications.
Miraglia, R. A. (2012). Nuove tendenze nei sistemi di controllo e di misurazione delle performance. *Management Control*, 5–14.
Mohammad, W. M. W., & Wasiuzzaman, S. (2021). Environmental, social and governance (ESG) disclosure, competitive advantage and performance of firms in Malaysia. *Cleaner Environmental Systems, 2*, 100015.
Morioka, S. N., & de Carvalho, M. M. (2016). A systematic literature review towards a conceptual framework for integrating sustainability performance into business. *Journal of Cleaner Production, 136*, 134–146.
Pondeville, S., Swaen, V., & De Rongé, Y. (2013). Environmental management control systems: The role of contextual and strategic factors. *Management Accounting Research, 24*(4), 317–332.
Porter, M. E., & Kramer, M. R. (2011). Creating shared value: Redefining capitalism and the role of the corporation in society. *Harvard Business Review, 89*(1/2), 62–77.
Qu, S. Q., & Dumay, J. (2011). The qualitative research interview. *Qualitative Research in Accounting & Management, 8*(3), 238–264.
Raimo, N., Caragnano, A., Zito, M., Vitolla, F., & Mariani, M. (2021). Extending the benefits of ESG disclosure: The effect on the cost of debt financing. *Corporate Social Responsibility and Environmental Management, 28*(4), 1412–1421.
Rodríguez-Olalla, A., & Avilés-Palacios, C. (2017). Integrating sustainability in organisations: An activity-based sustainability model. *Sustainability, 9*(6), 1072.
Russo, M. V., & Fouts, P. A. (1997). A resource-based perspective on corporate environmental performance and profitability. *Academy of Management Journal, 40*(3), 534–559.
Schöggl, J. P., Fritz, M. M., & Baumgartner, R. J. (2016). Toward supply chain-wide sustainability assessment: A conceptual framework and an aggregation method to assess supply chain performance. *Journal of Cleaner Production, 131*, 822–835.
Simons, R., Dévila, A., & Kaplan, R. S. (2000). *Performance measurement & control systems for implementing strategy: Text & cases*. Prentice Hall.
Suchman, M. C. (1995). Managing legitimacy: Strategic and institutional approaches. *Academy of Management Review, 20*(3), 571–610.
Vitale, G., Cupertino, S., Rinaldi, L., & Riccaboni, A. (2019). Integrated management approach towards sustainability: An Egyptian business case study. *Sustainability, 11*(5), 1244.
Williamson, D., Lynch-Wood, G., & Ramsay, J. (2006). Drivers of environmental behaviour in manufacturing SMEs and the implications for CSR. *Journal of Business Ethics, 67*, 317–330.
Windolph, S. E., Harms, D., & Schaltegger, S. (2014). Motivations for corporate sustainability management: Contrasting survey results and implementation. *Corporate Social Responsibility and Environmental Management, 21*(5), 272–285.
Yin, R. K. (2017). *Case study research and applications: Design and methods*. Sage Publications.

Part V
ESG Implementation and Practices: Challenges, Strategies and Case Studies

Chapter 30
ESG Regulation and Accountability: Shall We Really Imagine Sisyphus Happy?

Rosanna Spanò, Alessandra Allini, Francesca Salerno, and Edoardo Marcenaro

30.1 Background

The chapter at hand acknowledges that the breadth of change relating to environmental, social, and governance (ESG)–related matters poses several challenges, especially due to the marked increase in efforts to strengthen the legal provisions

---

Camus tells the story of Sisyphus, who defied the Gods and bound Death so that no human would have to die. When Death was finally freed and it was time for Sisyphus to die, he devised a deception that allowed him to escape the underworld. After finally apprehending Sisyphus, the Gods decreed that his punishment would last forever. He would have to push a rock up a mountain; once there, the rock would roll back down, forcing Sisyphus to start all over again. Camus portrays Sisyphus as an absurd hero who lives life to the fullest, despises Death, and is sentenced to a meaningless task. Camus uses Sisyphus' never-ending and pointless toil as a metaphor for modern lives which is tragic only in the rare instances when it becomes conscious. Camus is intrigued by Sisyphus' thoughts as he marches down the mountain to begin again. This is the truly tragic moment when the hero becomes aware of his plight. He has no hope, but "there is no fate that cannot be overcome by scorn." Sisyphus, like the absurd man, keeps pushing. Camus claims that when Sisyphus recognizes the futility of his task and the certainty of his fate, he is liberated to recognize the absurdity of his situation and achieves contented acceptance. Camus concludes that "all is well," and that "one must imagine Sisyphus happy."

R. Spanò (✉) · A. Allini
Department of Economics, Management, Institutions (DEMI), University of Naples "Federico II", Naples, Italy
e-mail: rosanna.spano@unina.it; alessandra.allini@unina.it

F. Salerno
Company: ENEL S.p.A, Rome, Italy
e-mail: francesca.salerno@enel.com

E. Marcenaro
Enel Grids srl, Rome, Italy
e-mail: edoardo.marcenaro@enel.com

N. Castellano et al. (eds.), *Environmental, Social, Governance (ESG)*, SIDREA Series in Accounting and Business Administration,
https://doi.org/10.1007/978-3-031-76618-3_30

concerning ESG, toward plenty and possibly overlapping requirements, also impinging internal processes and dynamics of organizations. Recent attempts by multiple institutions (GRI, EFRAG, ISSB, etc.) wish to define and standardize the ESG metrics for external reporting, disclosure, ESG scores, ESG materiality, ESG performance, and so forth. Considering the many standards and guidelines, some of which still in draft, and the different theoretical foundations and practical perspectives that they embraced, a problem arises for companies on what to measure and how, and on what to report and how. Furthermore, multiple accountability pressures leading voluntary adherence by companies to become quasi-mandatory, especially in sensitive industries, may lead to the creation of potential *loci* for overlapping issues and gaps broadly speaking for ESG as a holistic organizational process.

However, despite the rising importance of the theme highlighted above, literature is still scant, and results are jeopardized. Over the last few years, several studies have devoted attention to materiality conceptualizations and applications, focusing on diverse sets of standards (GRI, ISSB, EFRAG) and various regulatory sources. Multiple contributions have focused on archival analyses and variously examined the quantity of ESG disclosure (Arif et al., 2022; Arvidsson & Dumay, 2022; Chen & Xie, 2022; Guthrie et al., 2017; Karpoff et al., 2022; Nicolò et al., 2021; Yoo & Managi, 2022). Other papers look at the main topics to be disclosed (Agostini et al., 2022; Bebbington & Larrinaga, 2014; Bebbington et al., 2021; Busco et al., 2020; Cordazzo et al., 2020; Farneti et al., 2011; Laine et al., 2021; Lokuwaduge & Heenetigala, 2017; Merkl-Davies & Brennan, 2017; Michelon et al., 2022; Romolini et al., 2014). Yet, other papers focus more specifically on financial materiality issues (Bolt & Tregidga, 2023; Busco et al., 2020; Gerwanski et al., 2019; Sepúlveda-Alzate et al., 2022; Schiehll & Kolahgar, 2021; Torelli et al., 2020).

Although interesting insights can be gained from a cross-reading of the flourishing debate, current studies have addressed mainly what questions, while limitedly dealing with ESG disclosure as an organizational process. This, in turn, is crucial to better comprehend the complex, multifaceted, and interplayed perspectives of double materiality that are nowadays at the core of the changes in place. This makes the substantive application of ESG in organizations still a quite fuzzy domain of investigation. Companies may well face in short time opportunities but also challenges and threats relating to ESG. This includes new and upcoming risks deriving from an increase in compliance efforts, possibly paving the way for a greater risk of reputational impairment in the marketplace stemming from perceived inaccurate ESG information or deficient performance (Hackett et al., 2020).

The regulatory burden, which on paper seems to be intended to support social integration for ESG, may well unveil an ongoing *juridification* process, with the new requirements possibly ending up achieving the opposite of their wished aims (Power & Laughlin, 1996). In the current chapter, therefore, we aim to answer the following research question: *does ESG-related regulation really improve ESG corporate processes toward substantive accountability?*

This chapter focuses on the European context. We examine the current and upcoming regulation (broadly conceived as a mixture of hard and soft laws) to discuss whether it provides adequate ground for an ESG-based holistic management of the firms able to assure greater accountability toward value creation. For this purpose, and to ensure rigorous theoretical inquiry into a domain subject to strong contrasting beliefs, following Spanò et al. (2016) we employ a theoretical framework derived from Habermas' theory of communicative action (1984) as advanced by Broadbent and Laughlin (2013). Spanò et al. (2016) already used such an approach focusing on the regulatory issues pertaining to the management of entities seized from mafia-type associations, offering more ground for a greater understanding of the neglected relationship between accounting and the law (Power & Laughlin, 1996).

Broadbent and Laughlin (2013), leveraging Habermas' (1987) views, argue against the increase in formal, positive, and written law, which Habermas labels as a juridification process. Habermas' critical concern is with the colonizing, constitutive, and (con)densing force that law (as a medium) exerts over social action, in contrast to its potential for a facilitating, regulative one (law as institution, which is seen as an enabler). Habermas' view is that if it is possible to understand the constituent elements of "good" and "bad" law, it is also possible to understand the constituent elements of "good" and "bad" steering mechanisms (Broadbent & Laughlin, 2013). To understand whether current regulations about ESG are effective, also building on previous approaches in literature (Spanò et al., 2016), we thus follow Laughlin and Broadbent (1993) and include Teubner's (1987) criteria to judge good and bad laws, by reference to the concept of structural coupling. Reference to such a framework is valuable as it provides conceptual ground for a rigorous inquiry, detached from time-specific political views, to interpret the regulatory dilemma affecting the European setting: that is comprehending whether and how a juridified law on ESG could have destroying effects on the political designers of the law, even though there will be all manner of powers to prevent this from occurring, and for organizations.

Methodologically, to gather data that allow an operational discussion of the theoretical conceptions derived from the framework, the chapter embraces a quite novel approach. Due to the characteristics of the team of authors, all with both research and practice experience in the field consolidated over the years, the chapter is rooted in the Accidental Ethnography (AccE), which is a praxis-oriented methodology for practitioner-based research. AccE is a method in which practitioners who have become researchers use previously collected data to investigate important phenomena. AccE is a reflexive, reflective, and praxical method of inquiry in which the researcher examines data collected from day-to-day workplace processes to share important findings and provide insights into educational research and practice.

The findings allow us to answer the research question, advancing the scarce knowledge of practically rooted implications of the ESG regulatory proliferation, giving voice to practitioners in the field. Moreover, the study will provide critical conclusions and basis for further inquiry of special relevance to practice and for policymaking. The chapter is organized as follows. Section 30.2 presents the theoretical framework. Section 30.3 describes the research design. The fourth section summarizes the regulatory landscape and provides the practitioners' perspectives. Finally, Sect. 30.5 discusses the findings and provides some concluding remarks.

30.2 Theoretical Framework

This chapter relies upon Habermas' theory of communicative action (1984), in the operationalization put forth by Broadbent and Laughlin (2013). This skeletal framework acknowledges that society is a combination of the lifeworld (a symbolic dynamic space, a normative context within which culture, tradition, and identity can be reproduced); systems (a functionally definable arrangement of operations, such as organizations, which represent the tangible expressions of the lifeworld); and steering media (mechanisms such as power, money, or law), which steer the interface and interaction between lifeworld and systems and play a role in ensuring that the latter reflect the former. The theory identifies several changing pathways.

Morphostatic ones take the shape of rebuttal or reorientation, which respectively consist in the rejection or in the weak response by systems to the steering media, keeping a separation between them and the lifeworld.

Morphogenetic changes, instead, can take the form of colonization, which result from a decoupling with steering media possibly following the systems instead of the lifeworld, or evolution, that align systems and the lifeworld. An important basis to closely interpret these dynamics is, according to Habermas, in the understanding of the difference between the types of legal norms.

He distinguishes "law as medium," which is justified solely by appeal to procedure, and "law as institutions," which still admits of substantive justification at the level of the lifeworld. In highlighting this distinction, Habermas criticizes the increase in formal, positive, and written law, which he defines as a juridification process, that is not simply an expansion of the volume of regulation, but a specific manifestation of the dialectic of the Enlightenment, in which welfarist intentions culminate in the "violent abstraction" of regulation (Power & Laughlin, 1992). Juridification, in his view, translates in the loss of substantive justification, through a (excessive) proceduralization of relations that are morally substantive, which is corrosive to lifeworld values. Distinguishing law as a medium (seen as a constitutive and colonizing force) from law as an institution (seen as an enabler), Habermas argues that if it is possible to understand the constituent elements of "good" and "bad" laws, it is also possible to understand the constituent elements of "good" and "bad" steering mechanisms (Broadbent & Laughlin, 2013).

To understand whether current regulations about ESG are effective, we follow Laughlin and Broadbent's (1993) including Teubner's (1987) criteria to judge good and bad laws, by reference to a structural coupling examination. The notion of structural coupling refers to the relationship between systems and their environments, in terms of a dynamic interaction between various elements. Structural coupling creates a situation that is opposite to the decoupling one.

Structural coupling is breached when either relevance criteria are not met or the conditions of self-reproductive organizations are endangered.

Teubner's first condition ("relevance") relies on Habermas' conception of law as a medium that has the potential to move societal systems into new domains of activity and concern independently of the societal lifeworld, thus breaking the "relevance" criteria.

The second aspect of the breach of structural coupling relates to the disturbance of the self-reproductive processes of politics, law, and social systems. The self-reproductive capacity of an organization can be explained as the ability of an organization to continue to survive and operate by reproducing its lifeworld over time. Once an organization has been created, and a degree of autonomy of action has been granted, there needs to be a demonstrable abuse defined in the context of a full democratic debate (Laughlin & Broadbent, 1993). When this intrusion comes from a societal steering medium, such as the law, without the backing or the expression of the societal lifeworld, then it is not justifiable, and the repercussions are uncertain. Laughlin and Broadbent (1993) highlight that it is inevitable that juridified law, which, by implication, is material law, conforms to political guidance. At the same time, mutual indifference is unlikely to occur, as the desire to live within the law is a dominant, although not universal, characteristic of members of society. However, organizations can manage to appear compliant, for the sake of legitimacy, while pursuing alternative strategies.

Thus, on the one hand, juridified law can have destroying effects on the political designers of the law, even though there will be all manner of powers to prevent this from occurring. On the other hand, juridified law either can have disintegrating effects on the organizations being regulated or can be absorbed (albeit in costly ways) by these organizations (Laughlin & Broadbent, 1993).

Broadbent and Laughlin (2013) argue that enabling discursive processes are carried out and that, despite this reflexive law being far from reality, there are potential alternatives to excessive legal regulation, mainly based on participation and co-operation between different groups.

This articulated theoretical lens is employed in the current chapter as a lens to interpret the results and not as a rigid model to be confirmed/refuted. Thus, we take the conceptions of relevance and self-reproductive capacity explained above, as a means to comprehend the characteristics of an increasingly complex regulatory framework at the same time focusing on the impacts on ESG practices to discuss whether the approach in place can fulfill the aspirations of greater accountability and value creation surrounding the ESG transition in place.

30.3 Methodology

Thanks to the peculiar composition of the research team, made of two practitioners with more than 15 years of experience in the practice of litigation and ESG, and two researchers with consolidated project expertise in the ESG domain, plus several experiences as advisors for firms on these issues, the chapter befits from a praxis-oriented methodology for practitioner-based research, namely, AccE (Levitan et al., 2020). The approach used in this chapter is based on the development of AccE, which is a method in which practitioners who have become researchers use previously collected data to investigate important phenomena. We contend that AccE can help bridge the gap between research and practice (Fuji, 2015; Poulos, 2009).

AccE is the systematic study of previous practitioners' experience, which includes the collection and analysis of existing data from practitioners' organization (school, nonprofit, or business) to serve an ethnographic purpose in reporting on an educational experience, culture, or innovation of significant merit and contribution to the field. Practitioners' deep and diverse field-based experiences continue to be an underutilized source of data that can contribute to innovation and organizational improvement (Bensimon, 2007; Zeichner, 2007). Practitioners' vast and varied experiences remain largely untapped and unable to contribute to the broader research community, in part because practitioners do not typically plan scholarly research while embarking on a new project. However, during their work, practitioners frequently discover important phenomena that, if rigorously, reflectively, and pragmatically investigated, could contribute to research knowledge and organizational improvement (Eady et al., 2015). To ensure the trustworthiness of the results, these data require refocused and methodologically rigorous methods, which we begin to develop here. This is accomplished, for the most part, through a reorientation and recasting of traditional ethnographic strategies, resulting in a different approach to data collection. This reorientation and recasting of ethnographic methods creates an opportunity to use data collected as part of normal organizational operating procedures in the field.

AccE uses the unintentional and coincidental findings of previous researcher experiences to contribute to theory and practice, rather than as a supplement to a more traditional research intention and method (Fuji, 2015). The AccE approach allows practitioners to capitalize on unanticipated learning that occurs in practice, but it also includes specific data collection methods and analytical approaches that will provide more robust evidence about the learning that occurs in practice. AccE broadens the scope of action research because the researcher is first a practitioner and then conducts research after the fact. AccE is based on the premise that important research is frequently "accidental"—but not anecdotal or journalistic (Levitan et al., 2020).

From an operational perspective, it should be noted that even if a research project did not start with the usual prerequisites, the findings and lessons from deep, reflective, and systematic data analysis can still be a legitimate, significant contribution to knowledge for the organization, other practitioners, and theory. For this reason, extant yet few contributions mobilizing AccE highlight that its practices align with the eight "big tent" criteria advanced by Tracy (2010). Based on Tracy's (2010) work, we discover that AccE practices align with the eight "big tent" criteria: "(a) worthy topic, (b) rich rigor, (c) sincerity, (d) credibility, (e) resonance, (f) significant contribution, (g) ethics, and (h) meaningful coherence."

Moreover, as Levitan et al. (2020) argue, AccE is a method for sharing practitioner contributions based on previous experiences and practices; therefore, AccE practices are designed to provide guidelines that ensure scholarly rigor to practitioner-scholars. For this reason, the authors suggest embracing a set of practices required to conduct AccE rigorously, providing trustworthiness, and ensuring quality in the researcher's interpretations and broader contributions to the field. These are not necessarily to be intended as sequential steps, but as a means to improve the internal validity of any piece of research.

Thus, drawing from Levitan et al. (2020) for the purposes of the current study, the research team considered the following relevant issues.

Initiation. In this regard, it is worth noting that AccE is typically initiated by a significant experience sparking a connection between research learned by the practitioner and their experiences in the field. For our purpose, we considered a conversation among the team members about the issues of possible procedural excess and lacking accountability.

Reflection and reexamination. This phase involved all the researchers in reflecting on their knowledge, assumptions, and the implications of their work on ESG matters, also reexamining whether and how there could be room for their experiences that could enhance theory or practice.

Data collection, coding, and recursive consultation. Upon finding a particular focus thanks to the reflexive process briefly described above, the accidental ethnographer collected all possible extant data (both preexisting and new ones) for deeper analysis, also employing a predetermined coding scheme based on the researcher's reflective understanding of the topic and ensuring regular reflection back and forth.

30.4 Findings

The analysis has been carried out with a view to assess the characteristics of the regulatory framework and to gather insights into the practical experience of the team. Therefore, Sect. 30.4.1 presents the landscape from a regulatory perspective, while Sect. 30.4.2 gives evidence to several relevant practical issues related to the increasing regulatory requirements that researchers-participants have experienced over the last years. In particular, as per Sect. 30.4.2, the four team members discussed multiple times their points of view, and thus, they obtain an encompassing view of the phenomena under scrutiny. The results presented below are then interpolated and discussed trough the theoretical lens in the fifth section of this chapter, to provide a broad interpretation and gain insights into the current circumstances.

30.4.1 The Regulatory Landscape of ESG

To examine the issues relating to ESG disclosure that companies must provide, it is useful to review existing regulatory landscape to better set the context of the problem. The regulatory landscape is classified in regulations, standards, and guidelines, which are briefly summarized in Table 30.1.

Table 30.1 Regulatory landscape

Year	Name	Type	Main subjects	Main content
2000 (updated in 2016)	*GRI Global Initiative Reporting Standards*	Standard	Organizations of any size, type, sector, or geographic location that voluntarily intend to report on impacts related to specific economic, social, and/or environmental topics	Nonfinancial disclosure in annual report or in a stand-alone report (e.g., sustainability report, CSR) The GRI system is divided into three categories: universal standards that apply to all types of organizations; sectoral standards; and thematic standards
2014	*Directive 2014/95/EU—NFRD*	Regulation	Requires large undertakings which are public-interest entities, exceeding on their balance sheet dates the criterion of the average number of 500 employees during the financial year, to include nonfinancial disclosure in their annual report or in a stand-alone report (e.g., sustainability report, integrated annual report)	Minimum disclosure has to be provided on the following categories: environmental, social, employee matters, respect for human rights, anti-corruption, and bribery matters It neither imposes compliance with particular reporting standards, nor contains a detailed list of disclosure requirements
2017 (updated in 2021)	*Recommendations of Task Force on Climate-related Financial Disclosure*	Guideline	Suggests that all organizations (public and private entities in each jurisdiction) should include nonfinancial disclosure in financial filings	Minimum disclosure has to be provided on the following categories: governance, strategy, risk management, metrics, and targets It does not impose compliance with particular reporting standards, but it contains a detailed list of minimum disclosure requirements
2020	*Regulation (EU) 2020/852 (Taxonomy)*	Regulation	Requires large undertakings which are subject to the obligation to publish NFRD, to include information about eco-sustainable investments in nonfinancial disclosure reports	Minimum disclosure about environmental activities has to be provided on the following categories: climate change mitigation; climate change adaptation; sustainable use and protection of water and marine resources; transition to a circular economy; pollution prevention and control; and protection and restoration of biodiversity and ecosystems

2023	*ISSB Standards*	Standard	Organizations of any size, type, sector, or geographic location to include nonfinancial information about sustainable-related risks and opportunities into any documents also toward cross-reference, provided that the information is available to users of general-purpose financial reporting (e.g., also in a financial statement)	Minimum disclosure has to be provided on the following categories: governance, strategy, risk management, metrics, and targets Includes consistent metrics and standardized qualitative information, to help entities assess how climate-related issues and associated risks and opportunities affect entities
2023	*Directive 2022/2464 (EU)—CSRD*		Extends to all listed companies (including SMEs) and large companies that exceeds on their balance sheet dates the criterion of the average number of 250 employees during the financial year, to include nonfinancial disclosure in their annual report or in a stand-alone report (e.g., sustainability report)	Minimum disclosure has to be provided on the following categories: environmental factors (including Taxonomy disclosure), social factors, and governance factors It suggests compliance with ESRS
2023	*ESRS*	Standard	Requires all organizations to include nonfinancial disclosure in their annual report or in a stand-alone report	The organizations shall disclose material sustainability-related information comprising sector-agnostic, sector-specific, and entity-specific information The undertakings shall cover the following sustainability topics: environmental matters; social matters; and governance matters Prescribes the mandatory concepts and principles to apply for the preparation of sustainability statements under the Corporate Sustainability Reporting Directive (CSRD)

Over the last few years, there has been an increase in regulatory attempts by several bodies, both governmental and nongovernmental ones, as for ESG-related matters. This on the one hand has brought about an important focus on these issues, while this on the other hand increases complexity due to overlaps and partial mutual influence among several normative and non-normative sources (Laine et al., 2021). As said, the growing ESG challenges have generated pressures on companies to adopt a more systematic approach toward ESG reporting, but this heterogeneity in the regulatory landscape implies that organizations may struggle in mobilizing and mixing regulations, standards, and guidelines (Lokuwaduge & Heenetigala, 2017; Romolini et al., 2014). To better tap into this complex picture that Table 30.1 summarizes, we provide below a brief explanation of possible elements deriving from regulations enacted by EU and national institutions and from standards/guidelines enacted by standard setters and task force. The list (summarized and compiled in Table 30.1) constitutes a partial yet powerful illustration of the level of fragmentation and confusion that characterizes ESG reporting.

The EU is committed to achieving an accounting harmonization process of the regulatory landscape for ESG reporting to provide adequate disclosures to meet the stakeholders' information needs. The process started several years ago with Directive 2014/95/EU, which presented several issues and gaps. The latest directive, named Corporate Sustainability Reporting Directive (CSRD), aims to overcome the limitations of previous Directive 2014/95/EU, laying the groundwork for the harmonization of ESG reporting standards, clarifying the content of ESG reporting, and setting out the principles of ESG reporting. However, various limitations and shortcomings remain.

The first limitation is the lack of detailed disclosure requirements for each thematic area, a limitation in the previous directive, replicated in the current one. The absence of detailed information required leads companies to draw from the standards and guidelines the detailed information to be reported for each thematic area (e.g., the CSRD introduces the double materiality but does not define how to measure financial and impact materiality and how to monitor the dynamic development of materiality, so companies draw the information from standards and guidelines). The areas of discretion in the directive lead to heterogeneity of disclosure and a lack of harmonization of accounting because standards and guidelines have many inconsistencies compared to the thematic areas required by the regulations.

The second limitation is the danger related to the lack of comparability even if the recent updates suggest the mandatory adoption of the ESRS. Indeed, the co-existence of a set of complex and heterogeneous standards already in use (GRI, ISSB, EFRAG) may well lead to confusion due to the mobilization and mixing of standards or frameworks with substantially different approaches. Therefore, commitment to harmonize and find common pathways will become paramount in the foreseeable future.

In fact, there are underlying differences between enacted standards. The main differences are outlined as follows. The ISSB proposal is aimed to satisfy the investors' information needs, while the EFRAG and GRI proposals are aimed to meet stakeholders' information needs. The ISSB standards require to be reported general principles, with a focus on sector-specific climate-related risks and opportunities, the EFRAG standards require not only general principles but also specific metrics on the ESG approach, and the GRI requires not only general disclosures but also specific information on economic, social, and environmental impacts (TBL approach). ISSB material topics are based on financial materiality, EFRAG material topics are based on double materiality, and GRI topics are based on impact materiality. In order to favor the harmonization process, there needs greater co-operation among standard setters about drivers for defining standards to achieve uniformity and comparability of disclosure.

In addition, in order to improve disclosure by making it more specific and detailed to meet the information needs of stakeholders resulting from an increasing awareness of ESG issues, the EU has issued further regulations such as the Taxonomy Regulation (Regulation 2020/852/EU). This regulation requires companies to report additional information on sustainable investments beyond that already required by Directive 2014/95/EU. Taxonomy Regulation establishes an EU-wide classification system or "framework" intended to provide businesses and investors with a common language to identify to what degree economic activities can be considered environmentally sustainable. The Taxonomy Regulation imposes large public-interest entities to include information about how their activities align with the Taxonomy in the nonfinancial disclosure part of their financial statements. The Taxonomy Regulation brings new disclosure requirements for large listed companies that are already required to provide a nonfinancial statement under the Non-Financial Reporting Directive (NFRD). They will have to start disclosing how their business activities align with the climate objectives (adaptation and mitigation) under the EU Taxonomy Regulation in the course of 2022 (covering the financial year 2021) and all six environmental objectives in the course of 2023 (covering the financial year 2022). This regulation has objectives, primary users, and minimum disclosure requirements totally opposite to NFRD, so the motivation behind including the Taxonomy information in the nonfinancial disclosure is unclear. The resulting nonfinancial disclosure is a melting pot of disparate information with different aims and primary users. The last CSRD according to the multistakeholder approach was supposed to also regulate the disclosure of eco-sustainable investments, as well as provide a tool to achieve a systematization of nonfinancial disclosure regulations by reducing the still unresolved "ambiguities." The CSRD has included the detailed information requirements of Taxonomy in environmental matters, but it is not enough because it is a merely reference to the Taxonomy Regulation without a concrete intervention. A concrete intervention to regulate eco-sustainable investments may also lead to improve reporting, increase trust, and encourage more sustainable behaviors. Despite the intentions to improve ESG disclosure and to support companies in ESG reporting, the regulatory landscape is still complex and entangled.

Another limitation is connected to the legal instrument of the directive. The directive is the legal instrument used in the harmonization process, which must be transposed into national law to render its enforcement easier. The states are given some flexibility in transposing the directive. Thus, despite the directive's promise of harmonizing ESG disclosure in practice, the regulatory European landscape results are differentiated. To assist companies in ESG reporting, nongovernmental bodies have enacted frameworks. Several initiatives and frameworks have emerged, such as TFCD guidelines applicable to public and private entities in each jurisdiction to reach an alignment of accounting. However, the TFCD is structured around four thematic areas (governance, strategy, risk management, and metrics and targets) totally opposite to the NFRD's one (environmental, social, employee matters, respect for human rights, anti-corruption, and bribery matters). Moreover, TFCD requires to include nonfinancial disclosure in financial filings, compared to NFRD which requires to include nonfinancial disclosure in the annual report or in a standalone report (e.g., sustainability report, integrated annual report). These substantial differences lead large undertakings to produce more than one report at the end of the year, both according to TFCD and according to NFRD, attempting to fulfill multiple requirements. Despite the good intentions of nongovernmental initiatives, large undertakings are obligated to use a multitude of international and national regulations and reporting frameworks for a lack of alignment between guidelines and regulations, which is unlikely to improve the comparability and transparency of the information reported.

30.4.2 Practitioners' Taste on ESG Regulation and Accountability

From a more practical perspective, and bearing in mind all the above, what should be noted is that ESG reporting is indeed key for corporations' accountability toward their stakeholders. Increasingly, also at a mid-managerial level there is awareness (and commitment) on the idea that investors, consumers, NGOs, and analysts are more and more using a company's ESG performance as an indicator of business value and of management strength. This trend underpins the current shift from shareholder capitalism to stakeholder capitalism that companies are called to address and implement in their daily management and business planning.

Doing business in a sustainable way requires companies to sail through a multilayered and multifaceted prism of duties and responsibilities, which depart from the ordinary rules of profitability and the business judgment rule to embrace a new corporate vision which sees corporations as players who minimize their environmental and societal negative impact while bringing added value for the development of society. Corporations are fully cognizant of their "new role" in society, as drivers for change, and are conscious of the need to be accountable also for this toward not only shareholders, but also employees, customers, suppliers, governments, communities, etc.

The main corporate reaction to this has been an increased stakeholder engagement, achieved, among others, through increasing transparency and broadening the scope of reporting to the economic, environmental, and social impacts of corporations' activities, to allow for an increased trustworthiness and operational integrity in a company's business. To respond to the society's call for an increased sustainable business conduct, corporations are required to embed ESG concerns and activities "externally," that is, in their doing business, and "internally," that is, in their corporate governance and internal policy organization, and to measure and report all of such activities in compliance with the metrics available for sustainability reporting in order to be accountable toward the stakeholders.

Stakeholders appear to be more and more interested in ESG performance measurement through reporting, triggering a phenomenon whereby sustainability reporting is perceived as being at least as important as sustainability in business itself. While the principle "*you can manage only what you can measure*" can be successfully applied also to sustainability matters and activities, the *status quo* is showing that the methodology currently applied to sustainability measurement and reporting is very burdensome for companies and far from being flawless.

Firstly, the public call for an increased regulation of sustainability reporting has led corporations to the need to cope with an ESG reporting regulatory framework that, rather than being organic, structured, and corporate-friendly—in a word "sustainable"—is instead a highly complex, multifaceted, and overwhelming set or rules and standards, often overlapping, seldom mandatory, being the result of a continued stream of enactment of guidelines, regulations, soft and hard laws, best practices, reporting standards, rating instructions, nice-to-have requirements, certifications, etc. This overlegislation (or extreme juridification) of the ESG regulatory framework calls for corporations, and in-house counsels first, as frontrunners, to abandon the traditional Taxonomy applicable to legal hierarchy and instead implement a "mix & match" methodology whereby it is mainly up to the company management to choose the sustainability metrics to apply to its reporting, applying a wide discretionary power that companies still retain.

While a good degree of flexibility and discretion is desirable to ensure that ESG reporting provides a true picture of a company's sustainability activities, the proliferation of normative and quasi-normative set of rules with blurry boundaries and scope of application does not help either corporations or stakeholders to act in a predictable and reliable legal environment, casting doubts to the consistency of the current sustainability legal framework with the rule of law.

It is worth noting that the United Nations Global Compact realized that to face the actual moment of converging crises, "business has an important role to play by promoting ethical leadership and building trust between public and private institutions and in these institutions by civil society. Through Transformational Governance, this vision can be translated into business action, (...), as it provides a framework to address the rising stakeholder and shareholder expectations by adopting a broader approach to the G – governance dimension – in ESG – environmental, social governance. (..,)." Thus, business has to be "more accountable, ethical, inclusive and transparent to drive responsible business conduct, improve ESG performance and strengthen public institutions, laws and systems. This means fostering a culture of integrity, fairness and inclusion beyond legal formality — asking not just what is legal but what is right."[1]

As things stand, companies are required to make an effort that goes far beyond the application of a set of legal provisions, being required to act proactively to anticipate market needs, often reflected only in market uses, in market trends, or at most in soft law tools or best practices collated by internationally recognized institutions or bodies. As a matter of fact, the so-called hard law regulations reflect processes and evolutions that at company level were often already applied, transposed, and metabolized to a large extent. The absence of an organic upstream hard and mandatory legislation, however, leads to a proliferation of nonregulatory or para-regulatory instruments that make it extremely difficult if not impossible for companies that do not have an adequate organizational structure to navigate the panorama of rules to be followed in order to tell their business to the market.

This imposes a significant social cost on companies that cannot be ignored. Companies are required not only to operate in a sustainable manner, but also to equip themselves with an organizational structure and adequate IT tools in order to be able to monitor and analyze the regulatory context of reference, to collect, measure, and report on all values and activities that are relevant in a sustainability perspective according to a metric system that should be both reliable and flexible enough to adapt to an ever-changing regulatory framework. And this is not enough. Even if an organization implements a robust data collection system and an accurate sustainability reporting process, it shall also act on the data collected and measured, integrating them into the management decision-making process through a lesson-learned improvement process. This cost shift from governments to companies has to be computed in the overall assessment of a corporation ESG impact.

The strive for greater or even radical transparency by corporations on sustainability-related matters, moreover, has the raising of greenwashing concerns as flipping sides of the coin. The more sustainability reporting and communication assumes an autonomous value separate from the value of the sustainability of that company business, the more the risk of greenwashing distortive effects on fair competition among companies exists.

30.5 Conclusions

Drawing from the theoretical framework, the findings of the analysis unveil that ESG-related changes in progress in the European Union appear dangerously identifiable with what Broadbent and Laughlin indicate as reorientation, a change that cannot be rebutted but that risks being played in parallel with previous routines and practices. A cross-reading of the regulatory landscape analysis and the practitioners'

[1] https://unglobalcompact.org/what-is-gc/our-work/governance/transformational-governance.

views allow us to highlight several relevant issues as per the danger of a juridification process affecting ESG in the European setting.

The analysis carried out compounding both the turbulent and slippery regulatory framework and the perspectives of those involved within companies strategically and operationally making it effective demonstrate that the two conditions of relevance and self-reproductive capacity, which are crucial to guarantee the structural coupling of organizations, that determines whether laws are mediums or institutions, are actually not achievable under the current circumstances.

An important dimension to consider, in this regard, relates to the understanding of the manifold risks connected to the European Union posture. It is no coincidence that as far back as 1992, Pietro Perlingieri stated that the need for unity must not lead one to believe that the future is one of uniform and flattened legislation, which overcomes contrasts, discrepancies, and antinomies: suffice it to think of the diversity of the Constitutions, inspired by often peculiar principles and values, of cultural differences, of the actual functioning of the institutions, of the different ways of conceiving the interest of individuals and the general interest, and of the diversity of the *extra ordinem* sources of statutes and creative applications. The society of the future, and of Europe in particular, characterized by a unitary and rigidly uniform legislation, is, rather, a myth or utopia, which has no counterpart in other, much more established federative experiences.

From the cross-reading of regulatory analysis and practitioners' taste of the issues under scrutiny, we can grasp a tough attempt at legislative uniformity on ESG (at any cost, not necessarily in a functional way) that to a certain extent can constitute an unnecessary violence to the diversities that exist both on the cultural and on the economic level, which per se induces a breach of the structural coupling.

Indeed, the relevance criteria are weakened because the regulatory landscape is featured with uncertain boundaries and overlaps between norms, likely to induce a proliferating inhomogeneity due to multiple reports and overlapping/lacking disclosures. Moreover, huge spaces of discretion affect the "*how issues*" of compliance, possibly leading to inconsistencies over time and space. Here, even if most recent advice may well lead toward progressively ridding these limitations by reference to ESRS, doubts remain as per the substantive chances that this process, coupled with harmonization among different guidelines, is achievable in a decent timeline and with effective results. Although it is widely recognized that ample effort should be devoted to this exercise of harmonization of the various sources of guidelines, the process will face several difficulties due to their profound differences in terms of main declared recipients (investors for ISSB and stakeholders for EFRAG and GRI) and focus, with varying degrees of pervasiveness of sector-specific vs more general issues, and different balance between the E, S, and G matters.

The picture becomes even more worrying when dealing with practitioners' views, which highlight several warnings and endanger the self-reproductive capacities of organizations. A first set of problems moves from what we already recalled above, that is not only the unclear definitional, but also operational boundaries of the E, S, and G. This poses challenges also in terms of organizational culture, effort to interpret, convey, and align organizational levels, and means to transpose shared meanings into organic strategic postures.

This has also extreme relevance when dealing with more or less prescriptive themes, metrics, and disclosure requirements spread in different sources and pushing multiple action and disclosures. Also, it has important consequences as per the dialogue between the organization and its stakeholders, being in turn reflected in materiality-related decision-making. What should be noted here is the pushing need for an adequate commitment to rethink and adapt performance management and control systems to avoid detachment and decoupling. Moreover, this is even more challenging for those companies of smaller dimensions that, willy-nilly, are increasingly called to answer markets' calls for ESG.

Our analysis therefore sheds light on the long pathway that is still needed to make of regulators capable guide the various subjects involved toward a process of convergence and harmonization to satisfy the stakeholders' information needs of ESG reporting. The multiple limitations remain as per the complexity and high costs of the ESG transformation. The current landscape may dangerously endure the "repeat of the same meaningless task of pushing a boulder up a mountain, only to see it roll down again." Camus reminds us, however, that "the struggle itself... is enough to fill a man's heart. One must imagine Sisyphus happy."

To imagine Sisyphus happy, we need more struggle to incorporate the red flags we highlight as per the current norms to support substantive ESG accountability. Improvements will only be possible through a broader view and a more co-operative approach by regulators. Regulators and policymakers should consider these enhancements a priority. They need real improvement to give managers and accountants the tools to make a better ESG disclosure toward broad value creation. Otherwise, any effort to regulate ESG shall only be considered as a juridification process rather than a constitutive enabling process.

References

Agostini, M., Costa, E., & Korca, B. (2022). Non-financial disclosure and corporate financial performance under directive 2014/95/EU: Evidence from Italian listed companies. *Accounting in Europe, 19*(1), 78–109.

Arif, M., Gan, C., & Nadeem, M. (2022). Regulating non-financial reporting: Evidence from European firms' environmental, social and governance disclosures and earnings risk. *Meditari Accountancy Research, 30*(3), 495–523.

Arvidsson, S., & Dumay, J. (2022). Corporate ESG reporting quantity, quality and performance: Where to now for environmental policy and practice? *Business Strategy and the Environment, 31*(3), 1091–1110.

Bebbington, J., & Larrinaga, C. (2014). Accounting and sustainable development: An exploration. *Accounting, Organizations and Society, 39*(6), 395–413.

Bebbington, J., Larrinaga, C., O'Dwyer, B., & Thomson, I. (Eds.). (2021). *Routledge handbook of environmental accounting*. Routledge.

Bensimon, E. M. (2007). The underestimated significance of practitioner knowledge in the scholarship on student success. *The Review of Higher Education, 30*(4), 441–469.

Bolt, R., & Tregidga, H. (2023). Methodological insights "materiality is…": Sensemaking and sensegiving through storytelling. *Accounting, Auditing & Accountability Journal, 36*(1), 403–427.
Broadbent, J., & Laughlin, R. (2013). *Accounting control and controlling accounting: Interdisciplinary and critical perspectives*. Emerald Group Publishing.
Busco, C., Consolandi, C., Eccles, R. G., & Sofra, E. (2020). A preliminary analysis of SASB reporting: Disclosure topics, financial relevance, and the financial intensity of ESG materiality. *Journal of Applied Corporate Finance, 32*(2), 117–125.
Chen, Z., & Xie, G. (2022). ESG disclosure and financial performance: Moderating role of ESG investors. *International Review of Financial Analysis, 83*, 102291.
Cordazzo, M., Bini, L., & Marzo, G. (2020). Does the EU directive on non-financial information influence the value relevance of ESG disclosure? Italian evidence. *Business Strategy and the Environment, 29*(8), 3470–3483.
Eady, S., Drew, V., & Smith, A. (2015). Doing action research in organizations: Using communicative spaces to facilitate (transformative) professional learning. *Action Research, 13*(2), 105–122.
Farneti, F., Guthrie, J., & Siboni, B. (2011). Social and sustainability reporting in Italian local governments: What is not reported? In A. Ball & S. P. Osborne (Eds.), *Social accounting and public management. Accountability for the common good*. Routledge.
Fuji, L. A. (2015). Five stories of accidental ethnography: Turning unplanned moments in the field into data. *Qualitative Research, 15*(4).
Gerwanski, J., Kordsachia, O., & Velte, P. (2019). Determinants of materiality disclosure quality in integrated reporting: Empirical evidence from an international setting. *Business Strategy and the Environment, 28*(5), 750–770.
Guthrie, J., Manes-Rossi, F., & Orelli, R. L. (2017). Integrated reporting and integrated thinking in Italian public sector organisations. *Meditari Accountancy Research, 25*(4), 553–573.
Habermas, J. (1984). *The theory of communicative action, Vol. 1, reason and the rationalization of society*. (T. McCarthy, Trans.). Polity Press.
Habermas, J. (1987). *The theory of communicative action*., (T. McCarthy, Trans.). Polity Press.
Hackett, D., Demas, R., Sanders, D., Wicha, J., & Fowler, A. (2020). Growing ESG risks: The rise of litigation. *Environmental Law Reporter, 50*, 10849.
Karpoff, J. M., Litan, R., Schrand, C., & Weil, R. L. (2022). What ESG-related disclosures should the SEC mandate? *Financial Analysts Journal, 78*(2), 9–18.
Laine, M., Tregidga, H., & Unerman, J. (2021). *Sustainability accounting and accountability*. Routledge.
Laughlin, R., & Broadbent, J. (1993). Accounting and law: Partners in the Juridification of the public sector in the UK? *Critical Perspectives on Accounting, 4*(4), 337–368.
Levitan, J., Carr-Chellman, D., & Carr-Chellman, A. (2020). Accidental ethnography: A method for practitioner-based education research. *Action Research, 18*(3), 336–352.
Lokuwaduge, C. S. D. S., & Heenetigala, K. (2017). Integrating environmental, social and governance (ESG) disclosure for a sustainable development: An Australian study. *Business Strategy and the Environment, 26*(4), 438–450.
Merkl-Davies, D. M., & Brennan, N. M. (2017). A theoretical framework of external accounting communication: Research perspectives, traditions, and theories. *Accounting, Auditing & Accountability Journal, 30*(2), 433–469.
Michelon, G., Trojanowski, G., & Sealy, R. (2022). Narrative reporting: State of the art and future challenges. *Accounting in Europe, 19*(1), 7–47.
Nicolò, G., Zanellato, G., Manes-Rossi, F., & Tiron-Tudor, A. (2021). Corporate reporting metamorphosis: Empirical findings from state-owned enterprises. *Public Money & Management, 41*(2), 138–147.
Poulos, C. N. (2009). *Accidental ethnography: An inquiry into family secrecy*. Left Coast Press.
Power, M., & Laughlin, R. (1992). Critical theory and accounting. *Critical Management Studies, 21*(5), 441–465.

Power, M., & Laughlin, R. (1996). Habermas, law and accounting. *Accounting, Organizations and Society, 21*(5), 441–465.

Romolini, A., Fissi, S., & Gori, E. (2014). Scoring CSR reporting in listed companies–evidence from Italian best practices. *Corporate Social Responsibility and Environmental Management, 21*(2), 65–81.

Schiehll, E., & Kolahgar, S. (2021). Financial materiality in the informativeness of sustainability reporting. *Business Strategy and the Environment, 30*(2), 840–855.

Sepúlveda-Alzate, Y. M., García-Benau, M. A., & Gómez-Villegas, M. (2022). Materiality assessment: The case of Latin American listed companies. *Sustainability Accounting, Management and Policy Journal, 13*(1), 88–113.

Spanò, R., Paola, N. D., Caldarelli, A., & Vona, R. (2016). Accountants' hybridization and juridification: A critical reflection on the fight against organized crime. *Public Money & Management, 36*(6), 441–446.

Teubner, G. (1987). Juridification—Concepts, aspects limits, solutions. In G. Teubner (Ed.), *Juridification of social spheres*. Walter de Gruyter.

Torelli, R., Balluchi, F., & Furlotti, K. (2020). The materiality assessment and stakeholder engagement: A content analysis of sustainability reports. *Corporate Social Responsibility and Environmental Management, 27*(2), 470–484.

Tracy, S. (2010). Qualitative quality: Eight "big-tent" criteria for excellent qualitative research. *Qualitative Inquiry, 16*(10), 837–851.

Yoo, S., & Managi, S. (2022). Disclosure or action: Evaluating ESG behavior towards financial performance. *Finance Research Letters, 44*, 102108.

Zeichner, K. (2007). Accumulating knowledge across self-studies in teacher education. *Journal of Teacher Education, 58*(1), 36–46.

Chapter 31
Tools for Implementing ESG Factors in Asset Management Banking Policies: The Case of Fideuram-Intesa Sanpaolo Private Banking S.p.A.

Annalisa Baldissera

31.1 Introduction

The aim of this research is to analyze the integration of environmental, social, and governance (ESG) factors into the asset management policies of banks in order to identify significant actions for sustainability objectives. Because of their intermediary position in the economic system (Jeucken, 2004), banks can play a key role in achieving objectives of sustainable development (Fiordelisi et al., 2023; Menicucci & Paolucci, 2023) by being able to channel financial resources toward sustainable sectors. While considering that financing and investments are the two lines of intervention through which this role is implemented, this study focuses on the second line. Within this second line, the most useful actions in ESG terms are (a) the offer of sustainable financial products and (b) raising awareness among investors so that they direct their capital toward the products under (a). As highlighted by Birindelli et al. (2015), banks can contribute to sustainability through their commitment to creating and disseminating sustainable finance investment instruments. This study's analysis of the types of instruments that are useful for this purpose and of the functional measures for their diffusion among the public represents a significant step toward understanding the actual role of banks. To this end, the research used a single case study methodology, applying it to Fideuram-Intesa Sanpaolo Private Banking S.p.A. (hereinafter Fideuram). The choice of Fideuram, the primary Italian investment bank that is also relevant abroad and dedicated par excellence to asset management, is particularly suitable for this research. The structure of the case study report is based on the linear-analytic

A. Baldissera (✉)
Department of Law, University of Brescia, Brescia, Italy
e-mail: annalisa.baldissera@unibs.it

N. Castellano et al. (eds.), *Environmental, Social, Governance (ESG)*, SIDREA Series in Accounting and Business Administration,
https://doi.org/10.1007/978-3-031-76618-3_31

model indicated by Yin (2009), which, as observed by Runeson and Höst (2009), is the most widespread in the academic field.

According to La Torre et al. (2021), the centrality of banks is also recognized by institutions and lawmakers who trust in this role in pursuing countries' sustainable economic growth. This consideration forms the basis of policymakers' interventions aimed at encouraging the integration of ESG factors into banks' investment strategies. Among these interventions, the relevance of the two groups of actions on which this study has chosen to focus is confirmed by the numerous measures adopted by the European Union. Two components of the European Union legal framework are particularly significant. Regarding the first component, a fundamental measure is the Action Plan on Sustainable Finance (APSF), adopted by the European Commission on March 8, 2018 (European Commission, 2018). Based on the APSF, on July 6, 2021, the European Commission, following the European Green Deal of June 2019, adopted the new Strategy for Financing the Transition to a Sustainable Economy (European Commission, 2021). This consists of a complete package of measures to encourage the channeling of capital flows toward financing the transition to a sustainable economy, in line with European climate and environmental targets. The new strategy defines the Sustainable Finance Framework, which will play a key role in achieving ESG targets through three pillars: (1) a classification system or "taxonomy" of sustainable activities, (2) an external disclosure framework, and (3) a set of investment instruments.

Pillar 1 identifies a list of economic activities that are sustainable for the environment, with the aim of providing a common definition of sustainability that is useful for counteracting greenwashing phenomena. Therefore, the European Union adopted EU Regulation 2020/852 or Taxonomy Regulation, published in the Official Journal of the European Union on June 22, 2020. The taxonomy defined by the Regulation classifies as eco-compatible the economic activities aligned with the six European environmental objectives (mitigation of climate change, adaptation to climate change, sustainable use and protection of waters and marine resources, transition toward a circular economy, the prevention and reduction of pollution, and the protection and restoration of biodiversity and ecosystems). Based on the provisions of Article 8 of EU Regulation 2020/852, financial companies subject to the Corporate Sustainability Reporting Directive are required to disclose information regarding alignment with the taxonomy. These companies must also publish key performance indicators, expressing the percentage extent to which the assets under management (AUM) are aligned with the taxonomy. The second pillar concerns the definition of a disclosure framework for financial and nonfinancial companies aimed at providing investors with the information necessary to make updated investment choices. Within this pillar, EU Regulation 2019/2088 or Sustainable Finance Disclosure Regulation (SFDR) on sustainability-related disclosures in the financial services sector represents a fundamental act. It introduces, for some types of intermediaries, new obligations of information transparency on the procedures adopted to integrate sustainability factors into investment choices and consultancy activities. The third pillar consists of a set of investment tools, which includes benchmarks and standards, aimed at facilitating the alignment of the investment strategies of companies, financial market participants, and financial intermediaries with the EU's climate and environmental goals. In this regard, the European Union adopted Regulation (EU) 2023/2631 of November 22, 2023, which establishes uniform requirements for issuers who intend to offer investors bonds labeled "EuGB" (European Green Bonds).

Regarding the second component, the European Commission published some delegated acts on August 2, 2021, with which the implementation provisions of some disciplines were amended. In particular, the amendments concern MiFID II (Markets in Financial Instruments Directive II) referred to in Directive 2014/65/EU; IDD (Insurance Distribution Directive) referred to in EU Directive 2016/97; UCITS (Undertakings for the Collective Investment in Transferable Securities) pursuant to Directive 2014/91/EU; and Alternative Investment Fund Managers Directive pursuant to Directive 2011/61/EU. These acts are aimed at encouraging the integration of sustainability profiles in the product governance processes of intermediaries and in customer preferences for ESG factors. This integration must involve the provision of investment services, the distribution of Insurance-Based Investment Products, and the assessment of suitability.

As the European Union interventions demonstrate, the two issues analyzed in this study—the offer of an adequate range of sustainable products and investor preferences—constitute, from a legal point of view, two essential pillars for achieving sustainable finance. Subsequent sections of this study are organized as follows: Sect. 31.2 focuses on related literature, Sect. 31.3 presents the methodology, Sect. 31.4 is dedicated to analysis and discussion, and Sect. 31.5 outlines the conclusions and the study's main limitations.

31.2 Related Literature

As noted by Yin (2003), developing a theoretical framework for the case study is an essential phase that generally uses the literature review. The literature on corporate sustainability is particularly vast (Bruno & Lagasio, 2021) and encompasses multiple profiles, ranging from operations, strategies, and business routines (Aldowaish et al., 2022; Badunenko et al., 2021; Lozano, 2018; Schalock et al., 2016). In defining the theoretical framework, this survey focuses on studies relating to investment policies through which banks contribute to sustainability. In particular, the study selects two relevant profiles of asset management: the ability to offer an adequate range of sustainable financial products and the ability to channel capital to those products through appropriate customer awareness policies.

Regarding the first profile, Chaurasia (2014) examined the types of green banking financial products, and Schaltegger and Figge (2017) analyzed the available tools for banks to contribute to sustainable development and highlighted that "if investors and asset managers considered sustainability issues more thoroughly in their allocation of funds, they could exert a far greater influence on corporate environmental management" (p. 204). It follows that banks must be able to offer their customers environmentally friendly products, as financial instruments are crucial to applying green finance to real life (Wang & Zhi, 2016). This aspect was also underlined by Raut et al. (2017), who highlighted how unlike other sectors, which generally react to pressure from stakeholders, banks take on a proactive role because of their products. The UBS case (*Union des Banques Suisses* or Union Bank of Switzerland), studied by Hugenschmidt et al. (1999), is particularly close to this research because it analyzes, inter alia, the bank's asset management and the implementation of sustainable investment tools—"Eco Performance portfolios"—aimed both at responding to the growing customer interest in environmental aspects and at supporting its own environmental commitments.

The importance of providing sustainable financial products was also considered by Sahoo and Nayak (2007), who highlighted how environmental management by banking institutions was feasible not only through lending processes but also through the possibilities for customers to invest in environmentally friendly banking products. Similarly, Islam and Das (2013) noted that green finance—which included funds for green financing among its activities—was a branch of green banking that contributed significantly to the transition to resource-efficient and low-carbon industries. Dalal et al. (2015) highlighted the need to innovate banks' business models through banking products that generated environmental and social benefits. In fact, banks can manage customers' capital, particularly those of private equity investors, and create useful innovative financial products for preserving the ecosystem and supporting sustainable companies. In examining the financial and social objectives of institutional asset owners and the tools to achieve those objectives, Bose et al. (2019a) underlined the need to take into account a set of factors—much broader than those considered by modern portfolio theories—to offer solutions to financial intermediation agents and support investors. Bose et al. (2019b) illustrated the contribution that the financial system can make to sustainable development, through allocating scarce capital and matching savers to investors. To achieve these goals, the financial system must identify and evaluate the sources of long-term value creation and develop appropriate investment products for responsible investors.

Weber (2012) underlined the active role of banks in promoting sustainability by analyzing the history of ethical and socially responsible banking and highlighting how the latest developments in the financial sector have shifted the focus from managing sustainability risks to generating a positive impact on sustainability through offering appropriate products and services. Weber and Feltmate (2016) also noted that creating sustainable products and services demonstrated the increased investor demand for sustainably managed investments and the willingness of asset managers to integrate sustainability into their investment-selection strategies. Thus, the authors found that in the United States, "Between 1995 and 2012, assets of SRI [Sustainable Responsible Investments] funds increased by nearly 500 per cent" (p. 142).

Folqué et al. (2022) reported that the asset management sector was central to strengthening the European Commission's strategies to integrate Sustainable Development Goals (SDGs) into the financial markets. This role was implemented mainly through investment products and the influence exerted on investing companies, given that banks are also "called upon to contribute to the 2030 Agenda by issuing green and social Bonds, distributing sustainable investment products to their clients" (p. 30). Weber (2005) analyzed European banks and stressed that sustainability integration strategies in the financial sector transcended the mere measure of financial success and integrated the impact on sustainable development. Peeters (2005) highlighted how the banking and insurance sectors, as well as the capital market and the stock market, in the early 2000s began to fully understand the power of their role as intermediaries in sustainable development. Even then, investors could choose from various SRI products, including "negatively screened, positively screened, best in class, stakeholder activist and engagement based portfolios" (p. 221).

Regarding the second profile, this study considers that an essential element for the success of sustainable financial products and the channeling of capital to them is investor awareness and knowledge of the beneficial effects of these products on the environment, and on the whole society. Although the factors on which this awareness depends are many and largely linked to the individuality of investors, according to this study, a central role can and must be played by banks, which, through appropriate information and awareness-raising policies, can direct investment toward sustainable products. Given that banks, particularly investment banks, link debt and equity issuers with investors and promote the transmission of newly issued securities from issuers to asset managers (Urban & Wójcik, 2019), their sustainable investment policies can only be successful if accompanied by adequate investor awareness of the opportunities that green finance offers to the environment and society at large. From these considerations emerges the centrality of customer awareness as an essential action to direct capital toward sustainable activities. Raj and Rajan (2017) noted that although green banking was crucial for both banks and the economy, introducing various green banking products was insufficient in itself. It was necessary that the same products were used correctly by developing an adequate level of customer understanding and satisfaction.

De Clerck (2009) stressed that a high degree of transparency that informed savers about what the bank financed with their money meant that customers were encouraged to develop their interest and their participation in the positive actions implemented by social entrepreneurs. At the same time, customers must change their habits (Sudhalakshmi & Chinnadorai, 2014), and this change, according to Gimeno and Sols (2020), could be achieved where investors considered sustainability as an additional factor of return and risk in the selection of their portfolios. In this case, investors could choose according to their propensity for sustainability, that is, on the basis of the profitability they are willing to lose or the risk they are willing to accept in favor of sustainability.

The Nepal survey conducted by Devkota et al. (2022) found that customers were positive about sustainable banking practices and ready to support them. However, banks and financial institutions should educate and inform their clients about green financial instruments and their derivable benefits. Similarly, the Pakistan study by Ellahi et al. (2023) showed that customers were receptive and willing to invest in banks' sustainable policies. However, factors that determined customer awareness included not only the customers' education, age, gender, and employment but also the banks' sustainable practices. This was also confirmed by Nweke et al. (2020), who analyzed the Nigerian banking system, noting that the level of education, age, lack of basic ICT knowledge, and illiteracy had a negative impact on the awareness and functioning of green banks. This situation was mainly due to a lack of adequate educational and financial infrastructure and advanced information communication technologies. The results of the study show that although Nigerian banks are able to offer various green products, the lack of knowledge of these products by both customers and banks is a barrier to the necessary sustainability awareness. Anis et al. (2023) made similar observations regarding Indonesian banks that have low levels of innovation, in terms of both sustainability motivation and communication, and recommended that they urgently develop proactive sustainable strategies. In India, Chitra and Gokilavani (2020) found a considerable lack of awareness of green banking policies and inadequate knowledge of their implementation. As a developing country, financial inclusion has been achieved through a wider range of government initiatives and grants. Still in India, Taneja and Ali (2021) studied the determinants of customer intentions toward environmentally sustainable banking based on a sample of 440 Indian bank customers and identified attitude as the most influential factor on customers' intentions.

As the above literature demonstrates, the topic of integrating ESG factors into banking business models is widely covered. However, this study can make an additional contribution that is relevant to both theory and practice. From a theoretical point of view, given that existing studies recognize the centrality of both financial products and customer awareness, they can draw valid support from investigations, such as the one conducted here, which deal more specifically with operational aspects. A large part of the most widespread investigations has focused on ESG performance, that is, on a profile that considers the results obtained by companies in terms of sustainability. Drempetic et al. (2020) observed the presence of over 2200 studies on the relationships between financial and ESG performance in different sectors. Although these investigations are less widespread in the banking sector (Ersoy et al., 2022), this study, compared to them, shifts the investigation to a different level as it moves from the assumption that performance is the output of a process that began upstream through the adoption of tools and strategies aimed at obtaining this output. This study focuses precisely on the upstream phases, that is, on the products and actions that are useful for achieving ESG objectives. Moreover, this study proposes an analysis that is not particularly widespread in the literature, consisting of the joint examination of two aspects—supply and demand—which should not be separated. In fact, the offer of sustainable products (supply) should be as complete and adequate as possible; however, this offer is destined to remain unused and unproductive if there are no investors (demand) willing to take advantage of the products that this offer makes available.

From a practical point of view, using a concrete case of excellence can more effectively highlight the ways in which the integration of ESG factors into asset management strategies leads to successful results. Therefore, this study provides added value to practice, as it can suggest effective operational solutions for the banking sector as a whole. This analysis does not present a list of tools that are adequate in the abstract but have yet to be tested in practice. On the contrary, it indicates solutions that have actually been applied and tested, which have made Fideuram the leading Italian company in private banking.

31.3 Methodology

31.3.1 Case Study Approach and Theoretical Framework Development

Among the possible research approaches, an adequate and effective perspective combines the observation of practice with the analysis of theory through case studies (Yip & Bocken, 2018), whether they are individual or collective, as defined by Crowe et al. (2011). In analyzing the concrete implementation of sustainable asset management, the reality of the companies cannot be overlooked. Therefore, using case studies, which are based on the direct verification of facts, is particularly productive. This survey applied the case study methodology to Fideuram, a private bank. Based on Yin's (2012) classification, which distinguishes case studies as exploratory, explanatory, and descriptive, this research is descriptive because it responds to a "descriptive question (what happened?)" (Yin, 2006, p. 112). In particular, it does not aim to be a "prelude to social research," as in exploratory case studies (Tellis, 1997a, p. 1), nor does it aim to reconstruct, as in explanatory case studies, causal links allowing answers to questions such as "how" and "why" the observed facts have occurred. Instead, the research aims to describe the Fideuram case in order to facilitate—through an example of excellence in the Italian and European banking scenes—the understanding of some of the main aspects necessary for the success of sustainable finance.

To develop the theoretical framework, this research selected—within the literature analyzed above—Weber's (2005) benchmark study of European banks and financial service organizations, which seemed particularly suitable for the purpose of the investigation. On the one hand, this study analyzes European banks and financial service organizations and therefore the context to which Italy belongs. On the other hand, it also includes in the investigated profiles the sustainable products and services offered by the banks observed. Furthermore, Weber's study asks the research question, "Which European banks and financial service institutions have strategies, processes, services and products that promote sustainable development and what are their characteristics?" (p. 74). This raises a similar issue to the subject of this investigation, which aims to describe the actions through which Fideuram develops sustainable asset management.

Weber (2005) studied the theme of the integration of sustainability in European intermediaries in a holistic way by screening 127 banks, examining the asset management of 17 organizations—of which the author analyzed 24 equity funds—and investigating customer involvement in sustainable policymaking. The above study divided banking management into three areas—internal processes, credit business, and asset management—and analyzed them both through the selected organizations' business reports, for which he drew a dedicated checklist, and through questionnaires aimed at understanding the reasons why the selected organizations had implemented sustainable strategies. Finally, it identified, for each of the three areas mentioned above, how organizations have integrated sustainability into management. In line with Weber's approach, this research has given central importance to financial products as essential elements for the implementation of effective sustainable banking strategies, and considered the tools used by Fideuram to raise awareness of sustainable products.

The analysis of this case study was based on the methodology indicated by Yin (2009) and was divided into the following four phases:

1. Designing the case study
2. Preparing for the collection of case study evidence
3. Collecting the case study evidence
4. Analyzing the case study evidence

The individual phases are illustrated in the following sections.

31.3.2 Designing the Case Study

To design the case study, three of the five components indicated by Yin (2003) were selected as applicable:

- Study question
- Unit of analysis
- Criteria for interpreting the findings

Formulating the study question started by considering that the implementation of ESG factors requires adopting multiple measures involving different aspects of banking management and reporting to stakeholders. Among these aspects, the study focused on the investment policies implemented by Fideuram and, in particular, on two of its essential components: the sustainable products offered to investors and the policies for raising sustainability awareness among customers. Therefore, the study questions (SQs) were formulated as follows:

SQ1: How are the financial products through which Fideuram integrates ESG factors into its asset management policies?

SQ2: What tools does Fideuram use to raise customer awareness of sustainability?

Regarding the selection of the unit of analysis, Tellis (1997b) stressed that this generally corresponds to a system of actions rather than to an individual or group of individuals. Case studies should be selective and focus on one or two issues. Therefore, this research referred to the tripartite banking management proposed by Weber (2005). First, the selected unit of analysis was the asset management area.

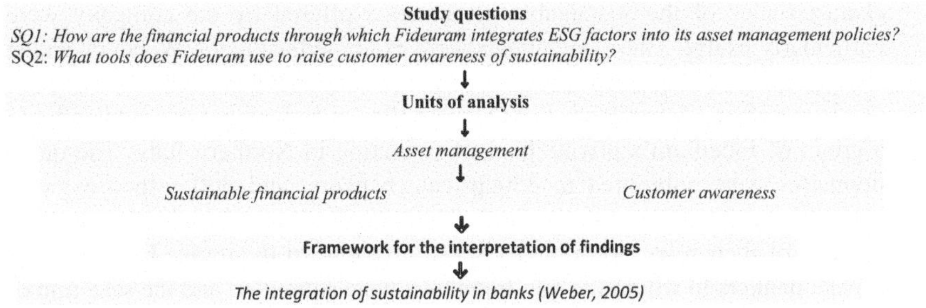

Fig. 31.1 Framework for the interpretation of findings

Second, within this area, the selected subunit of analysis was the sustainable financial products offered by Fideuram and the actions through which the company sensitizes its customers in order to channel capital toward sustainable investments.

Finally, regarding the criteria for interpreting the findings, while the literature on case study methodology is almost endless, few studies have illustrated this subject. Given the indicated gap, this investigation started by considering that "interpretation is a response to the question 'what does this mean?'" (Willig, 2014, p. 137) and built its own interpretive framework (Fig. 31.1), linking study questions (Rashid et al., 2019), as formulated above, with Weber's theory (2005) and his vision of financial products and customer engagement as tools to understanding the integration of sustainability within banks.

31.3.3 Preparing for the Collection of Case Study Evidence

According to Yin (2009), preparations for collecting case study evidence involve defining a case study protocol that identifies, inter alia, field procedures regarding data collection (Tellis, 1997b). Therefore, analyzing Fideuram involved the following sources:

(i) *Documents*—Responding to SQ1 involved using the main documentation available on the company's website, consisting of documents published by law, including the integrated report as of December 2022, and voluntary documents, such as information for investors and the general public. In particular, the 2022 Integrated Report was used to collect information relating to the types of sustainable financial products offered by the company, the volumes of capital invested in these products, the trends in AUM within the 3-year period 2020–2022, and the awareness-raising tools among customers and operators. Further documentation published by the company was used to acquire information regarding general data and the network of private bankers, agencies, and offices located throughout the national territory. Of these documents, the financial product information prospectuses that illustrated the technical characteristics of the sustainable investments offered by the company were particularly useful. These documents were examined using the Weber checklist component (2005) corresponding to sustainable financial products.

(ii) *Questionnaires*—In response to SQ2, an online questionnaire was addressed to a group of Fideuram's private bankers operating in Northern Italy. The questionnaires were submitted to 330 private bankers, and 300 responses were obtained (over 90% response rate). This demonstrates that these operators, because of their roles, were highly sensitivity toward the topic. The choice of private bankers to whom the questionnaires were submitted and the selection of Northern Italy were made based on convenience sampling. To obtain a high response rate, the research was aimed at private bankers who were easiest to contact and reach. For confidentiality reasons, the study does not provide information regarding the demographic characteristics of the participants (age, gender, professional experience, and experience in ESG products). The questionnaire comprised 11 questions and divided into two sections.

In the first section, the questions were designed to gather information regarding the level of awareness and interest of customer-investors toward sustainability. All questions had an answer grid, and for each one, the questionnaire also allowed the formulation of free answers. The second section concerned the tools that private bankers, based on their experience, considered useful for enhancing the level of awareness and interest of customer-investors toward sustainability. In this section, alongside the list of a series of possible answers, the questionnaire is provided for participants' considerations. The choice to address the questionnaire to private bankers was determined by two main reasons. First, their proximity to customers, particularly through direct and personal relationships and continuous advice, has been important. The closeness of the relationship is demonstrated by the rule that every Fideuram customer can rely on only one consultant, who assists in the management of assets in the financial, insurance, and social security fields. Fideuram's private bankers are financial advisers that are qualified for off-site offers and can meet customers both remotely, at home, and in the company's offices and subsidiaries. Second, in addition to maintaining a close relationship with savers, Fideuram's private bankers are highly professional, carefully selected and trained, are able to provide high-profile advice, and can rely on the support of a specialized management structure. The commitment of the private bankers consists mainly in the complete management of assets to identify customized solutions according to client needs. Therefore, private bankers are in a privileged position to raise customer awareness of sustainability, to understand the client's needs with respect to ESG factors, and to submit to them the sustainable investment opportunities offered by the company. The questionnaire, through which preliminary information on customer consciousness was also gathered, required private bankers to indicate, within a given range, which instruments they considered best suited to raising customer awareness and in what order of effectiveness.

31.3.4 Collecting the Case Study Evidence

Regarding Phase 3, the data were collected based on the following three principles indicated by Yin (2009):

- Using multiple sources
- Creating a database of collected materials
- Maintaining a chain of evidence

To this end, the study used the two data sources—the 2022 Integrated Report and the questionnaire—described above and created a database for each. Specifically, for the 2022 Integrated Report, both the full text published on the Fideuram website and the Excel and Word worksheets developed for data analysis were included in the database. For the questionnaire, the database contains statistics and graphs processed by Google Forms software, as well as Excel worksheets containing detailed information on the answers. Finally, in relation to the chain of evidence, the link between the collected data and the achieved results was based, for the Integrated Report, on the coding of information according to the cluster indicated in the field procedures (i.e., sustainable financial products). This coding helps to verify, through the database built by the study, whether the conclusions correspond to the information of the 2022 Integrated Report. For questionnaires, the chain of evidence is represented by the correspondence between the conclusions and the quantitative data contained in the statistics database.

31.4 Analysis and Discussion

31.4.1 Fideuram-Intesa Sanpaolo Private Banking S.p.A

Fideuram belongs to the Intesa Sanpaolo Group, which, with 13.6 million customers and over 45 billion Euros of market capitalization as of August 2023, is the Italian leader in all business sectors (retail, corporate, and wealth management) and is among the main realities at the European level. The Fideuram case was chosen for its economic representativeness in the banking sector and for its marked orientation toward sustainability. First, the company is a case of excellence, as it is not only a leader in the domestic market but also a leading private bank in the Euro area. Second, the company employs 4185 people and has a capillary organization consisting of 399 offices, 6648 private bankers, and 268 branches (as of December 2022). Third, the choice considered the performance of the company, which as of December 2022, was €327.2 billion assets under management (AUM), €49 million AUM for private bankers, €12.9 billion of total net inflows, and €1.1 billion consolidated net profit.

Regarding the sustainable orientation, Fideuram pays considerable attention to ESG problems, in turn supported in this path, by belonging to a group placed in the highest positions in the world for social impact. The Intesa Sanpaolo Group is in fact present in the major indices and in the most relevant sustainability rankings, including Dow Jones Sustainability Indices, FTSE4Good Index Series, MSCI ESG Indexes, CDP 2022, Corporate Knights-2023 Global 100 Most Sustainable Corporations in the World Index, MIB ESG Index, Solactive ESG Indices, STOXX® Sustainability Indices, Standard Ethics Indices, ECPI Indices, and Bloomberg Gender-Equality Index (GEI) 2023.

31.4.2 The Sustainable Offer

The data analysis followed Stake (1995), who distinguished two main methods of examining information—categorical aggregation and direct interpretation—and suggested making the choice by considering the type of case study and research questions. This survey used categorical aggregation, as this best suited both the nature of the case study, which aims to better understand the phenomenon of sustainability in the financial sector, and the focus of the research questions, which, by requiring the analysis of two profiles of asset management policies—sustainable financial products and customer awareness—have made it necessary to aggregate information around these two categories of research. Thus, the study carried out a two-step qualitative analysis.

The first phase identified sustainable financial products by analyzing the information contained in the Integrated Report as at 12/31/2022, and the documentation made available on the company's website. The choice to consider only the 2022 annuity was determined by the desire to have data as updated as possible based on the assumption that the path to sustainability is evolutionary and incremental and not regressive. Therefore, the consideration of recent data allows us to exclude from the analysis any actions implemented in the past and then abandoned, as exceeded by other more advanced ones. In particular, the Integrated Report was subjected to a content analysis using the following keywords: sustainab*, to intercept the terms sustainability and sustainable; ESG; and fund* and product* to intercept the offer of sustainable investment solutions.

The development of this first phase led to the identification of Fideuram's sustainable offer, which was divided in December 2022 into 197 products, comprising 94 discretionary accounts, 81 mutual funds, and 22 insurance and pension funds, with a total AUM of €46.4 billion. Specifically, sustainable products are classified by Fideuram on the basis of Articles 8 and 9 of the SFDR, depending on whether they are instruments that promote environmental or social characteristics (Art. 8) or products with ESG objectives (Art. 9). Table 31.1 summarizes the types of sustainable solutions offered by Fideuram and their volumes expressed in terms of AUM.

The areas of discretionary accounts and insurance offer product, both owned and international investment companies, aimed at supporting environmental or social factors, or pursuing sustainable investment objectives.

Table 31.1 Fideuram sustainable offer as of December 31, 2022

Type	SFDR Article	Product	No. of products	AUM (€ million)
Discretionary accounts			*94*	*17.226*
	Art. 8	Fogli	43	6.072
	Art. 8	Omnia	35	10.008
	Art. 8	ISPB[a] Wealth Collection	9	965
	Art. 8	Direct Valore +	5	0
	Art. 9	Fogli	2	181
Mutual funds			*81*	*26.599*
	Art. 8	Ailis SICAV[b]	3	1.307
	Art. 8	Fideuram Fund	2	997
	Art. 8	Fonditalia	39	13.539
	Art. 8	Interfund SICAV	21	8.954
	Art. 8	Willerfunds—Private Suite	8	937
	Art. 8	Fideuram Master Selection	3	172
	Art. 8	Fondi Alternativi–FAI Mercati Privati Sostenibili	1	394
	Art. 9	Fonditalia	1	255
	Art. 9	Willerfunds Private Suite	3	44
Insurance and pension funds			*22*	*2.616*
	Art. 8	Fideuram Vita	9	160
	Art. 8	Intesa Sanpaolo Life	6	27
	Art. 8	Fondo Pensione Fideuram	6	2.387
	Art. 9	Fideuram Vita	1	42
Total			*197*	*46.441*

[a]Intesa Sanpaolo Private Banking
[b]Società di Investimento a Capitale Variabile
Source: Fideuram 2022 Integrated Report

As for discretionary accounts, through the Fogli, Fideuram-Intesa Sanpaolo Private Banking Asset Management manages portfolios in securities, Exchange-Traded Funds (ETFs), and funds particularly sensitive to ESG issues. These products include the following:

The "Foglio Impact Allocation," which balances funds and ETFs and contributes to the SDGs adopted by all United Nations Member States in 2015 as part of the 2030 Agenda for Sustainable Development

The "Foglio Equity Net Zero Emission," aimed at supporting the transition to a green economy through the reduction of carbon emissions

The "Foglio Sustainable Infrastructure Balanced Solution," predominantly equity, that invests in funds and ETFs for the promotion of infrastructure investments useful for achieving the ecological and digital transition

The "Foglio Next Generation Winners," equity, aimed at promoting ESG factors through national and European recovery and infrastructure plans

Fideuram Omnia includes lines activated in 2022, with step-in and step-in dynamic mechanisms, through which a gradual entry into the equity strategy of the Active Beta 100 line is achieved. ISPB Wealth Collection is portfolio management services of Fideuram Asset Management SGR ("Società di Gestione del Risparmio") S.p.A. and promotes environmental and social characteristics, using integration criteria for ESG factors that mainly take into account issuers' ESG scoring. In relation to Direct Value +, the five sustainable management lines introduced in 2022 promote environmental and social characteristics and are divided into "Direct Value + Cauta," "Direct Value + Costruttiva," "Direct Value + Proattiva," "Direct Value + Decisa," and "Direct Value + Intraprendente."

The Asset Management of Fideuram includes an offer of mutual funds that can meet different performance needs through investments in the equity and bond sectors. The funds with sustainability features include "Ailis," a SICAV under Luxembourg law, which accesses the most renowned fund managers and pursues a sustainable strategy through a policy of portfolio diversification in line with ESG principles. With regard to "Fonditalia," which is the first fund under Luxembourg law to be located in Italy, the 40 sustainable sectors constitute the majority (65%) of the total sectors and include, inter alia, "Fonditalia 4Children" (Art. 9, SFDR) managed by the ESG and Strategic Activism team of Fideuram Asset Management SGR. The fund, with a strong social vocation (decent work, economic growth, quality education, and sustainable cities and communities), selects companies that are active in the sustainable transition and in the protection of children. Interfund SICAV is an investment company under Luxembourg law that adopts a sustainable and responsible investment policy, which integrates ESG, and sustainability factors, risks, and opportunities in analysis and investment decisions. "Willerfunds Private Suite," developed in 2022 by Fideuram Asset Management (Ireland), is divided into 11 compartments, three of which—"Eurizon Multi-Asset Circular Economy," "Lombard Odier Natural Capital," and "Vontobel Equity Global Impact"—have sustainable investment objectives, with the remaining eight promoting, among others, environmental and/or social characteristics (Art. 8, SFDR). "Willerfunds Private Suite Eurizon Multi-Asset Circular Economy" (Art. 9, SFDR) adopts a diversified investment strategy in line with the ESG criteria. "Willerfunds Private Suite Lombard Odier Natural Capital" invests in equity issued by companies in sectors related to the circular economy and natural capital optimization, such as the circular bioeconomy, resource efficiency, and Zero Waste. "Willerfunds Private Suite Vontobel Equity Global Impact" is also characterized by a diversified equity portfolio consistent with ESG principles. "Fideuram Master Selection" is a multimanager fund of funds for investment strategies in the main financial markets, thanks to a fund selection service managed by the most renowned international management companies. "Fideuram Alternative Investments (FAI) Mercati Privati Sostenibili," created for the Italian market by Fideuram Asset Management SGR in collaboration with Blackrock, is among the first closed-ended alternative investment funds that invest in unlisted companies and promote environmental and social characteristics.

Regarding the insurance sector, it is essential to remember the two Unit Linked policies promoting environmental and social characteristics: "Fideuram Vita Futura"

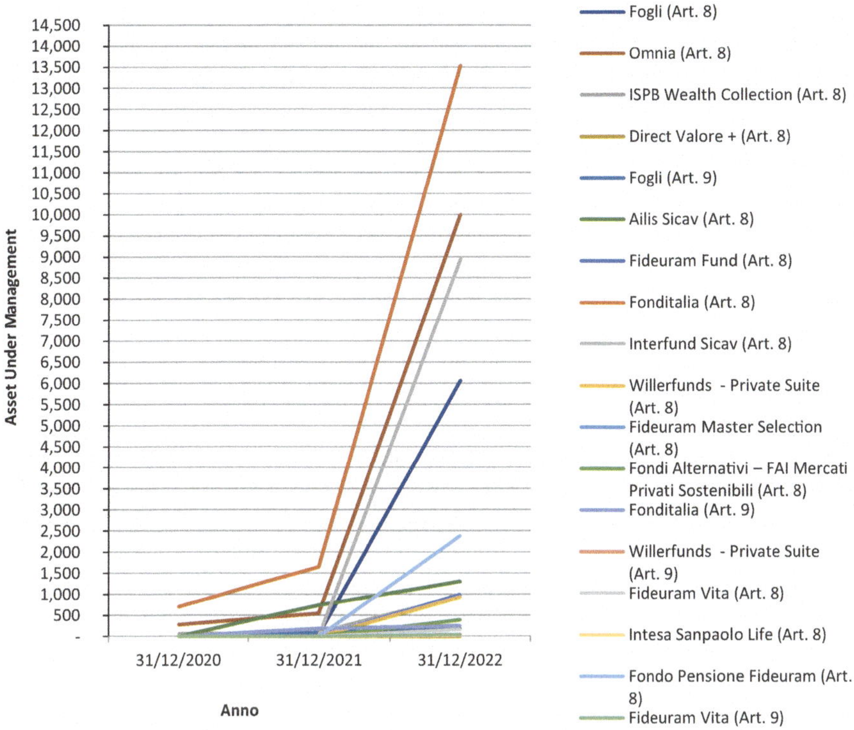

Fig. 31.2 Sustainable Products 2020–2022 (AUM million Euro). *Source*: own elaboration based on Fideuram 2022 Integrated Report

for Fideuram Networks, Sanpaolo Invest, and IW Private Investments, and "Selezione Private Pro" for Intesa Sanpaolo Private Banking. For pension, the "Fondo Pensione Aperto Fideuram" is one of the ESG solutions. In relation to the intertemporal dynamics of sustainable solutions offered to client-investors, Fig. 31.2 shows the trends expressed in terms of AUM value (Euro million).

In addition, the Group's range of sustainable products is complemented by the offer of third-party ESG products, in collaboration with leading international investment houses. As of December 31, 2022, 57% of the AUM were classified pursuant to Articles 8 and 9 of the SFDR, compared to 27% in 2021.

The data analysis reveals some significant aspects to appreciate the integration of sustainability in the asset management policies adopted by Fideuram. As Table 31.1 shows, the sustainable offering consists of many products targeted by Fideuram customers. Funds—77 of which are classified according to Article 8 SFDR and four according to Article 9—constitute the sector with the highest volume of assets. This volume represents over 60% of the total assets invested by Fideuram customers in the 183 Funds of 2022. First, this result indicates the ability of the company to adapt its offer to the requests for sustainable channeling of capital from major international institutions. Second, as Fig. 31.2 shows, this ability has considerably strengthened over time, with the trends increasing significantly on all products. In addition, annual increases are substantial, indicating a strong trajectory of financial capital toward a sustainable economy. This progress is clearly visible if we consider that the AUM corresponding to sustainable solutions has increased from €1039 million in 2020 to €3362 million in 2021, and €46,441 in 2022.

The wide range of sustainable products is certainly a clear sign of how Fideuram has integrated sustainability into its management. In addition, in a broader view of the problem, Fideuram's strategy shows it to be a winning tool even at the macro-economic level, allowing to move significant capital masses toward sectors in line with ESG principles. In this regard, it is also relevant to note that Fideuram, under the pressure of institutions and stakeholders, is currently accelerating the implementation of its ESG programs, most of which involve precisely the topics covered by this research. Specifically, these programs include the integration of ESG factors within the main asset management processes; the revision of the service model in order to integrate ESG factors into the adequacy engine and consulting platforms; the implementation of new offer strategies focused on sustainable products; and the definition and implementation of ESG training initiatives for all private banker networks. The above-mentioned programs are therefore aimed, on the one hand, at strengthening the sustainable offer and, on the other, at enhancing the role of private bankers, for whom, in addition to continuing training on green issues, the progressive introduction of ESG factors in incentive schemes is also envisaged.

The results of the research are consistent with existing studies (Dalal et al., 2015; Hugenschmidt et al., 1999; Islam & Das, 2013; Raut et al., 2017; Sahoo & Nayak, 2007; Weber & Feltmate, 2016), particularly in showing the importance of sustainable products for achievement of ESG objectives. In addition to this observation, the study conducted here has concretely demonstrated how these products progressively acquire a growing diffusion in the financial markets. The data collected show a rapid increase in the volumes of savings managed according to sustainable criteria and also indicate the composition of these volumes in terms of product type.

31.4.3 Customer Awareness

The second phase of the analysis has previously evaluated the customers' sustainable consciousness perceived by private bankers and then derived from the answers to the questionnaire a ranking of effectiveness of the tools to raise client awareness of sustainability. In relation to customers' sustainable consciousness, the questionnaire, while indicating a low level of sustainable sensitivity, highlighted the presence of important signs of progress toward sustainability, as summarized in Table 31.2.

The degree of satisfaction for sustainable investments cannot yet be assessed in the opinion of 77% of respondents, while 13% notes the presence of expectations of better performance of sustainable products in the medium to long term. The remaining issues are shared by about a quarter of the participants, denoting the presence of a sufficiently informed customer segment on sustainability.

Table 31.2 Customer orientation toward sustainability (%)

Subject	Answer	%
Level of knowledge of the concept of sustainability owned by customers	Medium	26%
Customer perception of the obligation to answer sustainability questions when profiling	Incentive to invest in sustainable products	23%
	Opportunity to raise awareness about sustainable investments	23%
Reasons for customers to invest in sustainable financial products	Best performance in the medium to long term	13%
Customer satisfaction with investing in sustainable financial products	Investments too recent to allow an assessment	77%
Increasing customer awareness of sustainability after MIFID II	Sufficient to make informed investment choices	26

Source: own elaboration

The signals emerging from the questionnaire regarding the level of customer sensitivity toward sustainability must be enhanced. Although the level of sensitivity has not yet reached a critical threshold, it should be considered that a group of customers has already developed a sustainable consciousness. In particular, if we look at the figures in Fig. 31.2 together with those in Table 31.2, we see an extremely relevant aspect, namely, that the propensity of customers to invest in sustainable products is a very recent phenomenon. This conclusion is reached considering, on the one hand, that the sudden increase in the volume of sustainable investments occurred in 2022 (Fig. 31.2), and on the other hand, 77% of the private bankers surveyed found that the investments are too recent to make performance judgments (Table 31.2). Considering that Fideuram is the largest private bank in Italy, it is likely to conclude that at the national level, the real movement toward sustainable finance has begun and represents a concrete and rapid response to the equally recent increase in pressure exerted in this direction by policymakers.

As for the effectiveness of customer awareness tools, the results of the questionnaire come from the perception of private bankers who, with regard to the topic, represent key figures, being the only subjects authorized to maintain direct relationships with the subjects who intend to invest in Fideuram products. The main results are shown in Table 31.3.

The majority of respondents attribute a good level of effectiveness to the presentation of the theme at the meeting, while the distribution of information materials is considered limited and good in equal measure. The simple reference to the Fideuram website does not attain a high level of effectiveness for any respondent, and according to almost half (48.8%), its effectiveness is limited. Customer participations in meetings with experts on sustainable finance are considered the awareness-raising tool with the highest degree of effectiveness by 43.6% of participants, followed by 41% by social networks. With regard to the latter data, it is interesting to note that the answers to the open questions showed first of all the tendency of older customers, generally over 40 years, to adopt a less active attitude toward

Table 31.3 Effectiveness of customer awareness tools on sustainability (% of respondents)

Tool	Level of effectiveness (% of respondents)			
	None	Limited	Good	High
Illustration of sustainable financial products when meeting customers	5.1	17.9	53.9	23.10
Distribution of information materials to customers	10.2	38.5	38.5	12.8
Reference to the Fideuram website	25.6	48.8	25.6	0
Meetings with customers and experts in sustainable finance	7.7	12.8	35.9	43.6
Information through the newspapers	7.7	46.2	41.0	5.1
Information by television	10.3	23.10	48.7	17.9
Information via radio stations	17.9	48.8	28.2	5.10
Social network	15.4	2.6	41.0	41.0

Source: own elaboration

sustainability, showing to have not always full awareness of the topic and to be more inclined to acquire information on it and its potential through the advice of private bankers. The younger clientele instead shows a much more marked sensitivity and proactive behavior, thanks to which it spontaneously acquires information, especially through social networks. Finally, between newspapers, television, and radio stations, the level of effectiveness varies mainly between limited and good.

To appreciate the relevance of these data, it is necessary to consider that the offer of a diversified and wide range of sustainable products, such as that of Fideuram, would not in itself be able to achieve success if it were not accompanied by sound placement and customer interaction activities. For this reason, the study selected private bankers as key figures, who, through the questionnaire, provided information from which significant, current, and prospective elements can be inferred. Since the massive placement of sustainable products requires an equally large demand, awareness-raising tools can also be of decisive importance. In this regard, the questionnaire indicated that in addition to social networks, which are mainly used by younger generations, a position of primary importance is held by meetings with customer participation in events attended by experts in sustainable finance. In line with this trend and with the objectives of customer awareness and engagement, Fideuram held, in 2022, 47 events—of which 28 in presence and 19 in digital—attended by 11,150 participants (5000 in presence and 6150 in digital).

The overall results of this survey suggest that there is still room for further strengthening of sustainable awareness and that the path taken by Fideuram is moving in the right direction. First, the boost that the private banker network can give to the placement of sustainable products is enhanced by Fideuram both through training and thanks to incentive forecasts. In this regard, with the aim of adequately training its professionals, Fideuram launched a comprehensive training program for the ESG certification of private bankers, with the provision of more than 51,000 h of teaching to 3057 participants. In addition, the relevance of the training is also accentuated by a further finding from the questionnaire, particularly the observation that the older generations tend to rely almost entirely on the advice of Fideuram to improve their knowledge of sustainable finance. The training of private bankers thus becomes even more significant, as it is necessary to convey the transmission of complete and updated information that promotes financial education to sustainability.

From this point of view, the study is also aligned with existing literature, which widely recognizes the centrality of customer awareness (De Clerck, 2009; Devkota et al., 2022; Ellahi et al., 2023; Gimeno & Sols, 2020; Raj & Rajan, 2017; Sudhalakshmi & Chinnadorai, 2014). However, in addition to this observation, the study reconstructed two further aspects. On the one hand, by highlighting the growth of sustainable investments, it demonstrated how customer awareness is also gradually improving and is resulting in the directing of growing masses of financial resources toward ESG factors. Moreover, a further distinctive element of this study is the analysis of the tools through which the objective of increasing the sustainable awareness of investors can be achieved and has actually been achieved by a company of excellence. This information was obtained on the one hand through the responses to the questionnaires, and on the other by considering the training and information initiatives adopted by Fideuram.

31.5 Conclusions and Limitations

Although the study presents numerous points of contact with the existing literature and reaches shared results, it nevertheless offers additional insights useful for both theory and practice. In theoretical terms, this study analyzes the topic by jointly considering the supply and demand of sustainable products. Much of the literature on the banking sector considers the integration of ESG factors, focusing on the actions through which banks enhance their sustainable offerings in order to compose technically adequate and sufficiently structured investment portfolios. In other words, these analyses focus on the management processes that produce effects internal to the organization and that seek to make it as ESG performing as possible. Alternatively, other studies focus their attention on the awareness and preferences of savers, analyzing the determining factors of their investment choices. Both aspects are relevant, but equally significant is their combined analysis, which highlights the strengths of an ESG strategy capable of operating simultaneously on the supply of sustainable financial instruments and on the demand that wants to invest in them. Consequently, this research can be considered an integration of Weber's (2005) theoretical model, which examined in detail the technical characteristics of the products offered by a large sample of European banks. The value of this study consists of having identified and combined two strategic elements—sustainable supply and awareness of demand—that represent essential success factors for the largest Italian investment bank. Moreover, the relevance of this research lies in the centrality that ESG themes assume in the banking sector and in the centrality that, in turn, the banking sector assumes for the progress of sustainability. The study can provide a contribution to the literature dedicated to the integration of sustainability in the business models of banking companies, also thanks to the empirical analysis of a case of absolute importance in the national and foreign panorama.

In practical terms, this study offers an empirical example of how the connection between supply and demand is not only an ideal objective, but can also be concretely implemented. An evolved ESG strategy is effectively applied by Fideuram in the search for a long-lasting balance between supply and demand. On the one hand, the offer is broad and characterized by the presence of sustainable products in the three areas—financial, insurance, and social security—in which investments are structured. On the other hand, demand is stimulated both through high-profile counseling, which acts as a vehicle for the transfer of sustainability concepts, and through awareness-raising tools that, as the evidence gathered shows, are among the most effective in the perception of private bankers. The analysis of the tools adopted to achieve this balance offers practice a virtuous and replicable example, and above all, it can raise awareness among directors, managers, and operators of the need for active involvement of investors. In the absence of appropriate knowledge of the ESG opportunities and risks that investors should possess, the resulting actions could only be partial.

The results emerging from the analysis show the existence of a significant integration of sustainability into Fideuram's asset management policies. The selected company has therefore assumed marked relevance with respect to this study. The findings showed a strong ESG commitment, thanks to which the company integrated sustainable factors into the investment process and investment advisory service, combining the financial evaluation of products with ESG metrics to measure ESG performance. In this context, the network of private bankers, to whom requests for information have been addressed, occupies a privileged position, since, thanks to the direct relationship with customers, it can be a channel for the transmission of sustainable consciousness and a tool for the perception of sustainable investor expectations. On the basis of these observations, it is therefore possible to conclude that ESG factors are well integrated in asset management and that Fideuram represents a reality of excellence, with a business model strongly oriented toward sustainability, as well as effective in financial performance results. In this sense, the company can represent an exemplary case, able to enrich the existing management schemes, suggesting valid directions of development in terms of sustainability. For all the reasons described, Fideuram represents a model of action for other companies that can implement similar operational solutions based on the same guiding principles.

With regard to the limits of this research, the literature has long highlighted critical issues related to case-based research methodology. Verschuren (2003) brings these limits back to the methodological aspect, highlighting how the case study—which he proposes is renamed case research—uses an indiscriminate set of methods and procedures. Similarly, the problem is methodological, according to Hyett et al. (2014), who in the case studies examined reveal inconsistencies in the methodology and design and confusion among researchers on the distinction between methodology and method, as well as between case studies and case reports, with the risk that the flexibility of the approach results in random reporting and limited applicability.

On the contrary, other scholars recognize the usefulness of case studies as valid tools for deepening a theme through real-life observations. According to Eisenhardt (1989), the theory resulting from the case studies is often new, verifiable, and empirically valid. Similarly, Tellis (1997a) believes that the case study represents an ideal methodology in which holistic and in-depth analysis is required. Gerring (2004) considers the case study method a particular way of defining cases, not a way of analyzing cases, and notes an insufficient appreciation of the methodological compromises that this method requires, whereas the perceived contrast between case study and noncase research is largely unjustified and the result of a misunderstanding. Although this research has adhered closely to the methods most widely recognized in the literature, its main limitation lies in the generalization of the results. The reference to a single case study leads, in fact, to conclusions that are largely affected by the specificities and singularity of the case in question. However, although the generalization to other companies in the sector of the results achieved here requires maximum caution, the limitation indicated is, at least in part, attenuated by the relevance of the case analyzed.

References

Aldowaish, A., Kokuryo, J., Almazyad, O., & Goi, H. C. (2022). Environmental, social, and governance integration into the business model: Literature review and research agenda. *Sustainability, 14*(5), 2959.

Anis, I., Gani, L., Fauzi, H., Hermawan, A. A., & Adhariani, D. (2023). The sustainability awareness of banking institutions in Indonesia, its implication on profitability by the mediating role of operational efficiency. *Asian Journal of Accounting Research, 8*(4), 356–372.

Badunenko, O., Kumbhakar, S. C., & Lozano-Vivas, A. (2021). Achieving a sustainable cost-efficient business model in banking: The case of European commercial banks. *European Journal of Operational Research, 293*(2), 773–785.

Birindelli, G., Ferretti, P., Intonti, M., & Iannuzzi, A. P. (2015). On the drivers of corporate social responsibility in banks: Evidence from an ethical rating model. *Journal of Management and Governance, 19*(2), 303–340.

Bose, S., Dong, G., & Simpson, A. (2019a). Sustainable investing and asset allocation at global scale. In S. Bose, G. Dong, & A. Simpson (Eds.), *The financial ecosystem: The role of finance in achieving sustainability* (pp. 225–251). Palgrave Macmillan.

Bose, S., Dong, G., & Simpson, A. (2019b). The role of finance in achieving sustainability. In S. Bose, G. Dong, & A. Simpson (Eds.), *The financial ecosystem: The role of finance in achieving sustainability* (pp. 1–18). Palgrave Macmillan.

Bruno, M., & Lagasio, V. (2021). An overview of the European policies on ESG in the banking sector. *Sustainability, 13*(22), 12641.

Chaurasia, A. K. (2014). Green banking practices in Indian banks. *The Journal of Management and Social Science, 1*(1), 41–54.

Chitra, V., & Gokilavani, R. (2020). Green banking trends: Customer knowledge and awareness in India. *Shanlax International Journal of Management, 8*(1), 54–60.

Crowe, S., Cresswell, K., Robertson, A., Huby, G., Avery, A., & Sheikh, A. (2011). The case study approach. *Medical Research Methodology, 11*(100), 1471–2288.

Dalal, S. P., Bonham, C., & Silvani, A. (2015). An investigation on ecosystem services, the role of investment banks, and investment products to foster conservation. In K. Wendt (Ed.), *Responsible investment banking: CSR, sustainability, ethics and governance* (pp. 285–300). Springer.

De Clerck, F. (2009). Ethical banking. In L. Zsolnai, Z. Boda, & L. Fekete (Eds.), *Ethical prospects. Economy, society, and environment* (pp. 209–227). Springer.
Devkota, N., Rai, R., Khanal, G., Padda, I. U. H., Paudel, U. R., Parajuli, S., & Bhandari, U. (2022). Customer perception and awareness of green banking practices: An alternative strategy of environmental sustainability. In U. Akkucuk (Ed.), *Disruptive technologies and eco-innovation for sustainable development* (pp. 20–41). IGI Global.
Drempetic, S., Klein, C., & Zwergel, B. (2020). The influence of firm size on the ESG score: Corporate sustainability ratings under review. *Journal of Business Ethics, 167*(2), 333–360.
Eisenhardt, K. M. (1989). Building theories from case study research. *Academy of Management Review, 14*(4), 532–550.
Ellahi, A., Jillani, H., & Zahid, H. (2023). Customer awareness on Green banking practices. *Journal of Sustainable Finance and Investment, 13*(3), 1377–1393.
Ersoy, E., Swiecka, B., Grima, S., Özen, E., & Romanova, I. (2022). The impact of ESG scores on bank market value? Evidence from the US banking industry. *Sustainability, 14*(15), 9527.
European Commission. (2018). *Communication from the Commission to the European Parliament, the European Council, the Council, the European Central Bank, the European Economic and Social Committee and the Committee of the Regions. Action plan: Financing sustainable growth.* COM(2018) 97 final.
European Commission. (2021). *Communication from the Commission to the European Parliament, the Council, the European Economic and Social Committee and the Committee of the Regions. Strategy for financing the transition to a sustainable economy.* COM(2021) 390 final.
Fiordelisi, F., Ricci, O., & Santilli, G. (2023). Environmental engagement and stock price crash risk: Evidence from the European banking industry. *International Review of Financial Analysis, 88*, 102689.
Folqué, M., Escrig-Olmedo, E., & Corzo Santamaría, M. T. (2022). Contribution of sustainable investment to sustainable development within the framework of the SDGS: The role of the asset management industry. *Sustainability Accounting, Management and Policy Journal, 14*(5), 1075–1100.
Gerring, J. (2004). What is a case study and what is it good for? *American Political Science Review, 98*(2), 341–354.
Gimeno, R., & Sols, F. (2020). Incorporating sustainability factors into asset management. *Financial Stability Review, 39*, 179–199.
Hugenschmidt, H., Kermode, Y., Schumacher, I., & Janssen, J. (1999). Sustainable banking at UBS. *Greener Management International, 27*, 37–48.
Hyett, N., Kenny, A., & Dickson-Swift, V. (2014). Methodology or method? A critical review of qualitative case study reports. *International Journal of Qualitative Studies on Health and Well-Being, 9*(1), 23606.
Islam, M. S., & Das, P. C. (2013). Green banking practices in Bangladesh. *IOSR Journal of Business and Management, 8*(3), 39–44.
Jeucken, M. (2004). *Sustainability in finance: Banking on the planet*. Eburon.
La Torre, M., Leo, S., & Panetta, I. C. (2021). Banks and environmental, social and governance drivers: Follow the market or the authorities? *Corporate Social Responsibility and Environmental Management, 28*(6), 1620–1634.
Lozano, R. (2018). Sustainable business models: Providing a more holistic perspective. *Business Strategy and the Environment, 27*(8), 1159–1166.
Menicucci, E., & Paolucci, G. (2023). ESG dimensions and bank performance: An empirical investigation in Italy. *Corporate Governance: The International Journal of Business in Society, 23*(3), 563–586.
Nweke, C., Ugwuoke, C., & Idume, G. (2020). Green banking awareness, challenges and sustainability in Nigeria. *Technology, 11*(3), 30–54.
Peeters, H. (2005). Sustainable development and the role of the financial world. In L. Hens & B. Nath (Eds.), *The world summit on sustainable development* (pp. 241–274). Springer.

Raj, G. P., & Rajan, A. P. (2017). A study on the customer awareness on green banking initiatives. *Intercontinental Journal of Finance Research Review, 5*(7), 54–65.
Rashid, Y., Rashid, A., Warraich, M. A., Sabir, S. S., & Waseem, A. (2019). Case study method: A step-by-step guide for business researchers. *International Journal of Qualitative Methods, 18*, 1–13.
Raut, R., Cheikhrouhou, N., & Kharat, M. (2017). Sustainability in the banking industry: A strategic multi-criterion analysis. *Business Strategy and the Environment, 26*(4), 550–568.
Runeson, P., & Höst, M. (2009). Guidelines for conducting and reporting case study research in software engineering. *Empirical Software Engineering, 14*, 131–164.
Sahoo, P., & Nayak, B. P. (2007). Green banking in India. *The Indian Economic Journal, 55*(3), 82–98.
Schalock, R. L., Verdugo, M., & Lee, T. (2016). A systematic approach to an organization's sustainability. *Evaluation and Program Planning, 56*, 56–63.
Schaltegger, S., & Figge, F. (2017). Sustainable development funds: Progress since the 1970s. In J. J. Bouma, M. Jeucken, & L. Klinkers (Eds.), *Sustainable banking. The greening of finance* (pp. 203–210). Routledge.
Stake, R. E. (1995). *The art of case study research*. Sage.
Sudhalakshmi, K., & Chinnadorai, K. (2014). Green banking practices in Indian banks. *International Journal of Management and Commerce Innovations, 2*(1), 232–235.
Taneja, S., & Ali, L. (2021). Determinants of customers' intentions towards environmentally sustainable banking: Testing the structural model. *Journal of Retailing and Consumer Services, 59*(102418), 1–14.
Tellis, W. (1997a). Application of a case study methodology. *The Qualitative Report, 3*(3), 1–19.
Tellis, W. (1997b). Introduction to case study. *The Qualitative Report, 3*(2), 1–14.
Urban, M. A., & Wójcik, D. (2019). Dirty banking: Probing the gap in sustainable finance. *Sustainability, 11*(6), 1745.
Verschuren, P. (2003). Case study as a research strategy: Some ambiguities and opportunities. *International Journal of Social Research Methodology, 6*(2), 121–139.
Wang, Y., & Zhi, Q. (2016). The role of green finance in environmental protection: Two aspects of market mechanism and policies. *Energy Procedia, 104*, 311–316.
Weber, O. (2005). Sustainability benchmarking of European banks and financial service organizations. *Corporate Social Responsibility and Environmental Management, 12*(2), 73–87.
Weber, O. (2012). Sustainable banking–history and current developments. *Available at SSRN 2159947*.
Weber, O., & Feltmate, B. (2016). *Sustainable banking: Managing the social and environmental impact of financial institutions*. University of Toronto Press.
Willig, C. (2014). Interpretation and analysis. In U. Flick (Ed.), *The sage handbook of qualitative data analysis* (pp. 136–150). Sage.
Yin, R. K. (2003). Case study research. In *Design and methods* (3rd ed.). Sage.
Yin, R. K. (2006). Case study methods. In J. L. Green, G. Camilli, & P. B. Elmore (Eds.), *Handbook of complementary methods in education research* (pp. 111–122). American Educational Research Association.
Yin, R. K. (2009). *Case study research. Design and methods* (Vol. 5, 4th ed.).
Yin, R. K. (2012). *Applications of case study research* (3rd ed.).
Yip, A. W., & Bocken, N. M. (2018). Sustainable business model archetypes for the banking industry. *Journal of Cleaner Production, 174*, 150–169.

Chapter 32
The Integration of ESG Issues in Community Banking: Contextual Factors and Strategic Managerial Perceptions

Francesca Bartolacci, Andrea Cardoni, and Michela Soverchia

32.1 Introduction

The process of integrating environmental, social and governance (ESG) factors in community banking is a critical issue from the theoretical and practical standpoints, as banks play a relevant role in steering countries and their economic systems toward sustainable development.

From the theoretical standpoint, in the last few years, many studies have demonstrated the strategic role of the banking system (Weber, 2012; Weber et al., 2008) and the need to further investigate the new wave of green banking, which is drawing significant attention from actors in the financial and productive sectors (Hummel et al., 2021). Green banking aims to spread the issue of sustainability to all economic players by activating the 'sustainability cycle' even in the regulated financial markets, in the context of the traditional banking system and Small Medium Enterprise (SMEs) (Cardoni & Kiseleva, 2023). This challenge involves various actors, including community banks, which primarily engage in activities that focus on retail savers, borrowers and SMEs in local communities and have always played a fundamental role in supporting the economic growth of these areas (D'Onza et al., 2022; Kim & McKillop, 2019). It follows that the integration of ESG factors in community banks and the relevant impacts of such an integration on strategic choices made in this specific socio-economic context is an important question that literature should deeply analyse.

F. Bartolacci (✉) · M. Soverchia
University of Macerata, Macerata, Italy
e-mail: francesca.bartolacci@unimc.it

A. Cardoni
University of Perugia, Perugia, Italy

N. Castellano et al. (eds.), *Environmental, Social, Governance (ESG)*, SIDREA Series in Accounting and Business Administration,
https://doi.org/10.1007/978-3-031-76618-3_32

From the practical standpoint, in May 2020, the European Banking Authority (EBA, 2020) issued new guidelines on credit lending and monitoring that mandated the integration of ESG factors into the credit policies of all European banks with regard to both these banks' strategic and organisational profiles as well as their financing and monitoring operations. Policymakers and bank managers are therefore strongly interested in the strategic and operational challenges that the integration can present, paying particular attention to the role of the contextual aspects with which they have to deal. Nevertheless, to the best of our knowledge, the integration of ESG factors into the strategies of community banks is still little explored in the literature (Campbell & Slack, 2011; Gangi et al., 2019; Scholtens, 2009; Weber, 2012). In particular, there is a lack of empirical analysis of the factors that guide the aforementioned integration process.

To fill this gap, this study aims to improve the understanding of what are the factors that impact most the ESG integration process in a community bank, paying particular attention to the strategic implications perceived by the bank's managers. For this purpose, a qualitative analysis was conducted that followed specific steps. First, the analysis was contextualised in the field of green banking, an increasingly relevant topic in the scientific landscape at the national and international levels. In particular, the current institutional context in which European banks operate was illustrated, considering the peculiar characteristics of community banking. Then, the ESG integration process was analysed, with particular reference to the main exogenous and endogenous factors that influence proactive strategic planning. To achieve these goals, a case study was conducted in which a small cooperative bank operating in two regions of central Italy was analysed. The case study offered interesting insights because of its attention to the surrounding socio-economic system.

The rest of this paper is organised as follows: In the next section, the literature is reviewed and the institutional context is analysed; in Sect. 32.3, the research methodology is described; in Sect. 32.4, the main research results are presented; and in Sect. 32.5, such results are discussed and this paper is concluded.

32.2 Literature Review and Institutional Context

32.2.1 Impact of Environmental, Social and Governance (ESG) Factors on the Banking Industry: The Green Banking Revolution

The banking system has always played a fundamental role in corporate finance as the most important source of external funds, especially loans (Mishkin, 2001), which ensure the flow of credit to firms and thus provide a solid foundation for economic growth (Cuevas et al., 1993). This aspect is now even more relevant with the advent of green banking (Zhang et al., 2022), a new approach whereby banks take the initiative to act as fundamental players in stimulating the implementation of responsible investments and sustainability strategies in society.

The literature on green banking and sustainable banking focused on banks that voluntary started such a path has significantly developed since the beginning of this century, as highlighted in some literature reviews (Aracil et al., 2021; Nájera-Sánchez, 2020; Sarma & Roy, 2020). Green banking and sustainable banking are almost overlapping concepts and refer to the activities of banks that are aimed at achieving environmental sustainability directly, by adapting their investment choices and operations to reduce or eliminate environmental impacts, and indirectly, by financing companies and other clients that have environmentally friendly behavior. In other words, green and sustainable banks attempt to contribute to the development of sustainable business practices and to mitigate the negative effects of banking activities on the environment by supporting ecologically favourable initiatives.

The stream of studies focused on green financing highlights that the essence of this approach is to provide loans to companies that implement environmentally friendly strategies without neglecting the financial solvency of such companies (Xing et al., 2021). If banks follow this kind of green credit policy, polluting companies would not be able to obtain loans to finance their investment projects. The aim of this policy is to push firms to incorporate environmental protection into their strategies and activities. The success of this green banking policy is seen as twofold: on the one hand, banks receive information on corporate environmental and social initiatives, which enables them to evaluate whether to support such initiatives financially; and on the other hand, firms are motivated to actively implement green strategies and to communicate their investment projects and the impacts thereof (He et al., 2019). In other words, clients are pushed toward green innovation and to improve their environmental disclosure (Amore & Bennedsen, 2016). As for the expected impacts, the literature highlights that while the direct involvement of banks in environmentally sustainable initiatives seems to have had minimal effects on environmental protection, if financial institutions motivate and sustain companies to realise environmentally friendly behaviour, a leverage effect can be generated (Esteban-Sanchez et al., 2017).

These considerations pose a very important question for scholars: *What reasons and factors could push banks to decide to operate responsibly?* And, therefore, *what factors drive the aforementioned integration process*? It is well known that financial intermediaries may act sustainably not only to generate benefits for their target communities but also to address the increasing pressure from regulators and to achieve satisfactory economic results (Gangi et al., 2019). In fact, some empirical studies have found that more environmentally friendly banks can also realise higher levels of operational efficiency and thereby reduce their risks as well as improve both their customers' loyalty and their reputation (Clarkson et al., 2011; Fiordelisi et al., 2011; Gatzert, 2015; Weber, 2012), but that good environmental performance is not yet a relevant factor of depositors' choice of banks (Galletta et al., 2021). However, in more recent years, one of the main factors that determined banks' adherence to green banking strategies and practices, at least in Europe, was undoubtedly the significant intervention of regulators, as detailed in the next section (Park & Kim, 2020).

32.2.2 *European and Italian Institutional Contexts for Green Banking*

The abundant green regulations in the last decade highlight the growing attention of policymakers and supervisory authorities around the world to ESG issues. At the institutional level, several ESG initiatives have been launched in recent years, from the most developed countries to emerging markets (Dikau & Volz, 2020).

Among the various areas in the world, the European Union (EU) has moved forward in a more determined and structured way on the topics of sustainability and ESG factors. Table 32.1 lists a series of regulations issued on the topic of sustainability. These regulations generally refer to governance and disclosure issues or focus on aspects of the environment and society for the banking and finance sector.

Two regulations are certainly topical for the next evolution of the sector, which refer to the EBA position and the EU Taxonomy defined in 2020.

As highlighted in the previous section, EBA (2020) issued new guidelines on credit lending and monitoring, which mandated the integration of ESG factors into the credit policies of all European banks, with clear consequences for the credit access conditions for SMEs. Specifically, the guidelines established that the banking institutions 'should incorporate ESG factors and associated risks in their credit risk appetite and risk management policies, credit risk policies and procedures, adopting a holistic approach' (EBA, 2020, art. 56). Moreover, in the next article, it is specified that 'institutions should take into account the risks associated with ESG factors on the financial conditions of borrowers, and in particular, the potential impact of environmental factors and climate change, in their credit risk appetite, policies and procedures' (EBA, 2020, art. 57). The integration of ESG factors is also explicitly mentioned in the sections concerning credit lending to micro and small enterprises and medium-sized and large enterprises.

The EU Taxonomy (EU Regulation 2020/852) is a classification system that determines whether an activity can be considered environmentally sustainable (that is, 'eco-sustainable'). An economic activity is considered eco-sustainable if it is

Table 32.1 Road map to sustainability and green banking integration in the European context

Date	Institution	Topic	Focus/ field
March 2018	European Commission	Action plan for sustainable finance	ESG/ finance
May 2020	European Banking Authority	Loan origination and monitoring guidelines	ESG/ finance
June 2020	European Parliament & Council	Framework for sustainable investments (EU Taxonomy)	ESG/ finance
November 2020	European Central Bank	Guidance on climate and environmental risks	E/ finance
June 2021	European Banking Authority	ESG risk management and oversight for credit institutions and investment firms	ESG/ finance

Note: Source: Esposito et al. (2022)

carried out in compliance with the established minimum safeguards and complies with the technical screening criteria set by the European Commission, and if the investments pursue (and do not significantly harm) one or more of the following six environmental goals: (1) climate change mitigation; (2) climate change adaptation; (3) the sustainable use and protection of water and marine resources; (4) the transition to a circular economy; (5) pollution prevention and control; and (6) the protection and restoration of biodiversity and ecosystems.

The EU Regulation 2021/2139 defines the sectors covered by the first two macro-objectives (with specific reference to the Nomenclature Statistique Activites Economiques (NACE) classification, when applicable). The very recent EU Regulation 2023/2486, issued in November 2023, completes the analysis and classification of the sectors covered by the remaining environmental goals (i.e. 3, 4, 5 and 6). These two regulations specify the application criteria identified by the main decree, that is, the EU Taxonomy. They also propose key performance indicators of a company's alignment with eco-sustainable activities. Companies are required to publish the proportions of their turnover, capital expenditure and operational expenditure related to activities covered by the Taxonomy, using the disclosure standards defined by EU Regulation 2021/2178. Specifically, banks are required to calculate and disclose a specific indicator, their Green Asset Ratio, which represents the ratio of the funds they provided for eco-sustainable investments aligned with the EU Taxonomy to their total credit assets (with some exclusions provided for in the regulation, such as loans to other banks).

In light of the new ESG regulations, at the national level, the Bank of Italy published in April 2022 a first set of supervisory expectations of climate risks for both less significant institutions (LSIs) and other non-banking financial institutions under its direct supervision. The document contains non-binding indications of how the Bank of Italy expects banking and financial firms to address climate and environmental risks in their risk management framework, considering the impacts on: (i) governance and control; (ii) the business model and the corporate strategy; (iii) the organisational system and operating processes; (iv) the risk management system; and (v) disclosure to the market. Currently, supervised banks' governance is asked to prepare a three-year action plan aimed at aligning their operations with the indications mentioned above. Each bank is required to conduct its own assessment; apply solutions that are most responsive to its exposure to physical and transaction risks, depending on the type, size and complexity of the bank's business; and present a plan of initiatives by the first quarter of 2023. Furthermore, in the second quarter of 2022, the Bank of Italy (2022b) conducted a thematic review of a sample of LSIs to monitor and assess the degree of their alignment with the Bank's supervisory expectations published in April 2022. According to the results of the review, intermediaries showed a widespread and growing awareness of the importance of the issue of sustainability in their business model and risks associated with climate change, but they had a low degree of alignment with the expectations of their full dissemination of their good practices in integrating such an issue in their corporate strategies. One of the most critical issues, as expected, was the unavailability of data and information systems capable of handling that risk appropriately (Loizzo & Schimperna, 2022).

32.2.3 Sustainability and ESG Factors in Community Banking

Community banking is a complex phenomenon with specific characteristics that make community banks peculiar (D'Onza et al., 2022; DeYoung et al., 2004; Lux & Green, 2015). As recently clarified (Berger et al., 2019), community banks have different typologies and organisational forms (i.e. commercial banks, cooperative banks, credit unions and savings banks) and differ from the larger and most affirmed financial institutions in terms of their following features: (i) locally based owners and directors or members; (ii) local funding sources through core deposits and (iii) local informational advantages through cultivation of long-term relationships (Kim & McKillop, 2019). According to Yellen (2015), community can identify their customers' needs and the local economic trends and, therefore, can be more receptive to local loan requests than large financial institutions.

Indeed, community banks can provide vital financial services to key segments of the local economy and thus fill this void left by larger non-community banks by addressing the difficult challenges brought about by the fast-changing banking landscape, evolving technologies and ever-increasing regulatory burdens (Fayman et al., 2022). The main characteristics of community banks are as follows:

- They are relatively small and autonomous entities that are typically focused on providing basic and personalised banking services to a local community;
- They have a privileged relationship with their territory and the local actors, as their local ownership gives them historical ties to the town or region and to its industries and consumers, who comprise their 'community';
- They are generally 'relationship banks', whose competitive advantages are their connection with their customers and knowledge of their history;
- Their financials are different from those of larger banks, with less leverage and less robust returns, less involvement in capital and securitisation markets than larger banks and a less diversified earnings stream, which makes them more vulnerable to disruption;
- They tend to use less technology; and
- They are characterised by management flexibility due to their mixed strategic approach (emergent and deliberate).

Based on all these features, community banks' business model is characterised by a high capacity to serve families and SMEs with flexible and highly customised services (D'Onza et al., 2022). However, they are less flexible today than in the past, given their recent regulatory constraints and limited territorial and sectoral diversification, which make these banks less resilient. The current regulatory system is more suited to the characteristics of large banks, which are transactional, dimensionally relevant and suitable for standardisation and mark-to-market accounting practices. For these reasons, the significant decrease in the number of community banks has been a cause for concern by policymakers, regulators and academics. The literature highlights that community banks have experienced a structural decline in the last 30 years (Petach et al., 2021), accentuated by the increase in the costs of compliance with supervisory regulations (Dahl et al., 2016). This has raised questions about the ability of community banks to remain competitive and sustainable and about the potential consequences of the gradual demise of these institutions (Kim & McKillop, 2019).

Considering this strategic evolution of the banking sector, it is important to analyse the potential impact of green banking on community banks' business model. This topic is particularly relevant because, by offering important financial services, including agricultural and small-business lending as well as residential mortgage origination, community banks are important financial institutions that can promote local growth but also ecological and social sustainability. As entities rooted in the territory that have strong connections with local businesses, they can exploit their specialised knowledge of specific local sectors and their greater understanding of local companies' corporate objectives. Moreover, with community banks' close relationships with their customers, they can provide personalised services that support these customers' social and ecological well-being.

It is very important to reflect on how community banks will develop in the near future, and in particular, on whether the green transition will represent a strategic risk or opportunity for them. This development significantly depends on what characteristics green banking will take on for community banks and what strategies these banks will be able to adopt in the face of the great transition toward sustainability.

Community banks, based on their identity and founding mission, already have elements of sustainability rooted in their DNA (Caldarelli et al., 2016; D'Onza et al., 2022). As recently argued (Győri et al., 2021), community banks support the fundamental pillars of sustainable value embedded in the following principles of the Global Alliance for Banking Values: (i) the triple bottom line approach; (ii) focus on the real economy; (iii) client orientation; (iv) long-term resiliency; (v) transparency; and (vi) culture. This study demonstrates how the founding characteristics of community banks that incorporate sustainability and long-term value creation—namely, social inclusion, collaboration with local institutions and support for SMEs and families—make them strategically oriented toward the integration of ESG factors into the business model. However, the topic of sustainability is assuming specific characteristics due to the evolution of the economic, social and regulatory contexts. Thus, community banks also need to define a strategic approach to green banking and integrate the ESG factors into their strategic decisions.

This study aims to contribute to filling the gap in the empirical literature and to validate the first experimental studies, thereby opening up avenues for further research on this critical subject (Durden, 2008; Pondeville et al., 2013).

32.3 Research Methodology and Selected Case Study

To achieve our research aim, a qualitative research method was implemented, namely, a single-case study, through which we were able to perform an in-depth analysis of a specific topic (Yin, 2014), especially one that is evolving and has not yet been analysed in depth. Indeed, our case study allowed for a complete understanding of a specific community bank by providing access to variables in such a real-life setting that may be difficult to examine through other research methods. Moreover, through case studies' connection of scientific research and corporate operativity, they broaden the understanding and replicability of best practices (Dal Mas et al., 2022).

Our research design and protocol followed an exploratory and descriptive approach. The exploratory research design is a preliminary investigation of an unfamiliar problem on which the literature has developed little (Neuman, 2003). It is designed to satisfy the researcher's interest, gain a better understanding of the investigated issue and pave the way for subsequent research. The present study is regarded as exploratory in the sense that little research has been conducted on ESG integration into community banks. Consequently, this study attempted to bridge professional practices with academic practices in exploring the topic and to provide a certain level of familiarity with it (Rubin & Babbin, 2001). The exploratory design in this study was further undertaken to guide research toward a descriptive design. The main purpose of this study remains descriptive in nature to favour the dialogue with the community of practitioners and stakeholders. Bless et al. (1995) advocated the intention of a researcher to employ a descriptive research design to determine the opinions of a group of people on a particular issue at a particular time. Neuman (2003) viewed the descriptive design as representing 'a picture of the specific details of a situation, social setting or relationship' (pp. 21–22). The discussion that developed as an outcome of the exploratory phase was subsequently used to identify the possible pivotal framework of the further investigation of the topic.

Our case study is on a small cooperative bank (hereafter, 'Bank') operating in central Italy, which has the following features: total assets below $1 billion, with a prevalent incidence of credit lending; focus on traditional banking services; flexibility; and strong relationship with the local community. As the Bank is a cooperative bank that is owned and controlled by its local customers (i.e. around 3000 shareholders) and operates according to the principle of mutuality, it aims to meet the needs of its members and of its surrounding communities.

The selected case offered interesting insights because its attention to the surrounding socio-economic context was considered a distinctive mark of its identity. Our analysis investigated how such a characteristic could impact the Bank's integration of ESG factors, with particular reference to contextual factors and managerial perceptions of such integration. The Bank represents a relevant case for the following reasons: (i) it involves the typical issues related to ESG integration in the banking sector; (ii) as a community bank, it is an under-investigated case in the scientific literature, especially with reference to green and sustainable banking; and (iii) it allows for the analysis of the subjects in a different scenario, as such subjects usually concern large banks (Campbell & Slack, 2011; Gangi et al., 2019; Scholtens, 2009; Weber, 2012). The selected case is especially unique in its very limited size compared to that of other community banks. This created the possibility of capturing all the signals from the Bank's interaction with its territory, also from the perspective of the Bank's key managers. The case is additionally unique due to its territories, which are two regions in central Italy with social and productive ecosystems characterised by the high presence of families and SMEs.

The Bank's business model is based on the traditional processes of banking intermediation. Its deposits (€373 million as of December 31, 2022) are mostly collected from families, businesses and other local actors, integrated with interbank and financing operations with the Central Bank. In terms of its credit assets (€305 million as of December 31, 2022), the main share is related to loans to families and businesses in the area, mainly represented by SMEs. Currently, the Bank has around 80 employees and serves its territories through ten branches. It implements the typical approach of a relationship bank characterised by strong attention to customer needs, high customisation of value propositions, operational flexibility of processes and constant consideration of its economic and social impacts on its territory. As already mentioned, the Bank operates under the mutuality principle of carrying out its business activities inspired by the so-called 'duality of purpose' (Caldarelli et al., 2016) that encompasses economic and social profitability.

In the last few years, sustainability factors have been gaining growing attention from the Banks' Board of Directors and Management, with greater emphasis on financial services and products related to sustainable investments and asset allocation. The Bank's collaboration with Banca Etica, activated in 2019, gave the Bank the opportunity to raise its customers' awareness of its ethical investments and to propose sustainable solutions to asset allocation. With the evolution of legislation and the increased relevance of the green transition, the sustainability topic has become more strategic, and the Bank's elaboration of a systematic plan of sustainable initiatives focused on climate risks was stimulated by the requests of the Bank of Italy (2022a, b), which supervises LSIs, of which the Bank is one. The Bank's 2023–2025 plan was presented according to the schedule set by the Bank of Italy and included a specific set of initiatives to be implemented in the next years to ensure the progressive alignment of the Bank's policies and processes with the Bank of Italy's supervisory expectations.

The Bank considered its underlying challenge in this scenario as supporting its customers and local actors in the green transition, a very relevant role that is being increasingly emphasised and stimulated at the European institutional level, as demonstrated by the recent Recommendation 2023/1425 issued by the European Commission on facilitating finance for the transition toward a sustainable economy. As clearly stated in the Commission Recommendation 2023/1425: 'Financial intermediaries can contribute to the financing of the transition by reflecting transition financing objectives in their lending or investment strategy' and are 'encouraged to engage with clients and investee undertakings in transition, especially where there is a significant need for transition finance' (pp. 11–12).

Following the holistic approach proposed by Hummel et al. (2021), we devoted our analysis to observing the impact of contextual factors on ESG integration, with particular reference to the strategic perspective. In many cases, ESG strategies represent a response to external pressures, such as new regulations, risk conditions to be countered or opportunities to seize (Epstein & Wisner, 2005).

Furthermore, the integration of ESG factors into business models is a highly topical question (Aldowaish et al., 2022), given the growing attention to social and environmental issues of companies that need funds. Business strategies and operational processes increasingly incorporate, sometimes in an impromptu and unplanned manner, social and environmental purposes that may affect the company's activities and performance measurement systems. As already pointed out, banks have a crucial role in promoting the sustainable development of companies by financially supporting their investments. It follows that the integration of ESG factors into the strategic and operational processes of community banks, especially referring to their lending activities, generates the double impact of stimulating the virtuous initiatives of companies toward their final consumers and generating relevant economic and social impacts (Borgers & Pownall, 2014; Brooks & Oikonomou, 2018).

Following the research approach, the topic is explored through the lenses of the Bank managers, the interviewers and the aforementioned official documents to gain a better understanding of the perceptions of ESG integration issues in the context of a community bank. Using the aforementioned literature, we prepared a questionnaire and conducted semi-structured interviews with the following three key actors of the Bank to capture their strategic managerial perceptions of the issue: the General Manager (coded as 'I_1'), the Commercial Director (coded as 'I_2') and the Risk Manager (coded as 'I_3'). These actors were selected for the following reasons: (i) their relevant organisational positions; (ii) the remarkable differences in their perspectives; and (iii) the impact, whether current or prospective, of ESG issues in their different professional roles.

The interviews, carried out in August 2023, were aimed at exploring the contextual factors that mainly impact ESG integration mechanisms and considering their possible effect on the Banks' strategy, as perceived by the three managers. Semi-structured interviews are often used in qualitative research to obtain information in a personalised setting, as they are organised with a set of questions that leave some room for flexibility to focus on certain topics, allowing the interviewees to share their opinions and experiences about those specific issues (Dearnley, 2005).

The interviews were recorded, and all the collected data were manually systematised. The reports that contained the interview results were shared with all the members of the research group and submitted to the interviewees to ensure their correctness, consistency and replicability.

We also had the opportunity to analyse some of the Bank's internal documents and plans, which allowed us to enrich and deepen our analysis. Utilising multiple sources of data allows researchers to realise triangulation and, thus, increase the validity of their research (Eisenhardt, 1989). In addition to enabling triangulation, different sources of data, due to their distinct natures, can generate different insights and thus can add rigour, depth and richness to a study (Rashid et al., 2019).

32.4 Case Analysis Results

As already mentioned, we investigated, through interviews, what are the contextual factors that most significantly impact ESG integration into the Bank's strategy, as perceived by the Banks' key managers.

One of the most important issues that emerged from the interviews concerns the different substantial or formal impacts of contextual factors on strategic planning (I_1). In other words, it was emphasised that the introduction of new ESG principles and rules can have a real impact on the definition of future strategies or, conversely, can represent a mere fulfilment of the pertinent regulation with a limited effect on the definition of future strategies. Furthermore, it was difficult to clearly distinguish a real effect from a narrative one. For example, for the media and press factor, for which the narrative effect is very important, the Bank must communicate its alignment with ESG principles so as not to be excluded from a new context following a 'trend', beyond the real impact produced.

According to I_1, one of the most relevant factors to consider is the Bank's customers. The Bank must decide whether and how to offer specific financial services and under what conditions, and it must also consider its competitive pressures. Together with the media factor—which maximises narrative impact—and the customer factor—which maximises real impact—other factors have a sort of 'intermediate' impact due to the combined presence of both impacts. For example, public administrations (PAs) must consider both the narrative impact—their necessary reporting of how they comply with the national and supranational ESG rules in their institutional decisions—and the real impact of their decisions on society and the environment, which derive from their interpretation and implementation of the ESG rules.

Along with the public sector, whose wishes increasingly derive from supranational contexts, there are standard setters who respond to the same logic. Principles and practices are decided at the global, European and American levels: PAs carry out the principle and standard setters establish the rules. Thus, also in this case, we can say that there is both a narrative impact—messages to be transmitted to the world—and a real impact.

Regulators, such as the Bank of Italy, facilitate the application of the standard setters' rules by financial intermediaries. I_1 complained that the objective for the development of the real economy seems to be losing value in those rules. Often, a chain is created that starts from a principle (often defined by a supranational institution), which is then replicated by others, in some cases losing contact with the real world, which is made by companies and people (often the subjects who close the chain). However, often without understanding what the initial principle was, regulators execute it and verify that it is accomplished.

Competitors can also be considered a relevant contextual factor in that a bank that wants to be competitive must adapt to certain principles and rules. Thus, following the mainstream can be a necessity. Employees are also a relevant factor, but it is necessary to underline that everyone has their own sensitivity to ESG integration, linked to personal and cultural factors that are subjective and determine different levels of awareness, so the top management message can be more or less effective. It is difficult to convey certain values in a working context and find personalities who are propulsive toward innovative projects. However, the Bank is trying to involve new professionals.

When the interviewees were asked to rank contextual factors according to their importance, I_1 put customers first, employees second, the media third, competitors fourth and PAs, standard setters and regulators fifth.

According to I_2, all the contextual factors indicated in Hummel et al. (2021) should be considered relevant, but they can be grouped into three levels in decreasing order of importance. At the first level are regulators, as a hefty legislative and monitoring system launched in recent years had a significant impact on both the diffusion and management of ESG integration. At the second level are institutional shareholders and the media, as linking a bank's reputation to its adoption of ESG issues is very important. Finally, at the third level are competitors, as there are still marked differences in banks' approaches to ESG integration at the strategic and operational levels, due to both their different sizes and their different degrees of sensitivity to ESG integration, so their best practices can certainly constitute important points of reference for other companies. Customers and employees can also be considered relevant, but to a lesser degree.

I_3 named the main influencing factors in order of relevance as follows: standard setters, regulators, media and press, competitors, customers, private shareholders and PAs. For each of these factors, one or more ESG factors should be considered more important. For standard setters and regulators, the more important elements are E and G; for the media and press, competitors and customers, E; and for private shareholders and PAs, S. The S factor has particularly always received attention from the Bank, but the Bank's attention to ESG factors has progressively increased following the growing importance attributed to these issues by regulators and the supervisory authority. I_3 added that the implementation of ESG initiatives also requires the strong commitment of the Bank's organisational structures.

I_3 also highlighted that the strategic relevance of ESG issues is demonstrated by the publication of a 'new' planning document, the 2023–2025 ESG Initiative Plan, as requested by the Bank of Italy, which will be updated annually. The growing importance of these issues to the Bank can also be seen in the Bank's 2022–2024 strategic business plan, which envisions, among other things, the acceleration of the Bank's green transition through its offering of specific products.

We asked the interviewees to indicate how relevant the most influential contextual factors are to the environmental (E), social (S) and governance (G) elements of sustainability and how they influence the Bank's identification of its strategic objectives and its strategic planning. Moreover, we asked the interviewees whether the Bank's strategic planning regards key E, S and G factors as risks and/or opportunities.

According to I_1, the Bank's strategic choices have a real repercussion on its clients' company management plans. In this case, all three ESG factors are involved: E (alignment with best practices related to the conscious use of resources), G (decisions that influence corporate governance and several management aspects) and S (choices that influence the development of a territory, its industrial settlement and the work offered). In fact, the Bank's strategic decisions influence the investment choices of its client companies, as well as their financial performance and thus, their community development opportunities. The people who work in those companies and their choices of where and how to live are also influenced—for example, their movement and the way in which they aggregate and choose to live: whether in large towns or small towns, in the suburbs and so on.

I_1 highlighted that for the social component, two main aspects must be considered: the Bank's need to make strategic choices that can favour its client companies and its even more ambitious need to create the conditions that will enable its client companies to deal with change—for example, the ecological transition—through innovative and effective projects.

According to I_1, the strategic objective of a community bank is not only to grant credit and offer other financial services but also to become an important reference for the development of its community—that is, to be considered fundamental for the birth of new businesses and supply chains or for the facilitation of the community's real estate investments—by supporting businesses and families with adequate tools, especially when they are in difficulty, and even by encouraging the creation of new businesses or the development of new projects when market opportunities arise.

I_2 declared that employees can have an important role in banks' pursuit of sustainability and of their relevant strategic objectives. While large banks are often characterised by a sort of depersonalisation, community banks aim to put themselves at the service of their community's economic development, which prevails over mere compliance with a rule that can lead to decisions to reduce or interrupt some services.

According to I_2, regulators are also extremely relevant in community banks' strategic planning. Although community banks are aware that their adherence to ESG regulations enhances their reputation, which they consider very important, they are hardly aware that such adherence also develops their commercial opportunities and ultimately enhances their financial performance. Regulators are relevant particularly to E and S, with S also referring to responsibility toward employees by improving working conditions and gender equality and by promoting financial inclusion. However, the assessment of risks prevails over that of the opportunities offered by ESG factors.

I_2 affirmed that the impact of the influencing factors on the definition of strategic objectives and planning occurs, above all, with regard to risk assessment. Furthermore, the E and S factors are not always simultaneously considered in strategic objectives and, therefore, in decisions. For example, the Bank reports its carbon dioxide emissions but is not concerned about the closure of 1500 of its branches. This is a case in which E receives greater attention than S. In addition, the Bank has an industrial strategy and an ESG strategy, but they are often not integrated, at least not completely.

According to I_3, the Bank considers the main ESG risks and opportunities in its strategic planning, and the Bank's ability to adequately consider these factors will develop further in the coming months, together with the improvement of the Bank's metrics for measuring ESG risks, which, as highlighted by the Bank of Italy, should be enhanced given the limited availability of data. In the Bank's future strategic business plan updates, further refinement of its assessments of risks and opportunities connected to ESG factors can be expected, starting from which the Bank will set commercial and risk objectives, including the related tolerance thresholds.

32.5 Discussion and Conclusions

Given the growing importance of sustainability, the link between its contextual factors, strategic planning and operational processes has been significantly strengthened (Hummel et al., 2021). ESG issues have been widely demonstrated and increasingly consolidated from the theoretical and regulatory perspectives and have been newly contextualised in local entrepreneurial environments. They have developed in a specific financial ecosystem represented by financial markets, in the context of circular relationships between large companies, consultants and institutions. In this area, regulation has found a strong interaction with the spontaneous behaviour of operators, who have become increasingly aware of the strategic importance of sustainability.

In economic and social ecosystems, often composed of small operators, the phenomenon presents different features (Cardoni & Kiseleva, 2023). As demonstrated in the previous section, the integration logics are currently characterised by a strong regulatory push in an attempt to increasingly influence the orientations and behaviours of operators.

The development of green banking is conditioned by this scenario, and the integration of ESG factors into banks can profoundly differ depending on the banks' size, economic and social contexts, and relevant markets. The analysis in this paper highlighted that the relationships between the contextual factors and the strategic managerial perceptions of ESG integration into community banking have particular characteristics and features.

To facilitate the interpretation of the different opinions that emerged from the interviews on ESG integration into community banking, the most influential contextual factors perceived by the key managers are listed in Table 32.2.

As shown in Table 32.2, the managerial perspectives are heterogeneous. From the perspective of the General Manager (I_1), attention to customers and employees prevails, with the impact extended to all the people employed by the local businesses. The substantial long-term impacts of ESG integration are considered more strategically relevant than the actual top-down pressures of such integration, which must be carefully managed to avoid the risk of producing only a symbolic impact. Therefore, in these perceptions, a strategic entrepreneurial attitude emerges, with strong attention to the long-term effects of the ESG integration on value creation. Paradoxically, the Commercial Director (I_2) presented a rather different order of influencing factors, which emphasises the institutional external pressures and considers customers and employees (in this case, limited to the banks' staff) less relevant

Table 32.2 Most influential contextual factors of ESG integration into community banks as perceived by the focus bank's key managers (listed in the order of their mentions by the interviewees)

General Manager (I_1)	Commercial Director (I_2)	Risk Manager (I_3)
Customers	Standard setters and regulators	Standard setters and regulators
Employees	Institutional shareholders	Media and press
Media and press	Media and press	Competitors
Competitors	Competitors	Customers
Standard setters and regulators	Customers	Private shareholders
	Employees	Public administration

at present. This position seems to confirm the strong top-down characterisation of the ESG integration into the local productive ecosystems, in which local actors, in particular, SMEs, still have a very distant attitude toward sustainability issues. The Commercial Director, who comes into close contact with this type of customers, feels limited pressure in a bottom-up logic and therefore expressed the contingent and pragmatic perspective of staying aligned with current customer needs while complying at best with the new institutional framework. Finally, the Risk Manager (I_3) expressed a seemingly more holistic position by judging the influences of standard setters and regulators as having maximum impact but also immediately considering the market and strategic effects in relation to competitors' pressures and customers' inclusion. In this case, the tensions between the top-down and bottom-up factors are carefully evaluated from the perspective of risks and opportunities for a community bank, following a systemic and risk-based approach. To summarise, in light of the interactions between the contextual factors and the strategic managerial perceptions of ESG integration into community banking, the ESG process in a community bank can be distinguished in terms of the E, S and G triad.

The integration of E is certainly the most urgent and was the most strongly considered by the Bank's managers, based on finance institutions' possible leverage effect to guide sustainable investments in local production systems. This is demonstrated by the following circumstances:

- The evolution of the legislation has mainly focused on climate risks;
- A taxonomy was created with exclusive reference to environmental aspects; and
- The supervising authorities have particularly focused on such issues.

The interview results confirm the strong impact of these recommendations on strategic planning that addresses climate and transition risks. This involves a top-down process, with the external environment having a strong influence through the supervisory authorities and the pressures generated by the mass media, and with the risk that the integration would remain only 'narrative', as highlighted by I_1. However, the effects are much more significant, and these can derive from the contemporary integration with customers and the community expectations. Considering the credit leverage, I_1 underlined that it is essential for the Bank to support local companies in the transition, although I_2 warned that many companies are not yet ready, either to formulate a sustainability strategy or to undertake disclosure, as also discussed in the literature (Cardoni et al., 2023; O'Reilly et al., 2023). From the customer perspective, according to I_2, more opportunities for ESG integration arise in the Bank's investment services by enhancing investors' awareness of sustainable bonds.

In such a scenario, in the short term, the integration of the E factor in the credit leverage does not seem to significantly influence the components of the company business model (i.e. value proposition, value creation system and value capture) but seems to have a greater impact on risk management and value protection. Not surprisingly, the supervisory expectations dedicate the main attention to the topic of risks, as demonstrated by the prevalence of the points related to risk management, including a comprehensive list of elements to consider:

- Mapping of events and their related integration into the risk management system;
- Creation of a high-quality database on climate and environmental risk profiles;
- Materiality analysis to incorporate climate and environmental risks into the processes of assessing the adequacy of internal capital and liquidity through the integration of the risk limit system;
- Periodic review of decisions and tools to preserve their validity and significance, considering the dynamic nature of climate risks; and.
- Specific focus on credit risks, market risks, operational risks and liquidity risks derived from the possible impact of climate transition.

The integration of S is certainly the most stimulating, as it is not limited to the implementation of social factors into a single organisation but also considers the leverage effects of the Bank's activities on the community. However, by moving from a single bottom line to a triple bottom line, the role of the Bank is no longer limited to supporting the economy, but it can already have significant social impacts.

I_2 underlined the occurrence of bank desertification and the concentration of credit provision in a limited number of large financial players. In these contexts, ESG integration presents both risks and opportunities to community banks, considering the limited possibility of such banks to diversify their sectors and territories but also their particular ability to manage the informal approaches and unstructured information that characterise SMEs (Berger et al., 2019; D'Onza et al., 2022). From this perspective, the interaction between E and S can be difficult to realise. To manage the climate and environmental risk according to green financing policies, the Bank should select the most deserving companies, that is, those engaged in the implementation of sustainability transition and transparent disclosure. More generally, the EBA lines observation will entail the need for the Bank to request much more structured information from companies, not only at the financial level but also concerning sustainability issues. As already highlighted, local companies, especially SMEs, still show limited awareness of, and limited readiness to undertake, the green transition (Cardoni et al., 2023; O'Reilly et al., 2023), and this can lead to adverse borrower selection that could negatively impact the business model and mission of a community bank. As underlined by the I_3, the Bank can have a strategic role in raising the awareness of, and educating, the local economic operators on ESG issues, acting with an 'inclusive' logic and not using the lever of sustainability selectively.

However, the integration of an inclusive approach into the business model and its implementation have to be seen from a long-term perspective. This is the component of strategic planning that I_1 defined as 'substantial' and that requires strong social interaction, with particular attention to customers. This component presents several difficulties in developing, as it is more emergent and incremental, but it is the most relevant for the evolution of the business model into one that integrates ESG factors. From the theoretical and regulatory viewpoints, the following two actions can accelerate the evolution of the business model:

- Reformulation of the concept of S to consider the possible leverage effect of banks on their community and territory; and.
- Definition of a taxonomy that standardises all the types of activities that produce social value and that can incorporate the aforementioned leverage effect, similar to the taxonomy established for the E factor.

The integration of G is the most complex and challenging task for a community bank. From the individual perspective of the bank as an organisation, the process of G integration is similar to that of any other entity: strengthening corporate governance in the direction of inclusiveness and transparency. However, due to banks' stringent regulation and careful supervision by the authorities, their governance is already very structured and close to the criteria for sustainable governance (Cardoni & Kiseleva, 2023). Furthermore, the Bank of Italy has recently shared with its supervised institutions best practices aimed at making their governance sustainable.

Even for G, however, the leverage effect is a crucial aspect, considering the possible strategic role of the governance of community banks in the broader context of local governance. The challenge is merging the E and S issues by: (i) finding the balance point between the effects of the ecological transition and social sustainability; and (ii) maintaining a high standard of social inclusiveness and realising the aforementioned equilibrium in the strategic planning and business model.

In conclusion, from the main results of the analysis, the following implications are derived. At the theoretical level, the case analysed contributes to the literature on the integration of ESG factors (Aldowaish et al., 2022) into a context often ignored by scientific literature and analyses different forces that can influence the integration process, distinguishing each of them with a single ESG factor (E, S or G). A contribution is also made to the literature related to community banks (Lux & Green, 2015), a line of research that has recently received less attention from scholars due to the constant decline of these organisations as a result of the phenomena of aggregation and crisis of the traditional banking system. To fill the research gap, this paper demonstrates that the advent of green banking designs a new scenario for community banking institutions that allows them to reevaluate their strategic role and provide new development opportunities. This could be considered a starting point for further developing the topic by adopting the pivotal frameworks that are mostly used in the ESG integration literature. Based on the results of this study, in future research, it would be particularly useful to test the institutional theory—especially to interpret the organisational reactions of community banks to the coercive, normative and mimetic pressures (Greenwood & Hinings, 1996) imposed on them by the contextual factors and the process of isomorphism (Powell & DiMaggio, 2001) that could characterise these particular entities, which are so closely linked to their surrounding ecosystem. Another interesting perspective is the legitimacy theory when considering the tensions that could emerge between the symbolic and substantive approaches (Crossley et al., 2021; Romero et al., 2018). These two approaches present very different characteristics at the strategic and organisational levels (Cormier & Magnan, 2015) and have significant impacts on thc quality of ESG integration. Following the substantive approach, the ESG integration can generate real changes in the process or practice to respond to stakeholders' expectations, whereas the symbolic approach is mainly aimed at enhancing a company's image and reputation (Crossley et al., 2021). This issue was particularly addressed by the General Manager when describing the possible narrative or real impact of the various contextual factors on the community bank strategy and business model.

At the practical level, this research can provide community bank managers a perspective for finding a balance between the E, S and G factors, thereby avoiding an uncritical transposition of integration models applied to other contexts. In particular, this research highlights the need to manage the strong tensions that can arise between the selective approach, derived from the management of environmental risks, and the inclusive approach that the bank must maintain with respect to its community and territory. At the policy level, this paper encourages regulators acting on the institutional levers of green banking to avoid standardised approaches and to maintain a strong consideration of the crucial role of community banks. On this site, it is important that: (i) the 'social taxonomy' contemplate and stimulate the leverage effects of community banks on their territory, and (ii) mechanisms are introduced to incentivise the achievement of 'integrated' ESG performance with an adequate balance between the environmental and social dimensions, especially with reference to SMEs.

This study had the following limitations: Its use of the exploratory and descriptive approaches to facilitate dialogue with the community of practitioners and stakeholders might have limited the preliminary structuration of this research at the theoretical level, as explained in the Methodology section. Additionally, case study research presents limitations as it may not be generalisable because it focuses on specific instances or organisations. Its findings are not always applicable to larger populations in different contexts. In fact, to achieve generalisability, statistical significance across the entire population is required, which would necessitate a different research protocol.

References

Aldowaish, A., Kokuryo, J., Almazyad, O., & Goi, H. C. (2022). Environmental, social, and governance integration into the business model: Literature review and research agenda. *Sustainability, 2022*(14), 2959. https://doi.org/10.3390/su14052959

Amore, M. D., & Bennedsen, M. (2016). Corporate governance and green innovation. *Journal of Environmental Economics and Management, 75*, 54–72. https://doi.org/10.1016/j.jeem.2015.11.003

Aracil, E., Nájera-Sánchez, J. J., & Forcadell, F. J. (2021). Sustainable banking: A literature review and integrative framework. *Finance Research Letters, 42*, 101932. https://doi.org/10.1016/j.frl.2021.101932

Bank of Italy. (2022a). *Supervisory expectations on climate and environmental risks*. Bank of Italy.

Bank of Italy. (2022b). *Climate risk for Italian banks: An update based on a sample survey*. Bank of Italy.

Berger, A. N., Molyneux, P., & Wilson, J. O. S. (2019). *The Oxford handbook of banking*. Oxford University Press.

Bless, C., Higson-Smith, C., & Kagee, A. (1995). *Fundamental of social research methods. An African perspective*. Juta and Co. Ltd.

Borgers, C. T., & Pownall, R. A. J. (2014). Attitudes towards socially and environmentally responsible investment. *Journal of Behavioral and Experimental Finance, 1*, 27–44. https://doi.org/10.1016/j.jbef.2014.01.005

Brooks, C., & Oikonomou, I. (2018). The effects of environmental, social and governance disclosures and performance on firm value: A review of the literature in accounting and finance. *The British Accounting Review, 50*(1), 1–15. https://doi.org/10.1016/j.bar.2017.11.005

Caldarelli, A., Fiondella, C., Maffei, M., & Zagaria, C. (2016). Managing risk in credit cooperative banks: Lessons from a case study. *Management Accounting Research, 32*.

Campbell, D., & Slack, R. (2011). Environmental disclosure and environmental risk: Sceptical attitudes of UK sell-side bank analysts. *The British Accounting Review, 43*(1), 54–64. https://doi.org/10.1016/j.bar.2010.11.002

Cardoni, A., & Kiseleva, E. (2023). *Sustainable governance*. Springer Nature., ISBN: 978-3-031-37491-3. https://doi.org/10.1007/978-3-031-37492-0

Cardoni, A., Kiseleva, E., & Bellucci, A. (2023). The quality of SMEs stakeholder communication during strategic crises: The case of Italian unlisted SMEs. *Business Strategy and the Environment, 32*(6), 3292–3308. https://doi.org/10.1002/bse.3300

Clarkson, P., Li, Y., Richardson, G., & Vasvari, F. (2011). Does it pay to be green? Determinants and consequences of proactive environmental strategies. *Journal of Accounting and Public Policy, 30*(2), 122–144. https://doi.org/10.1016/j.jaccpubpol.2010.09.013

Cormier, D., & Magnan, M. (2015). The economic relevance of environmental disclosure and its impact on corporate legitimacy: An empirical investigation. *Business Strategy and the Environment, 24*, 431–450. https://doi.org/10.1002/bse.1829

Crossley, R. M., Elmagrhi, M. H., & Ntim, C. G. (2021). Sustainability and legitimacy theory: The case of sustainable social and environmental practices of small and medium-sized enterprises. *Business Strategy and the Environment, 1*(23). https://doi.org/10.1002/bse.2837

Cuevas, C., Fafchamps, M., Hanson, R., Moll, P., & Srivastava, P. (1993). *Case studies of enterprise finance in Ghana* (Final report, Regional Program on Enterprise Development, The World Bank).

D'Onza, G., Formisano, V., Landi, A., & Modina, M. (2022). *Il credito cooperativo: modello di business, governance e sostenibilità*. AIDEA Position Paper, n. 1, Accademia Italiana di Economia Aziendale, Bologna.

Dahl, D., Meyer, A., & Neely, M. (2016), Scale Matters: Community Banks and Compliance Costs, *The Regional Economist*, July 2016.

Dal Mas, F., Tucker, W., Massaro, M., & Bagnoli, C. (2022). Corporate social responsibility in the retail business: A case study. *Corporate Social Responsibility and Environmental Management, 29*(1), 223–232. https://doi.org/10.1002/csr.2198

Dearnley, C. (2005). A reflection on the use of semi-structured interviews. *Nurse Researcher, 13*(1), 19–28. https://doi.org/10.7748/nr2005.07.13.1.19.c5997

DeYoung, R., Hunter, W. C., & Udell, G. F. (2004). The past, present, and probable future for community banks. *Journal of Financial Services Research, 25*, 85–133. https://doi.org/10.1023/B:FINA.0000020656.65653.79

Dikau, S., & Volz, U. (2020). *Central Bank mandates, sustainability objectives and the promotion of Green finance; SOAS Department of economics working paper no. 232*. School of Asian and African Studies.

Durden, C. (2008). Towards a socially responsible management control system. *Accounting, Auditing & Accountability Journal, 21*(5), 671–694. https://doi.org/10.1108/09513570810872969

Eisenhardt, K. M. (1989). Building theories from case study research. *The Academy of Management Review, 14*(4), 532–550. https://doi.org/10.2307/258557

Epstein, M. J., & Wisner, P. S. (2005). *Managing and Controlling Environmental Performance: Evidence from Mexico*. https://doi.org/10.1016/S1474-7871(05)14005-2

Esposito, D., Cacchin, M., & Ghilardi, B. (2022). *Bank of Italy: Supervisory Expectations on Climate and Environmental Risks*, Iason Research Paper Series.

Esteban-Sanchez, P., de la Cuesta-Gonzalez, M., & Paredes-Gazquez, J. D. (2017). Corporate social performance and its relation with corporate financial performance: International evidence in the banking industry. *Journal of Cleaner Production, 162*, 1102–1110. https://doi.org/10.1016/j.jclepro.2017.06.127

European Banking Authority. (2020). *Guidelines on loan origination and monitoring*. EBA.

Fayman, A., Chen, S., & Mayes, T. (2022). Community banks versus non-community banks: Post the great recession. *EconomicNotes, 51*(2), 1–20. https://doi-org.aurarialibrary.idm.oclc.org/10.1111/ecno.12196

Fiordelisi, F., Marques-Ibanez, D., & Molyneux, P. (2011). Efficiency and risk in European banking. *Journal of Banking & Finance, 35*(5), 1315–1326. https://doi.org/10.1016/j.jbankfin.2010.10.005

Galletta, S., Mazzù, S., Naciti, V., & Vermiglio, C. (2021). Sustainable development and financial institutions: Do banks' environmental policies influence customer deposits? *Business Strategy and the Environment, 30*, 643–656. https://doi.org/10.1002/bse.2644

Gangi, F., Meles, A., D'Angelo, E., & Daniele, L. M. (2019). Sustainable development and corporate governance in the financial system: Are environmentally friendly banks less risky? *Corporate Social Responsibility and Environmental Management, 26*, 529–547. https://doi.org/10.1002/csr.1699

Gatzert, N. (2015). The impact of corporate reputation and reputation damaging events on financial performance: Empirical evidence from the literature. *European Management Journal, 33*(6), 485–499. https://doi.org/10.1016/j.emj.2015.10.001

Greenwood, R., & Hinings, C. R. (1996). Understanding radical organizational change: Bringing together the old and the new institutionalism. *Academy of Management Review, 21*, 1022–1054.

Győri, Z., Khan, Y., & Szegedi, K. (2021). Business model and principles of a values-based Bank—Case study of MagNet Hungarian community Bank. *Sustainability, 13*, 9239. https://doi.org/10.3390/su13169239

He, L., Zhang, L., Zhong, Z., Wang, D., & Wang, F. (2019). Green credit, renewable energy investment and green economy development: Empirical analysis based on 150 listed companies of China. *Journal of Cleaner Production, 208*, 363–372. https://doi.org/10.1016/j.jclepro.2018.10.119

Hummel, K., Laun, U., & Krauss, A. (2021). Management of environmental and social risks and topics in the banking sector. An empirical investigation. *The British Accounting Review, 53*(1), 1–26. https://doi.org/10.1016/j.bar.2020.100921

Kim, D., & McKillop, D. G. (2019). Community, commercial, mutual and cooperative banking. In A. Berger, P. Molyneux, & J. O. S. Wilson (Eds.), *Oxford handbook of banking* (3rd ed.). Oxford University Press.

Loizzo, T., & Schimperna, F. (2022). *ESG Disclosure: regulatory framework and challenges for Italian banks*, Bank of Italy, Occasional Paper n.744.

Lux, M., & Green, R. (2015). *The state and fate of community banking, M-RCBG associate working paper series, no. 37*. Harvard Kennedy School.
Mishkin, F. S. (2001). *The economics of money, banking and financial markets* (6th ed., p. 186). Addison Wesley.
Nájera-Sánchez, J. J. (2020). A systematic review of sustainable banking through a co-word analysis. *Sustainability, 12*(1), 278. https://doi.org/10.3390/su12010278
Neuman, W. L. (2003). *Social research methods: Qualitative and quantitative approaches*. Allyn and Bacon.
O'Reilly, S., Gorman, L., Mac An Bhaird, C., & Brennan, N. M. (2023). *Implementing the European Union Green Taxonomy: implications for small-and-medium-seized enterprises*, Accounting Forum, (24 Nov. 2023).
Park, H., & Kim, J. D. (2020). Transition towards green banking: Role of financial regulators and financial institutions. *Asian Journal of Sustainability and Social Responsibility, 5*(5), 1–25. https://doi.org/10.1186/s41180-020-00034-3
Petach, L., Weiler, S., & Conroy, T. (2021). It's a wonderful loan: Local financial composition, community banks, and economic resilience. *Journal of Banking and Finance, 126*.
Pondeville, S., Swaen, V., & De Rongé, Y. (2013). Environmental management control systems: The role of contextual and strategic factors. *Management Accounting Research, 24*(4), 317–332. https://doi.org/10.1016/j.mar.2013.06.007
Powell, W., & DiMaggio, P. (Eds.). (2001). *The new institutionalism in organizational analysis* (p. 1991). Chicago.
Rashid, Y., Rashid, A., Warraich, M. A., Sabir, S. S., & Waseem, A. (2019). Case study method: a step-by-step guide for business researchers. *International Journal of Qualitative Methods, 18*, 1–13. https://doi.org/10.1177/160940691986242
Romero, S., Ruiz, S., & Fernandez-Feijoo, B. (2018). Sustainability reporting and stakeholder engagement in Spain: Different instruments, different quality. *Business Strategy and the Environment, 28*, 221–232. https://doi.org/10.1002/bse.2251
Rubin, A., & Babbin, R. B. (2001). *Research method for social work*. Cengage Learning.
Sarma, P., & Roy, A. (2020). A Scientometric analysis of literature on Green banking (1995-march 2019). *Journal of Sustainable Finance & Investment, 1711500*, 1–20. https://doi.org/10.1080/20430795.2020
Scholtens, B. (2009). Corporate social responsibility in the international banking industry. *Journal of Business Ethics, 86*, 159–175. https://doi.org/10.1007/s10551-008-9841-x
Weber, O. (2012). Environmental credit risk management in banks and financial service institutions. *Business Strategy and the Environment, 21*, 248–263. https://doi.org/10.1002/bse.737
Weber, O., Fenchel, M., & Scholz, R. W. (2008). Empirical analysis of the integration of environmental risks into the credit risk management process of European banks. *Business Strategy and the Environment, 17*(3), 149–159. https://doi.org/10.1002/bse.507
Xing, C., Zhang, Y., & Tripe, D. (2021). Green credit policy and corporate access to bank loans in China: The role of environmental disclosure and green innovation. *International Review of Financial Analysis, 77*, 101838. https://doi.org/10.1016/j.irfa.2021.101838
Yellen, J. (2015). *Some thoughts on community banking: a conversation with chair Chair Janet Yellen*, Community bank connections, 2nd Quarter.
Yin, R. K. (2014). *Case study research: Design and methods*. SAGE.
Zhang, X., Wang, Z., Zhong, X., Yang, S., & Siddik, A. B. (2022). Do Green banking activities improve the banks' environmental performance? The mediating effect of Green financing. *Sustainability, 14*, 989.

Chapter 33
Integrating ESG into a Business Model: A Case Study from a Non-profit Organization

Alberto Romolini, Silvia Fissi, Elena Gori, and Michele Sances

33.1 Introduction

The environmental, social and governance (ESG) (Gillan et al., 2010) and sustainability integration into a business model of an organization is currently debated in the literature, often under the concept of the sustainable business model (SBM) (Bocken et al., 2014; Schaltegger et al., 2016). As Geissdoerfer et al. (2018b) state, a sustainable business model is a 'business model that incorporate pro-active multistakeholder management, the creation of monetary and non-monetary value for a broad range of stakeholders, and hold a long-term perspective'.

Considering previous studies, ESG integration with a more traditional business model is analyzed under different views. For example, scholars have analyzed different typologies of SBMs and strategies for transforming a traditional business into a sustainable one (Bocken et al., 2014). Other perspectives are related to the creation of a circular business model characterized by the aim to close, slow, intensify, dematerialize and narrow the resource loops (Bocken et al., 2014; Geissdoerfer et al., 2018a) and to the analysis of socially responsible investments. However, in this field of study, there remains a general lack of knowledge concerning the on-field transformation of a traditional business model into a different one based on sustainable and ESG principles.

Moreover, the non-profit sector also represents an underdeveloped subject in the general study of business models, as Nielsen et al. (2019) observed, even though this industry constitutes an important part of the national economies of a country.

A. Romolini (✉) · M. Sances
International Telematic University Uninettuno, Rome, Italy
e-mail: alberto.romolini@uninettunouniversity.net

S. Fissi · E. Gori
University of Florence, Florence, Italy

N. Castellano et al. (eds.), *Environmental, Social, Governance (ESG)*, SIDREA Series in Accounting and Business Administration,
https://doi.org/10.1007/978-3-031-76618-3_33

According to some scholars (Foster et al., 2009; Knutsen, 2013; Laurett & Ferreira, 2018), it is possible to find different academic papers focused on non-profit organizations that mention business models in their studies without analyzing in depth the connection with ESG. However, the business model should be adapted to not-for-profit organizations considering different challenges like the difference from for-profit entities (Sanderse et al., 2020), the complexity of multiple incomes and stakeholders (Anheier, 2000), and long-term value creation.

This lack of knowledge needs to be addressed if we consider that the non-profit sector represents a crucial part of an important number of national economies. In fact, this industry appears highly developed in Western economies, especially in the EU, the USA and Canada. If we consider the EU environment, Italy represents an interesting environment for analyzing non-profit organizations. More specifically, in Italy, according to the Italian National Institute of Statistics (Istat, 2022), this sector is highly developed, with entities operating in different activities from charities to social and health services. The total number of non-profit entities is about 363,600, with 870,000 staff employed. Indeed, between 2019 and 2020, non-profit institutions grew by 0.2%, less than what was recorded between 2018 and 2019 (+0.9%), while the increase in employees remained around 1% in both years.

To summarize, as previous studies on SBMs are mainly focused on companies operating in private industries (Nosratabadi et al., 2019), few researchers have considered the integration of ESG and sustainability principles into the business model of a non-profit organization. Consequently, this chapter aims to fill this literature gap with an explorative case study of a non-profit organization group that has realized a real integration of the ESG perspective into its business model.

The paper is organized as follows: After the introduction, the second section presents a literature review of the integration of ESG into the business model of a non-profit organization. The third section presents the research method applied in the study. Then, the fourth section describes the case study analyzed while the fifth section discusses the research results. Finally, the paper ends with concluding remarks and discussions of limitations and future development of this study.

33.2 Literature Review

The concept of the business model appeared for the first time in the literature in the 1950s–1960s (Jones, 1960), but acquired importance only in the late 1990s (Osterwalder et al., 2005). Numerous definitions exist of the business model. According to Breuer and Lüdeke-Freund (2017), a business model is a representation of the way in which businesses create value for their customers. Timmers (1998) presents a business model as a description of sources of revenue, while Casadesus-Masanell and Ricart (2010) describe this concept as a cognitive scheme or a narrative about how a business works. Finally, Demil et al. (2015) claim that a business model encompasses ideas of how businesses work but also relate them to the practical implementation of value creation and the capture of value exchange.

With the growing importance of sustainable transition, the idea of a business model has also changed. Specifically, a sustainable transition is a transition from an unsustainable system into a more sustainable state (Rotmans et al., 2001). In recent years, the concept of a SBM as the key to the creation of sustainable businesses and sustainable transition has gained increasing prominence. According to Schaltegger et al. (2016), it requires a clear link between societal change and the business model. A SBM can be considered a sustainable means of production and consumption (Loorbach et al., 2017). According to Stubbs and Cocklin (2008), it needs to incorporate the pillars of economic, environmental and social sustainability as an integral part of a company's proposal and creation of value.

Geissdoerfer et al. (2018a) describe a SBM as a modified business model with specific characteristics and goals integrating sustainability in the value-capture mechanism of a company, which aims at creating monetary and non-monetary value for a broad range of stakeholders and holding a long-term perspective. Bocken et al. (2014) propose a categorization of SBMs into eight archetypes: (1) maximize material and energy efficiency; (2) create value from 'waste'; (3) substitute with renewables and natural processes; (4) deliver functionality rather than ownership; (5) adopt a stewardship role; (6) encourage sufficiency; (7) repurpose the business for society/environment; and (8) develop scale-up solutions.

Lozano (2018) instead states that a SBM is one that uses inputs and resources efficiently and provides added value and service, thus contributing to a more sustainable society. Ritala et al. (2018) see it as a way of maximizing material and energy efficiency, closing resource loops, using renewable forms of energy and natural processes, delivering functionality, encouraging sufficiency and developing and proposing sustainable scale-up solutions.

There is little literature available on specifically SBMs in social enterprises or the voluntary sector.

Yunus et al. (2010) developed the idea of a social business model, namely, a particular business model for social businesses which include a value-proposition, a value-constellation and an economic-profit equation. Regarding this issue, Michelini and Fiorentino (2012) proposed the addition of specific features such as reliance on innovative products and the use of non-conventional channels related to the value proposition. Moreover, a small number of other studies have explored the issue further, leaving this model in its infancy therefore (e.g. Seelos & Mair, 2007; Wilson & Post, 2013; Bocken et al., 2014; Seelos et al., 2011).

Still unexplored, it is evident that, whereas pioneering studies consistently highlighted that social business models should follow a clear social mission and should configure resources in a way that allows the organization to be economically self-sustaining (Seelos & Mair, 2007; Wilson & Post, 2013; Yunus et al., 2010), social business's underlying value drivers have not yet been identified (Spieth et al., 2019).

Except from these studies on social business model which have a strong profit component, to the best of our knowledge, something specific regarding SBMs within the voluntary sector has yet to appear in research about the voluntary sector. A limited number of studies have addressed the issue as a subsidiary feature of their analyses. For example, Beisland et al. (2022) examine the impact of ESG on microfinance, while Crespy and Miller (2011) and Simaens and Koster (2013) investigate the extent to which non-governmental organizations (NGOs) disclose their sustainability activities. Moreover, Traxler et al. (2020) discuss the importance of sustainability when it comes to the legitimacy, the quality of work and the trust enjoyed by international non-profit organizations. However, nothing specific concerning the integration of ESG into the business model of the voluntary sector has been found to date. This represents a gap that this research project attempts to fill.

A few final words need to be spent on how we represent a business model.

There are many ways to represent business models, such as the triple bottom line (TBL) Canvas, SBM Canvas, causal maps and so on (Steinhöfel et al., 2016). However, the best suited for our case study is the SBM Canvas described by Osterwalder and Pigneur (2010). This Canvas was created using nine building blocks that cover four main areas of a business, allowing users to align profit with concerns involving environmental and social issues (Joyce & Paquin, 2016). The Ecocanvas was created as a unique and simple visual tool that allows the user to creatively explore a more inclusive and holistic business model (Cerantola, 2019).

According to some scholars, the Osterwalder and Pigneur Canvas should be integrated by adding another element. For example, Rodrigues and Lopes (2018) argue that it is necessary to integrate additional tools, methodologies and techniques to make the business model canvas more dynamic, while Breuer et al. (2018) point to the necessity of adding social and ecological aspects to an existing planning tool, which is not sufficient to realize socially or environmentally friendly business activities in a practice tool.

Leaving aside this debate, the Osterwalder and Pigneur Canvas model is a useful one and will be used in the final section of this work.

33.3 Research Method

This research is exploratory in nature and, consequently, adopts the case study method, selecting the experience of Fondazione Dynamo Camp (Dynamo Camp Foundation), a pioneering non-profit entity well known not only in Italy but also in the rest of the world. Dynamo Camp Foundation was established in 2003 to work in the social sector, such as education, health, personal services and environmental care. Its mission is to create a 'venture philanthropy' model (Grossman et al., 2013; Moody, 2008) that generates new forms and opportunities for connecting 'profit' and 'non-profit' areas, proposing an alternative to public funding.

To collect data, we performed semi-structured interviews with key personnel from the Foundation: the president, the general manager and the business development manager (two interviews). The semi-structured interviews were managed in two different steps. Initially, the survey involved preliminary mail and telephone contacts to introduce the study's aim and scope. Later, the authors organized online interviews with the selected people. The interviews were recorded on a digital device for a total duration of about 145 min and then transcribed on paper. In this final step, the information was submitted to content analysis.

Finally, the research is enriched with information obtained by collecting secondary data (i.e. the official website, social media profiles, official corporate reports and documents and newspaper and magazine articles available online). We triangulated the data collection by using secondary data to support the information obtained through the interviews and improve the validity of the results (Bryman, 2015).

33.4 Case Study Overview

Dynamo Camp Foundation was established in 2003 with the mission of supporting the strategy and development of business organizations addressing social issues such as education, healthcare, social services and the environment while simultaneously promoting new employment opportunities. Replying to the American philanthropic model, Dynamo Camp Foundation has established companies aimed at financially supporting its social mission and generating employment, serving as a vehicle for the positive values underlying the very concept of Dynamo Camp Foundation.

Dynamo Camp Foundation is currently composed of non-profit entities operating in different sectors with a variety of organizations, such as foundations, associations and private companies (Fig. 33.1). While remaining connected to Dynamo Camp

Fig. 33.1 Dynamo Camp foundation

Foundation projects, the 'Dynamo Companies' are autonomous and distinct entities that target different users and markets compared to Fondazione Dynamo. For example, Pro Dynamo S.r.l. and Acqua Dynamo, under the Dynamo Companies umbrella, engage in the technical sportswear market, striving to convey social and environmental messages through their clothing. Dynamo Academy, on the other hand, promotes the social vision of Dynamo through training and consulting activities aimed at educating students, businesses and top managers in value-creation projects, effectively balancing business and social responsibility in the realm of corporate philanthropy.

The Foundation's vision is based on three different but connected sustainability concepts: economic, social and environmental. The specific values of Dynamo Camp Foundation are highlighted by the president as 'if from a legal point of view these entities are completely separate, from the ideological one the sustainability is the common thread'.

According to the group vision, during 20 years of activity, different forms of non-profit business were established. In 2006, an area of 1000 hectares historically reserved for hunting and belonging to Dynamo Camp Foundation became the World Wide Fund for Nature (WWF)-affiliated nature reserve called 'Oasi Dynamo'. Within the Oasi Dynamo, the agricultural society ('Oasi Dynamo FoodCo') was created in 2015, while the Oasyhotel was established in 2019. These companies owned by the Dynamo Foundation were created with two different purposes: to increase philanthropic issues and to raise profits in order to develop the Dynamo Foundation Group's mission.

In 2007, Fondazione Dynamo Camp ETS (hereinafter, Dynamo Camp ETS) was created to support, with dedicated projects, families and their children with severe or chronic illnesses. Dynamo Camp ETS was founded by Fondazione Dynamo Motore di Filantropia (Dynamo Foundation Philanthropy Engine); today it is part of the American SeriousFun Children's Network, established in 1988 by Paul Newman under the name Association of Hole in the Wall Camps, now SeriousFun. Each camp has a distinct and independent legal structure and is financially autonomous, even though they all share the same processes and perspectives regarding recreational therapies. The mission of Dynamo Camp ETS is to offer free recreational therapy programs, built on the Dynamo recreational therapy model, to children and young people with serious and chronic illnesses.

Dynamo Camp ETS hosts, with free-of-charge services, children from 6 to 17 years who are both in therapy and post-hospitalization. It also offers programs tailored to the needs of the whole family, admitting children affected by neurological diseases, diabetes and rare syndromes (those indicated by the Dynamo Camp Scientific and Medical Committee). All the guests are welcome for holidays lasting a maximum of 9 days, organized into 18 sessions. In 2010, Dynamo Academy was created. It is a social enterprise focused on corporate engagement, research, consulting and training that aims to spread the Dynamo Camp Foundation's know-how and experiences.

In summary, the Dynamo business model promotes 360-degree environmental and social values, adding to the promotion of local employment and the economy. An illustrative example is the Dynamo Camp project, which, through the creation of 'camps' for children with disabilities and degenerative diseases, promotes the inclusion of children often marginalized because of their condition and contributes to the revitalization and transition of the local economy towards sustainability. Furthermore, Dynamo Camp has revitalized and transformed the declining economy of the Apennine Pistoiese, once characterized by the manufacturing sector, making it a tourist destination. This occurred through the strong demand generated by Dynamo for accommodation related to projects and events associated with Dynamo Camp, as well as for employment related to the facility's operation and projects and for the goods required by the facility and events.

As for revenues, donations currently represent the most significant component. According to the 2021 social balance sheet of Dynamo Camp Onlus, more than 90% of revenues came from donations. However, the increasing importance of the Dynamo Companies cannot be denied, as their activities are increasingly making Dynamo economically sustainable. In this regard, the strategic use of reporting and sustainability by Dynamo should be highlighted, as it has become a leader in the sector, providing advice and updates to other companies and building a relationship of trust with donors and customers. Finally, expenses mainly involve the implementation of projects and the associated expenses.

33.5 Results and Discussion

Dynamo Camp Foundation has developed a unique organization of diversified social entities with distinct missions and legal forms aimed at serving different purposes. The group is structured as follows: Dynamo Camp focuses primarily on children with social and socio-health problems; Dynamo Academy focuses on education; and Oasis Dynamo aims at environmental conservation. Dynamo Camp Foundation has thus decided to address all possible aspects of sustainability, from social to environmental, as well as community investments, using different legal forms and 'enterprises', each with its own strategic orientation.

Dynamo Camp Foundation's particular view of sustainability is one of the core values underpinning the creation of the group. It goes beyond the simple delivery of the service for which it was founded, which is to provide occasions of happiness and well-being to children and young people affected by severe and chronic illnesses. The project has evolved over time with the purpose of promoting well-being within society, not just within the specific community where the camp is located (Schaltegger et al., 2016). In particular, the group is endowed with a shared system of values and a sustainability-oriented view from which each entity draws up its own development plan, including its specific ethical code.

Considering the sustainability perspectives, the social issues are more evident in Dynamo Camp ETS. Indeed, the services offered have evolved since the two sessions held in 2007 when only children and teenagers were permitted to take part. Over time, these services have been expanded to encompass the entire family unit, considering that, as stated by the head of the advisory area, '*when a child becomes ill, the family is also affected, especially healthy siblings*'. Recognizing the fact that Dynamo Camp ETS cannot meet the demands of all children, including those with less severe neurological conditions, the campsites project, currently active in Milan and Rome, has been developed to overcome the main facilities' hosting limitations. The primary recipients of these services are children affected by certain pathologies, their families and, more broadly speaking, all caregivers, including those who are in contact with children or young people, such as teachers and sports coaches operating within educational contexts. In short, as emphasized by the head of the advisory area, *'The Dynamo Camp ETS approach to sustainability prioritizes the social aspect with a proactive logic that seeks to anticipate emerging needs among stakeholders, even through innovative services'*. Dynamo Camp ETS is one of Italy's centres of excellence in recreational therapy, and this approach was applied here, ahead of its adoption internationally. In other words, as the head of the advisory area continues, '*Dynamo Camp ETS anticipated a need that had not yet emerged, which is to provide caregivers with a tool that can complement medical or psychological treatment'*.

It is thus evident that through its activities, Dynamo Camp ETS is guiding the society where it is located towards greater sustainability (Lozano, 2018). Sustainability is indeed the goal of Dynamo Camp Foundation. It encompasses multiple perspectives, with a particular focus on both environmental and social issues. From a social perspective, sustainability at Dynamo Camp ETS is also viewed based on its relationship with the local territory and community to provide services that address previously unmet needs. Examples are the construction of a nursery school and the organization of sports activities in collaboration with municipal authorities.

Furthermore, the activities of Dynamo Camp ETS have also been directed towards the revitalization of the Apennine Pistoiese region after the decline of the manufacturing industry there. This decline caused a transition from industrial production to tourism, as exemplified by the restructuring of spaces currently occupied by the Oasis Hotel, a luxury hotel that sources its supplies locally for the most part. This initiative has triggered an economic and social transition towards more sustainable sectors and economic models. In short, Dynamo Camp Foundation's view of sustainability extends beyond its core activities to engage with the local community and environment, with the aim of having a positive impact on and contributing towards sustainable economic and social development (Rotmans et al., 2001).

Another aspect of Dynamo Camp Foundation's sustainability is the environment. The camp of Dynamo Camp ETS has an ongoing parallel project involving the opening to the public of a private oasis, covering approximately 1000 hectares, that is affiliated with the WWF. Within this area, environmental conservation projects have been initiated. Additionally, a luxury hotel has been set up with a view to funding these environmental projects. Furthermore, an agricultural company whose products are sold under the Dynamo Camp Foundation brand has been created. The proceeds of this enterprise support environmental sustainability. The Foundation is also active in research, conducting studies on indigenous animal species within the oasis, thereby creating qualified employment opportunities in the scientific field.

To summarize, sustainability is interpreted as a long-term investment in the territory and the idea of creating companies, including commercial ones, that both promote the Dynamo brand and contribute their profits to Dynamo Camp Foundation to help it achieve its social goals. An example of this strategy is the creation of the 'Dynamo Good Company' clothing brand, which, thanks to its commercial activities, spreads awareness of the Foundation's projects and, operating as a charity (B Corp), simultaneously channels its profits toward institutional ends. The underlying message of Dynamo Camp Foundation's sustainability strategy is that '*it is possible to conduct business and create development while being socially sustainable and responsible; in particular, it is possible to strategically consider social sustainability, community investments, and the inclusion of disadvantaged and disabled individuals*' (President).

This perfectly represents a business strategy that, with the efficient and responsible use of resources, the creation of an oasis and the provision of integrated services, incorporates the principles of cost-effectiveness and environmental and social sustainability (Stubbs & Cocklin, 2008), ultimately serving as a successful example within the non-profit sector.

Over time, Dynamo Camp ETS has accumulated significant experience in reporting sustainability, particularly employing social reporting tools. '*We decided to approach the topic of social reporting as if we were a business, and, therefore, we no longer have the issue of 'obligation' from the perspective of the third sector. However, unlike a public trading company, we have not got a specific governance structure for oversights in sustainability, even though we consider ourselves organizations that should report just like businesses do*' (President). The experience of social reporting has led Dynamo Camp ETS to become a leader in the field and to establish, through Dynamo Academy, a consultancy and service structure for businesses. This same structure also provides internal consultancy services to companies within the group.

Its experience in social reporting has caused Dynamo Camp ETS to become a leader in the field. It has established Dynamo Academy, which serves as a consulting and service structure for businesses. This entity also provides internal consulting services to other companies within Dynamo Camp Foundation. From the point of view of competency, this represents an organizational innovation. As the president explains: '*We are the Academy but also the Dynamo Camp ETS research and development office. This permits us to have continuously updated expertise and overcome the real limitation of the third sector, which does not strategically address this issue*'. In other words, reporting at Dynamo Camp ETS stems from a strategic orientation towards sustainability and is not seen as mere compliance with the social reporting regulations for ETS (entities of the third sector).

In short, from an organizational standpoint, there is a unique competence centre for sustainability across the entire Dynamo Camp Foundation, represented by Dynamo Academy, with its distinct degree of experience even among international camps. From a methodological perspective, the reporting process has been developed concerning key international standards (Global Reporting Initiative), with a particular focus on materiality analysis. With this purpose in mind, a survey was conducted to understand who the external stakeholders were and the activities where Dynamo Camp ETS had the greatest impact. Specifically, the materiality assessment was carried out using a survey that involved internal stakeholders first and external ones later. The research was further expanded through the organization of online focus groups involving both categories. Users in the focus groups were hosted in two different rooms to avoid contamination between internal and external stakeholders. It is worth noting that a relevant stakeholder for Dynamo Camp ETS is the families, for whom communities have been created using Facebook. This permits families with children suffering from pathologies the opportunity to enter into contact with each other and feel stronger when dealing with challenges. In addition to families, other significant stakeholders include doctors and healthcare professionals, hospitals and volunteers.

The choice of a reporting model is also one of the results of the strong managerial organization of both the Foundation and its social enterprises. The social reporting process has had a positive impact on stakeholders in terms of stakeholder engagement and fundraising.

However, looking ahead, '*what all donors feel the need for is the desire to understand the impact of resources, even going beyond the social balance sheet that already reports activities extensively*' (Business Development Manager). In this regard, Dynamo Camp ETS has developed an experimental analysis based on the social return on investment (SROI) method, which allows for a deeper exploration of the social impact of the resources collected. This shows that the integration of ESG aspects into corporate strategies can have positive outcomes capable of attracting investors and promoting fundraising (Abdi et al., 2021; Ahmad et al., 2021; Ashwin Kumar et al., 2016; Chouaibi et al., 2021), while sustainability reporting builds trust within society and among the end users of the services provided (Crespy & Miller, 2011).

Finally, summarizing the results of this study, it became possible to develop a brief picture of the Dynamo Camp Foundation (Fig. 33.2).

Key Partners
- Local companies
- Local Health Authority "ASL Toscana Centro"
- San Marcello Piteglio Municipality
- Tuscany Region
- Union of Mountain Municipalities "Appennino Pistoiese"

Key Activities
Supporting child with severe and chronic illness through free recreational therapy programs

Key Resources
- A suitable structure to accommodate and meet the needs of children with severe and chronic illness
- Proactive logic that seeks to anticipate emerging needs
- Innovative services
- Qualified operators and caregivers
- Donations
- Sustainability reporting

Value Propositions
- Inclusion (of marginalized children for their health condition)
- Diversity
- Sustainability (also through the transition of the local economy towards sustainability)

Customer Relationships
- Long-lasting and fruitful relationships, not only with the user of the service but also with families' users
- The trust built with children and families affects also the donors

Channels
- Social media
- Email
- Website
- Corporate events

Customer Segments
- Families and children with severe or chronic illnesses
- Caregiver
- Teachers
- Sports coaches operating within the educational context

Cost Structure
- Implementation of projects and associated expenses
- Human resources costs
- Fix and assets (buildings)

Revenue Streams
- Donations (more than 90% of the organisation's revenues)
- Dynamo companies (group) different activities

Fig. 33.2 Dynamo Camp Foundation business model

33.6 Conclusions

The results discuss a case of transition from a traditional business model to a sustainable one with the integration of the ESG principles. This chapter provides one of the first studies about this topic applied in the non-profit sector, describing how managers could apply in practice the ESG approaches in managing non-profit entities. In this case, the ESG integration with the traditional business model is realized from different perspectives: the social approach that is traditional for this type of industry and the environmental one that represents a commitment to Dynamo Camp Foundation. The results contribute to reinforcing the academic debate about the integration of sustainability and business models in sectors different from private companies. Consequently, the originality of this study can be identified as an issue still little debated in the literature.

'Sustainable business models in entities of the third sector' indeed are a relatively new stream of research. This paper has examined the field through the study of Dynamo Camp Foundation's experience. Drawing our conclusions, the study shows that even entities in the third sector can successfully integrate sustainability into their business models by implementing social and environmental criteria while adhering to the principle of cost-effectiveness. In short, they can be sustainable and efficient (Ritala et al., 2018).

Another interesting aspect that emerged from the research is that Dynamo Camp Foundation's unique approach to doing business, based on a business model whose purpose is to create both monetary and non-monetary value in the long term (Geissdoerfer et al., 2018a), in addition to the strategic use of sustainability criteria, seems to have triggered a sustainability shift in the entire society where Dynamo Camp ETS is located, fostering a green and social transition (Schaltegger et al., 2016) and revitalizing the economy. This is of utmost importance and could be a useful result to reconsider green, social and industrial transitions. While eco-innovations, eco-efficiency and corporate social responsibility laws define much of the current sustainability agenda, they appear to be insufficient in themselves to achieve the holistic changes necessary for long-term social and environmental sustainability. On the contrary, the example of the Apennine Pistoiese, a region once dominated by a declining manufacturing industry, has reached a more sustainable and flourishing dimension thanks to Dynamo Camp ETS and its sustainable business practices, which could serve as a leading example.

Last but not least, integrating ESG into the business model and implementing sustainability reporting systems help build trust with donors and end users. Donors feel the need to know-how their money is being spent and whether it aligns with environmental and human rights principles. The Dynamo Camp Foundation case demonstrates that through a responsible and up-to-date business reporting system, these questions can be answered, building trust and promoting fundraising.

This research has limitations that represent, at the same time, opportunities for future development of this topic. Currently, the research is based on the analysis of a best practice. In particular, the choice derives from the necessity to explore a relatively new issue in academic studies and on-field experience. In the future, the study could be enlarged to consider other companies for a comparative analysis, expanding the research objective. Moreover, future studies could also use different research approaches with quantitative methods.

References

Abdi, Y., Li, X., & Càmara-Turull, X. (2021). Exploring the impact of sustainability (ESG) disclosure confirm value and financial performance (FP) in airline industry: The moderating role of size and age. *Environment, Development and Sustainability, 24*, 5052–5079. https://doi.org/10.1007/s10668-021-01649-w

Ahmad, N., Mobarek, A., & Roni, N. N. (2021). Revisiting the impact of ESG on financial performance of FTSE350 UK firms: Static and dynamic panel data analysis. *Cogent Business & Management, 8*(1), 1900500. https://doi.org/10.1080/23311975.2021.1900500

Anheier, H. K. (2000). *Managing non-profit organisations: Towards a new approach. Civil society working paper series 1.* Centre for civil society, London School of Economics and Political Science.

Ashwin Kumar, N. C., Smith, C., Badis, L., Wang, N., Ambrosy, P., & Tavares, R. (2016). ESG factors and risk-adjusted performance: A new quantitative model. *Journal of Sustainable Finance & Investment, 6*(4), 292–300. https://doi.org/10.1080/20430795.2016.1234909

Beisland, L. A., Zamore, S., & Mersland, R. (2022). Does it pay to be green? A study of the global microfinance industry. *Nonprofit and Voluntary Sector Quarterly*. https://doi.org/10.1177/08997640221110209

Bocken, N. M. P., Short, S. W., Rana, P., & Evans, S. (2014). A literature and practice review to develop sustainable business model archetypes. *Journal of Cleaner Production, 65*, 42–56. https://doi.org/10.1016/j.jclepro.2013.11.039

Breuer, H., & Lüdeke-Freund, F. (2017). Values-based network and business model innovation. *International Journal of Innovation Management, 21*(3), 1–13. https://doi.org/10.1142/S1363919617500281

Breuer, H., Fichter, K., Lüdeke-Freund, F., & Tiemann, I. (2018). Sustainability-oriented business model development: Principles, criteria, and tools. *International Journal of Entrepreneurial Venturing, 10*(2), 256–286.

Bryman, A. (2015). *Social research methods* (5th ed.). Oxford University Press.

Casadesus-Masanell, R., & Ricart, J. E. (2010). Competitiveness: Business model reconfiguration for innovation and internationalization. *Management Research, 8*(2), 123–149. https://doi.org/10.1108/1536-541011066470

Cerantola, N. (2019). *Ecologing: Circular Economy.*

Chouaibi, S., Chouaibi, J., & Rossi, M. (2021). ESG and corporate financial performance: The mediating role of green innovation: UK common law versus Germany civil law. *EuroMed Journal of Business, 17*(1), 46–71. https://doi.org/10.1108/EMJB-09-2020-0101

Crespy, C. T., & Miller, V. V. (2011). Sustainability reporting: A comparative study of NGOs and MNCs. *Corporate Social Responsibility and Environmental Management, 18*(5), 275–284. https://doi.org/10.1002/csr.248

Demil, B., Lecocq, X., Ricart, J. E., & Zott, C. (2015). Introduction to the SEJ special issue on business models: Business models within the domain of strategic entrepreneurship. *Strategic Entrepreneurship Journal, 9*(1), 1–15. https://doi.org/10.1002/sej.1194

Foster, W. L., Kim, P., & Christiansen, B. (2009). Ten nonprofit funding models. *Stanford Social Innovation Review, 7*(2), 32–39.

Geissdoerfer, M., Morioka, S. N., de Carvalho, M. M., & Evans, S. (2018a). Business models and supply chains for the circular economy. *Journal of Cleaner Production, 190*, 712–721. https://doi.org/10.1016/j.jclepro.2018.04.159

Geissdoerfer, M., Vladimirova, D., & Evans, S. (2018b). Sustainable business model innovation: A review. *Journal of Cleaner Production, 198*, 401–416. https://doi.org/10.1016/j.jclepro.2018.06.240

Gillan, S. L., Hartzell, J. C., Koch, A., & Starks, L. (2010). *Firms' environmental, social and governance (ESG) choices, performance and managerial motivation*. Unpublished working paper. Texas Tech University and University of Texas at Austin. http://www.pitt.edu/~awkoch/ESG%20Nov%202010.pdf

Grossman, A., Appleby, S., & Reimers, C. (2013). Venture philanthropy: Its evolution and its future. *Harvard Business School, 9*, 1–25.

Istat. (2022). *Struttura e profili del settore non profit*, Rome, https://www.istat.it/it/files//2022/10/REPORT-NON-PROFIT-2022.pdf

Jones, G. M. (1960). Educators, electrons, and business models: A problem in synthesis. *Accounting Review, 35*(4), 619–626.

Joyce, A., & Paquin, R. L. (2016). The triple layered business model canvas: A tool to design more sustainable business models. *Journal of Cleaner Production, 135*, 1474–1486. https://doi.org/10.1016/j.jclepro.2016.06.067

Knutsen, W. L. (2013). Value as a self-sustaining mechanism: Why some nonprofit organizations are different from and similar to private and public organizations. *Nonprofit and Voluntary Sector Quarterly, 42*(5), 985–1005.

Laurett, R., & Ferreira, J. J. (2018). Strategy in nonprofit organizations: A systematic literature review and agenda for future research. *Voluntas: International Journal of Voluntary and Nonprofit Organizations, 29*, 881–897.

Loorbach, D., Frantzeskaki, N., & Avelino, F. (2017). Sustainability transitions research: Transforming science and practice for societal change. *Annual Review of Environment and Resources, 42*, 599–626. https://doi.org/10.1146/annurev-environ-102014-021340

Lozano, R. (2018). Sustainable business models: Providing a more holistic perspective. *Business Strategy and the Environment, 27*(8), 1159–1166. https://doi.org/10.1002/bse.2059

Michelini, L., & Fiorentino, D. (2012). New business models for creating shared value. *Social Responsibility Journal, 8*(4), 561–577. https://doi.org/10.1108/17471111211272129

Moody, M. (2008). "Building a culture": The construction and evolution of venture philanthropy as a new organizational field. *Nonprofit and Voluntary Sector Quarterly, 37*(2), 324–352. https://doi.org/10.1177/0899764007310419

Nielsen, C., Lund, M., Montemari, M., Paolone, F., Massaro, M., & Dumay, J. (2019). *Business models: A research overview*. Routledge.

Nosratabadi, S., Mosavi, A., Shamshirband, S., Zavadskas, E. K., Rakotonirainy, A., & Chau, K. W. (2019). Sustainable business models: A review. *Sustainablity, 11*(6), 1663. https://doi.org/10.3390/su11061663

Osterwalder, A., & Pigneur, Y. (2010). *Business model generation: A handbook for visionaries, game changers, and challengers*. Wiley.

Osterwalder, A., Pigneur, Y., & Tucci, C. (2005). Clarifying business models: Origins, present, and future of the concept. *Communications of the Association for Information Systems, 16*, 1–28. https://doi.org/10.17705/1CAIS.01601

Ritala, P., Huotari, P., Albareda, L., Puumalainen, K., & Bocken, N. (2018). Sustainable business model adoption among S&P 500 firms: A longitudinal content analysis study. *Journal of Cleaner Production, 170*, 216–226. https://doi.org/10.1016/j.jclepro.2017.09.159

Rodrigues, V., & Lopes, H. E. G. (2018). The limits of the business model canvas as a dynamic framework. In *Proceedings of the SMS Sao Paulo Conference, Sao Paulo, Brazil* (pp. 15–17).

Rotmans, J., Kemp, R., & van Asselt, M. (2001). More evolution than revolution: Transition management in public policy. *Foresight, 3*(1), 15–31. https://doi.org/10.1108/14636680110803003

Sanderse, J., de Langen, F., & Perez Salgado, F. (2020). Proposing a business model framework for nonprofit organizations. *Journal of Applied Economics and Business Research, 10*(1), 40–53.

Schaltegger, S., Hansen, E. G., & Lüdeke-Freund, F. (2016). Business models for sustainability: Origins, present research, and future avenues. *Organization & Environment, 29*(1), 3–10. https://doi.org/10.1177/1086026615599806

Seelos, C., & Mair, J. (2007). Profitable business models and market creation in the context of deep poverty: A strategic view. *Academy of Management Perspectives, 21*, 49–63. https://doi.org/10.5465/AMP.2007.27895339

Seelos, C., Mair, J., Battilana, J., & Tina Dacin, M. (2011). The Embeddedness of social entrepreneurship: Understanding variation across local communities. In C. Marquis, M. Lounsbury, & R. Greenwood (Eds.), *Communities and organizations (Research in the sociology of organizations)* (Vol. 33, pp. 333–363). Emerald Group Publishing Limited. https://doi.org/10.1108/S0733-558X(2011)0000033013

Simaens, A., & Koster, M. (2013). Reporting on sustainable operations by third sector organizations: A signalling approach. *Public Management Review, 15*(7), 1040–1062. https://doi.org/10.1080/14719037.2012.757350

Spieth, P., Schneider, S., Clauß, T., & Eichenberg, D. (2019). Value drivers of social businesses: A business model perspective. *Long Range Planning, 52*(3), 427–444., ISSN 0024-6301. https://doi.org/10.1016/j.lrp.2018.04.004

Steinhöfel, E., Kohl, H., & Orth, R. (2016). *Business Model Innovation: A Comparative Analysis, conference paper*, 11th European Conference on Innovation and Entrepreneurship At The JAMK University of Applied Science, Jyväskylä, Finland.

Stubbs, W., & Cocklin, C. (2008). Conceptualizing a "sustainability business model". *Organization & Environment, 21*(2), 103–127. https://doi.org/10.1177/1086026608318042

Timmers, P. (1998). *Business models for electronic markets*. Research Note, September 9. https://citeseerx.ist.psu.edu/document?repid=rep1&type=pdf&doi=df8bf13f58c65394fdb1353957c1b90edf45fac4

Traxler, A. A., Greiling, D., & Hebesberger, H. (2020). GRI sustainability reporting by INGOs: A way forward for improving accountability? *VOLUNTAS: International Journal of Voluntary and Nonprofit Organizations, 31*, 1294–1310. https://doi.org/10.1007/s11266-018-9976-z

Wilson, F., & Post, J. (2013). Business models for people, planet (& profits): Exploring the phenomena of social business, a market-based approach to social value creation. *Small Business Economics, 40*(3), 715–737. https://doi.org/10.1007/s11187-011-9401-0

Yunus, M., Moingeon, B., & Lehmann-Ortega, L. (2010). Building social business models: Lessons from the Grameen experience. *Long Range Planning, 43*(2–3), 201. https://doi.org/10.1016/j.lrp.2009.12.005

Chapter 34
Integrating ESG into the Business Model Through a Network Approach. Insights from a Case Study

Federica Palazzi, Annalisa Sentuti, Francesca Maria Cesaroni, and Mara Del Baldo

34.1 Introduction

Several events and forces are encouraging firms to integrate sustainability into their strategies and business models (Bagnoli et al., 2019; Calandra et al., 2023). In this respect, the COVID-19 pandemic has played a major role, as it *'has highlighted the interconnectedness between people, planet and profits – and particularly between health, poverty, climate change and the stability of the global financial system'* (Adams & Abhayawansa, 2022, p. 1).

Sustainable development (SD), in which firms are called to play a major role, balances economic, environmental and social aspects and involves every part of a company, such as operations and production, organization, governance, assessment and communication (Lozano, 2012).

The European Banking Authority (EBA) (2021, p. 31) defines ESG factors as 'environmental, social or governance issues that can positively or negatively impact the financial performance or solvency of an entity, sovereign or individual'. When discussing ESG, we refer to an investment philosophy seeking long-term value growth (Eccles & Viviers, 2011) or integrating ESG into firm operations regarding SD (Lozano, 2012). ESG principles were formally proposed in 2004; since then, they have been practiced in Europe, America and other developed countries and have stimulated an extensive debate in the literature (Li et al., 2021; Savio et al., 2023).

For a company, integrating sustainability into its operations means introducing several changes (EY and DNV GL, 2017, p. 7) including: 1. drive for operational

F. Palazzi · A. Sentuti · F. M. Cesaroni (✉) · M. Del Baldo
Department of Economics, Society, Politics, University of Urbino, Urbino (PU), Italy
e-mail: francesca.cesaroni@uniurb.it

N. Castellano et al. (eds.), *Environmental, Social, Governance (ESG)*, SIDREA Series in Accounting and Business Administration,
https://doi.org/10.1007/978-3-031-76618-3_34

excellence; 2. integrated thinking; 3. innovation engine; 4. response to a changing world; and 5. new social impact models. Drive for operational excellence means improving process capacity to achieve the results (for example, introducing sustainability clauses for selection/management of suppliers or integrating sustainability risks in the risk enterprise management). Integrated thinking is a holistic way of thinking, which implies the creation of value thanks to the interaction of tangible and intangible capital. Innovation engine means that product/process innovation has to include environmental and social aspects from the beginning. Response to a changing world is the capacity to face social and environmental challenges through a proactive approach concerning operational practices and corporate purpose. New business models of social impact are emerging, oriented to the common good and positive social impact.

Sustainability integration would guarantee several advantages to companies: greater attractiveness for investors, risk reduction, customer commitment, reputation improvement and better human resource management (Du et al., 2013; Eccles et al., 2014; Janney & Gove, 2011).

Despite the increasing attention paid to ESG issues, few studies discuss how they can be integrated into the business model (Aldowaish et al., 2022) and contribute to value creation and proposition, value delivery and value capture (Bocken et al., 2014). Furthermore, while relationships with primary stakeholders—such as employees, suppliers, customers and communities—are recognized as crucial for high ESG performance (Zumente & Bistrova, 2021), how these relationships can contribute to strengthening business models by spreading consciousness about sustainability is still unclear.

ESG sustainability goals do not only affect large companies but should also involve small and medium-sized enterprises (SMEs). Given their widespread presence in the economic landscape of Italy and many other countries, also beyond the European Union, SMEs' contribution to SD can be particularly remarkable. The corporate social responsibility philosophy is translated and contextualized into various concrete actions and instruments in SMEs. These companies can adopt a sustainability-oriented approach through various actions and tools, involving strategies, corporate culture, accountability processes and governance systems (Del Baldo, 2009).

This study aims to analyse how a company's business model can integrate ESG issues to develop a sustainable business model, with a focus on the role of networks.

34.2 Theoretical Background: ESG and the Role of Networks

Integrating ESG into core business operations refers to a company's SD. SD balances economic, environmental and social aspects, considering all companies' systems, such as operations and production, the organizational system, governance, assessment and communication (Lozano, 2012). For SD concerning SMEs, the social dimension regards issues about the well-being of employees as well as job creation and education (Jenkins, 2006). Environmental issues include the effects of human activities on nature (pollution, depletion of natural resources and a decrease in biodiversity) (Baker, 2006).

The transition toward sustainability requires incremental and transformational changes in the production, consumer and business success concepts (Bruntland, 1987; Ryan et al., 2012). Furthermore, SD cannot be achieved by a single company in a stand-alone manner; it requires companies to interact with each other. In this line, changes for sustainability take their roots in the relationships' development among stakeholders and in the learning process, which activates inside the network (Ballard, 2005). Firms are interdependent actors within complex networks. Networks are constructed by organizational interactions (Håkansson & Snehota, 1995). Firms, as actors, can create change and stability in response to change. Additionally, the actions of actors involved in a network can change organizations, relationships and networks (Ryan et al., 2012). Moreover, actors co-create knowledge (Ballantyne, 2004) through interaction (Easton & Araujo, 1994). Sharing information and resources allows the creation of new knowledge applicable to face problems, also concerning environmental and social issues. But sharing information and resources needs trust between parties (Doz & Hamel, 1998).

Operating inside a network can allow SMEs to go beyond their limits due to a lack of resources and skills (Chaston & Mangles, 2000). Networks are extraordinary tools for SMEs to reach numerous goals, such as acquiring market knowledge, obtaining resources, learning from other parties, increasing cost efficiency and developing skills (Bosworth, 2009; Carson et al., 2004; Jämsä et al., 2011). A network is also where social capital develops, representing the value embedded in the social relationships of individuals and collectives (Adler & Kwon, 2002; Payne et al., 2011). Social capital is the sum of actual and potential resources, embedded within, available through and derived from the network of relationships (Ciambotti & Palazzi, 2015; Nahapiet & Ghoshal, 1998).

The values of entrepreneurs and top management can make a difference. The presence of entrepreneurs/top management 'brave' and ethical-oriented can favour pathways to sustainability. SMEs have several features that make them potential tools for sustainability spread. They are connoted by a substantial incidence of subjective variables that manifest through the entrepreneur/entrepreneurial family centrality and his/her/its values system, which facilitates the convergence around the corporate mission; a simple organizational structure that makes effective the coordination thanks to informal mechanisms and relationships; the social rooting and the proximity to social-economic context, inside and outside the company (Del Baldo, 2009). These characteristics common to many SMEs can facilitate the adoption of an ESG sustainability-oriented approach. According to Aldowaish et al. (2022), an ESG adoption prompted by external pressure can result in a hesitant sustainable approach. On the contrary, the decision to adopt a sustainability-oriented approach should be consistent with the value system of the entrepreneur or top management value system and corporate culture.

An integration process of ESG into every corporate level and all company's systems is necessary, with a holistic approach, starting with corporate strategy to single operations, from top management to all employees, in accordance with the value system and corporate culture. It implies the need for the integration of ESG into the business model.

According to Bocken et al. (2014), the main elements of business models are three: value propositions, value creation and delivery and value capture dimensions (Teece, 2018). A value proposition describes the firm's products or services that address customers' needs or wants (Zott & Amit, 2010). Value creation and delivery concern activities, partners and suppliers are devoted to providing what is promised to stakeholders. Finally, value capture represents the economic-financial link between value proposition and value delivery, which is how to earn revenues and cover the costs (Teece, 2018). A business model describes how firms create, deliver and capture value (Kraus et al., 2022).

Innovation makes a business model of success in the form of value creation innovation, new proposition innovation and value capture innovation (Clauss, 2017). The network of relationships each company can establish with external partners represents a key source of innovation for the business model. Partners allow a company to obtain resources, market opportunities and benefits that it could not access (Clauss, 2017). Thus, external support and collaboration with other subjects can allow a company to renovate its business model. So, each company must care about the quality of the established relationships (Kraus et al., 2022). Today, empowering a conventional business model means combining innovation with SD goals while maintaining and enhancing productivity and profitability. Sustainable business models employ proactive multi-stakeholder management, innovation and a long-term perspective to meet sustainability goals (Charles Jr. et al., 2017).

Gond et al. (2012) explain how to integrate sustainability into the business model, identifying eight possible configurations, distinguishing between sustainability and management controls (diagnostic vs. interactive), and the level of integration that includes technical, organizational and cognitive dimensions. The 'dormant decoupled strategy' and the 'integrated strategy' are the two extreme positions along the axe of sustainability integration. The first configuration displays parallel systems of control for management and sustainability, which are not employed to carry out the strategy. The 'integrated strategy' configuration corresponds to an ideal interactive use of both integrated systems; it represents the highest level of sustainability implementation and integration. In the intermediate positions, the level of integration varies from low (decoupling) to high (coupling).

Evans et al. (2017) argue that a sustainable business model fulfils through several steps (Nosratabadi et al., 2019): designing a sustainable value that integrates economic, social and environmental benefits; realizing a system of sustainable value flows among multiple stakeholders; generating a value network with a new aim, design and governance; considering the stakeholder interests and responsibilities for mutual value creation.

Thus, the business network approach could help understand how an innovative and sustainable business orientation can spread among firms embedded in the network through sharing values, norms, information and resources, thanks to relationships, interactions and exchanges (Håkansson et al., 2009; Håkansson & Snehota, 2017). Furthermore, the participation of SMEs in a network characterized by several private and public stakeholders could favour implementing actions and programs for SD (Del Baldo, 2009; Spence & Schmidpeter, 2003).

Although several authors emphasize the importance of stakeholder relationships in realizing a sustainable business model, the role that a network of relationships can play has not yet been explored. We argue that this is an important point, especially for SMEs, which, precisely through networks, could overcome a lack of resources and competencies also in relation to sustainability issues.

To effectively explore the integration of ESG issues in the business model through a sustainable networking approach, we employ the actor-resource-activity (ARA) framework (Håkansson & Snehota, 1995) developed by the Industrial Marketing and Purchasing (IMP) group. The IMP approach defines business networking as 'the conscious attempts of an actor to change or develop the process of interaction or the structure of relationships in which it is directly or indirectly involved and has suggested that networking is at the core of management in the business landscape' (Ford & Mouzas, 2013, p. 433). According to Ford and Mouzas (2013), relationships are the prime assets of a business actor. Relationships represent its own and its counterparts' prime assets. All actors depend on the resources and activities of others they do not control. These resources and activities are activated and modified in relationships. Thus, the ARA framework identifies three critical elements of a network: actors, which are nodes in the network; activities, which are actions implemented by actors; and resources, which are activated and combined in the network (Fortezza et al., 2021). We argue that this approach can be helpful to understand how the network of relationships in which a company is involved can contribute to creating and maintaining a sustainable business model that generates value for all stakeholders. It will be used to examine more in depth the variety of actors involved, the type of activities carried out and the specific resources interchanged within the network.

34.3 Methodology

34.3.1 Method

This study is exploratory in nature and adopts a qualitative research perspective. Based on an inductive and interpretive approach, empirical research is conducted on a single-case study (Eisenhardt & Graebner, 2007; Miles et al., 2014; Yin, 2003), selected through a purposive sampling (Patton, 1990). The case analysis method is recommended for understanding complex and little-known phenomena (Eisenhardt, 1989). Single-case studies help the researchers richly describe a phenomenon and get a deeper understanding of remarkably revelatory cases (Yin, 2003), useful for the investigation of a 'transparently observable' phenomenon (Eisenhardt, 1989, p. 537) and particularly suitable for gaining new theoretical insights (Eisenhardt & Graebner, 2007). Among the purposeful sampling strategies suggested by Patton (1990, p. 182), intensity sampling was employed to select an information-rich case that manifests the phenomenon intensely. The logic of this strategy is to investigate excellent or rich examples of the phenomenon of interest but not unusual cases.

34.3.2 Characteristics of the Case Study

The selected case refers to the 'Gino Girolomoni Cooperativa Agricola'. Its roots back to 1977, when Gino Girolomoni—recognized as the most influential pioneer in organic farming (Migliorini et al., 2018)—established the first organic cooperative in the Marche region based on clear principles of ethical production, environmental sustainability and peasants' tradition conservation, well before the first EU regulation on organic agriculture was established (Reg. EC 2092/91). Nowadays, the Girolomoni cooperative is run by the second generation—the founder's offspring—involves 30 farms and produces and commercializes organic agricultural products (mainly pasta, around 90 thousand quintals per year).

Over time, the cooperative has built a strong network. As stated on the company website, it represents an '*ecosystem*' which involves around 400 members and carries out the following activities: production and milling of wheat, production of organic pasta, sale of organic products, tourist reception and educational farm. Long before it began to be discussed globally, this cooperative has always adopted a sustainability perspective and put environmental, social and governance issues into practice by integrating them into corporate values, choices, strategies and behaviours. Moreover, the cooperative has always operated through a network perspective as an effect of a deep-rooted culture of sustainability spread at all levels. This culture is the basis of its competitive advantage, with significant consequences in terms of financial performance. At the same time, the cooperative has progressively spread its sensitivity towards sustainability among primary stakeholders (e.g. employees, suppliers, customers, etc.), contributing to a growing green and social consciousness throughout the supply chain and in the target market. For all these reasons, we believe that 'Gino Girolomoni Cooperativa Agricola' can be considered an excellent and rich case for understanding how ESG can be integrated into the business model and to analyse the role of the network in this regard.

Furthermore, the company can be classified as a small enterprise in accordance with the definition provided by the European Commission (2020). SMEs represent 99% of all businesses in the EU (European Commission, 2023). Given their relevance, the contribution of SMEs towards SD can be decisive. Therefore, studying how they incorporate ESG into their business model is important to understand how to facilitate the transition of the entire economic system towards sustainability.

Finally, the food industry is an emblematic sector characterized by increasing attention to social and environmental sustainability (Aureli et al., 2020; Cortese et al., 2021; Palazzi & Sentuti, 2021), both from governments and consumers. With regard to governments, just consider the profound relationships between the food industry and the various Sustainable Development Goals (SDGs), as highlighted by the Food Systems Summit for SDGs 2021 and the central role that the European Union has given, as part of the Green Deal, to the creation of sustainable food systems. Furthermore, consumers are increasingly attentive to the sustainability of products and production processes, as well as to the ethical behaviour of companies (Savelli & Murmura, 2023; Van Bussel et al., 2022).

34.3.3 Data Collection and Data Analysis

To collect and triangulate data, we selected several data sources. First, two semi-structured interviews with Giovanni Battista Girolomoni (#1), the current president of the cooperative. While the first interview was conducted online, the second was at the cooperative's headquarters. To further explore the role of the network, we interviewed two other key actors of the Girolomoni ecosystem: Pierfrancesco Fattori (#2), the president of the Montebello cooperative and Maria Girolomoni (#3), the president of Girolomoni Foundation.

The interview's total length is about 5 h, and all were transcribed verbatim. Field notes taken during the interviews are also considered part of the empirical material. Furthermore, documents provided by the company were also collected, as well as information gathered from magazines, newspaper articles, online news, interviews, blogs, social networks and official websites.

We carried out a thematic analysis using the six steps described by Braun and Clarke (2006) to identify the main themes within our qualitative data. We manually coded all data from multiple sources, including interviews, internal documents and field notes. The other data were used to further the authors' knowledge of the case. Furthermore, we mapped the Girolomoni network and adopted the ARA framework (Håkansson & Snehota, 1995) to identify the main actors, activities and resources involved in the network with peculiar attention to their role in ESG and sustainability.

The findings are described below. To support our results, we have extensively referenced the most emblematic excerpts from the interviews and other analysed data directly quoted in the text. Then, according to the ARA framework, we identified actors, activities and resources (Fortezza et al., 2021) of the Girolomoni ecosystem.

34.4 Integrating ESG Issues into the Business Model

The analysed company's approach to ESG and sustainability issues is very peculiar: '*We do not have a formalized system to measure and pursue ESG goals, but most of them are intrinsic to our DNA from the company creation*' (#1). The founder, in fact, in his vision, believed from the very beginning—and already in the 1970s—that all economic activities carried out by the company had to be combined with a strong concern for the environment and society. This imprinting, aimed to combine profit and ethics, is still firmly present within the cooperative, which continues to pursue what the founder outlined in one of his writings from the 1970s: '*Some argue that companies must produce profits and based on those profits we will talk about ethical destinations. No, it is the ethical choices that have to become economically sound, not the economic choices that have to become ethically sound, get this into your heads*'. Giovanni confirmed that '*This is the core issue of how to put together ESG purposes with those of the economic-financial principle, environmental and social sustainability with economic sustainability. It is not that you first pursue the economic one and then figure out how to allocate profits for ethical purposes. It is that the environmentally and socially sound activity must be economically sustainable. The paradigm must be reversed*'.

This, over the years, entailed concrete choices aimed at building—and innovating over time—a business model that could embrace these aspects simultaneously and be competitive. In other words, a sustainable business model. It relies on two fundamental aspects.

On the one hand, some cornerstones have always and still characterize the company's business model. These include: choosing a corporate governance model (predominantly mutual agricultural cooperative, established with the main objective of fostering agriculture in marginal areas) that favours the valorization of all partners and the whole territory, and not just the founding family; offering to the supplier farmers much more favourable raw materials purchase price and payment conditions terms than the market ones; guaranteeing all workers fair working conditions, timely wage payments and proper contractual grading; and paying attention to the environment. This last point deserves a closer look. Let us not forget, in fact, that the Girolomoni cooperative contributed to the birth of organic farming in Italy and continues to support it today. The cooperative has always adopted policies aimed at 'preserving soil fertility, respecting biodiversity, rebuilding the rural and peasant world, and creating an economy that is fair and linked to the land' (Report on the Fair Trade e Human Right Due Diligence, 2022). Furthermore, it has invested heavily in renewable energy funds.

On the other hand, major innovations have become necessary to keep the business model competitive over time. The most important change, in this regard, resulted in value creation innovation through the development of new partnerships, new capabilities, new processes, new technologies and new equipment. Specifically, they include the following.

In 2008–2009, the transformation and commercialization activities were separated from the agricultural production by establishing the Montebello cooperative: '*We needed to grow the agricultural part because the pasta factory had grown a lot and wheat was no longer enough for us. We should have gone to the market to buy it, but we wanted to maintain close contact with the farmers and opted for the creation of a new cooperative*' (#2). Between the two cooperatives, a partnership relationship was created: they are both joint members of the other. The new cooperative currently consists of around 300 members, who cultivate organic cereals that are then supplied to the Girolomoni cooperative for pasta production. In this way, the Girolomoni Cooperative has been able to expand production volumes and, at the same time, focus on its core business, always aiming for greater process quality and efficiency.

In 2010, the Girolomoni cooperative launched a second important partnership with other cooperatives in the sector to form the Marche Bio Consortium. The goal, in this case, is to access some funding lines provided at the regional level for agricultural supply chains. '*All the important investments made in the last few years have been made with supply chain projects carried out through Marche Bio and it is the only way we have, besides the production of cash, of course, to make important investments such as those faced in recent years. In addition, the Consortium today also provides professional advice to members regarding their investment projects and possible calls for tenders to access*' (#1). In this way, Girolomoni cooperative can access non-repayable or low-interest loans (and thus lower financial costs or none from an economic point of view) and rely on specific expertise otherwise unavailable internally.

The most important investment was made in 2019 and was related to the acquisition of a mill. The cooperative decided to internalize the entire grain milling process '*to have complete control over the supply chain and to be 100 per cent sure of managing the entire milling process. Managing all stages in-house is an important issue for a dedicated organic pasta mill like we do. Most of the products on the market are not made by dedicated plants: there are no durum wheat mills that make only organic pasta at the industrial level, just as at the production level there are no companies that make only organic pasta. This, for us, is an important, very important element of distinctiveness from other companies that, over time, have begun to produce organic pasta! Having now integrated the entire supply chain, we have no problem with contamination of the raw material*'. But this investment also aimed to create a more efficient supply chain, reduce transport and related costs, and thus helping to make the choices made from the environmental and social points of view more sustainable from an economic point of view. '*Making the supply chain as efficient as possible allows us to be competitive in the market, even if we sell a product that always costs a little more than others. So, there is a balance between consumer price and supply chain efficiency*'. This investment was made in 2019, even though the cooperative had already been in operation for several decades, because it was only then that the critical mass was reached, at the level of grain production with the Montebello cooperative, to use the mill efficiently and enable the Girolomoni cooperative to balance the fair price of raw materials with the need to remain competitive: '*To date, the mill is economically efficient and it is the one that allows us to stay in business even if we pay a little more for grain to our members than the market average. Internalization has made it possible to make the entire supply chain economically sustainable, also from a social and environmental point of view*'.

Furthermore, to formalize the company's commitment to sustainability, recently the company decided to join the Global Community of Fair Trade Enterprises. Namely, in January 2023, the cooperative was recognized as '*a 'Fair Trade' guaranteed enterprise by the World Fair Trade Organisation (WFTO), having verified compliance with fair trade standards*' (Report on the Fair Trade e Human Right Due diligence, 2022). It is an international guarantee system that verifies that companies that decide to join are truly fair trade enterprises and, as reported on the World Fair Trade Organisation (WFTO) website, '*This means they pioneer models of business that put people and planet first*'. '*This is as close as we get to a possible formalization of ESG in our company*', Giovanni pointed out. The guarantee system is based on the pursuit of ten objectives: (1) creating opportunities for economically marginalised producers; (2) transparency and accountability; (3) fair trading practices; (4) fair payment; (5) ensuring no child labour and forced labour; (6) commitment to non-discrimination, gender equity and women's economic empowerment and freedom of association; (7) ensuring good working conditions, (8) providing capacity building; (9) promoting fair trade; (10) climate action and protection of the environment. Specifically, '*this guarantee system assesses the entirety of a business, not just a specific product, and it includes an assessment of the whole enterprise's structure and business model, its operations and its supply chains*', specified Giovanni and added '*Being a predominantly mutual agricultural cooperative, established with the main objective of fostering agriculture in marginal areas, the pursuit of a fair trade goal is actually 'automatic'. But going to formalize it allowed us to go further and draft a Plan with an external audit on the ten fair trade goals. The various points invoke different ESGs, indeed, some of the ESGs are right inside the guarantee system'*.

Summing up, Gino Girolomoni Cooperativa Agricola integrates ESG issues in its business model at two levels, which are closely interlinked. One, value-based, which has always characterised the company and its entire businesses. The other, practical-based, aimed at giving concreteness to the values in the company's strategic choices and operational management.

In making values concrete, an inverse logic to the traditional one is followed: strategic and managerial choices are not to be profit-oriented, but ethical, environmental and social sustainability-oriented. Economic decisions are therefore made to choose the solutions that best support and realise these goals. '*Environmental and social sustainability are intrinsic to what we do. It's not that if organic product costs us more, we start introducing a traditional product line because it's convenient and helps us hold up the system! It is out of the question. If the organic market should disappear, we will also disappear and we will deal with it'*.

This obviously implies certain trade-offs, which in the case analysed release to two main aspects. First, executive remuneration is lower than the labour market average: '*One of the important issues is the ratio of the lowest salary to the highest salary within the company. The WFTO standard, recommended and not mandatory, is a one-to-five ratio. Some companies have a ratio of one to a thousand! So, when we talk about how we reconcile social sustainability with economic sustainability, maybe we need to start looking at these issues as well. The issue is equity! That has to be the starting point! [...] We have very talented managers, but we cannot afford managers who want one to ten. We must work with some equity. Otherwise, economic sustainability would not be reached*' (#1). Second, being a cooperative limits the decision-making autonomy of the Girolomoni family: '*The family has over the years given the guarantee of continuity to the cooperative, but then the decision-making mechanisms are not typical of a family business where there is an intrafamily succession. I am the president of the cooperative but there is a shareholders' meeting that appoints the board of directors every three years and the board of directors elects the president. Then, it is true that the associates do not intervene in the strategic decision process. But the shareholders elect the board of directors and the board of directors judges the managers*' (#1). However, this form of governance (predominantly mutual cooperative) provides some fiscal advantages, which also helps to make the business effectively sustainable thanks to lower tax burdens. In addition, there is no dividend distribution: '*profits remain in the cooperative and have allowed it to capitalize and partly self-finance the business over the years*' (#1).

34.5 The Role of the Network

Findings showed that the network created by Girolomoni is decisive in enabling the company to combine environmental and social sustainability issues with economic sustainability objectives. The 'Girolomoni ecosystem' (Fig. 34.1) is made up of multiple actors who, over time, have forged different kinds of relationships with the Girolomoni cooperative and have carried out various types of activities and resource exchanges to pursue sustainability (Table 34.1).

Namely, around Girolomoni cooperative, there are Montebello cooperative and Consorzio Marche Bio, which we have already mentioned in the previous section, Girolomoni Foundation, Granoturismo and Girolomoni Shops.

The Girolomoni Foundation was founded in 1996 '*at the behest of our parents and deals with all the cultural aspects: various events, conferences and activities. Today, its most important cultural activity is the publication of the magazine Mediterraneo Dossier*' (#3). It is a four-monthly magazine that '*discusses about organic and biodynamic agriculture, the environment, biodiversity, alternative energy, but also philosophy, theology, poetry and culture in general, linked to farming civilisation but not only*' (https://fondazionegirolomoni.it/mediterraneo-dossier/). The magazine is a virtual place for meeting, discussion and collaboration between the Foundation, the Cooperative, universities (the University of Urbino) and all those interested in the world of organic and more. The magazine is circulated '*among the cooperative's members, Girolomoni's customers through shops, subscribers, and with other agricultural cooperative that have embraced the magazine's aim and scope and use it as an information tool towards their members*' (#3). The Foundation also contributes to organize cultural initiatives aimed at disseminating the ethical and social values that characterize the whole ecosystem.

Granoturismo refers to the hospitality business and teaching activities realized through La locanda, Agriturismo Girolomoni and the related educational farm. These activities, owned by the Girolomoni family, help to promote the cooperative

Source: https://girolomoni.it/ecosistema/

Fig. 34.1 The Girolomoni ecosystem. *Source*: https://girolomoni.it/ecosistema/

products and also to spread the values that are at the heart of the cooperative, the importance of the land, the environment and rural life involving tourists and new generations in unique experiences in contact with unspoilt nature.

Finally, the two shops also play an essential role. Located in Urbino and Fossombrone, therefore always close to the area where the pasta factory is located, they have always been run by the family members: respectively, first by Giovanni's mother and aunt and currently by Giovanni's wife and cousin. The shops are not just a showcase for the cooperative's products but a tool through which the Girolomoni 'philosophy' is spread: '*They are very small businesses, we run them directly because otherwise they would not be economically viable. They only survive because they are family-run. But they are very important to us*' (#1). Even if a large part of the sale is through other distribution channels, with these two shops, the cooperative sells its products close to the production site (it does not have a shop inside the factory), distributes the Mediterraneo Dossier magazine and maintains direct contact with consumers.

At the heart of the network remains the Girolomoni cooperative, which '*is the engine of everything; without it, everything dies out*' (#3). However, there is one more actor not formalized in the ecosystem model depicted in Fig. 34.1 but whose presence is strongly felt in the case analysis: the Girolomoni family. Gino Girolomoni gave a strong and indelible imprint to the cooperative, which is still very much present today thanks to the effort everyone in the family makes to preserve it and ensure that it spreads in this direction. Because of the family, Gino Girolomoni's writings, initiatives and values still permeate every corner of the headquarters and every activity of the cooperative and still strongly guide the second generation in governing the company. Thus, the Girolomoni family is a key player that, over the years, has ensured the continuity and development of the cooperative, not only by providing values and human resources but also by making assets available and providing guarantees to banks when necessary.

Table 34.1 Actors, resources and activities of the 'Girolomoni Ecosystem'

Key actors	Key resources	Main activities
Girolomoni cooperative	Governance knowledge Technological knowledge Production process knowledge Marketing knowledge Financial resources	Production planning Transformation of raw materials, production of final goods and commercialization Fair remuneration Governance support Monitoring all the members through annual visits Formation and information about ESG
Montebello cooperative	Ownership of lands to grow Availability by farmers to the organic cultivations	Production of raw materials Quality assurance Supply security
Girolomoni foundation	Social relationships (with several stakeholders, e.g. consumers, tourists, universities, private or public organizations)	Publication of Mediterraneo dossier magazine Organization of cultural initiatives
Marche bioconsortium	Social and business relationships Professional expertise	Policy interface Search funding and tenders Participate in calls of tenders Consultancy services
La locanda Agriturismo Girolomoni	Relationships with tourists (national and foreign)	Communication and storytelling Spread the Girolomoni's values and culture
Girolomoni shops	Relationships with local consumers	Product sale in the neighbouring lands Mediterraneo dossier magazine distribution
Girolomoni family	Key values inherited by the founder Gino Girolomoni Human capital	Governance activities

Source: own elaboration

By analyzing the case, we found two dissemination mechanisms through which Girolomoni cooperative promotes and spreads the sustainability culture *among* and *through* the ecosystem actors.

With '*among* the ecosystem actors', we refer to all activities and exchanges of resources within the network, through which the Girolomoni cooperative raises awareness among all network actors and orients their behaviour towards sustainability, particularly regarding environmental and social issues. This mechanism concerns, first and foremost, the two cooperatives and, thus, the dissemination of ESG and sustainability orientation among all their members.

'*It is a path*', said Giovanni, pointing out that '*over time the characteristics of our members, and of the organic movement in general, have changed. In the early years, with few exceptions, those who made the choice of organic farming were part-time farmers, who had a guaranteed income because they were always doing another job and could afford to take risks. They had a strong belief, a strong personal quest component, on a value level perfectly coinciding with the cooperative. And they had economic peace of mind ensured by other sources of income*'. More recently, however, this sharing of values has to be constructed and, for the Girolomoni cooperative, all members must strive towards the goal of sustainability: '*In the last 10-15 years there has been an increase in companies that do organic farming as a profession: they are agricultural entrepreneurs who live only from farming. They are less idealistic; the economic issue is much more important and personal values play a marginal role. So the relationship with the cooperative, in these cases, is very important and must be built, in terms of training, supplying seeds, harvesting the product. But we aim to get there, by providing information, formation, conferences, initiatives, and slowly we see that certain messages start to get through. We hold at least two operational meetings a year with all our farmers, and we always take the opportunity to talk and train about sustainability issues. Last year, in view of the path we took with the WFTO, we explained what we were doing, why and what this would mean for them*' (#1).

All these activities and information exchange are necessary but insufficient: '*Another important activity we do is monitoring. Obviously, they are all companies controlled by the certifying bodies, but the control that we do with our agronomic staff, i.e. ten agronomists plus some internal members, is really monitoring: we visit all the companies, every year. For us, the concept of the supply chain is fundamental and should not be confused with the concept of traceability: it is one thing to know which farmer the grain comes from, it is another to know him and visit him. It is not the same thing! Monitoring concerns both the 300 members of the Montebello cooperative and another 100 suppliers from whom we buy wheat*' (#1).

With '*through* the ecosystem actors', we refer to all activities and exchanges of resources within the network and also from the network to external stakeholders. Specifically, this mechanism concerns the involvement of certain actors in the network to disseminate values to other actors and external stakeholders. These actors are, in particular, the Foundation, Girolomoni Agriturismo Girolomoni, La locanda and the Girolomoni shops. Within these actors, awareness of sustainability flows through entirely informal channels. It relies on belonging to the same family and related emotional aspects, on the profound sharing of values that binds family members together, and is passed on from the founder generation to the next. These actors and their activities are a means of disseminating these values, this 'Girolomoni's philosophy', inside and outside the network: cooperatives' members, consumers, tourists, young generations, universities, etc. In this way, the Girolomoni cooperative has spread the value of environmental and social sustainability far beyond its organization and ecosystem, involving large communities of external stakeholders.

Finally, turning our attention back to the Girolomoni ecosystem, it emerged that there is a two-way relationship between Girolomoni cooperative and the other network actors: if, on the one hand, the cooperative is committed to spreading awareness of ESG issues and sustainability in the network and through the network, especially on environmental and social aspects, on the other hand, the network—first of all, Montebello cooperative and Consorzio Marche Bio—helps Girolomoni cooperative to balance ESG objectives with the necessary economic sustainability. The whole network collaborates to make environmentally and socially ethical choices economical.

34.6 Discussions and Conclusions

This paper aimed to investigate how a company can embrace sustainability and integrate ESG issues to develop a sustainable business model, giving special attention to the role of networks.

The analysed case shows a very peculiar approach to integrating ESGs into the business model. Currently, most companies are trying to figure out how to make economic choices sustainable under the pressure of external global needs, that is, driven by worldwide considerations that animate the political debate and steer regulation toward more sustainable production models. In contrast, the company analysed has always posed the opposite question: how to make social and environmental choices sustainable from an economic point of view. In this case, the input is strictly internal, that is, related to the values that have always guided the establishment and development of the cooperative. Thus, the integration of ESG issues in the business model occurred, in this case, first of all at a value-based level: environmental issues, ethics and equity are overriding concepts that guide all economic choices at a practical level. Choosing a cooperative governance model, making the supply chain as efficient as possible, containing manager salaries and accessing subsidized sources of financing are some examples of how the cooperative seeks to make its business economically sustainable.

Furthermore, the networking approach proved to be central. The cooperative strives to ensure that ESG goals and sustainability awareness are increasingly shared and disseminated externally as well by the other actors who collaborate with them and, more generally, by its stakeholders. In this direction, the cooperative has, over time, built a network that currently involves about 400 companies through an integrated supply chain project. This network, called Girolomoni ecosystem, on the one hand, has helped the cooperative to remain competitive in the market and, on the other, to become a promoter of sustainability outside its organization as well. The established network became, thus, the recipient and amplifier of this dissemination.

This dissemination occurs through two mechanisms: *among* the ecosystem actors and *through* the ecosystem actors. Based on these two mechanisms, the Girolomoni cooperative has managed to build and consolidate a sustainable networking business model over time. Gino Girolomoni Cooperativa Agricola acts as a leading actor that promotes the sustainability culture, but all the actors involved can benefit and learn from the relationships that activate resources and activities valuable to meet sustainable goals.

The relationships within the network are bidirectional: Girolomoni cooperative disseminates ESG and sustainability to the network, but at the same time, the network enables the cooperative to be sustainable and combine environmental and social sustainability with economic sustainability.

We are contributing to the literature about ESG and business model (Aldowaish et al., 2022) through the empirical evidence of a case study by showing how the success of a sustainable business model of a small firm can result from a sustainable networking business model to create, deliver and capture value (Bocken et al., 2014) far beyond the boundaries of the individual enterprise. It involves multiple stakeholders, such as small companies, consumers, communities and universities, whose actions, resources and activities feed knowledge and culture about sustainability issues. Furthermore, our findings offer empirical evidence about how stakeholders can be recognized as powerful for high ESG performance (Zumente & Bistrova, 2021) and how these relationships can strengthen business models by spreading consciousness about sustainability.

We recognize that the analysed case could be called an exception, given the peculiar conception of ESG (How can social and environmental choices be made sustainable from an economic point of view?) that overturns the traditional paradigm underpinning an enterprise. But precisely because of its exceptionality, we hope it will inspire research and practice in thinking that another way of conceiving business is possible. It is exceptional, not impossible.

From a practical point of view, we contribute by highlighting how the shift from a sustainable business model to a sustainable networking business model can be a valuable tool to spread sensitivity towards environmental, social and governance issues among micro and small-sized firms. A sustainable networking business model contributes to sustainable goals thanks to resources and activities triggered by the relationships. Thus, leveraging the network can be useful for operational purposes and enhancing efforts towards sustainability in all dimensions. The sustainable network business model presented in this study can be considered a best practice, and we hope it can encourage companies to engage in sustainability. It could be replicated in other contexts to help spread awareness of ESG issues to the micro and small businesses that make up the backbone of the economy and thus foster the creation of systems that are increasingly attentive, responsible and proactive towards sustainability.

The study employs a holistic approach, which makes it possible to examine the company as a whole, to understand how ESG objectives coexist and integrate with those of an economic-financial nature, both at the corporate level and networking level, and analyse the relationship between networking strategy, sustainable business model and performance. Future steps in the research will include further interviews with some of the other actors in the network. This will make it possible to validate, improve and deepen the analysis to reach a model that can allow us to represent, even graphically, the different mechanisms that have been, or will be, identified.

Concerning the limitation, since the research deals with a single-case study, we recognize the need for a comparative study considering other experiences within the same industry and/or within different industries to carry out a cross-case analysis to investigate similarities and differences among cases as regards individual level (e.g. entrepreneurs' personal values, motivation, etc.), business level, networking and contextual factors.

References

Adams, C. A., & Abhayawansa, S. (2022). Connecting the COVID-19 pandemic, environmental, social and governance (ESG) investing and calls for 'harmonisation' of sustainability reporting. *Critical Perspectives on Accounting, 82*, 102309.

Adler, P. S., & Kwon, S.-W. (2002). Social capital: Prospects for a new concept. *The Academy of Management Review, 27*(1), 17–40. https://doi.org/10.2307/4134367

Aldowaish, A., Kokuryo, J., Almazyad, O., & Goi, H. C. (2022). Environmental, social, and governance integration into the business model: Literature review and research agenda. *Sustainability, 14*(5), 2959.

Aureli, S., Del, B., & Demartini, M. (2020). Accountability delle cooperative in tema di sostenibilità e sicurezza alimentare: l'esperienza di CAMST. In M. G. Baldarelli & M. M. Mattei (Eds.), *Liber Amicorum per Antonio Matacena, Collana Aziende pubbliche e imprenditorialità sociale* (pp. 61–76). Franco Angeli.

Bagnoli, C., Dal Mas, F., & Massaro, M. (2019). The 4th industrial revolution: Business models and evidence from the field. *International Journal of E-Services and Mobile Applications, 11*(3), 34–47.

Baker, S. (2006). *Sustainable development*. Routledge.

Ballantyne, D. (2004). Dialogue and its role in the development of relationship specific knowledge. *Journal of Business and Industrial Marketing, 19*(2), 114–123.

Ballard, D. (2005). Using learning processes to promote change for sustainable development. *Action Research, 3*(2), 135–156.

Bocken, N. M., Short, S. W., Rana, P., & Evans, S. (2014). A literature and practice review to develop sustainable business model archetypes. *Journal of Cleaner Production, 65*, 42–56.

Bosworth, G. (2009). Education, mobility and rural business development. *Journal of Small Business and Enterprise Development, 16*(4), 660–677.

Braun, V., & Clarke, V. (2006). Using thematic analysis in psychology. *Qualitative Research in Psychology, 3*(2), 77–101.

Bruntland, G. H. (1987). *Our Common Future*. Oxford University Press.

Calandra, D., Secinaro, S., Massaro, M., Dal Mas, F., & Bagnoli, C. (2023). The link between sustainable business models and Blockchain: A multiple case study approach. *Business Strategy and the Environment, 32*(4), 1403–1417.

Carson, D., Gilmore, A., & Rocks, S. (2004). SME marketing networking: A strategic approach. *Strategic Change, 13*(7), 369–382.
Charles, O. H., Jr., Schmidheiny, S., & Watts, P. (2017). *Walking the talk: The business case for sustainable development*. Routledge.
Chaston, I., & Mangles, T. (2000). Business networks: Assisting knowledge management and competence acquisition within UK manufacturing firms. *Journal of Small Business and Enterprise Development, 7*(2), 160–170.
Ciambotti, M., & Palazzi, F. (2015). Social capital and SMES: An exploratory case study. *Journal of International Business and Economics, 15*(2), 53–64.
Clauss, T. (2017). Measuring business model innovation: Conceptualization, scale development, and proof of performance. *R&D Management, 47*(3), 385–403.
Cortese, D., Rainero, C., & Cantino, V. (2021). Stakeholders' social dialogue about responsibility and sustainability in the food sector. *British Food Journal, 123*(3), 1287–1301.
Del Baldo, M. (2009). I territori della responsabilità sociale. Un modello marchigiano di sviluppo sostenibile. In A. Matacena & M. Del Baldo (Eds.), *Responsabilità sociale d'impresa e territorio. L'esperienza delle piccole e medie imprese marchigiane*. FrancoAngeli.
Doz, Y. L., & Hamel, G. (1998). *Alliance advantage: The art of creating value through partnering*. Harvard Business School.
Du, S., Bhattacharya, C., & Sen, S. (2013). *Corporate Social Responsibility, Multi-Faceted Job-Products, and Employee Outcomes* (August 27, 2013). ESMT Working Paper No. 13–07.
Easton, G., & Araujo, L. (1994). Market exchange, social structures and time. *European Journal of Marketing, 28*(3), 72–84.
EBA European Banking Authority. (2021). *EBA report on management and supervision of ESG risks for credit institutions and investment firms*. https://www.eba.europa.eu/
Eccles, N. S., & Viviers, S. (2011). The origins and meanings of names describing investment practices that integrate a consideration of ESG issues in the academic literature. *Journal of Business Ethics, 104*(2011), 389–402.
Eccles, G. R., Ioannou, I., & Serafeim, G. (2014). The impact of corporate sustainability on organizational processes and performance. *Management Science, 60*(11), 2835–2857.
Eisenhardt, K. M. (1989). Building theories from case study research. *Academy of Management Review, 14*(4), 532–550.
Eisenhardt, K. M., & Graebner, M. E. (2007). Theory building from cases: Opportunities and challenges. *Academy of Management Journal, 50*(1), 25–32.
European Commission. (2020). *User guide to the SME definition*. European Union.
European Commission. (2023). *SME definition*. https://single-market-economy.ec.europa.eu/smes/sme-definition_en. Accessed 13.09.23.
Evans, S., Vladimirova, D., Holgado, M., Van Fossen, K., Yang, M., Silva, E. A., & Barlow, C. Y. (2017). Business model innovation for sustainability: Towards a unified perspective for creation of sustainable business models. *Business Strategy and the Environment, 26*, 597–608.
EY & DNV GL. (2017). *Seize the change. Integrare la sostenibilità nel core business*.
Ford, D., & Mouzas, S. (2013). The theory and practice of business networking. *Industrial Marketing Management, 42*, 433–442.
Fortezza, F., Pagano, A., & Bocconcelli, R. (2021). Serial crowdfunding in start-up development: A business network view. *Journal of Business & Industrial Marketing, 36*(13), 250–262.
Gond, J. P., Grubnic, S., Herzig, C., & Moon, J. (2012). Configuring management control systems: Theorizing the integration of strategy and sustainability. *Management Accounting Research, 23*(3), 205–223.
Håkansson, H., & Snehota, I. (1995). *Developing relationships in business networks*. Routledge.
Håkansson, H., & Snehota, I. (2017). *No business is an Island: Making sense of the interactive business world*. Emerald Publishing Limited.
Håkansson, H., Ford, D., Gadde, L.-E., Snehota, I., & Waluszewski, A. (2009). *Business in networks*. Wiley.

Jämsä, P., Tähtinen, J., Ryan, A., & Pallari, M. (2011). Sustainable SMEs network utilization: The case of food enterprises. *Journal of Small Business and Enterprise Development, 18*(1), 141–156.

Janney, J. J., & Gove, S. (2011). Reputation and corporate social responsibility aberrations, trends, and hypocrisy: Reactions to firm choices in the stock option backdating scandal. *Journal of Management Studies, 48*, 1562–1585.

Jenkins, H. (2006). Small business champions for corporate social responsibility. *Journal of Business Ethics, 67*(3), 241–256.

Kraus, S., Kanbach, D. K., Krysta, P. M., Steinhoff, M. M., & Tomini, N. (2022). Facebook and the creation of the metaverse: Radical business model innovation or incremental transformation? *International Journal of Entrepreneurial Behavior & Research, 28*(9), 52–77.

Li, T.-T., Wang, K., Sueyoshi, T., & Wang, D. D. (2021). ESG: Research Progress and future prospects. *Sustainability, 13*, 11663.

Lozano, R. (2012). Towards better embedding sustainability into companies' systems: An analysis of voluntary corporate initiatives. *Journal of Cleaner Production, 25*, 14–26.

Migliorini, P., Gkisakis, V., Gonzalvez, V., Raigón, M. D., & Bàrberi, P. (2018). Agroecology in Mediterranean Europe: Genesis, state and perspectives. *Sustainability, 10*(8), 2724.

Miles, M. B., Huberman, A. M., & Saldana, J. (2014). *Qualitative data analysis. A methods sourcebook*. Sage Publications.

Nahapiet, J., & Ghoshal, S. (1998). Social capital, intellectual capital, and the organizational advantage. *The Academy of Management Review, 23*(2), 242–266. https://doi.org/10.2307/259373

Nosratabadi, S., Mosavi, A., Shamshirband, S., Zavadskas, E. K., Rakotonirainy, A., & Chau, K. W. (2019). Sustainable business models: A review. *Sustainability, 11*(6), 1663. https://doi.org/10.3390/su11061663

Palazzi, F., & Sentuti, A. (2021). La sicurezza alimentare per le imprese italiane dell'agrifood: barriere, driver e benefici percepiti. *Argomenti, 18*.

Patton, M. Q. (1990). *Qualitative evaluation and research methods*. SAGE Publications, inc.

Payne, G. T., Moore, C. B., Griffis, S. E., & Autry, C. W. (2011). Multilevel challenges and opportunities in social capital research. *Journal of Management, 37*(2), 491–520.

Ryan, A., Kajzer Mitchell, I., & Daskou, S. (2012). An interaction and networks approach to developing sustainable organizations. *Journal of Organizational Change Management, 25*(4), 578–594.

Savio, R., D'Andrassi, E., & Ventimiglia, F. (2023). A systematic literature review on ESG during the COVID-19 pandemic. *Sustainability, 15*(3), 2020. https://doi.org/10.3390/su15032020

Savelli, E., & Murmura, F. (2023). The intention to consume healthy food among older gen-Z: Examining antecedents and mediators. *Food Quality and Preference, 105*, 104788.

Spence, L., & Schmidpeter, R. (2003). SMEs, social capital and the common good. *Journal of Business Ethics, 45*(1), 93–108.

Teece, D. J. (2018). Business models and dynamic capabilities. *Long Range Planning, 51*(1), 40–49.

Van Bussel, L. M., Kuijsten, A., Mars, M., & Van't Veer, P. (2022). Consumers' perceptions on food-related sustainability: A systematic review. *Journal of Cleaner Production, 341*, 130904.

Yin, R. K. (2003). *Case study research: Design and methods* (3rd ed.). Sage.

Zott, C., & Amit, R. (2010). Business model design: An activity system perspective. *Long Range Planning, 43*(2–3), 216–226.

Zumente, I., & Bistrova, J. (2021). ESG importance for long-term shareholder value creation: Literature vs. practice. *Journal of Open Innovation: Technology, Market, and Complexity, 7*(2), 127.

Chapter 35
Barriers and Benefits of Implementing Circular Economy Models: A Case Study Analysis

Filippo Vitolla, Nicola Raimo, Arcangelo Marrone, and Michele Rubino

35.1 Introduction

This study, in the context of environmental, social, and governance (ESG) issues, aims to examine the barriers and benefits of the circular economy in the food sector.

The importance of ESG issues is growing globally, as more and more investors and consumers are concerned about the environmental and social impacts of companies and demand more sustainable and responsible business practices. Additionally, many international organizations, governments, and regulators are pushing for the adoption of ESG standards to improve corporate transparency and accountability. In general, ESG issues have become increasingly relevant because they are a response to the social and environmental challenges of our time, such as climate change and social exclusion. Companies that adopt ESG practices can improve their reputation, minimize risk, and create long-term value for all stakeholders (Raimo et al., 2021a). The growing focus on ESG issues and the imperative ecological transition, underscored by the escalating significance of environmental considerations and recent regulatory interventions in environmental affairs, have spurred companies to seek innovative approaches to conducting their operations (Jabbour et al., 2020). In recent years, there has been an increasingly unanimous recognition that the path toward sustainable production and development necessitates a departure from the traditional linear industrial model toward embracing the principles of the circular economy (Esposito et al., 2023). This shift holds the promise of fostering a more environmentally responsible and socially equitable society (Marcon et al., 2023). The circular economy is capable of breaking the current unsustainable linear economic paradigm based on the extraction of raw materials, mass consumption, and

F. Vitolla · N. Raimo (✉) · A. Marrone · M. Rubino
LUM University, Casamassima, BA, Italy
e-mail: vitolla@lum.it; raimo@lum.it; marrone@lum.it; rubino@lum.it

N. Castellano et al. (eds.), *Environmental, Social, Governance (ESG)*, SIDREA Series in Accounting and Business Administration,
https://doi.org/10.1007/978-3-031-76618-3_35

waste disposal (Ghisellini & Ulgiati, 2020). Circular economy models promote production and consumption systems based on the reuse, recycling, reduction, and recovery of resources to ensure a self-renewing global ecosystem (Esposito et al., 2023; Geissdoerfer et al., 2016; L'Abate et al., 2024; Vitolla et al., 2023). From this perspective, the transition to a circular economy offers a transformative pathway toward achieving sustainable development goals, aligning with the broader objectives of ESG integration and ecological stewardship.

The adoption of circular economy models could guarantee important benefits to companies not only of a financial nature but also connected to greater legitimacy (Murray et al., 2017) and greater compliance with stakeholder expectations (Barnabè & Nazir, 2021; Korhonen et al., 2018). However, as suggested by Kumar et al. (2019), despite the potential of the circular economy, capable of guaranteeing a series of benefits to companies, the full adoption of this production model has not yet been achieved. Furthermore, there are still many companies that have started to implement circular economy models but have encountered different obstacles (Kumar et al., 2019).

In light of this, the obstacles and benefits of implementing circular economy models have attracted the attention of academics (Geng & Doberstein, 2008; Govindan & Hasanagic, 2018; Kumar et al., 2019; Mehmood et al., 2021; Rizos et al., 2016; Wijkman & Skånberg, 2017). However, an in-depth analysis of the actual problems and advantages connected to a wide adoption of circular economy models is necessary in order to guarantee companies a greater awareness of the potential obstacles and benefits of this production model. This study aims to fill this gap in the academic literature by identifying, under the lens of the stakeholder theory, the barriers and benefits of the circular economy in the food sector. This production model takes on particular importance in the food sector since consumers are increasingly eco-aware and evaluate the foods and drinks to be purchased with ever greater attention, consequently creating important pressures on food companies which are therefore increasingly called to integrate sustainable practices into every part of the supply chain. In this regard, this study aims to answer the following two research questions:

RQ1: What are the barriers to the implementation of circular models in the food sector?

RQ2: What are the benefits deriving from the implementation of circular models in the food sector?

This study, in order to fill the literature gap, adopts a qualitative approach (Marschan-Piekkari & Welch, 2004). In particular, it uses the single case study method (Yin, 2008) focused on the Andriani S.p.A. firm, which is considered one of the most important companies in the innovation food sector, with a plant entirely dedicated to gluten-free production and strongly active in the field of sustainability and in the implementation of circular economy models.

This study extends the academic literature relating to the obstacles and advantages associated with the implementation of circular economy strategies. It also offers important implications for policymakers and firms.

The remainder of this work is structured as follows: Sect. 35.2 provides an overview of the literature, while Sect. 35.3 presents the theoretical background. Section 35.4 outlines the research methodology, while Sect. 35.5 presents and discusses the results. Finally, Sect. 35.6 draws overarching conclusions.

35.2 Literature Review

The implementation of circular economy models horizontally includes urban infrastructure, industries, social consumption systems, and cultural environment (Yuan et al., 2006; Zhijun & Nailing, 2007), while vertically it includes three different levels—macro, meso, and micro—represented respectively by governments and international organizations, groups of companies and industrial parks, and consumers and firms (Kumar et al., 2019). In line with the objectives of this study, the literature review focuses attention on the barriers and benefits of the circular economy in the micro context of the firms. At the micro level, firms are encouraged to implement cleaner production models and eco-design (Kumar et al., 2019). Cleaner production models refer to a lower environmental impact of production deriving from a more efficient use of resources throughout the entire process (Su et al., 2013), while eco-design refers to the consideration of environmental issues in the product and service design (Kumar et al., 2019). The integration of these elements allows companies to form environmentally friendly supply chains with an efficient use of resources and materials (Zhijun & Nailing, 2007).

35.2.1 *Barriers to the Circular Economy*

The implementation of circular models by companies encounters different barriers. According to Kumar et al. (2019), it is possible to identify three different categories of barriers: sociopolitical, managerial-environmental, and financial.

From a sociopolitical point of view, a first important barrier identified by the literature is represented by the lack of awareness and knowledge of the principles of the circular economy (Benton et al., 2017; Geng et al., 2009, 2012; Naustdalslid, 2014; Su et al., 2013; Winans et al., 2017; Xue et al., 2010; Yap, 2005). A similar barrier is represented by the difficulty of understanding the circular economy phenomenon (Benton et al., 2017). These barriers exist despite the actions implemented by world governments to spread the concept of circular economy and its basic principles (Benton et al., 2017) and to create environmental education among citizens and firms (Kumar et al., 2019). Indeed, the commitment of governments is often ineffective due to their difficult understanding of circular economy practices (Benton et al., 2017; Geng & Doberstein, 2008; Naustdalslid, 2014). Poor environmental education then generates a further barrier represented by the absence of human resources in possession of capabilities and skills related to the implementation of circular models (Benton et al., 2017; Li & Yu, 2011; Su et al., 2013; Xue et al., 2010; Yap, 2005). This circumstance reduces the possibility for companies to engage in circular models and also limits the possibility for governments to promote circular economy principles among citizens (Benton et al., 2017; Li & Yu, 2011; Su et al., 2013). Fragmented legal systems and poor government accountability are additional barriers (Benton et al., 2017; Geng & Doberstien, 2008; Li & Yu, 2011; Naustdalslid, 2014; Su et al., 2013; Winans et al., 2017). In other words, the absence of circular economy laws and regulations and the low capacity to enforce environmental rules resulting from the weak political support of governments complicate the implementation of circular models by companies (Kumar et al., 2019). There are also barriers related to demand represented by the poor attitude of consumers to purchase regenerated products by virtue of their appearance (Naustdalslid, 2014; Pomponi & Moncaster, 2017; Singh & Ordoñez, 2016; Zhu & Tian, 2016). In other words, very often consumers are used to paying attention to the appearance of the products and not to the environmental impacts and this could reduce the propensity of companies to implement circular production models. Still on the demand side, a further barrier is represented by citizens' reluctance to replace end-of-life products (Park et al., 2010).

From a managerial-environmental point of view, a barrier is represented by the absence of environmental management facilities and programs (Geng & Doberstein, 2008; Su et al., 2013; Yap, 2005). Both academic institutions and governments struggle to develop these elements, complicating the adoption of circular models by companies (Kumar et al., 2019). Furthermore, very often waste resource management systems have a low degree of technological development, which complicates the reuse of materials (Li & Yu, 2011), and often, there is no possibility to create new fields for waste handling (Geng & Doberstien, 2008). These circumstances lead to major difficulties for companies in implementing circular models.

Finally, from a financial point of view, a first general barrier is represented by the cost of implementing circular economy strategies, which require a significant initial investment (Liu & Bai, 2014) and which guarantee returns only in the long term (Kumar et al., 2019). In this regard, the short terms of the manager's mandate and their orientation toward short-term results to which fame and salary are linked could lead companies not to consider the implementation of circular models (Benton et al., 2017; Liu & Bai, 2014; Park et al., 2010). Furthermore, circular economy strategies involve important financial risks that reduce the propensity of companies to transition from linear to circular production and consumption models (Kumar et al., 2019). Furthermore, the lack of financial support from governments and banks also complicates the implementation of circular models by companies (Geng & Doberstein, 2008; Liu & Bai, 2014; Su et al., 2013). In this regard, strong fiscal pressures also make the transition to circular models more difficult (Kumar et al., 2019). Furthermore, the absence of incentives aimed at reducing the use of resources and promoting environmentally friendly activities represents a further barrier to the adoption of circular strategies by companies (Geng et al., 2009; Su et al., 2013). Indeed, the absence of such incentives leads to a low propensity on the part of companies to replace equipment and machinery with strong environmental impacts in favor of new, more environmentally friendly technologies (Kumar et al., 2019). Finally, the circular economy requires collaborative business models aimed at achieving a regular flow of resources and customer satisfaction, which, however, require high costs and reliable information (Liu & Bai, 2014; Pan et al., 2015; Pomponi & Moncaster, 2017; Su et al., 2013; Winans et al., 2017).

35.2.2 Circular Economy Benefits

The circular economy is associated with different benefits. According to Kumar et al. (2019), it is possible to identify three different categories of benefits: sociopolitical, environmental, and financial. From a sociopolitical point of view, the implementation of circular economy strategies strengthens relationships and communication with society and other operators in the sector (Geng et al., 2012; MacArthur, 2013; Sehnem et al., 2019). Indeed, by closing the loop, it is possible to create broader collaborations between different members of the supply chain (Geng et al., 2012; Kumar et al., 2019; MacArthur, 2013). The implementation of circular economy strategies then allows for greater alignment between companies and their customers (MacArthur, 2013). This also results in increased customer satisfaction and attraction of new customers (Kumar et al., 2019). From a broader perspective, the implementation of circular models allows for the creation of new job opportunities for local communities (Geng et al., 2012; MacArthur, 2013; Park et al., 2010; Sehnem et al., 2019; Yuan et al., 2006) and ensures greater environmental awareness and better public health conditions (Geng et al., 2012; Park et al., 2010). In this regard, a greater commitment by companies to circular economy strategies guarantees society greater knowledge of hazardous materials and promotes the use of more environmentally friendly products (Kumar et al., 2019). Furthermore, the implementation of circular economy strategies allows companies greater alignment with laws and regulations (Park et al., 2010), thus guaranteeing greater legitimacy and a reduction in social pressures (Kumar et al., 2019).

From an environmental point of view, first of all the implementation of circular models allows a reduction in negative effects on the environment thanks to the lower consumption of resources (Zhu & Tian, 2016). In particular, circular economy strategies make it possible to reduce waste through an increase in the productivity of materials resulting from recycling and reprocessing and by extending the life cycle (Geng et al., 2012; MacArthur, 2013; Park et al., 2010). Furthermore, circular economy strategies guarantee the protection of different natural resources such as minerals, energy, and water (Kumar et al., 2019) as well as a reduction in emissions of toxic substances and greenhouse gases, along with decreased consumption of fossil fuels (Geng et al., 2012; MacArthur, 2013). In this regard, such strategies have less impact on climate change (Kumar et al., 2019).

Finally, from a financial point of view, if on the one hand circular economy strategies require important initial investments, in the long term they could increase the profitability of companies (Geng et al., 2012; MacArthur, 2013; Park et al., 2010;

Sehnem et al., 2019). This derives from the possibility of creating more sustainable supply chains, minimizing the risks of environmental sanctions, reducing the level of waste production and the cost of production factors (Kumar et al., 2019). Furthermore, closed loop models could allow companies to sell their waste and make profits (Kumar et al., 2019). Finally, the implementation of circular economy strategies also guarantees organizational resilience and allows penetration into new markets and growth of the company (Park et al., 2010). In this regard, circular models are able to ensure a competitive advantage for companies compared to their competitors (Geng et al., 2012; MacArthur, 2013; Park et al., 2010).

35.3 Theoretical Background

This study, in line with other past contributions (Jabbour et al., 2020; Marcon et al., 2023; Marjamaa et al., 2021; Moggi & Dameri, 2021), uses the stakeholder theory to frame companies' commitment to the transition toward the circular economy, specifically exploring the associated barriers and benefits. This theory emphasizes the importance of meeting the needs of a diverse range of individuals, referred to as stakeholders, who possess a vested interest in the operations of the firm (Freeman, 1984; Mitchell et al., 1997; Nicolò et al., 2022; Raimo, 2021). According to this theory, the actions and decisions of a firm are shaped by its stakeholders, defined by Freeman (1984, p. 46) as "any group or individual who can affect or is affected by the achievement of the firm's objectives." The stakeholders pertinent for an organization vary based on its strategies, priorities, and mission (Savage et al., 1991). Clarkson (1995) suggests categorizing stakeholders into primary and secondary groups. Primary stakeholders are essential for the organization's survival (Clarkson, 1995). Secondary stakeholders encompass individuals or entities that affect organizational performance but are not critical for its existence (Clarkson, 1995). Considering all stakeholders enables firms to gain deeper insight and understanding of the interconnected relationships and interdependencies within their ecosystem (Freeman et al., 2020). This interdependence encompasses the creation and exchange of values, encompassing value creation from the firm to stakeholders and vice versa (Marcon et al., 2023). From this perspective, stakeholders serve as both recipients and creators, or co-creators, of value within firms (Freudenreich et al., 2020). The stakeholder theory embodies a business perspective that embraces a comprehensive understanding of the role and purpose of firms, along with the societal repercussions in both the short and long term (Freeman et al., 2020). It represents a more human-centered approach to business, driven by collaborative efforts among individuals, aiming to achieve outcomes that might otherwise be unattainable (Freeman et al., 2020). Hence, establishing robust relationships with both internal and external stakeholders is indispensable for operating a successful business model, as they constitute the foundation of a value creation network (Freudenreich et al., 2020; Moggi & Dameri, 2021). Value creation should be mutually beneficial for all parties involved, ensuring benefits for the various stakeholders (Freudenreich et al., 2020).

Stakeholders are pivotal in the transition from a linear to a circular economy (Marjamaa et al., 2021). The collaborative effort among various stakeholders is paramount in enhancing the likelihood of success in this transition (Moggi & Dameri, 2021; Velter et al., 2020). Indeed, embedding circularity into business models necessitates a systemic approach that encompasses the entirety of the value network, acknowledging the diverse actors within the system and their interconnections (Marcon et al., 2023; Moggi & Dameri, 2021; Zucchella & Previtali, 2019). Sustainability issues are typically multifaceted and demand the engagement of a wide array of stakeholders, including suppliers, customers, local communities, regulatory and governmental authorities, nongovernmental organizations, industry associations, and universities (Marcon et al., 2023). In the circular economy, stakeholders pursue both their individual interests and shared objectives to promote its advancement simultaneously (Marjamaa et al., 2021). Sharing knowledge, resources, infrastructure, and common values, along with fostering mutual trust among stakeholders, is essential prerequisites for cultivating a circular ecosystem (Marcon et al., 2023; Moggi & Dameri, 2021). Thus, stakeholder theory allows to frame the barriers encountered by companies in the transition toward the circular economy, as stakeholders, through influencing strategic decisions, providing resources and collaboration, and shaping the regulatory and social context, are able to favor or hinder the implementation of circular models (Jabbour et al., 2020). Furthermore, the stakeholder theory allows to frame the benefits obtained by companies in the transition toward the circular economy, as the advantages tied to implementing circular models surpass mere shareholder value maximization, fostering shared and sustainable value for the company and a diverse range of stakeholders (Esposito et al., 2023).

35.4 Research Methodology

This study is based on the key elements of qualitative research (Marschan-Piekkari & Welch, 2004). More in detail, it is based on a single case study (Yin, 2008) conducted on the company Andriani S.p.A., which represents an important actor active in the production and marketing of gluten-free pasta and flours. It therefore represents a single case study (Siggelkow, 2007) conducted on a company of excellence with regard to its commitment to sustainability and in particular to the implementation of circular economy strategies. In line with what Eisenhardt (1989) stated, it is therefore reasonable to expect that the analysis of this case study will allow the construction of theoretical contributions of considerable interest and a real understanding of the barriers and benefits of the circular economy strategies. Qualitative research and in particular case study analyses are particularly suitable for the investigation of complex phenomena which have only recently established themselves as important lines of academic research (Eisenhardt, 1989). In this regard, the circular economy represents a particularly complex phenomenon which has become the subject of considerable interest from academics in recent years.

35.4.1 Case Study Selection

The case study conducted in this study focuses on the company Andriani S.p.A. It is considered among the most important companies in the innovation food sector, with a factory entirely dedicated to allergen-free production. Andriani S.p.A. develops and produces a complete range of innovative gluten-free pasta with a variety of naturally gluten-free ingredients. It is present in the major distribution chains and has commercial relationships with over 50 countries around the world. Andriani S.p.A. operates in the food sector both as a copacker for the main brands worldwide and on its own with the production of Felicia Bio® and Biori® brand products.

The Andriani S.p.A. project was born in 2009 with the precise idea of innovating the pasta production and marketing sector by creating a gluten-free, healthy product with an innovative flavor thanks to a variety of new ingredients. Product and process innovation has always characterized the management approach of the company which, since its origins, has been projected toward the multiple challenges that the food innovation sector imposes as a result of the growing competitive tension at an international level.

Flexibility, research, dynamic organization, and innovation represent the main factors that drive the company's performance. Andriani S.p.A. adopts concrete actions and good practices toward all stakeholders. Concreteness, awareness, commitment, sharing, innovation, quality, transparency, respect, culture, justice, and sustainability represent the fundamental values to which Andriani S.p.A. is inspired. The mission instead is to learn from consumers, to innovate food production, and to inspire the entire supply chain to achieve excellence.

In November 2020, the extraordinary assembly of the shareholders, with the aim of allocating new liquidity to innovative and sustainable projects, formalized the transformation of the firm into a Benefit Company. This choice represented for Andriani S.p.A. a precise position, as well as a profound evolution of the approach to business. In 2022, Andriani S.p.A. obtained B Corp certification. Joining the global community of B Corp organizations means pursuing the objectives of creating shared value with ever greater vigor, maximizing the positive impact on employees, communities, the environment, and other stakeholders. Andriani S.p.A. has chosen to contribute to a real transition through concrete projects. In particular, the company has focused attention on different impact areas, including: supply chain and sustainable agriculture, health and well-being, development and valorization of the territory, climate change and circular economy, and valorization of people and group identity.

Andriani S.p.A. provides an insightful case study for analyzing the circular economy. This is not only due to the company's clear commitment to sustainability, but also because of its unique characteristics, such as its limited size and local connotation. Firstly, Andriani S.p.A. has demonstrated a strong dedication to sustainability and the implementation of circular practices. The food sector is notorious for its significant environmental impact, with challenges related to food waste management, water resource usage, and greenhouse gas emissions. However,

Andriani S.p.A. has proactively embraced these challenges, seeking innovative solutions to reduce its environmental footprint. Secondly, the relatively small size of Andriani S.p.A. may make it easier to analyze its practices and impacts. Unlike large multinational corporations that may operate across various sectors and geographical regions, small- and medium-sized enterprises like Andriani S.p.A. tend to have leaner decision-making structures and greater operational transparency. This could facilitate data collection and access to information necessary for in-depth analysis of its circular practices.

Lastly, Andriani S.p.A.'s location in a specific territory provides an opportunity to evaluate the impact of its initiatives on the local community. Firms located in small towns or rural areas may have a closer connection with surrounding communities and can significantly affect the local economy and environment. Hence, the analysis of the barriers and benefits of the circular economy becomes especially intriguing within this specific business context.

35.4.2 Data Collection

In line with previous contributions (McLeod, 2008; Yin, 2006, 2008), this study uses a mixed methodological approach. Data were collected through primary and secondary sources. The primary sources are represented by interviews and direct observation. The interviews were addressed to the Corporate Social Responsibility Manager and the Sustainability Coordinator of the company. Among the different types of interviews, a focused interview was preferred. It "is designed to determine the responses of persons exposed to a situation previously analyzed by the investigator" (Merton & Kendall, 1946, p. 541). The focused interview is particularly suitable as it takes up a short period of time and takes on the characteristics of a small conversation. While leaving space for the interviewees, it follows a certain order of questions derived from the case study research protocol (Merton & Kendall, 1946). During the interviews, simple questions were formulated without any prejudice toward the topics covered (Enns et al., 2011). This circumstance allowed the interviewees, who already knew the topics of the interview in advance, to provide a spontaneous comment about it and to argue their answers freely (Enns et al., 2011). During the interviews, conducted at the company's headquarters, around 50 simple questions were posed to the Corporate Social Responsibility Manager and the Sustainability Coordinator of the company. The initial set of inquiries delved into the broader aspects of the company, seeking to thoroughly understand the intricacies of the corporate environment under examination. Subsequently, the questioning shifted toward actions and strategies pertaining to the circular economy, exploring both product- and process-related perspectives. Following this, the focus turned to barrier analysis, examining challenges encountered both internally and externally within the company. Finally, the last segment of questions centered on elucidating the benefits derived from the implementation of circular models. The selected quantity of questions facilitated a thorough exploration of diverse facets concerning the company's dedication to the circular economy. Simultaneously, it effectively managed the interview duration, ensuring it did not overly encroach upon the company's time or impose undue burden on the interviewees.

The authors conducted direct observations at the headquarters of Andriani S.p.A., specifically focusing on segments of the production process related to the phenomenon under investigation, namely, the circular economy. In particular, they observed aspects of the production process related to the cultivation of spirulina algae. Furthermore, the authors personally attended meetings held by the company with local universities. During these meetings, insights were shared and training was provided on topics related to the circular economy.

Secondary sources are represented by company documents. In particular, the Company Profile, the Sustainability Management Report 2022, and the Impact Report 2022 were examined. The primary function of documentary analysis is to corroborate and support the evidence collected through other sources (Raimo et al., 2021b; Ricciardelli et al., 2020; Yin, 2008). In practice, company documents serve several key purposes. Firstly, they allow for the verification of concepts and terms that have emerged during interviews. Secondly, they facilitate the enhancement of information gathered through interviews by providing additional context and supplementary data. Lastly, company documents enable the drawing of in-depth conclusions about the investigated phenomenon.

As part of the different company documents, the Company Profile is used by the company to present itself to the public in a professional manner and aims to inform users about the products and services offered, the competitive positioning, and growth prospects. The Sustainability Management Report 2022 contains an overview of the commitment and results achieved during the year by Andriani S.p.A. on the subject of corporate social responsibility. This is a document drawn up in accordance with different sustainability standards. Finally, the Impact Report 2022 not only aims to provide feedback through a comparative analysis of planned versus achieved goals for the year but also takes a forward-looking approach. It outlines future objectives and the corresponding planned actions for the upcoming year across various impact areas.

The use of multiple sources guarantees greater value and consistency to the case study analysis. The main advantage is the possibility of guaranteeing a triangulation process. In other words, the use of different sources, guaranteeing a mutual confirmation method, ensures greater accuracy to the results obtained (Morrone et al., 2021; Ricciardelli et al., 2020).

35.4.3 Data Validity and Analysis

The presence of qualitative data requires a process of aggregation and triangulation aimed at ensuring validity and credibility (Ricciardelli et al., 2020). This process corresponds to the reliability tests of quantitative studies (Creswell, 2007; Morrone et al., 2021). In particular, the different triangulations guarantee accuracy, credibility, and validity to the results of qualitative studies (Creswell, 2007; Stake, 2000). Triangulation is broadly defined as "the combination of methodologies in the study of the same phenomenon" (Kaulio & Karlsson, 1998, p. 104). It was born in military sciences and navigation and refers to the use of different reference points to identify the exact position of an element or object (Kaulio & Karlsson, 1998). Subsequently, it was extended to qualitative research and in particular to case study analysis (Kaulio & Karlsson, 1998; Patton, 1987; Yin, 2008). Four different kinds of triangulations are identified by Patton (1987) as having the potential to increase the case study analysis value: methodological triangulation, data triangulation, investigator triangulation, and theory triangulation. The first three triangulation types were used in this research. In particular, methodological triangulation—which draws from a variety of primary and secondary sources—was applied to improve the quality and reliability of the data gathered. By carefully comparing the gathered data, through data triangulation, the authors were able to gain a thorough grasp of the phenomenon under study. Ultimately, the investigator triangulation involved an independent analysis of the phenomenon by the authors who individually conducted direct observation and independently examined the corporate documents. Furthermore, although the authors conducted the interviews together, they examined the information collected separately. By using investigator triangulation, it was possible to improve the quality of the data collected and reduce any bias arising from the authors' beliefs, opinions, and ideas.

The data analysis phase involved a profound interaction between the authors and the data and information collected aimed at understanding their meaning (Strauss & Corbin, 1998). The qualitative nature of the data used made a grounded theory approach more appropriate (Charmaz, 1983). It suggests a procedure that begins with the identification of key points, subsequently evolving into codes, which, in turn, undergo transformation into concepts, rendering the data more usable (Katamba et al., 2016). Ultimately, this process entails utilizing these concepts to construct categories that serve as the foundation for describing and discussing the results (Katamba et al., 2016). The grounded theory approach has been extended with the suggestions provided by other contributions (Creswell, 2007; Katamba et al., 2016; Miles & Huberman, 1994; Strauss & Corbin, 1998; Yin, 2008) in order to optimize the level of analysis. Considering this, the data analysis process comprised organization across three distinct phases. These phases initially encompassed cross-analyzing the raw data with the objective of comprehending the analyzed phenomenon. This involved a meticulous examination of the raw data, leading to the identification of initial conclusions and facilitating the exclusion of data deemed incongruent with the objectives of the study. The second phase was represented by the extrapolation of arguments from the raw data. This phase involved the coding of the data through the identification, naming, extrapolation, and classification of the evidence collected. The general criterion followed for data classification is represented by the source. In particular, the data were classified in relation to the sources used for collection. Finally, the last phase was represented by the interpretation of the data. This phase involved the analysis, understanding, and extraction of meaning from the data collected.

35.5 Results and Discussion

Andriani S.p.A. is committed to the principles of the circular economy through three primary avenues. The first one involves a collaboration with the Apulian startup, ApuliaKundi S.r.l. These two companies have aligned their efforts based on shared values, uniting toward a common objective of environmental sustainability and circular economy. This collaboration represents an innovative entrepreneurial initiative focused on preserving the planet's natural resources, particularly water. The joint effort includes the cultivation of spirulina algae, achieved through the reuse of water resources from the Andriani plant. Specifically, the production of spirulina algae entails the reuse of water used in die washing, following meticulous purification and filtration processes. As can be seen from the Impact Report 2022, the plant, inaugurated in September 2021, allowed the reuse of 1,640,000 L of water for the cultivation of spirulina algae which, thanks to the natural process of photosynthesis, guaranteed the sequestration of CO2 from atmosphere, leading to a further benefit in environmental terms. Once harvested from the production tanks through fine mesh filters, the algae undergo a process of pressing, extrusion, and cold drying to preserve its nutritional qualities. A portion of the dried algae is then utilized by Andriani as an ingredient in the production of organic and naturally gluten-free pasta. The remaining portion is employed by ApuliaKundi for various formulations, including sticks, tablets, and functional products. The production of spirulina algae represents a sustainable alternative to conventional agriculture and, if carried out in a completely natural way, has no costs for the environment (Lim et al., 2021). Its cultivation does not cause pollution and contributes to the reduction of greenhouse gases by capturing CO2 (Lim et al., 2021). It does not cause soil erosion, water contamination, or forest destruction, does not require the use of toxic pesticides and herbicides, and requires less water and energy than any other food (Lafarga et al., 2020).

The second avenue involves Andriani S.p.A.'s installation of a biomass boiler as a measure to mitigate greenhouse gas emissions, which contribute to climate change. Biomass encompasses organic materials like buckwheat bran and virgin wood waste derived from various activities such as wood processing, agriculture, and forest maintenance. The primary objective of this intervention is to harness the potential of these organic materials, rather than discarding them as waste, by generating energy through a purpose-built biomass boiler. This approach can be viewed as a means of waste valorization, aiming to derive additional benefits, such as energy production, from these materials rather than treating them solely as disposable waste.

The third avenue concerns the participation of Andriani S.p.A. to training activities on the topic of the circular economy in collaboration with Apulian and national universities. In particular, Andriani S. p. A. has renewed its partnership with the University of Gastronomic Sciences over the years as Supporting Member, providing scholarships. This partnership allows Andriani S.p.A. to participate actively in the life of the University, joining research projects and sharing commitment and strategies to build new sustainable food production and consumption scenarios at a national and international level.

Concerning RQ1 and the barriers to the circular economy, interviews with the Corporate Social Responsibility Manager and the Sustainability Coordinator highlighted issues linked to a relative lack of knowledge within the specific context in which the firm operates (Rizos et al., 2016). This points toward a deficiency in information or awareness regarding circular economy practices in the food sector. Moreover, challenges related to inadequate implementation have emerged, suggesting that, despite possessing theoretical knowledge among operators in the food sector, this knowledge may not be effectively translated into tangible actions in practice. In essence, while there is awareness of circular economy practices in the food sector, there is a deficit in the adoption and execution of these practices. In this regard, the examined company encountered difficulties in formulating and disseminating a cohesive vision to all employees regarding the importance of the circular economy (Winans et al., 2017). Even during the focus groups organized with stakeholders and in particular with suppliers, it encountered difficulties in explaining the principles and logic of the circular economy. Another closely interconnected barrier is associated with the challenge of locating skilled workers in the area who possess the requisite knowledge and skills related to the circular economy, such as materials engineers. From this standpoint, the barrier emerges due to the necessity of engaging relevant stakeholders possessing specific characteristics in the development of a collaborative circular business model (De Angelis et al., 2018; Sousa-Zomer et al., 2018). Additional barriers are associated with legal and regulatory frameworks (Kazancoglu et al., 2021). In this context, the examined company faced challenges related to the utilization of the biomethane trigenerator. While legislation provides incentives for biomethane use in transportation, it appears less supportive of its use for generating other forms of energy. From this standpoint, government support is an absolute necessity for transitioning companies' linear business models into circular economy business models (Kumar et al., 2019). Lastly, Andriani S.p.A. encountered financial barriers associated with accessing funds offered by the National Recovery and Resilience Plan. These challenges are shared by numerous companies in the area, arising from the extensive and complex documentation requirements, alongside tight deadlines and prolonged waiting periods. Indeed, the implementation of circular models involves higher costs and exposes companies to greater financial risks (Kirchherr et al., 2018). Nevertheless, the impact of this barrier was mitigated through collaboration with various banking institutions, enabling the company to secure financial resources on favorable terms due to its commitment to sustainable development.

Despite the presence of these obstacles, several compelling factors have propelled the adoption of circular models within the examined company. The pivotal force and primary driver behind the commitment to circular economy strategies stem from the top management's strong orientation toward sustainability (Hina et al., 2022). Additionally, there is a groundswell of interest among lower level employees toward the implementation of circular models and sustainable practices, a momentum supported by Andriani S.p.A.'s commitment to creating value that transcends mere economic profit (Rizos et al., 2016). The analysis of competitors' circularity levels has further acted as a catalyst for embracing circular models, alongside the facilitative influence of the company's size. The geographical context in which the company operates has also played a supportive role in reinforcing the commitment to circular economy strategies, particularly considering the substantial agricultural connotation of the area.

Regarding RQ2, the commitment to adopting circular models has yielded notable advantages for the company. The conducted interviews primarily showcased benefits associated with corporate reputation. The integration of circular models has, indeed, resulted in the fortification of the brand value and corporate image (Tognetti et al., 2015). Specifically, communicating the commitment to the circular economy to customers and stakeholders at large has played a pivotal role in enhancing the perception of both the brand and the company. Moreover, the implementation of circular models has yielded relational benefits by fostering new collaborations with other industrial entities. Additionally, it has facilitated closer ties with various university institutions, aiming to establish new collaborations and partnerships (Sehnem et al., 2019). Further benefits are also related to human capital. The implementation of circular models has heightened awareness among human resources regarding the significance of sustainability principles (Sehnem et al., 2019). This heightened awareness translates into increased employee engagement and alignment with the company's sustainable initiatives, thereby contributing to a more conscious and sustainability-oriented organizational culture. From a financial standpoint, the examined company has incurred increased costs related to investments in circular economy practices, such as spirulina alga production plants. However, the examined company anticipates significant financial gains in the medium to long term, primarily tied to the aforementioned impacts of adopting circular models on the intangible aspects of company management.

The results obtained in relation to barriers to the circular economy are in line with previous studies conducted in other geographical areas and sectors. In particular, they confirm what has been found by previous studies in relation to the lack of awareness and knowledge of the principles of the circular economy (Benton et al., 2017; Geng et al., 2009, 2012; Naustdalslid, 2014; Su et al., 2013; Winans et al., 2017; Xue et al., 2010; Yap, 2005). They also confirm the problems related to regulations that limit the adoption and implementation of circular models (Benton et al., 2017; Geng & Doberstien, 2008; Li & Yu, 2011; Naustdalslid, 2014; Su et al., 2013; Winans et al., 2017; Kumar et al., 2019).

The results obtained regarding the benefits of the circular economy are also in line with what was found by previous studies conducted in other geographical areas and sectors. In particular, they confirm what previous studies have found regarding the ability of the circular economy to guarantee greater alignment between companies and their customers (MacArthur, 2013). Furthermore, they confirm the financial effects of circular economy strategies which, in the short term, lead to an increase in costs and in the medium to long term could increase the profitability of companies (Geng et al., 2012; MacArthur, 2013; Park et al., 2010).

35.6 Conclusions

The shift toward a circular economy presents a transformative route to realizing sustainable development objectives, harmonizing with the overarching aims of ESG integration and ecological stewardship. This study was positioned within this academic discourse and aimed to investigate the integration of circular models within the food sector. Specifically, it aimed to address two distinct research questions pertaining to the barriers and benefits of implementing circular economy strategies in this sector. To answer these research questions and provide a comprehensive understanding of the challenges faced by companies in the food sector when adopting circular models, as well as the associated benefits, a single case analysis was conducted. This approach aimed to offer a holistic overview of the landscape in which companies in the food sector operate concerning the implementation of circular models. Regarding the barriers, the findings revealed challenges linked to a relative lack of knowledge within the specific context. Moreover, difficulties were identified in securing qualified personnel in the field of circular economy. Additionally, obstacles associated with the impact of laws and regulations were identified. Concerning the benefits, the results highlighted positive effects stemming from the implementation of circular models, primarily impacting intangible aspects such as human and relational capitals.

This study guarantees an important contribution to the academic literature. In the first place it enriches the stream of literature relating to the circular economy which is still limited and needs further investigations. In particular, the focus of this analysis on the food sector represents a noteworthy novelty in view of the great importance that the circular economy assumes in this sector. Secondly, it shows an overview of the barriers and benefits connected to the implementation of circular models identifying specific classifications that can guide future research.

This study also provides important implications for policymakers and firms. In particular, the barriers identified by this study could guide policymakers called to facilitate the path of companies toward the implementation of circular models. In this context, it is imperative for authorities to enact laws and regulations, along with incentives, designed to encourage companies' engagement with circular economy strategies. Additionally, promoting targeted educational and awareness campaigns is essential to foster the adoption of sustainable practices and encourage adherence to the principles of the circular economy. Moreover, policymakers ought to nurture collaboration among firms, the public sector, nongovernmental organizations, and other stakeholders to cultivate integrated solutions for tackling the challenges associated with implementing circular economy models. Additionally, they should facilitate the provision of technical support and guidance to companies seeking to transition to circular business models. This could be achieved through initiatives such as training programs, mentoring, or assistance in navigating organizational change. For their part, rather than relying on conventional practices, firms should increasingly adopt circular models, particularly considering the substantial benefits identified in this study. In this context, they ought to commit earnestly to recycling, optimize processes, diminish dependence on virgin raw materials, and embrace reusing and reconditioning to prolong the lifespan of goods. Moreover, firms should actively pursue sustainable design principles to craft products and services that are more durable, recyclable, and easily repairable. Furthermore, incorporating the use of renewable energy should be a priority for firms.

However, this study is not without limitations. The main limitation is connected to the analysis of a single case study which could limit the generalization of the obtained results. However, the choice of a strategic case study (Seawright & Gerring, 2008), such as the one examined, makes possible an adequate extension of the results obtained. Therefore, this limitation does not reduce the general quality of the work and offers important starting points for future research. In this regard, they will be able to extend the analysis to more firms by adopting the multiple case study methodology.

References

Barnabè, F., & Nazir, S. (2021). Investigating the interplays between integrated reporting practices and circular economy disclosure. *International Journal of Productivity and Performance Management, 70*(8), 2001–2031.

Benton, D., Hazell, J., & Hill, J. (2017). *The guide to the circular economy: Capturing value and managing material risk*. Routledge.

Charmaz, K. (1983). The grounded theory method: An explication and interpretation. In *Contemporary field research* (pp. 109–126). Little, Brown and Company.

Clarkson, M. E. (1995). A stakeholder framework for analyzing and evaluating corporate social performance. *Academy of Management Review, 20*(1), 92–117.

Creswell, J. W. (2007). *Qualitative inquiry and research design: Choosing among five approaches*. Sage.

De Angelis, R., Howard, M., & Miemczyk, J. (2018). Supply chain management and the circular economy: Towards the circular supply chain. *Production Planning & Control, 29*(6), 425–437.

Eisenhardt, K. M. (1989). Building theories from case study research. *Academy of Management Review, 14*(4), 532–550.

Enns, H., McFarlin, D. B., & Sweeney, P. B. (2011). How CIOs overcome the competing values challenge: Irish CIOs' perspectives. *Communications of the Association for Information Systems, 28*(1), 549–560.

Esposito, B., Raimo, N., Malandrino, O., & Vitolla, F. (2023). Circular economy disclosure and integrated reporting: The role of corporate governance mechanisms. *Business Strategy and the Environment, 32*(8), 5403–5419.

Freeman, R. E. (1984). *Strategic management: A stakeholder approach*. Pitman.

Freeman, R. E., Phillips, R., & Sisodia, R. (2020). Tensions in stakeholder theory. *Business & Society, 59*(2), 213–231.

Freudenreich, B., Lüdeke-Freund, F., & Schaltegger, S. (2020). A stakeholder theory perspective on business models: Value creation for sustainability. *Journal of Business Ethics, 166*(1), 3–18.

Geissdoerfer, M., Bocken, N. M., & Hultink, E. J. (2016). Design thinking to enhance the sustainable business modelling process–a workshop based on a value mapping process. *Journal of Cleaner Production, 135*, 1218–1232.

Geng, Y., & Doberstein, B. (2008). Developing the circular economy in China: Challenges and opportunities for achieving 'leapfrog development'. *The International Journal of Sustainable Development & World Ecology, 15*(3), 231–239.

Geng, Y., Zhu, Q., Doberstein, B., & Fujita, T. (2009). Implementing China's circular economy concept at the regional level: A review of progress in Dalian, China. *Waste Management, 29*(2), 996–1002.

Geng, Y., Fu, J., Sarkis, J., & Xue, B. (2012). Towards a national circular economy indicator system in China: An evaluation and critical analysis. *Journal of Cleaner Production, 23*(1), 216–224.

Ghisellini, P., & Ulgiati, S. (2020). Circular economy transition in Italy. Achievements, perspectives and constraints. *Journal of Cleaner Production, 243*, 118360.

Govindan, K., & Hasanagic, M. (2018). A systematic review on drivers, barriers, and practices towards circular economy: A supply chain perspective. *International Journal of Production Research, 56*(1–2), 278–311.

Hina, M., Chauhan, C., Kaur, P., Kraus, S., & Dhir, A. (2022). Drivers and barriers of circular economy business models: Where we are now, and where we are heading. *Journal of Cleaner Production, 333*, 130049.

Jabbour, C. J. C., Seuring, S., de Sousa Jabbour, A. B. L., Jugend, D., Fiorini, P. D. C., Latan, H., & Izeppi, W. C. (2020). Stakeholders, innovative business models for the circular economy and sustainable performance of firms in an emerging economy facing institutional voids. *Journal of Environmental Management, 264*, 110416.

Katamba, D., Marvin Nkiko, C., & Ademson, C. (2016). Managing stakeholders' influence on embracing business code of conduct and ethics in a local pharmaceutical company: Case of Kampala pharmaceutical industries (KPI). *Review of International Business and Strategy, 26*(2), 261–290.

Kaulio, M. A., & Karlsson, I. M. (1998). Triangulation strategies in user requirements investigations: A case study on the development of an IT-mediated service. *Behaviour & Information Technology, 17*(2), 103–112.

Kazancoglu, I., Sagnak, M., Kumar Mangla, S., & Kazancoglu, Y. (2021). Circular economy and the policy: A framework for improving the corporate environmental management in supply chains. *Business Strategy and the Environment, 30*(1), 590–608.

Kirchherr, J., Piscicelli, L., Bour, R., Kostense-Smit, E., Muller, J., Huibrechtse-Truijens, A., & Hekkert, M. (2018). Barriers to the circular economy: Evidence from the European Union (EU). *Ecological Economics, 150*, 264–272.

Korhonen, J., Nuur, C., Feldmann, A., & Birkie, S. E. (2018). Circular economy as an essentially contested concept. *Journal of Cleaner Production, 175*, 544–552.

Kumar, V., Sezersan, I., Garza-Reyes, J. A., Gonzalez, E. D., & Al-Shboul, M. D. A. (2019). Circular economy in the manufacturing sector: Benefits, opportunities and barriers. *Management Decision, 57*(4), 1067–1086.

L'Abate, V., Raimo, N., Albergo, F., & Vitolla, F. (2024). Social media to disseminate circular economy information. An empirical analysis on twitter. *Corporate Social Responsibility and Environmental Management, 31*(1), 528–539.

Lafarga, T., Fernández-Sevilla, J. M., González-López, C., & Acién-Fernández, F. G. (2020). Spirulina for the food and functional food industries. *Food Research International, 137*, 109356.

Li, J., & Yu, K. (2011). A study on legislative and policy tools for promoting the circular economic model for waste management in China. *Journal of Material Cycles and Waste Management, 13*, 103–112.

Lim, H. R., Khoo, K. S., Chew, K. W., Chang, C. K., Munawaroh, H. S. H., Kumar, P. S., & Show, P. L. (2021). Perspective of Spirulina culture with wastewater into a sustainable circular bioeconomy. *Environmental Pollution, 284*, 117492.

Liu, Y., & Bai, Y. (2014). An exploration of firms' awareness and behavior of developing circular economy: An empirical research in China. *Resources, Conservation and Recycling, 87*, 145–152.

MacArthur, E. (2013). *Towards a Circular Economy—Opportunities for the consumer goods sector*. https://www.ellenmacarthurfoundation.org/towards-the-circular-economy-vol-2-opportunities-for-the-consumer-goods

Marcon, M., Provensi, T., Sehnem, S., Campos, L. M., & Queiroz, A. A. F. S. L. (2023). The internalisation of the circular economy and ESG in Brazilian B corps from the perspective of the stakeholder theory. *Sustainable Development, 31*(5), 3513–3527.

Marjamaa, M., Salminen, H., Kujala, J., Tapaninaho, R., & Heikkinen, A. (2021). A sustainable circular economy: Exploring stakeholder interests in Finland. *South Asian Journal of Business and Management Cases, 10*(1), 50–62.

Marschan-Piekkari, R., & Welch, C. (2004). *Handbook of qualitative research methods for international business*. Edward Elgar.

McLeod, S. A. (2008). *Simply psychology: case study method in psychology*. Retrieved from www.simplypsychology.org/case-study.html

Mehmood, A., Ahmed, S., Viza, E., Bogush, A., & Ayyub, R. M. (2021). Drivers and barriers towards circular economy in Agri-food supply chain: A review. *Business Strategy & Development, 4*(4), 465–481.

Merton, R. K., & Kendall, P. L. (1946). The focused interview. *American Journal of Sociology, 51*(6), 541–557.

Miles, M. B., & Huberman, A. M. (1994). *Qualitative data analysis: An expanded sourcebook*. Sage.

Mitchell, R. K., Agle, B. R., & Wood, D. J. (1997). Toward a theory of stakeholder identification and salience: Defining the principle of who and what really counts. *Academy of Management Review, 22*(4), 853–886.

Moggi, S., & Dameri, R. P. (2021). Circular business model evolution: Stakeholder matters for a self-sufficient ecosystem. *Business Strategy and the Environment, 30*(6), 2830–2842.

Morrone, D., Raimo, N., Tarulli, A., & Vitolla, F. (2021). Digitalisation in the hospitality industry: Motivations, effects and role of COVID-19. *International Journal of Digital Culture and Electronic Tourism, 3*(3–4), 257–270.

Murray, A., Skene, K., & Haynes, K. (2017). The circular economy: An interdisciplinary exploration of the concept and application in a global context. *Journal of Business Ethics, 140*, 369–380.

Naustdalslid, J. (2014). Circular economy in China–the environmental dimension of the harmonious society. *International Journal of Sustainable Development & World Ecology, 21*(4), 303–313.

Nicolò, G., Ricciardelli, A., Raimo, N., & Vitolla, F. (2022). Visual disclosure through integrated reporting. *Management Decision, 60*(4), 976–994.

Pan, S. Y., Du, M. A., Huang, I. T., Liu, I. H., Chang, E. E., & Chiang, P. C. (2015). Strategies on implementation of waste-to-energy (WTE) supply chain for circular economy system: A review. *Journal of Cleaner Production, 108*, 409–421.

Park, J., Sarkis, J., & Wu, Z. (2010). Creating integrated business and environmental value within the context of China's circular economy and ecological modernization. *Journal of Cleaner Production, 18*(15), 1494–1501.

Patton, M. Q. (1987). *How to use qualitative methods in evaluation*. Sage.

Pomponi, F., & Moncaster, A. (2017). Circular economy for the built environment: A research framework. *Journal of Cleaner Production, 143*, 710–718.

Raimo, N. (2021). *Integrated reporting: State of play, theoretical underpinnings and empirical insights: The role of corporate governance mechanisms*. FrancoAngeli.

Raimo, N., Caragnano, A., Zito, M., Vitolla, F., & Mariani, M. (2021a). Extending the benefits of ESG disclosure: The effect on the cost of debt financing. *Corporate Social Responsibility and Environmental Management, 28*(4), 1412–1421.

Raimo, N., De Turi, I., Ricciardelli, A., & Vitolla, F. (2021b). Digitalization in the cultural industry: Evidence from Italian museums. *International Journal of Entrepreneurial Behavior & Research, 28*(8), 1962–1974.

Ricciardelli, A., Raimo, N., Manfredi, F., & Vitolla, F. (2020). Urban civic network as practice of social change and innovation. A case-study analysis. *Corporate Social Responsibility and Environmental Management, 27*(5), 1989–2003.

Rizos, V., Behrens, A., Van der Gaast, W., Hofman, E., Ioannou, A., Kafyeke, T., & Topi, C. (2016). Implementation of circular economy business models by small and medium-sized enterprises (SMEs): Barriers and enablers. *Sustainability, 8*(11), 1212.

Savage, G. T., Nix, T. W., Whitehead, C. J., & Blair, J. D. (1991). Strategies for assessing and managing organizational stakeholders. *Academy of Management Perspectives, 5*(2), 61–75.

Seawright, J., & Gerring, J. (2008). Case selection techniques in case study research: A menu of qualitative and quantitative options. *Political Research Quarterly, 61*(2), 294–308.

Sehnem, S., Vazquez-Brust, D., Pereira, S. C. F., & Campos, L. M. (2019). Circular economy: Benefits, impacts and overlapping. *Supply Chain Management: An International Journal, 24*(6), 784–804.

Siggelkow, N. (2007). Persuasion with case studies. *Academy of Management Journal, 50*(1), 20–24.

Singh, J., & Ordoñez, I. (2016). Resource recovery from post-consumer waste: Important lessons for the upcoming circular economy. *Journal of Cleaner Production, 134*, 342–353.

Sousa-Zomer, T. T., Magalhães, L., Zancul, E., & Cauchick-Miguel, P. A. (2018). Exploring the challenges for circular business implementation in manufacturing companies: An empirical investigation of a pay-per-use service provider. *Resources, Conservation and Recycling, 135*, 3–13.

Stake, R. E. (2000). Case studies. In N. K. Denzin & Y. S. Lincoln (Eds.), *Handbook of qualitative research* (pp. 435–454). Sage.

Strauss, A., & Corbin, J. (1998). *Basics of qualitative research: Techniques and procedures for developing grounded theory*. Sage.

Su, B., Heshmati, A., Geng, Y., & Yu, X. (2013). A review of the circular economy in China: Moving from rhetoric to implementation. *Journal of Cleaner Production, 42*, 215–227.

Tognetti, A., Grosse-Ruyken, P. T., & Wagner, S. M. (2015). Green supply chain network optimization and the trade-off between environmental and economic objectives. *International Journal of Production Economics, 170*, 385–392.

Velter, M. G. E., Bitzer, V., Bocken, N. M. P., & Kemp, R. (2020). Sustainable business model innovation: The role of boundary work for multi-stakeholder alignment. *Journal of Cleaner Production, 247*, 119497.

Vitolla, F., L'Abate, V., Petruzzella, F., Raimo, N., & Salvi, A. (2023). Circular economy disclosure in sustainability reporting: The effect of firm characteristics. *Sustainability, 15*(3), 2200.

Wijkman, A., & Skånberg, K. (2017). *The Circular Economy and Benefits for Society-A study pertaining to Finland, France, the Netherlands, Spain and Sweden*. UN Environment Document Repository.

Winans, K., Kendall, A., & Deng, H. (2017). The history and current applications of the circular economy concept. *Renewable and Sustainable Energy Reviews, 68*, 825–833.

Xue, B., Chen, X. P., Geng, Y., Guo, X. J., Lu, C. P., Zhang, Z. L., & Lu, C. Y. (2010). Survey of officials' awareness on circular economy development in China: Based on municipal and county level. *Resources, Conservation and Recycling, 54*(12), 1296–1302.

Yap, N. T. (2005). Towards a circular economy. *Greener Management International, 50*, 11–24.

Yin, R. K. (2006). Mixed methods research: Are the methods genuinely integrated or merely parallel. *Research in the Schools, 13*(1), 41–47.

Yin, R. K. (2008). *Case study research: Design and methods (Applied social research methods)*. Sage.

Yuan, Z., Bi, J., & Moriguichi, Y. (2006). The circular economy: A new development strategy in China. *Journal of Industrial Ecology, 10*(1–2), 4–8.

Zhijun, F., & Nailing, Y. (2007). Putting a circular economy into practice in China. *Sustainability Science, 2*(1), 95–101.

Zhu, Q., & Tian, Y. (2016). Developing a remanufacturing supply chain management system: A case of a successful truck engine remanufacturer in China. *Production Planning & Control, 27*(9), 708–716.

Zucchella, A., & Previtali, P. (2019). Circular business models for sustainable development: A "waste is food" restorative ecosystem. *Business Strategy and the Environment, 28*(2), 274–285.

Chapter 36
Transforming ESG Accountability Practices into Managerial Ones

Antonio Leotta, Carmela Rizza, Daniela Ruggeri, and Mariastella Messina

36.1 Introduction

Over the past few years, there has been a significant increase in the number of organisations producing sustainability reports. Interest in why firms conduct environmental, social and governance (ESG) activity is longstanding and increasing (Huang, 2021). From the literature, the motivations for preparing ESG reports are predominantly to meet stakeholders' expectations (Burritt & Schaltegger, 2010). Indeed, the ESG report was originally designed for external purposes. However, certain scholars are now shifting their attention towards ESG potential to enhance the managerial decision-making process (Amir & Serafeim, 2018; Gatti et al., 2018). The environmental accounting information gathered for external reporting can serve as a starting point for organisations that have never attempted to collect environmental information for internal decision-making purposes (Qian et al., 2011). Scholars have recently begun to focus on the potential of this tool to support the managerial decision-making process, that is on its effects on decision-making processes, and on managerial practices (Chiucchi et al., 2018). According to this stream of research, empirical evidence has shown the increasing use of ESG reports, particularly for internal communication purposes and sustainability management.

However, internal communication management and external communication must be integrated to promote comprehensive environmental management and best address stakeholders' pressures (Burritt, 2012). By including ESG reports in internal decision-making processes, companies can signal a genuine commitment of the organisation, aligning it with its mission and values (Garcia-Torea et al., 2023; Passetti et al., 2018). Despite this, the integration of sustainability control tools

A. Leotta (✉) · C. Rizza · D. Ruggeri · M. Messina
Department of Economics and Business, University of Catania, Catania, Italy
e-mail: antonio.leotta@unict.it

N. Castellano et al. (eds.), *Environmental, Social, Governance (ESG)*, SIDREA Series in Accounting and Business Administration,
https://doi.org/10.1007/978-3-031-76618-3_36

into management control systems (MCS) is often lacking. The absence of such integration would suggest a conception of reporting and related sustainability efforts by companies primarily for greenwashing and/or for legitimacy, especially when a company adopts a sustainability strategy primarily for external purposes (Cinquini et al., 2016).

However, there is a lack of a clear picture, data and empirical evidence of the advantages of integrating sustainability reports in the decision-making process (Hristov et al., 2022). To the best of our knowledge, few studies have focused on internal mechanisms and processes carried out to implement the new approach to reporting, especially those studies focused on "why" or "what" rather than on "how" the ESG reports are managed and implemented. When ESG practices are deeply rooted in the organisation's values, they have the potential to influence a company's behaviour and promote organisational change in strategic planning, decision-making and performance measurement processes (Amir & Serafeim, 2018; Chiucchi et al., 2018; Ciccola et al., 2023; Cinquini et al., 2016; Clementino & Perkins, 2021; Contrafatto & Burns, 2013; Garcia-Torea et al., 2023; van Duuren et al., 2016). However, existing studies have not thoroughly investigated how and to what extent ESG practices drive change within organisations, indicating a need for further research in this area (Cinquini et al., 2016; Passetti et al., 2018).

This chapter aims to contribute to filling the research gap emerging from previous studies by addressing the following research question: how do ESG practices evolve from accountability practices to accountability and managerial practices able to support decision-making and control processes?

In addressing the research question raised above, we use the theoretical lens proposed by Burns and Scapens (2000) for studying organisational changes. Even though widely used in management accounting change literature, Burns and Scapens' (2000) framework has potentials in the field of sustainability accounting, which includes ESG. The framework underscores how each of the four stages (encoding, enacting, reproduction and institutionalisation) plays a crucial role in influencing the successful institutionalisation of the ESG report, emphasising the importance of both synchronic and diachronic elements. Understanding the transformation of ESG accountability practices into both accountability and managerial practices requires an examination of the interaction between institutional and practical realms within organisational processes.

To address the research question raised above, the authors conducted a longitudinal case study focusing on a company referred to as Greenlife, chosen for its significant commitment to sustainability. The data for this study were obtained through document analysis and interviews. The interpretation of the collected data was guided by Burns and Scapens' (2000) framework, which served as the "method theory" (Lukka & Vinnari, 2014).

The findings demonstrate how Burns and Scapens' (2000) framework has been utilised to illustrate the evolution of ESG practices. Initially, the ESG report started as a form of accountability. Then, it evolved into a combined accountability and managerial practice that supports decision-making and control processes.

The chapter contributes to the ESG literature, by exploring how ESG practices affect decision-making processes (Burritt & Schaltegger, 2010; Chiucchi et al., 2018; Ciccola et al., 2023), highlighting that the presence of managerial practices favours the transformation of the ESG report from accountability practices into accountability and managerial practices. Furthermore, the institutional perspective allows us to delve into how changes occurred and how the interplay between ESG and managerial practices stimulated an ongoing participative change process.

The remainder of the chapter is structured as follows: the next section provides a review of the relevant literature on the topic. Subsequently, we present the theoretical framework, research methodology and the company profile in the following two sections. We then describe the empirical findings. Finally, we conclude with remarks on the study's contributions and limitations in the last section.

36.2 Literature Background

In recent years, the increasing focus on transparency and accountability has led to the widespread adoption of ESG practices (Drempetic et al., 2020). Contributions have highlighted two main approaches. Firstly, the outside-in approach focuses on meeting stakeholders' expectations (Burritt & Schaltegger, 2010), providing data for external reporting to communicate information to various stakeholders and to ensure compliance in line with the regulatory issues. Considering ESG reporting as a compliance exercise (Cinquini et al., 2016), research in this field has primarily outlined the role of ESG practices as a tool for accountability (Aouadi & Marsat, 2018; Duque-Grisales & Aguilera-Caracuel, 2021; Fabrizio & Kim, 2019; Fatemi et al., 2018; Nirino et al., 2021; Zhou et al., 2022). Secondly, some scholars have started assigning more relevance to the inside-out effect of ESG practices. Despite ESG being initially developed for external purposes, scholars have begun to focus on this tool to support the managerial decision-making process (Amir & Serafeim, 2018; Gatti et al., 2018). Coherently, management control studies have investigated how and to what extent MCS can support companies in the achievement of sustainability strategies (Castellano & Felden, 2021). Molinari et al. (2021) provided evidence about the role of MCS in sustaining the implementation of sustainability strategies and in supporting nonfinancial reporting, confirming the findings of Burritt and Schaltegger (2010) which outlined the relevance of ESG practices for supporting internal communication and sustainable investment decisions (Sciarelli et al., 2021). Combining the inside-out and outside-in approaches may pose some challenges, in implementing both of them in a coherent way (Boiral, 2013; Bouten & Hoozée, 2013; Delmas & Burbano, 2011; Garcia-Torea et al., 2023; Graafland & Smid, 2016).

The incorporation of ESG into decision-making could be indicative of an authentic organisational commitment, with a concomitant reflection within the mission and values of the organisation (Garcia-Torea et al., 2023; Passetti et al., 2018). Embedded in the organisations' values, these practices can influence firms' behaviours and facilitate organisational changes (Cinquini et al., 2016; Contrafatto & Burns, 2013; van Duuren et al., 2016). In particular, Clementino and Perkins (2021) discussed companies' responses to ESG ratings, showing that firms may conform to or resist ratings, suggesting that ESG ratings can contribute to bringing new issues into the strategies of companies, promoting internal changes. Similarly, Chiucchi et al. (2018) investigated how Integrated Reporting was used as a tool for communicating company performance to entrepreneurs for enriching company MCS to visualise and measure overall company performance. Recently, Ciccola et al. (2023) investigated the internal use of Integrated Report and its relationships with decision-making, emphasising how the integration of sustainability-related goals within corporate strategy and decision-making processes leads to periodically monitoring sustainability information for strategic and operational reasons. All these studies suggest that ESG reporting can be a catalyst for organisational changes by integrating sustainability performance data into strategic planning, decision-making and performance measurement processes (Hristov et al., 2022; Passetti et al., 2018; Stubbs & Higgins, 2014). Contrafatto and Burns (2013) investigated the relationship between organisational change and social, environmental accounting and reporting, as well as the role of management accounting in facilitating such organisational dynamics. Crucial to this ongoing process of organisational change was the production, utilisation and evolution of the information system within the case company.

According to IFAC 2022, ESG should be integrated into the purpose and strategy of the company. Therefore, pushing companies to adopt sustainable strategies is not just embracing ethical responsibility; rather, the resulting positive returns in terms of economic performance, organisational efficiency, competitive ability and improved reputation make it particularly attractive (Naciti et al., 2022).

However, integrating sustainability into strategic decision-making necessitates a clear understanding of its benefits, key value drivers and potential solutions. Hristov et al. (2022) posed two research questions: "What are the advantages of incorporating sustainability initiatives into strategic decision-making?" and "How can sustainability be integrated into corporate strategy to promote sustainable development?" (p. 83). These research questions stem from the recognition that while some research suggests positive outcomes from integrating sustainability into corporate strategy, primarily in terms of financial benefits, little is known about the primary sustainability dimensions that managers consider in practice and how these dimensions might impact overall corporate performance. Consequently, sustainability issues have often remained disconnected from corporate strategy.

The findings by Passetti et al. (2018) revealed that some companies have made efforts to integrate environmental sustainability into their mission and values. However, the study emphasised the significance of prioritising internal changes, initiated through environmental planning, to facilitate organisational transformation. In alignment with Stubbs and Higgins' (2014) research, there is a need to foster a comprehensive understanding of the changes in MCS experienced by adopting Integrated Reporting (IR), or to ascertain the degree to which IR fosters innovative disclosure mechanisms. Previous research has not sufficiently addressed how and to what extent these practices drive changes within organisations needing further investigation (Cinquini et al., 2016; Passetti et al., 2018). The latter needs to shed light on how the process of developing ESG reports occurs, and how the ESG report becomes an internal decision-making tool, integrating the strategy formulation and implementation process (Naciti et al., 2022; Stubbs & Higgins, 2014).

To the best of our knowledge, few studies have focused on the impact of ESG practices on decision-making processes, management practices and management accounting information (Burritt & Schaltegger, 2010; Chiucchi et al., 2018; Ciccola et al., 2023). There has been limited attention to investigate the role played by ESG practices as managerial practices to support decision-making and control processes (Huang, 2021; Tsang et al., 2023; Vitolla et al., 2019). To overcome the literature gap, the chapter addresses the question of how ESG practices evolve from accountability practices to accountability and managerial practices able to support decision-making and control processes.

36.3 Theoretical Framework

In addressing the research question raised above, we use the theoretical lens proposed by Burns and Scapens (2000) for studying organisational changes. Several studies have already drawn on this framework (Bertz & Quinn, 2022; Contrafatto & Burns, 2013; Johansson & Baldvinsdottir, 2003; Nor-Aziah & Scapens, 2007; Siti-Nabiha & Scapens, 2005), applying it in various contexts (Muhammad et al., 2019; Rizza & Ruggeri, 2018). For instance, Rizza and Ruggeri (2018) demonstrated how the institutionalisation of management accounting tools occurs when three institutional logics (family, business and community) are in place. Some contributions have investigated the consequences of the introduction of new accounting systems (Biswas & Akroyd, 2022) and how management control practices are used to communicate and provide guidance to organisational members (Barros & da Ferreira, 2023). Despite the usefulness of the Burns and Scapens (2000) framework for explaining how organisational change occurs, no studies have utilised it to gain a deep understanding of organisational changes led by the introduction of ESG practices.

The Burns and Scapens (2000) framework combines Gidden's structuration theory (Giddens, 1979, 1984) and Old Institutional Economics (Burns et al., 2006), depicting the change through a correlation between institutional realm and the realm of action through four key elements (or stages): encoding, enacting, reproduction and institutionalisation.

A visual depiction of the framework developed by Burns and Scapens (2000) is reproduced in Fig. 36.1.

As depicted in Fig. 36.1, two realms have been identified: the institutional realm and the realm of action. At the top, we have the institutional realm, which refers to the taken-for-granted assumptions, comprising institutional principles, values and power (Burns & Scapens, 2000, p. 10). At the bottom, we identify the realm of action, "actions carried out over time by organisational actors" (ter Bogt & Scapens,

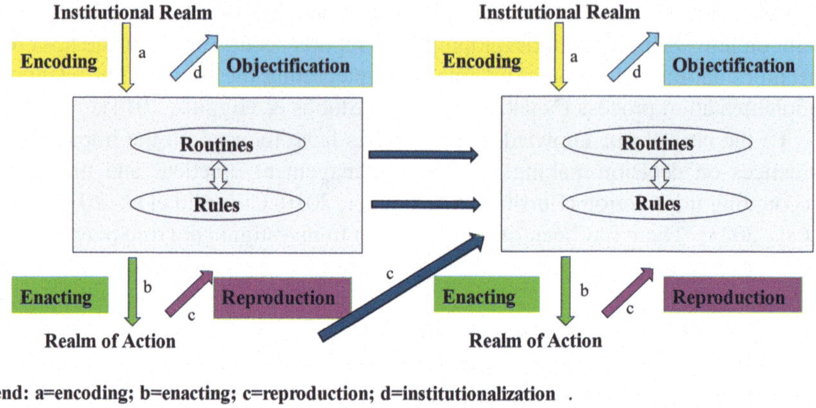

Fig. 36.1 Own elaboration based on Burns and Scapens' framework

2019, p. 1805). The two realms (institutional and action) are linked by rules and routines, which act as modalities, in line with Giddens' vocabulary. According to the framework, rules are the "formalised statement of procedures" while routines are the "procedures actually in use" (p. 7). In this framework, through encoding, enacting and reproduction of rules and routines, practices become institutionalised (Burns & Scapens, 2000).

A change is considered a process, which leads to shifts in organisational rules and routines in a recursive way between institutions (institutional realm) and actions (realm of actions) over time (Bertz & Quinn, 2022). In other words, "the rules and routines encode the institutions (i.e. the taken-for-granted assumptions) and are enacted through the actions" (ter Bogt & Scapens, 2019, p. 1805). Routines and rules are repeated and may change in a conscious or unconscious manner. Through encoding, enacting and reproduction of rules and routines, practices start being institutionalised (Burns & Scapens, 2000). New rules can be implemented, and new routines can emerge during the encoding and reproduction phases, shaping the change process.

Synchronic and diachronic elements characterise the two realms. The institutional realm and realm of action are characterised by synchronic elements when the institutional principles are encoded into rules and routines and the actors are involved in enacting them, while diachronic elements characterise the two realms when actions are reproduced into routines and routines are institutionalised, causing a cumulative process.

In general, studies have recognised that accounting and organisational change play a significant part in shaping organisational change processes (Scapens & Jazayeri, 2003; Senior & Swailes, 2010), highlighting that managing organisational change requires a comprehensive understanding of the existing context of the organisation (Alsharari, 2019). Even if widely used in management accounting change literature, Burns and Scapens' (2000) framework has potential in the field of sustainability accounting and ESG reporting. The framework highlights the role played by each of the four stages in affecting a successful ESG institutionalisation, distinguishing the relevance of synchronic and diachronic elements. The process of transforming ESG accountability practices into accountability and managerial ones needs to be understood by investigating how institutional and the practical realms interact within organisational processes, highlighting how the taken-for-granted assumptions influence, and are influenced by, actions carried out over time. The central role played by organisational rules and routines suggests that the process of transforming ESG accountability practices into accountability and managerial ones is affected by organisation-specific factors that need to be investigated through a longitudinal case research.

36.4 Research Method and Company Profile

This study used a longitudinal case study approach to closely examine the extent of organisational change led by the ESG report, introduced as accountability practice, becoming both a managerial and an accountability practice. The research explored the process through which this change occurred. Greenlife[1] was selected for this study based on its strong emphasis on sustainability. The company views sustainability as a continuous journey, ensuring that all members of the organisation are engaged and dedicated to implementing sustainability practices and embedding a culture that embraces sustainability values included in the mission and values of the company. The peculiarities of the business in which Greenlife operates sustain a strong commitment towards sustainability matters, involving all organisational members.

Greenlife, located in the south of Italy, is specialised in the production of standardised extracts derived from a variety of typical Mediterranean fruits and plants, utilising them for the creation of nutraceutical, cosmetic and veterinary products.

The founder of the company is a university professor who aimed to apply his pharmaceutical knowledge to address potential market needs and establish a business. Since 1997, Greenlife has been guided by a strong desire to return concrete value to the community and the planet in terms of health and well-being, which led it to adopt the first ESG report in 2021. The company's vision strongly emphasises sustainability values, as pointed out in the first ESG report: "*Sustainability is a pivotal element in our vision for the future*". Accordingly, sustainability is deeply implicated in the activity of the company, which is devoted to delivering high-quality extracts that offer numerous health and wellness benefits by carefully selecting and processing raw materials. Through its ongoing commitment to innovation and scientific excellence, Greenlife has experienced growth over the years and currently exports its products to other countries. Moreover, a path of

[1] An invented name was used to protect the privacy of the company.

managerialisation has been followed by the company, which recently introduced management accounting and control practices, by recruiting a controller who brought management accounting expertise into the organisation. The MCS adopted by the company was focused on cost monitoring to support decision-making processes.

In order to address the research question, data were gathered through document analysis and interviews. The research period extends from the beginning of 2019 up to thc middle of 2023, but the data collection process started from the beginning of 2022 and ended in the middle of 2023. The main data sources include documents describing Greenlife's profile and organisation, official financial documents, internal reports, product description documents, 2021 and 2022 ESG reports, and sustainability plans. The interviewees consisted of the founder, the general director, the sales manager, the human resources manager, one member of the administrative staff, the controller and the marketing manager. Eighteen interviews were conducted, each lasting around 1 h. Minutes of the interviews were sent to the company for approval. After receiving approval, certain extracts from the interviews were directly included in the text, while others were reported indirectly in the narrative form. All interviews were recorded and transcribed in full. Reflective questions were extensively used during the interviews. Asking for stories and/or anecdotes, for instance, encourages the interviewees to provide detailed information and triggers other stories and thoughts on the phenomena under investigation. We triangulated the data collected from the interviews with secondary sources to enhance the comprehensiveness of our analysis (Eisenhardt & Graebner, 2007).

The data collected were interpreted using the Burn and Scapens' (2000) framework employed as a "method theory" (Lukka & Vinnari, 2014), enhancing the analysis of the field evidence in order to understand processes that enabled ESG practices, initially introduced to meet accountability requests, to evolve into accountability and managerial practices capable of supporting decision-making.

36.5 Findings

Drawing on Burns and Scapens' (2000) framework, we analyse the organisational changes that occur by introducing an ESG report, outlining how this report, initially introduced as an accountability practice to meet market requests, also functions as a managerial practice. This change is depicted through a correlation between the institutional realm and the realm of action through the four stages: encoding, enacting, reproduction and institutionalisation. Each of these stages led to a deep investigation of organisational dynamics that shape the use of the ESG report, underlining how taken-for-granted assumptions influence, and are influenced by, actions carried out over time. Focusing on organisational ESG's rules and routines allowed us to explore how ESG evolves from accountability practices to accountability and managerial practices able to support decision-making and control processes.

Before delving into the description of the ESG report, it is important to emphasise the strategy pursued by the company to understand its commitment to sustainability even before the introduction of the ESG report.

36.5.1 Greenlife's Sustainability Values

The founder of the company was inspired to delve into and harness the botanical properties of Mediterranean flora through extensive international scientific research. This endeavour aimed to produce and certify natural ingredients for solutions promoting health and well-being which over the years led the company to receive various system and product certifications.

Greenlife employs a "product-market" approach-based strategy that encompasses building a specific branded ingredient portfolio tailored to each business unit; utilising specialised distribution channels and dedicated sales forces for each business area and geographical region; and implementing a targeted promotional and communication strategy aligned with the unique market needs of each business unit.

This holistic approach has been pivotal in driving growth across different markets following a circular economy approach. Greenlife R&D function identifies by-products from the agricultural industry as catalysts for a sustainable innovation system, repurposing raw materials such as olive leaves and fruit water that would otherwise go unused within the agricultural system. Employing a science-based innovation approach, these products are incorporated into nutraceutical and cosmetic solutions, effectively minimising resource wastefulness. Despite this strong sustainability commitment, the Greenlife MCS did not monitor sustainability activities that were checked and reported only upon customers' demands. Specifically, it was the customer office that was directly involved in fulfilling customers' assessment questionnaires related to sustainability issues, providing information for the required KPIs. This managerial practice was carried out solely by the customer office to meet the customers' sustainability requirements needed to place their orders.

36.5.1.1 The Introduction of ESG Report: Encoding Sustainability Values

The introduction of the first ESG report was promoted by the sales manager, who highlighted market pressures regarding the disclosure of sustainability initiatives, as he pointed out: "*in line with the market trend of disclosing more about sustainability policies, our customers demanded detailed information on this concern*".

Acknowledging this market request, and recognising the Greenlife's commitment to honesty, respect, sharing, well-being and sustainability, led the ownership to introduce the ESG report in 2021. Therefore, a consulting firm was directly involved in the designing of the ESG report, collaborating with the marketing manager who was familiar with customer requests.

Regarding this matter, the marketing manager stated: "*last year the ownership involved my team in developing a sustainability report that would disclose our sustainability strategies and initiatives to stakeholders. In this way, we were prepared to promptly respond to customer requests by systematically disseminating ESG information*".

Consequently, the ESG report was designed to depict how Greenlife worked to create value over time, providing a picture of the strategies, objectives and performance related to organisation's ability to create value. Initially, the ESG report served as an accountability tool, enabling stakeholders to discover Greenlife's strategies and initiatives on environmental and social issues.

The passion, energy and unconditional desire to create something beneficial for oneself and for others were pointed out by the human resources manager in the ESG report as follows: "*Today, we are ready to continue our journey, putting people at the centre and renewing our commitment to creating that shared social, economic and environmental well-being which has guided our choices over the years*".

According to the institutional theory, Greenlife's values and the market pressures to disclose environmental and social strategies and initiatives coherently to the IIR framework represented the institutional realm, which comprises the accumulation of beliefs, norms, power and interests (Jarzabkowski, 2008 p. 622). Consolidated Greenlife's values, the market pressures and IIR guidelines were the taken-for-granted assumptions that informed the consulting firm and the marketing manager who moulded the ESG report (Burns et al., 2003, 2006).

The ESG report was articulated in four sections: the first one briefly describes the organisation, its identity, history and ownership structure; the second part outlines the governance structure, the principles and procedures put in place by the company to ensure a proper management system; the third part details how the organisation manages its financial and nonfinancial capital to create value; and the fourth part gives details of the organisation's performance, activities and objectives described in ESG terms.

In order to define Greenlife's sustainability strategy, a process of stakeholder's engagement was activated involving each department manager in stakeholder selection and interactions. This modus operandi was explained by the founder as follows: "*We believe it is essential to engage our stakeholders in defining our strategy and goals, in order to meet the expectations of the people and organisations who choose us*".

The stakeholder engagement was depicted in the materiality matrix, which showed the matters that are actually "material" or relevant to the Company based on the scores assigned by stakeholders. The analysis of these material matters involved assessing their impacts on strategy, governance and performance of the organisation.

To guide the ESG strategy, the goals were broken down for each main area (environmental, social and governance), delineating specific matters, goals and the corresponding Sustainable Development Goals (SDG), as illustrated in Fig. 36.2.

Greenlife's strong commitment to sustainability values influenced, to some extent, the selection and implementation of new set of rules (Burns & Scapens,

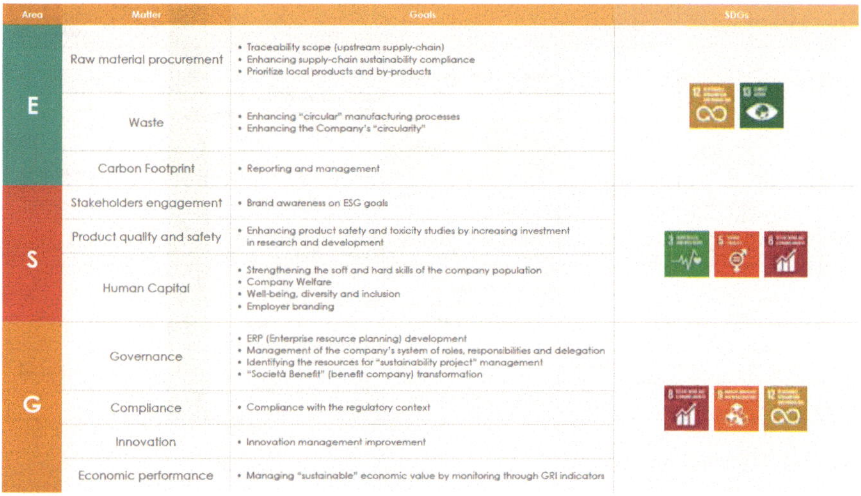

Area	Matter	Goals	SDGs
E	Raw material procurement	• Traceability scope (upstream supply-chain) • Enhancing supply-chain sustainability compliance • Prioritize local products and by-products	12, 13
	Waste	• Enhancing "circular" manufacturing processes • Enhancing the Company's "circularity"	
	Carbon Footprint	• Reporting and management	
S	Stakeholders engagement	• Brand awareness on ESG goals	3, 5, 8
	Product quality and safety	• Enhancing product safety and toxicity studies by increasing investment in research and development	
	Human Capital	• Strengthening the soft and hard skills of the company population • Company Welfare • Well-being, diversity and inclusion • Employer branding	
G	Governance	• ERP (Enterprise resource planning) development • Management of the company's system of roles, responsibilities and delegation • Identifying the resources for "sustainability project" management • "Società Benefit" (benefit company) transformation	8, 9, 12
	Compliance	• Compliance with the regulatory context	
	Innovation	• Innovation management improvement	
	Economic performance	• Managing "sustainable" economic value by monitoring through GRI indicators	

Fig. 36.2 ESG objectives

2000), which facilitated changes in Greenlife's organisational structure and managerial practices. Specifically, the introduction of the ESG report triggered the reconfiguration of the company's organisational structure and the restructuring of strategic planning.

Firstly, the introduction of the ESG report was accompanied by the establishment of a sustainability committee and the identification of a cross-functional team, called ESG coordinators. The sustainability committee was tasked with advising the executive board and making proposals primarily related to guidelines and initiatives aimed at embedding sustainability into business processes to create value in the short/medium and long term for all company stakeholders. The ESG coordinators were responsible for promoting and monitoring sustainability actions and the achievement of goals.

Secondly, concerning strategic planning, a sustainability plan was introduced. The sustainability plan aimed to break down the ESG areas into different matters. For each matter, the sustainability plan allowed for the definition of goals, objectives and actions. Additionally, for each action, KPIs were identified, specifying their timeline and the ESG coordinator responsible, as showed in Fig. 36.3.

The introduction of the sustainability plan was advocated for by the marketing manager and quality assurance manager, who believed it was essential to implement ESG strategies and develop initiatives. On this point, the marketing manager argued: "*We proposed the implementation of a sustainability plan to prevent the ESG report from devolving into a mere greenwashing initiative. We firmly believe that an ESG report should be accompanied by an action plan capable of furnishing quantifiable metrics to include in the report*". A new routine was introduced through the sustainability plan, fitting with established planning and control practices, involving not only the marketing manager but also all new organisational positions devoted to

AREA	MATTER	GOALS	OBJECTIVES	ACTIONS	KPI	Y1	Y2	Y3	ESG COORDINATORS
E	waste	Policies related to the management and reduction of waste products	Enhancing "circular" manufacturing processes	Start-up of the water reuse system in the production cycle	start-up monitoring of the new plant (KPI % of water recovered and reused - Amount of industrial water saved)	x			Quality manager and production manager
				Re-use of water in the production cycles			x	x	
				Measurement of the circularity degree of raw materials	(%) di MP by-Product su Tot MP	x	x	x	
				Check with customers via questionnaire availability of recycled plastic secondary pack -	% positive feedback	x			
				Engagement with supplier and customer to increase secondary pack circularity (with recycled plastic)	Sign supply agreement		x		
			Enhancing the Company's "circularity"	Reduction of plastic use and waste	num consumable items replaced with sustainable material	x			H&R manager
				Reduction of paper use and waste	reduction in purchase of paper compared to turnover		x		

Fig. 36.3 Sustainability plan

ESG issues. Designing the sustainability plan required individuals to identify goals, objectives, actions, KPIs and responsibilities. This routine shaped the company's strategic planning by introducing ESG areas and the related matters.

This was clearly reflected in new managerial practices planned in the sustainability plan, such as the reuse of water for the production cycle and the measurement of the circularity of raw materials.

The identification of the ESG committee and ESG coordinators, along with the introduction of the ESG report and the sustainability plan, represented the rules that defined the formal ways in which "things should be done" and they were necessary to coordinate and give meaning to ESG strategies and initiatives. The appointment of these new organisational roles led to the dissemination of ESG strategies throughout the company, involving organisational actors in gathering and monitoring information related to sustainability. In particular, the controller was directly involved for the first time in collecting and reconfiguring information related to sustainability planning. On this issue, he pointed out: *"Even though I always knew that the company was strongly committed to sustainability issues and that such KPIs were strategically relevant for our customers, before the ESG report, I was not involved in the measurement activities related to sustainability, governance, or the environment. Each of these aspects was entrusted to the marketing manager. Since the introduction of the sustainability plan, I have become involved. Therefore, ESG has also become a concern for the management control office"*. This evidence highlights that even though the management control office was involved in Greenlife's managerial practices, those related to sustainability issues were not under his responsibilities, requiring more effort in the identification of this kind of information and their reconfiguration for strategic planning purposes.

The "encoding" of Greenlife's existing institution and taken-for-granted assumptions and meanings into the new rules, routines and procedures activated a reshaping of Greenlife's ESG strategies and initiatives, leading to the implementation of ESG rules through current actions that also affected the ongoing routines.

Specifically, the reshaping of Greenlife's ESG strategies concerned the implementation of a stronger communication strategy aligned with the stakeholders' needs. In doing so, the company directly involved its main stakeholders in defining ESG strategies through the materiality analysis, moving towards more participative strategising process. At the same time, the formalisation of ESG strategies through the ESG report enhanced the company's bargaining power in managing customers' relationships. Customers were better informed about ESG initiatives, leading to increase trust in Greenlife.

The Greenlife's sustainability rules were "the formalised statement of procedures" such as the ESG report, the sustainability plan, the ESG committee and ESG coordinators, which enriched the Greenlife's managerial routines that were "the procedures actually in use" (Burns & Scapens, 2000, p. 7). These procedures were shaped by the organisational members to implement Greenlife's sustainability "rules" into everyday practices, such as in management control.

36.5.1.2 Enacting and Reproduction of ESG Rules and Routines

To fulfil sustainability rules, ESG coordinators organised meetings to discuss the implementation of ESG initiatives, monitor KPIs and analyse emerged criticalities. The implementation of the sustainability plan increased the involvement of the management control office and required middle managers to provide relevant information to ESG coordinators, stimulating further changes in organisational practices. For example, the controller argued: "*Since the sustainability plan was introduced, I had to collect and process new kinds of information such as the energy consumption. This required reconfiguring such information and including it in new reports*". This evidence highlighted that enacting ESG rules and routines stimulated the reconfiguration of people's responsibilities, involving middle managers in collecting and analysing information related to ESG initiatives, guided by the ESG coordinators. Their involvement entailed a reshaping of middle managers' practices to ensure the gathering of proper information for ESG reporting. Particularly, the management controller had to reconfigure cost accounting information for ESG purposes and collect nonfinancial information useful to monitor ESG activities.

Discussing the actions outlined in the sustainability plan prompted the revision of previously defined rules. On this point, the controller referred: "*In the process of gathering and analysing information for the necessary sustainability KPIs, I recommended an alternative method for calculating these indicators to more comprehensively capture the observed performance dimensions. Leveraging my experience, I engaged in discussions with ESG coordinators, presenting my proposal and articulating the reasons for the suggested change. I successfully persuaded them to adopt the modified indicator by providing practical examples to support my case*".

The enactment of ESG rules led organisational members to interpret them within the context of Greenlife and their own experiences, creating the opportunity to clarify and potentially change rules. This process questioned the validity of the existing rules and triggered a process of redefinition and reinterpretation (Oliveira & Quinn, 2015).

Accordingly, the introduction of the ESG report shaped organisational rules and routines that encoded the institutions (Greenlife's vision towards sustainability) and were enacted through actions defined in the sustainability plan. For instance, following the strategy on the environmental area, related to "waste" matter, the sustainability plan stated *"the policies related to the management and the reduction of waste"* as the goal to pursue. On this issue, the objective aimed to enhance circular manufacturing processes through five actions and the corresponding KPIs (see Fig. 36.3). On this point, the marketing manager pointed out: "*Great attention was placed on enhancing the circularity of waste to maximise the reusing and recycling of resources and materials as long as possible. For example, we invested in a machine designed to recycle production processes water cost-effectively, thereby recycling it back into our production processes. This investment aimed to improve efficiency and reduce water consumption, aligning with market requests for responsible use of natural resources*".

This evidence reveals that since the introduction of the ESG report and the related sustainability plan in 2021, significant changes have been initiated in the sustainability strategy, particularly in promoting the circularity of waste through internalising the recycling of production process water. This new direction led to the encoding of new rules and routines, which in turn activated various organisational and managerial practices. Specifically, the implementation of the water recycling machine required a reconfiguration of production processes, the assignment of new responsibilities and the establishment of new KPIs to monitor the effectiveness of the investment. Quarterly, the monitoring of these KPIs provided valuable insights, as noted by the controller: "*By monitoring the KPIs related to the % of water recovered and the related cost's savings, we were able to engage in discussion about further potential uses of the recovered water*". On this point, the general director further emphasised: "*Discussing the outcomes of the new investment in terms of the % of water recovered and of costs saved, I inquired with the production manager about the feasibility of utilizing the same water for additional purposes, thereby enhancing circularity and cost effectiveness. Upon receiving assurance from the production manager regarding the potability of the recovered water, I began contemplating its broader use*". In this scenario, the KPIs initiated a decision-making process involving all organisational actors in identifying potential future directions to strengthen the ESG strategy and enhance the company's circularity.

The introduction of the ESG report also stimulated new organisational practices, such as training courses aimed at promoting the engagement of Greenlife's organisational members and stimulating virtuous behaviours in addressing ESG strategies and initiatives. On this issue, the controller argued: "*we were accustomed with environmentally responsible behaviours; for example, we were used to have a coffee in a recycling paper cup. This practice allowed Greenlife to reduce the co2 emissions, supporting the achievement of Agenda 2030 objectives related to circularity*". Similarly, the marketing manager claimed: "*Greenlife's organisational members are young people who are very attentive to sustainability issues. That favoured the promotion of autonomous initiatives. For example, a member of my staff proposed using pens with a seed in the cap as a new marketing gadget to promote the Greenlife's commitment on sustainability. After testing it out, this initiative was successfully reintroduced".* This evidence of the implementation of sustainability strategies and initiatives highlighted how new routines emerged during the enacting and reproduction stages.

The reproduction of ESG rules and routines also informed on criticalities related to the use of sustainability plan for strategic decisions, as stated by the Controller: "*even though the ownership was highly committed on ESG issues, they were not previously considered in strategic and operational planning. As a result, managers did not have specific objectives related to sustainability issues, which made it difficult to compile the ESG report. For instance, if we aimed to report on supplier traceability, it was necessary to assign a specific objective to the purchasing manager regarding the percentage of sustainable suppliers*". The issue showed the need of integrating ESG strategies and initiatives into Greenlife's strategic and operational planning, suggesting revising the managerial performance measurement to adopt a management by objectives approach. Although the introduction of the ESG report reconfigured managers' responsibilities, it did not affect the managerial performance measurement.

Case evidence reveals that ESG practices introduced following the ESG report have provided external stakeholders with a tool to understand the Greenlife's sustainability strategies, aligning with the original intentions outlined in the report's introduction. At the same time, these practices have triggered a process of organisational change within the company, stimulating new sustainability practices and providing the opportunity to discover new directions. Consequently, the role of the ESG report has evolved, functioning as both an accountability and managerial tool, able to shape organisational practices, including those related to management control.

Analysing the process of enacting and reproduction of ESG rules and routines through the institutional framework allows us to investigate how institutional and the practical realms interacted within organisational processes, highlighting how the taken-for-granted assumptions influenced, and were influenced by, actions carried out over time.

In so doing, the interactions between institutional realm and realm of action were characterised by synchronic elements when the institutional principles were encoded into rules and routines and the actors were involved in enacting them, while diachronic elements characterised the two realms when actions were reproduced into routines, leading to a gradual reshaping of organisational processes.

36.5.1.3 Moving Towards the Institutionalisation of ESG Rules and Routines

In preparing both the ESG report and the sustainability plan in 2022, the sustainability strategies and initiatives undertaken in 2021 were pursued and further developed, whereas others were abandoned.

In particular, ESG practices allowed organisational actors to believe in ESG logics, providing them with cognitive structures to shape their attention, aid in problem solving and guide their behaviours (Thornton et al., 2013). This favoured the institutionalisation of such ESG rules and routines that were reproduced in the 2022 ESG report. This was the case of the reduction of plastic and paper, the recycling of production process water, the monthly ESG coordinator meetings and the use of pens with seed on the cup as a marketing gadget. Coherently, the sustainability plan in 2022 reinforced these initiatives and introduced new goals and actions aimed at enhancing the stakeholder engagement.

However, evidence indicates that certain strategies and initiatives were not included in the second ESG report because the ownership's commitment to them waned. For instance, discussing governance goals and actions included in the 2021 sustainability plan, the marketing manager highlighted: "*in 2021 the ownership proposed transforming Greenlife into a benefit company to not only pursue the purpose of profit, but also the specific purpose(s) of common benefit as outlined in its articles of association, in accordance with the stability law enacted in 2016. However, this request was not carried out because the ownership lost interest in it*".

Case evidence suggests that the introduction of the ESG report drove a process of change in Greenlife's rules and routines, prompting a reconfiguration of management control practices that initially focused on economic issues. Interviews revealed that the introduction of the ESG report was initially prompted by market requests for greater accountability regarding ESG topics. Consequently, the ESG report was conceived as a means to disclose to market in a systematic way what company made about ESG concerns, serving primarily as an accountability tool. However, the implementation of the ESG report also stimulated the introduction of the sustainability plan, which functioned as a managerial tool, involving functional managers in executing the ESG strategy by defining goals, objectives, actions and KPIs for each ESG dimension. This involvement required, on the one hand, functional managers to participate in data gathering for ESG reporting; and, on the other hand, the reconfiguring of such processes or activities. According to the theoretical framework, ESG rules and routines activated a reshaping of company's organisational structure and practices, enabling through the reproduction of the new rules and routines an ongoing process of change.

This occurrence explains how the ESG report, initially introduced for accountability purposes, can also function as both an accountability and managerial practice. It engages organisational actors in a renewed reporting process where economic objectives are combined with those related to environmental sustainability and governance. Figure 36.4 summarises the empirical findings through the Burns and Scapens framework.

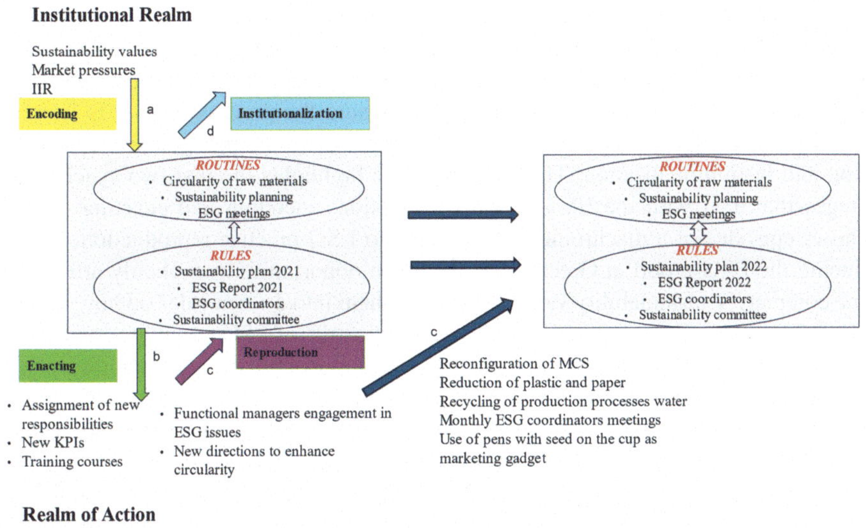

Fig. 36.4 Towards institutionalisation of ESG rules and routines in Greenlife

36.6 Concluding Remarks

The essence of ESG reporting lies in its ability to incorporate sustainability as a fundamental value that influences decision-making processes regarding environmental and social matters, while also shaping the governance structure of a firm. Embracing this perspective implies that ESG reporting should not merely consist of a set of standards for producing and delivering company reports; rather, it should be viewed as a mind-set that incorporates underlying assumptions. These assumptions, in order to be translated into practices, must align with the ingrained beliefs of the company where ESG practices are implemented. Nevertheless, studies have primarily highlighted the accountability role of ESG reporting, paying less attention to its potential to support managerial decision-making processes.

On this stream of research, this chapter seeks to explore how ESG practices evolve from accountability practices to accountability and managerial practices able to support decision-making and control processes. This evolution of ESG practices implies that they not only enter but also reshape the taken-for-granted assumptions of the organisation where they are introduced.

A case study was conducted at Greenlife, a company in its growth phase and deeply committed to sustainability values. The introduction of the ESG report was driven by market pressure aimed to satisfy the customers' requests, making accountability the primary concern behind its implementation. Examining how the ESG report evolved from being solely an accountability practice to also serving as a managerial practice requires an understanding of its impact on the decision-making process. To address this issue, Burns and Scapens' framework was adopted, as it focuses on the institutionalisation of organisational practices, particularly those introduced from external sources. The framework distinguishing four stages, two synchronic (encoding and enacting) and two diachronic (reproduction and institutionalisation), makes it suitable for analysing the process that starts from a set of taking-for-granted assumptions and reshapes them through practice reproduction and institutionalisation. The Greenlife case highlights the first two synchronic stages that deal with the ESG report introduction, encoding and enacting, while shows episodes of a diachronic stage, related to ESG practice reproduction. Introducing the ESG report at Greenlife provided an opportunity to explicitly articulate the company's sustainability values, encoding them into a set of rules on how things should be done. That was the case of the identification of ESG committee and ESG coordinators, and the introduction of the ESG report and the sustainability plan. From the case evidence, encoding meant producing new rules that reflected the main Greenlife's taken-for-granted assumptions on sustainability. The extent to which those rules were functioning was verified putting them into practices. The stage of enacting focused on integrating these ESG rules into the company's organisational practices. Greenlife already had operational practices geared towards efficiency, thanks to its culture of management accounting and control. The reduction of plastic and paper, the recycling of production process water, the monthly ESG coordinator meetings and the use of pens with seed on the cup as a marketing gadget represented episodes of ESG practice reproduction, which highlighted how ESG practices were directed towards operational decisions and management control purposes, facilitating the transition from accountability practices to accountability and managerial ones.

Case evidence indicates that the implementation of the ESG report led to significant changes in Greenlife's rules and routines, particularly in its management control practices, which shifted focus from purely economic issues. The integration of ESG rules and routines reshaped the company's organisational structure, facilitating an ongoing process of change that blended economic objectives with ESG goals. Thus, the ESG report, originally introduced for accountability purposes, evolved into a managerial practice that engaged organisational actors in a comprehensive reporting process.

The presence of pre-existing management accounting and control practices, along with Greenlife's ongoing path towards managerialisation, was significant organisational characteristics that influenced the transformation of ESG practices into managerial ones. Understanding how these ESG practices aligned with existing organisational practices is crucial in comprehending their evolution.

The field evidence reveals that Greenlife's peculiarities, such as its strong commitment to sustainability matters, accompanied the evolution of ESG practices in managerial practices. It was evident when KPIs were integrated into decision-making processes, such as in the case of the implementation of the water recycling machine. In particular, organisational actors, who were already aligned with sustainability values, were more inclined to pursue ESG goals and identify new business opportunities. The Greenlife's strong commitment on sustainability value influenced the selection and implementation of new set of rules, favouring the reconfiguration of the company's organisational structure and the restructuring of strategic planning.

The contribution of this chapter is mostly related to ESG literature, investigating the impact of these practices on decision-making processes, management practices and management accounting information (Burritt & Schaltegger, 2010; Chiucchi et al., 2018; Ciccola et al., 2023; Gatti et al., 2018). The field evidence indeed reveals that the transformation of the ESG report as accountability practices into accountability and managerial practices is facilitated by the presence of certain management accounting and control practices within the organisation. Additionally, Burns and Scapens' framework helped to explore how changes occurred at the introduction of the ESG report and how the interplay between ESG and managerial practices stimulated an ongoing participative change process.

Furthermore, the findings highlight that while companies may adopt ESG reports to impact their market reputation (Naciti et al., 2022), practising this report can also activate organisational changes that encourage using them as a managerial tool.

This research underscores multiple implications for managers, suggesting the integration of ESG concerns into MCS and advocating for regular monitoring of compliance between ESG practices and management control ones. Additionally, it emphasises the importance of engaging all organisational actors in ESG matters to discover new business opportunities.

However, the main research limitations stem from the limited period of observation, given that the ESG report was recently introduced. Further research can deal with analysing over time what factors can favour or hinder the whole process of institutionalising ESG reporting. Additionally, future research may investigate the interplay between management accounting practices and the managerial use of ESG reports.

References

Alsharari, N. M. (2019). Management accounting and organizational change: Alternative perspectives. *International Journal of Organizational Analysis, 27*(4), 1124–1147.

Amir, A. Z., & Serafeim, G. (2018). Why and how investors use ESG information: Evidence from a global survey. *Financial Analysts Journal, 74*(3), 87–103.

Aouadi, A., & Marsat, S. (2018). Do ESG controversies matter for firm value? Evidence from international data. *Journal of Business Ethics, 151*(4), 1027–1047.

Barros, R. S., & da Ferreira, A. M. D. S. C. (2023). Management control systems and innovation: A case study grounded in institutional theory. *Journal of Management Control, 34*(1), 109–133.

Bertz, J., & Quinn, M. (2022). Situated rationalities and management control change—An empirical note on key actors, situated rationalities and generalised practices. *Qualitative Research in Accounting and Management, 19*(1), 77–100.

Biswas, S., & Akroyd, C. (2022). Collaborative inter-organisational relationships and management control change. *Accounting and Finance, 62*(4), 4569–4586.

Boiral, O. (2013). Sustainability reports as simulacra? A counter-account of A and A+ GRI reports. *Accounting, Auditing & Accountability Journal, 26*(7), 1036–1071.

Bouten, L., & Hoozée, S. (2013). On the interplay between environmental reporting and management accounting change. *Management Accounting Research, 24*(4), 333–348.

Burns, J., & Scapens, R. W. (2000). Conceptualizing management accounting change: An institutional framework. *Management Accounting Research, 11*(1), 3–25.

Burns, J., Ezzamel, M., Scapens, R., & Scapens, R. W. (2003). *Challenge of management accounting change*. Elsevier.

Burns, J., Ribeiro, J. A., & Scapens, R. W. (2006). Institutional theories in management accounting change: Contributions, issues and paths for development. *Qualitative Research in Accounting & Management, 3*(2), 94–111.

Burritt, R. L. (2012). Environmental performance accountability: Planet, people, profits. *Accounting, Auditing and Accountability Journal, 25*(2), 370–405.

Burritt, R. L., & Schaltegger, S. (2010). Sustainability accounting and reporting: Fad or trend? *Accounting, Auditing & Accountability Journal, 23*(7), 829–846.

Castellano, N., & Felden, C. (2021). Management control Systems for Sustainability and Sustainability of management control systems. *Management Control, 2021*, 5–10.

Chiucchi, M. S., Montemari, M., & Gatti, M. (2018). The influence of integrated reporting on management control systems: A case study. *International Journal of Business and Management, 13*(7), 19.

Ciccola, R., Ascani, I., & Chiucchi, M. S. (2023). Relazioni tra Integrated Report e processi decisionali e di controllo: un'indagine empirica longitudinale. *Management Control, 2023*, 135–162.

Cinquini, L., Passetti, E., & Tenucci, A. (2016). La sostenibilità ambientale in azienda: quale relazione tra disclosure volontaria e gestione interna? *Management Control, 2016*, 15–32.

Clementino, E., & Perkins, R. (2021). How do companies respond to environmental, social and governance (ESG) ratings? Evidence from Italy. *Journal of Business Ethics, 171*(2), 379–397.

Contrafatto, M., & Burns, J. (2013). Social and environmental accounting, organisational change and management accounting: A processual view. *Management Accounting Research, 24*(4), 349–365.

Delmas, M. A., & Burbano, V. C. (2011). The drivers of greenwashing. *California Management Review, 54*(1), 64–87.

Drempetic, S., Klein, C., & Zwergel, B. (2020). The influence of firm size on the ESG score: Corporate sustainability ratings under review. *Journal of Business Ethics, 167*(2), 333–360.

Duque-Grisales, E., & Aguilera-Caracuel, J. (2021). Environmental, social and governance (ESG) scores and financial performance of Multilatinas: Moderating effects of geographic international diversification and financial slack. *Journal of Business Ethics, 168*(2), 315–334.

Eisenhardt, K. M., & Graebner, M. E. (2007). Theory building from cases: Opportunities and challenges. *Academy of Management Journal, 50*(1), 25–32.

Fabrizio, K. R., & Kim, E. H. (2019). Reluctant disclosure and transparency: Evidence from environmental disclosures. *Organization Science, 30*(6), 1207–1231.

Fatemi, A., Glaum, M., & Kaiser, S. (2018). ESG performance and firm value: The moderating role of disclosure. *Global Finance Journal, 38*, 45–64.

Garcia-Torea, N., Larrinaga, C., & Luque-Vílchez, M. (2023). Bridging the understanding of sustainability accounting and organizational change. *Organization and Environment, 36*(1), 17–38.

Gatti, M., Chiucchi, M. S., & Montemari, M. (2018). Management control systems and integrated reporting: Which relationships? The case of the Azienda Ospedaliero Universitaria Ospedali Riuniti Ancona. *International Journal of Business and Management, 13*(9), 169.

Giddens, A. (1979). *Central problems in social theory: Action, structure, and contradiction in social analysis* (Vol. 241). Univ of California Press.

Giddens, A. (1984). *The constitution of society: Outline of the theory of structuration*. Univ of California Press.

Graafland, J., & Smid, H. (2016). Environmental impacts of SMEs and the effects of formal management tools: Evidence from EU's largest survey. *Corporate Social Responsibility and Environmental Management, 23*(5), 297–307.
Hristov, I., Chirico, A., & Ranalli, F. (2022). Corporate strategies oriented towards sustainable governance: Advantages, managerial practices and main challenges. *Journal of Management and Governance, 26*(1), 75–97.
Huang, D. Z. X. (2021). Environmental, social and governance (ESG) activity and firm performance: A review and consolidation. *Accounting and Finance, 61*(1), 335–360.
Jarzabkowski, P. (2008). Shaping strategy as a structuration process. *Academy of Management Journal, 51*(4), 621–650.
Johansson, I. L., & Baldvinsdottir, G. (2003). Accounting for trust: Some empirical evidence. *Management Accounting Research, 14*(3), 219–234.
Lukka, K., & Vinnari, E. (2014). Domain theory and method theory in management accounting research. *Accounting, Auditing and Accountability Journal, 27*(8), 1308–1338.
Molinari, M., Maraghini, M. P., & Riccaboni, A. (2021). Reporting di Sostenibilità e Controllo Manageriale: L'esperienza di Edison S.p.A. *Management Control, 2021*, 61–86.
Muhammad, K., Mastuki, N., Darus, F., & Ghani, E. K. (2019). Accounting information system change in an agriculture company: Examination using Burns and Scapens framework. *Journal of International Studies, 12*(1), 105–118.
Naciti, V., Cesaroni, F., & Pulejo, L. (2022). Corporate governance and sustainability: A review of the existing literature. *Journal of Management and Governance, 26*(1), 55–74.
Nirino, N., Santoro, G., Miglietta, N., & Quaglia, R. (2021). Corporate controversies and company's financial performance: Exploring the moderating role of ESG practices. *Technological Forecasting and Social Change, 162*(September 2020), 120341.
Nor-Aziah, A. K., & Scapens, R. W. (2007). Corporatisation and accounting change. The role of accounting and accountants in a Malaysian public utility. *Management Accounting Research, 18*(2), 209–247.
Oliveira, J., & Quinn, M. (2015). Interactions of rules and routines: Re-thinking rules. *Journal of Accounting and Organizational Change, 11*(4), 503–526.
Passetti, E., Cinquini, L., & Tenucci, A. (2018). Implementing internal environmental management and voluntary environmental disclosure: Does organisational change happen. *Accounting, Auditing and Accountability Journal, 31*(4), 1145–1173.
Qian, W., Burritt, R., & Monroe, G. (2011). Environmental management accounting in local government: A case of waste management. *Accounting, Auditing and Accountability Journal, 24*(1), 93–128.
Rizza, C., & Ruggeri, D. (2018). The institutionalization of management accounting tools in family firms: The relevance of multiple logics. *Journal of Management Control, 28*(4), 503–528.
Senior, B., & Swailes, S. (2010). *Organizational change* (4th ed.). Prentice Hall.
Scapens, R. W., & Jazayeri, M. (2003). ERP systems and management accounting change: Opportunities or impacts? A research note. *European Accounting Review, 12*(1), 201–233.
Sciarelli, M., Cosimato, S., Landi, G., & Iandolo, F. (2021). Socially responsible investment strategies for the transition towards sustainable development: The importance of integrating and communicating ESG. *TQM Journal, 33*(7), 39–56.
Siti-Nabiha, A. K., & Scapens, R. W. (2005). Stability and change: An institutionalist study of management accounting change. *Accounting, Auditing and Accountability Journal, 18*(1), 44–73.
Stubbs, W., & Higgins, C. (2014). Integrated reporting and internal mechanisms of change. *Accounting, Auditing and Accountability Journal, 27*(7), 1068–1089.
ter Bogt, H. J., & Scapens, R. W. (2019). Institutions, situated rationality and agency in management accounting: A research note extending the Burns and Scapens framework. *Accounting, Auditing and Accountability Journal, 32*(6), 1801–1825.
Thornton, P. H., Ocasio, W., & Lounsbury, M. (2013). *The institutional logics perspective* (pp. 1–22). Wiley.

Tsang, A., Frost, T., & Cao, H. (2023). Environmental, social, and governance (ESG) disclosure: A literature review. *British Accounting Review, 55*(1), 101149.

van Duuren, E., Plantinga, A., & Scholtens, B. (2016). ESG integration and the investment management process: Fundamental investing reinvented. *Journal of Business Ethics, 138*(3), 525–533.

Vitolla, F., Raimo, N., & Rubino, M. (2019). Appreciations, criticisms, determinants, and effects of integrated reporting: A systematic literature review. *Corporate Social Responsibility and Environmental Management, 26*(2), 518–528.

Zhou, G., Liu, L., & Luo, S. (2022). Sustainable development, ESG performance and company market value: Mediating effect of financial performance. *Business Strategy and the Environment, 31*(7), 3371–3387.

Chapter 37
Implementing ESG in a Family Business Operating in a Sensitive Industry in the Light of Institutional Theory

Roberto Aprile and Sergio Bovo

37.1 Introduction

This research analyses how the governance of a company operating in a sensitive industry as the bitumen one has been acting with reference to the implementation of environmental, social, and governance (ESG) elements within its organization. The case study is relevant since it addresses a family business (Fassin & Signori, 2023)—which represents a widely diffused ownership structure in the Italian context and at a global level (Villalonga & Amit, 2020)—that decided in 2016 to start with a managerialization process by appointing an external CEO with large experience in the OIL industry. The success of such process is certified by the Best Managed Companies Award (by Deloitte Private), received in the years 2021, 2022, 2023 and 2024.

This study is based on the institutional theory to better analyze the isomorphic process conducted by the company and the relevance of the different typologies of pressure on the path conducted by the company.

The company, named "Alma Petroli S.p.A.", is among the European leading companies in the production of high-quality bitumen, with a tailor-made business model and standards of excellence that stand out for both safety and environment. Its wide bitumen portfolio is entirely produced in the specifically designed and operated refinery located in the Ravenna industrial district.

Coauthor of Sections 4 and 5.

R. Aprile (✉)
University of Bergamo, Bergamo, Italy
e-mail: roberto.aprile@unibg.it

S. Bovo
Alma Petroli SpA, Ravenna, Italy

N. Castellano et al. (eds.), *Environmental, Social, Governance (ESG)*, SIDREA Series in Accounting and Business Administration,
https://doi.org/10.1007/978-3-031-76618-3_37

The analysis allows to understand, in particular, the sequence of the steps that the company has developed over time and planned to develop, putting in evidence which are the forms of institutional pressure that manly affect the implementation process of ESG parameters.

The understanding of the impact of institutional forces on ESG implementation within a professionalized family business operating in a sensitive industry should be of interest for the academic audience, not only for the regulators and standard setters, but also for professionals, as members of the Board and owners of family businesses.

The remainder of this chapter is articulated as follows: Sect. 37.2 contains the literature review and the theoretical background, Sect. 37.3 describes the methodology and the limitations of the study, Sect. 37.4 contains the description of the case study, Sect. 37.5 contains the analysis of collected data, and Sect. 37.6 contains the discussion and the final conclusions, together with the indication of possible future developments of this study.

37.2 Literature Review and Theoretical Background

ESG factors represent an important topic that companies are called to face in recent years (Hartzmark & Sussman, 2019; Syed, 2017). Such dimensions are considered the pillars of the sustainable development of global economy and society (Li et al., 2021; Morozova et al., 2019).

ESG regulation stems from the introduction of responsible investment concept. Eurosif (2014) defines ESG integration as "the explicit inclusion by asset managers of ESG risks and opportunities into traditional financial analysis and investment decisions based on a systematic process and appropriate research sources".

As evidenced by Amel-Zadeh and Serafeim (2018), the United Nations (UN) Principles for Responsible Investment (PRI)—launched in 2006—state the commitment to incorporating ESG issues into investment analysis and ownership policies and practices. Such approach has required, mainly to listed companies, to implement accountability with reference to the ESG dimensions. Such process has gradually spread to other companies, also driven by international documents and regulation, such as, in particular, the UN Sustainable Development Goals (SDGs) issued in 2015.

Now, we can freely consider it a global and comprehensive phenomenon. Morozova et al. (2019, p. 589) talk about the "Development of the modern global entrepreneurship", to indicate the important change in the managerial approach that companies are pursuing nowadays.

Notwithstanding the wide agreement on the adoption of this new approach, as evidenced by Clive (2007, p. 102), it is not easy for companies to face these challenging mutations. They state that "Sustainable development has become a widely accepted norm that still presents major problems of implementation".

This means that it is extremely useful to understand the path traced by companies to achieve these goals, especially not-listed companies that, being subject to less stringent constraints in terms of obligations and reporting, represent an extremely interesting object of study, given their greater freedom in terms of reporting and therefore of management.

For such companies, main constraints can derive from the legislation, from relevant suppliers or clients, from the desire to go public, and from the requirements of different stakeholders. Other incentives can derive from the own desires of the ownership and of the management of the company.

The theoretical background is strongly rooted in the institutional theory (Di Maggio & Powell, 1991; Meyer & Rowan, 1977; Scott, 1987) and its different declinations. As evidenced by Fernando and Lawrence (2014), CSR practices have been analyzed adopting different theoretical perspectives (economic theories, and social and political ones), focusing on legitimacy theory, stakeholder theory, and institutional theory.

Institutionalization is a process by which individual actors transmit what is socially defined as real, and in the meantime, it represents a parameter of how much an action can be considered to be right in a given social reality (Zucher, 1991). From this perspective, institutionalization is strongly linked to legitimacy (Aprile & Bini, 2018), which is "a generalized perception or assumption that the actions of an entity are desirable, proper, or appropriate within some socially constructed system of norms, values, beliefs and definitions" (Suchman, 1995, p. 574). Searching for legitimacy and social acceptance, organizations, and in this case, companies, try to realize actions, structures, and practices that are perceived to be socially correct (Scott, 2001), reflecting in their behaviors the influences and constraints deriving from external environment (Scott, 1987).

According to the institutional theory, organizations face institutional pressures that lead them to adopt similar strategic activities with the aim to gain legitimacy (Suchman, 1995) and social acceptance (Bansal & Clelland, 2004; Berrone et al., 2013; Scott, 1987).

In particular, this wave of interest for ESG and sustainability recalls the theory of isomorphism (Di Maggio & Powell, 1983, 1991). Deephouse (1996) specifies that isomorphism is strictly related to organizational legitimacy, which means the acceptance of an organization by its external environment (Di Maggio & Powell, 1983; Meyer & Rowan, 1977; Meyer & Scott, 1983). Deephouse (1996, p. 1024) finds that "isomorphism in strategies is related to legitimacy conferred by regulators and media".

DiMaggio and Powell (1983) distinguish between two kinds of isomorphism, namely, "competitive isomorphism," which is driven by competitive pressures in the markets and stimulates companies to be effective and efficient; and "institutional isomorphism," which is more related to the social dimension of organizations.

The authors articulate institutional isomorphism in three categories: coercive, mimetic, and normative. The first is the result of "formal and informal pressures exerted on organizations by other organizations upon which they are dependent and by cultural expectations in the society within which organizations function" (DiMaggio & Powell, 1983, p. 155).

Mimetic isomorphism is based on the adoption of best practices, considered as a guarantee of success (Scott, 2001). In particular, when there is a high level of uncertainty, and difficulties to predict the future, imitation represents one of the most viable solutions, even if it is not able to grant success or to prevent relevant mistakes.

Normative isomorphism is related to the role played by professional and educational organizations, in particular, not only universities and professional networks, but also standard setters and professional bodies.

All three isomorphic forces have been playing a relevant role in the introduction of sustainable managerial behaviors.

Main organizations involved in this relevant process are here grouped in categories proposed by the authors of this research:

1. International, supernational, and national regulators, such as United Nations (UN), European Union (EU), and Italian Legislator, that can exert coercive power
2. Suppliers, customers, competitors, local communities and other stakeholders, media world, that can generate mimetic behaviors
3. Standard setters, professional bodies, such as Global Reporting Initiative (GRI), European Financial Reporting Advisory Group (EFRAG), International Sustainability Standards Board (ISSB), Task Force on Climate-Related Financial Disclosures (TCFD), created by the Financial Stability Board, United Nations Global Compact (UNGC), ESG rating providers, certification organizations, including International Organization for Standardization (ISO), scientist word and educational word, including scientific journals, and universities, and Stock exchange authorities, that can exert normative power

Each of the above-listed organizations is able to activate isomorphic processes toward sustainable approaches incentivizing the adoption of ESG best practices. In particular, regulatory obligations can be transformed into market opportunities. By this way, also behaviors not mandatory for all kinds of companies—for example, small and medium entities (SMEs), or not-listed companies—can be adopted anyway.

Among main regulations regarding ESG, we can recall the following ones:

- SFDR—Sustainable Finance Disclosure Regulation—Regulation (EU) 2019/2088 entered into force on March 10, 2021
- EU Taxonomy for Sustainable Activities—Regulation (EU) 2020/852—entered into force on July 12, 2020
- CSRD—Corporate Sustainability Reporting Directive—Directive (EU) 2022/2464 entered into force on January 5, 2023

The Commission adopted on July 31, 2023, the European Sustainability Reporting Standards (ESRS) for use by all companies subject to the Corporate Sustainability Reporting Directive (CSRD).

Due to the presence of several regulators and different organizations involved, there is not a specific standardization of the contents attributable to each of the three dimensions of ESG. For this research, we define a specific articulation of each parameter, useful to verify which ESG parameters have been achieved by the company, before and after the professionalization process, or are still to be achieved. We also analyze which are the main levers incentivizing the process of implementation of such parameters.

37.3 Methodology

The analysis is based on a case study (De Massis & Kotlar, 2014; Merkens, 2004; Yin, 1994), referred to "Alma Petroli S.p.A.", a company that has characteristics that can be relevant for this study.

Alma Petroli has been selected due to its own main characteristics: it is a family business (Kenyon-Rouvinez & Ward, 2005) that represents a significant share of all companies in the world (Astrachan & Kolenko, 1994; Lee, 2006; Allouche et al., 2008; Sharma et al., 2012), with particular regard to Italy, where it represents 65% of Italian firms[1], and it was awarded the Best Managed Company award by Deloitte Private for three consecutive years (2021, 2022, and 2023). It has started a process of professionalization (Chua et al., 2009) in 2016 hiring a General Manager, nonbelonging to the family (Klein & Bell, 2007), that has been appointed as CEO in 2018. Professionalization can be considered as "the process through which professional managers become involved in the family business management or ownership" (Giovannoni et al., 2011). Songini and Vola (2015) add another perspective, indicating that "expert managers" are academically qualified and/or have specific previous experience in business administration (Culasso et al., 2016).

As indicated by Klein and Bell (2007), we can classify the compositions of management teams in family businesses in three categories: pure family management; mixed constellation (cooperation with nonfamily executives); and total separation of ownership and management (pure nonfamily management). Alma Petroli can be included in the second typology, since the Board of Directors (BoD) is composed not only of members of the shareholding families, but also of external members, including the CEO.

The analysis has been based on semi-structured interviews (Schmidt, 2004) with the CEO, of 3 h each, held in September and October 2023, and in January 2024, articulated in four different moments in a way to understand the company, the steps that it has already done and the other steps it is in train to develop in the closest future, and the role of different institutional pressures. The final moment has been used to triangulate data from interviews with company documents. More in details, the first interview was focused on the recent history of Alma Petroli and on how the managerialization process has been designed, planned, and implemented; the second was focused on the analysis of each single process and initiative to address ESG

[1] https://www.econopoly.ilsole24ore.com/2021/02/16/family-business-successione/. Accessed 8.9.2023.

perspective; the third was focused on the role of different stakeholders and the relevance of the institutional pressure; and the last one, in January 2024, has been used to control information from previous interviews with company documents.

The interviewed CEO, Sergio Bovo, is also a coauthor of the chapter, in a way to control all information supplied in this contribution and to specifically describe the company.

Interviews have not been recorded since the interviewed CEO has had the opportunity to fully control and rectify the information included in this chapter. We also collected empirical documents (e.g., financial statements, contracts, minutes of the BoD meetings, remunerations policies), with the aim to verify the reliability of all information and data collected during the interviews and used within this research.

With reference to the three ESG dimensions, this study analyses the steps made by the company starting from the beginning, focusing especially on the period that can be classified as "mixed constellation" started with the appointment of an external CEO. The analysis includes further future steps, not yet completed but already started or planned. In particular, we focus on the logical order of intervention verifying whether the external reports have incentivized internal activities within the organization, or vice versa. In other words, we investigate whether external documents or practices represent a consequence of rooted internal activities or an incentive and in some ways an input that allows to start new internal procedures. Such approach allows to verify whether institutional pressure incentives the introduction of new internal procedures and activities.

As above explained, it is not easy to define a precise list of parameters for each ESG perspective. Evocative of this situation is the study of Berg et al. (2022), titled "Aggregate Confusion: The Divergence of ESG Ratings." Based on the existing norms, standards, and literature, we have defined a list of parameters useful to analyze the ESG perspective. This subjectivity can represent not only a limitation of the study, but also a point of strength. For example, SDGs could be theoretically useful to help the analysis of ESG dimensions, but they have been issued considering all global organizations and countries, and in some cases, they are not perfectly fitting with the context of Italian companies because SDGs may concern national and not corporate objectives, and because some of these objectives have been generally already met by Italian companies (e.g., Goal 8: *Decent work and economic growth*).

Selected parameters for this study are the following ones:

Environmental dimension:

- Certifications
- Renewable energy production
- Waste
- Recycling
- New units environmentally sustainable
- Prevention of pollution in each form
- Introduction of new environmentally friendly products and procedures

- Greenhouse gas emissions (GHG) and effluent emissions
- Community impacts.

Social dimension:

- Welfare
- Certifications
- Training and education
- Gender equality in the organization
- Support to the local community
- Other aspects.[2]

Governance dimension:

- Corporate culture
- Committees
- Independent directors
- Remuneration policy
- Internal audit
- Risk assessment and risk management
- Avoiding corruption and bribery
- Whistleblowing
- Codes of conduct and business principles
- Gender equality in the Board
- Accountability and transparency.

37.4 Case Study

Founded in 1957 and in operations since 1960, Alma Petroli is among the bitumen leading producers in Europe. The production site is located in Ravenna industrial district, and it has a throughput capacity of 550.000 tons/year of crude oils and heavy feedstocks. The bitumen production makes for approximately 70% of the yield, and it is useful to specify that Alma Petroli does not produce any fuel nor other products to be burned. In a few words, the company primary activity is the processing of crude oil and heavy semi-finished products specific for the production of bitumen for paving and industrial applications.

All the processes, units, structures, and assets have been designed, and are now managed and developed, to guarantee the highest degree of flexibility in serving the bitumen markets. Bitumen is a highly technological and sustainable product, whose diversified uses go from paving application in roads and runways to waterproofing or

[2]This parameter can be articulated as follows: workforce freedom of association; child labor; workplace health and safety; customer health and safety; avoidance of forced and compulsory labor; poverty and community impact; and discrimination, diversity, and equal opportunity.

soundproofing membranes to submarine cable coating (to mention just few examples). Bitumen is the only fully reusable building material and the only oil derivative that does not contribute to CO2 emissions in the atmosphere in its applications.

Each and every application requires a significantly different quality of the product, which is the result of long and professional R&D processes (whose relations with corporate governance (CG) have been studied by Ginesti et al., 2023), accurate raw material selection, and specific production unit setup. This is the essence of the Alma Petroli business model that has brought the company to have a refinery and a highly specialized laboratory that operates 24 h every day and to offer the most complete portfolio of bitumen in Europe.

The company was managed since its foundation by the founding family that led various stages of growth. Facing a significant change after some years with poor results, it has started a deep and thorough evolution in terms of structure and governance, which has led to a modern managerial approach successfully implemented. Since 2018, the CEO is an external manager that joined the company at the end of 2016 as General Manager, after a career in the oil and gas industry. Another peculiarity is that as of today, in the management team there are no shareholder representatives.

As affirmed by Sergio Bovo, to outline a quick picture of the recent successes, "Between 2018 and today Alma Petroli has always improved the economic and financial performance, with positive net results and starting from a NFP/EBITDA ratio of—6.6 in 2016 turning to cash positive (2022). It has already invested 20 million Euros mainly in new technologies, and has planned further 40 million Euros in assets and processes. Meantime, the company has grown in occupation with an increase of about 20% (from 82 to 99 employees), developed training activities, and has enlarged its business by incorporating two companies".

Alma Petroli has become in 2019 an official member of the Oil Companies International Marine Forum (OCIMF) and a core member of Eurobitume since 2018, granting access to primary networks of players and providing valuable contribution to both associations.

The following section analyzes the steps undertaken and planned in the transformation of the company, with a specific focus on the parameters listed in Sect. 37.3, also considering the underpinning logics and the impact of isomorphic pressures.

37.5 Analysis

37.5.1 The First Steps After the Introduction of the Managerialization Process

The CEO, Sergio Bovo, has specified that "The first driver in the managerial choices needed to be and has been to grant financial and nonfinancial sustainability in the long term". The first actions were therefore aimed at returning to profit and to cash generation, and to do so, market analysis and financial risk management (in particular, prices and forex hedging tools) have been developed (2017). Apart from such instruments that helped in assuming managerial decisions, the first actions have been:

- To formally define and share the corporate values (in 2017) and strategic guidelines (in 2018)
- To set up budgeting, multiyear plan, and control processes and tools (shared among management and directors at the Board)
- To define enterprise risk management (Maffei, 2021), helping both the strategic and managerial processes
- To reorganize processes by adopting a zero-base approach
- To reorganize both the structure and the governance starting from 2018.

With reference to the reorganization process, in the hiring phase Alma Petroli has concentrated on the aim of increasing and updating the competences available.

"The actions implemented following the above first steps created the conditions for a virtuous circle: good results, confidence in the plans, more resources to invest in development, better results, possibility to focus on the other priorities" (CEO comment).

In order to introduce and develop best practices in management and CG, in 2019 the company started to follow the Elite Euronext program, achieving the status of Elite company in January 2020, before any other company of the same lounge. This status is obtained at the end of a three-phase track, with various audits on economic and financial strength, governance, communication, planning, reporting, and social responsibility.

37.5.2 The Analysis of the ESG Parameters and Their Evolution Over Time

Moving to the parameters listed in Sect. 37.3, with reference to the first dimension (environmental), the starting point was already of a very high level, due to all the regulations strictly enforced for refineries (coercive isomorphism) and to the "no compromise attitude" of the management and ownership on these issues. To mention some of the most relevant achievements of Alma Petroli:

- All stationary source emissions are captured since more than 20 years as stated in the "Autorizzazione Integrata Ambientale" (AIA)
- All the liquid wastes are conveyed and treated by a cleaning and purification plant managed by an external consortium (AIA)
- Photovoltaic panels have been installed and in production since 2011.
- In 2007, it has voluntarily adhered to the Eco-Management and Audit Scheme (EMAS) Protocol that has the aim of promoting the best available standards in

environmental protection, as well as a transparent communication in the same field (example of normative isomorphism)

- In 2020, the soil cleaning and remediation was completed, verified, and certified by the Regional Environmental Authority (ARPAE).

Alma Petroli has achieved other certifications such as OHSAS, now ISO 45001, in 2017 and EN 13924 in 2020. Such certifications have been pursued with the aim to reach the best standards in safety for the workers.

More recently, the company has started to study the decarbonization plan, with the target of reducing first and resetting after the GHG emissions of the production units.

It is relevant to our discussion of the fact that the supply chain has played a very important role in developments of Alma Petroli approach toward environment and GHG: it has become common for the top-tier players to select their bitumen suppliers by evaluating not only the quality of the product but also its environmental impact and carbon footprint. In this respect, life-cycle inventory (LCI) and life-cycle assessment (LCA) analyses are conducted from the crude oil wells to the bitumen delivery (since 2020). In parallel, going well beyond the existing laws and regulations, most European players accept bitumen with a very low content in polycyclic aromatic hydrocarbons (PAH), which has led Alma Petroli, that is in full compliance with all the laws, to implement massive investments (e.g., full revamping of the crude oil distillation units, whose first phase was conducted between 2021 and 2023, and the second will be completed in 2025) in order to grant the best quality to its customers.

With reference to the second dimension (social), Alma Petroli has opted to redesign its positioning. A welfare program was developed and financed by the company, providing access for every employee to a number of benefits (from sports to leisure activities, from healthcare to books, etc.). The project started with preliminary steps in 2019 and evolved to its full extension in 2021.

In parallel, scholarships for employees' children, together with financial support to compensate the high inflation rate impact, have been delivered in 2020 (during the pandemic) and 2022.

The remuneration policy of the management and the workforce, in line with the findings of Kenyon-Rouvinez and Ward (2005), has been redesigned together with the introduction of individual target setting and performance evaluation. Such innovations are considered an extremely important pillar of a modernly managed company. The transition from a discretionary approach, typical of family business to a solid system, has gone through a series of steps. Organizationally, it started with the definition of a Management by Objectives (MBO) program in 2018, dedicated to the management team, and with a detailed plan that was completed in 2022 with the extension of objectives and incentives to most of the organization. It required the definition of a "cascading" process, where targets are selected consistently with the business plan, de-escalated along the organigram.

In parallel, a project to develop the job evaluation and the relevant compensation package definition for all the positions was developed, with a first release conducted internally (2018) and a thorough review completed in 2022 with external support of a highly specialized consulting company to achieve the best standards and to update the comparison with the external benchmark.

The next step, planned for 2025, is the setup and activation of an integrated performance evaluation system (MBO and competence review), in parallel with the creation of a "talent matrix" to monitor and help talents to develop.

A program to increase gender equality in the entire organization has been set, and its course is on track, as demonstrated by the percentage of new recruits of female gender and/or of non-Italian origin. The aim of the company is to obtain the certification in 2024, to have the possibility to be recognized for its commitment in this direction.

In the years, the company has significantly increased the investments on training, adding to the mandatory courses according to the existing laws on Health and Safety for Major Accident Hazard (MAH) industrial sites an intense program on both technical knowledge and soft skill/competency development.

Finally, initiatives to support the local communities have been planned with the following main targets:

- Improvement of the conditions of the families of the territory with health problems by support to specific projects (e.g., "Palestra della mente" with Alzheimer's Association, setting up remotely controlled intensive care units in the Local hospital, project that has started in 2023)
- Sponsorship to nonprofessional sports club, to develop children's teams and activities (rugby, football, fencing, since 2021).

With reference to the "other aspects" listed in footnote 5, we have to specify that Italian companies respectful of the law are already aligned with all the listed parameters. Only "poverty and community impact" represent something voluntary that, as explained before, is a dimension already included in its behaviors by Alma Petroli.

With reference to the third dimension (governance), relevant steps have been undertaken between 2018 and 2021. The main milestones can be summarized in:

- Updating the Ethics Code (the first release, dated 2012, has been following updated with the adoption of the General Confederation of Italian Industry guidelines in 2018)
- Setting up specific Managerial Committees as detailed below
- Setting up of a modern remuneration policy for the BoD (2018)
- Appointing of an independent director at the Board (2019)
- Setting up the organizational model against crimes and connected introduction of the supervisory body and whistleblowing procedures (2018).

With reference to the introduction of Managerial Committees, Management Committee has been created in 2017, the Investment Committee has been formed in 2018 (with guidelines and rules approved by the Board), and the Leadership Committee has been created in 2019 and composed of all the managers and with specific focus on organization and people development.

Communication plays an essential role in the success of a business and in improving stakeholder relationships (De Luca et al., 2022). Alma Petroli has planned to start with a structured presence in external communication, carefully selecting the channels (web and LinkedIn) and above all the "tone of voice." A Communication Committee was recently formed (2022), taking care of the planning and writing of all the contents, while visuals and graphics are managed with the support of external experts.

With reference to remuneration, the company reviewed in parallel both the remuneration policy for the Board members, introducing in 2018 short-term incentives based on economic performance, and the one for the management and the entire workforce based on a multidimensional approach.

The company has not created a Remuneration Policy Committee, but has approved the proposal made by the CEO during the shareholder meeting. In this case, the company has faced an important cultural barrier in the innovation of the remuneration of directors, in particular, introducing variable incentivizing components. Shareholders have showed some difficulties in accepting variable compensations deriving from the incentives and evaluation processes that might differ from their personal perceptions and feelings. This aspect can be rooted in the family business approach, strongly related to the entrepreneurial approach and intuition, and sometimes less related to final data. Till now, the inclusion in the remuneration policy of social and environmental aspects is limited to safety parameters (applied to the organization), being the remuneration of the Board based mainly on the financial performance of the company.

The appointment of an independent director has represented a relevant innovation, opening the Board to external figures. This innovation has not been the first and has benefitted from the fact that the Independent Director accepted to work for free and to share his wide knowledge in the industry (the Independent Director at that time was the Chairman of "Unione Petrolifera"—Oil Union). This evolution, consistent with the Italian code of governance, has been promoted by the CEO and benefitted of his relational network with experienced managers that have worked in the same industry.

Internal audit has not been formalized yet, since the company, for the moment, is based on external audit. Notwithstanding this situation, the company is working to implement specific controls of the different dimensions, based on the introduction of formalized control procedures and on the help of external consultants (e.g., for financial dimensions, and for the privacy), and the control of certification bodies.

With reference to risk management, the company has introduced specific controls, starting from the financial dimension (2017), and continuing (2018) developing other managerial aspects (operations, market, organization, culture, etc.).

With reference to codes of conduct and business principles, the analysis shows that many of the behaviors of the company are consistent with the principles indicated in the codes of governance. We have anyway to point out that since the company is not involved in a listing process in the short run, to be compliant with such codes do not represent a priority for the company.

A point to be outlined is linked to the fact that the attention paid to the whole organization and internal processes needs to be paired with an equal care toward all the elements of the supply chain, especially in the oil & gas international framework, where compliance to international rules (EU, US) is a complicate and extremely delicate matter (e.g., Russian sanctions, embargo on Venezuela, etc.). In general, the Know Your Customer (KYC) process has been implemented in order to grant safe and reliable checks on applicable laws and on each supplier's adherence to the values, principles, and procedures stated in Alma Petroli Code of Ethics and Model 231 against crimes. When possible critical issues are identified, the company makes recourse to the support of national and international specialized law firms.

Gender equality in the Board has not been reached yet, since the Board is completely composed of male members. This situation has historical roots, and it is not in the agenda in the short period.

Accountability and transparency represent a further evolution of the company and, starting from governance decisions, involve all ESG dimensions. At the moment, the company is compliant with all regulatory requirements, but has not supplied further reports or documents not specifically required by the law. It is expected to publish in 2024 its first sustainability report. Transparency is substantially affected mainly by the coercive isomorphic pressure.

37.6 Discussion and Conclusions

The study shows that the managerialization process of a family business requires to integrate several different parameters, taking care of the financial performance that represents the first step to grant long-term viability of the company. This aspect has been particularly required by shareholders represented by family members of the analyzed company. This research has shown that the path toward the implementation of a comprehensive and integrated ESG approach meets a first hurdle in cost constraints. Business expansion, stability, and organization growth represent, in substance, sort of prerequisites.

In this context, ESG parameters should be applied mainly for two reasons: regulatory requirements and mimetic isomorphic pressure made by the supply chain and strongly able to affect financial performance, since they can increase the reputation of the company (Othman et al., 2011). Such starting point is clearly relevant and leads to the introduction of a comprehensive culture of sustainability, articulated in the three ESG dimensions, but mainly rooted to environmental aspects and aspects related to the creation of a safe place for the employees of the company. That is due to the institutional pressure exerted by two important stakeholders, namely, customers and workforce. Another important dimension that has been substantially immediately introduced refers to the governance topic and consists of the risk assessment and management, related to the need to protect and preserve the financial performance of the company.

With the aim to create a pleasant and incentivizing working environment, welfare policies and incentivizing remuneration policies (MBO systems) have been of great importance. This is consistent with the resource-based view (Penrose, 1959; Wernerfelt, 1984; Barney, 1991; Wade & Hulland, 2004; Kristandl & Bontis, 2007) and the intellectual capital (IC) literature (Aisenberg Ferenhof et al., 2015; Bontis, 1998; Edvinsson & Malone, 1997), in which human resources are considered important factors for the value creation process of the company.

The above steps have been the first to be done by the company, consistently with the need to integrate financial and nonfinancial performance, maintaining an equilibrium among them and integrating each dimension within the value creation process.

With reference to the other ESG parameters that are less related to the financial performance, we can observe that the company is anyway doing many steps and others have been already planned.

One of the first to be applied has been the introduction of the organizational model aimed at preventing corporate crimes and bribes. This form of protection of the company from illegal behavior aims to safeguard the viability of the company and its reputation that represents an important competitive factor. Analogously, the introduction of green behaviors, green products, the reduction of emissions, and the production of renewable energy is contributing to be perceived by stakeholders as a well-managed company, acting correctly and taking care of several aspects related to nonfinancial performance. The CEO has clearly specified the importance of the role played by the supply chain, in this evolution process, that has required more stringent performance, compared to the law or other forms of regulations. This has an immediate relapse on Alma Petroli suppliers, to which the company needs to ask the same attention and guarantees.

In other words, mimetic isomorphism, integrated in the value creation process, is able to affect company's behaviors also more than the coercive or normative isomorphism, even if the coercive one represents the starting point, able to activate all the virtuous circle (Aprile & Bini, 2018).

With reference to the governance aspects, it emerges that many of the analyzed parameters do not represent a priority for the company, since they constitute necessary requirements mainly for listed companies. Their adoption is in general strongly related to the aim of introducing specific development paths, as going public, where coercive and normative pressure would become relevant. Mimetic isomorphism is less relevant for family businesses, even if the professionalization process, where the introduction of the connected experience and knowledge of best practice, can activate important steps also with reference to the governance dimension. Consistently, the steps made by the company, as the introduction of specific committees and independent directors, are related to the managerialization process of the company, which, benefitting of the professional culture of the CEO (Melis & Nawaz, 2023), has introduced best practices, generally rooted in the normative isomorphism (CG Codes).

Certifications and disclosure represent elements that can be introduced by the company in case of expected benefits, in particular, financial benefits. This means that if they are not required by the law, or are not required by the customers, they do not represent the first steps that a professional manager intends to perceive. Also in this case, market and financial incentives represent relevant forces able to activate the introduction of these elements.

An obstacle faced in the introduction of new forms of disclosure may arise in connection with the natural tendency of family business in keeping a low profile with reference to information sharing and communication, which can create a sort of viscosity in the assessment and reporting steps. In most of the cases, this is not due to an actual lack of transparency, but more to the tendency of managing the whole company with the same approach and care given to the family relations.

Another aspect that has emerged from this research is that both certification and disclosure (especially sustainability disclosure) can affect the organization and procedures of the company. Both of them do not represent the ending point of a path internally activated by the company, but the opportunity to activate processes that can generate useful pitfall also with reference to the organization and procedures of the company. This is fully consistent with the organizational learning theory (Chiva et al., 2014; Crossan et al., 1999; Duncan & Weiss, 1979). Levitt and March (1988) in fact show how the learning process or organizations are routine-based, history-dependent, and target-oriented, all aspects stimulated by external reporting. Consistently, also March (1991) developed the concepts of exploration and exploitation of routines (Aprile, 2021). External reporting, as the aim to obtain new certifications (e.g., gender equality certification), helps companies to internally reorganize in a way to meet the requirements functional to achieve the results that the company aims to communicate. In other words, certifications and disclosure represent leverages able to activate internal progress of the company.

The analyzed case study has evidenced useful findings, but cannot be generalized and requires further study to investigate the impact of institutional forces on the adoption of ESG parameters. It can be seen as a limitation of the present study. Anyway, it has been useful and interesting to test how institutional pressure is acting toward a family business that has started a professionalization process and to understand the strong relationship between ESG dimensions and financial performance, which continues to play a preponderant role. An example is represented by the investments made in favor of the local community. The authorization of such investments has been easier to be achieved by the Board, which is mainly composed of family members, due to the good financial performance achieved during the analyzed period. In other words, juridical requirements and financial performance represent one of the most important elements/incentives able to foster the introduction of ESG parameters within the company.

This study can be useful for academics, since it applies the institutional theory to the ESG parameter implementation in the context of a family business that has started a professionalization process. It can also be useful for practitioners since it shows a possible sequence in the implementation of ESG dimensions, consistent with the need to grant a good financial and nonfinancial performance.

Future developments of this study can be represented by a reproduction of this analysis with reference to a broader sample, for example, applying a questionnaire to an adequate number of companies that can be classified as family business that have started a professionalization process. It could be of value to extend the study to other typologies of companies and industries to compare and contrast the results of this study with other researches.

References

Aisenberg Ferenhof, A., Durst, S., Zaniboni Bialecki, M., & Selig, P. M. (2015). Intellectual capital dimensions: State of the art in 2014. *Journal of Intellectual Capital, 16*(1), 58–100. https://doi.org/10.1108/JIC-02-2014-0021

Allouche, J., Amann, B., Jaussaud, J., & Kurashina, T. (2008). The impact of family control on the performance and financial characteristics of family versus nonfamily businesses in Japan: A matched-pair investigation. *Family Business Review, 21*, 315–330. https://doi.org/10.1177/08944865080210040104

Amel-Zadeh, A., & Serafeim, G. (2018). Why and how investors use ESG information: Evidence from a global survey. *Financial Analysts Journal, 74*(3), 87–103. https://doi.org/10.2469/faj.v74.n3.2

Aprile, R. (2021). Implementazione dei sistemi ERP: errori e soluzioni sulla base dell'organizational learning. *Controllo di Gestione, 2*, 16–27.

Aprile, R., & Bini, L. (2018). The role of institutions in the process of global convergence to IFRS. *Financial Reporting, 2*, 111–134.

Astrachan, J. H., & Kolenko, T. A. (1994). A neglected factor explaining family business success: Human resource practices. *Family Business Review, 7*(3), 251–262.

Bansal, P., & Clelland, I. (2004). Talking trash: Legitimacy, impression management, and unsystematic risk in the context of the natural environment. *Academy of Management Journal.*

Barney, J. (1991). Firm resources and sustained competitive advantage. *Journal of Management, 17*(1), 99–120.

Berg, F., Koelbel, J. F., & Rigobon, R. (2022). Aggregate confusion: The divergence of ESG ratings. *Review of Finance, 26*(6), 1315–1344.

Berrone, P., Fosfuri, A., Gelabert, L., & Gomez-Mejia, L. R. (2013). Necessity as the mother of 'green' inventions: Institutional pressures and environmental innovations. *Strategic Management Journal, 34*, 891–909.

Bontis, N. (1998). Intellectual capital: An exploratory study that develops measures and models. *Management Decision, 36*(2), 63–76. https://doi.org/10.1108/00251749810204142

Chiva, R., Ghauri, P., & Alegre, J. (2014). Organizational learning, innovation and internationalization: A complex system model. *British Journal of Management, 25*, 687–705.

Chua, J. H., Chrisman, J., & Bergiel, E. B. (2009). Defining the family business by behavior. *Entrepreneurship: Theory and Practice, 23*(4), 19–39.

Clive, G. (2007). Sustainable development and global governance. *The Journal of Environment & Development, 16*(1), 102–125.

Crossan, M. M., Lane, H. W., & White, R. E. (1999). An organizational learning framework: From intuition to institution. *Academy of Management Review, 24*, 522–537.

Culasso, F., Giacosa, E., Manzi, L. M., & Tuant, E. (2016). Professionalization in family firms versus non-family businesses in Italy. *Impresa Progetto, 3*, 1–21.

De Luca, F., Iaia, L., Mehmood, A., & Vrontis, D. (2022). Can social media improve stakeholder engagement and communication of sustainable development goals? A cross-country analysis. *Technological Forecasting and Social Change, 177*, 121525. https://doi.org/10.1016/j.techfore.2022.121525

De Massis, A., & Kotlar, J. (2014). The case study method in family business research. Guidelines for qualitative scholarship. *Journal of Family Business Strategy, 5*(1), 15–29., ISSN 1877-8585. https://doi.org/10.1016/j.jfbs.2014.01.007

Deephouse, D. L. (1996). Does isomorphism legitimate? *Academy of Management Journal, 39*(4), 1024–1039.

Di Maggio, P., & Powell, W. (1983). The iron cage revisited: Institutional isomorphism and collective rationality in organizational fields. *American Sociological Review, 48*(2), 147–160.

Di Maggio, P., & Powell, W. (1991). *The new institutionalism in organizational analysis*. University of Chicago Press.

Duncan, R., & Weiss, A. (1979). Organizational learning: Implications for organizational design. *Research in Organizational Behavior, 1*, 75–123.

Edvinsson, L., & Malone, M. (1997). *Intellectual capital: Realising your Company's true value by finding its hidden brainpower*. HarperCollins.

Eurosif. (2014). *European SRI study*. Eurosif.

Fassin, Y., & Signori, S. (2023). *Family firms*. https://doi.org/10.4337/9781800374249.ch24

Fernando, S., & Lawrence, S. (2014). A theoretical framework for CSR practices: Integrating legitimacy theory, stakeholder theory and institutional theory. *Journal of Theoretical Accounting Research, 10*(1), 149–178.

Ginesti, G., Campa, D., Spanò, R., Allini, A., & Maffei, M. (2023). The role of CSR committee characteristics on R&D investments, international business review, *32*(5), 102147. ISSN 0969-5931.

Giovannoni, E., Maraghini, M. P., & Riccaboni, A. (2011). Transmitting knowledge across generations: The role of management accounting practices. *Family Business Review, 24*(2), 126–150.

Hartzmark, S. M., & Sussman, A. B. (2019). Do investors value sustainability? A natural experiment examining ranking and fund flows. *The Journal of Finance, 74*(6), 2789–2837.

Kenyon-Rouvinez, D., & Ward, J. L. (2005). *Family business. Key issues*. Palgrave Macmillan.

Klein, S., & Bell, F.-A. (2007). Non-family executives in family businesses: A literature review. *Electronic Journal of Family Business Studies (EJFBS), 1*(1), 19–37.

Kristandl, G., & Bontis, N. (2007). Constructing a definition for intangibles using the resource-based view of the firm. *Management Decision, 45*(9), 1510–1524.

Lee, J. (2006). Family firm performance: Further evidence. *Family Business Review, 19*, 103–114.

Levitt, B., & March, J. G. (1988). Organizational learning. *Annual Review of Sociology, 14*, 319–340.

Li, T.-T., Wang, K., Sueyoshi, T., & Wang, D. D. (2021). ESG: Research Progress and future prospects, sustainability. *MDPI, 13*(11663), 1–28. https://doi.org/10.3390/su132111663

Maffei, M. (2021). *Enterprise risk management across Europe* (pp. 279–303). Emerald Publishing Limited. https://doi.org/10.1108/978-1-83867-245-420211016

March, J. G. (1991). Exploration and exploitation in organizational learning. *Organizational Science, 2*(1), 71–87.

Melis, A., & Nawaz, T. (2023). The impact of CEOs' personal traits on Organisational performance: Evidence from faith-based charity Organisations. *Journal of Business Ethics*, 1–21. https://doi.org/10.1007/s10551-023-05412-1

Merkens, H. (2004). Selection Procedures, sampling, case construction, chapter 4.4, 165, 171. In U. Flick, E. von Kardorff, & I. Steinke (Eds.), *A companion to qualitative research*. Sage.

Meyer, J. W., & Rowan, B. (1977). Institutional organizations: Formal structure as myth and ceremony. *American Journal of Sociology, 83*(2), 340–363.

Meyer, J. W., & Scott, W. R. (1983). *Organization and environments: Ritual and rationality*. Stanford University Press.

Morozova, I. A., Popkova, E. G., & Litvinova, T. N. (2019). Sustainable development of global entrepreneurship: Infrastructure and perspectives. *The International Entrepreneurship and Management Journal, 15*, 589–597.

Othman, S., Darus, F., & Arshad, R. (2011). The influence of coercive isomorphism on corporate social responsibility reporting and reputation. *Social Responsibility Journal, 7*(1), 118–135.
Penrose, E. T. (1959). *The theory of the growth of the firm*. John Wiley.
Schmidt, C. (2004). The analysis of semi-structured interviews, chapter 5.1. In U. Flick, E. von Kardorff, & I. Steinke (Eds.), *A companion to qualitative research* (p. 253, 258). Sage.
Scott, W. R. (1987). The adolescence of institutional theory. *Administrative Science Quarterly, 32*, 493–511.
Scott, W. R. (2001). *Institutions and organizations* (2nd ed.). Sage.
Sharma, P., Chrisman, J. J., & Gersick, K. E. (2012). 25 years of family business review: Reflections on the past and perspectives for the future. *Family Business Review, 25*, 5–15. https://doi.org/10.1177/0894486512437626
Songini, L., & Vola, P. (2015). The role of professionalization and Managerialization in family business succession. *Managament Control, 1*, 9–43.
Suchman, M. C. (1995). Managing legitimacy: Strategic and institutional approaches. *Academy of Management Review, 20*(3), 571–610.
Syed, A. M. (2017). Environment, social, and governance (ESG) criteria and preference of managers. *Cogent Business & Management, 4*(1), 1340820. https://doi.org/10.1080/23311975.2017.1340820
Villalonga, B., & Amit, R. (2020). Family ownership. *Oxford Review of Economic Policy, 36*, 241–257. https://doi.org/10.1093/oxrep/graa007
Wade, M., & Hulland, J. (2004). The resource-based view and information systems research: Review, extension, and suggestions for future research. *MIS Quarterly*, 107–142.
Wernerfelt, B. (1984). A resource-based view of the firm. *Strategic Management Journal, 5*(2), 171–180.
Yin, R. K. (1994). *Case study research: Design and methods* (2nd ed.). Sage.
Zucher, L. G. (1991). The role of institutionalization in cultural persistence. In W. Powell & P. J. Di Maggio (Eds.), *The new institutionalism in organizational analysis* (pp. 83–107). The University of Chicago Press.

Chapter 38
A Systems Perspective on Sustainability Management Systems: Lessons for SMEs

Silvia Testarmata, Alessandro Giosi, Beatrice Meo, Sandro Brunelli, and Maria Lisa Centini

38.1 Introduction

The rise in stakeholder expectations and demands for sustainable and responsible business practices has put increasing pressure on organizations to consider sustainability issues in their strategy and operations. Management systems may be effective for embedding sustainability into organizational strategy (Carmine & De Marchi, 2023; Eccles et al., 2014; Nawaz & Koç, 2018) and operations (Battaglia et al., 2016; Beusch et al., 2022; Gond et al., 2012; Johnstone, 2019).

The integration of sustainability into organizational strategy and operations is not solely a matter of compliance or risk mitigation; it presents an opportunity for organizations to gain a competitive edge and foster long-term value creation (Edmans, 2023a, b; Porter & Kramer, 2011). Some studies have shown a positive relationship between sustainability performance and financial performance (Hussain et al., 2018; Lu & Taylor, 2016; Martínez-Ferrero & Frías-Aceituno, 2015; Yilmaz, 2021), indicating that sustainability management systems can enhance shareholder value and drive organizational success throughout the value chain (Dharmayanti et al., 2023; El-Haggar & Samaha, 2019; Epstein, 2008).

In light of this potential for financial benefit, it is essential to examine how organizations effectively integrate sustainability into their management systems and value chain to optimize shared value creation. However, integrating

S. Testarmata (✉) · A. Giosi · B. Meo
Dipartimento di Scienze Umane, Università LUMSA, Roma, Italy
e-mail: s.testarmata@lumsa.it

S. Brunelli
Dipartimento di Management e Diritto, Università degli Studi di Roma Tor Vergata, Roma, Italy

M. L. Centini
KPMG, Roma, Italy

N. Castellano et al. (eds.), *Environmental, Social, Governance (ESG)*, SIDREA Series in Accounting and Business Administration,
https://doi.org/10.1007/978-3-031-76618-3_38

sustainability within organizational strategy and operations is not straightforward, since it requires a dense interconnection involving organizational, cognitive and technical dimensions of management control systems (Gond et al., 2012).

To date, only a few studies have analysed the roles of management systems in the integration of sustainability into organizational strategy and operations (El-Haggar & Samaha, 2019; Nawaz & Koç, 2018). However, a broad stream of literature focuses on the roles and uses of management control systems to integrate sustainability in organizational strategy and operations (Battaglia et al., 2016; Beusch et al., 2022; Busco et al., 2024; Gond et al., 2012, 2024; Tu Le et al., 2024).

In addition, while larger organizations have received significant attention regarding sustainability integration into management systems, the specific context of small and medium enterprises (SMEs) remains relatively underexplored (Ahmad & Mohamed Zabri, 2024; Battaglia et al., 2016; Cavicchi et al., 2023; Guidi et al., 2024). In particular, agricultural SMEs often face unique challenges, including limited resources and capabilities, which may impact their ability to effectively integrate sustainability considerations into organizational strategy and operations (FAO, CIHEAM, PRIMA Foundation, UfM, 2023; FAO, IFAD, UNICEF, WFP, WHO, 2023; Testarmata et al., 2023). Thus, investigating how agricultural SMEs navigate these challenges and embrace sustainability issues within their management systems may provide valuable insights for practitioners, policymakers and researchers.

Therefore, the purpose of this study is to investigate whether and how the development and use of sustainability management systems are able to integrate sustainability issues within organizational strategy and operations, in order to identify the factors that support the integration of sustainability into the strategic decision-making process. As a theoretical model, the research proposes a new conceptual framework that combines the systematic approach to corporate sustainability tensions of Hahn et al. (2015) with the configuration approach to management control systems of Gond et al. (2012) to explore the potential roles and the uses of sustainability management systems in the integration of sustainability within strategy and operations according to a systems perspective. To the best of the authors' knowledge, this study represents the first analysis that investigates the integration of sustainability into management systems through the lens of the systems perspective. In addition, the analysis is embedded in the context of agricultural SMEs.

The remaining sections of this study are organized as follows: the second section proposes the theoretical framework used to integrate sustainability issues into management systems. The third section highlights the core traits of agricultural SMEs. The fourth section describes the research method and introduces the case study. The fifth section presents the case study analysis and outlines the research findings. The sixth section discusses the research findings. The final section outlines the conclusions of the study.

38.2 A Systems Perspective on Sustainability Management Systems

Within the growing stream of research on sustainability integration into organizational strategy and operations, little research has investigated the interplay of sustainability concerns and management systems (MSs). However, the urgent need to integrate specific sustainability issues within the more traditional MSs has been highlighted as necessary for the effective alignment of business strategy and operations with a sustainable approach to business (Beusch et al., 2022; Guidi et al., 2024; Nawaz & Koç, 2018).

An MS is a holistic framework that enables an organization to achieve its objectives through a systemic approach. MSs encompass procedures, processes, structures and tools for planning, executing, controlling and monitoring organizational activities in line with a dialectical relationship with the competitive environment (Cafferata, 2018, 2000). The core intent is to ensure efficiency, effectiveness and alignment with the organization's strategic goals (Drucker, 1954; Kaplan & Norton, 1992; Mintzberg et al., 1998; Porter, 1996; Simons, 1995). The effectiveness of an MS is often measured by its ability to adapt to changes in the environment, integrate new processes and technologies and support continuous improvement and learning within the organization (Argyris & Schön, 1978; Eisenhardt & Martin, 2000; Teece et al., 1997). MSs may indeed be effective for integrating sustainability issues into organizational strategy and operations (El-Haggar & Samaha, 2019; Nawaz & Koç, 2018; Schaltegger & Burritt, 2018).

Since traditional MSs are oriented towards achieving the business and economic goals of organizations, they are viewed as limited in addressing environmental and social issues and their interrelationships with financial issues (Gond et al., 2012). Given the limitations of MSs in addressing sustainability issues, sustainability management systems (SMSs) have emerged to support organizational sustainability (Johnstone, 2019). An SMS is a holistic management framework that incorporates sustainability into an organization's strategy, operations and decision-making processes. It aims to optimize resource use and improve sustainability by evaluating, managing and enhancing an organization's performance in economic, environmental and social dimensions (Epstein & Roy, 2001; Lozano, 2012; Nawaz & Koç, 2018; Porter & Kramer, 2006; Schaltegger & Burritt, 2010).

SMSs are designed to create a systemic approach to managing sustainability practices, ensuring that they are not just ad-hoc initiatives but are central to the organization's strategic direction and operations (Gao & Bansal, 2013; Hahn et al., 2015). The systemic approach (or integrative perspective) to business sustainability is predicated on the idea that sustainable business practices should not be an add-on or merely a social responsibility initiative, but rather an integral part of every aspect of an organization's operations (Hahn et al., 2015). The integrative perspective promotes balancing economic, environmental and social aspects without prioritizing one over the others. It acknowledges the inherent contradictions and tensions in striving for sustainability (i.e. paradoxical thinking) and proposes embracing these paradoxes rather than avoiding them. This integrative perspective aspires to devise innovative solutions to transcend the tension between business and society and promotes behavioural complexity, acknowledging the innovative collaborations that arise and allowing the concurrent pursuit of goals that may initially appear to be at odds with each other (Hahn et al., 2015). This approach is deeply rooted in the concept that corporate financial performance and corporate commitment to social and environmental issues are interconnected and that long-term value creation depends on integrating these dimensions into the core strategy and operations of the organization (Eccles et al., 2014; Edmans, 2023b).

The systematic framework proposed by Hahn et al. (2015) is extremely useful for the analysis of the tension in corporate sustainability. The framework promotes a holistic approach to decision-making that does not prioritize one sustainability dimension over others but seeks to advance them concurrently and acknowledges that sustainability tensions can manifest at various levels, including individual, organizational and systemic levels. Each level has distinct characteristics and implications for how sustainability is understood and enacted, leading to potential conflicts or synergies between different levels. However, this framework fails to delve into the day-to-day activity of a business and the operation of its management control systems. To fill this gap and overcome the limits of the systematic framework proposed by Hahn et al. (2015), we suggest a theoretical framework that also incorporates in this systematic scheme the configuration approach to management control systems proposed by Gond et al. (2012) for integrating sustainability within organizational strategy and management control systems.

Gond et al. (2012) have derived the concept of the management control system (MCS) from Simons' levers of control framework, in which the MCS represents a set of formal, information-based routines and procedures managers use to maintain or alter patterns in organizational activities (Simons, 1995, p. 5). According to Gond et al. (2012), sustainability integration in management systems is perceived as a 'socio-technical' process (Emery & Trist, 1969) based on the level of overlap between the MCSs and SCSs. Since traditional MCSs are oriented towards achieving the business and economic goals of organizations, they are viewed as '*limited... in addressing environmental and social issues as well as their interrelationships with financial issues*' (Gond et al., 2012, p. 208). Given the limitations of MCSs in addressing sustainability issues, SCSs have emerged to support organizational sustainability goals (Battaglia et al., 2016; Gond et al., 2012; Johnstone, 2019). An SCS can be defined as a collection of '*management accounting tools that connect organisational strategy with operations in a given context by providing information and direction, as well as monitoring and motivating employees to continually develop sustainable practices and procedures for future improved sustainability performance*' (Johnstone, 2019, p. 34). Gond et al. (2012) argue that the SCS should be effectively integrated with the MCS to contribute to an effective integration of sustainability within corporate strategy. They focus on the various uses of both MCSs and SCSs—diagnostic vs. interactive—as well as their level of integration on three dimensions (technical, organizational and cognitive) to design eight effective organizational 'ideal-types' that, with differences and commonalities would configure an overall integrated system.

Diagnostic control systems are '*formal information systems that managers use to monitor organizational outcomes and correct deviations from pre-set standards of performance*' (Simons, 1995, p. 59). Interactive control systems on the other hand focus attention on strategic uncertainties, (i.e. the emerging threats and opportunities upon which the current strategy is based) and enable strategic renewal. They offer an opportunity for learning by stimulating attention and dialogue on internal and external aspects as well as encouraging the emergence of new strategic initiatives. According to Battaglia et al. (2016), diagnostic control systems are instrumental in ensuring compliance with external regulations and standards, enabling decision-making and providing information on an organization's social and environmental activities and performance for external stakeholders. Conversely, interactive systems play a crucial role in controlling and adjusting actors' actions, focusing the actors' attention on key goals and fostering changes aligned with strategic objectives. These systems require intensive dialogue, direct engagement and frequent personal interactions between top managers and subordinates.

Indeed, the integration of sustainability into MCSs is conceived as a dense interconnection involving organizational, cognitive and technical dimensions of sustainability (Gond et al., 2012).

Organizational integration refers to actors' practices in relation to both types of systems (Gond et al., 2012). This includes the overlap of financial and managerial accounting functions with sustainability reporting and control. In addition, organizational integration may encompass the inclusion of tactical and operational level management from various functional areas in the implementation of sustainability strategies (Parisi, 2013). This implies that all managers in the organization should assume a shared responsibility for sustainability, not just a designated group of specialists. Companies can facilitate organizational integration through their beliefs and boundary systems by seamlessly integrating economic and sustainability concerns into their values statements and codes of conduct.

Cognitive integration refers to a shared understanding among managers working on mainstream control and sustainability issues (Gond et al., 2012). Hahn et al. (2014) differentiate two different cognitive frames with regard to corporate sustainability, the business case and the paradoxical frame. Schaltegger and Burritt (2018) provide another perspective by differentiating four types of business case: reactionary, reputational, responsible and collaborative. The collaborative case shares many of the characteristics of the paradoxical frame described by Hahn et al. (2014). This case defines business success as the simultaneous creation of financial, environmental and social benefits. It calls for fostering innovation and organizational development through interaction with stakeholders. Schaltegger and Burritt (2018) describe the four types of sustainability business case from an organization-wide perspective; however, individuals within the same organization may adopt different business cases.

Technical integration involves methodological links between systems for generating and reporting sustainability data and financial information. Gond et al. (2012) define technical integration as the '*integration of regular MCSs with activities and systems that can be described as internal sustainability management control*'

(p. 209). They further state that '*technical integration involves methodological links between the two encompassing types of systems, such as the presence of a common calculability infrastructure to gather information for both systems*'. A broader view of technical integration does not require common calculability, unlike the view adopted in the sustainability-balanced scorecard research stream (Beusch et al., 2022).

In an organization that integrates sustainability in MCSs, organizational integration is achieved when every functional area assumes accountability for sustainability rather than relegating it to a distinct department. Additionally, cognitive integration can be realized even when managers from various functions have differing viewpoints on sustainability, provided there is a mechanism in place to facilitate consistent dialogue and debate among them. Technical integration is manifested when both financial and sustainability-related metrics are embedded within the control systems used for performance measurement and strategic planning. The interplay between these three dimensions of integration can mitigate deficiencies in one or another of them (Beusch et al., 2022).

38.3 Main Traits of Agricultural SMEs

Agricultural SMEs play a crucial role in driving economic growth, ensuring food security, promoting sustainable practices and supporting rural communities. Indeed, the agricultural sector emerges as a pivotal area in terms of sustainability, particularly given the increasing emphasis on product quality and animal welfare. This focus aligns with the broader shift towards responsible production practices, underscoring the need to integrate ethical and environmental considerations into the core strategies of agricultural businesses. Their role is increasingly recognized in policy-making, with many governments and international organizations focusing on supporting these enterprises for the purposes of overall economic and social development. Thus, the need to understand how they incorporate sustainability concerns into their MSs has become extremely pressing.

SMEs in the agricultural sector have unique attributes, making it essential to create a theoretical framework that links MSs to organizational strategy and operations, with a particular focus on sustainability integration. Testarmata et al. (2023) point out that agricultural SMEs exhibit outstanding flexibility and dynamics but often face barriers such as limited operational experience and management, small collateral values and weak financial reporting systems. Plana-Farran and Gallizo (2021) highlight the tendency of agricultural SMEs to preserve the main characteristics of a family farm when adopting structures suitable for larger enterprises, combining the roles of investor, manager and specialist all in one.

Furthermore, Zambon et al. (2019) discuss the challenges faced by SMEs in aligning with Industry 4.0, noting that while large enterprises may benefit from such developments, SMEs often encounter difficulties due to the need for continuous innovation and policies that support their competitive edge. Lastly, OECD/FAO

(2023) emphasizes the role of SMEs in agricultural-based economies like India or Vietnam, where they represent the majority of industrial units and are key contributors to GDP, manufacturing output, exports and employment, thus underscoring their economic and social significance.

Therefore, SMEs in the agricultural sector often embody characteristics such as flexibility, deep knowledge of local markets and a strong dependence on natural and seasonal cycles (OECD, 2023). Their management structures tend to be less formalized compared to larger entities, with strategic decisions frequently stemming from tradition or owner-managers' intuition (Plana-Farran & Gallizo, 2021). These enterprises usually face unique challenges in integrating sustainability into their organizational strategy and operations, largely due to resource constraints and the immediate pressures of market and climatic conditions (Tiscini et al., 2020). However, the close ties to their local environment and communities mean they are well-positioned to adopt sustainability practices that align closely with the social and ecological systems they are part of (Dias et al., 2021).

Thus, exploration of the organizational, strategic, managerial and operational aspects of agricultural SMEs presents a unique opportunity to set the stage for extending the systematic framework for managing sustainability tensions in organizations proposed by Hahn et al. (2015) by incorporating the configuration approach to sustainability control systems proposed by Gond et al. (2012), thereby creating a holistic theoretical framework that harmonizes traditional business objectives with sustainability imperatives within MSs.

38.4 Research Method and Case Study Presentation

This study adopts a case study approach (Yin, 1989), as it is considered a suitable research method to analyse MSs (McCutcheon & Meredith, 1993) and to investigate the interactions between MCSs and organizational contexts (Otley & Berry, 1994). In particular, the research aims to examine the extent and manner in which the creation and implementation of sustainable SMSs could integrate sustainability concerns into the strategic framework and operational procedures of an organization.

The study employs an explanatory case study to present a novel conceptual framework that amalgamates the systemic approach to sustainability tensions (Hahn et al., 2015) with the configuration approach to the MCS proposed by Gond et al. (2012). This hybrid framework aims to incorporate the multifaceted dimensions of sustainability integration within MSs. The rationale for selecting an explanatory case study is based on its inherent capacity to delve deeply into complex phenomena within their real-life context, particularly when the boundaries between the phenomenon and context are not clearly evident (Yin, 1989). In addition, this method is well-suited where a contemporary, in-depth and detailed examination is required, and where the researcher has little control over the events.

An explanatory case study is particularly appropriate for this research because it allows for the exploration of 'how' and 'why' questions, facilitating a thorough understanding of the processes by which sustainability issues are integrated into organizational strategy and operations. It is well-suited for elucidating the intricate dynamics and subtleties involved in the application of the conceptual framework, providing rich, qualitative insights that are essential for theory testing and development.

Furthermore, an agricultural SME represents an ideal context for such an analysis. This sector is inherently connected to sustainability issues due to its direct impact on environmental resources, social structures and economic systems (OECD, 2023). SMEs in agriculture are often more agile than larger corporations, offering a distinctive opportunity to observe the integration of sustainability into MSs in a more pronounced and observable manner (Dias et al., 2021). Their size and scope mean that they can implement and adapt new systems more rapidly and responsively, thus offering clear insights into the effectiveness and challenges of such integration (Darby et al., 2022).

The agricultural sector faces a unique set of sustainability-related tensions due to the dual challenge of maximizing output to meet global food demands while simultaneously minimizing environmental and social impacts (OECD/FAO, 2023). Examining an agricultural SME allows the study to capture the nuances of integrating sustainability within strategic and operational frameworks, which may include balancing long-term ecological stewardship with short-term financial objectives, adhering to strict regulatory requirements, managing supply chain responsibilities and meeting the expectations of a diverse set of stakeholders.

Moreover, agricultural SMEs are at the forefront of innovation when it comes to sustainable practices, from reducing waste to using alternative energy sources and sustainable farming practices (OECD/FAO, 2023). Observing the application of a holistic theoretical framework within such a setting provides valuable empirical evidence to support or refine the theory, offering transferable lessons and strategies for broader application in the field of sustainability management. The findings can contribute significantly to both academic literature and practical applications, ultimately supporting the broader goal of achieving sustainable development.

AGRIMAD was considered suitable for analysis because the firm is vocal about working towards sustainability in the agricultural sector. AGRIMAD private limited partnership is the principal subsidiary of MADEO holdings, a family business established in 1984 in Calabria. The MADEO group includes other important elements such as Madeo Industria Alimentare and Sant'Anna di Madeo Anna agricultural enterprise, all bound together by a comprehensive network agreement, with AGRIMAD at the helm. This family firm has earned acclaim as a pioneer in welfare and sustainability, culminating in the distinction of being named as a '2022 Sustainability Hero'.

The firm operates in the agriculture sector by producing, distributing and selling a variety of high-quality products, which are mainly made using local pork. AGRIMAD has 50 employees (Fiscal Year, 2022) and reported revenues of almost seven million euros (Fiscal Year, 2022), thus qualifying as an SME. AGRIMAD adopts a traditional model of governance with a Sole Director who is a member of the family that owns the firm. Indeed, AGRIMAD is a lean organization in which the roles of Chief Executive Officer (known as a Sole Director) and Chief Marketing Officer are held by the eldest daughter of the founder of the group. The senior managers, who report directly to the Sole Director, are the Product Manager, the Innovation Manager, the Quality and Control Manager and the Administration Manager, who constitute a sort of enlarged board of directors who work together to guide the organization to business success and outstanding performance. The workforce of AGRIMAD is very young: around 50% of employees are less than 35 years old, and more than 70% are women.

The main data included interviews and archival material. Semi-structured interviews represent a qualitative data collection approach (Ahlin, 2019). This technique entails a predetermined set of questions, supplemented by opportunities for in-depth analysis of topics which emerge during interactions between researcher and respondent. Such interviews are typically conducted individually, and commonly last from 30 minutes to over an hour (DiCicco-Bloom & Crabtree, 2006). For this case study, three semi-structured interviews were conducted, in addition to a preliminary interview with the firm's founder acting as a privileged witness. Semi-structured interviews were conducted among senior and middle managers to obtain a complete picture of whether and how sustainability issues were effectively integrated within strategic planning, management and organizational activities (Riccaboni & Leone, 2010).

Archival data, which includes legislation, codes of conduct, policy statements and management reports, were useful for understanding the contextual conditions under which the firm operates, its commitment to sustainability (policy statement, code of conduct) and to understand how MSs support organizational activities related to sustainability. In addition, archival analysis was used to triangulate the interview-based findings (Yin, 1989).

The interviews took place during the summer of 2023, from June to August, in two stages. The aim of the preliminary interview with the firm's founder was to gain insights into the main pillars of AGRIMAD's strategy and operations and its approach to sustainability practices. After establishing the general landscape of AGRIMAD's approach to SMSs, a second round of semi-structured interviews with senior and middle managers of AGRIMAD took place to explore, in the unique setting of an Italian agricultural SME, the issue of sustainability integration in MSs through the lens of the systems perspective.

The interviewees were the Sole Director, the Innovation Manager and the Quality and Control Manager. There follows a brief description of the interviewees' backgrounds.

38.4.1 The Founder

The firm's founder, born in 1960, with a background in Human Resource Management and Personnel Administration, founded the MADEO group in 1984. AGRIMAD, the first firm in the group, began with one herd of 200 animals, and then expanded, first with a butcher's shop and then with the first meat processing plant. In addition, since 2021, the founder has been mayor of the town where the firm is located, San Demetrio Corone (CZ).

38.4.2 The Sole Director

The eldest daughter of the founder is the Sole Director of AGRIMAD. She studied for a degree in business economics with a specialization in management, marketing, and sales force management, and immediately after graduating started to work in the family firm. Moreover, she has completed various master's degrees and training courses on different topics relating to animal welfare (she is accredited as a specialist by the University of Bristol), including internal courses on specific topics such as problem-solving.

38.4.3 The Quality and Control Manager

The AGRIMAD Quality and Control Manager is a young biologist specializing in agri-food quality MSs; she previously worked as an HCCP consultant for the Oreca organization. She entered the firm 4 years ago and immediately found a place where she could develop her career.

38.4.4 The Innovation Manager

The youngest son of the founder, the Innovation Manager of AGRIMAD, is a young professional who recently graduated with a degree in science and food technology from the University of Milan. He has been working at the family firm for almost a year. During the COVID-19 pandemic, he started taking an interest in firm issues, in particular the pig farm. Subsequently, he became involved with the biogas plant, which is fundamental to the livestock operation, and he currently manages this part of the firm.

To answer the research questions, an interview guide was prepared for the semi-structured interviews in order to gain insights into:

- the genesis of the firm's commitment to sustainability, and what role sustainability plays within the firm's strategy;
- the alignment of the interviewees' perspectives concerning the commitment to sustainability;
- how sustainability is linked with different organizational functions and operations throughout the value chain, especially concerning management control systems;

- the dimensions affecting the role and use of MSs in relation to the firm's strategic orientation;
- the extent to which interviewees were involved in monitoring sustainability practices through the use of MSs.

The questions were drafted by three members of the research unit and validated by the remaining two. Each question aims to identify and explore one or more features of sustainability integration into the MS.

Table 38.1 shows the questions asked in the semi-structured interviews and how they address specific issues. Two questions were put to both the Sole Director and the Innovation Manager. In order to capture the data more effectively, the interviews were recorded, transcribed and subsequently coded (Creswell, 2007).

The protocol referred to was designed to achieve several goals: an assessment of the overall integration of sustainability in the MS and its maturity; a deeper understanding of which specific dimensions of integration have been used to greater or lesser degrees by AGRIMAD on its journey through the sustainability landscape; and, finally, an overall understanding of the processes, mechanisms and tools incorporated in the business to meet the challenges posed by sustainability.

38.5 Research Findings

At the heart of AGRIMAD's ethos lies a profound commitment to sustainability, a principle that not only underpinned its inception but also harmonizes closely with the United Nations Sustainable Development Goals (UN SDGs), something which became clear during the initial interview. This discussion revealed the essence of AGRIMAD: an organization deeply rooted in sustainability and community engagement, reflecting these principles in its strategic direction and the collaborative relationships between the various entities making up the MADEO group.

AGRIMAD's founder emerges as the guiding star of MADEO's strategic vision, personifying the pursuit of excellence through a specialized and superior product offering. The founder's ambition of prudent expansion, without escalating the firm's scale unnecessarily, underscores a strategic vision of maintaining a niche market presence. '*Our firm's core business revolves around not just any product, but one of specialized, unmatched quality. Our goal is to scale our operations judiciously, without ballooning our firm footprint*', the founder disclosed. AGRIMAD's founder is pivotal, steering the entire production continuum of the value chain from raw material procurement to the crafting of high-value intermediate goods. In recent years alone, the firm has won several awards for its commitment to sustainability: *the 2019 Welfare Promoter Award went to Madeo Industira Alimentare* and the *2020 Welfare Champion Award* went to AGRIMAD, which was recognized as a *Sustainability Hero* in 2022.

The genesis of AGRIMAD's sustainability ethos is deeply embedded in its '*corporate identity and philosophy*', according to the founder. '*As a localized*

Table 38.1 Dimensions of sustainability integration into MS

Interviewee (s)	Organizational integration	Cognitive integration	Technical integration
Sole Director and Marketing Manager	What is sustainability? What is your sustainability philosophy? To what extent is sustainability impacting the firm's ethical values? How is sustainability integrated within the firm's decision-making process and into its organizational structure?	Do you think sustainability tactics would have a bigger impact on revenues (increasing them) or on costs (pushing them down)? Do you think there is a trade-off between economic return and sustainability, or can they be combined into a win-win strategy? How is the internal communications flow? Top-down or bottom-up?	With reference only to the dimension of sustainability, do delegation procedures exist? If so, to what degree are they developed?
Quality and Control Manager	What is the structure of the firm's MC and SC systems? Is it formal, informal or in between? How does the chain of command-and-control work? Who elaborates and monitors the sustainability KPIs?	Does the firm get third-party certification? If so which ones(s)? Has the firm received some kind of rating (sustainability, legal, other kind. . .)? If so, what are they and how do they impact the business?	How has sustainability entered (or is entering) into the overall reporting system?
Innovation Manager	Is there a relationship between product/process innovations and sustainability and, if so, what is it? How does the information flow about sustainability work?	To what extent do aspects such as new developments in the regulatory framework and market dynamics impact the firm's choices about sustainability? What is the employees' engagement with sustainability? To what extent are phenomena such as aggregations and networking relevant for implementing and achieving a sustainable business model within your full supply chain? What are the possibilities for your business in terms of contributing to the circular economy?	At the intersection between innovation and the firm's ethical values, how has sustainability been (or is going to be) integrated within the overall business strategy and organizational structure? What is the structure of your ICT systems? Which software is utilized? Are the MC and SC systems both fully automated? Do you check the sustainability of your suppliers? If so, how are these controls embedded in your SCSs
Sole Director and Innovation Manager		Were there some specific trigger events or points that pushed the firm towards sustainability? What does the firm do for the region? What does the	

(continued)

Table 38.1 (continued)

Interviewee (s)	Organizational integration	Cognitive integration	Technical integration
		firm do to enhance the individual and collective well-being of employees? What welfare policies does it implement?	

Source: Authors' Elaboration

small enterprise, sustainability is not just a principle but the foundation upon which our firm is built', he explained. This intrinsic value of sustainability has motivated the firm from one generation to the next, fostering a culture deeply attuned to sustainable practices.

Contrary to industry trends typically driving companies towards sustainability, AGRIMAD's approach is characterized by intrinsic motivation. '*External factors had negligible impact*', the founder asserts, emphasizing the decision to embrace sustainability was self-initiated, not a reactionary measure to external pressures. He argues that sustainability is crucial for SMEs aiming for international recognition, resonating with the concept that reputational strategies are pivotal for overseas market penetration.

The management's commitment to sustainability is absolutely clear, with the founder highlighting the firm's proactive stance towards education and training. '*Our commitment to sustainability extends to organizing voluntary, comprehensive training sessions on various subjects, eagerly attended by all*', he remarked, showcasing a deep commitment to the social aspect of sustainability which includes extensive training and skill development, integral to the firm's forward-looking management practices.

While the creation of a detailed sustainability report remains in the pipeline, AGRIMAD has actively sought third-party certifications, underscoring its unwavering commitment to sustainability and compliance with sustainability regulations. This reflects the firm's commitment to maintaining a reputable external image and integrating sustainability into the firm's strategic and operational blueprint.

AGRIMAD's attitude to sustainable performance is intricately woven into its management control system. '*We've adopted measures to ensure almost all water utilized in our operations is collected, recycled, and repurposed, aligning with our commitment to the environmental aspect of sustainability*', the founder noted, indicating strides towards operational self-sufficiency and sustainability integration across the board.

Technologically, AGRIMAD is at the forefront, leveraging a sophisticated information technology infrastructure, including an enterprise resource planning system interconnected with an accounting management software system. This demonstrates the firm's commitment to operational efficiency and effectiveness, harnessing the power of technology, including artificial intelligence, to optimize operating processes.

The founder's belief in the paramount importance of sustainability issues in decision-making underscores a strategic ethos. '*Ignoring sustainability is a significant competitive disadvantage for any business, whether new or established*', he stated a philosophy that extends to the firm's supply chain management, where AGRIMAD enforces stringent sustainability controls, beginning with exhaustive self-assessments for suppliers and prioritizing partnerships with environmentally certified entities.

In essence, AGRIMAD's narrative is a testament to its unwavering commitment to sustainability—a cornerstone of its firm identity, market strategy and operational philosophy.

Below are the findings obtained to date from the semi-structured interviews pertaining to each dimension of integration emphasized by Gond et al. (2012).

38.5.1 Organizational Integration

AGRIMAD conceives sustainability '*as a set of words that for us are represented by our core values. Sustainability is taking together our family, employees, territory with a balanced trade-off between tradition and innovation*'. In the local context, the day-to-day activities of the firm impact all stakeholders. Thus, the reasons for ongoing improvements are evident and very clear. According to the Sole Director, few businesses are carrying on their activities while being fully sustainable, and Italian SMEs are not able to team up and establish effective networks and synergies for common purposes.

Hence, the organizational integration necessary for implementing effective SMSs still seems far from being achieved by many existing businesses. As for AGRIMAD, the philosophy of sustainability is, to a large extent, already incorporated in the firm's daily activities and in the way these activities are carried on. The presence of welfare plans, energy, plastic and water policies, and even some monetary incentives all provide evidence of sustainability. For instance, the firm has introduced a monthly sustainability award to the employee who demonstrates having adopted the most sustainable behavior in his/her department. The people in the department vote every month to elect the winner. The criteria used for the award are based on the UN SDGs, sustainability factors and other sustainability features. The Sole Director, in line with the founder's view, does not see the journey into sustainability as something which will change or impact the firm's current ethical values simply because AGRIMAD was born sustainable. As often happens in micro and small entities one question that arises is: where is the tangible evidence of their convictions and/or public statements?

When it comes to discussion of how sustainability is integrated within the firm's decision-making process and into its organizational structure, the issue became even more apparent as when the Sole Director declared '*I think being sustainable is not something you can achieve with big projects if the whole firm, especially its human resources, do not know what it means*'. This point of view is understandable in that it reflects concerns about the risk of the firm's sustainability strategy not being widely disseminated and shared amongst the employees. Additionally, the firm's other sustainability endeavours include initiatives aimed at benefiting the local community and environment, as well as the establishment of a training centre designed to equip the workforce with relevant skills and provide educational resources for the broader community.

As for the structure of MCSs and SCSs, the Quality and Control Manager revealed that they are both overseen and led by the Quality Department that, in small concerns like AGRIMAD, covers the traditional internal audit functions and related tasks. The quality department, however, jointly works with the general administrative department alongside the Sole Director. The existing KPIs are elaborated by the quality department and are updated on a quarterly basis. They relate to two main areas: waste reduction and energy savings. In addition, the Innovation Manager, who has some relevant specific knowledge because of his previous studies, provides continuous advice. This allows him to monitor energy-saving KPIs more effectively. Finally, the Product Manager is responsible for undertaking the necessary investments when the KPIs suggest the need to take further steps to significantly improve the sustainability strategy and performance. The SCS is also connected with both product and process innovation, especially the latter. As revealed by the Innovation Manager the latest equipment purchased by the firm is both more efficient and sustainable, increasing production, reducing plastic waste and increasing the use of recyclable materials.

As for the interviewees' main thoughts, it might be said that organizational integration is underway and that, thanks to a lean organizational chain of command, the informative flow of both MCS and SCS is quite effective. The overall MS is moderately unstructured, but the clarity of intentions of the people in charge can lead the firm, by following a step-by-step approach, to proper sustainability integration in management functions.

38.5.2 Cognitive Integration

The cognitive integration of sustainability into MSs is probably the most challenging. It relies on the need to achieve a shared understanding among people of why the implementation of SCSs is beneficial for the firm itself and the fundamental reasons behind the sustainability strategy pursued.

Often sustainability is triggered by specific events, which seems not to be the case with AGRIMAD since the Sole Director said that '*. . .the main event is a person: my father, the founder. Indeed, people that have worked for a long time and still work in our firm are invaluable stores of knowledge who can transmit our values to the next generation of workers*'. That is why the information flow regarding not only the SCS but also any kind of control is transversal, and widely shared communications occur at all levels to keep everyone in the firm well-informed.

Work-life balance is a priority. In many cases, entire families work for the group to which AGRIMAD belongs. Therefore, the firm always tries to adapt the organizational workflow to their needs (working hours, shift-swaps, flexibility and so on). The firm supports the female workforce, and there is a youth committee that organizes a series of initiatives aimed at increasing the sense of community and healthy lifestyles such as local sports competitions, team-building events and so on. Hence, employee engagement not only relates to sustainability but all the activities carried on by the firm. This involvement is more than repaid in terms of employee commitment. For example, the Innovation Manager said '*our employees frequently give us important tips on how to make the machinery function better, simple energy saving strategies, water saving suggestions and so on...*'.

The cognitive path to sustainability leads the firm to become involved in multiple initiatives in the local community and region. For instance, the firm supports a farm education project at a primary school and supports the local Red Cross, to which it also donated an ambulance. Moreover, there are projects with churches and clergy to help poor people and, in the words of the Sole Director '*we sit on the youth committees of the small towns around here which are involved in developing the territory and supporting sport initiatives*'.

A cognitive shift would also consider the perceived current and future benefits for the firm itself. The Sole Director thinks that economic and financial returns and sustainability can be combined into a win-win strategy in the long run. As she said, this is an established approach: '*Never look at short term results if you want to make a change. The hardest task is to make others understand that sustainability interventions would not negatively impact the value of the product but, on the contrary, they enhance it*'. Reasons underlying these comments can be inferred from the current macroeconomic landscape: the inflation rate, interest rates and increasing commodity prices. Balancing these negative trends against the desire to implement sustainability strategies, it is obvious a few economic targets/returns must be postponed. In this sense, the firm's ultimate goal is to manifest both the obvious and the less obvious qualities of its products through a clear long-term strategy that reflects its owner's long-term vision for sustainability. However, in the short term, different kinds of returns can be achieved, such as improved reputation, visibility, social, environmental and enhanced financial ratings, alongside an improved internal culture and sense of community. However, some cost savings are already apparent such as, for example, those obtained by using an innovative photovoltaic panels system.

However, all these valuable initiatives would not give the hoped-for results without including all the firms included in the supply chain on the journey, from the cattle breeders to the quality certifiers. This is why the firm continuously advocates and struggles to engage all its partners in the sustainability paradigm shift. '*Grow together to avoid resource waste and negative returns*', said the Sole Director.

The reputational side of cognitive integration also involves achieving third-party certification. Indeed, AGRIMAD, as revealed by the Quality and Control Manager, has received several certifications concerning quality assurance, supply chain assurance, environmental assurance and even animal welfare assurance. At the request of an important commercial partner, AGRIMAD also obtained a mixed sustainability and legal rating from a specialized firm in the field. The same has happened with its partner bank, which asked for a specific certification to improve the firm's financial rating. *'Nowadays financial and non-financial reputation go together and their mutual relationship make each other either better or worse'*, declared the Sole Director. Thus, the Weighted Average Cost of Capital (WACC) depends on both dimensions. In addition, it can be argued that the WACC needs to incorporate the sustainability perspective to give the right message to capital markets.

Notwithstanding the proactive approach adopted by AGRIMAD, sustainable business is nowadays more and more driven by significant changes in the regulatory framework. During the interviews, we wondered whether the task environment of AGRIMAD is impacted by these changes and if so to what extent it is affecting sustainability strategies and related control systems. The evidence collected reinforces the apparent pro-activism of AGRIMAD since the changes and related new requirements that come from the regulatory direction had already been spontaneously incorporated into the business before they became compulsory. At the frontiers of its task environment, AGRIMAD is now studying a new packaging system able to completely eliminate plastic called 'Shelf Life', which is a beeswax cloth able to maintain food products in good and stable condition for 30 days. Similarly, AGRIMAD is now screening suppliers more than it did previously by asking them to certify the origins of their products and the materials used to make them.

Of course, there were some regulatory changes concerning health and food security and packaging systems that pushed AGRIMAD to make some updates in its production chain and on formal procedures needed for selling its products. However, these aspects are negligible in the context of the whole sustainability journey that the firm has undertaken and on which it continues.

Finally, the great ambition of the firm—as the Innovation Manager said—is to positively contribute to the circular economy. The products made by AGRIMAD would allow it to meet the challenge. Much of the animal waste can be used to produce natural fertilizers and clean and renewable energy in different ways. Additionally, the collection and re-use of rainwater can be tremendously helpful, especially because the firm's production sites are located in the South of Italy, an area with low rainfall. It is obvious that meeting these targets would, at the least, both enhance the reputation and the efficiency of the firm and achieve multiple SDGs.

38.5.3 Technical Integration

When discussing the integration between SCSs and MCSs, Gond et al. (2012) did not hypothesize a specific chronological order among organizational, cognitive and technical integrations that companies should follow. There can be a common point of departure: when integration begins, it begins and must progress at all levels.

However, as the AGRIMAD case reveals, in the case of SMEs it is possible that the three components of the unique integration process follow a recurring step-by-step approach that starts with organizational integration and ends with technical integration. Indeed, the interviewees devoted considerable time to answering questions about the organizational and cognitive aspects of integration while, with few exceptions, they said little about technical integration. However, we collected some important evidence.

As for delegation processes relating only to the dimension of sustainability, the Sole Director depicted a flat organization, observing that delegation on the issue is still largely unstructured and underlining that '*. . .what matters is that all people should have the same knowledge and style in approaching the issue of sustainability*'. This would be a logical consequence of the cognitive integration path described previously.

Questioned on the introduction of sustainability into the reporting system, the Quality and Control Manager reported evidence already known: the existence of some KPIs for waste reduction and recycling and energy savings that are monitored on a quarterly basis.

Conversely, we collected new insights when moving to deal with the ICT systems that, it must be said, are still in their early stages. AGRIMAD uses three software systems. The first, the oldest in use, is the internal auditing software used to implement the MCSs, which is gradually expanding its coverage to cope with sustainability issues. However, as the senior managers revealed, the incorporation of sustainability information into the software is still in its infancy. The other two software systems, instead, are used ad-hoc for selected plant and machinery (such as the photovoltaic panels) used in production. As noted, the integration of such valuable information into the traditional ICT infrastructure might be a long process. Thus, the SCSs are still far from being automated.

As further evidence, the Innovation Manager revealed and the Quality and Control Manager confirmed, the current measurement of KPIs is carried out manually, even if some of the information used to assess them comes from some of the aforementioned software used for selected plant, machinery and a variety of equipment.

A fourth software system with the ability to speed up production and reduce material waste is the 'MES' which, in the words of the Innovation Manager '*...is revolutionary because it connects in real time all the 4.0 machines used in different production sites to achieve predetermined targets – for raw materials, semi-finished products, finished goods – by precisely following specific parameters specified at the beginning of the process by human beings*'.

At the end of the interview process, the Innovation Manager told us that the entire workforce is travelling on the path to sustainability as a way of improving at all levels, both for the sake of the firm, with regard to both internal and external stakeholders, and to achieve a more viable world. By doing so the firm is taking care not only of how it behaves on a global scale but also of how all the parties involved in its supply chain (suppliers, external contractors, customers, territory and

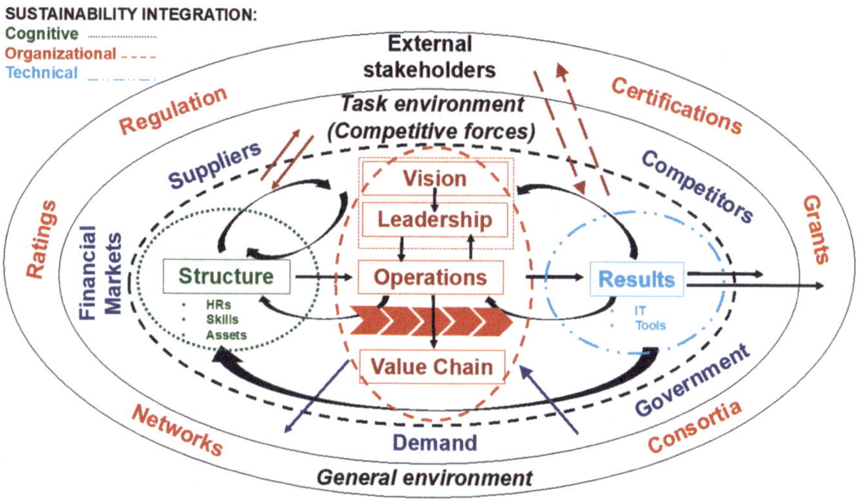

Fig. 38.1 SMSs: the case of AGRIMAD. *Source*: Authors' Elaboration

community) behave, to ensure that a robust sustainability networking process achieves sustainable global targets.

The research findings of this case study allow us to identify the main factors that support sustainability integration into the strategic decision-making process and their relationships with each other. As a result, we propose a holistic theoretical framework for sustainability integration into MSs according to a systems perspective. Figure 38.1 provides a graphical illustration of sustainability integration into AGRIMAD's MSs, the implications of which will be discussed in the subsequent section.

38.6 Discussion

Gond et al. (2012) emphasize the importance of sustainability rhetoric when organizations face the problem from an external perspective through reporting and a mission statement. The authors underline the lack of studies dealing with the intra-organizational impact of sustainability strategies. In this context, MCSs play an important role in strategy making as '*they shape the process of strategy emergence and support the implementation of deliberate strategies*' (Gond et al., 2012, p. 206). This emphasizes that MCSs are not just an instrumental tool used by executives as management by exception (diagnostic), but involve behaviour and activities that support changes aligned with higher strategic objectives (interactive).

The consideration of MCSs as a process and their use in an interactive manner require a more holistic approach in the discussion about the factors that support the integration of sustainability into the strategic decision-making process. Although integration has been discussed by authors in relation to the overlap between MCSs and SCSs, the dimensions of organizational, cognitive and technical integration could be used to investigate, in a holistic manner, the integration of sustainability into the whole MS, which requires multiple links between strategic vision, asset, process, organization and performance measurement. Considering vision, process and organization defines the context for achieving organizational and cognitive integration. In different ways, AGRIMAD's managers agree that 'value can be created through values'. Shared decision-making, employee engagement and youth committees are established within the firm. The absence of ownership and control separation appears to be a strong point, as all the managers are allowed by the owner to delegate in full all the aspects (and related decisions) that flow from their knowledge and expertise. The presence of formal and informal committees aimed at continuing to support the decision-making processes fully supports these managers' claims (Beusch et al., 2022).

Departments that have developed similar practices of reporting or management control can achieve organizational integration, even if they do not belong to the same part of the organizational structure. On the other hand, cognitive integration requires interaction and opportunities for discussion among individuals. It highlights the importance of dialogue and knowledge exchange as the basis for redefining cognitive boundaries. The model of Gond et al. (2012) underestimates the role of belief and boundary systems, even when the value of dialogue is emphasized, in our view.

In our case study, we found evidence of the sustainability-driven strategy pattern (Gond's configuration f) used by green start-ups or medium-sized enterprises that focus their business model on sustainability. The sustainability-driven strategy pattern (Gond's configuration f) used by green start-ups or medium-sized enterprises that focus their business model on sustainability is characterized by a high level of integration. Green start-ups or medium-sized enterprises that focus their business model on sustainability use SCS interactively to guide the strategy-making process, but the MCS is underdeveloped and lacks interactive use. Our findings reveal evidence of the context in which the pattern was developed and provide additional insights into the role of beliefs, strategic vision and dialogue.

Moreover, following Johnstone's (2019, p. 34) definition of SCS as a process that '*connects strategy with operations in a given context by providing information and direction, as well as monitoring and motivating employees to continually develop sustainable practices*', we move the control problem beyond accounting and number, incorporating the paradox approach, and provide empirically tested evidence about the context that characterizes SMEs. Our empirical findings are consistent with those of Beusch et al. (2022), who highlight the importance of dialogue in the integration process of sustainability. Dialogue between the strategic and tactical levels can mitigate difficulties caused by incomplete technical and organizational integration. Although even Beusch et al. (2022) focus on the relationship between MCS and SCS with integrated sustainability strategies, their references are to the value chain and external sustainability drivers. We should move to a holistic approach that considers all the MSs, not just the control process. The main findings of Beusch et al. (2022) are that '*committed CEOs and strategic-level management can avoid sustainability marginalization by communicating their beliefs through intensive dialogue' and 'extend the integration to include belief and boundary systems in addition to diagnostic and interactive LOC systems... beliefs and boundary systems are components of an organization's value system'.*

We found evidence that beliefs and boundary systems can facilitate organizational integration, even if we did not find a formal plan imposed by a value statement and code of conduct. SMEs use a flat and lean organizational structure with an emphasis on informal processes. That means diffusing the strategic vision. The integration of beliefs and boundaries can ensure the integration of sustainability into strategic processes, even if managers adopt a business case frame. Other than the interactive use of control, Arjaliès and Mundy (2013) and Rodriguez et al. (2013) suggest considering strategic validity controls. Strategic validity control includes monitoring the regulatory aspect and responding to stakeholder views regarding sustainable operations. While interactive control is more internally focused than a push for efficiency, strategic validity control is necessary to sustain a competitive advantage, promote innovation and redefine products and markets, ensuring effectiveness and value creation. Strategic validity control influences the cognitive frame (business case vs. paradoxical) (Hahn et al., 2014; Hahn & Aragón-Correa, 2015). The paradoxical situation requires the simultaneous creation of financial, environmental and social benefits (Carmine & De Marchi, 2023). It calls for fostering innovation and organizational development through interaction with stakeholders. Even if the tactical level may focus on the improvement of business processes and place emphasis on financial performance, the strategic level requires a collaborative approach involving stakeholders, promoting innovation and change and competitive advantage in the long term. Dialogue and debate are necessary to avoid the marginalization of sustainability while ensuring cognitive integration.

In our case, the market, consumers and other actors and stakeholders in the value chain drive the sensitivity and need for sustainability practices, rather than being driven by the law or imposed rules. It is born from the market, consumers and other actors and stakeholders in the value chain (Cheffi et al., 2021).

Beusch et al. (2022) propose a classification characterized by different levels of interactive use of control and focus posited on external sustainability demand drivers. The quadrant low-high usually refers to organizations at an early stage of maturity and focused on developing sustainability products, which can be conducted according to the sustainability-driven strategy of Gond et al. This configuration is largely consistent with the paradoxical frame that views sustainability concerns as an end in themselves. Under this configuration, the organization might not yet have a well-developed system for collecting diagnostic information about sustainability metrics related to its value chain. Without such information, the organization might not be able to conduct a detailed internal dialogue.

We believe that our case falls into this quadrant but with some differences.

The firm has worked hard to get third-party certifications to bolster its reputation and guarantee its overall compliance with all sustainability aspects. However, the development of full sustainability reports seems far from being achieved. Despite the developments in both external disclosure and internal control functions, there is still much room for improvement. The changes brought about by sustainability have impacts on other actors in the value chain of different magnitudes. AGRIMAD requires suppliers to self-assess their sustainability practices, obtain mandatory certifications and seek suppliers at the forefront of sustainability. The firm has chosen this route to continue its journey and to succeed within its sector.

Indeed, the firm felt strongly about the issue of sustainable packaging. While the firm recognizes the importance of reducing plastic usage by developing innovative packaging systems, it requires institutional help to succeed with this challenge. The cost of new sustainable packaging cannot be supported if it negatively affects profitability. The same considerations apply to circular economy issues. Recycling waste is possible, but it does have a cost. Further, even if the quantities of recycled materials are large for the firm, they are small in aggregate. Thus, the absence of a network logic within and across sectors and SMEs will hinder the pursuit of these valuable goals or result in slow progress. A network of cooperation between private sector, public sector and civil organizations and society can contribute to creating economies of scale and overcoming the problem (Brunelli et al., 2021). Therefore, sustainability is a matter of value co-creation.

Even if the AGRIMAD case is classified as a sustainability-driven strategy, we did not find the tension produced by the paradoxical frame because the firm's logic seems to be clear with regard to the long-term objectives expressed in terms of sustainability goals, counterbalanced by the short-term objectives based on efficiency and profitability.

Above all, it is clear that investing in sustainability and considering sustainability factors are ways to improve many areas: reputation, visibility and internal efficiency in the short term, sales, profitability, the cost of capital (both debt and equity) reduction and 360-degree growth in the long run (Beckmann & Schaltegger, 2021).

However, the evidence obtained demonstrates that forward-looking SMEs, with their leaner structure and inspired owners, can represent innovation hubs and a benchmark reference for the giants of the business world, demonstrating stronger activism that promotes sustainability.

38.7 Conclusion

Through an in-depth case study approach, this research has explored an example of best practice in the agricultural sector in Italy and examined the impact of sustainability integration on MSs. As a result, this study provides insights into how agriculture SMEs can effectively incorporate sustainability into their strategic and operational frameworks to enhance shared value creation.

Research findings indicate that agricultural SMEs embracing sustainability integration in their MSs can generate shared value through various mechanisms. The identified best practice encompasses a holistic approach to sustainability, incorporating sustainability factors into strategic planning, performance measurement systems, and employee engagement initiatives. This SME recognizes the interdependencies between financial success, social impact and environmental stewardship, leveraging sustainability integration to drive innovation, attract socially conscious customers and enhance stakeholder trust.

The contribution of this research lies in its empirical investigation of the integration of sustainability factors and their impact on MSs within agricultural SMEs. By examining an example of best practice in the Italian agricultural industry, the study offers practical insights and practical recommendations for organizations seeking to enhance shared value creation through sustainability integration. Furthermore, the research contributes to the broader literature on SMSs, expanding our understanding of the role of sustainability considerations in driving organizational success. In fact, the paper proposes a theoretical advancement by defining a new conceptual framework that combines a systematic approach to corporate sustainability tensions with the configuration approach to management control systems. This integration aids in understanding the roles and uses of SMS in embedding sustainability within business strategy and operations.

It is important to acknowledge that this study has certain limitations, such as the focus on a specific industry in Italy, which may limit the scope for generalizing the findings to other contexts. In addition, the data collected for this study relied on self-reported information from firm representatives, which may be subject to biases or inaccuracies that could impact the validity of the research findings. Moreover, the case study approach employed in this research involved only one firm, which may not fully represent the diversity and complexity of the entire industry. Furthermore, the study focused on a specific period of time and may not capture the dynamic nature of sustainability integration and its impact on MSs over the long term. Lastly, the study focused mostly on internal organizational factors and may not have taken into account all external factors, such as changes in regulations, market conditions or challenges that are unique to a certain industry, which could influence the implementation and effectiveness of sustainability practices.

In conclusion, this study seeks to shed light on the integration of sustainability factors into the MSs of agricultural SMEs. It seems that this integration can result in various benefits for SMEs in the agricultural sector. It can enhance their reputation, attract socially conscious customers, foster stakeholder trust, improve risk management and contribute to long-term financial performance. Understanding the potential advantages and associated mechanisms of sustainability integration in this specific context can guide organizations in adopting sustainable practices that align with their strategic goals and societal expectations. Moreover, by exploring the specific context of this SME and understanding the potential benefits and challenges the firm faces, this research has provided valuable insights for academics, practitioners and political institutions, contributing to the growing body of knowledge on sustainable business practices and MSs and ultimately encouraging the development of a more sustainable and responsible business environment. Finally, the research highlights how SMSs facilitate the alignment of sustainability goals with business operations, thus enhancing both organizational efficiency and sustainability outcomes. This integration supports SMEs in achieving competitive advantages and addresses the sustainability demands of stakeholders effectively.

Several promising directions for future research could further advance our understanding in this field. Firstly, conducting comparative studies across different industries and countries would enhance the generalizability of the findings and provide a broader perspective on the challenges and opportunities of sustainability integration. Secondly, investigating the role of stakeholder engagement and collaboration in shaping sustainability practices and outcomes could shed light on the mechanisms through which shared value can be effectively generated. Additionally, examining the influence of regulatory frameworks and industry-specific dynamics on the implementation and effectiveness of sustainability practices would offer valuable insights into the contextual factors that shape sustainability integration in SMEs. Future research should also consider the influence of external factors, such as regulatory changes and industry-specific dynamics, on sustainability implementation and outcomes. Moreover, exploring the role of technology and digitalization in facilitating sustainability integration and improving decision-making processes could yield practical ideas for leveraging digital tools and platforms to enhance sustainability performance.

In addition, to overcome the limitations of the research method used in this study, further research could employ a mixed-methods approach that combines self-reported data with objective measures to strengthen the validity of the research findings. Furthermore, expanding the sample size and diversifying the cases studied would offer a more comprehensive understanding of the complexities and variations in sustainability practices within the industry. Lastly, longitudinal studies could investigate the evolving nature of sustainability integration over time and its sustained impact on decision-making and MSs.

By addressing these limitations and pursuing these research directions, scholars and practitioners can contribute to the evolving field of sustainability and shared value in the context of service-based SMEs, facilitating the adoption of sustainable business practices and promoting positive societal outcomes.

References

Ahlin, E. M. (2019). Semi-structured interviews with expert practitioners: Their validity and significant contribution to translational research. In *Sage res methods cases Pt 2*. Sage Publications.

Ahmad, K., & Mohamed Zabri, S. (2024). The role of management accounting on the relationship between corporate social responsibility and performance in SMEs. *Measuring Business Excellence, 28*(1), 122–136.

Argyris, C., & Schön, D. A. (1978). *Organizational learning: A theory of action perspective*. Addison-Wesley.

Arjaliès, D. L., & Mundy, J. (2013). The use of management control systems to manage CSR strategy: A levers of control perspective. *Management Accounting Research, 24*(4), 284–300.

Battaglia, M., Passetti, E., Bianchi, L., & Frey, M. (2016). Managing for integration: A longitudinal analysis of management control for sustainability. *Journal of Cleaner Production, 136*, 213–225.

Beckmann, M., & Schaltegger, S. (2021). Sustainability in business: Integrated management of value creation and disvalue mitigation. In *Oxford research encyclopedia of business and management*. Oxford University Press.

Beusch, P., Frisk, J. E., Rosén, M., & Dilla, W. (2022). Management control for sustainability: Towards integrated systems. *Management Accounting Research, 54*, 1000777.

Brunelli, S., Carlino, C., Falivena, C., & Venuti, F. (2021). Accountability for climate change: A research synthesis through the lenses of the integrated thinking approach. *Meditari Accountancy Research, 29*(4), 1005–1038.

Busco, C., Giovannoni, E., Riccaboni, A., & Frigo, M. L. (2024). The micro-foundations of corporate purpose: Performance management in dynamic environments. *Management Accounting Research, 100890.*

Cafferata, R. (2000). *Sistemi, strutture, processi, persone*. Aracne.

Cafferata, R. (2018). *Management in adattamento. Tra razionalità economica, evoluzione e imperfezione dei sistemi*. Il Mulino.

Carmine, S., & De Marchi, V. (2023). Reviewing paradox theory in corporate sustainability toward a systems perspective. *Journal of Business Ethics, 184*, 139–158.

Cavicchi, C., Oppi, C., & Vagnoni, E. (2023). Mobilising management control systems to support sustainability strategy in SMEs: The case of a waste disposal firm. *Meditari Accountancy Research, 31*(4), 1015–1037.

Cheffi, W., Abdel-Maksoud, A., & Farooq, M. O. (2021). CSR initiatives, organizational performance and the mediating role of integrating CSR into management control systems: Testing an inclusive model within SMEs in an emerging economy. *Journal of Management Control, 32*(3), 333–367.

Creswell, J. W. (2007). *Qualitative inquiry and research design: Choosing among five approaches* (2nd ed.). Sage Publ. Inc..

Darby, J. L., Fugate, B. S., & Murray, J. B. (2022). The role of small and medium enterprise and family business distinctions in decision-making: Insights from the farm echelon. *Decision Sciences, 53*, 578–597.

Dharmayanti, N., Ismail, T., Hanifah, I. A., & Taqi, M. (2023). Exploring sustainability management control system and eco-innovation matter sustainable financial performance: The role of supply chain management and digital adaptability in Indonesian context. *Journal of Open Innovation: Technology, Market, and Complexity, 9*(3), 100119.

Dias, C., Gouveia, R. R., & Ferreira, J. J. (2021). Small agricultural businesses' performance - what is the role of dynamic capabilities, entrepreneurial orientation, and environmental sustainability commitment? *Business Strategy and the Environment, 30*(4), 1898–1912.

Dicicco-Bloom, B., & Crabtree, B. F. (2006). The qualitative research interview. *Medical Education, 40*, 314–321.

Drucker, P. F. (1954). *The practice of management*. Harper & Row.

Eccles, R. G., Ioannou, I., & Serafeim, G. (2014). The impact of corporate sustainability on organizational processes and performance. *Management Science, 60*(11), 2835–2857.

Edmans, A. (2023a). The end of ESG. *Financial Management, 52*(1), 3–17.

Edmans, A. (2023b). Applying economics—Not gut feel—To ESG. *Financial Analysts Journal, 79*(4), 16–29.

Eisenhardt, K. M., & Martin, J. A. (2000). Dynamic capabilities: What are they? *Strategic Management Journal, 21*(10–11), 1105–1121.

El-Haggar, S., & Samaha, A. (2019). Sustainability management system. In *Roadmap for global sustainability: Rise of the green communities*. Springer.

Emery, F. E., & Trist, E. L. (1969). Socio-technical systems. In F. E. Emery (Ed.), *Systems thinking* (pp. 281–296). Penguin.

Epstein, M. J. (2008). *Making sustainability work: Best practices in managing and measuring corporate social, environmental and economic impacts* (1st ed.). Routledge.

Epstein, M. J., & Roy, M.-J. (2001). Sustainability in action: Identifying and measuring the key performance drivers. *Long Range Planning, 34*(5), 585–604.

FAO, CIHEAM, PRIMA Foundation, UfM. (2023). *Sustainable agrifood systems in the Mediterranean—Levers for transformation*. FAO.

FAO, IFAD, UNICEF, WFP, WHO. (2023). *The state of food security and nutrition in the world 2023. Urbanization, agrifood systems transformation and healthy diets across the rural-urban continuum*. FAO.

Gao, J., & Bansal, P. (2013). Instrumental and integrative logics in business sustainability. *Journal of Business Ethics, 112*(2), 241–255.

Gond, J. P., Grubnic, S., Herzig, C., & Moon, J. (2012). Configuring management control systems: Theorizing the integration of strategy and sustainability. *Accounting Research., 23*(3), 205–223.

Gond, J.-P., Brès, L., & Mosonyi, S. (2024). Consultants as discreet corporate change agents for sustainability: Transforming organizations from the outside-in. *Business Ethics, the Environment & Responsibility, 33*, 157–169.

Guidi, M., Vitali, S., Giuliani, M., & Chiucchi, M. S. (2024). Understanding the interplay between sustainability strategy and the approach to sustainability reporting in SMEs. *Journal of Management & Organization*, 1–20. https://doi.org/10.1017/jmo.2023.65

Hahn, T., & Aragón-Correa, J. A. (2015). Toward cognitive plurality on corporate sustainability in organizations: The role of organizational factors. *Organization and Environment, 28*(3), 255–263.

Hahn, T., Preuss, L., Pinkse, J., & Figge, F. (2014). Cognitive frames in corporate sustainability: Managerial sensemaking with paradoxical and business case frames. *The Academy of Management Review, 39*(4), 463–487.

Hahn, T., Pinkse, J., Preuss, L., & Figge, F. (2015). Tensions in corporate sustainability: Towards an integrative framework. *Journal of Business Ethics, 127*(1), 297–316.

Hussain, N., Rigoni, U., & Cavezzali, E. (2018). Does it pay to be sustainable? Looking inside the black box of the relationship between sustainability performance and financial performance. *Corporate Social Responsibility and Environmental Management, 25*, 1198–1211.

Johnstone, L. (2019). Theorising and conceptualising the sustainability control system for effective sustainability management. *Journal of Management Control, 30*(1), 25–64.

Kaplan, R. S., & Norton, D. P. (1992). The balanced scorecard. Measures that drive performance. *Harvard Business Review, 1*, 71–79.

Lozano, R. (2012). Towards better embedding sustainability into companies' systems: An analysis of voluntary corporate initiatives. *Journal of Cleaner Production, 25*, 14–26.

Lu, W., & Taylor, M. E. (2016). Which factors moderate the relationship between sustainability performance and financial performance? A meta-analysis study. *Journal of International Accounting Research, 15*(1), 1–15.

Martínez-Ferrero, J., & Frías-Aceituno, J. V. (2015). Relationship between sustainable development and financial performance: International empirical research. *Business Strategy and the Environment, 24*(1), 20–39.

McCutcheon, D. M., & Meredith, J. R. (1993). Conducting case study research in operations management. *Journal of Operations Management, 11*(3), 239–256.

Mintzberg, H., Ahlstrand, B., & Lampel, J. (1998). *Strategy safari: A guided tour through the wilds of strategic management*. Free Press.

Nawaz, W., & Koç, M. (2018). Development of a systematic framework for sustainability management of organizations. *Journal of Cleaner Production, 171*, 1255–1274.

OECD. (2023). *Policies for the future of farming and food in the European Union, OECD agriculture and food policy reviews*. OECD Publishing.

OECD/FAO. (2023). *OECD-FAO Agricultural Outlook 2023–2032*. OECD Publishing.

Otley, D. T., & Berry, A. J. (1994). Case study research in management accounting and control. *Management Accounting Research, 5*(1): 45–65.

Parisi, C. (2013). The impact of organisational alignment on the effectiveness of firms' sustainability strategic performance measurement systems: An empirical analysis. *Journal of Management and Governance, 17*, 71–97.

Plana-Farran, M., & Gallizo, J. L. (2021). The survival of family farms: Socioemotional wealth (SEW) and factors affecting intention to continue the business. *Agriculture, 11*(6), 520.
Porter, M. E. (1996). What is strategy? *Harvard Business Review, 6*, 37–54.
Porter, M. E., & Kramer, M. R. (2006). Strategy & society: The link between competitive advantage and corporate social responsibility. *Harvard Business Review, 84*(12), 78–92.
Porter, M. E., & Kramer, M. R. (2011). The big idea: Creating shared value. *Harvard Business Review, 1*, 62–77.
Riccaboni, A., & Leone, L. E. (2010). Implementing strategies through management control systems: The case of sustainability. *International Journal of Productivity and Performance Management, 59*(2), 130–144.
Rodriguez, M., Magnan, M., & Boulianne, E. (2013). Stakeholders' influence on environmental strategy and performance indicators: A managerial perspective. *Management Accounting Research, 24*, 301–316.
Schaltegger, S., & Burritt, R. (2010). Sustainability accounting for companies: Catchphrase or decision support for business leaders? *Journal of World Business, 45*(4), 375–384.
Schaltegger, S., & Burritt, R. (2018). Business cases and corporate engagement with sustainability: Differentiating ethical motivations. *Journal of Business Ethics, 147*(2), 241–259.
Simons, R. (1995). *Levers of control: How managers use innovative control systems to drive strategic renewal*. Harvard Business School Press.
Teece, D. J., Pisano, G., & Shuen, A. (1997). Dynamic capabilities and strategic management. *Strategic Management Journal, 18*(7), 509–533.
Testarmata, S., Ferrari, E., & Grandis, F. G. (2023). Navigating the complexity: Challenges and opportunities of digitalizing Italian agriculture for sustainability. In A. Pezzi (Ed.), *Studi e ricerche del Dipartimento di Economia Aziendale* (Vol. 4, pp. 33–58). Roma Tre - Press.
Tiscini, R., Testarmata, S., Ciaburri, M., & Ferrari, E. (2020). Blockchain as sustainable business model innovation. *Management Decision, 58*(8), 1621–1642.
Tu Le, O. T., Hong Le, A. T., Thanh, V., Cam Tran, T. T., & Van Nguyen, C. (2024). Management control systems for sustainable development: A bibliographic study. *Cogent Business & Management, 11*(1), 2296699.
Yilmaz, I. (2021). Sustainability and financial performance relationship: International evidence. *World Review of Entrepreneurship, Management and Sustainable Development, 17*(3), 537–549.
Yin, R. K. (1989). *Case study research: Design and methods, applied social research methods series* (Vol. 5). Sage Publications.
Zambon, I., Cecchini, M., Egidi, G., Saporito, M. G., & Colantoni, A. (2019). Revolution 4.0: Industry vs. agriculture in a future development for SMEs. *PRO, 7*(1), 36.

Chapter 39
Towards the Identification of KPIs for 'Credible' Climate Transition Planning by EU Non-financial Borrowers in Hard-to-Abate Sectors

Riccardo Sallustio

39.1 Introduction

This chapter, first, aims to provide a summary of the origin, evolution and relevance of EU regulation on climate (or mitigation) transition plans for non-financial companies (NFCs), second, to identify common principles underpinning the credibility criteria of such plans based on a literature review of international sectoral standards and guidelines and, third, to define KPIs that can help enhance such credibility attributes in an EU context.

The outcome of this research could prove useful not only for the stakeholders of NFCs active in hard-to-abate sectors whose assets are more likely to become stranded, but also for EU credit institutions lending to such companies. These institutions, which are subject to a duty to prepare a prudential transition plan as further set out under the forthcoming EBA's Guidelines[1], face the difficult task of identifying the scope and attributes of their clients' climate transition plans that find their origin in enterprise risk management practices, climate science, monitoring of technological innovations, EU climate policy and legal sources.

The identification of transition indicators, i.e. KPIs that are capable of measuring the NFC's transition pathway as well as its governance of carbon transition risks, impacts and opportunities and '*how the transition and alignment is embedded within a business model*' is particularly relevant for credit institutions. KPIs could help

[1] European Banking Authority (EBA) (2024).

R. Sallustio (✉)
Green and Sustainable Finance at Luiss "Guido Carli" University, Rome, Italy
e-mail: rsallustio@luiss.it

N. Castellano et al. (eds.), *Environmental, Social, Governance (ESG)*, SIDREA Series in Accounting and Business Administration,
https://doi.org/10.1007/978-3-031-76618-3_39

avoid discrepancies between prudential and non-prudential transition plans and allow banks to evaluate how hard-to-abate borrowers are aligning with necessary technology transition, particularly in industries like automotive and power where specific technologies need to be developed or phased out.[2] In addition, KPIs should not just lead to an evaluation of how the company is aligning with Net Zero but also whether it is doing it consistently with EU Green Deal (EGD) objectives to maximize transition efforts by EU private and public institutions, as suggested also by the ECB in early 2024. In addition, the EBA has recently indicated '*that the most effective way forward to address greenwashing by EU banks is to focus on the finalisation and implementation of the existing and planned legislative initiatives. This includes rules on … transition plans*'.[3]

Notwithstanding various initiatives and contributions at the international level that have focused on the credibility of transition plans in the last 2 years, almost all initiatives are sector-agnostic. The recent setting of sectoral credibility criteria in the UK (Transition Plan Taskforce-TPT)[4] and France (ACT Initiative[5]) constitutes the gold standard for the definition of the key credibility attributes underpinning the preparation and implementation of climate transition plans by NFCs active in hard-to-abate sectors. However, these contributions fail to address the risk of misalignment from EGD and EU transition finance objectives and European Industrial Transition Pathways and could prove limited use to credit institutions subject to CRDVI and CRRIII.

The research plan will analyse, first, the relevance of transition plans of NFCs in the banking regulatory context; second, the minimum requirements of transition plans under EU law and key credibility criteria based on a literature review. Third, we will delve into the features of specific sectoral credibility attributes set by the ACT Initiative by considering a case study on the automotive sector and identifying which KPIs set by the ACT Initiative can address key credibility criteria identified in the literary review. Fourth, we will carry out a gap analysis of the benchmarks of selected KPIs to understand how they can be improved to capture alignment with key pillars of applicable European Industrial Transition Pathways and significant EGD policies, such as the recently adopted EU Net Zero Industry Act.

While the KPIs, for the purposes of this research, are focused on the automotive sector, the underlying principles could be used by shareholders, investors, lenders and regulators to assess performance of EU companies and directors' remuneration and be included in the emerging transition-linked bonds and loans for other hard-to-abate sectors.

---

[2]F. Schütze, F. Ballesteros et al. (2024), *Enhancing Comparability and Credibility of Transition Plans and Transition Risk Assessment with Standardized Net Zero Scenarios*, Wissenchaftsplattform Sustainable Finance, Policy Brief 2/2024.

[3]European Banking Authority (2024).

[4]Transition Plan Taskforce (2023).

[5]Accelerate Climate Transition (2024) and ACT Generic Methodology (2023).

39.2 Banking Regulatory Context

Following the implementation of the EBA's 'Draft Guidelines on the management of ESG risks' expected in 2025, credit institutions will need to evaluate the NFCs' ability to implement their mitigation actions and assess if and how the availability and allocation of resources at an affordable cost and for a sufficient duration impinge on the implementation of such actions. Banks should further assess the degree of vulnerability to transition risks of the NFC and its governance of the transition process, considering the relevance of opportunities from technological developments and impacts from environmental and climate regulations applicable or foreseeable to the sector of activity of the counterparty.

These evaluations are critical to assessing how an NFC can effectively manage its carbon lock-in risk, the soundness of its decarbonization pathway, and whether delayed decarbonization, failure to decarbonize, and the materialization of transition risks will impact the viability of its business model and the NFC's creditworthiness. The EBA is expressly demanding credit institutions assess mitigation opportunities, adaptive capacity and the soundness of the transition planning of the NFCs. Banks should not solely rely on corporate sustainability disclosures but expressly collect non-public data by engaging with at least NFCs in sectors and business lines that present material exposures to ESG risks (including climate risks), supplemented with information on the results and/or outcomes of such engagement.

The first line of defence that banks should set up is to establish a dialogue with counterparties about their transition plans and assess consistency with the institution's prudential transition planning. The consequence for credit institutions is that they will have to adjust their prudential frameworks with respect to exposure to counterparties that are failing to build up an adaptive capacity, to decarbonize fast enough or to prepare a sound transition plan. NFCs' climate transition planning acquires a specific role in credit decisions, and banks are permitted to ask their clients for transition plans, even if the latter NFCs are not bound to do so by operation of law. The EBA has further indicated the banks' duty to assess any reputational risks attached to the unsound transition plans of the banks' counterparties.

The results of NFCs' climate transition planning efforts allow banks[6] to especially assess the resilience and climate-related financial risks of NFCs operating in high-emitting sectors that are hard-to-abate, such as oil and gas, coal, power, steel, cement, shipping, chemical and automotive. These risks also include transition risks significantly impacting the corporate strategy, business model, risk management, investment and financial plans of these NFCs, hence indirectly impacting their creditworthiness.

The assessment by credit institutions of the NFCs' delay in transitioning to a low-carbon economy should not be made in a vacuum but rather consider as a benchmark the level of climate and nature restoration ambitions of the European

[6]McDaniels and Rismanchi (2023) and Di Maio et al. (2023).

Union and legal instruments such as the EU Climate Law[7] and the DNSH under the EU Taxonomy Regulation. As indicated by recital (54) of EU Regulation 2024/1623[8] (CRR3), '*[a]ssets or activities subject to impacts from environmental and/or social factors should be defined by reference to the ambition of the Union to become climate-neutral by 2050 as set out in the [EU Climate Law, the EU Nature Restoration Law], and the relevant sustainability goals of the Union. The technical screening criteria for 'do no significant harm' adopted in accordance with Article 17 of Regulation (EU) 2020/852 of the European Parliament and of the Council, as well as specific Union legislation to avert climate change, environmental degradation and biodiversity loss should be used to identify assets or exposures for the purpose of assessing dedicated prudential treatments and risk differentials*'. Hence, credit institutions' prudential plans should be based on the evaluation of clients' impacts from EU climate and sustainability goals and related policies.

This ultimately should translate into the deployment of transition finance by EU banks. The EU Commission has indicated that, in a European context, '*transition finance should be understood as the financing of climate- and environmental performance improvements to transition towards a sustainable economy, at a pace that is compatible with the climate and environmental objectives of the EU*',[9] therefore highlighting that the compatibility with EU Green Deal[10] objectives and with other EU policy initiatives is another relevant component of transition finance at the EU level. The EU Commission has also provided a definition of 'transition finance' as, inter alia, '*the financing of investments compatible with and contributing to the transition, that avoids lock-ins, including: . . . (c) investments in undertakings or economic activities with a credible transition plan at the level of the undertaking or at activity level; [or] (d) investments in undertakings or economic activities with credible science-based targets, where proportionate, that are supported by information ensuring integrity, transparency and accountability*'.[11]

The purpose of transition debt finance in an EU context is, hence, multifaceted and can be located in credit allocation seeking to achieve the avoidance of carbon lock-in risks, the assurance of credibility of transition plans, the enhancement and investment in science-based mitigation actions, and the pursuit of the EU Green

---

[7]Regulation (EU) 2021/1119 of 30 June 2019 of 30 June 2019 establishing the framework for achieving climate neutrality (European Climate Law) OJ L 243, 9.7.21.

[8]Regulation (EU) 2024/1623 of 31 May 2024 of the European Parliament and of the Council amending Regulation (EU) No 575/2013 as regards requirements for credit risk, credit valuation adjustment risk, operational risk, market risk and the output floor https://eur-lex.europa.eu/legal-content/EN/TXT/PDF/?uri=OJ:L_202401623, 19 June 2024, OJ L, 19.6.2024 p. 10/189, https://eur-lex.europa.eu/legal-content/EN/TXT/PDF/?uri=OJ:L_202401623.

[9]Commission Recommendation (EU) 2023/1425 of 27 June 2023 on facilitating finance for the transition to a sustainable economy, C/2023/3844, *OJ L 174, 7.7.2023, p. 19–46,* ELI: http://data.europa.eu/eli/reco/2023/1425/oj.

[10]Communication of the Commission of 11 December 2019 (COM(2019) 640 final).

[11]Ibid [9] at Article 2.2, p. 23.

Deal and of the EU climate and environmental objectives,[12] while taking into account environmental and social impacts.

Hence, there is a substantial connection that links climate transition plans with the EGD objectives, related policy measures and bank lending products. This connection is based on the EU-law-driven credibility of the attributes of NFCs' transition plans, the consistency of approaches between prudential and non-prudential plans, the quality of the NFC's transition governance, and the effectiveness of the engagement between the credit institution and the hard-to-abate client.

Traditionally, sustainable finance has dealt with the decarbonization of bank assets by solely evaluating the level of the financed emissions of a given loan or bond portfolio (i.e. the CO2 Kg for each € financed). While this metric is simple and usable and has its merits, it does not trigger real economy transition, unlike transition finance.

Now, given the significance of NFCs' transition plans, it is necessary to identify their origin and the existence of their credibility criteria.

39.3 EU Transition Plan Origin

Several EU large corporations and financial institutions have published in recent years, on a voluntary basis, climate transition plans and reports addressing their climate-related financial risks and potential decarbonization solutions. The intended purposes of these plans and reports, which should not be confused with sustainability reporting or non-financial disclosures, were to engage with and inform investors of, climate risks, and of the voluntary decarbonisation commitments made, in some cases, in the context of adherence to business coalition frameworks[13] and/or science-based target-setting initiatives.

As confirmed by the EBA,[14] the main legal source helping to define the concept of 'credibility' of transition plans is the Commission Recommendation (EU) 2023/1425 of 27 June 2023,[15] on facilitating finance for the transition to a sustainable economy (the 'EU Recommendation on Transition Finance'), which provides various recommendations that transition plans should be following both at entity and

[12] In particular, the EU Green Deal "*is a new growth strategy that aims to transform the EU into a fair and prosperous society, with a modern, resource-efficient and competitive economy where there are no net emissions of greenhouse gases in 2050 and where economic growth is decoupled from resource use. It also aims to protect, conserve and enhance the EU's natural capital, and protect the health and well-being of citizens from environment-related risks and impacts*". Ibid [10].

[13] See for example Leadership Group for Industry Transition's trackers, https://www.industrytransition.org and Responsible Steel's standards, https://www.responsiblesteel.org/resources/standard/.

[14] Ibid [3].

[15] Ibid [9].

activity levels. According to the EU Recommendation on Transition Finance, credible transition plans are a key tool for companies to articulate their targets and actions for transitioning to a climate-neutral or sustainable economy.

According to the EU Commission, these plans include information on milestones, activities, processes and resources and are encouraged to be time-bound, science-based and actionable. They should be integrated into the overall business strategy of the undertaking and cover the transition to environmental objectives. Additionally, as indicated above, credible transition plans should consider the integrity, transparency and accountability of the targets, avoid long-term lock-in to GHG-intensive (the so-called 'carbon lock-in')[16] or environmentally harmful activities, and ensure a robust governance process is in place to support their implementation and oversight.

EU law has very recently introduced mandatory reporting of these plans under the Corporate Sustainability Reporting Directive[17] (the 'CSRD') and, for selected NFCs, their mandatory adoption and implementation, on a best effort basis, under the Corporate Sustainability Due Diligence Directive adopted by the EU Council on 24 May 2024[18] (the 'CSDDD'), thus expanding the scope of climate transition plans published on a voluntary basis. Following the enactment of this EU legislation, the plans' role has been shifting from a pure marketing and social responsibility rationale to encompass separate legal, accounting, financial and regulatory requirements that engage with new issues commanding new governance and management approaches.

The CSRD, the ESRS E1,[19] the reporting standard on climate change adopted under the CSRD, and the CSDDD have not explicitly addressed the 'credibility' notion of climate transition plans[20] but rather established the minimum requirements that such plans must meet.

While there is no common definition of 'credible' transition plans in EU hard law—the only source being the EU Recommendation on Transition Finance, which is a soft law source—the most appropriate approach is to identify the relevance of credible transition plans within the CSRD framework and the minimum

---

[16] OECD (2023).

[17] Council Directive (EU) 2022/2464 of 14 December 2022 amending Regulation (EU) No 537/2014, Directive 2004/109/EC, Directive 2006/43/EC and Directive 2013/34/EU, as regards corporate sustainability reporting [2022], OJ L 322. https://eur-lex.europa.eu/legal-content/EN/TXT/?uri=CELEX:32022L2464.

[18] European Parliament legislative resolution of 24 April 2024 on the proposal for a directive of the European Parliament and of the Council on Corporate Sustainability Due Diligence and amending Directive (EU) 2019/1937 (COM(2022)0071—C9-0050/2022-2022/0051(COD)), https://www.europarl.europa.eu/doceo/document/TA-9-2024-0329_EN.html.

[19] Climate Change reporting standard ("ESRS E1") in Commission Delegated Regulation 2023/2772 (EU) of 31 July 2023 supplementing Directive 2013/34/EU, as regards sustainability reporting standards [2023], OJ L 22.12.23 (the "Delegated Regulation").

[20] Notably, when referring to transition plans, neither the CSRD nor the CSDDD mention the terms "credibility" or "credible". The ESRS E1 at AR21 uses the term credibility in the context of disclosing significant monetary amounts of CapEx and OpEx required to implement the mitigation actions, "*because as the purpose of this information is to demonstrate the credibility of its actions*".

requirements of transition plans, and the ESRS E1. Second, the scope of CSRD helps define the context: plans should engage with sustainability impacts, risks and opportunities; hence, in a transition context, the credibility of transaction plans should not just be risk-based, i.e. focused on addressing the transition risk component.

The literature on transition plans vouches for the importance of their credibility due to their impact on credit risk valuation,[21] capital allocation,[22] reputational risk and potentially defining the boundaries of greenwashing and related legal liability. Although the level of disclosure under ESRS E1 constitutes a significant improvement compared to the standards of reporting under the non-financial reporting legislation there is still '*a serious gap in the conceptualisation of credibility of transition plans*'.[23] Credibility is not just important for the near, medium and long-term prospects of NFCs but also for investors and credit institutions that rely on such plans to assess potential transmission channels impacting, especially, the reporting entity and the level of its alignment to warming objectives.

Incidentally, credibility also engages with accounting issues such as impairment, and a Net Zero transition commitment should be interpreted as a 'constructive obligation' for the purposes of recognising a provision in financial statements.[24]

The quest for credibility criteria in transition plans is an ongoing process. The implementation guidance for the climate transition plans expected in the summer of 2025 could be able to provide further guidance and identify additional data points and KPIs applicable to hard-to-abate sectors, as well as build up on the creation of new KPIs as recommended by GFANZ.[25] Another potential future source for credibility criteria could be the member states' national legislation or recommended practices that could integrate the minimum requirements set by ESRS E1 and ESRS G1. NFCs face a potential misalignment of guidance approaches to transition reporting between EU recommended minimum reporting standards[26] and those set out under practical national guidelines, which may raise to a higher reporting

[21] Association Europe Finances Régulations (2023). European Central Bank, *"Failing to plan is planning to fail"—why transition planning is essential for banks*, Supervisory blog 23 January 2024, https://www.bankingsupervision.europa.eu/press/blog/2024/html/ssm.blog240123~5471c5f63e.en.html#:~:text=Key%20findings%20from%20the%20ECB's,roughly%2090%25%20of%20these%20banks. European Central Bank, Risk of misalignments of banks' financings from EU climate objectives, January 2024, www.bankingsupervision.europa.eu/ecb/pub/pdf/ssm.bankingsectoralignmentreport202401~49c6513e71.en.pdf.

[22] United States Environmental Protection Agency (2024), Climate Transition Planning, https://www.epa.gov/climateleadership/climate-transition-planning. IIGCC (2023).

[23] Bingler et al. (2023).

[24] See in IFRS Interpretation Committee, Staff Paper (2023).

[25] OECD (2022).

[26] Commission Delegated Regulation (EU) 2023/2772 of 31 July 2023 published on 22 December 2023.

standard or set the best practice approach that also applies to the preparation and implementation of the climate transition plans.[27]

Credibility also relies on the enforceability of effective, proportionate and dissuasive[28] sanctions against NFCs and their directors and external auditors by Member States. A weak sanctions regime arguably fails to deter directors from disclosing impacts, risks and opportunities that could evidence pitfalls in the business model and the strategy. The gathering and management of this transition-related data can be costly for NFCs and require new skills; the imposition of administrative penalties that are not commensurate with the costs to be borne by the company would not be dissuasive. Furthermore, the lack of repressive action against NFCs impinges on the quality of the data, which could translate into potential financial stability issues and failure to reach the EGD objectives. Hence, the effectiveness of the sanctions is relevant as it ensures that the overall policy objectives can be pursued.

An area that could further impact the definition of credibility attributes is also the process of interoperability between ESRS E1 and ISSB S2.[29] This could be particularly relevant for listed companies reporting under both sustainability systems.

After having considered the development of climate transition planning, we should delve into the definition of the minimum requirements of climate transition plans to be prepared under ESRS E1 and into an analysis of the relevant related issues.

39.4 EU Law-Driven Minimum Requirements and Issues

39.4.1 Minimum Requirements

The origin of the elements of a plan under ESRS E1 can be identified in the Disclosure Requirement 'E1-1 -Transition Plan for Climate Change Mitigation', which focuses on the information as to the NFC's:

[27] The only relevant guidance contribution, to date, at national level in this respect has been issued by the AMF, the French financial market authority. See Autorité des Marchés Financières, "*Guide pédagogique à destination des entreprises pour rendre compte de leur plan de transition climatique* ", 9 February 2024, https://www.amf-france.org/fr/actualites-publications/publications/guides/guides-professionnels/guide-pedagogique-destination-des-entreprises-pour-rendre-compte-de-leur-plan-de-transition.

[28] The Court of Justice of the European Union (CJEU) has consistently emphasised that the severity of penalties should be proportionate to the gravity of the violations for which they are imposed, namely by guaranteeing a dissuasive effect. In this respect see judgment of 25 April 2013, Asociația Accept, C-81/12, EU:C:2013:275, par. 63. The Court further clarified that the enforcement provision must entail a significant likelihood that, in case of a violation of EU law provisions, appropriately severe penalties will be imposed. See Judgment of 12 July 2005, Commission / France, C-304/02, EU:C:2005:444, par. 37.

[29] EFRAG SRB meeting 23 August 2023, "*Interoperability between ESRS and ISSB standards EFRAG assessment at this stage and mapping table*", https://efrag.org/Assets/Download?assetUrl=%2Fsites%2Fwebpublishing%2FMeeting%20Documents%2F2307280747599961%2F04-02%20EFRAG%20SRB%20%20230823%20-%20EFRAG%20IFRS%20interoperability%20and%20mapping%20table.pdf.

(i) past, current and future mitigation efforts to ensure that its business model and strategic approach towards mitigating the impacts of climate change are compatible with the 1.5 °C warming limit and with the objective of achieving climate neutrality by 2050;
(ii) exposure to coal, oil and gas;
(iii) decarbonization levers and key actions planned, including changes in the undertaking’s products and services and its adoption of new technologies;
(iv) investments and funding supporting the implementation of the transition plan;
(v) potential locked-in GHG emissions from key assets and products;
(vi) turnover, CapEx and CapEx plans for future taxonomy alignment;
(vii) position in relation to the Paris-aligned Benchmarks, which refer to oil and gas companies, high-emitting power companies, etc., to assess whether it is included or excluded from such benchmarks;
(viii) integration of the transition plan into overall business strategy and financial planning;
(ix) progress on implementing its transition plan.

Notably, the above requirements relate to both qualitative and quantitative data that cannot be easily managed by applying current COSO-based reporting practices[30] and mainstream business plan methodologies such as SWOT analysis or Porter’s five forces model. Although these requirements ultimately have a financial impact, they interact with science and with regulatory, legal, risk management and technological issues. While these issues, depending on the circumstances, should be reported per se, in some cases they impinge on statements that have accounting relevance. For example, whether a Net Zero transition commitment should be interpreted as a ‘constructive obligation’ for the purposes of recognizing a provision in financial statements[31] requires a legal analysis of the effectiveness and bindingness of the commitment, while the stranding risk of an asset that could trigger its impairment should also be evaluated by reference to policy, scientific and technological considerations.

Identifying the nature and attributes of these scientific, regulatory, legal, risk management and technological issues is a critical first step in arranging effective transition governance that is transition plan-focused.

Based on the available literature, Table 39.1 sets out a preliminary list of novel issues faced by NFCs while engaging in the preparation of climate transition plans that bear relevance for the identification of ‘credibility’ criteria.

The definition of the minimum requirements set by ESRS E1 is an important step at EU level that needs to engage, however, with relevant other sources. Concurrently with the evolution of an EU concept of credible transition plans based on the cornerstone of ESRS E1, several additional approaches have been influencing Disclosure Requirement E1-1 and their interpretation. It is essential, also in light

[30] The latest opinion issued in March 2023 by COSO on internal controls for sustainability reporting fails to address internal control approaches to climate transition plans. See COSO (2023).
[31] Ibid [30].

Table 39.1 List of issues facing NFCs when preparing climate transition plans

Assessment of climate actual and future impacts on business model also based on climate scenarios and industrial pathways and implications for financial position, performance and cash flows	Identification and management of carbon lock-in risk	Identification and management of transition washing and greenwashing	Assessment of the impact of the change in consumers' preference	Identification and management of technology risks
Just transition considerations	Identification and management of biodiversity loss, dependencies and impacts	Assessment of drivers of change impacting sector at global and European level	Identification and cost/opportunity analysis of low-carbon technology advancements that surpass standard best available technologies	Reporting of forward-looking risks
Assessment of impact of carbon taxes	Assessment of the lifetime and the use of the assets by reference to sustainability and circularity criteria	Review of the corporate's adaptive capacity to deal with such new risks and climate-related opportunities and nature-based solutions	Identification of mitigation actions and related CapEx and OpEx investments	New abatement cost assessments and prioritization of investments in low-carbon technologies
New frontiers of directors' liability	Introduction of technology and asset life-based driven KPIs	Potential impact on provisioning and impairment in accounts	New role of internal controls and external assurance	Identification and management of climate change litigation risks and policy risks in the EU and the jurisdictions in which the NFC operates
Managed phase-out of brown assets	Reskilling and upskilling of workforce	Potential impact on existing contractual arrangements due to change in business model, value chain disruption, unavailability of critical raw materials and of usual energy sources	Increase in R&D capabilities and investments	Comparing planned production values against scenario-based targets for both emerging and declining technologies

of the preamble of the CSRD, that a teleological and historical interpretation of ESRS E1 be applied that considers the evolution of climate transition planning as a pillar of the global efforts to decarbonize enshrined in public international law and soft law that is recalled by the EU Treaties. Hence, the body of law derived from the EU Climate Law, the Green Deal, the sustainability objectives of Union and the EU Recommendation on Transition Finance underpins the interpretation of ESRS.

Non-EU approaches that bear relevance in the interpretation of ESRS E1 include, inter alia, the framework and guidance by the Assessing Transition Plan Collective[32] under the World Benchmarking Alliance, the OECD Guidance on Transition Finance,[33] the CBI's Guidance to Assess Transition Plans,[34] the 'A Tool for Developing Credible Transition Plans'[35] by the UN-convened Net Zero Asset Owners Alliance, the IGCC Corporate Climate Transition Plans,[36] the CDP Technical Note,[37] the GFANZ Technical Review Note on Transition Plans,[38] the ISO Net Zero Guidelines,[39] the UN HLEG Integrity Matters report,[40] the WWF Nature in Transition Plans,[41] the WBCSD Roadmaps to Nature Positive[42] and across-sectors transition plan requirements set by the ACT Initiative[43] and TPT.[44] These guidelines, which are sector-agnostic, have indicated approaches that should provide supplementary guidance in ascertaining credibility attributes for EU corporates subject to the CSRD (and, if applicable, the CSDDD). They are often related to the definition of action plans and steps that companies should undertake in order to implement credible transition plans rather than setting objective quantitative and qualitative criteria that would be able to set apart non-credible plans from credible ones. Notably, only WWF and WBCSD have published guidelines related to biodiversity loss and/or the integration of nature-based solutions in the plans.

By analysing the above EU and non-EU literature at this stage, we can derive the core principles that should underpin the preparation of 'credible' ESRS E1-compliant plans. The approach used to identify these core principles is based on a teleological interpretation of main transition finance guidelines, namely, ESRS

[32] World Benchmarking Alliance (2024).

[33] Ibid [25].

[34] CBI (2023).

[35] United Nations Environment Programme (2023).

[36] IIGCC (2023).

[37] CDP (2023).

[38] GFANZ (2023).

[39] International Organisation for Standardization (2022), https://www.iso.org/obp/ui/en/#iso:std:iso:iwa:42:ed-1:v1:en.

[40] United Nations High Level Expert Group on the Net Zero emission commitments of non-state entities (2022).

[41] WWF (2023).

[42] World Business Council for Sustainable Development (2023b).

[43] Accelerate Climate Transition (2024) and ACT Generic Methodology (2023).

[44] Ibid [4].

E1, ESRS G1, the EU Recommendation on Transition Finance, the 'IPSF Implementing Transition Finance Principles – Interim Report',[45] and the OECD Guidance on Transition Finance[46] by focusing on pivotal topics that are critical for decarbonization in the EU under these sources. The most representative recommendations set out by these sources in relation to such pivotal topics have been identified. Then, the other guidelines on transition plans set out above have been used to supplement these recommendations. Finally, the revised recommendations have been translated into actions for the NFC.

Table 39.2 sets out these core principles, the related actions and the underlying rationale underpinning these principles.

While the above principles are mainly qualitative, they could be translated into a quantitative KPI on credibility where all or most principles are satisfied as suggested by the ACT Initiative. Weighting, however, of the applicable answers might prove complex, as only a 100% score would pass a credibility test. The creation of additional quantitative KPIs to measure the credibility of transition plans is in its infancy, although the EER (Expected Emission Reduction) introduced by GFANZ could be a metric potentially applicable across sectors. Qualitative KPIs (especially when referring to the quality and credibility of new iterations of the NFC's transition plan to be published during the life of the loan) can be included in representations and warranties and in affirmative covenants in loan documentation.

The adoption of quantitative KPIs as a measure for assessing the credibility of transition plans has the benefit of creating a metric that can also be applied to sustainability-linked loans in a transition finance context and to the establishment of transition loan features capable of capturing borrowers' compliance with credible transition plans in general corporate purpose loans. This would help address the EBA's request for the integrity of the sustainability-linked loan market and greenwashing/transition washing concerns on the setting of KPIs and/or sustainability performance targets and/or penalties in these loans.[47]

39.5 Sectoral Credibility Criteria in ACT Initiative Methodology and Relevance of EGD

The literature review of available sector-agnostic guidelines for transition plans shows common traits: setting of targets, construction of action plans, definition of action plan components and timeline processes. While these guidelines are useful for lenders and investors for engagement purposes, however, they generally fail to provide sectoral quantitative credibility criteria that could be found in the sectoral

[45] IPSF Implementing Transition Finance Principles – Interim Report (2023).

[46] Ibid [25].

[47] Ibid [4] at para.92.

Table 39.2 Core principles for the preparation of 'credible' *ESRS* E1-compliant plans

Principle	Actions	Rationale
Wider scope	Cover not only mitigation but also adaptation, circular economy, zero pollution and biodiversity loss by considering EGD policies Assess the environmental impacts caused by the company on a life cycle assessment basis, including biodiversity impact assessments Regardless of whether the environmental impacts may be compliant with applicable law, identify impacts and whether such environmental impacts could be augmented by exceptional circumstances, such as unexpected climate conditions Assess if such environmental impacts can be reduced or removed altogether, identify appropriate actions, assess costs and the need for resources, and determine the timeline and measurability of the actions Prepare a response action plan to prevent, if possible or mitigate acute or chronic climate actions and adverse environmental impacts from emergency situations Assess dependencies and impacts from biodiversity losses As indicated by TPT,[a] consider the physical impacts of the changing climate, the regional and spatial implications of these, the effectiveness of adaptation efforts and possible limits to adaptation and the regional and spatial implications of these	According to the OECD, plans should also consider other environmental objectives (e.g. increasing adaptation and resilience, preventing biodiversity loss, limiting pollution, ensuring sustainable water management, waste management, circular economy considerations, etc.) and social considerations (e.g. pursuing gender equality and women's empowerment, quality jobs, preventing displacement, etc.) Ultimately, transition plans should aim to ascertain the NFC's resilience and its impacts on the earth's boundaries[b]
Transition governance	Identify and assess the impacts and dependencies of the transition plan on its stakeholders (e.g. its workforce, value chain counterparts, customers), society (e.g. local communities), the economy and the natural environment, throughout its value chain that may give rise to	Transition planning is not just an additional piece of reporting but rather a comprehensive risk management and strategic tool whose main underlying objective is to identify and address climate impacts, opportunity-specific transition risks, as well as other environmental impacts

(continued)

Table 39.2 (continued)

Principle	Actions	Rationale
	sustainability-related risks and opportunities Set objectives that relate to the resilience of the business to the changing climate and respond to the risks and opportunities that arise from the transition to a low-GHG emissions, climate-resilient economy Identify impacts hindering EU decarbonisation and environmental objectives or impinging on the feasibility of the transition pathways Provide evidence that the NFC possesses adaptive capacity to identify, assess, engage and has skills and applies methodologies to address each individual transition issue Identify need for skills, capabilities or resources that can prepare and implement the plan effectively Create responsible units dealing with each of the core areas and with sub-plans addressing impacts, risks and opportunities for each of the areas List the material impacts, risks and opportunities addressed by the administrative, management and supervisory bodies or their relevant committees, during the reporting period Explain (a) how the NFC carries out its risk assessment approach; (b) its risk prioritization methodology; and (c) the scope, main features and components of its risk management processes, and, more importantly, how the undertaking integrates the findings of its risk assessment for the key risks into relevant internal functions and processes Check if the plan enables stakeholders to evaluate clearly and effectively: The soundness of corporate strategy, the resilience	(potentially augmented by the compounding of physical risks) and related financial risks impacting the relevant NFC. This translates into the setting of mitigation actions based on a revised strategy that engages with the business model and the overall business strategy, as indicated by the EU Commission An effective transition plan, as outlined by the IPSF,[d] should have specific targets, demonstrate the ability to deliver, align with internal policies, have monitoring and correction processes, engage in external reporting and engagement, and undergo credible assessment procedures. It should be thorough in showcasing the organization's capacity and commitment to reaching decarbonization goals, yet succinct enough to avoid becoming too burdensome. The strategy should delineate specific short-term measures and remain flexible to accommodate unforeseen events. The strategy should strive to turn targets into a practical roadmap that the organization can use to evaluate its progress and improve its transition efforts. The plan should consider industry-specific strategies and include evaluations of upcoming technological advancements in a proactive manner to reflect the evolving nature of the transition For stakeholders to fully assess and trust the credibility of a transition plan, there must be comprehensive and transparent disclosure of all relevant data

(continued)

Table 39.2 (continued)

Principle	Actions	Rationale
	of the business model, the credibility of the mitigation actions, the effectiveness of the processes and internal competence for the supervision and monitoring of risk management vis-à-vis EGD objectives Ensure that the plan is translated into a practical roadmap containing targets or commitments with timescales to implement them, is time-constrained, or that the actions anticipated are time-constrained Ensure that the plan's measure of success is quantitative by introducing KPIs to this effect Ensure that the scope covers the entire business, and it is specific to that business Include detailed information on current emissions, the specific technologies that will be adopted, planned changes in production processes and the projected impact of these initiatives on reducing CO2 emissions Assess the implications of the plan for the value chain As indicated by TPT,[c] include as assumptions in the financial statements: (a) policy and regulatory change (b) the decarbonization trajectory of the global economy, relevant geographies and/or sectors, (c) macroeconomic trends (e.g. labour availability, cost of borrowing, etc.), (d) microeconomic and financial factors (e.g. availability of finance, relative prices), (e) technological developments access to counterparty data and reliability of data shifts in client and consumer demand, (f) the levels of warming over the short-, medium- and long-term, (g) the physical impacts of the changing climate, and the	

(continued)

Table 39.2 (continued)

Principle	Actions	Rationale
	regional and spatial implications of these and (h) the effectiveness of adaptation efforts and possible limits to adaptation, and the regional and spatial implications of these	
Taxonomy alignment	Indicate those NFC's activities that are aligned with the EU taxonomy regulation,[e] setting out an action plan to increase taxonomy alignment Carry out, where possible, a DNSH test and LCA of products to assess the level of misalignment from the EU taxonomy regulation	The taxonomy regulation introduces two additional criteria for defining an activity as 'sustainable', namely the do not significant harm ('DNSH') and the minimum social safeguards tests. By satisfying the DNSH test, the activity should not harm other environmental criteria set out by the taxonomy regulation using a life cycle assessment methodology ('LCA') For companies outside of Europe and companies whose activities are not entirely captured by the EU Taxonomy's existing criteria, it is for businesses and investors to conduct risk-based due diligence based on the OECD due diligence guidance for responsible business conduct (RBC)
1.5 °C compatibility	Set warming target at 1.5 °C above pre-industrial levels Disclose their current base year and baseline value, and, from 2030 onwards, update the base year for their GHG emission reduction targets after every five-year period thereafter Ensure the integrity of baselines and targets in accordance with science	Notably, the EU law minimum requirements and the OECD approach to transition planning are based on the requirement to ensure, on a best effort basis, that the business model and strategy are compatible with the transition to a sustainable economy and with the limiting of global warming to 1.5 °C and the Union's objective of achieving net zero by 2050 and a reduction of 90% by 2040 below 1990 levels As indicated by the EBA '[*p*] *ractices supporting credibility of transition plans include the use of scientifically grounded and regularly updated net-zero scenarios that provide pathways relevant to portfolio exposures, and ensuring that*

(continued)

Table 39.2 (continued)

Principle	Actions	Rationale
		the portfolio coverage of metrics and targets allows to draw conclusions on the institution's alignment with the net-zero trajectory...'[f]
Scope of GHG emission calculation methodologies	Cover both GHG intensity and absolute emissions. Set boundaries in line with best industry practices and coalition frameworks. Set a short-term target at 2–3 years and interim targets at a 5-year interval Determine its GHG emissions intensity for each unit of product at the facility level applying throughout its product life cycle, based on the most recent year, covering almost all sources of emissions within the sector-specific organizational boundaries, as well as indirect emissions under scope 3 Calculate GHG intensity with respect to each facility-specific product on a disaggregated basis, excluding any offsetting, CDR and any avoided emissions. Alongside a GHG intensity calculation, however, to enhance credibility and avoid greenwashing risks, the NFC should carry out an absolute emission assessment and disclose its total emissions Benchmark the absolute emission pathway by reference to a sector pathway or method approved by the Science-Based Targets initiative and the GHG emission absolute reduction of 90% compared to 1990 levels in line with the EU Commission Communication on Emission Targets of 6 February 2024[g] To enhance its credibility, in line with the GHG protocol that is adopted as a reference by ESRS, include separate targets for material non-CO2 greenhouse gas emissions (e.g. fossil	Despite projecting a rise in future absolute emissions due to rising demand, a company can still reduce its GHG intensity; hence, GHG intensity alone can be an incorrect measurement approach[h]

(continued)

Table 39.2 (continued)

Principle	Actions	Rationale
	methane and biogenic methane), if the NFC emits these types of GHGs through its operations Request third-party verification of the carbon baseline based on both carbon intensity and absolute emissions in accordance with the GHG protocol and organizational boundaries for GHG reporting based on sectoral best practices, covering the entire product and operations, regardless of the ownership of the relevant process	
Choice and use of climate scenarios and integrated assessment models (IAMs)	Evaluate and disclose the impacts, opportunities and risks associated with such scenarios Refer not only to the emissions produced by the energy used and the processes employed in the industry and the cost of carbon pricing but also include, as indicated by WBCSD[i] and GFANZ,[j] end-used energy demand for the industry and its mix, the low-carbon energy share, hydrogen cost, electrolyser capacity, CCS availability and investments, and the total production and demand for the relevant goods produced by the industry Apart from how much the NFC emits, consider, at minimum, choosing IAMs that are capable of capturing, on a forward-looking basis, additional variables such as how much energy and what type of energy the industry requires, and the actual demand for its products, materials or commodities, at the point of consumption or production, total capital expenditures, typically including low-carbon and non-low carbon in nature, for different activities within various sectors of the economy, and the total cost of producing some good or the price faced by consumers at a particular stage in the value chain	Evaluations of impacts, opportunities and risks according to these scenarios translate into a disclosure of how risks and opportunities may approximately significantly affect cash flows, performance, business position, research and development, cost of capital or access to credit in the short, medium and long term. A transition risk assessment, as a pre-requisite to a credible transition plan, requires, however, both a top-down approach, based on climate scenarios and, if available, biodiversity scenarios and a bottom-up approach (see 'drivers of change, transition risks and transmission channels'). These scenarios and models are unable to capture the complexity of all externalities, as indicated by Stern,[k] however, if properly applied, they can provide some indications for NFCs. The ESRS recommends that climate scenarios are prepared and disclosed in accordance with international standards such as the IPCC

(continued)

Table 39.2 (continued)

Principle	Actions	Rationale
Drivers of change, transition risks and transmission channels	Assess drivers of change in the sector. Drivers vary across different sectors, with some similarities such as market dynamics, adoption of new technologies, implementation of new policies and regulations, changes in consumer demand and disruptions in the supply chain. However, the way these drivers appear can differ greatly, even among hard-to-abate sectors Identify and classify transition risk based on the classification by NGFS (Network for greening the financial system) Identify drivers of change for each risk, assessing potential sources (technology, policy, legal, market) Provide a bottom-up transmission channel diagram to include categories of affected stakeholders and financial risks (credit, liquidity, market, refinancing and underwriting risks) for each of the transition risks	Analysis of drivers of change helps understand how future transition risks may materialize Identifying and understanding the interaction between these drivers and climate-related risks and transmission channels to financial risks helps define potential externalities and how impacts, risks and opportunities can present themselves Proper transition governance requires that the plan take into account climate-related financial risks and opportunities as well as the sectoral and individual peculiarities of the NFC by reference to its production inputs from a bottom-up perspective, e.g. existing applied technologies and technical processes by plant and by product, skill gaps in its personnel to be filled in to pursue decarbonization, sectoral industrial pathways, reasonably foreseeable innovation brought by new technologies impacting the company's markets, processes, new materials and the gradual unavailability of fossil fuel sources and the increasing availability of alternative fuels. Critical areas of attention are the positioning of the NFC vis-à-vis other peers and coalition frameworks, taking into account the adoption of new disruptive technologies by competitors, the availability of nature-based solutions and the compatibility of such technologies with the EGD policies. This information is unlikely to be obtained by investors and lenders through sustainability reporting or by third parties and it requires a specific engagement with the NFC

(continued)

Table 39.2 (continued)

Principle	Actions	Rationale
Technology risk	Assess technology developments by applying a technology readiness level methodology and mapping the decarbonization features of existing technologies and how new forthcoming technologies can transform production Identify the risk of early adoption of technology and consider gradual adoption and pilot cases Map current mainstream technology, existing technologies and forthcoming technologies against the net zero industry act and EU industrial pathways, if available for the sector Consider in the plan potential 'shocks' or stressors (sudden adverse changes) related to transition risks	The OECD guidance on transition finance[1] has set out ten criteria to ensure the credibility of transition plans. Among these criteria, OECD has indicated that plans should be based on available sectoral pathways and technological roadmaps and include an explanation as to how the plan's targets compare to relevant national-level frameworks, such as sector-specific transition pathways and roadmaps, where these are available
Policy risk	Identify climate-related policy factors (such as, e.g. new legislation on carbon pricing, eco-design, building efficiency or net zero industrial standards, expansion of reporting duties by corporates and directors' liability for climate change-related events, shift in consumer preference due to policy change, availability of raw materials due to deforestation or mining restrictions), creating obvious transition risks or opportunities for the NFC Assess how its assets and business activities may be exposed to these climate-related policy factors	Policies even if not translated into hard law have the possibility of seriously impacting corporate activities and operations. This can occur either directly or indirectly by impacting costs, revenues, raw material extraction, production and distribution processes. Policies can restrict the carrying out of certain business activities, e.g. by setting barriers to entry or stringent operational requirements, they can promote others by coordinating national policies such as the net zero industry act or the national plans on mitigation actions, setting incentives and providing grants. Other policies can require that industrial processes be adjusted so that they comply with sustainability objectives and standards
Legal risk	Assess the exposure to legal risk factors caused or augmented by climate risks (such as climate change litigation, contractual disputes related to disruption of the value chain due to climate	Operation legal risks for NFCs are traditionally linked to loss of material authorizations, breaches of contract and compensation for damages caused to third parties. Climate risks can

(continued)

Table 39.2 (continued)

Principle	Actions	Rationale
	events or the enactment of policies, compensation and losses from reputational risk)	augment these risks or create new types of legal risks
Consumer preference shift risk	Assess the likelihood of a consumer preference shift that could impact the company and/or the product based on potential drivers of change, such as peers' actions, technology, legal or policy changes Develop a risk response and a plan to deal with these potential factors based on the likelihood Update the likelihood assessment regularly Build up the predictive preferences of consumers or market participants by taking into account the circular and sustainability features of products when designing them	Depending on the sector, consumer preference may be extremely relevant. The environmental footprint of an intermediate material or of a consumer good, or of the energy intensity of a product may shift consumer preferences. Equally changes in policies, developments in technologies or legal actions on climate issues impacting the brand's reputation may cause a drop in revenues for the NFC
Business model impact	Assess how the company's value proposition and operating model engage with forward-looking transition impacts, risks and opportunities Assess how the company's business model benchmarks against 1.5 °C following different socioeconomic pathways (SSPs)[m] as well as against drivers of change, sectoral best practices, coalition frameworks and the adoption of innovative technologies and industrial processes by peers	Such assessment focuses on the evaluation of how scenarios and sectoral drivers might impact the resilience of the corporate borrower's business model and on whether such drivers can augment the consequences of climate-related externalities. This type of impact analysis bears relevance for the M&A strategy of the NFC, and, by taking historical performance into account, it can help prioritise acquisitions and dismissals of subsidiaries. NFCs can achieve emissions targets by winding down or retiring their own high-emitting assets rather than disposing of them to third-party buyers who may be less diligent owners The objective of this disclosure is to allow stakeholders to assess the extent and effectiveness of the NFC's strategic decisions and commitments and any changes to its business model(s) to foster material sustainability positive impacts or to

(continued)

Table 39.2 (continued)

Principle	Actions	Rationale
		prevent or mitigate material sustainability negative impacts, including a summarised description of the related policies, plans and targets
Stranding and carbon lock-in risks	Identify existing assets and infrastructure, as well as new investments, that are at risk of leading to emissions lock-in, and clearly set out the steps to be taken to prevent such lock-in. The plan should set out any strategy and process for the responsible retirement of high-emitting corporate assets	According to the WRI,[n] carbon lock-in occurs '*when fossil fuel-intensive systems perpetuate, delay or prevent the transition to low-carbon alternatives*'. In 2019, a study[o] calculated the greenhouse gas emissions produced by current infrastructure, industrial and personal assets. The study concluded that the world's remaining 'carbon budget', at 1.5 °C will be completely exhausted by the existing infrastructure. To limit temperature rise to the above levels, as indicated by the EU Recommendation on Transition Finance, the focus should be on building new carbon-intensive infrastructure and assets and seeking to retire existing high-emissions equipment early. To address the carbon lock-in risk, determine the life span of carbon-intensive infrastructure and equipment. Different infrastructure and types of assets ranging from 80 years for a building, 40 years for a cement plant, 35 years for a steel plant, 30 years for a ship and 18.5 years for an internal combustion (ICE) vehicle. Given that current investments in carbon-intensive projects are designed for long-term use, financial decisions made now impact the achievement of a low-carbon economy. Obviously, the availability and accessibility of alternatives, based on their Technology Readiness Level (TRL) that can substitute the high-emitting products or operations are also important factors to consider

(continued)

Table 39.2 (continued)

Principle	Actions	Rationale
Decarbonization levers	Introduce life cycle assessment, DNSH environmental product footprint processes and impact methodologies Identify opportunities by reference to peers' actions and coalition frameworks and EU industrial pathways[p]	Especially for hard-to-abate companies, the definition of the company's technological status quo and related impacts must be carried out, in an EU context, by reference to LCA and/or environmental product footprint processes and a DNSH approach and by comparing the outcome with technologies and industrial processes adopted by peers and coalition frameworks. Such data collection can be deemed credible as long as it is undertaken not only at the entity level but also at the plant and product level in order to capture the carbon lock-in risk of specific assets. In relation to quantitative data, this requires that directors verify the origin of the data and ensure that their approach to the analysis of this data is sound by reference to science-based scenarios
Quality of data	Describe the process used to identify and assess impacts, risks and opportunities under the disclosure requirement related to ESRS 2 IRO-1—Process to identify and assess material climate-related impacts, risks and opportunities	The acquisition of reliable and independent data regarding the climate-related drivers of change, impacts, risks and opportunities impacting the NFC is critical
Abatement costs calculation and prioritization of mitigation actions	Consider cost-benefit analysis of appropriate solutions To optimize emissions reductions with a budget of x million euros, it is advisable to select the abatement options with the lowest costs Prioritise mitigation solutions by also taking into account climate scenarios, the resilience of the business model and EU policy objectives Include all costs associated with the plan (e.g. write-downs, site remediation, contract penalties, regulatory costs)	The abatement cost refers to the expense incurred in lowering greenhouse gas (GHG) emissions by one tonne. Negative abatement costs refer to the potential to decrease emissions while still generating a positive economic outcome. The lowest abatement costs signify potential avenues for reducing emissions at a minimal expense. The use of marginal abatement cost curves (MACC) and MARCC[q] curves would also benefit the credibility of a plan. By using these curves, NFCs can assess where they stand in relation to the increase in cost abatement

(continued)

Table 39.2 (continued)

Principle	Actions	Rationale
		that transition risks, such as falling demand or asset devaluation, or regulatory shifts, will lead to. The creation of the MACC which sets out the potential for abatement for each cost that is considered feasible for transition purposes, can be elucidated as follows: When presented with a set of 20 emission reduction choices, each possessing distinct costs and potential benefits, it is possible to arrange them in ascending order of cost. An NFC should start with the most cost-effective alternatives and gradually increase its efforts until its emission reduction goal is achieved, allowing it to prioritize investments in light of potential cost increases. McKinsey[r] predicts a potential 60 percent supply-demand imbalance for net zero products in the steel, cement and chemicals industries by 2030. While shortages may momentarily hinder the shift to net zero, there is a chance for proactive participants to take advantage. Hence, as also indicated by GFANZ,[s] priority should be given to short- to medium-term emission reduction actions to achieve critical milestones by 2030 in order to reduce the risk of environmental tipping points
Investment and financial plan integration	As indicated by TPT, determine how the implementation of the plan is to affect the financial position over the short-, medium- and long-term, taking into consideration matters such as: (a) Investment and disposal plans (e.g. plans for capital expenditure, major acquisitions and divestments, joint ventures, business transformations,	The quality of the mitigation actions and any related investment and financial plans is another area where credibility is vital. To ensure the alignment of the mitigation actions with the strategy and policy drivers, the related capital and operating expenditure plans, research and development plans, and investments should be aligned with all strategy-driven and policy-

(continued)

Table 39.2 (continued)

Principle	Actions	Rationale
	innovation, new business areas, investments into research and development for climate solutions and asset retirements), including plans to which the entity is not contractually committed; and (b) Planned sources of funding to implement its plan As indicated by TPT, determine how the implementation of the plan is to affect the financial performance and cash flows over the short-, medium- and long-term (e.g. increased revenue from products and services aligned with low-GHG emissions, a climate-resilient economy and expenses associated with climate adaptation or mitigation) In accordance with ESRS E1 at AR21, the disclosure of significant monetary amounts of CapEx and OpEx required to implement the mitigation actions needs to be credible. This requires that these actions be identified, validated (also with the support of independent third-party experts) and expressly set out in the business plan, and that their related CapEx, OpEx, merger and acquisition activities, and research and development expenditures should identify potential equity, working capital and long-term financial needs and sources to meet the transition targets and relevant KPIs As indicated by the ACT initiative, include financial projections and a financial viability analysis in relation to the implementation of mitigation actions Establish mechanisms for financial support and incentives, including government grants, subsidies, tax reliefs, and access to green bonds or other green financing options	driven targets (e.g. capex-alignment with EU taxonomy or EGD objectives) and split between the underlying assets: New and legacy or stranded assets. This is to reflect progress in the areas of focus that they have identified in their strategic approach and business model impact analysis, while considering policy impacts. Depending on the sector and the position within the value chain, an NFC would focus on its plants vs. production process vs. product design vs. raw materials vs. embedded emissions

(continued)

Table 39.2 (continued)

Principle	Actions	Rationale
Just transition	Explain how the NFC is contributing to a just transition, i.e. the delivery of a net zero and climate-resilient economy in a way that delivers fairness and tackles inequality and injustice by maximizing positive economic, social and decent work gains and minimizing and mitigating negative impacts	Transition plans must consider and address the broader social consequences and impacts of mitigation actions, including on race, gender and intergenerational equity[u]
KPI setting	Set KPIs on: • Taxonomy and EU Green Deal alignment • Current and future production/revenue/CapEx and OpEx investments with respect to low-carbon products or services compared to the sector and its immediate peers • The reduction of emissions relative to the life of an asset. GFANZ[v] has introduced the expected emissions reduction (EER) indicator as an additional measure to existing key performance indicators (KPIs). The EER quantifies the unrealized emissions reduction potential of an asset or entity over a specific term, similar to how the 'expected return' quantifies the return of a financing decision • Carbon lock-in, energy and resource usage of each asset/plant • Integration of circular and sustainable practices at entity and asset/plant level • Internal KPIs and related control processes that are able to capture progress in all the relevant areas so enhancing the credibility features of a plan • Compliance with qualitative indicators on risk/impact/opportunities management related to the implementation of the plan	KPIs that can be used not only for the decarbonization performance under prudential and non-prudential plans but also for banking products such as sustainability-linked loans would allow for a convergence of indicators

[a]Ibid [4]
[b]Richardson et al. (2023)
[c]Ibid [4]
[d]IPSF, *Transition finance report - November 2022*. Available at: https://finance.ec.europa.eu/system/files/2022-11/221109-international-platform-sustainable-report-transition-finance_en.pdf

(continued)

[e]Regulation (EU) 2020/852 of 18 June 2020 on the establishment of a framework to facilitate sustainable investment, and amending Regulation (EU) 2019/2088, O*J L 198, 22.6.2020, p. 13–43*
[f]Ibid [3] at para. 122
[g]Commission Notice on securing our future Europe's 2040 climate target and path To climate neutrality by 2050 building a sustainable, just and prosperous society, (COM 2024/63 Final), https://eur-lex.europa.eu/legal-content/EN/TXT/?uri=COM%3A2024%3A63%3AFIN
[h]Zhang (2023), https://440megatonnes.ca/insight/companies-need-to-be-clear-emissions-reduction-targets/. P. Schreiber (2024). *Corporate Climate Transition Plans: What to look for*, Reclaim finance, January 2024, https://reclaimfinance.org/site/wp-content/uploads/2024/01/Report-Climate-Transition-Plan-Reclaim-Finance-January-2024.pdf
[i]World Business Council for Sustainable Development (2023a)
[j]Ibid. [38]
[k]Stern (2021)
[l]Ibid [16]
[m]Fujimori et al. (2017); Fricko et al. (2017); Riahi et al. (2017), pp. 153–168
[n]Sato et al. (2021)
[o]Tong et al. (2019), pp. 373–377
[p]EU Commission (2024)
[q]A Marginal Abatement Revenue Cost Curve (MARCC) is a MACC which also considers revenue items. See McKinsey (2023)
[r]Ibid [q]
[s]Ibid [38]
[t]Ibid [4]
[u]Ibid [40]
[v]Ibid [38]

standards from the TPT[48] and ACT Initiative.[49] In particular, the ACT Initiative defines a workable quantitative approach applicable to several criteria identified in the literature review. It identifies several KPIs for transition plan credibility that is critical in order to deal with carbon lock-in risk, retirement of high-emitting corporate assets and R&D on low-carbon assets and technologies. Such KPIs are then aggregated into a scoring system with a weighting of the relevant results.

A notable example of relevant sectoral quantitative KPIs is those set out in June 2024 by the ACT Initiative for the automotive sector below:

KPI	Explanation
AU 1.1 alignment of scope 1 + 2 emissions reduction targets	Assesses if the company's targets for direct (scope 1) and indirect (scope 2) emissions reductions align with industry standards and climate goals
AU 1.2 scope 3 upstream emissions reduction targets	Evaluates whether the scope 3 emissions reduction targets for the vehicle components are in line with global climate objectives
AU 1.3 alignment of scope 3 downstream emissions reduction targets	Evaluates whether the scope 3 emissions reduction targets for the vehicle usage are in line with global climate objectives

(continued)

[48]Ibid [4].
[49]Ibid [5].

KPI	Explanation
AU 1.4 time horizon of targets	Consider the timeframe over which the company's emissions reduction targets are set, ensuring they cover short, medium and long-term periods
AU 2.1 trend in past scope 1 + 2 emissions intensity	Looks at historical data to assess changes in emissions intensity over time
AU 2.2 and AU 3.1 share of low-carbon CapEx investments and R&D spending on low-carbon technologies	Assess the percentage of CapEx investments in low-carbon technologies in the company's total CapEx and the investment in research and development aimed at transitioning to low-carbon technologies
AU 4.1 and AU 4.2 trend in past scope 3 upstream and downstream emissions intensity	Analyse the projected trajectory of scope 3 emissions (upstream and downstream) over time
AU 4.3 locked-in emissions from sold products	Evaluates the extent to which current investments in for sold vehicles might lock in future emissions
AU 4.4 share of low-carbon vehicles	Measures the percentage of low-carbon vehicles in the company's total vehicle sales
AU 4.5 low-carbon vehicle efficiency performance	Assesses the average energy efficiency of electric vehicles
AU 5.1 oversight of climate change issues	Reviews how climate change issues are managed at the board or executive level
AU 5.2 climate change oversight capability	Evaluates the expertise and capability of the company's leadership to oversee climate-related issues
AU 5.3 low-carbon transition plan	Assesses the presence and quality of a strategic plan for transitioning to a low-carbon economy
AU 5.4 climate change management incentives	Measures if executive compensation is linked to climate performance targets
AU 5.5 climate change scenario testing	Evaluates if the company tests its business strategies against various climate scenarios
AU 6.1 and AU 6.2 strategy/activities to influence suppliers to reduce their GHG emissions	Assess the company's strategy and actual actions to engage suppliers in reducing emissions
AU 7.1 and AU 7.2 strategy/activities to influence clients to reduce their GHG emissions	Measures the company's strategy and actual actions to engage clients in reducing emissions
AU 8.1 company policy on engagement with associations, alliances, coalitions and think-tanks	Reviews the company's policy regarding its engagement with associations and other groups and their stance on climate issues
AU 8.2 associations, alliances, coalition and think-tanks supported do not have climate-negative activities or positions	Ensures that associations and other groups that the company supports do not engage in activities contrary to climate goals
AU 8.3 position on significant climate policies	Evaluates the company's stance and activities related to key climate policies
AU 9.1 revenue from low-carbon products and/or services	Looks at the revenues from the sale of low-emission vehicles and services
AU 9.2 changes to business model	Looks at the impact on the business model

In addition to AU 1.1 and AU 2.1 that deal with Scope 1 and 2 emissions and AU 1.2 and AU 1.3 that engage with Scope 3 upstream and downstream emissions, three KPIs can provide a comprehensive view of a manufacturer's efforts and effectiveness in transitioning to low-carbon technologies and reducing emissions in the sector: namely, 'AU 3.1 R&D Spending for Low-carbon technologies' which focuses on investment in innovative technologies, 'AU 4.3 Locked-in Emissions from Sold products' that evaluates the long-term impact of the sold vehicles on emissions and 'AU 4.4 Share of Low-carbon vehicles' that tracks the sale of sustainable vehicles.

Given the relevant impact of R&D for the decarbonisation of the automotive sector in the EU, 'AU 3.1 R&D Spending on Low-carbon technologies' measures the ratio of a company's R&D investments dedicated to developing low-carbon technologies to its total capital expenditures.

In line with transition finance's objective to reduce carbon lock-in risk, the 'AU 4.3 Locked-in emissions from sold products' KPI assesses the degree to which a manufacturer's fleet emissions are 'locked-in' based on the vehicles sold and their expected emissions over their lifetimes. It reflects how future-oriented is the NFC's sold vehicles portfolio in terms of emissions. Higher scores indicate a greater reliance on traditional, higher-emission vehicles, while lower scores signify a proactive shift towards low-emission alternatives, reducing long-term emissions commitments. The metric is gCO2/p.km multiplied by the average annual travel of vehicles (km) multiplied by the number of vehicles sold in a year.

KPI 'AU 4.4 Share of Low-carbon Vehicles' KPI evaluates the proportion of low-carbon vehicles in the manufacturer's overall vehicle sales. A higher percentage indicates a greater contribution to reducing fleet emissions and advancing the transition to sustainable transportation. This KPI is critical as it directly impacts the overall carbon footprint of the manufacturer's products and demonstrates market readiness and adoption of low-carbon technologies.

However, a review of the ACT Initiative's KPIs indicates that while its quantitative approach is sound and may constitute the most complete quantitative-based standard available for transition plans, the underlying benchmarks and scope of the KPIs are not updated to reflect the recent European Industrial Pathways on mobility under the EU Green Deal, the Critical Raw Material Act and the recent Net Zero Industry Act regarding batteries and EVs.

This bears relevance to the identification of the benchmarks for some KPIs introduced by the ACT Initiative for the automotive sector. A few examples of KPIs can be illustrative of this issue:

(i) in general, KPIs should also address specific targets of the upstream components (such as ratio of low-carbon steel, aluminium, and recycled plastic used in the vehicle);
(ii) KPI 'AU 4.3 Locked-in emissions from sold products' and AU 4.5 'Low-carbon vehicle efficiency performance' should ensure that the targets are more ambitious than targets under Regulation (EU) 2019/631, which sets a fleet-wide target of 95 g CO2/km for the years 2020–2024 for new passenger cars.

In addition, ambitious target-setting should consider that the following EU-wide fleet targets (WLTP) will apply: 93.6 g/km until 2029 (15% reduction compared to the 2021 baseline), 49.5 g/km from 2030 to 2034 (55% reduction) and 0 g/km from 2035 (100% reduction). The benchmarks used by ACT Initiative should be replaced with those set by the European Environment Agency[50];

(iii) in compliance with the 2024 EU Commission's 'Transition Pathway for the EU Mobility Industrial System' (the 'Transition Pathway'), the scope of the R&D for low-carbon technologies under AU 3.1 should not just be focused on Technology Readiness Level above 8, but should also include fuel-cell technologies to avoid reliance on a single technology such as EVs and on the development of new technologies that can reduce substantially the need of processing critical raw materials or even replace critical inputs with alternatives. In addition, the Transition Pathway requires investments in the recycling of batteries and fuel cells to recover strategic raw materials, in line with the targets of the Critical Raw Material Act. Hence, R&D for this recycling activity should be accounted for. The KPI should be used generally to capture R&D for all 'net zero technologies' under Article 3a of the recently adopted Net Zero Industry Act[51];

(iv) AU 4.4 should be assessed by reference to activities caught by 'Manufacture of automotive and mobility components' under the EU Taxonomy Regulation[52];

(v) given the relevance of the Circular Economy Action Plan, KPIs could be included in the 'Average recyclability of sold vehicles/products (% by sales-weighted metric tons)' as also evidenced in ICMA's Illustrative KPI Registry by reference to the benchmarks set by the Ellen McArthur Foundation New Plastics Economy Initiative, to be updated in line with the JRC report on recycled plastic content targets for new passenger cars[53] substantially reflected in an EU legislative proposal[54];

(vi) in line with the Just Transition objective of the Union, a KPI borrowed from the ICMA's Illustrative KPI Registry, could be applied to the manufacturers in transition, namely: Investment (m€ or number/share of trainees/people)

[50] See European Environment Agency (2024).

[51] See Final compromise text of Net Zero Industry Act https://data.consilium.europa.eu/doc/document/ST-6269-2024-INIT/en/pdf and https://ec.europa.eu/commission/presscorner/detail/en/ip_24_2309.

[52] See Taxonomy Compass, https://ec.europa.eu/sustainable-finance-taxonomy/activities/activity/283/view.

[53] Maury et al. (2023).

[54] Proposal for a Regulation of the European Parliament and of the Council on circularity requirements for vehicle design and on management of end-of-life vehicles, amending Regulations (EU) 2018/858 and 2019/1020 and repealing Directives 2000/53/EC and 2005/64/EC. See also EU Parliament briefing, www.europarl.europa.eu/RegData/etudes/BRIE/2023/754627/EPRS_BRI(2023)754627_EN.pdf.

dedicated to reskilling/upskilling workers from ICE specific/related capabilities or task to low-carbon vehicles necessary ones; and

(vii) in line with EU zero pollution objectives, KPIs could be introduced on level of 'Emissions for NOx, SOx and/or other pollutants (incl. PM) (absolute or intensity)' that are more ambitious than Euro 7 for ICE fleet.

39.6 Conclusion

In this chapter we have demonstrated that climate transition plans require NFCs active in hard-to-abate sectors to engage with new complex issues that require a novel approach to transition governance. While these issues may not vary among companies active in hard-to-abate sectors, they manifest in different ways, requiring a sectoral approach in addition to a general approach that deals with common features of transition plans. This is due to the drivers of change, transition risks, peculiar technologies, value chains and market dynamics of each industrial sector.

We have established that the quality of transition plans will depend on their credibility attributes, which are defined in accordance with both sector-agnostic and sector-specific standards, and on the commitment of the NFCs to pursuing transition governance effectively. However, the lack of established quantitative KPIs that can harmonise the credibility assessment of transition plans could jeopardise transition and give rise to greenwashing. In turn, this would impact the reliability of the prudential transition plans of EU credit institutions, which should not be based just on the 'financed emissions' metric, but also on their ability to help transition the real economy in line with forthcoming EBA Guidelines, CRD VI and CRR3. In this respect, the IPSF has warned that the mechanical use of the financed emission metric could inadvertently discourage financial institutions from engaging in transition finance.[55]

The key issues for the credibility of transition plans that will dictate the ability to decarbonise effectively are whether the relevant NFC will reduce the carbon lock-in risk of its production assets and products and will ensure a managed phase-out of high-emitting assets in line with the Union's EU Green Deal objectives as well as cause a reduction of emissions in its value chain. Such objectives should be captured by quantitative KPIs that are able to be updated by reference to the evolution of EU policies to ensure that the NFC is transitioning faster than the EU sectoral pathways to Net Zero and its transition is just and it does not harm other environmental objectives. Hence, evaluating the impact of financed emissions by reference to the locked-in emissions at asset and plant level would allow lenders and regulators to identify those financed emissions that are more at risk of becoming stranded and misaligned with EU climate and environmental goals.

[55] Ibid [40] at p. 35.

Other key issues for sectors such as the automotive one, where the main carbon lock-in risk is related to product usage, are the carbon emissions intensity of the vehicle production and components, the level of R&D on low-carbon technologies to be used by the vehicle, the choice of fuel technology and the timing for adopting new technologies in line with the EU Climate Law, the EU Green Deal and Net Zero Industry Act objectives. The application of key sectoral transition metrics to transition plans can enhance the latter's credibility. We considered the sectoral KPIs developed by ACT Initiative for the automotive sector and assessed their effectiveness from an EU policy standpoint and indicated possible solutions to foster their application for ESRS E1-compliant transition plans by automotive manufacturers. This approach can also be followed for other hard-to-abate sectors and could foster further research on the topic.

References

Accelerate Climate Transition. (2024). https://actinitiative.org/fr/act-methodologies/

ACT Generic Methodology. (2023). https://actinitiative.org/wp-content/uploads/pdf/act_generic_methodology_v2.0.pdf

Asociația Accept, C-81/12, EU:C:2013:275, par. 63.

Association Europe Finances Régulations. (2023). Transition plans: ensuring their comparability, credibility and effectiveness to accelerate the low carbon transition, Debate Paper, Issue n° 5/2023, November 2023, https://www.aefr.eu/en/debate-papers

Autorité des Marchés Financières. (9 February 2024). "Guide pédagogique à destination des entreprises pour rendre compte de leur plan de transition climatique", https://www.amf-france.org/fr/actualites-publications/publications/guides/guides-professionnels/guide-pedagogique-destination-des-entreprises-pour-rendre-compte-de-leur-plan-de-transition

Bingler, J., Colesanti Senni, C., Fixler, D., & Schimanski, T. (2023). *Net zero transition plans: Red flag indicators to assess inconsistencies and greenwashing*, wwfint.awsassets.panda.org/downloads/red-flag-indicators-for-transition-plan-inconsistencies-and-greenwashing-26-sept.pdf

CBI. (2023). *Guidance to assess transition plans*, https://www.climatebonds.net/files/reports/guidance_to_assess_transition_plans.pdf

CDP. (2023). *CDP Technical Note: Reporting on Transition Plans*, https://cdn.cdp.net/cdp-production/cms/guidance_docs/pdfs/000/003/101/original/CDP_technical_note_-_Climate_transition_plans.pdf

Commission Delegated Regulation (EU) 2023/2772 of 31 July 2023 published on 22 December 2023.

Commission Delegated Regulation 2023/2772 (EU) of 31 July 2023 supplementing Directive 2013/34/EU, as regards sustainability reporting standards [2023], OJ L 22.12.23.

Commission Notice (EU) – Technical guidance on the application of do no significant harm under the Recovery and Resilience Facility Regulation (C/2023/6454).

Commission Notice (EU) on the interpretation and implementation of certain legal provisions of the Disclosures Delegated Act under Article 8 of EU Taxonomy Regulation on the reporting of Taxonomy-eligible and Taxonomy-aligned economic activities and assets (second Commission Notice) (C/2023/305).

Commission Notice (EU) on the interpretation and implementation of certain legal provisions of the EU Taxonomy Climate Delegated Act establishing technical screening criteria for economic activities that contribute substantially to climate change mitigation or climate change adaptation and do no significant harm to other environmental objective (C/2023/267).

Commission Recommendation (EU) 2023/1425 of 27 June 2023 on facilitating finance for the transition to a sustainable economy, C/2023/3844, *OJ L 174, 7.7.2023, p. 19–46,* ELI: http://data.europa.eu/eli/reco/2023/1425/oj

COSO. (2023, March). "Achieving effective Internal Control Over Sustainability Reporting (ICSR): Building Trust and Confidence through the COSO Internal Control—Integrated Framework".

Council Directive (EU) 2022/2464 of 14 December 2022 amending Regulation (EU) No 537/2014, Directive 2004/109/EC, Directive 2006/43/EC and Directive 2013/34/EU, as regards corporate sustainability reporting [2022], OJ L 322. https://eur-lex.europa.eu/legal-content/EN/TXT/?uri=CELEX:32022L2464

Di Maio, C., & Dimitropouplou, M., et al. (2023). *An examination of net-zero commitments by the world's largest banks, ECB Occasional Paper Series No. 334*, www.ecb.europa.eu/pub/pdf/scpops/ecb.op334~4ddaea487d.en.pdf

EFRAG SRB meeting 23 August 2023, "Interoperability between ESRS and ISSB standards EFRAG assessment at this stage and mapping table", https://efrag.org/Assets/Download?assetUrl=%2Fsites%2Fwebpublishing%2FMeeting%20Documents%2F2307280747599961%2F04-02%20EFRAG%20SRB%20%20230823%20-%20EFRAG%20IFRS%20interoperability%20and%20mapping%20table.pdf

EU Commission. (2024). Transition pathways for European industrial ecosystems. https://single-market-economy.ec.europa.eu/industry/transition-pathways_en

European Banking Authority. (2024). Greenwashing Monitoring and Supervision, Final Report, EBA/REP/2024/09, at para.90, www.eba.europa.eu/sites/default/files/2024-05/a12e5087-8fd2-451f-8005-6d45dc838ffd/Report%20on%20greenwashing%20monitoring%20and%20supervision.pdf

European Commission, Directorate-General for Energy, De Vita, A., Kielichowska, I., Mandatowa, P., et al. (2020). *Technology pathways in decarbonisation scenarios*. Publications Office. https://data.europa.eu/doi/10.2833/994817

European Environment Agency. (2024). CO2 emissions performance of new passenger cars in Europe. https://www.eea.europa.eu/en/analysis/indicators/co2-performance-of-new-passenger?activeAccordion=546a7c35-9188-4d23-94ee-005d97c26f2b

European Parliament legislative resolution of 24 April 2024 on the proposal for a directive of the European Parliament and of the Council on Corporate Sustainability Due Diligence and amending Directive (EU) 2019/1937 (COM(2022)0071 – C9-0050/2022 – 2022/0051(COD)), https://www.europarl.europa.eu/doceo/document/TA-9-2024-0329_EN.html

Final compromise text of the Net Zero Industry Act. https://data.consilium.europa.eu/doc/document/ST-6269-2024-INIT/en/pdf and https://ec.europa.eu/commission/presscorner/detail/en/ip_24_2309

Fricko, P. H., et al. (2017). The marker quantification of the shared socioeconomic pathway 2: A middle-of-the-road scenario for the 21st century. *Global Environmental Change, 42*, 251–267. https://doi.org/10.1016/j.gloenvcha.2016.06.004. hdl:10044/1/78070. ISSN 0959-378.

Fujimori, S., Hasegawa, T., et al. (2017). SSP3: AIM implementation of shared socioeconomic pathways. *Global Environmental Change, 42*, 268–283. https://doi.org/10.1016/j.gloenvcha.2016.06.009. ISSN 0959-3780.O.

GFANZ. (2023). *Scaling transition finance and real-economy decarbonization, GFANZ Technical Review Note*, https://assets.bbhub.io/company/sites/63/2023/11/Transition-Finance-and-Real-Economy-Decarbonization-December-2023.pdf

IFRS Interpretation Committee, Staff Paper. (2023). Climate-related Commitments (IAS 37), 28–-29 November, 2023, https://www.ifrs.org/news-and-events/updates/ifric/2023/ifric-update-november-2023/

IIGCC. (2023). Investor expectations of corporate transition plans: from A to Zero, https://139838633.fs1.hubspotusercontent-eu1.net/hubfs/139838633/Past%20resource%20uploads/IIGCC_Investor-expectations-of-corporate-transition-plans_Final.pdf
International Energy Agency such as the Net Zero Emission scenario. https://www.iea.org/reports/global-energy-and-climate-model/net-zero-emissions-by-2050-scenario-nze
International Organisation for Standardization, Net Zero Guidelines. (IWA 42:2022). https://www.iso.org/obp/ui/en/#iso:std:iso:iwa:42:ed-1:v1:en
IPSF Implementing Transition Finance Principles – Interim Report. (2023). https://finance.ec.europa.eu/document/download/f332838d-a5da-4279-8986-dbb38a212432_en?filename=231204-ipsf-transition-finance-interim-report_en.pdf
Leadership Group for Industry Transition's trackers. at https://www.industrytransition.org
Maury, T., Tazi, N., Torres De Matos, C., Nessi, S., Antonopoulos, I., Pierri, E., Baldassarre, B., Garbarino, E., Gaudillat, P., & Mathieux, F. (2023). *Towards recycled plastic content targets in new passenger cars and light commercial vehicles*. Publications Office of the European Union, Luxembourg. https://doi.org/10.2838/834615. JRC129008. https://op.europa.eu/en/publication-detail/-/publication/0980feaf-2146-11ee-94cb-01aa75ed71a1/language-en
McDaniels, J., & Rismanchi, K. (2023). *The role of the financial sector in the net zero transition: Assessing implications for policy, supervision and market frameworks*. Institute of International Finance. www.iif.com/portals/0/Files/content/32370132_iif_transition_planning_report_2023_final_for_publication.pdf
McKinsey. (2023). *Decarbonize and create value: How incumbents can tackle the steep challenge*, https://www.mckinsey.com/capabilities/sustainability/our-insights/decarbonize-and-create-value-how-incumbents-can-tackle-the-steep-challenge
OECD. (2022). *OECD guidance on transition finance: Ensuring credibility of corporate climate transition plans, green finance and investment*. OECD Publishing. https://doi.org/10.1787/7c68a1ee-en
OECD. (2023). *Mechanisms to prevent carbon lock-in in transition finance, green finance and investment*. OECD Publishing. https://doi.org/10.1787/d5c49358-en
Proposal for a Regulation of the European Parliament and of the Council on circularity requirements for vehicle design and on management of end-of-life vehicles, amending Regulations (EU) 2018/858 and 2019/1020 and repealing Directives 2000/53/EC and 2005/64/EC.
Regulation (EU) 2020/852 of 18 June 2020 on the establishment of a framework to facilitate sustainable investment, and amending Regulation (EU) 2019/2088, O*J L 198, 22.6.*2020, *p. 13–.*
Regulation (EU) 2024/1623 of 31 May 2024 of the European Parliament and of the Council amending Regulation (EU) No 575/2013 as regards requirements for credit risk, credit valuation adjustment risk, operational risk, market risk and the output floor https://eur-lex.europa.eu/legal-content/EN/TXT/PDF/?uri=OJ:L_202401623, 19 June 2024, OJ L, 19.6.2024 p.10/189, https://eur-lex.europa.eu/legal-content/EN/TXT/PDF/?uri=OJ:L_202401623
Riahi, K., et al. (2017). The shared SocioEconomics pathways and their energy, land use, and greenhouse gas emissions implications: An overview. *Global Environmental Change, 42*, 153–168. https://doi.org/10.1016/j.gloenvcha.2016.05.009
Richardson, K., Steffen, W., Lucht, W., Bendtsen, J., Cornell, S. E., et al. (2023). Earth beyond six of nine planetary boundaries. *Science Advances, 9*(37). https://doi.org/10.1126/sciadv.adh2458
Sato, I., et al. (2021). *What is carbon lock-in and how can we avoid it?* World Resource Institute. https://www.wri.org/insights/carbon-lock-in-definition
Stern, N. (2021). *A time for action on climate change and a time for change in economics — Working paper 370 (PDF)*. Grantham Research Institute on Climate Change and the Environment. https://www.lse.ac.uk/granthaminstitute/wp-content/uploads/2021/10/working-paper-370-Stern.pdf. ISSN 2515-5717
Tong, D., Zhang, Q., Zheng, Y., et al. (2019). Committed emissions from existing energy infrastructure jeopardize 1.5 °C climate target. *Nature, 572*, 373–377. https://doi.org/10.1038/s41586-019-1364-3

Transition Plan Taskforce, Disclosure Framework. (2023, October). https://transitiontaskforce.net/wp-content/uploads/2023/10/TPT_Disclosure-framework-2023.pdf

United Nations Environment Programme. (2023). A Tool for Developing Credible Transition Plans: Public edition for asset owner pilot-testing. Geneva, https://www.unepfi.org/wordpress/wp-content/uploads/2023/12/NZAOA_A-Tool-for-Developing-Credible-Transition-Plans.pdf

United Nations High Level Expert Group on the Net Zero emission commitments of non-state entities. (2022). *Integrity matters*, https://www.un.org/sites/un2.un.org/files/high-level_expert_group_n7b.pdf .

World Benchmarking Alliance. (2024). *Assessing the credibility of a company's transition plan: Framework and guidance*. Assessing Transition Plan Collective (ATP-Col), version 1, September 2024, https://assets.worldbenchmarkingalliance.org/app/uploads/2024/09/ATP-Col-guidance-and-framework-document.pdf

World Business Council for Sustainable Development. (2023a). *Technical Documentation Energy Climate Scenario Catalogue*, www.wbcsd.org/download/file/13882

World Business Council for Sustainable Development. (2023b). *Roadmaps to Nature Positive*, www.wbcsd.org/contentwbc/download/17128/241711/1

WWF. (2023). *Nature in Transition Plans: Why and How?*, www.wwf.org.uk/sites/default/files/2023-02/WWF_Nature_In_Transition_Plans_Feb23.pdf

Zhang, A. (2023). *Companies need to absolutely clear about their emissions reporting targets*. Canadian Climate Institute. https://440megatonnes.ca/insight/companies-need-to-be-clear-emissions-reduction-targets/

The manufacturer's authorised representative in the EU is Springer Nature Customer Service Centre GmbH, Europaplatz 3, 69115 Heidelberg, Germany. If you have any concerns regarding our products, please contact ProductSafety@springernature.com

Printed and bound by CPI Group (UK) Ltd, Croydon, CR0 4YY
30/09/2026
02225596-0020